Who

A Directory of Prominent People

Detailed Contact Information for Noteworthy Individuals in Art, Business, Entertainment, Fashion, Government, Law, Literature, Media, Medicine, Politics, Religion, Science, Sports, and Other Areas

Second Edition

Edited by Kay Gill

615 Griswold Street • Detroit, MI 48226

ISBN 0-7808-0809-6

Printed in the United States of America

OMNIGRAPHICS, INC.
615 Griswold Street • Detroit, MI 48226
Phone Orders: 800-234-1340 • Fax Orders: 800-875-1340
Mail Orders: P.O. Box 625 • Holmes, PA 19043
www.omnigraphics.com

Table of Contents

Foreword 7

Introduction

Who's Included in *Who: A Directory of Prominent People* 9
About the Contact Information 10
Arrangement of Information in the Directory 10
Content of Individual Listings 10
Accuracy of Information in *Who: A Directory of Prominent People* 11

Who: A Directory of Prominent People 15

Subject Index 497

Actors 499
Advice Columnists
See: Columnists - Lifestyle & Features 529
Animators 505
Artists 505
See also:
Authors & Illustrators - Books for Young Readers 512
Cartoonists - Comic Strips & Panels 525
Cartoonists & Caricaturists - Editorial 527
Photographers 551
Association Executives
See: Organization Leaders 550
Astronauts 506
Attorneys & Judges 506
Authors - Fiction (Adult) 507
See also: Poets 553
Authors - Nonfiction 510
Authors & Illustrators - Books for Young Readers 512
Baseball Players & Managers 514
Basketball Players & Coaches 516
Bobsledders
See: Sports Personalities (Misc) 558
Bodybuilders
See: Fitness Personalities 536

Boxers
See: Sports Personalities (Misc) 558
Business Leaders 519
See also: Sports Team Owners 559
Cartoonists - Comic Strips & Panels 525
Cartoonists & Caricaturists - Editorial 527
Chefs 528
Choreographers
See: Dancers & Choreographers 532
Columnists - Commentary
See: Journalists (Print) 543
Columnists - Lifestyle & Features 529
Comedians 530
Conservationists
See: Organization Leaders 550
Corporate Trainers
See: Motivational Speakers 546
Critics (Art, Books, Film, Music) 531
Cyclists
See: Sports Personalities (Misc) 558
Dancers & Choreographers 532
Directors, Producers, Creators, Writers (Movies & TV) 533
See also: Animators 505
Disc Jockeys
See: Radio Personalities 554
Dramatists
See: Playwrights 553
Economists 535
Fashion Designers 535
Fashion Models 536
Figure Skaters
See: Sports Personalities (Misc) 558
First Ladies
See: US Presidents & Vice Presidents and Their Wives 565
Fitness Personalities 536
Football Players & Coaches 536
Golfers 539
Government & Political Figures (Misc) 540
See also:
Governors 541
Mayors 545
US Presidents & Vice Presidents and Their Wives 565
US Senators & Representatives 565
Governors 541
Gymnasts
See: Sports Personalities (Misc) 558
Hockey Players & Coaches 541
Inventors
See: Scientists & Inventors 556

Journalists (Broadcast)
See:
Radio Personalities....554
Sportscasters....560
Television Anchors & Reporters....560
Journalists (Print)....543
Judges
See: Attorneys & Judges....506
Lawyers
See: Attorneys & Judges....506
Magicians & Illusionists....545
Mayors....545
Models
See: Fashion Models....536
Motivational Speakers....546
Musicians, Singers, Songwriters....547
Olympic Athletes
See: Sports Personalities (Misc)....558
Organization Leaders....550
Photographers....551
Physicians....552
Playwrights....553
Poets....553
Politicians
See: Government & Political Figures (Misc)....540
Producers - Movies & TV
See: Directors, Producers, Creators, Writers (Movies & TV)....533
Race Car Drivers....554
Radio Personalities....554
See also: Sportscasters....560
Religious Leaders....556
Scientists & Inventors....556
Screenwriters
See: Directors, Producers, Creators, Writers (Movies & TV)....533
Singers & Songwriters
See: Musicians, Singers, Songwriters....547
Soccer Players....557
Speakers - Motivational
See: Motivational Speakers....546
Spiritual Leaders
See: Religious Leaders....556
Sports Personalities (Misc)....558
See also:
Baseball Players & Managers....514
Basketball Players & Coaches....516
Football Players & Coaches....536
Golfers....539
Hockey Players & Coaches....541
Race Car Drivers....554

Soccer Players 557
Tennis Players 564
Sports Team Owners....559
Sportscasters....560
See also:
Radio Personalities....554
Television Personalities 563
Swimmers
See: Sports Personalities (Misc) 558
Talk Show Hosts
See:
Radio Personalities....554
Television Personalities 563
Televangelists
See: Religious Leaders....556
Television Anchors & Reporters 560
Television Personalities 563
See also: Sportscasters 560
Tennis Players 564
Track & Field Athletes
See: Sports Personalities (Misc) 558
US Presidents & Vice Presidents and Their Wives 565
US Senators & Representatives 565
US Supreme Court Justices
See: Attorneys & Judges....506
Yoga
See: Fitness Personalities 536

Foreword

Never in recent memory has there been a time in which people are so acutely aware of the very many notable human beings who have distinguished themselves in different fields. Time was when our perception of men and women of fame was limited to the most eminent celebrities from not much beyond the worlds of entertainment, politics, and sports. Doubtless the universally easy access to, and the influence of modern media of every kind—from radio and television to magazine and newspapers, and most recently the Internet—have expanded the breadth of our celebrity recognition. The countless modern news and information outlets have profoundly fostered, heightened, and diffused ever more widespread awareness among us of the names and frequently the faces, and often the contributions and reputations, of outstanding achievers across a far wider span of accomplishment than ever before. Luminaries these days regularly surface in such formerly lesser followed activities as business, medicine, fashion, science, and religion, with renowned individuals from these worlds just as likely to be among today's household names.

The frequency of the need to know about the people who make and shape the news is one of the most recurring information requests in the nation's libraries. Just as it has so many times in the twenty years of its existence, Omnigraphics has sought the counsel and advice of practicing librarians in bringing forth an exemplary and strongly needed new reference source. I can foresee how this important work will therefore swiftly take its place on the ready reference shelves of public, school, and academic libraries. It will no doubt also prove to be a big hit with secondary school and college students who often find themselves casting about for some way to obtain first-hand information about a particular notable figure to fulfill a school assignment or personal interest.

I fully expect *Who: A Directory of Prominent People* to gain in popularity and to grow and expand as a dependable and indispensable element of the core reference collection of libraries of all kinds.

Dr. Paul Wasserman
Professor Emeritus
College of Information Studies
University of Maryland

Introduction

Who: A Directory of Prominent People provides detailed contact information for a wide range of newsworthy individuals, including those prominent in sports, entertainment, business, government, science, journalism, art, and literature. This directory contains more than 7,000 listings, including people who are well known to the general public as well as those whose names may be less familiar but who have distinguished themselves in their particular fields of expertise.

Most of the individuals listed here are living and still active in their fields of endeavor. A selected number of people who have died within the past 50 years are included as well, provided that the deceased person remains of current interest and there is a good source of information about him or her that can be given as the contact, such as a presidential library, hall of fame, or a museum or historical society with a special collection devoted to the individual.

Who's Included

This directory differs significantly from others of its type because its coverage is not limited to one particular area—it's not just a celebrity guide. The people listed in *Who: A Directory of Prominent People* represent a broad spectrum of interests and include:

- Actors, including those who perform in theater, film, and/or television
- Advice columnists
- Artists, photographers, and illustrators
- Attorneys, including those who've become well known through their involvement in high-profile criminal cases as well as those who may be less well known but have been ranked among the best in civil law
- Astronauts and others associated with the Space Program
- Business men and women, including heads of Fortune 500 companies and other corporate leaders and entrepreneurs, many of whom are among the wealthiest and most powerful people in the United States
- Cartoonists, including those who create comic strips and panels as well as editorial cartoonists and caricaturists whose work is seen primarily on op-ed pages of newspapers
- Chefs of famous restaurants, chefs seen regularly on television, and chefs who are noted cookbook authors (including individuals who might fit into all three of those categories)
- Comedians—standup comics who perform mainly in nightclubs or in comedy specials on TV as well as those who are comic actors
- Critics—art, book, film, music, and other media critics
- Dancers and choreographers
- Directors and producers of movies or television programs; creators of TV series; film and cartoon animators
- Economists
- Fashion models and fashion designers
- Fitness personalities whose faces have become familiar through television programs and/or videos
- Government and political leaders—current and former U.S. presidents, vice presidents, senators and congressional representatives, governors, and mayors; presidential advisors and cabinet secretaries and other agency heads; political campaign managers; and others

- Hosts of TV game shows, talent competitions, reality programs, or daytime talk shows
- Judges, including U.S. Supreme Court justices
- Magicians and illusionists
- Motivational speakers, many of whom also produce instructional videos, provide corporate training programs, and/or write best-selling how-to books
- News personalities from TV and radio, including news anchors, reporters, and correspondents; and hosts, moderators, and panelists of political discussion programs
- Organization founders, leaders, and activists who champion a range of causes
- Physicians and medical experts, including those known through syndicated columns featured in newspapers
- Psychics and astrologers
- Radio personalities—disc jockeys, talk show hosts, and other radio entertainers
- Religious and spiritual leaders, including members of the clergy, New Age philosophers, television evangelists, and other inspirational leaders
- Scholars and academics involved in studies at colleges or universities, think tanks, or other private organizations
- Scientists and inventors
- Singers, songwriters, musicians, and music groups representing all types of music—country, pop, rock, alternative, hip-hop, rap, rhythm & blues, Contemporary Christian, gospel, jazz, opera, classical
- Sports personalities—professional baseball, basketball, football, hockey, and soccer players; college and professional coaches and managers; pro golfers and tennis players; Olympic athletes; boxers and bicyclists; race car drivers; sportscasters; and others
- Writers of all types, including children's authors, novelists (all genres), essayists, and nonfiction authors; poets, playwrights, and screenwriters; and journalists, including syndicated and other columnists and noted contributors to political magazines

About the Contact Information

As a general rule, personal addresses and telephone numbers are not given for the people listed in this directory. For the most part, the contact data provided is for a relevant organization with which the person is closely associated, such as a talent agency, sports team, publisher, restaurant, television network, news syndicate, etc. The contact organization is chosen only if it's possible to obtain access to, or information about, the person listed by contacting that organization.

Arrangement of Information in the Directory

Listings in *Who* are organized in a single alphabetical sequence according to the listed person's last name. A **Subject Index** at the back of the directory enables users to identify all of the people who are listed in a particular field —e.g., all of the actors found in the directory, or all of the artists or astronauts, etc. A Subject Headings Table preceding the index outlines all of the subject headings used and includes *See* and *See also* references to help users identify all of the subject categories included in the index. This table also appears in the Contents section of the directory.

Content of Individual Listings

Names. Individuals listed in the directory are presented with the last name first. If a person is more widely known by an informal version of his or her name, then that is often the version given here (for example: Carter, Jimmy rather than Carter, James Earl). If known, titles such as MD or PhD are given with the person's name where applicable.

If a person is known by more than one name (e.g., Paul Reubens/Pee Wee Herman or Evan Hunter/Ed McBain), two listings are included for that individual, one for each name. However, if a person is known to the public only by the name under which he or she performs (e.g., 50 Cent or Ludacris), then just the single listing is included, but the person's real name usually is noted within the descriptive portion of the listing. For example, in the case of 50 Cent, the description identifies him as a singer/songwriter and includes a statement that his real name is Curtis Jackson.

Description. All entries in *Who* contain a brief description that "defines" the person listed and helps the reader to identify him or her. The amount of information given varies according to the nature of the individual or the field in which he or she is prominent. For example, most entertainers have a high level of name recognition, so the word "actor" or "singer" is sufficient to clearly define a particular individual. On the other hand, the head of a Fortune 500 company might be well known in the business world but not to the general public. Consequently, a little more detail, such as the individual's position within a particular company, is given as an aid to identifying that person. Some people have distinguished themselves in more than one area and may warrant a somewhat longer description as well. An example of this would be Hillary Rodham Clinton, who is identified as both a former First Lady of the United States and as a U.S. Senator (Democrat) from the state of New York; or Arnold Schwarzenegger, who is the Governor of California and is also an actor and a former bodybuilder.

Dates of Birth. Most listings in *Who: A Directory of Prominent People* provide the year in which the person was born (if the person is deceased, then both birth and death dates are given). These dates are presented next to the person's name, in parentheses.

Addresses. As noted above, nearly all of the addresses given in this directory are for organizations through which the persons listed may be contacted, or from which information about the person can be obtained. The address portion of each listing begins, then, with the name of the relevant contact organization, followed by its mailing address, city, state, and zip code. ***Although "c/o" usually does not precede the names of the contact organizations in this directory, it is implied in most cases and probably should be used when mailing an inquiry to a contact organization.***

Telephone Numbers. The phone numbers given in *Who: A Directory of Prominent People* usually are the main number of the contact organization and do not provide direct access to the person listed. Area codes are included with all phone numbers.

Other Contact Data. While many listings also provide the contact organization's general fax number, toll-free numbers are rarely included in this directory because they're not likely to be a successful means by which to communicate with or obtain information about the person listed. In those instances where a fax or toll-free number *is* provided, the area code is included with the number.

Websites. If the person listed has an official website, that is the one provided in this directory. If there is no official site but information about the individual can be found at the contact organization's site, then that is the web address listed. The information available at these sites can range from a detailed biography, to a brief sketch focusing mainly on the person's work history or accomplishments, to a descriptive sentence or two followed by a list of the person's writings or similar information.

The editors of *Who: A Directory of Prominent People* make every effort to provide the most useful websites they can find. Fan sites and other third-party sites are not listed.

The http:// that begins most website addresses is ***not*** included with that information here.

Accuracy of Information in *Who: A Directory of Prominent People*

The editors of this directory have made every effort to provide the most accurate and up to date information possible. However, the nature of the data is such that change is almost constant, and it's quite likely that some of the information given here will have changed before the directory is even in print—a basketball player may have been traded, a CEO resigned, or a favorite actor may have changed his or her manager or publicist. These sorts of changes are ongoing and, unfortunately, can't always be foreseen prior to publication.

Our Advisory Board

The editors are grateful to the following board members for their guidance in the development of this publication:

Paula M. Adams, Research and Information Technology Center Library, Nova Southeastern University, Fort Lauderdale, FL

Barbara J. Eichman, Southwest Regional Library, Pembroke Pines, FL

Mary "Mackie" Fritzmeier, North Regional/ BCC Library, Coconut Creek, FL

Susan L. Hill, Southwest Regional Library, Pembroke Pines, FL

Helene Palmer, Broward County Library, Fort Lauderdale, FL

Nuala Reynold, Broward County Library—Remote Operations Center, Lauderdale Lakes, FL

Comments & Suggestions Welcome

Critical comments about this directory are welcome, as are suggestions for additions or improvements. Please send all such comments to:

Editor – *Who: A Directory of Prominent People*
Omnigraphics, Inc.
615 Griswold St., Suite 1400
Detroit, MI 48226
editorial@omnigraphics.com

Who

A Directory of Prominent People

Who: A Directory of Prominent People

3 Doors Down
Alternative band
Agency Group — **Ph:** 212-581-3100
1775 Broadway Suite 515 — **Fax:** 212-581-0015
New York, NY 10019
www.3doorsdown.com

50 Cent (1976-)
Singer/songwriter; real name is Curtis Jackson
William Morris Agency — **Ph:** 212-586-5100
1325 Ave of the Americas — **Fax:** 212-246-3583
New York, NY 10019
www.50cent.com

Aaron, Hank (1934-)
Professional baseball player (retired); all-time major league home run leader
National Baseball Hall of Fame & Museum — **Ph:** 607-547-7200
Fax: 607-547-2044
25 Main St — **TF:** 888-425-5633
Cooperstown, NY 13326
www.baseballhalloffame.org

Abbott, Berenice (1898-1991)
Photographer
Edwynn Houk Gallery — **Ph:** 212-750-7070
745 5th Ave — **Fax:** 212-688-4848
New York, NY 10151

Abdul, Paula (1962-)
Singer and choreographer; judge on American Idol
Jeff Ballard Public Relations — **Ph:** 818-501-0889
4814 N Lemona Ave — **Fax:** 818-501-3310
Sherman Oaks, CA 91403
idolonfox.com

Abdul-Jabbar, Kareem (1947-)
Former professional basketball player; member of the Basketball Hall of Fame
Naismith Memorial Basketball Hall of Fame — **Ph:** 413-781-6500
Fax: 413-781-1939
1000 W Columbus Ave — **TF:** 877-446-6752
Springfield, MA 01105
www.hoophall.com

Abdur-Rahim, Shareef (1976-)
Professional basketball player
Sacramento Kings — **Ph:** 916-928-0000
ARCO Arena — **Fax:** 916-928-0727
1 Sports Pkwy
Sacramento, CA 95834
www.nba.com/kings

Abele, John
Co-Founder and Executive Director of Boston Scientific Corp
Boston Scientific Corp — **Ph:** 508-650-8000
1 Boston Scientific Pl
Natick, MA 01760
www.bostonscientific.com

Abercrombie, Neil (1938-)
US Representative from Hawaii (Democrat)
1502 Longworth Bldg — **Ph:** 202-225-2726
Washington, DC 20515 — **Fax:** 202-225-4580
www.house.gov/abercrombie

Abraham, F Murray (1939-)
Actor (Amadeus)
William Morris Agency — **Ph:** 310-859-4000
1 William Morris Pl — **Fax:** 310-859-4462
Beverly Hills, CA 90212

Abraham, John (1978-)
Professional football player
Atlanta Falcons **Ph:** 770-965-3115
4400 Falcon Pkwy **Fax:** 770-965-3185
Flowery Branch, GA 30542
www.atlantafalcons.com

Abraham, Spencer (1952-)
Former US Secretary of Energy and, prior to that, US Senator from Michigan; currently a distinguished visiting fellow at the Hoover Institution
Hoover Institution on War Revolution & Peace **Ph:** 650-723-1754 **Fax:** 650-723-1687
Stanford University
Stanford, CA 94305
www.hoover.org/bios

Abrams, Dan (1966-)
NBC News chief legal correspondent and host of The Abrams Report on MSNBC
MSNBC TV **Ph:** 201-583-5000
1 MSNBC Plaza
Secaucus, NJ 07094
www.msnbc.msn.com/id/3080263

Abramson, Jerry E (1946-)
Mayor of Louisville
527 W Jefferson St Suite 400 **Ph:** 502-574-2003
Louisville, KY 40202 **Fax:** 502-574-4303
www.loukymetro.org/mayor

Abramson, Larry
Telecommunications correspondent on National Public Radio
National Public Radio **Ph:** 202-513-2000
635 Massachusetts Ave NW **Fax:** 202-513-3329
Washington, DC 20001
www.npr.org

Abreu, Bobby (1974-)
Professional baseball player
Philadelphia Phillies **Ph:** 215-463-6000
Citizens Bank Park
1 Citizens Bank Park Way
Philadelphia, PA 19148
philadelphia.phillies.mlb.com

Abshire, David M (1926-)
President & CEO of the Center for Study of the Presidency; former US Ambassador to NATO; special counselor to President Reagan to coordinate the Iran-Contra investigation
Center for the Study of the Presidency **Ph:** 202-872-9800 **Fax:** 202-872-9811
1020 19th St NW Suite 250
Washington, DC 20036
www.thepresidency.org

Acevedo, Kirk (1974-)
Actor (Oz; Band of Brothers)
Abrams Entertainment **Ph:** 323-935-3333
5225 Wilshire Blvd Suite 515
Los Angeles, CA 90036
www.kirkacevedo.com

Acevedo-Vila, Anibal (1963-)
Governor of Puerto Rico (Popular Democratic Party)
La Fortaleza **Ph:** 787-725-7000
San Juan, PR 00901 **Fax:** 787-725-1472
www.fortaleza.gobierno.pr

Achebe, Chinua (1930-)
Nigerian novelist (Things Fall Apart)
Knopf Publishing/Author Mail **Ph:** 212-782-9000
1745 Broadway
New York, NY 10019
www.randomhouse.com/knopf/classics

Ackerman, F Duane (1942-)
Chairman & CEO of Bellsouth Corp
BellSouth Corp **Ph:** 404-249-2000
1155 Peachtree St NE **Fax:** 404-249-3839
Atlanta, GA 30309
bellsouthcorp.com/team

Ackerman, Gary L (1942-)
US Representative from New York (Democrat)
2243 Rayburn Bldg **Ph:** 202-225-2601
Washington, DC 20515 **Fax:** 202-225-1589
www.house.gov/ackerman

Acocella, Joan, PhD
Dance critic
New Yorker Magazine **Ph:** 212-286-5400
4 Times Sq **Fax:** 212-286-5735
New York, NY 10036

Ada, Alma Flor (1938-)
Cuban American author of books for children; she writes books both in Spanish and in English
Simon & Schuster Books for Young Readers **Ph:** 212-698-7000
1230 Ave of the Americas
New York, NY 10020
www.almaflorada.com

Adair, Charles E (1947-)
A partner in Cordova Ventures, a venture capital management company
Cordova Ventures **Ph:** 678-942-0300
2500 NorthWinds Pkwy **Fax:** 678-942-0301
3 NorthWinds Ctr Suite 475
Alpharetta, GA 30004
www.cordovaventures.com

Adami, Norman
President & CEO, Miller Brewing Co
Miller Brewing Co **Ph:** 414-931-2000
3939 W Highland Blvd **Fax:** 414-931-3735
Milwaukee, WI 53208
www.millerbrewing.com

Adams, Ansel (1902-1984)
Photographer
Ansel Adams Gallery **Ph:** 888-361-7622
PO Box 4185 **Fax:** 650-692-3512
Burlingame, CA 94011
www.anseladams.com

Adams, Bryan (1959-)
Pop/rock singer
International Creative Management **Ph:** 212-556-5600
40 W 57th St 17th Fl
New York, NY 10019
www.bryanadams.com

Adams, Jamie
Executive chef at Veni, Vidi, Vici
41 14th St **Ph:** 404-875-8424
Atlanta, GA 30309
www.buckheadrestaurants.com/venividivici

Adams, Jody
Rialto chef; cookbook author
Rialto at the Charles Hotel **Ph:** 617-661-5050
1 Bennett St **Fax:** 617-234-8093
Cambridge, MA 02138
www.rialto-restaurant.com

Adams, Julian, PhD
President and Chief Scientific Officer of Infinity Pharmaceuticals and an inventor of more than 40 patents; was responsible for the discovery and development of VELCADE, which is used in cancer therapy, and for the disovery of Viramune for HIV
Infinity Pharmaceuticals **Ph:** 617-453-1000
780 Memorial Dr **Fax:** 617-453-1001
Cambridge, MA 02139
www.ipi.com

Adams, KS "Bud" Jr (1923-)
Chairman, president, and CEO of Adams Resource & Energy Inc; founder & owner of the Tennessee Titans football franchise
Adams Resources & Energy Inc **Ph:** 713-881-3600
4400 Post Oak Pkwy Suite 2700 **Fax:** 713-881-3491
Houston, TX 77027
www.titansonline.com

Adams, Noah
NPR senior correspondent; former co-host of All Things Considered
National Public Radio **Ph:** 202-513-2000
635 Massachusetts Ave NW **Fax:** 202-513-3329
Washington, DC 20001
www.npr.org

Adams, Oleta (1962-)
Singer (various genres, including pop and gospel); songwriter
William Morris Agency **Ph:** 310-859-4000
1 William Morris Pl **Fax:** 310-859-4462
Beverly Hills, CA 90212
www.oletaadams.com

Adams, Orny
Comedian
Agency for the Performing Arts **Ph:** 310-888-4200
9200 Sunset Blvd Suite 900 **Fax:** 310-888-4242
Los Angeles, CA 90069
www.ornyadams.com

Adams, Richard (1920-)
Author of Watership Down
HarperCollins Publishers **Ph:** 212-207-7000
c/o Author Mail
10 E 53rd St
New York, NY 10022
www.harpercollins.com

Adams, Scott (1957-)
Creator of the Dilbert comic strip
United Feature Syndicate **Ph:** 212-293-8500
200 Madison Ave
New York, NY 10016
www.unitedfeatures.com

Adams, Thelma
Film critic
Us Weekly **Ph:** 212-484-1616
1290 Ave of the Americas 2nd Fl **Fax:** 212-651-7890
New York, NY 10104

Adams, Yolanda (1962-)
Gospel singer
N-House Management Inc **Ph:** 832-778-6774
4204 Bellaire Blvd Suite 220
West University, TX 77025
www.yolandaadams.net

Adamson, Rebecca (1950-)
Founder of First Nations Development Institute; a national advocate on local tribal issues (she is a Cherokee)
First Nations Development Institute — **Ph:** 540-371-5615 — **Fax:** 540-371-3505
2300 Fall Hill Ave Suite 412
Fredericksburg, VA 22401
www.firstnations.org

Adderley, Terence E (1933-)
Chairman of Kelly Services
Kelly Services Inc — **Ph:** 248-362-4444 — **Fax:** 248-244-5517
999 W Big Beaver
Troy, MI 48084
www.kellyservices.us

Addington, David S
Chief of Staff to Vice President Dick Cheney
1650 Pennsylvania Ave NW — **Ph:** 202-456-9000
Washington, DC 20501

Adelman, Rick (1946-)
Professional basketball coach
Sacramento Kings — **Ph:** 916-928-0000 — **Fax:** 916-928-0727
ARCO Arena
1 Sports Pkwy
Sacramento, CA 95834
www.nba.com/kings

Aderholt, Robert (1965-)
US Representative from Alabama (Republican)
1433 Longworth Bldg — **Ph:** 202-225-4876 — **Fax:** 202-225-5587
Washington, DC 20515
aderholt.house.gov

Adkins, Trace (1962-)
Country singer
William Morris Agency — **Ph:** 615-963-3000 — **Fax:** 615-963-3090
1600 Division St Suite 300
Nashville, TN 37203
traceadkins.com

Adler, Margot
Correspondent in NPR's New York bureau; host of Justice Talking; has been a Wicca priestess for more than 25 years
National Public Radio — **Ph:** 212-878-1430
New York Bureau
801 2nd Ave Suite 701
New York, NY 10017
www.npr.org

Adoff, Arnold (1935-)
Poet and anthologist; writes books for children and for young adults
Scholastic Inc — **Ph:** 212-343-6100
557 Broadway
New York, NY 10012
www.arnoldadoff.com

Adoff, Jaime
Author of books for young people (son of Arnold Adoff and Virginia Hamilton)
Scholastic Inc — **Ph:** 212-343-6100
557 Broadway
New York, NY 10012
www.jaimeadoff.com

Adu, Freddy (1989-)
Major League Soccer phenomenon
DC United — **Ph:** 703-478-6600 — **Fax:** 703-736-9451
14120 Newbrook Dr Suite 170
Chantilly, VA 20151
www.dcunited.com

Adubato, Richie (1937-)
Basketball coach (has coached both WNBA and NBA teams)
Washington Mystics — **Ph:** 202-266-2200 — **Fax:** 202-266-2220
Verizon Center
401 9th St NW Suite 750
Washington, DC 20004
www.wnba.com/mystics

Aebischer, David (1978-)
Professional hockey player
Montreal Canadiens — **Ph:** 514-932-2582 — **Fax:** 514-932-9296
1275 Saint Antoine St W
Montreal, QC H3C5L2
www.canadiens.com

Aerosmith
Rock band (Steven Tyler, Tom Hamilton, Brad Whitford, Joe Perry, Joey Kramer)
Monterey Peninsula Artists/Paradigm — **Ph:** 831-375-4889 — **Fax:** 831-375-2623
509 Hartnell St
Monterey, CA 93940
www.aerosmith.com

Affeldt, Jeremy (1979-)
Professional baseball player
Kansas City Royals — **Ph:** 816-921-8000 — **Fax:** 816-921-5775
Kauffman Stadium
1 Royal Way
Kansas City, MO 64129
kansascity.royals.mlb.com

Affleck, Ben (1972-)
Actor/screenwriter
Endeavor
9601 Wilshire Blvd 3rd Fl
Beverly Hills, CA 90210
Ph: 310-248-2000
Fax: 310-248-2020

Affleck, Casey (1975-)
Actor
Endeavor
9601 Wilshire Blvd 3rd Fl
Beverly Hills, CA 90210
Ph: 310-248-2000
Fax: 310-248-2020

Afkhami, Mahnaz
President and CEO of Women's Learning Partnership; former Iranian Minister of State for Women's Affairs
Women's Learning Partnership for Rights Development & Peace
4343 Montgomery Ave Suite 201
Bethesda, MD 20814
www.learningpartnership.org
Ph: 301-654-2774
Fax: 301-654-2775

Agam, Yaacov (1928-)
Fine artist
Gallery M
2830 E 3rd Ave
Denver, CO 80206
www.gallerym.com
Ph: 303-331-8400

Agar, Jerry
Radio talk show host (current issues)
KMBZ-AM
4935 Belinder Rd
Westwood, KS 66205
www.kmbz.com
Ph: 913-677-8998

Agarwal, Deborah A, PhD
Computer scientist
Lawrence Berkeley National Laboratory
1 Cyclotron Rd
Computational Research Div
MS50B-2239
Berkeley, CA 94720
dsd.lbl.gov/~deba
Ph: 510-486-4000
Fax: 510-486-6363

Agassi, Andre (1969-)
Professional tennis player
Andre Agassi Charitable Foundation
3960 Howard Hughes Pkwy Suite 750
Las Vegas, NV 89109
www.agassiopen.com
Ph: 702-227-5700
Fax: 702-866-2929

Agatston, Arthur S, MD (1947-)
South Beach Diet doctor; cardiologist and an associate professor of medicine at the University of Miami Medical School
4701 Meridian Ave
100 Tower
Miami Beach, FL 33140
www.southbeachdiet.com
Ph: 305-695-1404
Fax: 305-672-8711

Aguilera, Christina (1980-)
Singer
Creative Artists Agency
9830 Wilshire Blvd
Beverly Hills, CA 90212
www.christinaaguilera.com
Ph: 310-288-4545
Fax: 310-288-4800

Ai (1947-)
Poet
WW Norton & Co Inc
500 5th Ave
New York, NY 10110
www.nortonpoets.com
Ph: 212-354-5500
Fax: 212-869-0856

Aiken, Clay (1978-)
Singer
Creative Artists Agency
9830 Wilshire Blvd
Beverly Hills, CA 90212
www.clayaiken.com
Ph: 310-288-4545
Fax: 310-288-4800

Aikman, Troy (1966-)
Former professional football player (quarterback); member of the Pro Football Hall of Fame
SPRINGboard Agency
PO Box 581
Grapevine, TX 76099
www.aikman.com
Ph: 817-410-4702

Ailey, Alvin (1931-1989)
Dancer, choreographer, and founder of the Alvin Ailey American Dance Theater
Alvin Ailey American Dance Theater
Joan Weill Center for Dance
405 W 55th St
New York, NY 10019
www.alvinailey.org
Ph: 212-405-9000
Fax: 212-405-9001

Aislin (1942-)
Nom de plume & signature used by Terry Mosher, editorial cartoonist for the Montreal Gazette; Aislin is his daughter's name
Montreal Gazette
1010 Sainte Catherine St W Suite 200
Montreal, QC H3B5L1
www.aislin.com
Ph: 514-987-2222

Akaka, Daniel K (1924-)
US Senator from Hawaii (Democrat)
141 Hart Bldg — **Ph:** 202-224-6361
Washington, DC 20510 — **Fax:** 202-224-2126
akaka.senate.gov

Akers, David (1974-)
Professional football player
Philadelphia Eagles — **Ph:** 215-463-2500
NovaCare Complex — **Fax:** 215-339-5464
1 NovaCare Way
Philadelphia, PA 19145
www.philadelphiaeagles.com

Akin, Todd (1947-)
US Representative from Missouri (Republican)
117 Cannon Bldg — **Ph:** 202-225-2561
Washington, DC 20515 — **Fax:** 202-225-2563
www.house.gov/akin

Akinnuoye-Agbaje, Adewale (1967-)
Actor
Liebman Entertainment — **Ph:** 212-982-6666
235 Park Ave S 10th Fl — **Fax:** 212-982-2133
New York, NY 10003
abc.go.com/primetime/lost/show.html

Alba, Jessica (1981-)
Actor
Thruline Entertainment — **Ph:** 310-595-1500
9250 Wilshire Blvd — **Fax:** 310-595-1505
Ground Floor
Beverly Hills, CA 90212

Albee, Edward (1928-)
Playwright
William Morris Agency — **Ph:** 310-859-4000
1 William Morris Pl — **Fax:** 310-859-4462
Beverly Hills, CA 90212

Albom, Mitch (1958-)
Author (Tuesdays with Morrie; The Five People You Meet in Heaven); sports columnist for the Detroit Free Press; radio program host
Detroit Free Press — **Ph:** 313-222-6400
600 W Fort St — **Fax:** 313-222-5981
Detroit, MI 48226
www.albom.com

Albrecht, Chris
HBO chairman & CEO; president of HBO Original Programming
Home Box Office — **Ph:** 212-512-1000
1100 Ave of the Americas — **Fax:** 212-512-7020
New York, NY 10036
www.timewarner.com

Albrecht, Mark
President of International Launch Services; former Executive Secretary of the White House National Space Council
International Launch Services — **Ph:** 571-633-7400
1660 International Dr — **Fax:** 571-633-7500
Suite 800
McLean, VA 22102
www.ilslaunch.com

Albright, Chris (1979-)
Professional soccer player
Los Angeles Galaxy — **Ph:** 310-630-2200
Home Depot Center — **Fax:** 310-630-2250
18400 Avalon Blvd Suite 200
Carson, CA 90746
www.lagalaxy.com

Albright, Madeleine, PhD (1937-)
Former US Secretary of State (the first woman in history to hold this position)
Albright Group LLC — **Ph:** 202-842-7222
901 15th St NW Suite 1000
Washington, DC 20005
www.thealbrightgroupllc.com

Alcaraz, Lalo (1964-)
Editorial cartoonist; also creator of the politically themed Latino comic strip La Cucaracha
Universal Press Syndicate — **Ph:** 816-932-6600
4520 Main St
Kansas City, MO 64111
www.lacucaracha.com

Alda, Alan (1936-)
Actor
International Creative Management — **Ph:** 310-550-4000
8942 Wilshire Blvd
Beverly Hills, CA 90211

Alda, Arlene (1933-)
Photographer and children's book author (she illustrates her books using her own photographs); wife of actor Alan Alda
Tricycle Press — **Ph:** 510-559-1600
PO Box 7123
Berkeley, CA 94707
www.arlenealda.com

Aldrich, Lance
Co-creator (with Gary Wise) of the comic panel Real Life Adventures
Universal Press Syndicate — **Ph:** 816-932-6600
4520 Main St
Kansas City, MO 64111
www.amuniversal.com/ups/features

Aldrin, Buzz (1930-)
Former astronaut; now chairman of Starcraft Boosters Inc
Starcraft Boosters Inc **Ph:** 310-278-0384
10380 Wilshire Blvd Suite 703
Los Angeles, CA 90024
www.buzzaldrin.com

Alesio, Steven
Chairman and CEO of D & B
D & B Corp **Ph:** 973-921-5800
103 JFK Pkwy
Short Hills, NJ 07078
www.dnb.com/US/about/index.html

Alessandra, Tony
Motivational speaker (primarily to businesses, on marketing strategies and related issues)
5927 Balfour Ct Suite 103 **Ph:** 760-603-8110
Carlsbad, CA 92008 **Fax:** 760-603-8010
www.alessandra.com

Alexander, Duane F, MD
Director of the National Institute of Child Health & Human Development, National Institutes of Health
National Institute of Child Health & Human Development **Ph:** 301-496-3454 **Fax:** 301-402-1104
31 Center Dr Rm 2A03
Bethesda, MD 20892
www.nichd.nih.gov/about/director.htm

Alexander, Lamar (1940-)
US Senator from Tennessee (Republican)
302 Hart Bldg **Ph:** 202-224-4944
Washington, DC 20510 **Fax:** 202-228-3398
alexander.senate.gov

Alexander, Leslie
Owner of the Houston Rockets NBA team and the Houston Comets WNBA team
Houston Rockets **Ph:** 713-758-7200
Toyota Center **Fax:** 713-758-7396
1510 Polk St
Houston, TX 77002

Alexander, Lloyd (1924-)
Author of fantasy books for children
Dutton Children's Books Publicity **Ph:** 212-366-2000
345 Hudson St
New York, NY 10014
us.penguingroup.com

Alexander, Rodney M (1946-)
US Representative from Louisiana (Republican)
316 Cannon Bldg **Ph:** 202-225-8490
Washington, DC 20515 **Fax:** 202-225-5639
www.house.gov/alexander

Alexander, Shaun (1977-)
Professional football player
Seattle Seahawks **Ph:** 425-827-9777
11220 NE 53rd St **Fax:** 425-827-9008
Kirkland, WA 98033
www.seahawks.com

Alexis, Kim (1960-)
Model
Ford Models **Ph:** 212-219-6500
111 5th Ave **Fax:** 212-966-5028
New York, NY 10003
www.kimalexis.com

Alford, Harry C
President, CEO, and co-founder of the National Black Chamber of Commerce
National Black Chamber of Commerce **Ph:** 202-466-6888 **Fax:** 202-466-4918
1350 Connecticut Ave NW Suite 405
Washington, DC 20036
www.nationalbcc.org

Alfredsson, Daniel (1972-)
Professional hockey player
Ottawa Senators **Ph:** 613-599-0250
Corel Center **Fax:** 613-599-0358
1000 Palladium Dr
Kanata, ON K2V1A5
www.ottawasenators.com

Ali, Muhammad (1942-)
Boxing champion; born Cassius Clay
Muhammad Ali Center **Ph:** 502-584-9254
144 N Sixth St **Fax:** 502-589-4905
Louisville, KY 40202
www.ali.com

Alito, Samuel A Jr (1950-)
US Supreme Court justice
US Supreme Court Bldg **Ph:** 202-479-3000
1 1st St NE
Washington, DC 20543
www.supremecourtus.gov

Alkon, Amy
Writes the syndicated column The Advice Goddess
Creators Syndicate Inc **Ph:** 310-337-7003
5777 W Century Blvd Suite 700 **Fax:** 310-337-7625
Los Angeles, CA 90045
www.advicegoddess.com

Allan, Gary (1967-)
Country music singer
William Morris Agency **Ph:** 615-963-3000
1600 Division St Suite 300 **Fax:** 615-963-3090
Nashville, TN 37203
www.garyallan.com

Allard, Linda
Fashion designer (design director for Ellen Tracy)
Ellen Tracy Inc **Ph:** 212-944-6999
575 7th Ave 10th Fl
New York, NY 10018
www.ellentracy.com

Allard, Wayne (1943-)
US Senator from Colorado (Republican)
521 Dirksen Bldg **Ph:** 202-224-5941
Washington, DC 20510 **Fax:** 202-224-6471
allard.senate.gov

Allen, Debbie (1950-)
Dancer/choreographer; actor
Debbie Allen Dance Academy **Ph:** 310-280-9145
3623 Hayden Ave **Fax:** 310-280-0227
Culver City, CA 90232
www.debbieallendanceacademy.com

Allen, George (1952-)
US Senator from Virginia (Republican)
204 Russell Bldg **Ph:** 202-224-4024
Washington, DC 20510 **Fax:** 202-224-5432
allen.senate.gov

Allen, Joan (1956-)
Actor
International Creative Management **Ph:** 310-550-4000
8942 Wilshire Blvd
Beverly Hills, CA 90211

Allen, Larry (1971-)
Professional football player
San Francisco 49ers **Ph:** 408-562-4949
4949 Centennial Blvd **Fax:** 408-727-4937
Santa Clara, CA 95054
www.sf49ers.com

Allen, Marcus (1960-)
Former professional football player; member of the Pro Football Hall of Fame
Pro Football Hall of Fame **Ph:** 330-456-8207
2121 George Halas Dr NW **Fax:** 330-456-8175
Canton, OH 44708
www.profootballhof.com

Allen, Paul G (1953-)
Investor & philanthropist; co-founded Microsoft with Bill Gates in 1976; is also founder and chairman of Vulcan Inc and owner of the Portland Trail Blazers NBA team and Seattle Seahawks NFL franchise
Vulcan Inc **Ph:** 206-342-2000
505 5th Ave S Suite 900 **Fax:** 206-342-3000
Seattle, WA 98104
www.paulallen.com

Allen, Ray (1975-)
Professional basketball player
Seattle Supersonics **Ph:** 206-281-5800
351 Elliott Ave W Suite 500 **Fax:** 206-281-5839
Seattle, WA 98119
www.nba.com/sonics

Allen, Ron
NBC news correspondent
NBC News **Ph:** 212-664-4249
30 Rockefeller Plaza
New York, NY 10112
www.msnbc.msn.com/id/3689499

Allen, Ted (1965-)
Food & wine connoisseur on Queer Eye for the Straight Guy
William Morris Agency **Ph:** 310-859-4000
1 William Morris Pl **Fax:** 310-859-4462
Beverly Hills, CA 90212
www.bravotv.com

Allen, Thomas H (1945-)
US Representative from Maine (Democrat)
1717 Longworth Bldg **Ph:** 202-225-6116
Washington, DC 20515 **Fax:** 202-225-5590
tomallen.house.gov

Allen, Tim (1953-)
Comedian; actor
Messina Baker Entertainment **Ph:** 323-954-8600
955 Carrillo Dr Suite 100
Los Angeles, CA 90048
www.timallen.com

Allen, Woody (1935-)
Film director/writer/actor; also talented clarinettist
International Creative Management **Ph:** 212-556-5600
40 W 57th St 17th Fl
New York, NY 10019

Allende, Isabel (1942-)
Fiction writer (Daughter of Fortune)
HarperCollins Publishers **Ph:** 212-207-7000
c/o Author Mail
10 E 53rd St
New York, NY 10022
www.isabelallende.com

Alley, Kirstie (1955-)
Actor
William Morris Agency **Ph:** 310-859-4000
1 William Morris Pl **Fax:** 310-859-4462
Beverly Hills, CA 90212
www.sho.com/fatactress

Allison, Herbert M Jr
Chairman, president, and CEO of TIAA-CREF
TIAA-CREF **Ph:** 212-490-9000
750 3rd Ave 26th Fl **Fax:** 212-916-4840
New York, NY 10017
www.tiaa-cref.org

Allred, Gloria (1941-)
Feminist attorney noted for her legal work on women's rights and the rights of minorities
Allred Maroko & Goldberg **Ph:** 323-653-6530
6300 Wilshire Blvd Suite 1500 **Fax:** 323-653-1660
Los Angeles, CA 90048
www.gloriaallred.com

Almond, David (1951-)
British author of books for children & young adults (Skellig; Kit's Wilderness)
Random House Children's Books **Ph:** 212-782-9000
Publicity Dept
1745 Broadway
New York, NY 10019
www.randomhouse.com/kids

Almond, Joan
Photographer
Halsted Gallery **Ph:** 248-895-0204
PO Box 130 **Fax:** 248-332-0227
Bloomfield Hills, MI 48303
www.joanalmond.com

Alomar, Sandy (1966-)
Professional baseball player
Los Angeles Dodgers **Ph:** 323-224-1500
Dodger Stadium **Fax:** 323-224-1269
1000 Elysian Park Ave
Los Angeles, CA 90012
losangeles.dodgers.mlb.com

Alou, Felipe (1935-)
Baseball manager
San Francisco Giants **Ph:** 415-972-2000
AT & T Park
24 Willie Mays Plaza
San Francisco, CA 94107
sanfrancisco.giants.mlb.com

Alou, Moises (1966-)
Professional baseball player
San Francisco Giants **Ph:** 415-972-2000
AT & T Park
24 Willie Mays Plaza
San Francisco, CA 94107
sanfrancisco.giants.mlb.com

Alston, Rafer (1976-)
Professional basketball player
Houston Rockets **Ph:** 713-758-7200
Toyota Center **Fax:** 713-758-7396
1510 Polk St
Houston, TX 77002
www.nba.com/rockets

Alstott, Mike (1973-)
Professional football player
Tampa Bay Buccaneers **Ph:** 813-870-2700
1 Buccaneer Pl **Fax:** 813-878-0813
Tampa, FL 33607
www.buccaneers.com

Alt, Carol (1960-)
Model
Ford Models **Ph:** 212-219-6500
111 5th Ave **Fax:** 212-966-5028
New York, NY 10003
www.carolalt.com

Altabef, Peter
President & CEO of Perot Systems Corp
Perot Systems Corp **Ph:** 972-577-0000
2300 W Plano Pkwy
Plano, TX 75075
www.perotsystems.com/about/leadership.htm

Altea, Rosemary
Spiritual medium & healer
HarperCollins Publishers **Ph:** 212-207-7000
c/o Author Mail
10 E 53rd St
New York, NY 10022
www.rosemaryaltea.com

Alter, Jonathan
Newsweek senior editor; also writes a syndicated column
Washington Post Writers Group — **Ph:** 202-334-6375 **Fax:** 202-334-5669
1150 15th St NW 9th Fl
Washington, DC 20071
www.postwritersgroup.com

Alterman, Eric, PhD
Media columnist/critic, blogger, teacher, and author; a senior fellow at the Center for American Progress
Center for American Progress — **Ph:** 202-682-1611
1333 H St NW 10th Fl
Washington, DC 20005
www.americanprogress.org

Altman, Robert (1925-)
Movie director/writer/producer
International Creative Management — **Ph:** 310-550-4000
8942 Wilshire Blvd
Beverly Hills, CA 90211
www.robertaltman.com

Altman, Sidney, PhD (1939-)
Molecular biologist; 1989 Nobel Prize winner in Chemistry, with Thomas R. Cech, for their discovery of catalytic properties of RNA
Yale University — **Ph:** 203-432-3500 **Fax:** 203-432-5713
Dept of Molecular Cellular & Developmental Biology
KBT402
PO Box 208103
New Haven, CT 06520
www.biology.yale.edu

Altman, Stuart, PhD
Economist; professor of national health policy at the Heller School for Social Policy & Management at Brandeis
Brandeis University — **Ph:** 781-736-3801
Heller Graduate School
MS 035
Box 9110
Waltham, MA 02454
www.heller.brandeis.edu

Alvarado, Linda G (1953-)
Founder, president, and CEO of Alvarado Construction Inc; also a co-owner of the Colorado Rockies baseball club (she is the first minority to have an ownership stake in a major league baseball team)
Alvarado Construction Inc — **Ph:** 303-629-0783
1266 Santa Fe Dr
Denver, CO 80204

Alvarez, Antonio C II
CEO of Interstate Bakeries Corp
Interstate Bakeries Corp — **Ph:** 816-502-4000
12 E Armour Blvd
Kansas City, MO 64111
www.interstatebakeriescorp.com

Alvarez, Cesar L
Attorney; president & CEO of Greenberg Traurig law firm
Greenberg Traurig PA — **Ph:** 305-579-0668 **Fax:** 305-579-0717
1221 Brickell Ave 22nd Fl
Miami, FL 33131
www.gtlaw.com

Alvarez, Julia (1950-)
Novelist (How the García Girls Lost Their Accents)
Susan Bergholz Literary Services — **Ph:** 212-387-0545 **Fax:** 212-387-0546
17 W 10th St Suite 5B
New York, NY 10011
www.alvarezjulia.com

Amanpour, Christiane (1958-)
Chief international news correspondent for CNN
CNN — **Ph:** 404-827-1500
1 CNN Center
Atlanta, GA 30303
www.cnn.com/CNN/anchors_reporters

Amazing Kreskin (1935-)
Mentalist
Rubenstein Assoc — **Ph:** 212-843-8000 **Fax:** 212-843-9200
1345 Ave of the Americas
New York, NY 10105
www.amazingkreskin.com

Ambrose, Lauren (1978-)
Actor
United Talent Agency — **Ph:** 310-273-6700 **Fax:** 310-247-1111
9560 Wilshire Blvd 5th Fl
Beverly Hills, CA 90212
www.hbo.com/sixfeetunder

Amend, Bill (1962-)
Creator of the syndicated comic strip Fox Trot
Universal Press Syndicate — **Ph:** 816-932-6600
4520 Main St
Kansas City, MO 64111
homepage.mac.com/billamend

Amernick, Ann
Executive pastry chef and owner of Palena Restaurant
Palena Restaurant — **Ph:** 202-537-9250
3529 Connecticut Ave NW
Washington, DC 20008
www.palenarestaurant.com

Amis, Martin (1949-)
Author (London Fields novel & screenplay)
Random House Publicity **Ph:** 212-782-9000
1745 Broadway
New York, NY 10019
www.randomhouse.com

Amonte, Tony (1970-)
Professional hockey player
Calgary Flames **Ph:** 403-777-2177
Pengrowth Saddledome **Fax:** 403-777-2195
555 Saddledome Rise SE
Calgary, AB T2G2W1
www.calgaryflames.com

Amos, Daniel
Chairman and CEO of Aflac
Aflac Inc **Ph:** 706-323-3431
1932 Wynnton Rd
Columbus, GA 31999
www.aflac.com

Amos, Tori (1963-)
Singer-songwriter
Creative Artists Agency **Ph:** 310-288-4545
9830 Wilshire Blvd **Fax:** 310-288-4800
Beverly Hills, CA 90212
www.toriamos.com

Amos, Wally (1936-)
Founder of Famous Amos cookies; inspirational speaker
PO Box 897 **Ph:** 808-261-6075
Kailua, HI 96734 **Fax:** 808-263-6019
www.wallyamos.com

Ananiashvili, Nina (1963-)
Principal dancer for American Ballet Theatre
American Ballet Theatre **Ph:** 212-477-3030
890 Broadway **Fax:** 212-254-5938
New York, NY 10003
www.abt.org/dancers

Anderson, Brad (1924-)
Creator of the comic strip Marmaduke
United Feature Syndicate **Ph:** 212-293-8500
200 Madison Ave
New York, NY 10016
www.unitedfeatures.com

Anderson, Bradbury H
Vice Chairman and CEO of Best Buy Inc
Best Buy Co Inc **Ph:** 612-291-1000
7601 Penn Ave S
Richfield, MN 55423
www.bestbuy.com

Anderson, Derek (1974-)
Professional basketball player
Miami Heat **Ph:** 786-777-1000
American Airlines Arena **Fax:** 786-777-1609
601 Biscayne Blvd
Miami, FL 33132
www.nba.com/heat

Anderson, Garrett (1972-)
Professional baseball player
Los Angeles Angels of Anaheim **Ph:** 714-940-2000
Angel Stadium **Fax:** 714-940-2205
2000 Gene Autry Way
Anaheim, CA 92806
losangeles.angels.mlb.com

Anderson, Gillian (1968-)
Actor
Creative Artists Agency **Ph:** 310-288-4545
9830 Wilshire Blvd **Fax:** 310-288-4800
Beverly Hills, CA 90212
www.gilliananderson.ws

Anderson, Kevin J (1962-)
Science fiction/fantasy writer, including Star Wars and X-Files novels
Warner Books **Ph:** 212-522-7200
c/o Author Mail
1271 Ave of the Americas
New York, NY 10020
www.wordfire.com

Anderson, Kirk
Editorial cartoonist
Artizans **Ph:** 877-700-8666
11149 65th St NW **Fax:** 877-642-8666
Edmonton, AB T5W4K2
www.kirktoons.com

Anderson, Louie (1953-)
Comedian
International Creative Management **Ph:** 310-550-4000
8942 Wilshire Blvd
Beverly Hills, CA 90211
www.louieanderson.com

Anderson, Nick
Editorial cartoonist for the Houston Chronicle
Washington Post Writers Group **Ph:** 202-334-6375 **Fax:** 202-334-5669
1150 15th St NW 9th Fl
Washington, DC 20071
www.postwritersgroup.com/anderson.htm

Anderson, Pamela (1967-)
Actor
United Talent Agency **Ph:** 310-273-6700
9560 Wilshire Blvd 5th Fl **Fax:** 310-247-1111
Beverly Hills, CA 90212
www.pamelaanderson.com

Anderson, Paul M (1946-)
Chairman and CEO of Duke Energy Corp
Duke Energy Corp **Ph:** 704-382-7133
526 S Church St **Fax:** 704-382-8375
Charlotte, NC 28202
www.duke-energy.com

Anderson, Paul Thomas (1970-)
Film director/writer/producer (Magnolia, Boogie Nights)
Endeavor **Ph:** 310-248-2000
9601 Wilshire Blvd 3rd Fl **Fax:** 310-248-2020
Beverly Hills, CA 90210

Anderson, Richard Dean (1950-)
Actor
International Creative Management **Ph:** 310-550-4000
8942 Wilshire Blvd
Beverly Hills, CA 90211
rdanderson.com

Anderson, Rocky (1951-)
Mayor of Salt Lake City
451 S State St Suite 306 **Ph:** 801-535-7704
Salt Lake City, UT 84111 **Fax:** 801-535-6331
www.ci.slc.ut.us/mayor

Andreas, G Allen
Chairman, president, and CEO of Archer Daniels Midland Co
Archer Daniels Midland Co **Ph:** 217-424-5200
4666 E Faries Pkwy
Decatur, IL 62526
www.admworld.com/naen/about

Andreessen, Marc L
Co-founder & chairman of Opsware Inc
Opsware Inc **Ph:** 408-744-7300
599 N Mathilda Ave **Fax:** 408-744-7379
Sunnyvale, CA 94085
www.opsware.com

Andretti, John (1963-)
Race car driver
Sports Management Network **Ph:** 248-335-3535
1668 Telegraph Rd Suite 200 **Fax:** 248-335-3352
Bloomfield Hills, MI 48302
andretti.com

Andretti, Marco (1987-)
Race car driver
Sports Management Network **Ph:** 248-335-3535
1668 Telegraph Rd Suite 200 **Fax:** 248-335-3352
Bloomfield Hills, MI 48302
www.marcoandretti.com

Andretti, Mario (1940-)
Legendary race car driver
Sports Management Network **Ph:** 248-335-3535
1668 Telegraph Rd Suite 200 **Fax:** 248-335-3352
Bloomfield Hills, MI 48302
andretti.com

Andretti, Michael (1962-)
Race car driver and racing team owner
Sports Management Network **Ph:** 248-335-3535
1668 Telegraph Rd Suite 200 **Fax:** 248-335-3352
Bloomfield Hills, MI 48302
andretti.com

Andrews, Julie (1935-)
Actor/singer (Broadway and film)
William Morris Agency **Ph:** 212-586-5100
1325 Ave of the Americas **Fax:** 212-246-3583
New York, NY 10019
www.wma.com/julie_andrews/summary

Andrews, Naveen (1969-)
Actor (The English Patient; Lost)
Renee Jennett Management Ltd **Ph:** 310-287-9979
10028 Farragut Dr
Culver City, CA 90232
abc.go.com/primetime/lost/show.html

Andrews, Robert E (1957-)
US Representative from New Jersey (Democrat)
2439 Rayburn Bldg **Ph:** 202-225-6501
Washington, DC 20515 **Fax:** 202-225-6583
www.house.gov/andrews

Andrews, Wyatt (1952-)
National correspondent for CBS News
CBS News **Ph:** 212-975-4114
524 W 57th St
New York, NY 10019
www.cbsnews.com

Angelos, Peter G
Personal injury attorney; also chairman, CEO, and owner of the Baltimore Orioles baseball team
Law Offices of Peter G Angelos **Ph:** 410-649-2000
1 Charles Center **Fax:** 410-659-1780
100 N Charles St **TF:** 800-556-5522
Baltimore, MD 21201
www.lawpga.com

Angelou, Maya (1928-)
Poet
Random House Publicity **Ph:** 212-782-9000
1745 Broadway
New York, NY 10019
www.mayaangelou.com

Angle, Jim
Chief Washington correspondent for FOX News
FOX News Channel **Ph:** 202-824-6300
400 N Capitol St NW Suite 550
Washington, DC 20001
www.foxnews.com/fnctv

Aniston, Jennifer (1969-)
Actor
Creative Artists Agency **Ph:** 310-288-4545
9830 Wilshire Blvd **Fax:** 310-288-4800
Beverly Hills, CA 90212

Ankerberg, John
Televangelist
Ankerberg Theological Research Institute **Ph:** 423-892-7722
PO Box 8977
Chattanooga, TN 37414
www.ankerberg.org

Ann-Margret (1941-)
Actor; dancer
International Creative Management **Ph:** 310-550-4000
8942 Wilshire Blvd
Beverly Hills, CA 90211
www.ann-margret.com

Annan, Kofi (1938-)
Secretary General of the United Nations
Office of the Secretary General **Ph:** 212-963-4475
United Nations
New York, NY 10017
www.un.org

Annenberg, Walter H (1908-2002)
Publisher, broadcaster, diplomat, and philanthropist
Annenberg Foundation **Ph:** 610-341-9066
Radnor Financial Ctr **Fax:** 610-964-8688
150 N Radnor-Chester Rd Suite A200
Radnor, PA 19087
www.whannenberg.org

Ansay, A Manette (1964-)
Author (Vinegar Hill; Midnight Champagne)
HarperCollins Publishers **Ph:** 212-207-7000
c/o Author Mail
10 E 53rd St
New York, NY 10022
www.amanetteansay.com

Anschutz, Philip F (1939-)
Founder of Qwest and chairman of the Anschutz Co, Qwest's largest stockholder and the holding company for Anschutz's portfolio of companies, which include Qwest Communications and the Los Angeles Kings hockey club and LA Lakers basketball team
Anschutz Corp **Ph:** 303-298-1000
555 17th St Suite 2400 **Fax:** 303-298-8881
Denver, CO 80202
www.qwest.com

Ansen, David
Movie critic and senior editor for Newsweek
Newsweek Magazine **Ph:** 212-445-4000
251 W 57th St
New York, NY 10019

Ansin, Edmund Newton
One of America's wealthiest individuals; owns television stations in Miami and Boston
WSVN-TV **Ph:** 305-751-6692
1401 79th St Cswy **Fax:** 305-795-2266
Miami, FL 33141

Anthony, Carmelo (1984-)
Professional basketball player
Denver Nuggets **Ph:** 303-405-1100
Pepsi Center **Fax:** 303-575-1920
1000 Chopper Cir
Denver, CO 80204
www.nba.com/nuggets

Anthony, Marc (1968-)
Singer (Latin/pop)
Creative Artists Agency **Ph:** 310-288-4545
9830 Wilshire Blvd **Fax:** 310-288-4800
Beverly Hills, CA 90212
www.marcanthonyonline.com

Anthony, Piers (1934-)
Science fiction/fantasy author
Random House Publicity **Ph:** 212-782-9000
1745 Broadway
New York, NY 10019
www.hipiers.com

Antropov, Nik (1980-)
Professional hockey player
Toronto Maple Leafs **Ph:** 416-815-5700
Air Canada Center
40 Bay St Suite 400
Toronto, ON M5J2X2
www.mapleleafs.com

Antunes, Joel
Owner/chef of Joel restaurant; was previously the chef at the Ritz-Carlton Buckhead
Joel Restaurant **Ph:** 404-233-3500
3290 Northside Pkwy
Atlanta, GA 30327
www.joelrestaurant.com

Applebaum, Anne (1964-)
Op-ed columnist for the Washington Post; author
Washington Post **Ph:** 202-334-6000
1150 15th St NW
Washington, DC 20071
anneapplebaum.com

Applegate, Jane
Small business journalist; featured columnist on SBTV.com
Small Business Television Network **Ph:** 314-533-7288
20 Allen Ave Suite 344
Saint Louis, MO 63119
www.sbtv.com/about.asp

Applegate, KA (1956-)
Author of books for young readers (Animorphs)
Scholastic Inc **Ph:** 212-343-6100
555 Broadway
New York, NY 10012
www.scholastic.com/kaapplegate

Apted, Michael (1941-)
Film director; president of the Directors Guild of America
Directors Guild of America **Ph:** 310-289-2000
7920 W Sunset Blvd **Fax:** 310-289-2029
Los Angeles, CA 90046
www.dga.org

Aquino, Greg (1978-)
Professional baseball player
Arizona Diamondbacks **Ph:** 602-462-6500
Bank One Ballpark **Fax:** 602-462-6600
401 E Jefferson St
Phoenix, AZ 85004
arizona.diamondbacks.mlb.com

Archer, Dennis W (1942-)
Attorney; former mayor of Detroit and former president of the American Bar Assn
Dickinson Wright PLLC **Ph:** 313-223-3500
500 Woodward Ave Suite 4000 **Fax:** 313-223-3598
Detroit, MI 48226
www.dickinsonwright.com

Archer, Jeffrey (1940-)
British author of legal thrillers; former Member of Parliament and a convicted perjurer
St Martin's Press **Ph:** 212-674-5151
Attn: Publicity Dept
175 5th Ave
New York, NY 10010
www.stmartins.com

Archerd, Army (1922-)
Variety columnist for more than 50 years; now a blogger on variety.com
Variety Magazine **Ph:** 323-857-6600
5700 Wilshire Blvd Suite 120 **Fax:** 323-857-0742
Los Angeles, CA 90036
www.armyarcherd.com

Archibald, Nolan (1944-)
Chairman, president, and CEO of Black & Decker
Black & Decker Corp **Ph:** 410-716-3900
701 E Joppa Rd
Towson, MD 21286
www.bdk.com

Ardagh, Philip
Children's book author (Eddie Dickens Trilogy; Unlikely Exploits series)
Books for Young Readers **Ph:** 212-886-9200
Henry Holt & Co
115 W 18th St
New York, NY 10011
www.philipardagh.com

Arenas, Gilbert (1982-)
Professional basketball player
Washington Wizards **Ph:** 202-661-5000
Verizon Center **Fax:** 202-661-5094
601 F St NW
Washington, DC 20004
www.nba.com/wizards

Ariail, Robert
Editorial cartoonist for The State in Columbia, SC
United Feature Syndicate **Ph:** 212-293-8500
200 Madison Ave
New York, NY 10016
www.unitedfeatures.com

Arison, Micky
Owner, chairman, and CEO of Carnival Cruise Lines; also owns the Miami Heat basketball team
Carnival Corp — **Ph:** 305-599-2600
3655 NW 87th Ave — **Fax:** 305-471-4700
Miami, FL 33178
www.f-cca.com/pages/profiles/micky.html

Arkin, Alan (1934-)
Actor; also a noted children's book author
Endeavor — **Ph:** 310-248-2000
9601 Wilshire Blvd 3rd Fl — **Fax:** 310-248-2020
Beverly Hills, CA 90210

Arma, Tom
Baby photographer
Tom Arma Studio Inc — **Ph:** 520-398-8275
PO Box 3091
Tubac, AZ 85646
www.tomarma.com

Armani, Giorgio (1934-)
Fashion designer
114 5th Ave — **Ph:** 212-366-9720
New York, NY 10011
www.giorgioarmani.com

Armas, Chris (1972-)
Professional soccer player
Chicago Fire — **Ph:** 312-705-7200
980 N Michigan Ave Suite 1998 — **Fax:** 312-705-7393
Chicago, IL 60611
chicago.fire.mlsnet.com

Armey, Dick (1940-)
Former House Majority Leader, US Congress; chairman of FreedomWorks
FreedomWorks — **Ph:** 202-783-3870
1775 Pennsylvania Ave NW 11th Fl — **Fax:** 202-942-7649 — **TF:** 888-564-6273
Washington, DC 20006
www.freedomworks.org

Armstrong, Darrell (1968-)
Professional basketball player
Dallas Mavericks — **Ph:** 214-747-6287
The Pavilion — **Fax:** 214-658-7121
2909 Taylor St
Dallas, TX 75226
www.nba.com/mavericks

Armstrong, Kit (1992-)
Pianist & composer; also gifted in mathematics and science (child prodigy)
International Creative Management — **Ph:** 310-550-4000
8942 Wilshire Blvd
Beverly Hills, CA 90211
www.icmtalent.com/musperf/classical.html

Armstrong, Lance (1971-)
Cyclist; seven-time Tour de France winner
Capital Sports & Entertainment — **Ph:** 512-478-7211 — **Fax:** 512-476-0611
98 San Jacinto Blvd Suite 430
Austin, TX 78701
www.lancearmstrong.com

Armstrong, Robb
Creator of the comic strip Jump Start
United Feature Syndicate — **Ph:** 212-293-8500
200 Madison Ave
New York, NY 10016
www.unitedfeatures.com

Armstrong, Tom
Creator of the comic strip Marvin
King Features Syndicate Inc — **Ph:** 212-455-4000
888 7th Ave 2nd Fl
New York, NY 10019
www.kingfeatures.com

Arnaud, Davy (1980-)
Professional soccer player
Kansas City Wizards — **Ph:** 816-920-9300
2 Arrowhead Dr — **Fax:** 816-920-4774
Kansas City, MO 64129
kc.wizards.mlsnet.com

Arnet, Danielle
Writes the syndicated column on antique collecting, The Smart Collector
Tribune Media Services Inc — **Ph:** 312-222-4444
435 N Michigan Ave Suite 1500
Chicago, IL 60611
tmsfeatures.com/productlist.htm

Arnold, Elizabeth
National political correspondent on NPR
National Public Radio — **Ph:** 202-513-2000
635 Massachusetts Ave NW — **Fax:** 202-513-3329
Washington, DC 20001
www.npr.org

Arnold, Tom (1959-)
Comedian; actor; TV personality
International Creative Management — **Ph:** 310-550-4000
8942 Wilshire Blvd
Beverly Hills, CA 90211

Arnott, Jason (1974-)
Professional hockey player
Dallas Stars — **Ph:** 214-387-5500
2601 Ave of the Stars — **Fax:** 214-387-3599
Frisco, TX 75034
www.dallasstars.com

Arpey, Gerard J (1958-)
Chairman, president, and CEO of AMR Corp, the parent company of American Airlines
AMR Corp **Ph:** 817-963-1234
4333 Amon Carter Blvd **Fax:** 817-967-4162
Fort Worth, TX 76155
www.aa.com

Arpino, Gerald (1928-)
A founding member and artistic director of the Joffrey Ballet of Chicago; was a leading dancer for many years
Joffrey Ballet **Ph:** 312-739-0120
70 E Lake St Suite 1300 **Fax:** 312-739-0119
Chicago, IL 60601
www.joffrey.com

Arquette, Courteney Cox (1964-)
Actor
Brillstein-Grey Entertainment **Ph:** 310-275-6135
9150 Wilshire Blvd Suite 350 **Fax:** 310-275-6180
Beverly Hills, CA 90212

Arquette, David (1971-)
Actor
Gersh Agency **Ph:** 310-274-6611
232 N Canon Dr
Beverly Hills, CA 90210

Arrow, Kenneth J, PhD (1921-)
1972 Nobel Prize winner in Economics (while at MIT); Professor of Economics (Emeritus) at Stanford
Stanford University **Ph:** 650-725-3266
Landau Economics Bldg **Fax:** 650-725-5702
579 Serra Mall
Stanford, CA 94305
www-econ.stanford.edu

Arroyo, Carlos (1979-)
Professional basketball player
Detroit Pistons **Ph:** 248-377-0100
Palace at Auburn Hills **Fax:** 248-377-4262
4 Championship Dr
Auburn Hills, MI 48326
www.nba.com/pistons

Artest, Ron (1979-)
Professional basketball player
Sacramento Kings **Ph:** 916-928-0000
ARCO Arena **Fax:** 916-928-0727
1 Sports Pkwy
Sacramento, CA 95834
www.nba.com/kings

Artner, Alan
Art critic for the Chicago Tribune
Chicago Tribune **Ph:** 312-222-3232
435 N Michigan Ave **Fax:** 312-222-4674
Chicago, IL 60611

Arute, Jack
Sports commentator
ABC Sports **Ph:** 212-456-7777
77 W 66th St
New York, NY 10023

Asay, Chuck (1942-)
Editorial cartoonist for the Colorado Springs Gazette Telegraph
Creators Syndicate Inc **Ph:** 310-337-7003
5777 W Century Blvd Suite 700 **Fax:** 310-337-7625
Los Angeles, CA 90045
www.creators.com

Ash, Mary Kay (1918-2001)
Founder of Mary Kay Cosmetics
Mary Kay Inc **Ph:** 972-687-6300
PO Box 799045 **Fax:** 972-687-1609
Dallas, TX 75379
www.marykay.com

Ashanti (1980-)
Hip-hop/R&B singer
International Creative Management **Ph:** 310-550-4000
8942 Wilshire Blvd
Beverly Hills, CA 90211
www.ashantimusic.net

Ashbery, John (1927-)
Poet
Farrar Straus & Giroux **Ph:** 212-741-6900
19 Union Sq W
New York, NY 10003
www.fsgbooks.com

Ashbrook, Tom
Host of NPR's On Point
National Public Radio **Ph:** 202-513-2000
635 Massachusetts Ave NW **Fax:** 202-513-3329
Washington, DC 20001
www.npr.org

Ashe, Arthur (1943-1993)
First black man to be ranked number one in professional tennis
CMG Worldwide **Ph:** 317-570-5000
10500 Crosspoint Blvd **Fax:** 317-570-5500
Indianapolis, IN 46256
www.cmgww.com/sports/ashe

Asim, Jabari
Syndicated columnist
Washington Post Writers Group
1150 15th St NW 9th Fl
Washington, DC 20071
www.postwritersgroup.com
Ph: 202-334-6375
Fax: 202-334-5669

Askegard, Charles
A principal dancer with the New York City Ballet
New York City Ballet
New York State Theater
20 Lincoln Center
New York, NY 10023
www.nycballet.com/about/dancers.html
Ph: 212-870-5656
Fax: 212-870-7791

Askins, Renee (1959-)
Conservationist and author; founded the Wolf Fund and led the effort to reintroduce wolves into Yellowstone National Park
Vintage/Anchor Publicity
1745 Broadway 20th Fl
New York, NY 10019
www.reneeaskins.com
Ph: 212-572-2420

Asman, David
Host of Forbes on Fox
FOX News Channel
1211 Ave of the Americas
New York, NY 10036
www.foxnews.com/fnctv
Ph: 212-301-3000

Asmus, Barry, PhD
An advocate of free market economics; senior economist with the National Center for Policy Analysis and a noted public speaker
8777 E Via de Ventura Suite 175
Scottsdale, AZ 85258
www.barryasmus.com
Ph: 480-596-3442
Fax: 480-596-4054

Asner, Ed (1929-)
Actor
Innovative Artists
1505 10th St
Santa Monica, CA 90401
Ph: 310-656-0400
Fax: 310-656-0456

Aspell, Tom
NBC news foreign correspondent
NBC News
30 Rockefeller Plaza
New York, NY 10112
www.msnbc.msn.com/id/3689499
Ph: 212-664-4249

Assuras, Thalia
CBS News national correspondent for the Early Show
CBS News
524 W 57th St
New York, NY 10019
www.cbsnews.com
Ph: 212-975-4114

Atkinson, Rick
Investigative reporter for the Washington Post; author of the Pulitzer Prize winner An Army at Dawn: The War in North Africa 1942-1943
Henry Holt and Company
115 W 18th St
New York, NY 10011
www.anarmyatdawn.com
Ph: 212-886-9200
Fax: 212-633-0748

Attanasio, Mark
Chairman & principal owner of the Milwaukee Brewers baseball club
Milwaukee Brewers
Miller Park
1 Brewers Way
Milwaukee, WI 53214
milwaukee.brewers.mlb.com
Ph: 414-902-4400
Fax: 414-902-4515

Attell, Dave (1965-)
Comedian
3 Arts Entertainment
9460 Wilshire Blvd 7th Fl
Beverly Hills, CA 90212
www.daveattell.com
Ph: 310-888-3200
Fax: 310-888-3210

Attenborough, Richard (1923-)
Director, producer, actor
Creative Artists Agency
9830 Wilshire Blvd
Beverly Hills, CA 90212
Ph: 310-288-4545
Fax: 310-288-4800

Attkisson, Sharyl (1961-)
CBS News Capitol Hill correspondent
CBS News
2020 M St NW
Washington, DC 20036
www.cbsnews.com
Ph: 202-457-4481

Atwood, Margaret (1939-)
Author (The Handmaid's Tale)
Random House Publicity
1745 Broadway
New York, NY 10019
www.randomhouse.com
Ph: 212-782-9000

Aubry, Gabriel (1976-)
Male model
Wilhelmina Models Inc
300 Park Ave S 2nd Fl
New York, NY 10010
Ph: 212-473-0700
Fax: 212-473-3223

Auburn, David (1969-)
Playwright (Proof)
Paradigm **Ph:** 212-703-7540
500 5th Ave 37th Fl **Fax:** 212-764-8941
New York, NY 10110

Auchincloss, Louis (1917-)
Author; chronicler of New York's patrician upper class (Her Infinite Variety; East Side Story)
Houghton Mifflin Co **Ph:** 617-351-5000
Trade Div
Adult Editorial
222 Berkeley St 8th Fl
Boston, MA 02116
www.houghtonmifflinbooks.com

Auden, Bruce
Owner/chef of Biga on the Banks
Biga on the Banks **Ph:** 210-225-0722
203 S Saint Mary's Street
San Antonio, TX 78205
www.biga.com

Audioslave
Rock band formed by the merger of former lead singer/guitarist of Soundgarden (Chris Cornell) and band members from Rage Against the Machine
Creative Artists Agency **Ph:** 310-288-4545
9830 Wilshire Blvd **Fax:** 310-288-4800
Beverly Hills, CA 90212
www.audioslave.com

Auel, Jean (1936-)
Author of the Clan of the Cave Bear series (most recent is Shelters of Stone)
Bantam Dell Publicity **Ph:** 212-782-9000
1745 Broadway
New York, NY 10019
www.jeanauel.com

Auerbach, Red (1917-)
Former coach, now President of the Boston Celtics; member of the Basketball Hall of Fame
Naismith Memorial Basketball Hall of Fame **Ph:** 413-781-6500
1000 W Columbus Ave **Fax:** 413-781-1939
Springfield, MA 01105 **TF:** 877-446-6752
www.hoophall.com

Aun, Michael A
Motivational speaker, author, columnist, businessman
2901 E Irlo Bronson Memorial Hwy Suite D **Ph:** 407-870-0030
Kissimmee, FL 34744 **Fax:** 407-870-2088
TF: 800-356-0567
www.aunline.com

Auster, Paul (1947-)
Author (Book of Illusions; Timbuktu)
Henry Holt & Co **Ph:** 212-886-9200
115 W 18th St **Fax:** 212-633-0748
New York, NY 10011
www.paulauster.co.uk

Austin, Denise (1957-)
Fitness personality
Waterfront Media Inc **Ph:** 718-797-0722
45 Main St Suite 800 **Fax:** 718-797-0582
Brooklyn, NY 11201
www.deniseaustin.com

Austin, Emory
Professional speaker on business and leadership
Emory Austin & Co **Ph:** 704-333-9036
1131 S Kings Dr Suite 12 **Fax:** 704-377-0911
Charlotte, NC 28207
www.emoryaustin.com

Auth, Tony
Editorial cartoonist at the Philadelphia Inquirer
Universal Press Syndicate **Ph:** 816-932-6600
4520 Main St
Kansas City, MO 64111
www.amuniversal.com/ups/features

Autry, Alan (1952-)
Mayor of Fresno, CA; actor who played Captain Bubba Skinner on the TV series In The Heat of the Night
2600 Fresno St 2nd Fl **Ph:** 559-621-8000
Fresno, CA 93721 **Fax:** 559-621-7990
www.fresno.gov

Avanzini, John (1936-)
Televangelist; author and teacher on the subject of biblical economics and debt-free living
International Faith Center **Ph:** 817-222-0011
PO Box 917001 **Fax:** 817-222-0100
Fort Worth, TX 76117
www.avanzini.org

Avedon, Richard (1923-2004)
Photographer of celebrities
Richard Avedon Foundation **Ph:** 212-581-5040
25 W 53rd St
New York, NY 10019
www.richardavedon.com

Avent, Sharon Hoffman (1946-)
Owner, president, and CEO of Smead, a manufacturer of office products
Smead Mfg Co **Ph:** 651-437-4111
600 Smead Blvd **Fax:** 651-437-9134
Hastings, MN 55033
www.smead.com

Avery, Sid (1918-2002)
Celebrity photographer; founder and director of MPTV, a photo archives company
Motion Picture & Television Photo Archive **Ph:** 818-997-8292 **Fax:** 818-997-3998
16735 Saticoy St Suite 109
Van Nuys, CA 91406
www.mptv.net

Avi (1937-)
Children's book author (Crispin: The Cross of Lead)
Hyperion Books for Children **Ph:** 212-633-4400
114 5th Ave
New York, NY 10010
www.avi-writer.com

Avila, Jim
Investigative reporter and 20/20 correspondent
20/20 **Ph:** 212-456-7777
147 Columbus Ave
New York, NY 10023
abcnews.go.com/2020

Avondoglio, Kirk
Executive chef/owner of Perona Farms
Perona Farms **Ph:** 973-729-7878
350 Andover-Sparta Rd
Andover, NJ 07821
www.peronafarms.com

Ax, Emanuel (1949-)
Classical pianist
International Creative Management **Ph:** 212-556-5600
40 W 57th St 17th Fl
New York, NY 10019
www.emanuelax.com

Axel, Richard, MD (1946-)
Winner, with Linda B Buck, of the 2004 Nobel Prize in Physiology or Medicine for their discoveries of odorant receptors and the organization of the olfactory system
Axel Laboratory **Ph:** 212-305-6915
Columbia University **Fax:** 212-923-7249
College of Physicians & Surgeons
701 W 168th St 10th Fl
Box 134
New York, NY 10032
cpmcnet.columbia.edu/dept/neurobeh

Axelrod, Jim
Chief White House correspondent for CBS News
CBS News **Ph:** 212-975-4114
524 W 57th St
New York, NY 10019
www.cbsnews.com

Ayckbourn, Alan (1939-)
British playwright (Bedroom Farce); artistic director of the Stephen Joseph Theatre in Scarborough, England, where he premieres the majority of his plays
Grove/Atlantic Inc **Ph:** 212-614-7860
841 Broadway **Fax:** 212-614-7886
New York, NY 10003
www.alanayckbourn.net

Ayers, Chuck (1947-)
Draws the comic strip Crankshaft
King Features Syndicate Inc **Ph:** 212-455-4000
888 7th Ave 2nd Fl
New York, NY 10019
www.kingfeatures.com

Aykroyd, Dan (1952-)
Actor
Creative Artists Agency **Ph:** 310-288-4545
9830 Wilshire Blvd **Fax:** 310-288-4800
Beverly Hills, CA 90212

Azaria, Hank (1964-)
Actor
Endeavor **Ph:** 310-248-2000
9601 Wilshire Blvd 3rd Fl **Fax:** 310-248-2020
Beverly Hills, CA 90210

Azarian, Mary (1940-)
Woodcut artist and Caldecott medalist for Snowflake Bentley
Farmhouse Press **Ph:** 802-454-8087
258 Gray Rd
Plainfield, VT 05667
www.maryazarian.com

Azinger, Paul (1960-)
Professional golfer & broadcaster
PGA Tour **Ph:** 904-285-3700
100 PGA Tour Blvd
Ponte Vedra Beach, FL 32082
www.pgatour.com/players

Azria, Max
Fashion designer
BCBG MaxAzria **Ph:** 323-589-2224
2761 Fruitland Ave
Vernon, CA 90058
www.bcbg.com

Babbitt, Natalie (1932-)
Author of Tuck Everlasting
Books for Young Readers **Ph:** 212-741-6900
Farrar Straus & Giroux
19 Union Sq W
New York, NY 10003
www.fsgkidsbooks.com

Babcock, Mike (1963-)
Hockey coach
Detroit Red Wings **Ph:** 313-396-7544
Joe Louis Arena **Fax:** 313-567-0296
600 Civic Center Dr
Detroit, MI 48226
www.detroitredwings.com

Babin, Rex
Editorial cartoonist
Sacramento Bee **Ph:** 916-321-1911
PO Box 15779
Sacramento, CA 95852
www.sacbee.com/content/opinion

Babrowski, Claire
President, COO, and Acting CEO of RadioShack
RadioShack Corp **Ph:** 817-415-3011
300 RadioShack Cir
Fort Worth, TX 76102
www.radioshackcorporation.com

Baca, Joe (1947-)
US Representative from California (Democrat)
328 Cannon Bldg **Ph:** 202-225-6161
Washington, DC 20515 **Fax:** 202-225-8671
www.house.gov/baca

Bacall, Lauren (1924-)
Actor
William Morris Agency **Ph:** 310-859-4000
1 William Morris Pl **Fax:** 310-859-4462
Beverly Hills, CA 90212

Bach, David
Motivational speaker & author; creator of the FinishRich seminar series
Finish Rich Media **Ph:** 212-965-1972
295 Greenwich St Suite 529
New York, NY 10007
www.finishrich.com

Bacharach, Burt (1928-)
Singer/songwriter/composer
William Morris Agency **Ph:** 310-859-4000
1 William Morris Pl **Fax:** 310-859-4462
Beverly Hills, CA 90212
www.wma.com/burt_bacharach/summary

Bachus, Spencer (1947-)
US Representative from Alabama (Republican)
442 Cannon Bldg **Ph:** 202-225-4921
Washington, DC 20515 **Fax:** 202-225-2082
bachus.house.gov

Bacon, Kevin (1958-)
Actor; singer & songwriter
Endeavor **Ph:** 310-248-2000
9601 Wilshire Blvd 3rd Fl **Fax:** 310-248-2020
Beverly Hills, CA 90210
www.baconbros.com

Baddoo, Terry
Sports anchor on CNN International
CNN **Ph:** 404-827-1500
1 CNN Center
Atlanta, GA 30303
www.cnn.com/CNN/anchors_reporters

Badu, Erykah (1971-)
Singer
William Morris Agency **Ph:** 212-586-5100
1325 Ave of the Americas **Fax:** 212-246-3583
New York, NY 10019
www.erykahbadu.com

Baez, Danys (1977-)
Professional baseball player
Los Angeles Dodgers **Ph:** 323-224-1500
Dodger Stadium **Fax:** 323-224-1269
1000 Elysian Park Ave
Los Angeles, CA 90012
losangeles.dodgers.mlb.com

Bagwell, Jeff (1968-)
Professional baseball player
Houston Astros **Ph:** 713-259-8000
Minute Maid Park **Fax:** 713-259-8981
501 Crawford St
Houston, TX 77002
houston.astros.mlb.com

Baier, Bret
National security correspondent for FOX News
FOX News Channel **Ph:** 212-301-3000
1211 Ave of the Americas
New York, NY 10036
www.foxnews.com/fnctv

Bailey, Champ (1978-)
Professional football player
Denver Broncos **Ph:** 303-649-9000
13655 Broncos Pkwy **Fax:** 303-649-9354
Englewood, CO 80112
www.denverbroncos.com

Baird, Brian (1956-)
US Representative from Washington (Democrat)
1421 Longworth Bldg **Ph:** 202-225-3536
Washington, DC 20515 **Fax:** 202-225-3478
www.house.gov/baird

Baker, Dusty (1949-)
Baseball manager
Chicago Cubs **Ph:** 773-404-2827
Wrigley Field **Fax:** 773-404-4129
1060 W Addison St
Chicago, IL 60613
chicago.cubs.mlb.com

Baker, James A III (1930-)
Attorney; former Secretary of State under George HW Bush and Secretary of the Treasury under Ronald Reagan
Baker Botts LLP **Ph:** 713-229-1234
1 Shell Plaza **Fax:** 713-229-1522
910 Louisiana St
Houston, TX 77002
www.bakerbotts.com

Baker, Mark
Executive chef at the University Club of Chicago (a private club); formerly chef with Four Seasons Hotel Group for 23 years
University Club of Chicago **Ph:** 312-726-2840
76 E Monroe St **Fax:** 312-726-0620
Chicago, IL 60603
www.ucco.com

Baker, Richard (1948-)
US Representative from Louisiana (Republican)
341 Cannon Bldg **Ph:** 202-225-3901
Washington, DC 20515 **Fax:** 202-225-7313
baker.house.gov

Bakshi, Ralph (1938-)
Animator/animation director, producer, writer
Bakshi Productions Inc **Ph:** 626-441-1423
PO Box 2858
Silver City, NM 88061
www.ralphbakshi.com

Balanchine, George (1904-1983)
Regarded as the foremost contemporary choreographer in the world of ballet; founder (with Lincoln Kirstein) of the New York City Ballet
New York City Ballet **Ph:** 212-870-5656
New York State Theater **Fax:** 212-870-7791
20 Lincoln Center
New York, NY 10023
www.nycballet.com/about/staffart.html

Baldacci, David (1960-)
Author (Absolute Power)
Warner Books **Ph:** 212-522-7200
c/o Author Mail
1271 Ave of the Americas
New York, NY 10020
www.david-baldacci.com

Baldacci, John (1955-)
Governor of Maine (Democrat)
1 State House Stn **Ph:** 207-287-3531
Augusta, ME 04333 **Fax:** 207-287-1034
www.maine.gov/governor

Baldrige, Letitia
Writes on etiquette/protocol, manners
Simon & Schuster **Ph:** 212-698-7000
1230 Ave of the Americas
New York, NY 10020
www.letitia.com

Baldwin, Alec (1958-)
Actor
Creative Artists Agency **Ph:** 310-288-4545
9830 Wilshire Blvd **Fax:** 310-288-4800
Beverly Hills, CA 90212
www.alecbaldwin.com

Baldwin, Mike (1954-)
Creator of the syndicated comic panel Cornered
Universal Press Syndicate **Ph:** 816-932-6600
4520 Main St
Kansas City, MO 64111
cornered.co.nr

Baldwin, Tammy (1962-)
US Representative from Wisconsin (Democrat)
1022 Longworth Bldg **Ph:** 202-225-2906
Washington, DC 20515 **Fax:** 202-225-6942
tammybaldwin.house.gov

Bale, Christian (1974-)
Actor
Endeavor **Ph:** 310-248-2000
9601 Wilshire Blvd 3rd Fl **Fax:** 310-248-2020
Beverly Hills, CA 90210

Ball, Alan (1957-)
Writer/creator; producer (American Beauty; Six Feet Under)
United Talent Agency **Ph:** 310-273-6700
9560 Wilshire Blvd 5th Fl **Fax:** 310-247-1111
Beverly Hills, CA 90212
www.hbo.com/sixfeetunder

Ball, Edward (1959-)
Author (Slaves in the Family)
Simon & Schuster **Ph:** 212-698-7000
1230 Ave of the Americas
New York, NY 10020
www.simonsays.com

Ball, Jim
Motivational speaker (goal setting/achievement)
The Goals Institute **Ph:** 703-264-2000
PO Box 3736
Reston, VA 20195
www.goalsinstitute.com

Ballard, Robert, PhD (1942-)
Marine explorer who discovered the Titanic shipwreck
Mystic Aquarium & Institute for Exploration **Ph:** 860-572-5955
55 Coogan Blvd
Mystic, CT 06355
www.mysticaquarium.org

Ballmer, Steven A (1956-)
CEO of Microsoft Corp
Microsoft Corp **Ph:** 425-882-8080
1 Microsoft Way **Fax:** 425-706-7329
Redmond, WA 98052
www.microsoft.com

Ballou, Tyson (1976-)
Male model
IMG Models **Ph:** 212-228-9866
304 Park Ave S 12th Fl **Fax:** 212-979-0276
New York, NY 10010
www.imgmodels.com

Ban Breathnach, Sarah
Author of Simple Abundance
Warner Books **Ph:** 212-522-7200
c/o Author Mail
1271 Ave of the Americas
New York, NY 10020
www.simpleabundance.com

Bana, Eric (1968-)
Actor
William Morris Agency **Ph:** 310-859-4000
1 William Morris Pl **Fax:** 310-859-4462
Beverly Hills, CA 90212

Banderas, Antonio (1960-)
Actor
Creative Artists Agency **Ph:** 310-288-4545
9830 Wilshire Blvd **Fax:** 310-288-4800
Beverly Hills, CA 90212

Banks, Doug
Urban radio host; his show is a mix of music, humor, news, and commentary
ABC Radio Networks **Ph:** 212-456-7777
444 Madison Ave
New York, NY 10022
www.dougbanksshow.com

Banks, Lynne Reid (1929-)
Author of books for children (Indian in the Cupboard) and adults
HarperCollins Children's Books **Ph:** 212-261-6500
1350 Ave of the Americas
New York, NY 10019
www.lynnereidbanks.com

Banks, Russell (1940-)
Author (Affliction; Cloudsplitter; Continental Drift)
HarperCollins Publishers **Ph:** 212-207-7000
c/o Author Mail
10 E 53rd St
New York, NY 10022
www.harpercollins.com

Banks, Tyra (1973-)
Model, actor, television personality, television host
International Creative Management **Ph:** 310-550-4000
8942 Wilshire Blvd
Beverly Hills, CA 90211

Bantock, Nick
Author/illustrator/artist; titles include the Griffin & Sabine trilogy
Chronicle Books **Ph:** 415-537-4200
85 2nd St 6th Fl **Fax:** 415-537-4460
San Francisco, CA 94105
www.nickbantock.com

Banville, John (1945-)
Author (The Sea; The Book of Evidence)
Knopf Publishing/Author Mail **Ph:** 212-782-9000
1745 Broadway
New York, NY 10019
www.randomhouse.com/knopf

Baptiste, Baron
Fitness personality; teaches a program called Baptiste Power Vinyasa Yoga
Baptiste Power Yoga Institute **Ph:** 617-441-2144
PO Box 400279 **Fax:** 617-441-9891
Cambridge, MA 02140
www.baronbaptiste.com

Barbee, Victor
Dancer; is now Associate Artistic Director at American Ballet Theatre
American Ballet Theatre **Ph:** 212-477-3030
890 Broadway **Fax:** 212-254-5938
New York, NY 10003

Barber, Ronde (1975-)
Professional football player (Tiki Barber's twin)
Tampa Bay Buccaneers **Ph:** 813-870-2700
1 Buccaneer Pl **Fax:** 813-878-0813
Tampa, FL 33607
www.buccaneers.com

Barber, Tiki (1975-)
Professional football player (Ronde Barber's twin)
New York Giants **Ph:** 201-935-8111
Giants Stadium **Fax:** 201-939-4134
East Rutherford, NJ 07073
www.giants.com

Barbieri, Gato (1934-)
Jazz musician (tenor saxophone)
Central Entertainment Services Inc **Ph:** 609-522-0173 **Fax:** 609-522-0219
109 W Newark Ave
Wildwood Crest, NJ 08260
www.centralentertainment.com

Barbour, Haley (1947-)
Governor of Mississippi (Republican); former chairman of the Republican National Committee
PO Box 139 **Ph:** 601-359-3150
Jackson, MS 39205 **Fax:** 601-359-3741
www.governorbarbour.com

Barclay, Dolores
Movie/video critic
Associated Press **Ph:** 212-621-1500
450 W 33rd St 14th Fl **Fax:** 212-621-7046
New York, NY 10020

Barenaked Ladies
Alternative rock band
Nettwerk Management **Ph:** 604-654-2929
1650 W 2nd Ave **Fax:** 604-654-1993
Vancouver, BC V6J4R3
www.bnlmusic.com

Barfield, Claude E
Former consultant to the Office of the US Trade Representative; a resident scholar at the American Enterprise Institute
American Enterprise Institute for Public Policy Research **Ph:** 202-862-5800 **Fax:** 202-862-7177
1150 17th St NW Suite 1100
Washington, DC 20036
www.aei.org

Barker, Ben
Executive chef/owner of Magnolia Grill with his wife, Karen, who is the pastry chef
Magnolia Grill **Ph:** 919-286-3609
1002 9th St
Durham, NC 27705
www.uncpress.unc.edu/magnoliagrillcookbook

Barker, Bob (1923-)
Host of the television game show The Price is Right
CBS Studios **Ph:** 323-575-2345
The Price is Right
7800 Beverly Blvd
Los Angeles, CA 90036
www.cbs.com/daytime/price/about/bios

Barker, Clive (1952-)
Writer, artist, filmmaker (Hellraiser)
PO Box 691829 **Ph:** 310-550-4000
West Hollywood, CA 90069
www.clivebarker.com

Barker, Karen
Pastry chef and owner (with her husband, Ben) of the Magnolia Grill
Magnolia Grill **Ph:** 919-286-3609
1002 9th St
Durham, NC 27705
www.uncpress.unc.edu/magnoliagrillcookbook

Barkin, Ellen (1954-)
Actor
Creative Artists Agency **Ph:** 310-288-4545
9830 Wilshire Blvd **Fax:** 310-288-4800
Beverly Hills, CA 90212

Barkley, Charles (1963-)
Former basketball player, now an NBA studio analyst
IMG Inc **Ph:** 216-522-1200
1360 E 9th St Suite 100 **Fax:** 216-522-1145
Cleveland, OH 44114

Barlow, John Perry (1947-)
Retired cattle rancher, writer, and lyricist for the Grateful Dead; co-founder of the Electronic Frontier Foundation
Electronic Frontier Foundation **Ph:** 415-436-9333
454 Shotwell St **Fax:** 415-436-9993
San Francisco, CA 94110
www.eff.org/~barlow

Barlow, Kevan (1979-)
Professional football player
San Francisco 49ers **Ph:** 408-562-4949
4949 Centennial Blvd **Fax:** 408-727-4937
Santa Clara, CA 95054
www.sf49ers.com

Barnaby, Matthew (1973-)
Professional hockey player
Chicago Blackhawks **Ph:** 312-455-7000
United Center **Fax:** 312-455-7041
1901 W Madison St
Chicago, IL 60612
www.chicagoblackhawks.com

Barnes, Brenda C
Chairman & CEO of Sara Lee Corp
Sara Lee Corp **Ph:** 312-726-2600
70 W Madison St **Fax:** 312-558-4995
Chicago, IL 60602
www.saralee.com

Barnes, Clive (1927-)
Theater critic for the New York Post
New York Post **Ph:** 212-930-8000
1211 Ave of the Americas **Fax:** 212-930-8540
New York, NY 10036

Barnes, Fred
Executive editor of The Weekly Standard and co-host of The Beltway Boys on FOX; formerly the senior editor and White House correspondent for New Republic magazine
The Weekly Standard **Ph:** 202-293-4900
1150 17th St NW Suite 505 **Fax:** 202-293-4901
Washington, DC 20036
www.weeklystandard.com

Barnes, Jhane
Fashion and textile designer
119 W 40th St **Ph:** 212-575-2448
New York, NY 10018 **Fax:** 212-575-1332
www.jhanebarnes.com

Barnes, Kay
Mayor of Kansas City, Missouri
414 E 12th St 29th Fl **Ph:** 816-513-3500
Kansas City, MO 64106 **Fax:** 816-513-3518
www.kcmo.org

Barnes, Linda (1949-)
Author of the detective Carlotta Carlyle mystery series
St Martin's Press **Ph:** 212-674-5151
Attn: Publicity Dept
175 5th Ave
New York, NY 10010
www.lindabarnes.com

Barnes, Michael D (1943-)
Former US Congressman; president of the Brady Campaign to Prevent Gun Violence (formerly Handgun Control)
Brady Campaign to Prevent Gun Violence **Ph:** 202-898-0792
1225 'I' St NW Suite 1100
Washington, DC 20005
www.bradycampaign.org

Barnett, Nick (1981-)
Professional football player
Green Bay Packers **Ph:** 920-569-7500
PO Box 10628 **Fax:** 920-569-7201
Green Bay, WI 54307
www.packers.com

Barnett, Tommy
Televangelist and senior pastor of the Phoenix First Assembly of God church
Phoenix First Assembly of God **Ph:** 602-867-7117
13613 N Cave Creek Rd **Fax:** 602-493-9390
Phoenix, AZ 85022
www.phoenixfirst.org

Barney, Tina (1945-)
Photographer
Janet Borden Inc **Ph:** 212-431-0166
560 Broadway Suite 61 **Fax:** 212-274-1679
New York, NY 10012
www.janetbordeninc.com

Barnhart, Jo Anne B
Commissioner of the US Social Security Administration
Social Security Administration **Ph:** 410-965-3120
6401 Security Blvd **Fax:** 410-966-1463
Baltimore, MD 21235
www.ssa.gov/barnhart.htm

Baron, Frederick M
Founder of Baron & Budd PC, one of the largest toxic tort litigation firms in the US
Baron & Budd PC **Ph:** 214-521-3605
3102 Oak Lawn Ave Suite 1100 **Fax:** 214-520-1181
Dallas, TX 75219
www.baronandbudd.com

Barone, Michael
Senior writer for US News & World Report; syndicated columnist
US News & World Report **Ph:** 202-955-2000
1050 Thomas Jefferson St NW **Fax:** 202-955-2685
Washington, DC 20007
www.usnews.com

Barr, Roseanne (1952-)
Comedian; actor
United Talent Agency **Ph:** 310-273-6700
9560 Wilshire Blvd 5th Fl **Fax:** 310-247-1111
Beverly Hills, CA 90212
www.roseanneworld.com

Barreto, Hector V
Administrator of the US Small Business Administration
Small Business Administration **Ph:** 202-205-6605
409 3rd St SW **Fax:** 202-205-6802
Washington, DC 20416
www.sbaonline.sba.gov

Barrett, Andrea (1954-)
Author (Ship Fever)
WW Norton & Co Inc **Ph:** 212-354-5500
500 5th Ave **Fax:** 212-869-0856
New York, NY 10110
www.wwnorton.com

Barrett, Colleen
President of Southwest Airlines
Southwest Airlines Co **Ph:** 214-792-4000
PO Box 36611 **Fax:** 214-792-5015
2702 Love Field Dr
Dallas, TX 74235
www.swamedia.com

Barrett, Craig R, PhD (1939-)
Chairman of the Board of Intel
Intel Corp **Ph:** 408-765-8080
2200 Mission College Blvd
Santa Clara, CA 95052
www.intel.com/pressroom/execbios.htm

Barrett, J Gresham (1961-)
US Representative from South Carolina (Republican)
1523 Longworth Bldg **Ph:** 202-225-5301
Washington, DC 20515 **Fax:** 202-225-3216
www.house.gov/barrett

Barrett, Tom (1953-)
Mayor of Milwaukee
200 E Wells St Suite 201 **Ph:** 414-286-2200
Milwaukee, WI 53202 **Fax:** 414-286-3191
www.milwaukee.gov

Barrett, Wade (1976-)
Professional soccer player
Houston Dynamo **Ph:** 713-276-7500
1415 Louisiana St Suite 3400 **Fax:** 713-276-7580
Houston, TX 77002
houston.mlsnet.com

Barrow, Andrea
A host of In the Mix, a reality series for teens on PBS
In the Mix **Ph:** 212-684-3940
114 E 32nd St Suite 903 **Fax:** 212-684-4015
New York, NY 10016
www.pbs.org/inthemix

Barrow, John (1955-)
US Representative from Georgia (Democrat)
226 Cannon Bldg **Ph:** 202-225-2823
Washington, DC 20515 **Fax:** 202-225-3377
barrow.house.gov

Barrows, Allison
Creator of the comic strip Preteena
Universal Press Syndicate **Ph:** 816-932-6600
4520 Main St
Kansas City, MO 64111
www.amuniversal.com/ups/features

Barry, Brent (1971-)
Professional basketball player
San Antonio Spurs **Ph:** 210-444-5000
1 SBC Center **Fax:** 210-444-5003
San Antonio, TX 78219
www.nba.com/spurs

Barry, Dave (1947-)
Humor columnist (syndicated) and author
Miami Herald **Ph:** 305-350-2111
1 Herald Plaza **Fax:** 305-376-5287
Miami, FL 33132
www.davebarry.com

Barrymore, Drew (1975-)
Actor
Creative Artists Agency **Ph:** 310-288-4545
9830 Wilshire Blvd **Fax:** 310-288-4800
Beverly Hills, CA 90212

Bart, Peter (1932-)
Editor-in-Chief of Variety magazine; also writes a column for the magazine called The Backlot
Variety Magazine **Ph:** 323-857-6600
5700 Wilshire Blvd Suite 120 **Fax:** 323-857-0742
Los Angeles, CA 90036
www.variety.com

Barth, John (1930-)
Author (The Sot-Weed Factor)
Houghton Mifflin Co **Ph:** 617-351-5000
Trade Div
Adult Editorial
222 Berkeley St 8th Fl
Boston, MA 02116
www.houghtonmifflinbooks.com

Barth, John
Chairman, president, and CEO of Johnson Controls
Johnson Controls Inc **Ph:** 414-524-1200
5757 N Green Bay Ave
Milwaukee, WI 53201
www.johnsoncontrols.com

Bartimus, Tad
Writes the syndicated commentary column Among Friends
United Feature Syndicate **Ph:** 212-293-8500
200 Madison Ave
New York, NY 10016
www.unitedfeatures.com

Bartiromo, Maria (1967-)
Host and managing editor of the Wall Street Journal Report and Closing Bell on CNBC
CNBC **Ph:** 201-735-2622
900 Sylvan Ave
Englewood Cliffs, NJ 07632
moneycentral.msn.com/cnbc/tv

Bartlett, Bruce
Syndicated columnist who writes about economic policy; is also a Senior Fellow at the National Center for Policy Analysis and has held several economy-related positions in the US Government
Creators Syndicate Inc **Ph:** 310-337-7003
5777 W Century Blvd Suite 700 **Fax:** 310-337-7625
Los Angeles, CA 90045
www.creators.com/opinion.html

Bartlett, Roscoe G (1926-)
US Representative from Maryland (Republican)
2412 Rayburn Bldg **Ph:** 202-225-2721
Washington, DC 20515 **Fax:** 202-225-2193
www.bartlett.house.gov

Bartley, Dick
Creator, producer, and host of oldies radio programs
ABC Radio Networks **Ph:** 212-456-7777
444 Madison Ave
New York, NY 10022
www.dickbartley.com

Bartlit, Fred H Jr (1932-)
Trial lawyer specializing in product liability defense; represented President Bush in Tallahassee election litigation
Bartlit Beck Herman **Ph:** 312-494-4400
Palenchar & Scott LLP **Fax:** 312-494-4440
Courthouse Pl
54 W Hubbard St Suite 300
Chicago, IL 60610
www.bartlit-beck.com

Barton, Joe (1949-)
US Representative from Texas (Republican)
2109 Rayburn Bldg **Ph:** 202-225-2002
Washington, DC 20515 **Fax:** 202-225-3052
joebarton.house.gov

Baryshnikov, Mikhail (1948-)
Dancer and choreographer; actor
Creative Artists Agency **Ph:** 310-288-4545
9830 Wilshire Blvd **Fax:** 310-288-4800
Beverly Hills, CA 90212
www.baryshnikovdancefoundation.org

Bash, Dana
CNN's Congressional correspondent
CNN **Ph:** 202-898-7900
CNN Bldg
820 1st St NE
Washington, DC 20002
www.cnn.com/CNN/anchors_reporters

Bashir, Martin
Co-anchor on Nightline and a correspondent for 20/20
20/20 **Ph:** 212-456-7777
147 Columbus Ave
New York, NY 10023
abcnews.go.com/2020

Basinger, Kim (1953-)
Actor
Creative Artists Agency **Ph:** 310-288-4545
9830 Wilshire Blvd **Fax:** 310-288-4800
Beverly Hills, CA 90212

Basquiat, Jean-Michel (1960-1988)
Artist
Broad Art Foundation **Ph:** 310-399-4004
3355 Barnard Way
Santa Monica, CA 90405
www.basquiat.net

Bass, Charles F (1952-)
US Representative from New Hampshire (Republican)
2421 Rayburn Bldg **Ph:** 202-225-5206
Washington, DC 20515 **Fax:** 202-225-2946
www.house.gov/bass

Bass, Clarence (1938-)
Fitness personality/bodybuilder
Ripped Enterprises **Ph:** 505-266-5858
528 Chama NE **Fax:** 505-266-9123
PO Box 51236
Albuquerque, NM 87181
www.cbass.com

Basset, Brian (1957-)
Creator of the comic strips Red & Rover and Adam@Home
Washington Post Writers Group
1150 15th St NW 9th Fl
Washington, DC 20071
www.postwritersgroup.com
Ph: 202-334-6375
Fax: 202-334-5669

Bassett, Angela (1958-)
Actor
Creative Artists Agency
9830 Wilshire Blvd
Beverly Hills, CA 90212
Ph: 310-288-4545
Fax: 310-288-4800

Batali, Mario
Host of Molto Mario on the Food Network; owns Babbo Ristorante e Enoteca, a New York Italian restaurant; cookbook author
Babbo Ristorante e Enoteca
110 Waverly Pl
New York, NY 10011
www.babbonyc.com/mariob2.html
Ph: 212-777-0303
Fax: 212-777-3365

Bateman, Jason (1969-)
Actor
International Creative Management
8942 Wilshire Blvd
Beverly Hills, CA 90211
www.fox.com/arresteddev
Ph: 310-550-4000

Bates, Kathy (1948-)
Actor
International Creative Management
8942 Wilshire Blvd
Beverly Hills, CA 90211
Ph: 310-550-4000

Batista, Miguel (1971-)
Professional baseball player
Arizona Diamondbacks
Bank One Ballpark
401 E Jefferson St
Phoenix, AZ 85004
arizona.diamondbacks.mlb.com
Ph: 602-462-6500
Fax: 602-462-6600

Batiuk, Tom (1947-)
Creator of the comic strips Funky Winkerbean and Crankshaft
King Features Syndicate Inc
888 7th Ave 2nd Fl
New York, NY 10019
www.kingfeatures.com
Ph: 212-455-4000

Battey, James F Jr, MD, PhD
Director of the National Institute on Deafness & Other Communication Disorders, National Institutes of Health
National Institute on Deafness & Other Communication Disorders
31 Center Dr Bldg 31 Rm 3C02
Bethesda, MD 20892
www.nidcd.nih.gov
Ph: 301-402-0900
Fax: 301-402-1590

Battista, Bobbie
Former CNN anchor and host; now does media training & communications consulting with Atamira
Atamira Communications
3400 Peachtree Rd Suite 300
Atlanta, GA 30326
www.atamira.com
Ph: 404-262-5223
Fax: 404-814-1779

Battista, Richard
CEO and Acting CFO of Gemstar-TV Guide
Gemstar-TV Guide International Inc
6922 Hollywood Blvd
Hollywood, CA 90028
ir.gemstartvguide.com
Ph: 323-817-4600

Battle, Kathleen (1948-)
Opera singer (soprano)
Columbia Artists Management
1790 Broadway
New York, NY 10019
sonyclassical.com/artists/battle
Ph: 212-841-9500
Fax: 212-841-9744

Baucus, Max (1941-)
US Senator from Montana (Democrat)
511 Hart Bldg
Washington, DC 20510
baucus.senate.gov
Ph: 202-224-2651
Fax: 202-224-4700

Bauer, Gary (1946-)
Former president of the Family Research Council; founder & chairman of the Campaign for Working Families; served as President Reagan's domestic policy advisor and was a Republican presidential candidate in 2000
Campaign for Working Families
2800 Shirlington Rd Suite 930
Arlington, VA 22206
www.cwfpac.com
Ph: 703-671-8800
Fax: 703-671-8899

Bauer, Joan (1951-)
Writer of novels for young adults (Squashed; Thwonk; Rules of the Road; Hope Was Here)
GP Putnam's Sons Books for Young Readers **Ph:** 212-366-2000
Publicity Dept
345 Hudson St
New York, NY 10014
www.joanbauer.com

Bay, Austin
Writes a weekly syndicated column on national issues and foreign affairs
Creators Syndicate Inc **Ph:** 310-337-7003
5777 W Century Blvd Suite 700 **Fax:** 310-337-7625
Los Angeles, CA 90045
www.creators.com/opinion.html

Bay, Jason (1978-)
Professional baseball player
Pittsburgh Pirates **Ph:** 412-323-5000
PNC Park **Fax:** 412-323-5009
115 Federal St
Pittsburgh, PA 15212
pittsburgh.pirates.mlb.com

Bayh, Evan (1955-)
US Senator from Indiana (Democrat)
463 Russell Bldg **Ph:** 202-224-5623
Washington, DC 20510 **Fax:** 202-224-1377
bayh.senate.gov

Bayliss, Rick (1953-)
Chef; his specialty is Mexican cuisine, and he also owns Topolobampo, one of America's only fine-dining Mexican restaurants
Frontera Grill **Ph:** 312-661-1434
445 N Clark St
Chicago, IL 60610
www.fronterakitchens.com

Bazell, Robert
NBC News' chief health and science correspondent
NBC News **Ph:** 212-664-4249
30 Rockefeller Plaza
New York, NY 10112
www.msnbc.msn.com/id/3689499

Bazer, Mark
Writes a syndicated humor column
Tribune Media Services Inc **Ph:** 312-222-4444
435 N Michigan Ave Suite 1500
Chicago, IL 60611
tmsfeatures.com/productlist.htm

Beals, Jennifer (1963-)
Actor
Agency for the Performing Arts **Ph:** 310-273-0744
9200 Sunset Blvd Suite 900 **Fax:** 310-888-4242
Los Angeles, CA 90069

Beamer, Lisa
Author of Let's Roll!, which were her husband Todd's last words before the crash of United Flight 93, the only one of the hijacked planes that didn't reach its target on 9/11
Tyndale House Publishers Inc **Ph:** 630-668-8300
351 Executive Dr **Fax:** 800-684-0247
Carol Stream, IL 60188 **TF:** 800-323-9400
www.tyndale.com

Bean, Melissa L (1962-)
US Representative from Illinois (Democrat)
512 Cannon Bldg **Ph:** 202-225-3711
Washington, DC 20515 **Fax:** 202-225-7830
www.house.gov/bean

Beard, Alana (1982-)
Professional basketball player
Washington Mystics **Ph:** 202-266-2200
Verizon Center **Fax:** 202-266-2220
401 9th St NW Suite 750
Washington, DC 20004
www.wnba.com/mystics

Beard, Peter (1938-)
Photographer; much of his work has focused on Africa and African wildlife, as well as portraiture
Peter Beard Studio **Ph:** 212-757-3320
205 W 57th St Suite 2B **Fax:** 212-757-6275
New York, NY 10019
www.peterbeard.com

Bearden, Romare (1914-1988)
Visual artist whose work focused primarily on Black American life
Romare Bearden Foundation **Ph:** 212-924-0455
305 7th Ave **Fax:** 212-924-7107
New York, NY 10001
www.beardenfoundation.org

Beattie, Ann (1947-)
Short story writer & novelist; writes about the generation of Americans who grew up in the 60s (Perfect Recall)
Simon & Schuster **Ph:** 212-698-7000
1230 Ave of the Americas
New York, NY 10020
www.simonsays.com

Beattie, Bruce
Editorial cartoonist
Daytona Beach News-Journal **Ph:** 386-252-1511
901 6th St
Daytona Beach, FL 32117
www.news-journalonline.com/column/beattie

Beattie, Melody
Author of Codependent No More and other books published by Hazelden
Hazelden Publishing & Educational Services **Ph:** 651-213-4000 **Fax:** 651-213-4590
15251 Pleasant Valley Rd
PO Box 176
Center City, MN 55012
www.melodybeattie.com

Beatty, Warren (1937-)
Actor; producer/director/writer
Creative Artists Agency **Ph:** 310-288-4545
9830 Wilshire Blvd **Fax:** 310-288-4800
Beverly Hills, CA 90212

Beauprez, Bob (1948-)
US Representative from Colorado (Republican)
504 Cannon Bldg **Ph:** 202-225-2645
Washington, DC 20515 **Fax:** 202-225-5278
www.house.gov/beauprez

Becerra, Xavier (1958-)
US Representative from California (Democrat)
1119 Longworth Bldg **Ph:** 202-225-6235
Washington, DC 20515 **Fax:** 202-225-2202
becerra.house.gov

Bechtel, Riley P (1952-)
Chairman and CEO of Bechtel Group
Bechtel Corp **Ph:** 415-768-1234
50 Beale St **Fax:** 415-768-9038
San Francisco, CA 94105
www.bechtel.com

Beck (1970-)
Singer/songwriter Beck Hansen
Creative Artists Agency **Ph:** 310-288-4545
9830 Wilshire Blvd **Fax:** 310-288-4800
Beverly Hills, CA 90212
www.beck.com

Beck, Glenn (1964-)
Syndicated talk radio host; focuses on national issues
Premiere Radio Networks Inc **Ph:** 818-377-5300
15260 Ventura Blvd 5th Fl **Fax:** 818-377-5333
Sherman Oaks, CA 91403
www.glennbeck.com

Beck, Marilyn
Writes the syndicated showbiz column Hollywood Exclusive with Stacy Jenel Smith
Creators Syndicate Inc **Ph:** 310-337-7003
5777 W Century Blvd Suite 700 **Fax:** 310-337-7625
Los Angeles, CA 90045
www.creators.com

Becker, Gary S (1930-)
Winner of the 1992 Nobel Prize in Economics for having extended microeconomic analysis to a wide range of human behavior and interaction, including nonmarket behavior
University of Chicago **Ph:** 773-702-8168
Dept of Economics
1126 E 59th St
Chicago, IL 60637
home.uchicago.edu/~gbecker

Becker, Rob
Comedian; creator of the Broadway hit, Rob Becker's Defending the Caveman
William Morris Agency **Ph:** 212-586-5100
1325 Ave of the Americas **Fax:** 212-246-3583
New York, NY 10019
www.cavemania.com

Beckerman, Kyle (1982-)
Professional soccer player
Colorado Rapids **Ph:** 303-405-1100
Pepsi Center **Fax:** 720-931-2022
1000 Chopper Cir
Denver, CO 80204
www.coloradorapids.com

Becket, Candace
President of Religious Science International
Religious Science International **Ph:** 509-624-6700
901 E 2nd Ave Suite 302 **Fax:** 509-624-9322
Spokane, WA 99202 **TF:** 800-662-1348
www.rsintl.org

Beckett, Josh (1980-)
Professional baseball player
Boston Red Sox **Ph:** 617-267-9440
Fenway Park **Fax:** 617-236-6797
4 Yawkey Way
Boston, MA 02215
boston.redsox.mlb.com

Beckinsale, Kate (1973-)
Actor
Creative Artists Agency **Ph:** 310-288-4545
9830 Wilshire Blvd **Fax:** 310-288-4800
Beverly Hills, CA 90212

Beem, Rich (1970-)
Professional golfer
Gaylord Sports Management **Ph:** 480-483-9500
13845 N Northsight Blvd
Suite 200
Scottsdale, AZ 85260
www.gaylordsports.com

Begala, Paul (1961-)
Political contributor and Democratic strategist on CNN's The Situation Room; previously served as counselor in the Clinton Administration
CNN **Ph:** 202-898-7900
CNN Bldg
820 1st St NE
Washington, DC 20002
www.cnn.com/CNN/anchors_reporters

Begich, Mark
Mayor of Anchorage, Alaska
632 W 6th Ave Suite 840 **Ph:** 907-343-4431
Anchorage, AK 99501 **Fax:** 907-343-4499
www.muni.org/mayor

Behar, Joy (1943-)
Comedian; also co-host of The View
The View **Ph:** 212-456-7777
320 W 66th St
New York, NY 10023
abc.go.com/daytime/theview

Belafonte, Harry (1927-)
Singer (especially noted for his calypso music) and composer; human rights activist
William Morris Agency **Ph:** 310-859-4000
1 William Morris Pl **Fax:** 310-859-4462
Beverly Hills, CA 90212
www.wma.com/harry_belafonte/summary

Belda, Alain JP (1945-)
Chairman and CEO of Alcoa
Alcoa Inc **Ph:** 412-553-4545
201 Isabella St **Fax:** 412-553-4498
Pittsburgh, PA 15212
www.alcoa.com

Belfour, Ed (1965-)
Professional hockey player
Toronto Maple Leafs **Ph:** 416-815-5700
Air Canada Center
40 Bay St Suite 400
Toronto, ON M5J2X2
www.mapleleafs.com

Belichick, Bill (1952-)
Football coach
New England Patriots **Ph:** 508-543-8200
1 Patriots Pl **Fax:** 508-543-0285
Foxboro, MA 02035
www.patriots.com

Belkin, Steven
Founder and chairman of Trans National Group; an owner of Atlanta Spirit LLC, the parent company of the NBA's Atlanta Hawks, NHL's Atlanta Thrashers, and Philips Arena
Atlanta Hawks **Ph:** 404-827-3800
Centennial Tower **Fax:** 404-827-3880
101 Marietta St NW Suite 1900
Atlanta, GA 30303
www.nba.com/hawks

Bell, Buddy (1951-)
Baseball manager
Kansas City Royals **Ph:** 816-921-8000
Kauffman Stadium **Fax:** 816-921-5775
1 Royal Way
Kansas City, MO 64129
kansascity.royals.mlb.com

Bell, Darrin (1975-)
Cartoonist and editorial illustrator; draws the syndicated comic strip Rudy Park (which is written by Theron Heir) and is also the creator of Candorville
United Feature Syndicate **Ph:** 212-293-8500
200 Madison Ave
New York, NY 10016
www.bellcartoons.com

Bell, David (1972-)
Professional baseball player
Philadelphia Phillies **Ph:** 215-463-6000
Citizens Bank Park
1 Citizens Bank Park Way
Philadelphia, PA 19148
philadelphia.phillies.mlb.com

Bell, Griffin B (1918-)
US Attorney General 1977-1979; was senior partner of King & Spalding law firm, now Senior Counsel to the firm
King & Spalding LLP **Ph:** 404-572-4879
191 Peachtree St **Fax:** 404-572-5100
Atlanta, GA 30303
www.kslaw.com

Bell, Joshua (1967-)
Classical violinist
IMG Artists **Ph:** 212-994-3500
Carnegie Hall Tower **Fax:** 212-994-3550
152 W 57th St 5th Fl
New York, NY 10019
www.joshuabell.com

Bell, Raja (1976-)
Professional basketball player
Phoenix Suns **Ph:** 602-379-7900
America West Arena **Fax:** 602-379-7990
201 E Jefferson St
Phoenix, AZ 85004
www.nba.com/suns

Bell-Lundy, Sandra
Creator of the comic strip Between Friends
King Features Syndicate Inc **Ph:** 212-455-4000
888 7th Ave 2nd Fl
New York, NY 10019
www.kingfeatures.com

Bellisario, Donald (1935-)
Television writer and producer
Belisarius Productions **Ph:** 323-468-4500
Sunset Gower Studios
1438 N Gower St Box 25
Bldg 35 4th Fl
Los Angeles, CA 90028

Bello, Maria (1967-)
Actor
Creative Artists Agency **Ph:** 310-288-4545
9830 Wilshire Blvd **Fax:** 310-288-4800
Beverly Hills, CA 90212

Bellow, Saul (1915-2005)
Author (Adventures of Augie March; Herzog; Humboldt's Gift)
Penguin Publicity **Ph:** 212-366-2000
375 Hudson St
New York, NY 10014
us.penguingroup.com

Bellucci, Monica (1964-)
Italian actor
Creative Artists Agency **Ph:** 310-288-4545
9830 Wilshire Blvd **Fax:** 310-288-4800
Beverly Hills, CA 90212

Beltran, Carlos (1977-)
Professional baseball player
New York Mets **Ph:** 718-507-6387
Shea Stadium **Fax:** 718-507-6395
123-01 Roosevelt Ave
Flushing, NY 11368
newyork.mets.mlb.com

Beltre, Adrian (1979-)
Professional baseball player
Seattle Mariners **Ph:** 206-346-4000
Safeco Field **Fax:** 206-346-4050
1250 1st Ave S
Seattle, WA 98134
seattle.mariners.mlb.com

Belushi, Jim (1954-)
Actor
International Creative Management **Ph:** 310-550-4000
8942 Wilshire Blvd
Beverly Hills, CA 90211
www.jimbelushi.ws

Belzer, Richard (1944-)
Comedian; actor
Don Buchwald & Assoc **Ph:** 323-655-7400
6500 Wilshire Blvd Suite 2200 **Fax:** 323-655-7470
Los Angeles, CA 90048
www.nbc.com/Law_&_Order:_Special_Victims_Unit

Ben-Veniste, Richard (1943-)
Attorney; member of the 9/11 Commission and one of the principal prosecutors of the Watergate Special Prosecution Force
Mayer Brown Rowe & Maw LLP **Ph:** 202-263-3333
Fax: 202-263-3300
1909 K St NW
Washington, DC 20006
www.mayerbrownrowe.com

Benchley, Peter (1940-)
Author of Jaws
Random House Publicity **Ph:** 212-782-9000
1745 Broadway
New York, NY 10019
www.peterbenchley.com

Bender, Carole
Writes the comic strip Alley Oop (Jack Bender draws it)
Newspaper Enterprise Assn **Ph:** 212-293-8500
200 Madison Ave
New York, NY 10016
www.unitedfeatures.com

Bender, Jack
Draws the comic strip Alley Oop (Carole Bender writes the strip)
Newspaper Enterprise Assn **Ph:** 212-293-8500
200 Madison Ave
New York, NY 10016
www.unitedfeatures.com

Bender, Lawrence (1958-)
Movie producer (films include Good Will Hunting, Pulp Fiction, Reservoir Dogs); has also produced for television
William Morris Agency **Ph:** 310-859-4000
1 William Morris Pl **Fax:** 310-859-4462
Beverly Hills, CA 90212

Bendixen, Sergio
President of Bendixen and Assoc, a public opinion research, management, and communications consulting firm; a noted expert in Hispanic public opinion research
Bendixen & Assoc **Ph:** 305-529-9916
2800 Ponce de Leon Blvd **Fax:** 305-774-3578
Suite 1111
Coral Gables, FL 33134
www.bendixenandassociates.com

Benedetto, Richard
USA Today's national political correspondent/columnist
USA Today **Ph:** 703-854-3400
7950 Jones Branch Dr
McLean, VA 22108
www.usatoday.com/news/opinion/index.htm

Benedict XVI (1927-)
The Pope; born Joseph Ratzinger
Holy See **Ph:** 202-333-7121
Apostolic Nunciature **Fax:** 202-333-4036
3339 Massachusetts Ave NW
Washington, DC 20008
www.vatican.va

Benhamou, Eric (1956-)
Founder, chairman, and CEO of Benhamou Global Ventures, which invests and plays a role in high technology firms around the world
Benhamou Global Ventures LLC **Ph:** 650-324-3680 **Fax:** 650-473-1347
540 Cowper St Suite 200
Palo Alto, CA 94301
benhamouglobalventures.com

Benigni, Roberto (1952-)
Actor, director, writer
Nancy Seltzer & Assoc **Ph:** 323-938-3562
6220 Del Valle Dr **Fax:** 323-938-0589
Los Angeles, CA 90048

Bening, Annette (1958-)
Actor
Creative Artists Agency **Ph:** 310-288-4545
9830 Wilshire Blvd **Fax:** 310-288-4800
Beverly Hills, CA 90212

Benitez, Armando (1972-)
Professional baseball player
San Francisco Giants **Ph:** 415-972-2000
AT & T Park
24 Willie Mays Plaza
San Francisco, CA 94107
sanfrancisco.giants.mlb.com

Benmosche, Robert H (1945-)
Chairman & CEO of Metropolitan Life Insurance Co
MetLife Inc **Ph:** 212-578-2211
1 Madison Ave **Fax:** 212-578-3320
New York, NY 10010
www.metlife.com

Bennett, Cherie
Writes the syndicated column Hey Cherie! in which she answers questions from teens; has also written books and plays for teens
Copley News Service **Ph:** 619-293-1818
PO Box 120190
San Diego, CA 92112
www.cheriebennett.com

Bennett, Clay (1958-)
Editorial cartoonist for The Christian Science Monitor
Christian Science Monitor **Ph:** 617-450-2000
1 Norway St
Boston, MA 02115
www.claybennett.com

Bennett, Drew (1978-)
Professional football player
Tennessee Titans **Ph:** 615-565-4000
460 Great Circle Rd **Fax:** 615-565-4006
Nashville, TN 37228
www.titansonline.com

Bennett, Olivia (1989-)
Art prodigy known for her floral watercolor paintings
Olivia Bennett Art Gallery **Ph:** 817-442-8866
1228 Prospect St
Southlake, TX 76092
www.oliviabennett.com

Bennett, Robert F (1933-)
US Senator from Utah (Republican)
431 Dirksen Bldg **Ph:** 202-224-5444
Washington, DC 20510 **Fax:** 202-228-1168
bennett.senate.gov

Bennett, Robert S
Trial lawyer; former federal prosecutor
Skadden Arps Slate Meagher & Flom LLP **Ph:** 202-371-7180 **Fax:** 202-661-8205
1440 New York Ave NW
Washington, DC 20005
www.skadden.com

Bennett, Tony (1926-)
Singer
Creative Artists Agency **Ph:** 310-288-4545
9830 Wilshire Blvd **Fax:** 310-288-4800
Beverly Hills, CA 90212

Bennett, William J (1943-)
Author of The Book of Virtues; has served as US Secretary of Education, chairman of the National Endowment for the Humanities, and the first US Drug Czar; is currently the Washington Fellow at the Claremont Institute
Claremont Institute **Ph:** 909-621-6825
937 W Foothill Blvd Suite E **Fax:** 909-626-8724
Claremont, CA 91711
www.claremont.org

Benson, George (1943-)
Jazz guitarist; soul-pop singer
International Creative Management **Ph:** 310-550-4000
8942 Wilshire Blvd
Beverly Hills, CA 90211
www.georgebenson.com

Benson, Kevin E
President & CEO of Laidlaw International, a holding company for providers of school and intercity bus transportation and public transit services
Laidlaw International Inc **Ph:** 905-336-1800
3221 N Service Rd **Fax:** 905-336-3976
Burlington, ON L7R3Y8
www.laidlaw.com

Benson, Steve
Editorial cartoonist for The Arizona Republic
Arizona Republic **Ph:** 602-444-8000
200 E Van Buren St
Phoenix, AZ 85004
www.azcentral.com/arizonarepublic/opinions/benson

Benson, Tom
Owner of the New Orleans Saints football team & Arena Football League's New Orleans VooDoo
New Orleans Saints **Ph:** 504-733-0255
5800 Airline Dr **Fax:** 504-731-1888
Metairie, LA 70003
www.neworleanssaints.com

Bentas, Lily H
Chairman, president, and CEO of Cumberland Farms Inc
Cumberland Farms Inc **Ph:** 781-828-4900
777 Dedham St **Fax:** 781-828-9012
Canton, MA 02021

Bentley, Dierks (1975-)
Country singer
William Morris Agency **Ph:** 615-963-3000
1600 Division St Suite 300 **Fax:** 615-963-3090
Nashville, TN 37203
www.dierks.com

Bentley, Stephen (1954-)
Creator of the comic strip Herb & Jamaal
Creators Syndicate Inc **Ph:** 310-337-7003
5777 W Century Blvd Suite 700 **Fax:** 310-337-7625
Los Angeles, CA 90045
www.creators.com

Bentley, Wes (1978-)
Actor
Creative Artists Agency **Ph:** 310-288-4545
9830 Wilshire Blvd **Fax:** 310-288-4800
Beverly Hills, CA 90212

Berard, Bryan (1977-)
Professional hockey player
Columbus Blue Jackets **Ph:** 614-246-4625
Nationwide Arena **Fax:** 614-246-4007
200 W Nationwide Blvd 3rd Fl
Columbus, OH 43215
www.bluejackets.com

Berendt, John (1966-)
Author (Midnight in the Garden of Good and Evil)
Random House Publicity **Ph:** 212-782-9000
1745 Broadway
New York, NY 10019
www.randomhouse.com

Berenstain, Jan (1923-)
Author (with husband Stan) of the Berenstain Bears books
HarperCollins Children's Books **Ph:** 212-261-6500
1350 Ave of the Americas
New York, NY 10019
www.berenstainbears.com/sjbio.html

Berenstain, Stan (1923-)
Author (with wife Jan) of the Berenstain Bears books
HarperCollins Children's Books **Ph:** 212-261-6500
1350 Ave of the Americas
New York, NY 10019
www.berenstainbears.com/sjbio.html

Berg, A Scott (1949-)
Author of biographies (Lindbergh; Kate Remembered)
Putnam Publicity **Ph:** 212-366-2000
375 Hudson St
New York, NY 10014
us.penguingroup.com

Berg, Elizabeth
Author (Talk Before Sleep; The Art of Mending)
Ballantine Books Publicity **Ph:** 212-782-9000
1745 Broadway
New York, NY 10019
www.randomhouse.com/BB

Berg, Jeffrey
Chairman and CEO of International Creative Management
International Creative Management Inc **Ph:** 310-550-4000 **Fax:** 310-550-4100
8942 Wilshire Blvd
Beverly Hills, CA 90211
www.icmtalent.com

Berg, Jeremy, PhD
Director of the National Institute of General Medical Sciences, National Institutes of Health
National Institute of General Medical Sciences **Ph:** 301-594-2172 **Fax:** 301-402-0156
Natcher Bldg
45 Center Dr
Bethesda, MD 20892
www.nigms.nih.gov

Bergen, Candice (1946-)
Actor
William Morris Agency **Ph:** 310-859-4000
1 William Morris Pl **Fax:** 310-859-4462
Beverly Hills, CA 90212
www.wma.com/candice_bergen/summary

Berger, Dan
Writes a syndicated column on wine
Creators Syndicate Inc **Ph:** 310-337-7003
5777 W Century Blvd Suite 700 **Fax:** 310-337-7625
Los Angeles, CA 90045
www.creators.com

Berger, Thomas (1924-)
Novelist (Little Big Man)
Simon & Schuster **Ph:** 212-698-7000
1230 Ave of the Americas
New York, NY 10020
www.simonsays.com

Bergeron, Tom (1955-)
Television host (America's Funniest Home Videos; Dancing with the Stars)
America's Funniest Home Videos **Ph:** 818-460-7477
PO Box 4333
Hollywood, CA 90078
abc.go.com/primetime/americasfunniest

Bergman, Marilyn (1929-)
Songwriter; president & chairman of the board of the American Society of Composers, Authors, and Publishers (ASCAP)
ASCAP **Ph:** 212-621-6000
1 Lincoln Plaza **Fax:** 212-724-9064
New York, NY 10023 **TF:** 800-952-7227
www.ascap.com

Berkley, Shelley (1951-)
US Representative from Nevada (Democrat)
439 Cannon Bldg **Ph:** 202-225-5965
Washington, DC 20515 **Fax:** 202-225-3119
www.house.gov/berkley

Berkman, Lance (1976-)
Professional baseball player
Houston Astros **Ph:** 713-259-8000
Minute Maid Park **Fax:** 713-259-8981
501 Crawford St
Houston, TX 77002
houston.astros.mlb.com

Berko, Malcolm
Writes Taking Stock, a syndicated column on investment
Copley News Service **Ph:** 619-293-1818
PO Box 120190
San Diego, CA 92112
www.copleynews.com

Berman, Chris (1955-)
Sports broadcaster
ESPN **Ph:** 860-585-2000
ESPN Plaza
935 Middle St
Bristol, CT 06010
sports.espn.go.com/espntv/espnGuide

Berman, Howard L (1941-)
US Representative from California (Democrat)
2221 Rayburn Bldg **Ph:** 202-225-4695
Washington, DC 20515 **Fax:** 202-225-3196
www.house.gov/berman

Berman, John
ABC News correspondent
ABC News **Ph:** 212-456-7777
77 W 66th St
New York, NY 10023
www.abcnews.go.com/WNT

Berman, Steve W
Attorney; has served as lead or co-lead counsel for plaintiffs in securities, consumer, products liability & antitrust, and employment class actions (including litigation on behalf of Enron employees)
Hagens Berman Sobol Shapiro **Ph:** 206-623-7292
1301 5th Ave Suite 2900 **Fax:** 206-623-0594
Seattle, WA 98101
www.hagens-berman.com

Bern, Dorrit J
Chairman, president, and CEO of Charming Shoppes Inc
Charming Shoppes Inc **Ph:** 215-633-4918
450 Winks Ln **Fax:** 215-633-6759
Bensalem, PA 19020
www.charmingshoppes.com

Bernanke, Ben S, PhD (1953-)
Chairman of the Board of Governors of the Federal Reserve System
Federal Reserve System **Ph:** 202-452-3201
20th St & Constitution Ave NW **Fax:** 202-452-3819
Washington, DC 20551
www.federalreserve.gov/bios

Bernauer, David W
Chairman and CEO of Walgreen Co
Walgreen Co **Ph:** 847-940-2500
200 Wilmot Rd
Deerfield, IL 60015
www.walgreens.com/about/press

Berners-Lee, Tim (1955-)
Inventor of the World Wide Web
MIT Computer Science & Artificial Intelligence Laboratory **Ph:** 617-253-5851 **Fax:** 617-258-8682
Stata Center 32 Vassar St
Cambridge, MA 02139
www.w3.org/Consortium

Bernhard, Lisa
Entertainment correspondent for FOX News
FOX News Channel **Ph:** 212-301-3000
1211 Ave of the Americas
New York, NY 10036
www.foxnews.com/fnctv

Bernhard, Ruth (1905-)
Photographer
Peter Fetterman Gallery **Ph:** 310-453-6463
Bergamot Stn
2525 Michigan Ave Suite A7
Santa Monica, CA 90404
www.peterfetterman.com

Bernhard, Sandra (1955-)
Comedian, actor, singer
Fifteen Minutes **Ph:** 323-656-2700
8027 Briar Summit Dr **Fax:** 323-659-5582
Los Angeles, CA 90046
www.sandrabernhard.com

Bernick, David M
National trial counsel in mass tort litigation in the areas of abestos liability, tobacco cost recovery, pharmaceutical products, breast implants, and radiation exposure
Kirkland & Ellis LLP **Ph:** 312-861-2248
200 E Randolph Dr **Fax:** 312-861-2200
Chicago, IL 60601
www.kirkland.com

Bernick, Howard B
President and CEO of Alberto-Culver
Alberto-Culver Co **Ph:** 708-450-3400
2525 Armitage Ave **Fax:** 708-450-3435
Melrose Park, IL 60160
www.alberto.com/investing.cfm

Bernstein, Bonnie (1970-)
Former sports reporter
Velvet Hammer Media **Ph:** 212-975-4321
230 Park Ave Suite 840
New York, NY 10169
www.bonniebernstein.com

Bernstein, Leonard (1918-1990)
Conductor, composer
Leonard Bernstein Office Inc **Ph:** 212-315-0640
121 W 27th St Suite 1104 **Fax:** 212-315-0643
New York, NY 10001
www.leonardbernstein.com

Bernstein, Steven
Founder and Chairman of the Board of SBA Communications, an independent owner and operator of wireless communications infrastructure
SBA Communications Corp **Ph:** 561-995-7670
5900 Broken Sound Pkwy NW **Fax:** 561-998-3448
Boca Raton, FL 33487
sbasite.com

Berriault, Gina (1926-)
Author of stories, novels, and screenplays
Shoemaker & Hoard Publishers **Ph:** 202-364-4464
3704 Macomb St NW Suite 4 **Fax:** 202-364-4484
Washington, DC 20016
www.shoemakerhoard.com

Berry, Chuck (1926-)
Rock 'n' roll singer/guitarist
William Morris Agency **Ph:** 310-859-4000
1 William Morris Pl **Fax:** 310-859-4462
Beverly Hills, CA 90212
www.chuckberry.com

Berry, Halle (1966-)
Actor; former model
William Morris Agency **Ph:** 310-859-4000
1 William Morris Pl **Fax:** 310-859-4462
Beverly Hills, CA 90212
www.hallewood.com

Berry, Marion (1942-)
US Representative from Arkansas (Democrat)
2305 Rayburn Bldg **Ph:** 202-225-4076
Washington, DC 20515 **Fax:** 202-225-5602
www.house.gov/berry

Bertolucci, Bernardo (1940-)
Italian film writer and director
International Creative Management **Ph:** 310-550-4000
8942 Wilshire Blvd
Beverly Hills, CA 90211

Bertuzzi, Todd (1975-)
Professional hockey player
Vancouver Canucks **Ph:** 604-899-4600
General Motors Pl **Fax:** 604-899-4640
800 Griffiths Way
Vancouver, BC V6B6G1
www.canucks.com

Bethel, Sheila Murray, PhD
Motivational speaker, entrepreneur, and author; has also hosted public TV specials on Making a Difference
Bethel Institute **Ph:** 925-935-5258
155 Las Juntas Way
Walnut Creek, CA 94597
www.sheilamurraybethel.com

Bettany, Paul (1971-)
Actor
International Creative Management **Ph:** 310-550-4000
8942 Wilshire Blvd
Beverly Hills, CA 90211

Bettman, Gary (1952-)
NHL commissioner
National Hockey League **Ph:** 212-789-2000
1251 Ave of the Americas 47th Fl **Fax:** 212-789-2020
New York, NY 10020

Betty, Garry
President & CEO of Earthlink
Earthlink Inc **Ph:** 404-815-0770
1375 Peachtree St NE
Atlanta, GA 30309
www.earthlink.net/about

Bewkes, Jeffrey L
President and COO of Time Warner Inc
Time Warner Inc **Ph:** 212-484-8000
75 Rockefeller Plaza **Fax:** 212-489-6183
New York, NY 10019
www.timewarner.com

Beyster, J Robert, PhD
A champion of the employee-ownership philosophy; founded Science Applications International Corp, Beyster Institute for Entrepreneurial Employee Ownership, and the Foundation for Enterprise Development
Science Applications International Corp **Ph:** 858-826-6658 **Fax:** 858-826-6634
10260 Campus Point Dr L-1
San Diego, CA 92121
www.saic.com

Bezos, Jeffrey P (1964-)
Founder, president, CEO, and chairman of the board of Amazon.com
Amazon.com Inc **Ph:** 206-266-1000
PO Box 81226
Seattle, WA 98108
www.amazon.com

Bianculli, David
A TV critic and regular contributor to NPR's Fresh Air
National Public Radio **Ph:** 202-513-2000
635 Massachusetts Ave NW **Fax:** 202-513-3329
Washington, DC 20001
www.npr.org

Bibby, Mike (1978-)
Professional basketball player
Sacramento Kings **Ph:** 916-928-0000
ARCO Arena **Fax:** 916-928-0727
1 Sports Pkwy
Sacramento, CA 95834
www.nba.com/kings

Bickerstaff, Bernie (1944-)
Basketball coach
Charlotte Bobcats **Ph:** 704-357-0252
100 Hive Dr **Fax:** 704-357-0289
Charlotte, NC 28217
www.nba.com/bobcats

Biden, Joseph R Jr (1942-)
US Senator from Delaware (Democrat)
201 Russell Bldg **Ph:** 202-224-5042
Washington, DC 20510 **Fax:** 202-224-0139
biden.senate.gov

Bidwell, William V (1932-)
Owner of the Arizona Cardinals football club
Arizona Cardinals **Ph:** 602-379-0101
8701 S Hardy Dr **Fax:** 602-379-1819
Tempe, AZ 85284
www.azcardinals.com

Biel, Jessica (1982-)
Actor
Creative Artists Agency **Ph:** 310-288-4545
9830 Wilshire Blvd **Fax:** 310-288-4800
Beverly Hills, CA 90212
www.jessebiel.com

Bies, Susan Schmidt, PhD (1947-)
Member of the Board of Governors of the Federal Reserve System
Federal Reserve System **Ph:** 202-452-3217
20th St & Constitution Ave NW **Fax:** 202-452-2611
Washington, DC 20551
www.federalreserve.gov/bios

Biffle, Greg (1969-)
NASCAR driver
Roush Racing **Ph:** 704-720-4100
4600 Roush Pl NW
Concord, NC 28027
www.roushracing.com

Big Boy (1969-)
LA radio show host/dj; has also appeared in several movies, including Charlies Angels 2 and Deuce Bigelow
KPWR-FM **Ph:** 818-953-4200
2600 W Olive Ave 8th Fl **Fax:** 818-848-0961
Burbank, CA 91505
www.power106.fm

Big & Rich
Country music duo Big Kenny and John Rich
William Morris Agency **Ph:** 615-963-3000
1600 Division St Suite 300 **Fax:** 615-963-3090
Nashville, TN 37203
www.bigandrich.com

Big Tigger
Disc jockey (hip hop); also hosts a program on BET
Premiere Radio Networks Inc **Ph:** 818-377-5300
15260 Ventura Blvd 5th Fl **Fax:** 818-377-5333
Sherman Oaks, CA 91403
www.liveintheden.com

Bigar, Jacqueline
Astrologer; writes the syndicated daily horoscope column Jacqueline Bigar's Stars
King Features Syndicate Inc **Ph:** 212-455-4000
888 7th Ave 2nd Fl
New York, NY 10019
www.jacquelinebigar.com

Biggert, Judy (1937-)
US Representative from Illinois (Republican)
1317 Longworth Bldg **Ph:** 202-225-3515
Washington, DC 20515 **Fax:** 202-225-9420
judybiggert.house.gov

Biggio, Craig (1965-)
Professional baseball player
Houston Astros **Ph:** 713-259-8000
Minute Maid Park **Fax:** 713-259-8981
501 Crawford St
Houston, TX 77002
houston.astros.mlb.com

Biletnikoff, Fred (1943-)
Raiders receivers coach; former player (was a wide receiver for the Raiders himself); member Pro Football Hall of Fame
Oakland Raiders **Ph:** 510-864-5000
1220 Harbor Bay Pkwy **Fax:** 510-864-5134
Alameda, CA 94502
www.raiders.com

Bilirakis, Michael (1930-)
US Representative from Florida (Republican)
2408 Rayburn Bldg **Ph:** 202-225-5755
Washington, DC 20515 **Fax:** 202-225-4085
www.house.gov/bilirakis

Billick, Brian (1964-)
Football coach
Baltimore Ravens **Ph:** 410-547-8100
1101 Russell St **Fax:** 410-547-8112
Baltimore, MD 21230
www.baltimoreravens.com

Billingsley, Ray (1957-)
Creator of the comic strip Curtis
King Features Syndicate Inc **Ph:** 212-455-4000
888 7th Ave 2nd Fl
New York, NY 10019
www.kingfeatures.com

Billups, Chauncey (1976-)
Professional basketball player
Detroit Pistons **Ph:** 248-377-0100
Palace at Auburn Hills **Fax:** 248-377-4262
4 Championship Dr
Auburn Hills, MI 48326
www.nba.com/pistons

Binchy, Maeve (1940-)
Author (Circle of Friends)
Penguin Publicity **Ph:** 212-366-2000
375 Hudson St
New York, NY 10014
www.maevebinchy.com

Binder, Alan, PhD
Lunar and planetary scientist and former NASA researcher; founder, director, and president of the board of the Lunar Research Institute
Lunar Research Institute **Ph:** 520-663-5870
9040 S Rita Rd Suite 2360 **Fax:** 520-663-4023
Tucson, AZ 85747
www.lunar-research-institute.org

Bingaman, Jeff (1943-)
US Senator from New Mexico (Democrat)
703 Hart Bldg **Ph:** 202-224-5521
Washington, DC 20510 **Fax:** 202-224-2852
bingaman.senate.gov

Binoche, Juliette (1964-)
Actor
Endeavor **Ph:** 310-248-2000
9601 Wilshire Blvd 3rd Fl **Fax:** 310-248-2020
Beverly Hills, CA 90210

Birch, Glynn
President of MADD (Mothers Against Drunk Driving); the first male and first minority president in the organization's 25-year history
MADD **Ph:** 214-744-6233
511 E John Carpenter Fwy Suite 700 **Fax:** 972-869-2207 **TF:** 800-438-6233
Irving, TX 75062
www.madd.org/aboutus

Bird, Larry (1956-)
Former NBA player and coach; now president of basketball operations for the Indiana Pacers
Naismith Memorial Basketball Hall of Fame **Ph:** 413-781-6500 **Fax:** 413-781-1939
1000 W Columbus Ave **TF:** 877-446-6752
Springfield, MA 01105
www.hoophall.com

Bird, Sue (1980-)
Professional basketball player
Seattle Storm **Ph:** 206-281-5800
351 Elliott Ave W Suite 500
Seattle, WA 98119
www.wnba.com/storm

Birnbach, Lisa
Author (The Official Preppy Handbook)
Andrews McMeel Publishing **Ph:** 800-851-8923
4520 Main St
Kansas City, MO 64111
www.andrewsmcmeel.com

Birnbaum, Sheila L
Considered one of the top female lawyers in the US; represents corporations in complex mass tort and insurance litigation
Skadden Arps Slate Meagher & Flom LLP **Ph:** 212-735-2450
4 Times Sq
New York, NY 10036
www.skadden.com

Bisciotti, Steve (1960-)
Majority owner of the Baltimore Ravens football club
Baltimore Ravens **Ph:** 410-547-8100
1101 Russell St **Fax:** 410-547-8112
Baltimore, MD 21230
www.baltimoreravens.com

Bish, Randy
Editorial cartoonist
Pittsburgh Tribune-Review **Ph:** 412-321-6460
DL Clark Bldg
503 Martindale St 3rd Fl
Pittsburgh, PA 15212
www.pittsburghlive.com/x/tribune-review/opinion

Bishop, J Michael, MD (1936-)
Winner, with Harold E Varmus, of the 1989 Nobel Prize in Physiology or Medicine for the discovery of the cellular origin of retroviral oncogenes; is currently the Chancellor of the University of California San Francisco
University of California at San Francisco **Ph:** 415-476-3211 **Fax:** 415-476-6185
Box 0552
San Francisco, CA 94143
cc.ucsf.edu/people

Bishop, Rob (1951-)
US Representative from Utah (Republican)
124 Cannon Bldg **Ph:** 202-225-0453
Washington, DC 20515 **Fax:** 202-225-5857
www.house.gov/robbishop

Bishop, Sanford D Jr (1947-)
US Representative from Georgia (Democrat)
2429 Rayburn Bldg **Ph:** 202-225-3631
Washington, DC 20515 **Fax:** 202-225-2203
www.house.gov/bishop

Bishop, Timothy (1950-)
US Representative from New York (Democrat)
1133 Longworth Bldg **Ph:** 202-225-3826
Washington, DC 20515 **Fax:** 202-225-3143
wwwc.house.gov/timbishop

Bittermann, Jim
Senior European correspondent for CNN
CNN **Ph:** 404-827-1500
1 CNN Center
Atlanta, GA 30303
www.cnn.com/CNN/anchors_reporters

Bittman, Mark
Chef and food journalist (New York Times food critic); is also a cookbook author
New York Times **Ph:** 212-556-1234
229 W 43rd St
New York, NY 10036

Bjork (1965-)
Icelandic singer & composer; full name is Bjork Gudmundsdottir
William Morris Agency **Ph:** 310-859-4000
1 William Morris Pl **Fax:** 310-859-4462
Beverly Hills, CA 90212
www.bjork.com

Black, Cathleen P
President of Hearst Magazines Div at the Hearst Corp
Hearst Magazines Div **Ph:** 212-649-2000
1345 Ave of the Americas 42nd Fl **Fax:** 212-977-4148
New York, NY 10105
www.hearstcorp.com

Black, Clint (1962-)
Country music singer
William Morris Agency **Ph:** 615-963-3000
1600 Division St Suite 300 **Fax:** 615-963-3090
Nashville, TN 37203
www.clintblack.com

Black, Holly (1971-)
Author of fantasy novels for young adult readers (Tithe: A Modern Faerie Tale; The Spiderwick Chronicles)
Simon & Schuster Books for Young Readers **Ph:** 212-698-7000
1230 Ave of the Americas
New York, NY 10020
www.blackholly.com

Black, Jack (1969-)
Actor; composer/writer (Jack Black & Kyle Gass are the music group Tenacious D)
United Talent Agency **Ph:** 310-273-6700
9560 Wilshire Blvd 5th Fl **Fax:** 310-247-1111
Beverly Hills, CA 90212
www.tenaciousd.com

Black, Linda
Writes a daily horoscope column (syndicated)
Tribune Media Services Inc **Ph:** 312-222-4444
435 N Michigan Ave Suite 1500
Chicago, IL 60061
tmsfeatures.com/productlist.htm

Black, Roy
Nationally known trial lawyer (mainly criminal defense)
Black Srebnick Kornspan & Stumpf **Ph:** 305-371-6421
201 S Biscayne Blvd Suite 1300
Miami, FL 33131
www.royblack.com

Black Eyed Peas
Hip-hop music group
Monterey Peninsula Artists/ Paradigm **Ph:** 831-375-4889 **Fax:** 831-375-2623
509 Hartnell St
Monterey, CA 93940
www.blackeyedpeas.com

Blackburn, Marsha W (1952-)
US Representative from Tennessee (Republican)
509 Cannon Bldg **Ph:** 202-225-2811
Washington, DC 20515 **Fax:** 202-225-3004
www.house.gov/blackburn

Blagojevich, Rod R (1956-)
Governor of Illinois (Democrat)
State Capitol Bldg Rm 207 **Ph:** 217-782-6830
Springfield, IL 62706 **Fax:** 217-782-1853
www.illinois.gov/gov

Blahnik, Manolo (1943-)
Shoe designer
31 W 54th St **Ph:** 212-582-1583
New York, NY 10019

Blaine, David (1973-)
Magician
Creative Artists Agency **Ph:** 310-288-4545
9830 Wilshire Blvd **Fax:** 310-288-4800
Beverly Hills, CA 90212
www.davidblaine.com

Blake, Bud (1918-)
Creator of the comic strip Tiger
King Features Syndicate Inc **Ph:** 212-455-4000
888 7th Ave 2nd Fl
New York, NY 10019
www.kingfeatures.com

Blake, James (1979-)
Professional tennis player
ATP **Ph:** 904-285-8000
201 ATP Blvd **Fax:** 904-285-5966
Ponte Vedra Beach, FL 32082
www.atptennis.com

Blake, Jonathan D
Attorney; heads Covington & Burling's Technology, Media and Communications group and has represented clients in radio & television, cable, satellite, telephone, cellular & wireless generally, the Internet, and various new technologies
Covington & Burling **Ph:** 202-662-5506
1201 Pennsylvania Ave NW **Fax:** 202-662-6291
Washington, DC 20004
www.cov.com

Blake, Rob (1969-)
Professional hockey player
Colorado Avalanche **Ph:** 303-405-1100
Pepsi Center
1000 Chopper Cir
Denver, CO 80204
www.coloradoavalanche.com

Blakemore, Bill
ABC News war correspondent
ABC News **Ph:** 212-456-7777
77 W 66th St
New York, NY 10023
www.abcnews.go.com/WNT

Blakey, Marion C
Administrator of the Federal Aviation Administration
Federal Aviation Administration **Ph:** 202-267-3111
800 Independence Ave SW **Fax:** 202-267-5047
Washington, DC 20591
www.faa.gov/about/key_officials/blakey

Blalock, Hank (1980-)
Professional baseball player
Texas Rangers **Ph:** 817-273-5222
Ameriquest Field in Arlington **Fax:** 817-273-5294
1000 Ballpark Way **TF:** 888-968-3927
Arlington, TX 76011
texas.rangers.mlb.com

Blanchard, Ken
Corporate trainer & motivational speaker; author of The One Minute Manager
Ken Blanchard Cos **Ph:** 760-839-8070
125 State Pl **Fax:** 760-489-8407
Escondido, CA 92029 **TF:** 800-728-6000
www.blanchardtraining.com

Blanchard, Mark
Yoga instructor and a leader of the Power Yoga movement
Progressive Power Yoga Inc **Ph:** 818-676-0053
21800 Burbank Blvd Suite 225
Woodland Hills, CA 91367
progressivepoweryoga.com

Blanchett, Cate (1969-)
Actor
Creative Artists Agency **Ph:** 310-288-4545
9830 Wilshire Blvd **Fax:** 310-288-4800
Beverly Hills, CA 90212

Blanco, Kathleen (1942-)
Governor of Louisiana (Democrat)
PO Box 94004 **Ph:** 225-342-7015
Baton Rouge, LA 70804 **Fax:** 225-342-7099
www.gov.state.la.us

Blank, Arthur M (1952-)
Owner & CEO of the Atlanta Falcons football team; co-founder of Home Depot, from which he retired in 2001
Atlanta Falcons **Ph:** 770-965-3115
4400 Falcon Pkwy **Fax:** 770-965-3185
Flowery Branch, GA 30542
www.atlantafalcons.com

Blankfein, Lloyd (1954-)
President and COO of Goldman Sachs, a global investment banking, securities, and investment management firm
Goldman Sachs Co **Ph:** 212-902-1000
85 Broad St
New York, NY 10004
www.gs.com

Blankley, Tony
Writer of conservative commentary; a member of the McLaughlin Group
Conservative Chronicle **Ph:** 800-888-3039
9 2nd St NW
PO Box 317
Hampton, IA 50441
www.conservativechronicle.com

Blanks, Billy (1956-)
Tae-bo creator and instructor
Billy Blanks Foundation **Ph:** 818-325-0335
14708 Ventura Blvd **Fax:** 818-325-0369
Sherman Oaks, CA 91403
www.billyblanks.com

Blasingame, Jim
Creator and host of the nationally syndicated weekday radio/Internet talk show, The Small Business Advocate
Small Business Network **Ph:** 256-760-8402
503 E Tuscaloosa St **TF:** 888-823-2366
Florence, AL 35630
www.jbsba.com

Bledsoe, Drew (1972-)
Professional football player
Dallas Cowboys **Ph:** 972-556-9900
1 Cowboys Pkwy **Fax:** 972-556-9304
Irving, TX 75063
www.dallascowboys.com

Bleier, Rocky (1946-)
Motivational speaker (businesses, organizations, universities); former NFL player
Rocky Bleier Inc **Ph:** 412-621-2351
711 Filbert St **Fax:** 412-682-2334
Pittsburgh, PA 15232
www.rockybleier.com

Bleier, Scott
Business analyst for FOX News
FOX News Channel **Ph:** 212-301-3000
1211 Ave of the Americas
New York, NY 10036
www.foxnews.com/fnctv

Blige, Mary J (1970-)
R&B singer
Creative Artists Agency **Ph:** 310-288-4545
9830 Wilshire Blvd **Fax:** 310-288-4800
Beverly Hills, CA 90212
www.mjblige.com

Blitz, Marty
Owner/chef of Mise en Place Restaurant
Mise en Place Restaurant **Ph:** 813-254-5373
442 W Kennedy Blvd Suite 110 **Fax:** 813-254-3392
Tampa, FL 33606
www.miseonline.com

Blitzer, Wolf (1948-)
Anchor of CNN'S The Situation Room and host of Late Edition with Wolf Blitzer
CNN **Ph:** 202-898-7900
CNN Bldg
820 1st St NE
Washington, DC 20002
www.cnn.com/CNN/anchors_reporters

Bloch, Henry (1922-)
Co-founder and honorary chairman of the board of H&R Block Inc; he and his brother, Richard, founded the company in 1955
H & R Block Inc **Ph:** 816-753-6900
4400 Main St
Kansas City, MO 64111
hrblock.com/presscenter/about/executiveProfiles.jsp

Block, Francesca Lia
Author of books (including Weetzie Bat) for young readers
HarperCollins Children's Books **Ph:** 212-261-6500
1350 Ave of the Americas
New York, NY 10019
www.francescaliablock.com

Block, Melissa
Host of NPR's All Things Considered
National Public Radio **Ph:** 212-878-1430
New York Bureau
801 2nd Ave Suite 701
New York, NY 10017
www.npr.org

Blonz, Ed
Scientist/nutritionist and writer; does the syndicated newspaper column On Nutrition
United Feature Syndicate **Ph:** 212-293-8500
200 Madison Ave
New York, NY 10016
www.unitedfeatures.com

Bloom, Lisa (1961-)
Attorney; co-anchor for Court TV's daytime trial coverage program Trial Heat
Courtroom Television Network **Ph:** 212-973-2800
600 3rd Ave
New York, NY 10016
www.courttv.com/anchors

Bloom, Orlando (1977-)
Actor
International Creative Management **Ph:** 310-550-4000
8942 Wilshire Blvd
Beverly Hills, CA 90211
www.theofficialorlandobloomsite.com

Bloomberg, Michael R (1942-)
Mayor of New York City; founder of Bloomberg LP
City Hall **Ph:** 212-788-3000
New York, NY 10007 **Fax:** 212-788-2460
www.nyc.gov

Blos, Joan W (1928-)
Author of books for young readers (A Gathering of Days)
Simon & Schuster Books for Young Readers **Ph:** 212-698-7000
1230 Ave of the Americas
New York, NY 10020
www.simonsays.com

Blount, Mark (1975-)
Professional basketball player
Minnesota Timberwolves **Ph:** 612-673-1600
Target Center **Fax:** 612-673-1699
600 1st Ave N
Minneapolis, MN 55403
www.nba.com/timberwolves

Blum, Deborah (1954-)
Journalism professor and science writer (The Monkey Wars)
University of Wisconsin **Ph:** 608-263-3690
5154 Vilas Communication Hall
821 University Ave
Madison, WI 53706
www.journalism.wisc.edu

Blume, Judy (1938-)
Author best known for her books for young readers (Are You There God? It's Me, Margaret; Superfudge; Tales of a Fourth Grade Nothing)
Dutton Children's Books Publicity **Ph:** 212-366-2000
345 Hudson St
New York, NY 10014
www.judyblume.com

Blumenauer, Earl (1948-)
US Representative from Oregon (Democrat)
2446 Rayburn Bldg **Ph:** 202-225-4811
Washington, DC 20515 **Fax:** 202-225-8941
blumenauer.house.gov

Blumer, Bob
Food personality who uses the nom de plume The Surreal Gourmet
Food Network **Ph:** 212-398-8836
75 9th Ave **Fax:** 212-736-7716
New York, NY 10011
www.surrealgourmet.com

Blumner, Robyn (1961-)
Syndicated columnist with the St Petersburg Times; a civil liberties expert who writes about individual freedom as it relates to laws, current events, and social trends
Tribune Media Services Inc **Ph:** 312-222-4444
435 N Michigan Ave Suite 1500
Chicago, IL 60611
tmsfeatures.com/productlist.htm

Blunt, James (1974-)
Singer/songwriter
High Road Touring **Ph:** 415-332-9292
751 Bridgeway 3rd Fl **Fax:** 415-332-4692
Sausalito, CA 94965
www.jamesblunt.com

Blunt, Matt (1970-)
Governor of Missouri (Republican)
PO Box 720 **Ph:** 573-751-3222
Jefferson City, MO 65102 **Fax:** 573-751-1495
gov.missouri.gov

Blunt, Roy (1950-)
US Representative from Missouri (Republican); House Majority Whip
217 Cannon Bldg **Ph:** 202-225-6536
Washington, DC 20515 **Fax:** 202-225-5604
www.blunt.house.gov

Bly, Dre (1977-)
Professional football player
Detroit Lions **Ph:** 313-216-4000
222 Republic Dr **Fax:** 313-216-4069
Allen Park, MI 48101
www.detroitlions.com

Bocca, Julio (1967-)
A principal dancer with the American Ballet Theatre
American Ballet Theatre **Ph:** 212-477-3030
890 Broadway **Fax:** 212-254-5938
New York, NY 10003
www.abt.org/dancers

Bocelli, Andrea (1958-)
Opera/concert singer
Creative Artists Agency **Ph:** 212-277-9000
162 5th Ave 6th Fl **Fax:** 212-277-9099
New York, NY 10010
www.andreabocelli.org

Bochco, Steven (1943-)
TV writer/creator and producer
Creative Artists Agency **Ph:** 310-288-4545
9830 Wilshire Blvd **Fax:** 310-288-4800
Beverly Hills, CA 90212

Bochy, Bruce (1955-)
Baseball manager
San Diego Padres **Ph:** 619-795-5000
Petco Park **Fax:** 619-497-5339
PO Box 122000
San Diego, CA 92112
sandiego.padres.mlb.com

Bodenheimer, George
President of ESPN and of ABC Sports
ESPN **Ph:** 860-766-2000
ESPN Plaza **Fax:** 860-766-2213
935 Middle St
Bristol, CT 06010
corporate.disney.go.com

Bodman, Samuel, PhD (1938-)
US Secretary of Energy
US Dept of Energy **Ph:** 202-586-6210
1000 Independence Ave SW
Washington, DC 20585
www.energy.gov

Boehlert, Sherwood L (1936-)
US Representative from New York (Republican)
2246 Rayburn Bldg **Ph:** 202-225-3665
Washington, DC 20515 **Fax:** 202-225-1891
www.house.gov/boehlert

Boehner, John A (1949-)
US Representative from Ohio (Republican); replaced Tom DeLay as House majority leader
1011 Longworth Bldg **Ph:** 202-225-6205
Washington, DC 20515 **Fax:** 202-225-0704
johnboehner.house.gov

Bogans, Keith (1980-)
Professional basketball player
Houston Rockets **Ph:** 713-758-7200
Toyota Center **Fax:** 713-758-7396
1510 Polk St
Houston, TX 77002
www.nba.com/rockets

Boggs, Thomas Hale Jr
Attorney; considered one of the most effective and creative lawyers in Washington
Patton Boggs LLP **Ph:** 202-457-6040
2550 M St NW **Fax:** 202-457-6315
Washington, DC 20037
www.pattonboggs.com

Bogosian, Eric (1953-)
Actor, playwright, screenwriter
Creative Artists Agency **Ph:** 212-277-9000
162 5th Ave 6th Fl **Fax:** 212-277-9099
New York, NY 10010
www.ericbogosian.com

Bogues, Muggsy (1965-)
Basketball coach; former NBA player
Charlotte Sting **Ph:** 704-357-0252
100 Hive Dr **Fax:** 704-335-0289
Charlotte, NC 28217
www.wnba.com/sting

Bohannon, Jim
Radio talk show host and radio hall of famer; his show features special guests and callers discussing topics that range from current events and politics to entertainment and pop culture
Westwood One **Ph:** 212-641-2000
40 W 57th St 5th Fl **Fax:** 212-641-2172
New York, NY 10019
www.westwoodone.com

Boies, David (1941-)
Attorney; was special trial counsel for the US Dept of Justice in its antitrust suit against Microsoft; also served as lead counsel for former Vice President Al Gore in connection with litigation related to the election 2000 Florida vote count
Boies Schiller & Flexner LLP **Ph:** 914-749-8200
333 Main St **Fax:** 914-749-8300
Armonk, NY 10504
www.boies-schiller.com

Bok, Chip (1952-)
Editorial cartoonist for the Akron Beacon Journal
Creators Syndicate Inc **Ph:** 310-337-7003
5777 W Century Blvd Suite 700 **Fax:** 310-337-7625
Los Angeles, CA 90045
www.creators.com

Boldin, Anquan (1980-)
Professional football player
Arizona Cardinals **Ph:** 602-379-0101
8701 S Hardy Dr **Fax:** 602-379-1819
Tempe, AZ 85284
www.azcardinals.com

Boldman, Craig
Writes the comic strip Archie, which is drawn by Henry Scarpelli; Boldman has also written and drawn thousands of greeting cards for Hallmark, American Greetings, and other companies
Creators Syndicate Inc **Ph:** 310-337-7003
5777 W Century Blvd Suite 700 **Fax:** 310-337-7625
Los Angeles, CA 90045
www.creators.com

Boles, Anita
Executive Director of the National Healthy Mothers Healthy Babies Coalition
National Healthy Mothers Healthy Babies Coalition **Ph:** 703-836-6110 **Fax:** 703-836-3470
2001 N. Beauregard St
Alexandria, VA 22311

Bolle, Frank (1924-)
Artist who currently draws the comic strip Apartment 3-G, which is now written by Margaret Schulock
King Features Syndicate Inc **Ph:** 212-455-4000
888 7th Ave 2nd Fl
New York, NY 10019
www.kingfeatures.com

Bollenbach, Stephen F
Co-chairman and CEO of Hilton Hotels Corp
Hilton Hotels Corp **Ph:** 310-278-4321
9336 Civic Center Dr
Beverly Hills, CA 90210
www.hilton.com

Boller, Kyle (1981-)
Professional football player
Baltimore Ravens **Ph:** 410-547-8100
1101 Russell St **Fax:** 410-547-8112
Baltimore, MD 21230
www.baltimoreravens.com

Bolles, Richard Nelson
Author of What Color is Your Parachute?
Ten Speed Press **Ph:** 510-559-1600
PO Box 7123 **Fax:** 510-559-1629
Berkeley, CA 94707
www.jobhuntersbible.com

Bolling, Ruben
Creator of the syndicated comic strip Tom the Dancing Bug, a hybrid of editorial and comic strip cartooning
Universal Press Syndicate **Ph:** 816-932-6600
4520 Main St
Kansas City, MO 64111
www.amuniversal.com/ups/features

Bolten, Joshua B (1955-)
White House Chief of Staff (as of April 14, 2006; before that was Director, Office of Management & Budget)
Chief of Staff **Ph:** 202-456-6798
White House **Fax:** 202-456-1907
1600 Pennsylvania Ave NW
Washington, DC 20500
www.whitehouse.gov/government/cabinet.html

Bolton, John R (1948-)
Permanent US Representative to the United Nations
US Mission to the UN **Ph:** 212-415-4050
140 E 45th St
New York, NY 10017
www.un.int/usa

Bolton, Michael (1954-)
Singer
Creative Artists Agency **Ph:** 310-288-4545
9830 Wilshire Blvd **Fax:** 310-288-4800
Beverly Hills, CA 90212
www.michaelbolton.com

Bon Jovi, Jon (1962-)
Singer/singwriter; actor
Gersh Agency **Ph:** 310-274-6611
232 N Canon Dr
Beverly Hills, CA 90210
www.islandrecords.com/bonjovi

Bond, Julian (1940-)
NAACP chairman and civil rights activist
NAACP **Ph:** 410-580-5777
4805 Mt Hope Dr
Baltimore, MD 21215
www.naacp.org

Bond, Kit (1939-)
US Senator from Missouri (Republican)
274 Russell Bldg **Ph:** 202-224-5721
Washington, DC 20510 **Fax:** 202-224-8149
bond.senate.gov

Bond, Michael (1926-)
Paddington Bear author
Houghton Mifflin Children's Books **Ph:** 617-351-5000
222 Berkeley St 8th Fl
Boston, MA 02116
www.paddingtonbear.com

Bondra, Peter (1968-)
Professional hockey player
Atlanta Thrashers **Ph:** 404-827-5300
Centennial Tower **Fax:** 404-827-5909
101 Marietta St NW Suite 1900
Atlanta, GA 30303
www.atlantathrashers.com

Bonds, Barry (1964-)
Professional baseball player
San Francisco Giants **Ph:** 415-972-2000
AT & T Park
24 Willie Mays Plaza
San Francisco, CA 94107
www.barrybonds.com

Bonilla, Henry (1954-)
US Representative from Texas (Republican)
2458 Rayburn Bldg **Ph:** 202-225-4511
Washington, DC 20515 **Fax:** 202-225-2237
bonilla.house.gov

Bonner, Jo (1959-)
US Representative from Alabama (Republican)
315 Cannon Bldg **Ph:** 202-225-4931
Washington, DC 20515 **Fax:** 202-225-0562
bonner.house.gov

Bonners, Susan
Children's books author (A Silver Balloon)
Books for Young Readers **Ph:** 212-741-6900
Farrar Straus & Giroux
19 Union Sq W
New York, NY 10003
www.fsgkidsbooks.com

Bonnie, Shelby
Co-founder, chairman, and CEO of CNET Networks
CNET Networks Inc **Ph:** 415-344-2000
235 2nd St
San Francisco, CA 94105
www.cnet.com/aboutcnet

Bono (1960-)
Singer/composer (lead singer in U2); social activist. Real name is Paul Hewson.
Principle Management **Ph:** 212-765-2330
250 W 57th St Suite 2120
New York, NY 10107
www.u2.com

Bono, Mary (1961-)
US Representative from California (Republican)
405 Cannon Bldg **Ph:** 202-225-5330
Washington, DC 20515 **Fax:** 202-225-2961
www.house.gov/bono

Boone, Aaron (1973-)
Professional baseball player
Cleveland Indians **Ph:** 216-420-4200
Jacobs Field **Fax:** 216-420-4624
2401 Ontario St
Cleveland, OH 44115
cleveland.indians.mlb.com

Boortz, Neal (1945-)
Radio talk show host (political topics)
Cox Radio Syndication **Ph:** 404-962-2078
1601 W Peachtree St NE **Fax:** 404-897-2226
Atlanta, GA 30309
coxradiosyndication.com

Boozer, Carlos (1981-)
Professional basketball player
Utah Jazz **Ph:** 801-325-2500
Delta Center **Fax:** 801-325-2578
301 W South Temple St **TF:** 800-358-7328
Salt Lake City, UT 84101
www.nba.com/jazz

Boozman, John (1950-)
US Representative from Arkansas (Republican)
1519 Longworth Bldg **Ph:** 202-225-4301
Washington, DC 20515 **Fax:** 202-225-5713
www.boozman.house.gov

Bordallo, Madeleine Z (1933-)
US Delegate from Guam (Democrat)
427 Cannon Bldg **Ph:** 202-225-1188
Washington, DC 20515 **Fax:** 202-226-0341
www.house.gov/bordallo

Borden, Enid
CEO of Meals on Wheels Association of America
Meals on Wheels Assn of America **Ph:** 703-548-5558 **Fax:** 703-548-8024
203 S Union St
Alexandria, VA 22314
www.mowaa.org

Boren, Dan (1973-)
US Representative from Oklahoma (Democrat)
216 Cannon Bldg **Ph:** 202-225-2701
Washington, DC 20515 **Fax:** 202-225-3038
www.house.gov/boren

Borger, Gloria
A contributing editor at US News & World Report (writes the magazine's On Politics column)
US News & World Report **Ph:** 202-955-2000
1050 Thomas Jefferson St NW **Fax:** 202-955-2685
Washington, DC 20007
www.usnews.com

Borgman, Jim (1954-)
Editorial cartoonist; co-creator (with Jerry Scott) of the syndicated comic strip Zits
Cincinnati Enquirer **Ph:** 513-721-2700
312 Elm St
Cincinnati, OH 45202
borgman.enquirer.com

Borysenko, Joan, PhD
Psychologist, medical scientist, and author whose work is aimed at bringing science, medicine, psychology, and spirituality together in the service of healing
Mind-Body Health Sciences **Ph:** 303-440-8460
393 Dixon Rd **Fax:** 303-440-7580
Boulder, CO 80302
joanborysenko.com

Bosh, Chris (1984-)
Professional basketball player
Toronto Raptors **Ph:** 416-366-3865
40 Bay St Suite 400 **Fax:** 416-359-9198
Toronto, ON M5J2X2
www.nba.com/raptors

Boswell, Leonard L (1934-)
US Representative from Iowa (Democrat)
1427 Longworth Bldg **Ph:** 202-225-3806
Washington, DC 20515 **Fax:** 202-225-5608
www.house.gov/boswell

Bosworth, Kate (1983-)
Actor
United Talent Agency **Ph:** 310-273-6700
9560 Wilshire Blvd 5th Fl **Fax:** 310-247-1111
Beverly Hills, CA 90212

Boucher, Rick (1946-)
US Representative from Virginia (Democrat)
2187 Rayburn Bldg **Ph:** 202-225-3861
Washington, DC 20515 **Fax:** 202-225-0442
www.house.gov/boucher

Bouley, David
Chef/owner of Bouley and Danube restaurants, as well as Bouley Bakery and Bouley Market
Bouley **Ph:** 212-964-2525
120 W Broadway **Fax:** 212-219-3443
New York, NY 10013
www.thedanube.net

Boulot, Philippe
Executive chef of the Heathman Restaurant & Bar
Heathman Restaurant & Bar **Ph:** 503-790-7752
Heathman Hotel **Fax:** 503-790-7112
1001 SW Broadway
Portland, OR 97205
www.heathmanhotel.com

Boulud, Daniel
Chef and restaurateur; owns several restaurants, in New York and elsewhere in the US
Daniel Restaurant **Ph:** 212-288-0033
60 E 65th St **Fax:** 212-396-9014
New York, NY 10021
www.danielnyc.com

Bourdain, Anthony (1956-)
Executive chef of Brasserie Les Halles restaurants; also an author who has written crime novels, cookbooks, his memoir, and a restaurant expose
Brasserie Les Halles **Ph:** 212-679-4111
411 Park Ave S **Fax:** 212-779-0679
New York, NY 10016
www.anthonybourdain.com

Bourgeois, Louise (1911-)
Abstract Expressionist sculptor
Cheim & Read Gallery **Ph:** 212-242-7727
547 W 25th St **Fax:** 212-242-7737
New York, NY 10001

Bourguignon, Francois
Chief Economist and Senior Vice President, Development Economics, at the World Bank
World Bank **Ph:** 202-473-1000
1818 H St NW Rm MC4-315 **Fax:** 202-477-6391
Washington, DC 20433
www.worldbank.org

Bourke-White, Margaret (1904-1971)
Photographer
Gallery M **Ph:** 303-331-8400
2830 E 3rd Ave
Denver, CO 80206
www.gallerym.com

Bourne, Matthew (1960-)
Choreographer
William Morris Agency **Ph:** 310-859-4000
1 William Morris Pl **Fax:** 310-859-4462
Beverly Hills, CA 90212
www.matthewbournesnutcracker.com

Boustany, Charles W Jr (1956-)
US Representative from Louisiana (Republican)
1117 Longworth Bldg **Ph:** 202-225-2031
Washington, DC 20515 **Fax:** 202-225-5724
boustany.house.gov

Bouwer, Marc
Fashion designer
27 W 20th St **Ph:** 212-242-7510
New York, NY 10011
marcbouwer.com

Bouwmeester, Jay (1983-)
Professional hockey player
Florida Panthers **Ph:** 954-835-7000
BankAtlantic Center **Fax:** 954-835-7700
1 Panther Pkwy
Sunrise, FL 33323
www.floridapanthers.com

Bova, Ben, PhD (1932-)
Writer of science fiction as well as nonfiction about science, technology, and the future
National Space Society **Ph:** 202-429-1600
1620 'I' St NW Suite 615 **Fax:** 202-463-8497
Washington, DC 20006
www.benbova.net

Bovender, Jack O Jr (1945-)
Chairman and CEO of HCA Inc
HCA Inc **Ph:** 615-344-9551
1 Park Plaza **Fax:** 615-344-5722
Nashville, TN 37203
hcahealthcare.com

Bowden, Bobby (1929-)
College football coach
Florida State University Athletic Department
PO Box 2341
Tallahassee, FL 32306
seminoles.collegesports.com
Ph: 850-644-1465
Fax: 850-644-1356

Bowen, Bruce (1971-)
Professional basketball player
San Antonio Spurs
1 SBC Center
San Antonio, TX 78219
www.nba.com/spurs
Ph: 210-444-5000
Fax: 210-444-5003

Bowie, David (1947-)
Singer/composer; actor
International Creative Management
8942 Wilshire Blvd
Beverly Hills, CA 90211
www.davidbowie.com
Ph: 310-550-4000

Bowlen, Pat (1945-)
President & CEO of the Denver Broncos football franchise & co-owner of the Arena Football League's Colorado Crush
Denver Broncos
13655 Broncos Pkwy
Englewood, CO 80112
www.coloradocrush.com
Ph: 303-649-9000
Fax: 303-649-9354

Bowman, Richard A (1940-)
Attorney; product liability lawyer who spends about half of each year in catastrophic loss trials
Bowman & Brooke LLP
150 S 5th St Suite 2600
Minneapolis, MN 55402
www.bowmanandbrooke.com
Ph: 612-672-3233
Fax: 612-672-3200

Bowman, Scotty (1933-)
Long-time hockey coach (retired) who is now serving as a consultant to the Detroit Red Wings organization
Detroit Red Wings
Joe Louis Arena
600 Civic Center Dr
Detroit, MI 48226
www.detroitredwings.com
Ph: 313-396-7544
Fax: 313-567-0296

Boxer, Barbara (1940-)
US Senator from California (Democrat)
112 Hart Bldg
Washington, DC 20510
boxer.senate.gov
Ph: 202-224-3553

Boyd, Allen (1945-)
US Representative from Florida (Democrat)
1227 Longworth Bldg
Washington, DC 20515
www.house.gov/boyd
Ph: 202-225-5235
Fax: 202-225-5615

Boyd, Jeffery H
President & CEO of Priceline.com
Priceline.com Inc
800 Connecticut Ave
Norwalk, CT 06854
travel.priceline.com
Ph: 203-299-8000
Fax: 203-299-8948

Boyd, Ty
Motivational speaker (leadership training)
Ty Boyd Executive Learning Systems
1727 Garden Terr
Charlotte, NC 28203
www.tyboyd.com
Ph: 704-333-9999
Fax: 704-333-0207
TF: 800-336-2693

Boyer, Paul D, PhD (1918-)
1997 Nobel Laureate in Chemistry; biochemist; professor emeritus at UCLA
University of California
Dept of Chemistry & Biochemistry
607 Charles E Young Dr
Box 951569
Los Angeles, CA 90095
www.chem.ucla.edu
Ph: 310-825-4219
Fax: 310-206-4038

Boykins, Earl (1976-)
Professional basketball player
Denver Nuggets
Pepsi Center
1000 Chopper Cir
Denver, CO 80204
www.nba.com/nuggets
Ph: 303-405-1100
Fax: 303-575-1920

Boyle, Dan (1976-)
Professional hockey player
Tampa Bay Lightning
St Pete Times Forum
401 Channelside Dr
Tampa, FL 33602
www.tampabaylightning.com
Ph: 813-301-6600
Fax: 813-301-1487

Boyle, Father Gregory J
Jesuit priest; founder of Homeboy Industries/Jobs For A Future, a center where gang members and other at-risk youth can get help with job placement, tattoo removal, counseling, and other services
Homeboy Industries
1916 E 1st St
Los Angeles, CA 90033
www.homeboy-industries.org
Ph: 800-526-1254

Boyle, Gertrude
Chairman of the Board of Columbia Sportswear (she portrays the cantankerous Mother Boyle in Columbia commercials)
Columbia Sportswear Co **Ph:** 503-985-4000
14375 NW Science Park Dr **Fax:** 503-985-5960
Portland, OR 97229
www.columbia.com

Boyle, Lara Flynn (1970-)
Actor
United Talent Agency **Ph:** 310-273-6700
9560 Wilshire Blvd 5th Fl **Fax:** 310-247-1111
Beverly Hills, CA 90212

Boyle, Peter (1935-)
Actor
Innovative Artists **Ph:** 310-656-0400
1505 10th St **Fax:** 310-656-0456
Santa Monica, CA 90401
www.everybodylovesray.com

Boyle, Timothy
President & CEO of Columbia Sportswear (Gertrude Boyle's son)
Columbia Sportswear Co **Ph:** 503-985-4000
14375 NW Science Park Dr **Fax:** 503-985-5960
Portland, OR 97229
www.columbia.com

Boynton, Sandra (1953-)
Children's books author
Workman Publishing **Ph:** 212-254-5900
708 Broadway
New York, NY 10003
www.workman.com

Bozell, L Brent III (1956-)
Syndicated columnist, lecturer, television commentator, publisher, activist, businessman; founder and president of the Media Research Center, the largest media watchdog organization in America
Media Research Center **Ph:** 703-683-9733
325 S Patrick St **Fax:** 703-683-9736
Alexandria, VA 22314
www.mediaresearch.org/bios/lbb

Bracco, Lorraine (1954-)
Actor
Innovative Artists **Ph:** 310-656-0400
1505 10th St **Fax:** 310-656-0456
Santa Monica, CA 90401
www.hbo.com/sopranos/cast

Bradbury, Ray (1920-)
Author of fantasy fiction (Fahrenheit 451; The Illustrated Man)
HarperCollins Publishers **Ph:** 212-207-7000
c/o Author Mail
10 E 53rd St
New York, NY 10022
www.raybradbury.com

Bradford, Barbara Taylor (1933-)
Romance novelist (A Woman of Substance)
HarperCollins Publishers **Ph:** 212-207-7000
c/o Author Mail
10 E 53rd St
New York, NY 10022
www.barbarataylorbradford.com

Bradley, Ed (1941-)
Veteran broadcast journalist and 60 Minutes correspondent
60 Minutes **Ph:** 212-975-2006
555 W 57th St **Fax:** 212-975-1893
New York, NY 10019
www.cbsnews.com

Bradley, Jeb E (1952-)
US Representative from New Hampshire (Republican)
1218 Longworth Bldg **Ph:** 202-225-5456
Washington, DC 20515 **Fax:** 202-225-5822
www.house.gov/bradley

Bradley, Milton (1978-)
Professional baseball player
Oakland Athletics **Ph:** 510-638-4900
Network Assoc Coliseum **Fax:** 510-568-3770
7000 Coliseum Way
Oakland, CA 94621
oakland.athletics.mlb.com

Bradley Hagerty, Barbara
NPR religion correspondent
National Public Radio **Ph:** 202-513-2000
635 Massachusetts Ave NW **Fax:** 202-513-3329
Washington, DC 20001
www.npr.org

Bradshaw, John (1933-)
Author of several books on dysfunctional family issues and has done several PBS shows on the subject; pioneered the concept of the inner child
PO Box 720947 **Ph:** 713-771-1300
Houston, TX 77272
www.bradshawcassettes.com

Bradshaw, Terry (1948-)
Former professional football player (quarterback) and member of the Pro Football Hall of Fame; NFL studio analyst
FOX Sports Net **Ph:** 310-369-1000
10201 W Pico Blvd
Bldg 101
Los Angeles, CA 90035
msn.foxsports.com/nflonfox

Brady, James (1940-)
Former White House Press Secretary who was shot and seriously wounded in the assassination attempt on President Reagan; since then has been an activist for control of handguns
Brady Campaign to Prevent Gun Violence **Ph:** 202-898-0792
1225 'I' St NW Suite 1100
Washington, DC 20005
www.bradycampaign.org

Brady, Kevin (1955-)
US Representative from Texas (Republican)
428 Cannon Bldg **Ph:** 202-225-4901
Washington, DC 20515 **Fax:** 202-225-5524
www.house.gov/brady

Brady, Pat (1947-)
Creator of the comic strip Rose is Rose
United Feature Syndicate **Ph:** 212-293-8500
200 Madison Ave
New York, NY 10016
www.unitedfeatures.com

Brady, Robert A (1945-)
US Representative from Pennsylvania (Democrat)
206 Cannon Bldg **Ph:** 202-225-4731
Washington, DC 20515 **Fax:** 202-225-0088
www.house.gov/robertbrady

Brady, Sarah (1942-)
Wife of James Brady and a leader in the gun control movement
Brady Campaign to Prevent Gun Violence **Ph:** 202-898-0792
1225 'I' St NW Suite 1100
Washington, DC 20005
www.bradycampaign.org

Brady, Tom (1977-)
Professional football player
New England Patriots **Ph:** 508-543-8200
1 Patriots Pl **Fax:** 508-543-0285
Foxboro, MA 02035
www.patriots.com

Brady, Wayne (1972-)
Comedic entertainer
William Morris Agency **Ph:** 310-859-4108
1 William Morris Pl **Fax:** 310-248-5953
Beverly Hills, CA 90212
www.wma.com/wayne_brady/summary

Brafman, Ben
Criminal lawyer (clients have included Michael Jackson and Sean "Diddy" Combs)
Brafman & Associates **Ph:** 212-750-7800
767 3rd Ave 26th Fl **Fax:** 212-750-3906
New York, NY 10017

Brailer, David J, MD, PhD (1959-)
US National Coordinator for Health Information Technology
Office of the National Coordinator for Health Information Technology **Ph:** 202-690-7151
US Dept of Health & Human Services
200 Independence Ave SW Rm 517D
Washington, DC 20201
www.hhs.gov/healthit/bios.html

Branagh, Kenneth (1960-)
Actor; also film director/writer/producer
Special Artists Agency **Ph:** 310-859-9688
9465 Wilshire Blvd Suite 890
Beverly Hills, CA 90212

Brancaccio, David (1960-)
Host of Now on PBS
WNET **Ph:** 212-560-8600
450 W 33rd St 6th Fl
New York, NY 10001
www.pbs.org/now

Branch, John
Editorial cartoonist of the San Antonio Express-News
King Features Syndicate Inc **Ph:** 212-455-4000
888 7th Ave 2nd Fl
New York, NY 10019
www.kingfeatures.com

Branch, Michelle (1983-)
Pop singer
William Morris Agency **Ph:** 310-859-4000
1 William Morris Pl **Fax:** 310-859-4462
Beverly Hills, CA 90212
www.michellebranch.com

Brand, Elton (1979-)
Professional basketball player
Los Angeles Clippers **Ph:** 213-742-7100
Staples Center **Fax:** 213-742-7550
1111 S Figueroa St Suite 1100
Los Angeles, CA 90015
www.nba.com/clippers

Brando, Tim (1956-)
Sports broadcaster
CBS Sports **Ph:** 212-975-4321
51 W 52nd St
New York, NY 10019
cbs.sportsline.com/cbssports/team

Brandon, David A
Chairman & CEO of Domino's Pizza
Domino's Pizza LLC **Ph:** 734-930-3030
30 Frank Lloyd Wright Dr **Fax:** 734-747-6210
Ann Arbor, MI 48106
www.dominos.com

Brandt, Bill (1904-1983)
Photographer
Edwynn Houk Gallery **Ph:** 212-750-7070
745 5th Ave **Fax:** 212-688-4848
New York, NY 10151
www.houkgallery.com

Brantley, Ben (1954-)
Theater critic
New York Times **Ph:** 212-556-1234
229 W 43rd St
New York, NY 10036

Brashares, Ann
Author of books for young readers (Sisterhood of the Traveling Pants)
Random House Children's Books **Ph:** 212-782-9000
Publicity Dept
1745 Broadway
New York, NY 10019
www.randomhouse.com/kids

Brassai (1899-1984)
Photographer
Edwynn Houk Gallery **Ph:** 212-750-7070
745 5th Ave **Fax:** 212-688-4848
New York, NY 10151
www.houkgallery.com

Bratt, Benjamin (1963-)
Actor
Endeavor **Ph:** 310-248-2000
9601 Wilshire Blvd 3rd Fl **Fax:** 310-248-2020
Beverly Hills, CA 90210

Braugher, Andre (1962-)
Actor
Creative Artists Agency **Ph:** 310-288-4545
9830 Wilshire Blvd **Fax:** 310-288-4800
Beverly Hills, CA 90212

Braun, Lilian Jackson (1916-)
Author of the Cat Who... mystery series
Putnam Publicity **Ph:** 212-366-2000
375 Hudson St
New York, NY 10014
us.penguingroup.com

Braun, Matt
Writes Western fiction
St Martin's Press **Ph:** 212-674-5151
Attn: Publicity Dept
175 5th Ave
New York, NY 10010
www.mattbraun.com

Braver, Rita
National news correspondent
CBS News Sunday Morning **Ph:** 212-975-4114
Box O
524 W 57th St
New York, NY 10019
www.cbsnews.com

Bravo, Rose Marie
CEO of Burberry; highest paid woman in European business
Burberry Ltd **Ph:** 212-407-7100
9 E 57th St **Fax:** 212-355-9870
New York, NY 10022
www.burberryplc.com

Braxton, Toni (1967-)
Singer (R&B/pop)
Brokaw Co **Ph:** 310-273-2060
9255 Sunset Blvd Suite 804 **Fax:** 310-276-4037
Los Angeles, CA 90069
www.wma.com/toni_braxton/summary

Brazelton, T Berry, MD
Pediatrician; writes the syndicated column Family Today with Dr Joshua Sparrow, a child psychiatrist
New York Times Syndicate **Ph:** 212-556-1234
229 W 43rd St
New York, NY 10036
www.nytsyn.com/lifestyle.html

Breathed, Berkeley (1957-)
Cartoonist and children's book author/illustrator; creator of the comic strips Bloom County (1980-1989), Outland (1989-1995), and Opus
Washington Post Writers Group **Ph:** 202-334-6375 **Fax:** 202-334-5669
1150 15th St NW 9th Fl
Washington, DC 20071
www.berkeleybreathed.com

Bredesen, Phil (1943-)
Governor of Tennessee (Democrat)
State Capitol 1st Fl **Ph:** 615-741-2001
Nashville, TN 37243 **Fax:** 615-532-9711
www.tennesseeanytime.org/governor

Breen, Edward (1956-)
Chairman & CEO of Tyco
Tyco International Ltd **Ph:** 609-720-4200
9 Roszel Rd **Fax:** 609-720-4208
Princeton, NJ 08540
www.tyco.com

Breen, Steve
Creator of the comic strip Grand Avenue; also an editorial cartoonist
United Feature Syndicate **Ph:** 212-293-8500
200 Madison Ave
New York, NY 10016
www.unitedfeatures.com

Brees, Drew (1979-)
Professional football player
New Orleans Saints **Ph:** 504-733-0255
5800 Airline Dr **Fax:** 504-731-1768
Metairie, LA 70003
www.neworleanssaints.com

Bren, Donald L
Real estate developer and philanthropist
Irvine Co Inc **Ph:** 949-720-2000
550 Newport Center Dr
Newport Beach, CA 92660
www.donald-bren.com

Brenneman, Amy (1964-)
Actor
Creative Artists Agency **Ph:** 310-288-4545
9830 Wilshire Blvd **Fax:** 310-288-4800
Beverly Hills, CA 90212

Brenneman, Greg
Chairman & CEO of Burger King Corp
Burger King Corp **Ph:** 305-378-3000
5505 Blue Lagoon Dr
Miami, FL 33126
www.bk.com

Breslin, Jimmy (1930-)
Columnist for New York Newsday and author of The Gang That Couldn't Shoot Straight
Newsday **Ph:** 631-843-4000
235 Pinelawn Rd **Fax:** 631-843-2953
Melville, NY 11747
www.newsday.com

Brett, Jan
Author and illustrator of children's books
GP Putnam's Sons Books for Young Readers **Ph:** 212-366-2000
Publicity Dept
345 Hudson St
New York, NY 10014
www.janbrett.com

Brewer, Eric A, PhD
Founder of the Federal Search Foundation, which built FirstGov, the portal for the US government; was also the founder & Chief Scientist of Inktomi Corp, which is now part of Yahoo!
University of California at Berkeley **Ph:** 510-642-8143 **Fax:** 510-642-5775
Computer Science Div
623 Soda Hall
Berkeley, CA 94720
www.cs.berkeley.edu/~brewer

Brey-Casiano, Carol A
Director of the El Paso Public Library and past president of the American Library Association
El Paso Public Library **Ph:** 915-541-4098
501 N Oregon **Fax:** 915-541-4945
El Paso, TX 79901
www.carolbrey.com

Breyer, Stephen G (1938-)
US Supreme Court justice
US Supreme Court Bldg **Ph:** 202-479-3000
1 1st St NE
Washington, DC 20543
www.supremecourtus.gov

Brickman, Jim (1961-)
Composer/songwriter; concert performer
International Creative Management **Ph:** 310-550-4000
8942 Wilshire Blvd
Beverly Hills, CA 90211
www.jimbrickman.com

Bridges, Beau (1941-)
Actor
Creative Artists Agency **Ph:** 310-288-4545
9830 Wilshire Blvd **Fax:** 310-288-4800
Beverly Hills, CA 90212

Bridges, Jeff (1949-)
Actor
Special Artists Agency **Ph:** 310-859-9688
9465 Wilshire Blvd Suite 890
Beverly Hills, CA 90212
www.jeffbridges.com

Bridgewater, Dee Dee (1950-)
Jazz vocalist and host of JazzSet with Dee Dee Bridgewater on NPR
Ted Kurland Assoc **Ph:** 617-254-0007
173 Brighton Ave **Fax:** 617-782-3577
Boston, MA 02134
www.deedeebridgewater.com

Bridwell, Norman (1928-)
Author of Clifford the Big Red Dog
Scholastic Inc **Ph:** 212-343-6100
555 Broadway
New York, NY 10012
www2.scholastic.com

Briggs, Lance (1980-)
Professional football player
Chicago Bears **Ph:** 847-295-6600
Halas Hall at Conway Park **Fax:** 847-295-8986
1000 Football Dr
Lake Forest, IL 60045
www.chicagobears.com

Bright, Bobby N (1952-)
Mayor of Montgomery, Alabama
103 N Perry St **Ph:** 334-241-2000
Montgomery, AL 36104 **Fax:** 334-241-2266
www.ci.montgomery.al.us

Brightman, Sara (1960-)
Singer (pop, opera, musical theater)
Creative Artists Agency **Ph:** 212-277-9000
162 5th Ave 6th Fl **Fax:** 212-277-9099
New York, NY 10010
www.sarah-brightman.com

Brigman, June (1960-)
Current artist for the comic strip Brenda Starr
Tribune Media Services Inc **Ph:** 312-222-4444
435 N Michigan Ave Suite 1500
Chicago, IL 60611
www.comicspage.com

Brin, Sergey (1973-)
Google co-founder (with Larry Page) and president
Google Inc **Ph:** 650-623-0000
1600 Amphitheatre Pkwy **Fax:** 650-623-0001
Mountain View, CA 94043
www.google.com/corporate/execs.html

Brind'Amour, Rod (1970-)
Professional hockey player
Carolina Hurricanes **Ph:** 919-467-7825
RBC Center **Fax:** 919-462-7030
1400 Edwards Mill Rd
Raleigh, NC 27607
www.carolinahurricanes.com

Brinker, Bob
Host of the weekend financial talk radio program MoneyTalk
ABC Radio Networks **Ph:** 212-456-7777
444 Madison Ave
New York, NY 10022
www.bobbrinker.com

Brinkley, Christie (1954-)
Model
William Morris Agency **Ph:** 212-586-5100
1325 Ave of the Americas **Fax:** 212-246-3583
New York, NY 10019

Briscoe, Connie (1952-)
Author (Big Girls Don't Cry; PG County)
Random House Publicity **Ph:** 212-782-9000
1745 Broadway
New York, NY 10019
www.conniebriscoe.com

Brisebois, Patrice (1971-)
Professional hockey player
Colorado Avalanche **Ph:** 303-405-1100
Pepsi Center
1000 Chopper Cir
Denver, CO 80204
www.coloradoavalanche.com

Britt, Chris
Editorial cartoonist for the State Journal-Register in Springfield, IL
State Journal-Register **Ph:** 217-788-1300
1 Copley Plaza
9th St & Capitol Ave
PO Box 219
Springfield, IL 62705
www.copleynews.com

Broad, Eli (1934-)
Philanthropist and business leader; was founder-chairman of both SunAmerica Inc and KB Home (formerly Kaufman and Broad Home Corp)
The Broad Foundation **Ph:** 310-954-5050
10900 Wilshire Blvd 12th Fl **Fax:** 310-954-5051
Los Angeles, CA 90024
www.broadfoundation.org

Brock, Lou (1939-)
Former baseball player and Hall of Famer, now Special Instructor for the Cardinals team
Saint Louis Cardinals **Ph:** 314-421-3060
250 Stadium Plaza **Fax:** 314-425-0640
Saint Louis, MO 63102
stlouis.cardinals.mlb.com

Broder, David (1929-)
Syndicated columnist (political commentary)
Washington Post Writers Group **Ph:** 202-334-6375
Fax: 202-334-5669
1150 15th St NW 9th Fl
Washington, DC 20071
www.postwritersgroup.com

Broderick, Matthew (1962-)
Actor
Creative Artists Agency **Ph:** 310-288-4545
9830 Wilshire Blvd **Fax:** 310-288-4800
Beverly Hills, CA 90212
www.matthewbroderick.net

Brodesser, Claude
Entertainment journalist/columnist and host of the weekly radio program The Business on NPR
National Public Radio **Ph:** 202-513-2000
635 Massachusetts Ave NW **Fax:** 202-513-3329
Washington, DC 20001
www.npr.org

Brodeur, Martin (1972-)
Professional hockey player
New Jersey Devils **Ph:** 201-935-6050
Continental Airlines Arena **Fax:** 201-935-2127
50 Rt 120N
East Rutherford, NJ 07073
www.newjerseydevils.com

Brody, Adrien (1973-)
Actor
Creative Artists Agency **Ph:** 310-288-4545
9830 Wilshire Blvd **Fax:** 310-288-4800
Beverly Hills, CA 90212

Brogan, Stephen J
Attorney; represents corporations in complex litigation matters, including contests for corporate control, corporate criminal investigations, product liability, independent counsel investigations, and qui tam actions
Jones Day **Ph:** 202-879-3939
51 Louisiana Ave NW **Fax:** 202-626-1700
Washington, DC 20001
www.jonesday.com

Brokaw, Tom (1940-)
Veteran NBC journalist and former anchor of NBC Nightly News, a position from which he retired in 2004; now reporting and producing long-form documentaries and providing expertise during breaking news events
NBC News **Ph:** 212-664-4249
30 Rockefeller Plaza
New York, NY 10112
www.msnbc.msn.com/id/3689499

Brolin, James (1940-)
Actor
International Creative Management **Ph:** 310-550-4000
8942 Wilshire Blvd
Beverly Hills, CA 90211

Brooking, Keith (1975-)
Professional football player
Atlanta Falcons **Ph:** 770-965-3115
4400 Falcon Pkwy **Fax:** 770-965-3185
Flowery Branch, GA 30542
www.atlantafalcons.com

Brookins, Gary
Editorial cartoonist for the Richmond Times-Dispatch; also produces the cartoon panel Pluggers and works with Chris Cassatt on the comic strip Shoe
King Features Syndicate Inc **Ph:** 212-455-4000
888 7th Ave 2nd Fl
New York, NY 10019
www.kingfeatures.com

Brooks, Aaron (1976-)
Professional football player
Oakland Raiders **Ph:** 510-864-5000
1220 Harbor Bay Pkwy **Fax:** 510-864-5134
Alameda, CA 94502
www.raiders.com

Brooks, David (1961-)
New York Times op-ed columnist; also a commentator on PBS's Newshour with Jim Lehrer
New York Times **Ph:** 212-556-1234
229 W 43rd St
New York, NY 10036
www.nytimes.com/pages/opinion

Brooks, Derrick (1973-)
Professional football player
Tampa Bay Buccaneers **Ph:** 813-870-2700
1 Buccaneer Pl **Fax:** 813-878-0813
Tampa, FL 33607
www.buccaneers.com

Brooks, Garth (1962-)
Country music singer
Nancy Seltzer & Assoc **Ph:** 323-938-3562
6220 Del Valle Dr **Fax:** 323-938-0589
Los Angeles, CA 90048
www.garthbrooks.com

Brooks, James L (1940-)
Film director, producer, and writer; executive producer of The Simpsons
International Creative Management **Ph:** 310-550-4000
8942 Wilshire Blvd
Beverly Hills, CA 90211
www.thesimpsons.com

Brooks, Mel (1926-)
Writer, producer, director, actor
Brooksfilms **Ph:** 310-202-3292
9336 W Washington Blvd
Culver City, CA 90232

Brooks, Terry (1944-)
Author of science fiction & fantasy (Shannara series; Landover books)
Ballantine Books Publicity **Ph:** 212-782-9000
1745 Broadway
New York, NY 10019
www.terrybrooks.net

Brooks & Dunn
Country music duo (Kix Brooks and Ronnie Dunn)
William Morris Agency **Ph:** 615-963-3000
1600 Division St Suite 300 **Fax:** 615-963-3090
Nashville, TN 37203
www.brooks-dunn.com

Broome, Michael
Motivational speaker
1450 S Beersheba Rd **Ph:** 803-628-1290
Clover, SC 29710
www.motivationalmichael.com

Broome, Paul (1976-)
Professional soccer player
Real Salt Lake **Ph:** 801-924-8585
515 S 700 East Suite 2R **Fax:** 801-933-4713
Salt Lake City, UT 84102
www.mlsnet.com/MLS/rsl/

Brosnan, Pierce (1953-)
Actor
Creative Artists Agency **Ph:** 310-288-4545
9830 Wilshire Blvd **Fax:** 310-288-4800
Beverly Hills, CA 90212
www.piercebrosnan.com

Brothers, Joyce, PhD (1928-)
Psychologist; writes a syndicated advice column
King Features Syndicate Inc **Ph:** 212-455-4000
888 7th Ave 2nd Fl
New York, NY 10019
www.kingfeatures.com

Brown, Alton
Chef; host of Good Eats on Food TV
Food Network **Ph:** 212-398-8836
75 9th Ave **Fax:** 212-736-7716
New York, NY 10011
www.altonbrown.com

Brown, Bob
News correspondent for 20/20
20/20 **Ph:** 212-456-7777
147 Columbus Ave
New York, NY 10023
abcnews.go.com/2020

Brown, Byron
Mayor of Buffalo, New York
65 Niagra Sq Suite 201 **Ph:** 716-851-4841
Buffalo, NY 14202 **Fax:** 716-851-4360
www.ci.buffalo.ny.us

Brown, Campbell
NBC News correspondent and co-anchor of Today Weekend Edition
NBC News **Ph:** 212-664-4249
30 Rockefeller Plaza
New York, NY 10112
www.msnbc.msn.com/id/3689499

Brown, Chester (1960-)
Cartoonist for Drawn & Quarterly comic books
Drawn & Quarterly **Ph:** 514-279-2221
PO Box 48056
Montreal, QC H2V4S8
www.drawnandquarterly.com/artHome.php

Brown, Chris (1981-)
Professional football player
Tennessee Titans **Ph:** 615-565-4000
460 Great Circle Rd **Fax:** 615-565-4006
Nashville, TN 37228
www.titansonline.com

Brown, Colin W
President & CEO of JM Family Enterprises
JM Family Enterprises Inc **Ph:** 954-429-2031
100 Jim Moran Blvd **Fax:** 954-429-2222
Deerfield Beach, FL 33442

Brown, Corrine (1946-)
US Representative from Florida (Democrat)
2444 Rayburn Bldg **Ph:** 202-225-0123
Washington, DC 20515 **Fax:** 202-225-2256
www.house.gov/corrinebrown

Brown, Curtis (1976-)
Professional hockey player
Chicago Blackhawks **Ph:** 312-455-7000
United Center **Fax:** 312-455-7041
1901 W Madison St
Chicago, IL 60612
www.chicagoblackhawks.com

Brown, Dan (1964-)
Author of The DaVinci Code
Doubleday Publicity **Ph:** 212-782-9000
1745 Broadway
New York, NY 10019
www.danbrown.com

Brown, Dara
Anchor and senior producer for MSNBC.com's original programming
MSNBC TV **Ph:** 201-583-5000
1 MSNBC Plaza
Secaucus, NJ 07094
www.msnbc.msn.com/id/3080263

Brown, David (1916-)
Movie producer
International Creative Management **Ph:** 212-556-5600
40 W 57th St 17th Fl
New York, NY 10019

Brown, Harold, PhD (1927-)
Former US Secretary of Defense
Warburg Pincus LLC **Ph:** 212-878-0600
466 Lexington Ave **Fax:** 212-878-9100
New York, NY 10017
www.warburgpincus.com

Brown, Henry E Jr (1935-)
US Representative from South Carolina (Republican)
1124 Longworth Bldg **Ph:** 202-225-3176
Washington, DC 20515 **Fax:** 202-225-3407
wwwc.house.gov/henrybrown

Brown, James (1933-)
Singer known as the godfather of soul
William Morris Agency **Ph:** 310-859-4000
1 William Morris Pl **Fax:** 310-859-4462
Beverly Hills, CA 90212
www.godfatherofsoul.com

Brown, James (1951-)
Sportscaster; hosts sports programs and is a regular contributor to Real Sports with Bryant Gumbel on HBO
HBO Sports **Ph:** 212-512-1000
1100 Ave of the Americas
New York, NY 10036
www.hbo.com/realsports

Brown, Jerry (1938-)
Mayor of Oakland, California; former governor of the state
1 Frank H Ogawa Plaza **Ph:** 510-238-3141
Suite 321 **Fax:** 510-238-4731
Oakland, CA 94612
www.oaklandnet.com

Brown, Joe (1947-)
Judge on a courtroom TV show who is known for his creative alternative sentencing
Paramount Television **Ph:** 323-956-5000
Judge Joe Brown
5555 Melrose Ave
Hollywood, CA 90038
www.judgejoebrown.com

Brown, Josh (1979-)
Professional football player
Seattle Seahawks **Ph:** 425-827-9777
11220 NE 53rd St **Fax:** 425-827-9008
Kirkland, WA 98033
www.seahawks.com

Brown, Kris (1976-)
Professional football player
Houston Texans **Ph:** 832-667-2000
2 Reliant Park **Fax:** 832-667-2100
Houston, TX 77054
www.houstontexans.com

Brown, Larry (1940-)
Basketball coach
New York Knicks **Ph:** 212-465-6471
Madison Square Garden **Fax:** 212-465-6498
2 Pennsylvania Plaza
New York, NY 10121
www.nba.com/knicks

Brown, Les (1945-)
Speaker, entrepreneur, author
Les Brown Enterprises **Ph:** 800-733-4226
PO Box 27380 **TF:** 800-733-4226
Detroit, MI 48227
www.lesbrown.com

Brown, Marc (1946-)
Creator of the Arthur Adventure children's book series
Little Brown & Co **Ph:** 212-522-7200
Author Mail
1271 Ave of the Americas
New York, NY 10020
www.twbookmark.com

Brown, Marcia (1918-)
Children's book illustrator & author (Shadow; Stone Soup)
Simon & Schuster Books for Young Readers **Ph:** 212-698-7000
1230 Ave of the Americas
New York, NY 10020
www.simonsays.com

Brown, Margaret Wise (1910-1952)
Children's books author (Goodnight Moon)
WaterMark Inc **Ph:** 205-670-0710
8318 Hwy 26
Columbiana, AL 35051
www.margaretwisebrown.com

Brown, Michael
Owner of the Cincinnati Bengals football team
Cincinnati Bengals **Ph:** 513-621-3550
1 Paul Brown Stadium **Fax:** 513-621-3570
Cincinnati, OH 45202
www.bengals.com

Brown, Michael S, MD (1941-)
Winner (with Joseph L Goldstein) of the 1985 Nobel Prize in Physiology or Medicine for their discoveries concerning the regulation of cholesterol metabolism
Dept of Molecular Genetics **Ph:** 214-648-3111
University of Texas
Southwestern Medical Center at Dallas
5323 Harry Hines Blvd
Dallas, TX 75390
www.utsouthwestern.edu

Brown, Mike
Basketball coach
Cleveland Cavaliers **Ph:** 216-420-2000
Quicken Loans Arena **Fax:** 216-420-2298
1 Center Ct
Cleveland, OH 44115
www.nba.com/cavaliers

Brown, PJ (1969-)
Professional basketball player
New Orleans/Oklahoma City Hornets **Ph:** 405-208-4800
Oklahoma Tower
210 Park Ave Suite 1850
Oklahoma City, OK 73102
www.nba.com/hornets

Brown, Rita Mae (1944-)
Novelist; her books include the Mrs. Murphy mystery series (Mrs. Murphy is a cat), also called the Sneaky Pie Mysteries (Sneaky Pie is Brown's cat, who supposedly collaborates on the Mrs. Murphy books)
Bantam Dell Publicity **Ph:** 212-782-9000
1745 Broadway
New York, NY 10019
www.ritamaebrown.org

Brown, Sandra
Author of romance/suspense fiction
Simon & Schuster **Ph:** 212-698-7000
1230 Ave of the Americas
New York, NY 10020
www.sandrabrown.net

Brown, Sheldon (1979-)
Professional football player
Philadelphia Eagles **Ph:** 215-463-2500
NovaCare Complex **Fax:** 215-339-5464
1 NovaCare Way
Philadelphia, PA 19145
www.philadelphiaeagles.com

Brown, Sherrod (1952-)
US Representative from Ohio (Democrat)
2332 Rayburn Bldg **Ph:** 202-225-3401
Washington, DC 20515 **Fax:** 202-225-2266
www.house.gov/sherrodbrown

Brown, Trisha (1936-)
Modern dance choreographer; artistic director of Trisha Brown Dance Co
Trisha Brown Dance Co **Ph:** 212-582-0040
625 W 55th St 2nd Fl
New York, NY 10019
www.trishabrowncompany.org

Brown, Willie (1940-)
Hall of Fame football player; played for the Oakland Raiders and is now the squad development coach for the team
CMG Worldwide **Ph:** 317-570-5000
10500 Crosspoint Blvd **Fax:** 317-570-5500
Indianapolis, IN 46256
www.cmgworldwide.com/football/brown

Brown-Waite, Ginny (1943-)
US Representative from Florida (Democrat)
414 Cannon Bldg **Ph:** 202-225-1002
Washington, DC 20515 **Fax:** 202-226-6559
www.house.gov/brown-waite

Brownback, Sam (1956-)
US Senator from Kansas (Republican)
303 Hart Bldg **Ph:** 202-224-6521
Washington, DC 20510 **Fax:** 202-228-1265
brownback.senate.gov

Browne, Chance (1948-)
Draws the comic strip Hi & Lois with Brian Walker & Greg Walker (sons of Mort Walker; Chance Browne is the son of the strip's original co-creator, Dik Browne)
King Features Syndicate Inc **Ph:** 212-455-4000
888 7th Ave 2nd Fl
New York, NY 10019
www.kingfeatures.com

Browne, Chris (1952-)
Writes and draws the comic strip Hagar the Horrible, which was originally created by his father, Dik Browne
King Features Syndicate Inc **Ph:** 212-455-4000
888 7th Ave 2nd Fl
New York, NY 10019
www.kingfeatures.com

Browne, David
Music critic and author
Entertainment Weekly **Ph:** 212-522-5600
1675 Broadway **Fax:** 212-522-0059
New York, NY 10019
www.david-browne.com

Browne, Joy, PhD
Radio psychologist
WOR Radio Network **Ph:** 212-642-4500
111 Broadway 3rd Fl **Fax:** 212-642-4549
New York, NY 10006
www.drjoy.com

Browne, Patti Ann
News anchor on FOX News Channel
FOX News Channel **Ph:** 212-301-3000
1211 Ave of the Americas
New York, NY 10036
www.foxnews.com/fnctv

Browne, Sylvia (1936-)
Psychic and spiritual adviser
Sylvia Browne Corp **Ph:** 408-379-7070
Society of Novus Spiritus **Fax:** 408-871-2328
35 Dillon Ave
Campbell, CA 95008
www.sylvia.org

Browner, Carol (1955-)
Former head of the US Environmental Protection Agency
Albright Group LLC **Ph:** 202-842-7222
901 15th St NW Suite 1000
Washington, DC 20005
www.thealbrightgroupllc.com

Browning, Kurt (1966-)
Figure skater
Stars on Ice **Ph:** 216-436-3708
IMG
1360 E 9th St Suite 100
Cleveland, OH 44114
www.kurtfiles.com

Bruce, Carol Elder
Attorney; was Independent Counsel in a case involving President Clinton's pardon of financier Marc Rich, and her investigation of charges against Interior Secretary Bruce Babbitt resulted in his exoneration
Venable LLP **Ph:** 202-344-4717
575 7th St NW **Fax:** 202-344-8300
Washington, DC 20004
www.venable.com

Bruce, Isaac (1972-)
Professional football player
Saint Louis Rams **Ph:** 314-982-7267
1 Rams Way **Fax:** 314-770-9261
Earth City, MO 63045
www.stlouisrams.com

Bruckheimer, Jerry (1945-)
Filmmaker; also executive producer of several TV programs & series
Creative Artists Agency **Ph:** 310-288-4545
9830 Wilshire Blvd **Fax:** 310-288-4800
Beverly Hills, CA 90212
www.jbfilms.com

Brun, Christine
Interior designer; writes the syndicated column Small Spaces, which offers advice on how to live well in a small home
Copley News Service **Ph:** 619-293-1818
PO Box 120190
San Diego, CA 92112
www.copleynews.com

Brundege, Barbara
Photographer
Summit Photographic Workshops **Ph:** 831-440-0124
PO Box 67459
Scotts Valley, CA 95067
www.summitphotographic.com

Brunell, Mark (1970-)
Professional football player
Washington Redskins **Ph:** 703-726-7000
21300 Redskin Park Dr **Fax:** 703-726-7086
Ashburn, VA 20147
www.redskins.com

Bruner, Joseph P, MD
Fetal surgeon
Vanderbilt Medical Center **Ph:** 615-322-0122
1211 22nd Ave S **Fax:** 615-343-8881
Nashville, TN 37232

Bruno, Tony
Hosts a radio sports talk program
KMPC **Ph:** 310-452-7100
2800 28th St Suite 308 **Fax:** 310-452-5950
Los Angeles, CA 90405
www.1540theticket.com

Bruschi, Tedy (1973-)
Professional football player
New England Patriots **Ph:** 508-543-8200
1 Patriots Pl **Fax:** 508-543-0285
Foxboro, MA 02035
www.patriots.com

Bryan, Bob (1978-)
Professional tennis player
SFX Sports Group **Ph:** 202-686-2000
5335 Wisconsin Ave NW Suite 850 **Fax:** 202-686-5050
Washington, DC 20015
www.bobandmike.com

Bryan, Mike (1978-)
Professional tennis player
SFX Sports Group **Ph:** 202-686-2000
5335 Wisconsin Ave NW Suite 850 **Fax:** 202-686-5050
Washington, DC 20015
www.bobandmike.com

Bryant, Joe (1954-)
Basketball coach; former NBA player
Los Angeles Sparks **Ph:** 310-341-1000
2151 E Grand Ave Suite 100 **Fax:** 310-341-1029
El Segundo, CA 90245
www.wnba.com/sparks

Bryant, Kobe (1978-)
Professional basketball player
Los Angeles Lakers **Ph:** 310-426-6000
555 N Nash St **Fax:** 310-426-6105
El Segundo, CA 90245
www.nba.com/lakers

Bryant, Paul W (1913-1983)
Legendary University of Alabama football coach; was known as Bear Bryant
Paul Bryant Museum **Ph:** 205-348-4668
300 Paul W Bryant Dr **Fax:** 205-348-8883
Tuscaloosa, AL 35487 **TF:** 866-772-2327
www.bryantmuseum.com

Bryson, Bill (1951-)
Author (A Walk in the Woods; A Short History of Nearly Everything)
Broadway Books Publicity **Ph:** 212-782-9000
1745 Broadway
New York, NY 10019
www.randomhouse.com/features/billbryson

Brzezinski, Mika (1967-)
CBS News correspondent
CBS News **Ph:** 212-975-4114
524 W 57th St
New York, NY 10019
www.cbsnews.com

Brzezinski, Zbigniew, PhD (1928-)
National Security Advisor to President Jimmy Carter
Center for Strategic & International Studies **Ph:** 202-887-0200 **Fax:** 202-775-3199
1800 K St NW Suite 400
Washington, DC 20006
csis.org/experts

Buble, Michael (1975-)
Singer (swing music)
William Morris Agency **Ph:** 310-859-4000
1 William Morris Pl **Fax:** 310-859-4462
Beverly Hills, CA 90212
www.michaelbuble.com

Buchanan, Angela "Bay" (1949-)
Pat Buchanan's sister; served as his campaign chairman when he was a candidate for US President and is president of The American Cause, which he founded
The American Cause **Ph:** 703-255-2632
501 Church St Suite 217 **Fax:** 703-255-2219
Vienna, VA 22180
www.theamericancause.org

Buchanan, James M Jr, PhD (1919-)
Winner of the 1986 Nobel Prize in Economics for his development of the contractual and constitutional bases for the theory of economic and political decision-making
George Mason University **Ph:** 703-993-2327
Dept of Economics **Fax:** 703-993-1133
MSN 3G4
Fairfax, VA 22030
www.gmu.edu/departments/economics

Buchanan, Patrick J (1938-)
Political conservative and former candidate for US president; founder/chairman of The American Cause; also a syndicated columnist
The American Cause **Ph:** 703-255-2632
501 Church St Suite 217 **Fax:** 703-255-2219
Vienna, VA 22180
www.theamericancause.org

Buchanon, Phillip (1980-)
Professional football player
Houston Texans **Ph:** 832-667-2000
2 Reliant Park **Fax:** 832-667-2100
Houston, TX 77054
www.houstontexans.com

Buchman, Dana
Fashion designer
1441 Broadway 2nd Fl **Ph:** 212-626-3000
New York, NY 10018
www.danabuchman.com

Buchwald, Art (1925-)
Humorist; syndicated columnist/author
Tribune Media Services Inc **Ph:** 312-222-4444
435 N Michigan Ave Suite 1500
Chicago, IL 60611
tmsfeatures.com/productlist.htm

Buck, Joe (1969-)
Sports broadcaster
Fox Sports Net **Ph:** 310-369-9160
10201 W Pico Blvd **Fax:** 310-969-6049
Bldg 101
Los Angeles, CA 90035

Buck, Linda B, PhD (1947-)
Winner (with Richard Axel) of the 2004 Nobel Prize in Physiology or Medicine for discoveries of odorant receptors and the organization of the olfactory system
Buck Laboratory **Ph:** 206-667-6316
Fred Hutchinson Cancer Research Center **Fax:** 206-667-1031
1100 Fairview Ave N
MS A3-020
Seattle, WA 98109
www.hhmi.org/research/nobel

Buckley, Christopher (1952-)
Social & political satirist and editor of Forbes FYI magazine
Random House Publicity **Ph:** 212-782-9000
1745 Broadway
New York, NY 10019
www.randomhouse.com

Buckley, George W
Chairman, president, and CEO of 3M
3M Inc **Ph:** 651-737-4542
3M Center **Fax:** 651-733-9973
Saint Paul, MN 55144
www.3m.com

Buckley, William F Jr (1925-)
Author and founder and editor of The National Review
National Review **Ph:** 212-679-7330
215 Lexington Ave
New York, NY 10016
www.nationalreview.com

Buddle, Edson (1981-)
Professional soccer player
New York Red Bulls **Ph:** 201-583-7000
1 Harmon Plaza 3rd Fl **Fax:** 201-583-7055
Secaucus, NJ 07094
redbull.newyork.mlsnet.com

Buffett, Jimmy (1946-)
Singer/songwriter
Margaritaville Inc **Ph:** 305-296-9089
424A Fleming St **Fax:** 305-296-1084
Key West, FL 33040
www.margaritaville.com

Buffett, Warren E (1930-)
Billionaire stock market investor known as the Oracle of Omaha; chairman & CEO of Berkshire Hathaway
Berkshire Hathaway Inc **Ph:** 402-346-1400
1440 Kiewit Plaza
Omaha, NE 68131
www.berkshirehathaway.com

Bugliosi, Vincent (1934-)
Attorney who prosecuted Charles Manson; also writes books (Helter Skelter)
3699 Wilshire Blvd Suite 850 **Ph:** 310-273-9013
Los Angeles, CA 90010

Bulger, Marc (1977-)
Professional football player
Saint Louis Rams **Ph:** 314-982-7267
1 Rams Way **Fax:** 314-770-9261
Earth City, MO 63045
www.stlouisrams.com

Bullock, Sandra (1964-)
Actor; also produces movies
Creative Artists Agency **Ph:** 310-288-4545
9830 Wilshire Blvd **Fax:** 310-288-4800
Beverly Hills, CA 90212

Bulluck, Keith (1977-)
Professional football player
Tennessee Titans **Ph:** 615-565-4000
460 Great Circle Rd **Fax:** 615-565-4006
Nashville, TN 37228
www.titansonline.com

Bundchen, Gisele (1980-)
Model
IMG Models **Ph:** 212-253-8884
304 Park Ave S 12th Fl **Fax:** 212-253-8883
New York, NY 10010
www.imgmodels.com

Bunning, Jim (1931-)
US Senator from Kentucky (Republican)
316 Hart Bldg **Ph:** 202-224-4343
Washington, DC 20510 **Fax:** 202-224-1373
bunning.senate.gov

Bunting, Eve
Author of books for young readers, including picture books, middle grade novels, and novels for young adults
Boyds Mills Press **Ph:** 570-253-1164
815 Church St
Honesdale, PA 18431
www.boydsmillspress.com/authors.tpl

Burchfield, Bobby R
Trial lawyer; practices in the area of complex corporate litigation
McDermott Will & Emery LLP **Ph:** 202-756-8003
600 13th St NW **Fax:** 202-756-8087
Washington, DC 20005
www.mwe.com

Burd, Steven A (1950-)
Chairman, president & CEO of Safeway Inc
Safeway Inc **Ph:** 925-467-3000
5918 Stoneridge Mall Rd **Fax:** 925-467-3321
Pleasanton, CA 94588
www.safeway.com/Investor_Relations

Burgess, Michael C (1950-)
US Representative from Texas (Republican)
1721 Longworth Bldg **Ph:** 202-225-7772
Washington, DC 20515 **Fax:** 202-225-2919
burgess.house.gov

Burke, Brooke (1971-)
Model and television host
William Morris Agency **Ph:** 310-859-4000
1 William Morris Pl **Fax:** 310-859-4462
Beverly Hills, CA 90212
www.brookeburke.com

Burke, Chris (1965-)
Actor (first actor with Down's Syndrome to star in a television series)
CJJ Enterprises **Ph:** 609-581-2651
48 Hempstead Rd
Trenton, NJ 08610
www.chrisburke.org

Burke, James Lee (1936-)
Author (Dixie City Jam, Bitterroot, Purple Cane Road)
Simon & Schuster **Ph:** 212-698-7000
1230 Ave of the Americas
New York, NY 10020
www.jamesleeburke.com

Burke, Sean (1967-)
Professional hockey player
Tampa Bay Lightning **Ph:** 813-301-6600
St Pete Times Forum **Fax:** 813-301-1487
401 Channelside Dr
Tampa, FL 33602
www.tampabaylightning.com

Burleson, Nate (1981-)
Professional football player
Seattle Seahawks **Ph:** 425-827-9777
11220 NE 53rd St **Fax:** 425-827-9008
Kirkland, WA 98033
www.seahawks.com

Burness, Tad
Writes Auto Album, a syndicated column about vintage automobiles
King Features Syndicate Inc **Ph:** 212-455-4000
888 7th Ave 2nd Fl
New York, NY 10019
www.kingfeatures.com

Burnett, AJ (1977-)
Professional baseball player
Toronto Blue Jays **Ph:** 416-341-1000
1 Blue Jays Way **Fax:** 416-341-1250
Toronto, ON M5V1J1
toronto.bluejays.mlb.com

Burnett, Carol (1933-)
Comedic entertainer; actor
International Creative Management **Ph:** 310-550-4000
8942 Wilshire Blvd
Beverly Hills, CA 90211

Burns, Conrad (1935-)
US Senator from Montana (Republican)
187 Dirksen Bldg **Ph:** 202-224-2644
Washington, DC 20510 **Fax:** 202-224-8594
burns.senate.gov

Burns, Edward (1968-)
Screenwriter/producer/director/actor
Creative Artists Agency **Ph:** 310-288-4545
9830 Wilshire Blvd **Fax:** 310-288-4800
Beverly Hills, CA 90212

Burns, Eric
Host of Fox News Watch
FOX News Channel **Ph:** 212-301-3000
1211 Ave of the Americas
New York, NY 10036
www.foxnews.com/fnctv

Burns, Harmon E (1946-)
Senior General Partner of the San Francisco Giants baseball club
San Francisco Giants **Ph:** 415-972-2000
AT & T Park
24 Willie Mays Plaza
San Francisco, CA 94107
sanfrancisco.giants.mlb.com

Burns, Ken (1953-)
Documentary filmmaker
Florentine Films **Ph:** 603-756-3038
Maple Grove Rd **Fax:** 603-756-4389
PO Box 613
Walpole, NH 03608
www.florentinefilms.com

Burns, Scott
Writes a syndicated business column for The Dallas Morning News
Universal Press Syndicate **Ph:** 816-932-6600
4520 Main St
Kansas City, MO 64111
www.amuniversal.com/ups/features

Burr, Richard (1955-)
US Senator from North Carolina (Republican)
B40C Dirksen Bldg **Ph:** 202-224-3154
Washington, DC 20510
burr.senate.gov

Burrell, Pat (1976-)
Professional baseball player
Philadelphia Phillies **Ph:** 215-463-6000
Citizens Bank Park
1 Citizens Bank Park Way
Philadelphia, PA 19148
philadelphia.phillies.mlb.com

Burress, Plaxico (1977-)
Professional football player
New York Giants **Ph:** 201-935-8111
Giants Stadium **Fax:** 201-939-4134
East Rutherford, NJ 07073
www.giants.com

Burros, Marian
New York Times reporter and food columnist (syndicated)
New York Times Syndicate **Ph:** 212-556-1234
229 W 43rd St
New York, NY 10036
www.nytsyn.com/lifestyle.html

Burrough, Bryan
Author (Barbarians at the Gate)
HarperCollins Publishers **Ph:** 212-207-7000
c/o Author Mail
10 E 53rd St
New York, NY 10022
www.harpercollins.com

Burrows, Edwin G
Author of historical books (Gotham)
Oxford University Press **Ph:** 212-726-6000
198 Madison Ave
New York, NY 10016
www.oup.com

Burrus, Daniel
Motivational speaker; a leading technology forecaster, business strategist, and author whose writings include Technotrends
Burrus Research Assoc Inc **Ph:** 262-367-0949
557 Cottonwood Ave Suite 106 **Fax:** 262-367-7163
PO Box 47
Hartland, WI 53029
www.burrus.com

Burstyn, Ellen (1932-)
Actor
Creative Artists Agency **Ph:** 310-288-4545
9830 Wilshire Blvd **Fax:** 310-288-4800
Beverly Hills, CA 90212

Burton, Dan (1938-)
US Representative from Indiana (Republican)
2185 Rayburn Bldg **Ph:** 202-225-2276
Washington, DC 20515 **Fax:** 202-225-0016
www.house.gov/burton

Burton, Jeff (1967-)
NASCAR driver
Richard Childress Racing **Ph:** 336-731-3334
236 Industrial Dr
PO Box 1189
Welcome, NC 27374
www.rcrracing.com

Burton, Lance (1960-)
Magician/illusionist
Monte Carlo Resort & Casino **Ph:** 702-730-7777
3770 Las Vegas Blvd S **Fax:** 702-730-7229
Las Vegas, NV 89109
www.lanceburton.com

Burton, Tim (1958-)
Film director/writer/producer
William Morris Agency **Ph:** 310-859-4000
1 William Morris Pl **Fax:** 310-859-4462
Beverly Hills, CA 90212

Bury, Chris
Nightline correspondent
ABC News Nightline **Ph:** 202-222-7700
1717 DeSales St NW
Washington, DC 20036
www.abcnews.go.com/Nightline

Buscemi, Steve (1957-)
Actor
Endeavor **Ph:** 310-248-2000
9601 Wilshire Blvd 3rd Fl **Fax:** 310-248-2020
Beverly Hills, CA 90210

Busch, August A III (1963-)
Chairman of the Board of the Anheuser-Busch Companies
Anheuser-Busch Cos Inc **Ph:** 314-577-2000
1 Busch Pl **Fax:** 314-577-2900
Saint Louis, MO 63118
www.anheuser-busch.com

Busch, Jon (1976-)
Professional soccer player
Columbus Crew **Ph:** 614-447-2739
Columbus Crew Stadium **Fax:** 614-447-4109
1 Black & Gold Blvd
Columbus, OH 43211
columbus.crew.mlsnet.com

Busch, Kurt (1978-)
NASCAR driver
Penske Racing South **Ph:** 704-664-2300
200 Penske Way
Mooresville, NC 28115
www.penskeracing.com

Bush, Barbara (1925-)
Former First Lady of the US (wife of George HW Bush)
10000 Memorial Dr Suite 900 **Ph:** 713-686-1188
Houston, TX 77024

Bush, Fredy
Vice Chairman & CEO of Xinhua Finance
Xinhua Finance **Ph:** 212-669-6400
40 Fulton St 5th Fl **Fax:** 212-608-3024
New York, NY 10038
www.xfnn.com

Bush, George HW (1924-)
41st US President
10000 Memorial Dr Suite 900 **Ph:** 713-686-1188
Houston, TX 77024

Bush, George W (1946-)
43rd US President
President of the US **Ph:** 202-456-1414
1600 Pennsylvania Ave NW
Washington, DC 20500
www.whitehouse.gov/president

Bush, Jeb (1953-)
Governor of Florida (Republican)
State Capitol **Ph:** 850-488-4441
Tallahassee, FL 32399 **Fax:** 850-487-0801
www.flgov.com

Bush, Laura Welch (1946-)
First Lady of the United States (wife of President George W Bush)
First Lady **Ph:** 202-456-7064
1600 Pennsylvania Ave NW **Fax:** 202-456-6771
200 East Wing
Washington, DC 20500
www.whitehouse.gov/firstlady

Bush, Reggie (1985-)
USC football player drafted by the New Orleans Saints in 2006
New Orleans Saints **Ph:** 504-733-0255
5800 Airline Dr **Fax:** 504-731-1768
Metairie, LA 70003
www.neworleanssaints.com

Bushnell, Candace
Author of Sex and the City
Warner Books **Ph:** 212-522-7200
c/o Author Mail
1271 Ave of the Americas
New York, NY 10020
www.twbookmark.com

Buss, Jerry, PhD
Owner of the Los Angeles Lakers basketball team; also plays on the World Poker Tour
Los Angeles Lakers **Ph:** 310-426-6000
555 N Nash St **Fax:** 310-426-6106
El Segundo, CA 90245
www.nba.com/lakers

Butler, Brett (1958-)
Comedian; actor
International Creative Management **Ph:** 310-550-4000
8942 Wilshire Blvd
Beverly Hills, CA 90211
www.brettbutler.com

Butler, Caron (1980-)
Professional basketball player
Washington Wizards — **Ph:** 202-661-5000
Verizon Center — **Fax:** 202-661-5094
601 F St NW
Washington, DC 20004
www.nba.com/wizards

Butler, Jerametrius (1978-)
Professional football player
Saint Louis Rams — **Ph:** 314-982-7267
1 Rams Way — **Fax:** 314-770-9261
Earth City, MO 63045
www.stlouisrams.com

Butler, Octavia E (1947-)
Writer of science fiction & fantasy books (Patternmaster)
Warner Books — **Ph:** 212-522-7200
c/o Author Mail
1271 Ave of the Americas
New York, NY 10020
www.twbookmark.com

Butler, Robert Olen (1945-)
Author of A Good Scent from a Strange Mountain, a collection of stories about the aftermath of the Vietnam War and its enduring impact on the Vietnamese
Grove/Atlantic Inc — **Ph:** 212-614-7860
841 Broadway — **Fax:** 212-614-7886
New York, NY 10003
www.groveatlantic.com

Butt, Charles C
Chairman & CEO of the HE Butt Grocery Co
HE Butt Grocery Co — **Ph:** 210-938-8000
646 S Main Ave — **Fax:** 210-938-8169
San Antonio, TX 78204
www.heb.com

Butte, Amy S (1968-)
Executive Vice President and CFO of the New York Stock Exchange
New York Stock Exchange Inc — **Ph:** 212-656-3000
11 Wall St
New York, NY 10005
www.nyse.com

Butterfield, GK Jr (1947-)
US Representative from North Carolina (Democrat)
413 Cannon Bldg — **Ph:** 202-225-3101
Washington, DC 20515 — **Fax:** 202-225-3354
www.house.gov/butterfield

Buttner, Brenda
Senior business correspondent at FOX News Channel
FOX News Channel — **Ph:** 212-301-3000
1211 Ave of the Americas
New York, NY 10036
www.foxnews.com/fnctv

Buyer, Steve (1958-)
US Representative from Indiana (Republican)
2230 Rayburn Bldg — **Ph:** 202-225-5037
Washington, DC 20515 — **Fax:** 202-225-2267
stevebuyer.house.gov

Byars, Betsy (1928-)
Author of books for young readers
Puffin Books Publicity — **Ph:** 212-366-2000
345 Hudson St
New York, NY 10014
www.betsybyars.com

Byatt, AS (1936-)
British novelist & critic
Steven Barclay Agency — **Ph:** 707-773-0654
12 Western Ave — **Fax:** 707-778-1868
Petaluma, CA 94952 — **TF:** 888-965-7323
www.asbyatt.com

Bynes, Amanda (1986-)
Actor
United Talent Agency — **Ph:** 310-273-6700
9560 Wilshire Blvd 5th Fl — **Fax:** 310-247-1111
Beverly Hills, CA 90212

Byrd, Robert C (1917-)
US Senator from West Virginia (Democrat)
311 Hart Bldg — **Ph:** 202-224-3954
Washington, DC 20510 — **Fax:** 202-228-0002
byrd.senate.gov

Byrd, Tracy (1966-)
Country singer
William Morris Agency — **Ph:** 615-963-3000
1600 Division St Suite 300 — **Fax:** 615-963-3090
Nashville, TN 37203
www.tbyrd.com

C

Caan, James (1939-)
Actor
Endeavor — **Ph:** 310-248-2000
9601 Wilshire Blvd 3rd Fl — **Fax:** 310-248-2020
Beverly Hills, CA 90210

Cabot, Meg (1967-)
Author of The Princess Diaries books
HarperCollins Children's Books **Ph:** 212-261-6500
1350 Ave of the Americas
New York, NY 10019
www.megcabot.com

Cabraser, Elizabeth J
Attorney; principal practice areas include consumer protection, international and human rights, personal injury/torts, and defective products
Lieff Cabraser Heimann & Bernstein LLP **Ph:** 415-956-1000 **Fax:** 415-956-1008
Embarcadero Center W
275 Battery St Suite 3000
San Francisco, CA 94111
www.lieffcabraser.com

Cabrera, Miguel (1983-)
Professional baseball player
Florida Marlins **Ph:** 305-626-7400
Dolphins Stadium **Fax:** 305-626-7428
2267 Dan Marino Blvd
Miami, FL 33056
florida.marlins.mlb.com

Cabrera, Rob
Creator of the comic strip Silo Roberts
United Feature Syndicate **Ph:** 212-293-8500
200 Madison Ave
New York, NY 10016
www.unitedfeatures.com

Caedmon's Call
Contemporary Christian music group (folk-rock style)
Breen Agency **Ph:** 615-777-2227
110 30th Ave N Suite 3 **Fax:** 615-321-4656
Nashville, TN 37203
www.caedmonscall.com

Cafaro, Debra A (1957-)
Chairman, president, and CEO of Ventas Inc, a leading healthcare real estate investment trust
Ventas Inc **Ph:** 502-357-9000
10350 Ormsby Pk Pl Suite 300 **Fax:** 502-357-9001
Louisville, KY 40223
www.ventasreit.com

Cafferty, Jack
Anchor of CNN's In the Money
CNN **Ph:** 404-827-1500
1 CNN Center
Atlanta, GA 30303
www.cnn.com/CNN/anchors_reporters

Cage, Nicolas (1964-)
Actor
Creative Artists Agency **Ph:** 310-288-4545
9830 Wilshire Blvd **Fax:** 310-288-4800
Beverly Hills, CA 90212

Caggiano, Biba
Chef/owner of Biba Restaurant; also a cookbook author
Biba Restaurant **Ph:** 916-455-2422
2801 Capitol Ave **Fax:** 916-455-0542
Sacramento, CA 95816
biba-restaurant.com

Cagle, Daryl
Editorial/political cartoonist for MSNBC
Cagle Cartoons Inc **Ph:** 805-969-2829
PO Box 22342
Santa Barbara, CA 93121
www.caglecartoons.com

Cahill, Thomas
Author of nonfiction/historical works (Sailing the Wine-Dark Sea: Why the Greeks Matter)
Nan A Talese/Doubleday **Ph:** 212-782-8918
1745 Broadway 22nd Fl **Fax:** 212-782-8448
New York, NY 10019
www.thomascahill.com

Caine, Michael (1933-)
Actor
International Creative Management **Ph:** 310-550-4000
8942 Wilshire Blvd
Beverly Hills, CA 90211

Calcavecchia, Mark (1960-)
Professional golfer
Gaylord Sports Management **Ph:** 480-483-9500
13845 N Northsight Blvd Suite 200
Scottsdale, AZ 85260
www.gaylordsports.com

Calder, Alexander (1898-1976)
Sculptor; inventor of the mobile
Calder Foundation **Ph:** 212-334-2424
207 W 25th St 12th Fl **Fax:** 212-334-2423
New York, NY 10001
www.calder.org

Calfee, John E, PhD
Economist; resident scholar at the American Enterprise Institute
American Enterprise Institute for Public Policy Research **Ph:** 202-862-5800 **Fax:** 202-862-7177
1150 17th St NW Suite 1100
Washington, DC 20036
www.aei.org

Calhoun, Coyote
Country music disc jockey
WAMZ-FM **Ph:** 502-479-2222
4000 1 Radio Dr **Fax:** 502-479-2227
Louisville, KY 40218
www.wamz.com

Callahan, Bill (1956-)
College football coach
University of Nebraska Athletic Dept **Ph:** 402-472-3116
217 South Stadium
PO Box 880125
Lincoln, NE 68588
www.coachcallahan.com

Callahan, Robert F Jr
Chairman & CEO of Ziff Davis Media Inc; former President of ABC Television Network
Ziff Davis Media Inc **Ph:** 212-503-3500
28 E 28th St **Fax:** 212-503-5696
New York, NY 10016
www.ziffdavis.com

Calomiris, Charles, PhD
Economist
American Enterprise Institute for Public Policy Research **Ph:** 202-862-5800 **Fax:** 202-862-7177
1150 17th St NW Suite 1100
Washington, DC 20036
www.aei.org

Calvert, Ken (1953-)
US Representative from California (Republican)
2201 Rayburn Bldg **Ph:** 202-225-1986
Washington, DC 20515 **Fax:** 202-225-2004
calvert.house.gov

Camacho, Felix (1957-)
Governor of Guam (Republican)
238 Archbishop Flores St Suite 405 **Ph:** 671-472-8931 **Fax:** 671-477-4826
PO Box 2950
Hagatna, GU 96910
www.nga.org/governors

Camby, Marcus (1974-)
Professional basketball player
Denver Nuggets **Ph:** 303-405-1100
Pepsi Center **Fax:** 303-575-1920
1000 Chopper Cir
Denver, CO 80204
www.nba.com/nuggets

Cameron, Carl (1961-)
Chief White House correspondent for FOX News
FOX News Channel **Ph:** 202-824-6300
400 N Capitol St NW Suite 550
Washington, DC 20001
www.foxnews.com/fnctv

Cameron, James (1954-)
Producer/director/writer
Lightstorm Entertainment **Ph:** 310-656-6100
919 Santa Monica Blvd **Fax:** 310-656-6102
Santa Monica, CA 90401

Cameron, Mike (1973-)
Professional baseball player
San Diego Padres **Ph:** 619-795-5000
Petco Park **Fax:** 619-497-5339
PO Box 122000
San Diego, CA 92112
sandiego.padres.mlb.com

Cameron, W Bruce
Writes a syndicated humor column about daily life
Creators Syndicate Inc **Ph:** 310-337-7003
5777 W Century Blvd Suite 700 **Fax:** 310-337-7625
Los Angeles, CA 90045
www.creators.com

Camilleri, Louis C
Chairman and CEO of Altria Group, the parent company of Kraft Foods, Philip Morris International, Philip Morris USA, and Philip Morris Capital Corp
Altria Group Inc **Ph:** 917-663-5000
120 Park Ave **Fax:** 917-663-2167
New York, NY 10017
www.altria.com

Cammarata, Bernard (1941-)
Chairman of the Board and Acting CEO of TJX Cos, the off-price retailer whose businesses include TJ Maxx, Marshall's, HomeGoods, and AJ Wright
TJX Cos Inc **Ph:** 508-390-1000
770 Cochituate Rd
Framingham, MA 01701
www.tjx.com

Camp, Dave (1953-)
US Representative from Michigan (Republican)
137 Cannon Bldg **Ph:** 202-225-3561
Washington, DC 20515 **Fax:** 202-225-9679
wwwc.house.gov/camp

Camp, Jeremy (1978-)
Singer (Contemporary Christian music)
Third Coast Artists Agency **Ph:** 615-297-2021
2021 21st Ave S Suite 220 **Fax:** 615-297-2776
Nashville, TN 37212
www.jeremycamp.com

Campbell, Ben
Co-host (with Brian Egan) of a country music radio show
Premiere Radio Networks Inc — **Ph:** 818-377-5300
Ben & Brian — **Fax:** 818-377-5333
15260 Ventura Blvd 5th Fl
Sherman Oaks, CA 91403
www.benandbrian.com

Campbell, Glen (1936-)
Country singer
William Morris Agency — **Ph:** 615-963-3000
1600 Division St Suite 300 — **Fax:** 615-963-3090
Nashville, TN 37203
www.glencampbellshow.com

Campbell, James
President & CEO of GE Consumer & Industrial, a $14 billion global business
GE Consumer & Industrial Systems — **Ph:** 860-747-7397
41 Woodford Ave
Plainville, CT 06062
www.geconsumerproducts.com/pressroom

Campbell, Jenny
Illustrator; draws the comic strip Flo & Friends
Creators Syndicate Inc — **Ph:** 310-337-7003
5777 W Century Blvd Suite 700 — **Fax:** 310-337-7625
Los Angeles, CA 90045
www.creators.com

Campbell, John (1955-)
US Representative from California (Republican)
2402 Rayburn House Office Bldg — **Ph:** 202-225-5611 — **Fax:** 202-225-9177
Washington, DC 20515
campbell.house.gov

Campbell, Kirk
President & CEO of International Data Corp
International Data Corp — **Ph:** 508-935-4707
5 Speen St — **Fax:** 508-935-4015
Framingham, MA 01701
www.idc.com

Campbell, Neve (1973-)
Actor
International Creative Management — **Ph:** 310-550-4000
8942 Wilshire Blvd
Beverly Hills, CA 90211
www.official.nevecampbell.org

Canadas, Esther (1977-)
Fashion model
Wilhelmina Models Inc — **Ph:** 212-473-0700
300 Park Ave S 2nd Fl — **Fax:** 212-473-3223
New York, NY 10010

Canfield, Jack
Motivational speaker; co-author of the Chicken Soup for the Soul book series and founder of Self Esteem Seminars
PO Box 30880 — **Ph:** 805-563-2935
Santa Barbara, CA 93130 — **Fax:** 805-563-2945
www.chickensoup.com

Canin, Ethan
Author (Carry Me Across the Water; The Palace Thief, a short story that is being made into a movie called The Emperor's Club)
Random House Publicity — **Ph:** 212-782-9000
1745 Broadway
New York, NY 10019
www.randomhouse.com

Cannell, Stephen J (1941-)
TV writer/producer; novelist
Creative Artists Agency — **Ph:** 310-288-4545
9830 Wilshire Blvd — **Fax:** 310-288-4800
Beverly Hills, CA 90212
www.cannell.com

Cannon, Christopher (1950-)
US Representative from Utah (Republican)
2436 Rayburn Bldg — **Ph:** 202-225-7751
Washington, DC 20515 — **Fax:** 202-225-5629
www.house.gov/cannon

Cannon, Janell
Author & illustrator of children's picture books (Crickwing, Verdi, Stellaluna)
Harcourt Children's Books — **Ph:** 212-592-1000
15 E 26th St
New York, NY 10010
www.harcourtbooks.com

Cannon, Joe (1975-)
Professional soccer player
Colorado Rapids — **Ph:** 303-405-1100
Pepsi Ctr — **Fax:** 720-931-2022
1000 Chopper Cir
Denver, CO 80204
www.coloradorapids.com

Canton, James, PhD
Social scientist, author, and speaker; founder of the Institute for Global Futures, a San Francisco-based think tank that forecasts innovations and trends
Institute for Global Futures **Ph:** 415-563-0720
2084 Union St **Fax:** 415-563-0219
San Francisco, CA 94123
www.futureguru.com

Cantone, Mario (1960-)
Actor (theater, film, TV); comedian
Innovative Artists **Ph:** 310-656-0400
1505 10th St **Fax:** 310-656-0456
Santa Monica, CA 90401
www.mariocantone.com

Cantor, Eric (1963-)
US Representative from Virginia (Republican)
329 Cannon Bldg **Ph:** 202-225-2815
Washington, DC 20515 **Fax:** 202-225-0011
cantor.house.gov

Cantu, Hector
Writes the syndicated comic strip Baldo, which is drawn by Carlos Castellanos; Baldo was the first comic strip to feature Latino characters and themes
Universal Press Syndicate **Ph:** 816-932-6600
4520 Main St
Kansas City, MO 64111
www.amuniversal.com/ups/features

Cantwell, Maria (1958-)
US Senator from Washington (Democrat)
717 Hart Bldg **Ph:** 202-224-3441
Washington, DC 20510 **Fax:** 202-228-0514
cantwell.senate.gov

Capito, Shelley Moore (1953-)
US Representative from West Virginia (Republican)
1431 Longworth Bldg **Ph:** 202-225-2711
Washington, DC 20515 **Fax:** 202-225-7856
capito.house.gov

Caplan, Arthur, PhD (1950-)
Bioethicist
Center for Bioethics **Ph:** 215-898-7136
University of Pennsylvania
3401 Market St Suite 320
Philadelphia, PA 19104
www.bioethics.upenn.edu

Cappiello, Frank
Financial analyst, speaker/lecturer, frequent talk-show guest; chairman of Cappiello-Rushmore Funds
Cappiello-Rushmore Funds **Ph:** 301-657-1500
4922 Fairmont Ave 3rd Fl **Fax:** 301-343-3355
Bethesda, MD 20814

Capps, Lois (1938-)
US Representative from California (Democrat)
1707 Longworth Bldg **Ph:** 202-225-3601
Washington, DC 20515 **Fax:** 202-225-5632
www.house.gov/capps

Capriati, Jennifer (1976-)
Professional tennis player
WTA Tour **Ph:** 727-895-5000
1 Progress Plaza Suite 1500
Saint Petersburg, FL 33701
www.wtatour.com

Capuano, Michael E (1952-)
US Representative from Massachusetts (Democrat)
1530 Longworth Bldg **Ph:** 202-225-5111
Washington, DC 20515 **Fax:** 202-225-9322
www.house.gov/capuano

Carbonneau, Guy (1960-)
Former pro hockey player, now a special assistant to the General Manager of the Dallas Stars hockey team
Dallas Stars **Ph:** 214-387-5500
2601 Ave of the Stars **Fax:** 214-387-3599
Frisco, TX 75034
www.dallasstars.com

Carcieri, Don (1942-)
Governor of Rhode Island (Republican)
State House **Ph:** 401-222-2080
Providence, RI 02903 **Fax:** 401-273-5729
www.governor.state.ri.us

Card, Orson Scott (1951-)
Author of fantasy & science fiction novels (Shadow Puppets; Lost Boys)
Tor Books **Ph:** 212-388-0100
175 5th Ave
New York, NY 10010
www.hatrack.com

Cardin, Benjamin L (1943-)
US Representative from Maryland (Democrat)
2207 Rayburn Bldg **Ph:** 202-225-4016
Washington, DC 20515 **Fax:** 202-225-9219
www.cardin.house.gov

Cardoza, Dennis (1959-)
US Representative from California (Democrat)
435 Cannon Bldg **Ph:** 202-225-6131
Washington, DC 20515 **Fax:** 202-225-0819
www.house.gov/cardoza

Carell, Monroe J Jr
Chairman and CEO of Central Parking Corp
Central Parking Corp **Ph:** 615-297-4255
2401 21st Ave S Suite 200 **Fax:** 615-297-6240
Nashville, TN 37212
www.parking.com

Carell, Steve (1963-)
Actor
Endeavor **Ph:** 310-248-2000
9601 Wilshire Blvd 3rd Fl **Fax:** 310-248-2020
Beverly Hills, CA 90210
www.nbc.com/The_Office

Carey, Chase
President & CEO of the DIRECTV Group
DIRECTV Group Inc **Ph:** 310-964-0700
2230 E Imperial Hwy **Fax:** 310-535-5225
El Segundo, CA 90245
www.directv.com

Carey, Drew (1958-)
Comedian; actor
Messina Baker Entertainment **Ph:** 323-954-8600
955 Carrillo Dr Suite 100
Los Angeles, CA 90048
www.messinabaker.com

Carey, Mariah (1970-)
Singer
Creative Artists Agency **Ph:** 310-288-4545
9830 Wilshire Blvd **Fax:** 310-288-4800
Beverly Hills, CA 90212
www.mariahcarey.com

Carey, Peter (1943-)
Novelist (Oscar & Lucinda)
Random House Publicity **Ph:** 212-782-9000
1745 Broadway
New York, NY 10019
www.randomhouse.com

Carillo, Mary (1957-)
Former professional tennis player, now tennis analyst; also a correspondent on Real Sports with Bryant Gumbel on HBO
CBS Sports **Ph:** 212-975-4321
51 W 52nd St
New York, NY 10019
cbs.sportsline.com/cbssports/team

Carle, Eric (1929-)
Creator of picture books for very young children, including The Very Hungry Caterpillar
Simon & Schuster Books for Young Readers **Ph:** 212-698-7000
1230 Ave of the Americas
New York, NY 10020
www.eric-carle.com

Carlin, George (1936-)
Comedian
International Creative Management **Ph:** 310-550-4000
8942 Wilshire Blvd
Beverly Hills, CA 90211
www.georgecarlin.com

Carlisle, Rick (1959-)
Basketball coach
Indiana Pacers **Ph:** 317-917-2500
Conseco Fieldhouse **Fax:** 317-917-2599
125 S Pennsylvania St
Indianapolis, IN 46204
www.nba.com/pacers

Carlson, Gretchen (1967-)
FOX News anchor
FOX News Channel **Ph:** 212-301-3000
1211 Ave of the Americas
New York, NY 10036
www.foxnews.com/fnctv

Carlson, Stuart
Editorial cartoonist for the Milwaukee Sentinel
Universal Press Syndicate **Ph:** 816-932-6600
4520 Main St
Kansas City, MO 64111
www.amuniversal.com/ups/features

Carlson, Tucker (1969-)
Host of MSNBC's The Situation with Tucker Carlson
MSNBC TV **Ph:** 201-583-5000
1 MSNBC Plaza
Secaucus, NJ 07094
www.msnbc.msn.com/id/3080263

Carlyle, Randy (1956-)
Hockey coach
Mighty Ducks of Anaheim **Ph:** 714-704-2700
Arrowhead Pond of Anaheim **Fax:** 714-940-2953
2695 Katella Ave
Anaheim, CA 92806
www.mightyducks.com

Carmona, Richard H, MD (1949-)
US Surgeon General and a Vice Admiral
Dept of Health & Human Services **Ph:** 301-443-4000
Fax: 301-443-8590
5600 Fishers Ln Rm 18-67
Rockville, MD 20857
www.surgeongeneral.gov

Carnahan, Russ (1958-)
US Representative from Missouri (Democrat)
1232 Longworth Bldg **Ph:** 202-225-2671
Washington, DC 20515 **Fax:** 202-225-7452
www.house.gov/carnahan

Carney, John (1964-)
Professional football player
New Orleans Saints **Ph:** 504-733-0255
5800 Airline Dr **Fax:** 504-731-1768
Metairie, LA 70003
www.neworleanssaints.com

Caro, Mark
Movie critic for the Chicago Tribune
Chicago Tribune **Ph:** 312-222-3232
435 N Michigan Ave **Fax:** 312-222-4674
Chicago, IL 60611

Caro, Robert A (1935-)
Author of Master of the Senate, which is about Lyndon Johnson's years in the Senate
Knopf Publishing/Author Mail **Ph:** 212-782-9000
1745 Broadway
New York, NY 10019
www.robertcaro.com

Carpenter, Chris (1975-)
Professional baseball player
Saint Louis Cardinals **Ph:** 314-421-3060
250 Stadium Plaza **Fax:** 314-425-0640
Saint Louis, MO 63102
stlouis.cardinals.mlb.com

Carpenter, John (1948-)
Movie director
William Morris Agency **Ph:** 310-859-4000
1 William Morris Pl **Fax:** 310-859-4462
Beverly Hills, CA 90212
www.theofficialjohncarpenter.com

Carpenter, Mary Chapin (1958-)
Country music singer/songwriter
William Morris Agency **Ph:** 615-963-3000
1600 Division St Suite 300 **Fax:** 615-963-3090
Nashville, TN 37203
www.marychapincarpenter.com

Carper, Thomas (1947-)
US Senator from Delaware (Democrat)
513 Hart Bldg **Ph:** 202-224-2441
Washington, DC 20510 **Fax:** 202-228-2190
carper.senate.gov

Carr, David (1979-)
Professional football player
Houston Texans **Ph:** 832-667-2000
2 Reliant Park **Fax:** 832-667-2100
Houston, TX 77054
www.houstontexans.com

Carr, Howie (1952-)
Host of a syndicated talk radio show on political issues
WRKO-AM **Ph:** 617-779-5800
20 Guest St 3rd Fl
Boston, MA 92135
www.howiecarr.org

Carr, Lloyd (1945-)
Football coach
University of Michigan Athletic Dept **Ph:** 734-647-2583
Fax: 734-764-3221
1000 S State St
Ann Arbor, MI 48109
mgoblue.com

Carrell, Al
Writes the syndicated Super Handyman do-it-yourself column with his daughter Kelly
King Features Syndicate Inc **Ph:** 212-455-4000
888 7th Ave 2nd Fl
New York, NY 10019
www.kingfeatures.com

Carrell, Kelly
Writes the syndicated Super Handyman do-it-yourself column with her father Al
King Features Syndicate Inc **Ph:** 212-455-4000
888 7th Ave 2nd Fl
New York, NY 10019
www.kingfeatures.com

Carreno, Jose Manuel
A principal dancer for American Ballet Theatre
American Ballet Theatre **Ph:** 212-477-3030
890 Broadway **Fax:** 212-254-5938
New York, NY 10003
www.abt.org/dancers

Carreras, Jose (1946-)
Opera singer
William Morris Agency **Ph:** 310-859-4000
1 William Morris Pl **Fax:** 310-859-4462
Beverly Hills, CA 90212
www.wma.com/jose_carreras/summary

Carrey, Jim (1962-)
Actor and comedian
United Talent Agency **Ph:** 310-273-6700
9560 Wilshire Blvd 5th Fl **Fax:** 310-247-1111
Beverly Hills, CA 90212

Carroll, Brian (1981-)
Professional soccer player
DC United **Ph:** 202-587-5000
RFK Stadium **Fax:** 202-587-5400
2400 E Capitol St SE
Washington, DC 20003
dcunited.mlsnet.com

Carroll, Diahann (1925-)
Singer; actor
William Morris Agency **Ph:** 310-859-4000
1 William Morris Pl **Fax:** 310-859-4462
Beverly Hills, CA 90212
www.wma.com/diahann_carroll/summary

Carroll, James (1943-)
Author (An American Requiem; Madonna Red; Prince of Peace); a former priest, he also writes on religion and politics
Houghton Mifflin Co **Ph:** 617-351-5000
Trade Div
Adult Editorial
222 Berkeley St 8th Fl
Boston, MA 02116
www.houghtonmifflinbooks.com

Carroll, Jason
CNN national correspondent
CNN New York **Ph:** 212-275-7800
Time Warner Ctr
10 Columbus Cir
New York, NY 10019
www.cnn.com/CNN/anchors_reporters

Carroll, Pete (1951-)
Football coach
University of Southern California Athletic Dept **Ph:** 213-740-2311 **Fax:** 213-740-6364
University Park
Los Angeles, CA 90089
usctrojans.collegesports.com

Carrot Top (1967-)
Comedian (his real name is Scott Thompson)
International Creative Management **Ph:** 310-550-4000
8942 Wilshire Blvd
Beverly Hills, CA 90211
www.carrottop.com

Carruth, Hayden (1921-)
Poet and author
Copper Canyon Press **Ph:** 360-385-4925
PO Box 271 **Fax:** 360-385-4985
Port Townsend, WA 98368
haydencarruth.netfirms.com

Carsberg, Scott
Chef/owner of Lampreia Restaurant
Lampreia Restaurant **Ph:** 206-443-3301
2400 1st Ave
Seattle, WA 98121
www.lampreiarestaurant.com

Carsey, Marcy (1944-)
Independent TV producer; partner & co-founder (with Tom Werner) of Carsey-Werner
Carsey-Werner LLC **Ph:** 818-655-5598
12001 Ventura Pl 6th Fl
Studio City, CA 91604
www.cwm.com

Carson, Ben, MD (1951-)
Pediatric neurosurgeon
Carson Scholars Fund **Ph:** 410-828-1005
305 W Chesapeake Ave Suite L-020 **Fax:** 410-828-1007
Towson, MD 21204
www.carsonscholars.org

Carson, Julia (1938-)
US Representative from Indiana (Democrat)
1535 Longworth Bldg **Ph:** 202-225-4011
Washington, DC 20515 **Fax:** 202-225-5633
www.juliacarson.house.gov

Carter, Chip
Writes the syndicated column Inside the Video Games with his son Jonathan Carter
Tribune Media Services Inc **Ph:** 312-222-4444
435 N Michigan Ave Suite 1500
Chicago, IL 60611
tmsfeatures.com/productlist.htm

Carter, Cris (1965-)
Former professional football player; now a host on Inside the NFL on HBO
HBO Sports **Ph:** 212-512-1000
1100 Ave of the Americas
New York, NY 10036
www.hbo.com/infl

Carter, Deana (1966-)
Country singer
Creative Artists Agency **Ph:** 310-288-4545
9830 Wilshire Blvd **Fax:** 310-288-4800
Beverly Hills, CA 90212
www.deanacarter.net

Carter, Helena Bonham (1966-)
Actor
Endeavor **Ph:** 310-248-2000
9601 Wilshire Blvd 3rd Fl **Fax:** 310-248-2020
Beverly Hills, CA 90210

Carter, Jimmy (1924-)
39th US president; Nobel Peace Prize winner
Carter Center **Ph:** 404-420-5117
1 Copenhill **Fax:** 404-420-5100
453 Freedom Pkwy
Atlanta, GA 30307
www.cartercenter.org

Carter, John R (1941-)
US Representative from Texas (Republican)
408 Cannon Bldg **Ph:** 202-225-3864
Washington, DC 20515 **Fax:** 202-225-5886
www.house.gov/carter

Carter, Jonathan
Writes the syndicated column Inside the Video Games with his father, Chip Carter
Tribune Media Services Inc **Ph:** 312-222-4444
435 N Michigan Ave Suite 1500
Chicao, IL 60611
tmsfeatures.com/productlist.htm

Carter, Keith (1948-)
Photographer
Howard Greenberg Gallery **Ph:** 212-334-0010
41 E 57th St Suite 1406 **Fax:** 212-941-7479
New York, NY 10022
www.keithcarterphotographs.com

Carter, Rosalynn (1927-)
Former First Lady of the US (wife of President Jimmy Carter)
Carter Center **Ph:** 404-420-5117
1 Copenhill **Fax:** 404-420-5100
453 Freedom Pkwy
Atlanta, GA 30307
www.cartercenter.org

Carter, Tim
Former contractor who writes the syndicated column Ask the Builder
Tribune Media Services Inc **Ph:** 312-222-4444
435 N Michigan Ave Suite 1500
Chicago, IL 60611
tmsfeatures.com/productlist.htm

Carter, Vince (1977-)
Professional basketball player
New Jersey Nets **Ph:** 201-935-8888
Nets Champion Center **Fax:** 201-935-1088
390 Murray Hill Pkwy
East Rutherford, NJ 07073
www.nba.com/nets

Cartier-Bresson, Henri (1908-2004)
Photographer
Magnum Photos **Ph:** 212-929-6000
151 W 25th St **Fax:** 212-929-9325
New York, NY 10001
www.henricartierbresson.org

Caruso, David (1956-)
Actor
International Creative Management **Ph:** 310-550-4000
8942 Wilshire Blvd
Beverly Hills, CA 90211
www.cbs.com/primetime/csi_miami

Caruso-Cabrera, Michelle
Anchor of Worldwide Exchange on CNBC
CNBC **Ph:** 201-735-2622
900 Sylvan Ave
Englewood Cliffs, NJ 07632
moneycentral.msn.com/cnbc/tv

Carvey, Dana (1955-)
Comedian
Creative Artists Agency **Ph:** 310-288-4545
9830 Wilshire Blvd **Fax:** 310-288-4800
Beverly Hills, CA 90212

Carville, James (1944-)
Political strategist and international political/corporate consultant; political contributor and Democratic strategist on CNN's The Situation Room
Gaslight Inc **Ph:** 703-739-7777
424 S Washington St **Fax:** 703-739-7766
Lower Level
Alexandria, VA 22314
www.carville.info

Cary, Kathy
Chef/owner of Lilly's Restaurant
Lilly's **Ph:** 502-451-0447
1147 Bardstown Rd
Louisville, KY 40204
www.lillyslapeche.com

Casablanca, Ted
Gossip columnist; hosts The Awful Truth, covering celebrity news & gossip, on E!
E! Entertainment Television **Ph:** 323-954-2400
5700 Wilshire Blvd **Fax:** 323-954-2660
Los Angeles, CA 90036
www.eonline.com/On/People

Case, Ed (1952-)
US Representative from Hawaii (Democrat)
115 Cannon Bldg **Ph:** 202-225-4906
Washington, DC 20515 **Fax:** 202-225-4987
wwwc.house.gov/case

Case, Stephen M (1958-)
Co-founder and former chairman & CEO of America Online (AOL) and, later, chairman of AOL Time Warner; has now left the company and is involved primarily in philanthropy
Case Foundation **Ph:** 202-467-5788
1717 Rhode Island Ave NW 7th Fl **Fax:** 202-775-8513
Washington, DC 20036
www.casefoundation.org

Casey, Dwane (1957-)
Basketball coach
Minnesota Timberwolves **Ph:** 612-673-1600
Target Center **Fax:** 612-673-1699
600 1st Ave N
Minneapolis, MN 55403
www.nba.com/timberwolves

Casey, Sean (1974-)
Professional baseball player
Pittsburgh Pirates **Ph:** 412-323-5000
PNC Park **Fax:** 412-323-5009
115 Federal St
Pittsburgh, PA 15212
pittsburgh.pirates.mlb.com

Cashell, Robert
Mayor of Reno, Nevada
400 S Center St **Ph:** 775-334-2001
PO Box 1900 **Fax:** 775-334-4241
Reno, NV 89505
www.ci.reno.nv.us

Casper, Stephen P
Managing Director & CEO of Fischer Francis Trees & Watts Inc (fixed income portfolio management)
Dir/CEO **Ph:** 212-681-3000
Fischer Francis Trees & Watts Inc
200 Park Ave 46th Fl
New York, NY 10166
www.fftw.com

Cassavetes, Nick (1959-)
Film director; actor
International Creative Management **Ph:** 310-550-4000
8942 Wilshire Blvd
Beverly Hills, CA 90211

Cassell, Sam (1969-)
Professional basketball player
Los Angeles Clippers **Ph:** 213-742-7100
Staples Center **Fax:** 213-742-7550
1111 S Figueroa St Suite 1100
Los Angeles, CA 90015
www.nba.com/clippers

Casson, Mel
Writes and illustrates the comic strip Redeye
King Features Syndicate Inc **Ph:** 212-455-4000
888 7th Ave 2nd Fl
New York, NY 10019
www.kingfeatures.com

Castagna, Vanessa (1950-)
Executive Chairwoman of Mervyns' Board of Directors; also a senior member of Cerberus Capital Management
Exec Chm **Ph:** 510-727-3000
Mervyns **Fax:** 972-431-1362
22301 Foothill Blvd **TF:** 800-222-6161
Hayward, CA 94541
www.mervyns.com/corp

Castellanos, Carlos
Draws the syndicated comic strip Baldo, which is written by Hector Cantu; Baldo was the first comic strip to feature Latino characters and themes
Universal Press Syndicate **Ph:** 816-932-6600
4520 Main St
Kansas City, MO 64111
www.amuniversal.com/ups/features

Castilla, Vinny (1967-)
Professional baseball player
San Diego Padres **Ph:** 619-795-5000
Petco Park **Fax:** 619-497-5339
PO Box 122000
San Diego, CA 92112
sandiego.padres.mlb.com

Castillo, Luis (1975-)
Professional baseball player
Minnesota Twins **Ph:** 612-375-1366
Hubert H Humphrey Metrodome **Fax:** 612-375-7473
34 Kirby Puckett Pl
Minneapolis, MN 55415
minnesota.twins.mlb.com

Castle, Michael N (1939-)
US Representative from Delaware (Republican)
1233 Longworth Bldg **Ph:** 202-225-4165
Washington, DC 20515 **Fax:** 202-225-2291
www.house.gov/castle

Castle-Hughes, Keisha (1990-)
Actor
Creative Artists Agency **Ph:** 310-288-4545
9830 Wilshire Blvd **Fax:** 310-288-4800
Beverly Hills, CA 90212
www.keishacastlehughes.com

Castro-Wright, Eduardo
President and CEO of Wal-Mart Stores USA
Wal-Mart Stores USA **Ph:** 479-273-4000
702 SW 8th St
Bentonville, AR 72716
www.walmartstores.com

Castroneves, Helio (1975-)
Brazilian race car driver (Indy Racing League; Formula racing)
Penske Racing North **Ph:** 610-376-2966
366 Penske Plaza
Reading, PA 19602
www.heliocastroneves.com.br

Catalino, Ken
Editorial cartoonist
Creators Syndicate Inc **Ph:** 310-337-7003
5777 W Century Blvd Suite 700 **Fax:** 310-337-7625
Los Angeles, CA 90045
www.creators.com

Catchings, Tamika (1979-)
Professional basketball player
Indiana Fever **Ph:** 317-917-2500
Conseco Fieldhouse **Fax:** 317-917-2899
125 S Pennsylvania St
Indianapolis, IN 46204
www.tamikacatchings.com

Catlett, Elizabeth (1915-)
Sculptor
June Kelly Gallery **Ph:** 212-226-1660
591 Broadway
New York, NY 10012
www.junekellygallery.com

Catmull, Ed, PhD (1946-)
President and co-founder of Pixar Animation Studios
Pixar Animation Studios **Ph:** 510-752-3000
1200 Park Ave **Fax:** 510-752-3151
Emeryville, CA 94608
www.pixar.com

Cato, Kelvin (1974-)
Professional basketball player
Detroit Pistons **Ph:** 248-377-0100
Palace at Auburn Hills **Fax:** 248-377-4262
4 Championship Dr
Auburn Hills, MI 48326
www.nba.com/pistons

Cattrall, Kim (1956-)
Actor
International Creative Management **Ph:** 310-550-4000
8942 Wilshire Blvd
Beverly Hills, CA 90211
www.hbo.com/city

Catz, Safra
President and CFO of Oracle Corp
Oracle Corp **Ph:** 650-506-7000
500 Oracle Pkwy **Fax:** 650-506-7200
Redwood Shores, CA 94065
www.oracle.com/corporate

Caviezel, Jim (1968-)
Actor
International Creative Management **Ph:** 310-550-4000
8942 Wilshire Blvd
Beverly Hills, CA 90211

Cavuto, Neil (1958-)
Vice President of business news for FOX and anchor of Your World With Cavuto
FOX News Channel **Ph:** 212-301-3000
1211 Ave of the Americas
New York, NY 10036
www.foxnews.com/fnctv

Cech, Thomas R, PhD (1947-)
Winner of the 1989 Nobel Prize in Chemistry (with Sidney Altman) for their discovery of catalytic properties of RNA; president of Howard Hughes Medical Institute
Howard Hughes Medical Institute **Ph:** 301-215-8500
4000 Jones Bridge Rd
Chevy Chase, MD 20815
www.hhmi.org/research/nobel

Cedric the Entertainer (1964-)
Actor/comedian
Creative Artists Agency **Ph:** 310-288-4545
9830 Wilshire Blvd **Fax:** 310-288-4800
Beverly Hills, CA 90212
www.ceddybear.com

Cellini, Vince (1959-)
Sports broadcaster
Golf Channel **Ph:** 407-363-4653
7580 Commerce Center Dr
Orlando, FL 32819
www.thegolfchannel.com

Centanni, Steve
National correspondent for FOX News
FOX News Channel **Ph:** 212-301-3000
1211 Ave of the Americas
New York, NY 10036
www.foxnews.com/fnctv

Cerf, Vinton G, PhD (1943-)
Vice President and Chief Internet Evangelist for Google and Chairman of the Board of ICANN; was awarded the National Medal of Technology for founding and developing the Internet with his partner, Robert E Kahn
ICANN **Ph:** 310-823-9358
4676 Admiralty Way Suite 330 **Fax:** 310-823-8649
Marina del Rey, CA 90292
www.icann.org/biog/cerf.htm

Chabon, Michael (1963-)
Author (The Amazing Adventures of Kavalier and Clay); has also written screenplays, including for Spiderman 2
Steven Barclay Agency **Ph:** 707-773-0654
12 Western Ave **Fax:** 707-778-1868
Petaluma, CA 94952 **TF:** 888-965-7323
www.michaelchabon.com

Chabot, Steve (1953-)
US Representative from Ohio (Republican)
129 Cannon Bldg **Ph:** 202-225-2216
Washington, DC 20515 **Fax:** 202-225-3012
www.house.gov/chabot

Chabraja, Nicholas
Chairman and CEO of General Dynamics
General Dynamics Corp **Ph:** 703-876-3000
2941 Fairview Park Dr
Suite 100
Falls Church, VA 22042
www.gendyn.com

Chacon, Shawn (1977-)
Professional baseball player
New York Yankees **Ph:** 718-293-4300
Yankee Stadium **Fax:** 718-293-8414
161st St & River Ave
Bronx, NY 10451
newyork.yankees.mlb.com

Chadwick, Alex
Host of Day to Day on NPR
National Public Radio **Ph:** 202-513-2000
635 Massachusetts Ave NW **Fax:** 202-513-3329
Washington, DC 20001
www.npr.org

Chafee, Lincoln D (1953-)
US Senator from Rhode Island (Republican)
141A Russell Bldg **Ph:** 202-224-2921
Washington, DC 20510 **Fax:** 202-228-2853
chafee.senate.gov

Chagall, Marc (1887-1985)
Artist
Solomon R Guggenheim **Ph:** 212-423-3500
Museum
1071 5th Ave
New York, NY 10128
www.guggenheimcollection.org

Chakiris, George (1934-)
Dancer; actor
Scott Stander & Assoc Inc **Ph:** 818-905-7000
13701 Riverside Dr Suite 201 **Fax:** 818-990-0582
Sherman Oaks, CA 91423
www.scottstander.com

Chambers, Aidan (1934-)
British novelist; best known are his books for young adults (Dance On My Grave; Postcards from No Man's Land)
Dutton Children's Books **Ph:** 212-366-2000
Publicity
345 Hudson St
New York, NY 10014
www.aidanchambers.co.uk

Chambers, Chris (1978-)
Professional football player
Miami Dolphins **Ph:** 954-452-7000
7500 SW 30th St **Fax:** 954-452-7055
Davie, FL 33314
www.miamidolphins.com

Chambers, John T
President & CEO of Cisco Systems Inc
Cisco Systems Inc **Ph:** 408-526-8222
170 W Tasman Dr **Fax:** 408-526-4100
San Jose, CA 95134
www.cisco.com/en/US/about

Chambliss, Saxby (1943-)
US Senator from Georgia (Republican)
416 Russell Bldg **Ph:** 202-224-3521
Washington, DC 20510 **Fax:** 202-224-0103
chambliss.senate.gov

Chan, Jackie (1954-)
Actor
Creative Artists Agency **Ph:** 310-288-4545
9830 Wilshire Blvd **Fax:** 310-288-4800
Beverly Hills, CA 90212
www.jackie-chan.com

Chancellor, Van (1943-)
Women's professional basketball coach
Houston Comets **Ph:** 713-758-7200
Toyota Center **Fax:** 713-758-7396
1510 Polk St
Houston, TX 77002
www.wnba.com/comets

Chandler, Ben (1959-)
US Representative from Kentucky (Democrat)
1504 Longworth Bldg **Ph:** 202-225-4706
Washington, DC 20515 **Fax:** 202-225-2122
chandler.house.gov

Channing, Carol (1921-)
Singer, actor (primarily Broadway)
William Morris Agency **Ph:** 310-859-4000
1 William Morris Pl **Fax:** 310-859-4462
Beverly Hills, CA 90212
www.wma.com/carol_channing/summary

Channing, Stockard (1944-)
Actor
International Creative Management **Ph:** 310-550-4000
8942 Wilshire Blvd
Beverly Hills, CA 90211
www.nbc.com/The_West_Wing

Chao, Elaine L (1953-)
US Secretary of Labor
US Dept of Labor **Ph:** 202-693-6000
200 Constitution Ave NW **Fax:** 202-693-6111
Washington, DC 20210
www.dol.gov

Chapman, Steve (1954-)
Syndicated columnist (commentary)
Creators Syndicate Inc **Ph:** 310-337-7003
5777 W Century Blvd Suite 700 **Fax:** 310-337-7625
Los Angeles, CA 90045
www.creators.com/opinion.html

Chapman, Steven Curtis (1962-)
Singer (Contemporary Christian music)
CAA Nashville **Ph:** 615-383-8787
3310 West End Ave 5th Fl **Fax:** 615-383-4937
Nashville, TN 37203
www.scchapman.com

Chappelle, Dave (1972-)
Comedian
Gersh Agency **Ph:** 310-274-6611
232 N Canon Dr
Beverly Hills, CA 90210

Chara, Zdeno (1977-)
Professional hockey player
Ottawa Senators **Ph:** 613-599-0250
Corel Center **Fax:** 613-599-0358
1000 Palladium Dr
Kanata, ON K2V1A5
www.ottawasenators.com

Charen, Mona
Syndicated columnist & political analyst
Creators Syndicate Inc **Ph:** 310-337-7003
5777 W Century Blvd Suite 700 **Fax:** 310-337-7625
Los Angeles, CA 90045
www.creators.com/opinion.html

Charles, Ray (1930-2004)
Blues singer & musician
Ray Charles Enterprises **Ph:** 323-737-8000
2107 W Washington Blvd Suite 200
Los Angeles, CA 90018
www.raycharles.com

Chase, Chevy (1943-)
Comic actor
International Creative Management **Ph:** 310-550-4000
8942 Wilshire Blvd
Beverly Hills, CA 90211

Chase, David (1945-)
Producer/director/writer; creator of The Sopranos
United Talent Agency **Ph:** 310-273-6700
9560 Wilshire Blvd 5th Fl **Fax:** 310-247-1111
Beverly Hills, CA 90212
www.hbo.com/sopranos

Chast, Roz
New Yorker Magazine cartoonist
Cartoon Bank **Ph:** 914-478-5527
New Yorker Magazine **Fax:** 914-478-5604
28 Wells Ave Bldg 3 4th Fl
Yonkers, NY 10701
www.cartoonbank.com

Chavez, Cesar E (1927-1993)
Latino labor organizer and civil rights leader who founded the United Farm Workers of America
Cesar E Chavez Foundation **Ph:** 818-265-0300
500 N Brand Blvd Suite 1650 **Fax:** 818-265-0312
Glendale, CA 91203
www.cesarechavezfoundation.org

Chavez, Eric (1977-)
Professional baseball player
Oakland Athletics **Ph:** 510-638-4900
Network Assoc Coliseum **Fax:** 510-568-3770
7000 Coliseum Way
Oakland, CA 94621
oakland.athletics.mlb.com

Chavez, Linda (1947-)
Syndicated columnist (commentary)
Creators Syndicate Inc **Ph:** 310-337-7003
5777 W Century Blvd Suite 700 **Fax:** 310-337-7625
Los Angeles, CA 90045
www.creators.com/opinion.html

Chavez, Martin J (1952-)
Mayor of Albuquerque
PO Box 1293 **Ph:** 505-768-3000
Albuquerque, NM 87103 **Fax:** 505-768-3019
www.cabq.gov/mayor

Chaya, Masazumi
Dancer, choreographer, master teacher; associate artistic director of the Alvin Ailey American Dance Theater
Alvin Ailey American Dance Theater **Ph:** 212-405-9000 **Fax:** 212-405-9001
Joan Weill Center for Dance
405 W 55th St
New York, NY 10019
www.alvinailey.org

Cheadle, Don (1964-)
Actor
United Talent Agency **Ph:** 310-273-6700
9560 Wilshire Blvd 5th Fl **Fax:** 310-247-1111
Beverly Hills, CA 90212
www.doncheadle.com

Cheaney, Calbert (1971-)
Professional basketball player
Golden State Warriors **Ph:** 510-986-2200
1011 Broadway **Fax:** 510-452-0132
Oakland, CA 94607
www.nba.com/warriors

Cheechoo, Jonathan (1980-)
Professional hockey player
San Jose Sharks **Ph:** 408-287-7070
HP Pavilion at San Jose **Fax:** 408-999-5797
525 W Santa Clara St
San Jose, CA 95113
www.sjsharks.com

Cheeks, Maurice (1956-)
Basketball coach
Philadelphia 76ers **Ph:** 215-339-7600
Wachovia Center **Fax:** 215-339-7632
3601 S Broad St
Philadelphia, PA 19148
www.nba.com/sixers

Cheever, Eddie Jr (1958-)
Race car driver
Cheever Racing **Ph:** 317-824-5777
8266 Zionsville Rd **Fax:** 317-824-5780
Indianapolis, IN 46268
www.cheeverracing.com

Chelios, Chris (1962-)
Professional hockey player
Detroit Red Wings **Ph:** 313-396-7544
Joe Louis Arena **Fax:** 313-567-0296
600 Civic Center Dr
Detroit, MI 48226
www.detroitredwings.com

Chen, Julie (1970-)
An anchor of CBS News' The Early Show
The Early Show **Ph:** 212-975-2824
524 W 57th St
New York, NY 10019
www.cbsnews.com

Chenault, Kenneth I
Chairman and CEO of American Express
American Express Co **Ph:** 212-640-2000
200 Vesey St
3 World Financial Ctr
New York, NY 10285
home3.americanexpress.com/corp

Cheney, Lynne V (1941-)
Wife of Vice President Dick Cheney; also former chairman of the National Endowment for the Humanities
1650 Pennsylvania Ave NW **Ph:** 202-456-7458
Washington, DC 20501 **Fax:** 202-456-7489
www.whitehouse.gov/mrscheney

Cheney, Richard (1941-)
Vice President of the United States
Vice President of the US **Ph:** 202-456-7549
1650 Pennsylvania Ave NW
Washington, DC 20501
www.whitehouse.gov/vicepresident

Cher (1946-)
Singer; actor
International Creative Management **Ph:** 310-550-4000
8942 Wilshire Blvd
Beverly Hills, CA 90211
www.cher.com

Cherkasky, Michael G (1950-)
President & CEO of MMC, a global professional services firm (insurance, investment, consulting)
Marsh & McLennan Cos Inc **Ph:** 212-345-5000
1611 Ave of the Americas
New York, NY 10036
www.marshmac.com

Chernin, Peter
President & CEO of News Corporation
News Corp **Ph:** 212-852-7000
1211 Ave of the Americas 8th Fl **Fax:** 212-852-7145
New York, NY 10036
www.newscorp.com/management

Cherryh, CJ (1942-)
Author of science fiction/fantasy books
DAW Books Publicity **Ph:** 212-366-2000
375 Hudson St
New York, NY 10014
www.cherryh.com

Chertoff, Michael (1953-)
US Secretary of Homeland Security
US Dept of Homeland Security **Ph:** 202-282-8000
Naval Security Stn
Washington, DC 20528
www.dhs.gov

Chesley, Stanley M (1936-)
Senior attorney at Cincinnati's oldest law firm (est 1860); lead counsel in such high-profile cases as those involving tort litigation related to Agent Orange, Bendectin, Bhopal, the Bjork-Shiley heart valve, and breast implants
Waite Schneider Bayless & Chesley Co LPA **Ph:** 513-621-0267 **Fax:** 513-381-2375
1513 4th & Vine Tower
Cincinnati, OH 45202
www.wsbclaw.com

Chestnutt, Mark (1963-)
Country singer
Buddy Lee Attractions **Ph:** 615-244-4336
38 Music Sq East Suite 300 **Fax:** 615-726-0429
Nashville, TN 37204
www.markchesnutt.com

Chetry, Kiran
News update and weekend co-anchor for Fox News
FOX News Channel **Ph:** 212-301-3000
1211 Ave of the Americas
New York, NY 10036
www.foxnews.com/fnctv

Chiarello, Michael (1962-)
Host of Easy Entertaining with Michael Chiarello on Food Network; also the creator of NapaStyle specialty foods & handcrafted products and founding chef of Tra Vigne Restaurant in Napa Valley
Food Network **Ph:** 212-398-8836
75 9th Ave **Fax:** 212-736-7716
New York, NY 10011
www.napastyle.com

Chiklis, Michael (1963-)
Actor
Endeavor **Ph:** 310-248-2000
9601 Wilshire Blvd 3rd Fl **Fax:** 310-248-2020
Beverly HIlls, CA 90210

Child, Fred
Host of Performance Today, NPR's classical music radio program
National Public Radio **Ph:** 202-513-2000
635 Massachusetts Ave NW **Fax:** 202-513-3329
Washington, DC 20001
www.npr.org

Child, Lee
Author of mystery/thrillers/Jack Reacher books (The Killing Floor)
Bantam Dell Publicity **Ph:** 212-782-9000
1745 Broadway
New York, NY 10019
www.leechild.com

Childress, Brad (1956-)
Football coach
Minnesota Vikings **Ph:** 952-828-6500
9520 Viking Dr **Fax:** 952-828-6540
Eden Prairie, MN 55344
www.vikings.com

Chimerine, Lawrence, PhD
Economic consultant; president of Radnor International Consulting and co-founder of iGrandparents.com; also does public speaking
Radnor International Consulting Inc **Ph:** 610-356-1638 **Fax:** 610-668-8421
50 Belmont Ave Suite 810
Bala Cynwyd, PA 19004
larrychimerine.com

Chittister, Joan
A Benedictine Sister of Erie; author, lecturer, and founder/executive director of Benetvision: A Resource and Research Center for Contemporary Spirituality
Benetvision — **Ph:** 814-459-5994
355 E 9th St — **Fax:** 814-459-8066
Erie, PA 16503
www.benetvision.org

Cho, Frank (1971-)
Creator of the comic strip Liberty Meadows
Creators Syndicate Inc — **Ph:** 310-337-7003
5777 W Century Blvd Suite 700 — **Fax:** 310-337-7625
Los Angeles, CA 90045
www.creators.com

Cho, Margaret (1968-)
Comedian
William Morris Agency — **Ph:** 310-859-4000
1 William Morris Pl — **Fax:** 310-859-4462
Beverly Hills, CA 90212
www.margaretcho.net

Chocola, Chris (1962-)
US Representative from Indiana (Republican)
510 Cannon Bldg — **Ph:** 202-225-3915
Washington, DC 20515 — **Fax:** 202-225-6798
chocola.house.gov

Choi, Sophia
News anchor for CNN's Headline News
CNN — **Ph:** 404-827-1500
1 CNN Center
Atlanta, GA 30303
www.cnn.com/CNN/anchors_reporters

Chong, Tommy (1938-)
Comedian (Cheech & Chong)
Gersh Agency — **Ph:** 310-274-6611
232 N Canon Dr
Beverly Hills, CA 90210
www.cheechandchong.com

Chopra, Deepak, MD (1947-)
A leader in mind-body medicine, focusing on the connection between body, mind, spirit, and healing; also is author/speaker/health practitioner
Chopra Center at La Costa Resort & Spa — **Ph:** 760-931-7566
2013 Costa del Mar Rd — **Fax:** 760-931-7572
Carlsbad, CA 92009 — **TF:** 888-424-6772
www.chopra.com

Chow, Yun-Fat (1955-)
Actor
William Morris Agency — **Ph:** 310-859-4000
1 William Morris Pl — **Fax:** 310-859-4462
Beverly Hills, CA 90212

Choy, Sam
Hawaiian chef, restaurateur, cookbook author, and TV host
Sam Choy's Diamond Head Restaurant — **Ph:** 808-732-8645
449 Kapahulu Ave 2nd Fl — **Fax:** 808-732-8682
Honolulu, HI 96815
www.samchoy.com

Chrebet, Wayne (1973-)
Professional football player
New York Jets — **Ph:** 516-560-8100
1000 Fulton Ave — **Fax:** 516-560-8198
Hempstead, NY 11550
www.newyorkjets.com

Christensen, Donna (1945-)
US Delegate from the Virgin Islands (Democrat)
1510 Longworth Bldg — **Ph:** 202-225-1790
Washington, DC 20515 — **Fax:** 202-225-5517
www.house.gov/christian-christensen

Chu, James
Founder, chairman, and CEO of ViewSonic Corp, a leading global provider of visual display products
ViewSonic Corp — **Ph:** 909-444-8888
381 Brea Canyon Rd — **Fax:** 909-468-1202
Walnut, CA 91789
www.viewsonic.com

Chu, Morgan
A top trial lawyer
Irell & Manella LLP — **Ph:** 310-203-7000
1800 Ave of the Stars Suite 900 — **Fax:** 310-203-7199
Los Angeles, CA 90067
www.irell.com

Chu, Steven, PhD (1948-)
Director of Lawrence Berkeley National Laboratory; 1997 Nobel Laureate in Physics for development of methods to cool and trap atoms with laser light
Lawrence Berkeley National Laboratory — **Ph:** 510-486-4000
1 Cyclotron Rd
Berkeley, CA 94720
www.lbl.gov

Church, Charlotte (1986-)
Classical singer who also crosses over into Broadway musicals, opera, chamber music, Gaelic airs, and contemporary songs
William Morris Agency **Ph:** 310-859-4000
1 William Morris Pl **Fax:** 310-859-4462
Beverly Hills, CA 90212
www.charlottechurch.com

Church, Jok
Creator of the comic strip You Can with Beakman & Jax, a weekly feature that answers children's questions in an interactive way
Universal Press Syndicate **Ph:** 816-932-6600
4520 Main St
Kansas City, MO 64111
www.amuniversal.com/ups/features

Cicilline, David N (1961-)
Mayor of Providence, Rhode Island
25 Dorrance St **Ph:** 401-421-7740
Providence, RI 02903
www.providenceri.com

Ciresi, Michael V
Attorney; trial practice focuses in the areas of product liability, intellectual property, business and commercial litigation
Robins Kaplan Miller & Ciresi LLP **Ph:** 612-349-8500 **Fax:** 612-339-4181
2800 LaSalle Plaza
800 LaSalle Ave
Minneapolis, MN 55402
www.rkmc.com

Cisneros, Sandra (1954-)
Writer (poetry, stories, novels)
Susan Bergholz Literary Services **Ph:** 212-387-0545 **Fax:** 212-387-0546
17 W 10th St Suite 5B
New York, NY 10011
www.sandracisneros.com

Citret, Mark (1949-)
Photographer
PO Box 3493 **Ph:** 650-994-2420
Daly City, CA 94015 **Fax:** 650-994-1797
www.mcitret.com

CK, Louis (1967-)
Comedian
3 Arts Entertainment **Ph:** 310-888-3200
9460 Wilshire Blvd 7th Fl **Fax:** 310-888-3210
Beverly Hills, CA 90212

Claflin, Bruce L
President & CEO of 3Com Corp
3Com Corp **Ph:** 508-323-5000
350 Campus Dr **Fax:** 508-323-1111
Marlborough, MA 01752
www.3com.com

Claman, Liz
Co-anchor of CNBC's Morning Call and anchor of the primetime program Cover to Cover
CNBC **Ph:** 201-735-2622
900 Sylvan Ave
Englewood Cliffs, NJ 07632
moneycentral.msn.com/cnbc/tv

Clancy, Tom (1947-)
Author of popular fiction (Hunt for Red October, Patriot Games, etc.)
Ballantine Books Publicity **Ph:** 212-782-9000
1745 Broadway
New York, NY 10019
www.randomhouse.com/BB

Clapton, Eric (1945-)
Blues guitarist and singer
Creative Artists Agency **Ph:** 310-288-4545
9830 Wilshire Blvd **Fax:** 310-288-4800
Beverly Hills, CA 90212
www.claptononline.com

Clark, Anthony (1964-)
Stand-up comedian and television actor (Yes, Dear)
Gersh Agency **Ph:** 310-274-6611
232 N Canon Dr
Beverly Hills, CA 90210

Clark, Carol Higgins (1956-)
Author of suspense novels
Simon & Schuster **Ph:** 212-698-7000
1230 Ave of the Americas
New York, NY 10020
www.carolhigginsclark.com

Clark, Danny (1977-)
Professional football player
Oakland Raiders **Ph:** 510-864-5000
1220 Harbor Bay Pkwy **Fax:** 510-864-5134
Alameda, CA 94502
www.raiders.com

Clark, Dick (1929-)
American Bandstand host in the 1950s; his company is an independent producer of television programming
Dick Clark Productions Inc **Ph:** 310-786-8900
9200 Sunset Blvd 10th Fl
Los Angeles, CA 90069
www.dickclarkproductions.com

Clark, Mary Higgins (1929-)
Author of mystery/suspense novels
Simon & Schuster **Ph:** 212-698-7000
1230 Ave of the Americas
New York, NY 10020
www.simonsays.com

Clark, Richard (1946-)
President and CEO of Merck & Co Inc
Merck & Co Inc **Ph:** 908-423-1000
1 Merck Dr
PO Box 100
Whitehouse Station, NJ 08889
www.merck.com/about

Clark, Todd
Co-creator, with Steve Dickenson, of the comic strip Lola
Newspaper Enterprise Assn **Ph:** 212-293-8500
200 Madison Ave
New York, NY 10016
www.unitedfeatures.com

Clark, Wesley (1944-)
Retired four-star general and former NATO Supreme Allied Commander; ran for US President in 2004
James Lee Witt Assoc LLC **Ph:** 202-585-0780
701 13th St NW Suite 850 **Fax:** 202-585-0792
Washington, DC 20005
www.wittassociates.com

Clarke, Arthur C (1917-)
Scientist whose work led to the global satellite systems in use today; also a prolific science fiction writer (author of 2001: A Space Odyssey). Title is Sir.
Arthur C Clarke Foundation **Ph:** 202-736-1816
1627 I St Suite 1200
Washington, DC 20006
www.clarkefoundation.org

Clarke, Darren (1968-)
Professional golfer
Gaylord Sports Management **Ph:** 480-483-9500
13845 N Northsight Blvd
Suite 200
Scottsdale, AZ 85260
www.gaylordsports.com

Clarke, Richard (1951-)
Security expert and former senior White House Adviser; areas of expertise include homeland security, national security, cyber security, and counterterrorism
Good Harbor Consulting LLC **Ph:** 703-812-9199
1902 N Monroe St **Fax:** 703-243-5207
Arlington, VA 22203
www.goodharbor.net

Clarkson, Kelly (1982-)
Singer
Creative Artists Agency **Ph:** 310-288-4545
9830 Wilshire Blvd **Fax:** 310-288-4800
Beverly Hills, CA 90212
www.kellyclarksonweb.com

Clarkson, Patricia (1959-)
Actor
Creative Artists Agency **Ph:** 310-288-4545
9830 Wilshire Blvd **Fax:** 310-288-4800
Beverly Hills, CA 90212

Claxton, Speedy (1978-)
Professional basketball player
New Orleans/Oklahoma City Hornets **Ph:** 405-208-4800
Oklahoma Tower
210 Park Ave Suite 1850
Oklahoma City, OK 73102
www.nba.com/hornets

Clay, William L (1956-)
US Representative from Missouri (Democrat)
131 Cannon Bldg **Ph:** 202-225-2406
Washington, DC 20515 **Fax:** 202-225-1725
www.house.gov/clay

Claybrook, Joan
President of Public Citizen, a nonprofit consumer advocacy organization
Public Citizen **Ph:** 202-588-1000
1600 20th St NW **Fax:** 202-588-7796
Washington, DC 20009
www.citizen.org

Clayburgh, Jill (1944-)
Actor
International Creative Management **Ph:** 310-550-4000
8942 Wilshire Blvd
Beverly Hills, CA 90211

Clayton, Michael (1982-)
Professional football player
Tampa Bay Buccaneers **Ph:** 813-870-2700
1 Buccaneer Pl **Fax:** 813-878-0813
Tampa, FL 33607
www.buccaneers.com

Cleary, Beverly (1916-)
Author of books for children (Dear Mr. Henshaw; Ramona Quimby books)
HarperCollins Children's Books **Ph:** 212-261-6500
1350 Ave of the Americas
New York, NY 10019
www.beverlycleary.com

Cleaver, Emanuel (1944-)
US Representative from Missouri (Democrat)
1641 Longworth Bldg **Ph:** 202-225-4535
Washington, DC 20515 **Fax:** 202-225-4403
www.house.gov/cleaver

Cleese, John (1939-)
Comedic actor and member of Monty Python's Flying Circus
Creative Artists Agency **Ph:** 310-288-4545
9830 Wilshire Blvd **Fax:** 310-288-4800
Beverly Hills, CA 90212
www.thejohncleese.com

Clemens, Roger (1962-)
Professional baseball player
Houston Astros **Ph:** 713-259-8000
Minute Maid Park **Fax:** 713-259-8981
501 Crawford St
Houston, TX 77002
houston.astros.mlb.com

Clement, Bill (1950-)
NHL analyst; former professional hockey player
Outdoor Life Network **Ph:** 203-406-2500
2 Stamford Plaza **Fax:** 203-406-2534
281 Tresser Blvd
Stamford, CT 06901

Clements, Andrew (1949-)
Children's books author (Frindle)
Simon & Schuster Books for Young Readers **Ph:** 212-698-7000
1230 Ave of the Americas
New York, NY 10020
www.simonsays.com

Clements, Nate (1979-)
Professional football player
Buffalo Bills **Ph:** 716-648-1800
Ralph Wilson Stadium **Fax:** 716-649-6446
1 Bills Dr
Orchard Park, NY 14127
www.buffalobills.com

Clifford, Robert A
A top personal injury attorney specializing in aviation litigation
Clifford Law Offices **Ph:** 312-899-9090
120 N Lasalle St Suite 3100 **Fax:** 312-251-1160
Chicago, IL 60602
www.cliffordlaw.com

Clift, Eleanor
Contributing editor for Newsweek magazine; has also appeared as a panelist on such programs as The McLaughlin Group
Newsweek Magazine **Ph:** 212-445-4000
251 W 57th St
New York, NY 10019
www.eleanorclift.com

Clifton, Lucille (1936-)
Poet
BOA Editions Ltd **Ph:** 585-546-3410
260 East Ave **Fax:** 585-546-3913
Rochester, NY 14604
www.boaeditions.org

Clijsters, Kim (1983-)
Professional tennis player
WTA Tour **Ph:** 727-895-5000
1 Progress Plaza Suite 1500 **Fax:** 727-894-1982
Saint Petersburg, FL 33701
www.kimclijsters.be

Clinton, Bill (1946-)
42nd US President
William J Clinton Foundation **Ph:** 212-348-8882
55 W 125th St **Fax:** 212-348-9245
New York, NY 10027
www.clintonfoundation.org

Clinton, Hillary Rodham (1947-)
US Senator from New York (Democrat); former First Lady of the US (wife of President Bill Clinton)
476 Russell Bldg **Ph:** 202-224-4451
Washington, DC 20510 **Fax:** 202-228-0282
clinton.senate.gov

Clohessy, David (1957-)
Executive Director of SNAP (Survivors Network of those Abused by Priests)
Survivors Network of Those Abused by Priests **Ph:** 314-566-9790
Fax: 314-645-2017
7234 Arsenal St
Saint Louis, MO 63143
www.snapnetwork.org

Clooney, George (1961-)
Actor
Creative Artists Agency **Ph:** 310-288-4545
9830 Wilshire Blvd **Fax:** 310-288-4800
Beverly Hills, CA 90212

Close, Glenn (1947-)
Actor
PMK/HBH **Ph:** 310-289-6200
700 San Vicente Blvd Suite G910 **Fax:** 310-289-6677
West Hollywood, CA 90069

Cloutier, Dan (1976-)
Professional hockey player
Vancouver Canucks **Ph:** 604-899-4600
General Motors Pl **Fax:** 604-899-4640
800 Griffiths Way
Vancouver, BC V6B6G1
www.canucks.com

Clowes, Daniel (1961-)
Comic book artist; creator of the graphic novel Ghost World and Eightball
Fantagraphics Books **Ph:** 206-524-1967
7563 Lake CIty Way NE **Fax:** 206-524-2104
Seattle, WA 98115
www.fantagraphics.com

Clyburn, James E (1940-)
US Representative from South Carolina (Democrat)
2135 Rayburn Bldg **Ph:** 202-225-3315
Washington, DC 20515 **Fax:** 202-225-2313
www.house.gov/clyburn

Coase, Ronald H (1910-)
Winner of the 1991 Noble Prize in Economics for his discovery and clarification of the significance of transaction costs and property rights for the institutional structure and functioning of the economy
University of Chicago Law School **Ph:** 773-702-9494
1111 E 60th St
Chicago, IL 60637
coase.org

Coben, Harlan
Author of mystery/suspense novels (Gone for Good, Tell No One)
Bantam Dell Publicity **Ph:** 212-782-9000
1745 Broadway
New York, NY 10019
www.harlancoben.com

Coble, Howard (1931-)
US Representative from North Carolina (Republican)
2468 Rayburn Bldg **Ph:** 202-225-3065
Washington, DC 20515 **Fax:** 202-225-8611
coble.house.gov

Coburn, Tom, MD (1948-)
US Senator from Oklahoma (Republican); is also a physician specializing in family medicine, obstetrics, and the treatment of allergies
B40D Dirksen Bldg **Ph:** 202-224-5754
Washington, DC 20510 **Fax:** 202-224-6008
coburn.senate.gov

Cocco, Marie
Columnist (political commentary)
Washington Post Writers Group **Ph:** 202-334-6375
Fax: 202-334-5669
1150 15th St NW 9th Fl
Washington, DC 20071
www.postwritersgroup.com

Cochran, John
Senior Washington correspondent for ABC News
ABC News **Ph:** 202-222-7700
1717 DeSales St NW
Washington, DC 20036
www.abcnews.go.com/WNT

Cochran, Thad (1937-)
US Senator from Mississippi (Republican)
113 Dirksen Bldg **Ph:** 202-224-5054
Washington, DC 20510 **Fax:** 202-224-9450
cochran.senate.gov

Cochran, Tony
Creator of the comic strip Agnes
Creators Syndicate Inc **Ph:** 310-337-7003
5777 W Century Blvd Suite 700 **Fax:** 310-337-7625
Los Angeles, CA 90045
www.creators.com

Cockburn, Alexander (1941-)
Syndicated columnist (commentary); is also editor (with Jeffrey Saint Clair) of the biweekly muckraking newsletter CounterPunch
Creators Syndicate Inc **Ph:** 310-337-7003
5777 W Century Blvd Suite 700 **Fax:** 310-337-7625
Los Angeles, CA 90045
www.creators.com/opinion.html

Codrescu, Andrei (1946-)
Romanian-born poet and essayist; his commentary is featured on NPR's All Things Considered
National Public Radio **Ph:** 202-513-2000
635 Massachusetts Ave NW **Fax:** 202-513-3329
Washington, DC 20001
www.npr.org

Coelho, Paulo (1947-)
Brazilian writer (The Alchemist)
HarperCollins Publishers **Ph:** 212-207-7000
c/o Author Mail
10 E 53rd St
New York, NY 10022
www.paulocoelho.com.br

Coen, Ethan (1957-)
Movie producer/screenwriter with brother Joel
United Talent Agency **Ph:** 310-273-6700
9560 Wilshire Blvd 5th Fl **Fax:** 310-247-1111
Beverly Hills, CA 90212
www.coenbrothers.net

Coen, Joel (1954-)
Film writer/director with brother Ethan
United Talent Agency **Ph:** 310-273-6700
9560 Wilshire Blvd 5th Fl **Fax:** 310-247-1111
Beverly Hills, CA 90212
www.coenbrothers.net

Cofer, Judith Ortiz (1952-)
Author; her work includes books for young adults (The Meaning of Consuelo)
University of Georgia **Ph:** 706-542-2223
Dept of English
130 Park Hall
Athens, GA 30602
www.english.uga.edu/~jcofer

Coffee, John C Jr
Attorney & law professor; principal interests are corporations, securities regulation, class actions, criminal law, and white-collar crime
Columbia University **Ph:** 212-854-2640
School of Law
435 W 116th St
New York, NY 10027
www.law.columbia.edu

Cohan, Christopher
Owner and CEO of the Golden State Warriors basketball franchise
Golden State Warriors **Ph:** 510-986-2200
1011 Broadway **Fax:** 510-452-0132
Oakland, CA 94607

Cohen, Alan
General partner, chairman, and CEO of the Florida Panthers hockey franchise
Florida Panthers **Ph:** 954-835-7000
BankAtlantic Center **Fax:** 954-835-7700
1 Panther Pkwy
Sunrise, FL 33323

Cohen, Ben (1951-)
Co-founder/co-owner, with Jerry Greenfield, of Ben & Jerry's Ice Cream
Ben & Jerry's Homemade Holdings Inc **Ph:** 802-846-1500
Fax: 802-846-1520
30 Community Dr
South Burlington, VT 05403
www.benjerry.com

Cohen, Betty
President & CEO of Lifetime Television
Lifetime Television **Ph:** 212-424-7000
309 W 49th St
New York, NY 10019
www.lifetimetv.com

Cohen, Harlan
Writes the syndicated column Help Me Harlan!, which offers advice from a male perspective
King Features Syndicate Inc **Ph:** 212-455-4000
888 7th Ave 2nd Fl
New York, NY 10019
www.kingfeatures.com

Cohen, Randy
Writes the syndicated column The Ethicist
Universal Press Syndicate **Ph:** 816-932-6600
4520 Main St
Kansas City, MO 64111
www.amuniversal.com/ups/features

Cohen, Richard
Syndicated op-ed columnist
Washington Post Writers Group **Ph:** 202-334-6375
Fax: 202-334-5669
1150 15th St NW 9th Fl
Washington, DC 20071
www.postwritersgroup.com

Cohen, Richard B
Chairman and CEO of C & S Wholesale Grocers Inc
C & S Wholesale Grocers Inc **Ph:** 603-354-7000
7 Corporate Dr **Fax:** 603-354-4690
Keene, NH 03431
www.cswg.com

Cohen, Sasha (1984-)
Figure skater
US Figure Skating **Ph:** 719-635-5200
20 1st St
Colorado Springs, CO 80906
www.sashacohen.com

Cohen, William S (1940-)
Former US Secretary of Defense; former US Senator and Representative; in 1974, cast the deciding vote to impeach President Richard Nixon
Cohen Group **Ph:** 202-689-7900
1200 19th St NW Suite 400 **Fax:** 202-689-7910
Washington, DC 20036
www.cohengroup.net

Cohn, Linda (1959-)
ESPN sports news anchor
ESPN **Ph:** 860-585-2000
ESPN Plaza
935 Middle St
Bristol, CT 06010
sports.espn.go.com/espntv/espnGuide

Cohn, Scott
CNBC senior correspondent
CNBC **Ph:** 201-735-2622
900 Sylvan Ave
Englewood Cliffs, NJ 07632
moneycentral.msn.com/cnbc/tv

Coker, Larry (1948-)
Football coach
University of Miami Athletic Dept **Ph:** 305-284-4323 **Fax:** 305-284-2507
5821 San Amaro Dr
Coral Gables, FL 33146
hurricanesports.ocsn.com

Colangelo, Jerry J (1943-)
Chairman & CEO of the Phoenix Suns basketball team and of the Arizona Diamondbacks baseball club
Phoenix Suns **Ph:** 602-379-7900
America West Arena **Fax:** 602-379-7990
201 E Jefferson St
Phoenix, AZ 85004
www.nba.com/suns/news/jerry_colangelo_bio.html

Colbert, Keary (1982-)
Professional football player
Carolina Panthers **Ph:** 704-358-7000
Bank of America Stadium **Fax:** 704-358-7618
800 S Mint St
Charlotte, NC 28202
www.panthers.com

Cole, Erik (1978-)
Professional hockey player
Carolina Hurricanes **Ph:** 919-467-7825
RBC Center **Fax:** 919-462-7030
1400 Edwards Mill Rd
Raleigh, NC 27607
www.carolinahurricanes.com

Cole, Harriette
Writes the syndicated advice column Sense & Sensitivity
United Feature Syndicate **Ph:** 212-293-8500
200 Madison Ave
New York, NY 10016
www.unitedfeatures.com

Cole, Joanna (1944-)
Author of the Magic School Bus series
Scholastic Inc **Ph:** 212-343-6100
557 Broadway
New York, NY 10012
www2.scholastic.com

Cole, Natalie (1950-)
Jazz/pop singer (daughter of Nat 'King' Cole)
William Morris Agency **Ph:** 310-859-4000
1 William Morris Pl **Fax:** 310-859-4462
Beverly Hills, CA 90212
www.nataliecole.com

Cole, Paula (1968-)
Singer/songwriter, instrumentalist, and music producer
Monterey Peninsula Artists/ Paradigm **Ph:** 831-375-4889 **Fax:** 831-375-2623
509 Hartnell St
Monterey, CA 93940
www.paulacole.com

Cole, Scott
Fitness/wellness expert, author, and motivational speaker
Holiday Entertainment **Ph:** 310-396-6243
PO Box 25951
Los Angeles, CA 90025
www.scottcole.com

Cole, Tom (1949-)
US Representative from Oklahoma (Republican)
236 Cannon Bldg **Ph:** 202-225-6165
Washington, DC 20515 **Fax:** 202-225-3512
www.house.gov/cole

Coleman, Michael B (1954-)
Mayor of Columbus, Ohio
90 W Broad St Suite 247 **Ph:** 614-645-7671
Columbus, OH 43215 **Fax:** 614-645-1970
mayor.ci.columbus.oh.us

Coleman, Norm (1949-)
US Senator from Minnesota (Republican)
320 Hart Bldg **Ph:** 202-224-5641
Washington, DC 20510 **Fax:** 202-224-1152
coleman.senate.gov

Coles, Laveranues (1977-)
Professional football player
New York Jets **Ph:** 516-560-8100
1000 Fulton Ave **Fax:** 516-560-8198
Hempstead, NY 11550
www.newyorkjets.com

Coles, Robert, MD
Child psychiatrist, Harvard professor, and author of more than 50 books, including the Children of Crisis series and the Inner Life of Children series
Random House Publicity **Ph:** 212-782-9000
1745 Broadway
New York, NY 10019
www.randomhouse.com

Colfer, Eoin (1965-)
Children's books author (Artemis Fowl)
Hyperion Books for Children **Ph:** 212-633-4400
114 5th Ave
New York, NY 10010
www.eoincolfer.com

Colicchio, Tom
Chef/owner of Gramercy Tavern
Gramercy Tavern **Ph:** 212-477-0777
42 E 20th St **Fax:** 212-477-1160
New York, NY 10003
www.gramercytavern.com

Collette, Toni (1972-)
Actor
Endeavor **Ph:** 310-248-2000
9601 Wilshire Blvd 3rd Fl **Fax:** 310-248-2020
Beverly Hills, CA 90210

Collier, Bryan
Illustrator of books for young readers (awards winner for Martin's Big Words)
Books for Young Readers **Ph:** 212-886-9200
Henry Holt & Co
115 W 18th St
New York, NY 10011
www.bryancollier.com

Colligan, Ed
President and CEO of Palm Inc, a maker of mobile computing products
Palm Inc **Ph:** 408-617-7000
950 W Maude Ave **Fax:** 408-617-0100
Sunnyvale, CA 94085
www.palm.com/us/company/corporate/executive.html#ed

Collins, Billy (1941-)
US Poet Laureate 2001-2003; New York State Poet Laureate 2004-06
Steven Barclay Agency **Ph:** 707-773-0654
12 Western Ave **Fax:** 707-778-1868
Petaluma, CA 94952 **TF:** 888-965-7323
www.bigsnap.com/billy.html

Collins, Bobby
Comedian
On the Inside Productions **Ph:** 310-393-3378
PO Box 3644 **Fax:** 310-393-3454
Santa Monica, CA 90408
www.bobbycollins.com

Collins, Eileen (1956-)
Astronaut; first woman to command a Space Shuttle mission
Johnson Space Center **Ph:** 281-483-0123
2101 NASA Rd 1
Houston, TX 77058
www.jsc.nasa.gov/Bios/htmlbios/collins.html

Collins, Francis, MD, PhD (1950-)
Director of the National Human Genome Research Institute at the National Institutes of Health
National Human Genome Research Institute **Ph:** 301-402-0911
31 Center Dr Bldg 31 Rm 4B09
MSC 2152
Bethesda, MD 20892
www.genome.gov/About

Collins, Gail (1945-)
New York Times editorial page editor
New York Times **Ph:** 212-556-1234
229 W 43rd St
New York, NY 10036
www.nytco.com/company-executives.html

Collins, Heidi
CNN news anchor and correspondent
CNN New York **Ph:** 212-275-7800
Time Warner Ctr
10 Columbus Cir
New York, NY 10019
www.cnn.com/CNN/anchors_reporters

Collins, Jackie (1941-)
Author of best-sellers
Simon & Schuster **Ph:** 212-689-7000
1230 Ave of the Americas
New York, NY 10020
www.jackiecollins.com

Collins, James C
Author of Built to Last and Good to Great: Why Some Companies Make the Leap...And Others Don't
HarperCollins Publishers **Ph:** 212-207-7000
c/o Author Mail
10 E 53rd St
New York, NY 10022
www.jimcollins.com

Collins, Susan (1952-)
US Senator from Maine (Republican)
172 Russell Bldg **Ph:** 202-224-2523
Washington, DC 20510 **Fax:** 202-224-2693
collins.senate.gov

Collinsworth, Cris (1959-)
Former professional football player; now a host on Inside the NFL on HBO
HBO Sports **Ph:** 212-512-1000
1100 Ave of the Americas
New York, NY 10036
www.hbo.com/infl

Colmes, Alan
Politically liberal radio talk show host; also the liberal counterpart on Hannity & Colmes, the FOX debate/talk show
FOX News Channel **Ph:** 212-301-3000
1211 Ave of the Americas
New York, NY 10036
www.alan.com

Colon, Bartolo (1973-)
Professional baseball player
Los Angeles Angels of Anaheim **Ph:** 714-940-2000
Angel Stadium **Fax:** 714-940-2205
2000 Gene Autry Way
Anaheim, CA 92806
losangeles.angels.mlb.com

Colson, Chuck (1931-)
Founder and chairman of Prison Fellowship and a born-again Christian; former Special Counsel to President Nixon who served prison time for Watergate-related charges
Prison Fellowship **Ph:** 703-478-0100
44180 Riverside Pkwy **Fax:** 703-478-0452
Lansdowne, VA 20176
www.prisonfellowship.org

Columbu, Franco (1941-)
Fitness personality/bodybuilder; chiropractor
Franco Columbu Productions Inc **Ph:** 310-234-1160 **Fax:** 310-234-3401
2265A Westwood Blvd
Los Angeles, CA 90064
www.columbu.com

Columbus, Chris (1958-)
Film producer, director
Creative Artists Agency **Ph:** 310-288-4545
9830 Wilshire Blvd **Fax:** 310-288-4800
Beverly Hills, CA 90212

Combs, Roberta
President of the Christian Coalition
Christian Coalition of America **Ph:** 202-479-6900
PO Box 37030 **Fax:** 202-479-4260
Washington, DC 20013
www.cc.org

Combs, Sean "Diddy" (1969-)
Hip-hop performer, producer, and businessman
Bad Boy Worldwide Entertainment Group **Ph:** 212-381-1540 **Fax:** 212-381-1599
1710 Broadway
New York, NY 10019

Comper, F Anthony (1946-)
President & CEO of BMO Financial Group
BMO Financial Group **Ph:** 514-877-7373
Bank of Montreal **Fax:** 514-877-6933
129 rue Saint Jacques
6200 Place d' Armes
Montreal, QC H2Y1L6
www.bmo.com

Comrie, Mike (1980-)
Professional hockey player
Phoenix Coyotes **Ph:** 623-463-8800
5800 W Glenn Dr Suite 350 **Fax:** 623-463-8810
Glendale, AZ 85301
www.phoenixcoyotes.com

Conan, Neal (1949-)
Host of Talk of the Nation on NPR
National Public Radio **Ph:** 202-513-2000
635 Massachusets Ave NW **Fax:** 202-513-3329
Washington, DC 20001
www.npr.org

Conason, Joe (1954-)
National correspondent for The New York Observer and a syndicated columnist
New York Observer **Ph:** 212-755-2400
54 E 64th St
New York, NY 10021
www.observer.com

Conaway, Mike (1948-)
US Representative from Texas (Republican)
511 Cannon Bldg **Ph:** 202-225-3605
Washington, DC 20515 **Fax:** 202-225-4951
conaway.house.gov

Condron, Bob (1968-)
Co-creator, with Patrick Roberts, of the comic strip Todd the Dinosaur!
King Features Syndicate Inc **Ph:** 212-455-4000
888 7th Ave 2nd Fl
New York, NY 10019
www.kingfeatures.com

Conley, Darby
Creator of the comic strip Get Fuzzy
United Feature Syndicate **Ph:** 212-293-8500
200 Madison Ave
New York, NY 10016
www.unitedfeatures.com

Conn, David
Lead prosecutor in the successful retrial of Erik and Lyle Menendez; now practices criminal defense law
Law Office of David P Conn **Ph:** 310-571-2815
12400 Wilshire Blvd Suite 400 **Fax:** 310-207-0954
Los Angeles, CA 90025
www.davidconn.com

Connell, Evan S
Author of both fiction and nonfiction books
Counterpoint Press **Ph:** 212-340-8100
387 Park Ave S 12th Fl
New York, NY 10016
www.counterpointpress.com

Connelly, Jennifer (1970-)
Actor
International Creative Management **Ph:** 310-550-4000
8942 Wilshire Blvd
Beverly Hills, CA 90211

Connelly, Michael (1956-)
Mystery writer; several of his novels feature LAPD Detective Hieronymus (Harry) Bosch
Little Brown & Co **Ph:** 212-522-7200
Author Mail
1271 Ave of the Americas
New York, NY 10020
www.michaelconnelly.com

Connery, Sean (1930-)
Actor
Creative Artists Agency **Ph:** 310-288-4545
9830 Wilshire Blvd **Fax:** 310-288-4800
Beverly Hills, CA 90212
www.seanconnery.com

Connick, Harry Jr (1967-)
Jazz/swing musician/singer/songwriter; actor
Creative Artists Agency **Ph:** 310-288-4545
9830 Wilshire Blvd **Fax:** 310-288-4800
Beverly Hills, CA 90212
www.harryconnickjr.com

Connolly, John
Author of thrillers
Simon & Schuster **Ph:** 212-698-7000
1230 Ave of the Americas
New York, NY 10020
www.johnconnolly.co.uk

Connor, Christopher
Chairman, president, and CEO of Sherwin-Williams
Sherwin-Williams Co **Ph:** 216-566-2000
101 Prospect Ave NW
Cleveland, OH 44115
www.sherwin.com/about

Conrad, Jimmy (1977-)
Professional soccer player
Kansas City Wizards **Ph:** 816-920-9300
2 Arrowhead Dr **Fax:** 816-920-4774
Kansas City, MO 64129
kc.wizards.mlsnet.com

Conrad, Kent (1948-)
US Senator from North Dakota (Democrat)
530 Hart Bldg **Ph:** 202-224-2043
Washington, DC 20510 **Fax:** 202-224-7776
conrad.senate.gov

Conrad, Paul (1924-)
Editorial cartoonist; also creates bronze sculptures of political leaders
Tribune Media Services Inc **Ph:** 312-222-4444
435 N Michigan Ave Suite 1500
Chicago, IL 60611
www.comicspage.com

Conroy, Craig (1971-)
Professional hockey player
Los Angeles Kings **Ph:** 213-742-7100
Staples Center
1111 S Figueroa St
Los Angeles, CA 90015
www.lakings.com

Conroy, Frances (1953-)
Actor
International Creative Management **Ph:** 310-550-4000
8942 Wilshire Blvd
Beverly Hills, CA 90211
www.hbo.com/sixfeetunder

Conroy, Pat (1945-)
Author (The Great Santini; The Prince of Tides)
Doubleday Publicity **Ph:** 212-782-9000
1745 Broadway
New York, NY 10019
www.patconroy.com

Conyers, John Jr (1929-)
US Representative from Michigan (Democrat)
2426 Rayburn Bldg **Ph:** 202-225-5126
Washington, DC 20515 **Fax:** 202-225-0072
www.house.gov/conyers

Cook, John (1946-)
Mayor of El Paso, Texas
2 Civic Center Plaza 10th Fl **Ph:** 915-541-4145
El Paso, TX 79901 **Fax:** 915-541-4501
www.elpasotexas.gov/mayor

Cook, Richard
Chairman of Walt Disney Studios
Walt Disney Studios **Ph:** 818-560-1000
500 S Buena Vista St **Fax:** 818-560-1930
Burbank, CA 91521
disney.go.com/corporate

Cook, Robin, MD (1940-)
Physician and author of medical thrillers (Coma)
Berkley Books Publicity **Ph:** 212-366-2000
375 Hudson St
New York, NY 10014
penguinputnam.com

Cook, Scott D
Co-founder & chairman of Intuit
Intuit Inc **Ph:** 650-944-6000
2632 Marine Way
Mountain View, CA 94043
www.intuit.com

Cook, Thomas H (1947-)
Author of mystery/suspense novels (The Chatham School Affair)
Bantam Dell Publicity **Ph:** 212-782-9000
1745 Broadway
New York, NY 10019
www.randomhouse.com/bantamdell

Cooley, Denton A, MD (1926-)
Heart surgeon who performed the first successful human heart transplant in the United States and the first implantation of a total artificial heart in a human
Texas Heart Institute **Ph:** 713-791-4932
PO Box 20345 **Fax:** 713-791-3424
MC 3-258
Houston, TX 77225
texheartsurgeons.com

Coolidge, Martha (1946-)
Movie/television director
Paradigm **Ph:** 310-288-8000
360 N Crescent Dr **Fax:** 310-288-2000
North Bldg
Beverly Hills, CA 90210

Cooney, Caroline B (1947-)
Author of books for young adults
Random House Children's Books **Ph:** 212-782-9000
Publicity Dept
1745 Broadway
New York, NY 10019
www.randomhouse.com/kids

Coonts, Stephen (1946-)
Author (Flight of the Intruder)
St Martin's Press **Ph:** 212-674-5151
Attn: Publicity Dept
175 5th Ave
New York, NY 10010
www.stephencoonts.com

Cooper, Anderson (1967-)
Anchor of Anderson Cooper 360
CNN New York **Ph:** 212-275-7800
Time Warner Ctr
10 Columbus Cir
New York, NY 10019
www.cnn.com/CNN/anchors_reporters

Cooper, Jim (1954-)
US Representative from Tennessee (Democrat)
1536 Longworth Bldg **Ph:** 202-225-4311
Washington, DC 20515 **Fax:** 202-226-1035
www.cooper.house.gov

Cooper, Kenneth H, MD (1931-)
Founder of the Cooper Aerobics Center and host of the syndicated call-in radio show Healthy Living Radio; first coined the term aerobics
Cooper Ventures **Ph:** 972-233-4832
12200 Preston Rd **Fax:** 972-239-6649
Dallas, TX 75230
www.cooperaerobics.com

Cooper, Matthew T (1935-)
Lt General Matthew T Cooper USMC (Ret). President and CEO of the Marine Toys for Tots Foundation
Marine Toys for Tots Foundation **Ph:** 703-640-9433
Fax: 703-640-0917
PO Box 1947
Quantico, VA 22134

Cooper, Susan (1935-)
Children's book writer; author of the fantasy sequence, The Dark is Rising
Simon & Schuster Books for Young Readers **Ph:** 212-698-7000
1230 Ave of the Americas
New York, NY 10020
www.thelostland.com

Copeland, Kenneth (1937-)
Televangelist
Kenneth Copeland Ministries **Ph:** 817-252-2700
Fort Worth, TX 76192 **Fax:** 817-252-3499
www.kcm.org **TF:** 800-600-7395

Copperfield, David (1956-)
Illusionist
Polaris PR **Ph:** 323-939-7535
8135 W 4th St 2nd Fl **Fax:** 323-939-1566
Los Angeles, CA 90048
www.davidcopperfield.com

Coppola, Francis Ford (1939-)
Film producer/director
International Creative Management **Ph:** 310-550-4000
8942 Wilshire Blvd
Beverly Hills, CA 90211

Coppola, Michael
President and CEO of Advance Auto Parts Inc
Advance Auto Parts Inc **Ph:** 540-362-4911
5673 Airport Rd
Roanoke, VA 24012
www.advance-auto.com

Coppola, Sofia (1971-)
Film director/writer/producer; actor
Creative Artists Agency **Ph:** 310-288-4545
9830 Wilshire Blvd **Fax:** 310-288-4800
Beverly Hills, CA 90212

Corbett, John (1961-)
Actor; singer/musician
Creative Artists Agency **Ph:** 310-288-4545
9830 Wilshire Blvd **Fax:** 310-288-4800
Beverly Hills, CA 90212
www.johncorbettband.com

Corbett, Luke (1946-)
Chairman and CEO of Kerr-McGee Corp
Kerr-McGee Corp **Ph:** 405-270-1313
123 Robert S Kerr Ave
Oklahoma City, OK 73102
www.kerr-mcgee.com/about/abo_officers.htm

Corderi, Victoria
Dateline NBC correspondent
Dateline NBC **Ph:** 212-664-4249
30 Rockefeller Plaza
New York, NY 10112
www.msnbc.msn.com/id/3360263

Cordero, Francisco (1975-)
Professional baseball player
Texas Rangers **Ph:** 817-273-5222
Ameriquest Field in Arlington **Fax:** 817-273-5294
1000 Ballpark Way **TF:** 888-968-3927
Arlington, TX 76011
texas.rangers.mlb.com

Cordova, France, PhD (1947-)
Astronomer/astrophysicist and former NASA Chief Scientist; Chancellor of the University of California Riverside
Office of the Chancellor **Ph:** 951-827-5201
University of California Riverside **Fax:** 951-827-3866
900 University Ave
Riverside, CA 92521
www.chancellor.ucr.edu

Corea, Chick (1941-)
Jazz musician (piano, keyboards)
Ted Kurland Assoc **Ph:** 617-254-0007
173 Brighton Ave **Fax:** 617-782-3577
Boston, MA 02134
www.chickcorea.com

Corella, Angel (1975-)
A principal dancer for American Ballet Theatre
American Ballet Theatre **Ph:** 212-477-3030
890 Broadway **Fax:** 212-254-5938
New York, NY 10003
www.abt.org/dancers

Corey, Elias James, PhD (1928-)
Winner of the 1990 Nobel Prize in Chemistry for his development of the theory and methodology of organic synthesis
Harvard University **Ph:** 617-495-4033
Dept of Chemistry & Chemical Biology **Fax:** 617-495-0376
12 Oxford St
Cambridge, MA 02138
www.chem.harvard.edu

Corgan, Billy (1967-)
Former lead singer with the Smashing Pumpkins; now performing solo
William Morris Agency **Ph:** 310-859-4000
1 William Morris Pl **Fax:** 310-859-4462
Beverly Hills, CA 90212
www.billycorgan.com

Corley, Cheryl
NPR Senior Reporter (a general assignment reporter but with a special interest in housing issues)
National Public Radio **Ph:** 312-516-3360
Chicago Bureau **Fax:** 312-516-3377
65 E Wacker Pl Suite 1401
Chicago, IL 60601
www.npr.org

Corliss, Richard
Time Magazine senior writer; writes about movies, show business, and sports
Time Magazine **Ph:** 212-522-1212
Rockefeller Center
Time & Life Bldg
New York, NY 10020
www.time.com/time/columnist

Cormier, Robert (1925-)
Writer of books for young adults (The Chocolate War)
Random House Children's Books **Ph:** 212-782-9000
Publicity Dept
1745 Broadway
New York, NY 10019
www.randomhouse.com/teens

Cornett, Mick
Mayor of Oklahoma City
200 N Walker Ave Suite 302 **Ph:** 405-297-2424
Oklahoma City, OK 73102 **Fax:** 405-297-3759
www.okc.gov

Cornwell, Patricia (1956-)
Author of the Kay Scarpetta mystery series
Putnam Publicity **Ph:** 212-366-2000
375 Hudson St
New York, NY 10014
www.patricia-cornwell.com

Cornyn, John (1952-)
US Senator from Texas (Republican)
517 Hart Bldg **Ph:** 202-224-2934
Washington, DC 20510 **Fax:** 202-228-2856
cornyn.senate.gov

Correll, AD
Chairman of Georgia-Pacific Corp
Georgia-Pacific Corp **Ph:** 404-652-5248
133 Peachtree St NE **Fax:** 404-654-4789
Atlanta, GA 30303
www.gp.com/center/newsroom/correll.html

Corrigan, Maureen
Book critic on NPR's Fresh Air
National Public Radio **Ph:** 202-513-2000
635 Massachusetts Ave NW **Fax:** 202-513-3329
Washington, DC 20001
www.npr.org

Corrigan, Patrick (1951-)
Editorial cartoonist
Toronto Star **Ph:** 416-367-2000
1 Yonge St
Toronto, ON M5E1E6
corrigan.ca

Corso, Lee (1935-)
Sports broadcaster
ESPN **Ph:** 860-585-2000
ESPN Plaza
935 Middle St
Bristol, CT 06010
sports.espn.go.com/espntv/espnGuide

Corzine, Jon (1947-)
Governor of New Jersey (Democrat)
125 W State St Box 001 **Ph:** 609-292-6000
Trenton, NJ 08625 **Fax:** 609-292-3454
www.state.nj.us/governor

Cosby, Bill (1937-)
Comedian; actor
William Morris Agency **Ph:** 310-859-4000
1 William Morris Pl **Fax:** 310-859-4462
Beverly Hills, CA 90212
www.wma.com/bill_cosby/summary

Cosby, Rita (1964-)
Host of MSNBC's Rita Cosby Live & Direct
MSNBC TV **Ph:** 201-583-5000
1 MSNBC Plaza
Secaucus, NJ 07094
www.msnbc.msn.com/id/3080263

Costa, Jim (1952-)
US Representative from California (Democrat)
1004 Longworth Bldg **Ph:** 202-225-3341
Washington, DC 20515 **Fax:** 202-225-9308
www.house.gov/costa

Costas, Bob (1952-)
Veteran sportscaster; host of On The Record With Bob Costas and one of the hosts of Inside the NFL on HBO Sports
HBO Sports **Ph:** 212-512-1000
1100 Ave of the Americas
New York, NY 10036
www.hbo.com/infl

Costello, Carol
CNN anchor and reporter
CNN **Ph:** 404-827-1500
1 CNN Center
Atlanta, GA 30303
www.cnn.com/CNN/anchors_reporters

Costello, Elvis (1954-)
Singer/songwriter
Shore Fire Media **Ph:** 718-522-7171
32 Court St Suite 1600 **Fax:** 718-522-7242
Brooklyn, NY 11201
www.elviscostello.com

Costello, Jerry F (1949-)
US Representative from Illinois (Democrat)
2269 Rayburn Bldg **Ph:** 202-225-5661
Washington, DC 20515 **Fax:** 202-225-0285
www.house.gov/costello

Costello, Tom
NBC news correspondent
NBC News **Ph:** 212-664-4249
30 Rockefeller Plaza
New York, NY 10112
www.msnbc.msn.com/id/3689499

Costner, Kevin (1955-)
Actor, producer, director
Creative Artists Agency **Ph:** 310-288-4545
9830 Wilshire Blvd **Fax:** 310-288-4800
Beverly Hills, CA 90212

Cote, David M (1952-)
Chairman and CEO of Honeywell International
Honeywell International Inc **Ph:** 973-455-6768
101 Columbia Rd **Fax:** 973-455-4807
Morristown, NJ 07960
www.honeywell.com

Coughlin, Daniel (1934-)
Chaplain for the US House of Representatives (the first Catholic priest to hold this position since it was created in 1774)
US House of Representatives **Ph:** 202-225-2509
HB 25 US Capitol Bldg
Washington, DC 20515
chaplain.house.gov

Coughlin, Tom (1946-)
Football coach
New York Giants **Ph:** 201-935-8111
Giants Stadium **Fax:** 201-939-4134
East Rutherford, NJ 07073
www.giants.com

Coulier, Dave (1959-)
Comedian
Special Artists Agency **Ph:** 310-859-9688
9465 Wilshire Blvd Suite 890
Beverly Hills, CA 90212
www.cutitout.net

Coulter, Ann
Conservative political analyst & attorney; writes a nationally syndicated newspaper column
Universal Press Syndicate **Ph:** 816-932-6600
4520 Main St
Kansas City, MO 64111
www.anncoulter.com

Coulter, Catherine
Author of suspense thrillers, romantic thrillers, and historical romance novels
Jove Publicity **Ph:** 212-366-2000
375 Hudson St
New York, NY 10014
www.catherinecoulter.com

Counsell, Craig (1970-)
Professional baseball player
Arizona Diamondbacks **Ph:** 602-462-6500
Bank One Ballpark **Fax:** 602-462-6600
401 E Jefferson St
Phoenix, AZ 85004
arizona.diamondbacks.mlb.com

Coupland, Douglas (1961-)
Novelist (Hey Nostradamus!: A Novel; All Families are Psychotic)
Bloomsbury USA **Ph:** 212-674-5151
175 5th Ave Suite 300 **Fax:** 212-780-0115
New York, NY 10010
www.coupland.com

Couples, Fred (1959-)
Professional golfer
PGA Tour **Ph:** 904-285-3700
100 PGA Tour Blvd
Ponte Vedra Beach, FL 32082
www.pgatour.com/players

Couric, Katie (1957-)
Today Show co-anchor; has announced that she will leave Today at the end of May and is to replace Bob Schieffer as the anchor of CBS Evening News beginning in September 2006
Today Show **Ph:** 212-664-4249
30 Rockefeller Plaza
New York, NY 10112
www.msnbc.msn.com/id/3079108

Cousteau, Jacques (1910-1997)
Marine explorer & filmmaker; also an inventor
Cousteau Society **Ph:** 757-722-9300
710 Settlers Landing Rd **Fax:** 757-722-8185
Hampton, VA 23669
www.cousteau.org

Cousteau, Jean-Michel (1938-)
Ocean explorer, environmentalist, and founder/president of Ocean Futures Society; son of Jacques Cousteau
Ocean Futures Society **Ph:** 805-899-8899
325 Chapala St **Fax:** 805-899-8898
Santa Barbara, CA 93101
www.oceanfutures.org

Coverly, Dave
Creator of the comic strip Speed Bump
Creators Syndicate Inc **Ph:** 310-337-7003
5777 W Century Blvd Suite 700 **Fax:** 310-337-7625
Los Angeles, CA 90045
www.creators.com

Covey, Stephen R (1932-)
Author of The 7 Habits of Highly Effective People; also a speaker and the co-founder of FranklinCovey, a global professional services firm
3355 N University Ave **Ph:** 801-377-9515
Suite 200 **TF:** 800-254-8152
Provo, UT 84604
www.stephencovey.com

Cowan, Lee (1965-)
News correspondent
CBS News **Ph:** 212-975-4114
524 W 57th St
New York, NY 10019
www.cbsnews.com

Cowell, Simon (1959-)
A judge on American idol
Creative Artists Agency **Ph:** 310-288-4545
9830 Wilshire Blvd **Fax:** 310-288-4800
Beverly Hills, CA 90212

Cowens, Dave (1948-)
General manager & coach of the Chicago Sky WNBA team; former NBA player & coach and member of the NBA Hall of Fame
Chicago Sky **Ph:** 312-828-9550
20 W Kinzie St Suite 1000
Chicago, IL 60610
www.wnba.com/sky

Cowher, Bill (1956-)
Football coach
Pittsburgh Steelers **Ph:** 412-432-7800
3400 S Water St **Fax:** 412-432-7878
Pittsburgh, PA 15203
www.pittsburghsteelers.com

Cox, Bobby (1941-)
Baseball manager
Atlanta Braves **Ph:** 404-522-7630
PO Box 4064 **Fax:** 404-614-1392
Atlanta, GA 30302
atlanta.braves.mlb.com

Cox, Christopher (1952-)
Chairman of the Securities & Exchange Commission
Securities & Exchange Commission **Ph:** 202-551-2100
100 F St NE
Washington, DC 20549
www.sec.gov

Coxe, Tench
Managing Director of Sutter Hill Ventures, which finances technology-based start-ups
Sutter Hill Ventures **Ph:** 650-493-5600
755 Page Mill Rd Suite A-200 **Fax:** 650-858-1854
Palo Alto, CA 94304
www.shv.com

Coyle, Pat
Professional women's basketball coach
New York Liberty **Ph:** 212-564-9622
Madison Square Garden **Fax:** 212-465-6250
2 Pennsylvania Plaza
New York, NY 10121
www.wnba.com/liberty

Craig, Greg
Attorney who successfully represented Elian Gonzalez's father in his effort to regain custody of his son; was also part of the team that defended President Clinton against impeachment
Williams & Connolly LLP **Ph:** 202-434-5506
725 12th St NW **Fax:** 202-434-5760
Washington, DC 20005
www.wc.com

Craig, Jenny
Co-Founder of Jenny Craig International (weight loss centers)
Jenny Craig International **Ph:** 760-696-4000
5770 Fleet St
Carlsbad, CA 92008
www.jennycraig.com

Craig, Larry E (1945-)
US Senator from Idaho (Republican)
520 Hart Bldg **Ph:** 202-224-2752
Washington, DC 20510 **Fax:** 202-228-1067
craig.senate.gov

Cramer, Bud (1947-)
US Representative from Alabama (Democrat)
2368 Rayburn Bldg **Ph:** 202-225-4801
Washington, DC 20515 **Fax:** 202-225-4392
cramer.house.gov

Cramer, Charles
Photographer
Ansel Adams Gallery **Ph:** 800-568-7398
Yosemite National Park
Village Mall PO Box 455
Yosemite, CA 95389
www.charlescramer.com

Cramer, James
Host of CNBC's Mad Money
CNBC **Ph:** 201-735-2622
900 Sylvan Ave
Englewood Cliffs, NJ 07632
moneycentral.msn.com/cnbc/tv

Cramer, Richard Ben
Author of biographical books (Joe DiMaggio: The Hero's Life) and books about politics (What It Takes: The Way to the White House)
Simon & Schuster **Ph:** 212-698-7000
1230 Ave of the Americas
New York, NY 10020
www.simonsays.com

Crane, Brian (1949-)
Creator of the comic strip Pickles
Washington Post Writers Group **Ph:** 202-334-6375 **Fax:** 202-334-5669
1150 15th St NW 9th Fl
Washington, DC 20071
www.postwritersgroup.com

Crane, David (1957-)
Movie & TV writer and producer
International Creative Management **Ph:** 310-550-4000
8942 Wilshire Blvd
Beverly Hills, CA 90211

Crapo, Mike (1951-)
US Senator from Idaho (Republican)
239 Dirksen Bldg **Ph:** 202-224-6142
Washington, DC 20510 **Fax:** 202-228-1375
crapo.senate.gov

Cravens, Greg
Illustrates the comic strip The Buckets
United Feature Syndicate **Ph:** 212-293-8500
200 Madison Ave
New York, NY 10016
www.unitedfeatures.com

Crawford, Cindy (1966-)
Fashion model; entrepreneur
Creative Artists Agency **Ph:** 310-288-4545
9830 Wilshire Blvd **Fax:** 310-288-4800
Beverly Hills, CA 90212
www.cindy.com

Crawford, Jamal (1980-)
Professional basketball player
New York Knicks **Ph:** 212-465-6471
Madison Square Garden **Fax:** 212-465-6498
2 Pennsylvania Plaza
New York, NY 10121
www.nba.com/knicks

Crawford, Matt (1980-)
Professional soccer player
Colorado Rapids **Ph:** 303-405-1100
Pepsi Center **Fax:** 720-931-2022
1000 Chopper Cir
Denver, CO 80204
www.coloradorapids.com

Crawford, Michael (1942-)
Singer/actor (theatrical)
William Morris Agency **Ph:** 212-586-5100
1325 Ave of the Americas **Fax:** 212-246-3583
New York, NY 10019
www.mcifa.com

Cray, Robert (1953-)
Blues guitarist/singer
Fitzgerald Hartley Co **Ph:** 805-641-6441
34 N Palm St Suite 100 **Fax:** 805-641-6444
Ventura, CA 93001
www.robertcray.com

Cray, Seymour (1925-1996)
Designer of large-scale computers; developed the first supercomputer
Cray Inc **Ph:** 206-701-2000
411 1st Ave S Suite 600 **Fax:** 206-701-2500
Seattle, WA 98104
www.cray.com/about_cray/seymourcray.html

Craybas, Jill (1974-)
Professional tennis player
WTA Tour **Ph:** 727-895-5000
1 Progress Plaze Suite 1500 **Fax:** 727-894-1982
Saint Petersburg, FL 33701
www.wtatour.com

Creamer, Paula (1986-)
Professional golfer
Ladies Professional Golf Assn **Ph:** 386-274-6200
100 International Golf Dr **Fax:** 386-274-1099
Daytona Beach, FL 32124
www.lpga.com

Creavalle, Laura (1962-)
Professional bodybuilder and trainer
Club Creavalle Fitness **Ph:** 905-619-9480
41 Hester Ave
Ajax, ON L1T3Y6
www.clubcreavalle.com

Creech, Sharon (1945-)
Author of children's books (Walk Two Moons, The Wanderer, Love That Dog)
HarperCollins Children's Books **Ph:** 212-261-6500
1350 Ave of the Americas
New York, NY 10019
www.sharoncreech.com

Creeley, Robert (1926-)
Poet; one of the originators of the Black Mountain school of poetry
New Directions Publishing Corp **Ph:** 212-255-0230 **Fax:** 212-255-0231
80 8th Ave
New York, NY 10011
www.wwnorton.com/nd

Crennel, Romeo (1947-)
Football coach
Cleveland Browns **Ph:** 440-891-5000
76 Lou Groza Blvd **Fax:** 440-891-5009
Berea, OH 44017
www.clevelandbrowns.com

Crenshaw, Ander (1944-)
US Representative from Florida (Republican)
127 Cannon Bldg **Ph:** 202-225-2501
Washington, DC 20515 **Fax:** 202-225-2504
crenshaw.house.gov

Crews, Harry (1935-)
Writer
Simon & Schuster **Ph:** 212-698-7000
1230 Ave of the Americas
New York, NY 10020
www.harrycrews.com

Crichton, Michael, MD (1942-)
Author of techno-thrillers; filmmaker; creator of the TV series ER
HarperCollins Publishers **Ph:** 212-207-7000
c/o Author Mail
10 E 53rd St
New York, NY 10022
www.michaelcrichton.net

Crier, Catherine (1954-)
Journalist, attorney, and author of The Case Against Lawyers; hosts Catherine Crier Live on Court TV
Courtroom Television Network **Ph:** 212-973-2800
600 3rd Ave
New York, NY 10016
www.criercommunications.com

Criqui, Don
Sports broadcaster
CBS Sports **Ph:** 212-975-4321
51 W 52nd St
New York, NY 10019
cbs.sportsline.com/cbssports/team

Cromwell, James (1940-)
Actor
SDB Partners Inc **Ph:** 310-785-0060
1801 Ave of the Stars Suite 902 **Fax:** 310-785-0071
Los Angeles, CA 90067
www.hbo.com/sixfeetunder

Cronin, John (1950-)
Environmentalist & writer; director of the Pace Academy for the Environment
Pace Academy for the Environment **Ph:** 914-773-3738 **Fax:** 914-773-3265
861 Bedford Rd
Choate 221N
Pleasantville, NY 10570
www.pace.edu

Cronkite, Walter (1916-)
Former CBS newsman; writes a syndicated opinion column
King Features Syndicate Inc **Ph:** 212-455-4000
888 7th Ave 2nd Fl
New York, NY 10019
www.kingfeatures.com

Croom, Sylvester (1954-)
College football coach
Mississippi State University Athletic Dept **Ph:** 662-325-2323 **Fax:** 662-325-7360
PO Box 5327
Missisissippi State Univ, MS 39762
www.mstateathletics.com

Crosby, Norm (1927-)
Comedian; actor
William Morris Agency **Ph:** 310-859-4000
1 William Morris Pl **Fax:** 310-859-4462
Beverly Hills, CA 90212

Crosby, Sidney (1987-)
Professional hockey player
Pittsburgh Penguins **Ph:** 412-642-1300
1 Chatham Center Suite 400 **Fax:** 412-642-1859
Pittsburgh, PA 15219
www.pittsburghpenguins.com

Croshere, Austin (1975-)
Professional basketball player
Indiana Pacers — **Ph:** 317-917-2500
Conseco Fieldhouse — **Fax:** 317-917-2599
125 S Pennsylvania St
Indianapolis, IN 46204
www.nba.com/pacers

Cross, Marcia (1962-)
Actor
Framework Entertainment — **Ph:** 310-858-0333
9057 Nemo St Suite C — **Fax:** 310-858-1357
West Hollywood, CA 90069
abc.go.com/primetime/desperate

Cross, Randy (1954-)
NFL game analyst; former professional football player
CBS Sports — **Ph:** 212-975-4321
51 W 52nd St
New York, NY 10019
cbs.sportsline.com/cbssports/team

Crouch, Andrae (1942-)
Gospel music performer; pastor of the New Christ Memorial Church of God in Christ
New Christ Memorial Church of God in Christ — **Ph:** 818-361-1087
13333 Vaughn St
PO Box 1248
San Fernando, CA 91341
www.newcmc.org

Crow, Sheryl (1962-)
Pop/rock singer
William Morris Agency — **Ph:** 310-859-4000
1 William Morris Pl — **Fax:** 310-859-4462
Beverly Hills, CA 90212
www.sherylcrow.com

Crowe, Cameron (1957-)
Screenwriter/producer/director
Creative Artists Agency — **Ph:** 310-288-4545
9830 Wilshire Blvd — **Fax:** 310-288-4800
Beverly Hills, CA 90212

Crowe, James
CEO of Level 3 Communications Inc
Level 3 Communications Inc — **Ph:** 720-888-1000
1025 Eldorado Blvd
Broomfield, CO 80021
www.level3.com

Crowe, Russell (1964-)
Actor
PMK/HBH — **Ph:** 310-289-6200
700 San Vicente Blvd Suite G910 — **Fax:** 310-289-6677
West Hollywood, CA 90069

Crowell, Andrew E
Managing Partner & CEO of Crowell, Weedon & Co, a stock brokerage and money management firm
Crowell Weedon & Co — **Ph:** 213-620-1850
624 S Grand Ave
1 Wilshire Bldg Suite 2600
Los Angeles, CA 90017
www.crowellweedon.com

Crowley, Candy
CNN senior political correspondent
CNN — **Ph:** 202-898-7900
CNN Bldg
820 1st St NE
Washington, DC 20002
www.cnn.com/CNN/anchors_reporters

Crowley, Joseph (1962-)
US Representative from New York (Democrat)
312 Cannon Bldg — **Ph:** 202-225-3965
Washington, DC 20515 — **Fax:** 202-225-1909
crowley.house.gov

Crowley, Monica
Co-host of MSNBC's Connected: Coast to Coast
MSNBC TV — **Ph:** 201-583-5000
1 MSNBC Plaza
Secaucus, NJ 07094
www.msnbc.msn.com/id/3080263

Crudup, Billy (1968-)
Actor
Creative Artists Agency — **Ph:** 310-288-4545
9830 Wilshire Blvd — **Fax:** 310-288-4800
Beverly Hills, CA 90212

Cruise, Jorge
Diet and fitness expert
Jorge Cruise Co — **Ph:** 619-523-3035
PO Box 6220 — **Fax:** 619-374-2004
San Diego, CA 92166
www.jorgecruise.com

Cruise, Sister Tricia
President of Covenant House, an organization that provides shelter and services to homeless and runaway youth
Covenant House — **Ph:** 212-727-4000
346 W 17th St
New York, NY 10011
www.covenanthouse.org

Cruise, Tom (1962-)
Actor
Creative Artists Agency — **Ph:** 310-288-4545
9830 Wilshire Blvd — **Fax:** 310-288-4800
Beverly Hills, CA 90212

Crum, Thomas
Motivational speaker on the Magic of Conflict approach; conducts workshops worldwide for management and employees at all levels in corporations, government, and non-profit organizations
Aiki Works Inc **Ph:** 970-925-7099
PO Box 7845 **Fax:** 970-925-4532
Aspen, CO 81612
www.aikiworks.com

Crumb, Robert (1943-)
Comic book artist; his work includes Fritz the Cat
Fantagraphics Books **Ph:** 206-524-1967
7563 Lake City Way NE **Fax:** 206-524-2104
Seattle, WA 98115
www.fantagraphics.com

Crumpler, Alge (1977-)
Professional football player
Atlanta Falcons **Ph:** 770-965-3115
4400 Falcon Pkwy **Fax:** 770-965-3185
Flowery Branch, GA 30542
www.atlantafalcons.com

Cruz, Humberto
Personal finance columnist (The Savings Game); also, with his wife Georgina, writes the syndicated column Retire Smart
Tribune Media Services Inc **Ph:** 312-222-4444
435 N Michigan Ave Suite 1500
Chicago, IL 60611
tmsfeatures.com/productlist.htm

Cruz, Jose Jr (1974-)
Professional baseball player
Los Angeles Dodgers **Ph:** 323-224-1500
Dodger Stadium **Fax:** 323-224-1269
1000 Elysian Park Ave
Los Angeles, CA 90012
losangeles.dodgers.mlb.com

Cruz, Penelope (1974-)
Actor
Dart Group **Ph:** 212-277-7555
90 Park Ave 19th Fl **Fax:** 212-277-7550
New York, NY 10016

Cryer, Jon (1965-)
Actor
Paradigm **Ph:** 310-288-8000
360 N Crescent Dr **Fax:** 310-288-2000
North Bldg
Beverly Hills, CA 90210
www.cbs.com/primetime/two_and_a_half_men

Crystal, Billy (1947-)
Comedian, actor, writer/director/producer
International Creative Management **Ph:** 310-550-4000
8942 Wilshire Blvd
Beverly Hills, CA 90211

Csupo, Gabor (1952-)
Animator; co-creator & executive producer of Rugrats and other animated TV shows
Klasky Csupo Inc **Ph:** 323-463-0145
6353 Sunset Blvd **Fax:** 323-463-2569
Hollywood, CA 90028
www.klaskycsupo.com

Cuban, Mark (1958-)
Owner of the Dallas Mavericks basketball team; co-founded Broadcast.com, which he sold to Yahoo!
Dallas Mavericks **Ph:** 214-747-6287
The Pavilion **Fax:** 214-752-3860
2909 Taylor St
Dallas, TX 75226
www.nba.com/mavericks

Cubin, Barbara (1946-)
US Representative from Wyoming (Republican)
1114 Longworth Bldg **Ph:** 202-225-2311
Washington, DC 20515 **Fax:** 202-225-3057
www.house.gov/cubin

Cuellar, Henry (1955-)
US Representative from Texas (Democrat)
1404 Longworth Bldg **Ph:** 202-225-1640
Washington, DC 20515 **Fax:** 202-225-1641
www.house.gov/cuellar

Culberson, John (1956-)
US Representative from Texas (Republican)
1728 Longworth Bldg **Ph:** 202-225-2571
Washington, DC 20515 **Fax:** 202-225-4381
www.culberson.house.gov

Culkin, Macaulay (1980-)
Actor
Endeavor **Ph:** 310-248-2000
9601 Wilshire Blvd 3rd Fl **Fax:** 310-248-2020
Beverly Hills, CA 90210

Culp, H Lawrence
President and CEO of Danaher Corp
Danaher Corp **Ph:** 202-828-0850
2099 Pennsylvania Ave NW 12th Fl
Washington, DC 20006
www.danaher.com/about/officers.htm

Culpepper, Daunte (1977-)
Professional football player
Miami Dolphins **Ph:** 954-452-7000
7500 SW 30th St **Fax:** 954-452-7055
Davie, FL 33314
www.miamidolphins.com

Culvahouse, Arthur B Jr (1948-)
White House Counsel to President Ronald Reagan 1987-1989; now chairman of O'Melveny & Myers, an international law firm
O'Melveny & Myers LLP **Ph:** 202-383-5388
1625 'I' St NW **Fax:** 202-383-5414
Washington, DC 20006
www.omm.com

Cumming, Alan (1965-)
Actor
Creative Artists Agency **Ph:** 310-288-4545
9830 Wilshire Blvd **Fax:** 310-288-4800
Beverly Hills, CA 90212
www.alancumming.com

Cummings, EE (1894-1962)
Poet (EE stands for Edward Estlin)
WW Norton & Co Inc **Ph:** 212-354-5500
500 5th Ave **Fax:** 212-869-0856
New York, NY 10110
www.nortonpoets.com

Cummings, Elijah (1951-)
US Representative from Maryland (Democrat)
2350 Rayburn Bldg **Ph:** 202-225-4741
Washington, DC 20515 **Fax:** 202-225-3178
www.house.gov/cummings

Cummins, Jim
Correspondent and chief of NBC News Southwest Bureau
NBC News **Ph:** 212-664-4249
30 Rockefeller Plaza
New York, NY 10112
www.msnbc.msn.com/id/3689499

Cummuta, John
Motivational speaker; teaches working people that the way to financial independence is not through trying to manage their debt, but through eliminating it completely
Debt-FREE & Prosperous Living Inc **Ph:** 608-875-5908
310 2nd St
Boscobel, WI 53805
www.johncummuta.com

Cundiff, Billy (1980-)
Professional football player
Green Bay Packers **Ph:** 920-569-7500
PO Box 10628 **Fax:** 920-569-7201
Green Bay, WI 54307
www.packers.com

Cunningham, Imogen (1883-1976)
Photographer
Howard Greenberg Gallery **Ph:** 212-334-0010
41 E 57th St Suite 1406 **Fax:** 212-941-7479
New York, NY 10022
www.imogencunningham.com

Cunningham, Jeff (1976-)
Professional soccer player
Real Salt Lake **Ph:** 801-924-8585
515 S 700 East Suite 2R **Fax:** 801-933-4713
Salt Lake City, UT 84102
www.mlsnet.com/MLS/rsl/

Cunningham, Merce
Dancer/choreographer; founder and artistic director of Merce Cunningham Dance Co
Merce Cunningham Dance Co **Ph:** 212-255-8240
55 Bethune St **Fax:** 212-633-2453
New York, NY 10014
www.merce.org

Cunningham, Michael (1952-)
Author of The Hours
Steven Barclay Agency **Ph:** 707-773-0654
12 Western Ave **Fax:** 707-778-1868
Petaluma, CA 94952 **TF:** 888-965-7323
www.barclayagency.com

Cuomo, Christopher (1970-)
Senior legal correspondent for ABC News; also co-anchors Primetime
ABC News **Ph:** 212-456-7777
147 Columbus Ave
New York, NY 10023
www.abcnews.go.com/WNT

Cuomo, Mario (1932-)
Former governor of New York; Of Counsel to Willkie Farr & Gallagher
Willkie Farr & Gallagher LLP **Ph:** 212-728-8260
787 7th Ave **Fax:** 212-728-9260
New York, NY 10019
www.willkie.com/MarioCuomo

Curfman, Greg
Creator of the syndicated comic strip Meg!
United Media **Ph:** 212-293-8500
200 Madison Ave
New York, NY 10016
www.comics.com

Curl, Robert F, PhD (1933-)
1996 Nobel Laureate in Chemistry; he won the prize, which he shared with two other scientists, for their discovery of fullerenes
Rice University **Ph:** 713-348-4082
Space Science Bldg **Fax:** 713-348-5155
6100 Main St Rm 211
Houston, TX 77005
www.chem.rice.edu

Curry, Ann (1956-)
Co-anchor of Dateline NBC and news anchor for the Today Show
Dateline NBC **Ph:** 212-664-4249
30 Rockefeller Plaza
New York, NY 10112
www.msnbc.msn.com/id/3360263

Curry, Eddy (1982-)
Professional basketball player
New York Knicks **Ph:** 212-465-6471
Madison Square Garden **Fax:** 212-465-6498
2 Pennsylvania Plaza
New York, NY 10121
www.nba.com/knicks

Curry, Susie (1972-)
Champion bodybuilder
JMP Management **Ph:** 412-257-4555
PO Box 293 **Fax:** 412-257-1337
Presto, PA 15142
www.jmpmanagement.com/csc

Curry, Tim (1946-)
Actor
Innovative Artists **Ph:** 310-656-0400
1505 10th St **Fax:** 310-656-0456
Santa Monica, CA 90401

Curtin, Jim (1979-)
Professional soccer player
Chicago Fire **Ph:** 312-705-7200
980 N Michigan Ave Suite 1998 **Fax:** 312-705-7393
Chicago, IL 60611
chicago.fire.mlsnet.com

Curtis, Christopher Paul
Author of books for young readers (Bud, Not Buddy)
Random House Children's Books **Ph:** 212-782-9000
Publicity Dept
1745 Broadway
New York, NY 10019
www.randomhouse.com/kids

Curtis, Edward S (1868-1952)
Photographer & ethnologist; known for his work with American Indians
Edward S Curtis Gallery **Ph:** 530-964-2966
PO Box 759 **Fax:** 530-964-2606
McCloud, CA 96057
www.edwardscurtis.com

Curtis, Jamie Lee (1958-)
Actor; also author of books for children
Creative Artists Agency **Ph:** 310-288-4545
9830 Wilshire Blvd **Fax:** 310-288-4800
Beverly Hills, CA 90212

Curtis, Stacy
Free-lance editorial cartoonist
Artizans **Ph:** 877-700-8666
11149 6th St NW **Fax:** 877-642-8666
Edmonton, AB T5W4K2
www.stacycurtis.com

Curwood, Steve
Host and executive producer of NPR's Living On Earth
National Public Radio **Ph:** 202-513-2000
635 Massachusetts Ave NW **Fax:** 202-513-3329
Washington, DC 20001
www.npr.org

Cusack, Joan (1962-)
Actor
United Talent Agency **Ph:** 310-273-6700
9560 Wilshire Blvd 5th Fl **Fax:** 310-247-1111
Beverly Hills, CA 90212

Cusack, John (1966-)
Actor
William Morris Agency **Ph:** 310-859-4000
1 William Morris Pl **Fax:** 310-859-4462
Beverly Hills, CA 90212

Cushman, Karen (1941-)
Author of books for young adults (The Midwife's Apprentice; Catherine, Called Birdy)
Houghton Mifflin Children's Books **Ph:** 617-351-5000
222 Berkeley St 8th Fl
Boston, MA 02116
www.houghtonmifflinbooks.com

Cussler, Clive (1931-)
Adventure author (Raise the Titanic!; Dirk Pitt novels)
Simon & Schuster **Ph:** 212-698-7000
1230 Ave of the Americas
New York, NY 10020
www.numa.net

Cuthbert, Elisha (1982-)
Actor
Gersh Agency **Ph:** 310-274-6611
232 N Canon Dr
Beverly Hills, CA 90210

Cyrus, Billy Ray (1961-)
Country/gospel singer; actor (stars in Doc on PAX TV)
William Morris Agency **Ph:** 615-963-3000
1600 Division St Suite 300 **Fax:** 615-963-3090
Nashville, TN 37203
www.billyraycyrus.com

D'Adamo, Peter J, MD
Naturopathic doctor and author of diet books based on blood type (Eat Right 4 Your Type)
Putnam Publicity **Ph:** 212-366-2000
375 Hudson St
New York, NY 10014
www.dadamo.com

Daelemans, Kathleen
Chef & cookbook author (Cooking Thin)
Houghton Mifflin Co **Ph:** 617-351-5000
Trade Div
Adult Editorial
222 Berkeley St 8th Fl
Boston, MA 02116
www.kathleendaelemans.com

Dafoe, Willem (1955-)
Actor
Endeavor **Ph:** 310-248-2000
9601 Wilshire Blvd 3rd Fl **Fax:** 310-248-2020
Beverly Hills, CA 90210

Dahl, Roald (1916-1990)
Children's book author
Random House Children's Books **Ph:** 212-782-9000
Publicity Dept
1745 Broadway
New York, NY 10019
www.roalddahl.com

Dahlberg, Ken (1944-)
Chairman, president, and CEO of Science Applications International Corp
Science Applications International Corp **Ph:** 858-826-6658 **Fax:** 858-826-6634
10260 Campus Point Dr L-1
San Diego, CA 92121
www.saic.com

Dahler, Don
ABC News correspondent
ABC News **Ph:** 212-456-7777
77 W 66th St
New York, NY 10023
www.abcnews.go.com/Nightline

Dailey, Janet
Romance novelist
Kensington Publishing Corp **Ph:** 212-407-1500
850 3rd Ave
New York, NY 10022
www.janetdailey.com

Dailey, Jim (1942-)
Mayor of Little Rock, Arkansas
500 W Markham Suite 203 **Ph:** 501-371-4791
Little Rock, AR 72201 **Fax:** 501-371-4498
www.littlerock.org/MayorsOffice

Dalai Lama (1935-)
Exiled leader of Tibet
Wisdom Publications Inc **Ph:** 617-776-7416
199 Elm St **Fax:** 617-776-7841
Somerville, MA 02144
www.tibet.com/DL

Dale, Steve
Writes the syndicated column My Pet World
Tribune Media Services Inc **Ph:** 312-222-4444
435 N Michigan Ave Suite 1500
Chicago, IL 60611
tmsfeatures.com/productlist.htm

D'Alessandro, David F
President and CEO of Manulife Financial
Manulife Financial Corp **Ph:** 416-926-3000
200 Bloor St E **Fax:** 416-926-3503
Toronto, ON 02117
www.manulife.com

Daley, Richard M (1942-)
Mayor of Chicago
121 N La Salle St Rm 507 **Ph:** 312-744-3300
Chicago, IL 60602 **Fax:** 312-744-2324
www.cityofchicago.org

Dali, Salvador (1904-1989)
Surrealist painter
Salvador Dali Museum **Ph:** 727-823-3767
1000 3rd St S **Fax:** 727-894-6068
Saint Petersburg, FL 33701 **TF:** 800-442-3254
www.salvadordalimuseum.org

Daly, Carson (1973-)
Host of Last Call with Carson Daly, a late night talk show on NBC, and of the nationally syndicated radio program Carson Daly Most Requested; was formerly an MTV veejay and host of Total Request Live
NBC Television Network **Ph:** 212-664-4444
Last Call with Carson Daly
30 Rockefeller Plaza
New York, NY 10112
www.nbc.com/Last_Call_with_Carson_Daly

Daly, John (1966-)
Professional golfer
SFX Sports Group **Ph:** 202-686-2000
5335 Wisconsin Ave NW
Suite 850
Washington, DC 20015
www.johndaly.com

Daly, Tyne (1946-)
Actor
Hartig Hilepo Agency Ltd **Ph:** 212-929-1772
54 W 51st St Suite 610 **Fax:** 212-929-1266
New York, NY 10010

D'Amato, Alfonse (1937-)
Former US Senator; political analyst for FOX News
FOX News Channel **Ph:** 212-301-3000
1211 Ave of the Americas
New York, NY 10036
www.foxnews.com/fnctv

Damon, Johnny (1973-)
Professional baseball player
New York Yankees **Ph:** 718-293-4300
Yankee Stadium **Fax:** 718-293-8414
161st St & River Ave
Bronx, NY 10451
newyork.yankees.mlb.com

Damon, Matt (1970-)
Actor; screenwriter (Good Will Hunting)
PMK/HBH **Ph:** 310-289-6200
700 San Vicente Blvd **Fax:** 310-289-6677
Suite G910
West Hollywood, CA 90069

Dan, Michael
Chairman, president, and CEO of Brink's Co
Brink's Co **Ph:** 804-289-9600
1801 Bayberry Ct
PO Box 18100
Richmond, VA 23226
www.brinkscompany.com

Danes, Claire (1979-)
Actor
International Creative Management **Ph:** 310-550-4000
8942 Wilshire Blvd
Beverly Hills, CA 90211

Daniel, Beth (1956-)
Professional golfer
Ladies Professional Golf Assn **Ph:** 386-274-6200
100 International Golf Dr **Fax:** 386-274-1099
Daytona Beach, FL 32124
www.lpga.com

Daniels, Antonio (1975-)
Professional basketball player
Washington Wizards **Ph:** 202-661-5000
Verizon Center **Fax:** 202-661-5094
601 F St NW
Washington, DC 20004
www.nba.com/wizards

Daniels, Charlie (1936-)
Singer, musician, and leader of the Charlie Daniels Band
William Morris Agency **Ph:** 615-963-3000
1600 Division St Suite 300 **Fax:** 615-963-3090
Nashville, TN 37203
www.charliedaniels.com

Daniels, Jeff (1955-)
Actor
International Creative Management **Ph:** 310-550-4000
8942 Wilshire Blvd
Beverly Hills, CA 90211

Daniels, Mitch (1949-)
Governor of Indiana (Republican)
State House **Ph:** 317-232-4567
200 W Washington St Rm 206 **Fax:** 317-232-3443
Indianapolis, IN 46204
www.state.in.us/gov

Danko, William, PhD
Business author (wrote The Millionaire Next Door with Thomas J. Stanley)
Simon & Schuster **Ph:** 212-698-7000
1230 Ave of the Americas
New York, NY 10020
www.albany.edu/~danko

Danner, Blythe (1943-)
Actor
Creative Artists Agency **Ph:** 310-288-4545
9830 Wilshire Blvd **Fax:** 310-288-4800
Beverly Hills, CA 90212

Dannhauser, Stephen J (1950-)
A leading attorney in mergers & acquisitions
Weil Gotshal & Manges LLP **Ph:** 212-310-8326
767 5th Ave **Fax:** 212-310-8007
New York, NY 10153
www.weil.com

Danson, Ted (1947-)
Actor
Creative Artists Agency **Ph:** 310-288-4545
9830 Wilshire Blvd **Fax:** 310-288-4800
Beverly Hills, CA 90212

Danticat, Edwidge (1969-)
Author (Breath, Eyes, Memory; Krik? Krak!; The Dew Breaker)
Knopf Publishing/Author Mail **Ph:** 212-782-9000
1745 Broadway
New York, NY 10019
www.randomhouse.com/knopf

Danto, Arthur C (1924-)
Art critic for The Nation magazine
The Nation **Ph:** 212-209-5400
33 Irving Pl 8th Fl **Fax:** 212-982-9000
New York, NY 10003
www.thenation.com

D'Antoni, Mike (1958-)
Basketball coach
Phoenix Suns **Ph:** 602-379-7900
America West Arena **Fax:** 602-379-7990
201 E Jefferson St
Phoenix, AZ 85004
www.nba.com/suns

Danza, Tony (1951-)
Actor
William Morris Agency **Ph:** 310-859-4000
1 William Morris Pl **Fax:** 310-859-4462
Beverly Hills, CA 90212
www.tonydanza.com

Danziger, Paula (1944-2004)
Author of The Cat Ate My Gymsuit
GP Putnam's Sons Books for Young Readers **Ph:** 212-366-2000
Publicity Dept
345 Hudson St
New York, NY 10014
us.penguingroup.com

Darabont, Frank (1959-)
Writer/director/producer
Creative Artists Agency **Ph:** 310-288-4545
9830 Wilshire Blvd **Fax:** 310-288-4800
Beverly Hills, CA 90212

Darbee, Peter (1953-)
Chairman, president, and CEO of PG & E Corp
PG & E Corp **Ph:** 415-267-7000
1 Market Plaza **Fax:** 415-267-7265
Spear Tower Suite 2400
San Francisco, CA 94105
www.pgecorp.com

Darden, Christopher (1956-)
Attorney; OJ Simpson prosecutor
Law Offices of Christopher Darden & Assoc Inc **Ph:** 310-568-1804 **Fax:** 310-568-1806
5757 W Century Blvd Suite 700
Los Angeles, CA 90045
www.wma.com/christopher_darden/summary

Darling, James (1974-)
Professional football player
Arizona Cardinals **Ph:** 602-379-0101
8701 S Hardy Dr **Fax:** 602-379-1819
Tempe, AZ 85284
www.azcardinals.com

Daschle, Tom (1947-)
Former Senate Majority Leader (Democratic); now serves as a Senior Policy Advisor for the Washington law firm Alston and Bird
Alston & Bird LLP **Ph:** 202-756-3156
601 Pennsylvania Ave NW **Fax:** 202-756-3333
North Bldg 10th Fl
Washington, DC 20004
www.alston.com

Dass, Ram (1931-)
Teaches and writes about the nature of consciousness, and about service as a spiritual path (born Richard Alpert)
Ram Dass Tape Library Foundation **Ph:** 415-499-8586
524 San Anselmo Ave Suite 203
San Anselmo, CA 94960
www.ramdasstapes.org

Datsyuk, Pavel (1978-)
Professional hockey player
Detroit Red Wings **Ph:** 313-396-7544
Joe Louis Arena **Fax:** 313-567-0296
600 Civic Center Dr
Detroit, MI 48226
www.detroitredwings.com

Dauten, Dale
Writes The Corporate Curmudgeon, a syndicated column on job-related issues; also co-writes Kate & Dale Talk Jobs, with Kate Wendleton
King Features Syndicate Inc **Ph:** 212-455-4000
888 7th Ave 2nd Fl
New York, NY 10019
www.dauten.com

Davenport, Lindsay (1976-)
Professional tennis player
WTA Tour **Ph:** 727-895-5000
1 Progress Plaza Suite 1500 **Fax:** 727-894-1982
Saint Petersburg, FL 33701
www.wtatour.com

Davenport, Lynn P
President & CEO of MAXIMUS Inc, which provides government program operations and management services, consulting, and systems technology
MAXIMUS Inc **Ph:** 703-251-8500
11419 Sunset Hills Rd
Reston, VA 20190
www.maximus.com

David, George A
Chairman and CEO of United Technologies Corp
United Technologies Corp **Ph:** 860-728-7085
1 Financial Plaza **Fax:** 860-493-4165
Hartford, CT 06101
www.utc.com

David, Larry (1947-)
Comedy writer (Curb Your Enthusiasm; Seinfeld; Saturday Night Live); actor
Endeavor **Ph:** 310-248-2000
9601 Wilshire Blvd 3rd Fl **Fax:** 310-248-2020
Beverly Hills, CA 90210
www.hbo.com/larrydavid

David, Ted
Senior anchor on CNBC Business Radio; also continues to anchor on CNBC TV on a fill-in basis
CNBC **Ph:** 201-735-2622
900 Sylvan Ave
Englewood Cliffs, NJ 07632
moneycentral.msn.com/cnbc/tv

Davidson, Bruce (1933-)
Photographer
Magnum Photos **Ph:** 212-929-6000
151 W 25th St **Fax:** 212-929-9325
New York, NY 10001
www.magnumphotos.com

Davidson, Gordon K (1948-)
Attorney and chairman of Fenwick & West; advises technology companies (clients have included Cisco, Intuit, and Symantec)
Fenwick & West LLP **Ph:** 650-335-7237
Silicon Valley Center **Fax:** 650-938-5200
801 California St
Mountain View, CA 94041
www.fenwick.com

Davidson, John (1953-)
Former NHL goaltender; now an NHL television commentator
Outdoor Life Network **Ph:** 203-406-2500
2 Stamford Plaza **Fax:** 203-406-2534
281 Tresser Blvd
Stamford, CT 06901

Davidson, Richard K
Chairman of Union Pacific Corp
Union Pacific Corp **Ph:** 402-544-5000
1416 Dodge St
Omaha, NE 68179
www.up.com/investors

Davidson, William M (1922-)
President & CEO of Guardian Industries; also managing partner of the Detroit Pistons basketball team
Guardian Industries Corp **Ph:** 248-340-1800
2300 Harmon Rd **Fax:** 248-340-9988
Auburn Hills, MI 48326
www.wdi.bus.umich.edu

Davies, Matt
Editorial cartoonist for The Journal News (Westchester, NY)
Tribune Media Services Inc **Ph:** 312-222-4444
435 N Michigan Ave Suite 1500
Chicago, IL 60611
www.comicspage.com

Davies, Rob
Animator; co-founder & director of Atomic Cartoons Inc (creator of Atomic Betty)
Atomic Cartoons Inc **Ph:** 604-734-2866
1125 Howe St Suite 250 **Fax:** 604-734-2869
Vancouver, BC V6Z2K8
www.atomiccartoons.com

Davis, Al (1930-)
Owner of the Oakland Raiders football team
Oakland Raiders **Ph:** 510-864-5000
1220 Harbor Bay Pkwy **Fax:** 510-864-5160
Alameda, CA 94502
www.raiders.com

Davis, Artur (1967-)
US Representative from Alabama (Democrat)
208 Cannon Bldg **Ph:** 202-225-2665
Washington, DC 20515 **Fax:** 202-226-9567
www.house.gov/arturdavis

Davis, Baron (1979-)
Professional basketball player
Golden State Warriors **Ph:** 510-986-2200
1011 Broadway **Fax:** 510-452-0132
Oakland, CA 94607
www.nba.com/warriors

Davis, Chip (1947-)
Composer/musician; creator and leading member of the recording group Mannheim Steamroller
American Gramaphone LLC **Ph:** 402-457-4341
9130 Mormon Bridge Rd **Fax:** 402-457-4332
Omaha, NE 68152
www.mannheimsteamroller.com

Davis, Claude E
President & CEO of First Financial Bancorp
First Financial Bancorp **Ph:** 513-867-4700
300 High St
Hamilton, OH 45011
www.ffbc-oh.com

Davis, Clive (1934-)
Chairman and CEO of J Records; a long-time record executive known as a major hitmaker
J Records **Ph:** 646-840-5600
745 5th Ave 6th Fl
New York, NY 10151
www.jrecords.com

Davis, Danny (1941-)
US Representative from Illinois (Democrat)
1526 Longworth Bldg **Ph:** 202-225-5006
Washington, DC 20515 **Fax:** 202-225-5641
www.house.gov/davis

Davis, Domanick (1980-)
Professional football player
Houston Texans **Ph:** 832-667-2000
2 Reliant Park **Fax:** 832-667-2100
Houston, TX 77054
www.houstontexans.com

Davis, Doug (1975-)
Professional baseball player
Milwaukee Brewers **Ph:** 414-902-4400
Miller Park **Fax:** 414-902-4515
1 Brewers Way
Milwaukee, WI 53214
milwaukee.brewers.mlb.com

Davis, Erroll B Jr (1945-)
Chairman of Alliant Energy Corp
Alliant Energy Corp **Ph:** 608-458-3137
4902 N Biltmore Ln **Fax:** 608-458-3397
Madison, WI 53718
www.alliantenergy.com

Davis, Geena (1956-)
Actor
Creative Artists Agency **Ph:** 310-288-4545
9830 Wilshire Blvd **Fax:** 310-288-4800
Beverly Hills, CA 90212
abc.go.com/primetime/commanderinchief

Davis, Geoff (1958-)
US Representative from Kentucky (Republican)
1541 Longworth Bldg **Ph:** 202-225-3465
Washington, DC 20515 **Fax:** 202-225-0003
geoffdavis.house.gov

Davis, Jim (1957-)
US Representative from Florida (Democrat)
409 Cannon Bldg **Ph:** 202-225-3376
Washington, DC 20515 **Fax:** 202-225-5652
www.house.gov/jimdavis

Davis, Jim (1945-)
Garfield creator
Universal Press Syndicate **Ph:** 816-932-6600
4520 Main St
Kansas City, MO 64111
www.amuniversal.com/ups/features

Davis, Jo Ann (1950-)
US Representative from Virginia (Republican)
1123 Longworth Bldg **Ph:** 202-225-4261
Washington, DC 20515 **Fax:** 202-225-4382
joanndavis.house.gov

Davis, Kenneth C (1954-)
Author of the Don't Know Much About... book series
HarperCollins Children's Books **Ph:** 212-261-6500
1350 Ave of the Americas
New York, NY 10019
www.dontknowmuch.com

Davis, Kristin (1965-)
Actor
Endeavor **Ph:** 310-248-2000
9601 Wilshire Blvd 3rd Fl **Fax:** 310-248-2020
Beverly Hills, CA 90210
www.hbo.com/city

Davis, Lincoln (1940-)
US Representative from Tennessee (Democrat)
410 Cannon Bldg **Ph:** 202-225-6831
Washington, DC 20515 **Fax:** 202-226-5172
www.house.gov/lincolndavis

Davis, Lynn (1944-)
Photographer
Edwynn Houk Gallery **Ph:** 212-750-7070
745 5th Ave **Fax:** 212-688-4848
New York, NY 10151
www.houkgallery.com

Davis, Mark
Talk radio show host; is also an op-ed columnist for the Dallas Morning News
WBAP **Ph:** 817-695-0800
2221 E Lamar Blvd Suite 300
Arlington, TX 76006
www.wbap.com

Davis, Paige (1969-)
Host of Trading Spaces on The Learning Channel
The Learning Channel **Ph:** 240-662-2000
Trading Spaces
8516 Georgia Ave
Silver Spring, MD 20910
tlc.discovery.com

Davis, Raymond Jr, PhD (1914-)
2002 Nobel Prize winner in Physics for pioneering contributions to astrophysics
Brookhaven National Laboratory **Ph:** 631-344-8000
PO Box 5000
Upton, NY 11973
www.bnl.gov/bnlweb/raydavis

Davis, Ricky (1979-)
Professional basketball player
Minnesota Timberwolves **Ph:** 612-673-1600
Target Center **Fax:** 612-673-1699
600 1st Ave N
Minneapolis, MN 55403
www.nba.com/timberwolves

Davis, Susan A (1944-)
US Representative from California (Democrat)
1224 Longworth Bldg **Ph:** 202-225-2040
Washington, DC 20515 **Fax:** 202-225-2948
www.house.gov/susandavis

Davis, Tom (1949-)
US Representative from Virginia (Republican)
2348 Rayburn Bldg **Ph:** 202-225-1492
Washington, DC 20515 **Fax:** 202-225-3071
tomdavis.house.gov

Dawkins, Brian (1973-)
Professional football player
Philadelphia Eagles **Ph:** 215-463-2500
NovaCare Complex **Fax:** 215-339-5464
1 NovaCare Way
Philadelphia, PA 19145
www.philadelphiaeagles.com

Dawson, Pat
NBC news correspondent
NBC News **Ph:** 212-664-4249
30 Rockefeller Plaza
New York, NY 10112
www.msnbc.msn.com/id/3689499

Dawson, Phil (1975-)
Professional football player
Cleveland Browns **Ph:** 440-891-5000
76 Lou Groza Blvd **Fax:** 440-891-5009
Berea, OH 44017
www.clevelandbrowns.com

Day, Bill
Political cartoonist for the Memphis Commercial Appeal
United Feature Syndicate **Ph:** 212-293-8500
200 Madison Ave
New York, NY 10016
www.unitedfeatures.com

Day-Lewis, Daniel (1957-)
Actor
Parseghian/Planco Management **Ph:** 212-777-7786
23 E 22nd St **Fax:** 212-777-8642
New York, NY 10010

Dayne, Ron (1978-)
Professional football player
Denver Broncos **Ph:** 303-649-9000
13655 Broncos Pkwy **Fax:** 303-649-9354
Englewood, CO 80112
www.denverbroncos.com

Dayton, Mark (1947-)
US Senator from Minnesota (Democrat)
346 Russell Bldg **Ph:** 202-224-3244
Washington, DC 20510 **Fax:** 202-228-2186
dayton.senate.gov

Dayton, Sky
Founder of EarthLink and CEO of SK-Earthlink, a joint venture of Earthlink and SK Telecom
Earthlink Inc **Ph:** 404-815-0770
1375 Peachtree St NE
Atlanta, GA 30309
www.earthlink.net/about

De Angelis, Barbara, PhD (1951-)
Self-improvement author/speaker (expert on relationships and personal growth)
12021 Wilshire Blvd Suite 607 **Ph:** 310-535-0988
Los Angeles, CA 90025 **Fax:** 310-996-5587
www.barbaradeangelis.com

de Bont, Jan (1943-)
Cinematographer; also produces & directs
International Creative Management **Ph:** 310-550-4000
8942 Wilshire Blvd
Beverly Hills, CA 90211

de Cavel, Jean-Robert
Chef and owner of Jean-Robert at Pigall's
Jean-Robert at Pigall's **Ph:** 513-721-1345
127 W 4th St **Fax:** 513-352-6010
Cincinnati, OH 45202
www.jean-robertatpigalls.com

De la Hoya, Oscar (1973-)
Boxer (middleweight)
Golden Boy Promotions **Ph:** 213-489-5631
626 Wilshire Blvd Suite 350
Los Angeles, CA 90017
www.goldenboypromotions.com

de Kooning, Willem (1904-1997)
Abstract Expressionist painter
Solomon R Guggenheim Museum **Ph:** 212-423-3500
1071 5th Ave
New York, NY 10128
www.guggenheimcollection.org

De Laurentiis, Giada
A private chef and caterer in Los Angeles and the founder of GDL Foods; host of Everyday Italian on the Food Network
Food Network **Ph:** 212-398-8836
75 9th Ave **Fax:** 212-736-7716
New York, NY 10011
www.foodtv.com

De Matteo, Drea (1973-)
Actor
Dart Group **Ph:** 212-277-7555
90 Park Ave 19th Fl **Fax:** 212-277-7550
New York, NY 10016
www.nbc.com/Joey

De Mornay, Rebecca (1962-)
Actor
William Morris Agency **Ph:** 310-859-4000
1 William Morris Pl **Fax:** 310-859-4462
Beverly Hills, CA 90212

De Palma, Brian (1940-)
Film director, screenwriter
International Creative Management **Ph:** 310-550-4000
8942 Wilshire Blvd
Beverly Hills, CA 90211

De La Renta, Oscar (1932-)
Fashion designer
550 7th Ave **Ph:** 212-282-0500
New York, NY 10018
www.oscardelarenta.com

De Rosario, Dwayne (1978-)
Professional soccer player
Houston Dynamo **Ph:** 713-276-7500
1415 Louisiana St Suite 3400 **Fax:** 713-276-7580
Houston, TX 77002
houston.mlsnet.com

Deal, Nathan (1942-)
US Representative from Georgia (Republican)
2133 Rayburn Bldg **Ph:** 202-225-5211
Washington, DC 20515 **Fax:** 202-225-8272
www.house.gov/deal

Dean, Howard, MD (1948-)
Chairman of the Democratic National Committee; former governor of Vermont and 2004 presidential candidate
Democratic National Committee **Ph:** 202-863-8000
430 S Capitol St SE
Washington, DC 20003
www.democrats.org

Deaton, Chad C
Chairman and CEO of Baker Hughes (an oilfield services company)
Baker Hughes Inc **Ph:** 713-439-8600
3900 Essex Ln Suite 1200
Houston, TX 77027
www.bakerhughes.com/investor

Deaver, Jeffery (1950-)
Mystery/suspense writer; his books include the Lincoln Rhyme series (The Bone Collector)
Simon & Schuster **Ph:** 212-698-7000
1230 Ave of the Americas
New York, NY 10020
www.jefferydeaver.com

DeBakey, Michael E, MD (1908-)
Heart surgeon
Michael E DeBakey Dept of Surgery **Ph:** 713-798-8070
Baylor College of Medicine
1 Baylor Plaza
Houston, TX 77030
www.debakeydepartmentofsurgery.org

Debnam, Betty
Writes the syndicated feature The Mini Page, an educational activity page for children
Universal Press Syndicate **Ph:** 816-932-6600
4520 Main St
Kansas City, MO 64111
www.amuniversal.com/ups/features

Debreu, Gerard (1921-)
Winner of the 1983 Nobel Prize in Economics for having incorporated new analytical methods into economic theory and for his rigorous reformulation of the theory of general equilibrium
University of California at Berkeley **Ph:** 510-642-0822
Dept of Economics
549 Evans Hall Rm 3880
Berkeley, CA 94720
emlab.berkeley.edu/facdir/debreu.html

Decker, Dwight W, PhD
Chairman and CEO of Conexant Systems Inc
Conexant Systems Inc **Ph:** 949-483-4600
4000 MacArthur Blvd
Newport Beach, CA 92660
www.conexant.com

Decker, Susan
CFO and Executive Vice President, Finance & Administration, of Yahoo!
Yahoo! Inc **Ph:** 408-349-3300
701 1st Ave **Fax:** 408-349-3301
Sunnyvale, CA 94089
docs.yahoo.com/info/pr

Deen, Paula
Host of Paula's Home Cooking on the Food Network and owner of Lady & Sons restaurant in Savannah; is also a cookbook author (Southern cooking)
Lady & Sons **Ph:** 912-233-2600
102 W Congress St
Savannah, GA 31401
www.ladyandsons.com

Deering, John (1956-)
Chief editorial cartoonist for the Arkansas Democrat-Gazette; also creates the comic panel Strange Brew
Creators Syndicate Inc **Ph:** 310-337-7003
5777 W Century Blvd Suite 700 **Fax:** 310-337-7625
Los Angeles, CA 90045
www.creators.com

Dees, Morris S (1936-)
Founder (with Joe Levin) of the Southern Poverty Law Center and chief trial counsel for the Center
Southern Poverty Law Center **Ph:** 334-956-8200
400 Washington Ave
Montgomery, AL 36104
www.splcenter.org

Dees, Rick (1950-)
Comedic host of the nationally syndicated Rick Dees Weekly Top 40 radio show
X Radio **Ph:** 212-419-2926
Candler Bldg **Fax:** 212-896-5341
220 W 42nd St
New York, NY 10036
www.rick.com

DeFazio, Peter A (1947-)
US Representative from Oregon (Democrat)
2134 Rayburn Bldg **Ph:** 202-225-6416
Washington, DC 20515 **Fax:** 202-225-0032
www.house.gov/defazio

Deford, Frank (1938-)
Sports commentator
HBO Sports **Ph:** 212-512-1000
1100 Ave of the Americas
New York, NY 10036
www.hbo.com/infl

DeForge, Anna (1976-)
Professional basketball player
Indiana Fever **Ph:** 317-917-2500
Conseco Fieldhouse **Fax:** 317-917-2899
125 S Pennsylvania St
Indianapolis, IN 46204
www.wnba.com/fever

DeGeneres, Ellen (1958-)
Comedian; talk show host; actor
International Creative Management **Ph:** 310-550-4000
8942 Wilshire Blvd
Beverly Hills, CA 90211
ellen.warnerbros.com

DeGette, Diana (1957-)
US Representative from Colorado (Democrat)
1527 Longworth Bldg **Ph:** 202-225-4431
Washington, DC 20515 **Fax:** 202-225-5657
www.house.gov/degette

Deisenhofer, Johann, PhD (1943-)
Winner (with two other scientists) of the 1988 Nobel Prize in Chemistry for determining the three-dimensional structure of a photosynthetic reaction center
Southwestern Medical Center Dallas **Ph:** 214-648-5058
5323 Harry Hines Blvd
Dallas, TX 75390
www.utsouthwestern.edu

Deitz, Susan
Writes a syndicated advice column for singles
Creators Syndicate Inc **Ph:** 310-337-7003
5777 W Century Blvd Suite 700 **Fax:** 310-337-7625
Los Angeles, CA 90045
www.creators.com

Del Grande, Robert
Executive chef of Cafe Annie, one of four restaurants owned by the Schiller Del Grande Restaurant Group
Schiller Del Grande Restaurant Group **Ph:** 713-977-1922 **Fax:** 713-784-5089
5858 Westheimer Rd Suite 110 **TF:** 800-550-1922
Houston, TX 77057
www.schiller-delgrande.com

Del Rio, Jack (1963-)
Football coach
Jacksonville Jaguars **Ph:** 904-633-6000
1 Alltel Stadtium Pl **Fax:** 904-633-6050
Jacksonville, FL 32202
www.jaguars.com

Del Toro, Benicio (1967-)
Actor
Special Artists Agency **Ph:** 310-859-9688
9465 Wilshire Blvd Suite 890
Beverly Hills, CA 90212
www.beniciodeltoro.com

Delahunt, William (1941-)
US Representative from Massachusetts (Democrat)
2454 Rayburn Bldg **Ph:** 202-225-3111
Washington, DC 20515 **Fax:** 202-225-5658
www.house.gov/delahunt

Delainey, Gary
Writes the comic strip Betty; Gerry Rasmussen draws it
United Feature Syndicate **Ph:** 212-293-8500
200 Madison Ave
New York, NY 10016
www.unitedfeatures.com

Delaney, Samuel R (1942-)
Science fiction author (Dhalgren)
Vintage/Anchor Publicity **Ph:** 212-572-2420
1745 Broadway 20th Fl
New York, NY 10019
www.randomhouse.com/vintage

DeLauro, Rosa (1943-)
US Representative from Connecticut (Democrat)
2262 Rayburn Bldg **Ph:** 202-225-3661
Washington, DC 20515 **Fax:** 202-225-4890
www.house.gov/delauro

DeLay, Tom (1947-)
US Representative from Texas (Republican) and former House Majority Leader; has announced his intention to resign from Congress, probably in mid-June 2006
242 Cannon Bldg **Ph:** 202-225-5951
Washington, DC 20515 **Fax:** 202-225-5241
tomdelay.house.gov

Delgado, Carlos (1972-)
Professional baseball player
New York Mets **Ph:** 718-507-6387
Shea Stadium **Fax:** 718-507-6395
123-01 Roosevelt Ave
Flushing, NY 11368
newyork.mets.mlb.com

Delhomme, Jake (1975-)
Professional football player
Carolina Panthers **Ph:** 704-358-7000
Bank of America Stadium **Fax:** 704-358-7618
800 S Mint St
Charlotte, NC 28202
www.panthers.com

DeLillo, Don (1936-)
Novelist (Cosmopolis); has also written plays
Simon & Schuster **Ph:** 212-698-7000
1230 Ave of the Americas
New York, NY 10020
www.simonsays.com

Delk, Tony (1974-)
Professional basketball player
Detroit Pistons **Ph:** 248-377-0100
Palace at Auburn Hills **Fax:** 248-377-4262
4 Championship Dr
Auburn Hills, MI 43216
www.nba.com/pistons

Dell, Michael (1965-)
Dell founder and chairman
Dell Inc **Ph:** 512-338-4400
1 Dell Way
Round Rock, TX 78682
www.dell.com

DeLuise, Peter (1966-)
Actor; director (primarily television)
Agency for the Performing Arts **Ph:** 310-273-0744
9200 Sunset Blvd Suite 900 **Fax:** 310-888-4242
Los Angeles, CA 90069

Demarchelier, Patrick (1943-)
Photographer whose work is seen in print advertising and fashion editorial photography
Tony Shafrazi Gallery **Ph:** 212-274-9300
544 W 26th St **Fax:** 212-334-9499
New York, NY 10001
www.demarchelier.net

DeMille, Nelson (1943-)
Novelist (The General's Daughter)
Warner Books **Ph:** 212-522-7200
c/o Author Mail
1271 Ave of the Americas
New York, NY 10020
www.nelsondemille.net

DeMint, Jim (1951-)
US Senator from South Carolina (Republican)
825 Hart Bldg **Ph:** 202-224-6121
Washington, DC 20510
demint.senate.gov

Demitra, Pavol (1974-)
Professional hockey player
Los Angeles Kings **Ph:** 213-742-7100
Staples Center
1111 S Figueroa St
Los Angeles, CA 90015
www.lakings.com

Demme, Jonathan (1944-)
Film director/producer
International Creative Management **Ph:** 310-550-4000
8942 Wilshire Blvd
Beverly Hills, CA 90211

Dempsey, Clint (1983-)
Professional soccer player
New England Revolution **Ph:** 508-543-5001
Gillette Stadium **Fax:** 508-384-9128
1 Patriot Pl
Foxborough, MA 02035
www.revolutionsoccer.net

Dempsey, Patrick (1966-)
Actor
Creative Artists Agency **Ph:** 310-288-4545
9830 Wilshire Blvd **Fax:** 310-288-4800
Beverly Hills, CA 90212
abc.go.com/primetime/greysanatomy

DeMuth, Christopher
President of the American Enterprise Institute, where he is also a scholar (researches government regulation)
American Enterprise Institute for Public Policy Research **Ph:** 202-862-5800 **Fax:** 202-862-7177
1150 17th St NW Suite 1100
Washington, DC 20036
www.aei.org

Denby, David
Film critic and staff writer at The New Yorker
New Yorker Magazine **Ph:** 212-286-5400
4 Times Sq **Fax:** 212-286-5735
New York, NY 10036

Deng, Luol (1985-)
Professional basketball player
Chicago Bulls **Ph:** 312-455-4000
United Center **Fax:** 312-455-4198
1901 W Madison St
Chicago, IL 60612
www.nba.com/bulls

DeNiro, Robert (1943-)
Actor; producer
Creative Artists Agency **Ph:** 310-288-4545
9830 Wilshire Blvd **Fax:** 310-288-4800
Beverly Hills, CA 90212

Dennis, Carl (1939-)
Poet
Penguin Publicity **Ph:** 212-366-2000
375 Hudson St
New York, NY 10014
us.penguingroup.com

Dent, Charles W (1960-)
US Representative from Pennsylvania (Republican)
502 Cannon Bldg **Ph:** 202-225-6411
Washington, DC 20515 **Fax:** 202-226-0778
dent.house.gov

Dent, Harry S Jr (1930-)
Economic forecaster & public speaker
HS Dent Foundation **Ph:** 888-307-3368
309 S Jupiter Rd Suite 200 **Fax:** 214-644-2004
Allen, TX 75002
www.hsdent.com

Dent, Taylor (1981-)
Professional tennis player
ATP **Ph:** 904-285-8000
201 ATP Blvd **Fax:** 904-285-5966
Ponte Vedra Beach, FL 32082
www.taylordent.com

Denton, Eric (1978-)
Professional soccer player
Colorado Rapids **Ph:** 303-405-1100
Pepsi Center **Fax:** 720-931-2022
1000 Chopper Cir
Denver, CO 80204
www.coloradorapids.com

Denton, Jody
Celebrity chef and restauranteur
Merenda Restaurant **Ph:** 541-330-2304
900 NW Wall St
Bend, OR 97701
www.merendarestaurant.com

Denton, Stephanie
Expert on the subject of home and office organization; writes a syndicated column (Getting Organized) on the subject
Copley News Service **Ph:** 619-293-1818
PO Box 120190
San Diego, CA 92112
www.copleynews.com

dePaola, Tomie (1934-)
Author & illustrator of books for children
GP Putnam's Sons Books for Young Readers **Ph:** 212-366-2000
Publicity Dept
345 Hudson St
New York, NY 10014
www.tomie.com

Depp, Johnny (1963-)
Actor
United Talent Agency **Ph:** 310-273-6700
9560 Wilshire Blvd 5th Fl **Fax:** 310-247-1111
Beverly Hills, CA 90212

Dern, Laura (1967-)
Actor
Creative Artists Agency **Ph:** 310-288-4545
9830 Wilshire Blvd **Fax:** 310-288-4800
Beverly Hills, CA 90212

DeRogatis, Jim (1964-)
Pop music critic
Chicago Sun-Times **Ph:** 312-321-3000
401 N Wabash Ave **Fax:** 312-321-3084
Chicago, IL 60611
www.jimdero.com

Deromedi, Roger K
CEO of Kraft Foods
Kraft Foods Inc **Ph:** 847-646-2000
3 Lakes Dr
Northfield, IL 60093
www.kraft.com/profile

DeRosa, Mark (1975-)
Professional baseball player
Texas Rangers **Ph:** 817-273-5222
Ameriquest Field in Arlington **Fax:** 817-273-5294
1000 Ballpark Way **TF:** 888-968-3927
Arlington, TX 76011
texas.rangers.mlb.com

Derricks, Marguerite (1961-)
Choreographer (films, television, commercials, theater)
McDonald/Selznick Assoc Inc **Ph:** 323-957-6680
1611A N El Centro Ave
Hollywood, CA 90028
www.mcdonaldselznick.com

Dershowitz, Alan (1938-)
American civil rights libertarian, Harvard University law professor, and a leading defense attorney; clients have included: Claus von Bulow, Michael Milken, Mike Tyson, and Patricia Hearst
Harvard Law School **Ph:** 617-495-4617
1563 Massachusetts Ave **Fax:** 617-495-7855
Cambridge, MA 02138
www.law.harvard.edu/faculty/directory

Des Jardins, Traci
Chef & co-owner of Jardiniere
Jardiniere Restaurant **Ph:** 415-861-5555
300 Grove St **Fax:** 415-861-5580
San Francisco, CA 94102
www.jardiniere.com

Desaulniers, Marcel
Chef; author of cookbooks Death by Chocolate, Celebrate with Chocolate, and others
HarperCollins Publishers **Ph:** 212-207-7000
c/o Author Mail
10 E 53rd St
New York, NY 10022
www.harpercollins.com

Desjardins, Eric (1969-)
Professional hockey player
Philadelphia Flyers **Ph:** 215-465-4500
Wachovia Center **Fax:** 215-389-9403
3601 S Broad St
Philadelphia, PA 19148
www.philadelphiaflyers.com

Desmond-Hellmann, Susan, MD
President of Product Development at Genentech
Genentech Inc **Ph:** 650-225-1000
1 DNA Way **Fax:** 650-225-6000
South San Francisco, CA 94080
www.gene.com/gene/about/management

Dessen, Sarah (1970-)
Author of books for young adults
Viking Children's Books Publicity **Ph:** 212-366-2000
345 Hudson St
New York, NY 10014
www.sarahdessen.com

DeStefano, John Jr (1955-)
Mayor of New Haven, Connecticut
165 Church St **Ph:** 203-946-8200
New Haven, CT 06510 **Fax:** 203-946-7683
www.cityofnewhaven.com

Detorie, Rick
Illustrator, author of humorous books, and cartoonist, including the syndicated comic strip One Big Happy
Creators Syndicate Inc **Ph:** 310-337-7003
5777 W Century Blvd Suite 700 **Fax:** 310-337-7625
Los Angeles, CA 90045
www.creators.com

Deutsch, Donny
Chairman & CEO of Deutsch Inc, a marketing communications company; host of The Big Idea with Donny Deutsch on CNBC
Deutsch Inc **Ph:** 212-981-7600
111 8th Ave 14th Fl
New York, NY 10011
www.deutschinc.com

Devers, Gail (1966-)
Track & field athlete
Gail Devers Foundation Inc **Ph:** 770-822-4099
6555 Sugarloaf Pkwy Suite 307-137
Duluth, GA 30097
www.gaildevers.com

DeVito, Danny (1944-)
Actor/director/producer (film & TV)
Creative Artists Agency **Ph:** 310-288-4545
9830 Wilshire Blvd **Fax:** 310-288-4800
Beverly Hills, CA 90212

DeVos, Doug
President of Alticor Inc; he is the son of Rich DeVos, who founded Amway with Jay Van Andel, and he shares the Office of the Chief Executive with Jay's son, Steve Van Andel
Alticor Inc **Ph:** 616-787-1000
7575 Fulton St E
Ada, MI 49355
www.alticor.com/people/doug_devos.html

DeVos, Richard M (1926-)
Co-founded Amway Corp with Jay Van Andel in 1959; owns the Orlando Magic NBA team & the Orlando Miracle WNBA team
Amway Corp **Ph:** 616-787-1000
7575 Fulton St E
Ada, MI 49355
www.alticor.com/people/board_directors.html

DeWine, Mike (1947-)
US Senator from Ohio (Republican)
140 Russell Bldg **Ph:** 202-224-2315
Washington, DC 20510 **Fax:** 202-224-6519
dewine.senate.gov

DeWitt, William O Jr
Owner of the St Louis Cardinals baseball club
Saint Louis Cardinals **Ph:** 314-421-3060
Busch Stadium **Fax:** 314-425-0640
250 Stadium Plaza
Saint Louis, MO 63102

Dhue, Laurie
News update anchor for FOX News
FOX News Channel **Ph:** 212-301-3000
1211 Ave of the Americas
New York, NY 10036
www.foxnews.com/fnctv

Diamond, Jared, PhD (1937-)
Author of Guns, Germs, and Steel: The Fates of Human Societies; presently is a professor of geography at UCLA
UCLA **Ph:** 310-825-6177
Dept of Geography
Box 951524
1255 Bunche Hall
Los Angeles, CA 90095
www.edge.org/3rd_culture/bios/diamond.html

Diaz, Cameron (1972-)
Actor
Creative Artists Agency **Ph:** 310-288-4545
9830 Wilshire Blvd **Fax:** 310-288-4800
Beverly Hills, CA 90212

Diaz, Manuel A (1954-)
Mayor of the City of Miami, Florida
3500 Pan American Dr **Ph:** 305-250-5300
Miami, FL 33133 **Fax:** 305-854-4001
www.ci.miami.fl.us/mayor

Diaz, Nils J, PhD (1938-)
Chairman of the Nuclear Regulatory Commission
Nuclear Regulatory Commission **Ph:** 301-415-1759
Washington, DC 20555
www.nrc.gov

Diaz-Balart, Lincoln (1954-)
US Representative from Florida (Republican)
2244 Rayburn Bldg **Ph:** 202-225-4211
Washington, DC 20515 **Fax:** 202-225-8576
diaz-balart.house.gov

Diaz-Balart, Mario (1961-)
US Representative from Florida (Republican)
313 Cannon Bldg **Ph:** 202-225-2778
Washington, DC 20515 **Fax:** 202-226-0346
www.house.gov/mariodiaz-balart

DiCamillo, Kate
Author of books for young readers (The Tiger Rising; The Tale of Despereaux)
Candlewick Press **Ph:** 617-661-3330
2067 Massachusetts Ave **Fax:** 617-661-0565
Cambridge, MA 02140
www.candlewick.com

DiCaprio, Leonardo (1974-)
Actor
The Firm **Ph:** 310-860-8000
9465 Wilshire Blvd **Fax:** 310-860-8100
Beverly Hills, CA 90212
www.leonardodicaprio.com

Dick, Andy (1965-)
Actor; comedian
United Talent Agency **Ph:** 310-273-6700
9560 Wilshire Blvd 5th Fl **Fax:** 310-247-1111
Beverly Hills, CA 90212
www.andydick.com

Dickau, Dan (1978-)
Professional basketball player
Boston Celtics **Ph:** 617-854-8000
226 Causeway St 4th Fl **Fax:** 617-367-4286
Boston, MA 02114
www.nba.com/celtics

Dickenson, Steve
Co-creator, with Todd Clark, of the comic strip Lola
Newspaper Enterprise Assn **Ph:** 212-293-8500
200 Madison Ave
New York, NY 10016
www.unitedfeatures.com

Dickinson, Amy
Writes Ask Amy, a syndicated advice column
Tribune Media Services Inc **Ph:** 312-222-4444
435 N Michigan Ave Suite 1500
Chicago, IL 60611
tmsfeatures.com/productlist.htm

Dicks, Norman D (1940-)
US Representative from Washington (Democrat)
2467 Rayburn Bldg **Ph:** 202-225-5916
Washington, DC 20515 **Fax:** 202-226-1176
www.house.gov/dicks

Didion, Joan (1934-)
Author (The Year of Magical Thinking) & journalist
Knopf Publishing/Author Mail **Ph:** 212-782-9000
1745 Broadway
New York, NY 10019
www.randomhouse.com/knopf

Dido (1971-)
Singer
Nettwerk Management **Ph:** 310-855-0668
8730 Wilshire Blvd Suite 304 **Fax:** 310-855-0674
Beverly Hills, CA 90211
www.didomusic.com

Dierdorf, Dan (1949-)
TV sports commentator; former NFL player and member of the Pro Football Hall of Fame
CBS Sports **Ph:** 212-975-4321
51 W 52nd St
New York, NY 10019
cbs.sportsline.com/cbssports/team

Diesel, Vin (1967-)
Actor
The Firm **Ph:** 310-860-8000
9465 Wilshire Blvd **Fax:** 310-860-8100
Beverly Hills, CA 90212

Diffie, Joe (1958-)
Country singer
Buddy Lee Attractions **Ph:** 615-244-4336
38 Music Sq East Suite 300 **Fax:** 615-726-0429
Nashville, TN 37204
www.joediffie.com

Diggs, Taye (1972-)
Actor
Endeavor **Ph:** 310-248-2000
9601 Wilshire Blvd 3rd Fl **Fax:** 310-248-2020
Beverly Hills, CA 90210

Diller, Barry (1942-)
Chairman & CEO of IAC/InterActiveCorp and chairman of Expedia; a TV executive and Hollywood mogul who in the past has been head of Paramount Pictures, FOX, and QVC
IAC/InterActiveCorp **Ph:** 212-314-7300
152 W 57th St 42nd Fl **Fax:** 212-314-7309
New York, NY 10019
www.iac.com

Dillon, Corey (1974-)
Professional football player
New England Patriots **Ph:** 508-543-8200
1 Patriots Pl **Fax:** 508-543-0285
Foxboro, MA 02035
www.patriots.com

Dillon, David B
Chairman & CEO of Kroger Co
Kroger Co **Ph:** 513-762-4000
1014 Vine St **Fax:** 513-762-1400
Cincinnati, OH 45202
www.kroger.com

Dillon, Kate (1974-)
Plus-size model
Wilhelmina Models Inc **Ph:** 212-473-0700
300 Park Ave S 2nd Fl **Fax:** 212-473-3223
New York, NY 10010

Dillon, Matt (1964-)
Actor
Endeavor **Ph:** 310-248-2000
9601 Wilshire Blvd 3rd Fl **Fax:** 310-248-2020
Beverly Hills, CA 90210

DiMarco, Chris (1968-)
Professional golfer
PGA Tour **Ph:** 904-285-3700
100 PGA Tour Blvd
Ponte Vedra Beach, FL 32082
www.pgatour.com/players

Dimon, James
CEO of JP Morgan Chase & Co
JP Morgan Chase & Co **Ph:** 212-270-6000
270 Park Ave
New York, NY 10017
www.jpmorganchase.com

Dingell, John D (1926-)
US Representative from Michigan (Democrat)
2328 Rayburn Bldg **Ph:** 202-225-4071
Washington, DC 20515 **Fax:** 202-226-0371
www.house.gov/dingell

Dinklage, Peter (1969-)
Actor
SMS Talent Agency **Ph:** 310-289-0909
8730 Sunset Blvd Suite 440 **Fax:** 310-289-0990
Los Angeles, CA 90069

Dion, Celine (1968-)
Pop singer
Special Artists Agency **Ph:** 310-859-9688
9465 Wilshire Blvd Suite 890
Beverly Hills, CA 90212
www.celineonline.com

Dionne, EJ (1952-)
Syndicated columnist (op-ed)
Washington Post Writers Group **Ph:** 202-334-6375
Fax: 202-334-5669
1150 15th St NW 9th Fl
Washington, DC 20071
www.postwritersgroup.com

DiPietro, Rick (1981-)
Professional hockey player
New York Islanders **Ph:** 516-501-6700
1535 Old Country Rd **Fax:** 516-501-6729
Plainview, NY 11803
www.newyorkislanders.com

Dirda, Michael (1948-)
Writes syndicated book reviews & essays
Washington Post Book World **Ph:** 202-334-6375
1150 15th St NW 9th Fl **Fax:** 202-334-4536
Washington, DC 20071

Disney, Anthea
Executive Chairman of Gemstar-TV Guide
Gemstar-TV Guide International Inc **Ph:** 323-817-4600
6922 Hollywood Blvd
Hollywood, CA 90028
ir.gemstartvguide.com

Disney, Roy E (1930-)
Chairman of Shamrock Holdings, an investment company; a nephew of Walt Disney, he resigned from Disney Co in 2003 to protest Michael Eisner's management of the company
Shamrock Capital Advisors **Ph:** 818-845-4444
4444 Lakeside Dr **Fax:** 818-560-1930
Burbank, CA 91505
www.shamrock.com

DiSpirito, Rocco
Celebrity chef & cookbook author (Rocco's Five Minute Flavor)
Scribner Publicity Dept **Ph:** 212-698-7000
1230 Ave of the Americas
New York, NY 10020
www.roccodispirito.com

DiTerlizzi, Tony (1969-)
Illustrator/creator of children's picture books
Simon & Schuster Books for Young Readers **Ph:** 212-698-7000
1230 Ave of the Americas
New York, NY 10020
www.diterlizzi.com

Ditka, Mike (1939-)
Former professional football coach and hall-of-fame player; now a studio analyst on ESPN
ESPN **Ph:** 860-585-2000
ESPN Plaza
935 Middle St
Bristol, CT 06010
sports.espn.go.com/espntv/espnGuide

Dixie Chicks
Country music trio (Natalie Maines, Emily Robison, Martie Maguire)
CAA Nashville **Ph:** 615-383-8787
3310 West End Ave 5th Fl **Fax:** 615-383-4937
Nashville, TN 37203
www.dixiechicks.com

Dixon, Tamecka (1975-)
Professional basketball player
Houston Comets **Ph:** 713-758-7200
Toyota Center **Fax:** 713-758-7396
1510 Polk St
Houston, TX 77002
www.wnba.com/comets

Djorkaeff, Youri (1968-)
Professional soccer player
New York Red Bulls **Ph:** 201-583-7000
1 Harmon Plaza 3rd Fl **Fax:** 201-583-7055
Secaucus, NJ 07094
redbull.newyork.mlsnet.com

Dobbs, Lou (1945-)
Anchor and managing editor of Lou Dobbs Tonight; also does a financial news radio report and writes columns for Money magazine and for US News & World Report
CNN New York **Ph:** 212-275-7800
Time Warner Ctr
10 Columbus Cir
New York, NY 10019
www.cnn.com/CNN/anchors_reporters

Dobson, James C, PhD (1936-)
Founder of Focus on the Family; a lay religious leader, psychologist, and author
Focus on the Family **Ph:** 719-531-3400
Colorado Springs, CO 80995
www.family.org

Doctorow, EL (1931-)
Author of Ragtime, Billy Bathgate, and other novels
Random House Publicity **Ph:** 212-782-9000
1745 Broadway
New York, NY 10019
www.randomhouse.com

Dodd, Christopher J (1944-)
US Senator from Connecticut (Democrat)
448 Russell Bldg **Ph:** 202-224-2823
Washington, DC 20510 **Fax:** 202-224-1083
dodd.senate.gov

Doerr, Anthony (1973-)
Fiction writer (The Shell Collector, a short story collection; About Grace, a novel)
Simon & Schuster **Ph:** 212-698-7000
1230 Ave of the Americas
New York, NY 10020
myweb.cableone.net/adoerr

Doerr, L John (1952-)
Partner in Kleiner Perkins Caufield & Byers, a venture capital firm
Kleiner Perkins Caufield & Byers **Ph:** 650-233-2750 **Fax:** 650-233-0300
2750 Sand Hill Rd
Menlo Park, CA 94025
www.kpcb.com

Doggett, Lloyd (1946-)
US Representative from Texas (Democrat)
201 Cannon Bldg **Ph:** 202-225-4865
Washington, DC 20515 **Fax:** 202-225-3073
www.house.gov/doggett

Doherty, Peter C, PhD (1940-)
Winner (with Rolf M Zinkernagel) of the 1996 Nobel Prize in Physiology or Medicine for discoveries concerning the specificity of the cell-mediated immune defense
Saint Jude Children's Research Hospital **Ph:** 901-495-3300 **Fax:** 901-495-3107
332 N Lauderdale St
Memphis, TN 38105
www.stjude.org/faculty

Doherty, Shannen (1971-)
Actor
Endeavor **Ph:** 310-248-2000
9601 Wilshire Blvd 3rd Fl **Fax:** 310-248-2020
Beverly Hills, CA 90210

Dolan, Charles F (1926-)
Founder & chairman of Cablevision Systems Corp, which owns and operates Madison Square Garden, including the arena complex and its teams, the New York Knicks (NBA) and Liberty (WNBA) and the New York Rangers (NHL); was also the founder of HBO
Cablevision Systems Corp **Ph:** 516-803-1001
1111 Stewart Ave **Fax:** 516-803-2360
Bethpage, NY 11714
www.cablevision.com

Dolan, Lawrence
Owner of the Cleveland Indians baseball franchise
Cleveland Indians **Ph:** 216-420-4200
Jacobs Field **Fax:** 216-420-4624
2401 Ontario St
Cleveland, OH 44115

Dolan, Peter R
CEO of Bristol-Myers Squibb
Bristol-Myers Squibb Co **Ph:** 212-546-4000
345 Park Ave
New York, NY 10154
www.bms.com

Dole, Bob (1923-)
Former US Senator and Republican presidential candidate
Alston & Bird LLP **Ph:** 202-654-4848
601 Pennsylvania Ave NW
North Bldg
Washington, DC 20004
www.bobdole.org

Dole, Elizabeth H (1936-)
US Senator from North Carolina (Republican)
120 Russell Bldg **Ph:** 202-224-6342
Washington, DC 20510 **Fax:** 202-228-1100
dole.senate.gov

Doley, Harold E Jr (1948-)
Founder & CEO of Doley Securities Inc; the first and only African-American to own a seat on the New York Stock Exchange
Doley Securities Inc **Ph:** 504-561-1128
616 Baronne St **Fax:** 504-524-8382
New Orleans, LA 70113
www.doley.com

Dollar, Creflo A Jr
Televangelist
World Changers Ministries **Ph:** 770-210-5700
PO Box 490124 **Fax:** 770-210-5701
College Park, GA 30349 **TF:** 866-477-7683
www.worldchangers.org

Domenici, Pete (1932-)
US Senator from New Mexico (Republican)
328 Hart Bldg **Ph:** 202-224-6621
Washington, DC 20510 **Fax:** 202-228-3261
domenici.senate.gov

Domi, Tie (1969-)
Professional hockey player
Toronto Maple Leafs **Ph:** 416-815-5700
Air Canada Center
40 Bay St Suite 400
Toronto, ON M5J2X2
www.mapleleafs.com

Domingo, Placido (1941-)
Opera singer
Nancy Seltzer & Assoc **Ph:** 323-938-3562
6220 Del Valle Dr **Fax:** 323-938-0589
Los Angeles, CA 90048
www.placidodomingo.com

Donald, Arnold W
Chairman of the Board of Merisant, which makes tabletop sweeteners, including Equal
Merisant Worldwide Inc **Ph:** 312-840-6000
10 S Riverside Plaza Suite 850 **Fax:** 312-840-5101
Chicago, IL 60606
www.merisant.com

Donaldson, Colby (1974-)
Actor; former Survivor contestant
William Morris Agency **Ph:** 310-859-4000
1 William Morris Pl **Fax:** 310-859-4462
Beverly Hills, CA 90212
survivorhunks.com/ColbyDonaldson

Donna, Roberto
Chef; restauranteur
Galileo Restaurant **Ph:** 202-293-7191
1110 21st St NW **Fax:** 202-331-9364
Washington, DC 20036
www.robertodonna.com

Donnelly, Liza
New Yorker cartoonist (panels)
Cartoon Bank **Ph:** 914-478-5527
New Yorker Magazine **Fax:** 914-478-5604
28 Wells Ave Bldg 3 4th Fl
Yonkers, NY 10701
www.cartoonbank.com

Donner, Richard (1930-)
Movie producer/director
William Morris Agency **Ph:** 310-859-4000
1 William Morris Pl **Fax:** 310-859-4462
Beverly Hills, CA 90212

D'Onofrio, Vincent (1959-)
Actor
United Talent Agency **Ph:** 310-273-6700
9560 Wilshire Blvd 5th Fl **Fax:** 310-247-1111
Beverly Hills, CA 90212
www.nbc.com/Law_&_Order:_Criminal_Intent

Donohue, Paul, MD
Internal medicine specialist; writes To Your Good Health, a syndicated column on infectious diseases, public health, and sports medicine
King Features Syndicate Inc **Ph:** 212-455-4000
888 7th Ave 2nd Fl
New York, NY 10019
www.kingfeatures.com

Donovan, Anne (1961-)
Basketball coach
Seattle Storm **Ph:** 206-281-5800
351 Elliott Ave W Suite 500
Seattle, WA 98119
www.wnba.com/storm

Donovan, Landon (1982-)
Professional soccer player
Los Angeles Galaxy **Ph:** 310-630-2200
Home Depot Center **Fax:** 310-630-2250
18400 Avalon Blvd Suite 200
Carson, CA 90746
www.lagalaxy.com

Donvan, John
Nightline correspondent
ABC News Nightline **Ph:** 202-222-7700
1717 DeSales St NW
Washington, DC 20036
www.abcnews.go.com/Nightline

Doocy, Steve (1956-)
Co-anchor of Fox and Friends
FOX News Channel **Ph:** 212-301-3000
1211 Ave of the Americas
New York, NY 10036
www.foxnews.com/fnctv

Dooher, Donna
Chef at The Cookworks Cooking School and host of The Cookworks on Food Network Canada
The Cookworks **Ph:** 416-537-6464
99 Sudbury St Suite 8 **Fax:** 416-537-2653
Toronto, ON M6J3S7
www.thecookworks.com

Doolittle, John T (1950-)
US Representative from California (Republican)
2410 Rayburn Bldg **Ph:** 202-225-2511
Washington, DC 20515 **Fax:** 202-225-5444
www.house.gov/doolittle

Dooner, John
Chairman and CEO of McCann Worldgroup, which owns a global network of marketing communications companies
McCann Worldgroup **Ph:** 646-865-2000
622 3rd Ave **Fax:** 646-487-9610
New York, NY 10017
www.mccann.com

Dorgan, Byron L (1942-)
US Senator from North Dakota (Democrat)
322 Hart Bldg **Ph:** 202-224-2551
Washington, DC 20510 **Fax:** 202-224-1193
dorgan.senate.gov

Dotel, Octavio (1973-)
Professional baseball player
New York Yankees **Ph:** 718-293-4300
Yankee Stadium **Fax:** 718-293-8414
161st St & River Ave
Bronx, NY 10451
newyork.yankees.mlb.com

Dotson, Bob (1946-)
NBC News national correspondent
NBC News **Ph:** 212-664-4249
30 Rockefeller Plaza
New York, NY 10112
www.msnbc.msn.com/id/3689499

Dougan, Brady W (1959-)
President and CEO of Credit Suisse First Boston LLC
Credit Suisse First Boston LLC **Ph:** 212-325-2000
11 Madison Ave
New York, NY 10010
www.csfb.com

Douglas, James H (1951-)
Governor of Vermont (Republican)
109 State St 5th Fl **Ph:** 802-828-3333
Montpelier, VT 05609 **Fax:** 802-828-3339
www.vermont.gov/governor

Douglas, Katie (1979-)
Professional basketball player
Connecticut Sun **Ph:** 860-862-4000
1 Mohegan Sun Blvd **Fax:** 860-862-4010
Uncasville, CT 06382
www.wnba.com/sun

Douglas, Kirk (1916-)
Actor
Creative Artists Agency **Ph:** 310-288-4545
8930 Wilshire Blvd **Fax:** 310-288-4800
Beverly Hills, CA 90212

Douglas, Kyan (1970-)
Grooming guru on Queer Eye for the Straight Guy
Creative Artists Agency **Ph:** 310-288-4545
9830 Wilshire Blvd **Fax:** 310-288-4800
Beverly Hills, CA 90212
www.bravotv.com

Douglas, Michael (1944-)
Actor and film producer
Endeavor **Ph:** 310-248-2000
9601 Wilshire Blvd 3rd Fl **Fax:** 310-248-2020
Beverly Hills, CA 90210

Douglas, Tom
Chef; owns and operates four well-known restaurants in Seattle
Tom Douglas Restaurants **Ph:** 206-448-2001
2030 5th Ave **Fax:** 206-448-1979
Seattle, WA 98121
www.tomdouglas.com

Douglass, John W (1942-)
President & CEO of the Aerospace Industries Association
Aerospace Industries Assn **Ph:** 703-358-1000
1000 Wilson Blvd Suite 1700
Arlington, VA 22209
www.aia-aerospace.org

Douglass, Linda
Chief Capitol Hill correspondent for ABC News
ABC News **Ph:** 202-222-7700
1717 DeSales St NW
Washington, DC 20036
www.abcnews.go.com/WNT

Dove, Rita (1952-)
Former Poet Laureate of the US and consultant to the Library of Congress
UVA English Dept **Ph:** 434-924-7105
422A Bryan Hall **Fax:** 434-924-1478
PO Box 400121
Charlottesville, VA 22904
www.people.virginia.edu/~rfd4b

Dow, Harold (1947-)
48 Hours correspondent
48 Hours **Ph:** 212-975-4114
524 W 57th St
New York, NY 10019
www.cbsnews.com

Dowd, Maureen (1952-)
New York Times op-ed columnist (syndicated)
New York Times **Ph:** 202-862-0300
Washington Bureau **Fax:** 202-862-0340
1627 'I' St NW
Washington, DC 20006
www.nytimes.com/pages/opinion

Dower, John W, PhD
Professor of Japanese history and author of numerous historical books, including Embracing Defeat: Japan in the Wake of World War II
Massachusetts Institute of Technology **Ph:** 617-253-4445
77 Massachusetts Ave
Bldg E51-287
Cambridge, MA 02139
web.mit.edu/jdower/www/dower.htm

Downey, Robert Jr (1965-)
Actor
Creative Artists Agency **Ph:** 310-288-4545
9830 Wilshire Blvd **Fax:** 310-288-4800
Beverly Hills, CA 90212

Downs, Hugh (1921-)
President of the Board of Governors of the National Space Society; long-time television personality, now retired
National Space Society **Ph:** 202-429-1600
1620 'I' St NW Suite 615 **Fax:** 202-463-8497
Washington, DC 20006
www.nss.org/about/bog.html

Doyle, Jim (1945-)
Governor of Wisconsin (Democrat)
State Capitol **Ph:** 608-266-1212
PO Box 7863 **Fax:** 608-267-8983
Madison, WI 53707
www.wisgov.state.wi.us

Doyle, Mike (1953-)
US Representative from Pennsylvania (Democrat)
401 Cannon Bldg **Ph:** 202-225-2135
Washington, DC 20515 **Fax:** 202-225-3084
www.house.gov/doyle

Doyle, Roddy (1958-)
Irish comic novelist
Penguin Publicity **Ph:** 212-366-2000
375 Hudson St
New York, NY 10014
us.penguingroup.com

Dr Phil (1950-)
Talk show host, businessman, and author Phil McGraw
Dr Phil Show **Ph:** 323-956-3449
5482 Wilshire Blvd Suite 1902
Los Angeles, CA 90036
www.drphil.com

Dr Ruth (1928-)
Sex educator, therapist, and media psychologist Ruth Westheimer; her syndicated column Ask Dr. Ruth provides advice on sex, love, and relationships
King Features Syndicate Inc **Ph:** 212-455-4000
888 7th Ave 2nd Fl
New York, NY 10019
www.drruth.com

Dragila, Stacy (1971-)
Pole vaulter (first ever Olympic Gold Medalist in the women's pole vault)
USA Track & Field **Ph:** 317-261-0500
1 RCA Dome Suite 140
Indianapolis, IN 46225
www.usatf.com

Drake, Thelma D (1949-)
US Representative from Virginia (Republican)
1208 Longworth Bldg **Ph:** 202-225-4215
Washington, DC 20515 **Fax:** 202-225-4218
drake.house.gov

Draper, Dave (1942-)
Fitness personality/bodybuilder
PO Box 1335 **Ph:** 831-466-9182
Aptos, CA 95001 **Fax:** 831-466-9183
www.davedraper.com

Draper, Kris (1971-)
Professional hockey player
Detroit Red Wings **Ph:** 313-396-7544
Joe Louis Arena **Fax:** 313-567-0296
600 Civic Center Dr
Detroit, MI 48226
www.detroitredwings.com

Draper, Sharon M (1952-)
Professional educator (1997 Teacher of the Year) and author of books for young readers (The Battle of Jericho, Tears of a Tiger)
Simon & Schuster Books for Young Readers **Ph:** 212-698-7000
1230 Ave of the Americas
New York, NY 10020
sharondraper.com

Dreier, David (1952-)
US Representative from California (Republican)
233 Cannon Bldg **Ph:** 202-225-2305
Washington, DC 20515 **Fax:** 202-225-7018
www.dreier.house.gov

Drese, Ryan (1976-)
Professional baseball player
Washington Nationals **Ph:** 202-349-0400
RFK Stadium
2400 E Capitol St SE
Washington, DC 20003
washington.nationals.mlb.com

Drew, JD (1975-)
Professional baseball player
Los Angeles Dodgers **Ph:** 323-224-1500
Dodger Stadium **Fax:** 323-224-1269
1000 Elysian Park Ave
Los Angeles, CA 90012
losangeles.dodgers.mlb.com

Drexler, K Eric, PhD (1955-)
A pioneer in the study of nanotechnology; researcher, author, and policy advocate focused on emerging technologies and their consequences for the future; founder of the Foresight Institute and chief technical advisor for Nanorex
Nanorex **Ph:** 248-456-0700
PO Box 7188 **Fax:** 248-456-0701
Bloomfield Hills, MI 48302
www.e-drexler.com

Dreyfuss, Richard (1947-)
Actor
International Creative Management **Ph:** 310-550-4000
8942 Wilshire Blvd
Beverly Hills, CA 90211

Driscoll, Matthew J
Mayor of Syracuse, New York
203 City Hall **Ph:** 315-448-8005
Syracuse, NY 13202 **Fax:** 315-448-8067
www.syracuse.ny.us

Driver, Donald (1975-)
Professional football player
Green Bay Packers **Ph:** 920-569-7500
PO Box 10628 **Fax:** 920-569-7201
Green Bay, WI 54307
www.packers.com

Driver, Minnie (1970-)
Actor
Special Artists Agency **Ph:** 310-859-9688
9465 Wilshire Blvd Suite 890
Beverly Hills, CA 90212
www.minniedriver.com

Droughns, Reuben (1978-)
Professional football player
Cleveland Browns **Ph:** 440-891-5000
76 Lou Groza Blvd **Fax:** 440-891-5009
Berea, OH 44017
www.clevelandbrowns.com

Drudge, Matt (1967-)
Writes The Drudge Report (online); also hosts a political news and gossip radio show
Premiere Radio Networks Inc **Ph:** 818-377-5300
15260 Ventura Blvd 5th Fl **Fax:** 818-377-5333
Sherman Oaks, CA 91403
www.ksfo560.com/hosts.asp

Drummond, Eddie (1980-)
Professional football player
Detroit Lions **Ph:** 313-216-4000
222 Republic Dr **Fax:** 313-216-4069
Allen Park, MI 48101
www.detroitlions.com

Drury, Chris (1976-)
Professional hockey player
Buffalo Sabres **Ph:** 716-855-4100
HSBC Arena **Fax:** 716-855-4115
1 Seymour H Knox III Plaza
Buffalo, NY 14203
www.sabres.com

Duarte, Chris (1963-)
Contemporary blues-rock guitarist, singer, songwriter, bandleader (Chris Duarte Group)
Intrepid Artists International Inc **Ph:** 704-358-4777 **Fax:** 704-358-3171
1300 Baxter St Suite 405
Charlotte, NC 28204
www.intrepidartists.com

Ducasse, Alain (1956-)
Chef and owner of Alain Ducasse at the Essex House Restaurant in New York, as well as restaurants in Paris and Monaco
Alain Ducasse at the Essex House Restaurant **Ph:** 212-265-7300 **Fax:** 212-265-9300
155 W 58th St
New York, NY 10019
www.alain-ducasse.com

Duchovny, David (1960-)
Actor
United Talent Agency **Ph:** 310-273-6700
9560 Wilshire Blvd 5th Fl **Fax:** 310-247-1111
Beverly Hills, CA 90212

Duckett, TJ (1981-)
Professional football player
Atlanta Falcons **Ph:** 770-965-3115
4400 Falcon Pkwy **Fax:** 770-965-3185
Flowery Branch, GA 30542
www.atlantafalcons.com

Duff, Hilary (1987-)
Actor; singer
Creative Artists Agency **Ph:** 310-288-4545
9830 Wilshire Blvd **Fax:** 310-288-4800
Beverly Hills, CA 90212
www.hilaryduff.com

Duffy, Brian
Editorial cartoonist for the Des Moines Register
King Features Syndicate Inc **Ph:** 212-455-4000
888 7th Ave 2nd Fl
New York, NY 10019
www.kingfeatures.com

Duffy, JC
Creator of the comic strip The Fusco Brothers; also does the comic panel Go Fish, which is syndicated through United Feature Syndicate
Universal Press Syndicate **Ph:** 816-932-6600
4520 Main St
Kansas City, MO 64111
www.amuniversal.com/ups/features

Duffy, Karen (1962-)
Author of Model Patient: My Life As an Incurable Wise-Ass; has worked as an actress, model, journalist, and MTV veejay
HarperCollins Publishers **Ph:** 212-207-7000
c/o Author Mail
10 E 53rd St
New York, NY 10022
www.harpercollins.com

Duffy, Robert J
Mayor of Rochester, New York
30 Church St — **Ph:** 585-428-7045
Rochester, NY 14614 — **Fax:** 585-428-6059
www.cityofrochester.gov

Dugan, Dennis (1946-)
Movie/television director
United Talent Agency — **Ph:** 310-273-6700
9560 Wilshire Blvd 5th Fl — **Fax:** 310-247-1111
Beverly Hills, CA 90212

Duhon, Chris (1982-)
Professional basketball player
Chicago Bulls — **Ph:** 312-455-4000
United Center — **Fax:** 312-455-4198
1901 W Madison St
Chicago, IL 60612
www.nba.com/bulls

Dukakis, Olympia (1931-)
Actor
Parseghian/Planco Management — **Ph:** 212-777-7786
23 E 22nd St — **Fax:** 212-777-8642
New York, NY 10010

Duke, Patty (1946-)
Actor
CESD Voices — **Ph:** 310-475-2111
10635 Santa Monica Blvd
Suites 130/135
Los Angeles, CA 90025
www.pattyduke.net

Dulbecco, Renato, MD (1914-)
1975 Nobel Prize winner in Medicine; discovered that tumor viruses cause cancer by inserting their own genes into the chromosomes of infected cells, which was one of the first clues to the genetic nature of cancer
Salk Institute for Biological Studies — **Ph:** 858-453-4100 — **Fax:** 858-453-8534
PO Box 85800
San Diego, CA 92186
www.salk.edu/faculty

Dumas, Jerry (1930-)
Creator of the comic strip Sam & Silo
King Features Syndicate Inc — **Ph:** 212-455-4000
888 7th Ave 2nd Fl
New York, NY 10019
www.kingfeatures.com

Dunagin, Ralph
Editorial cartoonist; also writes the comic strip Grin & Bear It (with Fred Wagner) and is co-creator of The Middletons, with Dana Summers
King Features Syndicate Inc — **Ph:** 212-455-4000
888 7th Ave 2nd Fl
New York, NY 10019
www.kingfeatures.com

Dunaway, Faye (1941-)
Actor
Innovative Artists — **Ph:** 310-656-0400
1505 10th St — **Fax:** 310-656-0456
Santa Monica, CA 90401

Duncan, John J Jr (1947-)
US Representative from Tennessee (Republican)
2267 Rayburn Bldg — **Ph:** 202-225-5435
Washington, DC 20515 — **Fax:** 202-225-6440
www.house.gov/duncan

Duncan, Lois (1934-)
Writer of books for young adults (Summer of Fear; I Know What You Did Last Summer)
Random House Children's Books — **Ph:** 212-782-9000
Publicity Dept
1745 Broadway
New York, NY 10019
loisduncan.arquettes.com

Duncan, Michael Clarke (1957-)
Actor
Gersh Agency — **Ph:** 310-274-6611
232 N Canon Dr
Beverly Hills, CA 90210

Duncan, Tim (1976-)
Professional basketball player
San Antonio Spurs — **Ph:** 210-444-5000
1 SBC Center — **Fax:** 210-444-5003
San Antonio, TX 78219
www.slamduncan.com

Dungy, Tony (1955-)
Football coach
Indianapolis Colts — **Ph:** 317-297-2658
7001 W 56th St — **Fax:** 317-297-8971
Indianapolis, IN 46254
www.colts.com

Dunham, Chip
Creator of the syndicated comic strip Overboard
Universal Press Syndicate — **Ph:** 816-932-6600
4520 Main St
Kansas City, MO 64111
www.amuniversal.com/ups/features

Dunivant, Todd (1980-)
Professional soccer player
Los Angeles Galaxy **Ph:** 310-630-2200
Home Depot Center **Fax:** 310-630-2250
18400 Avalon Blvd Suite 200
Carson, CA 90746
www.lagalaxy.com

Dunleavy, Mike (1980-)
Professional basketball player
Golden State Warriors **Ph:** 510-986-2200
1011 Broadway **Fax:** 510-452-0132
Oakland, CA 94607
www.nba.com/warriors

Dunleavy, Mike Sr
Basketball coach
Los Angeles Clippers **Ph:** 213-742-7100
Staples Center **Fax:** 213-742-7550
1111 S Figueroa St Suite 1100
Los Angeles, CA 90015
www.nba.com/clippers

Dunn, Adam (1979-)
Professional baseball player
Cincinnati Reds **Ph:** 513-765-7000
Great American Ballpark **Fax:** 513-765-7342
100 Main St
Cincinnati, OH 45202
cincinnati.reds.mlb.com

Dunn, Stephen (1939-)
Poet
WW Norton & Co Inc **Ph:** 212-354-5500
500 5th Ave **Fax:** 212-869-0856
New York, NY 10110
www.nortonpoets.com

Dunn, Warrick (1975-)
Professional football player
Atlanta Falcons **Ph:** 770-965-3115
4400 Falcon Pkwy **Fax:** 770-965-3185
Flowery Branch, GA 30542
www.atlantafalcons.com

Dunne, Dominick (1926-)
Author (The Two Mrs. Grenvilles; An Inconvenient Woman); host of the Court TV show Dominick Dunne's Power, Privilege & Justice
Courtroom Television Network **Ph:** 212-286-8180
600 3rd Ave
New York, NY 10016
www.courttv.com/onair/shows/dunne

Dunne, John Gregory (1932-2003)
Novelist & screenwriter; collaborated with his wife, the writer Joan Didion, on Panic in Needle Park, True Confessions, and other screenplays
Vintage/Anchor Publicity **Ph:** 212-572-2420
1745 Broadway 20th Fl
New York, NY 10019
www.randomhouse.com/vintage

Dunner, Donald R (1931-)
Patent & trademark litigation specialist; currently focusing on intellectual property law
Finnegan Henderson Farabow Garrett & Dunner LLP **Ph:** 202-408-4062 **Fax:** 202-408-4400
901 New York Ave NW
Washington, DC 20001
www.finnegan.com

Dunning, Jennifer
New York Times dance critic
New York Times **Ph:** 212-556-1234
229 W 43rd St
New York, NY 10036

Dunseth, Brian (1977-)
Professional soccer player
Los Angeles Galaxy **Ph:** 310-630-2200
Home Depot Center **Fax:** 310-630-2250
18400 Avalon Blvd Suite 200
Carson, CA 90746
www.lagalaxy.com

Dunst, Kirsten (1982-)
Actor
PMK/HBH **Ph:** 310-289-6200
700 San Vicente Blvd **Fax:** 310-289-6677
Suite G910
West Hollywood, CA 90069

Duplantis, Jesse (1949-)
Evangelical Charismatic Christian minister; televangelist
Jesse Duplantis Ministries **Ph:** 985-764-2000
PO Box 2608 **Fax:** 985-764-0044
Hammond, LA 70404
www.jdm.org

DuPont, Pete (1935-)
Former US Congressman, Governor of Delaware, and Republican presidential candidate; now a law firm director & chairman of the National Center for Policy Analysis, and is a columnist on the Wall Street Journal's editorial page website
National Center for Policy Analysis **Ph:** 972-386-6272 **Fax:** 972-386-0924
12770 Coit Rd
Dallas, TX 75251
www.ncpa.org

Duques, Henry
Chairman and CEO of First Data Corp
First Data Corp **Ph:** 303-967-8000
6200 S Quebec St
Greenwood Village, CO 80111
ir.firstdata.com/directors.cfm

Durbin, Richard J (1944-)
US Senator from Illinois (Democrat)
332 Dirksen Bldg **Ph:** 202-224-2152
Washington, DC 20510 **Fax:** 202-228-0400
durbin.senate.gov

Durham, Ray (1971-)
Professional baseball player
San Francisco Giants **Ph:** 415-972-2000
AT & T Park
24 Willie Mays Plaza
San Francisco, CA 94107
sanfrancisco.giants.mlb.com

DuVall, Clea (1977-)
Actor
Endeavor **Ph:** 310-248-2000
9601 Wilshire Blvd 3rd Fl **Fax:** 310-248-2020
Beverly Hills, CA 90210
www.hbo.com/carnivale

Duvall, Robert (1931-)
Actor
Butcher's Run Films **Ph:** 310-246-4630
1041 N Formosa Ave
Santa Monica Bldg E200
West Hollywood, CA 90046

Dvorak, Radek (1977-)
Professional hockey player
Edmonton Oilers **Ph:** 780-414-4000
11230 110th St **Fax:** 780-409-5890
Edmonton, AB T5G3H7
www.edmontonoilers.com

Dwight, Tim (1975-)
Professional football player
New England Patriots **Ph:** 508-543-8200
1 Patriots Pl **Fax:** 508-543-0285
Foxboro, MA 02035
www.patriots.com

Dyer, Buddy (1958-)
Mayor of Orlando, Florida
400 S Orange Ave **Ph:** 407-246-2221
PO Box 4990 **Fax:** 407-246-2842
Orlando, FL 32802
www.cityoforlando.net

Dyer, Colin
President and Global CEO of Jones Lang LaSalle, a real estate services and investment management firm
Jones Lang LaSalle Inc **Ph:** 312-782-5800
200 E Randolph Dr
Chicago, IL 60601
www.joneslanglasalle.com

Dyer, Wayne, PhD (1940-)
Self-empowerment author (Your Erroneous Zones) & speaker
Hay House Inc **Ph:** 760-431-7695
PO Box 5100 **Fax:** 800-650-5115
Carlsbad, CA 92018
www.drwaynedyer.com

Dylan, Bob (1941-)
Singer, songwriter, composer
Creative Artists Agency **Ph:** 310-288-4545
9830 Wilshire Blvd **Fax:** 310-288-4800
Beverly Hills, CA 90212
www.bobdylan.com

Dyson, Esther (1951-)
Founding chairman of ICANN, now editor at large at CNET Networks (she sold her company, EDventure Holdings, to CNET Networks in early 2004)
Release 1.0 **Ph:** 212-924-8800
104 5th Ave 20th Fl **Fax:** 212-924-0240
New York, NY 10011
www.edventure.com

Dyson, Freeman (1923-)
Noted scientist and professor emeritus of physics at the Institute for Advanced Study; author of several books about science for the general public
Institute for Advanced Study **Ph:** 609-734-8055
School of Natural Sciences **Fax:** 609-951-4489
Einstein Dr
Princeton, NJ 08540
www.sns.ias.edu/~dyson

Dzerigian, Steve
Photographer
838 E University Ave **Ph:** 559-442-4868
Fresno, CA 93704
www.stevedzerigian.com

Eads, George (1967-)
Actor (CSI)
William Morris Agency **Ph:** 310-859-4000
1 William Morris Pl **Fax:** 310-859-4462
Beverly Hills, CA 90212
www.cbs.com/primetime/csi

Earl, Robert I
Founder, chairman, and CEO of Planet Hollywood
Planet Hollywood International **Ph:** 407-903-5500
7598 W Sand Lake Rd
Orlando, FL 32819

Earles, Johnny
Executive Chef and owner of Criolla's
Criolla's Restaurant **Ph:** 850-267-1267
170 E Scenic Hwy 30A **Fax:** 850-231-4568
Santa Rosa Beach, FL 32459
www.criollas.com

Earnhardt, Dale (1951-2001)
NASCAR legend
Dale Earnhardt Foundation **Ph:** 877-334-3253
1675 Dale Earnhardt Hwy 3
Mooresville, NC 28115
www.daleearnhardtinc.com

Earnhardt, Dale Jr (1974-)
NASCAR driver
Dale Earnhardt Inc **Ph:** 704-662-8000
1675 Dale Earnhardt Hwy 3
Mooresville, NC 28115
www.dalejr.com

Easley, Michael F (1950-)
Governor of North Carolina (Democrat)
166 W Jones St **Ph:** 919-733-5811
20301 MSC **Fax:** 919-733-2120
Raleigh, NC 27699
www.governor.state.nc.us

Eastman, Kevin (1962-)
Co-creator, with Peter Laird, of the Teenage Mutant Ninja Turtles (comic strip, comic books, movie, etc.)
Mirage Studios **Ph:** 413-586-7066
16 Market St
Northampton, MA 01060
www.ninjaturtles.com/origin/origin.htm

Eastwood, Clint (1930-)
Actor, director, producer
Malpaso Co **Ph:** 818-954-3367
4000 Warner Blvd
Bldg 81
Burbank, CA 91522
www.clinteastwood.net

Ebersol, Dick (1947-)
Chairman of NBC Universal Sports & Olympics
NBC Universal Sports & Olympics **Ph:** 212-664-4444
30 Rockefeller Plaza
New York, NY 10112
www.nbcuni.com

Eberstadt, Nicholas, PhD (1955-)
Economist; currently the Henry Wendt Scholar in Political Economy at the American Enterprise Institute
American Enterprise Institute for Public Policy Research **Ph:** 202-862-5800 **Fax:** 202-862-7177
1150 17th St NW Suite 1100
Washington, DC 20036
www.aei.org

Ebert, Roger (1942-)
Movie critic
Chicago Sun-Times **Ph:** 312-321-3000
350 N Orleans **Fax:** 312-321-3084
Chicago, IL 60654
rogerebert.suntimes.com

Eberts, Marge
Writes the syndicated newspaper column Dear Teacher (with Peggy Gisler)
King Features Syndicate Inc **Ph:** 212-455-4000
888 7th Ave 2nd Fl
New York, NY 10019
www.kingfeatures.com

Eckert, Robert A
Chairman of the board and CEO of Mattel
Mattel Inc **Ph:** 310-252-2000
333 Continental Blvd **Fax:** 310-252-2179
El Segundo, CA 90245
www.mattel.com

Eckhart, Aaron (1968-)
Actor
Creative Artists Agency **Ph:** 310-288-4545
9830 Wilshire Blvd **Fax:** 310-288-4800
Beverly Hills, CA 90212

Eco, Umberto (1932-)
Novelist (Foucault's Pendulum; The Name of The Rose)
Harcourt Trade Publishers **Ph:** 212-592-1000
15 E 26th St
New York, NY 10010
www.harcourtbooks.com

Ecohawk, John E
Attorney; executive director of the Native American Rights Fund (NARF) and a leading litigator in the field of Indian law
Native American Rights Fund **Ph:** 303-447-8760
1506 Broadway **Fax:** 303-443-7776
Boulder, CO 80302
www.narf.org

Edell, Dean, MD (1944-)
Host of a radio show on medical issues
Premiere Radio Networks Inc **Ph:** 818-377-5300
15260 Ventura Blvd 5th Fl **Fax:** 818-377-5333
Sherman Oaks, CA 91403
www.healthcentral.com

Edelman, Gerald M, MD, PhD (1929-)
Winner, with Rodney R Porter, of the 1972 Nobel Prize for Physiology or Medicine for discoveries concerning the chemical structure of antibodies
Dept of Neurobiology **Ph:** 858-784-2600
Scripps Research Institute
10500 N Torrey Pines Rd
SBR-14
La Jolla, CA 92037
www.scripps.edu/research

Edelman, Marian Wright (1939-)
Founder & president of the Children's Defense Fund and an advocate for disadvantaged Americans; first black woman admitted to the Mississippi Bar
Children's Defense Fund **Ph:** 202-628-8787
25 'E' St NW **Fax:** 202-662-3510
Washington, DC 20001 **TF:** 800-233-1200
www.childrensdefense.org/about/mwe.aspx

Edelman, Ric
Financial adviser, entrepreneur, and author; writes the syndicated column The Truth About Money and hosts weekly radio and TV talk shows
Edelman Financial Center Inc **Ph:** 703-818-0800
12450 Fair Lakes Cir Suite 200
Fairfax, VA 22033
www.ricedelman.com

Edelstein, David
Film critic on NPR's Fresh Air
National Public Radio **Ph:** 202-513-2000
635 Massachusetts Ave NW **Fax:** 202-513-3329
Washington, DC 20001
www.npr.org

Edgar, Robert W (1943-)
General Secretary of the National Council of Churches USA
National Council of Churches **Ph:** 212-870-2227
475 Riverside Dr Suite 880 **Fax:** 212-870-2030
New York, NY 10115
www.ncccusa.org

Edmonds, Jim (1970-)
Professional baseball player
Saint Louis Cardinals **Ph:** 314-421-3060
250 Stadium Plaza **Fax:** 314-425-0640
Saint Louis, MO 63102
stlouis.cardinals.mlb.com

Edmonds, Kenneth "Babyface" (1958-)
Singer/songwriter; music producer
Edmonds Entertainment **Ph:** 323-860-1550
1635 N Cahuenga Blvd 5th Fl **Fax:** 323-860-1558
Los Angeles, CA 90028
www.babyfacemusic.com

Edson, Margaret (1961-)
Dramatist (Wit)
Farrar Straus & Giroux **Ph:** 212-741-6900
19 Union Sq W
New York, NY 10003
www.fsgbooks.com

Edwards, Anthony (1962-)
Actor
United Talent Agency **Ph:** 310-273-6700
9560 Wilshire Blvd 5th Fl **Fax:** 310-247-1111
Beverly Hills, CA 90212

Edwards, Blake (1922-)
Movie producer/director/writer
Pitt Group **Ph:** 310-246-4800
9465 Wilshire Blvd Suite 470 **Fax:** 310-275-9258
Beverly Hills, CA 90212

Edwards, Carl (1979-)
NASCAR driver
Roush Racing **Ph:** 704-720-4100
4600 Roush Pl NW
Concord, NC 28027
www.roushracing.com

Edwards, Chet (1951-)
US Representative from Texas (Democrat)
2264 Rayburn Bldg **Ph:** 202-225-6105
Washington, DC 20515 **Fax:** 202-225-0350
edwards.house.gov

Edwards, Donnie (1973-)
Professional football player
San Diego Chargers **Ph:** 858-574-4500
4020 Murphy Canyon Rd **Fax:** 858-292-2760
San Diego, CA 92123
www.chargers.com

Edwards, Herm (1954-)
Football coach
Kansas City Chiefs **Ph:** 816-920-9300
Arrowhead Stadium **Fax:** 816-920-4315
1 Arrowhead Dr
Kansas City, MO 64129
www.kcchiefs.com

Edwards, John (1953-)
Former US Senator and trial lawyer; former candidate for Vice President of the US
Center on Poverty Work & Opportunity **Ph:** 919-843-8796
UNC Law School
Van Hecke-Wettach Hall
100 Ridge Rd CB 3380
Chapel Hill, NC 27599
www.law.unc.edu/Centers

Edwards, N Murray
Co-owner of the Calgary Flames hockey franchise
Calgary Flames **Ph:** 403-777-2177
Pengrowth Saddledome **Fax:** 403-777-2195
555 Saddledome Rise SE
Calgary, AB T2G2W1
www.calgaryflames.com

Edwards, Torri (1977-)
Track & field athlete (runner)
HSInternational **Ph:** 949-753-9153
9871 Irvine Center Dr
Irvine, CA 92618
www.hsi.net

Edwardson, John
Chairman of the Board of Directors and CEO of CDW Corp
CDW Corp **Ph:** 847-465-6000
200 N Milwaukee Ave
Vernon Hills, IL 60061
newsroom.cdw.com/executives/board.html

Egan, Brian
Co-host, with Ben Campbell, of Ben & Brian, a country music radio program
Premiere Radio Networks Inc **Ph:** 818-377-5300
Ben & Brian **Fax:** 818-377-5333
15260 Ventura Blvd 5th Fl
Sherman Oaks, CA 91403
www.benandbrian.com

Egielski, Richard (1952-)
Children's book writer and illustrator (The Tub People; Hey Al)
HarperCollins Children's Books **Ph:** 212-261-6500
1350 Ave of the Americas
New York, NY 10019
www.harperchildrens.com

Egoyan, Atom (1960-)
Independent filmmaker
Great North Artists Management **Ph:** 416-925-2051 **Fax:** 416-925-3904
350 Dupont St
Toronto, ON M5R1V9
www.egofilmarts.com

Ehlers, Vernon J (1934-)
US Representative from Michigan (Republican)
1714 Longworth Bldg **Ph:** 202-225-3831
Washington, DC 20515 **Fax:** 202-225-5144
www.house.gov/ehlers

Ehrlich, Robert L Jr (1957-)
Governor of Maryland (Republican)
State House **Ph:** 410-974-3901
100 State Cir **Fax:** 410-974-3275
Annapolis, MD 21401 **TF:** 800-811-8336
www.gov.state.md.us

Eichman, Erich
Books Editor of the Wall Street Journal
Wall Street Journal **Ph:** 212-416-2000
1 World Financial Center **Fax:** 212-416-4215
200 Liberty St
New York, NY 10281
www.opinionjournal.com/bios/bio_eichman.html

Eisenberg, Alan (1935-)
Executive Director of Actors' Equity Association, the labor union that represents American actors and stage managers working in the professional theatre
Actors' Equity Assn **Ph:** 212-869-8530
165 W 46th St **Fax:** 212-719-9815
New York, NY 10036
www.actorsequity.org

Eisenhower, Dwight D (1890-1969)
34th US President
Dwight D Eisenhower Library & Museum **Ph:** 785-263-6700 **TF:** 877-746-4453
200 SE 4th St
Abilene, KS 67410
www.dwightdeisenhower.com

Eisenhower, Mamie Doud (1896-1979)
Former First Lady of the US (wife of President Dwight D Eisenhower)
Dwight D Eisenhower Library & Museum **Ph:** 785-263-6700 **TF:** 877-746-4453
200 SE 4th St
Abilene, KS 67410
www.dwightdeisenhower.com

Eisenstaedt, Alfred (1898-1995)
Photojournalist
Gallery M **Ph:** 303-331-8400
2830 E 3rd Ave
Denver, CO 80206
www.gallerym.com

Eisman, Hy (1927-)
Writes and draws the classic comic strips Popeye & The Katzenjammer Kids (the world's oldest continuing comic strip)
King Features Syndicate Inc **Ph:** 212-455-4000
888 7th Ave 2nd Fl
New York, NY 10019
www.kingfeatures.com

Eismann, Jonathan
Chef & restauranteur
Pacific Time Restaurant **Ph:** 305-534-5979
915 Lincoln Rd
Miami Beach, FL 33139
www.pacifictimerestaurant.com

Ejabat, Mory
Co-founder, chairman, and CEO of Zhone Technologies
Zhone Technologies Inc **Ph:** 510-777-7000
7001 Oakport St **Fax:** 510-777-7001
Oakland, CA 94621
www.zhone.com

Elam, Jason (1970-)
Professional football player
Denver Broncos **Ph:** 303-649-9000
13655 Broncos Pkwy **Fax:** 303-649-9354
Englewood, CO 80112
www.denverbroncos.com

Elder, Larry (1952-)
Host of a radio talk show on current issues; also writes a nationally syndicated newspaper column
ABC Radio Networks **Ph:** 212-456-7777
444 Madison Ave
New York, NY 100222
www.larryelder.com

Eldredge, Todd (1971-)
Figure skater
Stars on Ice **Ph:** 216-436-3708
IMG
1360 E 9th St Suite 100
Cleveland, OH 44114
www.toddeldredge.net

Elfman, Jenna (1971-)
Actor
Creative Artists Agency **Ph:** 310-288-4545
9830 Wilshire Blvd **Fax:** 310-288-4800
Beverly Hills, CA 90212
www.jennaelfman.com

Elias, Patrik (1976-)
Professional hockey player
New Jersey Devils **Ph:** 201-935-6050
Continental Airlines Arena **Fax:** 201-935-2127
50 Rt 120N
East Rutherford, NJ 07073
www.newjerseydevils.com

Eliot, Jan
Creator of the comic strip Stone Soup
Universal Press Syndicate **Ph:** 816-932-6600
4520 Main St
Kansas City, MO 64111
www.amuniversal.com/ups/features

Elizondo, Hector (1936-)
Actor
William Morris Agency **Ph:** 310-859-4000
1 William Morris Pl **Fax:** 310-859-4462
Beverly Hills, CA 90212

Eller, Timothy
Chairman and CEO of Centex Corp, a leading home building company
Centex Corp **Ph:** 214-981-5000
2728 N Harwood St
Dallas, TX 75201
www.centex.com

Ellerbee, Linda (1944-)
Host of Nick News (which is produced by Lucky Duck Productions)
Lucky Duck Productions **Ph:** 212-463-0029
96 Morton St 4th Fl **Fax:** 212-463-7049
New York, NY 10014

Elliott, David James (1960-)
Actor
Creative Artists Agency **Ph:** 310-288-4545
9830 Wilshire Blvd **Fax:** 310-288-4800
Beverly Hills, CA 90212
www.cbs.com/primetime/jag

Elliott, Missy (1971-)
Hip-hop performer
Creative Artists Agency **Ph:** 310-288-4545
9830 Wilshire Blvd **Fax:** 310-288-4800
Beverly Hills, CA 90212
www.missy-elliott.com

Ellis, C Jack (1946-)
Mayor of Macon, Georgia
700 Poplar St **Ph:** 478-751-7170
Macon, GA 31201 **Fax:** 478-751-7931
www.cityofmacon.net

Ellis, Joseph
Nonfiction author
Knopf Publishing/Author Mail **Ph:** 212-782-9000
1745 Broadway
New York, NY 10019
www.randomhouse.com/knopf

Ellis, Rehema
NBC news correspondent
NBC News **Ph:** 212-664-4249
30 Rockefeller Plaza
New York, NY 10112
www.msnbc.msn.com/id/3689499

Ellison, Lawrence J (1944-)
Co-founder and CEO of Oracle Corp
Oracle Corp **Ph:** 650-506-7000
500 Oracle Pkwy **Fax:** 650-506-7200
Redwood Shores, CA 94065
www.oracle.com/corporate

Ellman, Steve
Chairman and CEO of the Phoenix Coyotes hockey team; chairman & CEO of the Ellman Companies
Coyotes Hockey LLC **Ph:** 623-463-8800
5800 W Glenn Dr Suite 350 **Fax:** 623-463-8810
Glendale, AZ 85301
www.phoenixcoyotes.com

Ellroy, James (1948-)
Writer of crime fiction (Black Dahlia; LA Confidential)
Warner Books **Ph:** 212-522-7200
c/o Author Mail
1271 Ave of the Americas
New York, NY 10020
www.twbookmark.com

Elrod, Jack (1924-)
Writes and draws the comic strip Mark Trail, which was originally created by artist and naturalist Ed Dodd in 1946
King Features Syndicate Inc **Ph:** 212-455-4000
888 7th Ave 2nd Fl
New York, NY 10019
www.kingfeatures.com

Els, Ernie (1969-)
Professional golfer
PGA Tour **Ph:** 904-285-3700
100 PGA Tour Blvd
Ponte Vedra Beach, FL 32082
www.ernieels.com

Elway, John (1960-)
Former professional football player (quarterback); co-owner and CEO of Arena Football's Colorado Crush
Colorado Crush **Ph:** 303-405-1100
Pepsi Center
1000 Chopper Cir
Denver, CO 80204
www.johnelway.com

Elwes, Cary (1962-)
Actor
United Talent Agency **Ph:** 310-273-6700
9560 Wilshire Blvd 5th Fl **Fax:** 310-247-1111
Beverly Hills, CA 90212

Emanuel, Rahm (1959-)
US Representative from Illinois (Democrat); chairman of the Democratic Congressional Campaign Committee
1319 Longworth Bldg **Ph:** 202-225-4061
Washington, DC 20515 **Fax:** 202-225-5603
www.house.gov/emanuel

Emberley, Ed (1931-)
Children's books writer & illustrator (drawing books and picture books)
Little Brown & Co **Ph:** 212-522-7200
Author Mail
1271 Ave of the Americas
New York, NY 10020
www.edemberley.com

Emerson, Jo Ann (1950-)
US Representative from Missouri (Republican)
2440 Rayburn Bldg **Ph:** 202-225-4404
Washington, DC 20515 **Fax:** 202-226-0326
www.house.gov/emerson

Emery, Ray (1982-)
Professional hockey player
Ottawa Senators **Ph:** 613-599-0250
Corel Center **Fax:** 613-599-0358
1000 Palladium Dr
Kanata, ON K2V1A5
www.ottawasenators.com

Eminem (1972-)
Actor, rapper; real name is Marshall Bruce Mathers III
United Talent Agency **Ph:** 310-273-6700
9560 Wilshire Blvd 5th Fl **Fax:** 310-247-1111
Beverly Hills, CA 90212
www.eminem.com

Emme (1964-)
Plus-size supermodel, writer, entrepreneur, and TV host
Emme Associates Inc **Ph:** 201-768-7592
PO Box 546 **Fax:** 201-768-5845
Closter, NJ 07624
www.emmesupermodel.com

Emmerich, Roland (1955-)
Movie producer/director/writer
Creative Artists Agency **Ph:** 310-288-4545
8930 Wilshire Blvd **Fax:** 310-288-4800
Beverly Hills, CA 90212

Enberg, Dick (1935-)
Sports broadcaster
CBS Sports **Ph:** 212-975-4321
51 W 52nd St
New York, NY 10019
cbs.sportsline.com/cbssports/team

Engel, Eliot L (1947-)
US Representative from New York (Democrat)
2161 Rayburn Bldg **Ph:** 202-225-2464
Washington, DC 20515 **Fax:** 202-225-5513
www.house.gov/engel

Engel, Richard
NBC News correspondent based in Baghdad
NBC News **Ph:** 212-664-4249
30 Rockefeller Plaza
New York, NY 10112
www.msnbc.msn.com/id/3689499

Engelbart, Douglas, PhD (1925-)
Inventor of the computer mouse
Bootstrap Institute **Ph:** 510-713-3550
6505 Kaiser Dr **Fax:** 510-792-3506
Fremont, CA 94555
www.bootstrap.org

Engelbreit, Mary (1952-)
Artist/illustrator & entrepreneur
Mary Engelbreit Studios **Ph:** 314-726-5646
6900 Delmar Blvd **Fax:** 314-726-5808
Saint Louis, MO 63130
www.maryengelbreit.com

Engen, Travis
President & CEO of Alcan Inc
Alcan Inc **Ph:** 514-848-8000
1188 Sherbrooke W **Fax:** 514-848-8115
Montreal, QC H3A3G2
www.alcan.com

Enger, Leif
Author (Peace Like a River)
Grove/Atlantic Inc **Ph:** 212-614-7860
841 Broadway **Fax:** 212-614-7886
New York, NY 10003
www.groveatlantic.com

Engibous, Thomas J
Chairman of Texas Instruments
Texas Instruments Inc **Ph:** 972-995-2011
12500 TI Blvd **Fax:** 972-995-4360
Dallas, TX 75243
www.ti.com

English, Diane (1948-)
Producer & writer; creator of Murphy Brown
International Creative Management **Ph:** 310-550-4000
8942 Wilshire Blvd
Beverly Hills, CA 90211

English, Phil (1956-)
US Representative from Pennsylvania (Republican)
1410 Longworth Bldg **Ph:** 202-225-5406
Washington, DC 20515 **Fax:** 202-225-3103
www.house.gov/english

English, Todd
Chef; owner of several restaurants (which make up the Olive Group)
Olive Group **Ph:** 617-242-9715
90 Main St **Fax:** 617-242-1333
Charlestown, MA 02129
www.toddenglish.com

Engvall, Bill (1957-)
Comedian
Parallel Entertainment **Ph:** 310-279-1123
9255 W Sunset Blvd Suite 1040 **Fax:** 310-279-1147
Los Angeles, CA 90069
www.billengvall.com

Ennico, Cliff
Expert on the legal & financial issues facing startup and growing companies; host of the PBS Money Hunt series and its spinoff, Money Hunt Small Business Challenge, and author of the syndicated column Succeeding in Your Business
Creators Syndicate Inc **Ph:** 310-337-7003
5777 W Century Blvd Suite 700 **Fax:** 310-337-7625
Los Angeles, CA 90045
www.creators.com

Ensign, John (1958-)
US Senator from Nevada (Republican)
364 Russell Bldg **Ph:** 202-224-6244
Washington, DC 20510 **Fax:** 202-228-2193
ensign.senate.gov

Ensler, Eve (1953-)
Playwright (The Vagina Monologues)
William Morris Agency **Ph:** 310-859-4000
151 El Camino Dr **Fax:** 310-859-4462
Beverly Hills, CA 90212
www.vday.org/contents/vday/aboutvday

Ensor, David
CNN's national security correspondent
CNN **Ph:** 202-898-7900
CNN Bldg
820 1st St NE
Washington, DC 20002
www.cnn.com/CNN/anchors_reporters

Enya (1961-)
Celtic music singer
Warner Bros Records **Ph:** 818-846-9090
PO Box 6868 **Fax:** 818-846-8474
Burbank, CA 91510
www.enya.com

Enzi, Mike (1944-)
US Senator from Wyoming (Republican)
379A Russell Bldg **Ph:** 202-224-3424
Washington, DC 20510 **Fax:** 202-228-0359
enzi.senate.gov

Ephron, Nora (1941-)
Screenwriter; also directs the movies (You've Got Mail, Sleepless in Seattle)
William Morris Agency **Ph:** 212-586-5100
1325 Ave of the Americas **Fax:** 212-246-3583
New York, NY 10019

Epperson, Sharon
CNBC personal finance correspondent
CNBC **Ph:** 201-585-2622
900 Sylvan Ave
Englewood Cliffs, NJ 07632
moneycentral.msn.com/cnbc/tv

Epps, Omar (1973-)
Actor
International Creative Management **Ph:** 310-550-4000
8942 Wilshire Blvd
Beverly Hills, CA 90211
www.fox.com/house

Epstein, Richard (1943-)
Law professor and a Senior Fellow at the Hoover Institution
University of Chicago Law School **Ph:** 773-702-9563
1111 E 60th St
Chicago, IL 60637
www.law.uchicago.edu/faculty/epstein

Erat, Martin (1981-)
Professional hockey player
Nashville Predators **Ph:** 615-770-7825
Gaylord Entertainment Center **Fax:** 615-770-2341
501 Broadway
Nashville, TN 37203
www.nashvillepredators.com

Erbe, Bonnie
Host of To the Contrary on PBS; is also a syndicated columnist
To the Contrary **Ph:** 202-973-2066
1825 K St NW Suite 501
Washington, DC 20006
www.pbs.org/ttc

Erdrich, Louise (1954-)
Novelist (Love Medicine; The Master Butchers Singing Club)
Andrew Wylie Agency **Ph:** 212-246-0069
250 W 57th St Suite 2114
New York, NY 10107
www.louiseerdrichbooks.com

Eresman, Randy
President & CEO of EnCana Corp, a leading oil and gas producer in North America
EnCana Corp **Ph:** 403-645-2000
1800-855 2nd St SW **Fax:** 403-645-3400
PO Box 2850
Calgary, AB T2P2S5
www.encana.com

Ergen, Charles W (1953-)
Founder, chairman, and CEO of EchoStar Communications, parent company of DISH Network
EchoStar Communications Corp **Ph:** 303-723-1000
9601 S Meridian Blvd
Englewood, CO 80112
www.echostar.com

Erickson, Donna
Writes the syndicated column Donna's Day, featuring creative ideas, activities, games, and projects designed to bring families together
King Features Syndicate Inc **Ph:** 212-455-4000
888 7th Ave 2nd Fl
New York, NY 10019
www.kingfeatures.com

Ernst, Mark (1959-)
Chairman, president, and CEO of H&R Block
H & R Block Inc **Ph:** 816-753-6900
4400 Main St
Kansas City, MO 64111
hrblock.com/presscenter

Ernst, Max (1891-1976)
German modernist painter (he was once married to Peggy Guggenheim)
Solomon R Guggenheim Museum **Ph:** 212-423-3500
1071 5th Ave
New York, NY 10128
www.guggenheimcollection.org

Erstad, Darin (1974-)
Professional baseball player
Los Angeles Angels of Anaheim **Ph:** 714-940-2000
Angel Stadium **Fax:** 714-940-2205
2000 Gene Autry Way
Anaheim, CA 92806
losangeles.angels.mlb.com

Erving, Julius (1950-)
Former professional basketball player; member of the Basketball Hall of Fame
Naismith Memorial Basketball Hall of Fame **Ph:** 413-781-6500
Fax: 413-781-1939
1000 W Columbus Ave **TF:** 877-446-6752
Springfield, MA 01105
www.hoophall.com

Erwitt, Elliott (1928-)
Photographer
Magnum Photos **Ph:** 212-929-6000
151 W 25th St **Fax:** 212-929-9325
New York, NY 10001
www.elliotterwitt.com

Esche, Robert (1978-)
Professional hockey player
Philadelphia Flyers **Ph:** 215-465-4500
Wachovia Center **Fax:** 215-389-9403
3601 S Broad St
Philadelphia, PA 19148
www.philadelphiaflyers.com

Eschenbach, Christoph (1940-)
Conductor and concert pianist; music director of the Philadelphia Orchestra
Philadelphia Orchestra **Ph:** 215-893-1900
260 S Broad St Suite 1600 **Fax:** 215-875-7649
Philadelphia, PA 19102
www.christoph-eschenbach.com

Escobar, Kelvim (1976-)
Professional baseball player
Los Angeles Angels of Anaheim **Ph:** 714-940-2000
Angel Stadium **Fax:** 714-940-2205
2000 Gene Autry Way
Anaheim, CA 92806
losangeles.angels.mlb.com

Eshoo, Anna G (1942-)
US Representative from California (Democrat)
205 Cannon Bldg **Ph:** 202-225-8104
Washington, DC 20515 **Fax:** 202-225-8890
www-eshoo.house.gov

Esiason, Boomer (1961-)
Sports commentator and former professional football player (quarterback)
CBS Sports **Ph:** 212-975-4321
51 W 52nd St
New York, NY 10019
cbs.sportsline.com/cbssports/team

Eskew, Michael L
Chairman and CEO of UPS
UPS Inc **Ph:** 404-828-6000
55 Glenlake Pkwy NE **Fax:** 404-828-6562
Atlanta, GA 30328
ups.com/pressroom/corp/board/board

Esquivel, Laura (1950-)
Author of Like Water for Chocolate
Vintage/Anchor Publicity **Ph:** 212-572-2420
1745 Broadway 20th Fl
New York, NY 10019
www.randomhouse.com/anchor

Essen, Richard J
Attorney; expert in the area of DUI defense
Essen Essen Susaneck Canet & Goodis PA **Ph:** 305-935-6680
Fax: 305-935-2314
Aventura Corporate Ctr **TF:** 888-303-7736
20801 Biscayne Blvd Suite 300
Aventura, FL 33180
www.richardessen.com

Essman, Susie
Comedian; actor
William Morris Agency **Ph:** 310-859-4000
1 William Morris Pl **Fax:** 310-859-4462
Beverly Hills, CA 90212
www.susieessman.com

Essner, Robert
Chairman, president, and CEO of the Wyeth Corp
Wyeth Corp **Ph:** 973-660-5000
5 Giralda Farms
Madison, NJ 07940
www.wyeth.com

Estefan, Gloria (1957-)
Latin singer
Creative Artists Agency **Ph:** 310-288-4545
9830 Wilshire Blvd **Fax:** 310-288-4800
Beverly Hills, CA 90212
www.gloriaestefan.com

Estrich, Susan (1952-)
Politician (was national campaign manager for Michael Dukakis), professor, lawyer, and writer; syndicated columnist
Creators Syndicate Inc **Ph:** 310-337-7003
5777 W Century Blvd Suite 700 **Fax:** 310-337-7625
Los Angeles, CA 90045
www.creators.com/opinion.html

Eszterhas, Joe (1944-)
Screenwriter (Showgirls, Basic Instinct, Flashdance, Jagged Edge)
William Morris Agency **Ph:** 310-859-4000
1 William Morris Pl **Fax:** 310-859-4462
Beverly Hills, CA 90212

Etheridge, Bob (1941-)
US Representative from North Carolina (Democrat)
1533 Longworth Bldg **Ph:** 202-225-4531
Washington, DC 20515 **Fax:** 202-225-5662
www.house.gov/etheridge

Etheridge, Melissa (1961-)
Singer
Creative Artists Agency **Ph:** 310-288-4545
9830 Wilshire Blvd **Fax:** 310-288-4800
Beverly Hills, CA 90212
www.melissaetheridge.com

Eugenides, Jeffrey (1960-)
Novelist (Middlesex)
Farrar Straus & Giroux **Ph:** 212-741-6900
19 Union Sq W
New York, NY 10003
www.jeffreyeugenides.com

Evanescence
Alternative band
Creative Artists Agency **Ph:** 212-277-9000
162 5th Ave 6th Fl **Fax:** 212-277-9099
New York, NY 10019
www.evanescence.com

Evans, Greg
Creator of the comic strip Luann
United Feature Syndicate **Ph:** 212-293-8500
200 Madison Ave
New York, NY 10016
www.unitedfeatures.com

Evans, Lane (1951-)
US Representative from Illinois (Democrat)
2211 Rayburn Bldg **Ph:** 202-225-5905
Washington, DC 20515 **Fax:** 202-225-5396
www.house.gov/evans

Evans, Lee (1981-)
Professional football player
Buffalo Bills **Ph:** 716-648-1800
Ralph Wilson Stadium **Fax:** 716-649-6446
1 Bills Dr
Orchard Park, NY 14127
www.buffalobills.com

Evans, Nicholas (1950-)
Author of The Horse Whisperer
Bantam Dell Publicity **Ph:** 212-782-9000
1745 Broadway
New York, NY 10019
www.randomhouse.com/bantamdell

Evans, Richard Paul (1962-)
Author of The Christmas Box
Richard Paul Evans Inc **Ph:** 801-532-6267
236 S 300 East **Fax:** 801-532-6358
Salt Lake City, UT 84111
www.richardpaulevans.com

Evans, Sara (1971-)
Country singer
William Morris Agency **Ph:** 615-963-3000
1600 Division St Suite 300 **Fax:** 615-963-3090
Nashville, TN 37203
www.saraevans.com

Evans, Tony
Senior pastor of Oak Cliff Bible Fellowship in Dallas; founder & president of The Urban Alternative, a national organization that seeks to bring about spiritual renewal in urban America through the church
Urban Alternative **Ph:** 214-943-3868
PO Box 4000 **Fax:** 214-943-2632
Dallas, TX 75208 **TF:** 800-800-3222
www.tonyevans.org

Evanson, Paul
Chairman, President and CEO of Allegheny Energy
Allegheny Energy Inc **Ph:** 724-837-3000
800 Cabin Hill Dr **Fax:** 724-830-5284
Greensburg, PA 15601 **TF:** 800-255-3443
www.alleghenyenergy.com

Eve (1978-)
Singer/rapper and actor; full name is Eve Jeffers
Creative Artists Agency **Ph:** 310-288-4545
9830 Wilshire Blvd **Fax:** 310-288-4800
Beverly Hills, CA 90212
www.upn.com/shows/eve

Everett, Rupert (1959-)
Actor
International Creative Management **Ph:** 310-550-4000
8942 Wilshire Blvd
Beverly Hills, CA 90211

Everett, Terry (1937-)
US Representative from Alabama (Republican)
2312 Rayburn Bldg **Ph:** 202-225-2901
Washington, DC 20515 **Fax:** 202-225-8913
wwwc.house.gov/everett

Everson, Mark W (1954-)
Commissioner of the Internal Revenue Service
Internal Revenue Service **Ph:** 202-622-9511
1111 Constitution Ave NW **Fax:** 202-622-5756
Washington, DC 20224
www.irs.gov/irs

Evert, Chris (1954-)
Former pro tennis player
7200 W Camino Real **Ph:** 561-394-2400
Boca Raton, FL 33433 **Fax:** 561-394-2479
www.chrisevert.org

F

Faber, David
Anchor and co-producer of CNBC's original documentaries and long form programming as well as a contributor to CNBC's Squawk on the Street; also does the Faber Report twice a week
CNBC **Ph:** 201-735-2622
900 Sylvan Ave
Englewood Cliffs, NJ 07632
moneycentral.msn.com/cnbc/tv

Fagan, Kevin (1956-)
Creator of the comic strip Drabble
United Feature Syndicate **Ph:** 212-293-8500
200 Madison Ave
New York, NY 10016
www.unitedfeatures.com

Fager, Jeffrey (1954-)
Executive Producer of 60 Minutes
CBS News **Ph:** 212-975-3247
524 W 57th St
New York, NY 10019
www.cbsnews.com

Fahey, John M Jr (1953-)
President & CEO of the National Geographic Society
National Geographic Society **Ph:** 202-857-7000
1145 17th St NW
Washington, DC 20036
press.nationalgeographic.com/pressroom

Fahey, Mike (1943-)
Mayor of Omaha, Nebraska
1819 Farnam St Suite 300 **Ph:** 402-444-5000
Omaha, NE 68183 **Fax:** 402-444-6059
www.ci.omaha.ne.us

Fahner, Tyrone C
Leading business lawyer and former attorney general of the state of Illinois
Mayer Brown Rowe & Maw LLP **Ph:** 312-701-7062 **Fax:** 312-706-8622
71 S Wacker Dr
Chicago, IL 60606
www.mayerbrownrowe.com

Fairbank, Richard
Founder, chairman, and CEO of Capital One
Capital One Financial Corp **Ph:** 703-720-1000
1680 Capital One Dr **Fax:** 703-720-1755
McLean, VA 22102 **TF:** 800-801-1164
www.capitalone.com/about/corpinfo

Falco, Edie (1963-)
Actor
Innovative Artists **Ph:** 310-656-0400
1505 10th St **Fax:** 310-656-0456
Santa Monica, CA 90401
www.hbo.com/sopranos/cast

Falco, Randy
President & COO of NBC Universal Television Group
NBC Universal Television Group **Ph:** 212-664-4444 **Fax:** 212-664-3720
30 Rockefeller Plaza 52nd Fl
New York, NY 10112
www.nbcuni.com

Falconer, Ian (1959-)
Author, illustrator, set designer; creator of the Olivia children's series
Simon & Schuster Books for Young Readers **Ph:** 212-698-7000
1230 Ave of the Americas
New York, NY 10020
www.simonsays.com

Faldo, Nick (1957-)
Professional golfer, businessman, and broadcaster
PGA Tour **Ph:** 904-285-3700
100 PGA Tour Blvd
Ponte Vedra Beach, FL 32082
www.nickfaldo.com

Faleomavaega, Eni FH (1943-)
US Delegate from American Samoa (Democrat)
2422 Rayburn Bldg **Ph:** 202-225-8577
Washington, DC 20515 **Fax:** 202-225-8757
www.house.gov/faleomavaega

Falk, Thomas (1958-)
Chairman and CEO of Kimberly-Clark
Kimberly-Clark Corp **Ph:** 972-281-1200
351 Phelps Dr
Irving, TX 75038
www.kimberly-clark.com

Fallon, Jimmy (1974-)
Comedian; actor
United Talent Agency **Ph:** 310-273-6700
9560 Wilshire Blvd 5th Fl **Fax:** 310-247-1111
Beverly Hills, CA 90212

Fallows, James (1949-)
National correspondent for The Atlantic Monthly
Atlantic Monthly **Ph:** 646-695-8500
711 3rd Ave 12th Fl **Fax:** 646-935-4157
New York, NY 10017
www.theatlantic.com

Falwell, Jerry (1933-)
A fundamentalist Baptist pastor, televangelist, and founder of the Moral Majority
Jerry Falwell Ministries **Ph:** 434-582-7618
Lynchburg, VA 24514
www.falwell.com

Fanning, Dakota (1994-)
Child actor
Osbrink Talent Agency **Ph:** 818-760-2488
4343 Lankershim Blvd Suite 100 **Fax:** 818-760-0991
Universal City, CA 91602

Faraci, John V
Chairman & CEO of International Paper Co
International Paper Co **Ph:** 203-541-8660
400 Atlantic St **Fax:** 203-541-8200
Stamford, CT 06921
www.internationalpaper.com

Farah, Joseph
Founder/CEO/editor of WorldNetDaily.com; non-fiction author; syndicated columnist; talk radio show host
Creators Syndicate Inc **Ph:** 310-337-7003
5777 W Century Blvd Suite 700 **Fax:** 310-337-7625
Los Angeles, CA 90045
www.creators.com/opinion.html

Farmer, Eunice
Writes the syndicated sewing advice column, Sew Simple; also runs Eunice Farmer Fabrics, a boutique fabric shop with sewing classes
King Features Syndicate Inc **Ph:** 212-455-4000
888 7th Ave 2nd Fl
New York, NY 10019
www.kingfeatures.com

Farmer, Nancy (1941-)
Author of books for young readers (The Ear the Eye and the Arm; A Girl Named Disaster; The House of the Scorpion)
Simon & Schuster Books for Young Readers **Ph:** 212-698-7000
1230 Ave of the Americas
New York, NY 10020
www.simonsays.com

Farnsworth, Elizabeth
Chief correspondent and principle substitute anchor for PBS's News Hour with Jim Lehrer
MacNeil/Lehrer Productions **Ph:** 703-998-2138
2700 S Quincy St Suite 250
Arlington, VA 22206
www.pbs.org/newshour/ww/farnsworth.html

Farr, David
Chairman, CEO, and president of Emerson Electric
Emerson Electric Co **Ph:** 314-553-2000
8000 W Florissant Ave
Saint Louis, MO 63136
www.gotoemerson.com/news/farr-bio.html

Farr, Sam (1941-)
US Representative from California (Democrat)
1221 Longworth Bldg **Ph:** 202-225-2861
Washington, DC 20515 **Fax:** 202-225-6791
www.farr.house.gov

Farrakhan, Louis (1933-)
Minister Farrakhan; leader of the Nation of Islam in the US; he was born Louis Eugene Walcott
Nation of Islam **Ph:** 773-324-6000
7531 S Stony Island Ave **Fax:** 773-324-6309
Chicago, IL 60649
www.noi.org

Farrell, Colin (1976-)
Actor
Creative Artists Agency **Ph:** 310-288-4545
9830 Wilshire Blvd **Fax:** 310-288-4800
Beverly Hills, CA 90212
www.colinfarrell.ie

Farrell, W James
Chairman of Illinois Toolworks
Illinois Tool Works Inc **Ph:** 847-724-7500
3600 W Lake Ave **Fax:** 847-657-4261
Glenview, IL 60025
www.itwinc.com

Farrelly, Bobby (1958-)
Producer/writer/director
Creative Artists Agency **Ph:** 310-288-4545
9830 Wilshire Blvd **Fax:** 310-288-4800
Beverly Hills, CA 90212

Farrelly, Peter (1956-)
Writer/director/producer
Creative Artists Agency **Ph:** 310-288-4545
9830 Wilshire Blvd **Fax:** 310-288-4800
Beverly Hills, CA 90212

Farrior, James (1975-)
Professional football player
Pittsburgh Steelers **Ph:** 412-432-7800
3400 S Water St **Fax:** 412-432-7878
Pittsburgh, PA 15203
www.pittsburghsteelers.com

Farris, G Steven
President, CEO, and COO of Apache Corp, an independent oil and gas exploration company
Apache Corp **Ph:** 713-296-6000
2000 Post Oak Blvd Suite 100
Houston, TX 77056
www.apachecorp.com

Fattah, Chaka (1956-)
US Representative from Pennsylvania (Democrat)
2301 Rayburn Bldg **Ph:** 202-225-4001
Washington, DC 20515 **Fax:** 202-225-5392
www.house.gov/fattah

Fauci, Anthony S, MD (1940-)
Director of the National Institute of Allergy & Infectious Diseases, National Institutes of Health
National Institute of Allergy & Infectious Diseases **Ph:** 301-496-2263 **Fax:** 301-496-4409
31 Center Dr Bldg 31 Rm 7A50
MSC 2520
Bethesda, MD 20892
www.niaid.nih.gov

Faulk, Marshall (1973-)
Professional football player
Saint Louis Rams **Ph:** 314-982-7267
1 Rams Way **Fax:** 314-770-9261
Earth City, MO 63045
www.marshallfaulk.com

Favre, Brett (1969-)
Professional football player
Green Bay Packers **Ph:** 920-569-7500
PO Box 10628 **Fax:** 920-569-7201
Green Bay, WI 54307
www.packers.com

Favreau, Jon (1966-)
Screenwriter; actor
Creative Artists Agency **Ph:** 310-288-4545
9830 Wilshire Blvd **Fax:** 310-288-4800
Beverly Hills, CA 90212
www.myspace.com/jonfavreau

Faw, Bob
NBC News national correspondent based in Washington, DC
NBC News **Ph:** 202-885-4200
4001 Nebraska Ave NW
Washington, DC 20016
www.msnbc.msn.com/id/3689499

Faxon, Brad (1961-)
Professional golfer
PGA Tour **Ph:** 904-285-3700
100 PGA Tour Blvd
Ponte Vedra Beach, FL 32082
www.pgatour.com/players

Feaster, Allison (1976-)
Professional basketball player
Charlotte Sting **Ph:** 704-357-0252
100 Hive Dr **Fax:** 704-335-0289
Charlote, NC 28217
www.wnba.com/sting

Federer, Roger (1981-)
Professional tennis player (Swiss)
ATP **Ph:** 904-285-8000
201 ATP Blvd **Fax:** 904-285-5966
Ponte Vedra Beach, FL 32082
www.rogerfederer.com

Fedorov, Sergei (1969-)
Professional hockey player
Columbus Blue Jackets **Ph:** 614-246-4625
Nationwide Arena **Fax:** 614-246-4007
200 W Nationwide Blvd 3rd Fl
Columbus, OH 43215
www.bluejackets.com

Fedotenko, Ruslan (1979-)
Professional hockey player
Tampa Bay Lightning **Ph:** 813-301-6600
St Pete Times Forum **Fax:** 813-301-1487
401 Channelside Dr
Tampa, FL 33602
www.tampabaylightning.com

Feeley, AJ (1977-)
Professional football player
San Diego Chargers **Ph:** 858-874-4500
4020 Murphy Canyon Rd **Fax:** 858-292-2760
San Diego, CA 92123
www.chargers.com

Feely, Jay (1976-)
Professional football player
New York Giants **Ph:** 201-935-8111
Giants Stadium **Fax:** 201-939-4134
East Rutherford, NJ 07073
www.giants.com

Feeney, Tom C (1958-)
US Representative from Florida (Republican)
323 Cannon Bldg **Ph:** 202-225-2706
Washington, DC 20515 **Fax:** 202-226-6299
www.house.gov/feeney

Fehr, Donald (1948-)
Executive director and general counsel of the Major League Baseball Player's Association
Major League Baseball Players Assn **Ph:** 212-826-0808
Fax: 212-752-4378
12 E 49th St 24th Fl
New York, NY 10017
mlbplayers.mlb.com/NASApp/mlb/pa/bios/fehr.jsp

Feiffer, Jules (1929-)
Cartoonist, author, playwright
Royce Carlton Inc **Ph:** 212-355-7700
866 United Nations Plaza **Fax:** 212-888-8659
New York, NY 10017
www.julesfeiffer.com

Feinberg, Kenneth R
Attorney and a leading expert in mediation and alternative dispute resolution; Special Settlement Master of the September 11th Victim Compensation Fund
Feinberg Group LLP **Ph:** 202-371-1110
Willard Office Bldg **Fax:** 202-962-9290
1455 Pennsylvania Ave NW Suite 390
Washington, DC 20004
www.thefeinberggroup.com

Feingold, Russell D (1953-)
US Senator from Wisconsin (Democrat)
506 Hart Bldg **Ph:** 202-224-5323
Washington, DC 20510 **Fax:** 202-224-2725
feingold.senate.gov

Feininger, Andreas (1906-1999)
Photographer
Gallery M **Ph:** 303-331-8400
2830 E 3rd Ave
Denver, CO 80206
www.gallerym.com

Feinstein, Dianne (1933-)
US Senator from California (Democrat)
331 Hart Bldg **Ph:** 202-224-3841
Washington, DC 20510 **Fax:** 202-228-3954
feinstein.senate.gov

Feinstein, Michael (1956-)
Singer/songwriter/pianist; considered one of the top interpreters of American popular song
William Morris Agency **Ph:** 310-859-4000
1 William Morris Pl **Fax:** 310-859-4462
Beverly Hills, CA 90212
www.michaelfeinstein.com

Feld, Kenneth
Chairman & CEO of Feld Entertainment Inc, which includes Ringling Bros Barnum & Bailey and Disney on Ice
Feld Entertainment Inc **Ph:** 703-448-4000
8607 Westwood Center Dr **Fax:** 703-448-4100
Vienna, VA 22182
www.feldentertainment.com

Feliz, Pedro (1975-)
Professional baseball player
San Francisco Giants **Ph:** 415-972-2000
AT & T Park
24 Willie Mays Plaza
San Francisco, CA 94107
sanfrancisco.giants.mlb.com

Feniger, Susan
Chef and restaurant owner-operator, with Mary Sue Milliken; the two have also hosted radio & TV food shows and are the creators of the Border Girls brand of fresh prepared foods
Border Grill **Ph:** 310-451-1655
1445 4th St
Santa Monica, CA 90401
www.marysueandsusan.com

Fenn, John B, PhD (1917-)
Winner of the 2002 Nobel Prize for Chemistry (one quarter of the prize) for the development of methods for identification and structure analyses of biological macromolecules
VCU Dept of Chemistry **Ph:** 804-828-1298
1001 W Main St **Fax:** 804-828-8599
PO Box 842006
Richmond, VA 23284
www.has.vcu.edu/che

Fennessy, Richard A
CEO of Insight, a leading IT solutions provider
Insight Enterprises Inc **Ph:** 480-333-3000
6820 S Harl Ave
Tempe, AZ 85283
www.insight.com

Ferdinand, Marie (1978-)
Professional basketball player
San Antonio Silver Stars **Ph:** 210-444-5050
1 SBC Center
San Antonio, TX 78219
www.wnba.com/silverstars

Ference, Andrew (1979-)
Professional hockey player
Calgary Flames **Ph:** 403-777-2177
Pengrowth Saddledome **Fax:** 403-777-2195
555 Saddledome Rise SE
Calgary, AB T2G2W1
www.calgaryflames.com

Ferguson, Mike (1970-)
US Representative from New Jersey (Republican)
214 Cannon Bldg **Ph:** 202-225-5361
Washington, DC 20515 **Fax:** 202-225-9460
www.house.gov/ferguson

Ferraro, Geraldine (1935-)
First woman vice-presidential candidate on a national party ticket (1984); TV analyst for FOX News
FOX News Channel **Ph:** 212-301-3000
1211 Ave of the Americas
New York, NY 10036
www.foxnews.com/fnctv

Ferrell, Will (1967-)
Actor & comedian
Creative Artists Agency **Ph:** 310-288-4545
9830 Wilshire Blvd **Fax:** 310-288-4800
Beverly Hills, CA 90212

Ferri, Alessandra (1963-)
A principal dancer for American Ballet Theatre
American Ballet Theatre **Ph:** 212-477-3030
890 Broadway **Fax:** 212-254-5938
New York, NY 10003
www.abt.org/dancers

Ferrigno, Lou (1952-)
Bodybuilder and personal trainer; portrayed The Incredible Hulk on television
Lou Ferrigno Enterprises Inc **Ph:** 310-395-2144
PO Box 1671
Santa Monica, CA 90406
www.louferrigno.com

Fetter, Trevor (1959-)
President and CEO of Tenet Healthcare
Tenet Healthcare Corp **Ph:** 469-893-2200
13737 Noel Rd
Dallas, TX 75240
www.tenethealth.com

Fettig, Jeff
Chairman and CEO of Whirlpool Corp
Whirlpool Corp **Ph:** 269-923-5000
2000 N M-63
Benton Harbor, MI 49022
www.whirlpoolcorp.com/governance

Feyerick, Deborah
CNN correspondent who specializes in criminal justice and terrorism
CNN New York **Ph:** 212-275-7800
Time Warner Ctr
10 Columbus Cir
New York, NY 10019
www.cnn.com/CNN/anchors_reporters

Fieger, Geoffrey (1950-)
Attorney; has represented Dr Jack Kevorkian and Jenny Jones
Fieger Fieger Kenney & Johnson PC **Ph:** 248-355-5555
Fax: 248-355-5148
19390 W 10-Mile Rd
Southfield, MI 48075
www.fiegerlaw.com

Field, Sally (1946-)
Actor
Creative Artists Agency **Ph:** 310-288-4545
9830 Wilshire Blvd **Fax:** 310-288-4800
Beverly Hills, CA 90212

Fielding, Fred F (1939-)
Attorney; former White House Counsel (1981-1986) and member of the 9/11 Commission
Wiley Rein & Fielding LLP **Ph:** 202-719-7320
1776 K St NW **Fax:** 202-719-7049
Washington, DC 20006
www.wrf.com

Fielding, Helen (1958-)
Author of the Bridget Jones books
Viking Publicity **Ph:** 212-366-2000
375 Hudson St
New York, NY 10014
us.penguingroup.com

Fields, Suzanne
Columnist and author
Creators Syndicate Inc **Ph:** 310-337-7003
5777 W Century Blvd Suite 700 **Fax:** 310-337-7625
Los Angeles, CA 90045
www.creators.com/opinion.html

Fiennes, Joseph (1970-)
Actor
Parseghian/Planco Management **Ph:** 212-777-7786
23 E 22nd St **Fax:** 212-777-8642
New York, NY 10010

Fiennes, Ralph (1962-)
Actor
Creative Artists Agency **Ph:** 310-288-4545
9830 Wilshire Blvd **Fax:** 310-288-4800
Beverly Hills, CA 90212

Filicia, Thom (1969-)
Design expert on Queer Eye for the Straight Guy
William Morris Agency **Ph:** 310-859-4000
1 William Morris Pl **Fax:** 310-859-4462
Beverly Hills, CA 90212
www.bravotv.com

Filner, Bob (1942-)
US Representative from California (Democrat)
2428 Rayburn Bldg **Ph:** 202-225-8045
Washington, DC 20515 **Fax:** 202-225-9073
www.house.gov/filner

Filo, David
Co-founder (with Jerry Yang) of Yahoo!
Yahoo! Inc **Ph:** 408-349-3300
701 1st Ave **Fax:** 408-349-3301
Sunnyvale, CA 94089
docs.yahoo.com/info/pr

Fineberg, Harvey V, MD, PhD (1945-)
President of the Institute of Medicine, National Academy of Sciences
Institute of Medicine **Ph:** 202-334-3300
National Academy of Sciences **Fax:** 202-334-3851
500 5th St NW
Washington, DC 20055
www.iom.edu

Finger, Alan
Yoga master; developed a form of yoga called ISHTA Yoga, the Integrated Science of Hatha Tantra and Ayurveda
Yoga Works **Ph:** 212-935-9642
160 E 56th 12th Fl **Fax:** 212-486-7775
New York, NY 10022
www.yogazone.com

Finley, Michael (1973-)
Professional basketball player
San Antonio Spurs **Ph:** 210-444-5000
1 SBC Center **Fax:** 210-444-5003
San Antonio, TX 78219
www.nba.com/spurs

Finley, Steve (1965-)
Professional baseball player
San Francisco Giants **Ph:** 415-972-2000
AT & T Park
24 Willie Mays Plaza
San Francisco, CA 94107
sanfrancisco.giants.mlb.com

Fireman, Paul B
Chairman and CEO of Reebok International
Reebok International Ltd **Ph:** 781-401-5000
1895 JW Foster Blvd **Fax:** 781-401-7402
Canton, MA 02021

Firth, Colin (1960-)
Actor
International Creative Management **Ph:** 310-550-4000
8942 Wilshire Blvd
Beverly Hills, CA 90211

Fischer, Jenna (1974-)
Actor
Odenkirk Talent Management **Ph:** 323-960-4777
650 N Bronson Ave Suite B-145
Los Angeles, CA 90004
www.nbc.com/The_Office

Fish, Mardy (1981-)
Professional tennis player
ATP **Ph:** 904-285-8000
201 ATP Blvd **Fax:** 904-285-5966
Ponte Vedra Beach, FL 32082
www.mardytennis.com

Fishburne, Laurence (1961-)
Actor
Paradigm **Ph:** 310-288-8000
360 N Crescent Dr **Fax:** 310-288-2000
North Bldg
Beverly Hills, CA 90210

Fisher, Carrie (1956-)
Actor; author
Creative Artists Agency **Ph:** 310-288-4545
9830 Wilshire Blvd **Fax:** 310-288-4800
Beverly Hills, CA 90212

Fisher, Donald G (1930-)
Founder and Chairman Emeritus of Gap Inc
Gap Inc **Ph:** 650-952-4400
2 Folsom St
San Francisco, CA 94105
www.gapinc.com

Fisher, Jeff (1958-)
Football coach
Tennessee Titans **Ph:** 615-555-4000
460 Great Circle Rd **Fax:** 615-565-4006
Nashville, TN 37228
www.titansonline.com

Fisher, Mary (1948-)
Speaker, author, and chronicler of the global AIDS epidemic; also an artist
Mary Fisher Productions Inc **Ph:** 561-832-9909
477 S Rosemary Ave Suite 325 **Fax:** 561-832-9668
West Palm Beach, FL 33401
www.maryfisher.com

Fishman, Steven
Chairman, CEO, and president of Big Lots
Big Lots Inc **Ph:** 614-278-6800
300 Phillipi Rd
Columbus, OH 43228
www.biglots.com

Fiske, Robert B Jr
Attorney; was independent counsel for the Whitewater investigation January-October 1994
Davis Polk & Wardwell **Ph:** 212-450-4090
450 Lexington Ave **Fax:** 212-450-3090
New York, NY 10017
www.dpw.com

Fitial, Benigno (1945-)
Governor of the Commonwealth of the Northern Mariana Islands; founder and member of the Covenant Party
Office of the Governor **Ph:** 670-664-2200
CB 10007 Capitol Hill **Fax:** 670-664-2211
Saipan, MP 96950
net.saipan.com/cftemplates/executive

Fittipaldi, Christian (1971-)
Race car driver; nephew of racing great Emerson Fittipaldi
Cheever Racing **Ph:** 317-824-5777
8266 Zionsville Rd **Fax:** 317-824-5780
Indianapolis, IN 46268
www.fittipaldionline.com

Fitzgerald, Larry (1983-)
Professional football player
Arizona Cardinals **Ph:** 602-379-0101
8701 S Hardy Dr **Fax:** 602-379-1819
Tempe, AZ 85284
www.azcardinals.com

Fitzgerald, Patrick J (1960-)
US Attorney for the Northern District of Illinois; currently serving as Special Counsel in the investigation of the alleged unauthorized disclosure of a CIA employee's identity
Dirksen Federal Bldg **Ph:** 312-353-5300
219 S Dearborn St 5th Fl
Chicago, IL 60604
www.usdoj.gov/usao/iln/osc

FitzGerald, Tom
San Francisco Chronicle columnist and writer of the syndicated column Open Season; both columns provide a compilation of recent humorous quotes from athletes, coaches, fans, columnists, and broadcasters
United Feature Syndicate **Ph:** 212-293-8500
200 Madison Ave
New York, NY 10016
www.unitedfeatures.com

Fitzpatrick, Mike (1963-)
US Representative from Pennsylvania (Republican)
1516 Longworth Bldg **Ph:** 202-225-4276
Washington, DC 20515 **Fax:** 202-225-9511
fitzpatrick.house.gov

FitzSimons, Dennis J (1950-)
Chairman, president, and CEO of the Tribune Co
Tribune Co **Ph:** 312-222-9100
435 N Michigan Ave **Fax:** 312-222-1573
Chicago, IL 60611
www.tribune.com/about

Flagg, Fannie (1941-)
Fiction writer (Fried Green Tomatoes at the Whistle Stop Cafe; Standing in the Rainbow)
Random House Publicity **Ph:** 212-782-9000
1745 Broadway
New York, NY 10019
www.randomhouse.com

Flake, Jeff (1962-)
US Representative from Arizona (Republican)
424 Cannon Bldg **Ph:** 202-225-2635
Washington, DC 20515 **Fax:** 202-226-4386
www.house.gov/flake

Flanders, Laura
Host of Radio Nation with Laura Flanders on Air America radio
Air America **Ph:** 646-274-4900
641 6th Ave
New York, NY 10011
www.airamericaradio.com

Flanery, Sean Patrick (1965-)
Actor
Gersh Agency **Ph:** 310-274-6611
232 N Canon Dr
Beverly Hills, CA 90210

Flatley, Michael (1958-)
Dancer, choreographer
Creative Artists Agency **Ph:** 310-288-4545
9830 Wilshire Blvd **Fax:** 310-288-4800
Beverly Hills, CA 90212
www.michaelflatley.com

Flatow, Ira (1949-)
NPR science correspondent; host of Talk of the Nation: Science Friday radio discussion show on science, technology, health, space, and the environment
National Public Radio **Ph:** 212-878-1430
New York Bureau
801 2nd Ave Suite 701
New York, NY 10017
www.sciencefriday.com

Flay, Bobby (1965-)
Chef; host of Food Network's BBQ with Bobby Flay, FoodNation, and Boy Meets Grill and is a regular on Iron Chef America
Food Network **Ph:** 212-398-8836
75 9th Ave **Fax:** 212-736-7716
New York, NY 10011
www.bobbyflay.com

Fleischman, John (1948-)
Science writer and author of the nonfiction book Phineas Gage: A Gruesome But True Story About Brain Science, a book for young adult readers
Houghton Mifflin Children's Books **Ph:** 617-351-5000
222 Berkeley St 8th Fl
Boston, MA 02116
www.houghtonmifflinbooks.com

Fleischman, Paul (1952-)
Author of fiction for young adults as well as children's picture books, poetry, and nonfiction works.
Candlewick Press **Ph:** 617-661-3330
2067 Massachusetts Ave **Fax:** 617-661-0565
Cambridge, MA 02140
www.paulfleischman.net

Fleischman, Sid (1920-)
Author of books for young readers (The Whipping Boy)
HarperCollins Children's Books **Ph:** 212-261-6500
1350 Ave of the Americas
New York, NY 10019
www.sidfleischman.com

Fleming, Denise (1950-)
Author/illustrator of children's picture books
Books for Young Readers **Ph:** 212-886-9200
Henry Holt & Co
115 W 18th St
New York, NY 10011
denisefleming.com

Fleming, Peggy (1948-)
Figure skater
IMG Inc **Ph:** 212-774-6732
825 7th Ave
New York, NY 10036
www.peggyfleming.net

Fleming, Renee (1959-)
Opera singer (soprano)
IMG Artists **Ph:** 212-994-3500
Carnegie Hall Tower **Fax:** 212-994-3550
152 W 57th St 5th Fl
New York, NY 10019
www.renee-fleming.com

Fletcher, Ernie (1952-)
Governor of Kentucky (Republican)
State Capitol Bldg **Ph:** 502-564-2611
700 Capitol Ave Rm 100 **Fax:** 502-564-2517
Frankfort, KY 40601
governor.ky.gov

Fletcher, London (1975-)
Professional football player
Buffalo Bills **Ph:** 716-648-1800
Ralph Wilson Stadium **Fax:** 716-649-6446
1 Bills Dr
Orchard Park, NY 14127
www.buffalobills.com

Fletcher, Martin
NBC News Tel Aviv bureau chief and correspondent
NBC News **Ph:** 212-664-4249
30 Rockefeller Plaza
New York, NY 10112
www.msnbc.msn.com/id/3689499

Fleury, Marc-Andre (1984-)
Professional hockey player
Pittsburgh Penguins **Ph:** 412-642-1300
1 Chatham Center Suite 400 **Fax:** 412-642-1859
Pittsburgh, PA 15219
www.pittsburghpenguins.com

Flintoff, Corey
NPR newscaster
National Public Radio **Ph:** 202-513-2000
635 Massachusetts Ave NW **Fax:** 202-513-3329
Washington, DC 20001
www.npr.org

Flockhart, Calista (1964-)
Actor
International Creative Management **Ph:** 310-550-4000
8942 Wilshire Blvd
Beverly Hills, CA 90211

Florence, Tyler
Chef; host of Food 911 and Tyler's Ultimate
Food Network **Ph:** 212-398-8836
75 9th Ave **Fax:** 212-736-7716
New York, NY 10011
www.foodnetwork.com

Flowers, Paulette
Writes the syndicated newspaper column Country Music Memo
King Features Syndicate Inc **Ph:** 212-455-4000
888 7th Ave 2nd Fl
New York, NY 10019
www.kingfeatures.com

Floyd, Cliff (1972-)
Professional baseball player
New York Mets **Ph:** 718-507-6387
Shea Stadium **Fax:** 718-507-6395
123-01 Roosevelt Ave
Flushing, NY 11368
newyork.mets.mlb.com

Flynn, Timothy P (1957-)
Chairman and CEO of KPMG LLP, an audit, tax, and risk advisory firm and the U.S. member firm of KPMG International, a Swiss cooperative
KPMG LLP **Ph:** 212-758-9700
345 Park Ave **Fax:** 212-758-9819
New York, NY 10154
www.kpmg.com/about/TPFlynn.asp

Flynt, Larry (1942-)
Chairman of Larry Flynt Publications and founder of Hustler Magazine for men
LFP Inc **Ph:** 323-651-5400
8484 Wilshire Blvd Suite 900 **Fax:** 323-651-3525
Beverly Hills, CA 90211
www.flyntdigital.com

Fo, Dario (1926-)
Italian playwright (political satires and farces), actor, and director
Grove/Atlantic Inc **Ph:** 212-614-7860
841 Broadway **Fax:** 212-614-7886
New York, NY 10003
www.groveatlantic.com

Fogel, Robert W (1926-)
Winner (with Douglass C North) of the 1993 Noble Prize in Economic Sciences
University of Chicago **Ph:** 773-708-7709
Dept of Economics **Fax:** 773-702-2901
1126 E 59th St
Chicago, IL 60637
economics.uchicago.edu

Fogerty, John (1945-)
Singer/songwriter; a founding member of Creedence Clearwater Revival
Creative Artists Agency **Ph:** 310-288-4545
9830 Wilshire Blvd **Fax:** 310-288-4800
Beverly Hills, CA 90212
www.johnfogerty.com

Fogg, Josh (1976-)
Professional baseball player
Colorado Rockies **Ph:** 303-292-0200
Coors Field **Fax:** 303-296-2066
2001 Blake St
Denver, CO 80205
colorado.rockies.mlb.com

Folbaum, Rick
Anchor for Fox News Live
FOX News Channel **Ph:** 212-301-3000
1211 Ave of the Americas
New York, NY 10036
www.foxnews.com/fnctv

Foley, Mark (1954-)
US Representative from Florida (Republican)
104 Cannon Bldg **Ph:** 202-225-5792
Washington, DC 20515 **Fax:** 202-225-3132
www.house.gov/foley

Foley, Thomas S (1929-)
Attorney; former Speaker of the US House of Representatives and former ambassador to Japan
Akin Gump Strauss Hauer & Feld LLP **Ph:** 202-887-4170 **Fax:** 202-887-4288
1333 New Hampshire Ave NW
Washington, DC 20036
www.akingump.com

Foley, William
Chairman of the Board and CEO of Fidelity National Financial Inc
Fidelity National Financial **Ph:** 904-854-8100
601 Riverside Ave
Jacksonville, FL 32204
www.fnf.com

Fonda, Bridget (1964-)
Actor
IFA Talent Agency **Ph:** 310-659-5522
8730 Sunset Blvd Suite 490 **Fax:** 310-659-3344
Los Angeles, CA 90069

Fonda, Jane (1937-)
Actor; activist
Creative Artists Agency **Ph:** 310-288-4545
9830 Wilshire Blvd **Fax:** 310-288-4800
Beverly Hills, CA 90212

Fonda, Peter (1940-)
Actor
Metropolitan Talent Agency **Ph:** 323-857-4500
4500 Wilshire Blvd 2nd Fl **Fax:** 323-857-4509
Los Angeles, CA 90010

Fontana, Tom (1951-)
Television series producer/writer (Homicide: Life on the Street; Oz; St Elsewhere)
United Talent Agency **Ph:** 310-273-6700
9560 Wilshire Blvd 5th Fl **Fax:** 310-247-1111
Beverly Hills, CA 90212
www.tomfontana.com

Foote, Adam (1971-)
Professional hockey player
Columbus Blue Jackets **Ph:** 614-246-4625
Nationwide Arena **Fax:** 614-246-4007
200 W Nationwide Blvd 3rd Fl
Columbus, OH 43215
www.bluejackets.com

Foote, Horton (1916-)
Playwright & screenwriter
International Creative Management **Ph:** 310-550-4000
8942 Wilshire Blvd
Beverly Hills, CA 90211

Foote, William
Chairman and CEO of USG Corp, a North American leader in the building materials industry
USG Corp **Ph:** 312-606-4000
125 S Franklin St
Chicago, IL 60606
www.usg.com

Forbes, J Randy (1952-)
US Representative from Virginia (Republican)
307 Cannon Bldg **Ph:** 202-225-6365
Washington, DC 20515 **Fax:** 202-226-1170
www.house.gov/forbes

Forbes, Steve (1947-)
President & CEO of Forbes and Editor-in-Chief of Forbes magazine; former candidate for US President
Forbes Inc **Ph:** 212-620-2200
60 5th Ave **Fax:** 212-206-5126
New York, NY 10011
www.forbes.com/columnists

Ford, Betty (1918-)
Former First Lady of the US (wife of President Gerald Ford); founder of the Betty Ford Center (drug & alcohol rehabilitation)
40365 Sand Dune Rd **Ph:** 760-324-1763
PO Box 927 **Fax:** 760-324-7289
Rancho Mirage, CA 92270
www.ford.utexas.edu

Ford, Cheryl (1981-)
Professional basketball player
Detroit Shock **Ph:** 248-377-0100
Palace at Auburn Hills **Fax:** 248-377-3260
4 Championship Dr
Auburn Hills, MI 48326
www.wnba.com/shock

Ford, Eileen (1922-)
Founder of Ford Models
Ford Models Inc **Ph:** 212-219-6500
111 5th Ave **Fax:** 212-966-5028
New York, NY 10003
www.fordmodels.com

Ford, Gerald R (1913-)
38th US President (born Leslie Lynch King Jr, adopted as Gerald Rudolph Ford Jr)
40365 Sand Dune Rd **Ph:** 760-324-1763
PO Box 927 **Fax:** 760-324-7289
Rancho Mirage, CA 92270
www.ford.utexas.edu

Ford, Harold Jr (1970-)
US Representative from Tennessee (Democrat)
325 Cannon Bldg **Ph:** 202-225-3265
Washington, DC 20515 **Fax:** 202-225-5663
www.house.gov/ford

Ford, Harrison (1942-)
Actor
United Talent Agency **Ph:** 310-273-6700
9560 Wilshire Blvd 5th Fl **Fax:** 310-247-1111
Beverly Hills, CA 90212

Ford, Jack
Attorney; has served as legal correspondent on NBC and ABC and currently has a program on Court TV
Courtroom Television Network **Ph:** 212-973-2800
600 3rd Ave
New York, NY 10016
www.courttv.com/anchors

Ford, Lew (1976-)
Professional baseball player
Minnesota Twins **Ph:** 612-375-1366
Hubert H Humphrey Metrodome **Fax:** 612-375-7473
34 Kirby Puckett Pl
Minneapolis, MN 55415
minnesota.twins.mlb.com

Ford, Richard (1944-)
Author of Independence Day
Knopf Publishing/Author Mail **Ph:** 212-782-9000
1745 Broadway
New York, NY 10019
www.randomhouse.com/knopf

Ford, Scott
President and CEO of Alltel Corp
ALLTEL Corp **Ph:** 501-905-8000
1 Allied Dr
Little Rock, AR 72202
www.alltel.com/corporate

Ford, William Clay (1925-)
Sole owner and chairman of the Detroit Lions football organization; the grandson of Henry Ford and Director Emeritus of Ford Motor Company's Board
Detroit Lions **Ph:** 313-216-4000
222 Republic Dr
Allen Park, MI 48101
www.detroitlions.com

Ford, William Clay Jr (1957-)
Chairman & CEO of Ford Motor Co; vice chairman of the Detroit Lions football organization
Ford Motor Co **Ph:** 313-322-3000
c/o Compliance Office
PO Box 685
Dearborn, MI 48126
www.ford.com/en/company

Foreman, George (1949-)
Former boxing champion
International Boxing Hall of Fame **Ph:** 315-697-7095
Fax: 315-697-5356
1 Hall of Fame Dr
Canastota, NY 13032
www.georgeforeman.com

Forman, Milos (1932-)
Film director
The Lantz Office **Ph:** 212-586-0200
200 W 57th St Suite 503
New York, NY 10019

Forsberg, Peter (1973-)
Professional hockey player
Philadelphia Flyers **Ph:** 215-465-4500
Wachovia Center **Fax:** 215-389-9403
3601 S Broad St
Philadelphia, PA 19148
www.philadelphiaflyers.com

Forsee, Gary D
President and CEO of Sprint Nextel Corp
Sprint Nextel Corp **Ph:** 913-624-3000
6200 Sprint Pkwy **Fax:** 913-624-3281
Overland Park, KS 66251
www2.sprint.com/mr/exList.do

Forsyth, Frederick (1938-)
Novelist (Day of the Jackal; Dogs of War)
St Martin's Press **Ph:** 212-674-5151
Attn: Publicity Dept
175 5th Ave
New York, NY 10010
www.stmartins.com

Fortenberry, Jeff (1960-)
US Representative from Nebraska (Republican)
1517 Longworth Bldg **Ph:** 202-225-4806
Washington, DC 20515 **Fax:** 202-225-5686
fortenberry.house.gov

Fortin, Judy
Weekend anchor for CNN's Headline News
CNN **Ph:** 404-827-1500
1 CNN Center
Atlanta, GA 30303
www.cnn.com/CNN/anchors_reporters

Fortson, Danny (1976-)
Professional basketball player
Seattle Supersonics **Ph:** 206-281-5800
351 Elliott Ave W Suite 500 **Fax:** 206-281-5839
Seattle, WA 98119
www.nba.com/sonics

Fortson, Tom, PhD
President and CEO of Promise Keepers (succeeds Bill McCartney, the organization's founder and first president)
Promise Keepers **Ph:** 303-964-7600
PO Box 11798
Denver, CO 80211
www.promisekeepers.org

Fortuno, Luis G (1962-)
US Representative from Puerto Rico (Republican)
126 Cannon Bldg **Ph:** 202-225-2615
Washington, DC 20515 **Fax:** 202-225-2154
www.house.gov/fortuno

Fossella, Vito J (1965-)
US Representative from New York (Republican)
1239 Longworth Bldg **Ph:** 202-225-3371
Washington, DC 20515 **Fax:** 202-226-1272
www.house.gov/fossella

Fossey, Dian, PhD (1932-1985)
World-famous expert on mountain gorillas
Dian Fossey Gorilla Fund International **Ph:** 404-624-5881
Fax: 404-624-5999
800 Cherokee Ave SE
Atlanta, GA 30315
www.gorillafund.org

Foster, DeShaun (1980-)
Professional football player
Carolina Panthers **Ph:** 704-358-7000
Bank of America Stadium **Fax:** 704-358-7618
800 S Mint St
Charlotte, NC 28202
www.panthers.com

Foster, Jodie (1962-)
Actor; also producer/director
International Creative Management **Ph:** 310-550-4000
8942 Wilshire Blvd
Beverly Hills, CA 90211

Fowler, Chris (1962-)
Sports broadcaster
ESPN **Ph:** 860-585-2000
ESPN Plaza
935 Middle St
Bristol, CT 06010
sports.espn.go.com/espntv/espnGuide

Fowles, John (1926-2005)
British novelist (The French Lieutenant's Woman; The Collector)
Warner Books **Ph:** 212-522-7200
c/o Author Mail
1271 Ave of the Americas
New York, NY 10020
www.fowlesbooks.com

Fox, John (1955-)
Football coach
Carolina Panthers **Ph:** 704-358-7000
Bank of America Stadium **Fax:** 704-358-7618
800 S Mint St
Charlotte, NC 28202
www.panthers.com

Fox, Jorja (1968-)
Actor
International Creative Management **Ph:** 310-550-4000
8942 Wilshire Blvd
Beverly Hills, CA 90211

Fox, Matthew (1966-)
Actor
International Creative Management **Ph:** 310-550-4000
8942 Wilshire Blvd
Beverly Hills, CA 90211
abc.go.com/primetime/lost/show.html

Fox, Michael, DVM, PhD
Author, veterinarian, and animal advocate and behaviorist; writes the syndicated animal advice column Animal Doctor and has written more than 40 books on animals for adults and children
United Feature Syndicate **Ph:** 212-293-8500
200 Madison Ave
New York, NY 10016
www.unitedfeatures.com

Fox, Michael J (1961-)
Actor; activist for Parkinson's research
Creative Artists Agency **Ph:** 310-288-4545
9830 Wilshire Blvd **Fax:** 310-288-4800
Beverly Hills, CA 90212
www.michaeljfox.org

Fox, Paula (1923-)
Author of books for young adults (The Slave Dancer); also writes adult fiction
Front Street Inc **Ph:** 828-221-2091
862 Haywood Rd **Fax:** 828-221-2112
Asheville, NC 28806
www.frontstreetbooks.com

Foxworthy, Jeff (1958-)
Comedian
Parallel Entertainment **Ph:** 310-279-1123
9255 W Sunset Blvd Suite 1040 **Fax:** 310-279-1147
Los Angeles, CA 90069
www.jefffoxworthy.com

Foxx, Jamie (1967-)
Actor; comedian
Creative Artists Agency **Ph:** 310-288-4545
9830 Wilshire Blvd **Fax:** 310-288-4800
Beverly Hills, CA 90212

Foxx, Virginia (1943-)
US Representative from North Carolina (Republican)
502 Cannon Bldg **Ph:** 202-225-2071
Washington, DC 20515 **Fax:** 202-225-2995
www.virginiafoxx.com

Foyt, AJ (1935-)
Former race car driver, now a racing team owner
Foyt Enterprises **Ph:** 936-372-3698
19480 Stokes Rd
Waller, TX 77484
www.foytracing.com

Francis, Bev (1955-)
Fitness personality; bodybuilder and former World Powerlifting Champion
Powerhouse Gym Bev Francis **Ph:** 516-933-1111
235-C Robbins Ln **Fax:** 516-933-1135
Syosset, NY 11791
www.bevfrancis.com

Francis, Dick (1920-)
Author of horse racing mysteries
Berkley Books Publicity **Ph:** 212-366-2000
375 Hudson St
New York, NY 10014
www.dickfrancis.com

Francis, Steve (1977-)
Professional basketball player
New York Knicks **Ph:** 212-465-6471
Madison Square Garden **Fax:** 212-465-6498
2 Pennsylvania Plaza
New York, NY 10121
www.nba.com/knicks

Franco, Julio (1958-)
Professional baseball player
New York Mets **Ph:** 718-507-6387
Shea Stadium **Fax:** 718-507-6395
123-01 Roosevelt Ave
Flushing, NY 11368
newyork.mets.mlb.com

Francona, Terry (1959-)
Baseball manager
Boston Red Sox **Ph:** 617-267-9440
Fenway Park **Fax:** 617-236-6797
4 Yawkey Way
Boston, MA 02215
boston.redsox.mlb.com

Frank, Barney (1940-)
US Representative from Massachusetts (Democrat)
2252 Rayburn Bldg **Ph:** 202-225-5931
Washington, DC 20515 **Fax:** 202-225-0182
www.house.gov/frank

Frank, Lawrence (1970-)
Basketball coach
New Jersey Nets **Ph:** 201-935-8888
Nets Champion Center **Fax:** 201-935-1088
390 Murray Hill Pkwy
East Rutherford, NJ 07073
www.nba.com/nets

Frank, Phil (1943-)
Co-creator, with Joe Troise, of the comic strip The Elderberries; Frank is the artist and Troise the writer
Universal Press Syndicate **Ph:** 816-932-6600
4520 Main St
Kansas City, MO 64111
www.amuniversal.com/ups/features

Frank, Robert (1924-)
Photographer & filmmaker (including a noted documentary of the Rolling Stones on tour)
Pace/MacGill Gallery **Ph:** 212-759-7999
32 E 57th St **Fax:** 212-759-8964
New York, NY 10022
www.pacemacgill.com/robertfrank.php

Frankel, Lois J (1948-)
Mayor of West Palm Beach, Florida
200 2nd St **Ph:** 561-822-1400
West Palm Beach, FL 33401 **Fax:** 561-822-1424
www.cityofwpb.com/mayor/mayor.htm

Franken, Al (1951-)
Television writer and producer, comedian, radio host, and bestselling author
William Morris Agency **Ph:** 310-859-4000
1 William Morris Pl **Fax:** 310-859-4462
Beverly Hills, CA 90212
www.al-franken.com

Franken, Bob
A CNN national correspondent
CNN **Ph:** 202-898-7900
CNN Bldg
820 1st St NE
Washington, DC 20002
www.cnn.com/CNN/anchors_reporters

Frankfort, Lew
Chairman and CEO of Coach, Inc
Coach Inc **Ph:** 212-594-1850
516 W 34th St **Fax:** 212-594-1682
New York, NY 10001 **TF:** 800-444-3611
www.coach.com/corporate/governance

Franklin, Aretha (1942-)
Singer known as the queen of soul
William Morris Agency **Ph:** 310-859-4000
1 William Morris Pl **Fax:** 310-859-4462
Beverly Hills, CA 90212
www.wma.com/aretha_franklin/summary

Franklin, Martin
Chairman and CEO of Jarden Corp, a leading provider of consumer home products
Jarden Corp **Ph:** 914-967-9400
555 Theodore Fremd Ave **Fax:** 914-967-9405
Suite B-302
Rye, NY 10580
www.jarden.com

Franklin, Nancy
TV critic
New Yorker Magazine **Ph:** 212-286-5400
4 Times Sq **Fax:** 212-286-5735
New York, NY 10036

Franklin, Shirley (1945-)
Mayor of Atlanta
55 Trinity Ave SW Suite 2400 **Ph:** 404-330-6100
Atlanta, GA 30303 **Fax:** 404-658-7361
www.atlantaga.gov/Mayor

Franks, Bubba (1978-)
Professional football player
Green Bay Packers **Ph:** 920-569-7500
PO Box 10628 **Fax:** 920-569-7201
Green Bay, WI 54307
www.packers.com

Franks, Trent (1957-)
US Representative from Arizona (Republican)
1237 Longworth Bldg **Ph:** 202-225-4576
Washington, DC 20525 **Fax:** 202-225-6328
www.house.gov/franks

Franz, Dennis (1944-)
Actor
Paradigm **Ph:** 212-703-7540
500 5th Ave 37th Fl
New York, NY 10110

Franz, Wanda, PhD
President of the National Right to Life Committee; a developmental psychologist and a professor of child development
National Right to Life Committee **Ph:** 202-626-8800
512 10th St NW
Washington, DC 20004

Franzen, Jonathan (1959-)
Novelist (The Corrections)
Farrar Straus & Giroux **Ph:** 212-741-6900
19 Union Sq W
New York, NY 10003
www.jonathanfranzen.com

Fraser, Brendan (1968-)
Actor
William Morris Agency **Ph:** 310-859-4000
1 William Morris Pl **Fax:** 310-859-4462
Beverly Hills, CA 90212
www.brendanfraser.com

Fratello, Mike
Basketball coach
Memphis Grizzlies **Ph:** 901-205-1234
FedExForum **Fax:** 901-205-1235
191 Beale St
Memphis, TN 38103
www.nba.com/grizzlies

Frayn, Michael (1933-)
Author & playwright (Noises Off and Copenhagen)
Henry Holt & Co **Ph:** 212-886-9200
115 W 18th St **Fax:** 212-633-0748
New York, NY 10011
www.henryholt.com

Frazier, Amy (1972-)
Professional tennis player
WTA Tour **Ph:** 727-895-5000
1 Progress Plaza Suite 1500 **Fax:** 727-894-1982
Saint Petersburg, FL 33701
www.wtatour.com

Frazier, Charles (1950-)
Author of Cold Mountain
Vintage/Anchor Publicity **Ph:** 212-572-2420
1745 Broadway 20th Fl
New York, NY 10019
www.randomhouse.com/vintage

Frazier, Stephen
CNN Headline News anchor
CNN **Ph:** 404-827-1500
1 CNN Center
Atlanta, GA 30303
www.cnn.com/CNN/anchors_reporters

Frazier, Walt (1945-)
Former professional basketball player; member of the Basketball Hall of Fame
Naismith Memorial Basketball Hall of Fame **Ph:** 413-781-6500
Fax: 413-781-1939
1000 W Columbus Ave **TF:** 877-446-6752
Springfield, MA 01105
www.hoophall.com

Frears, Stephen (1941-)
Film director
International Creative Management **Ph:** 310-550-4000
8942 Wilshire Blvd
Beverly Hills, CA 90211

Fredericks, Fred (1929-)
Draws the comic strip Mandrake the Magician, which was originally created by Lee Falk
King Features Syndicate Inc **Ph:** 212-455-4000
888 7th Ave 2nd Fl
New York, NY 10019
www.kingfeatures.com

Frederique (1967-)
Model; full name is Frederique van der Wal
Ford Models **Ph:** 212-219-6500
111 5th Ave **Fax:** 212-966-5028
New York, NY 10003

Freedman, Russell (1929-)
Author/illustrator of nonfiction children's books (Lincoln: A Photobiography)
Houghton Mifflin Children's Books **Ph:** 617-351-5000
222 Berkeley St 8th Fl
Boston, MA 02116
www.houghtonmifflinbooks.com

Freeman, Hunter (1985-)
Professional soccer player
Colorado Rapids **Ph:** 303-405-1100
Pepsi Center **Fax:** 720-931-2022
1000 Chopper Cir
Denver, CO 80204
www.coloradorapids.com

Freeman, Morgan (1937-)
Actor
Revelations Entertainment **Ph:** 310-394-3131
1221 2nd St 4th Fl **Fax:** 310-394-3133
Santa Monica, CA 90401
www.revelationsent.com

Frelinghuysen, Rodney (1946-)
US Representative from New Jersey (Republican)
2442 Rayburn Bldg **Ph:** 202-225-5034
Washington, DC 20515 **Fax:** 202-225-3186
frelinghuysen.house.gov

French, Marilyn (1929-)
Author of feminist novels (The Women's Room)
Random House Publicity **Ph:** 212-782-9000
1745 Broadway
New York, NY 10019
www.randomhouse.com

Freston, Thomas E
President & CEO of Viacom Inc; one of the founding members of the team that launched MTV
Viacom Inc **Ph:** 212-258-6000
1515 Broadway 52nd Fl **Fax:** 212-258-6100
New York, NY 10036
www.viacom.com

Freudenthal, David D (1950-)
Governor of Wyoming (Democrat)
State Capitol 200 W 24th St Rm 124 **Ph:** 307-777-7434
Fax: 307-632-3909
Cheyenne, WY 82002
wyoming.gov/governor

Fribourg, Paul J
Chairman, president, and CEO of ContiGroup Cos (poultry and pork production and cattle feeding)
ContiGroup Cos Inc **Ph:** 212-207-5100
277 Park Ave **Fax:** 212-207-2910
New York, NY 10172
www.contigroup.com

Friedkin, William (1935-)
Film director
William Morris Agency **Ph:** 310-859-4000
1 William Morris Pl **Fax:** 310-859-4462
Beverly Hills, CA 90212

Friedlander, Lee (1934-)
Photographer
National Gallery of Art **Ph:** 202-737-4215
2000B South Club Dr
Landover, MD 20785
www.nga.gov

Friedman, Amy (1952-)
Writes the syndicated Tell Me A Story newspaper feature
Universal Press Syndicate **Ph:** 816-932-6600
4520 Main St
Kansas City, MO 64111
www.amuniversal.com/ups/features

Friedman, Jane
President & CEO of HarperCollins
HarperCollins Publishers Inc **Ph:** 212-207-7000
10 E 53rd St **Fax:** 212-207-7145
New York, NY 10022

Friedman, Kinky
Candidate for Texas governor
Kinky Friedman for Governor 2006 **Ph:** 512-326-5115 **Fax:** 512-326-5116
5010 Burleson Rd
Austin, TX 78744
www.kinkyfriedman.com

Friedman, Milton (1912-)
Economist; winner of the 1976 Nobel Prize in Economic Sciences and has also been awarded the Presidential Medal of Freedom and the National Medal of Science
Hoover Institution on War Revolution & Peace **Ph:** 650-723-1754 **Fax:** 650-723-1687
Stanford University
Stanford, CA 94305
www-hoover.stanford.edu

Friedman, Rachelle
Co-CEO & president of J & R Electronics Inc
J & R Electronics Inc **Ph:** 212-238-9000
23 Park Row **Fax:** 212-238-9191
New York, NY 10038

Friedman, Thomas L (1953-)
New York Times foreign affairs columnist; syndicated
New York Times **Ph:** 202-862-0300
Washington Bureau **Fax:** 202-862-0340
1627 'I' St NW
Washington, DC 20006
www.nytimes.com/pages/opinion

Friedrich, Cathe
A pioneer in home exercise videos; creator of the Power Stepping fitness trend
Four Seasons Health Spa **Ph:** 856-881-9418
626 N Delsea Dr
Glassboro, NJ 08028
www.cathe.com

Friel, Brian (1929-)
Irish playwright (Dancing at Lughnasa)
Farrar Straus & Giroux **Ph:** 212-741-6900
19 Union Sq W
New York, NY 10003
www.fsgbooks.com

Friesen, Jeff (1976-)
Professional hockey player
Mighty Ducks of Anaheim **Ph:** 714-704-2700
Arrowhead Pond **Fax:** 714-940-2953
2695 Katella Ave
Anaheim, CA 92806
www.mightyducks.com

Fripp, Patricia (1945-)
Public speaker; also provides training in speaking and presentation skills for executives, professional speakers, and sales teams
527 Hugo St **Ph:** 415-753-6556
San Francisco, CA 94122 **Fax:** 415-753-0914
www.fripp.com **TF:** 800-634-3035

Frist, Bill, MD (1952-)
US Senator from Tennessee (Republican); Senate Majority Leader
461 Dirksen Bldg **Ph:** 202-224-3344
Washington, DC 20510 **Fax:** 202-228-1264
frist.senate.gov

Fritz, Jean (1915-)
Author of historical biographies for young readers
GP Putnam's Sons Books for Young Readers **Ph:** 212-366-2000
Publicity Dept
345 Hudson St
New York, NY 10014
us.penguingroup.com

Frommer, Arthur
Travel authority and author of travel guides; also writes the syndicated column Arthur Frommer's Budget Travel
King Features Syndicate Inc **Ph:** 212-455-4000
888 7th Ave 2nd Fl
New York, NY 10019
www.kingfeatures.com

Frontiere, Georgia (1932-)
Owner of the St Louis Rams football franchise
Saint Louis Rams **Ph:** 314-982-7267
1 Rams Way **Fax:** 314-770-9261
Saint Louis, MO 63045
www.stlouisrams.com/offthefield/teaminvolvement/frontiere

Frost, Richard W
CEO of Louisiana-Pacific, a major building products manufacturer
Louisiana-Pacific Corp **Ph:** 615-986-5600
414 Union St Suite 2000
Nashville, TN 37219
www.lpcorp.com

Fry, Michael
Co-creator (with T Lewis) of Over the Hedge
United Feature Syndicate **Ph:** 212-293-8500
200 Madison Ave
New York, NY 10016
www.unitedfeatures.com

Frye, Michael
Photographer (primarily nature)
Ansel Adams Gallery **Ph:** 888-361-7622
PO Box 4185 **Fax:** 650-692-3512
Burlingame, CA 94011
www.michaelfrye.com

Fu, Cary T
President & CEO of Benchmark Electronics
Benchmark Electronics Inc **Ph:** 979-849-6550
3000 Technology Dr
Angleton, TX 77515
www.bench.com

Fuchs, Victor, PhD (1924-)
Stanford economics professor (emeritus)
Stanford University Dept of Economics **Ph:** 650-326-7639
Fax: 650-328-4163
Launau Economics Bldg
579 Serra Mall
Stanford, CA 94305
www-econ.stanford.edu

Fudge, Ann (1952-)
Chairman & CEO of Young & Rubicam Brands
Young & Rubicam **Ph:** 212-210-3000
285 Madison Ave
New York, NY 10017
www.yr.com

Fuentes, Carlos (1928-)
Author (The Diary of Frida Kahlo)
Random House Publicity **Ph:** 212-782-9000
1745 Broadway
New York, NY 10019
www.randomhouse.com

Fugard, Athol (1932-)
Playwright (Master Harold and the Boys) and actor
William Morris Agency **Ph:** 212-586-5100
1325 Ave of the Americas **Fax:** 212-246-3583
New York, NY 10019

Fujita, Scott (1979-)
Professional football player
New Orleans Saints **Ph:** 504-733-0255
5800 Airline Dr **Fax:** 504-731-1768
Metairie, LA 70003
www.neworleanssaints.com

Fuld, Richard S Jr (1946-)
Chairman & CEO of Lehman Brothers Holdings
Lehman Brothers Holdings Inc **Ph:** 212-526-7000
745 7th Ave 30th Fl
New York, NY 10019
www.lehman.com/who/bios

Fuller, Linda
Co-founder, with her husband Millard, of Habitat for Humanity
Habitat for Humanity International **Ph:** 229-924-6935
121 Habitat St
Americus, GA 31709
www.habitat.org/how/linda.aspx

Fuller, Millard (1935-)
Co-founder, with his wife Linda, of Habitat for Humanity
Habitat for Humanity International **Ph:** 229-924-6935
121 Habitat St
Americus, GA 31709
www.habitat.org/how/millard.aspx

Furtado, Nelly (1978-)
Singer
Creative Artists Agency **Ph:** 310-288-4545
9830 Wilshire Blvd **Fax:** 310-288-4800
Beverly Hill, CA 90212
www.nellyfurtado.com

Furyk, Jim (1970-)
Professional golfer
PGA Tour **Ph:** 904-285-3700
100 PGA Tour Blvd
Ponte Vedra Beach, FL 32082
www.pgatour.com/players

Gabaldon, Diana (1952-)
Author of the Outlander series
Bantam Dell Publicity **Ph:** 212-782-9000
1745 Broadway
New York, NY 10019
www.dianagabaldon.com

Gaborik, Marian (1982-)
Professional hockey player
Minnesota Wild **Ph:** 651-222-9453
317 Washington St **Fax:** 651-222-1055
Saint Paul, MN 55102
www.wild.com

Gabriel, Peter (1950-)
Musician/singer/songwriter/composer
William Morris Agency **Ph:** 310-859-4000
1 William Morris Pl **Fax:** 310-859-4462
Beverly Hills, CA 90212
www.petergabriel.com

Gaddy, C Welton, PhD (1941-)
President of the Interfaith Alliance; a pastor and author who has a message of inclusion
Interfaith Alliance **Ph:** 202-639-6370
1331 H St NW 11th Fl **Fax:** 202-639-6375
Washington, DC 20005
www.interfaithalliance.org

Gadiesh, Orit
Chairman of Bain & Co, a global business consulting firm
Bain & Co **Ph:** 617-572-2000
131 Dartmouth St **Fax:** 617-572-2427
Boston, MA 02116
www.bain.com

Gagne, Eric (1976-)
Professional baseball player
Los Angeles Dodgers **Ph:** 323-224-1500
Dodger Stadium **Fax:** 323-224-1269
1000 Elysian Park Ave
Los Angeles, CA 90012
losangeles.dodgers.mlb.com

Gagne, Simon (1980-)
Professional hockey player
Philadelphia Flyers **Ph:** 215-465-4500
Wachovia Center **Fax:** 215-389-9403
3601 S Broad St
Philadelphia, PA 19148
www.philadelphiaflyers.com

Gaiman, Neil (1960-)
Creator/writer of the DC Comics horror-weird series, Sandman; also writes novels for adults (American Gods) and for children (Coraline)
HarperCollins Children's Books **Ph:** 212-261-6500
1350 Ave of the Americas
New York, NY 10019
www.neilgaiman.com

Gaines, Ernest J (1933-)
Novelist (A Lesson Before Dying; The Autobiography of Miss Jane Pittman)
Random House Publicity **Ph:** 212-782-9000
1745 Broadway
New York, NY 10019
www.bickley.com

Gainey, Bob (1953-)
Hockey coach
Montreal Canadiens **Ph:** 514-932-2582
1275 Saint Antoine St W **Fax:** 514-932-9296
Montreal, QC H3C5L2
www.canadiens.com

Galdikas, Birute, PhD (1946-)
Primatologist; leading researcher and authority on orangutans
Orangutan Foundation International **Ph:** 323-938-6046
Fax: 323-938-6047
4201 Wilshire Blvd Suite 407
Los Angeles, CA 90010
www.orangutan.org

Gallagher (1947-)
Comedian (real name is Leo Anthony Gallagher, but he goes only by Gallagher)
Sold Out Shows **Ph:** 561-791-0011
14984 Roan Ct **TF:** 800-791-0021
Wellington, FL 33414
www.gallaghersmash.com

Gallagher, Maggie (1960-)
Author and syndicated columnist (conservative commentary)
Universal Press Syndicate **Ph:** 816-932-6600
4520 Main St
Kansas City, MO 64111
www.amuniversal.com/ups/features

Gallagher, Mike
Talk radio host (conservative issues); also a regular contributor on FOX television news programs
Salem Radio Network **Ph:** 972-831-1920
6400 N Beltline Rd Suite 210 **Fax:** 972-831-8626
Irving, TX 76063
www.mikeonline.com

Gallant, Gerard (1963-)
Hockey coach
Columbus Blue Jackets **Ph:** 614-246-4625
Nationwide Arena **Fax:** 614-246-4007
200 W Nationwide Blvd 3rd Fl
Columbus, OH 43215
www.bluejackets.com

Gallegly, Elton (1944-)
US Representative from California (Republican)
2427 Rayburn Bldg **Ph:** 202-225-5811
Washington, DC 20515 **Fax:** 202-225-1100
www.house.gov/gallegly

Galloping Gourmet (1934-)
Celebrity chef Graham Kerr
Kerr Corp **Ph:** 360-387-3807
1020 N Sunset Dr **Fax:** 360-387-1898
Camano Island, WA 98282
www.grahamkerr.com

Gallup, Patricia
Co-founder, chairman, and CEO of PC Connection
PC Connection Inc **Ph:** 603-423-2000
730 Milford Rd **Fax:** 603-423-5748
Rt 101A
Merrimack, NH 03054
www.pcconnection.com

Gamble, Chris (1983-)
Professional football player
Carolina Panthers **Ph:** 704-358-7000
Bank of America Stadium **Fax:** 704-358-7618
800 S Mint St
Charlotte, NC 28202
www.panthers.com

Gamble, Ed
First ever editorial cartoonist at the Florida Times-Union in Jacksonville
King Features Syndicate Inc **Ph:** 212-455-4000
888 7th Ave 2nd Fl
New York, NY 10019
www.kingfeatures.com

Gammell, Stephen (1943-)
Illustrator of books for children (Song & Dance Man)
Simon & Schuster Books for Young Readers **Ph:** 212-698-7000
1230 Ave of the Americas
New York, NY 10020
www.simonsays.com

Gammons, Peter (1945-)
Sports broadcaster; also senior writer for ESPN the Magazine
ESPN **Ph:** 860-585-2000
ESPN Plaza
935 Middle St
Bristol, CT 06010
sports.espn.go.com/espntv/espnGuide

Gand, Gale
Executive pastry chef at Tru Restaurant
Tru Restaurant **Ph:** 312-202-0001
676 N Saint Clair St
Chicago, IL 60611
www.trurestaurant.com

Gandolfini, James (1961-)
Actor
United Talent Agency **Ph:** 310-273-6700
9560 Wilshire Blvd 5th Fl **Fax:** 310-247-1111
Beverly Hills, CA 90212
www.hbo.com/sopranos

Gandy, Kim (1954-)
President of the National Organization for Women (NOW)
National Organization for Women **Ph:** 202-628-8669
Fax: 202-785-8576
1100 H St NW
Washington, DC 20005
www.now.org/officers

Gangel, Jamie
National correspondent for the Today Show
Today Show **Ph:** 212-664-4249
30 Rockefeller Plaza
New York, NY 10112
www.msnbc.msn.com/id/3079108

Ganis, Sid (1940-)
President of the Board of Governors of the Academy of Motion Picture Arts & Sciences; a movie producer
Academy of Motion Picture Arts & Sciences **Ph:** 310-247-3000
8949 Wilshire Blvd
Beverly Hills, CA 90211

Gantos, Jack (1951-)
Author of children's books (picture books, middle-grade fiction, novels for young adults), including the Jack Henry books, Joey Piqza books, and Rotten Ralph books
Books for Young Readers **Ph:** 212-741-6900
Farrar Straus & Giroux
19 Union Sq W
New York, NY 10003
www.jackgantos.com

Ganzi, Victor
President & CEO of the Hearst Corp
Hearst Corp **Ph:** 212-649-2323
959 8th Ave
New York, NY 10019
www.hearstcorp.com/about

Garber, Don
Commissioner of Major League Soccer
Major League Soccer **Ph:** 212-450-1200
420 5th Ave 7th Fl **Fax:** 212-450-1300
New York, NY 10018
www.mlsnet.com/MLS/about/

Garcia, Andy (1956-)
Actor
Paradigm **Ph:** 310-288-8000
360 N Crescent Dr **Fax:** 310-288-2000
North Bldg
Beverly Hills, CA 90210

Garcia, Jeff (1970-)
Professional football player
Philadelphia Eagles **Ph:** 215-463-2500
NovaCare Complex **Fax:** 215-339-5464
1 NovaCare Way
Philadelphia, PA 19145
www.philadelphiaeagles.com

Garcia, Juan Pablo (1981-)
Professional soccer player
Club Deportivo Chivas USA **Ph:** 310-630-4550
Home Depot Center **Fax:** 310-630-4551
18400 Avalon Blvd
Carson, CA 90746
chivas.usa.mlsnet.com

Garcia, Nick (1979-)
Professional soccer player
Kansas City Wizards **Ph:** 816-920-9300
2 Arrowhead Dr **Fax:** 816-920-4774
Kansas City, MO 64129
kc.wizards.mlsnet.com

Garcia, Sergio (1980-)
Professional golfer
PGA Tour **Ph:** 904-285-3700
100 PGA Tour Blvd
Ponte Vedra Beach, FL 32082
www.pgatour.com/players

Garcia Marquez, Gabriel (1928-)
Winner of the 1982 Nobel Prize in Literature (One Hundred Years of Solitude; Love in the Time of Cholera)
Random House Publicity **Ph:** 212-782-9000
1745 Broadway
New York, NY 10019
www.randomhouse.com

Garciaparra, Nomar (1973-)
Professional baseball player
Los Angeles Dodgers **Ph:** 323-224-1500
Dodger Stadium **Fax:** 323-224-1269
1000 Elysian Park Ave
Los Angeles, CA 90012
losangeles.dodgers.mlb.com

Gardenhire, Ron (1957-)
Baseball manager
Minnesota Twins **Ph:** 612-375-1366
Hubert H Humphrey Metrodome **Fax:** 612-375-7473
34 Kirby Puckett Pl
Minneapolis, MN 55415
minnesota.twins.mlb.com

Gardner, David
Author, lecturer, and media personality; writes the syndicated investment advice column The Motley Fool with his brother Tom Gardner
Universal Press Syndicate **Ph:** 816-932-6600
4520 Main St
Kansas City, MO 64111
www.amuniversal.com/ups/features

Gardner, Tom
Author, lecturer, and media personality; writes the syndicated investment advice column The Motley Fool with his brother Tom Gardner
Universal Press Syndicate **Ph:** 816-932-6600
4520 Main St
Kansas City, MO 64111
www.amuniversal.com/ups/features

Garfunkel, Art (1941-)
Singer; actor
William Morris Agency **Ph:** 310-859-4000
1 William Morris Pl **Fax:** 310-859-4462
Beverly Hills, CA 90212
www.artgarfunkel.com

Garlick, Scott (1972-)
Professional soccer player
Real Salt Lake **Ph:** 801-924-8585
515 S 700 East Suite 2R **Fax:** 801-933-4713
Salt Lake City, UT 84102
www.mlsnet.com/MLS/rsl/

Garlin, Jeff (1962-)
Comedian; actor
3 Arts Entertainment **Ph:** 310-888-3200
9460 Wilshire Blvd 7th Fl **Fax:** 310-888-3210
Beverly Hills, CA 90212
www.hbo.com/larrydavid/cast

Garlington, Joseph
Bishop Garlington is founder & senior pastor of the Covenant Church of Pittsburgh and leader of Reconciliation Ministries; also hosts radio & TV programs, is the featured worship leader on several recordings, and is a Promise Keepers speaker
Covenant Church of Pittsburgh **Ph:** 412-731-6221
1111 Wood St **Fax:** 412-731-9610
Pittsburgh, PA 15221
www.ccop.org

Garner, Blair
Host of After MidNite, a syndicated radio show featuring country music
Premiere Radio Networks Inc **Ph:** 818-377-5300
15260 Ventura Blvd 5th Fl **Fax:** 818-377-5333
Sherman Oaks, CA 91403
www.aftermidnite.com

Garner, James (1928-)
Actor
Paradigm **Ph:** 310-288-8000
360 N Crescent Dr **Fax:** 310-288-2000
North Bldg
Beverly Hills, CA 90210

Garner, Jennifer (1972-)
Actor
Endeavor **Ph:** 310-248-2000
9601 Wilshire Blvd 3rd Fl **Fax:** 310-248-2020
Beverly Hills, CA 90210
abc.go.com/primetime/alias

Garner, Phil (1949-)
Baseball manager
Houston Astros **Ph:** 713-259-8000
Minute Maid Park **Fax:** 713-259-8981
501 Crawford St
Houston, TX 77002
houston.astros.mlb.com

Garnett, Kevin (1976-)
Professional basketball player
Minnesota Timberwolves **Ph:** 612-673-1600
Target Center **Fax:** 612-673-1699
600 1st Ave N
Minneapolis, MN 55403
www.nba.com/timberwolves

Garofalo, Janeane (1964-)
Comedian & actor; also co-hosts Minority Report on Air America radio
Gersh Agency **Ph:** 310-274-6611
232 N Canon Dr
Beverly Hills, CA 90210

Garrett, Brad (1960-)
Comedian; actor
International Creative Management **Ph:** 310-550-4000
8942 Wilshire Blvd
Beverly Hills, CA 90211
www.everybodylovesray.com

Garrett, Scott (1959-)
US Representative from New Jersey (Republican)
1318 Longworth Bldg **Ph:** 202-225-4465
Washington, DC 20515 **Fax:** 202-225-9048
www.house.gov/garrett

Garten, Ina
Owner of the Barefoot Contessa specialty food store and host of the Food Network show of the same name; also a cookbooks author
Food Network **Ph:** 212-398-8836
75 9th Ave **Fax:** 212-736-7716
New York, NY 10011
www.foodtv.com

Gary, Charlos (1968-)
Creator of the comic strip Working it Out
Creators Syndicate Inc **Ph:** 310-337-7003
5777 W Century Blvd Suite 700 **Fax:** 310-337-7625
Los Angeles, CA 90045
www.creators.com

Gary, Willie E (1947-)
Attorney; typically represents little known clients against major corporations, and he has won some of the biggest jury awards in US history
Gary Williams Parenti Finney Lewis McManus Watson & Sperando PL **Ph:** 772-283-8260 **Fax:** 772-220-3343 **TF:** 800-329-4279
Waterside Professional Bldg
221 E Osceola St
Stuart, FL 34994
www.williegary.com

Gasol, Pau (1980-)
Professional basketball player
Memphis Grizzlies **Ph:** 901-205-1234
FedExForum **Fax:** 901-205-1235
191 Beale St
Memphis, TN 38103
www.nba.com/grizzlies

Gasper, Gay
Personal trainer; a National Step Aerobic Champion
Image Planet **Ph:** 908-688-6675
1235F W Chestnut St
Union, NJ 07083
www.imageplanetclub.com

Gately, George (1928-)
Creator of the comic strip Heathcliff
Creators Syndicate Inc **Ph:** 310-337-7003
5777 W Century Blvd Suite 700 **Fax:** 310-337-7625
Los Angeles, CA 90045
www.creators.com

Gates, Antonio (1980-)
Professional football player
San Diego Chargers **Ph:** 858-574-4500
4020 Murphy Canyon Rd **Fax:** 858-292-2760
San Diego, CA 92123
www.chargers.com

Gates, Bill (1955-)
Microsoft co-founder, chairman, and chief software architect; wealthiest man in the world
Microsoft Corp **Ph:** 425-882-8080
1 Microsoft Way **Fax:** 425-706-7329
Redmond, WA 98052
www.microsoft.com/billgates

Gates, Henry Louis Jr, PhD (1950-)
Director of the WEB Du Bois Institute for African & African American Research at Harvard University
WEB Du Bois Institute for African & African American Research **Ph:** 617-495-8508
104 Mount Auburn St 3R
Cambridge, MA 02138
dubois.fas.harvard.edu

Gates, Melinda (1964-)
Wife of Bill Gates and co-founder/co-chair of the Bill & Melinda Gates Foundation
Bill & Melinda Gates Foundation **Ph:** 206-709-3100 **Fax:** 206-709-3180
PO Box 23350
Seattle, WA 98102
www.gatesfoundation.org

Gattinella, Wayne
President and CEO of WebMD
WebMD Corp **Ph:** 201-703-3400
669 River Dr
Center 2
Elmwood Park, NJ 07407
www.wbmd.com/waynegattinella.shtml

Gaven, Eddie (1986-)
Professional soccer player
Columbus Crew **Ph:** 614-447-2739
Columbus Crew Stadium **Fax:** 614-447-4109
1 Black & Gold Blvd
Columbus, OH 43211
columbus.crew.mlsnet.com

Gayle, Helene, MD (1955-)
Director of the Bill & Melinda Gates Foundation's HIV, TB, and Reproductive Health Program
Bill & Melinda Gates Foundation **Ph:** 206-709-3100 **Fax:** 206-709-3180
PO Box 23350
Seattle, WA 98102
www.gatesfoundation.org/globalhealth/relatedinfo

Gbandi, Chris (1979-)
Professional soccer player
FC Dallas **Ph:** 214-979-0303
14800 Quorum Dr Suite 300 **Fax:** 214-979-1118
Dallas, TX 75254
fc.dallas.mlsnet.com

Geddes, Anne
Baby photographer
Geddes Group/Nursery Room Ltd **Ph:** 206-374-9200 **Fax:** 206-374-9201
2101 4th Ave Suite 1010
Seattle, WA 98121
www.annegeddes.com

Geffen, David L (1943-)
Entertainment mogul: founder of Asylum and Geffen Records; movie and Broadway producer; a co-founder of Dreamworks SKG
DreamWorks SKG **Ph:** 818-733-7000
100 Universal City Plaza
Bldg 5121
Universal City, CA 91608

Geisel, Theodore (1904-1991)
Dr. Seuss
Random House Children's Books **Ph:** 212-782-9000
Publicity Dept
1745 Broadway
New York, NY 10019
www.randomhouse.com/kids

Geist, Bill (1945-)
News correspondent
CBS News Sunday Morning **Ph:** 212-975-4114
Box O
524 W 57th St
New York, NY 10019
www.cbsnews.com

Geldof, Bob (1951-)
Musician, composer, actor; organized both Live Aid and Live 8
William Morris Agency **Ph:** 310-859-4000
1 William Morris Pl **Fax:** 310-859-4462
Beverly Hills, CA 90212
www.bobgeldof.info

Gelinas, Martin (1970-)
Professional hockey player
Florida Panthers **Ph:** 954-835-7000
BankAtlantic Center **Fax:** 954-835-7700
1 Panther Pkwy
Sunrise, FL 33323
www.floridapanthers.com

Gellar, Sarah Michelle (1977-)
Actor
United Talent Agency **Ph:** 310-273-6700
9560 Wilshire Blvd 5th Fl **Fax:** 310-247-1111
Beverly Hills, CA 90212

Gellman, Marc, PhD
Rabbi; writes the syndicated God Squad column with Monsignor Tom Hartman
Tribune Media Services Inc **Ph:** 312-222-4444
435 N Michigan Ave Suite 1500
Chicago, IL 60611
tmsfeatures.com/productlist.htm

George, Bob (1938-)
Founder & CEO of People to People ministries and host of the People to People radio program; author of Classic Christianity
People to People Ministries **Ph:** 972-620-1755
1225 E Rosemeade Pkwy
Carrollton, TX 75007
www.realanswers.net

George, Elizabeth (1949-)
Author of mystery novels (A Place of Hiding)
Trident Media Group **Ph:** 212-262-4810
41 Madison Ave 36th Fl
New York, NY 10010
www.elizabethgeorgeonline.com

George, Jean Craighead (1919-)
Naturalist & author of books for young readers (Julie of the Wolves)
HarperCollins Children's Books **Ph:** 212-261-6500
1350 Ave of the Americas
New York, NY 10019
www.jeancraigheadgeorge.com

George, Richard L
President & CEO of Suncor Energy Inc
Suncor Energy Inc **Ph:** 403-269-8100
112 4th Ave SW **Fax:** 403-269-6200
PO Box 38
Calgary, AB T2P2V5
www.suncor.com

Geragos, Mark (1957-)
Criminal defense lawyer; has represented Susan McDougal (Whitewater), Scott Peterson, Michael Jackson, and other high-profile clients
Geragos & Geragos PC **Ph:** 213-625-3900
2 California Plaza **Fax:** 213-625-1600
350 S Grand Ave 39th Fl
Los Angeles, CA 90071
www.geragos.com

Gerard, Leo W
International president of United Steelworkers of America
United Steelworkers of America **Ph:** 412-562-2400
5 Gateway Ctr
Pittsburgh, PA 15222
www.uswa.org

Gerberding, Julie L, MD
Director of the Centers for Disease Control & Prevention
Centers for Disease Control & Prevention **Ph:** 404-639-7000 **Fax:** 404-639-7111
1600 Clifton Rd NE
Atlanta, GA 30333
www.cdc.gov/about/director.htm

Gere, Richard (1949-)
Actor; also published a book of his photography and has had several photo exhibitions
International Creative Management **Ph:** 310-550-4000
8942 Wilshire Blvd
Beverly Hills, CA 90211

Gergen, David (1942-)
Commentator, editor, teacher, author, and adviser to presidents for 30 years; is currently a professor of public service at Harvard's John F. Kennedy School of Government, Center for Public Leadership and also editor-at-large for US News & World Report
Center for Public Leadership **Ph:** 617-496-8866
JFK School of Government **Fax:** 617-496-3337
Harvard University
124 Mount Auburn St
Suite 165
Cambridge, MA 02138
www.davidgergen.com

Gerin, Jean-Louis (1957-)
Chef and owner of Restaurant Jean-Louis
Restaurant Jean-Louis **Ph:** 203-622-8450
61 Lewis St **Fax:** 203-622-5845
Greenwich, CT 06830
www.restaurantjeanlouis.com

Gerlach, Jim (1955-)
US Representative from Pennsylvania (Republican)
208 Cannon Bldg **Ph:** 202-225-4315
Washington, DC 20515 **Fax:** 202-225-8440
gerlach.house.gov

Gern, Francesca
Creator of Geri-Fit, a fitness program specifically designed for older adults
Geri-Fit Co Ltd **Ph:** 330-650-3539
PO Box 444
Hudson, OH 44236
www.gerifit.com/gerifounder.html

Geronimo, Don
Co-hosts (with Mike O'Meara) the Don & Mike Show, a radio program with a morning show type of format in the afternoon drive time slot
WJFK-FM **Ph:** 703-691-1900
10800 Main St
Fairfax, VA 22030
www.donandmikewebsite.com

Gerstein, Mordicai (1935-)
Children's books writer & illustrator (The Man Who Walked Between the Towers); also a painter, sculptor, and prize-winning designer and director of animated films
Craven Design Studios **Ph:** 212-696-4680
234 5th Ave **Fax:** 212-532-2626
New York, NY 10001
www.mordicaigerstein.com

Gertz, Bill (1952-)
Defense and national security reporter for the Washington Times
The Washington Times **Ph:** 202-636-3000
3600 New York Ave NE **Fax:** 202-269-3419
Washington, DC 20002
www.gertzfile.com

Geyer, Georgie Anne (1935-)
Foreign correspondent and syndicated columnist
Universal Press Syndicate **Ph:** 816-932-6600
4520 Main St
Kansas City, MO 64111
www.amuniversal.com/ups/features

Gharib, Susie
Co-anchor (with Paul Kangas) of the Nightly Business Report on PBS
Nightly Business Report **Ph:** 305-949-8321
PO Box 610002
Miami, FL 33261
www.nbr.com

Giacconi, Riccardo, PhD (1931-)
Winner of the 2002 Nobel Prize in Physics for pioneering contributions to astrophysics, which have led to the discovery of cosmic X-ray sources
Johns Hopkins University **Ph:** 410-516-0336
Dept of Physics & Astronomy **Fax:** 410-516-7239
3400 N Charles St
Bloomberg 233
Baltimore, MD 21218
astronomy.jhu.edu/people/faculty

Giacomelli, Mario (1925-)
Photographer
Robert Klein Gallery **Ph:** 617-267-7997
38 Newbury St 4th Fl **Fax:** 617-267-5567
Boston, MA 02116
www.robertkleingallery.com

Giamatti, Paul (1967-)
Actor
Endeavor **Ph:** 310-248-2000
9601 Wilshire Blvd 3rd Fl **Fax:** 310-248-2020
Beverly Hills, CA 90210

Giambi, Jason (1971-)
Professional baseball player
New York Yankees **Ph:** 718-293-4300
Yankee Stadium **Fax:** 718-293-8414
161st St & River Ave
Bronx, NY 10451
newyork.yankees.mlb.com

Gianni, Gary (1954-)
Illustrator; his work includes the comic strip Prince Valiant
King Features Syndicate Inc **Ph:** 212-455-4000
888 7th Ave 2nd Fl
New York, NY 10019
www.garygianni.com

Gibbons, Jim (1944-)
US Representative from Nevada (Republican)
100 Cannon Bldg **Ph:** 202-225-6155
Washington, DC 20515 **Fax:** 202-225-5679
wwwc.house.gov/gibbons

Gibbons, John (1977-)
Baseball manager
Toronto Blue Jays **Ph:** 416-341-1000
1 Blue Jays Way **Fax:** 416-341-1250
Toronto, ON M5V1J1
toronto.bluejays.mlb.com

Gibbons, Kaye (1960-)
Author of fiction (Ellen Foster; A Virtuous Woman)
Putnam Publicity **Ph:** 212-366-2000
375 Hudson St
New York, NY 10014
www.kayegibbons.com

Gibbs, Joe (1940-)
Football coach; also owns an auto racing team, Joe Gibbs Racing
Washington Redskins **Ph:** 703-726-7000
21300 Redskin Park Dr **Fax:** 703-726-7086
Ashburn, VA 20147
www.redskins.com

Giblin, James Cross (1933-)
Author of nonfiction books for young people
Houghton Mifflin Children's Books **Ph:** 617-351-5000
222 Berkeley St 8th Fl
Boston, MA 02116
www.houghtonmifflinbooks.com

Gibson, Bob (1935-)
Hall of Fame baseball pitcher, now a Special Instructor with the Cardinals
Saint Louis Cardinals **Ph:** 314-421-3060
250 Stadium Plaza **Fax:** 314-425-0640
Saint Louis, MO 63102
stlouis.cardinals.mlb.com

Gibson, Charles (1943-)
Co-anchor of Good Morning America on ABC
Good Morning America **Ph:** 212-456-7777
147 Columbus Ave
New York, NY 10023
www.abcnews.go.com/GMA

Gibson, John (1946-)
Hosts The Big Story with John Gibson on FOX News
FOX News Channel **Ph:** 212-301-3000
1211 Ave of the Americas
New York, NY 10036
www.foxnews.com/fnctv

Gibson, Mel (1956-)
Actor and film producer/director
International Creative Management **Ph:** 310-550-4000
8942 Wilshire Blvd
Beverly Hills, CA 90211

Gibson, William (1948-)
Science fiction author
Berkley Books Publicity **Ph:** 212-366-2000
375 Hudson St
New York, NY 10014
www.williamgibsonbooks.com

Giff, Patricia Reilly (1935-)
Author of books for young readers (Lily's Crossing; All the Way Home)
Random House Children's Books **Ph:** 212-782-9000
Publicity Dept
1745 Broadway
New York, NY 10019
www.randomhouse.com/kids

Gifford, Kathie Lee (1953-)
Entertainer
William Morris Agency **Ph:** 212-586-5100
1325 Ave of the Americas **Fax:** 212-246-3583
New York, NY 10019
www.kathieleegifford.com

Gigot, Paul A
Editor of the Wall Street Journal's editorial page
Wall Street Journal **Ph:** 609-520-4000
PO Box 300
Princeton, NJ 08543
www.opinionjournal.com

Giguere, Jean-Sebastien (1977-)
Professional hockey player
Mighty Ducks of Anaheim **Ph:** 714-704-2700
Arrowhead Pond **Fax:** 714-704-2913
2695 Katella Ave
Anaheim, CA 92806
www.mightyducks.com

Gilbert, Daniel
Chairman and founder of Quicken Loans; majority owner of the Cleveland Cavaliers basketball team
Cleveland Cavaliers **Ph:** 216-420-2000
Quicken Loans Arena **Fax:** 216-420-2298
1 Center Ct
Cleveland, OH 44115
www.nba.com/cavaliers/news

Gilbert, David (1971-)
Creator of the comic strip Buckles
King Features Syndicate Inc **Ph:** 212-455-4000
888 7th Ave 2nd Fl
New York, NY 10019
www.kingfeatures.com

Gilchrest, Wayne T (1946-)
US Representative from Maryland (Republican)
2245 Rayburn Bldg **Ph:** 202-225-5311
Washington, DC 20515 **Fax:** 202-225-0254
gilchrest.house.gov

Gilchrist, Brad
Produces the comic strip Nancy with Guy Gilchrist; the strip's original creator was Ernie Bushmiller, who died in 1982; the Gilchrists took it over in 1995
United Feature Syndicate **Ph:** 212-293-8500
200 Madison Ave
New York, NY 10016
www.unitedfeatures.com

Gilchrist, Guy (1957-)
Children's book author/illustrator and cartoonist; his work includes the comic strip Nancy (with Brad Gilchrist), which was originally created by Ernie Bushmiller, who died in 1982; the Gilchrists took over the strip in 1995
United Feature Syndicate **Ph:** 212-293-8500
200 Madison Ave
New York, NY 10016
gilchriststudios.com

Giles, Bill
Owner, chairman of Philadelphia Phillies baseball team
Philadelphia Phillies **Ph:** 215-463-6000
Citizens Bank Park **Fax:** 215-389-3050
1 Citizens Bank Park Way
Philadelphia, PA 19148
philadelphia.phillies.mlb.com

Giles, Brian (1971-)
Professional baseball player
San Diego Padres **Ph:** 619-795-5000
Petco Park **Fax:** 619-497-5339
PO Box 122000
San Diego, CA 92112
sandiego.padres.mlb.com

Giles, Marcus (1978-)
Professional baseball player
Atlanta Braves **Ph:** 404-522-7630
PO Box 4064 **Fax:** 404-614-1392
Atlanta, GA 30302
atlanta.braves.mlb.com

Gill, Vince (1957-)
Country singer
William Morris Agency **Ph:** 615-963-3000
1600 Division St Suite 300 **Fax:** 615-963-3090
Nashville, TN 37203
vincegill.com

Gillespie, Ed (1962-)
A top Republican strategist and former chairman of the Republican National Committee; co-founder (with Democrat Jack Quinn) of Quinn Gillespie & Assoc, considered one of Washington's top public affairs firms
Quinn Gillespie & Assoc LLC **Ph:** 202-457-1110
1133 Connecticut Ave NW **Fax:** 202-457-1130
5th Fl
Washington, DC 20036
www.quinngillespie.com

Gillett, George N Jr (1938-)
Owner of the Montreal Canadiens hockey team
Montreal Canadiens **Ph:** 514-932-2582
1275 Saint Antoine St W **Fax:** 514-932-9296
Montreal, QC H3C5L2
www.canadiens.com

Gilliam, Sam (1933-)
African-American painter
Marsha Mateyka Gallery **Ph:** 202-328-0088
2012 R St NW **Fax:** 202-332-0520
Washington, DC 20009
www.artline.com/galleries/mateyka

Gilligan, Paul
Creator of the comic strip Pooch Cafe
Universal Press Syndicate **Ph:** 816-932-6600
4520 Main St
Kansas City, MO 64111
www.amuniversal.com/ups/features

Gilliland, Jillian
Children's book illustrator; also illustrates the Tell Me A Story newspaper feature for children, which is written by Amy Friedman
Universal Press Syndicate **Ph:** 816-932-6600
4520 Main St
Kansas City, MO 64111
www.amuniversal.com/ups/features

Gilliland, Sam
Chairman and CEO of Sabre Holdings
Sabre Holdings Corp **Ph:** 682-605-1000
3150 Sabre Dr
Southlake, TX 76092
www.sabre-holdings.com

Gillings, Dennis B, PhD
Chairman & CEO of Quintiles Transnational Corp
Quintiles Transnational Corp **Ph:** 919-998-2000
4709 Creekstone Dr Suite 200
Durham, NC 27703
www.quintiles.com

Gillmor, Paul E (1939-)
US Representative from Ohio (Republican)
1203 Longworth Bldg **Ph:** 202-225-6405
Washington, DC 20515 **Fax:** 202-225-1985
www.house.gov/gillmor

Gilman, Kenneth
President and CEO of Asbury Automotive
Asbury Automotive Group Inc **Ph:** 212-885-2500
622 3rd Ave 37th Fl
New York, NY 10017
www.asburyauto.com

Gilpin, Laura (1891-1979)
Photographer
Amon Carter Museum **Ph:** 817-738-1933
3501 Camp Bowie Blvd
Fort Worth, TX 76107
www.cartermuseum.org

Ginepri, Robby (1982-)
Professional tennis player
ATP **Ph:** 904-285-8000
201 ATP Blvd **Fax:** 904-285-5966
Ponte Vedra Beach, FL 32082
www.robbyginepri.com

Gingrey, Phil, MD (1942-)
US Representative from Georgia (Republican)
1139 Cannon Bldg **Ph:** 202-225-2931
Washington, DC 20515 **Fax:** 202-225-2944
gingrey.house.gov

Gingrich, Candace (1967-)
Spokesperson for Gay & Lesbian rights
Youth Outreach Mgr **Ph:** 202-628-4160
Human Rights Campaign **Fax:** 202-347-5323
1640 Rhode Island Ave NW **TF:** 800-777-4723
Washington, DC 20036
www.hrc.org/Template.cfm?Section=Press_Room

Gingrich, Newt (1943-)
Former Speaker of the US House of Representatives; now a Senior Fellow at the American Enterprise Institute and CEO of the Gingrich Group, a communications and consulting firm that specializes in transformational change
American Enterprise Institute **Ph:** 202-862-5800
for Public Policy Research **Fax:** 202-862-7177
1150 17th St NW Suite 1100
Washington, DC 20036
www.newt.org

Ginobili, Manu (1977-)
Professional basketball player
San Antonio Spurs **Ph:** 210-444-5000
1 SBC Center **Fax:** 210-444-5003
San Antonio, TX 78219
www.nba.com/spurs

Ginsberg, Benjamin L
Attorney who served as national counsel to the Bush-Cheney presidential campaigns in 2000 and 2004, with a central role in the 2000 Florida recount; resigned after revealing that he had also advised the Swift Boat Veterans for Truth
Patton Boggs LLP **Ph:** 202-457-6405
2550 M St NW **Fax:** 202-457-6315
Washington, DC 20037
www.pattonboggs.com

Ginsburg, Art
Celebrity chef known as Mr Food
Ginsburg Enterprises Inc **Ph:** 954-938-0400
1770 NW 64th St Suite 500 **Fax:** 954-938-2005
Fort Lauderdale, FL 33309
www.mrfood.com

Ginsburg, Ruth Bader (1933-)
US Supreme Court justice
US Supreme Court Bldg **Ph:** 202-479-3000
1 1st St NE
Washington, DC 20543
www.supremecourtus.gov

Gionta, Brian (1979-)
Professional hockey player
New Jersey Devils **Ph:** 201-935-6050
Continental Airlines Arena **Fax:** 201-935-2127
50 Rt 120N
East Rutherford, NJ 07073
www.newjerseydevils.com

Giovanni, Nikki (1943-)
Poet & civil rights activist; also writer, commentator, and educator
HarperCollins Publishers **Ph:** 212-207-7000
c/o Author Mail
10 E 53rd St
New York, NY 10022
www.nikki-giovanni.com

Girardi, Joe (1964-)
Baseball manager
Florida Marlins **Ph:** 305-626-7400
Dolphins Stadium **Fax:** 305-626-7428
2267 Dan Marino Blvd
Miami, FL 33056
florida.marlins.mlb.com

Gisler, Peggy
With Marge Eberts, writes the syndicated newspaper column Dear Teacher
King Features Syndicate Inc **Ph:** 212-455-4000
888 7th Ave 2nd Fl
New York, NY 10019
www.kingfeatures.com

Giuliani, Rudy (1944-)
Chairman and CEO of Giuliani Partners, a consulting firm; former mayor of New York City who was in office at the time of the 9/11 crisis
Giuliani Partners LLC **Ph:** 212-931-7300
5 Times Sq **Fax:** 212-931-7310
New York, NY 10030
www.giulianipartners.com

Glasbergen, Randy (1957-)
Creator of the comic strip The Better Half
King Features Syndicate Inc **Ph:** 212-455-4000
888 7th Ave 2nd Fl
New York, NY 10019
www.glasbergen.com

Glaser, Robert
Founder, chairman, and CEO of RealNetworks, Inc.; RealAudio, followed by RealVideo & RealPlayer, were introduced under his direction
RealNetworks Inc **Ph:** 206-674-2700
2601 Eliot Ave **Fax:** 206-674-2699
Seattle, WA 98121
www.realnetworks.com/company

Glass, David D
Owner of the Kansas City Royals baseball club
Kansas City Royals **Ph:** 816-921-8000
Kauffman Stadium
1 Royal Way
Kansas City, MO 64129
kansascity.royals.mlb.com

Glass, Ira (1959-)
Host and producer of This American Life, a nationally syndicated radio show
WBEZ Radio **Ph:** 312-832-9150
This American Life
Navy Pier
848 E Grand Ave
Chicago, IL 60611
www.thislife.org

Glass, Julia
Author (Three Junes)
Vintage/Anchor Publicity **Ph:** 212-572-2420
1745 Broadway 20th Fl
New York, NY 10019
www.randomhouse.com/anchor

Glassman, James K
Former editor, publisher, and columnist, now a Resident Fellow at the American Enterprise Institute; author of two books on finance and host of tcsdaily.com
American Enterprise Institute for Public Policy Research **Ph:** 202-862-5800 **Fax:** 202-862-7177
1150 17th St NW Suite 1100
Washington, DC 20036
www.aei.org

Glauber, Roy J, PhD (1925-)
Winner of the 2006 Nobel Prize for Physics (one-half the prize with two other winners dividing the other half) for his contribution to the quantum theory of optical coherence; also Mallinckrodt Professor of Physics at Harvard University
Harvard University **Ph:** 617-495-2869
Dept of Physics
17 Oxford St
Lyman 331
Cambridge, MA 02138
www.physics.harvard.edu

Glaus, Troy (1976-)
Professional baseball player
Arizona Diamondbacks **Ph:** 602-462-6500
Bank One Ballpark **Fax:** 602-462-6600
401 E Jefferson St
Phoenix, AZ 85004
arizona.diamondbacks.mlb.com

Glavine, Tom (1966-)
Professional baseball player
New York Mets **Ph:** 718-507-6387
Shea Stadium **Fax:** 718-507-6395
123-01 Roosevelt Ave
Flushing, NY 11368
newyork.mets.mlb.com

Glazer, Malcolm I (1930-)
Owner of the Tampa Bay Buccaneers football franchise & Manchester United (UK) soccer team
Tampa Bay Buccaneers **Ph:** 813-870-2700
1 Buccaneer Pl **Fax:** 813-878-0813
Tampa, FL 33607
www.buccaneers.com

Gleiberman, Owen
EW movie/video critic
Entertainment Weekly **Ph:** 212-522-5600
1675 Broadway
New York, NY 10019

Glenn, Aaron (1972-)
Professional football player
Dallas Cowboys **Ph:** 972-556-9900
1 Cowboys Pkwy **Fax:** 972-556-9304
Irving, TX 75063
www.dallascowboys.com

Glenn, John (1921-)
Former astronaut and the first American to orbit Earth (Mercury 6, 1962); US Senator from Ohio 1975-1999
John Glenn Institute for Public Service & Public Policy **Ph:** 614-292-4545 **Fax:** 614-292-4868
Ohio State University
350 Page Hall
1810 College Rd
Columbus, OH 43210
www.glenninstitute.org

Glenn, Scott (1941-)
Actor
International Creative Management **Ph:** 310-550-4000
8942 Wilshire Blvd
Beverly Hills, CA 90211

Glenn, Terry (1974-)
Professional football player
Dallas Cowboys **Ph:** 972-556-9900
1 Cowboys Pkwy **Fax:** 972-556-9304
Irving, TX 75063
www.dallascowboys.com

Glickman, Dan (1944-)
President & CEO of the Motion Picture Association of America; former US Secretary of Agriculture
Motion Picture Assn of America **Ph:** 818-995-6600
15503 Ventura Blvd
Encino, CA 91436
www.mpaa.org/AboutUsGlickman.asp

Glink, Ilyce (1964-)
Expert on trends and issues in real estate & personal finance; writes a syndicated column Real Estate Matters with Samuel J. Tamkin ; has also written a number of books on the subject
Tribune Media Services Inc **Ph:** 312-222-4444
435 N Michigan Ave Suite 1500
Chicago, IL 60611
www.thinkglink.com

Glover, Danny (1946-)
Actor
International Creative Management **Ph:** 310-550-4000
8942 Wilshire Blvd
Beverly Hills, CA 90211

Glover, La'Roi (1974-)
Professional football player
Saint Louis Rams **Ph:** 314-982-7267
1 Rams Way **Fax:** 314-770-9261
Earth City, MO 63045
www.stlouisrams.com

Glover, Savion (1973-)
Dancer
William Morris Agency **Ph:** 310-859-4000
1 William Morris Pl **Fax:** 310-859-4462
Beverly Hills, CA 90212

Gluck, Louise (1943-)
Poet
HarperCollins Publishers **Ph:** 212-207-7000
c/o Author Mail
10 E 53rd St
New York, NY 10022
www.harpercollins.com

Godwin, Gail (1937-)
Author (The Odd Woman; Evenings at Five)
Ballantine Books Publicity **Ph:** 212-782-9000
1745 Broadway
New York, NY 10019
www.gailgodwin.com

Gohmert, Louie (1953-)
US Representative from Texas (Republican)
508 Cannon Bldg **Ph:** 202-225-3035
Washington, DC 20515 **Fax:** 202-225-5866
gohmert.house.gov

Goin, Suzanne
Chef and restaurant co-owner with sommelier Caroline Styne
AOC **Ph:** 323-653-6359
8022 W 3rd St
Los Angeles, CA 90048
www.aocwinebar.com

Goings, Nick (1978-)
Professional football player
Carolina Panthers **Ph:** 704-358-7000
Bank of America Stadium **Fax:** 704-358-7618
800 S Mint St
Charlotte, NC 28202
www.panthers.com

Goldberg, Bernard (1932-)
News reporter & writer; contributor to Real Sports with Bryant Gumbel on HBO
HBO Sports **Ph:** 212-512-1000
1100 Ave of the Americas
New York, NY 10036
www.hbo.com/realsports

Goldberg, Danny
Founder and chairman of Artemis Records
Artemis Records **Ph:** 212-414-1700
130 5th Ave 7th Fl **Fax:** 212-414-3188
New York, NY 10011
www.artemisrecords.com

Goldberg, Jonah
Conservative columnist (syndicated); a contributor to the Wall Street Journal, editor-at-large for the National Review Online, and a CNN commentator
Tribune Media Services Inc **Ph:** 312-222-4444
435 N Michigan Ave Suite 1500
Chicago, IL 60611
tmsfeatures.com/productlist.htm

Goldberg, Stan (1933-)
Comic books colorist and illustrator
Archie Comics Magazine **Ph:** 914-381-5155
325 Fayette Ave **Fax:** 914-381-2335
Mamaroneck, NY 10543
www.stangoldberg.com

Goldberg, Whoopi (1955-)
Actor; comedian
William Morris Agency **Ph:** 310-859-4000
1 William Morris Pl **Fax:** 310-859-4462
Beverly Hills, CA 90212
www.wma.com/whoopi_goldberg/summary

Goldin, Nan (1953-)
Photographer
Museum of Contemporary Photography **Ph:** 312-663-5554 **Fax:** 312-344-8067
Columbia College Chicago
600 S Michigan Ave
Chicago, IL 60605
mocp.org/collections/permanent

Goldman, Stan
FOX legal affairs editor
FOX News Channel **Ph:** 212-301-3000
1211 Ave of the Americas
New York, NY 10036
www.foxnews.com/fnctv

Goldman, William (1931-)
Novelist and screenwriter
Creative Artists Agency **Ph:** 310-288-4545
9830 Wilshire Blvd **Fax:** 310-288-4800
Beverly Hills, CA 90212

Goldsman, Akiva (1962-)
Film producer and writer
Creative Artists Agency **Ph:** 310-288-4545
9830 Wilshire Blvd **Fax:** 310-288-4800
Beverly Hills, CA 90212

Goldsmith, Jerry (1929-2004)
Composer
Kraft-Engel Management **Ph:** 818-380-1918
15233 Ventura Blvd Suite 200 **Fax:** 818-380-2609
Sherman Oaks, CA 91403
www.jerrygoldsmithonline.com

Goldstein, Joseph L, MD (1940-)
1985 Nobel Prize winner in Physiology or Medicine (with Michael S. Brown) for discoveries concerning the regulation of cholesterol metabolism
Dept of Molecular Genetics **Ph:** 214-648-3111
University of Texas
Southwestern Medical Center at Dallas
5323 Harry Hines Blvd
Dallas, TX 75390
www.utsouthwestern.edu

Goldthwait, Bobcat (1962-)
Comedian
Gersh Agency **Ph:** 310-274-6611
232 N Canon Dr
Beverly Hills, CA 90210

Goler, Wendell
A White House correspondent for FOX News
FOX News Channel **Ph:** 202-824-6300
400 N Capitol St NW Suite 550
Washington, DC 20001
www.foxnews.com/fnctv

Golisano, B Thomas (1941-)
Founder and chairman of Paychex; owner of the Buffalo Sabres hockey franchise
Paychex Inc **Ph:** 585-385-6666
911 Panorama Trail S **Fax:** 585-383-3449
Rochester, NY 14625
www.paychex.com

Gomes, Marcelo (1980-)
A principal dancer for American Ballet Theatre
American Ballet Theatre **Ph:** 212-477-3030
890 Broadway **Fax:** 212-254-5938
New York, NY 10003
www.abt.org/dancers

Gomez, Christian (1974-)
Professional soccer player
DC United **Ph:** 202-587-5000
RFK Stadium **Fax:** 202-587-5400
2400 E Capitol St SE
Washington, DC 20003
dcunited.mlsnet.com

Gomez, Herculez (1982-)
Professional soccer player
Los Angeles Galaxy **Ph:** 310-630-2200
Home Depot Center **Fax:** 310-630-2250
18400 Avalon Blvd Suite 200
Carson, CA 90746
www.lagalaxy.com

Gomez, Rebecca
Business correspondent for FOX News; provides daily market updates
FOX News Channel **Ph:** 212-301-3000
1211 Ave of the Americas
New York, NY 10036
www.foxnews.com/fnctv

Gomez, Scott (1979-)
Professional hockey player
New Jersey Devils **Ph:** 201-935-6050
Continental Airlines Arena **Fax:** 201-935-2127
50 Rt 120N
East Rutherford, NJ 07073
www.newjerseydevils.com

Gonchar, Sergei (1974-)
Professional hockey player
Pittsburgh Penguins **Ph:** 412-642-1300
1 Chatham Center Suite 400 **Fax:** 412-642-1859
Pittsburgh, PA 15219
www.pittsburghpenguins.com

Gonzales, Alberto (1955-)
Attorney General of the United States
US Dept of Justice **Ph:** 202-514-2000
950 Pennsylvania Ave NW **Fax:** 202-307-6777
Washington, DC 20530
www.usdoj.gov

Gonzales, Ron
Mayor of San Jose, California
801 N First St Suite 600 **Ph:** 408-277-4237
San Jose, CA 95110 **Fax:** 408-277-3755
www.sjmayor.org

Gonzalez, Charles A (1945-)
US Representative from Texas (Democrat)
327 Cannon Bldg **Ph:** 202-225-3236
Washington, DC 20515 **Fax:** 202-225-1915
gonzalez.house.gov

Gonzalez, Luis (1967-)
Professional baseball player
Arizona Diamondbacks **Ph:** 602-462-6500
Bank One Ballpark **Fax:** 602-462-6600
401 E Jefferson St
Phoenix, AZ 85004
arizona.diamondbacks.mlb.com

Gonzalez, Tony (1976-)
Professional football player
Kansas City Chiefs **Ph:** 816-920-9300
Arrowhead Stadium **Fax:** 816-920-4315
1 Arrowhead Dr
Kansas City, MO 64129
www.kcchiefs.com

Goo Goo Dolls
Rock band
William Morris Agency **Ph:** 310-859-4000
1 William Morris Pl **Fax:** 310-859-4462
Beverly Hills, CA 90212
www.googoodolls.org

Goodall, Jane, PhD (1934-)
Expert on chimpanzee behavior
Jane Goodall Institute for Wildlife Research Education & Conservation **Ph:** 703-682-9220 **Fax:** 703-682-9312
4245 N Fairfax Dr Suite 600
Arlington, VA 22203
www.janegoodall.org

Goode, Virgil H Jr (1946-)
US Representative from Virginia (Republican)
1520 Longworth Bldg **Ph:** 202-225-4711
Washington, DC 20515 **Fax:** 202-225-5681
www.house.gov/goode

Gooden, Drew (1981-)
Professional basketball player
Cleveland Cavaliers **Ph:** 216-420-2000
Quicken Loans Arena **Fax:** 216-420-2298
1 Center Ct
Cleveland, OH 44115
www.nba.com/cavaliers

Gooding, Cuba Jr (1968-)
Actor
Creative Artists Agency **Ph:** 310-288-4545
9830 Wilshire Blvd **Fax:** 310-288-4800
Beverly Hills, CA 90212

Goodlatte, Robert W (1952-)
US Representative from Virginia (Republican)
2240 Rayburn Bldg **Ph:** 202-225-5431
Washington, DC 20515 **Fax:** 202-225-9681
www.house.gov/goodlatte

Goodman, Ellen (1941-)
Syndicated columnist (commentary)
Washington Post Writers Group **Ph:** 202-334-6375 **Fax:** 202-334-5669
1150 15th St NW 9th Fl
Washington, DC 20071
www.postwritersgroup.com

Goodman, John (1952-)
Actor
Gersh Agency **Ph:** 310-274-6611
232 N Canon Dr
Beverly Hills, CA 90210

Goodman, John C, PhD
Founder & president of the National Center for Policy Analysis, a conservative think tank
National Center for Policy Analysis **Ph:** 972-386-6272 **Fax:** 972-386-0924
12770 Coit Rd
Dallas, TX 75251
www.ncpa.org/abo/staff/jcgoodman.html

Goodman, Oscar B
Mayor of Las Vegas
400 Stewart Ave 10th Fl **Ph:** 702-229-6241
Las Vegas, NV 89101 **Fax:** 702-385-7960
www.lasvegasnevada.gov

Goodnight, James H, PhD
CEO of SAS Institute Inc, a leader in business analytics software; also a co-founder of SAS Institute
SAS Institute Inc **Ph:** 919-677-8000
100 SAS Campus Dr **Fax:** 919-677-4444
Cary, NC 27513
www.sas.com

Goodson, Adrienne (1966-)
Professional basketball player
Charlotte Sting **Ph:** 704-357-0252
100 Hive Dr **Fax:** 704-335-0289
Charlotte, NC 28217
www.wnba.com/sting

Goodwin, Doris Kearns (1943-)
Historian; author of No Ordinary Time, a biography of Franklin & Eleanor Roosevelt
Simon & Schuster **Ph:** 212-698-7000
1230 Ave of the Americas
New York, NY 10020
www.simonsays.com

Goolsby, OB Jr
President & CEO of Pilgrim's Pride (poultry producers)
Pilgrim's Pride Corp **Ph:** 903-434-1000
4845 US Hwy 271 N
PO Box 93
Pittsburgh, TX 75686
www.pilgrimspride.com

Gordeeva, Ekaterina (1971-)
Figure skater
Stars on Ice **Ph:** 216-436-3708
IMG
1360 E 9th St Suite 100
Cleveland, OH 44114
www.starsonice.com

Gordimer, Nadine (1923-)
Winner of the 1991 Nobel Prize in Literature for novels and short stories in which the consequences of apartheid form the central theme
Penguin Publicity **Ph:** 212-366-2000
375 Hudson St
New York, NY 10014
us.penguingroup.com

Gordon, Bart (1949-)
US Representative from Tennessee (Democrat)
2304 Rayburn Bldg **Ph:** 202-225-4231
Washington, DC 20515 **Fax:** 202-225-6887
gordon.house.gov

Gordon, Bruce (1946-)
President and CEO of the NAACP
NAACP **Ph:** 410-580-5777
4805 Mt Hope Dr
Baltimore, MD 21215
www.naacp.org

Gordon, Ellen
President & COO of Tootsie Roll Industries Inc
Tootsie Roll Industries Inc **Ph:** 773-838-3400
7401 S Cicero Ave **Fax:** 773-838-3564
Chicago, IL 60629

Gordon, Jeff (1971-)
Race car driver
Hendrick Motorsports **Ph:** 704-455-3400
4400 Papa Joe Hendrick Blvd
Charlotte, NC 28262
www.jeffgordon.com

Gordon, Mary (1949-)
Author (fiction & nonfiction); books include Spending: A Novel and The Company of Women
Barnard College **Ph:** 212-854-2116
Dept of English **Fax:** 212-854-9498
417 Barnard Hall
3009 Broadway
New York, NY 10027
www.barnard.edu/english/faculty.html

Gordon, Phil (1951-)
Mayor of Phoenix, Arizona
200 W Washington St 11th Fl **Ph:** 602-262-7111
Phoenix, AZ 85003 **Fax:** 602-495-5583
phoenix.gov

Gore, Albert Jr (1948-)
Former Vice President of the United States
2100 West End Ave Suite 620 **Ph:** 615-327-2227
Nashville, TN 37203 **Fax:** 615-327-1323

Gore, Tipper (1948-)
Wife of former US Vice President Al Gore
2100 West End Ave Suite 620 **Ph:** 615-327-2227
Nashville, TN 37203 **Fax:** 615-327-1323

Gorelick, Jamie S (1950-)
Attorney; member of the 9/11 Commission and former Deputy Attorney General of the US
Wilmer Cutler Pickering Hale & Dorr LLP **Ph:** 202-663-6500 **Fax:** 202-663-6363
2445 M St NW
Washington, DC 20037
www.wilmerhale.com

Gorey, Edward (1925-2000)
Artist/illustrator
Edward Gorey House **Ph:** 508-362-3909
8 Strawberry Ln
Yarmouthport, MA 02675
www.edwardgoreyhouse.org

Gorman, Leon A
Chairman of LL Bean Inc
LL Bean Inc **Ph:** 207-865-4761
15 Casco St **Fax:** 207-552-6821
Freeport, ME 04033
www2.llbean.com

Gorog, Chris
Chairman and CEO of Napster
Napster LLC **Ph:** 310-281-5000
9044 Melrose Ave
Los Angeles, CA 90069
investor.napster.com

Gorrell, Bob (1955-)
Editorial cartoonist
Creators Syndicate Inc **Ph:** 310-337-7003
5777 W Century Blvd Suite 700 **Fax:** 310-337-7625
Los Angeles, CA 90045
www.creators.com

Gorton, Slade (1928-)
Attorney and former US senator from Washington; member of the 9/11 Commission
Preston Gates & Ellis LLP **Ph:** 206-623-7580
925 4th Ave Suite 2900 **Fax:** 206-623-7022
Seattle, WA 87104
www.prestongates.com

Gossett, Louis Jr (1936-)
Actor
CESD Voices **Ph:** 310-475-2111
10635 Santa Monica Blvd Suites 130/135
Los Angeles, CA 90025
www.louisgossett.info

Gott, Peter, MD (1935-)
A practicing internist; writes the syndicated column Dr. Gott in which he answers readers' medical questions
United Feature Syndicate **Ph:** 212-293-8500
200 Madison Ave
New York, NY 10016
www.unitedfeatures.com

Gottfried, Gilbert (1955-)
Comedian
William Morris Agency **Ph:** 212-586-5100
1325 Ave of the Americas **Fax:** 212-246-3583
New York, NY 10019
www.wma.com/gilbert_gottfried/summary

Gould, Elliott (1938-)
Actor
William Morris Agency **Ph:** 310-859-4000
1 William Morris Pl **Fax:** 310-859-4462
Beverly Hills, CA 90212
www.wma.com/elliott_gould/summary

Gourevitch, Philip (1961-)
Staff writer for New Yorker magazine and author of We Wish to Inform You That Tomorrow We Will Be Killed with Our Families: Stories from Rwanda
Farrar Straus & Giroux Inc **Ph:** 212-741-6900
19 Union Sq W
New York, NY 10003
www.fsgbooks.com

Grace, Bud
Creator of the comic strip Piranha Club
King Features Syndicate Inc **Ph:** 212-455-4000
888 7th Ave 2nd Fl
New York, NY 10019
www.kingfeatures.com

Grace, Nancy (1958-)
Host of the legal analysis program Nancy Grace on CNN's Headline Prime; also hosts Closing Arguments on Courtroom TV
CNN New York **Ph:** 212-275-7800
Time Warner Ctr
10 Columbus Cir
New York, NY 10019
www.cnn.com/CNN/anchors_reporters

Grace, Topher (1978-)
Actor
William Morris Agency Ph: 310-859-4000
1 William Morris Pl Fax: 310-859-4462
Beverly Hills, CA 90212
www.that70sshow.com

Gracin, Josh
Country singer; former contestant on American Idol
William Morris Agency Ph: 615-963-3000
1600 Division St Suite 300 Fax: 615-963-3090
Nashville, TN 37203
www.joshgracin.com

Grady, Patricia A, PhD
Director of the National Institute of Nursing Research and noted stroke researcher
National Institute of Nursing Research Ph: 301-496-8230
Fax: 301-594-3405
31 Ctr Dr
Bldg 31 Rm 5B05
Bethesda, MD 20892
ninr.nih.gov/ninr

Graedon, Joe
Writes the syndicated column The People's Pharmacy with his wife, Dr. Teresa Graedon
King Features Syndicate Inc Ph: 212-455-4000
888 7th Ave 2nd Fl
New York, NY 10019
www.kingfeatures.com

Graedon, Teresa, PhD
Writes the syndicated column The People's Pharmacy with her husband Joe Graedon
King Features Syndicate Inc Ph: 212-455-4000
888 7th Ave 2nd Fl
New York, NY 10019
www.kingfeatures.com

Graf, Steffi (1969-)
Professional tennis player (retired)
Andre Agassi Charitable Foundation Ph: 702-227-5700
Fax: 702-866-2929
3960 Howard Hughes Pkwy Suite 750
Las Vegas, NV 89109

Grafton, Sue (1940-)
Mystery writer (Kinsey Millhone/alphabet series, as in R is for Ricochet)
Putnam Publicity Ph: 212-366-2000
375 Hudson St
New York, NY 10014
www.suegrafton.com

Graham, Billy (1918-)
Evangelist
Billy Graham Evangelistic Assn Ph: 704-401-2432
1 Billy Graham Pkwy TF: 877-247-2426
Charlotte, NC 28201
www.billygraham.org

Graham, Franklin (1952-)
President of Samaritan's Purse; son of Billy Graham
Samaritan's Purse Ph: 828-262-1980
PO Box 3000 Fax: 828-266-1053
Boone, NC 28607
www.samaritanspurse.org

Graham, Fred (1931-)
Journalist, lawyer, broadcaster, and Court TV anchor
Courtroom Television Network Ph: 212-973-2800
600 3rd Ave
New York, NY 10016
www.courttv.com/anchors

Graham, Heather (1970-)
Actor
United Talent Agency Ph: 310-273-6700
9560 Wilshire Blvd 5th Fl Fax: 310-247-1111
Beverly Hills, CA 90212

Graham, Jack (1950-)
Creator of PowerPoint Ministries, a radio and television broadcast ministry of the Prestonwood Baptist Church in Plano, Texas, where he is pastor
PowerPoint Ministries Ph: 972-820-5000
PO Box 262627 TF: 800-779-7693
Plano, TX 75026
www.powerpoint.org

Graham, Jorie (1950-)
Poet
HarperCollins Publishers Ph: 212-207-7000
c/o Author Mail
10 E 53rd St
New York, NY 10022
www.harpercollins.com

Graham, Katharine (1917-2001)
Longtime publisher of the Washington Post & Pulitzer-Prize-winning writer
Knopf Publishing/Author Mail Ph: 212-782-9000
1745 Broadway
New York, NY 10019
www.randomhouse.com/knopf

Graham, Lauren (1967-)
Actor
International Creative Management **Ph:** 310-550-4000
8942 Wilshire Blvd
Beverly Hills, CA 90211

Graham, Lindsey (1955-)
US Senator from South Carolina (Republican)
290 Russell Bldg **Ph:** 202-224-5972
Washington, DC 20510 **Fax:** 202-224-3808
lgraham.senate.gov

Graham, Shayne (1977-)
Professional football player
Cincinnati Bengals **Ph:** 513-621-3550
1 Paul Brown Stadium **Fax:** 513-621-3570
Cincinnati, OH 45202
www.bengals.com

Grahame, John (1975-)
Professional hockey player
Tampa Bay Lightning **Ph:** 813-301-6600
St Pete Times Forum **Fax:** 813-301-1487
401 Channelside Dr
Tampa, FL 33602
www.tampabaylightning.com

Grammer, Kelsey (1955-)
Actor
Creative Artists Agency **Ph:** 310-288-4545
9830 Wilshire Blvd **Fax:** 310-288-4800
Beverly Hills, CA 90212

Granato, Cammi (1971-)
Olympic medalist in women's ice hockey
Granato Hockey **Ph:** 815-439-8293
PO Box 852
Plainfield, IL 60544
www.granatohockey.com

Granato, Tony (1964-)
Former hockey player, now assistant coach of the Colorado Avalanche hockey team
Colorado Avalanche **Ph:** 303-405-1100
Pepsi Center
1000 Chopper Cir
Denver, CO 80204
www.coloradoavalanche.com

Grandin, Temple, PhD (1947-)
Animal scientist; designer of systems & equipment for humane handling of livestock
Colorado State University **Ph:** 970-491-1442
Dept of Animal Sciences
Fort Collins, CO 80523
www.grandin.com

GrandPre, Mary (1954-)
Illustrator of the Harry Potter books; has also illustrated a number of children's picture books and is now creating her own characters and writing about them
Scholastic Inc **Ph:** 212-343-6100
557 Broadway
New York, NY 10012
www.marygrandpre.com

Granger, David
Editor-in-Chief of Esquire Magazine
Esquire Magazine **Ph:** 212-649-2000
250 W 55th St **Fax:** 212-977-3158
New York, NY 10019

Granger, Kay (1943-)
US Representative from Texas (Republican)
440 Cannon Bldg **Ph:** 202-225-5071
Washington, DC 20515 **Fax:** 202-225-5683
kaygranger.house.gov

Granholm, Jennifer (1959-)
Governor of Michigan (Democrat)
PO Box 30013 **Ph:** 517-373-3400
Lansing, MI 48909 **Fax:** 517-335-6863
www.michigan.gov/gov

Grant, Amy (1960-)
Singer (Christian music)
CAA Nashville **Ph:** 615-383-8787
3310 West End Ave 5th Fl **Fax:** 615-383-4937
Nashville, TN 37203
www.amygrant.com

Grant, Hugh (1960-)
Actor
Creative Artists Agency **Ph:** 310-288-4545
9830 Wilshire Blvd **Fax:** 310-288-4800
Beverly Hills, CA 90212

Grant, Hugh
Chairman, president, and CEO of Monsanto
Monsanto Co **Ph:** 314-694-1000
800 N Lindbergh Blvd
Saint Louis, MO 63167
www.monsanto.com

Granville, Laura (1981-)
Professional tennis player
WTA Tour **Ph:** 727-895-5000
1 Progress Plaza Suite 1500 **Fax:** 727-894-1982
Saint Petersburg, FL 33701
www.wtatour.com

Grass, Gunter (1927-)
German author (The Tin Drum) and winner of the 1999 Nobel Prize for Literature
Harcourt Trade Publishers **Ph:** 212-592-1000
15 E 26th St
New York, NY 10010
www.harcourtbooks.com

Grassley, Charles E (1933-)
US Senator from Iowa (Republican)
135 Hart Bldg **Ph:** 202-224-3744
Washington, DC 20510 **Fax:** 202-224-6020
grassley.senate.gov

Gratton, Robert
Chairman of Power Financial Corp, a management and holding company with controlling interests in financial services companies
Power Financial Corp **Ph:** 514-286-7430
751 Victoria Sq **Fax:** 514-286-7424
Montreal, QC H2Y2J3

Grau, Shirley Ann (1929-)
Southern novelist (The Keepers of the House)
Vintage/Anchor Publicity **Ph:** 212-572-2420
1745 Broadway 20th Fl
New York, NY 10019
www.randomhouse.com/vintage

Graves, Earl G Sr (1935-)
Founder and publisher of Black Enterprise Magazine
Earl G Graves Ltd **Ph:** 212-242-8000
130 5th Ave 10th Fl **Fax:** 212-886-9610
New York, NY 10011
www.blackenterprise.com

Graves, Sam (1963-)
US Representative from Missouri (Republican)
1513 Longworth Bldg **Ph:** 202-225-7041
Washington, DC 20515 **Fax:** 202-225-8221
www.house.gov/graves

Gray, John, PhD (1951-)
Author of Men are from Mars, Women are from Venus; writes a syndicated column on relationships
Creators Syndicate Inc **Ph:** 310-337-7003
5777 W Century Blvd Suite 700 **Fax:** 310-337-7625
Los Angeles, CA 90045
www.marsvenus.com

Gray, Macy (1970-)
Pop singer
William Morris Agency **Ph:** 310-859-4000
1 William Morris Pl **Fax:** 310-859-4462
Beverly Hills, CA 90212
www.macygray.com

Gray, Todd
Chef of Equinox Restaurant, which is located about one block from the White House
Equinox Restaurant **Ph:** 202-331-8118
818 Connecticut Ave NW
Washington, DC 20006
www.equinoxrestaurant.com

Gray, William M, PhD
Colorado State professor and researcher known for his annual hurricane predictions
Colorado State University **Ph:** 970-491-8681
Dept of Atmospheric Science **Fax:** 970-491-8449
200 W Lake St
Fort Collins, CO 80523
www.atmos.colostate.edu

Grazer, Brian (1951-)
Movie & TV writer and producer; with Ron Howard, co-founder and co-chairman of Imagine Entertainment
Imagine Entertainment **Ph:** 310-858-2000
9465 Wilshire Blvd 7th Fl **Fax:** 310-858-2020
Beverly Hills, CA 90212
www.imagine-entertainment.com

Greco, Michael S (1942-)
Trial lawyer in business, employment, and real estate law; 2005 president of the American Bar Association (will serve until August 2006)
Kirkpatrick & Lockhart **Ph:** 617-261-3232
Nicholson Graham LLP **Fax:** 617-261-3175
State Street Financial Center
1 Lincoln St
Boston, MA 02111
www.klng.com

Green, Ahman (1977-)
Professional football player
Green Bay Packers **Ph:** 920-569-7500
PO Box 10628 **Fax:** 920-569-7201
Green Bay, WI 54307
www.packers.com

Green, Al (1947-)
US Representative from Texas (Democrat)
1529 Longworth Bldg **Ph:** 202-225-7508
Washington, DC 20515 **Fax:** 202-225-2947
www.house.gov/algreen

Green, Dennis (1950-)
Football coach
Arizona Cardinals **Ph:** 602-379-0101
8701 S Hardy Dr **Fax:** 602-379-1819
Tempe, AZ 85284
www.dennisgreen.com

Green, Gene (1947-)
US Representative from Texas (Democrat)
2335 Rayburn Bldg **Ph:** 202-225-1688
Washington, DC 20515 **Fax:** 202-225-9903
www.house.gov/green

Green, Jeff (1962-)
NASCAR driver
Green Foundation **Ph:** 704-799-7053
137 Cedar Pointe Dr
Mooresville, NC 28117
www.jeffgreen.com

Green, Lauren
News update anchor on Fox and Friends
FOX News Channel **Ph:** 212-301-3000
1211 Ave of the Americas
New York, NY 10036
www.foxnews.com/fnctv

Green, Mark (1960-)
US Representative from Wisconsin (Republican)
1314 Longworth Bldg **Ph:** 202-225-5665
Washington, DC 20515 **Fax:** 202-225-5729
www.house.gov/markgreen

Green, Mike (1976-)
Professional football player
Seattle Seahawks **Ph:** 425-827-9777
11220 NE 53rd St **Fax:** 425-827-9008
Kirkland, WA 98033
www.seahawks.com

Green, Richard C
Chairman, president, and CEO of Aquila, which operates electricity and natural gas distribution utilities in six states
Aquila Inc **Ph:** 816-421-6600
20 W 9th St **Fax:** 816-467-3595
Kansas City, MO 64105
www.aquila.com

Green, Seth (1974-)
Actor
United Talent Agency **Ph:** 310-273-6700
9560 Wilshire Blvd 5th Fl **Fax:** 310-247-1111
Beverly Hills, CA 90212
www.sethgreenonline.com

Green, Shawn (1972-)
Professional baseball player
Arizona Diamondbacks **Ph:** 602-462-6500
Bank One Ballpark **Fax:** 602-462-6600
401 E Jefferson St
Phoenix, AZ 85004
arizona.diamondbacks.mlb.com

Green, Trent (1970-)
Professional football player
Kansas City Chiefs **Ph:** 816-920-9300
Arrowhead Stadium **Fax:** 816-920-4315
1 Arrowhead Dr
Kansas City, MO 64129
www.kcchiefs.com

Green, William (1979-)
Professional football player
Cleveland Browns **Ph:** 440-891-5000
76 Lou Groza Blvd **Fax:** 440-891-5009
Berea, OH 44017
www.clevelandbrowns.com

Green Day
Punk music band
Creative Artists Agency **Ph:** 310-288-4545
9830 Wilshire Blvd **Fax:** 310-288-4800
Beverly Hills, CA 90212
www.greenday.com

Greenberg, Jerry A
Co-founder, with Stuart Moore, of Sapient, a business consulting and technology services firm; both serve as CEO and chairman of Sapient's board
Sapient Corp **Ph:** 617-621-0200
25 1st St **Fax:** 617-621-1300
Cambridge, MA 02141
www.sapient.com

Greenberg, Paul (1937-)
Editor of the editorial pages of the Arkansas Democrat-Gazette and a syndicated columnist; gave Bill Clinton the sobriquet Slick Willie
Tribune Media Services Inc **Ph:** 312-222-4444
435 N Michigan Ave Suite 1500
Chicago, IL 60611
tmsfeatures.com/productlist.htm

Greene, Bob (1947-)
Author of Get With the Program! and other weight loss books/plans; was Oprah Winfrey's personal trainer
Westport Entertainment Assoc **Ph:** 203-319-4343
1700 Post Rd Suite C15
Fairfield, CT 06824
www.getwiththeprogram.org

Greene, Maurice (1974-)
Track & field athlete (runner)
HSInternational **Ph:** 949-753-9153
9871 Irvine Center Dr
Irvine, CA 92618
www.hsi.net

Greenfield, Eloise (1929-)
Poet and author of children's books (Africa Dream; Mary McLeod Bethune; Childtimes: A Three-Generation Memoir)
HarperCollins Children's Books **Ph:** 212-261-6500
1350 Ave of the Americas
New York, NY 10019
www.harperchildrens.com

Greenfield, Jeff (1943-)
CNN's senior analyst and a contributor to Inside Politics as well as other CNN programs
CNN **Ph:** 404-827-1500
1 CNN Center
Atlanta, GA 30303
www.cnn.com/CNN/anchors_reporters

Greenfield, Jerry (1951-)
Co-founder (with Ben Cohen) of Ben & Jerry's Ice Cream
Ben & Jerry's Homemade Holdings Inc **Ph:** 802-846-1500 **Fax:** 802-846-1520
30 Community Dr
South Burlington, VT 05403
www.benjerry.com

Greenfield, Lauren (1966-)
Photographer; author of Girl Culture
Chronicle Books **Ph:** 415-537-4200
85 2nd St 6th Fl **Fax:** 415-537-4460
San Francisco, CA 94105
www.chroniclebooks.com

Greengard, Paul, PhD (1925-)
Winner (with two other scientists) of the 2000 Nobel Prize in Medicine or Physiology for their discoveries concerning signal transduction in the nervous system
Rockefeller University **Ph:** 212-327-8000
Laboratory of Molecular & Cellular Neuroscience
1230 York Ave
New York, NY 10021
www.rockefeller.edu

Greenspan, Bud (1926-)
Filmmaker (sports films & documentaries)
Cappy Productions Inc **Ph:** 212-249-1800
118 E 57th St 3rd Fl **Fax:** 212-439-9165
New York, NY 10022
www.budgreenspan.com

Gregg, Judd (1947-)
US Senator from New Hampshire (Republican)
393 Russell Bldg **Ph:** 202-224-3324
Washington, DC 20510 **Fax:** 202-224-4952
gregg.senate.gov

Gregoire, Christine (1947-)
Governor of Washington (Democrat)
302 14th St SW **Ph:** 360-902-4111
PO Box 40002 **Fax:** 360-753-4110
Olympia, WA 98504
www.governor.wa.gov

Gregory, David
NBC News chief White House correspondent
NBC News **Ph:** 202-885-4200
4001 Nebraska Ave NW
Washington, DC 20016
www.msnbc.msn.com/id/3689499

Greider, William
National affairs correspondent for The Nation; also nonfiction author
The Nation **Ph:** 212-209-5400
33 Irving Pl 8th Fl **Fax:** 212-982-9000
New York, NY 10003
www.williamgreider.com

Greshes, Warren
Motivational speaker in the areas of personal & professional development
202 Telluride Trail **Ph:** 919-933-5900
Chapel Hill, NC 27514 **Fax:** 919-933-5711
www.greshes.com **TF:** 800-858-1516

Gretzky, Wayne (1961-)
Considered to be the greatest player in the history of hockey (retired); managing partner, alternate governor, and head coach of the Phoenix Coyotes NHL team
Phoenix Coyotes **Ph:** 623-463-8800
5800 W Glenn Dr Suite 350 **Fax:** 623-463-8810
Glendale, AZ 85301
www.phoenixcoyotes.com

Grey, Brad (1958-)
Chairman & CEO of Paramount Motion Pictures Group; co-founder of Brillstein-Grey Entertainment
Paramount Motion Pictures Group **Ph:** 323-956-5000
5555 Melrose Ave
Hollywood, CA 90038
www.viacom.com/management.jhtml

Grier, Mike (1975-)
Professional hockey player
Buffalo Sabres **Ph:** 716-855-4100
HSBC Arena **Fax:** 716-855-4115
1 Seymour H Knox III Plaza
Buffalo, NY 14203
www.sabres.com

Griese, Brian (1975-)
Professional football player
Chicago Bears **Ph:** 847-295-6600
Halas Hall at Conway Park **Fax:** 847-295-8986
1000 Football Dr
Lake Forest, IL 60045
www.chicagobears.com

Griffeth, Bill
Financial journalist and co-host of Power Lunch; was part of the production team that founded the Financial News Network, which NBC purchased in 1991
CNBC **Ph:** 201-735-2622
900 Sylvan Ave
Englewood Cliffs, NJ 07632
moneycentral.msn.com/cnbc/tv

Griffey, Ken Jr (1969-)
Professional baseball player
Cincinnati Reds **Ph:** 513-765-7000
Great American Ballpark **Fax:** 513-765-7342
100 Main St
Cincinnati, OH 45202
cincinnati.reds.mlb.com

Griffin, Eddie (1982-)
Professional basketball player
Minnesota Timberwolves **Ph:** 612-673-1600
Target Center **Fax:** 612-673-1699
600 1st Ave N
Minneapolis, MN 55403
www.nba.com/timberwolves

Griffin, Kathy (1961-)
Comedian
United Talent Agency **Ph:** 310-273-6700
9560 Wilshire Blvd 5th Fl **Fax:** 310-247-1111
Beverly Hills, CA 90212
www.kathygriffin.net

Griffith, Andy (1926-)
Actor
William Morris Agency **Ph:** 310-859-4000
1 William Morris Pl **Fax:** 310-859-4462
Beverly Hills, CA 90212

Griffith, Bill (1944-)
Creator of the comic strip Zippy the Pinhead
King Features Syndicate Inc **Ph:** 212-455-4000
888 7th Ave 2nd Fl
New York, NY 10019
www.kingfeatures.com

Griffith, Melanie (1957-)
Actor
William Morris Agency **Ph:** 310-859-4000
1 William Morris Pl **Fax:** 310-859-4462
Beverly Hills, CA 90212

Griffith, Robert (1970-)
Professional football player
Arizona Cardinals **Ph:** 602-379-0101
8701 S Hardy Dr **Fax:** 602-379-1819
Tempe, AZ 85284
www.azcardinals.com

Griffith, Yolanda (1970-)
Professional basketball player
Sacramento Monarchs **Ph:** 916-928-0000
ARCO Arena **Fax:** 916-928-8109
1 Sports Pkwy
Sacramento, CA 95834
www.wnba.com/monarchs

Griffiths, Rachel (1968-)
Actor
William Morris Agency **Ph:** 310-859-4000
1 William Morris Pl **Fax:** 310-859-4462
Beverly Hills, CA 90212
www.hbo.com/sixfeetunder/cast

Griggs, Andy (1973-)
Country singer
William Morris Agency **Ph:** 615-963-3000
1600 Division St Suite 300 **Fax:** 615-963-3090
Nashville, TN 37203
www.andygriggs.com

Grijalva, Raul M (1948-)
US Representative from Arizona (Democrat)
1440 Longworth Bldg **Ph:** 202-225-2435
Washington, DC 20515 **Fax:** 202-225-1541
www.house.gov/grijalva

Grimes, MaDonna
Founder and creative director of the MaDonna Grimes Dance Fitness Theatre Co, which offers classes that combine dance and exercise
MaDonna Grimes Dance Fitness Theatre Co **Ph:** 323-468-9000
6767 Sunset Blvd 2nd Level
Los Angeles, CA 90028
www.madonna-grimes.com

Grimes, Martha (1931-)
Mystery author; her work includes the series featuring the British detective Richard Jury
Viking Publicity **Ph:** 212-366-2000
375 Hudson St
New York, NY 10014
www.marthagrimes.com

Grimes, Nikki (1950-)
Poet of both children's and adult verse; author of books for children and young adults, including the novel Bronx Masquerade
Puffin Books Publicity **Ph:** 212-366-2000
345 Hudson St
New York, NY 10014
www.nikkigrimes.com

Grinney, Jay (1951-)
President & CEO of HealthSouth Corp
HealthSouth Corp **Ph:** 205-967-7116
1 HealthSouth Pkwy
Birmingham, AL 35243
www.healthsouth.com

Grinstein, Gerald
CEO of Delta Air Lines
Delta Airlines Inc **Ph:** 404-715-2600
1030 Delta Blvd **Fax:** 404-715-5042
Hartsfield-Atlanta Airport
Atlanta, GA 30320
www.delta.com

Grisham, John (1955-)
Author of legal thrillers
Doubleday Publicity **Ph:** 212-782-9000
1745 Broadway
New York, NY 10019
www.randomhouse.com/features/grisham

Griswold, Tom (1953-)
Co-host, with Bob Kevoian, of a comedy-based morning radio show
Bob & Tom Show **Ph:** 317-257-7565
6161 Fall Creek Rd **Fax:** 317-253-6501
Indianapolis, IN 46220
www.bobandtom.com

Groban, Josh (1981-)
Singer
William Morris Agency **Ph:** 310-859-4000
1 William Morris Pl **Fax:** 310-859-4462
Beverly Hills, CA 90212
www.joshgroban.com

Groening, Matt (1954-)
Creator of The Simpsons
Fox Broadcasting Co **Ph:** 310-369-1000
The Simpsons
10201 W Pico Blvd
Los Angeles, CA 90035
www.thesimpsons.com

Groopman, Jerome, MD
AIDS & cancer specialist/researcher who has written books about the spiritual lives of patients with serious illness
Harvard Institutes of Medicine **Ph:** 617-667-0070
4 Blackfan Circle Rm 351 **Fax:** 617-975-5244
Boston, MA 02115
www.jeromegroopman.com

Gros, Joshua (1982-)
Professional soccer player
DC United **Ph:** 202-587-5000
RFK Stadium **Fax:** 202-587-5400
2400 E Capitol St SE
Washington, DC 20003
dcunited.mlsnet.com

Gross, Bill
Founder, chairman, and CEO of Idealab
Idealab **Ph:** 626-585-6900
130 W Union St **Fax:** 626-535-2701
Pasadena, CA 91103
www.idealab.com

Gross, David J, PhD (1941-)
Winner (with two other scientists) of the 2004 Nobel Prize in Physics; director of the Kavli Institute for Theoretical Physics at the University of California, Santa Barbara
Kavli Institute for Theoretical Physics **Ph:** 805-893-7337
Fax: 805-893-2431
University of California Santa Barbara
Kohn Hall Rm 1219
Santa Barbara, CA 93106
www.kitp.ucsb.edu/inside

Gross, Terry (1951-)
Host of National Public Radio's Fresh Air, a guest-interview show
National Public Radio **Ph:** 212-878-1430
New York Bureau
801 2nd Ave Suite 701
New York, NY 10017
www.npr.org

Grosvenor, Gilbert (1931-)
Former president of the National Geographic Society (retired 1996), now chairman of the Society's Board of Trustees
National Geographic Society **Ph:** 202-857-7000
1145 17th St NW
Washington, DC 20036
press.nationalgeographic.com/pressroom

Grosvenor, Vertamae
Poet, actress, culinary anthropologist, and writer; as correspondent on NPR's Cultural Desk, provides stories on African American creativity, community, and citizenship, and is host of holiday specials about food and culture
National Public Radio **Ph:** 202-513-2000
635 Massachusetts Ave NW **Fax:** 202-513-3329
Washington, DC 20001
www.npr.org

Grousbeck, Wyc
Managing Partner and CEO of the Boston Celtics basketball club
Boston Celtics **Ph:** 617-854-8000
226 Causeway St 4th Fl **Fax:** 617-367-4286
Boston, MA 02114
www.nba.com/celtics

Grove, Amanda
Newsbreaks anchor on Court TV
Courtroom Television Network **Ph:** 212-973-2800
600 3rd Ave
New York, NY 10016
www.courttv.com/anchors

Grove, Andrew S (1936-)
Co-founder of Intel Corp; serves as Senior Advisor to executive management
Intel Corp **Ph:** 408-765-8080
2200 Mission College Blvd
Santa Clara, CA 95052
www.intel.com/pressroom/advisors.htm

Grove, Lloyd
Gossip columnist
Copley News Service **Ph:** 619-293-1818
PO Box 120190
San Diego, CA 92112
www.copleynews.com

Grubbs, Robert H, PhD (1942-)
Winner of the 2006 Nobel Prize for Chemistry (one third of the award with Richard P Schrock and Yves Chavrin) for the development of the metathesis method in organic synthesis
California Institute of Technology **Ph:** 626-395-6003
Fax: 626-568-8824
Div of Chemistry & Chemical Engineering
1200 E California Blvd
363 Crellin MC 164-30
Pasadena, CA 91125
www.cce.caltech.edu

Gruden, Jon (1963-)
Football coach
Tampa Bay Buccaneers **Ph:** 813-870-2700
1 Buccaneer Pl **Fax:** 813-878-0813
Tampa, FL 33607
www.buccaneers.com

Grumman, Cornelia
Editorial writer and member of the editorial board of the Chicago Tribune
Chicago Tribune **Ph:** 312-222-3232
435 N Michigan Ave **Fax:** 312-222-4674
Chicago, IL 60611
www.chicagotribune.com/news/opinion

Guardado, Eddie (1970-)
Professional baseball player
Seattle Mariners **Ph:** 206-346-4000
Safeco Field **Fax:** 206-346-4050
1250 1st Ave S
Seattle, WA 98134
seattle.mariners.mlb.com

Guare, John (1938-)
Playwright and screenwriter
International Creative Management **Ph:** 310-550-4000
8942 Wilshire Blvd
Beverly Hills, CA 90211

Guerin, Bill (1970-)
Professional hockey player
Dallas Stars **Ph:** 214-387-5500
2601 Ave of the Stars **Fax:** 214-387-3599
Frisco, TX 75034
www.dallasstars.com

Guerrero, Vladimir (1976-)
Professional baseball player
Los Angeles Angels of Anaheim **Ph:** 714-940-2000
Angel Stadium **Fax:** 714-940-2205
2000 Gene Autry Way
Anaheim, CA 92806
losangeles.angels.mlb.com

Guest, Christopher (1948-)
Actor; screenwriter; director
United Talent Agency **Ph:** 310-273-6700
9560 Wilshire Blvd 5th Fl **Fax:** 310-247-1111
Beverly Hills, CA 90212

Guevara, Amado (1976-)
Professional soccer player
New York Red Bulls **Ph:** 201-583-7000
1 Harmon Plaza 3rd Fl **Fax:** 201-583-7055
Secaucus, NJ 07094
redbull.newyork.mlsnet.com

Guevara, Susan
Illustrator of books for children
Puffin Books Publicity **Ph:** 212-366-2000
345 Hudson St
New York, NY 10014
www.susanguevara.com

Guilfoyle, Kimberly (1969-)
Legal analyst and host of The Lineup on Fox News
Fox News Channel **Ph:** 212-301-3000
1211 Ave of the Americas
New York, NY 10038
www.foxnews.com/fnctv

Guillemin, Roger, MD, PhD (1924-)
Winner of the 1977 Nobel Prize in Physiology or Medicine for discoveries concerning the peptide hormone production of the brain
Salk Institute for Biological Studies **Ph:** 858-453-4100 **Fax:** 858-453-8534
PO Box 85800
San Diego, CA 92186
www.salk.edu/faculty

Guillen, Carlos (1975-)
Professional baseball player
Detroit Tigers **Ph:** 313-962-4000
Comerica Park **Fax:** 313-471-2138
2100 Woodward Ave
Detroit, MI 48201
detroit.tigers.mlb.com

Guillen, Jose (1976-)
Professional baseball player
Washington Nationals **Ph:** 202-349-0400
RFK Stadium
2400 E Capitol St SE
Washington, DC 20003
washington.nationals.mlb.com

Guillen, Ozzie (1964-)
Baseball manager
Chicago White Sox **Ph:** 312-674-1000
US Cellular Field **Fax:** 312-674-5109
333 W 35th St
Chicago, IL 60616
chicago.whitesox.mlb.com

Guinn, Kenny (1936-)
Governor of Nevada (Republican)
101 N Carson St **Ph:** 775-684-5670
Carson City, NV 89701 **Fax:** 775-684-5683
gov.state.nv.us

Guisewite, Cathy
Creator of the comic strip Cathy
Universal Press Syndicate **Ph:** 816-932-6600
4520 Main St
Kansas City, MO 64111
www.amuniversal.com/ups/features

Gulati, Sunil (1960-)
President of US Soccer, the national governing body of soccer in the US
US Soccer Federation **Ph:** 312-808-1300
1801 S Prairie Ave **Fax:** 312-808-1301
Chicago, IL 60616
www.ussoccer.com

Gulbis, Natalie (1983-)
Professional golfer
Ladies Professional Golf Assn **Ph:** 386-274-6200
100 International Golf Dr **Fax:** 386-274-1099
Daytona Beach, FL 32124
www.nataliegulbis.com

Gumbel, Bryant (1948-)
Host of Real Sports with Bryant Gumbel on HBO; was long-time Today Show host
HBO Sports **Ph:** 212-512-1000
1100 Ave of the Americas
New York, NY 10036
www.hbo.com/realsports

Gumbel, Greg (1946-)
Studio host and sports commentator
CBS Sports **Ph:** 212-975-4321
51 W 52nd St
New York, NY 10019
cbs.sportsline.com/cbssports/team

Gunnarson, Dean (1964-)
Magician/escape artist
World Wide Talent Agency Ltd **Ph:** 204-255-6766
781 Silverstone Ave **Fax:** 204-669-0287
Winnipeg, MB R3T2W5
www.alwaysescaping.com

Gupta, Sanjay, MD (1972-)
Senior medical correspondent for CNN and co-host of Accent Health for Turner Private Networks; he is a practicing neurosurgeon & an assistant professor of neurosurgery
CNN **Ph:** 404-827-1500
1 CNN Center
Atlanta, GA 30303
www.cnn.com/CNN/anchors_reporters

Guren, Peter
Creator of the comic strip Ask Shagg
Creators Syndicate Inc **Ph:** 310-337-7003
5777 W Century Blvd Suite 700 **Fax:** 310-337-7625
Los Angeles, CA 90045
www.creators.com

Gustafson, Mark
Cartoonist and animator/animation director (directs humorous animation/live action mixes)
Laika **Ph:** 503-225-1130
1400 NW 22nd Ave **Fax:** 503-226-3746
Portland, OR 97210
www.markgustafson.com

Guterson, David (1956-)
Author (Snow Falling on Cedars)
Vintage/Anchor Publicity **Ph:** 212-572-2420
1745 Broadway 20th Fl
New York, NY 10019
www.randomhouse.com/vintage

Guthrie, Savannah
Journalist and attorney; the Washington correspondent for Court TV News
Courtroom Television Network **Ph:** 212-973-2800
600 3rd Ave
New York, NY 10016
www.courttv.com/anchors

Gutierrez, Carlos M (1953-)
US Secretary of Commerce
US Dept of Commerce **Ph:** 202-482-2112
1401 Constitution Ave NW **Fax:** 202-482-2741
Washington, DC 20230
www.commerce.gov

Gutierrez, Luis V (1953-)
US Representative from Illinois (Democrat)
2367 Rayburn Bldg **Ph:** 202-225-8203
Washington, DC 20515 **Fax:** 202-225-7810
luisgutierrez.house.gov

Gutknecht, Gil (1951-)
US Representative from Minnesota (Republican)
425 Cannon Bldg **Ph:** 202-225-2472
Washington, DC 20515 **Fax:** 202-225-3246
www.gil.house.gov

Guy, Rosa (1925-)
Novelist; co-founder of the Harlem Writers Guild
Coffee House Press **Ph:** 612-338-0125
27 N 4th St Suite 400 **Fax:** 612-338-4004
Minneapolis, MN 55401
www.coffeehousepress.org

Guzan, Brad (1984-)
Professional soccer player
Club Deportivo Chivas USA **Ph:** 310-630-4550
Home Depot Center **Fax:** 310-630-4551
18400 Avalon Blvd
Carson, CA 90746
chivas.usa.mlsnet.com

Guzy, Carol (1958-)
Photojournalist
Washington Post **Ph:** 202-334-6000
1150 15th St NW
Washington, DC 20071
www.washingtonpost.com

Gyllenhaal, Jake (1980-)
Actor
Creative Artists Agency **Ph:** 310-288-4545
9830 Wilshire Blvd **Fax:** 310-288-4800
Beverly Hills, CA 90212
www.jakegyllenhaal.com

Gyllenhaal, Maggie (1977-)
Actor
Creative Artists Agency **Ph:** 310-288-4545
9830 Wilshire Blvd **Fax:** 310-288-4800
Beverly Hills, CA 90212

H

Haas, Bob
Chairman of Levi Strauss & Co
Levi Strauss & Co **Ph:** 415-501-6000
1155 Battery St
San Francisco, CA 94111
www.levistrauss.com/about/bios

Habes, Bob
Movie critic; writes the syndicated column You Be the Critic
United Feature Syndicate **Ph:** 212-293-8500
200 Madison Ave
New York, NY 10016
www.unitedfeatures.com

Hackett, James
Chairman, president, and CEO of Anadarko
Anadarko Petroleum Corp **Ph:** 832-636-1000
1201 Lake Robbins Dr
The Woodlands, TX 77380
www.anadarko.com

Hackman, Gene (1930-)
Actor
Creative Artists Agency — **Ph:** 310-288-4545
9830 Wilshire Blvd — **Fax:** 310-288-4800
Beverly Hills, CA 90212

Haddix, Margaret Peterson (1964-)
Author of books for young adults (Running Out of Time; Among the Hidden; Among the Betrayed; Just Ella)
Simon & Schuster — **Ph:** 212-698-7000
1230 Ave of the Americas
New York, NY 10020
www.simonsays.com

Hadley, Stephen (1947-)
US National Security Advisor
1600 Pennsylvania Ave — **Ph:** 202-456-9491
Washington, DC 20504 — **Fax:** 202-456-2883
www.whitehouse.gov/nsc

Hafner, Travis (1977-)
Professional baseball player
Cleveland Indians — **Ph:** 216-420-4200
Jacobs Field — **Fax:** 216-420-4624
2401 Ontario St
Cleveland, OH 44115
cleveland.indians.mlb.com

Hagan, Michael J
Chairman & CEO of NutriSystem, Inc; was the co-founder of Verticalnet, Inc, a business-to-business internet and software company
NutriSystem Inc — **Ph:** 215-706-5300
200 Welsh Rd — **Fax:** 215-706-5388
Horsham, PA 19044 — **TF:** 800-321-8446
www.nutrisystem.com

Hagee, John (1940-)
President & CEO of Global Evangelism Television, which telecasts his national radio and television ministry throughout the US and Canada
John Hagee Ministries — **Ph:** 210-494-3900
239 N Loop 1604 W — **Fax:** 210-494-5536
San Antonio, TX 78232
www.jhm.org

Hagee, Michael W
General; Commandant of the US Marine Corps
US Marine Corps — **Ph:** 703-614-2500
2 Navy Annex — **Fax:** 703-697-7246
Washington, DC 20380
www.marines.mil/cmc

Hagel, Charles (1946-)
US Senator from Nebraska (Republican)
248 Russell Bldg — **Ph:** 202-224-4224
Washington, DC 20510 — **Fax:** 202-228-5213
hagel.senate.gov

Hagelin, John, PhD (1954-)
Quantum physicist, educator, author, and public policy expert; the Natural Law Party candidate for president in 2000
Institute of Science Technology & Public Policy — **Ph:** 641-472-1200 — **Fax:** 641-472-1165
Maharishi Univ of Management
1000 N 4th St
Fairfield, IA 52557
www.hagelin.org

Hagman, Larry (1931-)
Actor
Innovative Artists — **Ph:** 310-656-0400
1505 10th St — **Fax:** 310-656-0456
Santa Monica, CA 90401
www.larryhagman.com

Hahn, Robert W, PhD
Resident Scholar at the American Enterprise Institute and director of the AEI-Brookings Joint Center for Regulatory Studies
American Enterprise Institute for Public Policy Research — **Ph:** 202-862-5800 — **Fax:** 202-862-7177
1150 17th St NW Suite 1100
Washington, DC 20036
www.aei.org

Hahn, Scott (1957-)
Speaker, author, and teacher; founder and director of the Saint Paul Center for Biblical Theology and a Professor of Theology and Scripture at Franciscan University of Steubenville
Saint Paul Center — **Ph:** 740-264-7805
5A Hawthorne Ct
Steubenville, OH 43952
www.scotthahn.com

Haines, Mark
Anchor of CNBC's Squawk Box
CNBC — **Ph:** 201-735-2622
900 Sylvan Ave
Englewood Cliffs, NJ 07632
moneycentral.msn.com/cnbc/tv

Halberstam, David (1934-)
Author, journalist, historian
Hyperion Books — **Ph:** 212-456-0110
Editorial Dept
77 W 66th St 11th Fl
New York, NY 10023
www.hyperionbooks.com

Haley, Alex (1921-1992)
Author of Roots
Kunta Kinte-Alex Haley Foundation Inc
31 Old Solomons Island Rd
Suite 102
Annapolis, MD 21401
www.kintehaley.org
Ph: 410-841-6920
Fax: 410-841-6505

Haley, Gail E (1939-)
Children's book author (A Story, A Story; Post Office Cat; Mountain Jack Tales)
PO Box 1027
Blowing Rock, NC 28605
www.gailehaley.com
Ph: 828-262-2270

Hall, Barbara (1961-)
TV series producer/writer
Creative Artists Agency
9830 Wilshire Blvd
Beverly Hills, CA 90212
Ph: 310-288-4545
Fax: 310-288-4800

Hall, Dante (1978-)
Professional football player
Kansas City Chiefs
Arrowhead Stadium
1 Arrowhead Dr
Kansas City, MO 64129
www.kcchiefs.com
Ph: 816-920-9300
Fax: 816-920-4315

Hall, Donald (1928-)
Poet; also has written several nonfiction books, as well as children's books (including Ox-Cart Man), short stories, and plays, and has edited more than two dozen textbooks and anthologies
Houghton Mifflin Co
Trade Div
Adult Editorial
222 Berkeley St 8th Fl
Boston, MA 02116
www.houghtonmifflinbooks.com
Ph: 617-351-5000

Hall, Donald J Jr
President & CEO of Hallmark Cards; grandson of Hallmark's founder
Hallmark Cards Inc
PO Box 419034
Kansas City, MO 64141
www.hallmark.com
Ph: 816-274-5111

Hall, Jerry (1956-)
Model
Ford Models
111 5th Ave
New York, NY 10003
Ph: 212-219-6500
Fax: 212-966-5028

Hall, John (1974-)
Professional football player
Washington Redskins
21300 Redskin Park Dr
Ashburn, VA 20147
www.redskins.com
Ph: 703-726-7000
Fax: 703-726-7086

Hall, John L, PhD (1934-)
Winner of the 2006 Nobel Prize for Physics (sharing one-half of the award with Theodor W Hansch of Germany) for their contributions to the development of laser-based precision spectroscopy, including the optical frequency comb technique
JILA
University of Colorado
440 UCB
Boulder, CO 80309
jilawww.colorado.edu/hall
Ph: 303-492-7843
Fax: 303-492-5235

Hall, Michael C (1971-)
Actor
Gersh Agency
232 N Canon Dr
Beverly Hills, CA 90210
www.hbo.com/sixfeetunder
Ph: 310-274-6611

Hall, Ralph M (1923-)
US Representative from Texas (Republican)
2405 Rayburn Bldg
Washington, DC 20515
www.house.gov/ralphhall
Ph: 202-225-6673
Fax: 202-225-3332

Hall, Robert E
Economist; a senior fellow at the Hoover Institution and a professor in Stanford's economics department; is a frequent contributor to discussions of national economic policy
Hoover Institution on War Revolution & Peace
Stanford University
Stanford, CA 94305
www-hoover.stanford.edu
Ph: 650-723-1754
Fax: 650-723-1687

Halladay, Roy (1977-)
Professional baseball player
Toronto Blue Jays
1 Blue Jays Way
Toronto, ON M5V1J1
toronto.bluejays.mlb.com
Ph: 416-341-1000
Fax: 416-341-1250

Halmi, Robert Jr
President & CEO of Hallmark Entertainment and president of Hallmark Entertainment Holdings, the parent company of Hallmark Entertainment and Crown Media Holdings (of which he is chairman)
Hallmark Entertainment Inc
1325 Ave of the Americas
21st Fl
New York, NY 10019
Ph: 212-977-9001
Fax: 212-977-9049

Halperin, Mark (1965-)
Political Director of ABC News
ABC News **Ph:** 212-456-7777
77 W 66th St
New York, NY 10023
www.abcnews.go.com/WNT

Halperin, Morton, PhD (1938-)
A Senior Fellow at the Center for American Progress and Director of the Security and Peace Initiative, and is also the Executive Director of the Open Society Policy Center; served in government in the Clinton, Nixon, and Johnson administrations
Center for American Progress **Ph:** 202-682-1611
1333 H St NW 10th Fl
Washington, DC 20005
www.americanprogress.org

Halse Anderson, Laurie (1961-)
Writes novels for young adults as well as children's picture books
Viking Children's Books Publicity **Ph:** 212-366-2000
345 Hudson St
New York, NY 10014
www.writerlady.com

Hamersley, Gordon
Chef and owner of Hamersley's Bistro
Hamersley's Bistro **Ph:** 617-423-2700
553 Tremont St
Boston, MA 02116
www.hamersleysbistro.com

Hamilton, Gene
Writes a syndicated column on home improvement (Do It Yourself or Not?) with his wife Katie Hamilton
Tribune Media Services Inc **Ph:** 312-222-4444
435 N Michigan Ave Suite 1500
Chicago, IL 60611
tmsfeatures.com/productlist.htm

Hamilton, Jane (1957-)
Author of The Book of Ruth
Vintage/Anchor Publicity **Ph:** 212-572-2420
1745 Broadway 20th Fl
New York, NY 10019
www.randomhouse.com/anchor

Hamilton, Katie
Writes a syndicated column on home improvement (Do It Yourself or Not?) with her husband Gene Hamilton
Tribune Media Services Inc **Ph:** 312-222-4444
435 N Michigan Ave Suite 1500
Chicago, IL 60611
tmsfeatures.com/productlist.htm

Hamilton, Lee H (1931-)
Former US Representative from Indiana for 34 years and vice chair of the 9/11 Commission; director of the Woodrow Wilson International Center for Scholars
Woodrow Wilson International Center for Scholars **Ph:** 202-691-4000
1 Woodrow Wilson Plaza
1300 Pennsylvania Ave NW
Washington, DC 20004
wwics.si.edu

Hamilton, Linda (1956-)
Actor
Paradigm **Ph:** 310-288-8000
360 N Crescent Dr **Fax:** 310-288-2000
North Bldg
Beverly Hills, CA 90210

Hamilton, Richard (1978-)
Professional basketball player
Detroit Pistons **Ph:** 248-377-0100
Palace at Auburn Hills **Fax:** 248-377-4262
4 Championship Dr
Auburn Hills, MI 48326
www.nba.com/pistons

Hamilton, Virginia (1936-2002)
Children's book author who won nearly every major award in her field
Scholastic Inc **Ph:** 212-343-6100
557 Broadway
New York, NY 10012
www.virginiahamilton.com

Hamlisch, Marvin (1944-)
Music composer; principal pops conductor for the Pittsburgh Symphony Orchestra as well as the National Symphony Orchestra in Washington, DC
Pittsburgh Symphony Orchestra **Ph:** 412-392-4900
Heinz Hall
600 Penn Ave
Pittsburgh, PA 15222
www.pittsburghsymphony.org

Hamm, Mia (1972-)
Soccer player
Mia Hamm Foundation **Ph:** 919-544-9848
PO Box 56
Chapel Hill, NC 27514
www.miafoundation.org

Hammergren, John H
Chairman, president, and CEO of McKesson Corp
McKesson Corp **Ph:** 415-983-8862
1 Post St **Fax:** 415-983-7160
San Francisco, CA 94104
www.mckesson.com

Hammon, Becky (1977-)
Women's pro basketball player
New York Liberty **Ph:** 212-564-9622
Madison Square Garden **Fax:** 212-465-6250
2 Pennsylvania Plaza
New York, NY 10121
www.wnba.com/liberty

Hammond, Darrell (1960-)
Comedian
William Morris Agency **Ph:** 212-586-5100
1325 Ave of the Americas **Fax:** 212-246-3583
New York, NY 10019
www.nbc.com/Saturday_Night_Live/bios

Hammond, Mac
Televangelist
Mac Hammond Ministries **Ph:** 763-315-7200
PO Box 29469
Minneapolis, MN 55429
www.mac-hammond.org

Hampton, Christopher (1946-)
Playwright/screenwriter
Creative Artists Agency **Ph:** 310-298-4545
9830 Wilshire Blvd **Fax:** 310-288-4800
Beverly Hills, CA 90212

Hamre, John J, PhD (1950-)
President & CEO of the Center for Strategic and International Studies (CSIS)
Center for Strategic & International Studies **Ph:** 202-887-0200 **Fax:** 202-775-3199
1800 K St NW Suite 400
Washington, DC 20006
www.csis.org

Hamrlik, Roman (1974-)
Professional hockey player
Calgary Flames **Ph:** 403-777-2177
Pengrowth Saddledome **Fax:** 403-777-2195
555 Saddledome Rise SE
Calgary, AB T2G2W1
www.calgaryflames.com

Hanby, Mark (1946-)
Religious speaker, author, head of Mark Hanby Ministries
Mark Hanby Ministries **Ph:** 423-510-8383
PO Box 8093 **Fax:** 423-510-8765
Chattanooga, TN 37414
www.hanby.org

Handel, Bill (1951-)
Radio talk show host (a morning drive show and a week-end program on legal issues)
KFI-AM **Ph:** 818-559-2252
3400 W Olive Ave Suite 550
Burbank, CA 91505
www.handelonthelaw.com

Handelsman, Walt
Editorial cartoonist for Newsday
Tribune Media Services Inc **Ph:** 312-222-4444
435 N Michigan Ave Suite 1500
Chicago, IL 60611
www.comicspage.com

Handford, Martin (1956-)
Creator of the Where's Waldo series
Candlewick Press **Ph:** 617-661-3330
2067 Massachusetts Ave **Fax:** 617-661-0565
Cambridge, MA 02140
www.candlewick.com

Handzus, Michal (1977-)
Professional hockey player
Philadelphia Flyers **Ph:** 215-465-4500
Wachovia Center **Fax:** 215-389-9403
3601 S Broad St
Philadelphia, PA 19148
www.philadelphiaflyers.com

Haney, Lee (1959-)
Body builder and eight-time Mr Olympia; fitness professional and motivational speaker
Lee Haney World Class Fitness Center **Ph:** 404-892-6737
675 Ponce de Leon Ave NE
Atlanta, GA 30308
www.leehaney.com

Hanks, Tom (1956-)
Actor; producer/writer
Creative Artists Agency **Ph:** 310-288-4545
9830 Wilshire Blvd **Fax:** 310-288-4800
Beverly Hills, CA 90212

Hanlon, Glen (1957-)
Hockey coach
Washington Capitals **Ph:** 202-266-2200
401 9th St NW Suite 750 **Fax:** 202-266-2210
Washington, DC 20004
www.washingtoncaps.com

Hannah, Daryl (1960-)
Actor
Special Artists Agency **Ph:** 310-859-9688
9465 Wilshire Blvd Suite 890
Beverly Hills, CA 90212

Hannan, Peter (1941-)
Animator; creator of CatDog
Nickelodeon Animation **Ph:** 818-736-3000
231 W Olive Ave
Burbank, CA 91502
www.peterhannan.com

Hannemann, Mufi (1950-)
Mayor of Honolulu
530 S King St **Ph:** 808-523-4141
Honolulu, HI 96813 **Fax:** 808-527-5552
www.co.honolulu.hi.us/mayor

Hannity, Sean (1961-)
Co-host of Hannity & Colmes, a debate-driven talk show on FOX (he's the conservative, Colmes is the liberal); also hosts a radio talk show
FOX News Channel **Ph:** 212-301-3000
1211 Ave of the Americas
New York, NY 10036
www.hannity.com

Hanrahan, Paul
President and CEO of AES Corp, a leading electric power company
AES Corp **Ph:** 703-522-1315
4300 Wilson Blvd 11th Fl
Arlington, VA 22203
www.aes.com

Hansen, Chris
Dateline NBC correspondent and substitute anchor for NBC Nightly News
Dateline NBC **Ph:** 212-664-4249
30 Rockefeller Plaza
New York, NY 10112
www.msnbc.msn.com/id/3360263

Hansen, Liane
Host of Weekend Editon Sunday on NPR
National Public Radio **Ph:** 202-513-2000
635 Massachusetts Ave NW **Fax:** 202-513-3329
Washington, DC 20001
www.npr.org

Hansen, Mark Victor (1947-)
Motivational speaker, author, marketing consultant; co-author of Chicken Soup for the Soul
Mark Victor Hansen & Assoc Inc **Ph:** 949-764-2640 **Fax:** 949-722-6912
PO Box 7665
Newport Beach, CA 92658
www.markvictorhansen.com

Hanson, Jason (1970-)
Professional football player
Detroit Lions **Ph:** 313-216-4000
222 Republic Dr **Fax:** 313-216-4069
Allen Park, MI 48101
www.detroitlions.com

Hanway, H Edward
Chairman and CEO of CIGNA Corp
CIGNA Corp **Ph:** 215-761-1000
1 Liberty Pl **Fax:** 215-761-5518
Philadelphia, PA 19192
www.cigna.com

Haque, Promod
Managing Partner of Norwest Venture Partners
Norwest Venture Partners **Ph:** 650-321-8000
525 University Ave Suite 800 **Fax:** 650-321-8010
Palo Alto, CA 94301
www.norwestvc.com

Harang, Aaron (1978-)
Professional baseball player
Cincinnati Reds **Ph:** 513-765-7000
Great American Ballpark **Fax:** 513-765-7342
100 Main St
Cincinnati, OH 45202
cincinnati.reds.mlb.com

Harary, Franz (1963-)
Illusionist
David Belenzon Management Inc **Ph:** 619-462-6400 **Fax:** 619-462-2244
PO Box 3819
La Mesa, CA 91944
www.harary.com

Hardberger, Phil (1934-)
Mayor of San Antonio
PO Box 839966 **Ph:** 210-207-7060
San Antonio, TX 78283 **Fax:** 210-207-4168
www.sanantonio.gov/mayor

Harden, Marcia Gay (1959-)
Actor
International Creative Management **Ph:** 310-550-4000
8942 Wilshire Blvd
Beverly Hills, CA 90211

Harding, Scott
CEO of ADVO Inc.; also was co-founder of Newspaper Services of America (NSA), the nation's largest print media planning and buying agency
ADVO Inc **Ph:** 860-285-6100
1 Targeting Ctr
Windsor, CT 06095
www.advo.com/corpgovernance.html

Hare, David (1947-)
Playwright & screenwriter (wrote the screenplays for The Hours and for Alexander the Great)
Farrar Straus & Giroux **Ph:** 212-741-6900
19 Union Sq W
New York, NY 10003
www.fsgbooks.com

Hargitay, Mariska (1964-)
Actor; daughter of Jayne Mansfield and Mickey Hargitay
William Morris Agency **Ph:** 310-859-4000
1 William Morris Pl **Fax:** 310-859-4462
Beverly Hills, CA 90212
www.mariska.com

Hargrove, Mike (1949-)
Baseball manager
Seattle Mariners **Ph:** 206-346-4000
Safeco Field **Fax:** 206-346-4050
1250 1st Ave S
Seattle, WA 98134
seattle.mariners.mlb.com

Haring, Keith (1958-1990)
Avant-garde artist
Keith Haring Foundation **Ph:** 212-477-1579
676 Broadway **Fax:** 212-353-0843
New York, NY 10012
www.haring.com

Harkin, Tom (1939-)
US Senator from Iowa (Democrat)
731 Hart Bldg **Ph:** 202-224-3254
Washington, DC 20510 **Fax:** 202-224-9369
harkin.senate.gov

Harlan, Kevin (1960-)
Sports broadcaster
CBS Sports **Ph:** 212-975-4321
51 W 52nd St
New York, NY 10019
cbs.sportsline.com/cbssports/team

Harlow, Shalom (1973-)
Model
IMG Models **Ph:** 212-253-8884
304 Park Ave S 12th Fl **Fax:** 212-253-8883
New York, NY 10010
www.imgmodels.com

Harman, Jane (1945-)
US Representative from California (Democrat)
2400 Rayburn Bldg **Ph:** 202-225-8220
Washington, DC 20515 **Fax:** 202-226-7290
www.house.gov/harman

Harmon, Butch (1943-)
Golf instructor
Hambric Sports Management **Ph:** 214-720-7179
2 Turtle Creek Village **Fax:** 214-720-7787
3838 Oak Lawn Ave Suite 750
Dallas, TX 75219
www.butchharmon.com

Harmon, Mark (1951-)
Actor
Paradigm **Ph:** 310-288-8000
360 N Crescent Dr **Fax:** 310-288-2000
North Bldg
Beverly Hills, CA 90210
www.cbs.com/primetime/ncis

Harmon, Merle (1928-)
Sports broadcaster, now motivational speaker
2817 Shadow Dr W **Ph:** 817-652-1072
Arlington, TX 76006 **Fax:** 817-640-1811
merleharmon.com

Harney, Kenneth
Writes The Nation's Housing, a syndicated column on real estate
Washington Post Writers Group **Ph:** 202-334-6375
Fax: 202-334-5669
1150 15th St NW 9th Fl
Washington, DC 20071
www.postwritersgroup.com

Harpring, Matt (1976-)
Professional basketball player
Utah Jazz **Ph:** 801-325-2500
Delta Center **Fax:** 801-325-2578
301 W South Temple St
Salt Lake City, UT 84101
www.nba.com/jazz

Harrell, Keith
Keynote speaker; also does workshop programs on work performance, change, and teamwork (Attitude is Everything)
5927 Balfour Ct Suite 103 **Ph:** 760-603-8110
Carlsbad, CA 92008 **Fax:** 760-603-8010
www.keithharrell.com

Harrell, Rob
Creator of the comic strip Big Top
Universal Press Syndicate **Ph:** 816-932-6600
4520 Main St
Kansas City, MO 64111
www.amuniversal.com/ups/features

Harrelson, Woody (1961-)
Actor
Creative Artists Agency **Ph:** 310-288-4545
9830 Wilshire Blvd **Fax:** 310-288-4800
Beverly Hills, CA 90212

Harrigan, Irv
Co-hosts a morning radio drive-time show
KILT-FM **Ph:** 713-881-5100
24 Greenway Plaza Suite 1900 **Fax:** 713-881-5199
Houston, TX 77046
www.kilt.com

Harrington, Al (1980-)
Professional basketball player
Atlanta Hawks **Ph:** 404-827-3800
Centennial Tower **Fax:** 404-827-3880
101 Marietta St NW Suite 1900
Atlanta, GA 30303
www.nba.com/hawks

Harrington, Joey (1978-)
Professional football player
Detroit Lions **Ph:** 313-216-4000
222 Republic Dr **Fax:** 313-216-4069
Allen Park, MI 48101
www.detroitlions.com

Harrington, Richard J
President & CEO of the Thomson Corp
Thomson Corp **Ph:** 203-969-8700
1 Station Pl **Fax:** 203-977-8354
Metro Ctr
Stamford, CT 06902
www.thomson.com

Harris, Dan
ABC News correspondent
ABC News **Ph:** 212-456-7777
77 W 66th St
New York, NY 10023
www.abcnews.go.com/WNT

Harris, Ed (1950-)
Actor
Creative Artists Agency **Ph:** 310-288-4545
9830 Wilshire Blvd **Fax:** 310-288-4800
Beverly Hills, CA 90212

Harris, Emmylou (1947-)
Singer (pop, folk, country, alternative)
High Road Touring **Ph:** 415-332-9292
751 Bridgeway 3rd Fl **Fax:** 415-332-4692
Sausalito, CA 94965
www.emmylou.net

Harris, Jeff
Creator of Shortcuts, an educational cartoon page for children
United Feature Syndicate **Ph:** 212-293-8500
200 Madison Ave
New York, NY 10016
www.unitedfeatures.com

Harris, Julie (1925-)
Actor
William Morris Agency **Ph:** 310-859-4000
1 William Morris Pl **Fax:** 310-859-4462
Beverly Hills, CA 90212

Harris, Katherine (1979-)
US Representative from Florida (Republican); formerly Florida's Secretary of State and a figure in the controversy about vote counting in the 2000 presidential election
116 Cannon Bldg **Ph:** 202-225-5015
Washington, DC 20515 **Fax:** 202-226-0828
harris.house.gov

Harris, Quentin (1977-)
Professional football player
New York Giants **Ph:** 201-935-8111
Giants Stadium **Fax:** 201-939-4134
East Rutherford, NJ 07073
www.giants.com

Harris, Richard
Award-winning broadcast journalist; reports on science issues for NPR newsmagazines
National Public Radio **Ph:** 202-513-2000
635 Massachusetts Ave NW **Fax:** 202-513-3329
Washington, DC 20001
www.npr.org

Harris, Thomas (1940-)
Author of Silence of the Lambs
Dell Publicity **Ph:** 212-782-9000
1745 Broadway
New York, NY 10019
www.thomasharris.com

Harrison, Clifford
Chef and owner (with Anne Quatrano) of Bacchanalia, Quinones at Bacchanalia, and Floataway Cafe
Bacchanalia Restaurant **Ph:** 404-365-0410
1198 Howell Mill Rd
Atlanta, GA 30318
www.starprovisions.com

Harrison, E Hunter
President & CEO of the Canadian National Railway
Canadian National Railway Co **Ph:** 514-399-7212
935 de La Gauchetiere St **Fax:** 514-399-3779
West Montreal, QC H3B2M9
www.cn.ca

Harrison, Marvin (1972-)
Professional football player
Indianapolis Colts **Ph:** 317-297-2658
7001 W 56th St **Fax:** 317-297-8971
Indianapolis, IN 46254
www.colts.com

Harrison, Shelley A, PhD
Chairman of the Board of SPACEHAB, which provides support services for the space industry
SPACEHAB Inc **Ph:** 713-558-5000
12130 Hwy 3 Bldg 1 **Fax:** 713-558-5960
Webster, TX 77598
www.spacehab.com

Harrison, William B Jr
Chairman of JP Morgan Chase & Co
JP Morgan Chase & Co **Ph:** 212-270-4019
270 Park Ave **Fax:** 212-270-6522
New York, NY 10017
www.jpmorganchase.com

Hart, Betsy
Syndicated columnist (conservative commentary)
Scripps Howard News Service **Ph:** 202-408-1484
1090 Vermont Ave NW **Fax:** 202-408-5950
Suite 1000
Washington, DC 20005
www.shns.com

Hart, Johnny (1931-)
Creator of BC and (with Brant Parker) The Wizard of Id
Creators Syndicate Inc **Ph:** 310-337-7003
5777 W Century Blvd Suite 700 **Fax:** 310-337-7625
Los Angeles, CA 90045
www.creators.com

Hart, Mary (1950-)
Long-time anchor of ET entertainment newsmagazine
William Morris Agency **Ph:** 310-859-4000
1 William Morris Pl **Fax:** 310-859-4462
Beverly Hills, CA 90212
et.tv.yahoo.com/about

Hart, Melissa A (1962-)
US Representative from Pennsylvania (Republican)
1024 Longworth Bldg **Ph:** 202-225-2565
Washington, DC 20515 **Fax:** 202-226-2274
hart.house.gov

Hartley, Bob (1960-)
Hockey coach
Atlanta Thrashers **Ph:** 404-827-5300
Centennial Tower **Fax:** 404-827-5909
101 Marietta St NW Suite 1900
Atlanta, GA 30303
www.atlantathrashers.com

Hartman, Kevin (1974-)
Professional soccer player
Los Angeles Galaxy **Ph:** 310-630-2200
Home Depot Center **Fax:** 310-630-2250
18400 Avalon Blvd Suite 200
Carson, CA 90746
www.lagalaxy.com

Hartman, Steve (1963-)
CBS News correspondent
CBS News **Ph:** 212-975-4114
524 W 57th St
New York, NY 10019
www.cbsnews.com

Hartman, Tom
Monsignor; writes the syndicated God Squad column with Rabbi Marc Gellman
Tribune Media Services Inc **Ph:** 312-222-4444
435 N Michigan Ave Suite 1500
Chicago, IL 60611
tmsfeatures.com/productlist.htm

Hartmann, Thom
Radio talk show host (liberal) and author
The Thom Hartmann Show **Ph:** 212-584-5100
Sirius Satellite Radio
1221 Ave of the Americas
New York, NY 10020
www.thomhartmann.com

Hartnett, Josh (1978-)
Actor
Creative Artists Agency **Ph:** 310-288-4545
9830 Wilshire Blvd **Fax:** 310-288-4800
Beverly Hills, CA 90212

Harvey, Francis J, PhD
Secretary of the US Army
US Dept of the Army **Ph:** 703-695-4311
101 Army Pentagon **Fax:** 703-614-5520
Washington, DC 20310
www.army.mil/leaders

Harvey, Paul (1918-)
Radio show host (news and commentary)
ABC Radio Networks **Ph:** 212-456-7777
444 Madison Ave
New York, NY 10022
www.paulharvey.com

Harvey, Steve (1956-)
Comedian; radio DJ and host of The Steve Harvey Show
Creative Artists Agency — **Ph:** 310-288-4545
9830 Wilshire Blvd — **Fax:** 310-288-4800
Beverly Hills, CA 90212
www.steveharvey.com

Harvick, Kevin (1975-)
NASCAR driver
Richard Childress Racing — **Ph:** 336-731-3334
236 Industrial Dr
PO Box 1189
Welcome, NC 27374
www.rcrracing.com

Hasek, Dominik (1965-)
Professional hockey player
Ottawa Senators — **Ph:** 613-599-0250
Corel Center — **Fax:** 613-599-0358
1000 Palladium Dr
Kanata, ON K2V1A5
www.ottawasenators.com

Haslem, Udonis (1980-)
Professional basketball player
Miami Heat — **Ph:** 786-777-1000
American Airlines Arena — **Fax:** 786-777-1609
601 Biscayne Blvd
Miami, FL 33132
www.nba.com/heat

Hass, Robert (1941-)
US Poet Laureate 1995-97
Steven Barclay Agency — **Ph:** 707-773-0654
12 Western Ave — **Fax:** 707-778-1868
Petaluma, CA 94952 — **TF:** 888-965-7323
www.barclayagency.com

Hasselbeck, Elisabeth (1977-)
Co-host on The View
The View — **Ph:** 212-456-7777
320 W 66th St
New York, NY 10023
abc.go.com/daytime/theview

Hasselbeck, Matt (1975-)
Professional football player
Seattle Seahawks — **Ph:** 425-827-9777
11220 NE 53rd St — **Fax:** 425-827-9008
Kirkland, WA 98033
www.seahawks.com

Hasselhoff, David (1952-)
Actor
TalentWorks — **Ph:** 818-972-4300
3500 W Olive Ave Suite 1400 — **Fax:** 818-955-6411
Burbank, CA 91505

Hassett, Kevin A
Resident Scholar and Director of Economic Policy Studies at the American Enterprise Institute; a former senior economist at the Federal Reserve and Senator John McCain's chief economic adviser during his 2000 presidential campaign
American Enterprise Institute for Public Policy Research — **Ph:** 202-862-5800 — **Fax:** 202-862-7177
1150 17th St NW Suite 1100
Washington, DC 20036
www.aei.org

Hastert, J Dennis (1942-)
US Representative from Illinois (Republican); Speaker of the House of Representatives
235 Cannon Bldg — **Ph:** 202-225-2976
Washington, DC 20515 — **Fax:** 202-225-0697
www.house.gov/hastert

Hastings, Alcee L (1936-)
US Representative from Florida (Democrat)
2353 Rayburn Bldg — **Ph:** 202-225-1313
Washington, DC 20515 — **Fax:** 202-225-1171
alceehastings.house.gov

Hastings, Doc (1941-)
US Representative from Washington (Republican)
1323 Longworth Bldg — **Ph:** 202-225-5816
Washington, DC 20515 — **Fax:** 202-225-3251
hastings.house.gov

Hatch, Orrin G (1934-)
US Senator from Utah (Republican)
104 Hart Bldg — **Ph:** 202-224-5251
Washington, DC 20510 — **Fax:** 202-224-6331
hatch.senate.gov

Hatcher, Derian (1972-)
Professional hockey player
Philadelphia Flyers — **Ph:** 215-465-4500
Wachovia Center — **Fax:** 215-389-9403
3601 S Broad St
Philadelphia, PA 19148
www.philadelphiaflyers.com

Hatcher, Teri (1964-)
Actor
Paradigm — **Ph:** 310-288-8000
360 N Crescent Dr — **Fax:** 310-288-2000
North Bldg
Beverly Hills, CA 90210
abc.go.com/primetime/desperate

Hausfeld, Michael D (1946-)
A top civil litigator specializing in human rights, discrimination, antitrust, and international law
Cohen Milstein Hausfeld & Toll PLLC — **Ph:** 202-408-4600; **Fax:** 202-408-4699; **TF:** 888-347-4600
1100 New York Ave NW
West Tower Suite 500
Washington, DC 20005
www.cmht.com

Havel, Vaclav (1936-)
President of the Czech Republic; human rights activist; dramatist & writer
Vintage/Anchor Publicity — **Ph:** 212-572-2420
1745 Broadway 20th Fl
New York, NY 10019
www.randomhouse.com/vintage

Havlat, Martin (1981-)
Professional hockey player
Ottawa Senators — **Ph:** 613-599-0250; **Fax:** 613-599-0358
Corel Center
1000 Palladium Dr
Kanata, ON K2V1A5
www.ottawasenators.com

Havlicek, John (1940-)
Former professional basketball player; member of the Basketball Hall of Fame
Naismith Memorial Basketball Hall of Fame — **Ph:** 413-781-6500; **Fax:** 413-781-1939; **TF:** 877-446-6752
1000 W Columbus Ave
Springfield, MA 01105
www.hoophall.com

Hawk, Tony (1968-)
Skateboarder
Tony Hawk Inc — **Ph:** 760-477-2477
1611-A S Melrose Dr Suite 362
Vista, CA 92081
www.tonyhawk.com

Hawke, Ethan (1970-)
Actor
Creative Artists Agency — **Ph:** 310-288-4545; **Fax:** 310-288-4800
9830 Wilshire Blvd
Beverly Hills, CA 90212

Hawkins, Sophie B (1967-)
Singer/songwriter
Skyline Music — **Ph:** 683-586-7171; **Fax:** 683-586-7068
PO Box 38
Jefferson, NH 03583
www.sophiebhawkins.com

Hawn, Goldie (1945-)
Actor
Creative Artists Agency — **Ph:** 310-288-4545; **Fax:** 310-248-4800
9830 Wilshire Blvd
Beverly Hills, CA 90212

Hay, Lewis III
Chairman, president, and CEO of Florida Power & Light Co
FPL Group Inc — **Ph:** 561-694-4000; **Fax:** 561-694-4620
700 Universe Blvd
Juno Beach, FL 33408
www.fplgroup.com

Hay, Louise L (1926-)
Considered one of the founders of the self-help movement; a leader in the New Age movement and founder of Hay House publishers
Hay House Inc — **Ph:** 760-431-7695; **Fax:** 800-650-5115
PO Box 5100
Carlsbad, CA 92018
www.louisehay.com

Hayek, Salma (1966-)
Actor
William Morris Agency — **Ph:** 310-859-4000; **Fax:** 310-859-4462
1 William Morris Pl
Beverly Hills, CA 90212

Hayes, Eddie
Daytime anchor on Court TV and a practicing attorney (both civil and criminal defense law)
Courtroom Television Network — **Ph:** 212-973-2800
600 3rd Ave
New York, NY 10016
www.courttv.com/anchors

Hayes, Erin
ABC News correspondent
ABC News — **Ph:** 770-431-7770; **Fax:** 770-431-7800
2580 Cumberland Pkwy Suite 160
Atlanta, GA 30339
www.abcnews.go.com/WNT

Hayes, Jarvis (1981-)
Professional basketball player
Washington Wizards — **Ph:** 202-661-5000; **Fax:** 202-661-5094
Verizon Center
601 F St NW
Washington, DC 20004
www.nba.com/wizards

Hayes, Robin (1945-)
US Representative from North Carolina (Republican)
130 Cannon Bldg — **Ph:** 202-225-3715; **Fax:** 202-225-4036
Washington, DC 20515
www.hayes.house.gov

Hayes, Sean (1970-)
Actor (Jack on Will & Grace)
William Morris Agency **Ph:** 310-859-4000
1 William Morris Pl **Fax:** 310-859-4462
Beverly Hills, CA 90212
www.nbc.com/Will_&_Grace

Hayford, Jack (1954-)
Pastor of Living Way Ministries, which includes radio and television programs, book sales, a Pentecostal/Charismatic college & seminary, and the Hayford Bible Institute; is a speaker in many forums, including Promise Keepers
Jack Hayford Ministries **Ph:** 877-429-3673
14800 Sherman Way
Van Nuys, CA 91405
www.jackhayford.com

Hays, Kathleen
CNN Business News correspondent
CNN New York **Ph:** 212-275-7800
Time Warner Ctr
10 Columbus Cir
New York, NY 10019
www.cnn.com/CNN/anchors_reporters

Haysbert, Dennis (1954-)
Actor
Gersh Agency **Ph:** 310-274-6611
232 N Canon Dr
Beverly Hills, CA 90210
www.cbs.com/primetime/the_unit/bios

Hayward, Sam
Chef; owner of the Fore Street Restaurant
Fore Street Restaurant **Ph:** 207-775-2717
288 Fore Street
Portland, ME 04101

Hayworth, JD (1958-)
US Representative from Arizona (Republican)
2434 Rayburn Bldg **Ph:** 202-225-2190
Washington, DC 20515 **Fax:** 202-225-3263
hayworth.house.gov

Hazelton, Ron
Home improvement editor on Good Morning America; also hosts Ron Hazelton's HouseCalls
Good Morning America **Ph:** 212-456-7777
147 Columbus Ave
New York, NY 10023
www.ronhazelton.com

Heady, Robert K
Financial columnist & author (Complete Idiot's Guide to Managing your Money)
Alpha Books Publicity **Ph:** 212-366-2000
375 Hudson St
New York, NY 10014
us.penguingroup.com

Healy, Bernadine, MD (1944-)
Cardiologist and former director of the National Institutes of Health; writes the On Health column for US News & World Report
US News & World Report **Ph:** 202-955-2000
1050 Thomas Jefferson St NW **Fax:** 202-955-2685
Washington, DC 20007
www.usnews.com

Heaney, Seamus (1939-)
Irish poet
Farrar Straus & Giroux **Ph:** 212-741-6900
19 Union Sq W
New York, NY 10003
www.fsgbooks.com

Heaps, Jay (1976-)
Professional soccer player
New England Revolution **Ph:** 508-543-5001
Gillette Stadium **Fax:** 508-384-9128
1 Patriot Pl
Foxborough, MA 02035
www.revolutionsoccer.net

Hearn, Timothy J
Chairman, president, and CEO of Imperial Oil Ltd
Imperial Oil Ltd **Ph:** 416-968-5078
111 St Clair Ave W **Fax:** 416-968-5345
Toronto, ON M5W1K3
www.imperialoil.ca

Hearst, George R Jr
Chairman of the Hearst Corp (grandson of company founder William Randolph Hearst)
Hearst Corp **Ph:** 212-649-2323
959 8th Ave **Fax:** 212-765-3528
New York, NY 10019
www.hearstcorp.com

Heath, Mark (1960-)
Creator of the comic strip Spot the Frog
United Feature Syndicate **Ph:** 212-293-8500
200 Madison Ave
New York, NY 10016
www.unitedfeatures.com

Heatley, Dany (1981-)
Professional hockey player
Ottawa Senators — **Ph:** 613-599-0250
Corel Center — **Fax:** 613-599-0358
1000 Palladium Dr
Kanata, ON K2V1A5
www.ottawasenators.com

Heaton, Patricia (1958-)
Actor
United Talent Agency — **Ph:** 310-273-6700
9560 Wilshire Blvd 5th Fl — **Fax:** 310-247-1111
Beverly Hills, CA 90212
www.everybodylovesray.com

Heche, Anne (1969-)
Actor
Creative Artists Agency — **Ph:** 310-288-4545
9830 Wilshire Blvd — **Fax:** 310-288-4800
Beverly Hills, CA 90212

Hecht, Jochen (1977-)
Professional hockey player
Buffalo Sabres — **Ph:** 716-855-4100
HSBC Arena — **Fax:** 716-855-4115
1 Seymour H Knox III Plaza
Buffalo, NY 14203
www.sabres.com

Heckerling, Amy (1954-)
Movie writer/director
Creative Artists Agency — **Ph:** 310-288-4545
9830 Wilshire Blvd — **Fax:** 310-288-4800
Beverly Hills, CA 90212

Heckman, James J, PhD (1944-)
Winner of the 2000 Nobel Prize in Economics for his development of theory and methods for analyzing selective samples
University of Chicago — **Ph:** 773-702-0634
Dept of Economics — **Fax:** 773-702-8490
1126 E 59th St
Chicago, IL 60637
economics.uchicago.edu/faculty.shtml

Hedrick, Joan D
Author of the biographical work, Harriet Beecher Stowe: A Life
Oxford University Press — **Ph:** 212-726-6000
198 Madison Ave
New York, NY 10016
www.oup.com

Heeger, Alan J, PhD (1936-)
Winner (with two other scientists) of the 2000 Nobel Prize in Chemistry for the discovery and development of conductive polymers
University of California at Santa Barbara — **Ph:** 805-893-3184 — **Fax:** 805-893-4755
Dept of Physics
Broida Hall 6125
Santa Barbara, CA 93106
www.physics.ucsb.edu

Hefley, Joel (1935-)
US Representative from Colorado (Republican)
2372 Rayburn Bldg — **Ph:** 202-225-4422
Washington, DC 20515 — **Fax:** 202-225-1942
www.house.gov/hefley

Hefner, Christine (1952-)
Chairman and CEO of Playboy Enterprises
Playboy Enterprises Inc — **Ph:** 312-751-8000
680 N Lake Shore Dr — **Fax:** 312-751-2818
Chicago, IL 60611
www.playboyenterprises.com

Hefner, Hugh (1926-)
Founder & Editor-in-Chief of Playboy Magazine
Playboy Magazine — **Ph:** 310-246-4000
9242 Beverly Blvd — **Fax:** 310-246-4050
Beverly Hills, CA 90210
www.playboyenterprises.com

Hefter, Lee
Executive chef of Spago Beverly Hills and a partner in the Wolfgang Puck Fine Dining Group
Spago Beverly Hills — **Ph:** 310-385-0880
176 N Canon Dr — **Fax:** 310-385-9690
Beverly Hills, CA 90210
www.wolfgangpuck.com

Hegedus, Mike
Special features correspondent for CNBC's On the Money
CNBC — **Ph:** 201-735-2622
900 Sylvan Ave
Englewood Cliffs, NJ 07632
moneycentral.msn.com/cnbc/tv

Hegi, Ursula
Author (general fiction)
Simon & Schuster — **Ph:** 212-698-7000
1230 Ave of the Americas
New York, NY 10020
www.simonsays.com

Heimlich, Henry, MD (1920-)
Surgeon & researcher who developed the anti-choking procedure known as the Heimlich Maneuver
Heimlich Institute **Ph:** 513-559-2391
311 Straight St
Cincinnati, OH 45219
www.heimlichinstitute.org

Heineman, Dave (1948-)
Governor of Nebraska (Republican)
PO Box 94848 **Ph:** 402-471-2244
Lincoln, NE 68509 **Fax:** 402-471-6031
gov.nol.org

Heir, Theron
Writes the comic strip Rudy Park, which is drawn by Darrin Bell
United Feature Syndicate **Ph:** 212-293-8500
200 Madison Ave
New York, NY 10016
www.unitedfeatures.com

Heisley, Michael
Owner of the Memphis Grizzlies basketball franchise
Memphis Grizzlies **Ph:** 901-205-1234
FedExForum **Fax:** 901-205-1235
191 Beale St
Memphis, TN 38103
www.nba.com/grizzlies/about/media_guide.html

Hejduk, Frankie (1974-)
Professional soccer player
Columbus Crew **Ph:** 614-447-2739
Columbus Crew Stadium **Fax:** 614-447-4109
1 Black & Gold Blvd
Columbus, OH 43211
columbus.crew.mlsnet.com

Hejduk, Milan (1976-)
Professional hockey player
Colorado Avalanche **Ph:** 303-405-1100
Pepsi Center
1000 Chopper Cir
Denver, CO 80204
www.coloradoavalanche.com

Helgenberger, Marg (1958-)
Actor
International Creative Management **Ph:** 310-550-4000
8942 Wilshire Blvd
Beverly Hills, CA 90211
www.cbs.com/primetime/csi

Heller, Jane
Author of humorous mysteries
St Martin's Press **Ph:** 212-674-5151
Attn: Publicity Dept
175 5th Ave
New York, NY 10010
www.janeheller.com

Heller, Joe
Editorial cartoonist
Green Bay Press-Gazette **Ph:** 920-435-4411
PO Box 23430
Green Bay, WI 54305
www.hellertoon.com

Heller, Rachael F, PhD (1945-)
Author of The Carbohydrate Addict's Diet (with Dr. Richard F. Heller)
Dutton Publicity **Ph:** 212-366-2000
375 Hudson St
New York, NY 10014
us.penguingroup.com

Heller, Richard F, PhD
Author (with Dr. Rachael F. Heller) of The Carbohydrate Addict's Diet and related books
Dutton Publicity **Ph:** 212-366-2000
375 Hudson St
New York, NY 10014
www.carbohydrateaddicts.com

Helms, Jesse (1921-)
Former US Senator from North Carolina (retired in 2002 after 30 years in the Senate)
Jesse Helms Center Foundation **Ph:** 704-233-1776
PO Box 247
Wingate, NC 28174
www.jessehelmscenter.org

Helms, Robert P, PhD
Economist; Resident Scholar and Director of Health Policy Studies at the American Enterprise Institute
American Enterprise Institute for Public Policy Research **Ph:** 202-862-5800 **Fax:** 202-862-7177
1150 17th St NW Suite 1100
Washington, DC 20036
www.aei.org

Heloise
Writes the syndicated column Hints from Heloise
King Features Syndicate Inc **Ph:** 212-455-4000
888 7th Ave 2nd Fl
New York, NY 10019
www.heloise.com

Helprin, Mark (1947-)
Novelist and journalist; is a senior fellow of the Claremont Institute
Claremont Institute **Ph:** 909-621-6825
937 W Foothill Blvd Suite E **Fax:** 909-626-8724
Claremont, CA 91711
www.claremont.org

Helton, Mike
NASCAR president
NASCAR **Ph:** 386-253-0611
1801 W International Speedway Blvd
Daytona Beach, FL 32114

Helton, Todd (1973-)
Professional baseball player
Colorado Rockies **Ph:** 303-292-0200
Coors Field **Fax:** 303-296-2066
2001 Blake St
Denver, CO 80205
colorado.rockies.mlb.com

Hemmer, Bill (1964-)
FOX News weekday anchor and correspondent
FOX News Channel **Ph:** 212-301-3000
1211 Ave of the Americas
New York, NY 10036
www.foxnews.com/fnctv

Henderson, Chris (1970-)
Professional soccer player
New York Red Bulls **Ph:** 201-583-7000
1 Harmon Plaza 3rd Fl **Fax:** 201-583-7055
Secaucus, NJ 07094
redbull.newyork.mlsnet.com

Hendrickson, Ezra (1972-)
Professional soccer player
Columbus Crew **Ph:** 614-447-2739
Columbus Crew Stadium **Fax:** 614-447-4109
1 Black & Gold Blvd
Columbus, OH 43211
columbus.crew.mlsnet.com

Hendrie, Phil (1952-)
Call-in radio show host; does the voices of all of his guests
Premiere Radio Networks Inc **Ph:** 818-377-5300
15260 Ventura Blvd 5th Fl **Fax:** 818-377-5333
Sherman Oaks, CA 91403
www.philhendrieshow.com

Henin-Hardenne, Justine (1982-)
Professional tennis player
WTA Tour **Ph:** 727-895-5000
1 Progress Plaza Suite 1500 **Fax:** 727-894-1982
Saint Petersburg, FL 33701
www.henin-hardenne.be

Henkes, Kevin (1960-)
Author/illustrator of children's books, including picture books (Kitten's First Full Moon), mouse books, and novels
HarperCollins Children's Books **Ph:** 212-261-6500
1350 Ave of the Americas
New York, NY 10019
www.kevinhenkes.com

Henley, Don (1947-)
Singer and member of the Eagles band; environmentalist and founder of the Walden Woods Project and the Thoreau Institute
William Morris Agency **Ph:** 310-859-4000
1 William Morris Pl **Fax:** 310-859-4462
Beverly Hills, CA 90212
www.wbr.com/donhenley

Hennig, James F, PhD
Negotiations expert, author, and keynote speaker
JF Hennig Associates Inc **Ph:** 480-961-5050
721 N Lisbon Dr
Chandler, AZ 85226
www.jimhennig.com

Henry, Anthony (1976-)
Professional football player
Dallas Cowboys **Ph:** 972-556-9900
1 Cowboys Pkwy **Fax:** 972-556-9304
Irving, TX 75063
www.dallascowboys.com

Henry, Brad (1963-)
Governor of Oklahoma (Democrat)
2300 N Lincoln Blvd Rm 212 **Ph:** 405-521-2342
Oklahoma City, OK 73105 **Fax:** 405-521-3353
www.gov.ok.gov

Henry, Carol (1960-)
Photographer (mainly flowers)
Ansel Adams Gallery **Ph:** 888-361-7622
PO Box 4185 **Fax:** 650-692-3512
Burlingame, CA 94011
www.carolhenry.com

Henry, John W (1949-)
Principal owner of the Boston Red Sox baseball team
Boston Red Sox **Ph:** 617-267-9440
Fenway Park **Fax:** 617-236-6797
4 Yawkey Way
Boston, MA 02215
boston.redsox.mlb.com

Henry, Travis (1978-)
Professional football player
Tennessee Titans **Ph:** 615-565-4000
460 Great Circle Rd **Fax:** 615-565-4006
Nashville, TN 37228
www.titansonline.com

Hensarling, Jeb (1957-)
US Representative from Texas (Republican)
132 Cannon Bldg **Ph:** 202-225-3484
Washington, DC 20515 **Fax:** 202-226-4888
www.house.gov/hensarling

Henson, Drew (1980-)
Professional football player
Dallas Cowboys **Ph:** 972-556-9900
1 Cowboys Pkwy **Fax:** 972-556-9304
Irving, TX 75063
www.dallascowboys.com

Hentoff, Nat (1925-)
Journalist/syndicated columnist, an authority on the First Amendment, and a jazz expert
United Feature Syndicate **Ph:** 212-293-8500
200 Madison Ave
New York, NY 10016
www.unitedfeatures.com

Herbert, Bob (1945-)
New York Times op-ed columnist; prior to joining the Times, he was a news correspondent for NBC News
New York Times **Ph:** 212-556-1234
229 W 43rd St
New York, NY 10036
www.nytimes.com/pages/opinion

Herbert, Brian (1947-)
Science fiction author; co-author with Kevin J. Anderson of the Dune books (originated by his father, Frank Herbert)
Tor Books **Ph:** 212-388-0100
175 5th Ave
New York, NY 10010
www.dunenovels.com

Herenton, Willie W, PhD (1940-)
Mayor of Memphis, Tennessee
125 N Main St Suite 700 **Ph:** 901-576-6000
Memphis, TN 38103 **Fax:** 901-576-6012
www.cityofmemphis.org

Herera, Sue
Co-anchor of CNBC's PowerLunch; host and anchor of CNBC in India
CNBC **Ph:** 201-735-2622
900 Sylvan Ave
Englewood Cliffs, NJ 07632
moneycentral.msn.com/cnbc/tv

Herger, Wally (1945-)
US Representative from California (Republican)
2268 Rayburn Bldg **Ph:** 202-225-3076
Washington, DC 20515 **Fax:** 202-226-0852
www.house.gov/herger

Herman, Pee Wee (1952-)
Comedian; real name is Paul Reubens
United Talent Agency **Ph:** 310-273-6700
9560 Wilshire Blvd 5th Fl **Fax:** 310-247-1111
Beverly Hills, CA 90212

Hernandez, Ramon (1976-)
Professional baseball player
Baltimore Orioles **Ph:** 410-685-9800
Oriole Park at Camden Yards **Fax:** 410-547-6279
333 W Camden St
Baltimore, MD 21201
baltimore.orioles.mlb.com

Hernandez, Roger (1955-)
Nationally syndicated columnist; covers the Hispanic community and the issues and events that affect this ethnic group
King Features Syndicate Inc **Ph:** 212-455-4000
888 7th Ave 2nd Fl
New York, NY 10019
www.kingfeatures.com

Herrera, Carolina (1939-)
Fashion designer
501 7th Ave **Ph:** 212-944-5757
New York, NY 10018
www.carolinaherrera.com

Herridge, Catherine
FOX News's Homeland Defense correspondent
FOX News Channel **Ph:** 212-301-3000
1211 Ave of the Americas
New York, NY 10036
www.foxnews.com/fnctv

Herrmann, Edward (1943-)
Actor
Agency for the Performing Arts **Ph:** 310-273-0744
9200 Sunset Blvd Suite 900 **Fax:** 310-888-4242
Los Angeles, CA 90069

Herseth, Stephanie (1970-)
US Representative from South Dakota (Democrat)
331 Cannon Bldg **Ph:** 202-225-2801
Washington, DC 20515 **Fax:** 202-225-5823
www.house.gov/herseth

Hershey, Barbara (1948-)
Actor
International Creative Management
8942 Wilshire Blvd
Beverly Hills, CA 90211
Ph: 310-550-4000

Hertzfeldt, Don (1976-)
Animator and producer/director of animated short films; co-founder (with Mike Judge) of The Animation Show
Endeavor
9601 Wilshire Blvd 3rd Fl
Beverly Hills, CA 90210
www.bitterfilms.com
Ph: 310-248-2000
Fax: 310-248-2020

Hess, John
Chairman of the Board and CEO of Amerada Hess Corp
Amerada Hess Corp
1185 Ave of the Americas
New York, NY 10036
www.hess.com
Ph: 212-997-8500

Hesse, Karen (1952-)
Author of books for young readers (Out of the Dust; Aleutian Sparrow; Stowaway)
Simon & Schuster
1230 Ave of the Americas
New York, NY 10020
www.simonsays.com
Ph: 212-698-7000

Hession, Dennis P
Mayor of Spokane, Washington
808 W Spokane Falls Blvd
Spokane, WA 99201
www.spokanecity.org/government/mayor
Ph: 509-625-6250
Fax: 509-625-6789

Hewitt, Don (1922-)
Creator of 60 Minutes and its executive producer for 36 years; is now Executive Producer, CBS News
CBS News
524 W 57th St
New York, NY 10019
www.cbsnews.com
Ph: 212-975-3247

Hewitt, Jennifer Love (1979-)
Actor
Endeavor
9601 Wilshire Blvd 3rd Fl
Beverly Hills, CA 90210
Ph: 310-248-2000
Fax: 310-248-2020

Hewitt, Lleyton (1981-)
Professional tennis player
ATP
201 ATP Blvd
Ponte Vedra Beach, FL 32082
www.atptennis.com
Ph: 904-285-8000
Fax: 904-285-5966

Heyer, Steven J
CEO of Starwood Hotels & Resorts Worldwide, Inc.
Starwood Hotels & Resorts Worldwide Inc
1111 Westchester Ave
White Plains, NY 10604
www.starwoodhotels.com
Ph: 914-640-8100

Hiaasen, Carl (1953-)
Miami Herald columnist (syndicated); author
Miami Herald
1 Herald Plaza
Miami, FL 33132
www.carlhiaasen.com
Ph: 305-350-2111

Hiatt, Fred (1955-)
Editor of the Washington Post's editorial page
Washington Post
1150 15th St NW
Washington, DC 20071
www.washingtonpost.com
Ph: 202-334-6000

Hickenlooper, John
Mayor of Denver
1437 Bannock St Suite 350
Denver, CO 80202
www.denvergov.org
Ph: 720-865-9000
Fax: 720-865-8787

Hicks, Thomas O
Owner of the Texas Rangers baseball team, the Dallas Stars hockey club, and other sports interests
Southwest Sports Group LLC
1000 Ballpark Way Suite 400
Arlington, TX 76011
www.dallasstars.com
Ph: 817-273-5100

Hiepler, Mark
Attorney specializing in cases that involve personal injury, wrongful death, bad faith, and/or denial of insurance coverage
Hiepler & Hiepler
500 Esplanade Dr Suite 1550
Oxnard, CA 93036
www.hieplerlaw.com
Ph: 805-988-5833
Fax: 805-988-5828

Higgins, Brian (1959-)
US Representative from New York (Democrat)
431 Cannon Bldg
Washington, DC 20515
www.house.gov/higgins
Ph: 202-225-3306
Fax: 202-226-0347

Higgins, Greg
Co-owner and head chef at Higgins Restaurant & Bar
Higgins Restaurant & Bar
1239 SW Broadway
Portland, OR 97205
higgins.citysearch.com
Ph: 503-222-9070

Higgins, Jack
Editorial cartoonist for the Chicago Sun-Times
Chicago Sun-Times **Ph:** 312-321-3000
350 N Orleans **Fax:** 312-321-3084
Chicago, IL 60654
www.amuniversal.com/ups/features

Higgins, Jack (1929-)
Author of thrillers; Jack Higgins is a pseudonym for Harry Patterson
Putnam Publicity **Ph:** 212-366-2000
375 Hudson St
New York, NY 10014
us.penguingroup.com

Hijuelos, Oscar (1951-)
Novelist; his work includes The Mambo Kings Play Songs of Love, which was made into the movie The Mambo Kings
HarperCollins Publishers **Ph:** 212-207-7000
c/o Author Mail
10 E 53rd St
New York, NY 10022
www.oscarhijuelos.com

Hilfiger, Tommy (1951-)
Fashion designer
Tommy Hilfiger USA Inc **Ph:** 212-840-8888
25 W 39th St
New York, NY 10018
www.tommy.com

Hilgeman, Georgia K
Founder and executive director of the Vanished Children's Alliance
Vanished Children's Alliance **Ph:** 408-296-1113
991 W Hedding St Suite 101 **Fax:** 408-296-1117
San Jose, CA 95126
www.vca.org

Hill, Anita (1956-)
Attorney, professor, speaker; famous for her sexual harassment testimony in the Senate Confirmation hearings for Justice Clarence Thomas
MS 035 Brandeis University **Ph:** 781-736-3896
PO Box 549110
Waltham, MA 02454
my.brandeis.edu/profiles

Hill, Bob
Basketball coach
Seattle Supersonics **Ph:** 206-281-5800
351 Elliott Ave W Suite 500 **Fax:** 206-281-5839
Seattle, WA 98119
www.nba.com/sonics

Hill, Brian (1947-)
Basketball coach
Orlando Magic **Ph:** 407-916-2400
8701 Maitland Summit Blvd **Fax:** 407-916-2884
Orlando, FL 32810
www.nba.com/magic

Hill, David
Chairman & CEO of Fox Sports Television
Fox Sports Television Group **Ph:** 310-369-6000
10201 W Pico Blvd
FNC Bldg 101 5th Fl
Los Angeles, CA 90035

Hill, ED
An anchor on Fox & Friends
FOX News Channel **Ph:** 212-301-3000
1211 Ave of the Americas
New York, NY 10036
www.foxnews.com/fnctv

Hill, Eric (1927-)
Creator of the Spot books for very young children
GP Putnam's Sons Books for Young Readers **Ph:** 212-366-2000
Publicity Dept
345 Hudson St
New York, NY 10014
us.penguingroup.com

Hill, Faith (1967-)
Singer (country/pop)
CAA Nashville **Ph:** 615-383-8787
3310 West End Ave 5th Fl **Fax:** 615-383-4937
Nashville, TN 37203
www.faithhill.com

Hill, Grant (1972-)
Professional basketball player
Orlando Magic **Ph:** 407-916-2400
8701 Maitland Summit Blvd **Fax:** 407-916-2884
Orlando, FL 32810
www.nba.com/magic

Hill, Reynaldo (1982-)
Professional football player
Tennessee Titans **Ph:** 615-565-4000
460 Great Circle Rd **Fax:** 615-565-4006
Nashville, TN 37228
www.titansonline.com

Hillenbrand, Shea (1975-)
Professional baseball player
Toronto Blue Jays **Ph:** 416-341-1000
1 Blue Jays Way **Fax:** 416-341-1250
Toronto, ON M5V1J1
toronto.bluejays.mlb.com

Hillerman, Tony (1925-)
Author of mysteries featuring Navajo detectives
HarperCollins Publishers **Ph:** 212-207-7000
c/o Author Mail
10 E 53rd St
New York, NY 10022
www.tonyhillermanbooks.com

Hilton, Paris (1981-)
Socialite; model; actor
Endeavor **Ph:** 310-248-2000
9601 Wilshire Blvd 3rd Fl **Fax:** 310-248-2020
Beverly Hills, CA 90210

Hinchey, Maurice D (1938-)
US Representative from New York (Democrat)
2431 Rayburn Bldg **Ph:** 202-225-6335
Washington, DC 20515 **Fax:** 202-226-0774
www.house.gov/hinchey

Hinckley, Gordon B (1910-)
President and world leader of The Church of Jesus Christ of Latter-day Saints
Church of Jesus Christ of Latter-day Saints **Ph:** 801-240-1000
Fax: 801-240-2033
50 E North Temple St **TF:** 800-453-3860
Salt Lake City, UT 84150
www.lds.org

Hinds, Bill (1950-)
Created, writes, and draws the cartoon feature Buzz Beamer for Sports Illustrated for Kids; also draws Tank McNamara (which is written by Jeff Millar)
Universal Press Syndicate **Ph:** 816-932-6600
4520 Main St
Kansas City, MO 64111
www.amuniversal.com/ups/features

Hines, Cheryl (1965-)
Actor
International Creative Management **Ph:** 310-550-4000
8942 Wilshire Blvd
Beverly Hills, CA 90211
www.hbo.com/larrydavid/cast

Hingis, Martina (1980-)
Professional tennis player
Octagon Athlete Representation **Ph:** 703-905-3300
1751 Pinnacle Dr Suite 1500 **Fax:** 703-905-4495
McLean, VA 22102

Hinn, Benny (1952-)
Televangelist
Benny Hinn Ministries **Ph:** 817-722-2222
PO Box 162000 **Fax:** 817-722-1138
Irving, TX 75016 **TF:** 800-433-1900
www.bennyhinn.org

Hinojosa, Ruben (1940-)
US Representative from Texas (Democrat)
2463 Rayburn Bldg **Ph:** 202-225-2531
Washington, DC 20515 **Fax:** 202-225-5688
hinojosa.house.gov

Hinote, Dan (1977-)
Professional hockey player
Colorado Avalanche **Ph:** 303-405-1100
Pepsi Center
1000 Chopper Cir
Denver, CO 80204
www.coloradoavalanche.com

Hinrich, Kirk (1981-)
Professional basketball player
Chicago Bulls **Ph:** 312-455-4000
United Center **Fax:** 312-455-4198
1901 W Madison St
Chicago, IL 60612
www.nba.com/bulls

Hinton, SE (1948-)
Susan Eloise Hinton; author of young adult fiction (The Outsiders; Rumble Fish; That Was Then, This Is Now)
Random House Children's Books **Ph:** 212-782-9000
Publicity Dept
1745 Broadway
New York, NY 10019
www.sehinton.com

Hirsch, Lynda
Writes the syndicated column Lynda Hirsch on Soaps
Creators Syndicate Inc **Ph:** 310-337-7003
5777 W Century Blvd Suite 700 **Fax:** 310-337-7625
Los Angeles, CA 90045
www.creators.com

Hirschfeld, Al (1903-2003)
Artist famous for his line drawings/caricatures
Margo Feiden Galleries Ltd **Ph:** 212-677-5330
699 Madison Ave **Fax:** 212-979-0596
New York, NY 10021
www.alhirschfeld.com

Hirshfield, Jane (1953-)
Poet, translator, and essayist
Steven Barclay Agency **Ph:** 707-773-0654
12 Western Ave **Fax:** 707-778-1868
Petaluma, CA 94952 **TF:** 888-965-7323
www.barclayagency.com

Hitch, David
Editorial cartoonist for the Worcester Telegram and Gazette in Worcester, MA
King Features Syndicate Inc **Ph:** 212-455-4000
888 7th Ave 2nd Fl
New York, NY 10019
www.kingfeatures.com

Hitchcock, Ken (1951-)
Hockey coach
Philadelphia Flyers **Ph:** 215-465-4500
Wachovia Center **Fax:** 215-389-9403
3601 S Broad St
Philadelphia, PA 19148
www.philadelphiaflyers.com

Ho, David, MD (1952-)
Microbiologist; CEO and director of the Aaron Diamond AIDS Research Center
Aaron Diamond AIDS Research Center **Ph:** 212-448-5000 **Fax:** 212-725-1126
455 1st Ave
New York, NY 10016
www.adarc.org

Hoagland, Jim (1940-)
Columnist (syndicated) and senior foreign correspondent for the Washington Post
Washington Post Writers Group **Ph:** 202-334-6375 **Fax:** 202-334-5669
1150 15th St NW 9th Fl
Washington, DC 20071
www.postwritersgroup.com

Hoberman, J
Senior film critic at Village Voice; author
Village Voice **Ph:** 212-475-3300
36 Cooper Sq **Fax:** 212-475-8944
New York, NY 10003

Hobica, George
Travel writer; also writes a syndicated travel column, Ask George
Copley News Service **Ph:** 619-293-1818
PO Box 120190
San Diego, CA 92112

Hobson, David L (1936-)
US Representative from Ohio (Republican)
2346 Rayburn Bldg **Ph:** 202-225-4324
Washington, DC 20515
www.house.gov/hobson

Hobson, Mellody
Good Morning America's financial contributor; also is president of Ariel Capital Management, a Chicago-based investment management firm
Good Morning America **Ph:** 212-456-7777
147 Columbus Ave
New York, NY 10023
www.abcnews.go.com/GMA

Hoch, Scott (1955-)
Professional golfer
SFX Sports Group **Ph:** 202-686-2000
5335 Wisconsin Ave NW Suite 850
Washington, DC 20015
www.pgatour.com/players

Hockney, David (1937-)
British pop artist
Meyerovich Gallery **Ph:** 415-421-7171
251 Post St 4th Fl **Fax:** 415-421-2775
San Francisco, CA 94108
www.meyerovich.com

Hodes, Richard J, MD (1943-)
Director of the National Institute on Aging, National Institutes of Health
National Institute on Aging **Ph:** 301-496-9265
31 Center Dr Bldg 31 Rm 5C35 **Fax:** 301-496-2525
MSC 2292
Bethesda, MD 20892
www.nia.nih.gov

Hoekstra, Peter (1953-)
US Representative from Michigan (Republican)
2234 Rayburn Bldg **Ph:** 202-225-4401
Washington, DC 20515 **Fax:** 202-226-0779
hoekstra.house.gov

Hoest, Bunny
Produces the syndicated comic strip The Lockhorns; also produces Laugh Parade for Parade magazine and Bumper Snickers for the National Enquirer
King Features Syndicate Inc **Ph:** 212-455-4000
888 7th Ave 2nd Fl
New York, NY 10019
www.kingfeatures.com

Hoeven, John (1957-)
Governor of North Dakota (Republican)
600 E Boulevard Ave **Ph:** 701-328-2200
Dept 101 **Fax:** 701-328-2205
Bismarck, ND 58505
governor.state.nd.us

Hoffa, James P (1941-)
President of the Teamsters Union
International Brotherhood of Teamsters
25 Louisiana Ave NW
Washington, DC 20001
www.teamster.org
Ph: 202-624-6800

Hoffman, Alice (1952-)
Author (Practical Magic)
Doubleday Publicity
1745 Broadway
New York, NY 10019
www.alicehoffman.com
Ph: 212-782-9000

Hoffman, Dustin (1937-)
Actor
Endeavor
9601 Wilshire Blvd 3rd Fl
Beverly Hills, CA 90210
Ph: 310-248-2000
Fax: 310-248-2020

Hoffman, Ken
Writes the syndicated column Drive-Thru Gourmet, a humorous review of fast-food specials
King Features Syndicate Inc
888 7th Ave 2nd Fl
New York, NY 10019
www.kingfeatures.com
Ph: 212-455-4000

Hoffman, Philip Seymour (1967-)
Actor
Paradigm
500 5th Ave 37th Fl
New York, NY 10110
Ph: 212-703-7540
Fax: 212-764-8941

Hoffman, Ronald
President and CEO of Dover Corp
Dover Corp
280 Park Ave 34th Fl
New York, NY 10017
www.dovercorporation.com
Ph: 212-922-1640

Hoffman, Ronald L, MD (1945-)
Complementary/alternative medicine practitioner; hosts the radio show Health Talk and has written several books on the subject
The Hoffman Center
40 E 30th St 10th Fl
New York, NY 10016
www.drhoffman.com
Ph: 212-779-1744
Fax: 212-779-0891

Hoffman, Trevor (1967-)
Professional baseball player
San Diego Padres
Petco Park
PO Box 122000
San Diego, CA 92112
sandiego.padres.mlb.com
Ph: 619-795-5000
Fax: 619-497-5339

Holbert, Jerry
Editorial cartoonist for The Boston Herald
Newspaper Enterprise Assn
200 Madison Ave
New York, NY 10016
www.unitedfeatures.com
Ph: 212-293-8500

Holbrook, Bill (1958-)
Creator of the comic strips On the Fastrack and Safe Havens
King Features Syndicate Inc
888 7th Ave 2nd Fl
New York, NY 10019
www.kevinandkell.com
Ph: 212-455-4000

Holbrook, Hal (1925-)
Actor
cedvoices.com
10635 Santa Monica Blvd Suites 130/135
Los Angeles, CA 90025
www.cedvoices.com
Ph: 310-475-2111
Fax: 310-475-1929

Holden, Kip (1952-)
Mayor of Baton Rouge, Louisiana
222 Saint Louis St 3rd Fl
Baton Rouge, LA 70802
www.brgov.com/dept/Mayor
Ph: 225-389-3100
Fax: 225-389-5203

Holden, Stephen (1941-)
Movie critic
New York Times
229 W 43rd St
New York, NY 10036
Ph: 212-556-1234

Holden, Tim (1957-)
US Representative from Pennsylvania (Democrat)
2417 Rayburn Bldg
Washington, DC 20515
www.holden.house.gov
Ph: 202-225-5546
Fax: 202-226-0996

Holdsclaw, Chamique (1977-)
Professional basketball player
Los Angeles Sparks
2151 E Grand Ave Suite 100
El Segundo, CA 90245
www.wnba.com/sparks
Ph: 310-341-1000
Fax: 310-341-1029

Holeman, Linda (1949-)
Author of short stories as well as historic and contemporary novels for both adults and young adults
Tundra Books
481 University Ave Suite 900
Toronto, ON M5G2E9
www.lindaholeman.com
Ph: 416-598-4786
Fax: 416-598-0247
TF: 800-788-1074

Holik, Bobby (1971-)
Professional hockey player
Atlanta Thrashers **Ph:** 404-827-5300
Centennial Tower **Fax:** 404-827-5909
101 Marietta St NW Suite 1900
Atlanta, GA 30303
www.atlantathrashers.com

Holland, Bernard
Classical music critic
New York Times **Ph:** 212-556-1234
229 W 43rd St
New York, NY 10036

Hollander, Joel
Chairman & CEO of CBS Radio Inc
CBS Radio Inc **Ph:** 212-846-3939
1515 Broadway 46th Fl **Fax:** 212-314-9228
New York, NY 10036

Hollander, Nicole (1939-)
Creator of the comic strip Sylvia
Tribune Media Services Inc **Ph:** 312-222-4444
435 N Michigan Ave Suite 1500
Chicago, IL 60611
www.nicolehollander.com

Holliday, Charles O Jr (1948-)
Chairman and CEO of DuPont
DuPont **Ph:** 302-774-1000
1007 Market St **Fax:** 302-774-4399
Wilmington, DE 19898
www2.dupont.com

Holloway, Josh (1969-)
Actor
Diverse Talent Group **Ph:** 310-201-6565
1875 Century Park E **Fax:** 310-201-6572
Suite 2250
Los Angeles, CA 90067
www.joshholloway.com

Holm, Ian (1931-)
British actor
International Creative Management **Ph:** 310-550-4000
8942 Wilshire Blvd
Beverly Hills, CA 90211

Holmes, Earl (1973-)
Professional football player
Detroit Lions **Ph:** 313-216-4000
222 Republic Dr **Fax:** 313-216-4069
Allen Park, MI 48101
www.detroitlions.com

Holmes, Joan
President of The Hunger Project
The Hunger Project **Ph:** 212-251-9100
15 E 26th St Suite 1401 **Fax:** 212-532-9785
New York, NY 10010
www.thp.org

Holmes, Katie (1978-)
Actor
Creative Artists Agency **Ph:** 310-288-4545
9830 Wilshire Blvd **Fax:** 310-288-4800
Beverly Hills, CA 90212

Holmes, Priest (1973-)
Professional football player
Kansas City Chiefs **Ph:** 816-920-9300
Arrowhead Stadium **Fax:** 816-920-4315
1 Arrowhead Dr
Kansas City, MO 64129
www.kcchiefs.com

Holmgren, Mike (1948-)
Football coach
Seattle Seahawks **Ph:** 425-827-9777
11220 NE 53rd St **Fax:** 425-827-9008
Kirkland, WA 98033
www.seahawks.com

Holst, Art
Motivational speaker (on handling change, problem solving, discipline, teamwork, communicating effectively, how to laugh at yourself); was an NFL line judge for 15 years
Promotivation Inc **Ph:** 760-603-8110
c/o SpeakersOffice Inc **Fax:** 760-603-8010
5927 Balfour Ct Suite 103
Carlsbad, CA 92008
www.artholst.com

Holt, Kimberly Willis
Author of books for young adults (Keeper of the Night; When Zachary Beaver Came to Town)
Books for Young Readers **Ph:** 212-886-9200
Henry Holt & Co
115 W 18th St
New York, NY 10011
www.kimberlyholt.com

Holt, Lester (1959-)
News anchor on MSNBC
MSNBC TV **Ph:** 201-583-5000
1 MSNBC Plaza
Secaucus, NJ 07094
www.msnbc.msn.com/id/3080263

Holt, Rush (1948-)
US Representative from New Jersey (Democrat)
1019 Longworth Bldg **Ph:** 202-225-5801
Washington, DC 20515 **Fax:** 202-225-6025
holt.house.gov

Holt, Torry (1976-)
Professional football player
Saint Louis Rams **Ph:** 314-982-7267
1 Rams Way **Fax:** 314-770-9261
Earth City, MO 63045
www.stlouisrams.com

Holyfield, Evander (1962-)
Boxer (the only four-time heavyweight champion of the world)
Holyfield Management Inc **Ph:** 770-460-6807
794 Evander Holyfield Hwy
Fairburn, GA 30213
www.evanderholyfield.com

Honda, Michael M (1941-)
US Representative from California (Democrat)
1713 Longworth Bldg **Ph:** 202-225-2631
Washington, DC 20515 **Fax:** 202-225-2699
www.honda.house.gov

Honeycutt, Van B
Chairman and CEO of Computer Sciences Corp
Computer Sciences Corp **Ph:** 310-615-1726
2100 E Grand Ave **Fax:** 310-640-2648
El Segundo, CA 90245
www.csc.com

Hooley, Darlene (1939-)
US Representative from Oregon (Democrat)
2430 Rayburn Bldg **Ph:** 202-225-5711
Washington, DC 20515 **Fax:** 202-225-5699
hooley.house.gov

Hopkins, Anthony (1937-)
Actor
Creative Artists Agency **Ph:** 310-288-4545
9830 Wilshire Blvd **Fax:** 310-288-4800
Beverly Hills, CA 90212

Hopkins, Tom
Dynamic speaker who provides how-to seminars and other training products to enhance sales skills
Tom Hopkins International **Ph:** 480-949-0786
7531 E 2nd St **Fax:** 480-949-1590
Scottsdale, AZ 85251 **TF:** 800-528-0446
www.tomhopkins.com

Hopper, Dennis (1936-)
Actor
International Creative Management **Ph:** 310-550-4000
8942 Wilshire Blvd
Beverly Hills, CA 90211

Horn, Alan
President & COO of Warner Bros. Entertainment
Warner Bros Entertainment Inc **Ph:** 818-954-6000
4000 Warner Blvd
Burbank, CA 91522
www.timewarner.com

Horn, Joe (1972-)
Professional football player
New Orleans Saints **Ph:** 504-733-0255
5800 Airline Dr **Fax:** 504-731-1768
Metairie, LA 70003
www.neworleanssaints.com

Horner, Jack, PhD (1946-)
Paleontology curator at the Museum of the Rockies; expert on dinosaurs
Museum of the Rockies **Ph:** 406-994-3170
Montana State University
600 W Kagy Blvd
Bozeman, MT 59717
www.montana.edu/wwwmor

Horner, James (1953-)
Film composer
Gorfaine-Schwartz Agency **Ph:** 818-260-8500
4111 W Alameda Ave Suite 509
Burbank, CA 91505
www.james-horner.com

Hornish, Sam Jr (1979-)
Race car driver (Indy Racing League)
Sports Management Network Inc **Ph:** 248-335-3535
Fax: 248-335-3352
1668 Telegraph Rd Suite 200
Bloomfield Hills, MI 48302
www.samhornish.com

Hornsby, Bruce
Musician
Monterey Peninsula Artists/Paradigm **Ph:** 831-375-4889
Fax: 831-375-2623
509 Hartnell St
Monterey, CA 93940
www.brucehornsby.com

Horowitz, David (1937-)
Journalist and host of the Fight Back! Talk Back! radio program and the Fight Back! with David Horowitz television series
Fight Back! **Ph:** 310-820-1188
PO Box 49915
Los Angeles, CA 90049
www.fightback.com

Horsey, David
Editorial cartoonist and columnist for the Seattle Post-Intelligencer
Tribune Media Services Inc **Ph:** 312-222-4444
435 N Michigan Ave Suite 1500
Chicago, IL 60611
www.comicspage.com

Horton, Nathan (1985-)
Professional hockey player
Florida Panthers **Ph:** 954-835-7000
BankAtlantic Center **Fax:** 954-835-7700
1 Panther Pkwy
Sunrise, FL 33323
www.floridapanthers.com

Horvath, Polly (1957-)
Author of books for children (The Canning Season, Everything on a Waffle, The Pepins and Their Problems)
Books for Young Readers **Ph:** 212-741-6900
Farrar Straus & Giroux
19 Union Sq W
New York, NY 10003
www.pollyhorvath.com

Horvitz, H Robert, PhD (1947-)
Winner (with two other scientists) of the 2002 Nobel Prize in Medicine or Physiology for discoveries concerning genetic regulation of organ development and programmed cell death
Massachusetts Institute of Technology **Ph:** 617-253-4671 **Fax:** 617-253-8126
Dept of Biology Rm 68-425
Cambridge, MA 02139
www.hhmi.org/research/nobel

Horwitz, Jane
Movie reviewer/syndicated columnist (The Family Filmgoer)
Washington Post Writers Group **Ph:** 202-334-6375 **Fax:** 202-334-5669
1150 15th St NW 9th Fl
Washington, DC 20071
www.postwritersgroup.com

Hossa, Marian (1979-)
Professional hockey player
Atlanta Thrashers **Ph:** 404-827-5300
Centennial Tower **Fax:** 404-827-5909
101 Marietta St NW
Atlanta, GA 30303
www.atlantathrashers.com

Hostettler, John N (1961-)
US Representative from Indiana (Republican)
1214 Longworth Bldg **Ph:** 202-225-4636
Washington, DC 20515 **Fax:** 202-225-3284
www.house.gov/hostettler

Hotchkiss, Harley (1927-)
A co-owner of the Calgary Flames hockey franchise and chairman of the NHL Board of Governors
Calgary Flames **Ph:** 403-777-2177
Pengrowth Saddledome **Fax:** 403-777-2195
555 Saddledome Rise SE
Calgary, AB T2G2W1
www.calgaryflames.com

Houdini, Harry (1874-1926)
Legendary magician and escape artist
Houdini Museum **Ph:** 570-342-5555
1433 Main St
Scranton, PA 18508
houdini.org

Houghton, James R
Chairman of Corning Inc.
Corning Inc **Ph:** 607-974-9000
1 Riverfront Plaza
Corning, NY 14831
www.corning.com

Hounsou, Djimon (1964-)
Actor
Gersh Agency **Ph:** 310-274-6611
232 N Canon Dr
Beverly Hills, CA 90210

House, Yoanna (1980-)
Model
IMG Models **Ph:** 212-253-8884
304 Park Ave S 12th Fl **Fax:** 212-253-8883
New York, NY 10010
www.imgmodels.com

Houshmandzadeh, TJ (1977-)
Professional football player
Cincinnati Bengals **Ph:** 513-621-3550
1 Paul Brown Stadium **Fax:** 513-621-3570
Cincinnati, OH 45202
www.bengals.com

Houston, Whitney (1963-)
Singer; actor
William Morris Agency **Ph:** 310-859-4000
1 William Morris Pl **Fax:** 310-859-4462
Beverly Hills, CA 90212
www.wma.com/whitney_houston/summary

Howard, Clark
Radio show host (a call-in show about consumer issues)
Cox Radio Syndication **Ph:** 404-962-2078
1601 W Peachtree St NE **Fax:** 404-897-2226
Atlanta, GA 30309
clarkhoward.com

Howard, Dwight (1985-)
Professional basketball player
Orlando Magic **Ph:** 407-916-2400
8701 Maitland Summit Blvd **Fax:** 407-916-2884
Orlando, FL 32810
www.nba.com/magic

Howard, Josh (1980-)
Professional basketball player
Dallas Mavericks **Ph:** 214-747-6287
The Pavilion **Fax:** 214-658-7121
2909 Taylor St
Dallas, TX 75226
www.nba.com/mavericks

Howard, Margo
Writes the Dear Margo (formerly Dear Prudence) advice column; daughter of Eppie Lederer (Ann Landers)
Creators Syndicate Inc **Ph:** 310-337-7003
5777 W Century Blvd Suite 700 **Fax:** 310-337-7625
Los Angeles, CA 90045
www.creators.com

Howard, Ron (1954-)
Movie director and co-founder/co-chairman (with Brian Grazer) of Imagine Entertainment; actor
Imagine Entertainment **Ph:** 310-858-2000
9465 Wilshire Blvd 7th Fl **Fax:** 310-858-2020
Beverly Hills, CA 90212
www.imagine-entertainment.com

Howe, Gordie (1928-)
NHL great known as Mr Hockey
Power Play International Inc **Ph:** 248-356-4300
2000 Easy St
Commerce Township, MI 48390
www.mrandmrshockey.com

Howe, Neil (1951-)
Author and national speaker, historian, economist, and demographer; an authority on generations in America
LifeCourse Associates **Ph:** 703-759-2649
9080 Eaton Park Rd **Fax:** 703-759-9356
Great Falls, VA 22066 **TF:** 866-537-4999
www.lifecourse.com

Howse, Jennifer L, PhD
President of the March of Dimes Birth Defects Foundation
March of Dimes Birth Defects Foundation **Ph:** 914-428-7100 **Fax:** 914-428-8203
1275 Mamaroneck Ave
White Plains, NY 10605

Hoyer, Steny H (1939-)
US Representative from Maryland (Democrat); House Democratic Whip
1705 Longworth Bldg **Ph:** 202-225-4131
Washington, DC 20515 **Fax:** 202-225-4300
www.hoyer.house.gov

Hubbard, Barbara Marx (1929-)
Futurist, author, lecturer
New World Library **Ph:** 415-884-2100
14 Pamaron Way **Fax:** 415-884-2199
Novato, CA 94949
www.newworldlibrary.com

Hubbard, R Glenn, PhD (1958-)
Economist; former (2001-2003) chairman of the President's Council of Economic Advisers
American Enterprise Institute for Public Policy Research **Ph:** 202-862-5800 **Fax:** 202-862-7177
1150 17th St NW Suite 1100
Washington, DC 20036
www.aei.org

Hubbe, Nikolaj (1967-)
A principal dancer with the New York City Ballet; also has appeared as a guest artist with companies around the world
New York City Ballet **Ph:** 212-870-5656
New York State Theater **Fax:** 212-870-7791
20 Lincoln Center
New York, NY 10023
www.nycballet.com/about/dancers.html

Huber, David R, PhD
Chairman and CEO of Broadwing Corp, which provides networking solutions through its nationwide all-optical network
Broadwing Corp **Ph:** 443-259-4000
7015 Albert Einstein Dr **Fax:** 443-259-4444
Columbia, MD 21046
www.broadwing.com

Huckabee, Michael D (1955-)
Governor of Arkansas (Republican)
State Capitol Bldg **Ph:** 501-682-2345
Little Rock, AR 72201 **Fax:** 501-682-1382
www.accessarkansas.org/governor

Huddy, Juliet (1962-)
Co-host of FNC's Dayside and of Fox & Friends weekend edition
FOX News Channel **Ph:** 212-301-3000
1211 Ave of the Americas
New York, NY 10036
www.foxnews.com/fnctv

Hudson, Kate (1979-)
Actor
Creative Artists Agency **Ph:** 310-288-4545
9830 Wilshire Blvd **Fax:** 310-288-4800
Beverly Hills, CA 90212

Hudson, Mac
Co-hosts a morning drive show on the radio; does character & celebrity impersonations
KILT-FM **Ph:** 713-881-5100
24 Greenway Plaza Suite 1900 **Fax:** 713-881-5199
Houston, TX 77046
www.kilt.com

Hudson, Tim (1975-)
Professional baseball player
Atlanta Braves **Ph:** 404-522-7630
PO Box 4064 **Fax:** 404-614-1392
Atlanta, GA 30302
atlanta.braves.mlb.com

Hudson, Troy (1976-)
Professional basketball player
Minnesota Timberwolves **Ph:** 612-673-1600
Target Center **Fax:** 612-673-1699
600 1st Ave N
Minneapolis, MN 55403
www.nba.com/timberwolves

Huey, John
Editor-in-Chief of Time Inc
Time Inc **Ph:** 212-522-0023
Time & Life Bldg
1271 Ave of the Americas
New York, NY 10020
www.timewarner.com

Huff, Aubrey (1976-)
Professional baseball player
Tampa Bay Devil Rays **Ph:** 727-825-3137
Tropicana Field **Fax:** 727-825-3111
1 Tropicana Dr
Saint Petersburg, FL 33705
tampabay.devilrays.mlb.com

Huffington, Arianna (1950-)
Political columnist & author
Tribune Media Services Inc **Ph:** 312-222-4444
435 N Michigan Ave Suite 1500
Chicago, IL 60611
ariannaonline.com

Huffman, Felicity (1962-)
Actor
International Creative Management **Ph:** 310-550-4000
8942 Wilshire Blvd
Beverly Hills, CA 90211
abc.go.com/primetime/desperate

Hughes, Catherine L
Founder of Radio One (urban radio programming)
Radio One Inc **Ph:** 301-306-1111
5900 Princess Garden Pkwy 7th Fl **Fax:** 301-306-9426
Lanham, MD 20706
www.radio-one.com

Hughes, Dan
Basketball coach
San Antonio Silver Stars **Ph:** 210-444-5050
1 SBC Center
San Antonio, TX 78219
www.wnba.com/silverstars

Hughes, John (1950-)
Film writer/producer/director
William Morris Agency **Ph:** 310-859-4000
1 William Morris Pl **Fax:** 310-859-4462
Beverly Hills, CA 90212

Hughes, Larry (1979-)
Professional basketball player
Cleveland Cavaliers **Ph:** 216-420-2000
Quicken Loans Arena **Fax:** 216-420-2298
1 Center Ct
Cleveland, OH 44115
www.nba.com/cavaliers

Hughley, DL (1963-)
Comedian; actor
International Creative Management **Ph:** 310-550-4000
8942 Wilshire Blvd
Beverly Hills, CA 90211
www.icmtalent.com/musperf/comedy.html

Huizenga, H Wayne (1939-)
Chairman of Huizenga Holdings and Boca Resorts, Inc.; also owns the Miami Dolphins football team, Dolphins Stadium, and is involved in real estate
Huizenga Holdings — **Ph:** 954-627-5000
450 E Las Olas Blvd Suite 1500 — **Fax:** 954-627-5050
Fort Lauderdale, FL 33301
www.miamidolphins.com/contacts/administration/administration.asp

Hulme, Etta
Editorial cartoonist for the Star-Telegram
Fort Worth Star-Telegram — **Ph:** 817-390-7400
400 W 7th
Fort Worth, TX 76102
www.unitedfeatures.com

Hulshof, Kenny (1958-)
US Representative from Missouri (Republican)
412 Cannon Bldg — **Ph:** 202-225-2956
Washington, DC 20515 — **Fax:** 202-225-5712
hulshof.house.gov

Hume, Brit (1943-)
FNC's Washington, DC managing editor and host of Special Report With Brit Hume
FOX News Channel — **Ph:** 202-824-6300
400 N Capitol St NW Suite 550
Washington, DC 20001
www.foxnews.com/fnctv

Humphries, Rusty (1967-)
Host of an issue-oriented, caller-driven radio talk show (politically conservative)
Talk Radio Network — **Ph:** 541-664-8827
PO Box 3755 — **Fax:** 541-664-6250
Central Point, OR 97502
www.talkradionetwork.com

Hunt, Bonnie (1961-)
Actor
International Creative Management — **Ph:** 310-550-4000
8942 Wilshire Blvd
Beverly Hills, CA 90211

Hunt, Helen (1963-)
Actor
Creative Artists Agency — **Ph:** 310-288-4545
9830 Wilshire Blvd — **Fax:** 310-288-4800
Beverly Hills, CA 90212

Hunt, Helen LaKelly (1949-)
Founder and president of The Sister Fund, a private women's fund dedicated to the social, political, economic, and spiritual empowerment of women and girls
The Sister Fund — **Ph:** 212-260-4446
79 5th Ave 4th Fl — **Fax:** 212-260-4633
New York, NY 10003
www.sisterfund.org

Hunt, Lamar (1932-)
Founder of the American Football League (AFL) and founder/owner of the Kansas City Chiefs football franchise
Kansas City Chiefs — **Ph:** 816-920-9300
Arrowhead Stadium — **Fax:** 816-923-4719
1 Arrowhead Dr
Kansas City, MO 64129
www.kcchiefs.com

Hunt, Linda (1945-)
Actor
William Morris Agency — **Ph:** 310-859-4000
1 William Morris Pl — **Fax:** 310-859-4462
Beverly Hills, CA 90212

Hunt, Mary
Author and creator of The Cheapskate monthly newsletter; writes the syndicated newspaper column Everyday Cheapskate: Budget-Conscious Tips for Every Household
United Feature Syndicate — **Ph:** 212-293-8500
200 Madison Ave
New York, NY 10016
www.unitedfeatures.com

Hunter, Bill (1943-)
Executive Director of the National Basketball Players Association
National Basketball Players Assn — **Ph:** 212-655-0880 — **Fax:** 212-655-0881
2 Penn Plaza Suite 2430
New York, NY 10121
www.nbpa.com

Hunter, Duncan (1948-)
US Representative from California (Republican)
2265 Rayburn Bldg — **Ph:** 202-225-5672
Washington, DC 20515 — **Fax:** 202-225-0235
www.house.gov/hunter

Hunter, Evan (1926-)
Novelist (Blackboard Jungle) and screenwriter (Alfred Hitchcock's The Birds); writes mysteries as Ed McBain
Gelfman Schneider Literary Agency — **Ph:** 212-245-1993 — **Fax:** 212-245-8678
250 W 57th St Suite 2515
New York, NY 10107
www.edmcbain.com

Hunter, Holly (1958-)
Actor
William Morris Agency — **Ph:** 310-859-4000 — **Fax:** 310-859-4462
1 William Morris Pl
Beverly Hills, CA 90212

Hunter, Rachel (1969-)
Model and actor
Ford Models — **Ph:** 212-219-6500 — **Fax:** 212-966-5028
111 5th Ave
New York, NY 10003
rachelhunter.com

Hunter, Torii (1975-)
Professional baseball player
Minnesota Twins — **Ph:** 612-375-1366 — **Fax:** 612-375-7473
Hubert H Humphrey Metrodome
34 Kirby Puckett Pl
Minneapolis, MN 55415
minnesota.twins.mlb.com

Huntsman, Jon M
Founder & chairman of Huntsman LLC, the world's largest privately held chemical company
Huntsman LLC — **Ph:** 801-584-5700 — **Fax:** 801-584-5781
500 Huntsman Way
Salt Lake City, UT 84108
www.huntsman.com

Huntsman, Jon M Jr (1960-)
Governor of Utah (Republican)
210 State Capitol Complex Suite 220 — **Ph:** 801-538-1000 — **Fax:** 801-538-1528
Salt Lake City, UT 84114
www.utah.gov/governor

Hurd, Mark V
President and CEO of Hewlett-Packard
Hewlett-Packard Co — **Ph:** 650-857-1501
3000 Hanover St
Palo Alto, CA 94304
www.hp.com/hpinfo

Hurdle, Clint (1957-)
Baseball manager
Colorado Rockies — **Ph:** 303-292-0200 — **Fax:** 303-296-2066
Coors Field
2001 Blake St
Denver, CO 80205
colorado.rockies.mlb.com

Hurt, William (1950-)
Actor
Creative Artists Agency — **Ph:** 310-288-4545 — **Fax:** 310-288-4800
9830 Wilshire Blvd
Beverly Hills, CA 90212

Husni, Samir A, PhD
Journalism professor who reviews and rates consumer magazines (known as Mr Magazine)
University of Mississippi Journalism Dept — **Ph:** 662-915-1414 — **Fax:** 662-915-7765
PO Box 2906
123 Lester Hall
University, MS 38677
www.mrmagazine.com

Huston, Anjelica (1951-)
Actor
International Creative Management — **Ph:** 310-550-4000
8942 Wilshire Blvd
Beverly Hills, CA 90211

Hutchison, Kay Bailey (1943-)
US Senator from Texas (Republican)
284 Russell Bldg — **Ph:** 202-224-5922 — **Fax:** 202-224-0776
Washington, DC 20510
hutchison.senate.gov

Hutson, Don
Corporate consultant/speaker on high performance selling, leadership, customer service, personal growth
Don Hutson Organization — **Ph:** 901-767-0000 — **Fax:** 901-767-5959 — **TF:** 800-647-9166
516 Tennessee St Suite 219
Memphis, TN 38103
www.donhutson.com

Hutton, Lauren (1943-)
Model and actor
IMG Models — **Ph:** 212-253-8884 — **Fax:** 212-253-8883
304 Park Ave S 12th Fl
New York, NY 10010
www.laurenhutton.com

Hyde, Henry J (1924-)
US Representative from Illinois (Republican)
2110 Rayburn Bldg — **Ph:** 202-225-4561 — **Fax:** 202-225-1166
Washington, DC 20515
www.house.gov/hyde

Hyman, Trina Schart (1939-)
Illustrator of books for young readers (Saint George & the Dragon, retold by Margaret Hodges)
Simon & Schuster Books for Young readers **Ph:** 212-698-7000
1230 Ave of the Americas
New York, NY 10020
www.ortakales.com/illustrators/Hyman.html

Hynes, Patricia M
Trial lawyer who specializes in complex securities and commercial litigation
Milberg Weiss Bershad & Schulman LLP **Ph:** 212-594-5300 **Fax:** 212-868-1229
1 Pennsylvania Plaza 49th Fl
New York, NY 10019
www.milbergweiss.com

Iacocca, Lee (1924-)
A former chairman of Chrysler, which he's credited with saving from bankruptcy, and a one-time president of Ford, where he became known as the Father of the Mustang; now retired, his activities include support for diabetes research through the Iacocca Foundation
Iacocca Foundation **Ph:** 617-267-7747
17 Arlington St 4th Fl
Boston, MA 02116
www.iacoccafoundation.org

Ibanez, Raul (1972-)
Professional baseball player
Seattle Mariners **Ph:** 206-346-4000
Safeco Field **Fax:** 206-346-4050
1250 1st Ave S
Seattle, WA 98134
seattle.mariners.mlb.com

Icahn, Carl (1936-)
American billionaire financier who earned a reputation as a corporate raider after a hostile takeover of TWA in 1985; currently serves as chairman of the board and/or director of several companies, including XO Communications
XO Communications **Ph:** 703-547-2000
11111 Sunset Hills Rd **Fax:** 703-547-2881
Reston, VA 20190
www.xo.com

Ice Cube (1969-)
Rap/hip-hop singer; composer; actor. Real name is O'Shea Jackson
William Morris Agency **Ph:** 310-859-4000
1 William Morris Pl **Fax:** 310-859-4462
Beverly Hills, CA 90212
www.icecubemusic.com

Ice-T (1958-)
Actor; singer (rap)/composer. Real name is Tracy Morrow.
United Talent Agency **Ph:** 310-273-6700
9560 Wilshire Blvd 5th Fl **Fax:** 310-247-1111
Beverly Hills, CA 90212
www.icet.com

Idle, Eric (1943-)
Comedian; actor (was in Monty Python's Flying Circus)
William Morris Agency **Ph:** 310-859-4000
1 William Morris Pl **Fax:** 310-859-4462
Beverly Hills, CA 90212
www.pythonline.com

Ifill, Gwen (1955-)
Senior correspondent on PBS's NewsHour with Jim Lehrer; also moderator on Washington Week
MacNeil/Lehrer Productions **Ph:** 703-998-2138
2700 S Quincy St Suite 250
Arlington, VA 22206
www.pbs.org/newshour/ww/ifill.html

Iger, Robert A (1951-)
President & CEO of Walt Disney Co
Walt Disney Co **Ph:** 818-560-1000
500 S Buena Vista St **Fax:** 818-560-1930
Burbank, CA 91521
disney.go.com/corporate

Iginla, Jarome (1977-)
Professional hockey player
Calgary Flames **Ph:** 403-777-2177
Pengrowth Saddledome **Fax:** 403-777-2195
555 Saddledome Rise SE
Calgary, AB T2G2W1
www.calgaryflames.com

Iglesias, Enrique (1975-)
Singer (Latin, pop)
Creative Artists Agency **Ph:** 310-288-4545
9830 Wilshire Blvd **Fax:** 310-288-4800
Beverly Hills, CA 90212
www.enriqueiglesias.com

Iglesias, Julio (1943-)
Latin singer
Creative Artists Agency **Ph:** 310-288-4545
9830 Wilshire Blvd **Fax:** 310-288-4800
Beverly Hills, CA 90212
www.julioiglesias.net

Ignarro, Louis J, PhD (1941-)
Winner (with two other scientists) of the 1998 Nobel Prize in Medicine or Physiology for discoveries concerning nitric oxide as a signalling molecule in the cardiovascular system; his research indirectly led to the development of Viagra
University of California at Los Angeles **Ph:** 310-825-5159
Fax: 310-206-0589
Dept of Molecular & Medical Pharmacology
650 Charles Young Dr
Los Angeles, CA 90095
www.ucla.edu/about/nobelwinners

Ignatius, David (1950-)
Syndicated columnist (commentary)
Washington Post Writers Group **Ph:** 202-334-6375
Fax: 202-334-5669
1150 15th St NW 9th Fl
Washington, DC 20071
www.postwritersgroup.com

Iguodala, Andre (1984-)
Professional basketball player
Philadelphia 76ers **Ph:** 215-339-7600
Wachovia Center **Fax:** 215-339-7632
3601 S Broad St
Philadelphia, PA 19148
www.nba.com/sixers

Ilgauskas, Zydrunas (1975-)
Professional basketball player
Cleveland Cavaliers **Ph:** 216-420-2000
Quicken Loans Arena **Fax:** 216-420-2298
1 Center Ct
Cleveland, OH 44115
www.nba.com/cavaliers

Ilitch, Marian
With her husband Michael is co-founder/owner of Little Caesars Pizza and co-owner of the Detroit Red Wings hockey club & Detroit Tigers baseball club, as well as several other businesses
Ilitch Holdings Inc **Ph:** 313-983-6000
2211 Woodward Ave **Fax:** 313-983-6494
Fox Office Center
Detroit, MI 48201
www.ilitchholdings.com

Ilitch, Michael
With his wife Marian is co-founder/owner of Little Caesars Pizza and co-owner of the Detroit Red Wings hockey club & Detroit Tigers baseball club, as well as several other businesses
Ilitch Holdings Inc **Ph:** 313-983-6000
2211 Woodward Ave **Fax:** 313-983-6494
Fox Office Center
Detroit, MI 48201
www.ilitchholdings.com

Immelt, Jeffrey R (1956-)
Chairman of the Board and CEO of GE
General Electric Co **Ph:** 203-373-2211
3135 Easton Tpke **Fax:** 203-373-3131
Fairfield, CT 06828
www.ge.com/en/company/companyinfo

Imperioli, Michael (1966-)
Actor
United Talent Agency **Ph:** 310-273-6700
9560 Wilshire Blvd 5th Fl **Fax:** 310-247-1111
Beverly Hills, CA 90212
www.hbo.com/sopranos

Imus, Don (1940-)
Radio personality; disc jockey and host of Imus in the Morning
WFAN-AM **Ph:** 718-706-7690
34-12 36th St **Fax:** 718-383-5734
Astoria, NY 11106
www.wfan.com

Inaba, Carrie Ann
Dancer/choreographer; CEO & president of EnterMediArts Inc; a judge on Dancing with the Stars
EnterMediArts Inc **Ph:** 818-971-5044
11333 Moorpark St Suite 86
Studio City, CA 91602
www.carrieanninaba.com

Indigo Girls
Singers (Amy Ray and Emily Saliers); also activists for various causes
Russell Carter Artist Management **Ph:** 404-377-9900
315 W Ponce de Leon Ave Suite 755
Decatur, GA 30030
www.indigogirls.com

Indyk, Martin S, PhD (1951-)
Director of the Saban Center for Middle East Policy and Senior Fellow, Foreign Policy Studies, at the Brookings Institution; former Ambassador to Israel and has also held other government positions
Saban Center for Middle East Policy **Ph:** 202-797-6000 **Fax:** 202-797-6003
Brookings Institution
1775 Massachusetts Ave NW
Washington, DC 20036
www.brookings.edu/scholars/mindyk.htm

Inglis, Bob (1959-)
US Representative from South Carolina (Republican)
330 Cannon Bldg **Ph:** 202-225-6030
Washington, DC 20515 **Fax:** 202-226-1177
www.house.gov/inglis

Ingraham, Laura (1963-)
Radio talk show host (politics, the news media, Hollywood)
Talk Radio Network **Ph:** 541-664-8827
PO Box 3755 **Fax:** 541-664-6250
Central Point, OR 97502
www.talkradionetwork.com

Ingram, Martha R (1935-)
One of the wealthiest active businesswomen in the US; chairman of the board of Ingram Industries, a distribution conglomerate
Ingram Industries Inc **Ph:** 615-298-8200
1 Belle Meade Pl 4400 Harding Rd
Nashville, TN 37205

Inhofe, James M (1934-)
US Senator from Oklahoma (Republican)
453 Russell Bldg **Ph:** 202-224-4721
Washington, DC 20510 **Fax:** 202-228-0380
inhofe.senate.gov

Inkster, Juli (1960-)
Professional golfer
SFX Sports Group **Ph:** 202-686-2000
5335 Wisconsin Ave NW Suite 850
Washington, DC 20015
www.sfxsports.com

Inman, Bobby R (1931-)
Admiral. Former Director of Naval Intelligence and former Director of the National Security Agency
Public Agenda **Ph:** 212-686-6610
6 E 39th St **Fax:** 212-889-3461
New York, NY 10016
www.publicagenda.org

Innes, Laura (1959-)
Actor
Creative Artists Agency **Ph:** 310-288-4545
9830 Wilshire Blvd **Fax:** 310-288-4800
Beverly Hills, CA 90212
www.nbc.com/ER

Innes, Scott (1966-)
Morning radio talk show host (country music); also does voice work for movies (Scooby Doo)
WYNK-FM **Ph:** 225-231-1860
5555 Hilton Ave **Fax:** 225-231-1869
Baton Rouge, LA 70808
www.scottinnes.com

Inouye, Daniel K (1924-)
US Senator from Hawaii (Democrat)
722 Hart Bldg **Ph:** 202-224-3934
Washington, DC 20510 **Fax:** 202-224-6747
inouye.senate.gov

Insana, Ron (1961-)
Anchor of CNBC's Street Signs; also hosts a nationally syndicated radio show
CNBC **Ph:** 201-735-2622
900 Sylvan Ave
Englewood Cliffs, NJ 07632
moneycentral.msn.com/cnbc/tv

Insel, Thomas R, MD
Director, National Institute of Mental Health, National Institutes of Health
National Institute of Mental Health **Ph:** 301-443-3673 **Fax:** 301-443-2578
6001 Executive Blvd Rm 8235
MSC 9669
Bethesda, MD 20892
www.nimh.nih.gov/about/director.cfm

Inslee, Jay (1951-)
US Representative from Washington (Democrat)
403 Cannon Bldg **Ph:** 202-225-6311
Washington, DC 20515 **Fax:** 202-226-1606
www.house.gov/inslee

Insulza, Jose Miguel (1943-)
Secretary General of the Organization of American States
Organization of American States **Ph:** 202-458-3000 **Fax:** 202-458-3967
17th St & Constitution Ave NW
Washington, DC 20006
www.oas.org

Iorio, Pam (1959-)
Mayor of Tampa, Florida
306 E Jackson St **Ph:** 813-274-8251
Tampa, FL 33602 **Fax:** 813-274-7050
www.tampagov.net

Iovanna, Carol
Weekend/overnight anchor on FOX News
FOX News Channel **Ph:** 212-301-3000
1211 Ave of the Americas
New York, NY 10036
www.foxnews.com/fnctv

Irani, Ray, PhD
Chairman, president, and CEO of Occidental Petroleum
Occidental Petroleum Corp **Ph:** 310-208-8800
10889 Wilshire Blvd **Fax:** 310-443-6690
Los Angeles, CA 90024
www.oxy.com

Ireland, Jay
President of NBC Universal Television Stations
NBC Universal Television Stations **Ph:** 212-664-4444 **Fax:** 212-664-3720
30 Rockefeller Plaza
New York, NY 10112
www.nbcuni.com

Ireland, Kathy (1963-)
Fashion model; clothing designer
Sterling/Winters Co & Kathy Ireland Worldwide **Ph:** 310-557-2700 **Fax:** 310-557-1722
10900 Wilshire Blvd Suite 1550
Los Angeles, CA 90024
www.kathyireland.com

Irons, Jeremy (1948-)
Actor
Creative Artists Agency **Ph:** 310-288-4545
9830 Wilshire Blvd **Fax:** 310-288-4800
Beverly Hills, CA 90212

Irsay, James
Owner of the Indianapolis Colts football team
Indianapolis Colts **Ph:** 317-297-2658
7001 W 56th St **Fax:** 317-297-8971
Indianapolis, IN 46254
www.colts.com

Irvin, Michael (1966-)
Former professional football player (wide receiver); now a studio analyst for ESPN
ESPN **Ph:** 860-585-2000
ESPN Plaza
935 Middle St
Bristol, CT 06010
sports.espn.go.com/espntv/espnGuide

Irving, John (1942-)
Novelist (The World According to Garp; The Ciderhouse Rules)
Ballantine Books Publicity **Ph:** 212-782-9000
1745 Broadway
New York, NY 10019
www.randomhouse.com/BB

Irwin, Hale (1945-)
Professional golfer
Gaylord Sports Management **Ph:** 480-483-9500
13845 N Northsight Blvd Suite 200
Scottsdale, AZ 85260
www.gaylordsports.com

Irwin, Steve (1962-)
The Crocodile Hunter on Animal Planet
Animal Planet **Ph:** 240-662-2000
Crocodile Hunter
8516 Georgia Ave
Silver Spring, MD 20910
www.crocodilehunter.com

Isaac, Teresa Ann
Mayor of Lexington, Kentucky
200 E Main St **Ph:** 859-258-3100
Lexington, KY 40507 **Fax:** 859-258-3194
www.lfucg.com/Mayor

Isaacs, Amy
National Director, Americans for Democratic Action
Americans for Democratic Action **Ph:** 202-785-5980 **Fax:** 202-785-5969
1625 K St NW Suite 210
Washington, DC 20006
www.adaction.org

Isaacs, Susan (1943-)
Novelist (Compromising Positions; Long Time No See)
Scribner Publicity Dept **Ph:** 212-698-7000
1230 Ave of the Americas
New York, NY 10020
www.susanisaacs.com

Isaacson, Walter (1952-)
President & CEO of the Aspen Institute; former CEO & chairman of CNN and managing editor of Time Magazine; author of several biographies
Aspen Institute **Ph:** 202-736-5800
1 Dupont Circle NW Suite 700 **Fax:** 202-467-0790
Washington, DC 20036
www.aspeninstitute.org

Isaak, Chris (1956-)
Singer/songwriter and musician
Special Artists Agency **Ph:** 310-859-9688
9465 Wilshire Blvd Suite 890
Beverly Hills, CA 90212

Isakson, Johnny (1944-)
US Senator from Georgia (Republican)
C4 Russell Bldg **Ph:** 202-224-3643
Washington, DC 20510 **Fax:** 202-228-0724
isakson.senate.gov

Isdell, E Neville
Chairman & CEO of Coca-Cola
Coca-Cola Co **Ph:** 404-676-3808
1 Coca-Cola Plaza **Fax:** 404-676-6792
Atlanta, GA 30313
www2.coca-cola.com

Ishiguro, Kazuo (1954-)
Author (The Remains of the Day; Never Let Me Go)
Knopf Publishing/Author Mail **Ph:** 212-782-9000
1745 Broadway
New York, NY 10019
www.randomhouse.com/knopf

Isikoff, Michael (1952-)
Investigative correspondent for Newsweek magazine
Newsweek Washington Bureau **Ph:** 202-626-2000
1750 Pennsylvania Ave NW **Fax:** 202-626-2011
Suite 1220
Washington, DC 20006
msnbc.msn.com/id/4863599

Israel, Steve (1958-)
US Representative from New York (Democrat)
432 Cannon Bldg **Ph:** 202-225-3335
Washington, DC 20515 **Fax:** 202-225-4669
www.house.gov/israel

Isringhausen, Jason (1972-)
Professional baseball player
Saint Louis Cardinals **Ph:** 314-421-3060
250 Stadium Plaza **Fax:** 314-425-0640
Saint Louis, MO 63102
stlouis.cardinals.mlb.com

Issa, Darrell E (1953-)
US Representative from California (Republican)
211 Cannon Bldg **Ph:** 202-225-3906
Washington, DC 20515 **Fax:** 202-225-3303
www.issa.house.gov

Istook, Ernest Jim (1950-)
US Representative from Oklahoma (Republican)
2404 Rayburn Bldg **Ph:** 202-225-2132
Washington, DC 20515 **Fax:** 202-226-1463
www.house.gov/istook

Iverson, Allen (1975-)
Professional basketball player
Philadelphia 76ers **Ph:** 215-339-7600
Wachovia Center **Fax:** 215-339-7632
3601 S Broad St
Philadelphia, PA 19148
www.nba.com/sixers

Ivins, Molly (1944-)
Journalist/syndicated columnist & essayist
Creators Syndicate Inc **Ph:** 310-337-7003
5777 W Century Blvd Suite 700 **Fax:** 310-337-7625
Los Angeles, CA 90045
www.creators.com/opinion.html

Ivory, James (1928-)
Movie director/producer
Merchant Ivory Productions **Ph:** 212-582-8049
250 W 57th St Suite 1825 **Fax:** 212-459-9201
New York, NY 10107
www.merchantivory.com/ivory.html

Izzard, Eddie (1962-)
Comedian
Creative Artists Agency **Ph:** 310-288-4545
8930 Wilshire Blvd **Fax:** 310-288-4800
Beverly Hills, CA 90212
www.izzard.com

J

Ja Rule (1976-)
Rap artist; actor
Creative Artists Agency **Ph:** 310-288-4545
9830 Wilshire Blvd **Fax:** 310-288-4800
Beverly Hills, CA 90212
www.jarule.com

Jablonski, Patrick
Photographer
Ansel Adams Gallery **Ph:** 888-361-7622
PO Box 4185 **Fax:** 650-692-3512
Burlingame, CA 94011
www.anseladams.com

Jackman, Hugh (1968-)
Actor
Endeavor **Ph:** 310-248-2000
9601 Wilshire Blvd 3rd Fl **Fax:** 310-284-2020
Beverly Hills, CA 90210

Jackson, Alan (1958-)
Country singer/songwriter
CAA Nashville **Ph:** 615-383-8787
3310 West End Ave 5th Fl **Fax:** 615-383-4937
Nashville, TN 37203
www.alanjackson.com

Jackson, Alphonso R (1946-)
US Secretary of Housing & Urban Development (HUD)
US Dept of Housing & Urban Development **Ph:** 202-708-0417
Fax: 202-708-2476
451 7th St SW
Washington, DC 20410
www.hud.gov/about

Jackson, Bobby (1973-)
Professional basketball player
Memphis Grizzlies **Ph:** 901-205-1234
FedExForum **Fax:** 901-205-1235
191 Beale St
Memphis, TN 38103
www.nba.com/grizzlies

Jackson, Darrell (1978-)
Professional football player
Seattle Seahawks **Ph:** 425-827-9777
11220 NE 53rd St **Fax:** 425-827-9008
Kirkland, WA 98033
www.seahawks.com

Jackson, Frank G (1946-)
Mayor of Cleveland
601 Lakeside Ave NE **Ph:** 216-664-3990
Cleveland, OH 44114 **Fax:** 216-664-2815
www.city.cleveland.oh.us

Jackson, Janet (1966-)
Soul/R&B singer
Creative Artists Agency **Ph:** 310-288-4545
9830 Wilshire Blvd **Fax:** 310-288-4800
Beverly Hills, CA 90212
www.janetjackson.com

Jackson, Jesse (1941-)
Civil rights, religious, and political figure; founder & president of Rainbow/PUSH Coalition; former presidential candidate
Rainbow/PUSH Coalition **Ph:** 773-373-3366
930 E 50th St **Fax:** 773-373-3571
Chicago, IL 60615
www.rainbowpush.org

Jackson, Jesse Jr (1965-)
US Representative from Illinois (Democrat)
2419 Rayburn Bldg **Ph:** 202-225-0773
Washington, DC 20515 **Fax:** 202-225-0899
www.house.gov/jackson

Jackson, Jim (1970-)
Professional basketball player
Phoenix Suns **Ph:** 602-379-7900
America West Arena **Fax:** 602-379-7990
201 E Jefferson St
Phoenix, AZ 85004
www.nba.com/suns

Jackson, Joshua (1978-)
Actor
William Morris Agency **Ph:** 310-859-4000
1 William Morris Pl **Fax:** 310-859-4462
Beverly Hills, CA 90212
www.dawsonscreek.com

Jackson, Lauren (1981-)
Professional basketball player
Seattle Storm **Ph:** 206-281-5800
351 Elliott Ave W Suite 500
Seattle, WA 98119
www.wnba.com/storm

Jackson, Lisa
Author of suspense/romance novels
Kensington Publishing Corp **Ph:** 212-407-1500
850 3rd Ave
New York, NY 10022
www.lisajackson.com

Jackson, Marc (1975-)
Professional basketball player
New Orleans/Oklahoma City Hornets **Ph:** 405-208-4800
Oklahoma Tower
210 Park Ave Suite 1850
Oklahoma City, OK 73102
www.nba.com/hornets

Jackson, Michael (1958-)
Singer, songwriter, dancer
Ziffren Brittenham Branca Fischer Gilbert-Lurie Stiffelman & Cook LLP **Ph:** 310-552-3388
Fax: 310-553-7068
1801 Century Park W
Los Angeles, CA 90067
www.mjjsource.com

Jackson, Mike
Chairman and CEO of AutoNation
AutoNation Inc **Ph:** 954-769-7000
110 SE 6th St **Fax:** 954-769-6537
Fort Lauderdale, FL 33301
corp.autonation.com

Jackson, Peter (1961-)
Film director/producer/writer
International Creative Management — **Ph:** 310-550-4000
8942 Wilshire Blvd
Beverly Hills, CA 90211
www.lordoftherings.net

Jackson, Phil (1945-)
Basketball coach; former NBA player
Los Angeles Lakers — **Ph:** 310-426-6000
555 N Nash St — **Fax:** 310-426-6105
El Segundo, CA 90245
www.nba.com/lakers

Jackson, Randy (1956-)
One of the judges on Fox's American Idol
Fox Television Studios — **Ph:** 310-369-1000
American Idol
PO Box 900
Beverly Hills, CA 90213
idolonfox.com

Jackson, Samuel L (1948-)
Actor
International Creative Management — **Ph:** 310-550-4000
8942 Wilshire Blvd
Beverly Hills, CA 90211

Jackson, Shirley Ann, PhD (1946-)
Theoretical physicist and former chairman of the US Nuclear Regulatory Commission; currently president of Rensselaer Polytechnic Institute
Rensselaer Polytechnic Institute — **Ph:** 518-276-6211
Office of the President
110 8th St
Troy, NY 12180
www.rpi.edu

Jackson, Stephen (1978-)
Professional basketball player
Indiana Pacers — **Ph:** 317-917-2500
Conseco Fieldhouse — **Fax:** 317-917-2599
125 S Pennsylvania St
Indianapolis, IN 46204
www.nba.com/pacers

Jackson, Steven (1983-)
Professional football player
Saint Louis Rams — **Ph:** 314-982-7267
1 Rams Way — **Fax:** 314-770-9261
Earth City, MO 63045
www.stlouisrams.com

Jackson Lee, Sheila (1950-)
US Representative from Texas (Democrat)
2435 Rayburn Bldg — **Ph:** 202-225-3816
Washington, DC 20515 — **Fax:** 202-225-3317
www.jacksonlee.house.gov

Jacobs, Irwin M, PhD
Co-founder and chairman of the board of QUALCOMM; a pioneer in Code Division Multiple Access (CDMA) digital wireless technology and holds several CDMA patents
QUALCOMM Inc — **Ph:** 858-587-1121
5775 Morehouse Dr — **Fax:** 858-658-2100
San Diego, CA 92121
www.qualcomm.com

Jacobs, Jeremy M
Chairman and CEO of Delaware North, an international foodservice and hospitality management company; also owns the Boston Bruins hockey team
Delaware North Cos Inc — **Ph:** 716-858-5000
40 Fountain Plaza
Buffalo, NY 14202
www.delawarenorth.com

Jacobs, Marc (1963-)
Fashion designer
72 Spring St — **Ph:** 212-343-0222
New York, NY 10012
www.marcjacobs.com

Jacobs, Paul E, PhD
CEO of QUALCOMM
QUALCOMM Inc — **Ph:** 858-587-1121
5775 Morehouse Dr — **Fax:** 858-658-2100
San Diego, CA 92121
www.qualcomm.com

Jacobson, Michael F, PhD
Co-founder and executive director of the Center for Science in the Public Interest; an advocate for accuracy in food labeling and disclosure of nutrition information
Center for Science in the Public Interest — **Ph:** 202-332-9110
1875 Connecticut Ave NW Suite 300 — **Fax:** 202-265-4954
Washington, DC 20009

Jacoby, Jeff
Op-ed columnist for the Boston Globe
Boston Globe — **Ph:** 617-929-2000
135 Morrissey Blvd
PO Box 55819
Boston, MA 02205
www.boston.com/news/globe/editorial_opinion

Jacques, Brian (1939-)
Author of the Redwall books for young readers
Philomel Books Publicity **Ph:** 212-366-2000
345 Hudson St
New York, NY 10014
www.redwall.org

Jagger, Mick (1943-)
Lead singer for the Rolling Stones rock group
International Creative Management **Ph:** 310-550-4000
8942 Wilshire Blvd
Beverly Hills, CA 90211
www.mickjagger.com

Jagr, Jaromir (1972-)
Professional hockey player
New York Rangers **Ph:** 212-465-6486
Madison Square Garden **Fax:** 212-465-6494
2 Pennsylvania Plaza
New York, NY 10121
www.newyorkrangers.com

Jakes, John (1932-)
Author of historical novels and family sagas
Dutton Publicity **Ph:** 212-366-2000
375 Hudson St
New York, NY 10014
www.johnjakes.com

Jamail, Joseph D III (1925-)
Attorney who won the largest verdict in US history ($10.5 billion plus interest) in the trial of Pennzoil vs Texaco
Jamail & Kolius **Ph:** 713-651-3000
1 Allen Center Suite 3434 **Fax:** 713-651-1957
500 Dallas St
Houston, TX 77002
www.joejamail.net

James, Edgerrin (1978-)
Professional football player
Arizona Cardinals **Ph:** 602-379-0101
8701 S Hardy Dr **Fax:** 602-379-1819
Tempe, AZ 85284
www.azcardinals.com

James, Kevin (1965-)
Comedian; actor
Jeff Sussman Management **Ph:** 310-244-3567
603 W 115th St Suite 282
New York, NY 10025
www.kevinjames.tv

James, LeBron (1984-)
Professional basketball player
Cleveland Cavaliers **Ph:** 216-420-2000
Quicken Loans Arena **Fax:** 216-420-2298
1 Center Ct
Cleveland, OH 44115
www.nba.com/cavaliers

James, PD (1920-)
Mystery writer
Knopf Publishing/Author Mail **Ph:** 212-782-9000
1745 Broadway
New York, NY 10019
www.randomhouse.com/knopf

James, Sara
Dateline NBC correspondent
Dateline NBC **Ph:** 212-664-4249
30 Rockefeller Plaza
New York, NY 10112
www.msnbc.msn.com/id/3360263

James, Sharpe (1936-)
Mayor of Newark
920 Broad St Suite 200 **Ph:** 973-733-6400
Newark, NJ 07102
www.ci.newark.nj.us

James, Tory (1973-)
Professional football player
Cincinnati Bengals **Ph:** 513-621-3550
1 Paul Brown Stadium **Fax:** 513-621-3570
Cincinnati, OH 45202
www.bengals.com

Jamieson, Bob (1943-)
ABC news correspondent
ABC News **Ph:** 212-456-7777
77 W 66th St
New York, NY 10023
www.abcnews.go.com/WNT

Jamiroquai
British band
William Morris Agency **Ph:** 310-859-4000
1 William Morris Pl **Fax:** 310-859-4462
Beverly Hills, CA 90212
www.jamiroquai.com

Jamison, Antawn (1976-)
Professional basketball player
Washington Wizards **Ph:** 202-661-5000
Verizon Center **Fax:** 202-661-5094
601 F St NW
Washington, DC 20004
www.nba.com/wizards

Jamison, Judith (1943-)
Dancer/choreographer; artistic director for the Alvin Ailey American Dance Theater
Alvin Ailey American Dance Theater **Ph:** 212-405-9000 **Fax:** 212-405-9001
Joan Weill Center for Dance
405 W 55th St
New York, NY 10019
www.alvinailey.org

Janikowski, Sebastian (1978-)
Professional football player
Oakland Raiders **Ph:** 510-864-5000
1220 Harbor Bay Pkwy **Fax:** 510-864-5134
Alameda, CA 94502
www.raiders.com

Janney, Allison (1960-)
Actor
Paradigm **Ph:** 310-288-8000
360 N Crescent Dr **Fax:** 310-288-2000
North Blvd
Beverly Hills, CA 90210
www.nbc.com/The_West_Wing

Jansen, JoAnn
Choreographer for feature films
International Creative Management **Ph:** 310-550-4000
8942 Wilshire Blvd
Beverly Hills, CA 90211
www.joannjansen.com

Jansing, Chris
MSNBC daytime anchor and a correspondent for MSNBC and NBC News
MSNBC TV **Ph:** 201-583-5000
1 MSNBC Plaza
Secaucus, NJ 07094
www.msnbc.msn.com/id/3080263

Janz, Matt (1970-)
Creator of the comic strip Out of the Gene Pool
Washington Post Writers Group **Ph:** 202-334-6375 **Fax:** 202-334-5669
1150 15th St NW 9th Fl
Washington, DC 20071
www.postwritersgroup.com

Jaric, Marko (1978-)
Professional basketball player
Minnesota Timberwolves **Ph:** 612-673-1600
Target Center **Fax:** 612-673-1699
600 1st Ave N
Minneapolis, MN 55403
www.nba.com/timberwolves

Jarmusch, Jim (1953-)
Independent filmmaker
International Creative Management **Ph:** 310-550-4000
8942 Wilshire Blvd
Beverly Hills, CA 90211

Jarreau, Al (1940-)
Jazz singer
Creative Artists Agency **Ph:** 310-288-4545
9830 Wilshire Blvd **Fax:** 310-288-4800
Beverly Hills, CA 90212
www.aljarreau.com

Jarrett, Dale (1956-)
Race car driver
Robert Yates Racing **Ph:** 704-662-9625
PO Box 3640
Mooresville, NC 28117
www.dalejarrett.com

Jarrett, Gregg
FOX News anchor
FOX News Channel **Ph:** 212-301-3000
1211 Ave of the Americas
New York, NY 10036
www.foxnews.com/fnctv

Jars of Clay
Music group (Contemporary Christian music)
CAA Nashville **Ph:** 615-383-8787
3310 West End Ave 5th Fl **Fax:** 615-383-4937
Nashville, TN 37203
www.jarsofclay.com

Jarvik, Robert, MD (1946-)
Inventor of the first permanent total artificial heart, the Jarvik-7; CEO of Jarvik Heart, Inc, a private company that develops miniaturized heart assist devices for the treatment of severe heart failure
Jarvik Heart Inc **Ph:** 212-397-3911
333 W 52nd St
New York, NY 10019
www.jarvikheart.com

Jasperse, John
Choreographer; artistic director of John Jasperse Co
John Jasperse Co **Ph:** 212-375-0187
Thin Man Dance Inc **Fax:** 212-375-8283
140 2nd Ave Suite 501
New York, NY 10003
www.johnjasperse.org

Jastrow, Robert, PhD (1925-)
Space scientist; founder & former director of NASA's Goddard Institute for Space Studies
George C Marshall Institute **Ph:** 202-296-9655
1625 K St NW Suite 1050 **Fax:** 202-296-9714
Washington, DC 20006
www.marshall.org

Jauron, Dick
Football coach
Buffalo Bills **Ph:** 716-648-1800
Ralph Wilson Stadium **Fax:** 716-649-6446
1 Bills Dr
Orchard Park, NY 14127
www.buffalobills.com

Jeanty, Philippe
Chef and owner of Bistro Jeanty
Bistro Jeanty **Ph:** 707-944-0103
6510 Washington St **Fax:** 707-944-0370
Yountville, CA 94599
www.bistrojeanty.com

Jefferson, Richard (1980-)
Professional basketball player
New Jersey Nets **Ph:** 201-935-8888
Nets Champion Center **Fax:** 201-935-1088
390 Murray Hill Pkwy
East Rutherford, NJ 07073
www.nba.com/nets

Jefferson, William J (1947-)
US Representative from Louisiana (Democrat)
2113 Rayburn Bldg **Ph:** 202-225-6636
Washington, DC 20515 **Fax:** 202-225-1988
www.house.gov/jefferson

Jeffords, James M (1934-)
US Senator from Vermont (Independent)
413 Dirksen Bldg **Ph:** 202-224-5141
Washington, DC 20510 **Fax:** 202-228-0776
jeffords.senate.gov

Jeffrey, Terrence (1958-)
Editor of Human Events in the National Conservative Weekly; also writes a syndicated newspaper column
Creators Syndicate Inc **Ph:** 310-337-7003
5777 W Century Blvd Suite 700 **Fax:** 310-337-7625
Los Angeles, CA 90045
www.creators.com/opinion.html

Jeffries, Michael (1944-)
Chairman and CEO of Abercrombie & Fitch Co
Abercrombie & Fitch Co **Ph:** 614-283-6500
6301 Fitch Pass **TF:** 800-666-2595
New Albany, OH 43054
www.abercrombie.com

Jemison, Mae, MD (1957-)
Former astronaut on the space shuttle Endeavor (first woman of color to go into space); physician; President, Jemison Group Inc.
Jemison Group Inc **Ph:** 281-486-7918
PO Box 591455 **Fax:** 281-486-7522
Houston, TX 77259
www.jsc.nasa.gov/Bios/htmlbios/jemison-mc.html

Jenkins, Charlie Jr
CEO of Publix Super Markets
Publix Super Markets Inc **Ph:** 863-688-1188
1936 George Jenkins Blvd **Fax:** 863-284-5532
Lakeland, FL 33815

Jenkins, Geoff (1974-)
Professional baseball player
Milwaukee Brewers **Ph:** 414-902-4400
Miller Park **Fax:** 414-902-4515
1 Brewers Way
Milwaukee, WI 53214
milwaukee.brewers.mlb.com

Jenkins, Jerry B (1949-)
Writer-at-large for the Moody Bible Institute; author of the Left Behind fiction series and of nonfiction books on marriage & family and as-told-to biographies
Christian Writers Guild **Ph:** 866-495-5177
PO Box 88196 **Fax:** 719-495-5181
Black Forest, CO 80908
www.jerryjenkins.com

Jenkins, Scoville (1986-)
Professional tennis player
ATP **Ph:** 904-285-8000
201 ATP Blvd **Fax:** 904-285-5966
Ponte Vedra Beach, FL 32082
www.sco93.com

Jenkins, Steve (1952-)
Author/illustrator of informational books for children (What Do You Do With a Tail Like This?)
Houghton Mifflin Children's Books **Ph:** 617-351-5000
222 Berkeley St 8th Fl
Boston, MA 02116
www.houghtonmifflinbooks.com

Jenkins, William (1936-)
US Representative from Tennessee (Republican)
1207 Longworth Bldg **Ph:** 202-225-6356
Washington, DC 20515 **Fax:** 202-225-5714
www.house.gov/jenkins

Jenness, James (1946-)
Chairman and CEO of Kellogg Co
Kellogg Co **Ph:** 269-961-2000
1 Kellogg Sq
Battle Creek, MI 49016
investor.kelloggs.com

Jennings, Gerald D (1948-)
Mayor of Albany, New York
City Hall **Ph:** 518-434-5100
Albany, NY 12207 **Fax:** 518-434-5013
www.albanyny.org

Jennings, Peter (1938-2005)
Long-time ABC anchorman
ABC News **Ph:** 212-456-7777
77 W 66th St
New York, NY 10023
www.abcnews.go.com/wnt

Jentzsch, Heber
President of the Church of Scientology International, the mother church for all Scientology
Church of Scientology International **Ph:** 323-960-3500 **TF:** 800-334-5433
6331 Hollywood Blvd Suite 1200
Los Angeles, CA 90028
www.scientology.org

Jerrick, Mike
Co-host of Dayside and a weekend host of Fox and Friends
FOX News Channel **Ph:** 212-301-3000
1211 Ave of the Americas
New York, NY 10036
www.foxnews.com/fnctv

Jeter, Derek (1974-)
Professional baseball player
New York Yankees **Ph:** 718-293-4300
Yankee Stadium **Fax:** 718-293-8414
161st St & River Ave
Bronx, NY 10451
newyork.yankees.mlb.com

Jewel (1974-)
Singer (performs as Jewel but her full name is Jewel Kilcher)
Creative Artists Agency **Ph:** 310-288-4545
9830 Wilshire Blvd **Fax:** 310-288-4800
Beverly Hills, CA 90212
www.jeweljk.com

Jewison, Norman (1926-)
Movie producer and director
International Creative Management **Ph:** 310-550-4000
8942 Wilshire Blvd
Beverly Hills, CA 90211

Jewsbury, Jack (1981-)
Professional soccer player
Kansas City Wizards **Ph:** 816-920-9300
2 Arrowhead Dr **Fax:** 816-920-4774
Kansas City, MO 64129
kc.wizards.mlsnet.com

Jin, Ha (1956-)
Writer of novels (Waiting), short story collections (Under the Red Flag), and poetry
Vintage/Anchor Publicity **Ph:** 212-572-2420
1745 Broadway 20th Fl
New York, NY 10019
www.randomhouse.com/vintage

Jindal, Bobby (1971-)
US Representative from Louisiana (Republican)
1205 Longworth Bldg **Ph:** 202-225-3015
Washington, DC 20515 **Fax:** 202-225-0739
jindal.house.gov

Jobs, Steve (1955-)
CEO & co-founder of Apple Computer; also co-founder, chairman, and CEO of Pixar Studios, which recently was purchased by Disney
Apple Computer Inc **Ph:** 408-996-1010
1 Infinite Loop **Fax:** 408-996-0275
Cupertino, CA 95014
www.apple.com/pr/bios

Joffrey, Robert (1930-1988)
Dancer; founder of the original Joffrey Ballet
Joffrey Ballet **Ph:** 312-739-0120
70 E Lake St Suite 1300
Chicago, IL 60601
www.joffrey.com

Johanns, Mike (1950-)
US Secretary of Agriculture; former governor of Nebraska
US Dept of Agriculture **Ph:** 202-720-3631
1400 Independence Ave SW **Fax:** 202-720-2166
Washington, DC 20250
www.usda.gov

Johanson, Sue
Sex expert; answers questions live on the TV show Talk Sex
Talk Sex **Ph:** 212-651-2000
Oxygen Media Inc
75 9th Ave 7th Fl
New York, NY 10011
www.oxygen.com

Johansson, Scarlett (1984-)
Actor
William Morris Agency **Ph:** 310-859-4000
1 William Morris Pl **Fax:** 310-859-4462
Beverly Hills, CA 90212

John, Elton (1947-)
Singer, musician
Howard Rose Agency **Ph:** 310-858-3838
9460 Wilshire Blvd Suite 310
Beverly Hills, CA 90212
www.eltonjohn.com

Johns, Joe
Congressional correspondent for CNN
CNN **Ph:** 202-898-7900
CNN Bldg
820 1st St NE
Washington, DC 20002
www.cnn.com/CNN/anchors_reporters

Johnson, Abigail (1962-)
President and heir apparent to Fidelity Investments (FMR Corp)
FMR Corp **Ph:** 617-563-7000
82 Devonshire St **Fax:** 617-476-6150
Boston, MA 02109

Johnson, Andre (1981-)
Professional football player
Houston Texans **Ph:** 832-667-2000
2 Reliant Park **Fax:** 832-667-2100
Houston, TX 77054
www.houstontexans.com

Johnson, Avery (1965-)
Basketball coach; former NBA player
Dallas Mavericks **Ph:** 214-747-6287
The Pavillion **Fax:** 214-658-7121
2909 Taylor St
Dallas, TX 75226
www.nba.com/mavericks

Johnson, Betsey (1942-)
Fashion designer
498 7th Ave **Ph:** 212-244-0843
New York, NY 10018
www.betseyjohnson.com

Johnson, Chad (1978-)
Professional football player
Cincinnati Bengals **Ph:** 513-621-3550
1 Paul Brown Stadium **Fax:** 513-621-3570
Cincinnati, OH 45202
www.bengals.com

Johnson, Don (1949-)
Actor
International Creative Management **Ph:** 310-550-4000
8942 Wilshire Blvd
Beverly Hills, CA 90211

Johnson, Dwayne (1972-)
Actor; professional wrestler
United Talent Agency **Ph:** 310-273-6700
9560 Wilshire Blvd 5th Fl **Fax:** 310-247-1111
Beverly Hills, CA 90212
www.wwe.com/superstars/raw/therock

Johnson, Eddie (1984-)
Professional soccer player
FC Dallas **Ph:** 214-979-0303
14800 Quorum Dr Suite 300 **Fax:** 214-979-1118
Dallas, TX 75254
fc.dallas.mlsnet.com

Johnson, Eddie Bernice (1935-)
US Representative from Texas (Democrat)
1511 Longworth Bldg **Ph:** 202-225-8885
Washington, DC 20515 **Fax:** 202-226-1477
www.house.gov/ebjohnson

Johnson, Edward C III
Chairman & CEO of FMR Corp, a financial services conglomerate better known as Fidelity Investments
FMR Corp **Ph:** 617-563-7000
82 Devonshire St **Fax:** 617-563-6150
Boston, MA 02109

Johnson, Eric (1979-)
Professional football player
San Francisco 49ers **Ph:** 408-562-4949
4949 Centennial Blvd **Fax:** 408-727-4937
Santa Clara, CA 95054
www.sf49ers.com

Johnson, Greg (1971-)
Professional hockey player
Nashville Predators **Ph:** 615-770-7825
Gaylord Entertainment Center **Fax:** 615-770-2341
501 Broadway
Nashville, TN 37203
www.nashvillepredators.com

Johnson, Gus (1967-)
Sports broadcaster
CBS Sports **Ph:** 212-975-4321
51 W 52nd St
New York, NY 10019
cbs.sportsline.com/cbssports/team

Johnson, H Fisk, PhD
Chairman and CEO of SC Johnson & Son
SC Johnson & Son Inc **Ph:** 262-260-2000
1525 Howe St **Fax:** 262-260-6004
Racine, WI 53403
www.scjohnson.com

Johnson, Jay
Comedian/ventriloquist
William Morris Agency **Ph:** 310-859-4000
1 William Morris Pl **Fax:** 310-859-4462
Beverly Hills, CA 90212
www.monkeyjoke.com

Johnson, Jill
Creator of Oxycise exercise and weight loss program
Oxycise International Inc **Ph:** 800-699-2473
PO Box 262022 **Fax:** 303-224-0130
Littleton, CO 80163
www.oxycise.com

Johnson, Jimmie (1975-)
Race car driver
Hendrick Motorsports **Ph:** 704-455-3400
4400 Papa Joe Hendrick Blvd
Charlotte, NC 28262
www.hendrickmotorsports.com

Johnson, Jimmy (1943-)
Former college & professional football coach; television NFL commentator
FOX Sports Net **Ph:** 310-369-1000
10201 W Pico Blvd
Bldg 101
Los Angeles, CA 90035

Johnson, Jimmy
Creator of the comic strip Arlo & Janis
Newspaper Enterprise Assn **Ph:** 212-293-8500
200 Madison Ave
New York, NY 10016
www.unitedfeatures.com

Johnson, Joe (1981-)
Professional basketball player
Atlanta Hawks **Ph:** 404-827-3800
Centennial Tower **Fax:** 404-827-3880
101 Marietta St NW Suite 1900
Atlanta, GA 30303
www.nba.com/hawks

Johnson, John D
President and CEO of CHS, a diversified energy, grains, and foods company
CHS Inc **Ph:** 651-355-6000
5500 Cenex Dr
Inner Grove Heights, MN 55077
www.chsinc.com

Johnson, Keyshawn (1972-)
Professional football player
Carolina Panthers **Ph:** 704-358-7000
Bank of America Stadium **Fax:** 704-358-7618
800 S Mint St
Charlotte, NC 28202
www.panthers.com

Johnson, Lady Bird (1912-)
Former First Lady of the US (wife of LBJ); born Claudia Alta Taylor
Lyndon Baines Johnson Library & Museum **Ph:** 512-721-0200
2313 Red River St
Austin, TX 78705
www.lbjlib.utexas.edu

Johnson, Lawrence (1974-)
Track & Field athlete (pole vault)
HSInternational **Ph:** 949-753-9153
9871 Irvine Center Dr
Irvine, CA 92618
www.hsi.net

Johnson, Lonnie (1949-)
Inventor of the Super Soaker water gun
Johnson Research & Development Co **Ph:** 404-584-2475 **Fax:** 404-584-6772
263 Decatur St
Atlanta, GA 30312
www.johnsonrd.com

Johnson, Lyndon B (1908-1973)
36th US President
Lyndon Baines Johnson Library & Museum **Ph:** 512-721-0200
2313 Red River St
Austin, TX 78705
www.lbjlib.utexas.edu

Johnson, Magic (1959-)
Former basketball player (retired) and businessman (chairman and CEO of Johnson Development Corp); real name is Earvin Johnson, Jr
Johnson Development Corp **Ph:** 310-247-1994
9100 Wilshire Blvd Suite 710 E **Fax:** 310-247-0733
Beverly Hills, CA 90212
www.johnsondevelopmentcorp.com

Johnson, Nancy L (1935-)
US Representative from Connecticut (Republican)
2409 Rayburn Bldg **Ph:** 202-225-4476
Washington, DC 20515 **Fax:** 202-225-4488
www.house.gov/nancyjohnson

Johnson, Randy (1963-)
Professional baseball player
New York Yankees **Ph:** 718-293-4300
Yankee Stadium **Fax:** 718-293-8414
161st St & River Ave
Bronx, NY 10451
newyork.yankees.mlb.com

Johnson, Robert L (1946-)
Founder and chairman of Black Entertainment Television; he left BET in 2005 after selling the company to Viacom and is now chairman of RLJ Companies, which invests in companies in the financial services, real estate, hospitality, professional sports, film production, gaming, and recording industries
RLJ Cos **Ph:** 301-280-7700
3 Bethesda Metro Center
Suite 1000
Bethesda, MD 20814
www.rljcompanies.com

Johnson, Robert Wood IV
Owner of the New York Jets football franchise
New York Jets **Ph:** 516-560-8100
1000 Fulton Ave **Fax:** 516-560-8198
Hempstead, NY 11550

Johnson, Rudi (1979-)
Professional football player
Cincinnati Bengals **Ph:** 513-621-3550
1 Paul Brown Stadium **Fax:** 513-621-3570
Cincinnati, OH 45202
www.bengals.com

Johnson, Sam (1930-)
US Representative from Texas (Republican)
1211 Longworth Bldg **Ph:** 202-225-4201
Washington, DC 20515 **Fax:** 202-225-1485
www.samjohnson.house.gov

Johnson, Shannon (1974-)
Professional basketball player
San Antonio Silver Stars **Ph:** 210-444-5050
1 SBC Center
San Antonio, TX 78219
www.wnba.com/silverstars

Johnson, Spencer, MD (1938-)
Author of Who Moved My Cheese and co-author of the One Minute Manager; motivational speaker who assists organizations in dealing with change
Spencer Johnson Partners **Ph:** 800-851-9311
1775 West 2300 S Suite B **Fax:** 801-428-0476
Salt Lake City, UT 84119 **TF:** 800-851-9311
www.whomovedmycheese.com

Johnson, Stephen L (1951-)
Administrator of the US Environmental Protection Agency
Environmental Protection Agency **Ph:** 202-564-4700
Fax: 202-564-1450
1200 Pennsylvania Ave NW
Washington, DC 20460
www.epa.gov

Johnson, Tim (1946-)
US Senator from South Dakota (Democrat)
136 Hart Bldg **Ph:** 202-224-5842
Washington, DC 20510 **Fax:** 202-228-5765
johnson.senate.gov

Johnson, Timothy, MD (1936-)
Medical commentator for Good Morning America and other ABC News shows
ABC News **Ph:** 212-456-7777
77 W 66th St
New York, NY 10023
www.abcnews.go.com/GMA

Johnson, Timothy V (1946-)
US Representative from Illinois (Republican)
1229 Longworth Bldg **Ph:** 202-225-2371
Washington, DC 20515 **Fax:** 202-226-0791
www.house.gov/timjohnson

Johnson, Traci Paige (1966-)
Illustrator of Blues Clues books; former animator and voice actor for Blues Clues on Nick Jr
Simon & Schuster **Ph:** 212-698-7000
1230 Ave of the Americas
New York, NY 10020
www.simonsays.com

Johnson, William R
Chairman, president, and CEO of HJ Heinz Co
HJ Heinz Co **Ph:** 412-456-5700
PO Box 57
Pittsburgh, PA 15230
www.heinz.com/jsp/management.jsp

Johnston, Larry (1948-)
Chairman & CEO of Albertson's Inc.
Albertson's Inc **Ph:** 208-395-6200
250 E Parkcenter Blvd **Fax:** 208-395-6631
Boise, ID 83706
www.albertsons.com

Johnston, Lynn (1947-)
Creator of the comic strip For Better or For Worse
Universal Press Syndicate **Ph:** 816-932-6600
4520 Main St
Kansas City, MO 64111
www.amuniversal.com/ups/features

Joho, Jean
Vice President of Lettuce Entertain You Enterprises and Chef/Proprietor of Everest, Brasserie Jo, and Eiffel Tower restaurants
Everest Restaurant **Ph:** 312-663-8920
440 S LaSalle St 40th Fl
Chicago, IL 60605
www.leye.com/company/bios/joho.htm

Joines, Allen
Mayor of Winston-Salem, North Carolina
101 N Main St Suite 150 **Ph:** 336-727-2058
Winston-Salem, NC 27101 **Fax:** 336-748-3241
www.cityofws.org/Mayor

Jokinen, Olli (1978-)
Professional hockey player
Florida Panthers **Ph:** 954-835-7000
BankAtlantic Center **Fax:** 954-835-7600
1 Panther Pkwy
Sunrise, FL 33323
www.floridapanthers.com

Jolie, Angelina (1975-)
Actor
Media Talent Group **Ph:** 310-275-7900
9200 Sunset Blvd Suite 550 **Fax:** 310-275-7910
Los Angeles, CA 90069

Jones, Andruw (1977-)
Professional baseball player
Atlanta Braves **Ph:** 404-522-7630
PO Box 4064 **Fax:** 404-614-1392
Atlanta, GA 30302
atlanta.braves.mlb.com

Jones, Bill T (1952-)
Dancer/choreographer
IMG Artists **Ph:** 212-994-3500
Carnegie Hall Tower **Fax:** 212-994-3550
152 W 57th St 5th Fl
New York, NY 10019
www.billtjones.org

Jones, Chipper (1972-)
Professional baseball player; real name is Larry Wayne Jones
Atlanta Braves **Ph:** 404-522-7630
PO Box 4064 **Fax:** 404-614-1392
Atlanta, GA 30302
atlanta.braves.mlb.com

Jones, Clay
Editorial cartoonist for the Free Lance-Star in Fredericksburg, VA
Creators Syndicate Inc **Ph:** 310-337-7003
5777 W Century Blvd Suite 700 **Fax:** 310-337-7625
Los Angeles, CA 90045
www.creators.com

Jones, Cobi (1970-)
Professional soccer player
Los Angeles Galaxy **Ph:** 310-630-2200
Home Depot Center **Fax:** 310-630-2250
18400 Avalon Blvd Suite 200
Carson, CA 90746
www.lagalaxy.com

Jones, Damon (1976-)
Professional basketball player
Cleveland Cavaliers **Ph:** 216-420-2000
Quicken Loans Arena **Fax:** 216-420-2298
1 Center Ct
Cleveland, OH 44115
www.nba.com/cavaliers

Jones, Dewitt
Photographer/photojournalist and lecturer/motivational speaker; freelanced with National Geographic
Dewitt Jones Productions Inc **Ph:** 707-838-4379
517 Quince St **Fax:** 509-351-0266
Windsor, CA 95492
www.dewittjones.com

Jones, Eddie (1971-)
Professional basketball player
Memphis Grizzlies **Ph:** 901-205-1234
FedExForum **Fax:** 901-205-1235
191 Beale St
Memphis, TN 38103
www.nba.com/grizzlies

Jones, George (1931-)
Country music singer
Bandit Records **Ph:** 615-242-1234
PO Box 41119 **Fax:** 615-242-2134
Nashville, TN 37204
www.georgejones.com

Jones, Jacque (1975-)
Professional baseball player
Chicago Cubs **Ph:** 773-404-2827
Wrigley Field **Fax:** 773-404-4129
1060 W Addison St
Chicago, IL 60613
chicago.cubs.mlb.com

Jones, James Earl (1931-)
Actor
Paradigm **Ph:** 212-703-7540
500 5th Ave 37th Fl **Fax:** 212-764-8941
New York, NY 10110

Jones, Jeanne
Syndicated columnist who writes the Cook It Light feature; has also written many cookbooks
King Features Syndicate Inc **Ph:** 212-455-4000
888 7th Ave 2nd Fl
New York, NY 10019
www.kingfeatures.com

Jones, Jerry (1942-)
Owner of the Dallas Cowboys football franchise
Dallas Cowboys **Ph:** 972-556-9900
1 Cowboys Pkwy **Fax:** 972-556-9304
Irving, TX 75063
www.dallascowboys.com

Jones, John P III (1950-)
Chairman, president, and CEO of Air Products & Chemicals Inc
Air Products & Chemicals Inc **Ph:** 610-481-4911
7201 Hamilton Blvd
Allentown, PA 18195
www.airproducts.com/AboutUs

Jones, Julius (1981-)
Professional football player
Dallas Cowboys **Ph:** 972-556-9900
1 Cowboys Pkwy **Fax:** 972-556-9304
Irving, TX 75063
www.dallascowboys.com

Jones, Kevin (1982-)
Professional football player
Detroit Lions **Ph:** 313-216-4000
222 Republic Dr **Fax:** 313-216-4069
Allen Park, MI 48101
www.detroitlions.com

Jones, Larry (1940-)
Founder (with his wife Frances) and president of Feed the Children, a Christian nonprofit organization that provides aid and assistance to needy children and families in the US and around the world
Feed the Children **Ph:** 405-942-0228
PO Box 36 **Fax:** 405-945-4177
Oklahoma City, OK 73101
www.feedthechildren.org

Jones, Marion (1975-)
Track & field athlete (sprints, long jump)
USA Track & Field **Ph:** 317-261-0500
1 RCA Dome Suite 140
Indianapolis, IN 46225
www.usatf.com

Jones, Norah (1979-)
Singer
Creative Artists Agency **Ph:** 212-277-9000
162 5th Ave 6th Fl **Fax:** 212-277-9099
New York, NY 10010
www.norahjones.com

Jones, Quincy (1933-)
Musician, conductor, arranger, composer, producer, and music publisher
William Morris Agency **Ph:** 310-859-4000
1 William Morris Pl **Fax:** 310-859-4462
Beverly Hills, CA 90212
www.quincyjonesmusic.com/QuincyJones

Jones, Robert G
President & CEO and a member of the board of directors of Old National Bancorp
Old National Bancorp **Ph:** 812-464-1494
1 Main St
Evanville, IN 47708
www.oldnational.com

Jones, Samuel L
Mayor of Mobile, Alabama
205 Government St 10th Fl **Ph:** 251-208-7395
Mobile, AL 36644 **Fax:** 251-208-7548
www.cityofmobile.org

Jones, Taylor
Caricature artist
Tribune Media Services Inc **Ph:** 312-222-4444
435 N Michigan Ave Suite 1500
Chicago, IL 60611
www.comicspage.com

Jones, Thomas (1978-)
Professional football player
Chicago Bears **Ph:** 847-295-6600
Halas Hall at Conway Park **Fax:** 847-295-8986
1000 Football Dr
Lake Forest, IL 60045
www.chicagobears.com

Jones, Tom (1940-)
Singer
William Morris Agency **Ph:** 310-859-4000
1 William Morris Pl **Fax:** 310-859-4462
Beverly Hills, CA 90212
www.tomjones.com

Jones, Tommy Lee (1946-)
Actor
William Morris Agency **Ph:** 310-859-4000
1 William Morris Pl **Fax:** 310-859-4462
Beverly Hills, CA 90212

Jones, Walter (1974-)
Professional football player
Seattle Seahawks **Ph:** 425-827-9777
11220 NE 53rd St **Fax:** 425-827-9008
Kirkland, WA 98033
www.seahawks.com

Jones, Walter B (1943-)
US Representative from North Carolina (Republican)
422 Cannon Bldg **Ph:** 202-225-3415
Washington, DC 20515 **Fax:** 202-225-3286
jones.house.gov

Jones Reynolds, Star (1962-)
Co-host of The View; a lawyer and former prosecutor, as well as a former news and legal correspondent
The View **Ph:** 212-456-7777
320 W 66th St
New York, NY 10023
abc.go.com/daytime/theview

Jong, Erica (1942-)
Author of Fear of Flying
WW Norton & Co Inc **Ph:** 212-354-5500
500 5th Ave **Fax:** 212-869-0856
New York, NY 10110
www.ericajong.com

Jonze, Spike (1969-)
Director of commercials, music videos, and movies
Creative Artists Agency **Ph:** 310-288-4545
9830 Wilshire Blvd **Fax:** 310-288-4800
Beverly Hills, CA 90212

Joos, David W
President & CEO of CMS Energy and CEO of its principal subsidiary, Consumers Energy
CMS Energy Corp **Ph:** 517-788-0550
1 Energy Plaza
Jackson, MI 49201
www.cmsenergy.com/CorporateGovernance

Jordan, Eddie (1955-)
Basketball coach
Washington Wizards **Ph:** 202-661-5000
Verizon Center **Fax:** 202-661-5094
601 F St NW
Washington, DC 20004
www.nba.com/wizards

Jordan, Gregory B (1959-)
Named by American Lawyer as one of the country's top 45 lawyers under 45 in 2003; his practice involves primarily banking and financial services litigation, securities and derivative litigation, trade secrets litigation, and media and first amendment litigation
Reed Smith LLP **Ph:** 412-288-4124
435 6th Ave **Fax:** 412-288-3063
Pittsburgh, PA 15219
www.reedsmith.com

Jordan, Mary
Author of The Prison Angel; a Washington Post correspondent
Penguin Press Publicity **Ph:** 212-366-2000
375 Hudson St
New York, NY 10014
us.penguingroup.com

Jordan, Michael (1963-)
Professional basketball player (retired)
SFX Sports Group **Ph:** 202-686-2000
5335 Wisconsin Ave NW **Fax:** 202-686-5050
Suite 850
Washington, DC 20015

Jordan, Michael H
Chairman and CEO of EDS
Electronic Data Systems Corp **Ph:** 972-605-2100
5400 Legacy Dr **Fax:** 972-605-6662
Plano, TX 75024
www.eds.com

Jordan, Vernon E Jr (1935-)
Attorney; has held several government advisory positions and is the former president of the National Urban League and former director of the United Negro College Fund; a figure in the Monica Lewinsky scandal
Akin Gump Strauss Hauer & Feld LLP **Ph:** 202-887-4000 **Fax:** 202-887-4288
1333 New Hampshire Ave NW
Washington, DC 20036
www.akingump.com

Josefowicz, Gregory
Chairman, president, and CEO of Borders Group
Borders Group Inc **Ph:** 734-477-1100
100 Phoenix Dr
Ann Arbor, MI 48108
www.bordersgroupinc.com

Joseph, Curtis (1967-)
Professional hockey player
Phoenix Coyotes — **Ph:** 623-463-8800
5800 W Glenn Dr Suite 350 — **Fax:** 623-463-8810
Glendale, AZ 85301
www.phoenixcoyotes.com

Joseph, Shalrie (1978-)
Professional soccer player
New England Revolution — **Ph:** 508-543-5001
Gillette Stadium — **Fax:** 508-384-9128
1 Patriot Pl
Foxborough, MA 02035
www.revolutionsoccer.net

Jovanovski, Ed (1976-)
Professional hockey player
Vancouver Canucks — **Ph:** 604-899-4600
General Motors Pl — **Fax:** 604-899-4640
800 Griffiths Way
Vancouver, BC V6B6G1
www.canucks.com

Jovovich, Milla (1975-)
Model, clothing designer, actor
International Creative Management — **Ph:** 310-550-4000
8942 Wilshire Blvd
Beverly Hills, CA 90211
www.millaj.com

Joyce, Brenda
Author of romance novels
St Martin's Press — **Ph:** 212-674-5151
Attn: Publicity Dept
175 5th Ave
New York, NY 10010
www.brendajoyce.com

Joyner, Tom
Host of the Tom Joyner Morning Show, an urban radio program that's a mix of music, talk, sports, gossip, and comedy bits
ABC Radio Networks — **Ph:** 212-456-7777
444 Madison Ave
New York, NY 10022
www.abcradio.com

Judd, Ashley (1968-)
Actor
William Morris Agency — **Ph:** 310-859-4000
1 William Morris Pl — **Fax:** 310-859-4462
Beverly Hills, CA 90212

Judge, Jonathan J
President and CEO of Paychex
Paychex Inc — **Ph:** 585-385-6666
911 Panorama Trail S
Rochester, NY 14625

Judge, Mike (1962-)
Animator; creator of King of the Hill and Beavis & Butthead; co-founder (with Don Hertzfeldt) of The Animation Show
3 Arts Entertainment — **Ph:** 310-888-3200
9460 Wilshire Blvd 7th Fl — **Fax:** 310-888-3210
Beverly Hills, CA 90212
www.animationshow.com

Judge Judy (1942-)
Judge on the courtroom TV show Judge Judy; real name is Judith Scheindlin
Paramount Television — **Ph:** 323-956-5000
Judge Judy
5555 Melrose Ave
Hollywood, CA 90038
www.judgejudy.com

June, Cato (1979-)
Professional football player
Indianapolis Colts — **Ph:** 317-297-2658
7001 W 56th St — **Fax:** 317-297-8971
Indianapolis, IN 46254
www.colts.com

Jung, Andrea (1959-)
Chairman and CEO of Avon
Avon Products Inc — **Ph:** 212-282-5124
1345 Ave of the Americas — **Fax:** 212-282-6220
New York, NY 10105
www.avoncompany.com

Junger, Sebastian (1962-)
Free-lance journalist; author of The Perfect Storm
HarperCollins Publishers — **Ph:** 212-207-7000
c/o Author Mail
10 E 53rd St
New York, NY 10022
www.harpercollins.com

Juster, Norton (1929-)
Author of books for young readers (The Phantom Tollbooth; The Hello, Goodbye Window)
Random House Children's Books — **Ph:** 212-782-9000
Publicity Dept
1745 Broadway
New York, NY 10019
www.randomhouse.com/kids

Kaberle, Tomas (1978-)
Professional hockey player
Toronto Maple Leafs **Ph:** 416-815-5700
Air Canada Center
40 Bay St Suite 400
Toronto, ON M5J2X2
www.mapleleafs.com

Kaczmarek, Jane (1955-)
Actor
PMK/HBH **Ph:** 310-289-6200
700 San Vicente Blvd **Fax:** 310-289-6677
Suite G910
West Hollywood, CA 90069
www.fox.com/malcolm

Kadohata, Cynthia (1956-)
Author of books for young readers (Kira-Kira)
Simon & Schuster Books for Young Readers **Ph:** 212-698-7000
1230 Ave of the Americas
New York, NY 10020
www.kira-kira.us

Kaeding, Nate (1982-)
Professional football player
San Diego Chargers **Ph:** 858-874-4500
4020 Murphy Canyon Rd **Fax:** 858-282-2760
San Diego, CA 92123
www.chargers.com

Kagan, Daryn (1964-)
Hosts CNN Live Today
CNN **Ph:** 404-827-1500
1 CNN Center
Atlanta, GA 30303
www.cnn.com/CNN/anchors_reporters

Kagan, Robert (1958-)
Senior associate at Carnegie Endowment for International Peace; writes a monthly column on world affairs for The Washington Post and is a contributing editor to New Republic magazine
Carnegie Endowment for International Peace **Ph:** 202-483-7600
Fax: 202-483-1840
1779 Massachusetts Ave NW
Washington, DC 20036
www.carnegieendowment.org

Kage, Jonas
Ballet dancer; artistic director of Ballet West
Ballet West **Ph:** 801-323-6900
50 W 200 South
Salt Lake City, UT 84101
www.balletwest.org

Kahan, Paul
Executive chef of Blackbird
Blackbird Restaurant **Ph:** 312-715-0708
619 W Randolph St **Fax:** 312-715-0774
Chicago, IL 60606
www.blackbirdrestaurant.com

Kahlo, Frida (1907-1954)
Mexican painter
National Museum of Women in the Arts **Ph:** 202-783-5000
TF: 800-222-7270
1250 New York Ave NW
Washington, DC 20005
www.nmwa.org/collection

Kahn, Robert E, PhD (1938-)
Developer of the system design of the Arpanet, the first packet-switched network, and co-inventer of the Internet's TCP-IP protocol; was awarded the National Medal of Technology in 1997
Corp for National Research Initiatives **Ph:** 703-620-8990
Fax: 703-620-0913
1895 Preston White Dr
Suite 100
Reston, VA 20191
www.cnri.reston.va.us/bios/kahn.html

Kahne, Kasey (1980-)
NASCAR driver
Evernham Motorsports **Ph:** 704-924-9404
320 Aviation Dr **Fax:** 704-924-9495
Statesville, NC 28677
www.evernhammotorsports.com

Kahneman, Daniel, PhD (1934-)
Winner of the 2002 Nobel Prize in Economic Sciences for having integrated insights from psychological research into economic science
Princeton University **Ph:** 609-258-2280
Woodrow Wilson School of Public & International Affairs **Fax:** 609-258-5974
324 Wallace Hall
Princeton, NJ 08544
webscript.princeton.edu/~psych/psychology/home/index.php

Kaine, Tim (1958-)
Governor of Virginia (Democrat)
Patrick Henry Bldg 3rd Fl **Ph:** 804-786-2211
Richmond, VA 23219 **Fax:** 804-371-6351
www.governor.virginia.gov

Kamali, Norma (1945-)
Fashion designer
11 W 56th St **Ph:** 212-957-9797
New York, NY 10019
www.normakamalicollection.com

Kamen, Al
Political columnist
Washington Post Ph: 202-334-6000
1150 15th St NW
Washington, DC 20071
www.washingtonpost.com

Kanakaredes, Melina (1967-)
Actor
Gersh Agency Ph: 212-997-1818
41 Madison Ave 33rd Fl Fax: 212-997-1978
New York, NY 10010
www.cbs.com/primetime/csi_ny

Kandel, Eric, MD (1929-)
Winner (with two other scientists) of the 2000 Nobel Prize in Physiology or Medicine for discoveries concerning signal transduction in the nervous system
Howard Hughes Medical Institute Ph: 301-215-8500
4000 Jones Bridge Rd
Chevy Chase, MD 20815
www.hhmi.org/research/nobel

Kane, Carol (1952-)
Actor
Creative Artists Agency Ph: 310-288-4545
8930 Wilshire Blvd Fax: 310-288-4800
Beverly Hills, CA 90212

Kangas, Paul
Co-anchor (with Susie Gharib) of the Nightly Business Report on PBS
Nightly Business Report Ph: 305-949-8321
PO Box 610002
Miami, FL 33261
www.nbr.com

Kanjorski, Paul E (1937-)
US Representative from Pennsylvania (Democrat)
2188 Rayburn Bldg Ph: 202-225-6511
Washington, DC 20515 Fax: 202-225-0764
kanjorski.house.gov

Kantor, Mickey (1939-)
National chair of the Clinton/Gore election campaign 1991-92; served as Secretary of Commerce and as US Trade Representative in the Clinton Administration
Mayer Brown Rowe & Maw LLP Ph: 202-263-3295
1909 K St NW Fax: 202-263-5295
Washington, DC 20006
www.mayerbrownrowe.com

Kapanen, Sami (1973-)
Professional hockey player
Philadelphia Flyers Ph: 215-465-4500
Wachovia Center Fax: 215-389-9403
3601 S Broad St
Philadelphia, PA 19148
www.philadelphiaflyers.com

Kapell, Dave (1962-)
Creator of Magnetic Poetry refrigerator magnets
Magnetic Poetry Ph: 612-638-1040
PO Box 14862 Fax: 612-638-1079
Minneapolis, MN 55414
www.magneticpoetry.com

Kaplan, Joel S
International President of B'nai B'rith
B'nai B'rith International Ph: 202-857-6600
2020 K St NW 7th Fl Fax: 202-857-6699
Washington, DC 20006
www.bnaibrith.org

Kapor, Mitchell (1950-)
Founder of Lotus Development Corp and designer of Lotus 1-2-3
Kapor Enterprises Inc Ph: 415-946-3019
543 Howard St Suite 500
San Francisco, CA 94115
www.kapor.com

Kaptur, Marcy (1946-)
US Representative from Ohio (Democrat)
2366 Rayburn Bldg Ph: 202-225-4146
Washington, DC 20515 Fax: 202-225-7711
www.kaptur.house.gov

Karan, Donna (1948-)
Fashion designer
Donna Karan International Inc Ph: 212-789-1500
550 7th Ave
New York, NY 10018
www.donnakaran.com

Karas, Beth
Court TV correspondent; legal analyst; former New York City prosecutor
Courtroom Television Network Ph: 212-973-2800
600 3rd Ave
New York, NY 10016
www.courttv.com/anchors

Karatassos, Pano
Executive Chef at Kyma; son of Pano Karatassos, founder of Buckhead Restaurant Life Group (which Kyma is part of)
Kyma Restaurant Ph: 404-262-0702
3085 Piedmont Rd
Atlanta, GA 30305
www.buckheadrestaurants.com/kyma

Karatassos, Pano
Founder and owner of Buckhead Life Restaurant Group; is considered one the premier restaurateurs in the US
Buckhead Life Restaurant Group **Ph:** 404-237-2060 **Fax:** 404-237-2160
265 Pharr Rd
Atlanta, GA 30305
www.buckheadrestaurants.com

Karaty, Dan
Choreographer for pop music performers & films
Bloc Agency **Ph:** 323-954-7730
5651 Wilshire Blvd Suite C
Los Angeles, CA 90036
www.dankaraty.com

Karatz, Bruce
Chairman & CEO of KB Home, builders of new homes
KB Home **Ph:** 310-231-4000
10990 Wilshire Blvd **Fax:** 310-231-4222
Los Angeles, CA 90024 **TF:** 800-344-6637
www.kbhome.com

Kariya, Paul (1974-)
Professional hockey player
Nashville Predators **Ph:** 615-770-7825
Gaylord Entertainment Center **Fax:** 615-770-2341
501 Broadway
Nashville, TN 37203
www.nashvillepredators.com

Karl, George (1951-)
Basketball coach
Denver Nuggets **Ph:** 303-405-1100
Pepsi Center **Fax:** 303-575-1920
1000 Chopper Cir
Denver, CO 80204
www.nba.com/nuggets

Karl, Jonathan
ABC News senior national security correspondent
ABC News **Ph:** 202-222-7700
1717 DeSales St NW
Washington, DC 20036
www.abcnews.go.com/WNT

Karmanos, Peter Jr
Chairman and CEO of Compuware, which he co-founded; owns the Carolina Hurricanes hockey team
Compuware Corp **Ph:** 248-737-7300
31440 Northwestern Hwy **Fax:** 248-737-7555
Farmington Hills, MI 48334
www.compuware.com

Karmazin, Mel (1944-)
CEO of Sirius Satellite Radio; formerly President & COO of Viacom
Sirius Satellite Radio Inc **Ph:** 212-584-5100
1221 Ave of the Americas **Fax:** 212-584-5200
New York, NY 10020
www.sirius.com

Karn, Richard (1956-)
Actor who played Al Borland on Home Improvement; host of the TV game show Family Feud
Innovative Artists **Ph:** 310-656-0400
1505 10th St **Fax:** 310-656-0456
Santa Monica, CA 90401
www.familyfeud.tv/richard.html

Karon, Jan (1937-)
Author of the Mitford series
Viking Publicity **Ph:** 212-366-2000
375 Hudson St
New York, NY 10014
www.mitfordbooks.com

Kasay, John (1969-)
Professional football player
Carolina Panthers **Ph:** 704-358-7000
Bank of America Stadium **Fax:** 704-358-7618
800 S Mint St
Charlotte, NC 28202
www.panthers.com

Kasell, Carl (1934-)
Newscaster and official judge/scorekeeper of the news quiz show Wait Wait...Don't Tell Me!
National Public Radio **Ph:** 202-513-2000
635 Massachusetts Ave NW **Fax:** 202-513-3329
Washington, DC 20001
www.npr.org

Kasem, Casey (1932-)
Host of American Top 20 with Casey Kasem (radio show)
Premiere Radio Networks Inc **Ph:** 818-377-5300
15260 Ventura Blvd 5th Fl **Fax:** 818-377-5333
Sherman Oaks, CA 91403
www.premrad.com

Kashiba, Shiro
Master chef; owner of Shiro's Sushi Restaurant in Seattle
Shiro's Sushi Restaurant **Ph:** 206-443-9844
2401 2nd Ave
Seattle, WA 98121
www.shiros.com

Kasich, John (1952-)
Former Congressman from Ohio; host of The Heartland with John Kasich on FOX News and substitute host for The O'Reilly Factor
FOX News Channel **Ph:** 212-301-3000
1211 Ave of the Americas
New York, NY 10036
www.foxnews.com/fnctv

Kasparaitis, Darius (1972-)
Professional hockey player
New York Rangers **Ph:** 212-465-6486
Madison Square Garden **Fax:** 212-465-6494
2 Pennsylvania Plaza
New York, NY 10121
www.newyorkrangers.com

Katen, Karen
Vice Chairman of Pfizer Inc and president, Pfizer Human Health
Pfizer Human Health **Ph:** 212-733-2323
235 E 42nd St **Fax:** 212-573-7851
New York, NY 10017
www.pfizer.com/pfizer/are/media/index.jsp

Katz, David L, MD
Internist, preventive medicine specialist, and nutrition expert; co-founder and director of the Yale Prevention Research Center and a medical contributor to ABC News programs
Yale University **Ph:** 203-785-6283
Yale School of Public Health **Fax:** 203-785-6980
60 College St
PO Box 208034
New Haven, CT 06520

Katz, Joel A
Entertainment lawyer (represents well-known entertainers, music producers, record companies, concert promoters, and Fortune 500 companies)
Greenberg Traurig LLP **Ph:** 678-553-2100
The Forum **Fax:** 678-553-2212
3290 Northside Pkwy Suite 400
Atlanta, GA 30327
www.gtlaw.com

Katz, Stephen I, MD, PhD (1941-)
Director of the National Institute of Arthritis & Musculoskeletal and Skin Diseases, National Institutes of Health
National Institute of Arthritis & Musculoskeletal & Skin Diseases **Ph:** 301-496-4353 **Fax:** 301-480-6069
31 Center Dr Bldg 31 Rm 4C32
MSC 2350
Bethesda, MD 20892
www.niams.nih.gov

Katzen, Mollie (1950-)
Illustrator and designer as well as an author and food/nutrition/cultural history scholar; author of the Moosewood Cookbook
Ten Speed Press **Ph:** 510-559-1600
PO Box 7123
Berkeley, CA 94707
www.molliekatzen.com

Katzenberg, Jeffrey (1950-)
Movie producer/director (animated films) and co-founder of Dreamworks SKG
DreamWorks SKG **Ph:** 818-733-7000
100 Universal City Plaza
Bldg 5121
Universal City, CA 91608

Kauffman, Marta (1956-)
TV writer/producer
International Creative Management **Ph:** 310-550-4000
8942 Wilshire Blvd
Beverly Hills, CA 90211

Kauffmann, Stanley (1916-)
Film critic for The New Republic magazine
New Republic **Ph:** 202-508-4444
1331 H St NW Suite 700
Washington, DC 20005

Kaufman, Philip (1936-)
Movie director/writer
William Morris Agency **Ph:** 310-859-4000
1 William Morris Pl **Fax:** 310-859-4462
Beverly Hills, CA 90212

Kaysen, Susanna (1948-)
Author of the biographical work Girl, Interrupted; also writes fiction
Vintage/Anchor Publicity **Ph:** 212-572-2420
1745 Broadway 20th Fl
New York, NY 10019
www.randomhouse.com/vintage

Keane, Bil (1922-)
Creator of the comic strip The Family Circus
King Features Syndicate Inc **Ph:** 212-455-4000
888 7th Ave 2nd Fl
New York, NY 10019
www.kingfeatures.com

Keane, Glen (1954-)
Animator for Walt Disney feature films, including The Little Mermaid, Beauty and the Beast, and Aladdin; son of cartoonist Bil Keane (Family Circus)
Walt Disney Feature Animation **Ph:** 818-560-1000
500 S Buena Vista St
Burbank, CA 91521

Kearney, Chistopher J (1955-)
President & CEO of SPX
SPX Corp Ph: 704-752-4400
13515 Ballantyne Corporate Pl
Charlotte, NC 28277
www.spx.com

Keating, Phil
National correspondent for FOX News
FOX News Channel Ph: 212-301-3000
1211 Ave of the Americas
New York, NY 10036
www.foxnews.com/fnctv

Keaton, Diane (1946-)
Actor
Endeavor Ph: 310-248-2000
9601 Wilshire Blvd 3rd Fl Fax: 310-248-2020
Beverly Hills, CA 90212

Keats, Ezra Jack (1916-1983)
Writer and illustrator of books for children (The Snowy Day)
Ezra Jack Keats Foundation Ph: 718-252-4047
450 14th St
Brooklyn, NY 11215
www.ezra-jack-keats.org

Keefe, Jim (1965-)
Cartoonist; currently the artist for the comic strip Flash Gordon, which was originally created by Alex Raymond and has been drawn by a series of artists since his death
King Features Syndicate Inc Ph: 212-455-4000
888 7th Ave 2nd Fl
New York, NY 10019
www.kingfeatures.com

Keefe, Mike
Editorial cartoonist for the Denver Post
Denver Post Ph: 303-820-1010
1560 Broadway
Denver, CO 80202
www.intoon.com

Keegan, Robert
Chairman, CEO, and president of Goodyear Tire & Rubber
Goodyear Tire & Rubber Co Ph: 330-796-2121
1144 E Market St
Akron, OH 44316
www.goodyear.com/corporate/bios

Keenan, Mike (1949-)
Hockey coach; currently General Manager of the Florida Panthers hockey club
Florida Panthers Ph: 954-835-7000
BankAtlantic Center Fax: 954-835-7600
1 Panther Pkwy
Sunrise, FL 33323
www.floridapanthers.com

Keenan, Terry
FOX News business correspondent and anchor of Cashin' In
FOX News Channel Ph: 212-301-3000
1211 Ave of the Americas
New York, NY 10036
www.foxnews.com/fnctv

Keene, David
Chairman of the American Conservative Union
American Conservative Union Ph: 703-836-8602
1007 Cameron St Fax: 703-836-8606
Alexandria, VA 22314
conservative.org

Keener, Catherine (1960-)
Actor
Gersh Agency Ph: 310-274-6611
232 N Canon Dr
Beverly Hills, CA 90210

Keibler, Stacy (1979-)
Wrestler and WWE cover girl; a contestant on Dancing With the Stars II
World Wrestling Entertainment Inc Ph: 203-352-8600
1241 E Main St
Stamford, CT 06902
www.wwe.com/superstars/raw

Keillor, Garrison (1942-)
Host of A Prairie Home Companion on National Public Radio
Minnesota Public Radio Ph: 651-290-1212
45 E 7th St Fax: 651-290-1260
Saint Paul, MN 55101
www.prairiehome.org

Keitel, Harvey (1939-)
Actor
International Creative Management Ph: 212-556-5600
40 W 57th St 17th Fl
New York, NY 10019

Keith, Harold (1903-1998)
Author of Rifles for Watie, a historical novel for young readers
HarperCollins Children's Books **Ph:** 212-261-6500
1350 Ave of the Americas
New York, NY 10019
www.harperchildrens.com

Keith, Toby (1961-)
Country singer
Monterey Peninsula Artists/ Paradigm **Ph:** 615-251-4400 **Fax:** 615-251-4401
124 12th Ave S Suite 410
Nashville, TN 37203
www.tobykeith.com

Kelis (1979-)
Singer (urban/alternative)
Creative Artists Agency **Ph:** 212-277-9000
162 5th Ave 6th Fl **Fax:** 212-277-9099
New York, NY 10010
www.kelisonline.com

Kelleher, Herbert D
A founder and Executive Chairman of Southwest Airlines
Southwest Airlines Co **Ph:** 214-792-4000
PO Box 36611 **Fax:** 214-792-5015
2702 Love Field Dr
Dallas, TX 75235
www.swamedia.com

Keller, Hubert
Chef and owner of the Fleur de Lys Restaurant in San Francisco
Fleur de Lys Restaurant **Ph:** 415-673-7779
777 Sutter St **Fax:** 415-673-4619
San Francisco, CA 94109
www.fleurdelyssf.com

Keller, Ric (1964-)
US Representative from Florida (Republican)
419 Cannon Bldg **Ph:** 202-225-2176
Washington, DC 20515 **Fax:** 202-225-0999
keller.house.gov

Kellerman, Faye (1952-)
Mystery writer (wife of author Jonathan Kellerman)
HarperCollins Publishers **Ph:** 212-207-7000
c/o Author Mail
10 E 53rd St
New York, NY 10022
www.harpercollins.com

Kellerman, Jonathan, PhD (1949-)
Author of the Alex Delaware mystery series; Kellerman is a child psychologist
Ballantime Books Publicity **Ph:** 212-782-9000
1745 Broadway
New York, NY 10019
www.randomhouse.com/BB

Kelley, David E (1956-)
Writer/producer, primarily for television (LA Law, Picket Fences, Ally McBeal, The Practice)
David E Kelley Productions **Ph:** 310-727-2200
1600 Rosecrans Ave
Bldg 4B
Manhattan Beach, CA 90266

Kelley, Steve
Editorial cartoonist for the Times-Picayune in New Orleans, LA; also a humorist & speaker
Creators Syndicate Inc **Ph:** 310-337-7003
5777 W Century Blvd Suite 700 **Fax:** 310-337-7625
Los Angeles, CA 90045
www.creators.com

Kellner, Larry
Chairman and CEO of Continental Airlines
Continental Airlines Inc **Ph:** 713-324-5000
1600 Smith St
Houston, TX 77002
www.continental.com

Kelly, Gary C (1955-)
Vice Chairman & CEO of Southwest Airlines
Southwest Airlines Co **Ph:** 214-792-4000
PO Box 36611 **Fax:** 214-792-5015
2702 Love Field Dr
Dallas, TX 75235
www.swamedia.com

Kelly, Greg
White House correspondent for FOX News
FOX News Channel **Ph:** 212-301-3000
1211 Ave of the Americas
New York, NY 10036
www.foxnews.com/fnctv

Kelly, Melissa
Executive Chef and co-owner/proprietor of Primo Restaurant in Rockland, Maine
Primo Restaurant **Ph:** 207-596-0770
2 S Main St
Rockland, ME 04841
www.primorestaurant.com

Kelly, Moira (1968-)
Actor
Gersh Agency **Ph:** 310-274-6611
232 N Canon Dr
Beverly Hills, CA 90210

Kelly, R (1967-)
R&B singer and songwriter
Creative Artists Ageny **Ph:** 310-288-4545
9830 Wilshire Blvd **Fax:** 310-288-4800
Beverly Hills, CA 90212
www.r-kelly.com

Kelly, Robert (1955-)
Chairman, president, and CEO of Mellon Financial Corp
Mellon Financial Corp **Ph:** 412-234-5000
1 Mellon Center
Pittsburgh, PA 15258
www.mellon.com/investorrelations

Kelly, Sarah
Contemporary Christian singer
CAA Nashville **Ph:** 615-383-8787
3310 West End Ave 5th Fl **Fax:** 615-383-4937
Nashville, TN 37203
www.sarahkellymusic.com

Kelly, Sue (1936-)
US Representative from New York (Republican)
2182 Rayburn Bldg **Ph:** 202-225-5441
Washington, DC 20515 **Fax:** 202-225-3289
suekelly.house.gov

Kemp, Jack (1935-)
Founder and chairman of Kemp Partners, a strategic consulting firm; former Congressman, Republican candidate for Vice President, and HUD secretary, and was at one time a professional football player
Kemp Partners **Ph:** 202-572-4022
1901 Pennsylvania Ave NW **Fax:** 202-833-0708
Suite 300
Washington, DC 20006
www.kemppartners.com

Kemp, Will (1977-)
Dancer, choreographer, actor
Creative Artists Agency **Ph:** 310-288-4545
9830 Wilshire Blvd **Fax:** 310-288-4800
Beverly Hills, CA 90212
www.willkemp.org

Kempthorne, Dirk (1951-)
Governor of Idaho (Republican); Secretary-Designate of the US Dept of the Interior (due to the resignation of Gale Norton April 1, 2006)
State Capitol Bldg 2nd Fl **Ph:** 208-334-2100
Boise, ID 83720 **Fax:** 208-334-3454
gov.idaho.gov

Kendall, David E (1944-)
President Clinton's attorney for Whitewater & fundraising scandals and for his 1998 impeachment proceedings
Williams & Connolly LLP **Ph:** 202-434-5145
725 12th St NW **Fax:** 202-434-5792
Washington, DC 20005
www.wc.com

Kendall, Jason (1974-)
Professional baseball player
Oakland Athletics **Ph:** 510-638-4900
Network Assoc Coliseum **Fax:** 510-568-3770
7000 Coliseum Way
Oakland, CA 94621
oakland.athletics.mlb.com

Kendall, Pete (1973-)
Professional football player
New York Jets **Ph:** 516-560-8100
1000 Fulton Ave **Fax:** 516-560-8198
Hempstead, NY 11550
www.newyorkjets.com

Keneally, Thomas (1935-)
Novelist (Schindler's List)
Nan A Talese/Doubleday **Ph:** 212-782-8918
1745 Broadway 22nd Fl **Fax:** 212-782-8448
New York, NY 10019
www.randomhouse.com/nanatalese

Kenna, Michael (1953-)
Landscape photographer
Stephen Wirtz Gallery **Ph:** 415-433-6879
49 Geary St 3rd Fl **Fax:** 415-433-1608
San Francisco, CA 94108
www.michaelkenna.net

Kennedy, Anthony M (1936-)
US Supreme Court justice
US Supreme Court Bldg **Ph:** 202-479-3000
1 1st St NE
Washington, DC 20543
www.supremecourtus.gov

Kennedy, D James (1930-)
Presbyterian minister and televangelist; also founder of the Center for Reclaiming America
Coral Ridge Ministries **Ph:** 954-772-0404
5555 N Federal Hwy **Fax:** 954-771-3187
Fort Lauderdale, FL 33308
www.coralridge.org

Kennedy, Danielle
Business speaker on such topics as sales, interview techniques, negotiation skills, goal setting and achievement, time management, and mental and physical fitness
Danielle Kennedy Productions **Ph:** 800-848-8070
17366 Sunset Blvd Suite 203-B **Fax:** 310-454-3464
Pacific Palisades, CA 90272
www.daniellekennedy.com

Kennedy, David M, PhD
History professor at Stanford and nonfiction author (Freedom From Fear: The American People in Depression and War)
Stanford University **Ph:** 650-723-2651
History Dept **Fax:** 650-725-0597
Bldg 200 Rm 207
Stanford, CA 94305
history.stanford.edu/faculty/dkennedy

Kennedy, Edward M (1932-)
US Senator from Massachusetts (Democrat)
317 Russell Bldg **Ph:** 202-224-4543
Washington, DC 20510 **Fax:** 202-224-2417
kennedy.senate.gov

Kennedy, Jamie (1970-)
Actor; comedian
3 Arts Entertainment **Ph:** 310-888-3200
9460 Wilshire Blvd 7th Fl **Fax:** 310-888-3210
Beverly Hills, CA 90212
www.jamiekennedyworld.com

Kennedy, John Fitzgerald (1917-1963)
35th US President
John F Kennedy Library & Museum **Ph:** 617-514-1600
Fax: 617-514-1652
Columbia Point **TF:** 866-535-1960
Boston, MA 02125
www.jfklibrary.org

Kennedy, Joyce Lain
Author of the nationally syndicated Careers Now column, which provides advice on jobs and career development
Tribune Media Services Inc **Ph:** 312-222-4444
435 N Michigan Ave Suite 1500
Chicago, IL 60611
tmsfeatures.com/productlist.htm

Kennedy, Mark R (1957-)
US Representative from Minnesota (Republican)
1415 Longworth Bldg **Ph:** 202-225-2331
Washington, DC 20515 **Fax:** 202-225-6475
markkennedy.house.gov

Kennedy, Parker
Chairman and CEO of First American Corp; also chairman of its principal subsidiary, First American Title Insurance Co
First American Corp **Ph:** 714-558-3211
1 First American Way
Santa Ana, CA 92707
www.firstam.com

Kennedy, Patrick (1967-)
US Representative from Rhode Island (Democrat)
407 Cannon Bldg **Ph:** 202-225-4911
Washington, DC 20515 **Fax:** 202-225-3290
www.patrickkennedy.house.gov

Kennedy, Paul (1945-)
Writes a syndicated column on international affairs; is a professor of history & director of international security studies at Yale University
Tribune Media Services Inc **Ph:** 312-222-4444
435 N Michigan Ave Suite 1500
Chicago, IL 60611
tmsfeatures.com/productlist.htm

Kennedy, Robert F Jr (1954-)
Attorney and host of Ring of Fire on Air America Radio; president of the Waterkeeper Alliance, and senior attorney for the Natural Resources Defense Council
Ring of Fire **Ph:** 866-389-3473
PO Box 12308 **Fax:** 850-436-6008
Pensacola, FL 32591
www.ringoffireradio.com

Kennedy, William (1928-)
Author of novels about life in Albany, NY (Ironweed); also co-wrote the screenplay for The Cotton Club and is the executive director and founder of the New York State Writer's Institute
New York State Writers Institute **Ph:** 518-442-5620
Fax: 518-442-5621
New Library LE 320
SUNY Albany
Albany, NY 12222
www.williamkennedy.com

Kenny G (1956-)
Saxophonist (various music genres)
Creative Artists Agency **Ph:** 310-288-4545
9830 Wilshire Blvd **Fax:** 310-288-4800
Beverly Hills, CA 90212
www.kennyg.com

Kenseth, Matt (1972-)
NASCAR driver
Roush Racing **Ph:** 704-720-4100
4600 Roush Pl NW
Concord, NC 28027
www.roushracing.com

Kent, Jeff (1968-)
Professional baseball player
Los Angeles Dodgers **Ph:** 323-224-1500
Dodger Stadium **Fax:** 323-224-1269
1000 Elysian Park Ave
Los Angeles, CA 90012
losangeles.dodgers.mlb.com

Kent, Julie (1969-)
A principal dancer with the American Ballet Theatre; is married to ABT's associate artistic director Victor Barbee
American Ballet Theatre **Ph:** 212-477-3030
890 Broadway **Fax:** 212-254-5938
New York, NY 10003
www.abt.org/dancers

Kent, Philip I
Chairman and CEO of Turner Broadcasting System Inc
Turner Broadcasting System Inc **Ph:** 404-827-1700
1 CNN Center
Andrew Young International Blvd
Atlanta, GA 30303
www.turner.com

Kerger, Paula
President & CEO of the Public Broadcasting Service (PBS)
PBS **Ph:** 703-739-5015
2100 Crystal Dr **Fax:** 703-739-7500
Arlington, VA 22202
www.pbs.org/aboutpbs

Kerkorian, Kirk (1917-)
Billionaire Nevada financier; owner of Tracinda Corp, which owns MGM Mirage
Tracinda Corp **Ph:** 310-271-0638
150 Rodeo Dr Suite 250 **Fax:** 310-271-3416
Beverly Hills, CA 90212

Kernan, Joe
Co-anchor of Squawk Box on CNBC
CNBC **Ph:** 201-735-2622
900 Sylvan Ave
Englewood Cliffs, NJ 07632
moneycentral.msn.com/cnbc/tv

Kerr, David W
Chairman of Falconbridge Ltd, an international mining and metals company
Falconbridge Ltd **Ph:** 416-982-7111
207 Queens Key W Suite 800 **Fax:** 416-982-7423
Toronto, ON M5J1A7
www.falconbridge.com

Kerr, Graham (1934-)
Celebrity chef known as the Galloping Gourmet
Kerr Corp **Ph:** 360-387-3807
1020 N Sunset Dr **Fax:** 360-387-1898
Camano Island, WA 98282
www.grahamkerr.com

Kerr, ME (1927-)
Author of numerous books for young adults (ME Kerr is one of several pen names used by Marijane Meaker; others are Ann Aldrich, Mary James, MJ Meaker, and Vin Packer)
HarperCollins Children's Books **Ph:** 212-261-6500
1350 Ave of the Americas
New York, NY 10019
www.mekerr.com

Kerrey, Bob (1943-)
Former governor of Nebraska, former US Representative and US Senator, and a member of the 9/11 Commission; president of New School University in New York
New School University **Ph:** 212-229-5600
66 W 12th St
New York, NY 10011
www.newschool.edu/admin/pres

Kerrigan, Nancy (1969-)
American figure skater and Olympic medalist
StarGames Inc **Ph:** 781-224-9655
40 Salem St Suite 7 **Fax:** 781-224-9656
Lynnfield, MA 01940
www.nancyfans.com

Kerry, John F (1943-)
US Senator from Massachusetts (Democrat)
304 Russell Bldg **Ph:** 202-224-2742
Washington, DC 20510 **Fax:** 202-224-8525
kerry.senate.gov

Kest, Bryan (1965-)
Power Yoga instructor
Power Yoga Studio - West **Ph:** 310-458-9510
1410 2nd St 1st Fl
Santa Monica, CA 90401
www.poweryoga.com

Ketchum, Mark D (1950-)
CEO of Newell Rubbermaid
Newell Rubbermaid Inc **Ph:** 770-407-3800
10-B Glenlake Pkwy **Fax:** 770-407-3970
Atlanta, GA 30328
www.newellco.com

Keteyian, Armen (1953-)
Chief investigative correspondent for CBS News; had previously been a special features reporter for CBS Sports
CBS News **Ph:** 212-975-4114
524 W 57th St
New York, NY 10019
www.cbsnews.com

Kevoian, Bob (1950-)
Co-host, with Tom Griswold, of a comedy-based morning radio show
Bob & Tom Show **Ph:** 317-257-7565
6161 Fall Creek Rd **Fax:** 317-254-9511
Indianapolis, IN 46220
www.bobandtom.com

Key, Ted (1912-)
Creator of the comic strip Hazel
King Features Syndicate Inc **Ph:** 212-455-4000
888 7th Ave 2nd Fl
New York, NY 10019
www.kingfeatures.com

Keyes, Daniel (1927-)
Author (Flowers for Algernon)
Harcourt Trade Publishers **Ph:** 212-592-1000
15 E 26th St
New York, NY 10010
www.danielkeyesauthor.com

Keys, Alicia (1981-)
Soul/R&B singer
William Morris Agency **Ph:** 310-859-4000
1 William Morris Pl **Fax:** 310-859-4462
Beverly Hills, CA 90212
www.aliciakeys.net

Khabibulin, Nikolai (1973-)
Professional hockey player
Chicago Blackhawks **Ph:** 312-455-7000
United Center **Fax:** 312-455-7041
1901 W Madison St
Chicago, IL 60612
www.chicagoblackhawks.com

Khosla, Vinod
Founding CEO of Sun Microsystems and a top technology venture investor; also co-founder of Daisy Systems
Kleiner Perkins Caufield & Byers **Ph:** 650-233-2750
Fax: 650-233-0300
2750 Sand Hill Rd
Menlo Park, CA 94025
www.kpcb.com

Kid Rock (1971-)
Singer (real name is Robert J. Ritchie)
Creative Artists Agency **Ph:** 310-299-4545
9830 Wilshire Blvd **Fax:** 310-288-4800
Beverly Hills, CA 90212
www.kidrock.com

Kidd, Jason (1973-)
Professional basketball player
New Jersey Nets **Ph:** 201-935-8888
Nets Champion Center **Fax:** 201-935-1088
390 Murray Hill Pkwy
East Rutherford, NJ 07073
www.nba.com/nets

Kidd, Sue Monk (1948-)
Novelist (The Secret Life of Bees)
Viking Publicity **Ph:** 212-366-2000
375 Hudson St
New York, NY 10014
www.suemonkkidd.com

Kidman, Nicole (1967-)
Actor
Creative Artists Agency **Ph:** 310-288-4545
9830 Wilshire Blvd **Fax:** 310-288-4800
Beverly Hills, CA 90212

Kiely, W Leo
President and CEO of Molson Coors
Molson Coors Brewing Co **Ph:** 303-277-6661
1225 17th St Suite 1875
Denver, CO 80202
www.molsoncoors.com

Kilby, Jack (1923-2005)
Inventor of the microchip; winner of the 2000 Nobel Prize in Physics for his part in the invention of the integrated circuit
Texas Instruments Inc **Ph:** 972-995-2011
12500 TI Blvd
Dallas, TX 95243
www.ti.com/corp/docs/company

Kildee, Dale E (1929-)
US Representative from Michigan (Democrat)
2107 Rayburn Bldg **Ph:** 202-225-3611
Washington, DC 20515 **Fax:** 202-225-6393
www.house.gov/kildee

Killian, Mike
Writes the comic strip Dick Tracy, which is illustrated by Dick Locher
Tribune Media Services Inc **Ph:** 312-222-4444
435 N Michigan Ave Suite 1500
Chicago, IL 60611
www.comicspage.com

Killinger, Kerry
Chairman and CEO of Washington Mutual
Washington Mutual Inc **Ph:** 206-461-2000
1201 3rd Ave
Seattle, WA 98101
www.wamu.com/about/corporateprofile

Kilmeade, Brian
FOX News's sports anchor and a co-host of Fox and Friends
FOX News Channel **Ph:** 212-301-3000
1211 Ave of the Americas
New York, NY 10036
www.foxnews.com/fnctv

Kilmer, Val (1959-)
Actor
International Creative Management **Ph:** 310-550-4000
8942 Wilshire Blvd
Beverly Hills, CA 90211
www.valkilmer.org

Kilpatrick, Carolyn C (1945-)
US Representative from Michigan (Democrat)
1610 Longworth Bldg **Ph:** 202-225-2261
Washington, DC 20515 **Fax:** 202-225-5730
www.house.gov/kilpatrick

Kilpatrick, James J (1920-)
Conservative columnist; writes the syndicated column Covering the Courts
Universal Press Syndicate **Ph:** 816-932-6600
4520 Main St
Kansas City, MO 64111
www.amuniversal.com/ups/features

Kilpatrick, Kwame M (1970-)
Mayor of Detroit
2 Woodward Ave Suite 1126 **Ph:** 313-224-3400
Detroit, MI 48226 **Fax:** 313-224-4128
www.ci.detroit.mi.us/mayor

Kim, Byung-Hyun (1979-)
Professional baseball player
Colorado Rockies **Ph:** 303-292-0200
Coors Field **Fax:** 303-296-2066
2001 Blake St
Denver, CO 80205
colorado.rockies.mlb.com

Kim, Daniel Dae (1968-)
Actor
Lighthouse Entertainment **Ph:** 310-246-0499
409 N Camden Dr Suite 202
Beverly Hills, CA 90210
abc.go.com/primetime/lost/show.html

Kim, James J (1936-)
Founder, chairman, and CEO of Amkor Technology, a contract manufacturer for semiconductor companies
Amkor Technology Inc **Ph:** 610-431-9600
1345 Enterprise Dr **Fax:** 610-431-5881
West Chester, PA 19380
www.amkor.com

Kimmel, Jimmy (1967-)
Late-night TV show host
Bragman/Nyman/Cafarelli **Ph:** 310-854-4800
8687 Melrose Ave 8th Fl **Fax:** 310-854-4848
Los Angeles, CA 90069
abc.go.com/primetime/jimmykimmel

Kimmel, Sidney
Chairman of the Jones Apparel Group Inc
Jones Apparel Group Inc **Ph:** 215-785-4000
250 Rittenshouse Cir **Fax:** 215-785-1228
Bristol, PA 19007
www.jny.com

Kincaid, Bernard, PhD (1945-)
Mayor of Birmingham, Alabama
City Hall **Ph:** 205-254-2277
710 N 20th St **Fax:** 205-254-2926
Birmingham, AL 35203
ci.bham.al.us

Kincaid, Jamaica (1949-)
Author of novels about life in Antigua
Farrar Straus & Giroux **Ph:** 212-741-6900
19 Union Sq W
New York, NY 10003
www.fsgbooks.com

Kind, Ron (1963-)
US Representative from Wisconsin (Democrat)
1406 Longworth Bldg **Ph:** 202-225-5506
Washington, DC 20515 **Fax:** 202-225-5739
www.house.gov/kind

King, BB (1925-)
Blues guitarist and singer
William Morris Agency **Ph:** 310-859-4000
1 William Morris Pl **Fax:** 310-859-4462
Beverly Hills, CA 90212
www.bbking.com

King, Bernice A (1963-)
Youngest daughter of Dr. Martin Luther King, Jr and Coretta Scott King; motivational speaker and a minister at New Birth Missionary Baptist Church in Lithonia, GA
First Kingdom Management **Ph:** 404-525-5464
PO Box 110277 **Fax:** 404-525-5461
Atlanta, GA 30311
www.berniceking.com

King, Billie Jean (1943-)
Former tennis player
IMG Inc **Ph:** 216-522-1200
IMG Center **Fax:** 216-522-1145
1360 E 9th St Suite 100
Cleveland, OH 44114

King, Carole (1942-)
Singer/songwriter
CK Productions **Ph:** 818-980-2773
11684 Ventura Blvd Suite 273 **Fax:** 818-980-2478
Studio City, CA 91604
www.caroleking.com

King, Colbert I (1939-)
Washington Post editorial columnist
Washington Post **Ph:** 202-334-6000
1150 15th St NW
Washington, DC 20071
www.washingtonpost.com

King, Coretta Scott (1927-2006)
Wife of Dr Martin Luther King, Jr and a leader in the US civil rights movement; founded the King Center as a living memorial to her husband's life and dream
Martin Luther King Jr Center for Nonviolent Social Change **Ph:** 404-526-8900
449 Auburn Ave NE
Atlanta, GA 30312
www.thekingcenter.org

King, Dexter Scott (1961-)
The son of Dr Martin Luther King Jr and Coretta Scott King, and the chairman of the King Center
Martin Luther King Jr Center for Nonviolent Social Change Inc **Ph:** 404-526-8900
449 Auburn Ave NE
Atlanta, GA 30312
www.thekingcenter.org

King, Don (1932-)
Boxing promoter
Don King Productions Inc **Ph:** 954-418-5800
501 Fairway Dr
Deerfield Beach, FL 33441
www.donking.com

King, John
CNN's chief national correspondent
CNN **Ph:** 202-898-7900
CNN Bldg
820 1st St NE
Washington, DC 20002
www.cnn.com/CNN/anchors_reporters

King, Larry (1933-)
Host of Larry King Live on CNN; the show is simulcast on Westwood One radio stations
CNN **Ph:** 202-898-7900
CNN Bldg
820 1st St NE
Washington, DC 20002
www.cnn.com/CNN/anchors_reporters

King, Mark
President and CEO of ACS
Affiliated Computer Services Inc **Ph:** 214-841-6111
2828 N Haskell Ave
Dallas, TX 75204
www.acs-inc.com/about/people.html

King, Martin Luther Jr, PhD (1929-1968)
Charismatic leader of the US civil rights movement during the 1950s & '60s and an advocate of nonviolent social change; an ordained minister and founder/president of the Southern Christian Leadership Conference; was assassinated in 1968
King Center **Ph:** 404-526-8900
449 Auburn Ave NE
Atlanta, GA 30312
www.thekingcenter.org

King, Michael Patrick (1954-)
TV writer and producer
Endeavor **Ph:** 310-248-2000
9601 Wilshire Blvd 3rd Fl **Fax:** 310-248-2020
Beverly Hills, CA 90210
www.hbo.com/city

King, Peter T (1944-)
US Representative from New York (Republican)
436 Cannon Bldg **Ph:** 202-225-7896
Washington, DC 20515 **Fax:** 202-226-2279
peteking.house.gov

King, Stephen (1947-)
Author of thriller-horror novels and stories
Creative Artists Agency **Ph:** 310-288-4545
9830 Wilshire Blvd **Fax:** 310-288-4800
Beverly Hills, CA 90212
www.stephenking.com

King, Steve (1949-)
US Representative from Iowa (Republican)
1432 Longworth Bldg **Ph:** 202-225-4426
Washington, DC 20515 **Fax:** 202-225-3193
www.house.gov/steveking

Kingsley, Ben (1943-)
Actor
International Creative Management **Ph:** 310-550-4000
8942 Wilshire Blvd
Beverly Hills, CA 90211
www.benkingsley.com

Kingsolver, Barbara (1955-)
Author of The Poisonwood Bible
HarperCollins Publishers **Ph:** 212-207-7000
c/o Author Mail
10 E 53rd St
New York, NY 10022
www.kingsolver.com

Kingston, Jack (1955-)
US Representative from Georgia (Republican)
2242 Rayburn Bldg **Ph:** 202-225-5831
Washington, DC 20515 **Fax:** 202-226-2269
www.house.gov/kingston

Kingston, Maxine Hong (1940-)
Author; her memoirs and fiction include The Woman Warrior, China Men, Tripmaster Monkey, and Hawai'i One Summer
Vintage/Anchor Publicity **Ph:** 212-572-2420
1745 Broadway 20th Fl
New York, NY 10019
www.randomhouse.com/vintage

Kinkade, Thomas (1958-)
Painter who is considered to be the top-selling artist in America; emphasizes inspirational messages through his paintings
Thomas Kinkade Co **Ph:** 800-366-3733
900 Lightpost Way
Morgan Hill, CA 95037
www.thomaskinkade.com

Kinkead, Bob
Chef and owner of Kinkead's, an American brasserie-style restaurant; also owns Colvin Run Tavern at Fairfax Square in Tyson's Corner, Virginia
Kinkead's Restaurant **Ph:** 202-296-7700
2000 Pennsylvania Ave NW **Fax:** 202-296-7688
Washington, DC 20006
www.kinkead.com

Kinnear, Greg (1963-)
Actor
Creative Artists Agency **Ph:** 310-288-4545
9830 Wilshire Blvd **Fax:** 310-288-4800
Beverly Hills, CA 90212

Kinnell, Galway (1927-)
Poet (former state poet of Vermont)
Houghton Mifflin Co **Ph:** 617-351-5000
Trade Div
Adult Editorial
222 Berkeley St 8th Fl
Boston, MA 02116
www.houghtonmifflinbooks.com

Kinsella, John (1963-)
Australian poet; also a novelist, essayist, critic, publisher, and journal editor
WW Norton & Co Inc **Ph:** 212-354-5500
500 5th Ave **Fax:** 212-869-0856
New York, NY 10110
www.johnkinsella.org

Kinsolving, Carey
Writes the syndicated column Kids Talk About God
Creators Syndicate Inc **Ph:** 310-337-7003
5777 W Century Blvd Suite 700 **Fax:** 310-337-7625
Los Angeles, CA 90045
www.creators.com

Kiprusoff, Miikka (1976-)
Professional hockey player
Calgary Flames **Ph:** 403-777-2177
Pengrowth Saddledome **Fax:** 403-777-2195
555 Saddledome Rise SE
Calgary, AB T2G2W1
www.calgaryflames.com

Kirilenko, Andrei (1981-)
Professional basketball player
Utah Jazz **Ph:** 801-325-2500
Delta Center **Fax:** 801-325-2578
301 W South Temple St **TF:** 800-358-7328
Salt Lake City, UT 84101
www.nba.com/jazz

Kirk, David (1955-)
Author of the Miss Spider series of children's books
Scholastic Inc **Ph:** 212-343-6100
555 Broadway
New York, NY 10012
www.scholastic.com/titles/missspider

Kirk, Mark Steven (1959-)
US Representative from Illinois (Republican)
1717 Longworth Bldg **Ph:** 202-225-4835
Washington, DC 20515 **Fax:** 202-225-0837
www.house.gov/kirk

Kirkman, Rick
Co-creator, with Jerry Scott, of the comic strip Baby Blues
King Features Syndicate Inc **Ph:** 212-455-4000
888 7th Ave 2nd Fl
New York, NY 10019
babyblues.com

Kirkpatrick, Jeane J (1926-)
Former US ambassador to the United Nations
American Enterprise Institute for Public Policy Research **Ph:** 202-862-5800 **Fax:** 202-862-7177
1150 17th St NW Suite 1100
Washington, DC 20036
www.aei.org

Kirsch, Steve
Founder, chairman, and CEO of Propel Software; also founded Infoseek, which was acquired by Disney in 1999
Propel Software Corp **Ph:** 408-571-6300
1010 Rincon Cir **Fax:** 408-577-1070
San Jose, CA 95131
www.propel.com

Kirsch, William S (1956-)
President & CEO of Conseco
Conseco Inc **Ph:** 317-817-6100
11815 N Pennsylvania St
Carmel, IN 46032
www.conseco.com

Kirstein, Lincoln (1907-1996)
Co-founder (with George Balanchine) and administrative head of New York City Ballet and its affiliated academy, the School of American Ballet
New York City Ballet **Ph:** 212-870-5656
New York State Theater **Fax:** 212-870-7791
20 Lincoln Center
New York, NY 10023
www.nycballet.com/about/staffart.html

Kisor, Henry (1940-)
Book editor and literary columnist of the Chicago Sun-Times
Chicago Sun-Times **Ph:** 312-321-3000
401 N Wabash Ave **Fax:** 312-321-3084
Chicago, IL 60611
www.henrykisor.com

KISS
Rock band
Creative Artists Agency **Ph:** 310-288-4545
9830 Wilshire Blvd **Fax:** 310-288-4800
Beverly Hills, CA 90212
www.kissonline.com

Kissinger, Henry, PhD (1923-)
Former US Secretary of State; winner of the Nobel Peace Prize in 1973 (with Le Duc Tho)
Kissinger McLarty Assoc **Ph:** 212-759-7919
350 Park Ave 26th Fl **Fax:** 212-759-0042
New York, NY 10022
www.tmsfeatures.com/productlist.htm

Kistler, Darci (1964-)
A principal dancer with the New York City Ballet
New York City Ballet **Ph:** 212-870-5656
New York State Theater **Fax:** 212-870-7791
20 Lincoln Center
New York, NY 10023
www.nycballet.com/about/dancers.html

Kitchen, Mike (1956-)
Hockey coach
Saint Louis Blues **Ph:** 314-622-2500
Savvis Center **Fax:** 314-622-2582
1401 Clark Ave
Saint Louis, MO 63103
www.stlouisblues.com

Kite, Tom (1949-)
Professional golfer (Champions Tour)
PGA Tour **Ph:** 904-285-3700
100 PGA Tour Blvd
Ponte Vedra Beach, FL 32082
www.pgatour.com/players

Kitman, Marvin (1929-)
TV critic for Newsday
Newsday **Ph:** 631-843-2020
235 Pinelawn Rd **Fax:** 631-843-2953
Melville, NY 11747
www.marvinkitman.com

Kiyosaki, Robert T (1947-)
Author, with Sharon Lechter, of the Rich Dad Poor Dad series
Rich Dad Co **Ph:** 480-998-6971
4330 N Civic Ctr Plaza
Suite 101
Scottsdale, AZ 85251
www.richdad.com

Klasky, Arlene
Co-creator and executive producer of Rugrats; works mainly on development of new animated products for film and television
Klasky Csupo Inc **Ph:** 323-468-2600
6353 Sunset Blvd
Hollywood, CA 90028
www.klaskycsupo.com

Klawans, Stuart
Film critic for The Nation
The Nation **Ph:** 212-209-5400
33 Irving Pl 8th Fl **Fax:** 212-982-9000
New York, NY 10003
www.thenation.com

Klein, Calvin (1942-)
Fashion designer
205 W 39th St **Ph:** 212-719-2600
New York, NY 10018

Klein, Chris (1979-)
Actor (American Pie)
William Morris Agency **Ph:** 310-859-4000
1 William Morris Pl **Fax:** 310-859-4462
Beverly Hills, CA 90212

Klein, Joe (1946-)
Time Magazine columnist; author of Primary Colors (as Anonymous)
Time Magazine **Ph:** 212-522-1212
Rockefeller Center
Time & Life Bldg
New York, NY 10020
www.time.com/time/columnist/klein

Klein, Lawrence R, PhD (1920-)
Winner of the 1980 Nobel Prize in Economics for the creation of econometric models and the application to the analysis of economic fluctuations and economic policies
University of Pennsylvania **Ph:** 215-898-7713
Economics Dept **Fax:** 215-573-2057
335 McNeil Bldg
3718 Locust Walk
Philadelphia, PA 19104
www.econ.upenn.edu

Klein, Naomi (1970-)
Nonfiction author; journalist
The Nation **Ph:** 212-209-5400
33 Irving Pl 8th Fl **Fax:** 212-982-9000
New York, NY 10003
www.thenation.com

Klein, Robert (1942-)
Comedian
William Morris Agency **Ph:** 310-859-4000
1 William Morris Pl **Fax:** 310-859-4462
Beverly Hills, CA 90212
www.wma.com/robert_klein/summary

Klein, Steven
Fashion photographer
Steven Klein Studio **Ph:** 212-675-7655
842 Greenwich St **Fax:** 212-675-7664
New York, NY 10014
www.stevenkleinstudio.com

Klein, Yves (1928-1962)
Artist whose early paintings were monochromatic, often in blue
Solomon R Guggenheim Museum **Ph:** 212-423-3500
1071 5th Ave
New York, NY 10128
www.guggenheimcollection.org

Kleinrock, Leonard, PhD (1934-)
Creator of the basic principles of packet switching, the technology underpinning the Internet
University of California at Los Angeles **Ph:** 310-825-2543 **Fax:** 310-597-1502
Dept of Computer Science
4732 Boelter Hall
Los Angeles, CA 90095
www.lk.cs.ucla.edu

Kline, Franz (1910-1962)
Abstract Expressionist painter
Solomon R Guggenheim Museum **Ph:** 212-423-3500
1071 5th Ave
New York, NY 10128
www.guggenheimcollection.org

Kline, John P (1947-)
US Representative from Minnesota (Republican)
1429 Longworth Bldg **Ph:** 202-225-2271
Washington, DC 20515 **Fax:** 202-225-2595
www.house.gov/kline

Kline, Kevin (1947-)
Actor
Creative Artists Agency **Ph:** 310-288-4545
9830 Wilshire Blvd **Fax:** 310-288-4800
Beverly Hills, CA 90212

Kline, Lowry
Chairman & CEO of Coca-Cola Enterprises
Coca-Cola Enterprises Inc **Ph:** 770-989-3000
2500 Windy Ridge Pkwy
Suite 900
Atlanta, GA 31139
ir.cokecce.com/governance/officers.cfm

Klose, Kevin
President & CEO of National Public Radio
National Public Radio **Ph:** 202-513-2000
635 Massachusetts Ave NW **Fax:** 202-513-3329
Washington, DC 20001
www.npr.org

Kluge, John W
Founder, chairman, and president of Metromedia Co
Metromedia Co **Ph:** 201-531-8000
1 Meadowlands Plaza **Fax:** 201-531-2804
East Rutherford, NJ 07073

Kluger, Richard
Journalist, editor, and author (fiction and social history)
Random House Publicity **Ph:** 212-751-2600
1745 Broadway
New York, NY 10019
www.randomhouse.com

Klugh, Earl (1954-)
Jazz guitarist
International Creative Management **Ph:** 310-550-4000
8942 Wilshire Blvd
Beverly Hills, CA 90211
www.earlklugh.com

Klum, Heidi (1973-)
Model
IMG Models **Ph:** 212-253-8884
304 Park Ave S 12th Fl **Fax:** 212-253-8883
New York, NY 10010
www.heidiklum.com

Knauss, Donald R
Executive Vice President of Coca-Cola Co and President/COO of Coca-Cola North America
Coca-Cola Co **Ph:** 404-676-2121
1 Coca-Cola Plaza
Atlanta, GA 30313
www.coca-cola.com

Knight, Bob (1940-)
Basketball coach
Texas Tech University Athletic Dept **Ph:** 806-742-3355
PO Box 43021
Lubbock, TX 79409
texastech.collegesports.com

Knight, Brevin (1975-)
Professional basketball player
Charlotte Bobcats **Ph:** 704-357-0252
100 Hive Dr **Fax:** 704-357-0289
Charlotte, NC 28217
www.nba.com/bobcats

Knight, Christopher (1950-)
Art critic
Los Angeles Times **Ph:** 213-237-5000
202 W 1st St **Fax:** 213-237-4712
Los Angeles, CA 90012

Knight, Philip H
Chairman of Nike
Nike Inc **Ph:** 503-671-6453
1 Bowerman Dr
Beaverton, OR 97005
www.nikebiz.com

Knightly, Keira (1985-)
Actor
Endeavor **Ph:** 310-248-2000
9601 Wilshire Blvd 3rd Fl **Fax:** 310-248-2020
Beverly Hills, CA 90210

Knollenberg, Joe (1933-)
US Representative from Michigan (Republican)
2349 Rayburn Bldg **Ph:** 202-225-5802
Washington, DC 20515 **Fax:** 202-226-2356
www.house.gov/knollenberg

Knoller, Mark
CBS News's White House correspondent
CBS News **Ph:** 202-457-4481
2020 M St NW
Washington, DC 20036
www.cbsnews.com

Knopfler, Mark (1949-)
Guitarist; songwriter/singer; now performs solo & in collaboration with other artists but previously was front man of rock band Dire Straits
William Morris Agency **Ph:** 310-859-4000
1 William Morris Pl **Fax:** 310-859-4462
Beverly Hills, CA 90212
www.mark-knopfler.com

Knowles, Beyonce (1981-)
Soul/R&B singer (solo and as part of Destiny's Child)
Creative Artists Agency **Ph:** 310-288-4545
9830 Wilshire Blvd **Fax:** 310-288-4800
Beverly Hills, CA 90212
www.beyonceonline.com

Koch, Charles G (1935-)
Chairman of the board and CEO of Koch Industries
Koch Industries Inc **Ph:** 316-828-5201
4111 E 37th St N **Fax:** 316-828-5739
Wichita, KS 67201
www.kochind.com/newsroom/bios.asp

Kochalka, James
Cartoonist and musician. Develops cartoons for Nickelodeon and is the creator of the graphic novel Monkey vs Robot and Sketchbook Diaries; creates alternative rock music under the name James Kochalka Superstar
Top Shelf Productions **Ph:** 770-425-0551
PO Box 1282
Marietta, GA 30061
www.topshelfcomix.com

Koehler, Robert (1928-)
Journalist/syndicated columnist, essayist, fiction writer, and poet
Tribune Media Services Inc **Ph:** 312-222-4444
435 N Michigan Ave Suite 1500
Chicago, IL 60611
tmsfeatures.com/productlist.htm

Koepp, David (1964-)
Screenwriter
Creative Artists Agency **Ph:** 310-288-4545
9830 Wilshire Blvd **Fax:** 310-288-4800
Beverly Hills, CA 90212

Koertge, Ron (1940-)
Author of novels for young adults; also writes poetry
Candlewick Press **Ph:** 617-661-3330
2067 Massachusetts Ave **Fax:** 617-661-0565
Cambridge, MA 02140
www.candlewick.com

Kohl, Herbert H (1935-)
US Senator from Wisconsin (Democrat); owner of the Milwaukee Bucks basketball team
330 Hart Bldg **Ph:** 202-224-5653
Washington, DC 20510 **Fax:** 202-224-9787
kohl.senate.gov

Kohler, Herbert V Jr
Chairman, CEO, and president of Kohler Co
Kohler Co **Ph:** 920-457-4441
444 Highland Dr **Fax:** 920-457-1271
Kohler, WI 53044
www.kohler.com

Kohn, Donald L, PhD (1942-)
Member of the Board of Governors of the Federal Reserve System
Federal Reserve System **Ph:** 202-452-3761
20th St & Constitution Ave NW **Fax:** 202-452-2611
Washington, DC 20551
www.federalreserve.gov/bios

Kohn, Walter, PhD (1923-)
Winner of the 1998 Nobel Prize in Chemistry for his development of the density-functional theory
University of California at Santa Barbara **Ph:** 805-893-3061 **Fax:** 805-893-5816
Dept of Physics
Broida Hall
Bldg 572
Santa Barbara, CA 93106
www.physics.ucsb.edu/~kohn

Koivu, Saku (1974-)
Professional hockey player
Montreal Canadiens **Ph:** 514-932-2582
1275 Saint Antoine St W **Fax:** 514-932-9296
Montreal, QC H3C5L2
www.canadiens.com

Kolb, Dan (1975-)
Professional baseball player
Milwaukee Brewers **Ph:** 414-902-4400
Miller Park **Fax:** 414-902-4515
1 Brewers Way
Milwaukee, WI 53214
milwaukee.brewers.mlb.com

Kolbe, Jim (1942-)
US Representative from Arizona (Republican)
237 Cannon Bldg **Ph:** 202-225-2542
Washington, DC 20515 **Fax:** 202-225-0378
www.house.gov/kolbe

Kolbrener, Bob (1942-)
Photographer
Fay Gold Gallery Ph: 404-233-3843
764 Miami Circle
Atlanta, GA 30324
www.faygoldgallery.com

Kolls, Rebecca
Gardening expert
Scripps Howard Broadcasting Ph: 248-827-9402
WXYZ-TV
2077 W Ten Mile
Southfield, MI 48037
www.rebeccasgarden.com

Kolzig, Olaf (1970-)
Professional hockey player
Washington Capitals Ph: 202-266-2200
401 9th St NW Suite 750 Fax: 202-266-2210
Washington, DC 20004
www.washingtoncaps.com

Komando, Kim
Radio talk show host (computer/technology), columnist, and author
WestStar Talk Radio Network Ph: 602-381-8200
2711 N 24th St Fax: 602-381-8221
Phoenix, AZ 85008
www.komando.com

Komunyakaa, Yusef (1947-)
Poet
Farrar Straus & Giroux Ph: 212-741-6900
19 Union Sq W
New York, NY 10003
www.fsgbooks.com

Kondracke, Morton (1939-)
Veteran journalist; a regular contributor to FOX News programs and co-host of The Beltway Boys
FOX News Channel Ph: 212-301-3000
1211 Ave of the Americas
New York, NY 10036
www.foxnews.com/bio

Konerko, Paul (1976-)
Professional baseball player
Chicago White Sox Ph: 312-674-1000
US Cellular Field Fax: 312-674-5109
333 W 35th St
Chicago, IL 60616
chicago.whitesox.mlb.com

Konigsburg, EL (1930-)
Author of books for young adults (From the Mixed-Up Files of Mrs. Basil E. Frankweiler; View from Saturday); has also written and illustrated picture books for children
Simon & Schuster Books for Young Readers Ph: 212-698-7000
1230 Ave of the Americas
New York, NY 10020
www.simonsays.com

Koontz, Dean (1945-)
Suspense/horror novelist
Bantam Dell Publicity Ph: 212-782-9000
1745 Broadway
New York, NY 10019
www.deankoontz.com

Koop, C Everett, MD (1916-)
Former surgeon general of the United States
C Everett Koop Institute Ph: 603-650-1450
7025 Strasenburgh Hall Fax: 603-650-1452
Dartmouth College
Hanover, NH 03755
www.dartmouth.edu/dms/koop

Koppel, Andrea
Congressional correspondent for CNN
CNN Ph: 202-898-7900
CNN Bldg
820 1st St NE
Washington, DC 20002
www.cnn.com/CNN/anchors_reporters

Korda, Michael (1933-)
Editor-in-chief of Simon & Schuster as well as the author of both fiction and nonfiction
HarperCollins Publishers Ph: 212-207-7000
c/o Author Mail
10 E 53rd St
New York, NY 10022
www.harpercollins.com

Korman, Gordon (1963-)
Author of books for young adults
Scholastic Inc Ph: 212-343-6100
557 Broadway
New York, NY 10012
www.gordonkorman.com

Korn
Rock group
William Morris Agency Ph: 310-859-4000
1 William Morris Pl Fax: 310-859-4462
Beverly Hills, CA 90212
www.korn.com

Kornberg, Arthur, MD (1918-)
Winner (with Severo Ochoa) of the 1959 Nobel Prize in Physiology or Medicine for their discovery of the mechanisms in the biological synthesis of RNA and DNA
Dept of Biochemistry **Ph:** 650-723-4000
Beckman Center for Molecular & Genetic Medicine
Stanford University School of Medicine
279 W Campus Dr Rm B400
MC 5307
Stanford, CA 94305
biochemistry.stanford.edu/research/faculty.html

Kornheiser, Tony
Sports columnist for the Washington Post
Washington Post **Ph:** 202-334-6000
1150 15th St NW
Washington, DC 20071

Kornick, Michael
Chef and owner of mk The Restaurant in Chicago
mk Restaurant **Ph:** 312-482-9179
868 N Franklin St **Fax:** 312-482-9171
Chicago, IL 60610
www.mkchicago.com

Korver, Kyle (1981-)
Professional basketball player
Philadelphia 76ers **Ph:** 215-339-7600
Wachovia Center **Fax:** 215-339-7632
3601 S Broad St
Philadelphia, PA 19148
www.nba.com/sixers

Koskie, Corey (1973-)
Professional baseball player
Milwaukee Brewers **Ph:** 414-902-4400
Miller Park **Fax:** 414-902-4515
1 Brewers Way
Milwaukee, WI 53214
milwaukee.brewers.mlb.com

Kosters, Marvin H, PhD (1933-)
Economist; a resident scholar at the American Enterprise Institute, where he studies labor issues and income inequality
American Enterprise Institute for Public Policy Research **Ph:** 202-862-5800 **Fax:** 202-862-7177
1150 17th St NW Suite 1100
Washington, DC 20036
www.aei.org

Kot, Greg
Rock music critic for the Chicago Tribune
Chicago Tribune **Ph:** 312-222-3232
435 N Michigan Ave **Fax:** 312-222-4674
Chicago, IL 60611

Kotb, Hoda
Dateline NBC correspondent and host of Your Total Health
Dateline NBC **Ph:** 212-664-4249
30 Rockefeller Plaza
New York, NY 10112
www.msnbc.msn.com/id/3360263

Koterba, Jeff
Editorial cartoonist for the Omaha World-Herald
King Features Syndicate Inc **Ph:** 212-455-4000
888 7th Ave 2nd Fl
New York, NY 10019
www.kingfeatures.com

Kotlikoff, Laurence J, PhD (1951-)
Professor of Economics at Boston University and Research Associate at the National Bureau of Economic Research
Boston University **Ph:** 617-353-4002
Dept of Economics **Fax:** 617-353-4001
270 Bay State Rd
Boston, MA 02215
people.bu.edu/kotlikoff

Kournikova, Anna (1981-)
Professional tennis player
Octagon Athlete Representation **Ph:** 703-905-3300
1751 Pinnacle Dr Suite 1500 **Fax:** 703-905-4495
McLean, VA 22102
www.kournikova.com

Kovacevich, Richard M (1943-)
Chairman and CEO of Wells Fargo
Wells Fargo & Co **Ph:** 800-869-3557
420 Montgomery St
San Francisco, CA 94104
www.wellsfargo.com

Kovalchuk, Ilya (1983-)
Professional hockey player
Atlanta Thrashers **Ph:** 404-827-5300
Centennial Tower **Fax:** 404-827-5909
101 Marietta St NW Suite 1900
Atlanta, GA 30303
www.atlantathrashers.com

Kovaleski, John
Cartoonist, animator, illustrator; creator of the comic strip Bo Nanas
Washington Post Writers Group **Ph:** 202-334-6375 **Fax:** 202-334-5669
1150 15th St NW 9th Fl
Washington, DC 20071
www.kovaleski.com

Kovalev, Alex (1973-)
Professional hockey player
Montreal Canadiens **Ph:** 514-932-2582
1275 Saint Antoine St W **Fax:** 514-932-9296
Montreal, QC H3C5L2
www.canadiens.com

Kovel, Ralph
Antiques expert; with his wife Terry writes a syndicated column on antiques and collectibles
King Features Syndicate Inc **Ph:** 212-455-4000
888 7th Ave 2nd Fl
New York, NY 10019
www.kingfeatures.com

Kovel, Terry
Antiques expert; with her husband Ralph writes a syndicated column on antiques and collectibles
King Features Syndicate Inc **Ph:** 212-455-4000
888 7th Ave 2nd Fl
New York, NY 10019
www.kingfeatures.com

Kozlov, Vyacheslav (1972-)
Professional hockey player
Atlanta Thrashers **Ph:** 404-827-5300
Centennial Tower **Fax:** 404-827-5909
101 Marietta St NW Suite 1900
Atlanta, GA 30303
www.atlantathrashers.com

Kraddick, Kidd
Radio disc jockey & host of Kidd Kraddick in the Morning
KHKS-FM **Ph:** 214-866-8000
14001 N Dallas Pkwy Suite 300 **Fax:** 214-866-8501
Dallas, TX 75240
www.kiddlive.com

Kraft, Robert J
Owner of the New England Patriots football team; also founder of International Forest Products
New England Patriots **Ph:** 508-543-8200
1 Patriot Pl **Fax:** 508-543-0285
Foxboro, MA 02035
www.patriots.com

Krakauer, Jon (1954-)
Outdoor/adventure author (Into Thin Air);editor-at-large of Outside Magazine
Vintage/Anchor Publicity **Ph:** 212-572-2420
1745 Broadway 20th Fl
New York, NY 10019
www.randomhouse.com/anchor

Krall, Diana (1964-)
Jazz singer
William Morris Agency **Ph:** 310-859-4000
1 William Morris Pl **Fax:** 310-859-4462
Beverly Hills, CA 90212
www.dianakrall.com

Krantz, Judith (1928-)
Novelist (Scruples)
St Martin's Press **Ph:** 212-674-5151
Attn: Publicity Dept
175 5th Ave
New York, NY 10010
www.stmartins.com

Krasinski, John (1979-)
Actor
Creative Artists Agency **Ph:** 310-288-4545
9830 Wilshire Blvd **Fax:** 310-288-4800
Beverly Hills, CA 90212
www.nbc.com/The_Office

Krasner, Lee (1908-1984)
Painter; wife of Jackson Pollock
Pollock-Krasner House & Study Center **Ph:** 631-324-4929 **Fax:** 631-324-8768
830 Fireplace Rd
East Hampton, NY 11937
naples.cc.stonybrook.edu/CAS/pkhouse.nsf

Krasny, Michael P
Founder and Chairman Emeritus of CDW Corp
CDW Corp **Ph:** 847-465-6000
200 N Milwaukee Ave
Vernon Hills, IL 60061
newsroom.cdw.com/executives/board.html

Krause, Peter (1965-)
Actor
Creative Artists Agency **Ph:** 310-288-4545
9830 Wilshire Blvd **Fax:** 310-288-4800
Beverly Hills, CA 90212
www.hbo.com/sixfeetunder

Krause, Roy G
President & CEO of Spherion
Spherion Corp **Ph:** 954-308-7600
2050 Spectrum Blvd **Fax:** 954-938-7666
Fort Lauderdale, FL 33309
www.spherion.com

Krauthammer, Charles (1950-)
Syndicated columnist (politics, foreign policy, culture); also writes essays for Time magazine and contributes to several other publications.
Washington Post Writers Group — **Ph:** 202-334-6375 — **Fax:** 202-334-5669
1150 15th St NW 9th Fl
Washington, DC 20071
www.postwritersgroup.com

Kravitz, Lenny (1964-)
Rock musician, singer/songwriter
Agency for the Performing Arts — **Ph:** 310-273-0744
9200 Sunset Blvd Suite 900 — **Fax:** 310-888-4242
Beverly Hills, CA 90069
www.lennykravitz.com

Krawcheck, Sallie L
CFO and Head of Strategy for Citigroup
Citigroup Inc — **Ph:** 212-559-1000
399 Park Ave — **Fax:** 212-793-3946
New York, NY 10043
www.citigroup.com/citigroup/profiles/krawcheck

Krayzelburg, Lenny (1975-)
Olympic swimmer
Octagon Athlete Representation — **Ph:** 207-775-1500
2 Union St Suite 3000
Portland, ME 04101
www.octagonoly.com

Krehbiel, Frederick A
Co-chairman of Molex Inc, a manufacturer of electronic, electrical, and fiber optic interconnection products and systems
Molex Inc — **Ph:** 630-969-4550
2222 Wellington Ct
Lisle, IL 60532
www.molex.com

Kreis, Jason (1972-)
Professional soccer player
Real Salt Lake — **Ph:** 801-924-8585
515 S 700 East Suite 2R — **Fax:** 801-933-4713
Salt Lake City, UT 84102
www.mlsnet.com/MLS/rsl/

Krentz, Jayne Ann
Author of romantic/suspense novels; also writes as Amanda Quick and Jayne Castle
Putnam Publicity — **Ph:** 212-366-2000
375 Hudson St
New York, NY 10014
www.krentz-quick.com

Kressley, Carson (1969-)
Fashion advisor on Queer Eye for the Straight Guy
International Creative Management — **Ph:** 310-550-4000
8942 Wilshire Blvd
Beverly Hills, CA 90211
www.bravotv.com

Kreutz, Olin (1977-)
Professional football player
Chicago Bears — **Ph:** 847-295-6600
Halas Hall at Conway Park — **Fax:** 847-295-8986
1000 Football Dr
Lake Forest, IL 60045
www.chicagobears.com

Kricfalusi, John (1955-)
Animator; original creator of the Ren & Stimpy Show on Nickelodeon
Endeavor — **Ph:** 310-248-2000
9601 Wilshire Blvd 3rd Fl — **Fax:** 310-248-2020
Beverly Hills, CA 90210
www.johnkricfalusi.net

Kriegel, Robert, PhD
Business speaker/author (If it ain't broke...BREAK IT!)
16344 Sharon Way — **Ph:** 530-272-1100
Grass Valley, CA 95949 — **Fax:** 530-272-7520
www.kriegel.com

Kries, Jennifer
Dancer, choreographer, and fitness instructor
Balance — **Ph:** 212-539-3528
Sage Fitness
80 E 11th St Suite 414
New York, NY 10014
www.jenniferkries.com

Krim, Mathilde, PhD (1926-)
Research scientist; founding chairman of the American Foundation for AIDS Research (AMFAR)
American Foundation for AIDS Research — **Ph:** 212-806-1600 — **Fax:** 212-806-1601
120 Wall St
New York, NY 10005
www.amfar.org

Kristof, Kathy
Syndicated financial columnist
Tribune Media Services Inc — **Ph:** 312-222-4444
435 N Michigan Ave Suite 1500
Chicago, IL 60611
tmsfeatures.com/productlist.htm

Kristof, Nicholas D (1959-)
New York Times op-ed columnist
New York Times **Ph:** 212-556-1234
229 W 43rd St
New York, NY 10036
www.nytimes.com/pages/opinion

Kristofferson, Kris (1936-)
Singer/songwriter; actor
International Creative Management **Ph:** 310-550-4000
8942 Wilshire Blvd
Beverly Hills, CA 90211
kriskristofferson.com

Kristol, William (1952-)
Editor of The Weekly Standard and a political contributor for FOX News programs; has been a Republican Party strategist and was Chief of Staff to Vice President Dan Quayle & to Education Secretary William Bennett
The Weekly Standard **Ph:** 202-293-4900
1150 17th St NW Suite 505 **Fax:** 202-293-4901
Washington, DC 20036
www.weeklystandard.com

Kroenke, E Stanley
Owner of the Denver Nuggets basketball team, the Colorado Avalanche hockey team, and the Pepsi Center; co-owner of the St Louis Rams football team
Kroenke Sports Enterprises LLC **Ph:** 303-405-1100 **Fax:** 303-575-1920
Pepsi Center
1000 Chopper Cir
Denver, CO 80204
www.nba.com/nuggets/staff_directory/kroenke_bio.html

Kroft, Steve (1945-)
60 Minutes correspondent
60 Minutes **Ph:** 212-975-2006
555 W 57th St
New York, NY 10019
www.cbsnews.com

Kroszner, Randall S, PhD (1962-)
Member of the Board of Governors of the Federal Reserve System
Federal Reserve System **Ph:** 202-452-3000
20th St & Constitution Ave NW **Fax:** 202-452-2611
Washington, DC 20551
www.federalreserve.gov/bios

Kruger, Barbara (1945-)
Conceptual artist
Mary Boone Gallery **Ph:** 212-752-2929
745 5th Ave **Fax:** 212-752-3939
New York, NY 10151
www.maryboonegallery.com

Krugman, Paul (1953-)
New York Times op-ed columnist; also a professor of economics and international affairs at Princeton University
New York Times **Ph:** 212-556-1234
229 W 43rd St
New York, NY 10036
www.nytimes.com/pages/opinion

Krulwich, Robert
ABC News correspondent
ABC News **Ph:** 212-456-7777
77 W 66th St
New York, NY 10023
www.abcnews.go.com/WNT

Kuba, Filip (1976-)
Professional hockey player
Minnesota Wild **Ph:** 651-222-9453
317 Washington St **Fax:** 651-222-1055
Saint Paul, MN 55102
www.wild.com

Kubiak, Gary
Football coach
Houston Texans **Ph:** 832-667-2000
2 Reliant Park **Fax:** 832-667-2100
Houston, TX 77054
www.houstontexans.com

Kubovy, Itamar
Theatrical producer, writer, director; executive director of Pilobolus Dance Theatre
Pilobolus Dance Theatre **Ph:** 860-868-0538
PO Box 388 **Fax:** 860-868-0530
Washington Depot, CT 06794
www.pilobolus.com

Kucinich, Dennis (1946-)
US Representative from Ohio (Democrat)
1730 Longworth Bldg **Ph:** 202-225-5871
Washington, DC 20515 **Fax:** 202-225-5745
kucinich.house.gov

Kudelka, James (1955-)
Resident choreographer of the National Ballet of Canada
Walter Carsen Centre for the National Ballet of Canada **Ph:** 416-345-9686 **Fax:** 416-345-8323
470 Queens Quay W
Toronto, ON M5V3K4
www.national.ballet.ca

Kudelka, Marty (1974-)
Hip-hop dancer/choreographer
Bloc Agency **Ph:** 323-954-7730
5651 Wilshire Blvd Suite C
Los Angeles, CA 90036

Kudlow, Lawrence (1947-)
CEO of Kudlow & Co, an economic and investment research firm; economics commentator and host of Kudlow & Company on CNBC
Kudlow & Co LLC **Ph:** 212-644-8610
1 Dag Hammarskjold Plaza **Fax:** 212-588-1636
885 2nd Ave at 48th St 26th Fl
New York, NY 10017
www.kudlow.com

Kudrow, Lisa (1963-)
Actor
Endeavor **Ph:** 310-248-2000
9601 Wilshire Blvd 3rd Fl **Fax:** 310-248-2020
Beverly Hills, CA 90210
www.hbo.com/comeback

Kuhl, John R "Randy" Jr (1943-)
US Representative from New York (Republican)
1505 Longworth Bldg **Ph:** 202-225-3161
Washington, DC 20515 **Fax:** 202-225-5574
kuhl.house.gov

Kukoc, Toni (1968-)
Professional basketball player
Milwaukee Bucks **Ph:** 414-227-0500
Bradley Center **Fax:** 414-227-0543
1001 N 4th St
Milwaukee, WI 53203
www.nba.com/bucks

Kullman, Ellen (1956-)
Group Vice President, DuPont Safety & Protection Div
Safety & Protection Div **Ph:** 302-774-1000
DuPont **Fax:** 302-774-4399
1007 Market St
Wilmington, DE 19898
www2.dupont.com

Kulongoski, Ted (1940-)
Governor of Oregon (Democrat)
900 Court St NE **Ph:** 503-378-3111
Salem, OR 97301 **Fax:** 503-378-6827
www.governor.state.or.us

Kumin, Maxine (1925-)
Poet; served as Consultant in Poetry to the Library of Congress before that post was renamed Poet Laureate of the United States, and as the poet laureate of New Hampshire from 1989 to 1994
Anderson Literary Agency **Ph:** 212-234-0692
435 Convent Ave Suite 5 **Fax:** 212-234-0693
New York, NY 10031
www.maxinekumin.com

Kundera, Milan (1929-)
Franco-Czech novelist (The Unbearable Lightness of Being)
HarperCollins Publishers **Ph:** 212-207-7000
c/o Author Mail
10 E 53rd St
New York, NY 10022
www.harpercollins.com

Kunhardt, Dorothy
Author of Pat the Bunny, the classic interactive book for babies
Golden Books Publicity **Ph:** 212-782-9000
1745 Broadway
New York, NY 10019
www.randomhouse.com/golden

Kunhardt, Edith (1937-)
Children's book author; daughter of Dorothy Kunhardt, who was the author of Pat the Bunny
Golden Books Publicity **Ph:** 212-782-9000
1745 Broadway
New York, NY 10019
www.randomhouse.com/golden

Kunitz, Stanley (1905-)
Poet; has served twice as Poet Laureate of the US and was State Poet of New York and Chancellor of the Academy of American Poets
WW Norton & Co Inc **Ph:** 212-354-5500
500 5th Ave **Fax:** 212-869-0856
New York, NY 10110
www.nortonpoets.com

Kurtis, Bill (1940-)
Anchor of American Justice on A&E TV; is also executive producer of Cold Case Files on A&E
A & E Television Networks **Ph:** 212-210-1400
235 E 45th St
New York, NY 10017
www.aetv.com/american_justice/index.jsp

Kurtz, Howard (1953-)
Host of CNN's Reliable Sources, which scrutinizes the media for fairness and objectivity
CNN **Ph:** 202-898-7900
CNN Bldg
820 1st St NE
Washington, DC 20002
www.cnn.com/CNN/anchors_reporters

Kurzweil, Ray (1948-)
Inventor; principal developer of the first omni-font optical character recognition, the first CCD flat-bed scanner, the first text-to-speech synthesizer, and other technological inventions
Kurzweil Technologies Inc **Ph:** 781-263-0000
15 Walnut St **Fax:** 781-263-9999
Wellesley Hills, MA 02481 **TF:** 877-263-8263
www.kurzweiltech.com

Kushner, Harold S (1935-)
Rabbi Laureate of Temple Israel in Natick, Massachusetts; author (When Bad Things Happen to Good People; Who Needs God; How Good Do We Have to Be?)
Temple Israel of Natick **Ph:** 508-650-3521
145 Hartford St
Natick, MA 01760
www.randomhouse.com/knopf

Kushner, Tony (1956-)
Playwright (Angels in America)
Steven Barclay Agency **Ph:** 707-773-0654
12 Western Ave **Fax:** 707-778-1868
Petaluma, CA 94952 **TF:** 888-965-7323
www.barclayagency.com

Kuskin, Karla
Poet/author of books for children (Soap Soup, Any Me I Want to Be, Roar and More)
HarperCollins Children's Books **Ph:** 212-261-6500
1350 Ave of the Americas
New York, NY 10019
www.harperchildrens.com

Kutcher, Ashton (1978-)
Actor
Endeavor **Ph:** 310-248-2000
9601 Wilshire Blvd 3rd Fl **Fax:** 310-248-2020
Beverly Hills, CA 90210

Kuttner, Robert (1943-)
Co-founder and co-editor of The American Prospect and regularly writes for the magazine; has written several books as well
The American Prospect **Ph:** 202-776-0730
2000 L St NW Suite 717 **Fax:** 202-776-0740
Washington, DC 20036
www.prospect.org

Kwan, Michelle (1980-)
Figure skater
US Figure Skating **Ph:** 719-635-5200
20 1st St
Colorado Springs, CO 80906
www.usfigureskating.org

Kyl, Jon (1942-)
US Senator from Arizona (Republican)
730 Hart Bldg **Ph:** 202-224-4521
Washington, DC 20510 **Fax:** 202-224-2207
kyl.senate.gov

L

La Lanne, Jack (1914-)
Fitness personality
BeFit Enterprises Inc **Ph:** 805-772-6000
430 Quintana Rd **Fax:** 805-772-2590
PMB 151
Morro Bay, CA 93442
www.jacklalanne.com

La Russa, Tony (1944-)
Baseball manager
Saint Louis Cardinals **Ph:** 314-421-3060
250 Stadium Plaza **Fax:** 314-425-0640
Saint Louis, MO 63102
stlouis.cardinals.mlb.com

LaBan, Terry
Creator (with input from his wife Patty) of the comic strip Edge City
King Features Syndicate Inc **Ph:** 212-455-4000
888 7th Ave 2nd Fl
New York, NY 10019
www.kingfeatures.com

LaBelle, Patti (1944-)
Singer (R&B/soul)
Pattonium Inc **Ph:** 610-645-9034
PO Box 506
Wynnewood, PA 19096
www.pattilabelle.com

Labiner, Norah (1967-)
Novelist (Miniatures; Our Sometime Sister)
Coffee House Press **Ph:** 612-338-0125
27 N 4th St Suite 400 **Fax:** 612-338-4004
Minneapolis, MN 55401
www.coffeehousepress.org

LaBonte, Bobby (1964-)
Race car driver
Petty Enterprises — **Ph:** 336-498-2156
311 Branson Mill Rd
Randleman, NC 27317
www.bobbylabonte.com

LaChapelle, David (1968-)
Photographer (magazine & album covers, advertising, celebrity portraits); in addition to still photography, directs music videos for selected artists
CXA - Creative Exchange Agency — **Ph:** 212-414-4100 **Fax:** 212-414-0100
416 W 13th St Suite 316
New York, NY 10014
www.davidlachapelle.com

Lachey, Nick (1973-)
Actor; singer
International Creative Management — **Ph:** 310-550-4000
8942 Wilshire Blvd
Beverly Hills, CA 90211
www.nicklachey.com

Lack, Andrew R (1947-)
Chairman of the board of Sony BMG Music Entertainment
Sony BMG Music Entertainment Inc — **Ph:** 212-833-8000 **Fax:** 212-833-4583
550 Madison Ave
New York, NY 10022
www.sonybmg.com

Lacroix, Jean-Marie
Executive chef and owner of of Lacroix at The Rittenhouse in Philadelphia
Lacroix at the Rittenhouse — **Ph:** 215-790-2533
Rittenhouse Hotel — **Fax:** 215-732-3364
210 W Rittenhouse Sq — **TF:** 800-635-1042
Philadelphia, PA 19103
www.lacroixrestaurant.com

Lacy, Alan J (1954-)
Vice Chairman of Sears Holdings Corp
Sears Holdings Corp — **Ph:** 847-286-2500
3333 Beverly Rd — **Fax:** 847-286-7829
Hoffman Estates, IL 60179
www.searsholdings.com

Lafley, Alan G (1947-)
Chairman of the board, president, and CEO of Procter & Gamble
Procter & Gamble Co — **Ph:** 513-983-1100
1 Procter & Gamble Pl — **Fax:** 513-562-4500
Cincinnati, OH 45202
www.pg.com/news/management/bios_photos.jhtml

LaFrentz, Raef (1976-)
Professional basketball player
Boston Celtics — **Ph:** 617-854-8000
226 Causeway St 4th Fl — **Fax:** 617-367-4286
Boston, MA 02114
www.nba.com/celtics

Lagasse, Emeril (1959-)
Celebrity chef, author, restaurant owner, and host of Emeril Live and Essence of Emeril on the Food Network; also appears regularly on ABC News's Good Morning America
Emeril's Homebase — **Ph:** 504-524-4241
829 St Charles Ave — **Fax:** 504-523-5888
New Orleans, LA 70130
www.emerils.com

Lagattuta, Bill (1956-)
48 Hours correspondent
48 Hours — **Ph:** 212-975-4114
524 W 57th St
New York, NY 10019
www.cbsnews.com

Lagerfeld, Karl (1938-)
Fashion designer (designs for Chanel, for his own label, and for Fendi)
Chanel Inc — **Ph:** 212-688-5055
9 W 57th St 44th Fl
New York, NY 10019

LaGravenese, Richard (1959-)
Film writer, director
Creative Artists Agency — **Ph:** 310-288-4545
9830 Wilshire Blvd — **Fax:** 310-288-4800
Beverly Hills, CA 90212

LaHaye, Tim (1926-)
Author, minister, and speaker on Bible prophecy; a founder of the Pre-Trib Research Center, which aims to expose ministers to the teachings of good Bible prophecy; co-author, with Jerry Jenkins, of the Left Behind series
AMG Publishers — **Ph:** 423-894-6060
6815 Shallowford Rd — **Fax:** 423-894-9511
Chattanooga, TN 37421
www.timlahaye.com

Lahiri, Jhumpa, PhD (1967-)
Author of the short story collection Interpreter of Maladies
Houghton Mifflin Co — **Ph:** 617-351-5000
Trade Div
Adult Editorial
222 Berkeley St 8th Fl
Boston, MA 02116
www.houghtonmifflinbooks.com

LaHood, Ray (1945-)
US Representative from Illinois (Republican)
1424 Longworth Bldg **Ph:** 202-225-6201
Washington, DC 20515 **Fax:** 202-225-9249
www.house.gov/lahood

Lahti, Christine (1950-)
Actor
International Creative Management **Ph:** 310-550-4000
8942 Wilshire Blvd
Beverly Hills, CA 90211

Laimbeer, Bill (1957-)
Former NBA All Star, now a WNBA coach
Detroit Shock **Ph:** 248-377-0100
Palace at Auburn Hills **Fax:** 248-377-3260
4 Championship Dr
Auburn Hills, MI 48326
www.wnba.com/shock

Laird, Peter (1954-)
Co-creator, with Kevin Eastman, of the Teenage Mutant Ninja Turtles (comic strip, comic books, movie, etc.)
Mirage Studios **Ph:** 413-586-7066
16 Market St
Northampton, MA 01060
www.ninjaturtles.com/origin/origin.htm

Lama His Holiness the Dalai (1935-)
Exiled leader of Tibet
Wisdom Publications Inc **Ph:** 617-776-7416
199 Elm St **Fax:** 617-776-7841
Somerville, MA 02144
www.tibet.com/DL

Lamb, Wally (1950-)
Novelist (She's Come Undone)
HarperCollins Publishers **Ph:** 212-207-7000
c/o Author Mail
10 E 53rd St
New York, NY 10022
www.harpercollins.com

Lambert, Miranda (1983-)
Country singer
Buddy Lee Attractions **Ph:** 615-244-4336
38 Music Sq East Suite 300 **Fax:** 615-726-0429
Nashville, TN 37203
www.mirandalambert.com

Lambro, Donald (1940-)
Chief political correspondent for The Washington Times (his column is syndicated nationwide)
United Feature Syndicate **Ph:** 212-293-8500
200 Madison Ave
New York, NY 10016
www.unitedfeatures.com

Lamoriello, Lou
CEO, president, general manager, and head coach of the New Jersey Devils hockey team
New Jersey Devils **Ph:** 201-935-6050
Continental Airlines Arena **Fax:** 201-935-2127
50 Rt 120N
East Rutherford, NJ 07073
www.newjerseydevils.com

Lamott, Anne (1954-)
Author, humorist, recovering alcoholic, and born-again Christian; writes both fiction and nonfiction
Steven Barclay Agency **Ph:** 707-773-0654
12 Western Ave **Fax:** 707-778-1868
Petaluma, CA 94952 **TF:** 888-965-7323
www.barclayagency.com

Lampert, Edward S (1963-)
Chairman, Sears Holdings Corp; also chairman & CEO of ESL Investments
Sears Holdings Corp **Ph:** 847-286-2500
3333 Beverly Rd **Fax:** 847-286-7829
Hoffman Estates, IL 60179
www.searsholdings.com

Lampley, Jim (1949-)
Veteran sportscaster
HBO Sports **Ph:** 212-512-1000
1100 Ave of the Americas
New York, NY 10036
www.hbo.com/boxing

Lana, Wai
Yoga instructor
Wai Lana Yoga **Ph:** 888-924-5262
PO Box 6146
Malibu, CA 90264
wailana.com

Lancaster, Ralph I Jr
Trial lawyer (both civil and criminal matters, at national and international levels)
Pierce Atwood LLP **Ph:** 207-791-1100
1 Monument Sq **Fax:** 207-791-1350
Portland, ME 04101
www.pierceatwood.com

Landau, Martin (1931-)
Actor
Diverse Talent Group **Ph:** 310-201-6565
1875 Century Park E Suite 2250 **Fax:** 310-201-6572
Los Angeles, CA 90067

Landers, Ann (1918-2002)
Advice columnist; although she is deceased, Classic Ann Landers columns are still in syndication
Creators Syndicate Inc **Ph:** 310-337-7003
5777 W Century Blvd Suite 700 **Fax:** 310-337-7625
Los Angeles, CA 90045
www.creators.com

Landgren, Don Jr
Political cartoonist for The Landmark and other Central Massachusetts newspapers
The Landmark **Ph:** 508-829-5981
PO Box 546 **Fax:** 508-529-5984
Holden, MA 01520
www.donlandgren.com

Landis, John (1950-)
TV series producer/film director (An American Werewolf in Paris)
Gersh Agency **Ph:** 310-274-6611
232 N Canon Dr
Beverly Hills, CA 90210

Landis, Robyn
Health, holistic writer (Body Fueling; Herbal Defense)
Warner Books **Ph:** 212-522-7200
c/o Author Mail
1271 Ave of the Americas
New York, NY 10020
www.bodyfueling.com

Landis, Story C, PhD
Director of the National Institute of Neurological Disorders & Stroke, National Institutes of Health
National Institute of Neurological Disorders & Stroke **Ph:** 301-496-9746 **Fax:** 301-496-0296
31 Center Dr Bldg 31 Rm 8A52
MSC 2540
Bethesda, MD 20892
www.ninds.nih.gov/find_people/ninds

Landon, Allan R
Chairman, president, and CEO of Bank of Hawaii Corp
Bank of Hawaii Corp **Ph:** 808-537-8272
130 Merchant St
Honolulu, HI 96813
www.boh.com

Landrieu, Mary (1955-)
US Senator from Louisiana (Democrat)
724 Hart Bldg **Ph:** 202-224-5824
Washington, DC 20510 **Fax:** 202-224-9735
landrieu.senate.gov

Lane, Anthony (1962-)
Movie critic for The New Yorker
New Yorker Magazine **Ph:** 212-286-5400
4 Times Sq **Fax:** 212-286-5735
New York, NY 10036

Lane, Diane (1965-)
Actor
Endeavor **Ph:** 310-248-2000
9601 Wilshire Blvd 3rd Fl **Fax:** 310-248-2020
Beverly Hills, CA 90210
www.dianelane.com

Lane, Nathan (1956-)
Actor (film and theater)
United Talent Agency **Ph:** 310-273-6700
9560 Wilshire Blvd 5th Fl **Fax:** 310-247-1111
Beverly Hills, CA 90212

Lane, Robert W (1949-)
Chairman & CEO of Deere & Co
Deere & Co **Ph:** 309-765-4114
1 John Deere Pl **Fax:** 309-765-5772
Moline, IL 61265
www.deere.com

lang, kd (1961-)
Singer
Monterey Peninsula Artists/ Paradigm **Ph:** 831-375-4889 **Fax:** 831-375-2623
509 Hartnell St
Monterey, CA 93940

Lang, Robert (1970-)
Professional hockey player
Detroit Red Wings **Ph:** 313-396-7544
Joe Louis Arena **Fax:** 313-567-0296
600 Civic Center Dr
Detroit, MI 48226
www.detroitredwings.com

Lange, Dorothea (1895-1965)
Photographer
Oakland Museum of California **Ph:** 510-238-2200
1000 Oak St
Oakland, CA 94607
www.museumca.org

Lange, Jessica (1949-)
Actor
Creative Artists Agency **Ph:** 310-288-4545
9830 Wilshire Blvd **Fax:** 310-288-4800
Beverly Hills, CA 90212

Langenbrunner, Jamie (1975-)
Professional hockey player
New Jersey Devils **Ph:** 201-935-6050
Continental Airlines Arena **Fax:** 201-935-2127
50 Rt 120N
East Rutherford, NJ 07073
www.newjerseydevils.com

Langer, Bernhard (1957-)
Professional golfer
PGA Tour **Ph:** 904-285-3700
100 PGA Tour Blvd
Ponte Vedra Beach, FL 32082
www.pgatour.com/players

Langevin, James R (1964-)
US Representative from Rhode Island (Democrat)
109 Cannon Bldg **Ph:** 202-225-2735
Washington, DC 20515 **Fax:** 202-225-5976
www.house.gov/langevin

Lank, Edith
Writes a syndicated real estate column
Creators Syndicate Inc **Ph:** 310-337-7003
5777 W Century Blvd Suite 700 **Fax:** 310-337-7625
Los Angeles, CA 90045
www.creators.com

Lanni, J Terrence (1943-)
Chairman and CEO of MGM Mirage
MGM Mirage Inc **Ph:** 702-693-7123
3600 Las Vegas Blvd S
Las Vegas, NV 89109
www.mgm-mirage.com

Lansbury, Angela (1925-)
Actor
International Creative Management **Ph:** 310-550-4000
8942 Wilshire Blvd
Beverly Hills, CA 90211

Lantos, Tom (1928-)
US Representative from California (Democrat)
2413 Rayburn Bldg **Ph:** 202-225-3531
Washington, DC 20515
lantos.house.gov

Lanza, Frank
Chairman and CEO of L-3 Communications Holdings Inc
L-3 Communications Holdings Inc **Ph:** 212-697-1111
600 3rd Ave
New York, NY 10016
www.l-3com.com/about_l3

LaPaglia, Anthony (1959-)
Actor
International Creative Management **Ph:** 310-550-4000
8942 Wilshire Blvd
Beverly Hills, CA 90211
www.cbs.com/primetime/without_a_trace

Lapham, Lewis H (1935-)
Editor & writer; has written several books of essays and writes a monthly essay for Harper's Magazine (Notebook)
Harper's Magazine **Ph:** 212-420-5720
666 Broadway 11th Fl **Fax:** 212-228-5889
New York, NY 10012
www.harpers.org/LewisLapham.html

LaPierre, Wayne Jr (1949-)
Executive Vice President of the National Rifle Association
National Rifle Assn **Ph:** 703-267-1000
11250 Waples Mill Rd **Fax:** 703-267-3957
Fairfax, VA 22030
www.nramemberscouncils.com/wayne

Lapointe, Martin (1973-)
Professional hockey player
Chicago Blackhawks **Ph:** 312-455-7000
United Center **Fax:** 312-455-7041
1901 W Madison St
Chicago, IL 60612
www.chicagoblackhawks.com

Larchet, Patti
Vice Chairman & CEO of Jenny Craig
Jenny Craig International **Ph:** 760-696-4000
5770 Fleet St
Carlsbad, CA 92008
www.jennycraig.com/corporate

Larry the Cable Guy (1963-)
Comedian; real name is Dan Whitney
Parallel Entertainment **Ph:** 310-279-1123
9255 Sunset Blvd Suite 1040 **Fax:** 310-279-1147
Los Angeles, CA 90069
www.larrythecableguy.com

Larsen, Blaine (1986-)
Country singer/songwriter
Monterey Peninsula Artists/Paradigm **Ph:** 615-251-4400
124 12th Ave S Suite 410 **Fax:** 615-251-4401
Nashville, TN 37203
www.blainelarsen.com

Larsen, Rick (1965-)
US Representative from Washington (Democrat)
107 Cannon Bldg **Ph:** 202-225-2605
Washington, DC 20515 **Fax:** 202-225-4420
www.house.gov/larsen

Larson, Edward J, PhD (1953-)
The first sitting law professor to receive the Pulitzer Prize in History, which he was awarded for his 1997 book, Summer for the Gods: The Scopes Trial and America's Continuing Debate Over Science and Religion
University of Georgia **Ph:** 706-542-5191
School of Law **Fax:** 706-542-5001
Rusk Hall 329
Athens, GA 30602
www.law.uga.edu/academics/profiles

Larson, John
Dateline NBC's West Coast correspondent
NBC News **Ph:** 818-840-4444
3000 W Alameda Ave
Burbank, CA 91523
www.msnbc.msn.com/id/3360263

Larson, John B (1948-)
US Representative from Connecticut (Democrat)
1005 Longworth Bldg **Ph:** 202-225-2265
Washington, DC 20515 **Fax:** 202-225-1031
www.house.gov/larson

Larson, Jonathan (1960-1996)
Composer-lyricist-librettist of the Broadway hit Rent (died from an aortic aneurysm two weeks before it opened on Broadway)
Jonathan Larson Performing Arts Foundation **Ph:** 212-529-0814 **Fax:** 212-253-7604
PO Box 672
Prince St Station
New York, NY 10012
www.jlpaf.org

Larson, Julie
Creator of the comic panel The Dinette Set
Creators Syndicate Inc **Ph:** 310-337-7003
5777 W Century Blvd Suite 700 **Fax:** 310-337-7625
Los Angeles, CA 90045
www.creators.com

Larson, Lars
Host of a call-in radio show on political and other issues
Westwood One **Ph:** 212-641-2000
40 W 57th St 5th Fl **Fax:** 212-641-2172
New York, NY 10019
www.larslarson.com

Lassen, Christian Riese (1949-)
Marine artist (painting & sculpture)
Lassen International 3500 Las Vegas Blvd S # Suite M7 **Ph:** 702-792-9292 **Fax:** 702-796-3707
Las Vegas, NV 89109
www.lassenart.com

Lasseter, John A (1957-)
Executive Vice President, Creative, and a founding member of Pixar Animation Studios; oversees all of Pixar's films and associated projects and was the director of Toy Story and A Bug's Life
Pixar Animation Studios **Ph:** 510-752-3000
1200 Park Ave **Fax:** 510-752-3151
Emeryville, CA 94608
www.pixar.com

Last, Eugenia
Astrologer who writes the syndicated column The Last Word in Astrology
Universal Press Syndicate **Ph:** 816-932-6600
4520 Main St
Kansas City, MO 64111
www.astroadvice.com

Latham, Tom (1948-)
US Representative from Iowa (Republican)
2447 Rayburn Bldg **Ph:** 202-225-5476
Washington, DC 20515 **Fax:** 202-225-3301
www.tomlatham.house.gov

LaTourette, Steve (1954-)
US Representative from Ohio (Republican)
2453 Rayburn Bldg **Ph:** 202-225-5731
Washington, DC 20515 **Fax:** 202-225-3307
www.house.gov/latourette

Lauder, Leonard A
Chairman of the Estee Lauder Cos and the son of Estee Lauder
Estee Lauder Cos Inc **Ph:** 212-572-4200
767 5th Ave **Fax:** 212-572-3941
New York, NY 10153
www.elcompanies.com

Lauder, William P
President and CEO of the Estee Lauder Companies; grandson of Estee Lauder
Estee Lauder Cos Inc **Ph:** 212-572-4200
767 5th Ave
New York, NY 10153
www.elcompanies.com

Lauer, Matt (1957-)
Today Show co-anchor
Today Show **Ph:** 212-664-4249
30 Rockefeller Plaza
New York, NY 10112
www.msnbc.msn.com/id/3079108

Laughlin, Natalie
Plus-size model
Wilhelmina Models Inc **Ph:** 212-473-0700
300 Park Ave S 2nd Fl **Fax:** 212-473-3223
New York, NY 10010
www.natalielaughlin.com

Laughlin, Robert B, PhD (1950-)
Winner (with two other scientists) of the 1998 Nobel Prize in Physics for the discovery of a new form of quantum fluid with fractionally charged excitations
Stanford University **Ph:** 650-723-4563
Dept of Physics **Fax:** 650-723-9389
McCullough Bldg Rm 342
Stanford, CA 94305
www.stanford.edu/dept/physics

Lauper, Cyndi (1953-)
Pop singer
United Talent Agency **Ph:** 310-273-6700
9560 Wilshire Blvd 5th Fl **Fax:** 310-247-1111
Beverly Hills, CA 90212
www.cyndilauper.com

Lauren, Ralph (1939-)
Fashion designer; chairman and CEO of Polo Ralph Lauren Corp
Polo Ralph Lauren Corp **Ph:** 800-377-7656
650 Madison Ave
New York, NY 10022
investor.polo.com

Laurie, Greg
Televangelist and senior pastor of Harvest Christian Fellowship in Riverside, California
Harvest Christian Fellowship **Ph:** 951-687-6902
6115 Arlington Ave **Fax:** 951-687-4102
Riverside, CA 92504
www.harvest.org

Laurie, Hugh (1959-)
Actor
Gersh Agency **Ph:** 310-274-6611
232 N Canon Dr
Beverly Hills, CA 90210
www.fox.com/house

Laurie, William J
Owner and chairman of Paige Sports Entertainment, which owns the St. Louis Blues hockey team
Saint Louis Blues **Ph:** 314-622-2500
Savvis Center **Fax:** 314-622-2582
1401 Clark Ave
Saint Louis, MO 63103
www.stlouisblues.com

Lautenberg, Frank R (1924-)
US Senator from New Jersey (Democrat)
324 Hart Bldg **Ph:** 202-224-3224
Washington, DC 20510 **Fax:** 202-228-4054
lautenberg.senate.gov

Lavigne, Avril (1984-)
Singer
Nettwerk Management **Ph:** 604-654-2929
1650 W 2nd Ave **Fax:** 604-654-1993
Vancouver, BC V6J4R3
www.avril-lavigne.com

Lavin, Cheryl
Writes Tales from the Front, a syndicated newspaper column on relationships
Tribune Media Services Inc **Ph:** 312-222-4444
435 N Michigan Ave Suite 1500
Chicago, IL 60611
tmsfeatures.com/productlist.htm

Lavin, Leonard H
Chairman Emeritus of Alberto-Culver
Alberto-Culver Co **Ph:** 708-450-3100
2525 W Armitage Ave **Fax:** 708-450-3435
Melrose Park, IL 60160
www.alberto.com/investing.cfm

Laviolette, Peter (1964-)
Hockey coach
Carolina Hurricanes **Ph:** 919-467-7825
RBC Center **Fax:** 919-462-7030
1400 Edwards Mill Rd
Raleigh, NC 27607
www.carolinahurricanes.com

Law, Jude (1972-)
Actor
Endeavor **Ph:** 310-248-2000
9601 Wilshire Blvd 3rd Fl **Fax:** 310-248-2020
Beverly Hills, CA 90210

Lawler, Jerry (1949-)
Wrestler
World Wrestling Entertainment Inc **Ph:** 203-352-8600
1241 E Main St
Stamford, CT 06902
www.kinglawler.com

Lawler, Joseph
President & CEO of CMGI
CMGI Inc **Ph:** 781-663-5001
1100 Winter St Suite 4600
Waltham, MA 02451
www.cmgi.com

Lawrence, Jacob (1917-2000)
African American artist
Phillips Collection **Ph:** 202-387-2151
1600 21st St NW **Fax:** 202-387-2436
Washington, DC 20009
www.phillipscollection.org/html/collect.html

Lawrence, Martha C
Author of an astrological mystery series that features psychic detective Elizabeth Chase
St Martin's Press **Ph:** 212-674-5151
Attn: Publicity Dept
175 5th Ave
New York, NY 10010
www.marthalawrence.com

Lawrence, Martin (1965-)
Comedian; actor
United Talent Agency **Ph:** 310-273-6700
9560 Wilshire Blvd 5th Fl **Fax:** 310-247-1111
Beverly Hills, CA 90212

Lawson, Terry
Entertainment columnist for the Detroit Free Press
Detroit Free Press **Ph:** 313-222-6400
600 W Fort St **Fax:** 313-222-5981
Detroit, MI 48226

Laybourne, Geraldine
Founder, chairman, and CEO of Oxygen Media; was also the creative and business force behind Nickelodeon and Nick at Nite
Oxygen Media Inc **Ph:** 212-651-2000
75 9th Ave **Fax:** 212-651-2099
New York, NY 10011
www.oxygen.com

Lazarus, Mell (1927-)
Creator of the comic strips Momma and Miss Peach; has also written novels
Creators Syndicate Inc **Ph:** 310-337-7003
5777 W Century Blvd Suite 700 **Fax:** 310-337-7625
Los Angeles, CA 90045
www.creators.com

Lazarus, Shelly (1947-)
Chairman & CEO of Ogilvy & Mather Worldwide
Ogilvy & Mather Worldwide **Ph:** 212-237-4000
309 W 49th St **Fax:** 212-237-5123
New York, NY 10019
www.ogilvy.com

Lazear, Edward P, PhD (1948-)
Chairman of the White House Council of Economic Advisers
Council of Economic Advisers **Ph:** 202-395-5084
1800 G St NW 8th Fl **Fax:** 202-395-6958
Washington, DC 20502
www.whitehouse.gov/cea

Le Batard, Dan
Sports columnist; also contributor to ESPN
Miami Herald **Ph:** 305-350-2111
1 Herald Plaza
Miami, FL 33132
www.miami.com/mld/miamiherald/news/columnists

Le Carre, John (1931-)
Author of espionage novels (The Spy Who Came in From the Cold)
Little Brown & Co **Ph:** 212-522-7200
Author Mail
1271 Ave of the Americas
New York, NY 10020
www.johnlecarre.com

Le Guin, Ursula K (1929-)
Author of science fiction and fantasy novels (including the Earthsea series) and stories; also writes children's books and poetry
Virginia Kidd Agency **Ph:** 570-296-6205
PO Box 278 **Fax:** 570-296-7266
Milford, PA 18337
www.ursulakleguin.com

Leach, Jim (1942-)
US Representative from Iowa (Republican)
2186 Rayburn Bldg **Ph:** 202-225-6576
Washington, DC 20515 **Fax:** 202-226-1278
www.house.gov/leach

Leahy, Patrick J (1940-)
US Senator from Vermont (Democrat)
433 Russell Bldg **Ph:** 202-224-4242
Washington, DC 20510 **Fax:** 202-224-3479
leahy.senate.gov

Leary, Denis (1957-)
Actor; comedian
Creative Artists Agency **Ph:** 310-288-4545
9830 Wilshire Blvd **Fax:** 310-288-4800
Beverly Hills, CA 90212

Leavitt, David (1961-)
Author of short stories and novels
Bloomsbury USA **Ph:** 646-307-5858
175 5th Ave Suite 300 **Fax:** 212-780-0115
New York, NY 10010
www.bloomsburyusa.com

Leavitt, Michael O (1951-)
US Secretary of Health & Human Services
US Dept of Health & Human Services **Ph:** 202-690-7000
Fax: 202-690-7203
200 Independence Ave SW
Washington, DC 20201
www.hhs.gov/about/bios

LeBlanc, Matt (1967-)
Actor
Endeavor — **Ph:** 310-248-2000
9601 Wilshire Blvd 3rd Fl — **Fax:** 310-248-2020
Beverly Hills, CA 90210
www.nbc.com/Joey

Leblang, Bonnie Tandy
Writes Supermarket Sampler (with Carolyn Wyman), a weekly column about new grocery store items
Universal Press Syndicate — **Ph:** 816-932-6600
4520 Main St
Kansas City, MO 64111
www.uexpress.com

Lebowitz, Fran (1950-)
Author (humor)
William Morris Agency — **Ph:** 212-586-5100
1325 Ave of the Americas — **Fax:** 212-246-3583
New York, NY 10019
www.wma.com/fran_lebowitz/summary

Lecavalier, Vincent (1980-)
Professional hockey player
Tampa Bay Lightning — **Ph:** 813-301-6600
St Pete Times Forum — **Fax:** 813-301-1487
401 Channelside Dr
Tampa, FL 33602
www.tampabaylightning.com

Lechter, Sharon L
Co-author (with Robert Kiyosaki) of the Rich Dad series of books and CEO of the Rich Dad Co.
Rich Dad Co — **Ph:** 480-998-6971
4330 N Civic Ctr Plaza
Suite 101
Scottsdale, AZ 85251
www.richdad.com

Leckey, Andrew
Syndicated columnist (Successful Investing) and author (Global Investing)
Warner Books — **Ph:** 212-522-7200
c/o Author Mail
1271 Ave of the Americas
New York, NY 10020
www.twbookmark.com

Leclair, John (1969-)
Professional hockey player
Pittsburgh Penguins — **Ph:** 412-642-1300
1 Chatham Center Suite 400 — **Fax:** 412-642-1859
Pittsburgh, PA 15219
www.pittsburghpenguins.com

Leder, Mimi (1957-)
Movie director
International Creative Management — **Ph:** 310-550-4000
8942 Wilshire Blvd
Beverly Hills, CA 90211

Ledger, Heath (1979-)
Actor
Creative Artists Agency — **Ph:** 310-288-4545
9830 Wilshire Blvd — **Fax:** 310-288-4800
Beverly Hills, CA 90212

LeDoux, Harold (1926-)
Draws the comic strip Judge Parker, which is written by Woody Wilson
King Features Syndicate Inc — **Ph:** 212-455-4000
888 7th Ave 2nd Fl
New York, NY 10019
www.kingfeatures.com

Lee, Ang (1954-)
Film director
Creative Artists Agency — **Ph:** 310-288-4545
9830 Wilshire Blvd — **Fax:** 310-288-4800
Beverly Hills, CA 90212

Lee, Barbara (1946-)
US Representative from California (Democrat)
1724 Longworth Bldg — **Ph:** 202-225-2661
Washington, DC 20515 — **Fax:** 202-225-9817
www.house.gov/lee

Lee, Carlos (1976-)
Professional baseball player
Milwaukee Brewers — **Ph:** 414-902-4400
Miller Park — **Fax:** 414-902-4515
1 Brewers Way
Milwaukee, WI 53214
milwaukee.brewers.mlb.com

Lee, Cyndi
Yoga teacher and director of the OM yoga center
OM Yoga — **Ph:** 212-254-9642
826 Broadway 6th Fl — **Fax:** 212-254-7884
New York, NY 10003
www.omyoga.com

Lee, David M, PhD (1931-)
Winner (with two other scientists) of the 1996 Nobel Prize in Physics for the discovery of superfluidity in helium-3
Cornell University — **Ph:** 607-255-5286
Laboratory of Atomic & Solid State Physics — **Fax:** 607-255-6428
610 Clark Hall
Ithaca, NY 14853
www.lassp.cornell.edu

Lee, Debra
Chairman and CEO of Black Entertainment Television (BET)
Black Entertainment Television Inc **Ph:** 202-608-2000
1900 W Place NE
Washington, DC 20018
www.bet.com

Lee, Derrek (1975-)
Professional baseball player
Chicago Cubs **Ph:** 773-404-2827
Wrigley Field **Fax:** 773-404-4129
1060 W Addison St
Chicago, IL 60613
chicago.cubs.mlb.com

Lee, Harper (1926-)
Author of To Kill a Mockingbird
HarperCollins Publishers **Ph:** 212-207-7000
c/o Author Mail
10 E 53rd St
New York, NY 10022
www.harpercollins.com

Lee, Jason (1970-)
Actor
United Talent Agency **Ph:** 310-273-6700
9560 Wilshire Blvd 5th Fl **Fax:** 310-247-1111
Beverly Hills, CA 90212
www.nbc.com/My_Name_Is_Earl

Lee, Jeanette (1971-)
Professional pool player known as the Black Widow
Octagon Athlete Representation **Ph:** 703-905-3300
1751 Pinnacle Dr Suite 1500 **Fax:** 703-905-4495
McLean, VA 22102
www.jeanettelee.com

Lee, Mike
ABC News correspondent; does Road to Anywhere reports for World News Tonight
ABC News **Ph:** 212-456-7777
77 W 66th St
New York, NY 10023
www.abcnews.go.com/WNT

Lee, Spike (1957-)
Movie director and producer
William Morris Agency **Ph:** 212-586-5100
1325 Ave of the Americas **Fax:** 212-246-3583
New York, NY 10019
www.wma.com/spike_lee/summary

Lee, Stan (1922-)
Chairman of Marvel Comics and Marvel Films and creator of comic book heroes such as Spiderman and The Incredible Hulk; the comic strip The Amazing Spider-Man is written by Lee and drawn by his brother, Larry Lieber
King Features Syndicate Inc **Ph:** 212-455-4000
888 7th Ave 2nd Fl
New York, NY 10019
www.kingfeatures.com

Lee, Tommy (1962-)
Rock music personality
Creative Artists Agency **Ph:** 310-288-4545
9830 Wilshire Blvd **Fax:** 310-288-4800
Beverly Hills, CA 90212
www.tommylee.tv

Lee, Vic
Creator of the comic panel Pardon My Planet
King Features Syndicate Inc **Ph:** 212-455-4000
888 7th Ave 2nd Fl
New York, NY 10019
www.kingfeatures.com

Lee, William F
Trial lawyer whose practice concentrates on intellectual property and commercial litigation; in the 1980s, served as associate counsel to Independent Counsel Lawrence E. Walsh in the Iran-Contra investigation
Wilmer Cutler Pickering Hale & Dorr LLP **Ph:** 617-526-6556 **Fax:** 617-526-5000
60 State St
Boston, MA 02109
www.wilmerhale.com

Leetch, Brian (1968-)
Professional hockey player
Boston Bruins **Ph:** 617-624-1900
1 FleetCenter Pl Suite 250 **Fax:** 617-523-7184
Boston, MA 02114
www.bostonbruins.com

Leftwich, Byron (1980-)
Professional football player
Jacksonville Jaguars **Ph:** 904-633-6000
1 Alltel Stadium Pl **Fax:** 904-633-6050
Jacksonville, FL 32202
www.jaguars.com

Legace, Manny (1973-)
Professional hockey player
Detroit Red Wings **Ph:** 313-396-7544
Joe Louis Arena **Fax:** 313-567-0296
600 Civic Center Dr
Detroit, MI 48226
www.detroitredwings.com

Leguizamo, John (1964-)
Actor and comedian
William Morris Agency **Ph:** 310-859-4000
1 William Morris Pl **Fax:** 310-859-4462
Beverly Hills, CA 90212

Lehane, Dennis (1966-)
Novelist (Mystic River)
HarperCollins Publishers **Ph:** 212-207-7000
c/o Author Mail
10 E 53rd St
New York, NY 10022
www.dennislehanebooks.com

Lehman, John F (1942-)
Former Secretary of the Navy; member of the 9/11 Commission
JF Lehman & Co **Ph:** 212-634-0100
450 Park Ave 6th Fl **Fax:** 212-634-1155
New York, NY 10022
www.johnflehman.com

Lehman, Tom (1959-)
Professional golfer
SFX Sports Group **Ph:** 202-686-2000
5335 Wisconsin Ave NW **Fax:** 202-686-5050
Suite 850
Washington, DC 20015
www.pgatour.com/players

Lehrer, Jim (1934-)
Anchor of The Newshour with Jim Lehrer on PBS
MacNeil/Lehrer Productions **Ph:** 703-998-2138
2700 S Quincy St Suite 250
Arlington, VA 22206
www.pbs.org/newshour/ww/jim_lehrer.html

Lehtinen, Jere (1973-)
Professional hockey player
Dallas Stars **Ph:** 214-387-5500
2601 Ave of the Stars **Fax:** 214-387-3599
Frisco, TX 75034
www.dallasstars.com

Lehtonen, Kari (1983-)
Professional hockey player
Atlanta Thrashers **Ph:** 404-827-5300
Centennial Tower **Fax:** 404-827-5909
101 Marietta St NW Suite 1900
Atlanta, GA 30303
www.atlantathrashers.com

Leibovitz, Annie (1949-)
Photographer (magazine/celebrity)
Art+Commerce **Ph:** 212-206-0737
755 Washington St **Fax:** 212-463-7267
New York, NY 10014
www.artandcommerce.com

Leifer, Carol (1956-)
Comedian & comedy writer
Creative Artists Agency **Ph:** 310-288-4545
9830 Wilshire Blvd **Fax:** 310-288-4800
Beverly Hills, CA 90212

Leigh, Jennifer Jason (1962-)
Actor
Endeavor **Ph:** 310-248-2000
9601 Wilshire Blvd 3rd Fl **Fax:** 310-248-2020
Beverly Hills, CA 90210

Leinart, Matt (1983-)
USC football player drafted by the Arizona Cardinals in 2006
Arizona Cardinals **Ph:** 602-379-0101
8701 S Hardy Dr **Fax:** 602-379-1819
Tempe, AZ 85284
www.azcardinals.com

Leipold, Craig L
Owner of the Nashville Predators hockey franchise
Nashville Predators **Ph:** 615-770-2300
Gaylord Entertainment Center **Fax:** 615-770-2309
501 Broadway
Nashville, TN 37203
www.nashvillepredators.com

Lelie, Ashley (1980-)
Professional football player
Denver Broncos **Ph:** 303-649-9000
13655 Broncos Pkwy **Fax:** 303-649-9354
Englewood, CO 80112
www.denverbroncos.com

Lemaire, Jacques (1945-)
Hockey coach
Minnesota Wild **Ph:** 651-222-9453
317 Washington St **Fax:** 651-222-1055
Saint Paul, MN 55102
www.wild.com

Lemieux, Mario (1965-)
Hall of fame hockey player (retired) and owner of the Pittsburgh Penguins hockey franchise
Pittsburgh Penguins **Ph:** 412-642-1300
1 Chatham Center Suite 400 **Fax:** 412-642-1859
Pittsburgh, PA 15219
www.pittsburghpenguins.com

Lenard, Voshon (1973-)
Professional basketball player
Portland Trail Blazers **Ph:** 503-234-9291
1 Center Ct Suite 200 **Fax:** 503-736-2187
Portland, OR 97227
www.nba.com/blazers

L'Engle, Madeleine (1918-)
Author of books for children and young adults (A Wrinkle in Time)
Random House Children's Books **Ph:** 212-782-9000
Publicity Dept
1745 Broadway
New York, NY 10019
www.madeleinelengle.com

Lennox, Annie (1954-)
Singer; also performs with Dave Stewart as the Eurythmics
Creative Artists Agency **Ph:** 310-288-4545
9830 Wilshire Blvd **Fax:** 310-288-4800
Beverly Hills, CA 90212
www.annielennox.co.uk

Lennox, Betty (1976-)
Professional basketball player
Seattle Storm **Ph:** 206-281-5800
351 Elliott Ave W Suite 500
Seattle, WA 98119
www.wnba.com/storm

Lenny, Richard H
Chairman, president, and CEO of the Hershey Co
Hershey Co **Ph:** 717-534-6799
100 Crystal A Dr
Hershey, PA 17033
www.hersheyfoods.com/about/directors.asp

Leno, Jay (1950-)
Comedian; host of The Tonight Show
NBC **Ph:** 818-840-4444
The Tonight Show with Jay Leno
3000 W Alameda Ave
Burbank, CA 91523
www.nbc.com/The_Tonight_Show_with_Jay_Leno

Lentz, Nathanael V
President & CEO of VerticalNet
VerticalNet Inc **Ph:** 610-407-3500
400 Chester Field Pkwy
Malvern, PA 19355
www.verticalnet.com

Leo, John (1935-)
Contributing editor and columnist at US News & World Report
US News & World Report **Ph:** 202-955-2000
1050 Thomas Jefferson St NW **Fax:** 202-955-2685
Washington, DC 20007
www.usnews.com

Leonard, Elmore (1925-)
Author of western novels & off-beat mysteries, several of which have been made into movies
HarperCollins Publishers **Ph:** 212-207-7000
c/o Author Mail
10 E 53rd St
New York, NY 10022
www.elmoreleonard.com

Leonard, John (1939-)
Critic for CBS News Sunday Morning
CBS News Sunday Morning **Ph:** 212-975-4114
Box O
524 W 57th St
New York, NY 10019
www.cbsnews.com

Leonard, Justin (1972-)
Professional golfer
Hambric Sports Management **Ph:** 214-720-7179
2 Turtle Creek Village **Fax:** 214-720-7787
3838 Oak Lawn Ave Suite 750
Dallas, TX 75219
www.justinleonard.com

Leoni, Tea (1966-)
Actor
United Talent Agency **Ph:** 310-273-6700
9560 Wilshire Blvd 5th Fl **Fax:** 310-247-1111
Beverly Hills, CA 90212

Leonsis, Ted
Vice Chairman of AOL LLC and president of AOL Audience Business; majority owner of the Washington Capitals NHL team
AOL LLC **Ph:** 703-265-1000
22000 AOL Way
Dulles, VA 20166
corp.aol.com

Lepore, Dawn G
Chairman, president, and CEO of drugstore.com
Drugstore.com Inc **Ph:** 425-372-3200
411 108th Ave NE Suite 1400 **Fax:** 425-372-3800
Bellevue, WA 98004
www.drugstore.com

Lerach, William S (1946-)
Considered one of the leading securities lawyers in the US; is chief counsel in some of the largest and highest profile securities class action and corporate derivative suits in recent years, including Enron, Dynegy, Qwest, WorldCom, and AOL/Time Warner
Lerach Coughlin Stoia Geller Rudman & Robbins LLP **Ph:** 619-231-1058
Fax: 619-231-7423
655 W Broadway Suite 1900 **TF:** 800-449-4900
San Diego, CA 92101
www.lerachlaw.com

Lerman, Robert, PhD
A professor of economics at American University and senior fellow in labor and social policy at the Urban Institute; a leading expert on how education, employment, and family structure work together to affect economic well-being
American University **Ph:** 202-885-3761
Dept of Economics **Fax:** 202-885-3790
4400 Massachusetts Ave NW
Washington, DC 20016
www.american.edu/cas/faculty.shtml

Lerner, Michael
Rabbi of Beyt Tikkun, author, and editor of TIKKUN magazine: A Bimonthly Jewish Critique of Politics, Culture and Society
Tikkun Magazine **Ph:** 510-644-1200
2342 Shattuk Ave Suite 1200
Berkeley, CA 94704
www.tikkun.org

Lerner, Nathan (1913-1999)
Illinois photographer
Stephen Daiter Gallery **Ph:** 312-787-3350
311 W Superior St Suite 404 **Fax:** 312-787-3354
Chicago, IL 60610
www.stephendaitergallery.com

Lerner, Randolph D (1962-)
Chairman of MBNA Corp; owner of the Cleveland Browns football team
Cleveland Browns **Ph:** 440-891-5000
76 Lou Groza Blvd **Fax:** 440-891-5009
Berea, OH 44017
www.clevelandbrowns.com

Lesar, David J (1954-)
Chairman of the Board, president, and CEO of Halliburton
Halliburton Co **Ph:** 713-759-2600
1401 McKinney St Suite 2400
Houston, TX 77010
www.halliburton.com/about/exec.jsp

Leslie, Lisa (1972-)
Professional basketball player
Los Angeles Sparks **Ph:** 310-341-1000
2151 E Grand Ave Suite 100 **Fax:** 310-341-1029
El Segundo, CA 90245
www.wnba.com/sparks

Lessig, Lawrence (1961-)
Professor of Law at Stanford Law School and founder of the school's Center for Internet and Society; argued against interpretations of copyright that could stifle innovation and discourse online in Eldred vs Ashcroft
Stanford University Law School **Ph:** 650-725-2565
Crown Quadrangle
559 Nathan Abbott Way
Stanford, CA 94305
www.lessig.org

Lessing, Doris (1919-)
Author of novels and short stories
HarperCollins Publishers **Ph:** 212-207-7000
c/o Author Mail
10 E 53rd St
New York, NY 10022
www.harpercollins.com

Lester, Julius (1939-)
Author of fiction, nonfiction (Autobiography of God), children's books (To Be A Slave), and poetry
Dial Publicity **Ph:** 212-366-2000
345 Hudson St
New York, NY 10014
us.penguingroup.com

Lethem, Jonathan
Fiction author (Motherless Brooklyn; Fortress of Solitude)
Vintage/Anchor Publicity **Ph:** 212-572-2420
1745 Broadway 20th Fl
New York, NY 10019
www.randomhouse.com/vintage

Letterman, David (1947-)
Host of the Late Show with David Letterman
CBS **Ph:** 212-975-5300
The Late Show with David Letterman **Fax:** 212-975-4780
1697 Broadway
New York, NY 10019
www.cbs.com

Letts, Billie
Fiction author (Where the Heart Is; The Honk & Holler Opening Soon)
Warner Books **Ph:** 212-522-7200
c/o Author Mail
1271 Ave of the Americas
New York, NY 10020
www.twbookmark.com

Levin, Carl (1934-)
US Senator from Michigan (Democrat)
269 Russell Bldg **Ph:** 202-224-6221
Washington, DC 20510 **Fax:** 202-224-1388
levin.senate.gov

Levin, Ira (1929-)
Novelist (The Stepford Wives, Rosemary's Baby); also wrote Deathtrap, the longest running thriller in Broadway history
HarperCollins Publishers **Ph:** 212-207-7000
c/o Author Mail
10 E 53rd St
New York, NY 10022
www.harpercollins.com

Levin, Joseph J Jr (1943-)
Founder (with Morris Dees) of the Southern Poverty Law Center
Southern Poverty Law Center **Ph:** 334-956-8200
400 Washington Ave
Montgomery, AL 36104
www.splcenter.org

Levin, Sander M (1931-)
US Representative from Michigan (Democrat)
2300 Rayburn Bldg **Ph:** 202-225-4961
Washington, DC 20515 **Fax:** 202-226-1033
www.house.gov/levin

Levine, Howard
Chairman and CEO of Family Dollar Stores Inc
Family Dollar Stores Inc **Ph:** 704-847-6961
10401 Monroe Rd
Matthews, NC 28105
www.familydollar.com

Levine, James (1943-)
Conductor and pianist; music director of the Boston Symphony Orchestra and of the Metropolitan Opera
Boston Symphony Orchestra **Ph:** 617-266-1492
301 Massachusetts Ave
Boston, MA 02115
www.bso.org

Levine, Philip (1928-)
Poet
Knopf Publishing/Author Mail **Ph:** 212-782-9000
1745 Broadway
New York, NY 10019
www.randomhouse.com/knopf

Leving, Jeffery M
Attorney who represents fathers in matters of joint custody; was the Chicago lawyer involved with the Elian Gonzalez case
Law Offices of Jeffery M Leving Ltd **Ph:** 312-807-3990
19 S LaSalle St Suite 450
Chicago, IL 60603
www.dadsrights.com

Levinson, Arthur, PhD
Chairman and CEO of Genentech Inc
Genentech Inc **Ph:** 650-225-1000
1 DNA Way **Fax:** 650-225-6000
South San Francisco, CA 94080
www.gene.com/gene/about/management

Levinson, Barry (1942-)
Director/screenwriter/producer
International Creative Management **Ph:** 310-550-4000
8942 Wilshire Blvd
Beverly Hills, CA 90211
www.levinson.com

Levitt, Zola
Jewish Christian televangelist
Zola Levitt Ministries **Ph:** 214-696-8844
PO Box 12268
Dallas, TX 75225
www.levitt.com

Levy, Eugene (1946-)
Actor, writer
United Talent Agency **Ph:** 310-273-6700
9560 Wilshire Blvd 5th Fl **Fax:** 310-247-1111
Beverly Hills, CA 90212

Levy, Robert W
Mayor of Atlantic City, New Jersey
1301 Bacharach Blvd Suite 706 **Ph:** 609-347-5400
Atlantic City, NJ 08401 **Fax:** 609-347-5638
www.cityofatlanticcity.org

Levy, Steve (1965-)
Sports broadcaster
ESPN **Ph:** 860-585-2000
ESPN Plaza
935 Middle St
Bristol, CT 06010
sports.espn.go.com/espntv/espnGuide

Lewent, Judy C
Executive Vice President, CFO, and President of Human Health Asia, Merck & Co.; considered one of the most powerful women in US business
Merck & Co Inc **Ph:** 908-423-1000
1 Merck Dr **Fax:** 908-735-3184
PO Box 100
Whitehouse Station, NJ 08889
www.merck.com

Lewinter, Mel
Chairman of Universal Motown Records Group
Universal Motown Records Group **Ph:** 212-373-0600
1755 Broadway 7th Fl
New York, NY 10019

Lewis, Aylwin B (1955-)
President & CEO, Sears Holdings Corp
Sears Holdings Corp **Ph:** 847-286-2500
3333 Beverly Rd **Fax:** 847-286-7829
Hoffman Estates, IL 60179
www.searsholdings.com

Lewis, Carl (1961-)
Track & field athlete
Cleve Lewis Management **Ph:** 303-531-4469
10940 S Parker Rd Suite 526
Parker, CO 80134
www.carllewis.com

Lewis, CS (1898-1963)
Author whose work encompassed literary criticism, children's literature, fantasy literature, and popular theology; his best-known works include: The Chronicles of Narnia, The Screwtape Letters, and Mere Christianity
HarperCollins Publishers **Ph:** 212-207-7000
c/o Author Mail
10 E 53rd St
New York, NY 10022
www.cslewisclassics.com

Lewis, Dana
Moscow correspondent for FOX News
FOX News Channel **Ph:** 212-301-3000
1211 Ave of the Americas
New York, NY 10036
www.foxnews.com/fnctv

Lewis, David Levering (1936-)
Author of several acclaimed books, including WEB Du Bois: Biography of a Race, 1868-1919
Henry Holt & Co Inc **Ph:** 212-886-9200
115 W 18th St **Fax:** 212-633-0748
New York, NY 10011
www.henryholt.com/owlbooks.htm

Lewis, Edward
Founder and chairman of Essence Communications Inc, which publishes Essence, a lifestyle magazine for African-American women
Essence Communications Inc **Ph:** 212-642-0600
1500 Broadway 6th Fl
New York, NY 10036
www.essence.com/essence

Lewis, George
NBC news correspondent
NBC News **Ph:** 212-664-4249
30 Rockefeller Plaza
New York, NY 10112
www.msnbc.msn.com/id/3689499

Lewis, Jamal (1979-)
Professional football player
Baltimore Ravens **Ph:** 410-547-8100
1101 Russell St **Fax:** 410-547-8112
Baltimore, MD 21230
www.baltimoreravens.com

Lewis, Jerry (1926-)
Comedian
William Morris Agency **Ph:** 310-859-4000
1 William Morris Pl **Fax:** 310-859-4462
Beverly Hills, CA 90212
www.jerrylewiscomedy.com

Lewis, Jerry (1934-)
US Representative from California (Republican)
2112 Rayburn Bldg **Ph:** 202-225-5861
Washington, DC 20515 **Fax:** 202-225-6498
www.house.gov/jerrylewis

Lewis, John (1940-)
US Representative from Georgia (Democrat)
343 Cannon Bldg **Ph:** 202-225-3801
Washington, DC 20515 **Fax:** 202-225-0351
www.house.gov/johnlewis

Lewis, Juliette (1973-)
Actor
Gersh Agency **Ph:** 310-274-6611
232 N Canon Dr
Beverly Hills, CA 90210

Lewis, Kenneth D (1947-)
Chairman, CEO, and president of Bank of America
Bank of America Corp **Ph:** 800-432-1000
100 N Tyron St
Charlotte, NC 28255
www.bankofamerica.com/newsroom

Lewis, Marvin (1958-)
Football coach
Cincinnati Bengals **Ph:** 513-621-3550
1 Paul Brown Stadium **Fax:** 513-621-3570
Cincinnati, OH 45202
www.bengals.com

Lewis, Ramsey (1935-)
Jazz pianist and composer
Ted Kurland Assoc **Ph:** 617-254-0007
173 Brighton Ave **Fax:** 617-782-3577
Boston, MA 02134
www.ramseylewis.com

Lewis, Rashard (1979-)
Professional basketball player
Seattle Supersonics **Ph:** 206-281-5800
351 Elliott Ave W Suite 500 **Fax:** 206-281-5839
Seattle, WA 98119
www.nba.com/sonics

Lewis, Ray (1975-)
Professional football player
Baltimore Ravens **Ph:** 410-547-8100
1101 Russell St **Fax:** 410-547-8112
Baltimore, MD 21230
www.raylewis52.com

Lewis, Ron (1946-)
US Representative from Kentucky (Republican)
2418 Rayburn Bldg **Ph:** 202-225-3501
Washington, DC 20515 **Fax:** 202-226-2019
www.house.gov/ronlewis

Lewis, T
Co-creator, with Michael Fry, of the comic strip Over the Hedge
United Feature Syndicate **Ph:** 212-293-8500
200 Madison Ave
New York, NY 10016
www.unitedfeatures.com

Leykis, Tom (1956-)
Radio talk show host (syndicated)
Westwood One **Ph:** 212-641-2000
40 W 57th St 5th Fl **Fax:** 212-641-2172
New York, NY 10019
www.blowmeuptom.com

Leyland, Jim (1944-)
Baseball manager
Detroit Tigers **Ph:** 313-962-4000
Comerica Park **Fax:** 313-471-2138
2100 Woodward Ave
Detroit, MI 48201
detroit.tigers.mlb.com

Li, Ting-Kai, MD (1934-)
Director of the National Institute on Alcohol Abuse & Alcoholism, National Institutes of Health
National Institute on Alcohol Abuse & Alcoholism **Ph:** 301-443-3885 **Fax:** 301-443-7043
5635 Fishers Ln
MSC 9304
Bethesda, MD 20892
www.niaaa.nih.gov

Liang, Christine
President & COO of Asian Source Inc (ASI)
ASI Corp **Ph:** 510-226-8000
48289 Fremont Blvd
Fremont, CA 94538

Liang, Edwaard
Dancer; performed in a leading role in Fosse on Broadway; is currently a soloist with the New York City Ballet
New York City Ballet **Ph:** 212-870-5656
New York State Theater **Fax:** 212-870-7791
20 Lincoln Center
New York, NY 10023
www.nycballet.com/about/dancers.html

Liasson, Mara
NPR's national political correspondent; is also a political correspondent for FOX News Channel
National Public Radio **Ph:** 202-513-2000
635 Massachusetts Ave NW **Fax:** 202-513-3329
Washington, DC 20001
www.npr.org

Libby, I Lewis (1950-)
Former Chief of Staff to Vice President Dick Cheney and Assistant to the Vice President for National Security Affairs; currently a senior advisor at Hudson Institute, a conservative think tank, and is under indictment in the so-called Valerie Plame affair
Hudson Institute **Ph:** 202-974-2400
1015 15th St NW 6th Fl **Fax:** 202-974-2410
Washington, DC 20005
www.hudson.org

Liddy, Edward M
Chairman, president, and CEO of Allstate Corp and Allstate Insurance Co
Allstate Corp **Ph:** 847-402-5000
2775 Sanders Rd Suite F7 **Fax:** 847-836-3998
Northbrook, IL 60062
www.allstate.com/media

Liddy, G Gordon (1930-)
Radio talk show host; was involved in the Watergate scandal
Radio America **Ph:** 202-408-0944
1030 15th St NW Suite 1040 **Fax:** 202-408-1087
Washington, DC 20005 **TF:** 800-807-4703
www.liddyshow.us

Lidge, Brad (1976-)
Professional baseball player
Houston Astros **Ph:** 713-259-8000
Minute Maid Park **Fax:** 713-259-8981
501 Crawford St
Houston, TX 77002
houston.astros.mlb.com

Lidle, Cory (1972-)
Professional baseball player
Philadelphia Phillies **Ph:** 215-463-6000
Citizens Bank Park
1 Citizens Bank Park Way
Philadelphia, PA 19148
philadelphia.phillies.mlb.com

Lidstrom, Nicklas (1970-)
Professional hockey player
Detroit Red Wings **Ph:** 313-396-7544
Joe Louis Arena **Fax:** 313-567-0296
600 Civic Center Dr
Detroit, MI 48226
www.detroitredwings.com

Lieber, Jon (1970-)
Professional baseball player
Philadelphia Phillies **Ph:** 215-463-6000
Citizens Bank Park
1 Citizens Bank Park Way
Philadelphia, PA 19148
philadelphia.phillies.mlb.com

Lieberman, Joseph I (1942-)
US Senator from Connecticut (Democrat)
706 Hart Bldg **Ph:** 202-224-4041
Washington, DC 20510 **Fax:** 202-224-9750
lieberman.senate.gov

Liebman, Wendy (1961-)
Comedian
Gersh Agency **Ph:** 310-274-6611
232 N Canon Dr
Beverly Hills, CA 90210
www.wendyliebman.com

Liesman, Steve
CNBC's senior economics reporter
CNBC **Ph:** 201-735-2622
900 Sylvan Ave
Englewood Cliffs, NJ 07632
moneycentral.msn.com/cnbc/tv

Ligon, Austin
Co-Founder, president, and CEO of CarMax
CarMax Inc **Ph:** 804-747-0422
4900 Cox Rd
Glen Allen, VA 23060
www.carmax.com

Lileks, James (1958-)
Syndicated political humor columnist for Newhouse News Service; is also a columnist for the Star-Tribune (Minneapolis-St Paul)
Newhouse News Service **Ph:** 202-383-7800
1101 Connecticut Ave NW **Fax:** 202-296-9537
Suite 300
Washington, DC 20036
www.lileks.com

Lilly, Kristine (1971-)
Soccer player on the US National Team
US Soccer Federation **Ph:** 312-808-1300
1801 S Prairie Ave **Fax:** 312-808-1301
Chicago, IL 60616
www.ussoccer.com

Lima, Adriana (1981-)
Model
DNA Model Management **Ph:** 212-226-0080
520 Broadway
New York, NY 10012

Liman, Doug (1965-)
Movie producer/director
Creative Artists Agency **Ph:** 310-288-4545
9830 Wilshire Blvd **Fax:** 310-288-4800
Beverly Hills, CA 90212

Limbaugh, David (1952-)
Syndicated columnist (commentary); brother of Rush Limbaugh
Creators Syndicate Inc **Ph:** 310-337-7003
5777 W Century Blvd Suite 700 **Fax:** 310-337-7625
Los Angeles, CA 90045
www.davidlimbaugh.com

Limbaugh, Rush (1951-)
Right-wing radio talk show host
Premiere Radio Networks Inc **Ph:** 818-377-5300
15260 Ventura Blvd 5th Fl **Fax:** 818-377-5333
Sherman Oaks, CA 91403
www.rushlimbaugh.com

Lin, Carol
Anchors CNN's weekend primetime news programs
CNN **Ph:** 404-827-1500
1 CNN Center
Atlanta, GA 30303
www.cnn.com/CNN/anchors_reporters

Lin, Lucia (1962-)
Violinist
Boston Symphony Orchestra **Ph:** 617-266-1492
301 Massachusetts Ave
Boston, MA 02115
www.bso.org

Lincoln, Blanche L (1960-)
US Senator from Arkansas (Democrat)
355 Dirksen Bldg **Ph:** 202-224-4843
Washington, DC 20510 **Fax:** 202-228-1371
lincoln.senate.gov

Lindberg, Donald AB, MD (1933-)
Director of the National Library of Medicine; a scientist who has pioneered in applying computer technology to health care
National Library of Medicine **Ph:** 301-496-6308
8600 Rockville Pike **Fax:** 301-496-4450
Bldg 38 Rm 2E17 **TF:** 888-346-3656
Bethesda, MD 20894
www.nlm.nih.gov

Lindell, Rian (1977-)
Professional football player
Buffalo Bills **Ph:** 716-648-1800
Ralph Wilson Stadium **Fax:** 716-649-6446
1 Bills Dr
Orchard Park, NY 14127
www.buffalobills.com

Linden, Trevor (1970-)
Professional hockey player
Vancouver Canucks **Ph:** 604-899-4600
General Motors Pl **Fax:** 604-899-4640
800 Griffiths Way
Vancouver, BC V6B6G1
www.canucks.com

Linder, John (1942-)
US Representative from Georgia (Republican)
1026 Longworth Bldg **Ph:** 202-225-4272
Washington, DC 20515 **Fax:** 202-225-4696
linder.house.gov

Lindner, Carl H
Founder, chairman, and principal shareholder of American Financial Group, Inc
American Financial Group Inc **Ph:** 513-579-6739
580 Walnut St 10th Fl W
Cincinnati, OH 45202
www.afginc.com

Lindros, Eric (1973-)
Professional hockey player
Toronto Maple Leafs **Ph:** 416-815-5700
Air Canada Center
40 Bay St Suite 400
Toronto, ON M5J2X2
www.mapleleafs.com

Lindsey, Lawrence B, PhD (1954-)
Former director of the National Economic Council; currently a visiting scholar at the American Enterprise Institute, where he researches tax policy, monetary policy, international economic development, and fiscal policy
American Enterprise Institute for Public Policy Research **Ph:** 202-862-5800 **Fax:** 202-862-7177
1150 17th St NW Suite 1100
Washington, DC 20036
www.aei.org

Linehan, Scott
Football coach
Saint Louis Rams **Ph:** 314-982-7267
1 Rams Way **Fax:** 314-770-9261
Earth City, MO 63045
www.stlouisrams.com

Lingle, Linda (1953-)
Governor of Hawaii (Republican)
State Capitol **Ph:** 808-586-0034
415 S Beretania St **Fax:** 808-586-0006
Honolulu, HI 96813
www.hawaii.gov/gov

Linkin Park
Music group (a blend of alternative metal & hip-hop)
Warner Bros Records **Ph:** 818-846-9090
PO Box 6868 **Fax:** 818-846-8474
Burbank, CA 91510
www.linkinpark.com

Linney, Laura (1964-)
Actor
International Creative Management **Ph:** 310-550-4000
8942 Wilshire Blvd
Beverly Hills, CA 90211

Lionel
Radio talk show host whose show combines discussions of current events and offbeat topics with humor; was previously the host of Snap Judgment on Court TV
WOR Radio Network **Ph:** 212-642-4500
1440 Broadway **Fax:** 212-642-4549
New York, NY 10018
www.lionelonline.com

Liotta, Ray (1955-)
Actor
Endeavor — **Ph:** 310-248-2000
9601 Wilshire Blvd 3rd Fl — **Fax:** 310-248-2020
Beverly Hills, CA 90210

Lipinski, William O (1937-)
US Representative from Illinois (Democrat)
1217 Longworth Bldg — **Ph:** 202-225-5701
Washington, DC 20515 — **Fax:** 202-225-1012
www.house.gov/lipinski

Lippman, Laura (1959-)
Mystery novelist (Every Secret Thing; the Tess Monaghan novels)
HarperCollins Publishers — **Ph:** 212-207-7000
c/o Author Mail
10 E 53rd St
New York, NY 10022
www.lauralippman.com

Lipsyte, Robert (1938-)
Journalist and writer of books for young adults (The Contender)
HarperCollins Children's Books — **Ph:** 212-261-6500
1350 Ave of the Americas
New York, NY 10019
www.robertlipsyte.com

Lipton, James (1926-)
Host of Inside the Actors Studio; is also a writer & producer
International Creative Management — **Ph:** 212-556-5600
40 W 57th St 17th Fl
New York, NY 10019
www.bravotv.com

Lipton, Martin (1931-)
Attorney specializing in advising major corporations on mergers and acquisitions and matters affecting corporate policy and strategy
Wachtell Lipton Rosen & Katz — **Ph:** 212-403-1200
51 W 52nd St — **Fax:** 212-403-2200
New York, NY 10019
www.wlrk.com

Lisovicz, Susan
Co-host of CNN's In the Money
CNN New York — **Ph:** 212-275-7800
Time Warner Ctr
10 Columbus Cir
New York, NY 10019
www.cnn.com/CNN/anchors_reporters

Lithgow, John (1945-)
Actor
Creative Artists Agency — **Ph:** 310-288-4545
9830 Wilshire Blvd — **Fax:** 310-288-4800
Beverly Hills, CA 90212

Litke, Mark
ABC News chief Asia correspondent
ABC News — **Ph:** 212-456-7777
77 W 66th St
New York, NY 10023
www.abcnews.go.com/WNT

Little, Grady (1950-)
Baseball manager
Los Angeles Dodgers — **Ph:** 323-224-1500
Dodger Stadium — **Fax:** 323-224-1269
1000 Elysian Park Ave
Los Angeles, CA 90012
losangeles.dodgers.mlb.com

Little, Tony (1957-)
Personal trainer known for his infomercials
Perigee Publicity — **Ph:** 212-366-2000
375 Hudson St
New York, NY 10014
www.tonylittle.com

Littlefield, Bill
Author and sports commentator; hosts NPR's weekly sports magazine Only A Game
National Public Radio — **Ph:** 202-513-2000
635 Massachusetts Ave NW — **Fax:** 202-513-3329
Washington, DC 20001
www.npr.org

Littlefield, Ron
Mayor of Chattanooga
101 E 11th St Suite 100 — **Ph:** 423-425-7800
Chattanooga, TN 37402
www.chattanooga.gov

Litton, Drew
Sports cartoonist at the Rocky Mountain News (Win, Lose & Drew)
Rocky Mountain News — **Ph:** 303-892-5000
400 W Colfax Ave
Denver, CO 80204
cfapp2.rockymountainnews.com/drew

Liu, Lucy (1968-)
Actor
Untitled Entertainment — **Ph:** 310-601-2100
331 N Maple Dr 3rd Fl — **Fax:** 310-601-2344
Beverly Hills, CA 90210

Liveris, Andrew N
Chairman, president, and CEO of Dow Chemical
Dow Chemical Co **Ph:** 989-636-1000
2030 Dow Ctr
Midland, MI 48642
www.dow.com/corpgov

LL Cool J (1968-)
Singer (rap/hip-hop); actor
William Morris Agency **Ph:** 212-586-5100
1325 Ave of the Americas **Fax:** 212-246-3583
New York, NY 10019
www.defjam.com

Lloyd, Christopher (1938-)
Actor
Gersh Agency **Ph:** 310-274-6611
232 N Canon Dr
Beverly Hills, CA 90210

Lo Duca, Paul (1972-)
Professional baseball player
New York Mets **Ph:** 718-507-6387
Shea Stadium **Fax:** 718-507-6395
123-01 Roosevelt Ave
Flushing, NY 11368
newyork.mets.mlb.com

Loaiza, Esteban (1971-)
Professional baseball player
Oakland Athletics **Ph:** 510-638-4900
Network Assoc Coliseum **Fax:** 510-568-3770
7000 Coliseum Way
Oakland, CA 94621
oakland.athletics.mlb.com

Lobel, Arnold (1933-1987)
Children's book author & illustrator (Fables; the Frog & Toad books)
HarperCollins Children's Books **Ph:** 212-261-6500
1350 Ave of the Americas
New York, NY 10019
www.harperchildrens.com

LoBiondo, Frank A (1946-)
US Representative from New Jersey (Republican)
225 Cannon Bldg **Ph:** 202-225-6572
Washington, DC 20510 **Fax:** 202-225-3318
www.house.gov/lobiondo

Locher, Dick (1929-)
Editorial cartoonist; also draws the Dick Tracy comic strip
Tribune Media Services Inc **Ph:** 312-222-4444
435 N Michigan Ave Suite 1500
Chicago, IL 60611
www.comicspage.com

Lockhart, Keith (1959-)
Boston Pops conductor
Boston Pops Orchestra **Ph:** 617-266-1492
Symphony Hall
301 Massachusetts Ave
Boston, MA 02115
www.bso.org

Locklear, Heather (1961-)
Actor
International Creative Management **Ph:** 310-550-4000
8942 Wilshire Blvd
Beverly Hills, CA 90211

Lodge, David (1935-)
Novelist; also writes literary criticism
Penguin Publicity **Ph:** 212-366-2000
375 Hudson St
New York, NY 10014
us.penguingroup.com

Lofgren, Zoe (1947-)
US Representative from California (Democrat)
102 Cannon Bldg **Ph:** 202-225-3072
Washington, DC 20515 **Fax:** 202-225-3336
www.house.gov/lofgren

Lofton, Kenny (1967-)
Professional baseball player
Los Angeles Dodgers **Ph:** 323-224-1500
Dodger Stadium **Fax:** 323-224-1269
1000 Elysian Park Ave
Los Angeles, CA 90012
losangeles.dodgers.mlb.com

Loggins, Kenny (1948-)
Singer/songwriter
William Morris Agency **Ph:** 310-859-4000
1 William Morris Pl **Fax:** 310-859-4462
Beverly Hills, CA 90212
www.kennyloggins.com

Logue, Ronald E
Chairman and CEO of State Street Corp (financial services)
State Street Corp **Ph:** 617-786-3000
225 Franklin St
Boston, MA 02110
www.statestreet.com

Lohan, Lindsay (1986-)
Actor
Creative Artists Agency **Ph:** 310-288-4545
9830 Wilshire Blvd **Fax:** 310-288-4800
Beverly Hills, CA 90212
www.llrocks.com

Lohman, Alison (1979-)
Actor
Creative Artists Agency **Ph:** 310-288-4545
9830 Wilshire Blvd **Fax:** 310-288-4800
Beverly Hills, CA 90212

Lomas Garza, Carmen (1948-)
Chicana artist whose principal subject is the everyday lives of Mexican Americans; her work includes creating/illustrating children's books
Children's Book Press **Ph:** 415-821-3080
2211 Mission St
San Francisco, CA 94110
www.carmenlomasgarza.com

Lomax, Michael, PhD (1948-)
President & CEO of the United Negro College Fund
United Negro College Fund Inc **Ph:** 703-205-3400
8260 Willow Oaks Corporate Dr **TF:** 800-331-2244
Fairfax, VA 22031
www.uncf.org

Lombardi, Vince (1913-1970)
Legendary football coach
Estate of Vince Lombardi **Ph:** 317-570-5000
CMG Worldwide **Fax:** 317-570-5500
10500 Crosspoint Blvd
Indianapolis, IN 46256
www.vincelombardi.com

Lomonaco, Michael
Chef at Guastavino's; formerly chef at Windows on the World and Noche
Guastavino's **Ph:** 212-980-2455
409 E 59th St **Fax:** 212-980-2904
New York, NY 10022
www.guastavinos.com/chef.asp

Lonergan, Kenneth (1963-)
Playwright and screenwriter; director
Creative Artists Agency **Ph:** 310-288-4545
9830 Wilshire Blvd **Fax:** 310-288-4800
Beverly Hills, CA 90212

Lonestar
Country music band
William Morris Agency **Ph:** 615-963-3000
1600 Division St Suite 300 **Fax:** 615-963-3090
Nashville, TN 37203
www.lonestar.mu

Long, Eddie L
Televangelist
Bishop Eddie L Long Ministries Inc **Ph:** 770-696-9600
Fax: 770-981-9430
PO Box 1019
Lithonia, GA 30058
www.newbirth.org/bio_bishop.asp

Long, Howie (1960-)
NFL studio analyst for Fox Sports; former professional football player (defensive lineman) and member of the Pro Football Hall of Fame
FOX Sports Net **Ph:** 310-369-1000
10201 W Pico Blvd
Bldg 101
Los Angeles, CA 90035
msn.foxsports.com/nflonfox

Longoria, Eva (1975-)
Actor
Warren Cowan & Assoc **Ph:** 310-275-0777
8899 Beverly Blvd Suite 919 **Fax:** 310-247-0810
Los Angeles, CA 90048
www.evalongoria.com

Longwell, Ryan (1974-)
Professional football player
Minnesota Vikings **Ph:** 952-828-6500
9520 Viking Dr **Fax:** 952-828-6540
Eden Prairie, MN 55344
www.vikings.com

Lopez, George (1961-)
Comedian
Gersh Agency **Ph:** 310-274-6611
232 N Canon Dr
Beverly Hills, CA 90210
www.georgelopez.com

Lopez, Javy (1970-)
Professional baseball player
Baltimore Orioles **Ph:** 410-685-9800
Oriole Park at Camden Yards **Fax:** 410-547-6279
333 W Camden St
Baltimore, MD 21201
baltimore.orioles.mlb.com

Lopez, Jennifer (1969-)
Actor; singer
International Creative Management **Ph:** 310-550-4000
8942 Wilshire Blvd
Beverly Hills, CA 90211
www.jenniferlopez.com

Lorberbaum, Jeffrey S
Chairman and CEO of Mohawk Industries
Mohawk Industries Inc **Ph:** 706-629-7721
160 S Industrial Blvd
Calhoun, GA 30701
www.mohawkind.com

Loren, Sophia (1934-)
Actor
CMG Worldwide **Ph:** 310-651-2000
8560 Sunset Blvd 10th Fl PH
West Hollywood, CA 90069
www.sophialoren.com

Lorenz, Lee (1933-)
Comic illustrator and artist; former art editor at the New Yorker magazine, where he has contributed more than 1,500 humorous drawings
Cartoon Bank **Ph:** 914-478-5527
New Yorker Magazine **Fax:** 914-478-5604
28 Wells Ave Bldg 3 4th Fl
Yonkers, NY 10701
www.cartoonbank.com

Loretta, Mark (1971-)
Professional baseball player
Boston Red Sox **Ph:** 617-267-9440
Fenway Park **Fax:** 617-236-6797
4 Yawkey Way
Boston, MA 02215
boston.redsox.mlb.com

Loria, Jeffrey H
Owner of the Florida Marlins baseball club
Florida Marlins **Ph:** 305-626-7400
Dolphins Stadium **Fax:** 305-626-7428
2267 Dan Marino Blvd
Miami, FL 33028
florida.marlins.mlb.com

Los Lobos
Mexican/rock band from East LA
Red Light Management **Ph:** 434-245-4900
PO Box 1467 **Fax:** 434-245-4933
Charlottesville, VA 22902
www.redlightmanagement.com/artists/loslobos

Lott, Ronnie (1959-)
Hall-of-fame football player (retired)
Pro Football Hall of Fame **Ph:** 330-456-8207
2121 George Halas Dr NW **Fax:** 330-456-8175
Canton, OH 44708
www.profootballhof.com

Lott, Trent (1941-)
US Senator from Mississippi (Republican)
487 Russell Bldg **Ph:** 202-224-6253
Washington, DC 20510 **Fax:** 202-224-2262
lott.senate.gov

Love, Courtney (1964-)
Singer (her band is Hole); actor
Special Artists Agency **Ph:** 310-859-9688
9465 Wilshire Blvd Suite 890
Beverly Hills, CA 90212
www.courtneylove.com

Love, Davis III (1964-)
Professional golfer
PGA Tour **Ph:** 904-285-3700
100 PGA Tour Blvd
Ponte Vedra Beach, FL 32082
www.pgatour.com

Love, Susan, MD (1948-)
President & medical director of the Dr. Susan Love Research Foundation and a leader in the breast cancer advocacy movement; author of books on breast cancer and menopause
Dr Susan Love Research Foundation **Ph:** 310-230-1712 **Fax:** 310-230-1612
PO Box 846
Pacific Palisades, CA 90272
www.susanlovemdfoundation.org

Loveless, Patty (1957-)
Country singer
William Morris Agency **Ph:** 615-963-3000
1600 Division St Suite 300 **Fax:** 615-963-3090
Nashville, TN 37203
www.pattyloveless.com

Lovell, James A Jr (1928-)
Former astronaut and commander of Apollo 13 (1970)
National Space Society **Ph:** 202-429-1600
1620 'I' St NW Suite 615 **Fax:** 202-463-8497
Washington, DC 20006
www.nss.org/about/bios/lovell.html

Loveman, Gary
Chairman, CEO, and president of Harrah's Entertainment
Harrah's Entertainment Inc **Ph:** 702-407-6000
1 Harrah's Ct
Las Vegas, NV 89119
investor.harrahs.com

Lovett, Lyle (1957-)
Singer; composer
Monterey Peninsula Artists/ Paradigm **Ph:** 831-375-4889 **Fax:** 831-375-2623
509 Hartnell St
Monterey, CA 93940

Lovett, Richard
President of Creative Artists Agency
Creative Artists Agency **Ph:** 310-288-4545
9830 Wilshire Blvd
Beverly Hills, CA 90212

Lovitz, Jon (1957-)
Comedian; actor
Agency for the Performing Arts **Ph:** 310-273-0744
9200 Sunset Blvd Suite 900 **Fax:** 310-888-4242
Beverly Hills, CA 90069

Lowe, Chan (1953-)
Editorial cartoonist for the Sun-Sentinel, South Florida
Tribune Media Services Inc **Ph:** 312-222-4444
435 N Michigan Ave Suite 1500
Chicago, IL 60611
www.comicspage.com

Lowe, Derek (1973-)
Professional baseball player
Los Angeles Dodgers **Ph:** 323-224-1500
Dodger Stadium **Fax:** 323-224-1269
1000 Elysian Park Ave
Los Angeles, CA 90012
losangeles.dodgers.mlb.com

Lowe, Rob (1964-)
Actor
Creative Artists Agency **Ph:** 310-288-4545
9830 Wilshire Blvd **Fax:** 310-288-4800
Beverly Hills, CA 90212

Lowell, Christopher (1955-)
TV host, decorating guru, entrepreneur, author
Rogers & Cowan PR **Ph:** 310-854-8100
Pacific Design Center **Fax:** 310-854-8101
8687 Melrose Ave 7th Fl
Los Angeles, CA 90069
www.christopherlowell.com

Lowell, Mike (1974-)
Professional baseball player
Boston Red Sox **Ph:** 617-267-9440
Fenway Park **Fax:** 617-236-6797
4 Yawkey Way
Boston, MA 02215
boston.redsox.mlb.com

Lowey, Nita M (1937-)
US Representative from New York (Democrat)
2329 Rayburn Bldg **Ph:** 202-225-6506
Washington, DC 20515 **Fax:** 202-225-0546
www.house.gov/lowey

Lowman, Meg, PhD (1953-)
Botanist known for her research on the rainforest canopy ecology
New College of Florida **Ph:** 941-359-4370
Natural Sciences Division
5700 N Tamiami Trail
Sarasota, FL 34243
www.ncf.edu

Lowry, Lois (1937-)
Author of books for young readers (The Giver; Number the Stars)
Houghton Mifflin Children's Books **Ph:** 617-351-5000
222 Berkeley St 8th Fl
Boston, MA 02116
www.loislowry.com

Lowry, Rich
Journalist/syndicated columnist (conservative commentary); editor of the National Review
King Features Syndicate Inc **Ph:** 212-455-4000
888 7th Ave 2nd Fl
New York, NY 10019
www.kingfeatures.com

Lucado, Max
Pastor, author, and host of the radio program UpWords
Oak Hills Church **Ph:** 210-698-6868
19595 IH-10W **Fax:** 210-698-1323
San Antonio, TX 78257
www.maxlucado.com

Lucas, Craig (1951-)
Playwright
Gersh Agency **Ph:** 310-274-6611
232 N Canon Dr
Beverly Hills, CA 90210

Lucas, Frank D (1960-)
US Representative from Oklahoma (Republican)
2342 Rayburn Bldg **Ph:** 202-225-5565
Washington, DC 20515 **Fax:** 202-225-8698
www.house.gov/lucas

Lucas, George (1944-)
Movie writer/producer; founder & chairman of Lucasfilm Ltd
Lucasfilm Ltd **Ph:** 415-662-1800
PO Box 29901
San Francisco, CA 94129
www.lucasfilm.com/inside/bio

Lucas, Ken (1979-)
Professional football player
Carolina Panthers **Ph:** 704-358-7000
Bank of America Stadium **Fax:** 704-358-7618
800 S Mint St
Charlotte, NC 28202
www.panthers.com

Lucas, Robert E Jr, PhD (1937-)
Winner of the 1995 Nobel Prize in Economics for developing and applying the hypothesis of rational expectations
University of Chicago **Ph:** 773-702-8179
Dept of Economics **Fax:** 773-702-8490
1126 E 59th St
Chicago, IL 60637
home.uchicago.edu/~sogrodow

Lucci, Susan (1947-)
Soap opera star known for having been nominated for an Emmy more than any other person before finally winning in 1999
Brownstein & Assoc Inc **Ph:** 212-265-3666
630 9th Ave Suite 217 **Fax:** 646-219-4340
New York, NY 10036
www.susanlucci.com

Lucid, Shannon, PhD (1943-)
Astronaut (active); the first American to live in space
Johnson Space Center **Ph:** 281-483-0123
2101 NASA Rd 1
Houston, TX 77058
www.jsc.nasa.gov/bios

Luck, Jo
President & CEO of Heifer International, an organization that works with communities in an effort to end hunger and poverty
Heifer Project International **Ph:** 501-907-2600
PO Box 8058 **Fax:** 501-907-2602
Little Rock, AR 72203
www.heifer.org

Luckovich, Mike
Editorial cartoonist for the Atlanta Constitution
Creators Syndicate Inc **Ph:** 310-337-7003
5777 W Century Blvd Suite 700 **Fax:** 310-337-7625
Los Angeles, CA 90045
www.creators.com

Ludacris (1977-)
Atlanta-based rapper (real name is Chris Bridges)
William Morris Agency **Ph:** 212-586-5100
1325 Ave of the Americas **Fax:** 212-246-3583
New York, NY 10019
www.defjam.com/ludacris

Lugar, Richard G (1932-)
US Senator from Indiana (Republican)
306 Hart Bldg **Ph:** 202-224-4814
Washington, DC 20510 **Fax:** 202-228-0360
lugar.senate.gov

Lukins, Sheila
Chef; Parade Magazine food editor (Simply Delicious column); cookbooks author
Parade Magazine **Ph:** 212-450-7000
711 3rd Ave **Fax:** 212-450-7284
New York, NY 10017
www.parade.com

Lumet, Sidney (1924-)
Movie director
International Creative Management **Ph:** 310-550-4000
8942 Wilshire Blvd
Beverly Hills, CA 90211

Lundgren, Terry
Chairman, president, and CEO of Federated Department Stores
Federated Department Stores Inc **Ph:** 513-579-7000
7 W 7th St
Cincinnati, OH 45202
www.federated-fds.com/company/exec.asp

Lundquist, Alex (1970-)
Male model
Wilhelmina Models Inc **Ph:** 212-473-0700
300 Park Ave S 2nd Fl **Fax:** 212-473-3223
New York, NY 10010

Lundquist, Verne (1940-)
Sports broadcaster
CBS Sports **Ph:** 212-975-4321
51 W 52nd St
New York, NY 10019
cbs.sportsline.com/cbssports/team

Lundqvist, Henrik (1982-)
Professional hockey player
New York Rangers **Ph:** 212-465-6486
Madison Square Garden **Fax:** 212-465-6494
2 Pennsylvania Plaza
New York, NY 10121
www.newyorkrangers.com

Lungren, Daniel E (1946-)
US Representative from California (Republican)
2448 Rayburn Bldg **Ph:** 202-225-5716
Washington, DC 20515 **Fax:** 202-226-1298
www.house.gov/lungren

Luongo, Roberto (1979-)
Professional hockey player
Florida Panthers **Ph:** 954-835-7000
BankAtlantic Center **Fax:** 954-835-7700
1 Panther Pkwy
Sunrise, FL 33323
www.floridapanthers.com

Lupone, Patti (1949-)
Actor (primarily stage); singer
Innovative Artists **Ph:** 212-253-6900
235 Park Ave S 7th Fl **Fax:** 212-253-6400
New York, NY 10003
www.pattilupone.net

Lurie, Alison (1926-)
Writer (novels include The Last Resort, The War Between the Tates, Imaginary Friends) & scholar
Cornell University **Ph:** 607-255-6800
263 Goldwin Smith Hall **Fax:** 607-255-6661
Ithaca, NY 14853
people.cornell.edu/pages/al28

Lurie, Jeffrey, PhD (1951-)
Owner of the Philadelphia Eagles football franchise
Philadelphia Eagles **Ph:** 215-463-2500
NovaCare Complex **Fax:** 215-339-5464
1 NovaCare Way
Philadelphia, PA 19145
www.philadelphiaeagles.com/team/frontoffice.jsp

Luskin, Robert D (1950-)
Attorney specializing in RICO actions, prosecutions under the federal money laundering statutes, civil and criminal forfeitures, and congressional investigations, with extensive experience defending cases involving allegations of official corruption; currently serving as Karl Rove's attorney in the Valerie Plame case
Patton Boggs LLP **Ph:** 202-457-6190
2550 M St NW **Fax:** 202-457-6315
Washington, DC 20037
www.pattonboggs.com

Lustig, Arnost (1926-)
Czech author (A Prayer for Katerina Horovitzova)
Smallmouth Press Corp **Ph:** 718-956-5764
PO Box 661
New York, NY 10185
www.smallmouthpress.com

Lynch, Barbara
Chef and owner of No. 9 Park restaurant in Boston
No 9 Park Restaurant **Ph:** 617-742-9991
9 Park St
Boston, MA 02108
www.no9park.com

Lynch, Chris (1962-)
Writer of books for young adults, primarily about teen-age boys (Freewill; Iceman; Slot Machine)
HarperCollins Children's Books **Ph:** 212-261-6500
1350 Ave of the Americas
New York, NY 10019
www.chrislynchbooks.com

Lynch, David (1946-)
Director, writer, producer
Creative Artists Agency **Ph:** 310-288-4545
9830 Wilshire Blvd **Fax:** 310-288-4800
Beverly Hills, CA 90212
www.davidlynch.com

Lynch, John (1952-)
Governor of New Hampshire (Democrat)
State House 107 N Main St Rm 208 **Ph:** 603-271-2121
Fax: 603-271-7680
Concord, NH 03301 **TF:** 800-852-3456
www.state.nh.us/governor

Lynch, Peter L
President & CEO of Winn-Dixie Stores Inc
Winn-Dixie Stores Inc **Ph:** 904-783-5000
5050 Edgewood Ct
Jacksonville, FL 32254
www.winn-dixie.com

Lynch, Stephen F (1955-)
US Representative from Massachusetts (Democrat)
319 Cannon Bldg **Ph:** 202-225-8273
Washington, DC 20515 **Fax:** 202-225-3984
www.house.gov/lynch

Lynch, Thomas (1948-)
Poet & essayist
WW Norton & Co Inc **Ph:** 212-354-5500
500 5th Ave **Fax:** 212-869-0856
New York, NY 10110
www.nortonpoets.com

Lyne, Adrian (1941-)
Movie producer/director
International Creative Management **Ph:** 310-550-4000
8942 Wilshire Blvd
Beverly Hills, CA 90211

Lyne, Susan (1950-)
President & CEO of Martha Stewart Living Omnimedia Inc
Martha Stewart Living Omnimedia Inc **Ph:** 212-827-8000
11 W 42nd St 23rd Fl
New York, NY 10036
www.marthastewart.com

Lynn, Jonathan (1943-)
Filmmaker, screenwriter, and novelist
Gersh Agency **Ph:** 310-274-6611
232 N Canon Dr
Beverly Hills, CA 90210
www.jonathanlynn.com

Lynn, Loretta (1935-)
Country singer
CAA Nashville **Ph:** 615-383-8787
3310 West End Ave 5th Fl **Fax:** 615-383-4937
Nashville, TN 37203
www.lorettalynn.com

Lynton, Michael
Chairman and CEO of Sony Pictures Entertainment
Sony Pictures Entertainment **Ph:** 310-244-4000
10202 W Washington Blvd **Fax:** 310-244-2626
Culver City, CA 90232
www.sonypictures.com/corp/aboutsonypictures.html

Lyon, Danny (1942-)
Photographer
Edwynn Houk Gallery **Ph:** 212-750-7070
745 5th Ave **Fax:** 212-688-4848
New York, NY 10151
www.houkgallery.com

Lyons, Gene (1943-)
Columnist for the Arkansas Democrat-Gazette (syndicated)
Newspaper Enterprise Assn **Ph:** 212-293-8500
200 Madison Ave
New York, NY 10016
www.unitedfeatures.com

Lyons, Jeffrey
Film and theater critic for WNBC-TV in New York; co-hosted the PBS series Sneak Preview
WNBC-TV **Ph:** 212-664-4444
30 Rockefeller Plaza **Fax:** 212-664-2994
New York, NY 10112
www.wnbc.com/meetthenewsteam

Ma, Yo-Yo (1955-)
Classical cellist
International Creative Management **Ph:** 212-556-5600
40 W 57th St 17th Fl
New York, NY 10019
www.yo-yoma.com

Mabika, Mwadi (1976-)
Professional basketball player
Los Angeles Sparks **Ph:** 310-341-1000
2151 E Grand Ave Suite 100 **Fax:** 310-341-1029
El Segundo, CA 90245
www.wnba.com/sparks

Mabrey, Vicki (1956-)
Nightline correspondent
Nightline **Ph:** 202-222-7700
1717 DeSales St NW
Washington, DC 20036
www.cbsnews.com

Mac, Bernie (1958-)
Comedian/actor
International Creative Management **Ph:** 310-550-4000
8942 Wilshire Blvd
Beverly Hills, CA 90211
www.fox.com/berniemac

Macatee, Bill (1955-)
Sports broadcaster
CBS Sports **Ph:** 212-975-4321
51 W 52nd St
New York, NY 10019
cbs.sportsline.com/cbssports/team

Macaulay, David (1946-)
Author and illustrator of books about building (Castle; Cathedral) and other books for young readers, including Black & White and The Way Things Work
Houghton Mifflin Children's Books **Ph:** 617-351-5000
222 Berkeley St 8th Fl
Boston, MA 02116
www.houghtonmifflinbooks.com/authors/macaulay

MacCallum, Martha
FOX News Live anchor
FOX News Channel **Ph:** 212-301-3000
1211 Ave of the Americas
New York, NY 10036
www.foxnews.com/fnctv

MacCormack, Charles F
President & CEO of Save the Children
Save the Children Federation Inc **Ph:** 203-221-4030 **TF:** 800-728-3843
54 Wilton Rd
Westport, CT 06880
www.savethechildren.org/news/experts.asp

MacDiarmid, Alan, PhD (1927-)
Winner (with two other scientists) of the 2000 Nobel Prize in Chemistry for the discovery and development of conductive polymers
University of Pennsylvania **Ph:** 215-898-8317
Dept of Chemistry
231 S 34th St
Pittsburgh, PA 19104
www.sas.upenn.edu/chem

MacDonald, Norm (1963-)
Comedian
Creative Artists Agency **Ph:** 310-288-4545
9830 Wilshire Blvd **Fax:** 310-288-4800
Beverly Hills, CA 90212

MacDonald, Richard (1946-)
Sculptor
Archive Gallery **Ph:** 800-972-5528
16 Lower Ragsdale Dr
Monterey, CA 93940
www.richardmacdonald.com

MacDowell, Andie (1958-)
Actor; former model
International Creative Management **Ph:** 310-550-4000
8942 Wilshire Blvd
Beverly Hills, CA 90211

Maceda, Jim
NBC news correspondent
NBC News **Ph:** 212-664-4249
30 Rockefeller Plaza
New York, NY 10112
www.msnbc.msn.com/id/3689499

MacFarlane, Seth (1973-)
Creator of the animated TV series The Family Guy
Endeavor **Ph:** 310-248-2000
9601 Wilshire Blvd 3rd Fl **Fax:** 310-248-2020
Beverly Hills, CA 90210
www.familyguy.com

Macha, Ken (1950-)
Baseball manager
Oakland Athletics **Ph:** 510-638-4900
Network Assoc Coliseum **Fax:** 510-568-3770
7000 Coliseum Way
Oakland, CA 94621
oakland.athletics.mlb.com

MacInnis, Frank
Chairman and CEO of EMCOR Group (mechanical and electrical construction, energy infrastructure, and facilities services businesses)
EMCOR Group Inc **Ph:** 203-849-7800
301 Merritt Seven Corporate Park 6th Fl
Norwalk, CT 06851
www.emcorgroup.com

MacIntosh, Craig (1943-)
Draws the comic strip Sally Forth
King Features Syndicate Inc **Ph:** 212-455-4000
888 7th Ave 2nd Fl
New York, NY 10019
www.kingfeatures.com

Mack, Connie IV
US Representative from Florida (Republican)
317 Cannon Bldg **Ph:** 202-225-2536
Washington, DC 20515 **Fax:** 202-225-6820
mack.house.gov

Mack, John
Chairman and CEO of Morgan Stanley
Morgan Stanley **Ph:** 212-761-4000
1585 Broadway **Fax:** 212-761-0086
New York, NY 10036
www.morganstanley.com

MacKay, Graeme (1968-)
Editorial cartoonist for the Hamilton Spectator; syndicated through Artizans
Hamilton Spectator **Ph:** 905-526-3439
44 Frid St
Hamilton, ON L8N3G3
www.mackaycartoons.net

Mackay, Harvey
Author of Swim with the Sharks Without Being Eaten Alive; is also a business speaker, a syndicated columnist, and chairman and CEO of Mackay Envelope Corp, a company he founded at the age of 26
Mackay Envelope Co **Ph:** 612-331-9311
2100 Elm St SE
Minneapolis, MN 55414
www.mackay.com

Mackenzie, Ross (1941-)
Syndicated columnist and editorial page editor for the Richmond Times-Dispatch
Tribune Media Services Inc **Ph:** 312-222-4444
435 N Michigan Ave Suite 1500
Chicago, IL 60611
tmsfeatures.com/productlist.htm

Mackey, John
Chairman and CEO of Whole Foods Market Inc
Whole Foods Market Inc **Ph:** 512-477-4455
550 Bowie St
Austin, TX 78703
www.wholefoodsmarket.com/company/leadership.html

MacKinnon, Catharine A (1946-)
Lawyer, teacher, writer, activist; specializes in sex equality issues under international and constitutional law
University of Michigan Law School **Ph:** 734-647-3595 **Fax:** 734-764-8309
624 S State St
Ann Arbor, MI 48109
www.law.umich.edu

MacKinnon, Roderick, MD (1956-)
Winner of the 2003 Nobel Prize in Chemistry for structural and mechanistic studies of ion channels in cell membranes
Howard Hughes Medical Institute **Ph:** 301-215-8500
4000 Jones Bridge Rd
Chevy Chase, MD 20815
www.hhmi.org/research/nobel

Macklin, David (1978-)
Professional football player
Arizona Cardinals **Ph:** 602-379-0101
8701 S Hardy Dr **Fax:** 602-379-1819
Tempe, AZ 85284
www.azcardinals.com

Mackowiak, Rob (1976-)
Professional baseball player
Chicago White Sox **Ph:** 312-674-1000
US Cellular Field **Fax:** 312-674-5109
333 W 35th St
Chicago, IL 60616
chicago.whitesox.mlb.com

MacLachlan, Kyle (1959-)
Actor
Gersh Agency **Ph:** 310-274-6611
232 N Canon Dr
Beverly Hills, CA 90210
www.kylemaclachlan.com

MacLachlan, Patricia (1938-)
Author of books for young readers (Sarah, Plain & Tall); also writes picture books
HarperCollins Children's Books **Ph:** 212-261-6500
1350 Ave of the Americas
New York, NY 10019
www.harperchildrens.com

MacLaine, Shirley (1934-)
Actor; dancer; author
International Creative Management **Ph:** 310-550-4000
8942 Wilshire Blvd
Beverly Hills, CA 90211
www.shirleymaclaine.com

MacLean, Doug (1954-)
President and General Manager of the Columbus Blue Jackets hockey team; has also coached hockey
Columbus Blue Jackets **Ph:** 614-246-4625
Nationwide Arena **Fax:** 614-246-4007
200 W Nationwide Blvd 3rd Fl
Columbus, OH 43215
www.bluejackets.com

Macpherson, Elle (1963-)
Model
International Creative Management **Ph:** 212-556-5600
40 W 57th St 17th Fl
New York, NY 10019

MacTavish, Craig (1958-)
Hockey coach
Edmonton Oilers **Ph:** 780-414-4000
11230 110th St **Fax:** 780-409-5890
Edmonton, AB T5G3H7
www.edmontonoilers.com

Macy, William H (1950-)
Actor
Creative Artists Agency **Ph:** 310-288-4545
9830 Wilshire Blvd **Fax:** 310-288-4800
Beverly Hills, CA 90212

Madden, John (1949-)
Film director
Creative Artists Agency **Ph:** 310-288-4545
9830 Wilshire Blvd **Fax:** 310-288-4800
Beverly Hills, CA 90212

Madden, John (1936-)
Sports broadcaster; former NFL coach
ESPN **Ph:** 860-585-2000
ESPN Plaza
935 Middle St
Bristol, CT 06010
sports.espn.go.com/nfl/madden

Madden, John (1973-)
Professional hockey player
New Jersey Devils **Ph:** 201-935-6050
Continental Airlines Arena **Fax:** 201-935-2127
50 Rt 120N
East Rutherford, NJ 07073
www.newjerseydevils.com

Madden, Steve (1958-)
Footwear designer
52-16 Barnett Ave **Ph:** 718-446-1800
Long Island City, NY 11104
www.stevemadden.com

Maddon, Joe (1954-)
Baseball manager
Tampa Bay Devil Rays — **Ph:** 727-825-3137
Tropicana Field — **Fax:** 727-825-3111
1 Tropicana Dr
Saint Petersburg, FL 33705
tampabay.devilrays.mlb.com

Maddux, Greg (1966-)
Professional baseball player
Chicago Cubs — **Ph:** 773-404-2827
Wrigley Field — **Fax:** 773-404-4129
1060 W Addison St
Chicago, IL 60613
chicago.cubs.mlb.com

Madonna (1958-)
Singer and actor; real name is Madonna Louise Veronica Ciccone
Creative Artists Agency — **Ph:** 310-288-4545
9830 Wilshire Blvd — **Fax:** 310-288-4800
Beverly Hills, CA 90212
www.madonna.com

Madsen, Michael (1958-)
Actor; poet
Paradigm — **Ph:** 310-288-8000
360 N Crescent Dr — **Fax:** 310-288-2000
North Bldg
Beverly Hills, CA 90210
www.michaelmadsen.com

Maffei, Gregory B
President and CEO of Liberty Media Corp, a holding company with interests in electronic retailing, media, communications, and entertainment businesses; its brands include QVC, Encore, Starz, and IAC/Interactive Corp
Liberty Media Corp — **Ph:** 720-875-5400
12300 Liberty Blvd — **Fax:** 720-875-5401
Englewood, CO 80112
www.libertymedia.com

Magee, Mike (1984-)
Professional soccer player
New York Red Bulls — **Ph:** 201-583-7000
1 Harmon Plaza 3rd Fl — **Fax:** 201-583-7055
Secaucus, NJ 07094
redbull.newyork.mlsnet.com

Magerko, Maggie H
President and owner of 84 Lumber (daughter of the company's founder and CEO, Joe Hardy III)
84 Lumber Co — **Ph:** 724-228-8820
1019 Rt 519 Bldg 7
Eighty Four, PA 15330
www.84lumber.com

Maggette, Corey (1979-)
Professional basketball player
Los Angeles Clippers — **Ph:** 213-742-7100
Staples Center — **Fax:** 213-742-7550
1111 S Figueroa St Suite 1100
Los Angeles, CA 90015
www.nba.com/clippers

Magliozzi, Ray (1949-)
Co-host (with his brother Tom) of Car Talk on NPR; they also write the syndicated column Click and Clack Talk Cars
National Public Radio — **Ph:** 202-513-2000
635 Massachusetts Ave NW — **Fax:** 202-513-3329
Washington, DC 20001
cartalk.cars.com

Magliozzi, Tom (1936-)
Co-host (with his brother Ray) of Car Talk on NPR; they also write the syndicated column Click and Clack Talk Cars
National Public Radio — **Ph:** 202-513-2000
635 Massachusetts Ave NW — **Fax:** 202-513-3329
Washington, DC 20001
cartalk.cars.com

Magloire, Jamaal (1978-)
Professional basketball player
Milwaukee Bucks — **Ph:** 414-227-0500
Bradley Center — **Fax:** 414-227-0543
1001 N 4th St
Milwauke, WI 53203
www.nba.com/bucks

Magnus, Edie
Dateline NBC correspondent
Dateline NBC — **Ph:** 212-664-4249
30 Rockefeller Plaza
New York, NY 10112
www.msnbc.msn.com/id/3360263

Magowan, Peter A
Managing General Partner of the San Francisco Giants baseball club
San Francisco Giants — **Ph:** 415-972-2000
AT & T Park
24 Willie Mays Plaza
San Francisco, CA 94107
sanfrancisco.giants.mlb.com

Magritte, Rene (1898-1967)
Surrealist painter
Solomon R Guggenheim Museum — **Ph:** 212-423-3500
1071 5th Ave
New York, NY 10128
www.guggenheimcollection.org

Maguire, Tobey (1975-)
Actor
Creative Artists Agency **Ph:** 310-288-4545
9830 Wilshire Blvd **Fax:** 310-288-4800
Beverly Hills, CA 90212

Maher, Bill (1956-)
Comedian and television personality
Creative Artists Agency **Ph:** 310-288-4545
9830 Wilshire Blvd **Fax:** 310-288-4800
Beverly Hills, CA 90212
www.billmaher.com

Mahfood, Robin
President, CEO, and one of the original founders of Food for the Poor
Food for the Poor Inc **Ph:** 954-427-2222
550 SW 12th Ave **TF:** 800-427-9104
Dept 9662
Deerfield Beach, FL 33442
www.foodforthepoor.org

Mahfouz, Naguib (1911-)
Novelist (The Cairo Trilogy); winner of the 1988 Nobel Prize for Literature
Random House Publicity **Ph:** 212-782-9000
1745 Broadway
New York, NY 10019
www.randomhouse.com

Mahoney, John (1940-)
Actor
International Creative Management **Ph:** 310-550-4000
8942 Wilshire Blvd
Beverly Hills, CA 90211

Maiellaro, Matt
Animator, producer; co-creator of Space Ghost:Coast to Coast and Aqua Teen Hunger Force for Cartoon Network; also created 12 oz. Mouse for Cartoon Network's Adult Swim
Cartoon Network **Ph:** 404-885-2263
Williams Street
1065 Williams St
Atlanta, GA 30309
www.aquateencentral.com

Mailer, Norman (1923-)
Author
Random House Publicity **Ph:** 212-782-9000
1745 Broadway
New York, NY 10019
www.randomhouse.com

Makin, John H, PhD
Economist; former consultant to the US Treasury, the Congressional Budget Office, and the International Monetary Fund; visiting scholar at the American Enterprise Institute, where he specializes in international finance and financial markets
American Enterprise Institute for Public Policy Research **Ph:** 202-862-5800 **Fax:** 202-862-7177
1150 17th St NW Suite 1100
Washington, DC 20036
www.aei.org

Malakhov, Vladimir (1968-)
A principal dancer for American Ballet Theatre
American Ballet Theatre **Ph:** 212-477-3030
890 Broadway **Fax:** 212-254-5938
New York, NY 10003
www.abt.org/dancers

Malcolm, Steven (1949-)
Chairman, president, and CEO of Williams Companies Inc (natural gas businesses)
Williams Cos Inc **Ph:** 918-573-2000
1 Williams Center
Tulsa, OK 74172
www.williams.com

Maldonado, Chuck
Dancer/choreographer (choreographed opening and closing ceremonies at the 1996 Olympic Games in Atlanta)
Bloc Agency **Ph:** 323-954-7730
5651 Wilshire Blvd Suite C
Los Angeles, CA 90036
www.dancersunlimited.org/~chuck

Malhotra, Manny (1980-)
Professional hockey player
Columbus Blue Jackets **Ph:** 614-246-4625
Nationwide Arena **Fax:** 614-246-4007
200 W Nationwide Blvd 3rd Fl
Columbus, OH 43215
www.bluejackets.com

Malkin, Michelle (1970-)
Syndicated columnist (op-ed)
Creators Syndicate Inc **Ph:** 310-337-7003
5777 W Century Blvd Suite 700 **Fax:** 310-337-7625
Los Angeles, CA 90045
www.creators.com/opinion.html

Malkovich, John (1953-)
Actor
Creative Artists Agency **Ph:** 310-288-4545
9830 Wilshire Blvd **Fax:** 310-288-4800
Beverly Hills, CA 90212

Mallett, Jef
Cartoonist and illustrator; creator of the comic strip Frazz
United Feature Syndicate **Ph:** 212-293-8500
200 Madison Ave
New York, NY 10016
www.unitedfeatures.com

Mallon, Meg (1963-)
Professional golfer
Ladies Professional Golf Assn **Ph:** 386-274-6200
100 International Golf Dr **Fax:** 386-274-1099
Daytona Beach, FL 32124
www.lpga.com

Mallory, Mark
Mayor of Cincinnati and former US Congressman from Ohio
801 Plum St Rm 150 **Ph:** 513-352-3250
Cincinnati, OH 45202 **Fax:** 513-352-5201
www.cincinnati-oh.gov

Malloy, Mike
Host of a politically liberal radio talk show
Air America **Ph:** 646-274-4900
641 6th Ave **TF:** 866-303-2270
New York, NY 10011
www.mikemalloy.com

Malone, Jena (1984-)
Actor
United Talent Agency **Ph:** 310-273-6700
9560 Wilshire Blvd 5th Fl **Fax:** 310-247-1111
Beverly Hills, CA 90212

Malone, John, PhD (1941-)
Chairman of Liberty Media
Liberty Media Corp **Ph:** 720-875-5400
12300 Liberty Blvd **Fax:** 720-875-5401
Englewood, CO 80112
www.libertymedia.com

Malone, Moses (1955-)
Hall-of-fame basketball player (retired)
Naismith Memorial Basketball Hall of Fame **Ph:** 413-781-6500
Fax: 413-781-1939
1000 W Columbus Ave **TF:** 877-446-6752
Springfield, MA 01105
www.hoophall.com

Maloney, Carolyn B (1948-)
US Representative from New York (Democrat)
2331 Rayburn Bldg **Ph:** 202-225-7944
Washington, DC 20515 **Fax:** 202-225-4709
www.house.gov/maloney

Maloof, Gavin
Vice chairman of Maloof Companies, the Maloof family's diversified business that includes ownership of the Sacramento Kings NBA team, the Monarchs WNBA team, and ARCO Arena
Sacramento Kings **Ph:** 916-455-4647
ARCO Arena **Fax:** 916-928-6912
1 Sports Pkwy
Sacramento, CA 95834
www.nba.com/kings

Maloof, Joe
President of Maloof Companies, the Maloof family's diversified business that includes ownership of the Sacramento Kings NBA team, the Monarchs WNBA team, and ARCO Arena
Sacramento Kings **Ph:** 916-455-4647
ARCO Arena **Fax:** 916-928-6912
1 Sports Pkwy
Sacramento, CA 95834
www.nba.com/kings

Malouf, Waldy
Chef and co-owner of the Beacon Restaurant & Bar in New York City
Beacon Restaurant **Ph:** 212-332-0500
25 W 56th St
New York, NY 10019
www.beaconnyc.com

Maltbie, Roger (1951-)
Professional golfer (Champions Tour)
PGA Tour **Ph:** 904-285-3700
100 PGA Tour Blvd
Ponte Vedra Beach, FL 32082
www.pgatour.com

Maltby, Kirk (1972-)
Professional hockey player
Detroit Red Wings **Ph:** 313-396-7544
Joe Louis Arena **Fax:** 313-567-0296
600 Civic Center Dr
Detroit, MI 48226
www.detroitredwings.com

Maltin, Leonard (1950-)
Film critic, historian, and author; resident movie buff on Entertainment Tonight
Paramount Television Group **Ph:** 323-956-5000
Entertainment Tonight **Fax:** 323-862-0282
5555 Melrose Ave
Los Angeles, CA 90038
www.leonardmaltin.com

Malveaux, Suzanne
CNN White House correspondent
CNN **Ph:** 202-898-7900
CNN Bldg
820 1st St NE
Washington, DC 20002
www.cnn.com/CNN/anchors_reporters

Mamet, David (1947-)
Writer and director of plays and movies
International Creative Management **Ph:** 310-550-4000
8942 Wilshire Blvd
Beverly Hills, CA 90211

Mammana, Dennis
Astronomer, lecturer, and celestial photographer; also writes the syndicated feature Stargazers, which is distributed through Copley News Service
Copley News Service **Ph:** 619-293-1818
PO Box 120190
San Diego, CA 92112
www.skyscapes.com

Manchin, Joe III (1947-)
Governor of West Virginia (Democrat)
State Capitol Bldg **Ph:** 304-558-2000
1900 Kanawha Blvd E **Fax:** 304-342-7025
Charleston, WV 25305
www.wvgov.org

Mandel, Howie (1955-)
Comedian
International Creative Management **Ph:** 310-550-4000
8942 Wilshire Blvd
Beverly Hills, CA 90211
www.howiemandel.com

Mangini, Eric (1971-)
Football coach
New York Jets **Ph:** 516-560-8100
1000 Fulton Ave **Fax:** 516-560-8198
Hempstead, NY 11550
www.newyorkjets.com

Manheim, Camryn (1961-)
Actor
CESD Talent Agency **Ph:** 310-475-2111
10635 Santa Monica Blvd Suites 130/135
Los Angeles, CA 90025
www.camryn.com

Manilow, Barry (1943-)
Musician, singer, composer, producer
William Morris Agency **Ph:** 310-859-4000
1 William Morris Pl **Fax:** 310-859-4462
Beverly Hills, CA 90212
www.manilow.com

Manion, John
Executive Chef at Mas Restaurant in Chicago (Nuevo Latino cuisine)
Mas Restaurant **Ph:** 773-276-8700
1670 W Division
Chicago, IL 60622
www.masrestaurant.com

Mankiewicz, Josh
Dateline NBC correspondent
NBC News **Ph:** 818-840-4444
3000 W Alameda Ave
Burbank, CA 91523
www.msnbc.msn.com/id/3360263

Mankoff, Robert
New Yorker Magazine cartoonist and cartoon editor
Cartoon Bank **Ph:** 914-478-5527
New Yorker Magazine **Fax:** 914-478-5604
28 Wells Ave Bldg 3 4th Fl
Yonkers, NY 10701
www.cartoonbank.com

Mann, Emily (1952-)
Theatrical writer, producer, director; artistic director of McCarter Theatre
McCarter Theatre **Ph:** 609-258-6500
91 University Pl **Fax:** 609-497-0369
Princeton, NJ 08540
www.mccarter.org

Mann, Michael (1943-)
Writer/producer/director (film & television)
Creative Artists Agency **Ph:** 310-288-4545
9830 Wilshire Blvd **Fax:** 310-288-4800
Beverly Hills, CA 90212

Mann, Sally (1951-)
Photographer
Edwynn Houk Gallery **Ph:** 212-750-7070
745 5th Ave **Fax:** 212-688-4848
New York, NY 10151
www.houkgallery.com

Mannheim Steamroller (1947-)
Recording group created by composer/musician Chip Davis
American Gramaphone LLC **Ph:** 402-457-4341
9130 Mormon Bridge Rd **Fax:** 402-457-4332
Omaha, NE 68152
www.mannheimsteamroller.com

Manning, Eli (1981-)
Professional football player; brother of Peyton Manning
New York Giants **Ph:** 201-935-8111
Giants Stadium **Fax:** 201-939-4134
East Rutherford, NJ 07073
www.giants.com

Manning, Peyton (1976-)
Professional football player
Indianapolis Colts **Ph:** 317-297-2658
7001 W 56th St **Fax:** 317-297-8971
Indianapolis, IN 46254
www.peytonmanning.com

Manoogian, Richard A
Chairman of Masco Corp, which manufactures brand-name consumer products for the home and family, including Delta faucets
Masco Corp **Ph:** 313-792-6266
21001 Van Born Rd **Fax:** 313-792-6135
Taylor, MI 48180

Manson, Marilyn (1969-)
Singer (metal)
Creative Artists Agency **Ph:** 310-288-4545
9830 Wilshire Blvd **Fax:** 310-288-4800
Beverly Hills, CA 90212
marilynmanson.com

Mantegna, Joe (1947-)
Actor
Peter Strain & Assoc **Ph:** 323-525-3391
5455 Wilshire Blvd Suite 1812 **Fax:** 323-525-0881
Los Angeles, CA 90036
www.joemantegna.com

Mantle, Mickey (1931-1995)
Legendary New York Yankees centerfielder & all-time sports hero
National Baseball Hall of Fame & Museum **Ph:** 607-547-7200
Fax: 607-547-2044
25 Main St **TF:** 888-425-5633
Cooperstown, NY 13326
www.baseballhalloffame.org

Manuel, Charlie (1944-)
Baseball manager
Philadelphia Phillies **Ph:** 215-463-6000
Citizens Bank Park
1 Citizens Bank Park Way
Philadelphia, PA 19148
philadelphia.phillies.mlb.com

Manzullo, Donald (1944-)
US Representative from Illinois (Republican)
2228 Rayburn Bldg **Ph:** 202-225-5676
Washington, DC 20515 **Fax:** 202-225-5284
manzullo.house.gov

Mapp, Justin (1984-)
Professional soccer player
Chicago Fire **Ph:** 312-705-7200
980 N Michigan Ave Suite 1998 **Fax:** 312-705-7393
Chicago, IL 60611
chicago.fire.mlsnet.com

Mapplethorpe, Robert (1946-1989)
Photographer
Art + Commerce **Ph:** 212-206-0737
755 Washington St **Fax:** 212-463-7267
New York, NY 10014
www.mapplethorpe.org

Mara, Wellington T (1916-)
Co-owner of the New York Giants football franchise
New York Giants **Ph:** 201-935-8111
Giants Stadium **Fax:** 201-935-8493
East Rutherford, NJ 07073
www.giants.com

Maravich, Pete (1947-1988)
Former professional basketball player; member of the Basketball Hall of Fame
Naismith Memorial Basketball Hall of Fame **Ph:** 413-781-6500
Fax: 413-781-1939
1000 W Columbus Ave **TF:** 877-446-6752
Springfield, MA 01105
www.hoophall.com

Marber, Patrick (1964-)
Playwright & screen writer
Creative Artists Agency **Ph:** 310-288-4545
9830 Wilshire Blvd **Fax:** 310-288-4800
Beverly Hills, CA 90212

Marbury, Stephon (1977-)
Professional basketball player
New York Knicks **Ph:** 212-476-5641
Madison Square Garden **Fax:** 212-465-6498
2 Pennsylvania Plaza
New York, NY 10121
www.nba.com/knicks

Marchant, Kenny (1951-)
US Representative from Texas (Republican)
501 Cannon Bldg **Ph:** 202-225-6605
Washington, DC 20515 **Fax:** 202-225-0074
www.marchant.house.gov

Marchant, Todd (1973-)
Professional hockey player
Mighty Ducks of Anaheim **Ph:** 714-704-2700
Arrowhead Pond **Fax:** 714-940-2953
2695 Katella Ave
Anaheim, CA 92806
www.mightyducks.com

Marciuliano, Francesco
Writes the comic strip Sally Forth
King Features Syndicate Inc **Ph:** 212-455-4000
888 7th Ave 2nd Fl
New York, NY 10019
www.kingfeatures.com

Marcus, Rudolph A, PhD (1923-)
Winner of the 1992 Nobel Prize in Chemistry for his contributions to the theory of electron transfer reactions in chemical systems
Arthur Amos Noyes Laboratory of Chemical Physics **Ph:** 626-395-6566
California Institute of Technology
MC 127-72
Pasadena, CA 91125
www.cce.caltech.edu/faculty

Mare, Olindo (1973-)
Professional football player
Miami Dolphins **Ph:** 954-452-7000
7500 SW 30th St **Fax:** 954-452-7055
Davie, FL 33314
www.miamidolphins.com

Margolis, Matthew
Dog training expert; writes the syndicated column Dogs, Cats and Other People
Creators Syndicate Inc **Ph:** 310-337-7003
5777 W Century Blvd Suite 700 **Fax:** 310-337-7625
Los Angeles, CA 90045
www.unclematty.com

Margulies, Donald (1954-)
Dramatist (Dinner with Friends)
Rosenstone/Wender **Ph:** 212-725-9445
38 E 29th St 10th Fl **Fax:** 212-725-9447
New York, NY 10016

Margulies, Jimmy
Caricaturist; editorial/political cartoonist for The Record in Hackensack, NJ
Creators Syndicate Inc **Ph:** 310-337-7003
5777 W Century Blvd Suite 700 **Fax:** 310-337-7625
Los Angeles, CA 90045
www.creators.com

Margulies, Julianna (1966-)
Actor
Special Artists Agency **Ph:** 310-859-9688
9465 Wilshire Blvd Suite 890
Beverly Hills, CA 90212

Margulis, Lynn, PhD (1938-)
Biologist best known for her theory of symbiogenesis
University of Massachusetts **Ph:** 413-545-2286
Dept of Geosciences **Fax:** 413-545-1200
611 N Pleasant St
233 Morrill Science Ctr
Amherst, MA 01003
www.geo.umass.edu

Marinelli, Rod
Football coach
Detroit Lions **Ph:** 313-216-4000
222 Republic Dr **Fax:** 313-216-4069
Allen Park, MI 48101
www.detroitlions.com

Marino, Dan (1961-)
Former NFL quarterback (retired) and hall of famer; NFL studio analyst and a host of Inside the NFL on HBO
CBS Sports **Ph:** 212-975-4321
51 W 52nd St
New York, NY 10019
danmarino.com

Marion, Shawn (1978-)
Professional basketball player
Phoenix Suns **Ph:** 602-379-7900
America West Arena **Fax:** 602-379-7990
201 E Jefferson St
Phoenix, AZ 85004
www.nba.com/suns

Mark, Reuben
Chairman and CEO of Colgate-Palmolive
Colgate-Palmolive Co **Ph:** 212-310-2000
300 Park Ave
New York, NY 10022
www.colgate.com

Markey, Edward J (1946-)
US Representative from Massachusetts (Democrat)
2108 Rayburn Bldg **Ph:** 202-225-2836
Washington, DC 20515 **Fax:** 202-226-0092
www.house.gov/markey

Marks, John
Mayor of Tallahassee, Florida
300 S Adams St **Ph:** 850-891-2000
Tallahassee, FL 32301 **Fax:** 850-891-8542
www.talgov.com

Markstein, Gary
Editorial/political cartoonist for the Milwaukee Journal-Sentinel
Copley News Service **Ph:** 619-293-1818
PO Box 120190
San Diego, CA 92112
www.copleynews.com

Marleau, Patrick (1979-)
Professional hockey player
San Jose Sharks **Ph:** 408-287-7070
HP Pavilion at San Jose **Fax:** 408-999-5797
525 W Santa Clara St
San Jose, CA 95113
www.sjsharks.com

Marlette, Doug
Editorial cartoonist; is also the creator of the comic strip Kudzu
Tribune Media Services Inc **Ph:** 312-222-4444
435 N Michigan Ave Suite 1500
Chicago, IL 60611
www.comicspage.com

Marley, Ziggy (1968-)
Jamaican reggae singer; son of legendary reggae artist Bob Marley
William Morris Agency **Ph:** 310-859-4000
1 William Morris Pl **Fax:** 310-859-4462
Beverly Hills, CA 90212
www.ziggymarley.com

Marlin, Sterling (1957-)
NASCAR driver
MB2 Motorsports **Ph:** 704-720-0733
1035 Mecklenburg Hwy
PO Box 270
Mooresville, NC 28115
www.mb2mbvmotorsports.com

Maron, Margaret
Mystery writer (Deborah Knott series)
Warner Books **Ph:** 212-522-7200
c/o Author Mail
1271 Ave of the Americas
New York, NY 10020
www.margaretmaron.com

Maroth, Mike (1977-)
Professional baseball player
Detroit Tigers **Ph:** 313-962-4000
Comerica Park **Fax:** 313-471-2138
2100 Woodward Ave
Detroit, MI 48201
detroit.tigers.mlb.com

Marquis, Jason (1978-)
Professional baseball player
Saint Louis Cardinals **Ph:** 314-421-3060
250 Stadium Plaza **Fax:** 314-425-0640
Saint Louis, MO 63102
stlouis.cardinals.mlb.com

Marr, Tom
Radio talk show host (conservative)
WCBM-AM **Ph:** 410-580-6800
1726 Reisterstown Rd
Suite 117
Baltimore, MD 21208
www.tommarr.com

Marriott, JW Jr (1932-)
Chairman & CEO of Marriott International (manages and franchises hotels)
Marriott International Inc **Ph:** 301-380-3000
1 Marriott Dr **Fax:** 301-380-8957
Washington, DC 20058
www.marriott.com

Marriott, Richard
Chairman of the Board of Host Marriott Corp (lodging real estate property owner)
Host Marriott Corp **Ph:** 240-744-1000
6903 Rockledge Dr Suite 1500
Bethesda, MD 20817
www.hostmarriott.com

Marron, Donald B, PhD
Acting Director of the Congressional Budget Office; previously was Chief Economist for the President's Council of Economic Advisers
Congressional Budget Office **Ph:** 202-226-2700
Ford House Office Bldg Rm 402 **Fax:** 202-225-7509
2nd & D Sts SW
Washington, DC 20515
www.cbo.gov

Mars, John F (1937-)
Chairman of Mars Inc; also co-owner, with siblings Forrest Jr. and Jacqueline, of Mars Inc
Mars Inc **Ph:** 703-821-4900
6885 Elm St **Fax:** 703-448-9678
McLean, VA 22101

Marsalis, Branford (1960-)
Jazz saxophonist
Wilkins Management **Ph:** 617-354-2736
323 Broadway **Fax:** 617-354-2396
Cambridge, MA 02139
www.branfordmarsalis.com

Marsalis, Wynton (1961-)
Jazz & classical musician (trumpet) and composer; artistic director of Jazz at Lincoln Center
Jazz at Lincoln Center **Ph:** 212-258-9800
33 W 60th St **Fax:** 212-258-9900
New York, NY 10023
www.wyntonmarsalis.net

Marshall, Donyell (1973-)
Professional basketball player
Cleveland Cavaliers **Ph:** 216-420-2000
Quicken Loans Arena **Fax:** 216-420-2298
1 Center Ct
Cleveland, OH 44115
www.nba.com/cavaliers

Marshall, Garry (1934-)
Film & TV producer/director/writer; actor
Creative Artists Agency **Ph:** 310-288-4545
9830 Wilshire Blvd **Fax:** 310-288-4800
Beverly Hills, CA 90212

Marshall, James C (1948-)
US Representative from Georgia (Democrat)
515 Cannon Bldg **Ph:** 202-225-6531
Washington, DC 20515 **Fax:** 202-225-3013
www.house.gov/marshall

Marshall, Jon A
President & CEO of GlobalSantaFe Corp, an oil and gas drilling contractor
GlobalSantaFe Corp **Ph:** 281-925-6000
15375 Memorial Dr **Fax:** 281-925-6010
Houston, TX 77079
www.gsfdrill.com

Marshall, Penny (1942-)
Movie director/producer; also actor
International Creative Management **Ph:** 310-550-4000
8942 Wilshire Blvd
Beverly Hills, CA 90211

Marshall, Thurgood (1908-1993)
First African American appointed to the Supreme Court of the United States; chief counsel in Brown vs. Board of Education, which ordered desegregation of public schools
Thurgood Marshall Scholarship Fund **Ph:** 212-573-8888
Fax: 212-573-8497
80 Maiden Ln Suite 2204
New York, NY 10038
www.thurgoodmarshallfund.org

Marshall, Tyrone (1974-)
Professional soccer player
Los Angeles Galaxy **Ph:** 310-630-2200
Home Depot Center **Fax:** 310-630-2250
18400 Avalon Blvd Suite 200
Carson, CA 90746
www.lagalaxy.com

Marsters, James (1962-)
Actor
Himber Entertainment **Ph:** 310-276-2500
211 S Beverly Dr **Fax:** 310-276-2538
Beverly Hills, CA 90212
www.jamesmarsters.com

Martin, Ann M (1955-)
Author of The Babysitters Club series
Scholastic Inc **Ph:** 212-343-6100
557 Broadway
New York, NY 10012
www.scholastic.com/annmartin

Martin, Bill Jr
Author of books for young children (Brown Bear, Brown Bear, What Do You See?)
Books for Young Readers **Ph:** 212-886-9200
Henry Holt & Co
115 W 18th St
New York, NY 10011
www.billmartinjr.com

Martin, Curtis (1973-)
Professional football player
New York Jets **Ph:** 516-560-8100
1000 Fulton Ave **Fax:** 516-560-8198
Hempstead, NY 11550
www.newyorkjets.com

Martin, David (1943-)
CBS News's National Security correspondent, covering the Pentagon and the State Dept
CBS News **Ph:** 202-457-4481
2020 M St NW
Washington, DC 20036
www.cbsnews.com

Martin, Ellen James
Writes the syndicated real estate column Smart Moves
Universal Press Syndicate **Ph:** 816-932-6600
4520 Main St
Kansas City, MO 64111
www.amuniversal.com/ups/features

Martin, Jacques (1952-)
Hockey coach
Florida Panthers **Ph:** 954-835-7000
BankAtlantic Center **Fax:** 954-835-7600
1 Panther Pkwy
Sunrise, FL 33323
www.floridapanthers.com

Martin, Joe
Creator of the comic strips Cats With Hands, Willy 'n Ethel, and Mr. Boffo
Neatly Chiseled Features **Ph:** 262-248-9460
1870 Loramoor Ln **Fax:** 262-248-3431
Lake Geneva, WI 53147
www.mrboffo.com

Martin, Judith (1938-)
Author of the Miss Manners etiquette-related advice column
United Feature Syndicate **Ph:** 212-293-8500
200 Madison Ave
New York, NY 10016
www.unitedfeatures.com

Martin, Kenyon (1977-)
Professional basketball player
Denver Nuggets **Ph:** 303-405-1100
Pepsi Center **Fax:** 303-575-1920
1000 Chopper Cir
Denver, CO 80204
www.nba.com/nuggets

Martin, Mark (1959-)
NASCAR driver
Roush Racing **Ph:** 704-720-4100
4600 Roush Pl NW
Concord, NC 28027
www.roushracing.com

Martin, Ricky (1971-)
Latin singer
Creative Artists Agency **Ph:** 310-288-4545
9830 Wilshire Blvd **Fax:** 310-288-4800
Beverly Hills, CA 90212
www.rickymartin.com

Martin, Roland S
Editor of BlackAmericaWeb.com and news editor for Savoy Magazine; also writes a syndicated column
Creators Syndicate Inc **Ph:** 310-337-7003
5777 W Century Blvd Suite 700 **Fax:** 310-337-7625
Los Angeles, CA 90045
www.creators.com/opinion.html

Martin, Steve (1945-)
Actor, comedian, and writer
International Creative Management **Ph:** 310-550-4000
8942 Wilshire Blvd
Beverly Hills, CA 90211
www.stevemartin.com

Martinez, Mel R (1946-)
US Senator from Florida (Republican); former US Secretary of Housing & Urban Development
C2 Russell Bldg **Ph:** 202-224-3041
Washington, DC 20510 **Fax:** 202-228-5172
martinez.senate.gov

Martinez, Pedro (1971-)
Professional baseball player
New York Mets **Ph:** 718-507-6387
Shea Stadium **Fax:** 718-507-6395
123-01 Roosevelt Ave
Flushing, NY 11368
newyork.mets.mlb.com

Martinez, Victor
Author of Parrot in the Oven: Mi Vida
HarperCollins Children's Books **Ph:** 212-261-6500
1350 Ave of the Americas
New York, NY 10019
www.harperchildrens.com

Martinez, Victor (1978-)
Professional baseball player
Cleveland Indians **Ph:** 216-420-4200
Jacobs Field **Fax:** 216-420-4624
2401 Ontario St
Cleveland, OH 44115
cleveland.indians.mlb.com

Martini, Steve (1946-)
Mystery writer (former attorney, administrative law judge, and supervising hearing officer)
Putnam Publicity **Ph:** 212-366-2000
375 Hudson St
New York, NY 10014
www.stevemartini.com

Martino, Tom
Radio show host/consumer advocate
Westwood One **Ph:** 212-641-2000
40 W 57th St 5th Fl **Fax:** 212-641-2172
New York, NY 10019
www.troubleshooter.com

Martins, Nilas (1967-)
A principal dancer with the New York City Ballet; has also performed on television and in film
New York City Ballet **Ph:** 212-870-5656
New York State Theater **Fax:** 212-870-7791
20 Lincoln Center
New York, NY 10023
www.nycballet.com/about/dancers.html

Martins, Peter (1946-)
Dancer & choreographer; Ballet Master in Chief for the New York City Ballet
New York City Ballet **Ph:** 212-870-5656
New York State Theater **Fax:** 212-870-7791
20 Lincoln Center
New York, NY 10023
www.nycballet.com/about/staffart.html

Martins, Thiago (1976-)
Professional soccer player
Colorado Rapids **Ph:** 303-405-1100
Pepsi Center **Fax:** 720-931-2022
1000 Chopper Cir
Denver, CO 80204
www.coloradorapids.com

Marzollo, Jean (1942-)
Children's book author (I Spy books, Shanna Show books); also illustrates some of her books (Ten Little Eggs)
Warner Books **Ph:** 212-522-7200
c/o Author Mail
1271 Ave of the Americas
New York, NY 10020
www.jeanmarzollo.com

Mas, Jorge
Chairman of the Board of MasTec, a provider of telecommunications-related engineering and construction services, and of Neff Corp, an equipment rental company; he is also chairman of the Cuban American National Foundation
MasTec Inc **Ph:** 305-599-1800
800 S Douglas Rd 12th Fl **Fax:** 305-406-1909
Coral Gables, FL 33134
www.mastec.com

Maslin, Janet (1949-)
New York Times book reviewer
New York Times **Ph:** 212-556-1234
229 W 43rd St
New York, NY 10036

Mason, Bobbie Ann (1942-)
Southern novelist (Feather Crowns; In Country)
HarperCollins Publishers **Ph:** 212-207-7000
c/o Author Mail
10 E 53rd St
New York, NY 10022
www.harpercollins.com

Mason, Derrick (1974-)
Professional football player
Baltimore Ravens **Ph:** 410-547-8100
1101 Russell St **Fax:** 410-547-8112
Baltimore, MD 21230
www.baltimoreravens.com

Mason, Desmond (1977-)
Professional basketball player
New Orleans/Oklahoma City Hornets **Ph:** 405-208-4800
Oklahoma Tower
210 Park Ave Suite 1850
Oklahoma City, OK 73102
www.nba.com/hornets

Mason, Jackie (1931-)
Comedian
William Morris Agency **Ph:** 310-859-4000
1 William Morris Pl **Fax:** 310-859-4462
Beverly Hills, CA 90212
www.jackiemason.com

Masry, Edward (1932-2005)
Personal injury/toxic tort attorney whose firm successfully handled the Hinkley case profiled in the movie Erin Brockovich
Masry & Vititoe **Ph:** 818-991-8900
5707 Corsa Ave 2nd Fl **Fax:** 818-991-6200
Westlake Village, CA 91362 **TF:** 800-561-5500
www.masryvititoe.com

Master P (1967-)
Hip-hop recording artist/manager (real name is Percy Miller)
Agency West Entertainment **Ph:** 323-933-8709
4401 Wilshire Blvd Suite 250 **Fax:** 323-933-8710
Los Angeles, CA 90010

Masters, Roy (1928-)
Talk radio show host; provides on-air counseling for callers to help them understand and reclaim control over their own lives
Talk Radio Network **Ph:** 541-664-8827
PO Box 3755 **Fax:** 541-664-6250
Central Point, OR 97502
www.talkradionetwork.com

Masterson, Mary Stuart (1966-)
Actor
Creative Artists Agency **Ph:** 310-288-4545
9830 Wilshire Blvd **Fax:** 310-288-4800
Beverly Hills, CA 90212

Matalin, Mary (1953-)
Conservative political adviser & commentator; married to James Carville
Gaslight Inc **Ph:** 703-739-6006
424 S Washington St **Fax:** 703-739-6171
Alexandria, VA 22314
www.matalin.info

matchbox twenty
Rock group
Creative Artists Agency **Ph:** 310-288-4545
9830 Wilshire Blvd **Fax:** 310-288-4800
Beverly Hills, CA 90212
www.matchboxtwenty.com

Matheny, Mike (1970-)
Professional baseball player
San Francisco Giants **Ph:** 415-972-2000
AT & T Park
24 Willie Mays Plaza
San Francisco, CA 94107
sanfrancisco.giants.mlb.com

Matheson, Jim (1960-)
US Representative from Utah (Democrat)
1222 Longworth Bldg **Ph:** 202-225-3011
Washington, DC 20515 **Fax:** 202-225-5638
matheson.house.gov

Mathis, Clint (1976-)
Professional soccer player
Colorado Rapids **Ph:** 303-405-1100
Pepsi Center **Fax:** 720-931-2022
1000 Chopper Cir
Denver, CO 80204
www.coloradorapids.com

Mathis, Johnny (1935-)
Singer
William Morris Agency **Ph:** 310-859-4000
1 William Morris Pl **Fax:** 310-859-4462
Beverly Hills, CA 90212
www.johnnymathis.com

Mathisen, Tyler
Managing Editor of CNBC Business News
CNBC **Ph:** 201-735-2622
900 Sylvan Ave
Englewood Cliffs, NJ 07632
moneycentral.msn.com/cnbc/tv

Matlin, Marlee (1965-)
Actor
Innovative Artists **Ph:** 310-656-0400
1505 10th St **Fax:** 310-656-0456
Santa Monica, CA 90401
www.marleeonline.com

Matsuhisa, Nobuyuki
Chef and restauranteur; his restaurants (most named either Nobu or Matsuhisa) are located in the US, Europe, and Asia
Matsuhisa Restaurant **Ph:** 310-659-9639
129 N La Cienega
Beverly Hills, CA 90211
www.nobumatsuhisa.com

Matsui, Doris (1944-)
US Representative from California (Democrat)
2310 Rayburn Bldg **Ph:** 202-225-7163
Washington, DC 20515 **Fax:** 202-225-0566
www.house.gov/matsui

Matsui, Hideki (1974-)
Professional baseball player
New York Yankees **Ph:** 718-293-4300
Yankee Stadium **Fax:** 718-293-8414
161st St & River Ave
Bronx, NY 10451
newyork.yankees.mlb.com

Matsui, Kazuo (1975-)
Professional baseball player
New York Mets **Ph:** 718-507-6387
Shea Stadium **Fax:** 718-507-6395
123-01 Roosevelt Ave
Flushing, NY 11368
newyork.mets.mlb.com

Matsui, Keiko (1963-)
Jazz keyboardist and composer
Ted Kurland Assoc **Ph:** 617-254-0007
173 Brighton Ave **Fax:** 617-782-3577
Boston, MA 02134
www.keikomatsui.com

Mattea, Kathy (1959-)
Country/gospel singer
International Music Network **Ph:** 978-283-2883
278 Main St **Fax:** 978-283-2330
Gloucester, MA 01930
www.kathymattea.com

Matthews, Chris (1945-)
Host of the MSNBC-TV talk show Hardball with Chris Matthews
MSNBC TV **Ph:** 201-583-5000
1 MSNBC Plaza
Secaucus, NJ 07094
www.msnbc.msn.com/id/3080263

Matthews, Dave
Vocalist/guitarist in the Dave Matthews Band (rock band)
Monterey Peninsula Artists/ Paradigm **Ph:** 831-375-4889 **Fax:** 831-375-2623
509 Hartnell St
Monterey, CA 93940
www.davematthewsband.com

Matthiessen, Peter (1927-)
Naturalist and explorer; author of The Snow Leopard (nonfiction), At Play in the Fields of the Lord (fiction), and numerous other works, primarily nonfiction
Farrar Straus & Giroux **Ph:** 212-741-6900
19 Union Sq W
New York, NY 10003
www.fsgbooks.com

Maughan, Rex
Founder, president, and CEO of Forever Living Products International (health & beauty products)
Forever Living Products International Inc **Ph:** 480-998-8888 **Fax:** 480-905-8451
7501 E McCormick Pkwy
Scottsdale, AZ 85258
www.foreverliving.com

Maupin, Armistead (1944-)
Novelist (Tales of the City series) and gay activist
Steven Barclay Agency **Ph:** 707-773-0654
12 Western Ave **Fax:** 707-778-1868
Petaluma, CA 94952 **TF:** 888-965-7323
www.barclayagency.com

Mauresmo, Amelie (1979-)
Professional tennis player
WTA Tour **Ph:** 727-895-5000
1 Progress Plaza Suite 1500 **Fax:** 727-894-1982
Saint Petersburg, FL 33701
www.ameliemauresmo.fr

Mavrothalassitis, George
Chef and proprietor of Chef Mavro restaurant in Honolulu; a founding member of Hawaii Regional Cuisine
Chef Mavro **Ph:** 808-944-4714
1969 S King St
Honolulu, HI 96826
www.chefmavro.com

Max, Peter (1937-)
Artist (pop art/neo-Expressionism)
Gallery M **Ph:** 303-331-8400
2830 E 3rd Ave **TF:** 877-331-8401
Denver, CO 80206
www.petermax.com

Maxwell, Carla (1945-)
Dancer; artistic director of the Limon Dance Co., a repertory dance ensemble founded by Jose Limon
Jose Limon Dance Foundation **Ph:** 212-777-3353
307 W 38th St Suite 1105 **Fax:** 212-777-4764
New York, NY 10018
www.limon.org

Maxwell, John C, PhD
Leadership expert, speaker, author, and founder of Maximum Impact, a people development company
Maximum Impact **Ph:** 678-225-3100
PO Box 7700 **Fax:** 678-225-3414
Atlanta, GA 30357 **TF:** 877-225-3311
www.maximumimpact.com/speakers

Maxwell, Kay J
President of the League of Women Voters
League of Women Voters **Ph:** 202-429-1965
1730 M St NW Suite 1000 **Fax:** 202-429-0854
Washington, DC 20036
www.lwv.org

May, Elaine (1932-)
Playwright/screenwriter (Primary Colors; The Birdcage); during the 1960s she did comedy routines with Mike Nichols (they were married at one time)
William Morris Agency **Ph:** 310-859-4000
1 William Morris Pl **Fax:** 310-859-4462
Beverly Hills, CA 90212

Mayans, Carlos (1948-)
Mayor of Wichita, Kansas
455 N Main St **Ph:** 316-268-4331
MS 1-135 **Fax:** 316-268-4333
Wichita, KS 67202
www.wichita.gov/Government

Mayfair, Billy (1966-)
Professional golfer
Gaylord Sports Management **Ph:** 480-483-9500
13845 N Northsight Blvd Suite 200
Scottsdale, AZ 85260
www.gaylordsports.com

Mayfield, Jeremy (1969-)
NASCAR driver
Evernham Motorsports **Ph:** 704-924-9404
320 Aviation Dr **Fax:** 704-924-9495
Statesville, NC 28677
www.jeremymayfield.com

Mayfield, Max
Director of the Tropical Prediction Center, National Hurricane Center
National Hurricane Center **Ph:** 305-229-4470
Tropical Prediction Center **Fax:** 305-553-1901
11691 SW 17th St
Miami, FL 33165
www.whitehouse.gov/government/m_mayfield-bio.html

Maynard, Joyce
Author of books for adults and for young adults (To Die For; The Usual Rules)
St Martin's Press **Ph:** 212-674-5151
Attn: Publicity Dept
175 5th Ave
New York, NY 10010
www.joycemaynard.com

Mayne, Kenny (1959-)
Sports news co-anchor & reporter
ESPN **Ph:** 860-585-2000
EPSN Plaza
935 Middle St
Bristol, CT 06010
sports.espn.go.com/espntv/espnGuide

Mays, L Lowry
Chairman of Clear Channel Communications
Clear Channel Communications Inc **Ph:** 210-822-2828 **Fax:** 210-822-2299
200 E Basse Rd
San Antonio, TX 78209
www.clearchannel.com

Mazer, Norma Fox (1931-)
Author of short story collections and novels for young adults (After the Rain, Missing Pieces, Out of Control)
HarperCollins Children's Books **Ph:** 212-261-6500
1350 Ave of the Americas
New York, NY 10019
www.harperchildrens.com

McAllister, Deuce (1978-)
Professional football player
New Orleans Saints **Ph:** 504-733-0255
5800 Airline Dr **Fax:** 504-731-1768
Metairie, LA 70003
www.neworleanssaints.com

McAllister, Rallie, MD
Writes a syndicated column on health & medicine (practices emergency medicine in a Level One trauma center)
Creators Syndicate Inc **Ph:** 310-337-7003
5777 W Century Blvd Suite 700 **Fax:** 310-337-7625
Los Angeles, CA 90045
www.creators.com

McBain, Ed (1926-)
Pen name of Evan Hunter, under which he writes mysteries
Gelfman Schneider Literary Agency **Ph:** 212-245-1993 **Fax:** 212-245-8678
250 W 57th St Suite 2515
New York, NY 10107
www.edmcbain.com

McBride, Jeff (1959-)
Magician
Tobias Beckwith Inc **Ph:** 702-697-7002
3960 Briarcrest Ct
Las Vegas, NV 89120
www.mcbridemagic.com

McBride, Martina (1966-)
Country singer
CAA Nashville **Ph:** 615-383-8787
3310 West End Ave 5th Fl **Fax:** 615-383-4937
Nashville, TN 37203
martina-mcbride.com

McCabe, Bryan (1975-)
Professional hockey player
Toronto Maple Leafs **Ph:** 416-815-5700
Air Canada Center
40 Bay St Suite 400
Toronto, ON M5J2X2
www.mapleleafs.com

McCaffrey, Anne (1926-)
Science fiction author (Dragonriders of Pern books)
Ballantine Books Publicity **Ph:** 212-782-9000
1745 Broadway
New York, NY 10019
www.annemccaffrey.org

McCain, John (1936-)
US Senator from Arizona (Republican)
241 Russell Bldg **Ph:** 202-224-2235
Washington, DC 20510 **Fax:** 202-228-2862
mccain.senate.gov

McCann, James F
Chairman and CEO of 1-800-flowers.com
1-800-FLOWERS.com Inc **Ph:** 516-237-6000
1 Old Country Rd
Carle Place, NY 11514
www.1800flowers.com

McCartan, Patrick F (1934-)
Attorney; works on complex antitrust, taxation, takeovers, and officer/director liability cases and various kinds of securities/shareholder litigation; is active in corporate governance matters and in product liability/consumer class actions
Jones Day **Ph:** 216-586-3939
North Point **Fax:** 216-579-0212
901 Lakeside Ave
Cleveland, OH 44114
www1.jonesday.com

McCarthy, Carolyn (1944-)
US Representative from New York (Democrat)
106 Cannon Bldg **Ph:** 202-225-5516
Washington, DC 20515 **Fax:** 202-225-5758
carolynmccarthy.house.gov

McCarthy, Colman (1938-)
Former Washington Post columnist and peace advocate; founder of the Center for Teaching Peace, which helps schools begin or broaden peace studies programs
Center for Teaching Peace **Ph:** 202-537-1372
4501 Van Ness St
Washington, DC 20016

McCarthy, Cormac (1933-)
Author (All the Pretty Horses)
International Creative Management **Ph:** 212-556-5600
40 West 57th St 17th Fl
New York, NY 10019
www.cormacmccarthy.com

McCarthy, Jenny (1972-)
Actor
William Morris Agency **Ph:** 310-859-4000
1 William Morris Pl **Fax:** 310-859-4462
Beverly Hills, CA 90212

McCarthy, Mike
Football coach
Green Bay Packers **Ph:** 920-569-7500
PO Box 10628 **Fax:** 920-569-7301
Green Bay, WI 54307
www.packers.com

McCartney, Paul (1942-)
Singer/songwriter/composer; former Beatle
Paul Freundlich Associates **Ph:** 212-334-6116
451 Greenwich St Suite 503 **Fax:** 212-334-6336
New York, NY 10013
www.paulmccartney.com

McCartney, Stella (1971-)
Fashion designer; daughter of Paul McCartney
Stella McCartney New York **Ph:** 212-255-1556
429 W 14th St
New York, NY 10014
www.stellamccartney.com

McCarty, Darren (1973-)
Professional hockey player
Calgary Flames **Ph:** 403-777-2177
Pengrowth Saddledome **Fax:** 403-777-2195
555 Saddledome Rise SE
Calgary, AB T2G2W1
www.calgaryflames.com

McCarver, Tim (1959-)
Former major league baseball player; TV sports analyst and interviewer
Fox Sports Net **Ph:** 310-369-9160
10201 W Pico Blvd **Fax:** 310-969-6049
Bldg 101
Los Angeles, CA 90035
www.timmccarver.com

McCaskey, Michael
Chairman of the Chicago Bears football franchise; grandson of team founder George Halas
Chicago Bears **Ph:** 847-295-6600
Halas Hall at Conway Park **Fax:** 847-295-8986
1000 Football Dr
Lake Forest, IL 60045

McCaslin, John
Journalist; writes the syndicated column The Beltway Beat
Tribune Media Services Inc **Ph:** 312-222-4444
435 N Michigan Ave Suite 1500
Chicago, IL 60611
tmsfeatures.com/productlist.htm

McCaughey, Gerald
President & CEO of the CIBC group of companies
Canadian Imperial Bank of Commerce **Ph:** 416-980-2211 **Fax:** 416-980-5026
Commerce Ct
Toronto, ON M5L1A2
www.cibc.com/ca

McCaul, Michael (1962-)
US Representative from Texas (Democrat)
415 Cannon Bldg **Ph:** 202-225-2401
Washington, DC 20515 **Fax:** 202-225-5955
www.house.gov/mccaul

McCaw, John E Jr
Chairman of Orca Bay Sports & Entertainment, NHL Governor, and an owner of the Vancouver Canucks hockey team; co-founder and a former director of McCaw Communications and McCaw Cellular Communications
Orca Bay Sports & Entertainment **Ph:** 604-899-4600 **Fax:** 604-899-4640
General Motors Pl
800 Griffiths Way
Vancouver, BC V6B6G1
www.canucks.com

McChesney, John
NPR technology correspondent
National Public Radio **Ph:** 415-503-3160
San Francisco Bureau **Fax:** 415-552-4467
2601 Mariposa St
San Franciso, CA 94110
www.npr.org

McClatchy, Kevin S
CEO & Managing General Partner of the Pittsburgh Pirates baseball club
Pittsburgh Pirates **Ph:** 412-323-5000
PNC Park **Fax:** 412-323-5009
115 Federal St
Pittsburgh, PA 15212
www.pittsburghpirates.com

McClellan, Mark B, MD, PhD (1963-)
Administrator of the Centers for Medicare & Medicaid Services, US Dept of Health & Human Services
Centers for Medicare & Medicaid Services **Ph:** 202-690-6726 **Fax:** 202-690-6262
200 Independence Ave SW Rm 445-G
Washington, DC 20201
www.cms.hhs.gov/CMSLeadership

McClelland, Frank
Chef/proprietor of L'Espalier restaurant in Boston
L'Espalier Restaurant **Ph:** 617-262-3023
30 Gloucester St
Boston, MA 02115
www.lespalier.com

McClintock, Jessica (1930-)
Fashion designer
1400 16th St **Ph:** 415-553-8200
San Francisco, CA 94103 **Fax:** 415-553-8329
www.jessicamcclintock.com

McClure, Charles G "Chip"
Chairman, president, and CEO of ArvinMeritor Inc, a supplier to the motor vehicle industry
ArvinMeritor Inc **Ph:** 248-435-1000
2135 W Maple Rd
Troy, MI 48084
www.arvinmeritor.com

McCollum, Betty (1954-)
US Representative from Minnesota (Democrat)
1029 Longworth Bldg **Ph:** 202-225-6631
Washington, DC 20515 **Fax:** 202-225-1968
www.mccollum.house.gov

McConaughey, Matthew (1969-)
Actor
Creative Artists Agency **Ph:** 310-288-4545
9830 Wilshire Blvd **Fax:** 310-288-4800
Beverly Hills, CA 90212

McConnell, John H
Majority owner, chairman, and governor of the Columbus Blue Jackets hockey franchise
Columbus Blue Jackets **Ph:** 614-246-4625
Nationwide Arena **Fax:** 614-246-4007
200 W Nationwide Blvd
Columbus, OH 43215
www.bluejackets.com

McConnell, Mitch (1942-)
US Senator from Kentucky (Republican)
361A Russell Bldg **Ph:** 202-224-2541
Washington, DC 20510 **Fax:** 202-224-2499
mcconnell.senate.gov

McConnell Serio, Suzie (1966-)
Basketball coach
Minnesota Lynx **Ph:** 612-673-1600
Target Center **Fax:** 612-673-1699
600 1st Ave N
Minneapolis, MN 55403
www.wnba.com/lynx

McCormack, Eric (1962-)
Actor
Endeavor **Ph:** 310-248-2000
9601 Wilshire Blvd 3rd Fl **Fax:** 310-248-2020
Beverly Hills, CA 90210
www.nbc.com/Will_&_Grace

McCotter, Thaddeus G (1965-)
US Representative from Michigan (Republican)
1632 Longworth Bldg **Ph:** 202-225-8171
Washington, DC 20515 **Fax:** 202-225-2667
mccotter.house.gov

McCourt, Frank
Owner and chairman of the Los Angeles Dodgers baseball franchise
Los Angeles Dodgers **Ph:** 323-224-1500
Dodger Stadium **Fax:** 323-224-2617
1000 Elysian Park Ave
Los Angeles, CA 90012
www.dodgers.com

McCourt, Frank (1931-)
Author of Angela's Ashes
Simon & Schuster **Ph:** 212-698-7000
1230 Ave of the Americas
New York, NY 10020
www.simonsays.com

McCown, Josh (1979-)
Professional football player
Detroit Lions **Ph:** 313-216-4000
222 Republic Dr **Fax:** 313-216-4069
Allen Park, MI 48101
www.detroitlions.com

McCown, Luke (1981-)
Professional football player
Tampa Bay Buccaneers **Ph:** 813-870-2700
1 Buccaneer Pl **Fax:** 813-878-0813
Tampa, FL 33607
www.buccaneers.com

McCoy, Dustan
Chairman and CEO of Brunswick Corp
Brunswick Corp **Ph:** 847-735-4700
1 N Field Ct **Fax:** 847-735-4765
Lake Forest, IL 60045
www.brunswick.com

McCoy, Glenn (1965-)
Creator of the syndicated comic strip The Duplex; also known for his editorial and magazine cartoons
Universal Press Syndicate **Ph:** 816-932-6600
4520 Main St
Kansas City, MO 64111
www.amuniversal.com/ups/features

McCracken, Craig (1971-)
Animator; creator, writer, producer of the Power Puff Girls TV series; animation director of the Power Puff Girls movie
Cartoon Network Studios **Ph:** 818-729-4000
300 N 3rd St
Burbank, CA 91502
www.cartoonnetworkla.com/english/tv_shows/ppg/index.html

McCrane, Paul (1961-)
Actor
Stone Manners Agency **Ph:** 323-655-1313
6500 Wilshire Blvd Suite 550 **Fax:** 323-655-7676
Los Angeles, CA 90048

McCrery, Jim (1949-)
US Representative from Louisiana (Republican)
2104 Rayburn Bldg **Ph:** 202-225-2777
Washington, DC 20515 **Fax:** 202-225-8039
mccrery.house.gov

McCrory, Patrick
Mayor of Charlotte, North Carolina
600 E 4th St **Ph:** 704-336-2241
Charlotte-Mecklenberg Government Center
Charlotte, NC 28202
www.charmeck.nc.us/Departments/Mayor

McCrumb, Sharyn (1948-)
Author of novels about the history and folklore of Appalachia (the Ballad novels)
Signet Publicity **Ph:** 212-366-2000
375 Hudson St
New York, NY 10014
www.sharynmccrumb.com

McCuddy, Bill
Entertainment correspondent for FOX News
FOX News Channel **Ph:** 212-301-3000
1211 Ave of the Americas
New York, NY 10036
www.foxnews.com/fnctv

McCullough, Colleen (1937-)
Australian novelist (The Thorn Birds)
Simon & Schuster **Ph:** 212-698-7000
1230 Ave of the Americas
New York, NY 10020
www.simonsays.com

McCullough, David (1933-)
Author of historical/biographical books
Simon & Schuster **Ph:** 212-698-7000
1230 Ave of the Americas
New York, NY 10020
www.simonsays.com

McCully, Emily Arnold (1939-)
Illustrator of children's books (other authors' books and her own picture books, including Mirette On the High Wire)
GP Putnam's Sons Books for Young Readers **Ph:** 212-366-2000
Publicity Dept
345 Hudson St
New York, NY 10014
us.penguingroup.com

McCurry, Mike (1954-)
Former White House Press Secretary
Grassroots Enterprise Inc **Ph:** 202-783-5910
1101 17th St NW Suite 1350 **Fax:** 202-783-5911
Washington, DC 20036
www.grassroots.com

McDaniel, Raymond
Chairman and CEO of Moody's
Moody's Corp **Ph:** 212-553-0300
99 Church St
New York, NY 10007
www.moodys.com

McDermott, Alice
Fiction author (Charming Billy)
Farrar Straus & Giroux **Ph:** 212-741-6900
19 Union Sq W
New York, NY 10003
www.fsgbooks.com

McDermott, Dylan (1961-)
Actor
Creative Artists Agency **Ph:** 310-288-4545
9830 Wilshire Blvd **Fax:** 310-288-4800
Beverly Hills, CA 90212

McDermott, Gerald (1941-)
Artist and creator of books and films that he has adapted into picture books for adults and for children (Anansi the Spider: A Tale from the Ashanti; Arrow to the Sun: A Tale from the Pueblo)
Harcourt Children's Books **Ph:** 212-592-1000
15 E 26th St
New York, NY 10010
www.geraldmcdermott.com

McDermott, Jim (1936-)
US Representative from Washington (Democrat)
1035 Longworth Bldg **Ph:** 202-225-3106
Washington, DC 20515 **Fax:** 202-225-6197
www.house.gov/mcdermott

McDonald, Audra (1970-)
Broadway & concert performer; recording artist; actor
Gersh Agency **Ph:** 310-274-6611
232 N Canon Dr
Beverly Hills, CA 90210

McDonald, Michael (1952-)
Singer
Vector Management **Ph:** 615-269-6600
PO Box 120479 **Fax:** 615-269-6002
Nashville, TN 37212
www.michaelmcdonald.com

McDonnell, Patrick (1956-)
Creator of the comic strip Mutts
King Features Syndicate Inc **Ph:** 212-455-4000
888 7th Ave 2nd Fl
New York, NY 10019
www.kingfeatures.com

McDonough, Kevin
Tune in Tonight columnist (highlights and commentary on broadcast and cable programming)
United Feature Syndicate **Ph:** 212-293-8500
200 Madison Ave
New York, NY 10016
www.unitedfeatures.com

McDormand, Frances (1957-)
Actor
Endeavor **Ph:** 310-248-2000
9601 Wilshire Blvd 3rd Fl **Fax:** 310-248-2020
Beverly Hills, CA 90210

McDowell, Dagen
FOX News business correspondent
FOX News Channel **Ph:** 212-301-3000
1211 Ave of the Americas
New York, NY 10036
www.foxnews.com/fnctv

McDowell, Josh (1939-)
Religious author & speaker
Josh McDowell Ministry **Ph:** 972-907-1000
660 International Pkwy **Fax:** 972-669-4053
Suite 100
Richardson, TX 75081
www.josh.org

McDowell, Malcolm (1943-)
Actor
Paradigm **Ph:** 310-288-8000
360 N Crescent Dr **Fax:** 310-288-2000
North Bldg
Beverly Hills, CA 90210

McDyess, Antonio (1974-)
Professional basketball player
Detroit Pistons **Ph:** 248-377-0100
Palace at Auburn Hills **Fax:** 248-377-4262
4 Championship Dr
Auburn Hills, MI 48326
www.nba.com/pistons

McEldowney, Brooke
Creator of the comic strip 9 Chickweed Lane
United Feature Syndicate **Ph:** 212-293-8500
200 Madison Ave
New York, NY 10016
www.unitedfeatures.com

McEnroe, John (1959-)
Former tennis player and member of the International Tennis Hall of Fame; tennis analyst
CBS Sports **Ph:** 212-975-4321
51 W 52nd St
New York, NY 10019
cbs.sportsline.com/cbssports/team

McEnroe, Patrick (1966-)
Former tennis player; tennis analyst/host
CBS Sports **Ph:** 212-975-4321
51 W 52nd St
New York, NY 10019
cbs.sportsline.com/cbssports/team

McEntire, Reba (1955-)
Country singer; actor
CAA Nashville **Ph:** 615-383-8787
3310 West End Ave 5th Fl **Fax:** 615-383-4937
Nashville, TN 37203
www.reba.com

McEwan, Ian (1948-)
Author of novels (Saturday; Atonement; Amsterdam) & short stories
Nan A Talese/Doubleday **Ph:** 212-782-8918
1745 Broadway 22nd Fl **Fax:** 212-782-8448
New York, NY 10019
www.ianmcewan.com

McFadden, Cynthia (1956-)
Co-anchor for ABC News's Prime Time Live and for Nightline
Prime Time Live **Ph:** 212-456-7777
147 Columbus Ave
New York, NY 10023
www.abcnews.go.com/Primetime

McFadden, Daniel L, PhD (1937-)
Economics professor and director of the Econometrics Laboratory at the University of California; winner of the 2000 Nobel Prize in Economics for his development of theory and methods for analyzing discrete choice
University of California at Berkeley **Ph:** 510-643-0822
Fax: 510-642-0638
Dept of Economics
549 Evans Hall Rm 3880
Berkeley, CA 94720
emlab.berkeley.edu/econ

McFarlane, Todd (1961-)
Comic book artist who created Spawn; co-founder of Image Comics and founder of McFarlane Toys
Image Comics Inc 1942 University Ave Suite 305 **Ph:** 510-644-4980
Fax: 510-644-4988
Berkeley, CA 94704
www.mcfarlane.com/info

McFerrin, Bobby (1950-)
Singer (jazz); classical conductor
Original Artists **Ph:** 212-254-1234
826 Broadway 4th Fl **Fax:** 212-254-3121
New York, NY 10003
www.bobbymcferrin.com

McG (1970-)
Director of commercials, music videos, and movies; full name is Joseph McGinty Nichol
Endeavor **Ph:** 310-248-2000
9601 Wilshire Blvd 3rd Fl **Fax:** 310-248-2020
Beverly Hills, CA 90210

McGahee, Willis (1981-)
Professional football player
Buffalo Bills **Ph:** 716-648-1800
Ralph Wilson Stadium **Fax:** 716-649-6446
1 Bills Dr
Orchard Park, NY 14127
www.buffalobills.com

McGahern, John (1934-)
Irish writer of novels & stories (Amongst Women; By the Lake)
Vintage/Anchor Publicity **Ph:** 212-572-2420
1745 Broadway 20th Fl
New York, NY 10019
www.randomhouse.com/vintage

McGarry, Steve
Cartoonist and illustrator; creator of Pop Culture and Badlands; writes and illustrates the syndicated feature KidCity
United Features Syndicate **Ph:** 212-293-8500
200 Madison Ave
New York, NY 10016
www.stevemcgarry.com

McGeary, Roderick C
Chairman of BearingPoint, a management consulting and systems integration firm
BearingPoint Inc **Ph:** 703-747-3000
1676 International Dr
McLean, VA 22102
www.bearingpoint.com

McGee, Terrence (1980-)
Professional football player
Buffalo Bills **Ph:** 716-648-1800
Ralph Wilson Stadium **Fax:** 716-649-6446
1 Bills Dr
Orchard Park, NY 14127
www.buffalobills.com

McGill, Steve
President & CEO of Eastern Financial Florida Credit Union
Eastern Financial Florida Credit Union — **Ph:** 954-704-5000
3700 Lakeside Dr
Miramar, FL 33027
www.effcu.org

McGinnis, Susan (1964-)
Anchor of CBS Morning News and a business contributor to The Early Show
CBS News — **Ph:** 212-975-4114
524 W 57th St
New York, NY 10019
www.cbsnews.com

McGovern, James P (1959-)
US Representative from Massachusetts (Democrat)
430 Cannon Bldg — **Ph:** 202-225-6101
Washington, DC 20515 — **Fax:** 202-225-5759
www.house.gov/mcgovern

McGovern, Patrick J
Founder and chairman of IDG
International Data Group — **Ph:** 617-534-1200
3 Post Office Sq 4th Fl — **Fax:** 617-262-2300
Boston, MA 02109
idg.com

McGrady, Tracy (1979-)
Professional basketball player
Houston Rockets — **Ph:** 713-758-7200
Toyota Center — **Fax:** 713-758-7396
1510 Polk St
Houston, TX 77002
www.t-mac.com

McGrath, Eugene
Chairman of the board of Consolidated Edison Inc
Consolidated Edison Inc — **Ph:** 212-460-4600
4 Irving Pl
New York, NY 10003
www.conedison.com/governance

McGrath, Joseph
President & CEO of Unisys Corp
Unisys Corp — **Ph:** 215-986-4011
Unisys Way
Blue Bell, PA 19424
www.unisys.com

McGrath, Judy
Chairman & CEO of MTV Networks
MTV Networks — **Ph:** 212-258-8712
1515 Broadway 25th Fl — **Fax:** 212-258-8100
New York, NY 10036

McGrath, Mark (1968-)
Lead singer in the rock group Sugar Ray
William Morris Agency — **Ph:** 310-859-4000
1 William Morris Pl — **Fax:** 310-859-4462
Beverly Hills, CA 90212
www.sugarray.com

McGrath, Robert
Chef and owner of the Roaring Fork restaurants in Scottsdale, Arizona, and Austin, Texas
Roaring Fork Restaurant — **Ph:** 480-947-0795
4800 N Scottsdale Rd
Scottsdale, AZ 85251
www.roaringfork.com

McGraw, Harold III (1949-)
Chairman, president, and CEO of McGraw-Hill
McGraw Hill Cos Inc — **Ph:** 212-512-2000
1221 Ave of the Americas 49th Fl — **Fax:** 212-512-3514
New York, NY 10020
www.mcgraw-hill.com

McGraw, Phil, PhD (1950-)
Dr Phil. Talk show host, businessman, author
Dr Phil Show — **Ph:** 323-956-3449
5482 Wilshire Blvd Suite 1902
Los Angeles, CA 90036
www.drphil.com

McGraw, Tim (1967-)
Country singer
CAA Nashville — **Ph:** 615-383-8787
3310 West End Ave 5th Fl — **Fax:** 615-383-4937
Nashville, TN 37203
www.timmcgraw.com

McGregor, Ewan (1971-)
Actor
Creative Artists Agency — **Ph:** 310-288-4545
9830 Wilshire Blvd — **Fax:** 310-288-4800
Beverly Hills, CA 90212

McGruder, Aaron
Creator of the syndicated comic strip The Boondocks
Universal Press Syndicate — **Ph:** 816-932-6600
4520 Main St
Kansas City, MO 64111
www.amuniversal.com/ups/features

McGuane, Thomas (1939-)
Author of novels (The Sporting Club), short stories, essays, and screenplays
Vintage/Anchor Publicity — **Ph:** 212-572-2420
1745 Broadway 20th Fl
New York, NY 10019
www.randomhouse.com/vintage

McGuire, Jack
Interim president & CEO of the American Red Cross
Interim Pres/CEO **Ph:** 202-303-4498
American Red Cross
2025 'E' St NW
Washington, DC 20006
www.redcross.org/aboutus

McGuire, William W, MD
Chairman and CEO of UnitedHealth Group; holds board certification in internal medicine and pulmonary medicine and is a member of the NIH National Cancer Policy Board
UnitedHealth Group **Ph:** 952-936-1300
9900 Bren Rd E
Minnetonka, MN 55343
www.unitedhealthgroup.com

McHale, Joel
Host of The Soup on E!
E! Entertainment Television **Ph:** 323-954-2400
5700 Wilshire Blvd **Fax:** 323-954-2660
Los Angeles, CA 90036
www.eonline.com/On/People

McHale, Kevin (1957-)
Former NBA player, now a basketball coach
Naismith Memorial Basketball Hall of Fame **Ph:** 413-781-6500
Fax: 413-781-1939
1000 W Columbus Ave **TF:** 877-446-6752
Springfield, MO 01105
www.hoophall.com

McHenry, Patrick (1975-)
US Representative from North Carolina (Republican)
224 Cannon Bldg **Ph:** 202-225-2576
Washington, DC 20515 **Fax:** 202-225-0316
mchenry.house.gov

McHugh, John M (1948-)
US Representative from New York (Republican)
2333 Rayburn Bldg **Ph:** 202-225-4611
Washington, DC 20515 **Fax:** 202-226-0621
mchugh.house.gov

McIntyre, Jamie
CNN's senior Pentagon correspondent
CNN **Ph:** 202-898-7900
CNN Bldg
820 1st St NE
Washington, DC 20002
www.cnn.com/CNN/anchors_reporters

McIntyre, Mike (1956-)
US Representative from North Carolina (Democrat)
2437 Rayburn Bldg **Ph:** 202-225-2731
Washington, DC 20515 **Fax:** 202-225-5773
www.house.gov/mcintyre

McIntyre, Vonda
Science fiction author
Simon & Schuster **Ph:** 212-698-7000
1230 Ave of the Americas
New York, NY 10020
www.sff.net/people/Vonda

McKay, Peter
Writes a syndicated humor column
Creators Syndicate Inc **Ph:** 310-337-7003
5777 W Century Blvd Suite 700 **Fax:** 310-337-7625
Los Angeles, CA 90045
www.creators.com

McKayle, Donald (1930-)
Dancer, choreographer, teacher; currently Artistic Mentor for the Limon Dance Co
Jose Limon Dance Foundation **Ph:** 212-777-3353
307 W 38th St Suite 1105 **Fax:** 212-777-4764
New York, NY 10018
www.limon.org

McKee, Rick
Editorial cartoonist for the Augusta Chronicle (GA)
King Features Syndicate Inc **Ph:** 212-455-4000
888 7th Ave 2nd Fl
New York, NY 10019
www.kingfeatures.com

McKellen, Ian (1939-)
Actor
International Creative Management **Ph:** 310-550-4000
8942 Wilshire Blvd
Beverly Hills, CA 90211
www.mckellen.com

McKelvey, Andrew J
Founder, chairman, and CEO of Monster Worldwide, the parent company of Monster
Monster Worldwide Inc **Ph:** 212-351-7000
622 3rd Ave **Fax:** 917-256-8511
New York, NY 10017
www.monsterworldwide.com

McKenna, Dennis
Chairman, president, and CEO of Silicon Graphics
Silicon Graphics Inc **Ph:** 650-960-1980
1500 Crittenden Ln
Mountain View, CA 94043
www.sgi.com/company_info

McKenzie, John
ABC News correspondent specializing in medical science reporting
ABC News **Ph:** 212-456-7777
77 W 66th St
New York, NY 10023
www.abcnews.go.com/WNT

McKenzie, Kevin (1954-)
Former dancer, now artistic director for the American Ballet Theatre
American Ballet Theatre **Ph:** 212-477-3030
890 Broadway **Fax:** 212-254-5938
New York, NY 10003
www.abt.org/insideabt/leadership.asp

McKeon, Buck (1938-)
US Representative from California (Democrat)
2351 Rayburn Bldg **Ph:** 202-225-1956
Washington, DC 20515 **Fax:** 202-226-0683
mckeon.house.gov

McKinley, Robin (1952-)
Author of fantasy fiction (The Hero & the Crown; The Blue Sword)
Puffin Books Publicity **Ph:** 212-366-2000
345 Hudson St
New York, NY 10014
www.robinmckinley.com

McKinnell, Henry A, PhD
Chairman and CEO of Pfizer
Pfizer Inc **Ph:** 212-573-2323
235 E 42nd St
New York, NY 10017
www.pfizer.com

McKinney, Cynthia (1955-)
US Representative from Georgia (Democrat)
320 Cannon Bldg **Ph:** 202-225-1605
Washington, DC 20515 **Fax:** 202-226-0691
www.house.gov/mckinney

McKissack, Frederick L (1939-)
Collaborates with his wife, Patricia C. McKissack, on historical fiction and books for young readers about African Americans
Random House Children's Books **Ph:** 212-782-9000
Publicity Dept
1745 Broadway
New York, NY 10019
www.randomhouse.com/kids

McKissack, Patricia C (1944-)
Author of historical fiction and African American books for young readers; often writes in collaboration with her husband, Frederick L McKissack
Random House Children's Books **Ph:** 212-782-9000
Publicity Dept
1745 Broadway
New York, NY 10019
www.randomhouse.com/kids

McLachlan, Sarah (1968-)
Singer/songwriter
Nettwerk Management **Ph:** 310-855-0668
8730 Wilshire Blvd Suite 304
Beverly Hills, CA 90211
www.sarahmclachlan.com

McLane, Drayton Jr
Owner, chairman, and CEO of the Houston Astros baseball team; a grocery wholesaler and entrepreneur (chairman of the McLane Group)
Houston Astros **Ph:** 713-259-8000
Minute Maid Park **Fax:** 713-259-8025
501 Crawford St
Houston, TX 77002
houston.astros.mlb.com

McLaughlin, Emma
Co-author (with Nicola Kraus) of The Nanny Diaries
St Martin's Press **Ph:** 212-674-5151
Attn: Publicity Dept
175 5th Ave
New York, NY 10010
www.stmartins.com

McLaughlin, John, PhD (1927-)
Creator, executive producer, and host of The McLaughlin Group
The McLaughlin Group **Ph:** 202-457-0870
1211 Connecticut Ave NW Suite 810
Washington, DC 20036
www.mclaughlin.com

McLaughlin, Sean
MSNBC's chief meteorologist
MSNBC TV **Ph:** 201-583-5000
1 MSNBC Plaza
Secaucus, NJ 07094
www.msnbc.msn.com/id/3080263

McLin, Rhine L
Mayor of Dayton, Ohio
101 W 3rd St 2nd Fl **Ph:** 937-333-3636
Dayton, OH 45402 **Fax:** 937-333-4297
www.cityofdayton.org

McMahon, Ed (1923-)
TV host/spokesman
McMahon Communications Inc **Ph:** 310-274-7411
12000 Crest Ct **Fax:** 310-274-0493
Beverly Hills, CA 90210
www.johnnycarson.com

McMahon, Tom
Writes Kid Tips, a syndicated advice column about parenting
King Features Syndicate Inc **Ph:** 212-455-4000
888 7th Ave 2nd Fl
New York, NY 10019
www.kingfeatures.com

McMahon, Vince
Chairman of World Wrestling Entertainment (WWE)
World Wrestling Entertainment Inc **Ph:** 203-352-8600 **Fax:** 203-359-5151
1241 E Main St
Stamford, CT 06902
corporate.wwe.com

McManus, Erwin
Lead pastor and cultural architect of Mosaic; a national & international speaker on issues of church growth, organizational change, leadership, postmodern culture, and urban & global issues
Mosaic **Ph:** 562-908-2200
13200 Crossroads Pkwy N Suite 325 **Fax:** 562-908-2772
City of Industry, CA 91746
www.mosaic.org

McMichael, Randy (1979-)
Professional football player
Miami Dolphins **Ph:** 954-452-7000
7500 SW 30th St **Fax:** 954-452-7055
Davie, FL 33314
www.miamidolphins.com

McMillan, Nate (1964-)
Basketball coach
Portland Trail Blazers **Ph:** 503-234-9291
1 Center Ct Suite 200 **Fax:** 503-736-2187
Portland, OR 97227
www.nba.com/blazers

McMillan, Terry (1951-)
Fiction author (Waiting to Exhale; How Stella Got Her Groove Back)
Viking Publicity **Ph:** 212-366-2000
375 Hudson St
New York, NY 10014
authors.aalbc.com/terry.htm

McMorris, Cathy (1969-)
US Representative from Washington (Republican)
1708 Longworth Bldg **Ph:** 202-225-2206
Washington, DC 20515 **Fax:** 202-225-3392
www.mcmorris.house.gov

McMurray, Jamie (1976-)
NASCAR driver
Roush Racing **Ph:** 704-720-4100
4600 Roush Pl NW
Concord, NC 28027
www.roushracing.com

McMurtry, Larry (1936-)
Fiction author (Lonesome Dove, Terms of Endearment, The Last Picture Show)
Simon & Schuster **Ph:** 212-698-7000
1230 Ave of the Americas
New York, NY 10020
www.simonsays.com

McNabb, Donovan (1976-)
Professional football player
Philadelphia Eagles **Ph:** 215-463-2500
NovaCare Complex **Fax:** 215-339-5464
1 NovaCare Way
Philadelphia, PA 19145
www.donovanmcnabb.com

McNair, Robert C
Owner of the Houston Texans football franchise; founder of Cogen Technologies
Houston Texans **Ph:** 832-667-2000
2 Reliant Park
Houston, TX 77054
www.houstontexans.com

McNair, Steve (1973-)
Professional football player
Tennessee Titans **Ph:** 615-565-4000
460 Great Circle Rd **Fax:** 615-565-4006
Nashville, TN 37228
www.titansonline.com

McNally, David
Inspirational/motivational speaker and personal branding expert
9717 Colorado Rd **Ph:** 952-835-0300
Bloomington, MN 55438 **Fax:** 952-835-0305
www.davidmcnally.com **TF:** 800-228-1218

McNally, Terrence (1939-)
Playwright (Love! Valour! Compassion!)
William Morris Agency **Ph:** 212-586-5100
1325 Ave of the Americas **Fax:** 212-246-3583
New York, NY 10019

McNealy, Scott
Co-founder and chairman of Sun Microsystems
Sun Microsystems Inc **Ph:** 650-960-1300
4150 Network Cir
Santa Clara, CA 95054
www.sun.com

McNerney, W James (1949-)
Chairman, president, and CEO of Boeing
Boeing Co **Ph:** 312-544-2000
100 N Riverside Plaza
Chicago, IL 60606
www.boeing.com

McNulty, Michael R (1947-)
US Representative from New York (Democrat)
2210 Rayburn Bldg **Ph:** 202-225-5076
Washington, DC 20515 **Fax:** 202-225-5077
www.house.gov/mcnulty

McPartland, Marian (1918-)
Jazz pianist and long-time host of Marian McPartland's Piano Jazz on NPR
National Public Radio **Ph:** 202-513-2000
635 Massachusetts Ave NW **Fax:** 202-513-3329
Washington, DC 20001
www.npr.org

McPhee, John (1931-)
Author (Coming into the Country; Annals of the Former World)
Farrar Straus & Giroux **Ph:** 212-741-6900
19 Union Sq W
New York, NY 10003
www.johnmcphee.com

McPherson, John
Cartoonist; work includes the syndicated comic panel Close to Home
Universal Press Syndicate **Ph:** 816-932-6600
4520 Main St
Kansas City, MO 64111
www.amuniversal.com/ups/features

McQueen, Alexander (1969-)
Fashion designer
417 W 14th St **Ph:** 212-645-1797
New York, NY 10014
www.alexandermcqueen.com

McShane, Ian (1942-)
Actor
International Creative Management **Ph:** 310-550-4000
8942 Wilshire Blvd
Beverly Hills, CA 90211
www.hbo.com/deadwood/cast

McWilliams-Franklin, Taj (1970-)
Professional basketball player
Connecticut Sun **Ph:** 860-862-4000
1 Mohegan Sun Blvd **Fax:** 860-862-4010
Uncasville, CT 06382
www.wnba.com/sun

Meade, Robin
Anchors CNN Headline News's Robin & Company and co-hosts Turner Private Network's AccentHealth with Dr Sanjay Gupta
CNN **Ph:** 404-827-1500
1 CNN Center
Atlanta, GA 30303
www.cnn.com/CNN/anchors_reporters

Means, Marianne
Nationally syndicated political columnist
King Features Syndicate Inc **Ph:** 212-455-4000
888 7th Ave 2nd Fl
New York, NY 10019
www.kingfeatures.com

Mears, Casey (1978-)
NASCAR driver
Chip Ganassi Racing **Ph:** 704-662-9642
8500 Westmoreland Dr
Concord, NC 28027
www.caseymears.com

Meddick, Jim
Creator of the comic strip Monty
Newspaper Enterprise Assn **Ph:** 212-293-8500
200 Madison Ave
New York, NY 10016
www.unitedfeatures.com

Medeski Martin & Wood
Music group (jazz-funk organ trio)
Monterey Peninsula Artists/Paradigm **Ph:** 831-375-4889 **Fax:** 831-375-2623
509 Hartnell St
Monterey, CA 93940
www.mmw.net

Mediate, Rocco (1962-)
Professional golfer
Gaylord Sports Management **Ph:** 480-483-9500
13845 N Northsight Blvd
Suite 200
Scottsdale, AZ 85260
www.gaylordsports.com

Medved, Michael (1948-)
Film critic, author, and radio talk show host (movies, politics, pop culture)
Salem Radio Network **Ph:** 972-831-1920
6400 N Beltline Rd Suite 210 **Fax:** 972-831-8626
Irving, TX 75063
www.michaelmedved.com

Meehan, Martin T (1956-)
US Representative from Massachusetts (Democrat)
2229 Rayburn Bldg **Ph:** 202-225-3411
Washington, DC 20515 **Fax:** 202-226-0771
www.house.gov/meehan

Meek, Kendrick (1966-)
US Representative from Florida (Democrat)
1039 Longworth Bldg **Ph:** 202-225-4506
Washington, DC 20515 **Fax:** 202-226-0777
kendrickmeek.house.gov

Meeks, Gregory W (1953-)
US Representative from New York (Democrat)
1710 Longworth Bldg **Ph:** 202-225-3461
Washington, DC 20515 **Fax:** 202-226-4169
www.house.gov/meeks

Meeks, Larry
Writes the syndicated minority advice column Ethnically Speaking
Creators Syndicate Inc **Ph:** 310-337-7003
5777 W Century Blvd Suite 700 **Fax:** 310-337-7625
Los Angeles, CA 90045
www.creators.com

Meese, Edwin III (1931-)
Former attorney general of the United States; was also President Reagan's chief policy advisor and currently is the Ronald Reagan Distringuished Fellow in Public Policy at the Heritage Foundation
Heritage Foundation **Ph:** 202-546-4400
214 Massachusetts Ave NE **Fax:** 202-546-8328
Washington, DC 20002
www.heritage.org/About/Staff/EdwinMeese.cfm

Mehta, Sonny (1942-)
Knopf president, publisher, and editor-in-chief
Alfred A Knopf Inc **Ph:** 212-782-9000
1745 Broadway **Fax:** 212-302-7985
New York, NY 10019

Mehta, Zubin (1936-)
Classical conductor
Sony Classical **Ph:** 212-833-8000
550 Madison Ave
New York, NY 10022
www.sonyclassical.com

Meier, Randy
MSNBC daytime anchor
MSNBC TV **Ph:** 201-583-5000
1 MSNBC Plaza
Secaucus, NJ 07094
www.msnbc.msn.com/id/3080263

Meijer, Doug
Co-chairman of Meijer Inc (retail supercenters)
Meijer Inc **Ph:** 616-791-3335
2929 Walker Ave NW **Fax:** 616-791-2437
Grand Rapids, MI 49544

Meijer, Hank
Co-chairman Meijer Inc (retail supercenters)
Meijer Inc **Ph:** 616-791-3333
2929 Walker Ave NW **Fax:** 616-791-2437
Grand Rapids, MI 49544

Melancon, Charlie (1952-)
US Representative from Louisiana (Republican)
404 Cannon Bldg **Ph:** 202-225-4031
Washington, DC 20515 **Fax:** 202-226-3944
www.house.gov/melancon

Mellanby, Scott (1966-)
Professional hockey player
Atlanta Thrashers **Ph:** 404-827-5300
Centennial Tower **Fax:** 404-827-5909
101 Marietta St NW Suite 1900
Atlanta, GA 30303
www.atlantathrashers.com

Mellencamp, John (1951-)
Singer
Creative Artists Agency **Ph:** 310-288-4545
9830 Wilshire Blvd **Fax:** 310-288-4800
Beverly Hills, CA 90212
www.mellencamp.com

Melman, Richard
Founder and chairman of Lettuce Entertain You Enterprises, a Chicago-based corporation that owns more than 50 restaurants nationwide
Lettuce Entertain You **Ph:** 773-878-7340
Enterprises
5419 N Sheridan Rd
Chicago, IL 60640
www.leye.com

Melnyk, Eugene (1959-)
Owner of the Ottawa Senators hockey team; also chairman and CEO of Biovail Corporation, a company he founded in 1989
Ottawa Senators **Ph:** 613-599-0250
Corel Center **Fax:** 613-599-0358
1000 Palladium Dr
Kanata, ON K2V1A5
www.ottawasenators.com

Meloni, Christopher (1961-)
Actor
Gersh Agency **Ph:** 212-997-1818
41 Madison Ave 33rd Fl **Fax:** 212-997-1978
New York, NY 10010
www.christopher-meloni.com

Melton, Howell W Jr
Managing partner of Holland & Knight law firm; his practice emphasizes contract and business torts litigation
Holland & Knight LLP **Ph:** 407-425-8500
200 S Orange Ave Suite 2600 **Fax:** 407-244-5288
Orlando, FL 32801
www.hklaw.com

Meltzer, Allan H, PhD (1928-)
Economist; a professor of political economy and public policy at Carnegie Mellon University and a visiting scholar at the American Enterprise Institute
American Enterprise Institute for Public Policy Research **Ph:** 202-862-5800 **Fax:** 202-862-7177
1150 17th St NW Suite 1100
Washington, DC 20036
www.aei.org

Meltzer, Milton (1915-)
Writer of social history for children and young adults
Random House Children's Books **Ph:** 212-782-9000
Publicity Dept
1745 Broadway
New York, NY 10019
www.randomhouse.com/kids

Melvin, Bob (1961-)
Baseball manager
Arizona Diamondbacks **Ph:** 602-462-6500
Bank One Ballpark **Fax:** 602-462-6600
401 E Jefferson St
Phoenix, AZ 85004
arizona.diamondbacks.mlb.com

Melvin, Chasity (1976-)
Women's professional basketball player
Washington Mystics **Ph:** 202-266-2200
Verizon Center **Fax:** 202-266-2220
401 9th St NW Suite 750
Washington, DC 20004
www.wnba.com/mystics

Menand, Louis, PhD
Author of The Metaphysical Club: A Story of Ideas in America; also a book critic for New Yorker magazine and a contributing editor of The New York Review of Books
Farrar Straus & Giroux **Ph:** 212-741-6900
19 Union Sq W
New York, NY 10003
www.fsgbooks.com

Mendelson, Alan C (1939-)
Attorney; his practice is primarily targeted toward the representation of emerging and public growth companies, with strong emphasis on companies in the life sciences industry
Latham & Watkins LLP **Ph:** 650-463-4693
Silicon Valley **Fax:** 650-463-2600
135 Commonwealth Dr
Menlo Park, CA 94025
www.lw.com

Mendenhall, Preston
Moscow correspondent for NBC News
NBC News **Ph:** 212-664-4249
30 Rockefeller Plaza
New York, NY 10112
www.msnbc.msn.com/id/3689499

Mendes, Sam (1965-)
Movie director
Creative Artists Agency **Ph:** 310-288-4545
9830 Wilshire Blvd **Fax:** 310-288-4800
Beverly Hills, CA 90212

Menees, Tim
Editorial cartoonist
Pittsburgh Post-Gazette **Ph:** 412-263-1100
34 Blvd of the Allies
Pittsburgh, PA 15222
www.post-gazette.com/timmenees

Menendez, Robert (1954-)
US Senator from New Jersey (Democrat)
502 Hart Bldg **Ph:** 202-224-4744
Washington, DC 20510 **Fax:** 202-228-2197
menendez.senate.gov

Menino, Thomas M (1942-)
Mayor of Boston
1 City Hall Plaza **Ph:** 617-635-4500
Boston, MA 02201 **Fax:** 617-635-3496
www.cityofboston.gov/mayor

Meola, Tony (1969-)
Professional soccer player
New York Red Bulls **Ph:** 201-583-7000
1 Harmon Plaza 3rd Fl **Fax:** 201-583-7055
Secaucus, NJ 07094
redbull.newyork.mlsnet.com

Mercer, Roy D
Comedic character created by Tulsa, Oklahoma radio announcers Brent Douglas and Phil Stone
Transparent Creative Management **Ph:** 615-385-4395
PO Box 121143
Nashville, TN 37212
www.roydmercer.com

Merchant, Larry (1931-)
Expert boxing analyst
HBO Sports **Ph:** 212-512-1000
1100 Ave of the Americas
New York, NY 10036
www.hbo.com/boxing

Merchant, Natalie (1963-)
Singer
Creative Artists Agency **Ph:** 310-288-4545
9830 Wilshire Blvd **Fax:** 310-288-4800
Beverly Hills, CA 90212
www.nataliemerchant.com

MercyMe
Music group (Christian/inspirational)
Third Coast Artists Agency **Ph:** 615-297-2021
2021 21st Ave S Suite 220 **Fax:** 615-297-2776
Nashville, TN 37212
www.mercyme.org

Meredith, William (1919-)
Poet
Northwestern University Press **Ph:** 847-491-2046
629 Noyes St
Evanston, IL 60208
nupress.northwestern.edu

Merin, Jennifer
Writes the syndicated travel column Around the World with Jennifer Merin
Creators Syndicate Inc **Ph:** 310-337-7003
5777 W Century Blvd Suite 700 **Fax:** 310-337-7625
Los Angeles, CA 90045
www.creators.com

Merrill, Christine
Artist who paints very expensive portraits of dogs belonging to wealthy and/or famous people
William Secord Gallery **Ph:** 212-249-0075
52 E 76th St **Fax:** 212-288-1938
New York, NY 10021
www.christinemerrill.com

Merton, Robert C, PhD (1944-)
Winner, with Myron S Scholes, of the 1997 Nobel Prize in Economic Sciences for a new method to determine the value of derivatives
Harvard Business School **Ph:** 617-495-6678
Morgan Hall 397 **Fax:** 617-495-8863
Boston, MA 02163
www.hbs.edu

Merullo, Roland
Novelist (In Revere; In Those Days)
Vintage/Anchor Publicity **Ph:** 212-572-2420
1745 Broadway 20th Fl
New York, NY 10019
www.randomhouse.com/vintage

Merwin, WS (1927-)
Poet and essayist
Steven Barclay Agency **Ph:** 707-773-0654
12 Western Ave **Fax:** 707-778-1868
Petaluma, CA 94952 **TF:** 888-965-7323
www.barclayagency.com

Mesa, Jose (1966-)
Professional baseball player
Colorado Rockies **Ph:** 303-292-0200
Coors Field **Fax:** 303-296-2066
2001 Blake St
Denver, CO 80205
colorado.rockies.mlb.com

Mesereau, Thomas
Defense attorney for Michael Jackson; also represented actor Robert Blake
Susan Yu & Tom Mesereau **Ph:** 310-284-3120
1875 Century Park E Suite 700
Los Angeles, CA 90067

Meserve, Jeanne
Homeland security correspondent for CNN
CNN **Ph:** 202-898-7900
CNN Bldg
820 1st St NE
Washington, DC 20002
www.cnn.com/CNN/anchors_reporters

Meserve, Richard A, PhD (1944-)
President of the Carnegie Institution and former chairman of the Nuclear Regulatory Commission; a scientist and lawyer whose legal practice was devoted to technical issues related to science, law, and public policy
Carnegie Institution **Ph:** 202-387-6400
1530 P St NW **Fax:** 202-387-8092
Washington, DC 20005
carnegieinstitution.org/president.html

Messina, Jo Dee (1970-)
Country singer
William Morris Agency **Ph:** 615-963-3000
1600 Division St Suite 300 **Fax:** 615-963-3090
Nashville, TN 37203
www.jodeemessina.com

Messing, Debra (1968-)
Actor
3 Arts Entertainment **Ph:** 310-888-3200
9460 Wilshire Blvd 7th Fl **Fax:** 310-888-3210
Beverly Hills, CA 90212
www.nbc.com/Will_&_Grace

Messman, Jack L
Chairman of the Board and CEO of Novell
Novell Inc **Ph:** 781-464-8000
404 Wyman St Suite 500
Waltham, MA 02451
www.novell.com/company/bios

Metcalfe, Walter L Jr (1938-)
Former chairman of Bryan Cave law firm, with an active corporate practice; represented owners in the purchase, restructuring, and resale of the New England Patriots NFL franchise
Bryan Cave LLP **Ph:** 314-259-2475
1 Metropolitan Sq **Fax:** 314-552-8475
211 N Broadway Suite 3600
Saint Louis, MO 63102
www.bryancave.com

Metheny, Pat (1954-)
Jazz guitarist/composer
Ted Kurland Assoc **Ph:** 617-254-0007
173 Brighton Ave **Fax:** 617-782-3577
Boston, MA 02134
www.patmethenygroup.com

Meyer, Barry M
Chairman & CEO of Warner Bros Entertainment
Warner Bros Entertainment Inc **Ph:** 818-954-6000
4000 Warner Blvd
Burbank, CA 91522
www.timewarner.com

Meyer, Edgar (1960-)
Classical bassist
Chamber Music Society of Lincoln Center **Ph:** 212-875-5775
70 Lincoln Center Plaza
New York, NY 10023
www.edgarmeyer.com

Meyer, Joyce (1942-)
Televangelist
Joyce Meyer Ministries **Ph:** 636-349-0303
PO Box 655 **TF:** 800-727-9673
Fenton, MO 63026
www.joycemeyer.org

Meyer, Laurence H, PhD (1944-)
A leading economic forecaster; a Distinguished Scholar at the Center for Strategic & International Studies, former member of the Board of Governors of the Federal Reserve System, and author of A Term at the Fed
Center for Strategic & International Studies **Ph:** 202-775-3284 **Fax:** 202-775-3199
1800 K St NW Suite 400
Washington, DC 20006
www.csis.org/experts

Meyer, Ron
President & CEO of Universal Studios; was a founder of Creative Artists Agency
Universal Studios **Ph:** 818-777-1000
100 Universal City Plaza **Fax:** 818-777-2500
Universal City, CA 91608
www.nbcuni.com

Meyer, Urban (1964-)
Head coach of the University of Florida football team (Florida Gators)
University of Florida Football Office **Ph:** 352-375-4683
PO Box 14485
Gainesville, FL 32604
www.gatorzone.com/football

Meyerson, Harold (1950-)
Editor-at-large of The American Prospect; also political editor & columnist for LA Weekly
The American Prospect **Ph:** 202-776-0730
2000 L St NW Suite 717 **Fax:** 202-776-0740
Washington, DC 20036
www.prospect.org

Mica, John L (1943-)
US Representative from Florida (Republican)
2313 Rayburn Bldg **Ph:** 202-225-4035
Washington, DC 20515 **Fax:** 202-226-0821
www.house.gov/mica

Michael, Judith
Judith Michael is the pseudonym of a husband-and-wife writing team, Judith Barnard and Michael Fain
Ballantine Books Publicity **Ph:** 212-782-9000
1745 Broadway
New York, NY 10019
www.randomhouse.com/BB

Michaels, Jack D (1938-)
Chairman, president, and CEO of Snap-on Inc
Snap-On Inc **Ph:** 262-656-5200
2801 80th St
Kenosha, WI 53141
www.snapon.com

Michaels, Lorne (1944-)
Television producer
Creative Artists Agency **Ph:** 310-288-4545
9830 Wilshire Blvd **Fax:** 310-288-4800
Beverly Hills, CA 90212
www.nbc.com

Michaud, Mike (1955-)
US Representative from Maine (Democrat)
437 Cannon Bldg **Ph:** 202-225-6306
Washington, DC 20515 **Fax:** 202-225-2943
michaud.house.gov

Mickelson, Phil (1970-)
Professional golfer
Gaylord Sports Management **Ph:** 480-483-9500
13845 N Northsight Blvd
Suite 200
Scottsdale, AZ 85260
www.philmickelson.com

Midler, Bette (1945-)
Actor and singer
Creative Artists Agency **Ph:** 310-288-4545
9830 Wilshire Blvd **Fax:** 310-288-4800
Beverly Hills, CA 90212

Midori (1971-)
Concert violinist
International Creative Management **Ph:** 212-556-5600
40 W 57th St 17th Fl
New York, NY 10019
www.gotomidori.com

Mighty Mighty Bosstones
Ska/punk band
Monterey Peninsula Artists/Paradigm **Ph:** 831-375-4889
Fax: 831-375-2623
509 Hartnell St
Monterey, CA 93940
www.3feetunder.com/bosstones

Mignola, Mike (1962-)
Comic book artist; creator of Hellboy
Dark Horse Comics Inc **Ph:** 503-652-8815
10956 SE Main St **Fax:** 503-654-9440
Milwaukie, OR 97222

Mihm, Chris (1979-)
Professional basketball player
Los Angeles Lakers **Ph:** 310-426-6000
555 N Nash St **Fax:** 310-426-6105
El Segundo, CA 90245
www.nba.com/lakers

Miklaszewski, Jim
NBC News's chief Pentagon correspondent
NBC News **Ph:** 202-885-4200
4001 Nebraska Ave NW
Washington, DC 20016
www.msnbc.msn.com/id/3689499

Mikulski, Barbara A (1936-)
US Senator from Maryland (Democrat)
709 Hart Bldg **Ph:** 202-224-4654
Washington, DC 20510 **Fax:** 202-224-8858
mikulski.senate.gov

Miles, Darius (1981-)
Professional basketball player
Portland Trail Blazers **Ph:** 503-234-9291
1 Center Ct Suite 200 **Fax:** 503-736-2187
Portland, OR 97227
www.nba.com/blazers

Miles, Jack (1942-)
Author (God: A Biography)
Random House Publicity **Ph:** 212-782-9000
1745 Broadway
New York, NY 10019
www.jackmiles.com

Millar, Jeff
Writes the comic strip Tank McNamara, which is drawn by Bill Hinds
Universal Press Syndicate **Ph:** 816-932-6600
4520 Main St
Kansas City, MO 64111
www.amuniversal.com/ups/features

Millar, Kevin (1971-)
Professional baseball player
Baltimore Orioles **Ph:** 410-685-9800
Oriole Park at Camden Yards **Fax:** 410-547-6279
333 W Camden St
Baltimore, MD 21201
baltimore.orioles.mlb.com

Millender-McDonald, Juanita (1938-)
US Representative from California (Democrat)
2445 Rayburn Bldg **Ph:** 202-225-7924
Washington, DC 20515 **Fax:** 202-225-7926
www.house.gov/millender-mcdonald

Miller, Alan
President and CEO of Universal Health Services
Universal Health Services Inc **Ph:** 610-768-3300
367 S Gulph Rd
King of Prussia, PA 19406
www.uhsinc.com/about_officers.php

Miller, Andre (1976-)
Professional basketball player
Denver Nuggets **Ph:** 303-405-1100
Pepsi Center **Fax:** 303-575-1920
1000 Chopper Cir
Denver, CO 80204
www.nba.com/nuggets

Miller, Arthur (1915-2005)
Playwright (Death of a Salesman)
Penguin Publicity **Ph:** 212-366-2000
375 Hudson St
New York, NY 10014
us.penguingroup.com

Miller, Avram
CEO of Avram Miller Co, a strategy and business development corporation
Avram Miller Co **Ph:** 415-276-1901
3053 Fillmore St **Fax:** 415-276-1901
San Francisco, CA 94123
www.avrammiller.com

Miller, Brad (1976-)
Professional basketball player
Sacramento Kings **Ph:** 916-928-0000
ARCO Arena **Fax:** 916-928-0727
1 Sports Pkwy
Sacramento, CA 95834
www.nba.com/kings

Miller, Brad (1953-)
US Representative from North Carolina (Democrat)
1722 Longworth Bldg **Ph:** 202-225-3032
Washington, DC 20515 **Fax:** 202-225-0181
www.house.gov/bradmiller

Miller, Candice S (1954-)
US Representative from Michigan (Republican)
228 Cannon Bldg **Ph:** 202-225-2106
Washington, DC 20515 **Fax:** 202-226-1169
candicemiller.house.gov

Miller, Dennis (1953-)
Comedian
William Morris Agency **Ph:** 212-586-5100
1325 Ave of the Americas **Fax:** 212-246-3583
New York, NY 10019
www.officialdennismiller.com

Miller, Gary G (1948-)
US Representative from California (Republican)
1037 Longworth Bldg **Ph:** 202-225-3201
Washington, DC 20515 **Fax:** 202-226-6962
www.house.gov/garymiller

Miller, George (1945-)
US Representative from California (Democrat)
2205 Rayburn Bldg **Ph:** 202-225-2095
Washington, DC 20515 **Fax:** 202-225-5609
www.house.gov/georgemiller

Miller, Gin
Creator of step training and Ramping
Gin Miller Fitness **Ph:** 770-720-8668
PO Box 1229 **Fax:** 770-345-8703
Canton, GA 30169
www.ginmiller.com

Miller, Jeff (1959-)
US Representative from Florida (Republican)
324 Cannon Bldg **Ph:** 202-225-4136
Washington, DC 20515 **Fax:** 202-225-3414
jeffmiller.house.gov

Miller, Johnny (1947-)
Professional golfer (Champions Tour)
PGA Tour **Ph:** 904-285-3700
100 PGA Tour Blvd
Ponte Vedra Beach, FL 32082
www.pgatour.com

Miller, Jonathan
Chairman and CEO of AOL
AOL LLC **Ph:** 703-265-1000
22000 AOL Way
Dulles, VA 20166
www.corp.aol.com

Miller, Keith
NBC News' senior foreign correspondent, based in London
NBC News **Ph:** 212-664-4249
30 Rockefeller Plaza
New York, NY 10112
www.msnbc.msn.com/id/3689499

Miller, Kelly (1978-)
Professional basketball player
Phoenix Mercury **Ph:** 602-514-8333
America West Arena **Fax:** 602-514-8303
201 E Jefferson St
Phoenix, AZ 85004
www.wnba.com/mercury

Miller, Larry (1953-)
Actor and comedian
Gersh Agency **Ph:** 310-274-6611
232 N Canon Dr
Beverly Hills, CA 90210

Miller, Larry H
Owns one of the largest retail auto operations in the US as well as several other businesses, including the Utah Jazz basketball team
Larry H Miller Group **Ph:** 801-563-4100
9350 S 150 East Suite 1000
Sandy, UT 84070
www.lhm.com

Miller, Laura (1958-)
Mayor of Dallas
1500 Marilla St Suite 5EN **Ph:** 214-670-4054
Dallas, TX 75201 **Fax:** 214-670-0646
www.dallascityhall.com

Miller, Marisa (1980-)
Model
IMG Models **Ph:** 212-253-8884
304 Park Ave S 12th Fl **Fax:** 212-253-8883
New York, NY 10010

Miller, Matt (1962-)
Political commentator, author, columnist, radio host, and consultant; a senior fellow at the Center for American Progress
Center for American Progress **Ph:** 202-682-1611
1333 H St NW 10th Fl
Washington, DC 20005
www.mattmilleronline.com

Miller, Mike (1980-)
Professional basketball player
Memphis Grizzlies **Ph:** 901-205-1234
FedExForum **Fax:** 901-205-1235
191 Beale St
Memphis, TN 38103
www.nba.com/grizzlies

Miller, Nicole (1951-)
Fashion designer; also designs home furnishings
Nicole Miller Showroom **Ph:** 212-719-9200
525 7th Ave 20th Fl
New York, NY 10018
www.nicolemiller.com

Miller, Rand (1959-)
Computer software designer; co-founder of Cyan, the company that created the Myst & Riven computer games
Cyan Worlds **Ph:** 509-468-0807
14617 Newport Hwy **Fax:** 509-467-2209
Mead, WA 99021
www.cyan.com

Miller, Ryan (1980-)
Professional hockey player
Buffalo Sabres **Ph:** 716-855-4100
HSBC Arena **Fax:** 716-855-4115
1 Seymour H Knox III Plaza
Buffalo, NY 14203
www.sabres.com

Miller, Stephanie (1961-)
Host of I've Got A Secret on Oxygen Media; also has a call-in talk radio show with a progressive viewpoint
Oxygen Media Inc **Ph:** 212-651-2000
75 9th Ave 7th Fl **Fax:** 212-651-2099
New York, NY 10011
www.stephaniemiller.com

Miller, Sue (1943-)
Novelist (The Good Mother)
Knopf Publishing/Author Mail **Ph:** 212-782-9000
1745 Broadway
New York, NY 10019
www.randomhouse.com/knopf

Miller, Wiley
Creator of the comic strip and panel Non Sequitur
Universal Press Syndicate **Ph:** 816-932-6600
4520 Main St
Kansas City, MO 64111
www.amuniversal.com/ups/features

Millhauser, Steven
Novelist (Edwin Mullhouse; Martin Dressler)
Vintage/Anchor Publicity **Ph:** 212-572-2420
1745 Broadway 20th Fl
New York, NY 10019
www.randomhouse.com/vintage

Milliken, Mary Sue
Restaurant owner-operator, with Susan Feniger; the two have also hosted radio & TV food shows and are the creators of the Border Girls brand of fresh prepared foods
Border Grill **Ph:** 310-451-1655
1445 4th St
Santa Monica, CA 90401
www.marysueandsusan.com

Millionaire, Tony
Cartoonist; creator of Sock Monkey and Maakies
Fantagraphics Books **Ph:** 206-524-1967
7563 Lake City Way NE **Fax:** 206-524-2104
Seattle, WA 98115
www.maakies.com

Millman, Dan (1946-)
Author of spiritual books (The Way of the Peaceful Warrior)
New World Library **Ph:** 415-884-2100
14 Pamaron Way **Fax:** 415-884-2199
Novato, CA 94949
www.danmillman.com

Millstein, Ira M (1926-)
Attorney; a senior partner at Weil, Gotshal & Manges, where he practices in the areas of government regulation and antitrust law; has also counseled boards on issues of corporate governance
Weil Gotshal & Manges LLP **Ph:** 212-310-8100
767 5th Ave **Fax:** 212-310-8006
New York, NY 10153
www.weil.com

Milone, Francis M
Attorney specializing in employment & labor law
Morgan Lewis & Bockius LLP **Ph:** 215-963-5000
1701 Market St **Fax:** 215-963-5001
Philadelphia, PA 19103
www.morganlewis.com

Milsap, Ronnie (1946-)
Country singer
Buddy Lee Attractions **Ph:** 615-244-4336
38 Music Sq East Suite 300 **Fax:** 615-726-0429
Nashville, TN 37203
www.ronniemilsap.com

Mina, Roberto (1984-)
Professional soccer player
FC Dallas **Ph:** 214-979-0303
14800 Quorum Dr Suite 300 **Fax:** 214-979-1118
Dallas, TX 75254
fc.dallas.mlsnet.com

Mineta, Norman Y (1931-)
Secretary of the US Department of Transporation
US Dept of Transportation **Ph:** 202-366-1111
400 7th St SW **Fax:** 202-366-7202
Washington, DC 20590
www.dot.gov

Ming, Jenny
President of Old Navy, a division of Gap Inc
Old Navy Inc **Ph:** 650-952-4400
2 Folsom St **Fax:** 415-427-2553
San Francisco, CA 94105
www.gapinc.com/public/About/abt_leader.shtml

Ming, Yao (1980-)
Professional basketball player
Houston Rockets **Ph:** 713-758-7200
Toyota Center **Fax:** 713-758-7396
1510 Polk St
Houston, TX 77002
www.nba.com/rockets

Minghella, Anthony (1954-)
Screenwriter/director/producer
Creative Artists Agency **Ph:** 310-288-4545
9830 Wilshire Blvd **Fax:** 310-288-4800
Beverly Hills, CA 90212

Minner, Ruth Ann (1935-)
Governor of Delaware (Democrat)
150 William Penn St 2nd Fl **Ph:** 302-577-3210
Dover, DE 19901 **Fax:** 302-739-2775
www.state.de.us/governor

Minsky, Marvin, PhD (1927-)
Robotics/artificial intelligence pioneer
Massachusetts Institute of Technology **Ph:** 617-253-0300
Media Laboratory
77 Massachusetts Ave Bldg E15
Cambridge, MA 02139
web.media.mit.edu/~minsky

Miro, Joan (1893-1983)
Painter, sculptor, printmaker, and decorative artist
Meyerovich Gallery **Ph:** 415-421-7171
251 Post St 4th Fl **Fax:** 415-421-2775
San Francisco, CA 94108
www.meyerovich.com

Mirren, Helen (1945-)
Actor
Creative Artists Agency **Ph:** 310-288-4545
9830 Wilshire Blvd **Fax:** 310-288-4800
Beverly Hills, CA 90212

Mischer, Don (1940-)
Director/producer of television and live events (award shows/specials)
William Morris Agency **Ph:** 310-859-4000
1 William Morris Pl **Fax:** 310-859-4462
Beverly Hills, CA 90212
www.donmischer.com

Miss Manners (1938-)
Name under which Judith Martin writes her etiquette-related advice column
United Feature Syndicate **Ph:** 212-293-8500
200 Madison Ave
New York, NY 10016
www.unitedfeatures.com

Missett, Judi Sheppard
Founder and CEO of Jazzercise Inc
Jazzercise Inc — **Ph:** 760-476-1750
2460 Impala Dr — **Fax:** 760-602-7180
Carlsbad, CA 92010
www.jazzercise.com

Mistry, Rohinton (1952-)
Author of novels (A Fine Balance; Family Matters) and short stories
Random House Publicity — **Ph:** 212-782-9000
1745 Broadway
New York, NY 10019
www.randomhouse.com

Mitchard, Jacquelyn (1953-)
Writes a syndicated column (The Rest of Us); is also a novelist best-known for Deep End of the Ocean
Penguin Publicity — **Ph:** 212-366-2000
375 Hudson St
New York, NY 10014
www.jackiemitchard.com

Mitchell, Andrea (1946-)
NBC News chief foreign affairs correspondent
NBC News — **Ph:** 202-885-4200
4001 Nebraska Ave NW
Washington, DC 20016
www.msnbc.msn.com/id/3689499

Mitchell, Arthur (1934-)
Founder & artistic director/school director of Dance Theatre of Harlem
Dance Theatre of Harlem Inc — **Ph:** 212-690-2800
466 W 152nd St — **Fax:** 212-690-8736
New York, NY 10031
www.dancetheatreofharlem.org

Mitchell, Brian Stokes (1958-)
Actor (primarily theatre) and concert performer
Brookside Artist Management — **Ph:** 212-489-4929
250 W 57th St Suite 2303
New York, NY 10107
www.brianstokes.com

Mitchell, David (1969-)
Author (Cloud Atlas)
Random House Publicity — **Ph:** 212-782-9000
1745 Broadway
New York, NY 10019
www.randomhouse.com

Mitchell, George J (1933-)
Former Senate Majority Leader; now an attorney with DLA Piper, he was recently appointed to lead an independent investigation into the past use of performance-enhancing drugs in Major League Baseball; he also serves as chairman of the board of the Walt Disney Company
DLA Piper Rudnick Gray Cary — **Ph:** 212-835-6000
1251 Ave of the Americas
New York, NY 10020
www.dlapiper.com

Mitchell, Joni (1943-)
Singer/songwriter
SL Feldman & Associates — **Ph:** 604-734-5945
1505 W 2nd Ave Suite 200
Vancouver, BC V6H3Y4
www.jonimitchell.com

Mitchell, Mary
Writes a weekly column on politics, society, personal issues
United Feature Syndicate — **Ph:** 212-293-8500
200 Madison Ave
New York, NY 10016
www.unitedfeatures.com

Mitchell, Russ (1960-)
Anchor of the CBS News Sunday Edition
CBS News — **Ph:** 212-975-4114
524 W 57th St
New York, NY 10019
www.cbsnews.com

Mitchell, Sam (1963-)
Basketball coach
Toronto Raptors — **Ph:** 416-366-3865
40 Bay St Suite 400 — **Fax:** 416-359-9198
Toronto, ON M5J2X2
www.nba.com/raptors

Mitchell, W
Motivational/inspirational speaker
12014 W 54th Dr Suite 100 — **Ph:** 303-425-1800
Arvada, CO 80002 — **Fax:** 303-425-9069
www.wmitchell.com — **TF:** 800-421-4840

Mitchell, William
President and CEO of Arrow Electronics
Arrow Electronics Inc — **Ph:** 516-391-1300
25 Hub Dr
Melville, NY 11747
www.arrow.com

Mittermeier, Russell A, PhD (1949-)
Primatologist, herpetologist, and wildlife conservationist
Conservation International **Ph:** 202-912-1000
1919 M St NW Suite 600 **TF:** 800-406-2306
Washington, DC 20036
www.conservation.org

Mize, Larry (1958-)
Professional golfer
SFX Sports Group **Ph:** 202-686-2000
5335 Wisconsin Ave NW **Fax:** 202-686-5050
Suite 850
Washington, DC 20015
www.pgatour.com

Mizrahi, Isaac (1961-)
Fashion designer
Creative Artists Agency **Ph:** 310-288-4545
9830 Wilshire Blvd **Fax:** 310-288-4800
Beverly Hills, CA 90212
target.com/isaac_group/index.jhtml

Mobley, Cuttino (1975-)
Professional basketball player
Los Angeles Clippers **Ph:** 213-742-7100
Staples Center **Fax:** 213-742-7550
1111 S Figueroa St Suite 1100
Los Angeles, CA 90015
www.nba.com/clippers

Mobley, Stacey J (1945-)
Senior Vice President, Chief Administrative Officer, and General Counsel of DuPont
DuPont **Ph:** 302-774-8051
1007 Market St **Fax:** 302-774-7321
Wilmington, DE 19898
www.dupont.com

Moby (1965-)
Techno/pop musician and recording artist; real name is Richard Melville Hall
MCT Management **Ph:** 212-563-0831
520 8th Ave Suite 2001 **Fax:** 212-563-5099
New York, NY 10018
www.moby.com

Modano, Mike (1970-)
Professional hockey player
Dallas Stars **Ph:** 214-387-5500
2601 Ave of the Stars **Fax:** 214-287-3599
Frisco, TX 75034
www.mikemodano.com

Modell, Art (1925-)
Minority owner of the Baltimore Ravens football franchise
Baltimore Ravens **Ph:** 410-547-8100
1101 Russell St **Fax:** 410-547-8112
Baltimore, MD 21230
www.baltimoreravens.com

Modin, Fredrik (1974-)
Professional hockey player
Tampa Bay Lightning **Ph:** 813-301-6600
St Pete Times Forum **Fax:** 813-301-1487
401 Channelside Dr
Tampa, FL 33602
www.tampabaylightning.com

Mohammed, Nazr (1977-)
Professional basketball player
San Antonio Spurs **Ph:** 210-444-5000
1 SBC Center **Fax:** 210-444-5003
San Antonio, TX 78219
www.nba.com/spurs

Molendorp, Dayton H
President & CEO of American United Life Insurance Co
American United Life **Ph:** 317-285-1877
Insurance Co
1 American Sq
PO Box 368
Indianapolis, IN 46206
www.aul.com

Mollohan, Alan B (1943-)
US Representative from West Virginia (Democrat)
2302 Rayburn Bldg **Ph:** 202-225-4172
Washington, DC 20515 **Fax:** 202-225-7564
www.house.gov/mollohan

Monaghan, Dominic (1976-)
Actor
Agency for the Performing Arts **Ph:** 310-888-4200
9200 Sunset Blvd Suite 900
Los Angeles, CA 90069
abc.go.com/primetime/lost

Moncrief, Mike (1943-)
Mayor of Fort Worth, Texas
1000 Throckmorton St 3rd Fl **Ph:** 817-392-6118
Fort Worth, TX 76102 **Fax:** 817-392-2409
www.fortworthgov.org

Mondale, Walter F (1928-)
Former Vice President of the US under Jimmy Carter; a practicing attorney and senior counsel at Dorsey & Whitney
Dorsey & Whitney LLP **Ph:** 612-340-6307
50 S 6th St Suite 1500 **Fax:** 612-340-2643
Minneapolis, MN 55402
www.dorsey.com

Mondello, Bob
NPR film critic
National Public Radio **Ph:** 202-513-2000
635 Massachusetts Ave NW **Fax:** 202-513-3329
Washington, DC 20001
www.npr.org

Mondrian, Piet (1872-1944)
Abstract painter
Mondrian/Holtzman Trust **Ph:** 540-428-3140
HCR International **Fax:** 540-428-3145
85 Waterloo St
Warrenton, VA 20186
www.mondriantrust.com

Monfort, Charles
Chairman and CEO of the Colorado Rockies baseball franchise
Colorado Rockies **Ph:** 303-292-0200
2001 Blake St **Fax:** 303-312-2219
Denver, CO 80205
colorado.rockies.mlb.com

Mo'Nique (1967-)
Comedian; actor
Gersh Agency **Ph:** 310-274-6611
232 N Canon Dr
Beverly Hills, CA 90210
www.1monique.com

Montague-Reyes, Karen
Creator of the comic strip Clear Blue Water
Universal Press Syndicate **Ph:** 816-932-6600
4520 Main St
Kansas City, MO 64111
www.amuniversal.com/ups/features

Montalban, Ricardo (1920-)
Actor
William Morris Agency **Ph:** 310-859-4000
1 William Morris Pl **Fax:** 310-859-4462
Beverly Hills, CA 90212

Montana, Joe (1956-)
Former NFL quarterback (retired) and member of the Pro Football Hall of Fame
Pro Football Hall of Fame **Ph:** 330-456-8207
2121 George Halas Dr NW **Fax:** 330-456-8175
Canton, OH 44708
www.profootballhof.com

Montgomery, David
General partner, president, and CEO of the Philadelphia Phillies baseball franchise
Philadelphia Phillies **Ph:** 215-463-6000
Citizens Bank Park
1 Citizens Bank Park Way
Philadelphia, PA 19148

Montgomery, John Michael (1965-)
Country singer
Buddy Lee Attractions **Ph:** 615-244-4336
38 Music Sq East Suite 300 **Fax:** 615-726-0429
Nashville, TN 37203
www.johnmichael.com

Montgomery, Larry
Chairman and CEO of Kohl's
Kohl's Corp **Ph:** 262-703-7000
N56 W17000 Ridgewood Dr
Menomonee Falls, WI 53051
www.kohlscorporation.com

Montgomery, Mike (1947-)
Basketball coach
Golden State Warriors **Ph:** 510-986-2200
1011 Broadway **Fax:** 510-452-0132
Oakland, CA 94607
www.nba.com/warriors

Montgomery Gentry
Country music duo (Eddie Montgomery and Troy Gentry)
Monterey Peninsula Artists/ Paradigm **Ph:** 615-251-4400
Fax: 615-251-4401
124 12th Ave S Suite 410
Nashville, TN 37203
www.montgomerygentry.com

Montrone, Paul
Chairman and CEO of Fisher Scientific
Fisher Scientific International Inc **Ph:** 603-929-2650
1 Liberty Ln
Hampton, NH 03842
www.fisherscientific.com

Moon, Marilyn, PhD (1947-)
An expert on Medicare and social insurance; vice president and Director of the Health Program at the American Institutes for Research
American Institutes for Research **Ph:** 202-403-5000
Fax: 202-403-5001
1000Thomas Jefferson St NW
Washington, DC 20007
www.air.org/health

Moonves, Leslie (1949-)
President & CEO of CBS Corp
CBS Corp **Ph:** 212-975-4321
51 W 52nd St **Fax:** 212-258-6100
New York, NY 10019
www.cbscorporation.com

Moore, Ann S
Chairman and CEO of Time Inc
Time Inc **Ph:** 212-484-8000
75 Rockefeller Plaza
New York, NY 10019
www.timewarner.com

Moore, Darla D
A partner at Rainwater, Inc, one of the largest private investment firms in America
Rainwater Inc **Ph:** 817-820-6600
777 Main St Suite 2250
Fort Worth, TX 76102
mooreschool.sc.edu/moore

Moore, Demi (1962-)
Actor
Creative Artists Agency **Ph:** 310-288-4545
9830 Wilshire Blvd **Fax:** 310-288-4800
Beverly Hills, CA 90212

Moore, Dennis (1945-)
US Representative from Kansas (Democrat)
1724 Longworth Bldg **Ph:** 202-225-2865
Washington, DC 20515 **Fax:** 202-225-2807
www.house.gov/moore

Moore, Gordon E, PhD (1929-)
Co-founder of Intel, now Chairman Emeritus; known for Moore's Law, in which he predicted that the number of transistors the industry would be able to place on a computer chip would double every couple of years
Intel Corp **Ph:** 408-765-8080
2200 Mission College Blvd
Santa Clara, CA 95052
www.intel.com

Moore, Gwen (1951-)
US Representative from Wisconsin (Democrat)
1400 Longworth Bldg **Ph:** 202-225-4572
Washington, DC 20515 **Fax:** 202-225-8135
www.house.gov/gwenmoore

Moore, J Stuart
Co-founder, with Jerry Greenberg, of Sapient, a business consulting and technology services firm; both serve as CEO and chairman of Sapient's board
Sapient Corp **Ph:** 617-621-0200
25 1st St **Fax:** 617-621-1300
Cambridge, MA 02141
www.sapient.com

Moore, Julianne (1960-)
Actor
Creative Artists Agency **Ph:** 310-288-4545
9830 Wilshire Blvd **Fax:** 310-288-4800
Beverly Hills, CA 90212

Moore, Mandy (1984-)
Singer/actor
The Firm **Ph:** 310-860-8000
9465 Wilshire Blvd **Fax:** 310-860-8100
Beverly Hills, CA 90212
mandymooremusic.com

Moore, Mary Tyler (1936-)
Actor
United Talent Agency **Ph:** 310-273-6700
9560 Wilshire Blvd 5th Fl **Fax:** 310-247-1111
Beverly Hills, CA 90212

Moore, Michael (1954-)
Filmmaker/director; author
Endeavor **Ph:** 310-248-2000
9601 Wilshire Blvd 3rd Fl **Fax:** 310-248-2020
Beverly Hills, CA 90210
www.MichaelMoore.com

Moore, Roy S
The judge who fought removal of the monument featuring the Ten Commandments from public display in the rotunda of the Alabama Judicial Building; former Chief Justice of Alabama and also has a Doctor of Divinity Ecclesiastical Degree
Foundation for Moral Law Inc **Ph:** 334-262-1245
PO Box 4086 **Fax:** 334-262-1708
Montgomery, AL 36103
www.morallaw.org

Moore, Steve
Creator of the syndicated comic panel In the Bleachers; also works in TV and feature animation
Universal Press Syndicate **Ph:** 816-932-6600
4520 Main St
Kansas City, MO 64111
www.amuniversal.com/ups/features

Moore, Thomas, PhD (1940-)
Author of Care of the Soul; former monk in a Catholic religious order and former professor of psychology; has an advice column on Beliefnet.com
HarperCollins Publishers **Ph:** 212-207-7000
c/o Author Mail
10 E 53rd St
New York, NY 10022
www.careofthesoul.net

Moores, John
Owner of the San Diego Padres baseball club
San Diego Padres **Ph:** 619-795-5000
Petco Park **Fax:** 619-497-5339
PO Box 122000
San Diego, CA 92108
sandiego.padres.mlb.com

Moos, Jeanne
National news correspondent for CNN
CNN New York **Ph:** 212-275-7800
Time Warner Ctr
10 Columbus Cir
New York, NY 10019
www.cnn.com/CNN/anchors_reporters

Mora, Gene
Creator of the comic panel Graffiti
United Feature Syndicate **Ph:** 212-293-8500
200 Madison Ave
New York, NY 10016
www.unitedfeatures.com

Mora, Jim (1961-)
Football coach
Atlanta Falcons **Ph:** 770-965-3115
4400 Falcon Pkwy **Fax:** 770-965-3185
Flowery Branch, GA 30542
www.atlantafalcons.com

Morales, Esai (1962-)
Actor
Innovative Artists **Ph:** 310-656-0400
1505 10th St **Fax:** 310-656-0456
Santa Monica, CA 90401

Moran, James (1945-)
US Representative from Virginia (Democrat)
2239 Rayburn Bldg **Ph:** 202-225-4376
Washington, DC 20515 **Fax:** 202-225-0017
moran.house.gov

Moran, James M
Founder and honorary chairman of JM Family Enterprises, one of the largest privately-held companies in the US
JM Family Enterprises Inc **Ph:** 954-429-2044
100 Jim Moran Blvd **Fax:** 954-429-2382
Deerfield Beach, FL 33442
www.jmfamily.com

Moran, Jerry (1954-)
US Representative from Kansas (Republican)
2443 Rayburn Bldg **Ph:** 202-225-2715
Washington, DC 20515 **Fax:** 202-225-5124
www.house.gov/moranks01

Moran, Patricia G
Chairman of JM Family Enterprises; daughter of founder Jim Moran
JM Family Enterprises Inc **Ph:** 954-429-2000
100 Jim Moran Blvd **Fax:** 954-429-2382
Deerfield Beach, FL 33442

Moran, Terry
Co-anchor of Nightline
Nightline **Ph:** 202-222-7700
1717 DeSales St NW
Washington, DC 20036
abcnews.go.com/Nightline

Moreno, Alejandro (1979-)
Professional soccer player
Houston Dynamo **Ph:** 713-276-7500
1415 Louisiana St Suite 3400 **Fax:** 713-276-7580
Houston, TX 77002
houston.mlsnet.com

Moreno, Arturo (1946-)
Self-made billionaire and owner of the Los Angeles Angels of Anaheim baseball club (the first Mexican-American to own a U.S. major league sports team)
Los Angeles Angels of Anaheim **Ph:** 714-634-2000
Angel Stadium **Fax:** 714-940-2001
2000 Gene Autry Way
Anaheim, CA 92806
losangeles.angels.mlb.com

Moreno, Jaime (1974-)
Professional soccer player
DC United **Ph:** 202-587-5000
RFK Stadium **Fax:** 202-587-5400
2400 E Capitol St SE
Washington, DC 20003
dcunited.mlsnet.com

Moreno, Rita (1931-)
Actor (the only female performer to have won all four of the most prestigious show business awards: the Oscar, the Emmy, the Grammy, and the Tony)
Agency for the Performing Arts **Ph:** 310-273-0744
9200 Sunset Blvd Suite 900 **Fax:** 310-888-4242
Los Angeles, CA 90069

Morgan, Dan (1978-)
Professional football player
Carolina Panthers **Ph:** 704-358-7000
Bank of America Stadium **Fax:** 704-358-7618
800 S Mint St
Charlotte, NC 28202
www.panthers.com

Morgan, James
Chairman of Applied Materials Inc
Applied Materials Inc **Ph:** 408-727-5555
3050 Bowers Ave
Santa Clara, CA 95054
www.appliedmaterials.com

Morgan, Joe (1943-)
Former baseball player/Hall of Fame member; TV analyst for major league baseball games
National Baseball Hall of Fame & Museum **Ph:** 607-547-7200 **Fax:** 607-547-2044
25 Main St **TF:** 888-425-5633
Cooperstown, NY 13326
www.baseballhalloffame.org

Morgan, Marlo
Author of Mutant Message Down Under
HarperCollins Publishers **Ph:** 212-207-7000
c/o Author Mail
10 E 53rd St
New York, NY 10022
www.harpercollins.com

Morgan, Mike (1957-)
Creator of the comic strip For Heaven's Sake
Creators Syndicate Inc **Ph:** 310-337-7003
5777 W Century Blvd Suite 700 **Fax:** 310-337-7625
Los Angeles, CA 90045
www.creators.com

Morgan, Robert (1944-)
Novelist (Gap Creek)
Algonquin Books of Chapel Hill **Ph:** 919-967-0108
PO Box 2225 **Fax:** 919-933-0272
Chapel Hill, NC 27515
www.algonquin.com/morgan

Morgenstern, Julie
Professional organizer and author of Organizing from the Inside Out
Julie Morgenstern Enterprises **Ph:** 212-544-8722
850 7th Ave **Fax:** 212-544-0755
New York, NY 10019 **TF:** 866-742-6473
www.juliemorgenstern.com

Morgenthau, Robert M (1919-)
District Attorney of New York County (borough of Manhattan)
District Attorney **Ph:** 212-335-9000
New York County
1 Hogan Pl
New York, NY 10013
www.manhattanda.org

Morgridge, John P
Chairman of Cisco Systems
Cisco Systems Inc **Ph:** 408-526-8229
170 W Tasman Dr **Fax:** 408-526-4100
San Jose, CA 95134
newsroom.cisco.com/dlls/corpfact.html

Moriarty, Erin
48 Hours correspondent
48 Hours **Ph:** 212-975-4114
524 W 57th St
New York, NY 10019
www.cbsnews.com

Morin, Jim (1953-)
Editorial cartoonist for the Miami Herald
Miami Herald **Ph:** 305-350-2111
1 Herald Plaza
Miami, FL 33132
www.miami.com/mld/miamiherald/news/opinion

Morissette, Alanis (1974-)
Singer/songwriter
Creative Artists Agency **Ph:** 310-288-4545
9830 Wilshire Blvd **Fax:** 310-288-4800
Beverly Hills, CA 90212
www.alanismorissette.com

Morrell, Geoff
ABC News White House correspondent
ABC News **Ph:** 202-222-7700
1717 DeSales St NW
Washington, DC 20036
www.abcnews.go.com/WNT

Morris, Doug
Chairman & CEO, Universal Music Group
Universal Music Group **Ph:** 212-841-8000
1755 Broadway 7th Fl
New York, NY 10019

Morris, Edmund (1940-)
Biographer (The Rise of Theodore Roosevelt; Dutch: A Memoir of Ronald Reagan)
Random House Publicity **Ph:** 212-782-9000
1745 Broadway
New York, NY 10019
www.randomhouse.com

Morris, Errol (1948-)
Documentary filmmaker (The Fog of War: Eleven Lessons from the Life of Robert S. McNamara; The Thin Blue Line)
Endeavor **Ph:** 310-248-2000
9601 Wilshire Blvd 3rd Fl **Fax:** 310-248-2020
Beverly Hills, CA 90210
www.sonyclassics.com/fogofwar

Morris, Kathryn (1969-)
Actor
Endeavor Ph: 310-248-2000
9601 Wilshire Blvd 3rd Fl Fax: 310-248-2020
Beverly Hills, CA 90210
www.cbs.com/primetime/cold_case

Morris, Mark (1956-)
Choreographer; founder and artistic director of the Mark Morris Dance Group
Mark Morris Dance Group Ph: 718-624-8400
Discalced Inc Fax: 718-624-8900
3 Lafayette Ave
Brooklyn, NY 11217
www.mmdg.org

Morris, Matt (1974-)
Professional baseball player
San Francisco Giants Ph: 415-972-2000
AT & T Park
24 Willie Mays Plaza
San Francisco, CA 94107
sanfrancisco.giants.mlb.com

Morris, Michael G
Chairman, president, and CEO of American Electric Power Co, the nation's largest electricity generator
American Electric Power Co Inc Ph: 614-716-1000
Fax: 614-716-1823
1 Riverside Plaza
Columbus, OH 43215
www.aep.com

Morris, Peter
Venture capitalist; general partner of New Enterprise Associates
New Enterprise Assoc Ph: 650-854-9499
2490 Sand Hill Rd Fax: 650-854-9397
Menlo Park, CA 94025
www.nea.com/Partners/Partners

Morrison, Keith
Dateline NBC correspondent
Dateline NBC Ph: 212-664-4249
30 Rockefeller Plaza
New York, NY 10112
www.msnbc.msn.com/id/3360263

Morrison, Lillian (1917-)
Poet, anthologist, folklorist, and author & editor of children's poetry collections; retired from the New York Public Library
Boyds Mills Press Ph: 570-253-1164
815 Church St
Honesdale, PA 18431
www.boydsmillspress.com

Morrison, Toni (1931-)
Author (Beloved); winner of the Nobel Prize for Literature in 1993
Knopf Publishing/Author Mail Ph: 212-782-9000
1745 Broadway
New York, NY 10019
www.randomhouse.com/knopf

Morse, Ralph (1917-)
Photographer
Gallery M Ph: 303-331-8400
2830 E 3rd Ave
Denver, CO 80206
www.gallerym.com

Mortensen, Viggo (1958-)
Actor
Creative Artists Agency Ph: 310-288-4545
9830 Wilshire Blvd Fax: 310-288-4800
Beverly Hills, CA 90212

Mos Def (1973-)
Underground hip-hop artist (real name is Dante Terrell Smith)
Brookside Artist Management Ph: 212-489-4929
250 W 57th St Suite 2303
New York, NY 10107
www.mosdefmusic.com

Mosbacher, Robert Jr
President and CEO of the Overseas Private Investment Corp
Overseas Private Investment Corp Ph: 202-336-8401
1100 New York Ave NW 12th Fl
Washington, DC 20527
www.opic.gov

Moseley, T Michael
General; Chief of Staff of the US Air Force
Chief of Staff Ph: 703-697-9225
Pentagon Rm 4E924
Washington, DC 20330
www.af.mil/library/afchain.asp

Mosher, Terry (1942-)
Editorial cartoonist for the Montreal Gazette; the nom de plume & signature he uses on cartoons is Aislin, which is his daughter's name
Montreal Gazette Ph: 514-987-2222
1010 Sainte Catherine St W Suite 200
Montreal, QC H3B5L1
www.aislin.com

Mosley, Walter (1952-)
Author; books include mysteries that feature Easy Rawlins (Devil in a Blue Dress)
Warner Books **Ph:** 212-522-7200
c/o Author Mail
1271 Ave of the Americas
New York, NY 10020
www.waltermosley.com

Moss, Carrie-Anne (1967-)
Actor (Matrix, Chocolat, Memento)
William Morris Agency **Ph:** 310-859-4000
1 William Morris Pl **Fax:** 310-859-4462
Beverly Hills, CA 90212

Moss, Geoffrey
Artist; does captionless editorial/political drawings
Creators Syndicate Inc **Ph:** 310-337-7003
5777 W Century Blvd Suite 700 **Fax:** 310-337-7625
Los Angeles, CA 90045
www.creators.com

Moss, Kate (1974-)
Model
IMG Models **Ph:** 212-253-8884
304 Park Ave S 12th Fl **Fax:** 212-253-8883
New York, NY 10010

Moss, Randy (1977-)
Professional football player
Oakland Raiders **Ph:** 510-864-5000
1220 Harbor Bay Pkwy **Fax:** 510-864-5134
Alameda, CA 94502
www.raiders.com

Moss, Santana (1979-)
Professional football player
Washington Redskins **Ph:** 703-726-7000
21300 Redskin Park Dr **Fax:** 703-726-7086
Ashburn, VA 20147
www.redskins.com

Mother Angelica (1923-)
Catholic nun and founder of Eternal Word Television Network (EWTN)
EWTN **Ph:** 205-271-2900
5817 Old Leeds Rd **Fax:** 205-271-2939
Irondale, AL 35210
www.ewtn.com

Motley, Ronald L (1944-)
Trial lawyer who is lead counsel for family members & survivors of the 9/11 terrorist attacks seeking justice against al Qaeda financiers; has won major cases against the asbestos & tobacco industries
Motley Rice LLC **Ph:** 843-216-9000
28 Bridgeside Blvd **Fax:** 843-216-9450
PO Box 1792
Mount Pleasant, SC 29465
www.motleyrice.com

Moulds, Eric (1973-)
Professional football player
Houston Texans **Ph:** 832-667-2000
2 Reliant Park **Fax:** 832-667-2100
Houston, TX 77054
www.houstontexans.com

Moulton, Sara
Host of Sara's Secrets on the Food Network
Food Network **Ph:** 212-398-8836
75 9th Ave **Fax:** 212-736-7716
New York, NY 10011
www.saramoulton.com

Mourning, Alonzo (1970-)
Professional basketball player
Miami Heat **Ph:** 786-777-1000
American Airlines Arena **Fax:** 786-777-1609
601 Biscayne Blvd
Miami, FL 33132
www.nba.com/heat

Moyer, Jamie (1962-)
Professional baseball player
Seattle Mariners **Ph:** 206-346-4000
Safeco Field **Fax:** 206-346-4050
1250 1st Ave S
Seattle, WA 98134
seattle.mariners.mlb.com

Mr Food
Celebrity chef Art Ginsburg
Ginsburg Enterprises Inc **Ph:** 954-938-0400
1770 NW 64th St Suite 500 **Fax:** 954-938-2005
Fort Lauderdale, FL 33309
www.mrfood.com

Mr Magazine
Name under which journalism professor Samir A Husni reviews and rates consumer magazines
University of Mississippi **Ph:** 662-915-1414
Journalism Dept **Fax:** 662-915-7765
PO Box 2906
123 Lester Hall
University, MS 38677
www.mrmagazine.com

Mudd, Daniel H
President and CEO of Fannie Mae
Fannie Mae **Ph:** 202-752-7000
3900 Wisconsin Ave NW
Washington, DC 20016
www.fanniemae.com

Mueller, Lisel (1924-)
Poet
Louisiana State University Press **Ph:** 225-578-8271
PO Box 25053
Baton Rouge, LA 70894
www.lsu.edu/lsupress

Mueller, Robert S III (1944-)
FBI Director
Federal Bureau of Investigation **Ph:** 202-324-3444
935 Pennsylvania Ave NW **Fax:** 202-324-4705
Washington, DC 20535
www.fbi.gov/aboutus.htm

Muench, David (1936-)
Landscape photographer
Muench Photography Inc **Ph:** 805-685-2825
142 Santa Felicia Dr
Goleta, CA 93117
www.muenchphotography.com

Muench, Marc (1966-)
Landscape photographer (son of David Muench); does photographs for magazines and for Canon Photo Safari on ESPN
Muench Photography Inc **Ph:** 805-685-2825
142 Santa Felicia Dr
Goleta, CA 93117
www.muenchphotography.com

Muhammad, Muhsin (1973-)
Professional football player
Chicago Bears **Ph:** 847-295-6600
Halas Hall at Conway Park **Fax:** 847-295-8986
1000 Football Dr
Lake Forest, IL 60045
www.chicagobears.com

Muir, David
ABC News correspondent
ABC News **Ph:** 212-456-7777
77 W 66th St
New York, NY 10023
www.abcnews.go.com/WNT

Mulcahy, Anne M (1952-)
Chairman & CEO of Xerox
Xerox Corp **Ph:** 203-968-3553
800 Long Ridge Rd **Fax:** 203-968-4566
Stamford, CT 06904
www.xerox.com

Mulder, Mark (1977-)
Professional baseball player
Saint Louis Cardinals **Ph:** 314-421-3060
250 Stadium Plaza **Fax:** 314-425-0640
Saint Louis, MO 63102
stlouis.cardinals.mlb.com

Muldoon, Paul (1951-)
Poet
Farrar Straus & Giroux **Ph:** 212-741-6900
19 Union Sq W
New York, NY 10003
www.paulmuldoon.net

Mullally, Megan (1958-)
Actor
Gersh Agency **Ph:** 310-274-6611
232 N Canon Dr
Beverly Hills, CA 90210
www.nbc.com/Will_&_Grace

Mullen, Jim
Writes the syndicated humor column The Village Idiot
United Feature Syndicate **Ph:** 212-293-8500
200 Madison Ave
New York, NY 10016
www.unitedfeatures.com

Mullen, Michael G
Admiral; Chief of Naval Operations, US Dept of the Navy
CNO **Ph:** 703-695-5664
US Dept of the Navy
2000 Navy Pentagon
Washington, DC 20350
www.navy.mil

Muller, Edward R
Chairman, president, and CEO of Mirant Corp, a company that produces and sells electricity
Mirant Corp **Ph:** 678-579-5000
1155 Perimeter Center W Suite 100 **Fax:** 678-579-5001
Atlanta, GA 30338
www.mirant.com

Muller, Judy
ABC News correspondent
ABC News **Ph:** 323-671-5261
4151 Prospect Ave **Fax:** 323-671-5210
Los Angeles, CA 90027
www.abcnews.go.com/WNT

Muller, Mancow (1967-)
Host of a morning radio show featuring a wacky/crude crew
WKQX - Q101 **Ph:** 312-527-8348
230 Merchandise Mart Plaza **Fax:** 312-527-3620
Chicago, IL 60654
www.q101.com

Mullis, Kary B, PhD (1944-)
1993 Nobel Laureate in Chemistry for his work in DNA research; serves on the advisory board of the National Organization to Reform Marijuana Laws
NORML Advisory Board **Ph:** 202-483-5500
1600 K St NW
Washington, DC 20006
www.karymullis.com

Mulroney, Dermot (1963-)
Actor
International Creative Management **Ph:** 310-550-4000
8942 Wilshire Blvd
Beverly Hills, CA 90211

Mulva, James J (1946-)
Chairman & CEO of ConocoPhillips
ConocoPhillips **Ph:** 281-293-1000
600 N Dairy Ashford Rd **Fax:** 281-293-1440
Houston, TX 77079
www.conocophillips.com

Mundell, Robert A, PhD (1932-)
Winner of the 1999 Nobel Prize in Economics for his analysis of monetary and fiscal policy under different exchange rate regimes and his analysis of optimum currency areas
Columbia University **Ph:** 212-854-3669
Dept of Economics **Fax:** 212-854-8059
International Affairs Bldg
420 W 118th St
New York, NY 10027
www.columbia.edu/~ram15

Munger, Charles T
Vice Chairman of Berkshire Hathaway
Berkshire Hathaway Inc **Ph:** 402-346-1400
1440 Kiewit Plaza
Omaha, NE 68131
www.berkshirehathaway.com

Muniz, Frankie (1985-)
Actor
International Creative Management **Ph:** 310-550-4000
8942 Wilshire Blvd
Beverly HIlls, CA 90211
www.celebritykidz.com/frankiemuniz

Munk, Peter
Founder and chairman of Barrick Gold Corp
Barrick Gold Corp **Ph:** 416-861-9111
Canada Trust Tower
161 Bay St Suite 3700
Toronto, ON M5J2S1
www.barrick.com

Munro, Alice (1931-)
Author of fiction (mostly short stories)
Knopf Publishing/Author Mail **Ph:** 212-782-9000
1745 Broadway
New York, NY 10019
www.randomhouse.com/knopf

Munsch, Robert (1945-)
Children's book author and storyteller
Scholastic Inc **Ph:** 212-343-6100
557 Broadway
New York, NY 10012
www.robertmunsch.com

Munson, David R (1942-)
Mayor of Sioux Falls, South Dakota
224 W 9th St **Ph:** 605-367-8800
Sioux Falls, SD 57104
www.siouxfalls.org/mayor

Murad, Ferid, MD, PhD (1936-)
Winner (with two other scientists) of the 1998 Nobel Prize in Medicine for discoveries concerning nitric oxide as a signalling molecule in the cardiovascular system
University of Texas Medical School **Ph:** 713-500-7501 **Fax:** 713-500-7444
6431 Fannin St Rm 4098
Houston, TX 77030
ibp.med.uth.tmc.edu/facresint.htm

Murakami, Haruki (1949-)
Author (After the Quake; Kafka on the Shore)
Knopf Publishing/Author Mail **Ph:** 212-782-9000
1745 Broadway
New York, NY 10019
www.randomhouse.com/knopf

Murdoch, K Rupert (1931-)
Chairman & CEO of News Corp, which owns numerous media companies (broadcast & print), including 20th Century Fox, FOX Broadcasting, and HarperCollins Publishers
News Corp **Ph:** 212-852-7000
1211 Ave of the Americas 8th Fl
New York, NY 10036
www.newscorp.com/management

Murillo, Mario
Evangelist
Mario Murillo Ministries **Ph:** 925-945-1151
PO Box 5027
San Ramon, CA 94583
www.mariomurillo.com

Murkoff, Heidi
Author of What to Expect When You're Expecting and related titles
Workman Publishing **Ph:** 212-254-5900
708 Broadway
New York, NY 10003
www.workman.com

Murkowski, Frank (1933-)
Governor of Alaska (Republican)
PO Box 110001 **Ph:** 907-465-3500
Juneau, AK 99811 **Fax:** 907-465-3532
www.gov.state.ak.us

Murkowski, Lisa (1957-)
US Senator from Alaska (Republican)
C1 Russell Bldg **Ph:** 202-224-6665
Washington, DC 20510 **Fax:** 202-224-5301
murkowski.senate.gov

Murphy, Ann Pleshette
Parenting contributor for ABC News's Good Morning America
Good Morning America **Ph:** 212-456-7777
147 Columbus Ave
New York, NY 10023
www.annpleshettemurphy.com

Murphy, Brittany (1977-)
Actor
Mosaic Media Group **Ph:** 310-786-4900
9200 W Sunset Blvd 10th Fl
Los Angeles, CA 90069

Murphy, Carolyn (1975-)
Model
Creative Artists Agency **Ph:** 310-288-4545
9830 Wilshire Blvd **Fax:** 310-288-4800
Beverly Hills, CA 90212

Murphy, Dennis
Dateline NBC correspondent
Dateline NBC **Ph:** 212-664-4249
30 Rockefeller Plaza
New York, NY 10112
www.msnbc.msn.com/id/3360263

Murphy, Eddie (1961-)
Comedian; actor
Rogers & Cowan PR **Ph:** 310-854-8100
Pacific Design Center **Fax:** 310-854-8101
8687 Melrose Ave 7th Fl
Los Angeles, CA 90069

Murphy, Jim (1947-)
Author of books for young readers that are based on actual historical events (The Great Fire)
Houghton Mifflin Co **Ph:** 617-351-5000
Trade Div
Adult Editorial
222 Berkeley St 8th Fl
Boston, MA 02116
www.houghtonmifflinbooks.com

Murphy, John V
Chairman, president, and CEO of OppenheimerFunds
OppenheimerFunds Inc **Ph:** 212-323-0200
2 World Financial Center **Fax:** 212-323-0558
225 Liberty St
New York, NY 10281
www.oppenheimerfunds.com

Murphy, Steve
President & CEO of Rodale (magazine, book, and online publisher)
Rodale Inc **Ph:** 610-967-8154
33 E Minor St **Fax:** 800-813-6627
Emmaus, PA 18098
www.rodale.com

Murphy, Tamara
Executive chef and owner of Brasa Restaurant in Seattle
Brasa Restaurant **Ph:** 206-728-4220
2107 3rd Ave
Seattle, WA 98121
www.brasa.com

Murphy, Timothy F (1952-)
US Representative from Pennsylvania (Republican)
322 Cannon Bldg **Ph:** 202-225-2301
Washington, DC 20515 **Fax:** 202-225-1844
murphy.house.gov

Murray, Bryan (1942-)
Hockey coach; has also been a general manager
Ottawa Senators **Ph:** 613-599-0250
Corel Center **Fax:** 613-599-0358
1000 Palladium Dr
Kanata, ON K2V1A5
www.ottawasenators.com

Murray, Chad Michael (1981-)
Actor
Creative Artists Agency **Ph:** 310-288-4545
9830 Wilshire Blvd **Fax:** 310-288-4800
Beverly Hills, CA 90212

Murray, Patty (1950-)
US Senator from Washington (Democrat)
173 Russell Bldg **Ph:** 202-224-2621
Washington, DC 20510 **Fax:** 202-224-0238
murray.senate.gov

Murray, Sabina
Author of The Caprices, a short story collection that revolves around the Pacific Campaign of World War II
Houghton Mifflin Co **Ph:** 617-351-5000
Trade Div
Adult Editorial
222 Berkeley St 8th Fl
Boston, MA 02116
www.houghtonmifflinbooks.com

Murtha, John P (1932-)
US Representative from Pennsylvania (Democrat)
2423 Rayburn Bldg **Ph:** 202-225-2065
Washington, DC 20515 **Fax:** 202-225-5709
www.house.gov/murtha

Musgrave, Marilyn N (1949-)
US Representative from Colorado (Republican)
1507 Longworth Bldg **Ph:** 202-225-4676
Washington, DC 20515 **Fax:** 202-225-5870
musgrave.house.gov

Mutombo, Dikembe (1966-)
Professional basketball player
Houston Rockets **Ph:** 713-758-7200
Toyota Center **Fax:** 713-758-7396
1510 Polk St
Houston, TX 77002
www.nba.com/rockets

Mydans, Carl (1907-2004)
Photographer
Gallery M **Ph:** 303-331-8400
2830 E 3rd Ave
Denver, CO 80206
www.gallerym.com

Myers, Bruce C
President and CEO of Advanced Marketing Services, a provider of customized wholesaling services to book retailers
Advanced Marketing Services Inc **Ph:** 858-457-2500
5880 Oberlin Dr Suite 400
San Diego, CA 92121
www.advmkt.com

Myers, Chris (1959-)
Sports broadcaster
FOX Sports Net **Ph:** 310-369-1000
10201 W Pico Blvd
Bldg 101
Los Angeles, CA 90035
msn.foxsports.com/CMI

Myers, David W
Writes the syndicated newspaper column, About Real Estate
King Features Syndicate Inc **Ph:** 212-455-4000
888 7th Ave 2nd Fl
New York, NY 10019
www.kingfeatures.com

Myers, Lisa
NBC News senior investigative correspondent
NBC News **Ph:** 202-885-4200
4001 Nebraska Ave NW
Washington, DC 20016
www.msnbc.msn.com/id/3689499

Myers, Mike (1963-)
Actor
Creative Artists Agency **Ph:** 310-288-4545
9830 Wilshire Blvd **Fax:** 310-288-4800
Beverly Hills, CA 90212

Myers, Russell (1938-)
Creator of the comic strip Broom-Hilda
Tribune Media Services Inc **Ph:** 312-222-4444
435 N Michigan Ave Suite 1500
Chicago, IL 60611
www.comicspage.com

Myers, Walter Dean (1937-)
Writer of books for young adults (Monster)
HarperCollins Children's Books **Ph:** 212-261-6500
1350 Ave of the Americas
New York, NY 10019
www.walterdeanmyersbooks.com

Mylrea, Mindy
Fitness instructor; creator and owner of FitFlixs Productions
FitFlixs Productions **Ph:** 877-348-3549
225 Esmeralda Dr
Santa Cruz, CA 95060
www.jumpincfitness.com/fitflixs

Myrick, Sue (1941-)
US Representative from North Carolina (Republican)
230 Cannon Bldg **Ph:** 202-225-1976
Washington, DC 20515 **Fax:** 202-225-3389
myrick.house.gov

Myss, Caroline
Author & speaker on the subjects of human consciousness, spirituality and mysticism, health, energy medicine, and advancing the science of medical intuition; also hosts a call-in radio program
CMED Institute **Ph:** 815-220-8723
1004 Brittany Rd
Highland Park, IL 60035
www.myss.com

Na, An (1972-)
Writer of books for young readers (A Step from Heaven)
Front Street Inc **Ph:** 828-221-2091
862 Haywood Rd **Fax:** 828-221-2112
Asheville, NC 28806
www.frontstreetbooks.com

Nabel, Elizabeth G, MD
Director of the National Heart, Lung, and Blood Institute, National Institutes of Health
National Heart Lung & Blood Institute **Ph:** 301-496-4236
9000 Rockville Pike
Bldg 31
Bethesda, MD 20892
www.nhlbi.nih.gov

Nabokov, Evgeni (1975-)
Professional hockey player
San Jose Sharks **Ph:** 408-287-7070
HP Pavilion at San Jose **Fax:** 408-999-5797
525 W Santa Clara St
San Jose, CA 95113
www.sjsharks.com

Nabors, Jim (1930-)
Actor; singer
William Morris Agency **Ph:** 310-859-4000
1 William Morris Pl **Fax:** 310-859-4462
Beverly Hills, CA 90212
www.jimnabors.com

Nadal, Rafael (1986-)
Professional tennis player
ATP **Ph:** 904-285-8000
201 ATP Blvd **Fax:** 904-285-5966
Ponte Vedra Beach, FL 32082
www.atptennis.com

Nader, Ralph (1934-)
Consumer activist; independent presidential candidate in 2000 and 2004
Center for Study of Responsive Law **Ph:** 202-387-8030 **Fax:** 202-234-5176
PO Box 19367
Washington, DC 20036
www.nader.org

Nadler, Jerrold (1947-)
US Representative from New York (Democrat)
2334 Rayburn Bldg **Ph:** 202-225-5635
Washington, DC 20515 **Fax:** 202-225-6923
www.house.gov/nadler

Naegele, Robert O Jr
Chairman of Minnesota Sports & Entertainment, the parent company of the Minnesota Wild hockey team
Minnesota Wild **Ph:** 651-602-6000
317 Washington St **Fax:** 651-222-1055
Saint Paul, MN 55102
www.wild.com/team/Naegele.asp

Nagin, C Ray
Mayor of New Orleans
1300 Perdido St Suite 2E04 **Ph:** 504-658-4900
New Orleans, LA 70112 **Fax:** 504-658-4938
www.cityofno.com

Naipaul, VS (1932-)
Winner of the 2001 Nobel Prize for Literature; writes both fiction & nonfiction
Knopf Publishing/Author Mail **Ph:** 212-782-9000
1745 Broadway
New York, NY 10019
www.randomhouse.com/knopf

Naisbitt, John (1929-)
Leading futurist; author (Megatrends), speaker, and technology expert/consultant
Megatrends Ltd **Ph:** 301-587-1409
1409 Woodside Pkwy **Fax:** 301-587-3744
Silver Spring, MD 20901
www.naisbitt.com

Najimy, Kathy (1957-)
Actor
International Creative Management **Ph:** 212-556-5600
40 W 57th St 17th Fl
New York, NY 10019
www.kathynajimy.com

Nakai, R Carlos (1946-)
Native American musician (flutist)
Herschel Freeman Agency **Ph:** 901-757-4567
7684 Apahon Ln
Germantown, TN 38138
www.canyonrecords.com/artists.htm

Nakamura, Kaori
A principal dancer with Pacific Northwest Ballet
Pacific Northwest Ballet **Ph:** 206-441-9411
301 Mercer St **Fax:** 206-441-2440
Seattle, WA 98109
www.kaorinakamura.com

Nance, John J (1946-)
Aviation analyst/consultant for ABC News's Good Morning America
Good Morning America **Ph:** 212-456-7777
147 Columbus Ave
New York, NY 10023
www.abcnews.go.com/GMA

Nantz, Jim (1959-)
Sports broadcaster
CBS Sports **Ph:** 212-975-4321
51 W 52nd St
New York, NY 10019
cbs.sportsline.com/cbssports/team

Napolitano, Andrew
Senior judicial analyst for FOX News
FOX News Channel **Ph:** 212-301-3000
1211 Ave of the Americas
New York, NY 10036
www.foxnews.com/fnctv

Napolitano, Grace Flores (1936-)
US Representative from California (Democrat)
1609 Longworth Bldg **Ph:** 202-225-5256
Washington, DC 20515 **Fax:** 202-225-0027
www.napolitano.house.gov

Napolitano, Janet (1957-)
Governor of Arizona (Democrat)
1700 W Washington St **Ph:** 602-542-4331
Executive Tower 9th Fl **Fax:** 602-542-7601
Phoenix, AZ 85007
www.governor.state.az.us

Nardelli, Robert L
Chairman, president, and CEO of Home Depot Inc
Home Depot Inc **Ph:** 770-384-3622
2455 Paces Ferry Rd **Fax:** 770-384-2051
Atlanta, GA 30339
corporate.homedepot.com

Narron, Jerry (1956-)
Baseball manager
Cincinnati Reds **Ph:** 513-765-7000
Great American Ballpark **Fax:** 513-765-7342
100 Main St
Cincinnati, OH 45202
cincinnati.reds.mlb.com

Nasar, Sylvia
Author of A Beautiful Mind
Simon & Schuster **Ph:** 212-698-7000
1230 Ave of the Americas
New York, NY 10020
www.jrn.columbia.edu/faculty/nasar.asp

Nash, Rick (1984-)
Professional hockey player
Columbus Blue Jackets **Ph:** 614-246-4625
Nationwide Arena **Fax:** 614-246-4007
200 W Nationwide Blvd 3rd Fl
Columbus, OH 43215
www.bluejackets.com

Nash, Steve (1974-)
Professional basketball player
Phoenix Suns **Ph:** 602-379-7900
America West Arena **Fax:** 602-379-7990
201 E Jefferson St
Phoenix, AZ 85004
www.nba.com/suns

Naslund, Markus (1973-)
Professional hockey player
Vancouver Canucks **Ph:** 604-899-4600
General Motors Pl **Fax:** 604-899-4640
800 Griffiths Way
Vancouver, BC V6B6G1
www.canucks.com

Nasr, Octavia E
CNN's senior editor for Arab affairs
CNN **Ph:** 404-827-1500
1 CNN Center
Atlanta, GA 30303
www.cnn.com/CNN/anchors_reporters

Nassetta, Christopher J
President and CEO of Host Marriott
Host Marriott Corp **Ph:** 240-744-1000
6903 Rockledge Dr Suite 1500
Bethesda, MD 20817
www.hostmarriott.com

Nathan, Alan
Radio talk show host (politics)
Radio America **Ph:** 202-408-0944
1030 15th St NW **Fax:** 202-408-1087
Washington, DC 20005
http://www.alannathan.com

Nathan, Joan
Host and executive producer of Jewish Cooking in America with Joan Nathan
Jewish Cooking in America with Joan Nathan **Ph:** 410-356-5600
Maryland Public Television
11767 Owings Mills Rd
Owings Mills, MD 21117
www.pbs.org/mpt/jewishcooking

Nathan, Joe (1974-)
Professional baseball player
Minnesota Twins **Ph:** 612-375-1366
Hubert H Humphrey Metrodome **Fax:** 612-375-7473
34 Kirby Puckett Pl
Minneapolis, MN 55415
minnesota.twins.mlb.com

Naughton, James (1945-)
Actor, singer, director
International Creative Management **Ph:** 212-556-5600
40 W 57th St 17th Fl
New York, NY 10019
www.icmtalent.com/musperf/contemporary.html

Navarrette, Ruben (1967-)
Syndicated columnist
Washington Post Writers Group **Ph:** 202-334-6375 **Fax:** 202-334-5669
1150 15th St NW 9th Fl
Washington, DC 20071
www.postwritersgroup.com

Naylor, Phyllis Reynolds (1933-)
Children's book author (Shiloh; the Boy-Girl Battle Books series)
Random House Children's Books **Ph:** 212-782-9000
Publicity Dept
1745 Broadway
New York, NY 10019
www.randomhouse.com/kids

Neal, Richard E (1949-)
US Representative from Massachusetts (Democrat)
2266 Rayburn Bldg **Ph:** 202-225-5601
Washington, DC 20515 **Fax:** 202-225-8112
www.house.gov/neal

Nealon, Kevin (1953-)
Comedian
Gersh Agency **Ph:** 310-274-6611
232 N Canon Dr
Beverly Hills, CA 90210
www.kevinnealon.com

Neas, Ralph G
President of People for the American Way
People for the American Way **Ph:** 202-467-4999
2000 M St NW Suite 400 **TF:** 800-326-7329
Washington, DC 20036
www.pfaw.org

Nechita, Alexandra (1985-)
Romanian-born art prodigy
Allucra LLC **Ph:** 818-990-5910
13908 3/4 Ventura Blvd
Sherman Oaks, CA 91423
www.nechita.info

Nedved, Petr (1971-)
Professional hockey player
Philadelphia Flyers **Ph:** 215-465-4500
Wachovia Center **Fax:** 215-389-9403
3601 S Broad St
Philadelphia, PA 19148
www.philadelphiaflyers.com

Neeson, Liam (1952-)
Actor
International Creative Management **Ph:** 310-550-4000
8942 Wilshire Blvd
Beverly Hills, CA 90211

Negroponte, John D (1939-)
Director of National Intelligence
Office of the Director of National Intelligence **Ph:** 202-201-1111
Washington, DC 20511
www.odni.gov

Neighmond, Patricia
Journalist; NPR's health policy correspondent
National Public Radio **Ph:** 202-513-2000
635 Massachusetts Ave NW **Fax:** 202-513-3329
Washington, DC 20001
www.npr.org

Neill, Sam (1947-)
Actor
International Creative Management **Ph:** 310-550-4000
8942 Wilshire Blvd
Beverly Hills, CA 90211

Neiman, LeRoy (1927-)
Artist; paints images of sporting events & leisure activities
Hammer Galleries LLC **Ph:** 212-644-4400
33 W 57th St **Fax:** 212-644-4407
New York, NY 10019
www.leroyneiman.com

Nelly (1974-)
Rap/hip-hop artist; actor
United Talent Agency **Ph:** 310-273-6700
9560 Wilshire Blvd 5th Fl **Fax:** 310-247-1111
Beverly Hills, CA 90212
www.nelly.net

Nelson, Ben (1941-)
US Senator from Nebraska (Democrat)
720 Hart Bldg **Ph:** 202-224-6551
Washington, DC 20510 **Fax:** 202-228-0012
bennelson.senate.gov

Nelson, Bill (1942-)
US Senator from Florida (Democrat)
716 Hart Bldg **Ph:** 202-224-5274
Washington, DC 20510 **Fax:** 202-228-2183
billnelson.senate.gov

Nelson, Kendall
Photographer (American West/cowboys)
Peter Fetterman Gallery **Ph:** 310-453-6463
Bergamot Stn
2525 Michigan Ave Suite A7
Santa Monica, CA 90404
www.peterfetterman.com

Nelson, Marilyn (1946-)
Poet; author of Carver: A Life in Poems
University of Connecticut **Ph:** 860-486-2141
English Dept
Box U-4025
215 Glenbrook Rd
Storrs, CT 06269
www.english.uconn.edu

Nelson, Marilyn Carlson
Chair and CEO of Carlson Companies
Carlson Cos Inc **Ph:** 763-212-1273
701 Carlson Pkwy **Fax:** 763-212-2219
Minnetonka, MN 55305
www.carlson.com

Nelson, Stephanie
Writes the syndicated column The Supermarket Shopper, a guide to supermarkets & grocery savings (she inherited the column from Martin Sloane, who retired from writing in December 2005)
United Feature Syndicate **Ph:** 212-293-8500
200 Madison Ave
New York, NY 10016
www.unitedfeatures.com

Nelson, Willie (1933-)
Singer/songwriter; actor; also president of Farm Aid
William Morris Agency **Ph:** 310-859-4000
1 William Morris Pl **Fax:** 310-859-4462
Beverly Hills, CA 90212
www.willienelson.com

Nemechek, Joe (1963-)
Race car driver
MB2 Motorsports **Ph:** 704-720-0733
1035 Mecklenburg Hwy
PO Box 270
Mooresville, NC 28115
www.mb2mbvmotorsports.com

Neubauer, Joseph
Chairman & CEO of ARAMARK
ARAMARK Corp **Ph:** 215-238-3880
1101 Market St **Fax:** 215-238-3333
Philadelphia, PA 19107
www.aramark.com/investor_relations.htm

Neufeld, Peter
Attorney; co-founder & co-director, with Barry Scheck, of the Innocence Project at the Cardozo School of Law, which only handles cases where postconviction DNA testing of evidence can yield conclusive proof of innocence
Innocence Project **Ph:** 212-364-5340
100 5th Ave 3rd Fl **Fax:** 212-364-5341
New York, NY 10011
www.innocenceproject.com

Neugebauer, Randy (1949-)
US Representative from Texas (Republican)
429 Cannon Bldg **Ph:** 202-225-4005
Washington, DC 20515 **Fax:** 202-225-9615
www.randy.house.gov

Neuharth, Al (1924-)
Founder of USA Today; writes a weekly column; founder and senior advisory chairman of the Freedom Forum
USA Today **Ph:** 703-854-3400
7950 Jones Branch Dr
McLean, VA 22108
www.usatoday.com/news/opinion/index.htm

Neuwirth, Bebe (1958-)
Actor
International Creative Management **Ph:** 310-550-4000
8942 Wilshire Blvd
Beverly Hills, CA 90211

Neville, Aaron (1941-)
Singer (jazz, pop, contemporary Christian/gospel)
William Morris Agency **Ph:** 310-859-4000
1 William Morris Pl **Fax:** 310-859-4462
Beverly Hills, CA 90212
www.aaronneville.com

Neville, Emily Cheney (1919-)
Children's book author (It's Like This, Cat)
HarperCollins Children's Books **Ph:** 212-261-6500
1350 Ave of the Americas
New York, NY 10019
www.harperchildrens.com

Nevin, Phil (1971-)
Professional baseball player
Texas Rangers **Ph:** 817-273-5222
Ameriquest Field in Arlington **Fax:** 817-273-5294
1000 Ballpark Way **TF:** 888-968-3927
Arlington, TX 76011
texas.rangers.mlb.com

Newell, Mike (1942-)
Movie director and producer
International Creative Management **Ph:** 310-550-4000
8942 Wilshire Blvd
Beverly Hills, CA 90211

Newhart, Bob (1929-)
Comedian; actor
William Morris Agency **Ph:** 310-859-4000
1 William Morris Pl **Fax:** 310-859-4462
Beverly Hills, CA 90212
www.bobnewhart.com

Newhouse, Donald E (1929-)
President of Advance Publications, a family-owned, privately held communications company that owns Conde Nast, Parade, and Fairchild Publications, American City Business Journals, the Golf Digest Companies, and newspapers in more than 20 US cities
Advance Publications Inc **Ph:** 718-981-1234
950 Fingerboard Rd
Staten Island, NY 10305

Newhouse, Samuel I Jr (1927-)
Chairman and CEO of Advance Publications, a family-owned, privately held communications company that owns Conde Nast, Parade, and Fairchild Publications, American City Business Journals, the Golf Digest Companies, and newspapers in more than 20 US cities
Advance Publications Inc **Ph:** 718-981-1234
950 Fingerboard Rd
Staten Island, NY 10305

Newman, Arnold (1918-)
Photographer (celebrity portraits)
Peter Fetterman Gallery **Ph:** 310-453-6463
Bergamot Stn
2525 Michigan Ave Suite A7
Santa Monica, CA 90404
www.peterfetterman.com

Newman, Paul (1925-)
Actor
International Creative Management **Ph:** 310-550-4000
8942 Wilshire Blvd
Beverly Hills, CA 90211

Newman, Randy (1943-)
Singer/songwriter; composer
Monterey Peninsula Artists/Paradigm **Ph:** 831-375-4889 **Fax:** 831-375-2623
509 Hartnell St
Monterey, CA 93940
www.randynewman.com

Newman, Ryan (1977-)
NASCAR driver
Penske Racing South **Ph:** 704-664-2300
200 Penske Way
Mooresville, NC 28115
www.penskeracing.com

Newman, Steve
Writes Earthweek, a syndicated column about natural and man-made events that affect the planet
Universal Press Syndicate **Ph:** 816-932-6600
4520 Main St
Kansas City, MO 64111
www.amuniversal.com/ups/features

Newman, Terence (1978-)
Professional football player
Dallas Cowboys **Ph:** 972-556-9900
1 Cowboys Pkwy **Fax:** 972-556-9304
Irving, TX 75063
www.dallascowboys.com

Newsboys
Contemporary Christian music group; lead singer is Peter Furler
H2O Artist Agency **Ph:** 770-736-5363
2422 Waterscape Trail **Fax:** 770-736-9389
Snellville, GA 30078
www.newsboys.com

Newsom, Gavin C (1967-)
Mayor of San Francisco
1 Dr Carlton B Goodlett Pl Rm 200 **Ph:** 415-554-6141
San Francisco, CA 94102 **Fax:** 415-554-6160
www.sfgov.org

Newton, Thandie (1972-)
Actor
William Morris Agency **Ph:** 310-859-4000
1 William Morris Pl **Fax:** 310-859-4462
Beverly Hills, CA 90212

Newton, Wayne (1942-)
Singer and musician
William Morris Agency **Ph:** 310-859-4000
1 William Morris Pl **Fax:** 310-859-4462
Beverly Hills, CA 90212
www.waynenewton.com

Ney, Bob (1954-)
US Representative from Ohio (Republican)
2438 Rayburn Bldg **Ph:** 202-225-6265
Washington, DC 20515 **Fax:** 202-225-3394
ney.house.gov

Nguyen, Betty
News anchor for CNN
CNN **Ph:** 404-827-1500
1 CNN Center
Atlanta, GA 30303
www.cnn.com/CNN/anchors_reporters

Nhat Hanh, Thich (1926-)
Buddhist monk/Zen master, poet, peace activist, and author
Parallax Press **Ph:** 510-525-0101
PO Box 7355 **Fax:** 510-525-7129
Berkeley, CA 94707
www.parallax.org

Niblock, Robert
Chairman, president, and CEO of Lowe's
Lowe's Cos Inc **Ph:** 704-758-1000
1000 Lowe's Blvd
Mooresville, NC 28117
www.lowes.com

Nichol, Joseph McGinty (1970-)
Director of commercials, music videos, and movies
Endeavor **Ph:** 310-248-2000
9601 Wilshire Blvd 3rd Fl **Fax:** 310-248-2020
Beverly Hills, CA 90210

Nichols, Joe (1976-)
Country singer
CAA Nashville **Ph:** 615-383-8787
3310 West End Ave 5th Fl **Fax:** 615-383-4937
Nashville, TN 37203
joenichols.com

Nichols, Kyra (1958-)
A principal dancer with the New York City Ballet; has also performed on national television and with other ballet groups around the world
New York City Ballet **Ph:** 212-870-5656
New York State Theater **Fax:** 212-870-7791
20 Lincoln Center
New York, NY 10023
www.nycballet.com/about/dancers.html

Nichols, Mike (1931-)
Director (film, theater, television) and producer
Creative Artists Agency **Ph:** 310-288-4545
9830 Wilshire Blvd **Fax:** 310-288-4800
Beverly Hills, CA 90212

Nicholson, Jack (1937-)
Actor
Bresler Kelly & Assoc **Ph:** 310-479-5611
11500 W Olympic Blvd Suite 352
Los Angeles, CA 90064

Nicholson, R James "Jim" (1938-)
US Secretary of Veterans Affairs; former chairman of the Republican National Committee and former US Ambassador to the Holy See
US Dept of Veterans Affairs **Ph:** 202-273-4809
810 Vermont Ave NW Rm 1000 **Fax:** 202-273-4877
Washington, DC 20420
www1.va.gov/opa/bios

Nicholson, Susan
Columnist, speaker, cookbook author, and a consultant in the area of food and nutrition; writes the syndicated column 7-Day Menu Planner
Universal Press Syndicate **Ph:** 816-932-6600
4520 Main St
Kansas City, MO 64111
www.amuniversal.com/ups/features

Nicholson, William (1948-)
Screenwriter
Creative Artists Agency **Ph:** 310-288-4545
9830 Wilshire Blvd **Fax:** 310-288-4800
Beverly Hills, CA 90212
williamnicholson.co.uk

Nickels, Greg (1955-)
Mayor of Seattle
600 4th Ave 7th Fl **Ph:** 206-684-4000
PO Box 94749 **Fax:** 206-684-5360
Seattle, WA 98124
www.ci.seattle.wa.us/mayor

Nicklaus, Jack (1940-)
Professional golfer; golf course designer
Nicklaus Design **Ph:** 561-227-0300
11780 US Hwy 1 Suite 500 **Fax:** 561-227-0548
North Palm Beach, FL 33408
www.nicklaus.com

Niedermayer, Scott (1973-)
Professional hockey player
Mighty Ducks of Anaheim **Ph:** 714-704-2700
Arrowhead Pond **Fax:** 714-940-2953
2695 Katella Ave
Anaheim, CA 92806
www.mightyducks.com

Nieporent, Drew
Restaurateur; creator of the Myriad Restaurant Group
Myriad Restaurant Group **Ph:** 212-941-1976
375 Greenwich St **Fax:** 212-334-4498
New York, NY 10013
www.myriadrestaurantgroup.com

Nieuwendyk, Joe (1966-)
Professional hockey player
Florida Panthers **Ph:** 954-835-7000
BankAtlantic Center **Fax:** 954-835-7700
1 Panther Pkwy
Sunrise, FL 33323
www.floridapanthers.com

Nimoy, Leonard (1931-)
Actor/director
Gersh Agency **Ph:** 310-274-6611
232 N Canon Dr
Beverly Hills, CA 90210
www.theofficialleonardnimoyfanclub.com

Nischan, Michel
Chef; is credited with creating a cuisine that focuses on pure ingredients and intense flavors, without the use of cream, butter, processed starches, or processed sugars
Miche Mache LLC **Ph:** 203-372-3680
201 Morehouse Hwy
Fairfield, CT 06432
www.michelnischan.com

Nissinen, Mikko (1962-)
Dancer, teacher, and artistic director of the Boston Ballet
Boston Ballet **Ph:** 617-695-6950
19 Clarendon St
Boston, MA 02116
www.bostonballet.org

Nixon, Cynthia (1966-)
Actor
William Morris Agency **Ph:** 212-586-5100
1325 Ave of the Americas **Fax:** 212-246-3583
New York, NY 10019
www.hbo.com/city

Nixon, Joan Lowery (1927-2003)
Author of mystery/suspense books for young adults; also writes historical and adventure stories
Random House Children's Books **Ph:** 212-782-9000
Publicity Dept
1745 Broadway
New York, NY 10019
www.randomhouse.com/kids

Nixon, Richard M (1913-1994)
37th US President
Richard Nixon Library & Birthplace **Ph:** 714-993-5075 **Fax:** 714-528-0544
18001 Yorba Linda Blvd
Yorba Linda, CA 92886
www.nixonfoundation.org

Noah, Yannick (1960-)
Professional tennis player
SFX Sports Group **Ph:** 202-686-2000
5335 Wisconsin Ave NW Suite 850 **Fax:** 202-686-5050
Washington, DC 20015
www.sfxsports.com

Noddle, Jeffrey
Chairman and CEO of SUPERVALU
SUPERVALU Inc **Ph:** 952-828-4000
11840 Valley View Rd
Eden Prairie, MN 55344
www.supervalu.com

Noel, Fabrice (1985-)
Professional soccer player
Colorado Rapids **Ph:** 303-405-1100
Pepsi Center **Fax:** 720-931-2022
1000 Chopper Cir
Denver, CO 80204
www.coloradorapids.com

Nolan, Beth (1951-)
Attorney; White House Counsel to President Bill Clinton from 1999-2001
Crowell & Moring LLP **Ph:** 202-624-2514
1001 Pennsylvania Ave NW **Fax:** 202-628-5116
Washington, DC 20004
www.crowell.com

Nolan, Deanna (1979-)
Professional basketball player
Detroit Shock **Ph:** 248-377-0100
Palace at Auburn Hills **Fax:** 248-377-3260
4 Championship Dr
Auburn Hills, MI 48326
www.wnba.com/shock

Nolan, Graham
Draws the comic strips Rex Morgan MD and The Phantom
King Features Syndicate Inc **Ph:** 212-455-4000
888 7th Ave 2nd Fl
New York, NY 10019
www.kingfeatures.com

Nolan, Han (1956-)
Author of books for young adults (Send Me Down a Miracle; Dancing on the Edge; If I Should Die Before I Wake)
Harcourt Children's Books **Ph:** 212-592-1000
15 E 26th St
New York, NY 10010
www.hannolan.com

Nolan, Mike (1959-)
Football coach
San Francisco 49ers **Ph:** 408-562-4949
4949 Centennial Blvd **Fax:** 408-727-4937
Santa Clara, CA 95054
www.sf49ers.com

Nolte, Nick (1941-)
Actor
Creative Artists Agency **Ph:** 310-288-4545
9830 Wilshire Blvd **Fax:** 310-288-4800
Beverly Hills, CA 90212

Noonan, Pat (1980-)
Professional soccer player
New England Revolution **Ph:** 508-543-5001
Gillette Stadium **Fax:** 508-384-9128
1 Patriot Pl
Foxborough, MA 02035
www.revolutionsoccer.net

Noonan, Peggy (1950-)
Author and Wall Street Journal editor & columnist; was a special assistant to President Reagan and chief speechwriter to Vice President George Bush during his presidential campaign
Wall Street Journal **Ph:** 609-520-4000
PO Box 300
Princeton, NJ 08543
www.peggynoonan.com

Noory, George
Has taken over from retiring Art Bell to become the host of Coast-to-Coast AM (a radio talk show about the paranormal)
Premiere Radio Networks Inc **Ph:** 818-377-5300
15260 Ventura Blvd 5th Fl **Fax:** 818-377-5333
Sherman Oaks, CA 91403
www.coasttocoastam.com

Nooyi, Indra K (1956-)
President & CFO of PepsiCo
PepsiCo Inc **Ph:** 914-253-2000
700 Anderson Hill Rd **Fax:** 914-253-2070
Purchase, NY 10577
www.pepsico.com

Norman, Bebo
Christian singer
Third Coast Artists Agency **Ph:** 615-297-2021
2021 21st Ave S Suite 220 **Fax:** 615-297-2776
Nashville, TN 37212
www.bebonorman.com

Norman, Greg (1955-)
Professional golfer & entrepreneur
Great White Shark Enterprises **Ph:** 561-743-8818
501 N AIA **Fax:** 561-743-8831
Jupiter, FL 33477
www.shark.com

Norman, Jessye (1945-)
Singer (primarily opera & concert, but also performs in jazz, gospel, and other genres)
Sony Classical **Ph:** 212-833-8000
550 Madison Ave
New York, NY 10022
www.sonyclassical.com

Norris, Michelle
Host of All Things Considered on NPR
National Public Radio **Ph:** 202-513-2000
635 Massachusetts Ave NW **Fax:** 202-513-3329
Washington, DC 20001
www.npr.org

North, Douglass C, PhD (1920-)
Winner, with Robert W Fogel, of the 1993 Nobel Prize in Economics for having renewed research in economic history by applying economic theory and quantitative methods in order to explain economic and institutional change
Hoover Institution on War Revolution & Peace **Ph:** 650-723-1754 **Fax:** 650-723-1687
Stanford University
Stanford, CA 94305
www-hoover.stanford.edu

North, Oliver (1943-)
Retired Marine Lt Colonel who is now a syndicated columnist and talk radio show host; became a public figure due to his involvement in the Iran-Contra scandal
Creators Syndicate Inc **Ph:** 310-337-7003
5777 W Century Blvd Suite 700 **Fax:** 310-337-7625
Los Angeles, CA 90045
olivernorth.com

Northcutt, Dennis (1977-)
Professional football player
Cleveland Browns **Ph:** 440-891-5000
76 Lou Groza Blvd **Fax:** 440-891-5009
Berea, OH 44017
www.clevelandbrowns.com

Northup, Anne Meagher (1948-)
US Representative from Kentucky (Republican)
2459 Rayburn Bldg **Ph:** 202-225-5401
Washington, DC 20515 **Fax:** 202-225-5776
northup.house.gov

Norton, Edward (1969-)
Actor
Endeavor **Ph:** 310-248-2000
9601 Wilshire Blvd 3rd Fl **Fax:** 310-248-2020
Beverly Hills, CA 90210

Norton, Eleanor Holmes (1937-)
US Delegate from the District of Columbia (Democrat)
2136 Rayburn Bldg **Ph:** 202-225-8050
Washington, DC 20515 **Fax:** 202-225-3002
www.norton.house.gov

Norville, Deborah (1958-)
Anchors the newsmagazine show Inside Edition
William Morris Agency **Ph:** 310-859-4000
1 William Morris Pl **Fax:** 310-859-4462
Beverly Hills, CA 90212
www.dnorville.com

Norwood, Charlie (1941-)
US Representative from Georgia (Republican)
2452 Rayburn Bldg **Ph:** 202-225-4101
Washington, DC 20515 **Fax:** 202-226-0776
www.house.gov/norwood

Noth, Chris (1954-)
Actor
United Talent Agency **Ph:** 310-273-6700
9560 Wilshire Blvd 5th Fl **Fax:** 310-247-1111
Beverly Hills, CA 90212
www.nbc.com/Law_&_Order:_Criminal_Intent

Novak, BJ (1979-)
Actor, writer, and stand-up comedian
William Morris Agency **Ph:** 310-859-4000
1 William Morris Pl **Fax:** 310-859-4462
Beverly Hills, CA 90212
www.bjnovak.com

Novak, David
Chairman, CEO, and president of Yum! Brands, a restaurant company (brands include KFC, Pizza Hut, Taco Bell, and Long John Silver's)
Yum! Brands Inc **Ph:** 502-874-8300
1441 Gardiner Ln **Fax:** 502-874-8790
Louisville, KY 40213
www.yum.com/investors/faqs.asp

Novak, Lindsey
Syndicated advice columnist (At Work) & career coach
Creators Syndicate Inc **Ph:** 310-337-7003
5777 W Century Blvd Suite 700 **Fax:** 310-337-7625
Los Angeles, CA 90045
www.creators.com

Novak, Michael (1933-)
Author, philosopher, and theologian; writes about religion, philosophy, capitalism/freedom
American Enterprise Institute for Public Policy Research **Ph:** 202-862-5800 **Fax:** 202-862-7177
1150 17th St NW Suite 1100
Washington, DC 20036
www.michaelnovak.net

Novak, Robert (1931-)
Nationally syndicated columnist
Creators Syndicate Inc **Ph:** 310-337-7003
5777 W Century Blvd Suite 700 **Fax:** 310-337-7625
Los Angeles, CA 90045
www.creators.com/opinion.html

Novelli, William D
CEO of AARP
AARP **Ph:** 202-434-2277
601 'E' St NW **TF:** 888-687-2277
Washington, DC 20049
www.aarp.org

Novello, Antonia, MD (1944-)
Former US Surgeon General, now Health Commissioner of New York State
New York State Dept of Health **Ph:** 518-474-2011
Empire State Plaza **Fax:** 518-474-5450
Corning II Tower
Albany, NY 12237
www.health.state.ny.us

Novotny, Monica
Correspondent for MSNBC's Countdown with Keith Olbermann
MSNBC TV **Ph:** 201-583-5000
1 MSNBC Plaza
Secaucus, NJ 07094
www.msnbc.msn.com/id/3080263

Nowitzki, Dirk (1978-)
Professional basketball player
Dallas Mavericks **Ph:** 214-747-6287
The Pavilion **Fax:** 214-658-7121
2909 Taylor St
Dallas, TX 75226
www.nba.com/mavericks

Nugent, Ted (1948-)
Rock singer/guitarist; outspoken advocate for shooting sports
Nugent USA **Ph:** 517-750-9060
4008 W Michigan Ave **Fax:** 517-750-3640
Jackson, MI 49202
www.tednugent.com

Nuland, Sherwin B, MD (1930-)
Physician, surgeon, teacher, medical historian, and author of How We Die; is also the author of the National Geographic publication, Incredible Voyage: Exploring the Human Body
Vintage/Anchor Publicity **Ph:** 212-572-2420
1745 Broadway 20th Fl
New York, NY 10019
www.randomhouse.com/vintage

Null, Gary (1945-)
Host of the radio program Natural Living with Gary Null
Gary Null & Assoc Inc **Ph:** 646-505-4660
2307 Broadway 2nd Fl **Fax:** 212-362-0216
New York, NY 10024
www.garynull.com

Numeroff, Laura (1953-)
Author of books for children, including the If You Give series (If You Give a Moose a Muffin; If You Give a Pig a Pancake, and others)
HarperCollins Children's Books **Ph:** 212-261-6500
1350 Ave of the Americas
New York, NY 10019
www.lauranumeroff.com

Nunes, Devin (1973-)
US Representative from California (Republican)
1017 Longworth Bldg **Ph:** 202-225-2523
Washington, DC 20515 **Fax:** 202-225-3404
www.nunes.house.gov

Nunez, Ramo (1985-)
Professional soccer player
FC Dallas **Ph:** 214-979-0303
14800 Quorum Dr Suite 300 **Fax:** 214-979-1118
Dallas, TX 75254
fc.dallas.mlsnet.com

Nunn, Sam (1938-)
US Senator from Georgia for 24 years; co-chair (with Ted Turner) & CEO of Nuclear Threat Initiative
Nuclear Threat Initiative **Ph:** 202-296-4810
1747 Pennsylvania Ave NW **Fax:** 202-296-4811
7th Fl
Washington, DC 20006
www.nti.org

Nussle, Jim (1960-)
US Representative from Iowa (Republican)
303 Cannon Bldg **Ph:** 202-225-2911
Washington, DC 20515 **Fax:** 202-225-9129
nussle.house.gov

Nye, Bill (1955-)
Engineer/scientist; host of Bill Nye the Science Guy
William Morris Agency **Ph:** 212-586-5100
1325 Ave of the Americas **Fax:** 212-246-3583
New York, NY 10019
www.billnye.com

Nye, Naomi Shihab (1952-)
Author of poetry for young people & for adults (19 Varieties of Gazelle: Poems of the Middle East) as well as picture books for children (Sitti's Secrets)
HarperCollins Children's Books **Ph:** 212-261-6500
1350 Ave of the Americas
New York, NY 10010
www.NaomiShihabNyebooks.com

Oates, Joyce Carol (1938-)
Fiction writer and a humanities professor at Princeton
HarperCollins Publishers **Ph:** 212-207-7000
c/o Author Mail
10 E 53rd St
New York, NY 10022
www.joycecaroloatesbooks.com

Obama, Barack (1961-)
US Senator from Illinois (Democrat)
B40B Dirksen Bldg **Ph:** 202-224-2854
Washington, DC 20510 **Fax:** 202-228-5417
obama.senate.gov

O'Beirne, Kate
National Review's Washington editor
National Review **Ph:** 202-543-9226
Washington Bureau **Fax:** 202-543-9341
219 Pennsylvania Ave SE
Washington, DC 20003
www.nationalreview.com

Oberndorf, Meyera E
Mayor of Virginia Beach
2401 Courthouse Dr Bldg 1 **Ph:** 757-427-4581
Virginia Beach, VA 23456 **Fax:** 757-426-5699
www.vbgov.com/city_hall/bios

Oberstar, James L (1934-)
US Representative from Minnesota (Democrat)
2365 Rayburn Bldg **Ph:** 202-225-6211
Washington, DC 20515 **Fax:** 202-225-0699
www.oberstar.house.gov

Obey, David (1938-)
US Representative from Wisconsin (Democrat)
2314 Rayburn Bldg **Ph:** 202-225-3365
Washington, DC 20515
obey.house.gov

O'Brien, Conan (1963-)
Late night TV talk show host
Late Night with Conan O'Brien **Ph:** 212-664-3737
30 Rockefeller Plaza
New York, NY 10112
www.nbc.com

O'Brien, Edna (1946-)
Novelist; writes about Ireland and writes mysteries
Houghton Mifflin Co **Ph:** 617-351-5000
Trade Div
Adult Editorial
222 Berkeley St 8th Fl
Boston, MA 02116
www.houghtonmifflinbooks.com

O'Brien, James J (1954-)
Chairman and CEO of Ashland Inc
Ashland Inc **Ph:** 859-815-3333
50 E River Ctr Blvd
Covington, KY 41012
www.ashland.com

O'Brien, Miles
Co-anchor of CNN's American Morning
CNN New York **Ph:** 212-275-7800
Time Warner Ctr
10 Columbus Cir
New York, NY 10019
www.cnn.com/CNN/anchors_reporters

O'Brien, Ronnie (1979-)
Professional soccer player
FC Dallas **Ph:** 214-979-0303
14800 Quorum Dr Suite 300 **Fax:** 214-979-1118
Dallas, TX 75254
fc.dallas.mlsnet.com

O'Brien, Soledad (1966-)
Co-anchor of American Morning on CNN
CNN New York **Ph:** 212-275-7800
Time Warner Ctr
10 Columbus Cir
New York, NY 10019
www.cnn.com/CNN/anchors_reporters

Ochsner, John L, MD
Physician whose expertise includes heart surgery and heart transplantation and vascular surgery
Ochsner Clinic Foundation **Ph:** 504-842-3000
1514 Jefferson Hwy
New Orleans, LA 70121
www.ochsner.org/Surgery/staff.html#no

O'Connell, Jerry (1974-)
Actor
Endeavor **Ph:** 310-248-2000
9601 Wilshire Blvd 3rd Fl **Fax:** 310-248-2020
Beverly Hills, CA 90210

O'Connell, Patrick
Chef and (with Reinhard Lynch) proprietor of The Inn at Little Washington
Inn at Little Washington **Ph:** 540-675-3800
389 Middle St
PO Box 300
Washington, VA 22747
www.theinnatlittlewashington.com

O'Connor, Bob
Mayor of Pittsburgh
414 Grant St Suite 512 **Ph:** 412-255-2626
Pittsburgh, PA 15219 **Fax:** 412-255-2687
www.city.pittsburgh.pa.us

Odland, Steve (1948-)
Chairman and CEO of Office Depot
Office Depot Inc **Ph:** 561-438-4800
2200 Old Germantown Rd **Fax:** 561-438-4001
Delray Beach, FL 33445
www.officedepot.com

Odom, Lamar (1979-)
Professional basketball player
Los Angeles Lakers **Ph:** 310-426-6000
555 N Nash St **Fax:** 310-426-6105
El Segundo, CA 90245
www.nba.com/lakers

O'Donnell, Chris (1970-)
Actor
Endeavor **Ph:** 310-248-2000
9601 Wilshire Blvd 3rd Fl **Fax:** 310-248-2020
Beverly Hills, CA 90210

O'Donnell, Kelly
NBC News White House correspondent
NBC News **Ph:** 212-664-4249
30 Rockefeller Plaza
New York, NY 10112
www.msnbc.msn.com/id/3689499

O'Donnell, Norah
MSNBC's chief Washington correspondent
NBC News **Ph:** 202-885-4200
4001 Nebraska Ave NW
Washington, DC 20016
www.msnbc.msn.com/id/3080263

O'Donnell, Pierce (1947-)
Leading trial lawyer; primarily represents corporate interests in such areas as entertainment, intellectual property, securities, toxic tort, real estate, constitutional law, and finance
O'Donnell & Schaeffer LLP **Ph:** 213-532-2000
550 S Hope St Suite 2000 **Fax:** 213-532-2020
Los Angeles, CA 90071
www.oslaw.com

O'Donnell, Rosie (1962-)
Comedian, actor, and former TV talk show host
International Creative Management **Ph:** 310-550-4000
8942 Wilshire Blvd
Beverly Hills, CA 90211
www.rosie.com

Oe, Kenzaburo (1935-)
Japanese writer who says he writes for a Japanese readership; won the Nobel Prize for Literature in 1994 for The Silent Cry, but his best-known novel is A Personal Matter
Grove/Atlantic Inc **Ph:** 212-614-7860
841 Broadway **Fax:** 212-614-7886
New York, NY 10003
www.groveatlantic.com

Ogden, Bradley
Chef and restauranteur; co-owner of the Lark Creek Restaurant Group
Bradley Ogden at Caesar's Palace **Ph:** 702-731-7110
Fax: 877-346-4642
3570 Las Vegas Blvd S
Las Vegas, NV 89109
www.larkcreek.com

Ogden, Jonathon (1974-)
Professional football player
Baltimore Ravens **Ph:** 410-547-8100
1101 Russell St **Fax:** 410-547-8112
Baltimore, MD 21230
www.baltimoreravens.com

Ogletree, Charles J (1952-)
Professor, legal theorist, attorney; counsel to Anita Hill during Senate confirmation hearings for Justice Clarence Thomas; co-chair of the Reparations Coordinating Committee, a group researching a lawsuit related to reparations for descendants of African slaves
Harvard Law School **Ph:** 617-495-5097
1563 Massachusetts Ave **Fax:** 617-496-3936
Cambridge, MA 02138
www.law.harvard.edu/faculty/directory

Oh, Sandra (1971-)
Actor
United Talent Agency **Ph:** 310-273-6700
9560 Wilshire Blvd 5th Fl **Fax:** 310-247-1111
Beverly Hills, CA 90212
abc.go.com/primetime/greysanatomy

Ohlde, Nicole (1982-)
Professional basketball player
Minnesota Lynx **Ph:** 612-673-1600
Target Center **Fax:** 612-673-1699
600 1st Ave N
Minneapolis, MN 55403
www.wnba.com/lynx

Ohman, Jack (1960-)
Editorial cartoonist for The Oregonian
Tribune Media Services Inc **Ph:** 312-222-4444
435 N Michigan Ave Suite 1500
Chicago, IL 60611
www.comicspage.com

Ohno, Apolo (1982-)
American speedskater
US Olympic Training Center **Ph:** 719-632-5551
1 Olympic Plaza
Colorado Springs, CO 80909
www.usoc.org

O'Hurley, John (1956-)
Actor (Seinfeld); businessman; celebrity dancer on Dancing with the Stars
Warren Cowan & Assoc **Ph:** 310-275-0777
8899 Beverly Blvd Suite 919
Los Angeles, CA 90048
www.johnohurley.com

Okafor, Emeka (1982-)
Professional basketball player
Charlotte Bobcats **Ph:** 704-357-0252
100 Hive Dr **Fax:** 704-357-0289
Charlotte, NC 28217
www.nba.com/bobcats

O'Keefe, Sean (1956-)
Former NASA Administrator; now Chancellor of LSU
Office of the Chancellor **Ph:** 225-578-6977
Louisiana State University **Fax:** 225-578-5982
156 Thomas Boyd Hall
Baton Rouge, LA 70803
www.lsu.edu/chancellor

O'Keeffe, Georgia (1887-1986)
Artist best known for her large-scale depictions of flowers
Georgia O'Keeffe Museum **Ph:** 505-946-1000
217 Johnson St
Santa Fe, NM 87501
www.okeeffemuseum.org

Okur, Mehmet (1979-)
Professional basketball player
Utah Jazz **Ph:** 801-325-2500
Delta Center **Fax:** 801-325-2578
301 W South Temple St **TF:** 800-358-7328
Salt Lake City, UT 84101
www.nba.com/jazz

Olah, George A, PhD (1927-)
Winner of the 1994 Nobel Prize in Chemistry for his contribution to carbocation chemistry
University of Southern California **Ph:** 213-740-5976
Fax: 213-740-5087
Loker Hydrocrbon Research Institute
837 Bloom Walk MC 1661 Rm 203
Los Angeles, CA 90089
chem.usc.edu/faculty/Olah.html

Olasky, Marvin, PhD (1950-)
Political journalist, syndicated columnist, and author; considered the father of compassionate conservatism
Creators Syndicate Inc **Ph:** 310-337-7003
5777 W Century Blvd Suite 700 **Fax:** 310-337-7625
Los Angeles, CA 90045
www.creators.com/opinion.html

Olbermann, Keith (1959-)
Host of Countdown with Keith Olbermann; was previously a sports anchor
MSNBC TV **Ph:** 201-583-5000
1 MSNBC Plaza
Secaucus, NJ 07094
www.msnbc.msn.com/id/3080263

Oldham, Todd (1962-)
Designer (fashion, product, interior, and graphic design)
120 Wooster St 3rd Fl **Ph:** 212-226-4668
New York, NY 10012 **Fax:** 212-226-4873
www.toddoldhamstudio.com

O'Leary, Dennis S, MD
President of the Joint Commission on Accreditation of Healthcare Organizations
Joint Commission on Accreditation of Healthcare Organizations **Ph:** 630-792-5000
Fax: 630-792-5005
1 Renaissance Blvd
Oakbrook Terrace, IL 60181
www.jointcommission.org

Oliphant, Pat (1935-)
Editorial cartoonist; also works in other media, including sculpture, etching, lithography, and monotype
Universal Press Syndicate **Ph:** 816-932-6600
4520 Main St
Kansas City, MO 64111
www.amuniversal.com/ups/features

Oliphant, Thomas
Correspondent and Washington columnist for the Boston Globe
Boston Globe **Ph:** 202-857-5050
1130 Connecticut Ave NW Suite 520 **Fax:** 202-857-3933
Washington, DC 20036
bostonglobe.com/newsroom

Oliva, Sergio (1941-)
Bodybuilding champion
Jack Merjimekian **Ph:** 561-394-2635
50 SW 3rd Ave Suite 302
Boca Raton, FL 33432
www.sergiooliva.com

Oliveira, Elmar (1950-)
Concert violinist; first and only American violinist to win the Gold Medal at Moscow's Tchaikovsky International Competition
Seldy Cramer Artists **Ph:** 925-299-0623
3436 Springhill Rd **Fax:** 925-299-0624
Lafayette, CA 94549
www.elmaroliveira.com

Oliver, Jamie (1975-)
Chef; host of The Naked Chef and Oliver's Twist on the Food Network
Food Network **Ph:** 212-398-8836
75 9th Ave **Fax:** 212-736-7716
New York, NY 10011
www.jamieoliver.net

Oliver, Meg
Anchor on Up to the Minute, CBS's late-night news show
Up to the Minute **Ph:** 212-975-4114
524 W 57th St
New York, NY 10019
www.cbsnews.com

Olmos, Edward James (1947-)
Actor; social activist
Creative Artists Agency **Ph:** 310-288-4545
9830 Wilshire Blvd **Fax:** 310-288-4800
Beverly Hills, CA 90212

Olsen, Ashley (1986-)
Actor & entrepreneur; co-founder (with twin Mary-Kate) of Dualstar Entertainment
Dualstar Entertainment Group **Ph:** 310-553-9000
1801 Century Park E 12th Fl
Los Angeles, CA 90067
www.mary-kateandashley.com

Olsen, Ben (1977-)
Professional soccer player
DC United **Ph:** 202-587-5000
RFK Stadium **Fax:** 202-587-5400
2400 E Capitol St SE
Washington, DC 20003
dcunited.mlsnet.com

Olsen, Mary-Kate (1986-)
Actor & entrepreneur; co-founder (with twin Ashley) of Dualstar Entertainment
Dualstar Entertainment Group **Ph:** 310-553-9000
1801 Century Park E 12th Fl
Los Angeles, CA 90067
www.mary-kateandashley.com

Olson, Mark W (1943-)
Member of the Board of Governors of the Federal Reserve System
Federal Reserve System **Ph:** 202-452-3271
20th St & Constitution Ave NW **Fax:** 202-452-2611
Washington, DC 20551
www.federalreserve.gov/bios

Olson, Peter
Chairman and CEO of Random House
Random House Inc **Ph:** 212-782-9000
1745 Broadway **Fax:** 212-302-7985
New York, NY 10019
www.bertelsmann.com

Olson, Ronald L (1941-)
Attorney specializing in commercial litigation, including antitrust, securities, commercial contracts, and business torts; was lead counsel for Edison International in the California electricity crisis
Munger Tolles & Olson LLP **Ph:** 213-683-9111
355 S Grand Ave 35th Fl **Fax:** 213-683-5111
Los Angeles, CA 90071
www.mto.com

Olson, Theodore B (1940-)
Attorney and former US Solicitor General (2001-2004); argued the Bush v Gore case stemming from the 2000 presidential election before the US Supreme Court
Gibson Dunn & Crutcher **Ph:** 202-955-8668
1050 Connecticut Ave NW **Fax:** 202-530-9575
Washington, DC 20036
www.gibsondunn.com

Olver, John W (1936-)
US Representative from Massachusetts (Democrat)
1111 Longworth Bldg **Ph:** 202-225-5335
Washington, DC 20515 **Fax:** 202-226-1224
www.house.gov/olver

Olyphant, Timothy (1968-)
Actor
Special Artists Agency **Ph:** 310-859-9688
9465 Wilshire Blvd Suite 890
Beverly Hills, CA 90212
www.hbo.com/deadwood

O'Malley, Martin
Mayor of Baltimore
100 N Holliday St Suite 250 **Ph:** 410-396-3835
Baltimore, MD 21202 **Fax:** 410-576-9425
www.baltimorecity.gov/mayor

O'Meara, Mike
Co-host (with Don Geronimo) of Don & Mike, an afternoon radio show with a morning drive format
WJFK-FM **Ph:** 703-691-1900
10800 Main St
Fairfax, VA 22030
www.donandmikewebsite.com

Omidyar, Pierre
Founder and chairman of eBay
eBay Inc **Ph:** 408-376-7400
2145 Hamilton Ave **Fax:** 408-376-7401
San Jose, CA 95125
pages.ebay.com/aboutebay.html

Ondaatje, Michael (1943-)
Author of The English Patient
Steven Barclay Agency **Ph:** 707-773-0654
12 Western Ave **Fax:** 707-778-1868
Petaluma, CA 94952 **TF:** 888-965-7323
www.barclayagency.com

O'Neal, Jermaine (1978-)
Professional basketball player
Indiana Pacers **Ph:** 317-917-2500
Conseco Fieldhouse **Fax:** 317-917-2599
125 S Pennsylvania St
Indianapolis, IN 46204
www.nba.com/pacers

O'Neal, Shaquille (1972-)
Professional basketball player
Miami Heat **Ph:** 786-777-1000
American Airlines Arena **Fax:** 786-777-1609
601 Biscayne Blvd
Miami, FL 33132
www.nba.com/heat

O'Neal, Stan
Chairman, CEO, and president of Merrill Lynch
Merrill Lynch & Co Inc **Ph:** 212-449-1000
4 World Financial Ctr
250 Vesey St
New York, NY 10080
www.ml.com

O'Neill, Beverly
Mayor of Long Beach, California
333 W Ocean Blvd 14th Fl **Ph:** 562-570-6801
Long Beach, CA 90802 **Fax:** 562-570-6538
www.longbeach.gov/mayor

O'Neill, Jeff (1976-)
Professional hockey player
Toronto Maple Leafs **Ph:** 416-815-5700
Air Canada Center
40 Bay St Suite 400
Toronto, ON M5J2X2
www.mapleleafs.com

O'Neill, Roger
NBC news correspondent
NBC News **Ph:** 212-664-4249
30 Rockefeller Plaza
New York, NY 10112
www.msnbc.msn.com/id/3689499

Ono, Yoko (1933-)
Artist
Elliott Mintz Public Relations **Ph:** 323-656-0680
2934 1/2 Beverly Glen Cir
Bel-Air, CA 90077
www.yoko-ono.com

Onstad, Pat (1968-)
Professional soccer player
Houston Dynamo **Ph:** 713-276-7500
1415 Louisiana St Suite 3400 **Fax:** 713-276-7580
Houston, TX 77002
houston.mlsnet.com

Opdyke, Irene Gut (1922-)
Author of the autobiographical In My Hands: Memories of a Holocaust Rescuer
Vintage/Anchor Publicity **Ph:** 212-572-2420
1745 Broadway 20th Fl
New York, NY 10019
www.randomhouse.com/anchor

Oppenheimer, Andres
Latin American correspondent for the Miami Herald and syndicated foreign affairs columnist (The Oppenheimer Report)
Miami Herald **Ph:** 305-350-2111
1 Herald Plaza
Miami, FL 33132
www.tmsfeatures.com/productlist.htm

O'Quinn, John M (1941-)
Leading trial lawyer; has won some of the largest verdicts and settlements in the U.S.
O'Quinn Laminack & Pirtle **Ph:** 713-223-1000
2300 Lyric Centre Bldg **Fax:** 713-222-6903
440 Louisiana St Suite 2300
Houston, TX 77002
www.oqlaw.com

O'Quinn, Terry (1952-)
Actor
Innovative Artists **Ph:** 310-656-0400
1505 10th St **Fax:** 310-656-0456
Santa Monica, CA 90401
abc.go.com/primetime/lost/show.html

Ordonez, Magglio (1974-)
Professional baseball player
Detroit Tigers **Ph:** 313-962-4000
Comerica Park **Fax:** 313-471-2138
2100 Woodward Ave
Detroit, MI 48201
detroit.tigers.mlb.com

O'Reilly, Bill (1949-)
Host of The O'Reilly Factor on FOX News; also hosts a syndicated radio talk show (Radio Factor) and writes a syndicated column
FOX News Channel **Ph:** 212-556-2500
1211 Ave of the Americas
New York, NY 10036
www.billoreilly.com

O'Reilly, David J (1947-)
Chairman and CEO of Chevron Corp
Chevron Corp **Ph:** 925-842-3232
6001 Bollinger Canyon Rd **Fax:** 925-842-6047
San Ramon, CA 94583
www.chevron.com/about/company_profile

Orfalea, Paul J
Founder of Kinko's (which was sold in 2004 and is now FedEx Kinko's); is now involved in investment and philanthropy
Orfalea Family Foundation **Ph:** 805-565-7550
1280 Coast Village Cir Suite A **Fax:** 805-565-7554
Santa Barbara, CA 93108
www.paulorfalea.com

O'Riley, Christopher
Pianist and host of NPR's From the Top
National Public Radio **Ph:** 202-513-2000
635 Massachusetts Ave NW **Fax:** 202-513-3329
Washington, DC 20001
www.christopheroriley.com

Oringer, Ken (1965-)
Executive chef and co-owner of Restaurant Clio in Boston
Restaurant Clio **Ph:** 617-536-7200
370 Commonwealth Ave
Boston, MA 02215
www.cliorestaurant.com

Orman, Suze
Finance expert; personal finance commentator and host of The Suze Orman Show on CNBC-TV
International Creative Management **Ph:** 212-556-5600
40 W 57th St 17th Fl
New York, NY 90211
www.suzeorman.com

Ormond, Paul A
Chairman, president, and CEO of Manor Care Inc, which owns and operates long-term care centers through its operating group, HCR Manor Care
Manor Care Inc **Ph:** 419-252-5500
333 N Summit St **Fax:** 419-252-5596
Toledo, OH 43699
www.hcr-manorcare.com/investor

Ornish, Dean, MD (1953-)
Author of Dr. Dean Ornish's Program for Reversing Heart Disease, as well as Eat More, Weigh Less and other titles
Preventive Medicine Research Institute **Ph:** 415-332-2525 **Fax:** 415-332-5730
900 Bridgeway
Sausalito, CA 94965
www.pmri.org

Ornstein, Norman J, PhD (1948-)
Political author & speaker; resident scholar at American Enterprise Institute, where he studies politics, Congress, and elections
American Enterprise Institute for Public Policy Research **Ph:** 202-862-5800 **Fax:** 202-862-7177
1150 17th St NW Suite 1100
Washington, DC 20036
www.aei.org

O'Rourke, PJ (1947-)
A senior fellow at the Cato Institute and a leading political satirist whose work is published in a wide variety of magazines; has also written bestselling books, including Parliament of Whores and Give War a Chance
Cato Institute **Ph:** 202-842-0200
1000 Massachusetts Ave NW **Fax:** 202-842-3490
Washington, DC 20001
www.cato.org/people/orourke.html

Orrico, Stacie (1986-)
Pop singer
CAA Nashville **Ph:** 615-383-8787
3310 West End Ave 5th Fl **Fax:** 615-383-4937
Nashville, TN 37203
www.stacieorrico.com

Ortega, Kenny
Director/choreographer (mostly film, including Dirty Dancing)
Paradigm **Ph:** 310-288-8000
360 N Crescent Dr **Fax:** 310-288-2000
North Bldg
Beverly Hills, CA 90210
www.schwartzmanpr.com/agency/kennyortega.asp

Ortiz, David (1975-)
Professional baseball player
Boston Red Sox **Ph:** 617-267-9440
Fenway Park **Fax:** 617-236-6797
4 Yawkey Way
Boston, MA 02215
boston.redsox.mlb.com

Ortiz, Russ (1974-)
Professional baseball player
Arizona Diamondbacks **Ph:** 602-462-6500
Bank One Ballpark **Fax:** 602-462-6600
401 E Jefferson St
Phoenix, AZ 85004
arizona.diamondbacks.mlb.com

Ortiz, Solomon P (1938-)
US Representative from Texas (Democrat)
2470 Rayburn Bldg **Ph:** 202-225-7742
Washington, DC 20515 **Fax:** 202-226-1134
www.house.gov/ortiz

Osborne, Mary Pope (1949-)
Author of the Magic Tree House series and other books for children
Random House Children's Books **Ph:** 212-782-9000
Publicity Dept
1745 Broadway
New York, NY 10019
www.randomhouse.com/kids

Osborne, Tom (1937-)
US Representative from Nebraska (Republican)
507 Cannon Bldg **Ph:** 202-225-6435
Washington, DC 20515 **Fax:** 202-226-1385
www.house.gov/osborne

Osbourne, Ozzy (1948-)
Singer (heavy metal music)
Creative Artists Agency **Ph:** 310-288-4545
9830 Wilshire Blvd **Fax:** 310-288-4800
Beverly Hills, CA 90212
www.ozzy.com

Osgood, Charles (1933-)
CBS News Sunday Morning anchor; also anchors and writes The Osgood File, his daily news commentary broadcast on the CBS Radio Network
CBS News Sunday Morning **Ph:** 212-975-4114
Box O
524 W 57th St
New York, NY 10019
www.cbsnews.com

Osheroff, Douglas D, PhD (1945-)
Winner (with two other scientists) of the 1996 Nobel Prize in Physics for the discovery of superfluidity in helium-3
Stanford University **Ph:** 650-723-4228
Dept of Physics **Fax:** 650-725-6544
382 Via Pueblo Mall Rm 150
Stanford, CA 94305
www.stanford.edu/dept/physics

Osment, Haley Joel (1988-)
Actor
Coast to Coast Talent Group Inc **Ph:** 323-845-9200
Fax: 323-845-9212
3350 Barham Blvd
Los Angeles, CA 90068
www.kidactors.com/haley

Osmond, Donny (1957-)
Singer; actor
William Morris Agency **Ph:** 310-859-4000
1 William Morris Pl **Fax:** 310-859-4462
Beverly Hills, CA 90212
www.donny.com

Osmond, Marie (1959-)
Singer
William Morris Agency **Ph:** 615-963-3000
1600 Division St Suite 300 **Fax:** 615-963-3090
Nashville, TN 37203
www.osmond.com/marie

O'Steen, David N, PhD
Executive Director of the National Right to Life Committee
National Right to Life Committee **Ph:** 202-626-8800
512 10th St NW
Washington, DC 20004

Osteen, Joel (1963-)
Senior Pastor of Lakewood Church and leader of Joel Osteen Ministries (including television outreach ministry)
Lakewood Church **Ph:** 713-635-4154
PO Box 23297 **Fax:** 713-635-4753
Houston, TX 77228
www.joelosteen.com

Osteen, Louis
Chef and owner of Louis's at Pawley's (new Southern cuisine)
Louis's at Pawley's **Ph:** 843-237-8757
10880 Ocean Hwy US 17
Pawleys Island, SC 29585
www.louisatpawleys.com

Osunsami, Steve
ABC News correspondent
ABC News **Ph:** 212-456-7777
77 W 66th St
New York, NY 10023
www.abcnews.go.com/WNT

Oswalt, Roy (1977-)
Professional baseball player
Houston Astros **Ph:** 713-259-8000
Minute Maid Park **Fax:** 713-259-8981
501 Crawford St
Houston, TX 77002
houston.astros.mlb.com

Otellini, Paul
President and CEO of Intel Corp
Intel Corp **Ph:** 408-765-8080
2200 Mission College Blvd
Santa Clara, CA 95052
www.intel.com/pressroom/execbios.htm

Otis, Clarence Jr
Chairman and CEO of Darden Restaurants; Darden brands include Red Lobster, Olive Garden, Smokey Bones, and Bahama Breeze restaurants
Darden Restaurants Inc **Ph:** 407-245-4000
5900 Lake Ellenor Dr
Orlando, FL 32809
www.dardenrestaurants.com

Otter, CL "Butch" (1942-)
US Representative from Idaho (Republican)
1711 Longworth Bldg **Ph:** 202-225-6611
Washington, DC 20515 **Fax:** 202-225-3029
www.house.gov/otter

Oughton, Duncan (1977-)
Professional soccer player
Columbus Crew **Ph:** 614-447-2739
Columbus Crew Stadium **Fax:** 614-447-4109
1 Black & Gold Ave
Columbus, OH 43211
columbus.crew.mlsnet.com

Outkast
Rap/hip-hop duo ("Andre 3000" Benjamin and Antwan "Big Boi" Patton)
William Morris Agency **Ph:** 212-586-5100
1325 Ave of the Americas **Fax:** 212-246-3583
New York, NY 10019

Ovechkin, Alexander (1985-)
Professional hockey player
Washington Capitals **Ph:** 202-266-2200
401 9th St NW Suite 750 **Fax:** 202-266-2210
Washington, DC 20004
www.washingtoncapitals.com

Overbay, Lyle (1977-)
Professional baseball player
Toronto Blue Jays **Ph:** 416-341-1000
1 Blue Jays Way **Fax:** 416-341-1250
Toronto, ON M5V1J1
toronto.bluejays.mlb.com

Overby, Peter
NPR correspondent; covers money, power, and political influence
National Public Radio **Ph:** 202-513-2000
635 Massachusetts Ave NW **Fax:** 202-513-3329
Washington, DC 20001
www.npr.org

Overmyer, Steve
Sports anchor for CNN's Headline News
CNN **Ph:** 404-827-1500
1 CNN Center
Atlanta, GA 30303
www.cnn.com/CNN/anchors_reporters

Owens, Bill (1950-)
Governor of Colorado (Republican)
136 State Capitol Bldg **Ph:** 303-866-2471
Denver, CO 80203 **Fax:** 303-866-2003
www.colorado.gov/governor

Owens, James W
Chairman and CEO of Caterpillar Inc
Caterpillar Inc **Ph:** 309-675-1000
100 NE Adams St **Fax:** 309-675-1182
Peoria, IL 61629
www.cat.com

Owens, Major R (1936-)
US Representative from New York (Democrat)
2309 Rayburn Bldg **Ph:** 202-225-6231
Washington, DC 20515 **Fax:** 202-226-0112
www.house.gov/owens

Owens, Ronn
San Francisco Bay area talk show host; show format covers a wide range of topics, including politics, popular culture, current events, personal issues, and gossip
KGO-AM **Ph:** 415-954-8100
900 Front St
San Francisco, CA 94111
www.ronn.com

Owens, Terrell (1973-)
Professional football player
Dallas Cowboys **Ph:** 972-556-9900
1 Cowboys Pkwy **Fax:** 972-556-9304
Irving, TX 75063
www.terrellowens.com

Oxley, Michael G (1944-)
US Representative from Ohio (Republican)
2308 Rayburn Bldg **Ph:** 202-225-2676
Washington, DC 20515
oxley.house.gov

Oz, Frank (1944-)
Sesame Street puppeteer who does various Muppets voices as well as voices of other characters in film (e.g., Yoda in Star Wars); is also a film director
Creative Artists Agency **Ph:** 310-288-4545
9830 Wilshire Blvd **Fax:** 310-288-4800
Beverly Hills, CA 90212

Ozick, Cynthia (1928-)
Writer of both fiction and criticism (essay collections); novels include The Puttermesser Papers
Houghton Mifflin Co **Ph:** 617-351-5000
Trade Div
Adult Editorial
222 Berkeley St 8th Fl
Boston, MA 02116
www.houghtonmifflinbooks.com

Ozolinsh, Sandis (1972-)
Professional hockey player
New York Rangers **Ph:** 212-465-6486
Madison Square Garden **Fax:** 212-465-6494
2 Pennsylvania Plaza
New York, NY 10121
www.newyorkrangers.com

Ozzie, Ray
Founder of Groove Networks, which is now a Microsoft subsidiary; he is one of three chief technical officers at Microsoft, reporting directly to Bill Gates; was also the creator of IBM Corp's Lotus Notes
Groove Networks Inc **Ph:** 978-720-2000
100 Cummings Ctr Suite 535Q **Fax:** 978-720-2001
Beverly, MA 01915
www.groove.net

P

Pace, Orlando (1975-)
Professional football player
Saint Louis Rams **Ph:** 314-982-7267
1 Rams Way **Fax:** 314-770-9261
Earth City, MO 63045
www.stlouisrams.com

Pace, Peter (1945-)
General (USMC); Chairman of the Joint Chiefs of Staff
Joint Chiefs of Staff **Ph:** 703-697-9121
9999 Joint Chiefs of Staff **Fax:** 703-697-8758
Pentagon
Washington, DC 20318
www.jcs.mil

Pacino, Al (1940-)
Actor
Creative Artists Agency **Ph:** 310-288-4545
9830 Wilshire Blvd **Fax:** 310-288-4800
Beverly Hills, CA 90212

Pacwa, Father Mitch, PhD
Catholic priest; lectures widely and hosts and appears as a guest on radio & TV programs
Ignatius Productions **Ph:** 866-289-7936
2256 Rocky Ridge Rd Suite 105 **Fax:** 205-979-8131
Birmingham, AL 35216
www.fathermitchpacwa.org

Page, Clarence (1947-)
Chicago Tribune columnist (syndicated); an essayist for the PBS NewsHour
Tribune Media Services Inc **Ph:** 312-222-4444
435 N Michigan Ave Suite 1500
Chicago, IL 60611
tmsfeatures.com/productlist.htm

Page, Larry (1973-)
Co-founder (with Sergey Brin) and president of Google
Google Inc **Ph:** 650-623-0000
1600 Amphitheatre Pkwy **Fax:** 650-623-0001
Mountain View, CA 94043
www.google.com/corporate/execs.html

Page, Robin
Author of nonfiction books for young readers (What Do You Do With a Tail Like This?); writes in collaboration with her husband, author/illustrator Steve Jenkins
Houghton Mifflin Children's Books — **Ph:** 617-351-5000
222 Berkeley St 8th Fl
Boston, MA 02116
www.houghtonmifflinbooks.com

Paglia, Camille (1947-)
Noted feminist and non-fiction author
Random House Publicity — **Ph:** 212-782-9000
1745 Broadway
New York, NY 10019
www.randomhouse.com

Paisley, Brad (1972-)
Country singer
William Morris Agency — **Ph:** 615-963-3000
1600 Division St Suite 300 — **Fax:** 615-963-3090
Nashville, TN 37203
www.bradpaisley.com

Pak, Se Ri (1977-)
Professional golfer
Ladies Professional Golf Assn — **Ph:** 386-274-6200
100 International Golf Dr — **Fax:** 386-274-1099
Daytona Beach, FL 32124
www.lpga.com

Palance, Jack (1919-)
Actor
William Morris Agency — **Ph:** 310-859-4000
1 William Morris Pl — **Fax:** 310-859-4462
Beverly Hills, CA 90212

Palatini, Margie
Children's books author (Earthquack!, Sweet Tooth, Bedhead)
Simon & Schuster Books for Young Readers — **Ph:** 212-698-7000
1230 Ave of the Americas
New York, NY 10020
www.margiepalatini.com

Palencia, Juan Francisco (1973-)
Professional soccer player
Club Deportivo Chivas USA — **Ph:** 310-630-4550
Home Depot Center — **Fax:** 310-630-4551
18400 Avalon Blvd
Carson, CA 90746
chivas.usa.mlsnet.com

Paley, Grace (1922-)
Poet, feminist, writer (short stories and essays), and antiwar activist
Farrar Straus & Giroux — **Ph:** 212-741-6900
19 Union Sq W
New York, NY 10003
www.fsgbooks.com

Pallone, Frank Jr (1951-)
US Representative from New Jersey (Democrat)
420 Cannon Bldg — **Ph:** 202-225-4671
Washington, DC 20515 — **Fax:** 202-225-9665
www.house.gov/pallone

Palmer, Arnold (1929-)
Professional golfer
IMG Inc — **Ph:** 216-522-1200
IMG Center — **Fax:** 216-522-1145
1360 E 9th St Suite 100
Cleveland, OH 44114
www.arnoldpalmer.com

Palmer, Carson (1979-)
Professional football player
Cincinnati Bengals — **Ph:** 513-621-3550
1 Paul Brown Stadium — **Fax:** 513-621-3570
Cincinnati, OH 45202
www.bengals.com

Palmer, Charlie
Chef/restaurateur known for his Progressive American cuisine
Charlie Palmer Group — **Ph:** 212-755-7050
34 E 61st St Suite 2A — **Fax:** 212-750-8613
New York, NY 10021
www.charliepalmer.com

Palmer, Douglas H (1951-)
Mayor of Trenton, New Jersey
319 E State St — **Ph:** 609-989-3030
Trenton, NJ 08608 — **Fax:** 609-989-3939
www.ci.trenton.nj.us

Palminteri, Chazz (1952-)
Actor
William Morris Agency — **Ph:** 310-859-4000
1 William Morris Pl — **Fax:** 310-859-4462
Beverly Hills, CA 90212

Palmisano, Samuel J
Chairman of the board, president, and CEO of IBM
IBM Corp — **Ph:** 914-766-1900
New Orchard Rd
Armonk, NY 10504
www.ibm.com/ibm/us

Paltrow, Gwyneth (1972-)
Actor
PMK/HBH **Ph:** 310-289-6200
700 San Vicente Blvd **Fax:** 310-289-6677
Suite G910
West Hollywood, CA 90069

Pamplin, Robert B Jr, PhD (1941-)
Oregon businessman, philanthropist, farmer, minister, and author
RB Pamplin Corp **Ph:** 503-248-1133
805 SW Broadway Suite 2400
Portland, OR 97205
www.pamplin.org

Panetta, Leon (1938-)
Chief of Staff to President Bill Clinton 1994-1997; prior to that was Director of the Office of Management & Budget
Leon & Sylvia Panetta Institute for Public Policy **Ph:** 831-582-4200 **Fax:** 831-582-4082
California State Univ Monterey Bay
100 Campus Center
Bldg 86E
Seaside, CA 93955
www.panettainstitute.org

Panter, Gary
Illustrator, painter, and designer. Creator of the cartoon character Jimbo as well as Pink Donkey and the Fly, an online animated series for Cartoon Network; was the graphic designer for the TV show Pee-Wee's Playhouse
Drawn & Quarterly **Ph:** 514-279-2221
PO Box 48056
Montreal, QC H2V4S8
www.garypanter.com

Pantoliano, Joe (1951-)
Actor
United Talent Agency **Ph:** 310-273-6700
9560 Wilshire Blvd 5th Fl **Fax:** 310-247-1111
Beverly Hills, CA 90212
www.joeypants.com

Papantonio, Mike (1953-)
Trial lawyer whose practice is limited to mass torts, product liability, and personal injury/wrongful death litigation; co-host of Ring of Fire with Robert F Kennedy, Jr on Air America Radio
Levin Papantonio **Ph:** 850-435-7000
316 S Baylen St Suite 600 **Fax:** 850-497-7057
PO Box 12308 **TF:** 888-435-7001
Pensacola, FL 32591
www.levinlaw.com

Paquin, Anna (1982-)
Actor
William Morris Agency **Ph:** 310-859-4000
1 William Morris Pl **Fax:** 310-859-4462
Beverly Hills, CA 90212

Parcells, Bill (1941-)
Football coach
Dallas Cowboys **Ph:** 972-556-9900
1 Cowboys Pkwy **Fax:** 972-556-9304
Irving, TX 75063
www.dallascowboys.com

Paretsky, Sara
Author of the VI Warshawski mysteries
Penguin Publicity **Ph:** 212-366-2000
375 Hudson St
New York, NY 10014
www.saraparetsky.com

Paris, Twila (1958-)
Singer/songwriter (Christian music)
Jeff Roberts & Associates **Ph:** 615-859-7040
206 Bluebird Dr **Fax:** 615-859-6504
Goodlettsville, TN 37072
www.twilaparis.com

Parish, Herman
Writes the Amelia Bedelia books for children, a series originally begun by his aunt, Peggy Parish
HarperCollins Children's Books **Ph:** 212-261-6500
1350 Ave of the Americas
New York, NY 10019
www.harperchildrens.com

Parisi, Mark
Creator of the comic panel Off the Mark
United Feature Syndicate **Ph:** 212-293-8500
200 Madison Ave
New York, NY 10016
www.unitedfeatures.com

Park, Barbara (1947-)
Author of the Junie B. Jones series for children
Random House Children's Books **Ph:** 212-782-9000
Publicity Dept
1745 Broadway
New York, NY 10019
www.randomhouse.com/kids

Park, CS, PhD
Chairman and CEO of Maxtor Corp, a supplier of hard disk drive storage products
Maxtor Corp **Ph:** 408-894-5000
500 McCarthy Blvd
Milpitas, CA 95035
www.maxtor.com

Park, Grace (1979-)
Professional golfer
Gaylord Sports Management **Ph:** 480-483-9500
13845 N Northsight Blvd
Suite 200
Scottsdale, AZ 85260
www.gracepark.us

Park, Linda Sue (1960-)
Author of books for young readers (A Single Shard)
Houghton Mifflin Children's Books **Ph:** 617-351-5000
222 Berkeley St 8th Fl
Boston, MA 02116
www.lindasuepark.com

Parker, Brant (1920-)
Co-creator (with Johnny Hart) of The Wizard of Id
Creators Syndicate Inc **Ph:** 310-337-7003
5777 W Century Blvd Suite 700 **Fax:** 310-337-7625
Los Angeles, CA 90045
www.creators.com

Parker, Douglas W
Chairman, president, and CEO of US Airways Group
US Airways Group Inc **Ph:** 480-693-5050
111 W Rio Salado Pkwy
Tempe, AZ 85281
www.usairways.com/about

Parker, Kathleen
Orlando Sentinel columnist (syndicated)
Tribune Media Services Inc **Ph:** 312-222-4444
435 N Michigan Ave Suite 1500
Chicago, IL 60611
tmsfeatures.com/productlist.htm

Parker, Mark
President and CEO of Nike Inc
Nike Inc **Ph:** 503-671-6453
1 Bowerman Dr **Fax:** 503-671-6300
Beaverton, OR 97005
www.nikebiz.com

Parker, Mary-Louise (1964-)
Actor
Parseghian/Planco Management **Ph:** 212-777-7786
23 E 22nd St **Fax:** 212-777-8642
New York, NY 10010

Parker, Robert B (1932-)
Author of crime fiction, including books that feature the Boston private-eye Spenser
Putnam Publicity **Ph:** 212-366-2000
375 Hudson St
New York, NY 10014
us.penguingroup.com

Parker, Sarah Jessica (1965-)
Actor
Creative Artists Agency **Ph:** 310-288-4545
9830 Wilshire Blvd **Fax:** 310-288-4800
Beverly Hills, CA 90212
www.hbo.com/city

Parker, Star (1956-)
Social activist and founder of the Coalition on Urban Renewal & Education, which advocates faith-based and free market alternatives as a cure for poverty
Coalition on Urban Renewal & **Ph:** 310-410-9981
Education **Fax:** 310-410-9982
6033 W Century Blvd Suite 950
Los Angeles, CA 90045
www.urbancure.org

Parker, Tony (1982-)
Professional basketball player
San Antonio Spurs **Ph:** 210-444-5000
1 SBC Center **Fax:** 210-444-5003
San Antonio, TX 78219
www.nba.com/spurs

Parker, Trey (1969-)
Co-creator and executive producer of South Park, with Matt Stone
William Morris Agency **Ph:** 310-859-4000
1 William Morris Pl **Fax:** 310-859-4462
Beverly Hills, CA 90212
www.southparkstudios.com

Parkhurst, Michael (1984-)
Professional soccer player
New England Revolution **Ph:** 508-543-5001
Gillette Stadium **Fax:** 508-384-9128
1 Patriot Pl
Foxborough, MA 02035
www.revolutionsoccer.net

Parks, Suzan-Lori (1964-)
Playwright; screenwriter
Creative Artists Agency **Ph:** 310-288-4545
9830 Wilshire Blvd **Fax:** 310-288-4800
Beverly Hills, CA 90212

Parrett, William G
CEO of Deloitte Touche Tohmatsu
Deloitte Touche Tohmatsu **Ph:** 212-489-1600
1633 Broadway
New York, NY 10019
www.deloitte.com/dtt

Parrish, Mark (1977-)
Professional hockey player
Los Angeles Kings **Ph:** 213-742-7100
Staples Center
1111 S Figueroa St
Los Angeles, CA 90015
www.lakings.com

Parshall, Janet
Host of Janet Parshall's America, a nationally syndicated conservative/Christian radio talk show originating from Washington, DC
Salem Radio Network **Ph:** 972-831-1920
6400 N Beltline Rd Suite 210 **Fax:** 972-831-8626
Irving, TX 75063
www.srnonline.com

Parsons, Benny (1941-)
Former race car driver
International Motorsports Hall of Fame **Ph:** 256-362-5002
PO Box 1018
Talladega, AL 35161
www.motorsportshalloffame.com

Parsons, David (1959-)
Dancer/choreographer/teacher; founder and artistic director of Parsons Dance Company
Parsons Dance Co **Ph:** 212-869-9275
229 W 42nd St Suite 800 **Fax:** 212-944-7417
New York, NY 10036
www.parsonsdance.org

Parsons, Richard D
Chairman and CEO of Time Warner
Time Warner Inc **Ph:** 212-484-8000
75 Rockefeller Plaza **Fax:** 212-489-6183
New York, NY 10019
www.timewarner.com

Parton, Dolly (1946-)
Country singer; actor
International Creative Management **Ph:** 310-550-4000
8942 Wilshire Blvd
Beverly Hills, CA 90211
www.dollywood.com/company-info/dollys_story.aspx

Pascal, Amy
Vice Chairman, Sony Pictures Entertainment; and chairman, Motion Picture Group, Sony Pictures Entertainment
Sony Pictures Entertainment **Ph:** 310-244-4000
10202 W Washington Blvd **Fax:** 310-244-2626
Culver City, CA 90232
www.sonypictures.com

Pascal, Francine (1938-)
Author of the Sweet Valley series for young adult readers
Simon & Schuster **Ph:** 212-698-7000
1230 Ave of the Americas
New York, NY 10020
www.simonsays.com

Pascrell, Bill (1937-)
US Representative from New Jersey (Democrat)
2464 Rayburn Bldg **Ph:** 202-225-5751
Washington, DC 20515 **Fax:** 202-225-5782
www.pascrell.house.gov

Pasierb, Steve
President & CEO of Partnership for a Drug Free America
Partnership for a Drug-Free America **Ph:** 212-922-1560 **Fax:** 212-922-1570
405 Lexington Ave Suite 1601
New York, NY 10174
www.drugfree.org

Pason, Greg
National Secretary, Socialist Party USA
Socialist Party USA **Ph:** 212-982-4586
339 Lafayette St Suite 303
New York, NY 10012

Pastis, Stephan (1968-)
Creator of the comic strip Pearls Before Swine
United Feature Syndicate **Ph:** 212-293-8500
200 Madison Ave
New York, NY 10016
www.unitedfeatures.com

Pastor, Ed (1943-)
US Representative from Arizona (Democrat)
2465 Rayburn Bldg **Ph:** 202-225-4065
Washington, DC 20515 **Fax:** 202-225-1655
www.house.gov/pastor

Pataki, George E (1945-)
Governor of New York (Republican)
State Capitol **Ph:** 518-474-8390
Executive Chamber **Fax:** 518-474-1513
Albany, NY 12224
www.state.ny.us/governor

Patchett, Ann (1963-)
Novelist (Bel Canto)
HarperCollins Publishers **Ph:** 212-207-7000
c/o Author Mail
10 E 53rd St
New York, NY 10022
www.annpatchett.com

Paterno, Joe (1926-)
Football coach
Penn State Athletic Dept **Ph:** 814-865-1086
101 Bryce Jordan Ctr
University Park, PA 16802
www.gopsusports.com/football

Paterson, Katherine
Author of books for children and young adults (Bridge to Terabithia, Jacob Have I Loved, The Master Puppeteer, The Great Gilly Hopkins)
HarperCollins Children's Books **Ph:** 212-261-6500
1350 Ave of the Americas
New York, NY 10019
www.terabithia.com

Patinkin, Mandy (1952-)
Actor; singer
International Creative Management **Ph:** 310-550-4000
8942 Wilshire Blvd
Beverly Hills, CA 90211
www.mandypatinkin.net

Patric, Jason (1966-)
Actor
United Talent Agency **Ph:** 310-273-6700
9560 Wilshire Blvd 5th Fl **Fax:** 310-247-1111
Beverly Hills, CA 90212

Patrick, Dan (1957-)
Sports Center anchor/host; ESPN radio host; ESPN the Magazine writer
ESPN **Ph:** 860-585-2000
ESPN Plaza
935 Middle St
Bristol, CT 06010
sports.espn.go.com/espntv/espnGuide

Patrick, Danica (1982-)
Race car driver
Rahal-Letterman Racing **Ph:** 614-529-7000
4601 Lyman Dr
Hilliard, OH 43026
www.danicaracing.com

Patterson, James (1947-)
Author of mystery/suspense novels, including the Alex Cross books
Little Brown & Co **Ph:** 212-522-7200
Author Mail
1271 Ave of the Americas
New York, NY 10020
www.jamespatterson.com

Patterson, Richard North (1947-)
Author of suspense/thriller novels (Balance of Power)
Random House Publicity **Ph:** 212-782-9000
1745 Broadway
New York, NY 10019
www.randomhouse.com

Patty, Sandi (1956-)
Gospel singer
William Morris Agency **Ph:** 615-963-3000
1600 Division St Suite 300 **Fax:** 615-963-3090
Nashville, TN 37203
www.sandipatty.com

Paul, Christi
Weekend anchor for CNN's Headline News
CNN **Ph:** 404-827-1500
1 CNN Center
Atlanta, GA 30303
www.cnn.com/CNN/anchors_reporters

Paul, Ron (1935-)
US Representative from Texas (Republican)
203 Cannon Bldg **Ph:** 202-225-2831
Washington, DC 20515
www.house.gov/paul

Pauley, Jane (1950-)
Veteran broadcast journalist and TV host
William Morris Agency **Ph:** 310-859-4000
1 William Morris Pl **Fax:** 310-859-4462
Beverly Hills, CA 90212

Paulison, R David (1947-)
Acting Director of the Federal Emergency Management Agency (FEMA); nominated in April 2006 to become the first DHS Under Secretary for Federal Emergency Management
Federal Emergency Management Agency **Ph:** 202-646-3900
Fax: 202-646-3930
500 C St SW
Washington, DC 20472
www.fema.gov

Paulk, Earl (1927-)
Televangelist and a bishop in the International Communion of Charismatic Churches; in the 1950s became known for his bold preaching against prejudice and racism through his television and radio programs
Cathedral at Chapel Hill **Ph:** 404-243-5020
4650 Flat Shoals Pkwy **Fax:** 404-243-5927
Decatur, GA 30034
www.col.tv

Paulsen, Gary (1939-)
Author of books for teens (Hatchet, Dogsong, The Winter Room)
Random House Children's Books **Ph:** 212-782-9000
Publicity Dept
1745 Broadway
New York, NY 10019
www.garypaulsen.com

Paulson, Henry M Jr
Chairman of the Board and CEO of Goldman Sachs
Goldman Sachs Co **Ph:** 212-902-1000
85 Broad St
New York, NY 10004
www.gs.com

Pavano, Carl (1976-)
Professional baseball player
New York Yankees **Ph:** 718-293-4300
Yankee Stadium **Fax:** 718-293-8414
161st St & River Ave
Bronx, NY 10451
newyork.yankees.mlb.com

Pawlenty, Tim (1960-)
Governor of Minnesota (Republican)
130 State Capitol **Ph:** 651-296-3391
Saint Paul, MN 55155 **Fax:** 651-296-2089
www.governor.state.mn.us

Paxton, Bill (1955-)
Actor
Endeavor **Ph:** 310-248-2000
9601 Wilshire Blvd 3rd Fl **Fax:** 310-248-2020
Beverly Hills, CA 90210
www.hbo.com/biglove/cast

Payne, Donald M (1934-)
US Representative from New Jersey (Democrat)
2209 Rayburn Bldg **Ph:** 202-225-3436
Washington, DC 20515 **Fax:** 202-225-4160
www.house.gov/payne

Payne, Henry
Editorial cartoonist for The Detroit News
United Feature Syndicate **Ph:** 212-293-8500
200 Madison Ave
New York, NY 10016
www.unitedfeatures.com

Payne, Les
Reporter, syndicated columnist, and associate managing editor at Newsday
Tribune Media Services Inc **Ph:** 312-222-4444
435 N Michigan Ave Suite 1500
Chicago, IL 60611
tmsfeatures.com/productlist.htm

Payton, Gary (1968-)
Professional basketball player
Miami Heat **Ph:** 786-777-1000
American Airlines Arena **Fax:** 786-777-1609
601 Biscayne Blvd
Miami, FL 33132
www.nba.com/heat

Payton, Sean (1963-)
Football coach
New Orleans Saints **Ph:** 504-733-0255
5800 Airline Dr **Fax:** 504-731-1768
Metairie, LA 70003
www.neworleanssaints.com

Peacock, Molly (1947-)
Poet
Anderson Grinberg Literary Management **Ph:** 212-620-5883
266 W 23rd St Suite 3
New York, NY 10011
www.mollypeacock.org

Pearce, Guy (1967-)
Actor
International Creative Management **Ph:** 310-550-4000
8942 Wilshire Blvd
Beverly Hills, CA 90211

Pearce, Steve (1947-)
US Representative from New Mexico (Republican)
1604 Longworth Bldg **Ph:** 202-225-2365
Washington, DC 20515 **Fax:** 202-225-9599
pearce.house.gov

Pearl, Bill (1930-)
Bodybuilder and former Mr Universe
Bill Pearl Enterprises Inc **Ph:** 541-535-3363
PO Box 1080 **Fax:** 541-535-5507
Phoenix, OR 97535
www.billpearl.com

Pearl Jam
Alternative band
Creative Artists Agency **Ph:** 310-288-4545
9830 Wilshire Blvd **Fax:** 310-288-4800
Beverly Hills, CA 90212
www.pearljam.com

Peavy, Jake (1981-)
Professional baseball player
San Diego Padres **Ph:** 619-795-5000
Petco Park **Fax:** 619-497-5339
PO Box 122000
San Diego, CA 92112
sandiego.padres.mlb.com

Peca, Michael (1974-)
Professional hockey player
Edmonton Oilers **Ph:** 780-414-4000
11230 110th St **Fax:** 780-409-5890
Edmonton, AB T5G3H7
www.edmontonoilers.com

Peck, Carole
Chef and restaurant owner; cookbook author
Good News Cafe **Ph:** 203-266-4663
694 Main St S
Woodbury, CT 06798
www.carolepeck.com

Peck, M Scott, MD (1936-)
Author of The Road Less Traveled
Simon & Schuster **Ph:** 212-698-7000
1230 Ave of the Americas
New York, NY 10020
www.mscottpeck.com

Peck, Richard (1934-)
Author of books for young adults (A Year Down Yonder; The River Between Us)
Puffin Books Publicity **Ph:** 212-366-2000
345 Hudson St
New York, NY 10014
us.penguingroup.com

Peck, Robert Newton (1928-)
Author of the young readers' classic, A Day No Pigs Would Die
HarperCollins Children's Books **Ph:** 212-261-6500
1350 Ave of the Americas
New York, NY 10019
my.athenet.net/~blahnik/rnpeck

Peek, Jeffrey M
Chairman and CEO of CIT Group Inc, a consumer and commercial finance company
CIT Group Inc **Ph:** 212-382-7000
1211 Ave of the Americas
New York, NY 10036
www.cit.com

Peel, Mark
Executive chef & owner of Campanile Restaurant in Los Angeles
Campanile Restaurant **Ph:** 323-938-1447
624 S La Brea Ave
Los Angeles, CA 90036
www.campanilerestaurant.com

Peet, Amanda (1972-)
Actor
Gersh Agency **Ph:** 310-274-6611
232 N Canon Dr
Beverly Hills, CA 90210

Peirce, Lincoln
Creator of the syndicated comic strip Big Nate
Newspaper Enterprise Assn **Ph:** 212-293-8500
200 Madison Ave
New York, NY 10016
www.unitedfeatures.com

Peirce, Neal (1932-)
Syndicated columnist (political commentary)
Washington Post Writers Group **Ph:** 202-334-6375 **Fax:** 202-334-5669
1150 15th St NW 9th Fl
Washington, DC 20071
www.postwritersgroup.com

Pellegrini, Luciano
Executive chef at Valentino Restaurant Las Vegas, one of several restaurants owned by Piero Selvaggio Restaurant Group
Valentino Las Vegas at the Venetian Resort Hotel & Casino **Ph:** 702-414-3000 **Fax:** 702-414-3099
3355 Las Vegas Blvd S
Las Vegas, NV 89109
pieroselvaggio.com

Pellett, Nancy C
Chairman and CEO of the Farm Credit Administration
Farm Credit Administration **Ph:** 703-883-4008
1501 Farm Credit Dr
McLean, VA 22102
www.fca.gov/nancypellettbio.htm

Pelley, Scott (1957-)
60 Minutes correspondent
60 Minutes **Ph:** 212-975-2006
555 W 57th St
New York, NY 10019
www.cbsnews.com

Pelosi, Nancy (1940-)
US Representative from California (Democrat); House Minority Leader
2371 Rayburn Bldg **Ph:** 202-225-4965
Washington, DC 20515 **Fax:** 202-225-8259
www.house.gov/pelosi

Peluso, Michelle
President & CEO of Travelocity
Travelocity **Ph:** 682-605-3000
3150 Sabre Dr
Southlake, TX 76092
svc.travelocity.com

Pelzer, Dave (1960-)
Author of A Child Called IT
PO Box 1846 **Ph:** 760-321-4452
Rancho Mirage, CA 92270 **Fax:** 760-321-6842
www.davepelzer.com

Pena, Wily Mo (1982-)
Professional baseball player
Boston Red Sox **Ph:** 617-267-9440
Fenway Park **Fax:** 617-236-6797
4 Yawkey Way
Boston, MA 02215
boston.redsox.mlb.com

Pence, Caprial
Celebrity chef, cookbook author, and owner, with husband John Pence, of Caprial's Bistro; they also offer cooking classes in conjunction with the restaurant
Caprial's Bistro **Ph:** 503-236-6457
7015 SE Milwaukie Ave
Portland, OR 97202
www.caprial.com

Pence, Mike (1959-)
US Representative from Indiana (Republican)
426 Cannon Bldg **Ph:** 202-225-3021
Washington, DC 20515 **Fax:** 202-225-3382
mikepence.house.gov

Penicheiro, Ticha (1974-)
Professional basketball player
Sacramento Monarchs **Ph:** 916-928-0000
ARCO Arena **Fax:** 916-928-8109
1 Sports Pkwy
Sacramento, CA 95834
www.wnba.com/monarchs

Penn, Irving (1917-)
Photographer; early work was as a fashion & celebrity photographer; later focused on indigenous peoples found on his travels around the world
Halsted Gallery **Ph:** 248-895-0204
PO Box 130 **Fax:** 248-332-0227
Bloomfield Hills, MI 48303
www.halstedgallery.com

Penn, Robin Wright (1966-)
Actor
Creative Artists Agency **Ph:** 310-288-4545
9830 Wilshire Blvd **Fax:** 310-288-4800
Beverly Hills, CA 90212
www.robinwrightpenn.net

Penn, Sean (1960-)
Actor; producer/director
Creative Artists Agency **Ph:** 310-288-4545
9830 Wilshire Blvd **Fax:** 310-288-4800
Beverly Hills, CA 90212

Penn & Teller (1955-)
Magicians
Rio All Suite Hotel & Casino **Ph:** 702-777-7777
3700 W Flamingo Rd **TF:** 888-746-7153
Las Vegas, NV 89103
www.pennandteller.com

Penner, Rudolph G, PhD
Economist; a senior fellow at the Urban Institute and a former director of the Congressional Budget Office (1983-1987)
Urban Institute **Ph:** 202-833-7200
2100 M St NW **Fax:** 202-223-3043
Washington, DC 20037
www.urban.org/about/seniorfellows.cfm

Pennington, Chad (1976-)
Professional football player
New York Jets **Ph:** 516-560-8100
1000 Fulton Ave **Fax:** 516-560-8198
Hempstead, NY 11550
www.newyorkjets.com

Pennington, Ty (1965-)
Design team leader/carpenter on ABC's Extreme Makeover: Home Edition
CESD Talent Agency **Ph:** 310-475-2111
10635 Santa Monica Blvd
Suites 130/135
Los Angeles, CA 90025
www.tythehandyguy.com

Penny, Brad (1978-)
Professional baseball player
Los Angeles Dodgers **Ph:** 323-224-1500
Dodger Stadium **Fax:** 323-224-1269
1000 Elysian Park Ave
Los Angeles, CA 90012
losangeles.dodgers.mlb.com

Penske, Roger (1937-)
Owner of the Penske Racing Team as well as several other businesses; former sports car driving champion
Penske Corp **Ph:** 248-648-2000
2555 Telegraph Rd
Bloomfield Hills, MI 48302

Pepin, Jacques
Chef, food columnist, cookbook author, and cooking teacher
KQED-TV **Ph:** 415-864-2000
2601 Mariposa St
San Francisco, CA 94110
www.jacquespepin.net

Percival, Troy (1969-)
Professional baseball player
Detroit Tigers **Ph:** 313-962-4000
Comerica Park **Fax:** 313-471-2138
2100 Woodward Ave
Detroit, MI 48201
detroit.tigers.mlb.com

Perdue, David A
Chairman and CEO of Dollar General Corp
Dollar General Corp **Ph:** 615-855-4000
100 Mission Ridge **Fax:** 615-855-5252
Goodlettsville, TN 37072
www.dollargeneral.com

Perdue, James A, PhD
Chairman & CEO of Perdue Farms
Perdue Farms Inc **Ph:** 410-543-3000
31149 Old Ocean City Rd **Fax:** 410-543-3292
Salisbury, MD 21804
www.perdue.com

Perdue, Sonny (1946-)
Governor of Georgia (Republican)
State Capitol Rm 203 **Ph:** 404-656-1776
Atlanta, GA 30334 **Fax:** 404-657-7332
www.gov.state.ga.us

Perelman, Ronald O (1943-)
Chairman and CEO of MacAndrews & Forbes Holdings and chairman of its subsidiary, Revlon Inc
MacAndrews & Forbes Holdings Inc **Ph:** 212-572-5956 **Fax:** 212-527-4400
35 E 62nd St
New York, NY 10021

Perenchio, Jerry
Chairman & CEO of Univision Communications
Univision Communications Inc **Ph:** 310-556-7600
1999 Ave of the Stars Suite 3050 **Fax:** 310-556-7615
Los Angeles, CA 90067
www.univision.net

Peretz, Martin
Editor-in-chief of The New Republic
New Republic **Ph:** 202-508-4444
1331 H St NW Suite 700
Washington, DC 20005
www.tnr.com

Perez, Antonio
Chairman & CEO of Eastman Kodak Co
Eastman Kodak Co **Ph:** 585-724-4000
343 State St **Fax:** 585-724-0633
Rochester, NY 14650
www.kodak.com

Perez, Eddie A (1957-)
Mayor of Hartford, Connecticut
550 Main St **Ph:** 860-543-8500
Hartford, CT 06103 **Fax:** 860-722-6606
www.hartford.gov/government/mayor

Perez, Miguel (1950-)
Cuban-American journalist; writes a syndicated column about the US Latino population, Latin America, and immigration issues
Creators Syndicate Inc **Ph:** 310-337-7003
5777 W Century Blvd Suite 700 **Fax:** 310-337-7625
Los Angeles, CA 90045
www.creators.com/opinion.html

Perez, Oliver (1981-)
Professional baseball player
Pittsburgh Pirates **Ph:** 412-323-5000
PNC Park **Fax:** 412-323-5009
115 Federal St
Pittsburgh, PA 15212
pittsburgh.pirates.mlb.com

Perkins, Ed
Founding editor (now retired) of the Consumer Reports Travel Letter; writes a syndicated travel advice column
Tribune Media Services Inc **Ph:** 312-222-4444
435 N Michigan Ave Suite 1500
Chicago, IL 60611
tmsfeatures.com/productlist.htm

Perkins, Lucian (1953-)
Photojournalist (staff photographer for the Washington Post)
Washington Post **Ph:** 202-334-6000
1150 15th St NW
Washington, DC 20071
www.lucianperkins.com

Perkins, Tony
President of the Family Research Council
Family Research Council **Ph:** 202-393-2100
801 G St NW **Fax:** 202-393-2134
Washington, DC 20001
www.frc.org

Perl, Martin L, PhD (1927-)
Winner, with Frederick Reines, of the 1995 Nobel Prize in Physics for pioneering experimental contributions to lepton physics
Stanford Linear Accelerator Center **Ph:** 650-926-4286 **Fax:** 650-926-5379
2575 Sand Hill Rd
Menlo Park, CA 94305
www.slac.stanford.edu/slac/faculty/hepfaculty.html

Perlman, Itzhak (1945-)
Classical violinist; is also a conductor, and is the Principal Guest Conductor for the Detroit Symphony Orchestra
IMG Artists **Ph:** 212-994-3500
Carnegie Hall Tower **Fax:** 212-994-3550
152 W 57th St 5th Fl
New York, NY 10019
www.imgartists.com

Perlozzo, Sam (1951-)
Baseball manager
Baltimore Orioles **Ph:** 410-685-9800
Oriole Park at Camden Yards **Fax:** 410-547-6279
333 W Camden St
Baltimore, MD 21201
baltimore.orioles.mlb.com

Pernot, Guillermo
Chef and owner of the Nuevo Latino restaurant, Pasion!, in Philadelphia
Pasion Restaurant **Ph:** 215-875-9895
211 S 15th St
Philadelphia, PA 19102
www.pasionrestaurant.com

Perot, Ross (1930-)
Founder and Chairman Emeritus of Perot Systems Corp; was also the founder of Electronic Data Systems (EDS) and was a candidate for US president in 1992 & 1996
Perot Systems Corp **Ph:** 972-577-0000
2300 W Plano Pkwy
Plano, TX 75075
www.perotsystems.com

Perreault, Yanic (1971-)
Professional hockey player
Nashville Predators **Ph:** 615-770-7825
Gaylord Entertainment Center **Fax:** 615-770-2341
501 Broadway
Nashville, TN 37203
www.nashvillepredators.com

Perricone, Nicholas, MD
Clinical and research dermatologist who is considered an anti-aging expert; author of several best-selling books on health and nutrition
639 Research Pkwy **Ph:** 203-379-0726
Meriden, CT 06450 **Fax:** 203-379-0817
www.nvperriconemd.com

Perrier, Georges
Chef and owner of Le Bec-Fin and other restaurants in Philadelphia
Le Bec-Fin Restaurant **Ph:** 215-567-1000
1523 Walnut St
Philadelphia, PA 19102
www.lebecfin.com

Perrineau, Harold (1968-)
Actor
Abrams Entertainment **Ph:** 323-935-3333
5225 Wilshire Blvd Suite 515
Los Angeles, CA 90036
abc.go.com/primetime/lost/bios

Perry, Anne (1938-)
Author of English mysteries
Ballantine Books Publicity **Ph:** 212-782-9000
1745 Broadway
New York, NY 10019
www.anneperry.net

Perry, Chris (1961-)
Professional golfer
SFX Sports Group **Ph:** 202-686-2000
5335 Wisconsin Ave NW Suite 850 **Fax:** 202-686-5050
Washington, DC 20015
www.pgatour.com

Perry, Matthew (1969-)
Actor
Creative Artists Agency **Ph:** 310-288-4545
9830 Wilshire Blvd **Fax:** 310-288-4800
Beverly Hills, CA 90212

Perry, Rick (1950-)
Governor of Texas (Republican)
PO Box 12428 **Ph:** 512-463-2000
Austin, TX 78711 **Fax:** 512-463-1849
www.governor.state.tx.us

Peters, Bernadette (1948-)
Actor (primarily stage); singer
William Morris Agency **Ph:** 212-586-5100
1325 Ave of the Americas **Fax:** 212-246-3583
New York, NY 10019
www.bernadettepeters.com

Peters, Mike (1943-)
Editorial cartoonist and creator of the comic strip Mother Goose & Grimm
King Features Syndicate Inc **Ph:** 212-455-4000
888 7th Ave 2nd Fl
New York, NY 10019
www.kingfeatures.com

Peters, Tom (1942-)
Management expert, speaker, and author (with Bob Waterman) of In Search of Excellence, which is considered one of the greatest business books of all time
Tom Peters Co **Ph:** 617-242-5522
1 First Ave 2nd Fl **Fax:** 617-242-5520
Charlestown Navy Yard
Boston, MA 02129
www.tompeters.com

Petersen, William (1953-)
Actor
United Talent Agency **Ph:** 310-273-6700
9560 Wilshire Blvd 5th Fl **Fax:** 310-247-1111
Beverly Hills, CA 90212
www.cbs.com/primetime/csi

Petersen, Wolfgang (1941-)
Movie producer/director
Creative Artists Agency **Ph:** 310-288-4545
8930 Wilshire Blvd **Fax:** 310-288-4800
Beverly Hills, CA 90212

Peterson, Bart (1958-)
Mayor of Indianapolis
200 E Washington St **Ph:** 317-327-3601
Suite 2501 **Fax:** 317-327-3980
Indianapolis, IN 46204
www.indygov.org/eGov/Mayor

Peterson, Collin C (1944-)
US Representative from Minnesota (Democrat)
2159 Rayburn Bldg **Ph:** 202-225-2165
Washington, DC 20515 **Fax:** 202-225-1593
collinpeterson.house.gov

Peterson, Donald K
Chairman and CEO of Avaya, a provider of communications networks and services for businesses
Avaya Inc **Ph:** 908-953-6000
211 Mt Airy Rd
Basking Ridge, NJ 07920
www.avaya.com

Peterson, George E, PhD
A senior fellow at the Urban Institute and an expert on public finance and urban development
Urban Institute **Ph:** 202-833-7200
2100 M St NW **Fax:** 202-223-3043
Washington, DC 20037
www.urban.org/about/seniorfellows.cfm

Peterson, John (1938-)
US Representative from Pennsylvania (Republican)
123 Cannon Bldg **Ph:** 202-225-5121
Washington, DC 20515 **Fax:** 202-225-5796
www.house.gov/johnpeterson

Peterson, Mike (1976-)
Professional football player
Jacksonville Jaguars **Ph:** 904-633-6000
1 Alltel Stadium Pl **Fax:** 904-633-6050
Jacksonville, FL 32202
www.jaguars.com

Peterson, Peter G (1926-)
Senior chairman & co-founder of the Blackstone Group, a private investment banking firm; has held a number of high-level business and government positions, including Secretary of Commerce in the Nixon Administration
The Blackstone Group **Ph:** 212-583-5000
345 Park Ave **Fax:** 212-583-5712
New York, NY 10154
www.blackstone.com

Petri, Thomas E (1940-)
US Representative from Wisconsin (Republican)
2462 Rayburn Bldg **Ph:** 202-225-2476
Washington, DC 20515 **Fax:** 202-225-2356
www.house.gov/petri

Pett, Joel
Editorial cartoonist for the Lexington Herald-Leader
Lexington Herald-Leader **Ph:** 859-231-3100
100 Midland Ave
Lexington, KY 40508
www.ucomics.com/joelpett

Pett, Mark
Editorial cartoonist
Universal Press Syndicate **Ph:** 816-932-6600
4520 Main St
Kansas City, MO 64111
www.amuniversal.com/ups/features

Pettigrew, Roderic I, MD, PhD
Director of the National Institute of Biomedical Imaging & Bioengineering, National Institutes of Health
National Institute of Biomedical Imaging & Bioengineering
6707 Democracy Blvd Rm 202
Bethesda, MD 20892
www.nibib.nih.gov
Ph: 301-496-8859
Fax: 301-480-4515

Pettitte, Andy (1972-)
Professional baseball player
Houston Astros
Minute Maid Park
501 Crawford St
Houston, TX 77002
houston.astros.mlb.com
Ph: 713-259-8000
Fax: 713-259-8981

Petty, Kyle (1960-)
Race car driver
Petty Enterprises
311 Branson Mill Rd
Randleman, NC 27317
www.pettyracing.com
Ph: 336-498-2156

Petty, Richard (1937-)
Hall of Fame race car driver (retired)
Petty Enterprises
311 Branson Mill Rd
Randleman, NC 27317
www.pettyracing.com
Ph: 336-498-2156

Petty, Tom (1950-)
Singer
William Morris Agency
1 William Morris Pl
Beverly Hills, CA 90212
www.tompetty.com
Ph: 310-859-4000
Fax: 310-859-4462

Peyton, John (1964-)
Mayor of Jacksonville, Florida
117 W Duval St Suite 400
Jacksonville, FL 32202
www.ci.jax.fl.us/Mayor
Ph: 904-630-1776
Fax: 904-630-2391

Pfaff, William (1928-)
Syndicated columnist (political commentary) and author; writes on international relations, contemporary history, and US policy
Tribune Media Services Inc
435 N Michigan Ave Suite 1500
Chicago, IL 60611
tmsfeatures.com/productlist.htm
Ph: 312-222-4444

Pfeiffer, Michelle (1958-)
Actor
Creative Artists Agency
9830 Wilshire Blvd
Beverly Hills, CA 90212
Ph: 310-288-4545
Fax: 310-288-4800

Phaneuf, Dion (1985-)
Professional hockey player
Calgary Flames
Pengrowth Saddledome
555 Saddledome Rise SE
Calgary, AB T2G2W1
www.calgaryflames.com
Ph: 403-777-2177
Fax: 403-777-2195

Phelps, Fred (1929-)
Pastor of the Westboro Baptist Church and rabid anti-gay activist
Westboro Baptist Church
3701 SW 12th St
Topeka, KS 66604
www.godhatesfags.com/main/phelpsbio.html
Ph: 785-273-0325

Philbin, Regis (1931-)
Host of Live with Regis & Kelly
William Morris Agency
1325 Ave of the Americas
New York, NY 10019
tvplex.go.com/buenavista/regisandkelly
Ph: 212-586-5100
Fax: 212-246-3583

Philbrick, Nathaniel
Nonfiction author (In the Heart of the Sea)
Viking Publicity
375 Hudson St
New York, NY 10014
us.penguingroup.com
Ph: 212-366-2000

Philippoussis, Mark (1976-)
Professional tennis player
ATP
201 ATP Blvd
Ponte Vedra Beach, FL 32082
www.atptennis.com
Ph: 904-285-8000
Fax: 904-285-5966

Phillippe, Ryan (1974-)
Actor
United Talent Agency
9560 Wilshire Blvd 5th Fl
Beverly Hills, CA 90212
Ph: 310-273-6700
Fax: 310-247-1111

Phillips, Bill
Author of Body for Life: 12 Weeks to Mental & Physical Strength; founder of the EAS Body for Life company/program
HarperCollins Publishers
c/o Author Mail
10 E 53rd St
New York, NY 10022
www.harpercollins.com
Ph: 212-207-7000

Phillips, Carter G (1952-)
Considered one of the top Washington, DC litigators; served as law clerk to Chief Justice Warren Burger on the US Supreme Court
Sidley Austin LLP **Ph:** 202-736-8270
1501 K St NW **Fax:** 202-736-8711
Washington, DC 20005
www.sidley.com

Phillips, Jeanne
Writes the Dear Abby advice column, which was founded by her mother, Pauline Phillips (writing as Abigail Van Buren)
Universal Press Syndicate **Ph:** 816-932-6600
4520 Main St
Kansas City, MO 64111
www.amuniversal.com/ups/features

Phillips, John R
Attorney who represents whistleblowers in qui tam lawsuits; lawsuits brought by his firm on behalf of whistleblowers have returned more than $2 billion to the US Treasury
Phillips & Cohen LLP **Ph:** 202-833-4567
2000 Massachusetts Ave NW 1st Fl **Fax:** 202-833-1815
Washington, DC 20036
www.phillipsandcohen.com

Phillips, Julian
An anchor of Fox & Friends Weekend
FOX News Channel **Ph:** 212-301-3000
1211 Ave of the Americas
New York, NY 10036
www.foxnews.com/fnctv

Phillips, Kyra
CNN news anchor and correspondent
CNN **Ph:** 404-827-1500
1 CNN Center
Atlanta, GA 30303
www.cnn.com/CNN/anchors_reporters

Phillips, Lou Diamond (1962-)
Actor
Global Artists Agency **Ph:** 323-836-0320
1648 N Wilcox Ave 2nd Fl
Los Angeles, CA 90028

Phillips, Stone (1954-)
Co-anchor of Dateline NBC
Dateline NBC **Ph:** 212-664-4249
30 Rockefeller Plaza
New York, NY 10112
www.msnbc.msn.com/id/3360263

Phillips, William D, PhD (1948-)
Winner (with two other scientists) of the 1997 Nobel prize in Physics for development of methods to cool and trap atoms with laser light
National Institute of Standards & Technology **Ph:** 301-975-6554 **Fax:** 301-975-8272
Atomic Physics Div
100 Bureau Dr
S-8424 Bldg 221 Rm A153
Gaithersburg, MD 20899

Phish
Alternative rock group
Monterey Peninsula Artists/ Paradigm **Ph:** 831-375-4889 **Fax:** 831-375-2623
509 Hartnell St
Monterey, CA 93940
www.phish.com

Phoenix, Joaquin (1974-)
Actor
Endeavor **Ph:** 310-248-2000
9601 Wilshire Blvd 3rd Fl **Fax:** 310-248-2020
Beverly Hills, CA 90210

Piazza, Mike (1968-)
Professional baseball player
San Diego Padres **Ph:** 619-795-5000
Petco Park **Fax:** 619-497-5339
PO Box 122000
San Diego, CA 92112
sandiego. padres.mlb.com

Picasso, Pablo (1881-1973)
Spanish painter
Solomon R Guggenheim Museum **Ph:** 212-423-3500
1071 5th Ave
New York, NY 10128
www.picasso.fr/anglais

Piccolo, Rina
Creator of the comic strip Tina's Groove; is also one of the Six Chix cartoonists
King Features Syndicate Inc **Ph:** 212-455-4000
888 7th Ave 2nd Fl
New York, NY 10019
www.kingfeatures.com

Pickering, Chip (1963-)
US Representative from Mississippi (Republican)
229 Cannon Bldg **Ph:** 202-225-5031
Washington, DC 20515 **Fax:** 202-225-5797
www.house.gov/pickering

Picoult, Jodi
Novelist
Simon & Schuster **Ph:** 212-698-7000
1230 Ave of the Americas
New York, NY 10020
www.jodipicoult.com

Pierce, Antonio (1978-)
Professional football player
New York Giants **Ph:** 201-935-8111
Giants Stadium **Fax:** 201-939-4134
East Rutherford, NJ 07073
www.giants.com

Pierce, David Hyde (1959-)
Actor
SMS Talent Inc **Ph:** 310-289-0909
8730 Sunset Blvd Suite 440 **Fax:** 310-289-0990
Los Angeles, CA 90069

Pierce, Harvey R
Chairman and CEO of American Family Insurance Group
American Family Insurance Group **Ph:** 608-249-2111
6000 American Pkwy
Madison, WI 53783

Pierce, Mary (1975-)
Professional tennis player
WTA Tour **Ph:** 727-895-5000
1 Progress Plaza Suite 1500 **Fax:** 727-894-1982
Saint Petersburg, FL 33701
www.wtatour.com

Pierce, Paul (1977-)
Professional basketball player
Boston Celtics **Ph:** 617-854-8000
226 Causeway St 4th Fl **Fax:** 617-367-4286
Boston, MA 02114
www.nba.com/celtics

Pierce, Tamora (1954-)
Author of juvenile fiction, including the fantasy series Song of the Lioness, The Circle of Mage, and The Protector of the Small
Random House Children's Books **Ph:** 212-782-9000
Publicity Dept
1745 Broadway
New York, NY 10019
www.tamora-pierce.com

Piercy, Marge (1936-)
Author of poetry & fiction and a political activist
Knopf Publishing/Author Mail **Ph:** 212-782-9000
1745 Broadway
New York, NY 10019
www.margepiercy.com

Pierre, Juan (1977-)
Professional baseball player
Chicago Cubs **Ph:** 773-404-2827
Wrigley Field **Fax:** 773-404-4129
1060 W Addison St
Chicago, IA 60613
chicago.cubs.mlb.com

Pike, Christopher (1954-)
Author of thrillers for young adults
Simon & Schuster **Ph:** 212-698-7000
1230 Ave of the Americas
New York, NY 10020
www.simonsays.com

Pilcher, Rosamunde (1924-)
Novelist (The Shell Seekers)
St Martin's Press **Ph:** 212-674-5151
Attn: Publicity Dept
175 5th Ave
New York, NY 10010
www.stmartins.com

Pilgrim, Bo
Co-founder & chairman of Pilgrim's Pride Corp
Pilgrim's Pride Corp **Ph:** 903-855-1000
110 S Texas St
Pittsburgh, TX 75686
www.pilgrimspride.com

Pilkey, Dav (1966-)
Author/illustrator of books for children, including the Captain Underpants series
Scholastic Inc **Ph:** 212-343-6100
557 Broadway
New York, NY 10012
www.pilkey.com

Pindell, Howardena (1943-)
African American Abstract painter
Art Dept **Ph:** 631-632-7250
Staller Center **Fax:** 631-632-7261
State University of New York at Stony Brook
Stony Brook, NY 11794
www.art.sunysb.edu/pindell.html

Pinker, Steven, PhD (1954-)
Harvard psychology professor; conducts research on language and cognition and is the author of several books on the subject
Harvard University **Ph:** 617-495-3800
Dept of Psychology
William James Hall
33 Kirkland St
Cambridge, MA 02138
pinker.wjh.harvard.edu

Pinkerton, Jim
Political analyst for FOX News, columnist, and author
FOX News Channel **Ph:** 202-824-6300
400 N Capitol St NW Suite 550
Washington, DC 20001
www.foxnews.com/fnctv

Pinkney, Andrea Davis (1963-)
Author of biographies for young readers about extraordinary African Americans
Scholastic Inc **Ph:** 212-343-6100
557 Broadway
New York, NY 10012
www.scholastic.com

Pinkney, Jerry (1939-)
Children's book illustrator
Dial Publicity **Ph:** 212-366-2000
345 Hudson St
New York, NY 10014
us.penguingroup.com

Pinkwater, Daniel (1941-)
Children's book author and commentator on NPR's All Things Considered
National Public Radio **Ph:** 202-513-2000
635 Massachusetts Ave NW **Fax:** 202-513-3329
Washington, DC 20001
www.npr.org

Pinsky, Robert (1940-)
US Poet Laureate 1997-2000, translator, essayist, and teacher
Steven Barclay Agency **Ph:** 707-773-0654
12 Western Ave **Fax:** 707-778-1868
Petaluma, CA 94952 **TF:** 888-965-7323
www.barclayagency.com

Pinter, Harold (1930-)
British playwright; also a screenwriter and political activist
Grove/Atlantic Inc **Ph:** 212-614-7860
841 Broadway **Fax:** 212-614-7886
New York, NY 10003
www.haroldpinter.org

Piraro, Dan
Creator of the comic strip Bizarro
King Features Syndicate Inc **Ph:** 212-455-4000
888 7th Ave 2nd Fl
New York, NY 10019
www.kingfeatures.com

Pirkey, Louis T (1937-)
A top trademark litigator
Fulbright & Jaworksi LLP **Ph:** 512-474-5201
600 Congress Ave Suite 2400 **Fax:** 512-320-4598
Austin, TX 78701
www.fulbright.com

Pitt, Brad (1963-)
Actor
Creative Artists Agency **Ph:** 310-288-4545
9830 Wilshire Blvd **Fax:** 310-288-4800
Beverly Hills, CA 90212

Pittman, Michael (1975-)
Professional football player
Tampa Bay Buccaneers **Ph:** 813-870-2700
1 Buccaneer Pl **Fax:** 813-878-0813
Tampa, FL 33607
www.buccaneers.com

Pitts, Joseph R (1939-)
US Representative from Pennsylvania (Republican)
221 Cannon Bldg **Ph:** 202-225-2411
Washington, DC 20515 **Fax:** 202-225-2013
www.house.gov/pitts

Pitts, Leonard Jr (1957-)
Miami Herald op-ed columnist who writes about culture, race, families, relationships, and the politics of the human condition; syndicated
Tribune Media Services Inc **Ph:** 312-222-4444
435 N Michigan Ave Suite 1500
Chicago, IL 60611
tmsfeatures.com/productlist.htm

Piven, Jeremy (1965-)
Actor
Creative Artists Agency **Ph:** 310-288-4545
9830 Wilshire Blvd **Fax:** 310-288-4800
Beverly Hills, CA 90212
www.hbo.com/entourage

Plain, Belva (1918-)
Romance novelist
Bantam Dell Publicity **Ph:** 212-782-9000
1745 Broadway
New York, NY 10019
www.randomhouse.com/features/belvaplain

Plank, Raymond
Founder and chairman of Apache Corp, an independent oil and gas exploration and development company
Apache Corp **Ph:** 713-296-6000
2000 Post Oak Blvd Suite 100
Houston, TX 77056
www.apachecorp.com

Plante, Bill (1938-)
CBS News White House correspondent
CBS News — **Ph:** 202-457-4481
2020 M St NW
Washington, DC 20036
www.cbsnews.com

Platts, Todd Russell (1962-)
US Representative from Pennsylvania (Republican)
1032 Longworth Bldg — **Ph:** 202-225-5836
Washington, DC 20515 — **Fax:** 202-226-1000
www.house.gov/platts

Plum-Ucci, Carol (1957-)
Author of mysteries for young adults (The Body of Christopher Creed)
Harcourt Children's Books — **Ph:** 212-592-1000
15 E 26th St
New York, NY 10010
www.harcourtbooks.com

Plummer, Christopher (1929-)
Actor
International Creative Management — **Ph:** 310-550-4000
8942 Wilshire Blvd
Beverly Hills, CA 90211
www.icmtalent.com/musperf/theater.html

Plummer, Jake (1974-)
Professional football player
Denver Broncos — **Ph:** 303-649-9000
13655 Broncos Pkwy — **Fax:** 303-649-9354
Englewood, CO 80112
www.denverbroncos.com

Podesta, Anthony T
Legislative and public relations strategist/lobbyist
PodestaMattoon — **Ph:** 202-393-1010
1001 G St NW Suite 900E — **Fax:** 202-393-5510
Washington, DC 20001
www.podestamattoon.com

Podesta, John (1949-)
Chief of Staff during the Clinton Administration; currently president & CEO of the Center for American Progess, a public policy research institute
Center for American Progress — **Ph:** 202-682-1611
1333 H St NW 10th Fl
Washington, DC 20005
www.americanprogress.org

Podhoretz, John (1961-)
Contributor for the FOX News Channel; is also a columnist for the New York Post, The Weekly Standard, and other publications and was a co-founder of The Weekly Standard
FOX News Channel — **Ph:** 212-301-3000
1211 Ave of the Americas
New York, NY 10036
www.foxnews.com/fnctv

Poe, Ted (1948-)
US Representative from Texas (Republican)
1605 Longworth Bldg — **Ph:** 202-225-6565
Washington, DC 20515 — **Fax:** 202-225-5547
www.house.gov/poe

Pogue, William R (1930-)
Former astronaut who was part of the Skylab 4 crew
National Space Society — **Ph:** 202-429-1600
1620 'I' St NW Suite 615 — **Fax:** 202-463-8497
Washington, DC 20003
www.nss.org

Pohlad, Carl R (1915-)
Owner of the Minnesota Twins baseball club
Minnesota Twins — **Ph:** 612-375-1366
Hubert H Humphrey Metrodome — **Fax:** 612-375-7473
34 Kirby Puckett Pl
Minneapolis, MN 55415
minnesota.twins.mlb.com

Point of Grace
Christian music group
Blanton Harrell Cooke & Corzine — **Ph:** 615-627-0444
5300 Virginia Way Suite 100 — **Fax:** 615-627-0449
Brentwood, TN 37027
www.pointofgrace.net

Poitier, Sidney (1927-)
Actor
Creative Artists Agency — **Ph:** 310-288-4545
9830 Wilshire Blvd — **Fax:** 310-288-4800
Beverly Hills, CA 90212

Polamalu, Troy (1981-)
Professional football player
Pittsburgh Steelers — **Ph:** 412-432-7800
3400 S Water St — **Fax:** 412-432-7878
Pittsburgh, PA 15203
www.pittsburghsteelers.com

Polanski, Roman (1933-)
Film director, writer, and producer
International Creative Management **Ph:** 310-550-4000
8942 Wilshire Blvd
Beverly Hills, CA 90211

Politan, Vinnie
Attorney and Court TV daytime trial anchor and program co-host
Courtroom Television Network **Ph:** 212-973-2800
600 3rd Ave
New York, NY 10016
www.courttv.com/anchors

Politzer, H David, PhD (1949-)
Winner (with two other scientists) of the 2004 Nobel Prize in Physics for the discovery of asymptotic freedom in the theory of the strong interaction
Particle Theory Group **Ph:** 626-395-4252
California Institute of Technology
1200 E California Blvd
Pasadena, CA 91125
theory.caltech.edu/~politzer

Pollack, Kenneth M, PhD (1966-)
Director of Research, Saban Center for Middle East Policy and a Brookings senior fellow for Foreign Policy Studies; has held several government positions, including with the National Security Council and the CIA
Saban Center for Middle East Policy **Ph:** 202-797-6462 **Fax:** 202-797-2481
Brookings Institution
1775 Massachusetts Ave NW
Washington, DC 20036
www.brookings.edu

Pollack, Sydney (1934-)
Movie producer/director
Creative Artists Agency **Ph:** 310-288-4545
9830 Wilshire Blvd **Fax:** 310-288-4800
Beverly Hills, CA 90212

Pollin, Abe
Owner of the Washington Wizards basketball team
Washington Sports & Entertainment LP **Ph:** 202-628-3200
601 F St NW
Washington, DC 20001
www.nba.com/wizards

Pollitt, Katha
Columnist for The Nation magazine; also a poet and essayist
The Nation **Ph:** 212-209-5400
33 Irving Pl 8th Fl **Fax:** 212-982-9000
New York, NY 10003
www.thenation.com

Pollock, Jackson (1912-1956)
Modern artist known for his spontaneous pouring technique
Pollock-Krasner House & Study Center **Ph:** 631-324-4929 **Fax:** 631-324-8768
830 Fireplace Rd
East Hampton, NY 11937
naples.cc.stonybrook.edu/CAS/pkhouse.nsf

Pollock, Robert B (1954-)
President and CEO of Assurant Inc, a provider of specialized insurance products and related services
Assurant Inc **Ph:** 212-859-7000
1 Chase Manhattan Plaza 41st Fl
New York, NY 10005
www.assurant.com

Pombo, Richard W (1961-)
US Representative from California (Republican)
2411 Rayburn Bldg **Ph:** 202-225-1947
Washington, DC 20515 **Fax:** 202-226-0861
www.house.gov/pombo

Pomeroy, Earl (1952-)
US Representative from North Dakota (Democrat)
1501 Longworth Bldg **Ph:** 202-225-2611
Washington, DC 20515 **Fax:** 202-226-0893
www.pomeroy.house.gov

Ponce, Carlos (1972-)
Latin singer and actor; also a correspondent for Entertainment Tonight
William Morris Agency **Ph:** 310-859-4000
1 William Morris Pl **Fax:** 310-859-4462
Beverly Hills, CA 90212
www.carlosponce.com

Poniewozik, James
Media & television critic for Time Magazine
Time Magazine **Ph:** 212-522-1212
Rockefeller Center
Time & Life Bldg
New York, NY 10020
www.time.com/time/columnist

Ponsot, Marie (1921-)
Poet
Knopf Publishing/Author Mail **Ph:** 212-782-9000
1745 Broadway
New York, NY 10019
www.randomhouse.com/knopf

Popcorn, Faith (1947-)
Trends forecaster and marketing consultant
Faith Popcorn's Brain Reserve **Ph:** 212-772-7778
1 Dag Hammarskjold Plaza **Fax:** 212-772-7787
885 2nd Ave 16th Fl
New York, NY 10017
www.faithpopcorn.com

Pope, Carl
Executive Director of the Sierra Club
Sierra Club **Ph:** 415-977-5500
85 2nd St 2nd Fl **Fax:** 415-977-5799
San Francisco, CA 94105
www.sierraclub.org/pressroom/leaders

Pope, Eddie (1973-)
Professional soccer player
Real Salt Lake **Ph:** 801-924-8585
515 S 700 East Suite 2R **Fax:** 801-933-4713
Salt Lake City, UT 84102
www.mlsnet.com/MLS/rsl/

Pope, Edwin
Sports columnist for the Miami Herald (has been there for more than 45 years)
Miami Herald **Ph:** 305-350-2111
1 Herald Plaza
Miami, FL 33132
www.miami.com/mld/miamiherald/sports

Pope, Lois
Philanthropist and founder of the Lois Pope LIFE Foundation and LIFE (Leaders in Furthering Education); widow of Generoso Pope, Jr, founder of The National Enquirer
Lois Pope LIFE Foundation **Ph:** 561-865-0955
6274 Linton Blvd Suite 103 **Fax:** 561-865-0938
Delray Beach, FL 33484
www.life-edu.org

Popeil, Ronald M
Founder of Ronco Inventions, the creator of Dial-O-Matic and similar products
Ronco Inventions Inc **Ph:** 818-775-4602
21344 Superior St
Chatsworth, CA 91311
www.ronco.com

Popeo, R Robert (1938-)
Trial lawyer; president and chairman of Mintz Levin
Mintz Levin Cohn Ferris Glovsky & Popeo PC **Ph:** 617-542-6000 **Fax:** 617-542-2241
1 Financial Center
Boston, MA 02111
www.mintz.com

Popovich, Gregg (1948-)
Basketball coach
San Antonio Spurs **Ph:** 210-444-5000
1 SBC Center **Fax:** 210-444-5003
San Antonio, TX 78219
www.nba.com/spurs

Portale, Alfred
Chef of the Gotham Bar & Grill
Gotham Bar & Grill **Ph:** 212-620-4020
12 E 12th St **Fax:** 212-627-7810
New York, NY 10003
www.gothambarandgrill.com

Porter, Jerry (1978-)
Professional football player
Oakland Raiders **Ph:** 510-864-5000
1220 Harbor Bay Pkwy **Fax:** 510-864-5134
Alameda, CA 94502
www.raiders.com

Porter, Jon (1955-)
US Representative from Nevada (Republican)
218 Cannon Bldg **Ph:** 202-225-3252
Washington, DC 20515 **Fax:** 202-225-2185
www.house.gov/porter

Porter, Michael E, PhD
Director of the Institute for Strategy & Competitiveness at Harvard Business School; a leading authority on competitive strategy and the competitiveness and economic development of nations, states, and regions
Institute for Strategy & Competitiveness **Ph:** 617-495-6309 **Fax:** 617-547-8543
Harvard Business School
Soldiers Field Rd
Ludcke House
Boston, MA 02163
www.people.hbs.edu/mporter

Portis, Clinton (1981-)
Professional football player
Washington Redskins **Ph:** 703-726-7000
21300 Redskin Park Dr **Fax:** 703-726-7086
Ashburn, VA 20147
www.redskins.com

Portman, Natalie (1981-)
Actor
Creative Artists Agency **Ph:** 310-288-4545
9830 Wilshire Blvd **Fax:** 310-288-4800
Beverly Hills, CA 90212

Portman, Rachel (1960-)
Composer
Kraft-Engel Management **Ph:** 818-380-1918
15233 Ventura Blvd Suite 200 **Fax:** 818-380-2609
Sherman Oaks, CA 91403
sonyclassical.com

Portman, Rob (1955-)
US Trade Representative
Office of the US Trade Representative **Ph:** 202-395-7360
600 17th St NW
Washington, DC 20508
www.ustr.gov

Posada, Jorge (1971-)
Professional baseball player
New York Yankees **Ph:** 718-293-4300
Yankee Stadium **Fax:** 718-293-8414
161st St & River Ave
Bronx, NY 10451
newyork.yankees.mlb.com

Posen, Zak
Fashion designer
House of Z LLC **Ph:** 212-925-1263
13-17 Laight St **Fax:** 212-925-1264
New York, NY 10013
www.zacposen.com

Poses, Frederic
Chairman & CEO of American Standard
American Standard Cos Inc **Ph:** 732-980-6000
1 Centennial Ave **Fax:** 732-980-3335
Piscataway, NJ 08854 **TF:** 800-223-0068
ir.americanstandard.com

Post, Jeffrey
President & CEO of CUNA Mutual Group, a provider of financial services to credit unions and their members
CUNA Mutual Group **Ph:** 608-238-5851
5910 Mineral Point Rd
Madison, WI 53705
www.cunamutual.com

Post, Peggy (1945-)
Primary spokesperson and author for the Emily Post Institute; also writes monthly columns in Good Housekeeping and Parents magazines
Good Housekeeping **Ph:** 212-649-2000
250 W 55th St
New York, NY 10019
www.emilypost.com/about/peggy.htm

Poti, Tom (1977-)
Professional hockey player
New York Rangers **Ph:** 212-465-6486
Madison Square Garden **Fax:** 212-465-6494
2 Pennsylvania Plaza
New York, NY 10121
www.newyorkrangers.com

Potok, Chaim (1929-2002)
Novelist (The Chosen; My Name is Asher Lev), philosopher, theologian, historian; was an ordained rabbi
Ballantine Books Publicity **Ph:** 212-782-9000
1745 Broadway
New York, NY 10019
www.randomhouse.com/BB

Potter, John E
Postmaster General & CEO of the US Postal Service
US Postal Service **Ph:** 202-268-2500
475 L'Enfant Plaza West SW **Fax:** 202-268-4860
Washington, DC 20260
www.usps.com/communications/organization/pmg.htm

Potter, Ned
Science correspondent for ABC News
ABC News **Ph:** 212-456-7777
77 W 66th St
New York, NY 10023
www.abcnews.go.com/WNT

Potter, Tom
Mayor of Portland, Oregon
1221 SW 4th Ave Suite 340 **Ph:** 503-823-4120
Portland, OR 97204 **Fax:** 503-823-3588
www.portlandonline.com/mayor

Potvin, Denis (1953-)
Hockey commentator and Hall of Fame defenseman (retired)
Florida Panthers **Ph:** 954-835-7000
BankAtlantic Center **Fax:** 954-835-7700
1 Panther Pkwy
Sunrise, FL 33323
www.floridapanthers.com

Pouillon, Nora (1943-)
Chef/restauranteur; owns Restaurant Nora and Asia Nora, both in Washington, DC
Restaurant Nora **Ph:** 202-462-5143
2132 Florida Ave NW
Washington, DC 20008
www.noras.com

Poundstone, Paula (1959-)
Comedian
William Morris Agency **Ph:** 310-859-4000
1 William Morris Pl **Fax:** 310-859-4462
Beverly Hills, CA 90212
www.paulapoundstone.com

Povich, Maury (1939-)
Host of the syndicated daytime TV talk show Maury
Maury Show **Ph:** 212-547-8400
Hotel Pennsylvania/Grand Ballroom **Fax:** 212-244-3548
15 Penn Plaza
New York, NY 10001
www.mauryshow.com

Powell, Colin (1937-)
Former US Secretary of State; a 4-Star General who is also a former Chairman of the Joint Chiefs of Staff; is currently a Strategic Limited Partner in the venture capital firm Kleiner Perkins Caufield & Byers
Kleiner Perkins Caufield & Byers **Ph:** 650-233-2750
Fax: 650-233-0300
2750 Sand Hill Rd
Menlo Park, CA 94025
www.kpcb.com

Powell, Dwane
Editorial cartoonist at the Raleigh News & Observer
Creators Syndicate Inc **Ph:** 310-337-7003
5777 W Century Blvd Suite 700 **Fax:** 310-337-7625
Los Angeles, CA 90045
www.creators.com

Powell, Elaine (1975-)
Professional basketball player
Chicago Sky **Ph:** 312-828-9550
20 W Kinzie St Suite 1000
Chicago, IL 60610
www.wnba.com/sky

Prager, Dennis (1948-)
Radio talk show host, author, and syndicated columnist
Creators Syndicate Inc **Ph:** 310-337-7003
5777 W Century Blvd Suite 700 **Fax:** 310-337-7625
Los Angeles, CA 90045
www.creators.com/opinion.html

Prather, Hugh (1938-)
Minister, lecturer, counselor, talk radio host (Living in the Light), and, with his wife Gayle, the author of numerous books, including Notes to Myself
Wisdom Radio **Ph:** 304-323-8000
PO Box 1546
Bluefield, WV 24701
www.beliefnet.com/author/author_92.html

Prelutsky, Jack (1940-)
Author of poetry books for children (The New Kid on the Block; The Dragons Are Singing Tonight)
HarperCollins Children's Books **Ph:** 212-261-6500
1350 Ave of the Americas
New York, NY 10019
www.harperchildrens.com

Prescott, Edward C, PhD (1940-)
Winner, with Finn E Kydland of Norway, of the 2004 Nobel Prize in Economics for contributions to dynamic macroeconomics: the time consistency of economic policy and the driving forces behind business
WP Carey School of Business **Ph:** 480-727-7977
Arizona State University **Fax:** 480-965-0748
PO Box 873806
Tempe, AZ 85287
wpcarey.asu.edu/ecn

Presley, Elvis (1935-1977)
Legendary singer known as the King of Rock and Roll
Elvis Presley Enterprises Inc **Ph:** 901-332-3322
3734 Elvis Presley Blvd
Memphis, TN 38116
www.elvis.com

Presley, Lisa Marie (1968-)
Singer; daughter of Elvis and sole owner & board chairperson of Elvis Presley Enterprises Inc.
William Morris Agency **Ph:** 310-859-4000
1 William Morris Pl **Fax:** 310-859-4462
Beverly HIlls, CA 90212
lisamariepresley.com

Press, Bill
Syndicated columnist; political analyst and radio & TV commentator
Tribune Media Services Inc **Ph:** 312-222-4444
435 N Michigan Ave Suite 1500
Chicago, IL 60611
tmsfeatures.com/productlist.htm

Pressler, Paul S
President & CEO of Gap Inc
Gap Inc **Ph:** 650-952-4400
2 Folsom St
San Francisco, CA 94105
www.gapinc.com

Preston, Kelly (1962-)
Actor
International Creative Management **Ph:** 310-550-4000
8942 Wilshire Blvd
Beverly Hills, CA 90211

Preston, Marilynn
A certified personal trainer and author of Energy Express, a syndicated column on sports & fitness; is also the creator/co-writer/co-executive producer of the syndicated Energy Express televison show
Creators Syndicate Inc **Ph:** 310-337-7003
5777 W Century Blvd Suite 700 **Fax:** 310-337-7625
Los Angeles, CA 90045
www.creators.com

Preston, Richard, PhD (1954-)
Author of The Hot Zone (considered non-fiction); also The Cobra Event (fiction)
Ballantine Books Publicity **Ph:** 212-782-9000
1745 Broadway
New York, NY 10019
www.richardpreston.net

Previn, Andre (1929-)
Musician, composer, conductor (classical and jazz)
Columbia Artists Management **Ph:** 212-841-9500
1790 Broadway **Fax:** 212-841-9744
New York, NY 10019
www.andre-previn.com

Price, Dave (1966-)
Weatherman and feature reporter for CBS News's The Early Show
The Early Show **Ph:** 212-975-2824
524 W 57th St
New York, NY 10019
www.cbsnews.com

Price, David (1940-)
US Representative from North Carolina (Democrat)
2162 Rayburn Bldg **Ph:** 202-225-1784
Washington, DC 20515 **Fax:** 202-225-2014
price.house.gov

Price, Deb
Writes a nationally syndicated column on gay and lesbian issues
Creators Syndicate Inc **Ph:** 310-337-7003
5777 W Century Blvd Suite 700 **Fax:** 310-337-7625
Los Angeles, CA 90045
www.creators.com

Price, Hilary (1969-)
Creator of the comic strip Rhymes With Orange
King Features Syndicate Inc **Ph:** 212-455-4000
888 7th Ave 2nd Fl
New York, NY 10019
www.rhymeswithorange.com

Price, Joan
Fitness speaker, writer, and instructor whose specialty is helping nonexercisers start and stick to an exercise program
Unconventional Moves **Ph:** 888-234-8837
454 Raspberry Ln
Sebastopol, CA 95472
www.joanprice.com

Price, Nick (1957-)
Professional golfer
PGA Tour **Ph:** 904-285-3700
100 PGA Tour Blvd
Ponte Vedra Beach, FL 32082
www.pgatour.com

Price, Reynolds (1933-)
Novelist, poet, and essayist; his nonfiction works often deal with religious/spiritual subjects
Duke University Dept of English **Ph:** 919-684-2741
Fax: 919-684-4871
Box 90014
Durham, NC 27708
fds.duke.edu/db/aas/English

Price, Richard (1949-)
Author of Clockers
Random House Publicity **Ph:** 212-782-9000
1745 Broadway
New York, NY 10019
www.randomhouse.com

Price, Tom (1954-)
US Representative from Georgia (Republican)
506 Cannon Bldg **Ph:** 202-225-4501
Washington, DC 20515 **Fax:** 202-225-4656
tomprice.house.gov

Prickett, Charlene
Fitness instructor
Charlene Prickett Inc — **Ph:** 403-244-6621
PO Box 4697 — **Fax:** 403-243-9980
Station C
Calgary, AB T2T5P1
www.charleneprickett.com

Priestley, Jason (1969-)
Actor; also drives race cars
United Talent Agency — **Ph:** 310-273-6700
9560 Wilshire Blvd 5th Fl — **Fax:** 310-247-1111
Beverly Hills, CA 90212

Primeau, Keith (1971-)
Professional hockey player
Philadelphia Flyers — **Ph:** 215-465-4500
Wachovia Center — **Fax:** 215-389-9403
3601 S Broad St
Philadelphia, PA 19148
www.philadelphiaflyers.com

Prince, Tayshaun (1980-)
Professional basketball player
Detroit Pistons — **Ph:** 248-377-0100
Palace at Auburn Hills — **Fax:** 248-377-4262
4 Championship Dr
Auburn Hills, MI 48326
www.nba.com/pistons

Prinze, Freddie Jr (1976-)
Actor
International Creative Management — **Ph:** 310-550-4000
8942 Wilshire Blvd
Beverly Hills, CA 90211
abc.go.com/primetime/freddie

Prior, Mark (1980-)
Professional baseball player
Chicago Cubs — **Ph:** 773-404-2827
Wrigley Field — **Fax:** 773-404-4129
1060 W Addison St
Chicago, IL 60613
chicago.cubs.mlb.com

Pritikin, Robert
Diet book author
Pritikin Longevity Center & Spa — **Ph:** 305-935-7100
Fax: 305-935-7371
19735 Turnberry Way — **TF:** 800-327-4914
Aventura, FL 33180

Probst, Jeff (1962-)
Host of Survivor
Endeavor — **Ph:** 310-248-2000
9601 Wilshire Blvd 3rd Fl — **Fax:** 310-248-2020
Beverly Hills, CA 90210
www.cbs.com/primetime/survivor12

Pronger, Chris (1974-)
Professional hockey player
Edmonton Oilers — **Ph:** 780-414-4000
11230 110th St — **Fax:** 780-409-5890
Edmonton, AB T5G3H7
www.edmontonoilers.com

Proulx, Annie (1935-)
Writes novels (The Shipping News) and short stories
Liz Darhansoff — **Ph:** 917-305-1300
Darhansoff Verrill & Feldman — **Fax:** 917-305-1400
236 W 26th St Suite 802
New York, NY 10001
www.annieproulx.com

Pruden, Wesley (1935-)
Editor-in-chief of the Washington Times
The Washington Times — **Ph:** 202-636-3000
3600 New York Ave NE — **Fax:** 202-636-8906
Washington, DC 20002
washingtontimes.com

Prudhomme, Paul
Chef, cookbook author, and owner of K-Paul's Louisiana Kitchen
K-Paul's Louisiana Kitchen — **Ph:** 504-524-7394
416 Chartres St
New Orleans, LA 70130
www.chefpaul.com

Prusiner, Stanley B, MD (1942-)
Winner of the 1997 Nobel Prize in Medicine for his discovery of Prions, a new biological principle of infection
University of California — **Ph:** 415-476-4482
Dept of Neurology — **Fax:** 415-476-8386
Box 0518
San Francisco, CA 94143
directory.ucsf.edu

Pryce, Deborah (1951-)
US Representative from Ohio (Republican)
204 Cannon Bldg — **Ph:** 202-225-2015
Washington, DC 20515
www.house.gov/pryce

Pryor, Mark (1963-)
US Senator from Arkansas (Democrat)
217 Russell Bldg — **Ph:** 202-224-2353
Washington, DC 20510 — **Fax:** 202-228-0908
pryor.senate.gov

Ptak, Frank
President & CEO of the Marmon Group, an international association of more than 100 companies that operate independently within diverse business sectors
Marmon Group Inc — **Ph:** 312-372-9500
225 W Washington St — **Fax:** 312-845-5305
Chicago, IL 60606

Puck, Wolfgang (1949-)
Chef, cookbook author, and restaurateur; owns several restaurants (including Spago) with his wife & partner, Barbara Lazaroff
Spago Beverly Hills — **Ph:** 310-385-0880
176 N Canon Dr — **Fax:** 310-385-9690
Beverly Hills, CA 90210
www.wolfgangpuck.com

Pujols, Albert (1980-)
Professional baseball player
Saint Louis Cardinals — **Ph:** 314-421-3060
250 Stadium Plaza — **Fax:** 314-425-0640
Saint Louis, MO 63102
stlouis.cardinals.mlb.com

Pullman, Bill (1953-)
Actor
One Entertainment — **Ph:** 310-550-9500
9220 Sunset Blvd Suite 306
Los Angeles, CA 90069

Pullman, Philip (1946-)
Author of the trilogy His Dark Materials, which ends with The Amber Spyglass, the first children's book to win the Whitbread Book of the Year Award
Random House Children's Books — **Ph:** 212-782-9000
Publicity Dept
1745 Broadway
New York, NY 10019
www.philip-pullman.com

Purcell, Bill
Mayor of Nashville
225 Polk Ave — **Ph:** 615-862-6000
Nashville, TN 37203 — **Fax:** 615-862-6040
www.nashville.gov/mayor

Putnam, Adam (1974-)
US Representative from Florida (Republican)
1213 Longworth Bldg — **Ph:** 202-225-1252
Washington, DC 20515 — **Fax:** 202-226-0585
www.house.gov/putnam

Putnam, Howard
Author, speaker, and advisor on business issues, change, leadership and ethics; former CEO of Southwest Airlines
SpeakersOffice Inc — **Ph:** 760-603-8110
5927 Balfour Ct Suite 103 — **Fax:** 760-603-8010
Carlsbad, CA 92008
www.howardputnam.com

Pynchon, Thomas (1937-)
Novelist (Gravity's Rainbow)
Penguin Publicity — **Ph:** 212-366-2000
375 Hudson St
New York, NY 10014
us.penguingroup.com

Q

Quaid, Dennis (1954-)
Actor
William Morris Agency — **Ph:** 310-859-4000
1 William Morris Pl — **Fax:** 310-859-4462
Beverly Hills, CA 90212

Quaid, Randy (1950-)
Actor
Gersh Agency — **Ph:** 310-274-6611
232 N Canon Dr
Beverly Hills, CA 90210

Quaranta, Santino (1984-)
Professional soccer player
DC United — **Ph:** 202-587-5000
RFK Stadium — **Fax:** 202-587-5400
2400 E Capitol St SE
Washington, DC 20003
dcunited.mlsnet.com

Quayle, Dan (1947-)
Former Vice President of the United States, under President George HW Bush
7001 N Scottsdale Rd Suite 2010 — **Ph:** 480-922-5700
Scottsdale, AZ 85253
www.vicepresidentdanquayle.com

Qubein, Nido
Keynote speaker, seminar leader, corporate consultant, author
Creative Services Inc — **Ph:** 336-889-3010
PO Box 6008 — **Fax:** 336-885-3001
High Point, NC 27262
www.nidoqubein.com

Queen Latifah (1970-)
Actor, singer, rapper; real name is Dana Owens
William Morris Agency **Ph:** 310-859-4000
1 William Morris Pl **Fax:** 310-859-4462
Beverly Hills, CA 90212
www.wma.com/queen_latifah/summary

Quenneville, Joel (1958-)
Hockey coach
Colorado Avalanche **Ph:** 303-405-1100
Pepsi Center
1000 Chopper Cir
Denver, CO 80204
www.coloradoavalanche.com

Quick, Becky
Co-anchor of Squawk Box on CNBC
CNBC **Ph:** 201-735-2622
900 Sylvan Ave
Englewood Cliffs, NJ 07632
moneycentral.msn.com/cnbc/tv

Quindlen, Anna (1953-)
Journalist (Newsweek columnist) and novelist (One True Thing)
International Creative Management **Ph:** 212-556-5600
40 W 57th St 17th Fl
New York, NY 10019
www.randomhouse.com/features/aquindlen

Quinn, Aidan (1959-)
Actor
Special Artists Agency **Ph:** 310-859-9688
9465 Wilshire Blvd Suite 890
Beverly Hills, CA 90212

Quinn, Brigitte
An anchor for FOX News Live
FOX News Channel **Ph:** 212-301-3000
1211 Ave of the Americas
New York, NY 10036
www.foxnews.com/fnctv

Quinones, John (1952-)
ABC News correspondent for Prime Time Live
Prime Time Live **Ph:** 212-456-7777
147 Columbus Ave
New York, NY 10023
www.abcnews.go.com/Primetime

Quivers, Robin (1952-)
Co-host of the Howard Stern Show
SIRIUS Satellite Radio **Ph:** 212-584-5100
1221 Ave of the Americas
New York, NY 10020
quivers.atspace.com

Rabe, David (1940-)
Playwright; has also written several screenplays
Creative Artists Agency **Ph:** 310-288-4545
9830 Wilshire Blvd **Fax:** 310-288-4800
Beverly Hills, CA 90212

Rackers, Neil (1976-)
Professional football player
Arizona Cardinals **Ph:** 602-379-0101
8701 S Hardy Dr **Fax:** 602-379-1819
Tempe, AZ 85284
www.azcardinals.com

Radanovich, George (1955-)
US Representative from California (Republican)
438 Cannon Bldg **Ph:** 202-225-4540
Washington, DC 20515 **Fax:** 202-225-3402
www.radanovich.house.gov

Raddatz, Martha
ABC News chief White House correspondent
ABC News **Ph:** 202-222-7700
1717 DeSales St NW
Washington, DC 20036
www.abcnews.go.com/WNT

Radke, Brad (1972-)
Professional baseball player
Minnesota Twins **Ph:** 612-375-1366
Hubert H Humphrey Metrodome **Fax:** 612-375-7473
34 Kirby Puckett Pl
Minneapolis, MN 55415
minnesota.twins.mlb.com

Radmanovic, Vladimir (1980-)
Professional basketball player
Los Angeles Clippers **Ph:** 213-742-7100
Staples Center **Fax:** 213-742-7550
1111 S Figueroa St Suite 1100
Los Angeles, CA 90015
www.nba.com/clippers

Raeside, Adrian (1957-)
Editorial cartoonist; also creator of the comic strip The Other Coast
Creators Syndicate Inc **Ph:** 310-337-7003
5777 W Century Blvd Suite 700 **Fax:** 310-337-7625
Los Angeles, CA 90045
www.creators.com

Rafalski, Brian (1973-)
Professional hockey player
New Jersey Devils — **Ph:** 201-935-6050
Continental Airlines Arena — **Fax:** 201-935-2127
50 Rt 120N
East Rutherford, NJ 07073
www.newjerseydevils.com

Rafter, Patrick (1972-)
Professional tennis player
SFX Sports Group — **Ph:** 202-686-2000
5335 Wisconsin Ave NW — **Fax:** 202-686-5050
Suite 850
Washington, DC 20015
www.sfxsports.com

Rahall, Nick (1949-)
US Representative from West Virginia (Democrat)
2307 Rayburn Bldg — **Ph:** 202-225-3452
Washington, DC 20515 — **Fax:** 202-225-9061
www.rahall.house.gov

Raichlen, Steven
Author of the Barbecue Bible series; also a journalist, cooking teacher, and TV host (Barbecue University)
Workman Publishing — **Ph:** 212-254-5900
708 Broadway
New York, NY 10003
www.barbecuebible.com

Rainwater, Gary
Chairman, CEO, and president of Ameren Corp, a provider of electric and natural gas services
Ameren Corp — **Ph:** 314-621-3222
1901 Chouteau Ave
Saint Louis, MO 63103
www.ameren.com

Raitt, Bonnie (1949-)
Singer/songwriter, guitarist
Capitol Records — **Ph:** 323-462-6252
1750 N Vine St — **Fax:** 323-469-0384
Hollywood, CA 90028
www.bonnieraitt.com

Rajamannar, MV
Chairman & CEO of Diners Club North America
Diners Club North America — **Ph:** 773-380-5100
8430 W Bryn Mawr Ave
Chicago, IL 60631
www.dinersclubnorthamerica.com

Rajapatirana, Sarath, PhD
Economist; visiting fellow at the American Enterprise Institute and an economic adviser to the World Bank
American Enterprise Institute for Public Policy Research — **Ph:** 202-862-5800 — **Fax:** 202-862-7177
1150 17th St NW Suite 1100
Washington, DC 20036
www.aei.org

Rakove, Jack N
Author of Original Meanings: Politics and Ideas in the Making of the Constitution
Vintage/Anchor Publicity — **Ph:** 212-572-2420
1745 Broadway 20th Fl
New York, NY 10019
www.randomhouse.com/vintage

Rall, Ted (1963-)
Editorial cartoonist; also an illustrator, columnist, and radio commentator
Universal Press Syndicate — **Ph:** 816-932-6600
4520 Main St
Kansas City, MO 64111
www.rall.com

Ralston, Steve (1974-)
Professional soccer player
New England Revolution — **Ph:** 508-543-5001
Gillette Stadium — **Fax:** 508-384-9128
1 Patriot Pl
Foxborough, MA 02035
www.revolutionsoccer.net

Ramirez, Aramis (1978-)
Professional baseball player
Chicago Cubs — **Ph:** 773-404-2827
Wrigley Field — **Fax:** 773-404-4129
1060 W Addison St
Chicago, IL 60613
chicago.cubs.mlb.com

Ramirez, Manny (1972-)
Professional baseball player
Boston Red Sox — **Ph:** 617-267-9440
Fenway Park — **Fax:** 617-236-6797
4 Yawkey Way
Boston, MA 02215
boston.redsox.mlb.com

Ramirez, Michael
Senior editor and editorial cartoonist for Investor's Business Daily's editorial page
Copley News Service — **Ph:** 619-293-1818
PO Box 120190
San Diego, CA 92112
www.copleynews.com

Ramirez, Ramon (1969-)
Professional soccer player
Club Deportivo Chivas USA **Ph:** 310-630-4550
Home Depot Center **Fax:** 310-630-4551
18400 Avalon Blvd
Carson, CA 90746
chivas.usa.mlsnet.com

Ramis, Harold (1944-)
Screenwriter/producer/director; actor
United Talent Agency **Ph:** 310-273-6700
9560 Wilshire Blvd 5th Fl **Fax:** 310-247-1111
Beverly Hills, CA 90212

Ramos, Jorge (1958-)
News anchor considered to be one of the most influential Latinos in the US; also writes a syndicated column and provides radio commentary to dozens of stations
Univision Television Network **Ph:** 305-471-4346
9405 NW 41st St
Miami, FL 33178
www.jorgeramos.com

Ramsey, Dave
Author (Financial Peace) and radio talk show host; writes and talks about financial issues related to removing debt
Lampo Group **Ph:** 615-371-8881
1749 Mallory Ln Suite 100 **Fax:** 615-371-5007
Brentwood, TN 37207
www.daveramsey.com

Ramsey, Marshall
Editorial cartoonist for the Clarion Ledger in Jackson, MS
Copley News Service **Ph:** 619-293-1818
PO Box 120190
San Diego, CA 92112
www.copleynews.com

Ramsey, Patrick (1979-)
Professional football player
Washington Redskins **Ph:** 703-726-7000
21300 Redskin Park Dr **Fax:** 703-726-7086
Ashburn, VA 20147
www.redskins.com

Ramstad, Jim (1946-)
US Representative from Minnesota (Republican)
103 Cannon Bldg **Ph:** 202-225-2871
Washington, DC 20515 **Fax:** 202-225-6351
www.house.gov/ramstad

Randi, James (1928-)
Magician & escape artist; also investigates & demystifies paranormal and pseudoscientific claims
James Randi Educational Foundation **Ph:** 954-467-1112 **Fax:** 954-467-1660
201 SE 12th St
Fort Lauderdale, FL 33316
www.randi.org

Randle El, Antwaan (1979-)
Professional football player
Washington Redskins **Ph:** 703-726-7000
21300 Redskin Park Dr **Fax:** 703-726-7086
Ashburn, VA 20147
www.redskins.com

Randolph, Willie (1954-)
Baseball manager
New York Mets **Ph:** 718-507-6387
Shea Stadium **Fax:** 718-507-6395
123-01 Roosevelt Ave
Flushing, NY 11368
newyork.mets.mlb.com

Randolph, Zach (1981-)
Professional basketball player
Portland Trail Blazers **Ph:** 503-234-9291
1 Center Ct Suite 200 **Fax:** 503-736-2187
Portland, OR 97227
www.nba.com/blazers

Rangel, Charles B (1930-)
US Representative from New York (Democrat)
2354 Rayburn Bldg **Ph:** 202-225-4365
Washington, DC 20515 **Fax:** 202-225-0816
www.house.gov/rangel

Ransome, James E (1964-)
Illustrator of children's books (The Creation; Uncle Jed's Barbershop)
107 Knollwood Rd **Ph:** 845-876-2148
Rhinebeck, NY 12572
www.jamesransome.com

Rascal Flatts
Country music group (Jay DeMarcus, Gary Levox, and Joe Don Rooney)
William Morris Agency **Ph:** 615-963-3000
1600 Division St Suite 300 **Fax:** 615-963-3090
Nashville, TN 37203
www.rascalflatts.com

Rasmussen, Gerry
Draws the comic strip Betty; Gary Delainey writes it
United Feature Syndicate **Ph:** 212-293-8500
200 Madison Ave
New York, NY 10016
www.unitedfeatures.com

Raspberry, William (1935-)
Washington Post columnist
Washington Post **Ph:** 202-334-6000
1150 15th St NW
Washington, DC 20071
www.washingtonpost.com

Ratcliffe, David M (1948-)
Chairman, president, and CEO of Southern Co (an energy company)
Southern Co **Ph:** 404-506-7903
270 Peachtree St NW **Fax:** 404-506-0598
Atlanta, GA 30303
www.southerncompany.com

Rathbun, Kent
Executive chef and proprietor of Abacus and Jasper's restaurants, both in the Dallas area
Abacus Restaurant **Ph:** 214-559-3111
4511 McKinney Ave
Dallas, TX 75205
www.abacus-restaurant.com

Rathbun, Kevin
Executive chef & owner of Rathbun's in Atlanta
Rathbun's at the Stove Works **Ph:** 404-524-8280
Inman Park **Fax:** 404-524-8580
112 Krog St Suite R
Atlanta, GA 30307
www.rathbunsrestaurant.com

Rather, Dan (1931-)
Veteran newsman and correspondent for 60 Minutes; former anchor for CBS Evening News
CBS News **Ph:** 212-975-4114
524 W 57th St
New York, NY 10019
www.cbsnews.com

Rathje, Mike (1974-)
Professional hockey player
Philadelphia Flyers **Ph:** 215-465-4500
Wachovia Center **Fax:** 215-389-9403
3601 S Broad St
Philadelphia, PA 19148
www.philadelphiaflyers.com

Rathmann, Peggy (1953-)
Children's book author/illustrator (Officer Buckle and Gloria)
GP Putnam's Sons Books for Young Readers **Ph:** 212-366-2000
Publicity Dept
345 Hudson St
New York, NY 10014
www.peggyrathmann.com

Ratigan, Dylan
Host of On the Money and an anchor of Business Day
CNBC **Ph:** 201-735-2622
900 Sylvan Ave
Englewood Cliffs, NJ 07632
moneycentral.msn.com/cnbc/tv

Ratner, Brett (1969-)
Movie director/producer
Creative Artists Agency **Ph:** 310-288-4545
9830 Wilshire Blvd **Fax:** 310-288-4800
Beverly Hills, CA 90212

Ratner, Bruce
Principal owner of the New Jersey Nets basketball team
New Jersey Nets **Ph:** 201-935-8888
Nets Champion Center **Fax:** 201-635-3268
390 Murray Hill Pkwy
East Rutherford, NJ 07073
www.nba.com/nets/news/bruce_ratner.html

Rattay, Tim (1977-)
Professional football player
Tampa Bay Buccaneers **Ph:** 813-870-2700
1 Buccaneer Pl **Fax:** 813-878-0813
Tampa, FL 33607
www.buccaneers.com

Ray, Man (1890-1976)
Artist (photographer, painter, sculptor, and filmmaker); born Emmanuel Radnitsky
Man Ray Trust **Ph:** 516-938-7373
225 Park Ave **Fax:** 516-931-8438
Hicksville, NY 11801
www.manraytrust.com

Ray, Rachael
Host of 30-Minute Meals (which is also the name of one of her cookbooks) and $40 a day; both shows are on Food Network
Food Network **Ph:** 212-398-8836
75 9th Ave **Fax:** 212-736-7716
New York, NY 10011
www.foodtv.com

Raycroft, Andrew (1980-)
Professional hockey player
Boston Bruins **Ph:** 617-624-1900
1 FleetCenter Pl Suite 250 **Fax:** 617-523-7184
Boston, MA 02114
www.bostonbruins.com

Razov, Ante (1974-)
Professional soccer player
Club Deportivo Chivas USA **Ph:** 310-630-4550
Home Depot Center **Fax:** 310-630-4551
18400 Avalon Blvd Suite 500
Carson, CA 90746
chivas.usa.mlsnet.com

Reagan, Michael (1946-)
Radio talk show host (conservative); oldest son of Ronald Reagan
Radio America **Ph:** 202-408-0944
1030 15th St NW **Fax:** 202-408-1087
Washington, DC 20005
www.radioamerica.org

Reagan, Nancy (1921-)
Former First Lady of the US; widow of President Ronald Reagan
Ronald Reagan Presidential Foundation **Ph:** 805-522-2977 **Fax:** 805-520-9702
40 Presidential Dr
Simi Valley, CA 93065
www.reaganfoundation.org

Reagan, Ron
Co-host of MSNBC's Connected: Coast to Coast
MSNBC TV **Ph:** 201-583-5000
1 MSNBC Plaza
Secaucus, NJ 07094
www.msnbc.msn.com/id/3080263

Reagan, Ronald (1911-2004)
40th US President; actor
Ronald Reagan Presidential Foundation **Ph:** 805-522-2977 **Fax:** 805-520-9702
40 Presidential Dr
Simi Valley, CA 93065
www.reaganfoundation.org

Reasoner, Harry M (1939-)
Attorney; principal area of practice is complex civil litigation and has represented major oil companies, investment bankers, chemical companies, pipeline companies, TV networks, and computer companies
Vinson & Elkins LLP **Ph:** 713-758-2358
First City Tower **Fax:** 713-615-5173
1001 Fannin St Suite 2300
Houston, TX 77002
www.velaw.com

Recchi, Mark (1968-)
Professional hockey player
Carolina Hurricanes **Ph:** 919-467-7825
RBC Center **Fax:** 919-462-7030
1400 Edwards Mill Rd
Raleigh, NC 27607
www.carolinahurricanes.com

Rechin, Bill
Co-creator, with Don Wilder, of the comic strip Crock
King Features Syndicate Inc **Ph:** 212-455-4000
888 7th Ave 2nd Fl
New York, NY 10019
www.kingfeatures.com

Red Hot Chili Peppers
Rock group
Creative Artists Agency **Ph:** 310-288-4545
9830 Wilshire Blvd **Fax:** 310-288-4800
Beverly Hills, CA 90212
www.redhotchilipeppers.com

Redd, Michael (1979-)
Professional basketball player
Milwaukee Bucks **Ph:** 414-227-0500
Bradley Center **Fax:** 414-227-0543
1001 N 4th St
Milwuakee, WI 53203
www.nba.com/bucks

Redden, Wade (1977-)
Professional hockey player
Ottawa Senators **Ph:** 613-599-0250
Corel Center **Fax:** 613-599-0358
1000 Palladium Dr
Kanata, ON K2V1A5
www.ottawasenators.com

Redfield, James (1950-)
Author of The Celestine Prophecy
Warner Books **Ph:** 212-522-7200
c/o Author Mail
1271 Ave of the Americas
New York, NY 10020
www.celestinevision.com

Redford, Robert (1936-)
Actor/producer/director
Creative Artists Agency **Ph:** 310-288-4545
9830 Wilshire Blvd **Fax:** 310-288-4800
Beverly Hills, CA 90212

Redgrave, Vanessa (1937-)
Actor
International Creative Management **Ph:** 310-550-4000
8942 Wilshire Blvd
Beverly Hills, CA 90211

Redstone, Shari
President of National Amusements Inc, which owns movie theater chains and is the parent company of both Viacom and CBS Corp
National Amusements Inc **Ph:** 781-461-1600
200 Elm St **Fax:** 781-407-0052
Dedham, MA 02026
www.national-amusements.com

Redstone, Sumner M (1923-)
Founder & Executive Chairman of Viacom and Chairman of CBS Corp
Viacom Inc **Ph:** 212-258-6000
1515 Broadway 52nd Fl **Fax:** 212-258-6354
New York, NY 10036
www.viacom.com

Reed, Ed (1978-)
Professional football player
Baltimore Ravens **Ph:** 410-547-8100
1101 Russell St **Fax:** 410-547-8112
Baltimore, MD 21230
www.baltimoreravens.com

Reed, Ishmael (1938-)
Poet, novelist, essayist, playwright, and editor, as well as a teacher and MacArthur fellow
University of Delaware Library **Ph:** 302-831-2229
Special Collections
Newark, DE 19717
www.lib.udel.edu/ud/spec/findaids/reed

Reed, Jack (1949-)
US Senator from Rhode Island (Democrat)
728 Hart Bldg **Ph:** 202-224-4642
Washington, DC 20510 **Fax:** 202-224-4680
reed.senate.gov

Reed, Jeff (1979-)
Professional football player
Pittsburgh Steelers **Ph:** 412-432-7800
3400 S Water St **Fax:** 412-432-7878
Pittsburgh, PA 15203
www.pittsburghsteelers.com

Reed, Lou (1942-)
Musician
CESD Talent Agency **Ph:** 310-475-2111
10635 Santa Monica Blvd
Suites 130/135
Los Angeles, CA 90025
www.loureed.org

Reed, Ralph E Jr, PhD (1961-)
PR consultant and a top political newsmaker; has worked on seven presidential campaigns and was executive director of the Christian Coalition from 1989-1997
Century Strategies **Ph:** 770-232-2929
3235 Satellite Blvd Suite 575
Duluth, GA 30096
www.censtrat.com

Reed, Rex (1938-)
Film critic (On the Town)
New York Observer **Ph:** 212-755-2400
54 E 64th St
New York, NY 10021
www.observer.com

Reed, Stephen R (1949-)
Mayor of Harrisburg, Pennsylvania
10 N Market Sq **Ph:** 717-255-3040
Harrisburg, PA 17101 **Fax:** 717-255-3036
www.harrisburgpa.gov

Reese, Charley (1937-)
Journalist/syndicated op-ed columnist (conservative)
King Features Syndicate Inc **Ph:** 212-455-4000
888 7th Ave 2nd Fl
New York, NY 10019
www.kingfeatures.com

Reese, Della (1931-)
Singer; actor; is also an ordained minister
William Morris Agency **Ph:** 310-859-4000
1 William Morris Pl **Fax:** 310-859-4462
Beverly Hills, CA 90212
www.dellareese.com

Reeve, Christopher (1952-2004)
Actor and advocate of spinal cord research
Christopher Reeve Paralysis Foundation **Ph:** 800-225-0292
636 Morris Tpke Suite 3A
Short Hills, NJ 07078
www.christopherreeve.org

Reeves, Keanu (1964-)
Actor
Creative Artists Agency **Ph:** 310-288-4545
9830 Wilshire Blvd **Fax:** 310-288-4800
Beverly Hills, CA 90212

Reeves, Richard (1936-)
Author and syndicated columnist
Universal Press Syndicate **Ph:** 816-932-6600
4520 Main St
Kansas City, MO 64111
www.richardreeves.com

Regula, Ralph (1924-)
US Representative from Ohio (Republican)
2306 Rayburn Bldg **Ph:** 202-225-3876
Washington, DC 20515 **Fax:** 202-225-3059
wwwc.house.gov/regula

Rehberg, Dennis (1955-)
US Representative from Montana (Republican)
516 Cannon Bldg **Ph:** 202-225-3211
Washington, DC 20515 **Fax:** 202-225-5687
www.house.gov/rehberg

Rehm, Diane (1936-)
Host of the Diane Rehm Show, a talk show on National Public Radio
National Public Radio **Ph:** 202-513-2000
635 Massachusetts Ave NW **Fax:** 202-513-3329
Washington, DC 20001
www.npr.org

Rehr, Henrik (1964-)
Draws the comic strip Ferd'nand, which was originally created in 1937 by Henning Dahl Mikkelsen (d. 1982)
United Feature Syndicate **Ph:** 212-293-8500
200 Madison Ave
New York, NY 10016
www.unitedfeatures.com

Reich, Howard (1954-)
Music critic (jazz)
Chicago Tribune **Ph:** 312-222-3232
435 N Michigan Ave **Fax:** 312-222-4674
Chicago, IL 60611

Reich, Robert B (1946-)
Co-founder and national editor of The American Prospect; Secretary of Labor in the Clinton Administration; nonfiction author
The American Prospect **Ph:** 617-570-8030
5 Broad St **Fax:** 617-570-8028
Boston, MA 02109
www.prospect.org

Reich, Steven F
Attorney; as Sr. Assoc. Counsel to President Clinton, duties included supervising the legal team that responded to investigations conducted by independent counsels, federal prosecutors, and congressional committees
Manatt Phelps & Phillips LLP **Ph:** 212-790-4500
7 Times Sq **Fax:** 212-790-4545
New York, NY 10036
www.manatt.com

Reichert, Dave (1950-)
US Representative from Washington (Republican)
1223 Longworth Bldg **Ph:** 202-225-7761
Washington, DC 20515 **Fax:** 202-225-8673
www.house.gov/reichert

Reid, Andy (1958-)
Football coach
Philadelphia Eagles **Ph:** 215-463-2500
NovaCare Complex **Fax:** 215-339-5464
1 NovaCare Way
Philadelphia, PA 19145
www.philadelphiaeagles.com

Reid, Chip
NBC News correspondent; covers Congress and politics
NBC News **Ph:** 202-885-4200
4001 Nebraska Ave NW
Washington, DC 20016
www.msnbc.msn.com/id/3689499

Reid, Harry (1939-)
US Senator from Nevada (Democrat); Senate Minority Leader
528 Hart Bldg **Ph:** 202-224-3542
Washington, DC 20510 **Fax:** 202-224-7327
reid.senate.gov

Reid, Travis
President & CEO, Loews Cineplex Theatres
Loews Cineplex Entertainment Corp **Ph:** 646-521-6200
711 5th Ave
New York, NY 10022
www.fandango.com/BoardOfDirectors.aspx

Rein, Jeffrey A
President & COO of Walgreen Co
Walgreen Co **Ph:** 847-940-2500
200 Wilmot Rd
Deerfield, IL 60015
www.walgreens.com/about/press

Reinemund, Steven S (1949-)
Chairman and CEO of PepsiCo
PepsiCo Inc **Ph:** 914-253-2000
700 Anderson Hill Rd
Purchase, NY 10577
www.pepsico.com

Reiner, John (1956-)
Cartoonist who took over writing and drawing The Lockhorns from the late Bill Hoest
King Features Syndicate Inc **Ph:** 212-455-4000
888 7th Ave 2nd Fl
New York, NY 10019
www.kingfeatures.com

Reiner, Rob (1947-)
Movie director & producer; actor
William Morris Agency **Ph:** 310-859-4000
1 William Morris Pl **Fax:** 310-859-4462
Beverly Hills, CA 90212

Reinhardt, Uwe E, PhD (1937-)
An authority on health care economics
Princeton University **Ph:** 609-258-4781
Woodrow Wilson School of Public & International Affairs **Fax:** 609-258-5974
351 Wallace Hall
Princeton, NJ 08544
www.wws.princeton.edu

Reinsdorf, Jerry (1936-)
Chairman/owner of the Chicago Bulls basketball team and the Chicago White Sox baseball club
Chicago Bulls **Ph:** 312-455-4000
United Center **Fax:** 312-455-4198
1901 W Madison St
Chicago, IL 60612
www.nba.com/bulls/news/jerry_reinsdorf.html

Reis, Matt (1975-)
Professional soccer player
New England Revolution **Ph:** 508-543-5001
Gillette Stadium **Fax:** 508-384-9128
1 Patriot Pl
Foxborough, MA 02035
www.revolutionsoccer.net

Reiser, Paul (1957-)
Actor, comedian, and writer
Creative Artists Agency **Ph:** 310-288-4545
9830 Wilshire Blvd **Fax:** 310-288-4800
Beverly Hills, CA 90212

Reitman, Ivan (1946-)
Movie producer and director
Creative Artists Agency **Ph:** 310-288-4545
9830 Wilshire Blvd **Fax:** 310-288-4800
Beverly Hills, CA 90212

Relient K
Music group (power pop/punk rock/Christian rock)
CAA Nashville **Ph:** 615-383-8787
3310 West End Ave 5th Fl **Fax:** 615-383-4937
Nashville, TN 37203
www.relientk.com

Rell, M Jodi (1946-)
Governor of Connecticut (Republican)
210 Capitol Ave **Ph:** 860-566-4840
Hartford, CT 06106 **Fax:** 860-524-7395
www.ct.gov/governorrell

Remnick, David (1958-)
Editor of The New Yorker and author of Lenin's Tomb and other books
New Yorker Magazine **Ph:** 212-286-5400
4 Times Sq **Fax:** 212-286-5735
New York, NY 10036

Rendell, Edward G (1944-)
Governor of Pennsylvania (Democrat)
225 Main Capitol Bldg **Ph:** 717-787-2500
Harrisburg, PA 17120 **Fax:** 717-772-8284
www.governor.state.pa.us

Rendell, Ruth (1930-)
British author of mystery/detective books
Random House Publicity **Ph:** 212-782-9000
1745 Broadway
New York, NY 10019
www.randomhouse.com

Renney, Tom
Hockey coach
New York Rangers **Ph:** 212-465-6486
Madison Square Garden **Fax:** 212-465-6494
2 Pennsylvania Plaza
New York, NY 10121
www.newyorkrangers.com

Rennison, Louise
British comedy writer and author of books written from the point of view of a 14-year-old (Georgia Nicolson)
HarperCollins Children's Books **Ph:** 212-261-6500
1350 Ave of the Americas
New York, NY 10019
www.georgianicolson.com

Renteria, Edgar (1975-)
Professional baseball player
Atlanta Braves **Ph:** 404-522-7630
PO Box 4064 **Fax:** 404-614-1392
Atlanta, GA 30302
atlanta.braves.mlb.com

Renwick, Glenn M (1955-)
President & CEO of Progressive Corp
Progressive Corp **Ph:** 440-461-5000
6300 Wilson Mills Rd
Mayfield Village, OH 44143
www.progressive.com/investors

Renzi, Rick (1958-)
US Representative from Arizona (Republican)
418 Cannon Bldg **Ph:** 202-225-2315
Washington, DC 20515 **Fax:** 202-226-9739
www.house.gov/renzi

Resnick, John
Host of Legends of Success, the talk radio show on which he interviews successful entrepreneurs and businessmen
Legends of Success **Ph:** 717-791-9774
3428 Lisburn Rd **Fax:** 717-791-9781
Mechanicsburg, PA 17055 **TF:** 800-458-5656
www.legendsofsuccess.com

Reubens, Paul (1952-)
Comedian (as Pee Wee Herman); actor
United Talent Agency **Ph:** 310-273-6700
9560 Wilshire Blvd 5th Fl **Fax:** 310-247-1111
Beverly Hills, CA 90212

Rey, HA (1898-1977)
Author of the Curious George books
Houghton Mifflin Children's Books **Ph:** 617-351-5000
222 Berkeley St 8th Fl
Boston, MA 02116
www.houghtonmifflinbooks.com/features/cgsite

Reyes, Silvestre (1944-)
US Representative from Texas (Democrat)
2433 Rayburn Bldg **Ph:** 202-225-4831
Washington, DC 20515 **Fax:** 202-225-2016
wwwc.house.gov/reyes

Reynolds, Alan (1942-)
A supply side economist; currently a senior fellow at the Cato Institute, a libertarian think tank
Cato Institute **Ph:** 202-842-0200
1000 Massachusetts Ave NW **Fax:** 202-842-3490
Washington, DC 20001
www.cato.org

Reynolds, Burt (1936-)
Actor
International Creative Management **Ph:** 310-550-4000
8942 Wilshire Blvd
Beverly Hills, CA 90211
www.burtreynolds.com

Reynolds, Dean
ABC News national correspondent
ABC News Chicago Bureau **Ph:** 312-899-4015
190 N State St 3rd Fl **Fax:** 312-899-4050
Chicago, IL 60601
www.abcnews.go.com/WNT

Reynolds, Debbie (1932-)
Actor
William Morris Agency **Ph:** 310-859-4000
1 William Morris Pl **Fax:** 310-859-4462
Beverly Hills, CA 90212
www.debbiereynolds.com

Reynolds, Don
Economic forecaster; a consulting economist, futurist, and professional speaker
1320 S University Dr Suite 1000 **Ph:** 817-882-4905
Fax: 817-882-4905
Fort Worth, TX 76109
www.donreynolds.com

Reynolds, Joey (1946-)
Host of a late-night radio talk show; the show is comedic, personality-based, non-political
WOR Radio Network **Ph:** 212-642-4500
1440 Broadway **Fax:** 212-642-4549
New York, NY 10018
www.worradionet.com

Reynolds, Peter H (1961-)
Children's book author & illustrator (the Judy Moody series and others); he also illustrates books written by other authors, including Judy Blume and Ellen Potter
Pippin Properties Inc **Ph:** 212-338-9310
155 E 38th St Suite 2H **Fax:** 212-338-9579
New York, NY 10016
www.peterhreynolds.com

Reynolds, Robert
Chairman, president, and CEO of Graybar Electric
Graybar Electric Co Inc **Ph:** 314-573-9200
34 N Meramec Ave
Saint Louis, MO 63105
www.graybar.com

Reynolds, Thomas M (1950-)
US Representative from New York (Republican); chairman of the National Republican Congressional Committee
332 Cannon Bldg **Ph:** 202-225-5265
Washington, DC 20515 **Fax:** 202-225-5910
www.house.gov/reynolds

Rhames, Ving (1959-)
Actor
International Creative Management **Ph:** 310-550-4000
8942 Wilshire Blvd
Beverly Hills, CA 90211

Rhea, Caroline (1964-)
Comedian, TV host, actor
William Morris Agency **Ph:** 310-859-4000
1 William Morris Pl **Fax:** 310-859-4462
Beverly Hills, CA 90212
www.nbc.com/The_Biggest_Loser

Rhee, Jhoon (1932-)
Martial artist credited as the Father of American Tae Kwon Do
Jhoon Rhee Institute **Ph:** 410-381-4999
9520 Gerwig Ln Suite T
Columbia, MD 21046
masterrhee.com

Rhodes, Arthur (1969-)
Professional baseball player
Philadelphia Phillies **Ph:** 215-463-6000
Citizens Bank Park
1 Citizens Bank Park Way
Philadelphia, PA 19148
philadelphia.phillies.mlb.com

Rhodes, Randi
Radio talk show host (liberal)
Air America **Ph:** 646-274-4900
641 6th Ave
New York, NY 10011
www.airamericaradio.com

Rhodes, William
President and CEO of AutoZone Inc
AutoZone Inc **Ph:** 901-495-6500
123 S Front St
Memphis, TN 38103
www.autozoneinc.com

Rhymes, Busta (1972-)
Rapper and hip-hop artist; real name is Trevor Smith Jr
Creative Artists Agency **Ph:** 310-288-4545
9830 Wilshire Blvd **Fax:** 310-288-4800
Beverly Hills, CA 90212
www.bustarhymes.com

Ribeiro, Caroline (1980-)
Brazilian model
Marilyn Model MGT Inc **Ph:** 212-260-6500
300 Park Ave S **Fax:** 212-260-0821
New York, NY 10010

Ribisi, Giovanni (1974-)
Actor
William Morris Agency **Ph:** 310-859-4000
1 William Morris Pl **Fax:** 310-859-4462
Beverly Hills, CA 90212

Ricci, Christina (1980-)
Actor
International Creative Management **Ph:** 310-550-4000
8942 Wilshire Blvd
Beverly Hills, CA 90211

Ricci, Mike (1971-)
Professional hockey player
Phoenix Coyotes **Ph:** 623-463-8800
5800 W Glenn Dr Suite 350 **Fax:** 623-463-8810
Glendale, AZ 85301
www.phoenixcoyotes.com

Rice, Anne (1941-)
Author of Interview with the Vampire
1239 1st St **Ph:** 504-522-8634
New Orleans, LA 70130
www.annerice.com

Rice, Condoleezza, PhD (1954-)
US Secretary of State
US Dept of State **Ph:** 202-647-9572
2201 C St NW **Fax:** 202-647-2283
Washington, DC 20520
www.state.gov

Rice, Jerry (1962-)
Former professional football player
SFX Sports Group **Ph:** 202-686-2000
5335 Wisconsin Ave NW Suite 850 **Fax:** 202-686-5050
Washington, DC 20015

Rice, Linda Johnson
President & CEO of Johnson Publishing, publishers of EBONY and JET magazines
Johnson Publishing Co Inc **Ph:** 312-322-9200
820 S Michigan Ave
Chicago, IL 60605
www.johnsonpublishing.com

Rich, Adrienne (1929-)
Poet, essayist, and activist
Steven Barclay Agency **Ph:** 707-773-0654
12 Western Ave **Fax:** 707-778-1868
Petaluma, CA 94952 **TF:** 888-965-7323
www.barclayagency.com

Rich, Frank (1949-)
New York Times associate editor and columnist
New York Times **Ph:** 212-556-1234
229 W 43rd St
New York, NY 10036
www.barclayagency.com

Richard, Margaret
Host and producer of Body Electric exercise program on public television, which introduced the concept of doing exercise to music
Body Electric Corp of America **Ph:** 716-662-0668
4329 S Buffalo St **Fax:** 716-662-5329
Orchard Park, NY 14127
www.bodyelectrictv.com

Richards, Ann (1933-)
Former governor of Texas; senior adviser to Public Strategies, a public relations firm
Public Strategies Inc **Ph:** 512-474-8848
98 San Jacinto Blvd Suite 1200 **Fax:** 512-474-0120
Austin, TX 78701
www.pstrategies.com

Richards, Brad (1980-)
Professional hockey player
Tampa Bay Lightning **Ph:** 813-301-6600
St Pete Times Forum **Fax:** 813-301-1487
401 Channelside Dr
Tampa, FL 33602
www.tampabaylightning.com

Richards, Cecile
President of the Planned Parenthood Federation of America; daughter of Ann Richards, former governor of Texas
Planned Parenthood Federation of America **Ph:** 212-541-7800 **Fax:** 212-245-1845
434 W 33rd St
New York, NY 10001
www.plannedparenthood.org

Richards, Keith (1943-)
Rock guitarist; member of the Rolling Stones
William Morris Agency **Ph:** 310-859-4000
1 William Morris Pl **Fax:** 310-859-4462
Beverly Hills, CA 90212
www.keithrichards.com

Richardson, Bill (1947-)
Governor of New Mexico (Democrat)
State Capitol Bldg 490 Old Santa Fe Trail Rm 400 **Ph:** 505-827-3000 **Fax:** 505-476-2226
Santa Fe, NM 87501
www.governor.state.nm.us

Richardson, Dot, MD (1961-)
Olympic softball gold medalist; physician and director of the USAT National Training Center
Progressive Sports Management **Ph:** 720-266-5007 **Fax:** 720-266-5011
385 Inverness Dr S Suite 370
Englewood, CO 80112
www.dotrichardson.com

Richardson, Jason (1981-)
Professional basketball player
Golden State Warriors **Ph:** 510-986-2200
1011 Broadway **Fax:** 510-452-0132
Oakland, CA 94607
www.nba.com/warriors

Richardson, Jerry
Owner/founder of the Carolina Panthers football franchise
Carolina Panthers **Ph:** 704-358-7000
Bank of America Stadium **Fax:** 704-358-7618
800 S Mint St
Charlotte, NC 28202
www.panthers.com

Richardson, Quentin (1980-)
Professional basketball player
New York Knicks **Ph:** 212-465-6471
Madison Square Garden **Fax:** 212-465-6498
2 Pennsylvania Plaza
New York, NY 10121
www.nba.com/knicks

Richardson, Robert C, PhD (1937-)
Winner (with two other scientists) of the 1996 Nobel Prize in Physics for the discovery of superfluidity in helium-3
Cornell University **Ph:** 607-255-6423
Laboratory of Atomic & Solid State Physics **Fax:** 607-255-6428
638 Clark Hall
Ithaca, NY 14853
www.lassp.cornell.edu

Richenhagen, Martin (1952-)
President and CEO of AGCO Corp (manufactures and distributes agricultural equipment)
AGCO Corp **Ph:** 770-813-9200
4205 River Green Pkwy
Duluth, GA 30096
www.agcocorp.com

Richeson, Clee (1969-)
Sculptor
Gallery M **Ph:** 303-331-8400
2830 E 3rd Ave
Denver, CO 80206
www.cleericheson.com

Rickles, Don (1926-)
Comedian
William Morris Agency **Ph:** 310-859-4000
1 William Morris Pl **Fax:** 310-859-4462
Beverly Hills, CA 90212
www.wma.com/don_rickles/summary

Rickman, Alan (1946-)
Actor
Endeavor **Ph:** 310-248-2000
9601 Wilshire Blvd 3rd Fl **Fax:** 310-248-2020
Beverly Hills, CA 90210

Ride, Sally, PhD (1951-)
Former astronaut; first American woman to orbit Earth
Sally Ride Science **Ph:** 858-638-1432
9191 Towne Centre Dr **Fax:** 858-638-1419
Suite L101 **TF:** 800-561-5161
San Diego, CA 92122
www11.jsc.nasa.gov/Bios/htmlbios/ride-sk.html

Ridley, John (1967-)
TV & film writer, producer, and director; author
Gotham Group **Ph:** 310-285-0001
9255 Sunset Blvd Suite 515 **Fax:** 310-285-0077
Los Angeles, CA 90069
www.twbookmark.com

Ridnour, Luke (1981-)
Professional basketball player
Seattle Supersonics **Ph:** 206-281-5800
351 Elliott Ave W Suite 500 **Fax:** 206-281-5839
Seattle, WA 98119
www.nba.com/sonics

Rigby, Cathy (1952-)
Actor best known for her performance as Peter Pan; former Olympic gymnast
McCoy Rigby Entertainment **Ph:** 714-525-8388
110 E Wilshire Ave Suite 201
Fullerton, CA 92832
www.mccoyrigby.com

Riggio, Leonard
Chairman of Barnes & Noble
Barnes & Noble Inc **Ph:** 212-633-3300
122 5th Ave **Fax:** 212-675-0413
New York, NY 10011
www.barnesandnobleinc.com

Riley, Dawn (1964-)
Yacht racer
America True **Ph:** 415-974-1018
Pier 40 **Fax:** 415-974-1024
San Francisco, CA 94107
www.americatrue.org

Riley, Joseph P Jr
Mayor of Charleston, South Carolina
PO Box 652 **Ph:** 843-577-6970
Charleston, SC 29402
www.ci.charleston.sc.us

Riley, Pat (1945-)
Former basketball player; now president & coach of the Miami Heat
Miami Heat **Ph:** 786-777-1000
American Airlines Arena **Fax:** 786-777-1609
601 Biscayne Blvd
Miami, FL 33132
www.nba.com/heat

Riley, Robert (1944-)
Governor of Alabama (Republican)
600 Dexter Ave Suite N-104 **Ph:** 334-242-7100
Montgomery, AL 36130 **Fax:** 334-353-0004
www.governor.state.al.us

Rill, James F (1933-)
A top antitrust attorney; has served as Assistant Attorney General in charge of the US Dept. of Justice's Antitrust Division
Howrey LLP **Ph:** 202-383-6562
1299 Pennsylvania Ave NW **Fax:** 202-383-6610
Washington, DC 20004
www.howrey.com

Rimando, Nick (1979-)
Professional soccer player
DC United **Ph:** 202-587-5000
RFK Stadium **Fax:** 202-587-5400
2400 E Capitol St SE
Washington, DC 20003
dcunited.mlsnet.com

Rimes, LeAnn (1982-)
Country singer
CAA Nashville **Ph:** 615-383-8787
3310 West End Ave 5th Fl **Fax:** 615-383-4937
Nashville, TN 37203
www.rimestimes.com

Rimm, Sylvia, PhD
Writes a syndicated column on parenting, Sylvia Rimm on Raising Kids
Creators Syndicate Inc **Ph:** 310-337-7003
5777 W Century Blvd Suite 700 **Fax:** 310-337-7625
Los Angeles, CA 90045
www.creators.com

Rinaldi, Ann (1934-)
Writer of historical fiction for young adults
Harcourt Children's Books **Ph:** 212-592-1000
15 E 26th St
New York, NY 10010
www.annrinaldi.com

Ringgold, Faith (1930-)
Artist best known for her painted story quilts (art that combines painting, quilted fabric, and storytelling); she is also an author of books for young readers
University of California at San Diego **Ph:** 858-534-2860
Dept of Visual Arts
9500 Gilman Dr
La Jolla, CA 92093
www.faithringgold.com

Rios, Delia M
Newhouse News Service reporter; writes on the American Identity
Newhouse News Service **Ph:** 202-383-7800
1101 Connecticut Ave NW **Fax:** 202-296-9537
Suite 300
Washington, DC 20036
www.newhousenews.com

Ripa, Kelly (1970-)
Actor/co-host of the syndicated TV show Live with Regis and Kelly
William Morris Agency **Ph:** 212-586-5100
1325 Ave of the Americas **Fax:** 212-246-3583
New York, NY 10019
tvplex.go.com/buenavista/regisandkelly

Ripert, Eric (1965-)
Chef at Le Bernardin, a New York City seafood restaurant
Le Bernardin Restaurant **Ph:** 212-554-1515
155 W 51st St **Fax:** 212-554-1100
New York, NY 10019
www.le-bernardin.com

Ripken, Cal Jr (1960-)
Played baseball with the Baltimore Orioles for 21 seasons (now retired)
Ripken Baseball **Ph:** 410-823-0808
1427 Clarkview Rd Suite 100 **Fax:** 410-823-0850
Baltimore, MD 21209
ripkenbaseball.com

Ritchie, Fiona (1960-)
Host of the music program Thistle and Shamrock on NPR
National Public Radio **Ph:** 202-513-2000
635 Massachusetts Ave NW **Fax:** 202-513-3329
Washington, DC 20001
www.npr.org

Ritter, Bill
ABC News correspondent on 20/20
20/20 **Ph:** 212-456-7777
147 Columbus Ave
New York, NY 10023
abcnews.go.com/2020

Ritter, Mike
Editorial cartoonist for The Tribune in Phoenix
King Features Syndicate Inc **Ph:** 212-455-4000
888 7th Ave 2nd Fl
New York, NY 10019
www.kingfeatures.com

Ritts, Herb (1952-2002)
Celebrity photographer
Fahey/Klein Gallery **Ph:** 323-934-2250
148 N La Brea **Fax:** 323-934-4243
Los Angeles, CA 90036
www.herbritts.com

Rivera, Geraldo (1943-)
Veteran reporter and talk show host; currently host of the nationally syndicated program Geraldo at Large
FOX News Channel **Ph:** 212-301-3000
1211 Ave of the Americas
New York, NY 10036
www.foxnews.com/fnctv

Rivera, Mariano (1969-)
Professional baseball player
New York Yankees **Ph:** 718-293-4300
Yankee Stadium **Fax:** 718-293-8414
161st St & River Ave
Bronx, NY 10451
newyork.yankees.mlb.com

Rivers, Doc (1961-)
Basketball coach
Boston Celtics **Ph:** 617-854-8000
226 Causeway St 4th Fl **Fax:** 617-367-4286
Boston, MA 02114
www.nba.com/celtics

Rivers, Joan (1933-)
Comedian; talk show host; entertainment personality
Joan Rivers Worldwide **Ph:** 212-751-2028
150 E 58th St 24th Fl **Fax:** 212-751-1967
New York, NY 10155
www.joanrivers.com

Rivet, Jeannine M
Executive Vice President, UnitedHealth Group
UnitedHealth Group **Ph:** 952-936-7213
9900 Bren Rd E **Fax:** 952-936-0044
Minnetonka, MN 55343
www.unitedhealthgroup.com

Robach, Amy
Daytime anchor for MSNBC
MSNBC TV **Ph:** 201-583-5000
1 MSNBC Plaza
Secaucus, NJ 07094
www.msnbc.msn.com/id/3080263

Robbins, Anthony (1961-)
Motivational speaker & author; considered an authority on the psychology of leadership, negotiations, organizational turnaround, and peak performance
9888 Carroll Centre Rd **Ph:** 858-535-9900
San Diego, CA 92126 **TF:** 800-445-8183
www.tonyrobbins.com

Robbins, Jerome (1918-1998)
Choreographer of ballets created for the New York City Ballet, Ballets USA, American Ballet Theatre, and other international companies; and a director of musicals, plays, movies, and television programs
New York City Ballet **Ph:** 212-870-5656
New York State Theater **Fax:** 212-870-7791
20 Lincoln Center
New York, NY 10023
www.nycballet.com/about/staffart.html

Robbins, Tim (1958-)
Actor, director, screenwriter
Creative Artists Agency **Ph:** 310-288-4545
9830 Wilshire Blvd **Fax:** 310-288-4800
Beverly Hills, CA 90212

Robbins, Tom (1936-)
Fiction writer (Even Cowgirls Get the Blues)
Random House Publicity **Ph:** 212-782-9000
1745 Broadway
New York, NY 10019
www.randomhouse.com

Roberts, Brian L (1960-)
Chairman and CEO of Comcast
Comcast Corp **Ph:** 215-665-1700
1500 Market St **Fax:** 215-981-7790
Philadelphia, PA 19102
www.cmcsk.com

Roberts, Carter
President and CEO of the World Wildlife Fund
World Wildlife Fund **Ph:** 202-293-4800
1250 24th St NW
Washington, DC 20037
www.worldwildlife.org

Roberts, Chuck
Weekday news anchor for CNN's Headline News
CNN **Ph:** 404-827-1500
1 CNN Center
Atlanta, GA 30303
www.cnn.com/CNN/anchors_reporters

Roberts, Cokie (1943-)
Senior news analyst on National Public Radio; also writes a syndicated column with her husband, Steve Roberts, and is a political commentator for TV news
National Public Radio **Ph:** 202-513-2000
635 Massachusetts Ave NW **Fax:** 202-513-3329
Washington, DC 20001
www.npr.org

Roberts, Deborah (1960-)
News correspondent for 20/20; also serves as substitute anchor on other ABC News programs
20/20 **Ph:** 212-456-7777
147 Columbus Ave
New York, NY 10023
abcnews.go.com/2020

Roberts, Doris (1929-)
Actor
International Creative Management **Ph:** 310-550-4000
8942 Wilshire Blvd
Beverly Hills, CA 90211
www.everybodylovesray.com

Roberts, Gary (1966-)
Professional hockey player
Florida Panthers **Ph:** 954-835-7000
BankAtlantic Center **Fax:** 954-835-7700
1 Panther Pkwy
Sunrise, FL 33323
www.floridapanthers.com

Roberts, John
CNN's senior national correspondent (was previously with CBS News for 14 years)
CNN **Ph:** 404-827-1500
1 CNN Center
Atlanta, GA 30303
www.cnn.com/CNN/anchors_reporters

Roberts, John G Jr (1955-)
Chief Justice of the US Supreme Court
US Supreme Court Bldg **Ph:** 202-479-3000
1 1st St NE
Washington, DC 20543
www.supremecourtus.gov

Roberts, Julia (1967-)
Actor
Creative Artists Agency **Ph:** 310-288-4545
9830 Wilshire Blvd **Fax:** 310-288-4800
Beverly HIlls, CA 90212

Roberts, Lawrence G, PhD (1937-)
An authority on packet switching and network architectures; was responsible for the design, initiation, planning, and development of the world's first major packet network, now called the Internet
Caspian Networks Inc **Ph:** 650-812-7900
2800A Bayshore Rd **Fax:** 650-812-7906
Palo Alto, CA 94303
www.packet.cc

Roberts, Leonard H
Chairman of RadioShack Corp
RadioShack Corp **Ph:** 817-415-3011
300 RadioShack Cir
Fort Worth, TX 76102
www.radioshackcorporation.com

Roberts, Monty (1935-)
Has developed a communication method for taming wild horses without inflicting pain; has written about these experiences in The Man Who Listens to Horses
Monty & Pat Roberts Inc **Ph:** 805-688-6288
PO Box 1700 **Fax:** 805-688-2242
Solvang, CA 93464
www.montyroberts.com

Roberts, Nora (1950-)
Author of romance & mainstream fiction; also writes as JD Robb
Jove Publicity **Ph:** 212-366-2000
375 Hudson St
New York, NY 10014
www.noraroberts.com

Roberts, Oral (1918-)
Televangelist and founder of Oral Roberts University
Oral Roberts Ministry **Ph:** 918-495-7777
Tulsa, OK 74171 **Fax:** 918-495-6033
www.orm.cc

Roberts, Pat (1936-)
US Senator from Kansas (Republican)
109 Hart Bldg **Ph:** 202-224-4774
Washington, DC 20510 **Fax:** 202-224-3514
roberts.senate.gov

Roberts, Patrick (1962-)
Co-creator, with Bob Condron, of the comic strip Todd the Dinosaur!
King Features Syndicate Inc **Ph:** 212-455-4000
888 7th Ave 2nd Fl
New York, NY 10019
www.kingfeatures.com

Roberts, Paul Craig (1939-)
Economist; also writes a syndicated column
Creators Syndicate Inc **Ph:** 310-337-7003
5777 W Century Blvd Suite 700 **Fax:** 310-337-7625
Los Angeles, CA 90045
www.creators.com/opinion.html

Roberts, Richard (1948-)
Evangelist; president & CEO of Oral Roberts University
Oral Roberts University **Ph:** 918-495-6161
7777 S Lewis Ave
Tulsa, OK 74171
www.orm.cc

Roberts, Robin (1960-)
Good Morning America co-anchor
Good Morning America **Ph:** 212-456-7777
147 Columbus Ave
New York, NY 10023
www.abcnews.go.com/GMA

Roberts, Steven V (1943-)
Syndicated columnist (with his wife, Cokie Roberts) and frequent participant in political discussion shows
United Feature Syndicate **Ph:** 212-293-8500
200 Madison Ave
New York, NY 10016
www.unitedfeatures.com

Roberts, Troy (1962-)
48 Hours correspondent
48 Hours **Ph:** 212-975-4114
524 W 57th St
New York, NY 10019
www.cbsnews.com

Roberts, Willo Davis (1928-2004)
Author of mystery/suspense books for young adults (Don't Hurt Laurie!; Twisted Summer) and for adults; also writes medical background and historical novels for adults
Simon & Schuster Books for Young Readers **Ph:** 212-698-7000
1230 Ave of the Americas
New York, NY 10020
www.simonsays.com

Robertson, Michael L
Founder & chairman of Linspire Inc., a consumer software company; also founder and former chairman/CEO of MP3.com
Linspire Inc **Ph:** 858-587-6700
9333 Genesee Ave 3rd Fl **Fax:** 858-587-8095
San Diego, CA 92121
www.linspire.com

Robertson, Nic
Senior international correspondent based in London
CNN **Ph:** 404-827-1500
1 CNN Center
Atlanta, GA 30303
www.cnn.com/CNN/anchors_reporters

Robertson, Pat (1930-)
Religious broadcaster; founder and chairman of the Christian Broadcasting Network (CBN) and host of the 700 Club
Christian Broadcasting Network Inc **Ph:** 757-226-7000 **Fax:** 757-226-2017
CBN Center
977 Centerville Tpke
Virginia Beach, VA 23463
www.patrobertson.com

Robinson, Cleo Parker (1949-)
Founder, executive artistic director, and choreographer of Cleo Parker Robinson Dance, a multi-cultural modern dance ensemble
Cleo Parker Robinson Dance **Ph:** 303-295-1759
119 Park Ave W **Fax:** 303-295-1328
Denver, CO 80205
www.cleoparkerdance.org

Robinson, Crystal (1974-)
Professional basketball player
Washington Mystics **Ph:** 202-266-2200
Verizon Center **Fax:** 202-266-2220
401 9th St NW Suite 750
Washington, DC 20004
www.wnba.com/mystics

Robinson, David (1965-)
Former NBA star, now retired (played for the San Antonio Spurs)
Octagon Athlete Representation **Ph:** 703-905-3300
1751 Pinnacle Dr Suite 1500 **Fax:** 703-905-4495
McLean, VA 22102

Robinson, Dunta (1982-)
Professional football player
Houston Texans **Ph:** 832-667-2000
2 Reliant Park **Fax:** 832-667-2100
Houston, TX 77054
www.houstontexans.com

Robinson, Fatima (1971-)
Choreographer (film; music videos)
Bloc Agency **Ph:** 323-954-7730
5651 Wilshire Blvd Suite C
Los Angeles, CA 90036

Robinson, Frank (1935-)
Baseball manager and, as a player, a Baseball Hall of Fame inductee
Washington Nationals **Ph:** 202-349-0400
RFK Stadium
2400 E Capitol St SE
Washington, DC 20003
washington.nationals.mlb.com

Robinson, Jackie (1919-1972)
Brooklyn Dodgers great who was the first African-American to play major league baseball
National Baseball Hall of Fame & Museum **Ph:** 607-547-7200 **Fax:** 607-547-2044
25 Main St **TF:** 888-425-5633
Cooperstown, NY 13326
www.baseballhalloffame.org

Robinson, Marilynne (1947-)
Author (Housekeeping; Gilead)
Farrar Straus & Giroux **Ph:** 212-741-6900
19 Union Sq W
New York, NY 10003
www.fsgbooks.com

Robinson, Ron
President of Young America's Foundation (YAF), a conservative organization
Young America's Foundation **Ph:** 703-318-9608
FM Kirby Freedom Center **Fax:** 703-318-9122
110 Elden St
Herndon, VA 20170
www.yaf.org

Robinson, Smokey (1935-)
Singer/songwriter
William Morris Agency **Ph:** 310-859-4000
1 William Morris Pl **Fax:** 310-859-4462
Beverly Hills, CA 90212
www.wma.com/smokey_robinson/summary

Robison, James
Televangelist
Life Outreach International **Ph:** 817-267-4211
PO Box 982000
Fort Worth, TX 76182
www.lifeoutreach.org

Robson, Wade (1982-)
Dancer; choreographer
Creative Artists Agency **Ph:** 310-288-4545
9830 Wilshire Blvd **Fax:** 310-288-4800
Beverly Hills, CA 90212

Rock, Chris (1965-)
Comedian; actor
Endeavor
9601 Wilshire Blvd 3rd Fl
Beverly Hills, CA 90210
www.chrisrock.com
Ph: 310-248-2000
Fax: 310-248-2020

Rockefeller, Jay (1937-)
US Senator from West Virginia (Democrat)
531 Hart Bldg
Washington, DC 20510
rockefeller.senate.gov
Ph: 202-224-6472
Fax: 202-224-7665

Rockenwagner, Hans
German chef, restaurant owner, and cookbook author
Rockenwagner Restaurant
2435 Main St
Santa Monica, CA 90405
www.rockenwagner.com
Ph: 310-399-6504
Fax: 310-399-7984

Rockwell, Norman (1894-1978)
Artist best known for his Saturday Evening Post covers
Norman Rockwell Museum at Stockbridge
9 Glendale Rd
Stockbridge, MA 01262
www.nrm.org
Ph: 413-298-4100
Fax: 413-298-4142

Rockwell, Sam (1968-)
Actor
Gersh Agency
41 Madison Ave 33rd Fl
New York, NY 10010
Ph: 212-997-1818
Fax: 212-997-1978

Rodale, Ardath
Chairman of Rodale Inc (magazine, book, and online publisher)
Rodale Inc
33 E Minor St
Emmaus, PA 18098
www.rodale.com
Ph: 610-967-5171
Fax: 610-967-8963

Roddick, Andy (1982-)
Professional tennis player
SFX Sports Group
5335 Wisconsin Ave NW Suite 850
Washington, DC 20015
www.andyroddick.com
Ph: 202-686-2000
Fax: 202-686-5050

Rodgers, Griffin P, MD
Acting Director of the National Institute of Diabetes and Digestive & Kidney Diseases, National Institutes of Health
National Institute of Diabetes & Digestive & Kidney Diseases
31 Center Dr
Bldg 31 Rm 9A52
Bethesda, MD 20892
www.niddk.nih.gov
Ph: 301-496-5877
Fax: 301-402-2125

Rodkin, Gary
President & CEO of ConAgra Foods
ConAgra Foods Inc
1 ConAgra Dr
Omaha, NE 68102
www.conagrafoods.com
Ph: 402-595-4000

Rodriguez, Alex (1975-)
Professional baseball player
New York Yankees
Yankee Stadium
161st St & River Ave
Bronx, NY 10451
newyork.yankees.mlb.com
Ph: 718-293-4300
Fax: 718-293-8414

Rodriguez, Arturo (1949-)
President of United Farm Workers
United Farm Workers of America
PO Box 62
Keene, CA 93531
www.ufw.org
Ph: 661-822-5571

Rodriguez, Eloy, PhD (1947-)
Biological chemist; founder of the scientific discipline of Zoopharmocognosy, which is the study of how animals medicate themselves
LH Bailey Hortrium
Cornell University
259 Biotechnology Bldg
Ithaca, NY 14853
www.plantbio.cornell.edu/people.php
Ph: 607-254-2956
Fax: 607-254-2952

Rodriguez, Freddy (1975-)
Actor
United Talent Agency
9560 Wilshire Blvd 5th Fl
Beverly Hills, CA 90212
www.hbo.com/sixfeetunder
Ph: 310-273-6700
Fax: 310-247-1111

Rodriguez, Ivan (1971-)
Professional baseball player
Detroit Tigers
Comerica Park
2100 Woodward Ave
Detroit, MI 48201
detroit.tigers.mlb.com
Ph: 313-962-4000
Fax: 313-471-2138

Rodriguez, Michelle (1978-)
Actor
International Creative Management **Ph:** 310-550-4000
8942 Wilshire Blvd
Beverly Hills, CA 90212
abc.go.com/primetime/lost/show.html

Rodriguez, Paul (1955-)
Comedian
International Creative Management **Ph:** 310-550-4000
8942 Wilshire Blvd
Beverly Hills, CA 90211
www.paulrodriguez.com

Rodriguez, Rene
Miami Herald movie critic
Miami Herald **Ph:** 305-350-2111
1 Herald Plaza
Miami, FL 33132

Rodriguez, Richard
An editor at Pacific News Service; essayist for the Newshour with Jim Lehrer on PBS
MacNeil/Lehrer Productions **Ph:** 703-998-2138
2700 S Quincy St Suite 250
Arlington, VA 22206
www.pbs.org/newshour/ww/essayists.html

Rodriguez, Robert (1968-)
Independent filmmaker
International Creative Management **Ph:** 310-550-4000
8942 Wilshire Blvd
Beverly Hills, CA 90211

Roemer, Timothy J (1956-)
Former Congressman and a member of the 9/11 Commission; president of the Center for National Policy (a think tank)
Center for National Policy **Ph:** 202-682-1800
1 Massachusetts Ave NW Suite 333 **Fax:** 202-682-1818
Washington, DC 20001
www.cnponline.org

Roenick, Jeremy (1970-)
Professional hockey player
Los Angeles Kings **Ph:** 213-742-7100
Staples Center
1111 S Figueroa St
Los Angeles, CA 90015
www.lakings.com

Roeper, Richard (1960-)
Chicago Sun-Times columnist; co-host of the Ebert & Roeper TV show (movie reviews)
Chicago Sun-Times **Ph:** 312-321-3000
401 N Wabash Ave **Fax:** 312-321-3084
Chicago, IL 60611
www.suntimes.com/index/roeper.html

Roethlisberger, Ben (1982-)
Professional football player
Pittsburgh Steelers **Ph:** 412-432-7800
3400 S Water St **Fax:** 412-432-7878
Pittsburgh, PA 15203
www.pittsburghsteelers.com

Rogel, Steven R
Chairman, president, and CEO of Weyerhaeuser
Weyerhaeuser Co **Ph:** 253-924-2345
PO Box 9777
Federal Way, WA 98063
investor.weyerhaeuser.com

Rogers, Adrian (1931-)
Televangelist
Love Worth Finding Ministries **Ph:** 901-382-7900
2941 Kate Bond Rd **Fax:** 901-388-8346
Memphis, TN 38133
www.lwf.org

Rogers, Edward S
President & CEO of Rogers Communications Inc (RCI); also owns the controlling interest in the Toronto Blue Jays baseball club
Rogers Communications Inc **Ph:** 416-935-7777
333 Bloor St E 10th Fl **Fax:** 416-935-3538
Toronto, ON M4W1G9
www.rogers.com

Rogers, Fred (1928-2003)
Host of Mr Rogers Neighborhood (which is still on PBS, despite his death in 2003)
Family Communications Inc **Ph:** 412-687-2990
4802 5th Ave **Fax:** 412-687-1226
Pittsburgh, PA 15213
www.fci.org

Rogers, Harold (1937-)
US Representative from Kentucky (Republican)
2406 Rayburn Bldg **Ph:** 202-225-4601
Washington, DC 20515 **Fax:** 202-225-0940
www.house.gov/rogers

Rogers, Kenny (1964-)
Professional baseball player
Detroit Tigers **Ph:** 313-962-4000
Comerica Park **Fax:** 313-471-2138
2100 Woodward Ave
Detroit, MI 48201
detroit.tigers.mlb.com

Rogers, Kenny (1938-)
Country/pop singer
William Morris Agency **Ph:** 615-963-3000
1600 Division St Suite 300 **Fax:** 615-963-3090
Nashville, TN 37203
www.kennyrogers.com

Rogers, Mike (1963-)
US Representative from Michigan (Republican)
133 Cannon Bldg **Ph:** 202-225-4872
Washington, DC 20515 **Fax:** 202-225-5820
www.mikerogers.house.gov

Rogers, Mike D (1958-)
US Representative from Alabama (Republican)
514 Cannon Bldg **Ph:** 202-225-3261
Washington, DC 20515 **Fax:** 202-226-8485
www.house.gov/mike-rogers

Rogers, Mimi (1956-)
Actor
The Firm **Ph:** 310-860-8000
9465 Wilshire Blvd **Fax:** 310-860-8100
Beverly Hills, CA 90212

Rogers, Neil
Talk radio show host
WQAM **Ph:** 305-770-1456
20295 NW 2nd Ave
Miami, FL 33169
www.neilrogers.com

Rogers, Rob
Editorial cartoonist for the Pittsburgh Post-Gazette
Pittsburgh Post-Gazette **Ph:** 412-263-1100
34 Blvd of the Allies
Pittsburgh, PA 15222
www.unitedfeatures.com

Rohmann, Eric (1957-)
Author and illustrator of books for young readers (Time Flies; My Friend Rabbit)
Random House Children's Books **Ph:** 212-782-9000
Publicity Dept
1745 Broadway
New York, NY 10019
www.randomhouse.com/kids

Rohn, Jim
Motivational speaker on the fundamentals of human behavior and personal motivation that affect professional performance
Jim Rohn International **Ph:** 817-442-5407
2835 Exchange Blvd Suite 200 **Fax:** 817-442-1390
Southlake, TX 76092 **TF:** 800-929-0434
www.jimrohn.com

Rohr, James E
Chairman and CEO of PNC Financial Services Group
PNC Financial Services Group Inc **Ph:** 412-762-2000
249 5th Ave
1 PNC Plaza
Pittsburgh, PA 15222
www.pnc.com

Rohrabacher, Dana (1947-)
US Representative from California (Republican)
2338 Rayburn Bldg **Ph:** 202-225-2415
Washington, DC 20515 **Fax:** 202-225-0145
rohrabacher.house.gov

Roizen, Michael, MD (1946-)
Author of the RealAge books and scientific adviser on the RealAge website
HarperCollins Publishers **Ph:** 212-207-7000
c/o Author Mail
10 E 53rd St
New York, NY 10022
www.realage.com

Roker, Al (1954-)
Today Show's weather and feature reporter
Today Show **Ph:** 212-664-4249
30 Rockefeller Plaza
New York, NY 10112
www.alroker.com

Rolen, Scott (1975-)
Professional baseball player
Saint Louis Cardinals **Ph:** 314-421-3060
250 Stadium Plaza **Fax:** 314-425-0640
Saint Louis, MO 63102
stlouis.cardinals.mlb.com

Rolfe, Chris (1983-)
Professional soccer player
Chicago Fire **Ph:** 312-705-7200
980 N Michigan Ave Suite 1998 **Fax:** 312-705-7393
Chicago, IL 60611
chicago.fire.mlsnet.com

Rolle, Samari (1976-)
Professional football player
Baltimore Ravens **Ph:** 410-547-8100
1101 Russell St **Fax:** 410-547-8112
Baltimore, MD 21230
www.baltimoreravens.com

Rollins, Jimmy (1978-)
Professional baseball player
Philadelphia Phillies **Ph:** 215-463-6000
Citizens Bank Park
1 Citizens Bank Park Way
Philadelphia, PA 19148
philadelphia.phillies.mlb.com

Roloson, Dwayne (1969-)
Professional hockey player
Edmonton Oilers **Ph:** 780-414-4000
11230 110th St **Fax:** 780-409-5890
Edmonton, AB T5G3H7
www.edmontonoilers.com

Rolston, Brian (1973-)
Professional hockey player
Minnesota Wild **Ph:** 651-222-9453
317 Washington St **Fax:** 651-222-1055
Saint Paul, MN 55102
www.wild.com

Rolston, Matthew
Photographer & video/commercial film director
HSI Productions **Ph:** 310-558-7100
3630 Eastham Dr **Fax:** 310-558-7101
Culver City, CA 90232
www.matthewrolston.com

Romanek, Mark (1959-)
Director (music videos, commercials, movies)
Creative Artists Agency **Ph:** 310-288-4545
9830 Wilshire Blvd **Fax:** 310-288-4800
Beverly Hills, CA 90212
www.markromanek.com

Romano, Michael
Chef of the Union Square Cafe and partner in the Union Square Hospitality Group, which includes five New York restaurants and a jazz club
Union Square Cafe **Ph:** 212-243-4020
21 E 16th St
New York, NY 10003
www.bluesmoke.com/blue/secondary/michael.html

Romano, Ray (1957-)
Comedian; actor
William Morris Agency **Ph:** 212-586-5100
1325 Ave of the Americas **Fax:** 212-246-3583
New York, NY 10019
www.rayromano.com

Rome, Jim
Sports talk show host & interviewer on radio & television
Premiere Radio Networks Inc **Ph:** 818-377-5300
15260 Ventura Blvd 5th Fl **Fax:** 818-377-5333
Sherman Oaks, CA 91403
www.jimrome.com

Romer, Paul M, PhD
Economist and lead developer of the New Growth Theory, which addresses the question of what sustains economic growth in a physical world characterized by diminishing returns and scarcity
Stanford University **Ph:** 650-723-3025
Graduate School of Business
518 Memorial Way
Stanford, CA 94305
www.stanford.edu/~promer

Romero, Anthony D
Executive Director of the American Civil Liberties Union (the first Latino & openly gay man to head the ACLU)
American Civil Liberties Union **Ph:** 212-549-2500
125 Broad St 18th Fl **Fax:** 212-549-2580
New York, NY 10004
www.aclu.org

Romero, JC (1976-)
Professional baseball player
Los Angeles Angels of Anaheim **Ph:** 714-940-2000
Angel Stadium **Fax:** 714-940-2205
2000 Gene Autry Way
Anaheim, CA 92806
losangeles.angels.mlb.com

Romero, John (1967-)
Computer programmer & game designer (including Doom)
Midway Home Entertainment **Ph:** 858-658-9500
10110 Mesa Rim Rd
San Diego, CA 92121
www.rome.ro

Romijn, Rebecca (1972-)
Model; actor
William Morris Agency **Ph:** 310-859-4000
1 William Morris Pl **Fax:** 310-859-4462
Beverly Hills, CA 90212

Romney, Mitt (1947-)
Governor of Massachusetts (Republican)
State House Executive Office **Ph:** 617-725-4000
Rm 360 **Fax:** 617-727-9725
Boston, MA 02133
www.mass.gov

Ronstadt, Linda (1946-)
Singer
William Morris Agency **Ph:** 310-859-4000
1 William Morris Pl **Fax:** 310-859-4462
Beverly Hills, CA 90212

Rooney, Andy (1919-)
60 Minutes essayist (usually humorous); writer
60 Minutes **Ph:** 212-975-2006
555 W 57th St
New York, NY 10019
www.cbsnews.com

Rooney, Brian
ABC News correspondent
ABC News **Ph:** 323-671-5261
4151 Prospect Ave **Fax:** 323-671-5210
Los Angeles, CA 90027
www.abcnews.go.com/WNT

Rooney, Daniel M (1932-)
Owner of the Pittsburgh Steelers football franchise
Pittsburgh Steelers **Ph:** 412-432-7800
3400 S Water St **Fax:** 412-432-7878
Pittsburgh, PA 15203
www.steelers.com/team/frontoffice

Rooney, Michael
Dancer; choreographer (music videos, commercials); son of actor Mickey Rooney
Bloc Agency **Ph:** 323-954-7730
5651 Wilshire Blvd Suite C
Los Angeles, CA 90036

Rooney, Therese A
Chairman of Golden Rule Insurance Co
Golden Rule Insurance Co **Ph:** 317-297-4123
7440 Woodlands **Fax:** 317-298-0875
Indianapolis, IN 46278

Ros-Lehtinen, Ileana (1952-)
US Representative from Florida (Republican)
2160 Rayburn Bldg **Ph:** 202-225-3931
Washington, DC 20515 **Fax:** 202-225-5620
www.house.gov/ros-lehtinen

Rose, Charlie (1942-)
Host of the Charlie Rose Show on PBS
731 Lexington Ave **Ph:** 212-617-1600
New York, NY 10022
www.charlierose.com

Rose, Irwin, PhD (1926-)
Winner (with two other scientists) of the 2004 Nobel Prize in Chemistry for the discovery of ubiquitin-mediated protein degradation
University of California at Irvine College of Medicine **Ph:** 949-824-5863 **Fax:** 949-824-8540
Dept of Physiology & Biophysics
Irvine, CA 92697
www.ucihs.uci.edu/pandb

Rose, Jalen (1973-)
Professional basketball player
New York Knicks **Ph:** 212-465-6471
Madison Square Garden **Fax:** 212-465-6498
2 Pennsylvania Plaza
New York, NY 10121
www.nba.com/knicks

Rose, John
Took over the comic strip Barney Google and Snuffy Smith after the death of its creator, Fred Lasswell
King Features Syndicate Inc **Ph:** 212-455-4000
888 7th Ave 2nd Fl
New York, NY 10019
www.kingfeatures.com

Rose, Robert E
Chairman of the Board of GlobalSantaFe
GlobalSantaFe Corp **Ph:** 281-925-6000
15375 Memorial Dr **Fax:** 281-925-6010
Houston, TX 77079
www.gsfdrill.com

Rosen, James
FOX News White House correspondent
FOX News Channel **Ph:** 202-824-6300
400 N Capitol St NW Suite 550
Washington, DC 20001
www.foxnews.com/fnctv

Rosen, Uzi
CEO of Bank Leumi USA, a subsidiary of Bank Leumi le-Israel, one of Israel's leading banks
Bank Leumi USA **Ph:** 917-542-2343
420 Lexington Ave
New York, NY 10170

Rosenblum, Walter (1919-2006)
Photographer
Gallery M **Ph:** 303-331-8400
2830 E 3rd Ave
Denver, CO 80206
www.gallerym.com

Rosenfeld, Isadore, MD (1926-)
A physician, Health Editor of Parade Magazine, and author of books on health
Warner Books **Ph:** 212-522-7200
c/o Author Mail
1271 Ave of the Americas
New York, NY 10020
www.twbookmark.com

Rosengarten, David, PhD
Travel writer, cookbook author, TV host, and an authority on food, wine, and cooking; is also editor-in-chief of The Rosengarten Report, a food & wine newsletter for consumers
Salt Pig Publishing LLC **Ph:** 703-394-4931
1750 Old Meadow Rd 3rd Fl **Fax:** 703-905-8100
McLean, VA 22102
www.davidrosengarten.com

Rosensweig, Dan
COO of Yahoo!
Yahoo! Inc **Ph:** 408-349-3300
701 1st Ave **Fax:** 408-349-3301
Sunnyvale, CA 94089
docs.yahoo.com/info/pr

Rosenthal, Daniel D
President & CEO of Downey Financial Corp
Downey Financial Corp **Ph:** 949-854-3100
3501 Jamboree Rd
Newport Beach, CA 92660
www.downeysavings.com

Roski, Edward P Jr
Chairman of the Board & CEO of Majestic Realty; also part owner of the Staples Center, Los Angeles Kings hockey team, and Los Angeles Lakers basketball team, and is the owner of the Silverton Hotel & Casino in Las Vegas
Majestic Realty Co **Ph:** 562-948-4301
13191 Crossroads Pkwy N 6th Fl **Fax:** 562-695-2329
City of Industry, CA 91746
www.majesticrealty.com

Ross, Alan
Photographer, master printer, and educator; was Ansel Adams' photographic assistant in Carmel from 1974 to 1979
Alan Ross Photography **Ph:** 505-466-2335
24 Estambre Rd **Fax:** 505-466-2336
Santa Fe, NM 87508
www.alanrossphotography.com

Ross, Brian (1948-)
Chief investigative correspondent for ABC News
ABC News **Ph:** 212-456-7777
77 W 66th St
New York, NY 10023
www.abcnews.go.com/WNT

Ross, Gary (1956-)
Writer/director/producer
Creative Artists Agency **Ph:** 310-288-4545
9830 Wilshire Blvd **Fax:** 310-288-4800
Beverly Hills, CA 90212

Ross, Mike (1961-)
US Representative from Arkansas (Democrat)
314 Cannon Bldg **Ph:** 202-225-3772
Washington, DC 20515 **Fax:** 202-225-1314
www.house.gov/ross

Ross, Scott
Founder, chairman, and CEO of Digital Domain
Digital Domain Inc **Ph:** 310-314-2800
300 Rose Ave **Fax:** 310-314-2888
Venice, CA 90291
www.digitaldomain.com

Rossellini, Isabella (1952-)
Actor; model
Parseghian/Planco Management **Ph:** 212-777-7786
23 E 22nd St **Fax:** 212-777-8642
New York, NY 10010

Rotenberg, Marc (1960-)
Executive Director of the Electronic Privacy Information Center; also teaches information privacy law at Georgetown University Law Center
Electronic Privacy Information Center **Ph:** 202-483-1140 **Fax:** 202-483-1248
1718 Connecticut Ave NW Suite 200
Washington, DC 20009
www.epic.org

Roth, Philip (1933-)
Novelist (Good-bye Columbus, Portnoy's Complaint, The Plot Against America)
Houghton Mifflin Co **Ph:** 617-351-5000
Trade Div
Adult Editorial
222 Berkeley St 8th Fl
Boston, MA 02116
www.houghtonmifflinbooks.com/authors/roth

Roth, Richard (1949-)
A CNN correspondent who works exclusively on the United Nations; hosts Diplomatic License on CNN International
CNN New York **Ph:** 212-275-7800
Time Warner Ctr
10 Columbus Cir
New York, NY 10019
www.cnn.com/CNN/anchors_reporters

Roth, Tim (1961-)
British actor
Special Artists Agency **Ph:** 310-859-9688
9465 Wilshire Blvd Suite 890
Beverly Hills, CA 90212

Rothko, Mark (1903-1970)
Russian-born artist
Solomon R Guggenheim Museum **Ph:** 212-423-3500
1071 5th Ave
New York, NY 10128
www.guggenheimcollection.org

Rothman, Steven R (1952-)
US Representative from New Jersey (Democrat)
2302 Rayburn Bldg **Ph:** 202-225-5061
Washington, DC 20515 **Fax:** 202-225-5851
www.house.gov/rothman

Rounds, Mike (1954-)
Governor of South Dakota (Republican)
500 E Capitol Ave **Ph:** 605-773-3212
Pierre, SD 57501 **Fax:** 605-773-5844
www.state.sd.us/governor

Rourke, Mickey (1956-)
Actor
International Creative Management **Ph:** 310-550-4000
8942 Wilshire Blvd
Beverly Hills, CA 90211

Roush, Jack (1942-)
NASCAR racing team owner
Roush Racing **Ph:** 704-720-4100
4600 Roush Pl NW
Concord, NC 28027
www.roushracing.com

Rove, Karl (1950-)
Deputy chief of staff and senior adviser to President George W Bush
1600 Pennsylvania Ave NW **Ph:** 202-456-2369
2nd Fl West Wing **Fax:** 202-456-2530
Washington, DC 20502

Rowand, Aaron (1977-)
Professional baseball player
Philadelphia Phillies **Ph:** 215-463-6000
Citizens Bank Park
1 Citizens Bank Park Way
Philadelphia, PA 19148
philadelphia.phillies.mlb.com

Rowe, John W, MD
Executive Chairman of Aetna (has announced his intention to retire from Aetna late in 2006)
Aetna Inc **Ph:** 860-273-0123
151 Farmington Ave **Fax:** 860-273-3971
Hartford, CT 06156
www.aetna.com/presscenter

Rowland, F Sherwood, PhD (1927-)
Winner (with two other scientists) of the 1995 Nobel Prize in Chemistry for work in atmospheric chemistry, particularly concerning the formation and decomposition of ozone
University of California at Irvine **Ph:** 949-824-6016 **Fax:** 949-824-2905
Dept of Chemistry
571 Rowland Hall
Irvine, CA 92697
www.chem.uci.edu

Rowlands, Gena (1930-)
Actor
International Creative Management **Ph:** 310-550-4000
8942 Wilshire Blvd
Beverly Hills, CA 90211

Rowley, Cynthia (1958-)
Fashion designer
376 Bleecker St **Ph:** 212-242-0847
New York, NY 10014
www.cynthiarowley.com

Rowling, JK (1965-)
Author of the Harry Potter books
Scholastic Inc **Ph:** 212-343-6100
557 Broadway
New York, NY 10012
www.jkrowling.com

Rowling, Robert B
Chairman and CEO of TRT Holdings Inc., a diversified holding company with holdings in energy, hotels (the Omni hotel chain), financial services, and consumer retailing
TRT Holdings Inc **Ph:** 972-871-5551
420 Decker St **Fax:** 972-871-5665
Irving, TX 75062

Roy, Patrick (1965-)
Co-owner of the junior hockey team the Quebec Remparts; former NHL goalie (retired) and all-time leader in NHL victories for a goaltender
Quebec Remparts **Ph:** 418-525-1212
Pepsi Coliseum **Fax:** 418-525-2242
250 Wilfrid-Hamel Blvd
Quebec, QC G1L5A7
www.remparts.qc.ca/eng/curriculum_patrick_roy.pdf

Roybal-Allard, Lucille (1941-)
US Representative from California (Democrat)
2330 Rayburn Bldg **Ph:** 202-225-1766
Washington, DC 20515 **Fax:** 202-226-0350
www.house.gov/roybal-allard

Royce, Ed (1951-)
US Representative from California (Republican)
2202 Rayburn Bldg **Ph:** 202-225-4111
Washington, DC 20515 **Fax:** 202-226-0335
www.royce.house.gov

Rozen, Leah
Movie critic at People Magazine
People Magazine **Ph:** 212-522-1212
Rockefeller Center **Fax:** 212-522-0331
Time & Life Bldg
New York, NY 10020

Rubenstein, Atoosa (1973-)
Writes Dear Seventeen, a syndicated advice column for teens
King Features Syndicate Inc **Ph:** 212-455-4000
888 7th Ave 2nd Fl
New York, NY 10019
www.kingfeatures.com

Rubin, Ellis S
Defense attorney who has gained national attention for his role in unusual cases
Law Offices of Ellis Rubin PA **Ph:** 305-576-5600
4141 NE 2nd Ave Suite 203 **Fax:** 305-576-3292
Miami, FL 33137
www.ellisrubin.com

Rubin, Leigh
Creator of the comic panel Rubes
Creators Syndicate Inc **Ph:** 310-337-7003
5777 W Century Blvd Suite 700 **Fax:** 310-337-7625
Los Angeles, CA 90045
www.creators.com

Rubin, Robert E (1938-)
US Secretary of the Treasury in the Clinton Administration; currently Director, Chairman of the Executive Committee, and Member of the Office of the Chairman of Citigroup Inc
Citigroup Inc **Ph:** 212-559-1000
399 Park Ave **Fax:** 212-793-3946
New York, NY 10043
www.citigroup.com/citigroup/corporategovernance

Rucinsky, Martin (1971-)
Professional hockey player
New York Rangers **Ph:** 212-465-6486
Madison Square Garden **Fax:** 212-465-6494
2 Pennsylvania Plaza
New York, NY 10121
www.newyorkrangers.com

Rudin, Scott (1958-)
Movie producer
Dart Group **Ph:** 212-277-7555
90 Park Ave 19th Fl **Fax:** 212-277-7550
New York, NY 10016

Rudman, Warren B (1930-)
Former US senator & founding co-chairman (with Bob Kerrey & Pete Peterson) of the Concord Coalition
Concord Coalition **Ph:** 703-894-6222
1011 Arlington Blvd Suite 300 **Fax:** 703-894-6231
Arlington, VA 22209
www.concordcoalition.org

Rudner, Rita (1956-)
Comedian
International Creative Management **Ph:** 310-550-4000
8942 Wilshire Blvd
Beverly Hills, CA 90211
www.ritafunny.com

Ruff, Lindy (1960-)
Hockey coach
Buffalo Sabres **Ph:** 716-855-4100
HSBC Arena **Fax:** 716-855-4115
1 Seymour H Knox III Plaza
Buffalo, NY 14203
www.sabres.com

Ruiz, Hector, PhD (1945-)
Chairman and CEO of Advanced Micro Devices
Advanced Micro Devices Inc **Ph:** 408-732-2400
1 AMD Pl **Fax:** 408-982-6164
PO Box 3453
Sunnyvale, CA 94088
www.amd.com

Rukeyser, Louis (1933-)
Economic commentator; has retired as a television host but is expected to continue his newsletters
PO Box 9605 **Ph:** 703-905-8000
McLean, VA 22102 **TF:** 800-892-9702
www.rukeyser.com

Rule, Ann (1935-)
True crime writer
Simon & Schuster **Ph:** 212-698-7000
1230 Ave of the Americas
New York, NY 10020
www.annrules.com

Rumsfeld, Donald H (1932-)
US Secretary of Defense
US Dept of Defense **Ph:** 703-692-7100
1000 Defense Pentagon **Fax:** 703-697-9080
Washington, DC 20301
www.defenselink.mil/osd/topleaders.html

Runyan, Marla (1969-)
Track & field runner; first legally-blind athlete to compete in the Olympic Games
Flynn Sports Management **Ph:** 423-753-0851
625-A Hales Chapel Rd
Gray, TN 37615
www.marlarunyan.com

Ruppersberger, Dutch (1946-)
US Representative from Maryland (Democrat)
1630 Longworth Bldg **Ph:** 202-225-3061
Washington, DC 20515 **Fax:** 202-225-3094
dutch.house.gov

Rush, Bobby L (1946-)
US Representative from Illinois (Democrat)
2416 Rayburn Bldg **Ph:** 202-225-4372
Washington, DC 20515 **Fax:** 202-226-0333
www.house.gov/rush

Rush, Geoffrey (1951-)
Actor
Creative Artists Agency **Ph:** 310-288-4545
9830 Wilshire Blvd **Fax:** 310-288-4800
Beverly Hills, CA 90212

Rushdie, Salman (1947-)
Anglo-Indian novelist (The Satanic Verses)
Random House Publicity **Ph:** 212-782-9000
1745 Broadway
New York, NY 10019
www.randomhouse.com

Rusher, William
Syndicated columnist; former publisher of the National Review
United Feature Syndicate **Ph:** 212-293-8500
200 Madison Ave
New York, NY 10016
www.unitedfeatures.com

Russell, Bill (1934-)
Former professional basketball player; member of the Basketball Hall of Fame
Naismith Memorial Basketball Hall of Fame **Ph:** 413-781-6500
Fax: 413-781-1939
1000 W Columbus Ave **TF:** 877-446-6752
Springfield, MA 01105
www.hoophall.com

Russell, Francia
Founding artistic director (with Kent Stowell) of the Pacific Northwest Ballet
Pacific Northwest Ballet **Ph:** 206-441-9411
301 Mercer St **Fax:** 206-441-2440
Seattle, WA 98109
www.pnb.org/company

Russell, Herman J
Atlanta entrepreneur
HJ Russell & Co **Ph:** 404-330-1000
504 Fair St SW **Fax:** 404-330-0922
Atlanta, GA 30313
www.hjrussell.com

Russell, Jay (1960-)
Film director
Creative Artists Agency **Ph:** 310-288-4545
9830 Wilshire Blvd **Fax:** 310-288-4800
Beverly Hills, CA 90212

Russell, Kurt (1951-)
Actor
Creative Artists Agency **Ph:** 310-288-4545
9830 Wilshire Blvd **Fax:** 310-288-4800
Beverly Hills, CA 90212

Russell, Mark (1932-)
Political satirist
Tribune Media Services Inc **Ph:** 312-222-4444
435 N Michigan Ave Suite 1500
Chicago, IL 60611
www.markrussell.net

Russert, Tim (1950-)
Moderator of Meet the Press; is also an anchor at MSNBC and CNBC and is NBC News Senior Vice President and Washington Bureau Chief
Meet the Press **Ph:** 202-885-4598
4001 Nebraska Ave NW **Fax:** 202-966-4544
Washington, DC 20016
www.msnbc.msn.com/id/4459759

Russo, Patricia F
Chairman and CEO of Lucent Technologies
Lucent Technologies Inc **Ph:** 908-582-8500
600 Mountain Ave **Fax:** 908-508-2576
Murray Hill, NJ 07974
www.lucent.com

Russo, Rene (1954-)
Actor & model
John Crosby Management **Ph:** 323-874-2400
1310 N Spaulding Ave **Fax:** 323-874-2500
Los Angeles, CA 90046

Russo, Richard (1949-)
Fiction author (novels and short stories)
Vintage/Anchor Publicity **Ph:** 212-572-2420
1745 Broadway 20th Fl
New York, NY 10019
www.randomhouse.com/vintage

Russo, Thomas A (1943-)
An executive vice president and the chief legal officer of Lehman Brothers Holdings Inc.; from 1975-1977 held legal positions with the Commodity Futures Trading Commission
Lehman Brothers Inc **Ph:** 212-526-7000
745 7th Ave 30th Fl
New York, NY 10019
www.lehman.com/who/bios/#TAR

Rust, Edward B Jr
Chairman and CEO of State Farm Insurance Companies
State Farm Insurance Cos **Ph:** 309-766-2311
1 State Farm Plaza
Bloomington, IL 61710
www.statefarm.com

Ruta, Frank A
Executive chef & owner of Palena Restaurant in Washington, DC; in the 1980s was personal lunch and dinner chef and executive sous chef at the White House for the Reagan and Bush families
Palena Restaurant **Ph:** 202-537-9250
3529 Connecticut Ave NW
Washington, DC 20008
www.palenarestaurant.com

Ryan, Arthur F
Chairman and CEO of Prudential Financial Inc
Prudential Financial Inc **Ph:** 973-802-6000
751 Broad St
Newark, NJ 07102

Ryan, Meg (1961-)
Actor
Creative Artists Agency **Ph:** 310-288-4545
9830 Wilshire Blvd **Fax:** 310-288-4800
Beverly Hills, CA 90212

Ryan, Nolan (1947-)
Major League Baseball Hall of Fame pitcher (retired); all-time leader in strikeouts
Nolan Ryan Foundation & Exhibit Center **Ph:** 281-388-1134 **Fax:** 281-388-1135
2925 S Bypass 35
Alvin, TX 77511
www.nolanryanfoundation.org

Ryan, Pam Munoz (1951-)
Author of books for children (picture books and novels)
Scholastic Inc **Ph:** 212-343-6100
557 Broadway
New York, NY 10012
www.pammunozryan.com

Ryan, Patrick G
Founder and Executive Chairman of Aon
Aon Corp **Ph:** 312-381-1000
200 E Randolph St
Chicago, IL 60601
www.aon.com

Ryan, Patrick T
President & CEO of PolyMedica
PolyMedica Corp **Ph:** 781-933-2020
11 State St
Woburn, MA 01801
www.polymedica.com

Ryan, Paul (1970-)
US Representative from Wisconsin (Republican)
1113 Longworth Bldg **Ph:** 202-225-3031
Washington, DC 20515 **Fax:** 202-225-3393
www.house.gov/ryan

Ryan, Thomas M
Chairman, president, and CEO of CVS Corp and president & CEO of CVS Pharmacy Inc
CVS Corp **Ph:** 401-765-1500
1 CVS Dr
Woonsocket, RI 02895
www.cvs.com/investorrelations

Ryan, Timothy J (1973-)
US Representative from Ohio (Democrat)
222 Cannon Bldg **Ph:** 202-225-5261
Washington, DC 20515 **Fax:** 202-225-3719
timryan.house.gov

Ryan, Tom K (1926-)
Creator of the comic strip Tumbleweeds
King Features Syndicate Inc **Ph:** 212-455-4000
888 7th Ave 2nd Fl
New York, NY 10019
www.tumbleweeds.com

Rybak, RT
Mayor of Minneapolis
350 S 5th St Suite 331 **Ph:** 612-673-2100
Minneapolis, MN 55415 **Fax:** 612-673-2305
www.ci.minneapolis.mn.us/mayor

Ryder, Thomas O
Chairman of Reader's Digest
Reader's Digest Assn Inc **Ph:** 914-238-1000
Reader's Digest Rd
Pleasantville, NY 10570
www.rd.com

Ryder, Winona (1971-)
Actor
Endeavor
9601 Wilshire Blvd 3rd Fl
Beverly Hills, CA 90210
Ph: 310-248-2000
Fax: 310-248-2020

Rylant, Cynthia (1954-)
Poet, novelist, and artist; her children's books include Missing May, When the Relatives Came, and the Henry & Mudge Ready-to-Read series
Simon & Schuster Books for Young Readers
1230 Ave of the Americas
New York, NY 10020
www.cynthiarylant.com
Ph: 212-698-7000

Ryun, Jim (1947-)
US Representative from Kansas (Republican)
1110 Longworth Bldg
Washington, DC 20515
www.ryun.house.gov
Ph: 202-225-6601
Fax: 202-225-7986

S

Saban, Nick (1951-)
Football coach
Miami Dolphins
7500 SW 30th St
Davie, FL 33314
www.miamidolphins.com
Ph: 954-452-7000
Fax: 954-452-7055

Sabbatini, Rory (1976-)
Professional golfer
SFX Sports Group
5335 Wisconsin Ave NW Suite 850
Washington, DC 20015
www.pgatour.com
Ph: 202-686-2000
Fax: 202-686-5050

Sabia, Michael J (1953-)
President & CEO of Bell Canada Enterprises (BCE) and CEO of Bell Canada
BCE Inc
1000 de la Gauchetiere W Suite 3700
Montreal, QC H3B4Y7
www.bce.ca/en
Ph: 514-870-8777
Fax: 514-786-3970

Sabine, Charles
NBC news correspondent
NBC News
30 Rockefeller Plaza
New York, NY 10112
www.msnbc.msn.com/id/3689499
Ph: 212-664-4249

Sabo, Martin Olav (1938-)
US Representative from Minnesota (Democrat)
2336 Rayburn Bldg
Washington, DC 20515
sabo.house.gov
Ph: 202-225-4755
Fax: 202-225-4886

Sachar, Louis (1954-)
Author of Holes and other popular books for young readers, including the Marvin Redpost books and There's a Boy in the Girls' Bathroom
Random House Children's Books
Publicity Dept
1745 Broadway
New York, NY 10019
www.louissachar.com
Ph: 212-782-9000

Sachs, Lloyd
Entertainment critic
Chicago Sun-Times
401 N Wabash Ave
Chicago, IL 60611
Ph: 312-321-3000
Fax: 312-321-3084

Sack, Steve (1953-)
Editorial cartoonist for the Minneapolis Star Tribune
Tribune Media Services Inc
435 N Michigan Ave Suite 1500
Chicago, IL 60611
www.comicspage.com
Ph: 312-222-4444

Sacks, Oliver, MD (1933-)
Physician (neurologist) & writer (author of Awakenings) concerned with ways in which individuals survive and adapt to neurological diseases/conditions, and what this can tell us about the human brain
Wylie Agency
250 W 57th St Suite 2114
New York, NY 10107
www.oliversacks.com
Ph: 212-246-0069

Sadler, Elliott (1975-)
Race car driver
Robert Yates Racing
PO Box 3640
Mooresville, NC 28117
www.ryr.com
Ph: 704-662-9625

Safer, Morley (1931-)
Veteran journalist and 60 Minutes correspondent
60 Minutes
555 W 57th St
New York, NY 10019
www.cbsnews.com
Ph: 212-975-2006

Saffell, Janis
Fitness expert who presents innovative kickbox/fitness programs; president & CEO of Fitness Express International, a consulting company that produces fitness educational events and product lines
Fitness Express International **Ph:** 888-685-2608
2333 Brickell Ave Suite 208 **Fax:** 305-860-0982
Miami, FL 33129
www.janissaffell.com

Safina, Dinara (1986-)
Professional tennis player
WTA Tour **Ph:** 727-895-5000
1 Progress Plaza Suite 1500 **Fax:** 727-894-1982
Saint Petersburg, FL 33701
www.wtatour.com

Sagal, Peter
Host of the NPR quiz show Wait Wait...Don't Tell Me; also writes plays
National Public Radio **Ph:** 202-513-2000
635 Massachusetts Ave NW **Fax:** 202-513-3329
Washington, DC 20001
www.npr.org

Saget, Bob (1956-)
Actor; comedian
William Morris Agency **Ph:** 310-859-4000
1 William Morris Pl **Fax:** 310-859-4462
Beverly Hills, CA 90212
www.wma.com/bob_saget/summary

Saint Laurent, Yves (1936-)
Fashion designer
3 E 57th St **Ph:** 212-223-7463
New York, NY 10022
www.ysl.com

Sajak, Pat (1946-)
Host of Wheel of Fortune game show
Wheel of Fortune **Ph:** 310-244-1234
Robert Young Bldg **Fax:** 310-244-2233
10202 W Washington Blvd
Suite 2000
Culver City, CA 90232
www.wheeloffortune.com

Sakai, Stan (1953-)
Comic book artist; creator of Usagi Yojimbo
Dark Horse Comics Inc **Ph:** 503-652-8815
10956 SE Main St **Fax:** 503-654-9440
Milwaukie, OR 97222
www.usagiyojimbo.com

Sakic, Joe (1969-)
Professional hockey player
Colorado Avalanche **Ph:** 303-405-1100
Pepsi Center
1000 Chopper Cir
Denver, CO 80204
www.coloradoavalanche.com

Salazar, John T (1953-)
US Representative from Colorado (Democrat)
1531 Longworth Bldg **Ph:** 202-225-4761
Washington, DC 20515 **Fax:** 202-226-0622
www.house.gov/salazar

Salazar, Ken (1955-)
US Senator from Colorado (Democrat)
B40A Dirksen Bldg **Ph:** 202-224-5852
Washington, DC 20510 **Fax:** 202-228-5036
salazar.senate.gov

Salei, Ruslan (1974-)
Professional hockey player
Mighty Ducks of Anaheim **Ph:** 714-704-2700
Arrowhead Pond **Fax:** 714-704-2913
2695 Katella Ave
Anaheim, CA 92806
www.mightyducks.com

Sales, Nykesha (1976-)
Professional basketball player
Connecticut Sun **Ph:** 860-862-4000
1 Mohegan Sun Blvd **Fax:** 860-862-4010
Uncasville, CT 06382
www.wnba.com/sun

Salinas, Maria Elena (1959-)
News anchor; also writes a syndicated column
Univision Television Network **Ph:** 305-471-4346
9405 NW 41st St
Miami, FL 33178
www.mariaesalinas.com

Salinger, JD (1919-)
Author of Catcher in the Rye
Warner Books **Ph:** 212-522-7200
c/o Author Mail
1271 Ave of the Americas
New York, NY 10020
www.twbookmark.com

Salk, Jonas, MD (1914-1995)
Developer of the polio vaccine
Salk Institute for Biological Studies **Ph:** 858-453-4100
Fax: 858-453-8534
PO Box 85800
San Diego, CA 92186
www.salk.edu

Sall, John
Co-founder & Executive Vice President of SAS (a software and services company)
SAS Institute Inc **Ph:** 919-677-8000
100 SAS Campus Dr **Fax:** 919-677-4444
Cary, NC 27513
www.sas.com

Salley, John (1964-)
Former pro basketball player and co-host of FOX's Best Damn Sports Show Period
Fox Sports **Ph:** 310-369-1000
10201 W Pico Blvd
Bldg 101
Los Angeles, CA 90035
msn.foxsports.com/bestdamn

Salvatore, RA (1959-)
Fantasy writer; besides his own books, he also novellized the Star Wars trilogy
Random House Publicity **Ph:** 212-782-9000
1745 Broadway
New York, NY 10019
www.rasalvatore.com

Sammons, Mary (1947-)
President & CEO of Rite Aid Corp
Rite Aid Corp **Ph:** 717-761-2633
30 Hunter Ln **Fax:** 717-731-3860
Camp Hill, PA 17011
www.riteaid.com

Sampras, Pete (1971-)
Professional tennis player
IMG Inc **Ph:** 216-522-1200
IMG Center **Fax:** 216-522-1145
1360 E 9th St Suite 100
Cleveland, OH 44114
www.petesampras.com

Sams, BJ (1980-)
Professional football player
Baltimore Ravens **Ph:** 410-547-8100
1101 Russell St **Fax:** 410-547-8112
Baltimore, MD 21230
www.baltimoreravens.com

Samsonov, Sergei (1978-)
Professional hockey player
Edmonton Oilers **Ph:** 780-414-4000
11230 110th St **Fax:** 780-409-5890
Edmonton, AB T5G3H7
www.edmontonoilers.com

Samueli, Henry, PhD (1954-)
Co-founder, chairman, & chief technology officer of Broadcom Corp and a named inventor in 22 US patents; owner of the Mighty Ducks of Anaheim hockey team
Broadcom Corp **Ph:** 949-450-8700
16215 Alton Pkwy
Irvine, CA 92618
www.broadcom.com/company/keyexec_samueli.php

Samuelson, Orion
Host of the National Farm Report; also does weekly editorial commentary on the world of agriculture
Tribune Radio Networks **Ph:** 312-222-3342
435 N Michigan Ave **Fax:** 312-222-4876
Chicago, IL 60611
www.tribuneradio.com

Samuelson, Paul A, PhD (1915-)
Winner of the 1970 Nobel Prize in Economic Sciences (while at MIT); writes a syndicated economic commentary column
Tribune Media Services Inc **Ph:** 312-222-4444
435 N Michigan Ave Suite 1500
Chicago, IL 60611
tmsfeatures.com/productlist.htm

Samuelson, Robert (1945-)
Syndicated columnist (commentary); also a Newsweek contributing editor
Washington Post Writers Group **Ph:** 202-334-6375
Fax: 202-334-5669
1150 15th St NW 9th Fl
Washington, DC 20071
www.postwritersgroup.com

Samuelsson, Marcus (1970-)
Chef and co-owner of Aquavit, a New York restaurant that specializes in Scandinavian food
Restaurant Aquavit **Ph:** 212-307-7311
65 E 55th St
New York, NY 10022
www.aquavit.org

Sanborn, David (1945-)
Jazz saxophonist
International Creative Management **Ph:** 310-550-4000
8942 Wilshire Blvd
Beverly Hills, CA 90211
www.davidsanborn.com

Sanborn, Mark
Motivational speaker on leadership, team building, customer service, and mastering change
Sanborn & Associates Inc **Ph:** 303-683-0714
818 Summer Dr **Fax:** 303-683-0825
Highlands Ranch, CO 80126 **TF:** 800-650-3343
www.marksanborn.com

Sanchez, Linda T (1969-)
US Representative from California (Democrat)
1007 Longworth Bldg **Ph:** 202-225-6676
Washington, DC 20515 **Fax:** 202-226-1012
www.house.gov/lindasanchez

Sanchez, Loretta (1960-)
US Representative from California (Democrat)
1230 Longworth Bldg **Ph:** 202-225-2965
Washington, DC 20515 **Fax:** 202-225-5859
www.lorettasanchez.house.gov

Sanchez, Marcela
Writes a weekly column on Latin America, available in both English & Spanish
Washington Post Writers Group **Ph:** 202-334-6375 **Fax:** 202-334-5669
1150 15th St NW 9th Fl
Washington, DC 20071
www.postwritersgroup.com

Sanders, Bernard (1941-)
US Representative from Vermont (Independent)
2233 Rayburn Bldg **Ph:** 202-225-4115
Washington, DC 20515 **Fax:** 202-225-6790
bernie.house.gov

Sanders, Jerry
Mayor of San Diego
202 C St 11th Fl **Ph:** 619-236-6330
San Diego, CA 92101 **Fax:** 619-236-7228
www.sandiego.gov

Sanders, Kerry
NBC News correspondent (based in Miami)
NBC News **Ph:** 212-664-4249
30 Rockefeller Plaza
New York, NY 10112
www.msnbc.msn.com/id/3689499

Sanders, Mark D
Songwriter and author whose work includes I Hope You Dance, a book based on the hit song (which he also wrote)
Rutledge Hill Press Publicity **Ph:** 615-902-2214
PO Box 14100
Nashville, TN 37214

Sanders, Reggie (1967-)
Professional baseball player
Kansas City Royals **Ph:** 816-921-8000
Kauffman Stadium **Fax:** 816-921-5775
1 Royal Way
Kansas City, MO 64129
kansascity.royals.mlb.com

Sanderson, Geoff (1972-)
Professional hockey player
Phoenix Coyotes **Ph:** 623-463-8800
5800 W Glenn Dr Suite 350 **Fax:** 623-463-8810
Glendale, AZ 85301
www.phoenixcoyotes.com

Sandford, John (1944-)
Author of the suspense series in which the titles include the word Prey (Lucas Davenport is the protagonist)
Ballantine Books Publicity **Ph:** 212-782-9000
1745 Broadway
New York, NY 10019
www.johnsandford.org

Sandler, Adam (1966-)
Actor and comedian
Endeavor **Ph:** 310-248-2000
9601 Wilshire Blvd 3rd Fl **Fax:** 310-248-2020
Beverly Hills, CA 90210
www.adamsandler.com

Sandler, Marion O
Chairman and CEO of Golden West Financial Corp; her husband, Herbert M Sandler, has the same titles and they operate as a husband-and-wife management team
Golden West Financial Corp **Ph:** 510-446-3420
1901 Harrison St
Oakland, CA 94612
www.gdw.com

Sandoval, Arturo (1949-)
Cuban jazz musician (trumpet)
Turi's Music Enterprises Inc **Ph:** 305-579-5130
801 Brickell Bay Dr Suite 870 **Fax:** 305-579-5135
Miami Beach, FL 33131
www.arturosandoval.com

Sanford, Mark (1960-)
Governor of South Carolina (Republican)
PO Box 12267 **Ph:** 803-734-2100
Columbia, SC 29211 **Fax:** 803-734-5167
www.scgovernor.com

Sanger, Stephen
Chairman of the Board and CEO of General Mills
General Mills Inc **Ph:** 763-764-7600
1 General Mills Blvd
Minneapolis, MN 55426
www.generalmills.com/corporate/investors

Sanneh, Tony (1971-)
Professional soccer player
Chicago Fire **Ph:** 312-705-7200
980 N Michigan Ave Suite 1998 **Fax:** 312-705-7393
Chicago, IL 60611
chicago.fire.mlsnet.com

Sansom, Chip (1951-)
Cartoonist for the comic strip The Born Loser, which was originally created by his father, Art Sansom
Newspaper Enterprise Assn — **Ph:** 212-293-8500
200 Madison Ave
New York, NY 10016
www.unitedfeatures.com

Sansone, Leslie
Fitness instructor; developer of In-Home Walking
Walk Aerobics Inc — **Ph:** 724-658-1400
2801 Wilmington Rd
New Castle, PA 16105
www.walkaerobics.com

Sansone, Maggie
New Age musician (Celtic music; dulcimer)
Maggie's Music — **Ph:** 410-867-0642
PO Box 490 — **Fax:** 410-867-0265
Shady Side, MD 20764 — **TF:** 877-624-4436
www.maggiesansone.com

Santana, Carlos (1947-)
Guitarist and leader of the band Santana
Creative Artists Agency — **Ph:** 310-288-4545
9830 Wilshire Blvd — **Fax:** 310-288-4800
Beverly Hills, CA 90212
www.santana.com

Santana, Johan (1979-)
Professional baseball player
Minnesota Twins — **Ph:** 612-375-1366
Hubert H Humphrey Metrodome — **Fax:** 612-375-7473
34 Kirby Puckett Pl
Minneapolis, MN 55415
minnesota.twins.mlb.com

Santana, Jose
President & CEO of Timex
Timex Corp — **Ph:** 203-346-5000
555 Christian Rd — **Fax:** 203-346-5139
Middlebury, CT 06762

Santoro, Gene
Music critic; also covers film and jazz for the New York Daily News
The Nation — **Ph:** 212-209-5400
33 Irving Pl 8th Fl — **Fax:** 212-982-9000
New York, NY 10003
www.thenation.com

Santorum, Rick (1958-)
US Senator from Pennsylvania (Republican)
511 Dirksen Bldg — **Ph:** 202-224-6324
Washington, DC 20510 — **Fax:** 202-228-0604
santorum.senate.gov

Sapp, Warren (1972-)
Professional football player
Oakland Raiders — **Ph:** 510-864-5000
1220 Harbor Bay Pkwy — **Fax:** 510-864-5134
Alameda, CA 94502
www.qbkilla.com

Saralegui, Cristina (1948-)
Host of a Spanish-language talk show
Creative Artists Agency — **Ph:** 310-288-4545
9830 Wilshire Blvd — **Fax:** 310-288-4800
Beverly Hills, CA 90212
www.cristinaonline.com

Saramago, Jose (1922-)
Portuguese writer (winner of the 1998 Nobel Prize for Literature)
Harcourt Trade Publishers — **Ph:** 212-592-1000
15 E 26th St
New York, NY 10010
www.harcourtbooks.com

Sarandon, Susan (1946-)
Actor
International Creative Management — **Ph:** 310-550-4000
8942 Wilshire Blvd
Beverly Hills, CA 90211

Sarbanes, Paul S (1933-)
US Senator from Maryland (Democrat)
309 Hart Bldg — **Ph:** 202-224-4524
Washington, DC 20510 — **Fax:** 202-224-1651
sarbanes.senate.gov

Sarcev, Milos (1964-)
Professional bodybuilder, fitness model, and consultant
PO Box 892242 — **Ph:** 714-680-8881
Temecula, CA 92589
www.milossarcev.com

Sargent, Ben (1948-)
Editorial cartoonist
Universal Press Syndicate — **Ph:** 816-932-6600
4520 Main St
Kansas City, MO 64111
www.amuniversal.com/ups/features

Sargent, Ronald
Chairman and CEO of Staples Inc
Staples Inc — **Ph:** 508-253-5000
500 Staples Dr
Framingham, MA 01702
investor.staples.com

Sartwell, Crispin (1958-)
Syndicated columnist (commentary on popular culture, religion, politics, education)
Creators Syndicate Inc **Ph:** 310-337-7003
5777 W Century Blvd Suite 700 **Fax:** 310-337-7625
Los Angeles, CA 90045
www.creators.com/opinion.html

Sarver, Robert
Majority owner of the Phoenix Suns basketball franchise
Phoenix Suns **Ph:** 602-379-7900
America West Arena **Fax:** 602-379-7990
201 E Jefferson St
Phoenix, AZ 85004
www.nba.com/suns/news/sarver_bio.html

Saskin, Ted
Executive Director of the National Hockey League Players Association
National Hockey League Players Assn **Ph:** 416-408-4040
777 Bay St Suite 2400
Toronto, ON M5G2C8
www.nhlpa.com

Satan, Miroslav (1974-)
Professional hockey player
New York Islanders **Ph:** 516-501-6700
1535 Old Country Rd **Fax:** 516-501-6729
Plainview, NY 11803
www.mirosatan.sk

Sather, Glen (1943-)
President & General Manager of the New York Rangers hockey club
New York Rangers **Ph:** 212-465-6486
Madison Square Garden **Fax:** 212-465-6494
2 Pennsylvania Plaza
New York, NY 10121
www.newyorkrangers.com

Sauerbrun, Todd (1973-)
Professional football player
Denver Broncos **Ph:** 303-649-9000
13655 Broncos Pkwy **Fax:** 303-649-9354
Englewood, CO 80112
www.denverbroncos.com

Saunders, Debra (1954-)
Syndicated op-ed columnist
Creators Syndicate Inc **Ph:** 310-337-7003
5777 W Century Blvd Suite 700 **Fax:** 310-337-7625
Los Angeles, CA 90045
www.creators.com/opinion.html

Saunders, Flip (1955-)
Basketball coach
Detroit Pistons **Ph:** 248-377-0100
Palace at Auburn Hills **Fax:** 248-377-4262
4 Championship Dr
Auburn Hills, MI 48326
www.nba.com/pistons

Saunders, Jeraldine
Writes the syndicated column Omarr's Astrological Forecast (she is the successor to astrologer Sydney Omarr)
Tribune Media Services Inc **Ph:** 312-222-4444
435 N Michigan Ave Suite 1500
Chicago, IL 60611
tmsfeatures.com/productlist.htm

Saunders, John (1955-)
Sports broadcaster
ESPN **Ph:** 860-585-2000
ESPN Plaza
935 Middle St
Bristol, CT 06010
sports.espn.go.com/espntv/espnGuide

Savage, Frank
CEO of Savage Holdings LLC, a global financial services company
Savage Holdings LLC **Ph:** 212-969-1000
1345 Ave of the Americas **Fax:** 212-969-2229
New York, NY 10105

Savage, Michael (1942-)
Drive time radio talk show host (right wing) and the person credited with creating the phrase Compassionate Conservative
Talk Radio Network **Ph:** 541-664-8827
PO Box 3755 **Fax:** 541-664-6250
Central Point, OR 95702
www.talkradionetwork.com

Savage, Terry
Nationally known expert on personal finance; author and syndicated columnist as well as a regular commentator on several television networks on issues related to investing and financial markets
Terry Savage Productions Ltd **Ph:** 312-266-1717
676 N Michigan Ave Suite 3610
Chicago, IL 60611
www.terrysavage.com

Savidge, Martin
NBC News correspondent (based in Atlanta)
NBC News **Ph:** 212-664-4249
30 Rockefeller Plaza
New York, NY 10112
www.msnbc.msn.com/id/3689499

Saving, Thomas R, PhD (1933-)
Economics professor and director of the Private Enterprise Research Center at Texas A&M University
Private Enterprise Research Center **Ph:** 979-845-7722 **Fax:** 979-845-6636
Texas A & M University
4231 TAMU
College Station, TX 77843
www.tamu.edu/perc

Sawhney, Mohanbir (1963-)
Scholar, teacher, consultant, and speaker on strategic marketing, e-business, and innovation
Kellogg School of Management **Ph:** 847-491-2713 **Fax:** 847-467-5605
Center for Research in Technology & Innovation
Jacobs Ctr Rm 5245B
2001 Sheridan Rd
Evanston, IL 60208
www.mohansawhney.com

Sawyer, Diane (1945-)
Co-anchor of ABC News's Good Morning America and of PrimeTime Live
Good Morning America **Ph:** 212-456-7777
147 Columbus Ave
New York, NY 10023
www.abcnews.go.com/GMA

Sawyer Brown
Country music group
Monterey Peninsula Artists/Paradigm **Ph:** 615-251-4400 **Fax:** 615-251-4401
124 12th Ave S Suite 410
Nashville, TN 37203
www.sawyerbrown.com

Saxton, Jim (1943-)
US Representative from New Jersey (Republican)
2217 Rayburn Bldg **Ph:** 202-225-4765
Washington, DC 20515 **Fax:** 202-225-0778
www.house.gov/saxton

Say, Allen (1937-)
Author and illustrator of children's books (Grandfather's Journey; Boy of the Three-Year Nap)
Houghton Mifflin Children's Books **Ph:** 617-351-5000
222 Berkeley St 8th Fl
Boston, MA 02116
www.houghtonmifflinbooks.com/authors/allensay

Sayler, Robert N (1940-)
Attorney; has been lead counsel representing major corporations for billion dollar-plus insurance coverage disputes for asbestos, DES, environmental cleanup, and breast implant liabilities
Covington & Burling **Ph:** 202-662-6000
1201 Pennsylvania Ave NW **Fax:** 202-662-6291
Washington, DC 20004
www.cov.com

Sayles, John (1950-)
Film director/producer/writer
Paradigm **Ph:** 310-288-8000
360 N Crescent Dr **Fax:** 310-288-2000
North Bldg
Beverly Hills, CA 90210

Scaduto, Al (1928-)
Produces the comic panel They'll Do It Every Time, which was originally created in 1929 by Jimmy Hatlo
King Features Syndicate Inc **Ph:** 212-455-4000
888 7th Ave 2nd Fl
New York, NY 10019
www.kingfeatures.com

Scalia, Antonin (1936-)
US Supreme Court justice
US Supreme Court Bldg **Ph:** 202-479-3000
1 1st St NE
Washington, DC 20543
www.supremecourtus.gov

Scancarelli, Jim
Writes & draws the comic strip Gasoline Alley; he is the third cartoonist to do so (the strip was originally created by Frank King)
Tribune Media Services Inc **Ph:** 312-222-4444
435 N Michigan Ave Suite 1500
Chicago, IL 60611
www.comicspage.com

Scarborough, Joe (1963-)
Host of Scarborough Country on MSNBC; former Republican Congressman from Florida
MSNBC TV **Ph:** 201-583-5000
1 MSNBC Plaza
Secaucus, NJ 07094
www.msnbc.msn.com/id/3080263

Scardino, Marjorie M (1947-)
Chief executive of Pearson (international media group)
Pearson Inc **Ph:** 212-641-2400
1330 Ave of the Americas
New York, NY 10019
www.pearson.com

Scarlett, Lynn
Deputy Secretary who is presently Acting Secretary of the Interior upon the resignation of Gale Norton April 1, 2006; the Secretary-Designate is Idaho Governor Dirk Kempthorne
Actg Secy **Ph:** 202-208-7351
US Dept of the Interior **Fax:** 202-208-5048
1849 C St NW
Washington, DC 20240
www.doi.gov/welcome.html

Scarpelli, Henry
Draws the comic strip Archie, which is written by Craig Boldman
Creators Syndicate Inc **Ph:** 310-337-7003
5777 W Century Blvd Suite 700 **Fax:** 310-337-7625
Los Angeles, CA 90045
www.creators.com

Schadler, Jay
Correspondent for Primetime
Prime Time Live **Ph:** 212-456-7777
147 Columbus Ave
New York, NY 10023
www.abcnews.go.com/Primetime

Schakowsky, Janice D (1944-)
US Representative from Illinois (Democrat)
1027 Longworth Bldg **Ph:** 202-225-2111
Washington, DC 20515 **Fax:** 202-226-6890
www.house.gov/schakowsky

Schar, Dwight
Chairman of NVR Inc, which operates business segments for homebuilding and mortgage banking
NVR Inc **Ph:** 703-956-4000
11700 Plaza America Dr **Fax:** 703-956-4750
Suite 500
Reston, VA 20190

Schatz, Howard
Photographer
Schatz/Ornstein Studio **Ph:** 212-334-6667
435 W Broadway **Fax:** 212-334-6669
New York, NY 10012
www.howardschatz.com

Schatz, Thomas
President of Citizens Against Government Waste and its lobbying arm, the Council for Citizens Against Government Waste
Citizens Against Government Waste **Ph:** 202-467-5300
Fax: 202-437-4253
1301 Connecticut Ave NW
Suite 400
Washington, DC 20036
www.cagw.org

Scheck, Barry (1949-)
Attorney & law professor; co-founder/co-director, with Peter Neufeld, of the Innocence Project at the Cardozo School of Law, which only handles cases where postconviction DNA testing of evidence can yield conclusive proof of innocence
Innocence Project **Ph:** 212-364-5340
100 5th Ave 3rd Fl **Fax:** 212-364-5341
New York, NY 10011
www.innocenceproject.com

Scheer, Robert (1936-)
Syndicated columnist; also co-hosts the radio program Left, Right and Center
Creators Syndicate Inc **Ph:** 310-337-7003
5777 W Century Blvd Suite 700 **Fax:** 310-337-7625
Los Angeles, CA 90045
www.robertscheer.com

Scheindlin, Judith (1942-)
Judge on the courtroom TV show Judge Judy
Paramount Television **Ph:** 323-956-5000
Judge Judy
5555 Melrose Ave
Hollywood, CA 90038
www.judgejudy.com

Schelling, Thomas C, PhD (1921-)
Winner (with Robert J Aumann of Israel) of the 2005 Nobel Prize in Economics for enhancing the understanding of conflict and cooperation through game-theory analysis
Maryland School of Public Policy **Ph:** 301-405-3494
Fax: 301-403-4675
University of Maryland
2101 Van Munching Hall
College Park, MD 20742
www.puaf.umd.edu/facstaff/faculty.html

Schenkenberg, Marcus (1968-)
Male model
Ford Models **Ph:** 212-219-6500
111 5th Ave **Fax:** 212-966-5028
New York, NY 10003

Schenkkan, Robert (1953-)
Actor (Star Trek: The Next Generation); also screenwriter & playwright (The Kentucky Cycle)
William Morris Agency **Ph:** 310-859-4000
1 William Morris Pl **Fax:** 310-859-4462
Beverly Hills, CA 90212

Scher, Laura
Co-founder & CEO of Working Assets Funding Service
Working Assets Funding Service **Ph:** 415-788-0777
101 Market St Suite 700
San Francisco, CA 94105

Scheuer, Michael
CIA official and author of Imperial Hubris: Why the West is Losing the War on Terror, which was published anonymously
Brassey's Inc — **Ph:** 703-661-1548
22841 Quicksilver Dr — **Fax:** 703-661-1547
Dulles, VA 20166

Schieffer, Bob (1937-)
Anchor and moderator of Face the Nation and interim anchor of the CBS Evening News
Face the Nation with Bob Schieffer — **Ph:** 202-457-4481
2020 M St NW
Washington, DC 20036
www.cbsnews.com

Schiff, Adam (1960-)
US Representative from California (Democrat)
326 Cannon Bldg — **Ph:** 202-225-4176
Washington, DC 20515 — **Fax:** 202-225-5828
schiff.house.gov

Schiff, Brad
Animator/director; specializes in action-packed and sports-related stop-motion animation
Laika — **Ph:** 503-225-1130
1400 NW 22nd Ave — **Fax:** 503-226-3746
Portland, OR 97210
www.laika.com/house

Schiff, Stacy
Author of Saint-Exupery: A Biography
Modern Library — **Ph:** 212-751-2600
Random House Publishing Group
Random House Inc
1745 Broadway
New York, NY 10171
www.randomhouse.com

Schiffer, Claudia (1970-)
Model
United Talent Agency — **Ph:** 310-273-6700
9560 Wilshire Blvd 5th Fl — **Fax:** 310-247-1111
Beverly Hills, CA 90212

Schilling, Curt (1966-)
Professional baseball player
Boston Red Sox — **Ph:** 617-267-9440
Fenway Park — **Fax:** 617-236-6797
4 Yawkey Way
Boston, MA 02215
boston.redsox.mlb.com

Schimmel, Robert (1950-)
Comedian
Gersh Agency — **Ph:** 310-274-6611
232 N Canon Dr
Beverly Hills, CA 90210
www.robertschimmel.com

Schlafly, Phyllis (1924-)
Conservative, pro-family advocate; founder & president of Eagle Forum, a pro-family organization; writes a syndicated column
Eagle Forum — **Ph:** 618-462-5415
PO Box 618 — **Fax:** 618-462-8909
Alton, IL 62002
www.eagleforum.org

Schlesinger, Chris
Chef, restauranteur, and cookbook author (The Thrill of the Grill)
East Coast Grill & Raw Bar — **Ph:** 617-491-6568
1271 Cambridge St Inman Sq — **Fax:** 617-868-4278
Cambridge, MA 02139
www.eastcoastgrill.net

Schlesinger, James R, PhD (1929-)
Former US Secretary of Defense, US Secretary of Energy, and CIA Director in the 1970s; has also served as chairman of the Atomic Energy Commission
MITRE Corp — **Ph:** 703-883-5358
7515 Colshire Dr Suite 1200
McLean, VA 22102
www.mitre.org/about/trustees.html

Schlesinger, Richard (1954-)
News correspondent for 48 Hours and other CBS News broadcasts
CBS News — **Ph:** 212-975-4114
524 W 57th St
New York, NY 10019
www.cbsnews.com

Schlessinger, Laura, PhD (1947-)
Radio talk show host and author; principal focus of her work is morals, values, and ethics (she is a licensed marriage, family, and child counselor)
Premiere Radio Networks Inc — **Ph:** 818-377-5300
15260 Ventura Blvd 5th Fl — **Fax:** 818-377-5333
Sherman Oaks, CA 91403
www.drlaura.com

Schleyer, William T
Chairman and CEO of Adelphia
Adelphia Communications Corp — **Ph:** 303-268-6300
5619 DTC Pkwy
Greenwood Village, CO 80111
www.adelphia.com

Schlosser, Eric
Investigative journalist, correspondent for Atlantic Monthly, and author of nonfiction; his books include Fast Food Nation
Atlantic Monthly **Ph:** 617-854-7700
77 N Washington St
Boston, MA 02114
www.houghtonmifflinbooks.com

Schlow, Michael
Chef and owner of Radius Restaurant in Boston
Radius Restaurant **Ph:** 617-426-1234
8 High St **Fax:** 617-426-2526
Boston, MA 02110
www.radiusrestaurant.com

Schmich, Mary
Writes the comic strip Brenda Starr with artist June Brigman
Tribune Media Services Inc **Ph:** 312-222-4444
435 N Michigan Ave Suite 1500
Chicago, IL 60611
www.comicspage.com

Schmidt, Eric E, PhD
Chairman of the Executive Committee and CEO of Google Inc; previously was Chairman & CEO of Novell and, earlier, was involved in the development of Java at Sun Microsystems
Google Inc **Ph:** 650-623-0000
1600 Amphitheatre Pkwy **Fax:** 650-623-0001
Mountain View, CA 94043
www.google.com/corporate/execs.html

Schmidt, Jason (1973-)
Professional baseball player
San Francisco Giants **Ph:** 415-972-2000
AT & T Park
24 Willie Mays Plaza
San Francisco, CA 94107
sanfrancisco.giants.mlb.com

Schmidt, Jean
US Representative from Ohio (Republican)
238 Cannon Bldg **Ph:** 202-225-3164
Washington, DC 20515 **Fax:** 202-225-1992
www.house.gov/schmidt **TF:** 800-784-6366

Schmitt, Harrison H, PhD (1935-)
Former astronaut (Lunar Module Pilot on Apollo 17, the last Apollo mission to the moon); former US Senator from New Mexico
Annapolis Center for Science Based Public Policy **Ph:** 410-268-3302 **Fax:** 410-268-4953
111 Forbes St Suite 200
Annapolis, MD 21401
www.annapoliscenter.org

Schnatter, John H
Founder and chairman of Papa John's International
Papa John's International Inc **Ph:** 502-261-7272
2002 Papa John Blvd
Louisville, KY 40299
www.papajohns.com/investor

Schneider, Donald J
Chairman of Schneider National, a leading provider of transportation, logistics, and related services
Schneider National Inc **Ph:** 920-592-2000
3101 S Packerland Dr
Green Bay, WI 54306

Schneider, Howie (1930-)
Creator of the comic strip The Sunshine Club
Newspaper Enterprise Assn **Ph:** 212-293-8500
200 Madison Ave
New York, NY 10016
www.unitedfeatures.com

Schneider, William (1955-)
Political commentator and senior political analyst for CNN; also a Resident Fellow at American Enterprise Institute and a contributing editor to various news publications
CNN **Ph:** 202-898-7900
820 1st St NE
Washington, DC 20002
www.cnn.com/CNN/anchors_reporters

Schnieders, Richard J (1949-)
Chairman, president, and CEO of SYSCO Corp
SYSCO Corp **Ph:** 281-584-1221
1390 Enclave Pkwy **Fax:** 281-584-2880
Houston, TX 77077
www.sysco.com/investor/governance.html

Schoenherr, John (1935-)
Illustrator of books for children (Owl Moon; Julie of the Wolves)
135 Upper Creek Rd **Ph:** 908-996-2203
Stockton, NJ 08559
www.embracingthechild.org/aschoenherr.html

Scholes, Myron S, PhD (1941-)
Winner (with Robert C Merton) of the 1997 Nobel Prize in Economic Sciences for a new method to determine the value of derivatives
Stanford University **Ph:** 650-723-2146
Graduate School of Business **Fax:** 650-725-0468
518 Memorial Way
Stanford, CA 94305
gsbapps.stanford.edu/facultybios

Schorr, Bill
Editorial cartoonist; also creates the comic strip The Grizzwells
United Feature Syndicate **Ph:** 212-293-8500
200 Madison Ave
New York, NY 10016
www.unitedfeatures.com

Schorr, Daniel (1916-)
Senior news analyst for NPR (a veteran reporter-commentator and the last of Edward R Murrow's CBS team still fully active in journalism)
National Public Radio **Ph:** 202-414-2000
635 Massachusetts Ave NW **Fax:** 202-414-3329
Washington, DC 20001
www.npr.org

Schorsch, Ismar, PhD (1935-)
Chancellor and President of the Faculties, as well as a professor of Jewish History, at the Jewish Theological Seminary, the intellectual and religious center of Conservative Judaism
Jewish Theological Seminary **Ph:** 212-678-8000
3080 Broadway **Fax:** 212-678-8947
New York, NY 10027
www.jtsa.edu

Schottenheimer, Marty (1943-)
Football coach
San Diego Chargers **Ph:** 858-874-4500
4020 Murphy Canyon Rd **Fax:** 858-282-2760
San Diego, CA 92123
www.chargers.com

Schrag, Jim
Executive Director of the Mennonite Church USA
Mennonite Church USA **Ph:** 574-294-7523
500 S Main St **Fax:** 574-293-1892
Elkhart, IN 46515
www.mennoniteusa.org

Schram, Martin (1942-)
Syndicated columnist (commentary)
Scripps Howard News Service **Ph:** 202-408-1484
1090 Vermont Ave NW **Fax:** 202-408-5950
Suite 1000
Washington, DC 20005
www.shns.com

Schreiber, Cory
Executive chef & owner of Wildwood Restaurant in Portland, Oregon
Wildwood Restaurant **Ph:** 503-248-9663
1221 NW 21st Ave
Portland, OR 97209
wildwoodrestaurant.com

Schrock, Richard R, PhD (1945-)
Winner of the 2006 Nobel Prize for Chemistry (one third of the award with Robert H Grubbs & Yves Chauvin) for the development of the metathesis method in organic synthesis
Massachusetts Institute of Technology **Ph:** 617-253-1596 **Fax:** 617-253-7670
Dept of Chemistry
77 Massachusetts Ave Rm 6-331
Cambridge, MA 02139
web.mit.edu/chemistry

Schroder, Rick (1970-)
Actor
Hofflund/Polone **Ph:** 310-859-1971
9465 Wilshire Blvd Suite 820
Beverly Hills, CA 90212

Schroeder, Pat (1940-)
Former US Congresswoman from Colorado (retired); now President and CEO of the Association of American Publishers
Assn of American Publishers **Ph:** 202-347-3375
50 F St NW Suite 400 **Fax:** 202-347-3690
Washington, DC 20001
www.publishers.org

Schuessler, John
Chairman, CEO, and president of Wendy's International Inc
Wendy's International Inc **Ph:** 614-764-3100
1 Dave Thomas Blvd
Dublin, OH 43017
www.wendys-invest.com

Schuller, Robert H (1926-)
Televangelist and senior pastor of the Crystal Cathedral in Garden Grove, California
Crystal Cathedral **Ph:** 714-971-4000
12141 Lewis St **Fax:** 714-750-3836
Garden Grove, CA 92842
www.crystalcathedral.org

Schultz, Howard
Founder and chairman of Starbucks; owner of the Seattle SuperSonics basketball team
Starbucks Coffee Co **Ph:** 206-447-1575
2401 Utah Ave S
Seattle, WA 98134
www.starbucks.com

Schultz, William F
Executive Director of Amnesty International (USA)
Amnesty International USA **Ph:** 212-807-8400
5 Penn Plaza 14th Fl **Fax:** 212-627-1451
New York, NY 10001
www.amnestyusa.org

Schulz, Charles (1922-2000)
Creator of the Peanuts comic strip
Charles M Schulz Museum **Ph:** 707-579-4452
2301 Hardies Ln **Fax:** 707-579-4436
Santa Rosa, CA 95403
www.schulzmuseum.org

Schulze, Richard M
Founder and chairman of Best Buy
Best Buy Co Inc **Ph:** 612-291-1000
7601 Penn Ave S
Richfield, MN 55423
www.bestbuy.com

Schumacher, Joel (1939-)
Movie director
Creative Artists Agency **Ph:** 310-288-4545
9830 Wilshire Blvd **Fax:** 310-288-4800
Beverly Hills, CA 90212

Schumer, Charles E (1950-)
US Senator from New York (Democrat); chairman of the Democratic Senatorial Campaign Committee
313 Hart Bldg **Ph:** 202-224-6542
Washington, DC 20510 **Fax:** 202-228-3027
schumer.senate.gov

Schutz, Stephen, PhD
Creator of the Blue Mountain Arts animated electronic greeting card website; illustrates greeting cards & books
Blue Mountain Arts Inc **Ph:** 303-449-0536
PO Box 4549 **Fax:** 800-545-8573
Boulder, CO 80306
www.sps.com

Schutz, Susan Polis (1944-)
Co-founder of Blue Mountain Arts; writes greeting card poetry
Blue Mountain Arts Inc **Ph:** 303-449-0536
PO Box 4549 **Fax:** 800-545-8573
Boulder, CO 80306
www.sps.com

Schwab, Charles R (1937-)
Founder, chairman, and CEO of Charles Schwab & Co Inc
Charles Schwab & Co Inc **Ph:** 415-627-7000
101 Montgomery St **Fax:** 415-636-7097
San Francisco, CA 94104
www.aboutschwab.com

Schwab, Leslie B
Founder & chairman of Les Schwab Tire Centers
Les Schwab Tire Centers **Ph:** 541-447-4136
646 NW Madras Hwy **Fax:** 541-416-5208
Prineville, OR 97754
www.lesschwab.com

Schwabach, Bob
Writes the syndicated column On Computers with wife Joy Schwabach
Universal Press Syndicate **Ph:** 816-932-6600
4520 Main St
Kansas City, MO 64111
www.amuniversal.com/ups/features

Schwabach, Joy
Writes the syndicated column On Computers with husband Bob Schwabach
Universal Press Syndicate **Ph:** 816-932-6600
4520 Main St
Kansas City, MO 64111
www.amuniversal.com/ups/features

Schwartz, Allyson Y (1948-)
US Representative from Pennsylvania (Democrat)
426 Cannon Bldg **Ph:** 202-225-6111
Washington, DC 20515 **Fax:** 202-226-0611
schwartz.house.gov

Schwartz, David A, MD
Director, National Institute of Environmental Health Sciences, National Institutes of Health
National Institute of Environmental Health Sciences **Ph:** 919-541-3201
PO Box 12233
Research Triangle Park, NC 27709
www.niehs.nih.gov

Schwartz, Herbert F (1935-)
Intellectual property lawyer; lead counsel for corporate clients in patent, trademark, copyright, and trade secret cases
Ropes & Gray **Ph:** 212-596-9010
1251 Ave of the Americas **Fax:** 212-596-9090
New York, NY 10020
www.ropesgray.com

Schwartz, Jonathan (1966-)
President & CEO of Sun Microsystems
Sun Microsystems Inc **Ph:** 650-960-1300
4150 Network Cir
Santa Clara, CA 95054
www.sun.com

Schwartz, Ted
Founder and chairman of APAC
APAC Customer Services Inc **Ph:** 847-374-4980
6 Parkway N **Fax:** 847-374-4991
Deerfield, IL 60015
apaccustomerservices.com

Schwarz, Christina (1962-)
Author of the bestseller Drowning Ruth
Ballantine Books Publicity **Ph:** 212-782-9000
1745 Broadway
New York, NY 10019
www.randomhouse.com/BB

Schwarz, Joe (1937-)
US Representative from Michigan (Republican)
128 Cannon Bldg **Ph:** 202-225-6276
Washington, DC 20515 **Fax:** 202-225-6281
schwarz.house.gov

Schwarzbaum, Lisa
Movie critic
Entertainment Weekly **Ph:** 212-522-5600
1675 Broadway **Fax:** 212-522-6104
New York, NY 10019

Schwarzenegger, Arnold (1947-)
Governor of California (Republican); actor; former bodybuilder and Mr. Universe
State Capitol 1st Fl **Ph:** 916-445-2841
Sacramento, CA 95814 **Fax:** 916-445-4633
www.governor.ca.gov

Schwarzkopf, H Norman (1934-)
Retired general who became well known during Desert Shield and Desert Storm; public speaker
International Creative Management **Ph:** 212-556-5600
40 W 57th St 17th Fl
New York, NY 10019
www.icmtalent.com/lect/lect.html

Schweitzer, Brian (1955-)
Governor of Montana (Democrat)
PO Box 200801 **Ph:** 406-444-3111
Helena, MT 59620 **Fax:** 406-444-4151
governor.mt.gov

Schwimmer, David (1966-)
Actor
Gersh Agency **Ph:** 310-274-6611
232 N Canon Dr
Beverly Hills, CA 90210

Scieszka, Jon (1954-)
Author of books for children and young adults (Math Curse; Science Verse; The True Story of the Three Little Pigs)
Viking Children's Books Publicity **Ph:** 212-366-2000
345 Hudson St
New York, NY 10014
us.penguingroup.com

Scioscia, Mike (1958-)
Baseball manager
Los Angeles Angels of Anaheim **Ph:** 714-940-2000
Angel Stadium **Fax:** 714-940-2205
2000 Gene Autry Way
Anaheim, CA 92806
losangeles.angels.mlb.com

Sciutto, Jim
ABC News London correspondent
ABC News **Ph:** 212-456-7777
77 W 66th St
New York, NY 10023
www.abcnews.go.com/WNT

Scobee, Josh (1982-)
Professional football player
Jacksonville Jaguars **Ph:** 904-633-6000
1 Alltel Stadium Pl **Fax:** 904-633-6050
Jacksonville, FL 32202
www.jaguars.com

Scorsese, Martin (1942-)
Film director
The Firm **Ph:** 310-860-8000
9465 Wilshire Blvd **Fax:** 310-860-8100
Beverly Hills, CA 90212

Scott, Bryan (1981-)
Professional football player
New Orleans Saints **Ph:** 504-733-0255
5800 Airline Dr **Fax:** 504-731-1768
Metairie, LA 70003
www.neworleanssaints.com

Scott, Byron (1961-)
Basketball coach
New Orleans/Oklahoma City Hornets **Ph:** 405-208-4800
Oklahoma Tower
210 Park Ave Suite 1850
Oklahoma City, OK 73102
www.nba.com/hornets

Scott, Carol
President of ECA World Fitness and creative director of group fitness for the Equinox fitness clubs; teaches and conducts national/international conference workshops, specializing in business and marketing, kickboxing, body sculpture, and aerobic choreography
East Coast Alliance World Fitness **Ph:** 516-432-6877
414 E Beech St **Fax:** 516-432-7044
Long Beach, NY 11561
www.ecaworldfitness.com

Scott, David (1945-)
US Representative from Georgia (Democrat)
417 Cannon Bldg **Ph:** 202-225-2939
Washington, DC 20515 **Fax:** 202-225-4628
davidscott.house.gov

Scott, Jerry (1955-)
Co-creator, with Rick Kirkman, of the comic strip Baby Blues; also collaborated with Jim Borgman on the creation of Zits and for several years he wrote and drew the comic strip Nancy
King Features Syndicate Inc **Ph:** 212-455-4000
888 7th Ave 2nd Fl
New York, NY 10019
babyblues.com

Scott, Jon
FOX News Live anchor
FOX News Channel **Ph:** 212-301-3000
1211 Ave of the Americas
New York, NY 10036
www.foxnews.com/fnctv

Scott, Larry (1938-)
The first Mr Olympia
Larry Scott Research Foundation **Ph:** 800-225-9752
Fax: 801-593-0911
451 N Main St
Kaysville, UT 84037
www.larryscott.com

Scott, Ridley (1937-)
Movie director and producer of advertising commercials
RSA USA Inc **Ph:** 310-659-1577
634 N La Peer Dr **Fax:** 310-659-1377
Los Angeles, CA 90069
www.rsafilms.com

Scott, Robert C (1947-)
US Representative from Virginia (Democrat)
1201 Longworth Bldg **Ph:** 202-225-8351
Washington, DC 20515 **Fax:** 202-225-8354
www.house.gov/scott

Scott, Stuart (1965-)
Sports Center anchor
ESPN **Ph:** 860-585-2000
ESPN Plaza
935 Middle St
Bristol, CT 06010
sports.espn.go.com/espntv/espnGuide

Scott, Tony (1944-)
Movie director and producer
Creative Artists Agency **Ph:** 310-288-4545
9830 Wilshire Blvd **Fax:** 310-288-4800
Beverly Hills, CA 90212

Scott, Walter Jr
Chairman of the Board of Level 3 Communications
Level 3 Communications Inc **Ph:** 720-888-1000
1025 Eldorado Blvd **Fax:** 720-888-5422
Broomfield, CO 80021
www.level3.com

Scott, Willard (1934-)
Today Show weather reporter
Today Show **Ph:** 212-664-4249
30 Rockefeller Plaza
New York, NY 10112
www.msnbc.msn.com/id/3079108

Scully, Vin (1927-)
Sportscaster; known as the Voice of the Dodgers, for whom he began covering games in 1950; member Radio Hall of Fame
Los Angeles Dodgers **Ph:** 323-224-1500
Dodger Stadium **Fax:** 323-224-1354
1000 Elysian Park Ave
Los Angeles, CA 90012
www.radiohof.org/sportscasters/vinscully.html

Scurry, Briana (1971-)
Goalkeeper on the US Women's National Soccer Team
US Soccer Federation **Ph:** 312-808-1300
1801 S Prairie Ave **Fax:** 312-808-1301
Chicago, IL 60616
www.ussoccer.com

Seacrest, Ryan (1974-)
Host of American Idol on TV; also a radio show host (top 40 and morning drive shows)
Premiere Radio Networks Inc **Ph:** 818-377-5300
15260 Ventura Blvd 5th Fl **Fax:** 818-377-5333
Sherman Oaks, CA 91403
www.ryanseacrest.com

Seagal, Steven (1951-)
Actor; producer
International Creative Management **Ph:** 310-550-4000
8942 Wilshire Blvd
Beverly Hills, CA 90211

Seager, John
President and CEO of Population Connection (formerly Zero Population Growth)
Population Connection **Ph:** 202-332-2200
1400 16th St NW Suite 320 **Fax:** 202-332-2302
Washington, DC 20036
www.populationconnection.org

Sealy, Scott (1981-)
Professional soccer player
Kansas City Wizards **Ph:** 816-920-9300
2 Arrowhead Dr **Fax:** 816-920-4774
Kansas City, MO 64129
kc.wizards.mlsnet.com

Seamans, Andy
Writes The Answer Man, a syndicated column on trivia
Creators Syndicate Inc **Ph:** 310-337-7003
5777 W Century Blvd Suite 700 **Fax:** 310-337-7625
Los Angeles, CA 90045
www.creators.com

Sears, Barry, PhD (1947-)
Scientist and researcher on the hormonal effects of food; author of The Zone books
HarperCollins Publishers **Ph:** 212-207-7000
c/o Author Mail
10 E 53rd St
New York, NY 10022
www.harpercollins.com

Sebelius, Kathleen (1948-)
Governor of Kansas (Democrat)
State Capitol Bldg 2nd Fl **Ph:** 785-296-3232
Topeka, KS 66612 **Fax:** 785-296-7973
www.ksgovernor.org

Sebold, Alice
Author of The Lovely Bones
Steven Barclay Agency **Ph:** 707-773-0654
12 Western Ave **Fax:** 707-778-1868
Petaluma, CA 94952 **TF:** 888-965-7323
www.barclayagency.com

Secada, Jon (1961-)
Latin singer
Big3 Entertainment **Ph:** 727-343-1840
6090 Central Ave **Fax:** 727-384-5195
Saint Petersburg, FL 33707
jonsecada.com

Sedaris, David (1956-)
Writer (essayist), social critic, and speaker
Steven Barclay Agency **Ph:** 707-773-0654
12 Western Ave **Fax:** 707-778-1868
Petaluma, CA 94952 **TF:** 888-965-7323
www.barclayagency.com

Sedin, Daniel (1980-)
Professional hockey player
Vancouver Canucks **Ph:** 604-899-4600
General Motors Pl **Fax:** 604-899-4640
800 Griffiths Way
Vancouver, BC V6B6G1
www.canucks.com

Sedin, Henrik (1980-)
Professional hockey player
Vancouver Canucks **Ph:** 604-899-4600
General Motors Pl **Fax:** 604-899-4640
800 Griffiths Way
Vancouver, BC V6B6G1
www.canucks.com

Seemungal, Martin
ABC News Africa correspondent
ABC News **Ph:** 212-456-7777
77 W 66th St
New York, NY 10023
www.abcnews.go.com/WNT

Segal, George (1924-2000)
Sculptor and artist
George & Helen Segal Foundation **Ph:** 732-951-0950 **Fax:** 732-821-5877
136 Davidsons Mill Rd
Monmouth Junction, NJ 08852
www.segalfoundation.org

Segal, Lewis
Dance critic
Los Angeles Times **Ph:** 213-237-5000
202 W 1st St **Fax:** 213-237-4712
Los Angeles, CA 90012

Seger, Bob (1945-)
Singer; composer
Creative Artists Agency **Ph:** 310-288-4545
9830 Wilshire Blvd **Fax:** 310-288-4800
Beverly Hills, CA 90212
www.bobseger.com

Seidenberg, Ivan
Chairman and CEO of Verizon Communications
Verizon Communications Inc **Ph:** 212-395-1000
1095 Ave of the Americas
New York, NY 10036
investor.verizon.com/profile

Seigenthaler, John
Anchors the week-end editions of NBC Nightly News; is also a contributing anchor for MSNBC and anchor of MSNBC Investigates
NBC News **Ph:** 212-664-4249
30 Rockefeller Plaza
New York, NY 10112
www.msnbc.msn.com/id/3689499

Seinfeld, Jerry (1954-)
Comedian
Shapiro/West & Assoc **Ph:** 310-278-8896
141 El Camino Dr Suite 205 **Fax:** 310-278-7238
Beverly Hills, CA 90212
www.sonypictures.com/tv/shows/seinfeld

Seitz, Matt Zoller
Film and television critic
New York Press **Ph:** 212-244-2282
333 7th Ave 14th Fl **Fax:** 212-244-9864
New York, NY 10001

Selanne, Teemu (1970-)
Professional hockey player
Mighty Ducks of Anaheim **Ph:** 714-704-2700
Arrowhead Pond **Fax:** 714-940-2953
2695 Katella Ave
Anaheim, CA 92806
www.mightyducks.com

Seles, Monica (1973-)
Professional tennis player
IMG Inc **Ph:** 216-522-1200
IMG Center **Fax:** 216-522-1145
1360 E 9th St Suite 100
Cleveland, OH 44114

Selick, Henry (1953-)
Animation director/producer/writer
Laika **Ph:** 503-225-1130
1400 NW 22nd Ave **Fax:** 503-226-3746
Portland, OR 97210
www.laika.com/entertainment

Selig, Allan H "Bud" (1934-)
Commissioner of Major League Baseball
Major League Baseball **Ph:** 212-931-7800
245 Park Ave 31st Fl
New York, NY 10167
www.mlb.com

Seliger, Mark (1959-)
Editorial photographer; former chief photographer for Rolling Stone magazine
Proof Photographic Agents **Ph:** 212-727-7445
247 W 16th St Suite 2F
New York, NY 10011
www.markseliger.com

Seligman, Nicole K (1956-)
General counsel for the Sony Corp. of America, where she oversees all legal, intellectual property, investor relations, governmental, regulatory, and general affairs activities for the company
Sony Corp of America **Ph:** 212-833-6800
550 Madison Ave
New York, NY 10022
www.sony.com/SCA/bios/seligman.shtml

Selleck, Tom (1945-)
Actor
Management 360 **Ph:** 310-272-7000
9111 Wilshire Blvd **Fax:** 310-272-0084
Beverly Hills, CA 90210

Sellers, Bob
A Fox News Live anchor
FOX News Channel **Ph:** 212-301-3000
1211 Ave of the Americas
New York, NY 10036
www.foxnews.com/fnctv

Semel, Terry
Chairman and CEO of Yahoo!
Yahoo! Inc **Ph:** 408-349-3300
701 1st Ave **Fax:** 408-349-3301
Sunnyvale, CA 94089
docs.yahoo.com/info/pr

Senay, Emily, MD (1960-)
Health & medical correspondent for CBS News's The Early Show
The Early Show **Ph:** 212-975-2824
524 W 57th St
New York, NY 10019
www.cbsnews.com

Sendak, Maurice (1928-)
Children's book illustrator and author (Where the Wild Things Are, In the Night Kitchen, Outside Over There)
Steven Barclay Agency **Ph:** 707-773-0654
12 Western Ave **Fax:** 707-778-1868
Petaluma, CA 94952 **TF:** 888-965-7323
www.barclayagency.com

Senge, Peter, PhD (1947-)
Business author and founder of the Society for Organizational Learning; a senior lecturer at MIT
Society for Organizational Learning **Ph:** 617-300-9500
Fax: 617-354-2093
25 1st St Suite 414
Cambridge, MA 02141
www.solonline.org/aboutsol/who/Senge

Seniuk, Lasha
Writes the weekly syndicated horoscope column Mystic Stars
Tribune Media Services Inc **Ph:** 312-222-4444
435 N Michigan Ave Suite 1500
Chicago, IL 60611
tmsfeatures.com/productlist.htm

Sensenbrenner, Jim Jr (1943-)
US Representative from Wisconsin (Republican)
2449 Rayburn Bldg **Ph:** 202-225-5101
Washington, DC 20515 **Fax:** 202-225-3190
www.house.gov/sensenbrenner

Sequeira, Douglas (1977-)
Professional soccer player
Real Salt Lake **Ph:** 801-924-8585
515 S 700 East Suite 2R **Fax:** 801-933-4713
Salt Lake City, UT 84102
www.mlsnet.com/MLS/rsl/

Serra, Matthew
Chairman, president, and CEO of Foot Locker Inc
Foot Locker Inc **Ph:** 212-720-3700
112 W 34th St
New York, NY 10120
www.footlocker-inc.com

Serrano, Jose E (1943-)
US Representative from New York (Democrat)
2227 Rayburn Bldg **Ph:** 202-225-4361
Washington, DC 20515 **Fax:** 202-225-6001
www.house.gov/serrano

Serrano, Julian
Executive Chef of Picasso at the Bellagio
Picasso Restaurant **Ph:** 877-234-6358
Bellagio Hotel & Casino
3600 Las Vegas Blvd
Las Vegas, NV 89109
www.bellagiolasvegas.com

Sesno, Frank
A CNN special correspondent
CNN **Ph:** 404-827-1500
1 CNN Center
Atlanta, GA 30303
www.cnn.com/CNN/anchors_reporters

Sessions, Jeff (1946-)
US Senator from Alabama (Republican)
335 Russell Bldg **Ph:** 202-224-4124
Washington, DC 20510 **Fax:** 202-224-3149
sessions.senate.gov

Sessions, Pete (1955-)
US Representative from Texas (Republican)
1514 Longworth Bldg **Ph:** 202-225-2231
Washington, DC 20515 **Fax:** 202-225-5878
sessions.house.gov

Seth, Vikram (1952-)
Author of poetry collections, novels, a libretto, and the travel memoir From Heaven Lake: Travels Through Sinkiang and Tibet
Vintage/Anchor Publicity **Ph:** 212-572-2420
1745 Broadway 20th Fl
New York, NY 10019
www.randomhouse.com/vintage

Setzer, Brian (1959-)
Musician & composer; heads up the Brian Setzer Orchestra and is lead singer/guitarist for Stray Cats
William Morris Agency **Ph:** 310-859-4000
1 William Morris Pl **Fax:** 310-859-4462
Beverly Hills, CA 90212
www.briansetzer.com

Severinsen, Doc (1927-)
Big band/jazz trumpeter and conductor; was leader of the band on The Tonight Show with Johnny Carson
International Creative Management **Ph:** 212-556-5600
40 W 57th St 17th Fl
New York, NY 10019
www.icmtalent.com/musperf/jazz_world.html

Sevigny, Chloe (1974-)
Actor
Endeavor **Ph:** 310-248-2000
9601 Wilshire Blvd 3rd Fl **Fax:** 310-248-2020
Beverly Hills, CA 90210
www.hbo.com/biglove/cast

Sexson, Richie (1974-)
Professional baseball player
Seattle Mariners **Ph:** 206-346-4000
Safeco Field **Fax:** 206-346-4050
1250 1st Ave S
Seattle, WA 98134
seattle.mariners.mlb.com

Seymour, Jane (1951-)
Actor
Gersh Agency **Ph:** 310-274-6611
232 N Canon Dr
Beverly Hills, CA 90210
www.friendsofjane.com

Shaara, Jeff (1952-)
Author of Civil War books; Gods and Generals and The Last Full Measure finish the story begun by his father, Michael Shaara, in The Killer Angels
Ballantine Books Publicity **Ph:** 212-782-9000
1745 Broadway
New York, NY 10019
www.jeffshaara.com

Shadegg, John (1949-)
US Representative from Arizona (Republican)
306 Cannon Bldg **Ph:** 202-225-3361
Washington, DC 20515 **Fax:** 202-225-3462
johnshadegg.house.gov

Shaffer, Peter (1926-)
Playwright and screenwriter (Equus and Amadeus)
HarperCollins Publishers **Ph:** 212-207-7000
c/o Author Mail
10 E 53rd St
New York, NY 10022
www.harpercollins.com

Shakira (1977-)
Latin singer; full name is Shakira Isabel Mebarak Ripoll
Rogers & Cowan PR **Ph:** 310-854-8100
Pacific Design Center **Fax:** 310-854-8101
8687 Melrose Ave 7th Fl
Los Angeles, CA 90069
www.shakira.com

Shales, Tom (1953-)
Washington Post television critic; also writes a syndicated column on what goes on behind the scenes at TV networks and cable channels
Washington Post Writers Group **Ph:** 202-334-6375
Fax: 202-334-5669
1150 15th St NW 9th Fl
Washington, DC 20071
www.postwritersgroup.com

Shalhoub, Tony (1953-)
Actor
Creative Artists Agency **Ph:** 310-288-4545
9830 Wilshire Blvd **Fax:** 310-288-4800
Beverly Hills, CA 90212
www.usanetwork.com/series/monk

Shalit, Gene (1932-)
Film critic; arts editor and critic for the Today Show
Today Show **Ph:** 212-664-4249
30 Rockefeller Plaza
New York, NY 10112
www.msnbc.msn.com/id/3079108

Shanahan, Brendan (1969-)
Professional hockey player
Detroit Red Wings **Ph:** 313-396-7544
Joe Louis Arena **Fax:** 313-567-0296
600 Civic Center Dr
Detroit, MI 48226
www.detroitredwings.com

Shanahan, Mike (1952-)
Football coach
Denver Broncos **Ph:** 303-649-9000
13655 Broncos Pkwy **Fax:** 303-649-9354
Englewood, CO 80112
www.denverbroncos.com

Shandling, Garry (1949-)
Comedian
Endeavor **Ph:** 310-248-2000
9601 Wilshire Blvd 3rd Fl **Fax:** 310-248-2020
Beverly Hills, CA 90210

Shankar, Ravi (1920-)
Sitar virtuoso; composer
International Creative Management **Ph:** 212-556-5600
40 W 57th St 17th Fl
New York, NY 10019
www.ravishankar.org

Shannon, David
Author & illustrator of children's books (No, David!; How Georgie Radbourn Saved Baseball)
Scholastic Inc **Ph:** 212-343-6100
555 Broadway
New York, NY 10012
www.scholastic.com/titles/nodavid

Shapira, David S
Chairman & CEO of Giant Eagle Inc, a retail grocery store chain
Giant Eagle Inc **Ph:** 412-963-6200
101 Kappa Dr
Pittsburgh, PA 15238

Shapiro, Ben (1984-)
At age 17 became the youngest nationally syndicated columnist in the US; his columns are printed nationwide in major newspapers and websites
Creators Syndicate Inc **Ph:** 310-337-7003
5777 W Century Blvd Suite 700 **Fax:** 310-337-7625
Los Angeles, CA 90045
benjaminshapiro.com

Shapiro, Robert L (1942-)
Criminal defense attorney; has defended OJ Simpson, Christian Brando, and Robert Evans
Christensen Miller Fink Glaser Weil & Shapiro LLP **Ph:** 310-556-7886
Fax: 310-556-2920
10250 Constellation Blvd 19th Fl
Los Angeles, CA 90067
chrismill.lawoffice.com

Shapiro, Steven
ACLU Legal Director
American Civil Liberties Union **Ph:** 212-549-2500
125 Broad St 18th Fl **Fax:** 212-549-2580
New York, NY 10004
www.aclu.org

Sharapova, Maria (1987-)
Professional tennis player
WTA Tour **Ph:** 727-895-5000
1 Progress Plaza Suite 1500 **Fax:** 727-894-1982
Saint Petersburg, FL 33701
www.wtatour.com

Sharer, Kevin
Chairman, president, and CEO of Amgen
Amgen Inc **Ph:** 805-447-1000
1 Amgen Center Dr **Fax:** 805-447-1010
Thousand Oaks, CA 91320
www.amgen.com

Sharpe, Shannon (1968-)
Former NFL player, now TV studio analyst for NFL games
CBS Sports **Ph:** 212-975-4321
51 W 52nd St
New York, NY 10019
cbs.sportsline.com/cbssports/team

Sharpe, William F, PhD (1934-)
Winner (with two other scientists) of the 1990 Nobel Prize in Economic Sciences for pioneering work in the theory of financial economics
Stanford University **Ph:** 650-723-2146
Graduate School of Business **Fax:** 650-725-0468
518 Memorial Way
Stanford, CA 94305
gsbapps.stanford.edu/facultybios

Sharper, Darren (1975-)
Professional football player
Minnesota Vikings **Ph:** 952-828-6500
9520 Viking Dr **Fax:** 952-828-6540
Eden Prairie, MN 55344
www.vikings.com

Shatner, William (1931-)
Actor
TalentWorks **Ph:** 818-972-4300
3500 W Olive Ave Suite 1400 **Fax:** 818-955-6411
Burbank, CA 91505
www.williamshatner.com

Shaughnessy, Meghann (1979-)
Professional tennis player
WTA Tour **Ph:** 727-895-5000
1 Progress Plaza Suite 1500 **Fax:** 727-894-1982
Saint Petersburg, FL 33701
www.wtatour.com

Shaw, Brad
Hockey coach
New York Islanders **Ph:** 516-501-6700
1535 Old Country Rd **Fax:** 516-501-6729
Plainview, NY 11803
www.newyorkislanders.com

Shaw, E Clay Jr (1939-)
US Representative from Florida (Republican)
1236 Longworth Bldg **Ph:** 202-225-3026
Washington, DC 20515 **Fax:** 202-225-8398
shaw.house.gov

Shaw, Jason (1973-)
Male model; former spokesmodel for Tommy Hilfiger
Wilhelmina Models Inc **Ph:** 212-473-0700
300 Park Ave S 2nd Fl **Fax:** 212-473-3223
New York, NY 10010

Shaw, Kathryn L, PhD
Economics researcher and professor of economics at Stanford; was a member of President Clinton's Council of Economic Advisors
Stanford University **Ph:** 650-725-4168
Graduate School of Business **Fax:** 650-725-0468
518 Memorial Way
Stanford, CA 94305
gsbapps.stanford.edu/facultybios

Shawn, Eric
FOX News senior correspondent
FOX News Channel **Ph:** 212-301-3000
1211 Ave of the Americas
New York, NY 10036
www.foxnews.com/fnctv

Shaye, Robert K
Founder, co-chairman, and co-CEO of New Line Cinema
New Line Cinema **Ph:** 310-854-5811
116 N Robertson Blvd **Fax:** 310-652-3421
Suite 400
Los Angeles, CA 90048
www.newline.com

Shays, Christopher (1945-)
US Representative from Connecticut (Republican)
1126 Longworth Bldg **Ph:** 202-225-5541
Washington, DC 20515 **Fax:** 202-225-9629
www.house.gov/shays

SHeDaisy
Country music group (Kassidy, Kelsi, and Kristyn Osborn)
William Morris Agency **Ph:** 615-963-3000
1600 Division St Suite 300 **Fax:** 615-963-3090
Nashville, TN 37203
www.shedaisy.com

Sheeler, Charles (1883-1965)
Precisionist painter and photographer
Edwynn Houk Gallery **Ph:** 212-750-7070
745 5th Ave **Fax:** 212-688-4848
New York, NY 10151

Sheen, Charlie (1965-)
Actor
Endeavor **Ph:** 310-248-2000
9601 Wilshire Blvd 3rd Fl **Fax:** 310-248-2020
Beverly Hills, CA 90210
www.cbs.com/primetime/two_and_a_half_men

Sheen, Martin (1940-)
Actor
International Creative Management **Ph:** 310-550-4000
8942 Wilshire Blvd
Beverly Hills, CA 90211
www.nbc.com/The_West_Wing

Sheets, Ben (1978-)
Professional baseball player
Milwaukee Brewers **Ph:** 414-902-4400
Miller Park **Fax:** 414-902-4515
1 Brewers Way
Milwaukee, WI 53214
milwaukee.brewers.mlb.com

Sheffield, Gary (1968-)
Professional baseball player
New York Yankees **Ph:** 718-293-4300
Yankee Stadium **Fax:** 718-293-8414
161st St & River Ave
Bronx, NY 10451
newyork.yankees.mlb.com

Shelby, Richard C (1934-)
US Senator from Alabama (Republican)
110 Hart Bldg **Ph:** 202-224-5744
Washington, DC 20510 **Fax:** 202-224-3416
shelby.senate.gov

Sheldon, Sidney (1917-)
Bestselling author and screenwriter
Warner Books **Ph:** 212-522-7200
c/o Author Mail
1271 Ave of the Americas
New York, NY 10020
www.twbookmark.com

Shell, Art (1946-)
Football coach
Oakland Raiders **Ph:** 510-864-5000
1220 Harbor Bay Pkwy **Fax:** 510-864-5134
Alameda, CA 94502
www.raiders.com

Shelton, Blake (1976-)
Country singer
William Morris Agency **Ph:** 615-963-3000
1600 Division St Suite 300 **Fax:** 615-963-3090
Nashville, TN 37203
www.blakeshelton.com

Shelton, Mike
Editorial cartoonist for the Orange County Register
King Features Syndicate Inc **Ph:** 212-455-4000
888 7th Ave 2nd Fl
New York, NY 10019
www.kingfeatures.com

Sheneman, Drew
Editorial cartoonist for The Star Ledger (Newark, NJ)
Tribune Media Services Inc **Ph:** 312-222-4444
435 N Michigan Ave Suite 1500
Chicago, IL 60611
www.comicspage.com

Shepard, Sam (1943-)
Playwright, actor, director
International Creative Management **Ph:** 310-550-4000
8942 Wilshire Blvd
Beverly Hills, CA 90211

Shepherd, Chuck (1945-)
Writes News of the Weird, a weekly syndicated humor column of strange-but-true news stories
Universal Press Syndicate **Ph:** 816-932-6600
4520 Main St
Kansas City, MO 64111
www.amuniversal.com/ups/features

Sheppard, Lito (1981-)
Professional football player
Philadelphia Eagles **Ph:** 215-463-2500
NovaCare Complex **Fax:** 215-339-5464
1 NovaCare Way
Philadelphia, PA 19145
www.philadelphiaeagles.com

Sheridan, Nicolette (1963-)
Actor
Gersh Agency **Ph:** 310-274-6611
232 N Canon Dr
Beverly Hills, CA 90210
abc.go.com/primetime/desperate

Sherman, Brad (1954-)
US Representative from California (Democrat)
1030 Longworth Bldg **Ph:** 202-225-5911
Washington, DC 20515 **Fax:** 202-225-5879
www.house.gov/sherman

Sherman, Cindy (1954-)
Photographer (makes photographs of herself that are not self-portraits)
Metro Pictures **Ph:** 212-206-7100
519 W 24th St **Fax:** 212-337-0070
New York, NY 10011
www.metropicturesgallery.com

Sherman, Mickey
Attorney for Michael Skakel, who was convicted of murdering Martha Moxley; appears regularly on various news programs
Sherman Richichi & Hickey LLC — **Ph:** 203-324-2296 — **Fax:** 203-348-7313
27 5th St
Stamford, CT 06905
www.srh-law.com

Sherman-Palladino, Amy (1966-)
TV series writer (Gilmore Girls)
Endeavor — **Ph:** 310-248-2000 — **Fax:** 310-248-2020
9601 Wilshire Blvd 3rd Fl
Beverly Hills, CA 90210

Shernoff, William
Attorney who has devoted his career to fighting insurance company abuse; is credited with setting the legal precedent that established bad faith law
Shernoff Bidart & Darras LLP — **Ph:** 909-621-4935 — **Fax:** 909-625-6915
600 S Indian Hill Blvd
Claremont, CA 91711
www.sbd-law.com

Sherr, Lynn (1942-)
News correspondent for 20/20
20/20 — **Ph:** 212-456-7777
147 Columbus Ave
New York, NY 10023
abcnews.go.com/2020

Sherwood, Don (1941-)
US Representative from Pennsylvania (Republican)
1131 Longworth Bldg — **Ph:** 202-225-3731 — **Fax:** 202-225-9594
Washington, DC 20515
www.house.gov/sherwood

Shestack, Jerome J (1925-)
Trial lawyer who has handled complex business litigation for ABC, NBC, CBS, Westinghouse, GAF, Hertz, RCA, Advanta, and Comcast
Wolf Block Schorr & Solis-Cohen LLP — **Ph:** 215-977-2290 — **Fax:** 215-977-2787
1650 Arch St 22nd Fl
Philadelphia, PA 19103
www.wolfblock.com

Shields, Brooke (1965-)
Actor
William Morris Agency — **Ph:** 310-859-4000 — **Fax:** 310-859-4462
1 William Morris Pl
Beverly Hills, CA 90212
www.wma.com/brooke_shields/summary

Shields, David
Writes essays (Body Politic) and stories
Dunow & Carlson Literary Agency — **Ph:** 212-645-7606 — **Fax:** 212-645-7614
27 W 20th St Suite 1003
New York, NY 10011
www.davidshields.com

Shields, Mark (1937-)
Journalist/syndicated columnist; also a political commentator/analyst on Newshour with Jim Lehrer on PBS
Creators Syndicate Inc — **Ph:** 310-337-7003 — **Fax:** 310-337-7625
5777 W Century Blvd Suite 700
Los Angeles, CA 90045
www.creators.com/opinion.html

Shields, Will (1971-)
Professional football player
Kansas City Chiefs — **Ph:** 816-920-9300 — **Fax:** 816-920-4315
Arrowhead Stadium
1 Arrowhead Dr
Kansas City, MO 64129
www.kcchiefs.com

Shilling, A Gary, PhD (1937-)
Author, columnist, and speaker known for his accurate economic forecasts (known as Doctor Disinflation)
A Gary Shilling & Co — **Ph:** 973-467-0070 — **Fax:** 973-467-4073
500 Morris Ave
Springfield, NJ 07081
www.agaryshilling.com

Shimkus, John (1958-)
US Representative from Illinois (Republican)
513 Cannon Bldg — **Ph:** 202-225-5271 — **Fax:** 202-225-5880
Washington, DC 20515
www.house.gov/shimkus

Shinn, George (1941-)
Owner of the New Orleans Hornets basketball team
New Orleans Hornets — **Ph:** 405-208-4800
Oklahoma Tower
210 Park Ave Suite 1850
Oklahoma City, OK 73102
www.nba.com/hornets

Shipman, Claire
Senior national correspondent and substitute anchor on news segments of ABC News's Good Morning America
Good Morning America — **Ph:** 212-456-7777
147 Columbus Ave
New York, NY 10023
www.abcnews.go.com/GMA

Shockey, Jeremy (1980-)
Professional football player
New York Giants **Ph:** 201-935-8111
Giants Stadium **Fax:** 201-939-4134
East Rutherford, NJ 07073
www.giants.com

Shore, Howard (1946-)
Film composer/conductor
Gorfaine/Schwartz Agency **Ph:** 818-260-8500
4111 W Alameda Ave Suite 509 **Fax:** 818-260-8522
Burbank, CA 91505
www.gsamusic.com/composers.html

Shore, Pauly (1968-)
Comedian
Gersh Agency **Ph:** 310-274-6611
232 N Canon Dr
Beverly Hills, CA 90210
www.paulyshore.com

Short, Martin (1950-)
Comedian; actor
William Morris Agency **Ph:** 310-859-4000
1 William Morris Pl **Fax:** 310-859-4462
Beverly Hills, CA 90212

Showalter, Buck (1956-)
Baseball manager
Texas Rangers **Ph:** 817-273-5222
Ameriquest Field in Arlington **Fax:** 817-273-5294
1000 Ballpark Way
Arlington, TX 76011
texas.rangers.mlb.com

Shreve, Anita (1946-)
Novelist (The Pilot's Wife)
Little Brown & Co **Ph:** 212-522-7200
Author Mail
1271 Ave of the Americas
New York, NY 10020
www.anitashreve.com

Shribman, David (1954-)
Executive editor of the Pittsburgh Post-Gazette; syndicated columnist (political)
Pittsburgh Post-Gazette **Ph:** 412-263-1100
34 Blvd of the Allies
Pittsburgh, PA 15222
www.amuniversal.com/ups/features

Shriver, Maria (1955-)
Former news correspondent and wife of California governor Arnold Schwarzenegger
First Lady **Ph:** 916-445-2841
State Capitol Bldg **Fax:** 916-445-4633
Sacramento, CA 95814
www.firstlady.ca.gov

Shriver, Pam (1962-)
Former professional tennis player, now a TV sportscaster
CBS Sports **Ph:** 212-975-4321
51 W 52nd St
New York, NY 10019
cbs.sportsline.com/cbssports/team

Shteyngart, Gary (1972-)
Author (The Russian Debutante's Handbook)
Riverhead Books Publicity **Ph:** 212-366-2000
375 Hudson St
New York, NY 10014
us.penguingroup.com

Shue, Elisabeth (1963-)
Actor
Creative Artists Agency **Ph:** 310-288-4545
9830 Wilshire Blvd **Fax:** 310-288-4800
Beverly Hills, CA 90212

Shula, Don (1930-)
Former NFL coach
Pro Football Hall of Fame **Ph:** 330-456-8207
2121 George Halas Dr NW **Fax:** 330-456-8175
Canton, OH 44708
www.profootballhof.com

Shulevitz, Uri (1935-)
Children's book author/illustrator (Snow); also illustrates books written by other authors (The Fool of the World and the Flying Ship by Arthur Ransome; The Golem by Isaac Bashevis Singer)
Books for Young Readers **Ph:** 212-741-6900
Farrar Straus & Giroux
19 Union Sq W
New York, NY 10003
www.fsgkidsbooks.com

Shulock, Margaret
Writes the comic strip Apartment 3-G, which is drawn by Frank Bolle; also one of the writers of Six Chix
King Features Syndicate Inc **Ph:** 212-455-4000
888 7th Ave 2nd Fl
New York, NY 10019
www.kingfeatures.com

Shuster, Bill (1961-)
US Representative from Pennsylvania (Republican)
1108 Longworth Bldg **Ph:** 202-225-2431
Washington, DC 20515 **Fax:** 202-225-2486
www.house.gov/shuster

Shuster, David
MSNBC correspondent based in Washington, DC; reports daily for Hardball with Chris Matthews
MSNBC TV **Ph:** 201-583-5000
1 MSNBC Plaza
Secaucus, NJ 07094
www.msnbc.msn.com/id/3080263

Shyamalan, M Night (1970-)
Film writer, director, producer
United Talent Agency **Ph:** 310-273-6700
9560 Wilshire Blvd 5th Fl **Fax:** 310-247-1111
Beverly Hills, CA 90212
www.mnight.com

Sichelman, Lew
Writes the syndicated column The Housing Scene, which features consumer-oriented information on housing and real estate
United Feature Syndicate **Ph:** 212-293-8500
200 Madison Ave
New York, NY 10016
www.unitedfeatures.com

Siddons, Anne Rivers (1936-)
Author of fiction (Fault Lines; Colony)
HarperCollins Publishers **Ph:** 212-207-7000
c/o Author Mail
10 E 53rd St
New York, NY 10022
anneriverssiddons.com

Sidhu, Sanjiv S
Founder and chairman of the board of i2 Technologies
i2 Technologies Inc **Ph:** 469-357-1000
1 i2 plaza
11701 Luna Rd
Dallas, TX 75234
www.i2.com

Sieberg, Daniel
CNN technology correspondent and host of Next@CNN
CNN **Ph:** 404-827-1500
1 CNN Center
Atlanta, GA 30303
www.cnn.com/CNN/anchors_reporters

Siegel, Bernie, MD (1932-)
Physician, author, motivational speaker, and advocate for individuals with chronic illnesses; his books include Love, Medicine and Miracles; and Peace, Love and Healing
Exceptional Cancer Patients **Ph:** 814-337-8192
522 Jackson Park Dr **Fax:** 814-337-0699
Meadville, PA 16335
www.ecap-online.org

Siegel, Joel (1943-)
Movie critic; entertainment editor on ABC News's Good Morning America
Good Morning America **Ph:** 212-456-7777
147 Columbus Ave
New York, NY 10023
www.abcnews.go.com/GMA

Siegel, Marc K, MD
Board certified internist who writes both fiction & nonfiction; Ask Dr. Marc is a regular online feature at thenation.com
The Nation **Ph:** 212-209-5400
33 Irving Pl 8th Fl **Fax:** 212-982-9000
New York, NY 10003
www.doctorsiegel.com

Siegel, Robert (1946-)
All Things Considered host
National Public Radio **Ph:** 202-513-2000
635 Massachusetts Ave NW **Fax:** 202-513-3329
Washington, DC 20001
www.npr.org

Siers, Kevin
Editorial cartoonist for the Charlotte Observer
Charlotte Observer **Ph:** 704-358-5000
600 S Tryon St
Charlotte, NC 28202
www.kingfeatures.com/features

Sieving, Paul A, MD
Director of the National Eye Institute, National Institutes of Health
National Eye Institute **Ph:** 301-496-2234
31 Center Dr Bldg 31 Rm 6A05
MSC 2510
Bethesda, MD 20892

Sikorsky, Bob
Automotive consultant; writes the syndicated column Drive It Forever
New York Times Syndicate **Ph:** 212-499-3300
609 Greenwich St 6th Fl
New York, NY 10014
www.nytsyn.com/lifestyle.html

Silver, Joel (1952-)
Producer of action/adventure movies
Silver Pictures **Ph:** 818-954-4490
c/o Warner Bros **Fax:** 818-954-3237
4000 Warner Blvd
Bldg 90
Burbank, CA 91522

Silverman, Henry R (1940-)
Chairman and CEO of Cendant Corp
Cendant Corp **Ph:** 212-413-1800
9 W 57th St **Fax:** 212-413-1923
New York, NY 10019
www.cendant.com/investors

Silverstein, Shel (1932-1999)
Poet, illustrator, and author of humorous books for young readers
HarperCollins Children's Books **Ph:** 212-261-6500
1350 Ave of the Americas
New York, NY 10019
shelsilverstein.com

Silverstone, Alicia (1976-)
Actor
Innovative Artists **Ph:** 310-656-0400
1505 10th St **Fax:** 310-656-0456
Santa Monica, CA 90401

Simeone, Lisa
Host of World of Opera on NPR
National Public Radio **Ph:** 202-513-2000
635 Massachusetts Ave NW **Fax:** 202-513-3329
Washington, DC 20001
www.npr.org

Simmons, Bobby (1980-)
Professional basketball player
Milwaukee Bucks **Ph:** 414-227-0500
Bradley Center **Fax:** 414-227-0543
1001 N 4th St
Milwaukee, WI 53203
www.nba.com/bucks

Simmons, Brian (1975-)
Professional football player
Cincinnati Bengals **Ph:** 513-621-3550
1 Paul Brown Stadium **Fax:** 513-621-3570
Cincinnati, OH 45202
www.bengals.com

Simmons, Henry (1970-)
Actor
Gersh Agency **Ph:** 310-274-6611
232 N Canon Dr
Beverly Hills, CA 90210

Simmons, Kimora Lee (1975-)
Fashion designer (Baby Phat line), model, actor, entrepreneur, and hip-hop socialite
eFashion Solutions **Ph:** 201-601-4283
80 Enterprise Ave S
Secaucus, NJ 07094
www.kimoraleesimmons.com

Simmons, Richard (1948-)
Fitness expert
William Morris Agency **Ph:** 310-859-4000
1 William Morris Pl **Fax:** 310-859-4462
Beverly Hills, CA 90212
www.richardsimmons.com

Simmons, Rob (1943-)
US Representative from Connecticut (Republican)
215 Cannon Bldg **Ph:** 202-225-2076
Washington, DC 20515 **Fax:** 202-225-4977
simmons.house.gov

Simmons, Russell (1957-)
Founder, chairman, president, and CEO of Rush Communications, one of the largest African-American-owned media firms in the US; he also started Def Jam Records and is responsible for Def Poetry and Def Comedy Jam
Rush Communications Inc **Ph:** 212-840-9399
512 7th Ave **Fax:** 212-840-9390
New York, NY 10018

Simms, Chris (1980-)
Professional football player
Tampa Bay Buccaneers **Ph:** 813-870-2700
1 Buccaneer Pl **Fax:** 813-878-0813
Tampa, FL 33607
www.buccaneers.com

Simms, Phil (1954-)
Former NFL quarterback, now lead analyst for NFL games on CBS
CBS Sports **Ph:** 212-975-4321
51 W 52nd St
New York, NY 10019
cbs.sportsline.com/cbssports/team

Simon, Bob (1941-)
60 Minutes correspondent
60 Minutes **Ph:** 212-975-2006
555 W 57th St
New York, NY 10019
www.cbsnews.com

Simon, Carly (1945-)
Singer
William Morris Agency **Ph:** 310-859-4000
1 William Morris Pl **Fax:** 310-859-4462
Beverly Hills, CA 90212
www.carlysimon.com

Simon, Chris (1972-)
Professional hockey player
Calgary Flames **Ph:** 403-777-2177
Pengrowth Saddledome **Fax:** 403-777-2195
555 Saddledome Rise SE
Calgary, AB T2G2W1
www.calgaryflames.com

Simon, Herbert
Co-owner of Pacers Sports & Entertainment Co and the Indiana Pacers basketball team
Indiana Pacers **Ph:** 317-917-2500
Conseco Fieldhouse
125 S Pennsylvania St
Indianapolis, IN 46204

Simon, Melvin
Co-owner of Pacers Sports & Entertainment Co and the Indiana Pacers basketball team
Indiana Pacers **Ph:** 317-917-2500
Conseco Fieldhouse
125 S Pennsylvania St
Indianapolis, IN 46204

Simon, Neil (1927-)
Playwright; also wrote the screenplays for some of his stage plays
William Morris Agency **Ph:** 310-859-4000
1 William Morris Pl **Fax:** 310-859-4462
Beverly Hills, CA 90212

Simon, Paul (1941-)
Singer/songwriter
Creative Artists Agency **Ph:** 310-288-4545
9830 Wilshire Blvd **Fax:** 310-288-4800
Beverly Hills, CA 90212
www.paulsimon.com

Simon, Scott (1952-)
Host of Weekend Edition Saturday on NPR
National Public Radio **Ph:** 202-513-2000
635 Massachusetts Ave NW **Fax:** 202-513-3329
Washington, DC 20001
www.npr.org

Simon, Seymour (1931-)
Author of science books for children; also writes children's mystery books and is the creator of Einstein Anderson, Science Detective
Scholastic Inc **Ph:** 212-343-6100
557 Broadway
New York, NY 10012
www.seymoursimon.com

Simpson, Ashlee (1984-)
Singer
Creative Artists Agency **Ph:** 310-288-4545
9830 Wilshire Blvd **Fax:** 310-288-4800
Beverly Hills, CA 90212
www.ashleesimpsonmusic.com

Simpson, Jessica (1980-)
Pop/rock singer; actor
Creative Artists Agency **Ph:** 310-288-4545
9830 Wilshire Blvd **Fax:** 310-288-4800
Beverly Hills, CA 90212
www.jessicasimpson.com

Simpson, Mike (1950-)
US Representative from Idaho (Republican)
1339 Longworth Bldg **Ph:** 202-225-5531
Washington, DC 20515 **Fax:** 202-225-8216
www.house.gov/simpson

Sims, Molly (1976-)
Model; actor
Next Management LLC **Ph:** 212-925-5100
15 Watts St **Fax:** 212-925-5931
New York, NY 10013
www.mollysims.com

Sinbad (1956-)
Comedian; actor
Creative Artists Agency **Ph:** 310-288-4545
9830 Wilshire Blvd **Fax:** 310-288-4800
Beverly Hills, CA 90212

Sinegal, James D
President and CEO of Costco; a co-founder of the company
Costco Wholesale Corp **Ph:** 425-313-8163
999 Lake Dr **Fax:** 425-313-6593
Issaquah, WA 98027
www.costco.com

Singer, Bryan (1965-)
Movie director/producer
William Morris Agency **Ph:** 310-859-4000
1 William Morris Pl **Fax:** 310-859-4462
Beverly Hills, CA 90212

Singer, Marilyn (1948-)
Author of books for children and young adults, including novels, poetry, nature books, picture books, fairy tales, and mysteries
Simon & Schuster Books for Young Readers **Ph:** 212-698-7000
1230 Ave of the Americas
New York, NY 10020
www.marilynsinger.net

Singh, Vijay (1963-)
Professional golfer
IMG Inc **Ph:** 216-522-1200
IMG Center **Fax:** 216-522-1145
1360 E 9th St Suite 100
Cleveland, OH 44114
www.pgatour.com

Singletary, Michelle
Writes the syndicated business column The Color of Money, which offers common-sense lessons about life and money
Washington Post Writers Group **Ph:** 202-334-6375 **Fax:** 202-334-5669
1150 15th St NW 9th Fl
Washington, DC 20071
www.postwritersgroup.com

Singleton, John (1968-)
Movie director
United Talent Agency **Ph:** 310-273-6700
9560 Wilshire Blvd 5th Fl **Fax:** 310-247-1111
Beverly Hills, CA 90212
www.john-singleton.com

Sinise, Gary (1955-)
Actor
Creative Artists Agency **Ph:** 310-288-4545
9830 Wilshire Blvd **Fax:** 310-288-4800
Beverly Hills, CA 90212
www.cbs.com/primetime/csi_ny

Sisto, Jeremy (1974-)
Actor
International Creative Management **Ph:** 310-550-4000
8942 Wilshire Blvd
Beverly Hills, CA 90211
www.hbo.com/sixfeetunder

Siu, Russell WJ
Co-owner and Executive Chef of 3660 on the Rise in Honolulu
3660 on the Rise **Ph:** 808-737-1177
3660 Waialae Ave **Fax:** 808-735-6105
Honolulu, HI 96816
www.3660.com

Sizemore, Tom (1961-)
Actor
Innovative Artists **Ph:** 310-656-0400
1505 10th St **Fax:** 310-656-0456
Santa Monica, CA 90401

Skaggs, Ricky (1954-)
Country singer (most recently focused on bluegrass)
Skaggs Family Records **Ph:** 615-264-8877
PO Box 2478 **Fax:** 615-264-8899
Hendersonville, TN 37077
www.skaggsfamilyrecords.com

Skelton, Ike (1931-)
US Representative from Missouri (Democrat)
2206 Rayburn Bldg **Ph:** 202-225-2876
Washington, DC 20515 **Fax:** 202-225-2695
www.house.gov/skelton

Skiles, Scott (1964-)
Basketball coach
Chicago Bulls **Ph:** 312-455-4000
United Center **Fax:** 312-455-4198
1901 W Madison St
Chicago, IL 60612
www.nba.com/bulls

Skinner, James A
Vice chairman and CEO of McDonald's Corp
McDonald's Corp **Ph:** 630-623-3000
1 McDonald's Plaza
Oak Brook, IL 60523
www.mcdonalds.com

Skoula, Martin (1979-)
Professional hockey player
Minnesota Wild **Ph:** 651-222-9453
317 Washington St **Fax:** 651-222-1055
Saint Paul, MN 55102
www.wild.com

Slater, Christian (1969-)
Actor
International Creative Management **Ph:** 310-550-4000
8942 Wilshire Blvd
Beverly Hills, CA 90211

Slatkin, Leonard (1944-)
Conductor; music director of the National Symphony Orchestra and principal guest conductor of the Royal Philharmonic Orchestra in London and of the Los Angeles Philharmonic
Office of Leonard Slatkin **Ph:** 202-416-8100
JFK Center for the Performing Arts **Fax:** 202-416-8123
2700 F St NW
Washington, DC 20566
www.leonardslatkin.com

Slaughter, John B, PhD (1934-)
President and CEO of the National Action Council for Minorities in Engineering; former director of the National Science Foundation
National Action Council for Minorities in Engineering **Ph:** 914-539-4010 **Fax:** 914-539-4032
440 Hamilton Ave Suite 302
White Plains, NY 10601
www.nacme.org

Slaughter, Louise M (1929-)
US Representative from New York (Democrat)
2469 Rayburn Bldg **Ph:** 202-225-3615
Washington, DC 20515 **Fax:** 202-225-7822
www.slaughter.house.gov

Slay, Francis G (1955-)
Mayor of St Louis
1200 Market St Suite 200 **Ph:** 314-622-3201
Saint Louis, MO 63103 **Fax:** 314-622-4061
stlouis.missouri.org

Slayton, Bobby (1955-)
Comedian (known as the Pit Bull of Comedy)
Gersh Agency **Ph:** 310-274-6611
232 N Canon Dr
Beverly Hills, CA 90210
www.bobbyslayton.com

Sleator, William (1945-)
Writer of science fiction books for children & young adults (Parasite Pig; Interstellar Pig)
Puffin Books Publicity **Ph:** 212-366-2000
345 Hudson St
New York, NY 10014
us.penguingroup.com

Sloan, Harry
Chairman and CEO of Metro-Goldwyn-Mayer; founder of SBS Broadcasting
Metro-Goldwyn-Mayer Inc **Ph:** 310-449-3000
10250 Constellation Blvd
Los Angeles, CA 90067

Sloan, Jerry (1942-)
Basketball coach
Utah Jazz **Ph:** 801-325-2500
Delta Center **Fax:** 801-325-2578
301 W South Temple St
Salt Lake City, UT 84101
www.nba.com/jazz

Slobodkina, Esphyr (1908-2002)
Artist and author/illustrator of children's books
Slobodkina Foundation Inc **Ph:** 516-674-0776
32 William St
Glen Head, NY 11545
www.slobodkina.com

Slouka, Mark
Author of God's Fool
Vintage/Anchor Publicity **Ph:** 212-572-2420
1745 Broadway 20th Fl
New York, NY 10019
www.randomhouse.com/vintage

Slutsky, Jeff
Motivational speaker on what he calls street fighter marketing
Street Fighter Marketing Inc **Ph:** 614-337-7474
467 Waterbury Ct **Fax:** 614-337-2233
Gahanna, OH 43230 **TF:** 800-758-8759
www.streetfightermarketing.net

Small, David (1945-)
Illustrator of children's books (Imogene's Antlers; So You Want to be President?)
Philomel Books Publicity **Ph:** 212-366-2000
345 Hudson St
New York, NY 10014
us.penguingroup.com

Smaltz, Donald
Served as Independent Counsel in the investigation of then-Secretary of Agriculture Mike Espy
Spiegel Liao & Kagay LLP **Ph:** 415-956-5959
388 Market St Suite 900 **Fax:** 415-362-1431
San Francisco, CA 94111
www.slksf.com

Smerconish, Michael (1962-)
Philadelphia lawyer turned political commentator; writes a weekly syndicated column and hosts a daily radio talk show
The Big Talker 1210 AM **Ph:** 610-668-5800
2 Bala Plaza **Fax:** 610-668-5885
Bala Cynwyd, PA 19004
www.mastalk.com

Smiley, Jane (1949-)
Novelist (A Thousand Acres; Good Faith)
Vintage/Anchor Publicity **Ph:** 212-572-2420
1745 Broadway 20th Fl
New York, NY 10019
www.randomhouse.com/anchor

Smiley, Tavis (1964-)
Host of talk/interview programs on radio and on television
The Smiley Group Inc **Ph:** 323-290-1888
3870 Crenshaw Blvd Suite 391 **Fax:** 323-290-3940
Los Angeles, CA 90008
tavistalks.com

Smirnoff, Yakov (1951-)
Russian comedian
William Morris Agency **Ph:** 310-859-4000
1 William Morris Pl **Fax:** 310-859-4462
Beverly Hills, CA 90212
www.yakov.com

Smith, Aaron (1976-)
Professional football player
Pittsburgh Steelers **Ph:** 412-432-7800
3400 S Water St **Fax:** 412-432-7878
Pittsburgh, PA 15203
www.pittsburghsteelers.com

Smith, Adam (1965-)
US Representative from Washington (Democrat)
227 Cannon Bldg **Ph:** 202-225-8901
Washington, DC 20515 **Fax:** 202-225-5893
www.house.gov/adamsmith

Smith, Anna Deavere (1950-)
Playwright, performance artist, actor, and teacher
Creative Artists Agency **Ph:** 310-288-4545
9830 Wilshire Blvd **Fax:** 310-288-4800
Beverly Hills, CA 90212

Smith, Christopher H (1953-)
US Representative from New Jersey (Republican)
2373 Rayburn Bldg **Ph:** 202-225-3765
Washington, DC 20515 **Fax:** 202-225-7768
www.house.gov/chrissmith

Smith, Daniel E
President & CEO of Sycamore Networks, a provider of optical switching products for telecommunications service providers
Sycamore Networks Inc **Ph:** 978-250-2900
220 Mill Rd **Fax:** 978-256-3434
Chelmsford, MA 01824
www.sycamorenet.com/corporate

Smith, Derek (1975-)
Professional football player
San Francisco 49ers **Ph:** 408-562-4949
4949 Centennial Blvd **Fax:** 408-727-4937
Santa Clara, CA 95054
www.sf49ers.com

Smith, Frederick W (1944-)
Founder, chairman, president, and CEO of FedEx Corp
FedEx Corp **Ph:** 901-818-7576
942 Shady Grove Rd **Fax:** 901-398-1111
Memphis, TN 38120
www.fedex.com/us/about/today/bios.html

Smith, Gordon (1952-)
US Senator from Oregon (Republican)
404 Russell Bldg **Ph:** 202-224-3753
Washington, DC 20510 **Fax:** 202-228-3997
gsmith.senate.gov

Smith, Hamilton O, MD (1931-)
Winner (with two other scientists) of the 1978 Nobel Prize in Physiology or Medicine; is currently involved in research at the Venter Insitute in the areas of synthetic biology and biological energy
J Craig Venter Institute **Ph:** 240-268-2605
9704 Medical Center Dr **Fax:** 240-268-4000
Rockville, MD 20850
www.venterinstitute.org/research

Smith, Harry (1951-)
An anchor of CBS News's The Early Show; also hosts a daily news and analysis feature on CBS Radio Network
The Early Show **Ph:** 212-975-2824
524 W 57th St
New York, NY 10019
www.cbsnews.com

Smith, Hugh C, MD
Professor of medicine at the Mayo Clinic College of Medicine; primary appointment is in cardiovascular diseases
Mayo Clinic **Ph:** 507-284-2511
200 1st St SW **Fax:** 507-284-0161
Rochester, MN 55905
mayoresearch.mayo.edu/mayo/research/staff/smith_hc.cfm

Smith, Jada Pinkett (1971-)
Actor
International Creative Management **Ph:** 310-550-4000
8942 Wilshire Blvd
Beverly Hills, CA 90211

Smith, Jeff
Creator of the comic book Bone
Cartoon Books **Ph:** 614-224-4487
PO Box 16973 **Fax:** 614-224-4488
Columbus, OH 43216
www.boneville.com/cartoonbooks/aboutjeff.shtml

Smith, Jimmy (1969-)
Professional football player
Jacksonville Jaguars **Ph:** 904-633-6000
1 Alltel Stadium Pl **Fax:** 904-633-6050
Jacksonville, FL 32202
www.jaguars.com

Smith, Joe (1975-)
Professional basketball player
Milwaukee Bucks **Ph:** 414-227-0500
Bradley Center **Fax:** 414-227-0543
1001 N 4th St
Milwuakee, WI 53203
www.nba.com/bucks

Smith, Katie (1974-)
Professional basketball player; most decorated women's player in the history of USA Basketball
Detroit Shock **Ph:** 248-377-0100
Palace at Auburn Hills **Fax:** 248-377-3260
4 Championship Pl
Auburn Hills, MI 48326
www.wnba.com/shock

Smith, Kevin (1970-)
Actor/director
View Askew Productions **Ph:** 732-842-6933
PO Box 400 **Fax:** 732-842-3772
Red Bank, NJ 07701
www.viewaskew.com

Smith, Lamar (1947-)
US Representative from Texas (Republican)
2184 Rayburn Bldg **Ph:** 202-225-4236
Washington, DC 20515 **Fax:** 202-225-8628
lamarsmith.house.gov

Smith, Larry
Sports anchor for CNN's Headline News
CNN **Ph:** 404-827-1500
1 CNN Center
Atlanta, GA 30303
www.cnn.com/CNN/anchors_reporters

Smith, Lee (1944-)
Fiction author (Saving Grace)
Ballantine Books Publicity **Ph:** 212-782-9000
1745 Broadway
New York, NY 10019
www.leesmith.com

Smith, Liz
Syndicated gossip columnist
Tribune Media Services Inc **Ph:** 312-222-4444
435 N Michigan Ave Suite 1500
Chicago, IL 60611
tmsfeatures.com/productlist.htm

Smith, Lovie (1958-)
Football coach
Chicago Bears **Ph:** 847-295-6600
Halas Hall at Conway Park **Fax:** 847-295-8986
1000 Football Dr
Lake Forest, IL 60045
www.chicagobears.com

Smith, Maggie (1934-)
Actor
International Creative Management **Ph:** 310-550-4000
8942 Wilshire Blvd
Beverly Hills, CA 90211

Smith, Michael W (1957-)
Singer (Contemporary Christian)
CAA Nashville **Ph:** 615-383-8787
3310 West End Ave 5th Fl **Fax:** 615-383-4937
Nashville, TN 37203
www.michaelwsmith.com

Smith, Mike (1960-)
Editorial cartoonist for the Las Vegas Sun; also draws StockcarToons, a weekly cartoon on NASCAR racing
Las Vegas Sun **Ph:** 702-385-3111
PO Box 98970 **Fax:** 702-383-7264
Las Vegas, NV 89193
www.kingfeatures.com/features

Smith, Roberta
Art critic
New York Times **Ph:** 212-556-1234
229 W 43rd St
New York, NY 10036

Smith, Rod (1970-)
Professional football player
Denver Broncos **Ph:** 303-649-9000
13655 Broncos Pkwy **Fax:** 303-649-9354
Englewood, CO 80112
www.denverbroncos.com

Smith, Shepard (1964-)
Anchors The Fox Report
FOX News Channel **Ph:** 212-301-3000
1211 Ave of the Americas
New York, NY 10036
www.foxnews.com/fnctv

Smith, Stacy Jenel
Writes the syndicated showbiz column Hollywood Exclusive with Marilyn Beck
Creators Syndicate Inc **Ph:** 310-337-7003
5777 W Century Blvd Suite 700 **Fax:** 310-337-7625
Los Angeles, CA 90045
www.creators.com

Smith, Stan (1946-)
Former tennis player
CMG Worldwide **Ph:** 317-570-5000
10500 Crosspoint Blvd
Indianapolis, IN 46256
www.cmgworldwide.com/sports/smith

Smith, Steve
Writes the syndicated automotive column Ridin' in Style
New York Times Syndicate **Ph:** 212-499-3300
609 Greenwich St 6th Fl
New York, NY 10014
www.nytsyn.com/lifestyle.html

Smith, Tangela (1977-)
Professional basketball player
Charlotte Sting **Ph:** 704-357-0252
100 Hive Dr **Fax:** 704-335-0289
Charlotte, NC 28217
www.wnba.com/sting

Smith, Vernon, PhD (1927-)
Winner of the 2002 Nobel Prize in Economics for having established laboratory experiments as a tool in empirical economic analysis, especially in the study of alternative market mechanisms
George Mason University **Ph:** 703-993-1151
Dept of Economics **Fax:** 703-993-1133
MSN 3G4
Fairfax, VA 22030
www.gmu.edu/departments/economics

Smith, Walter J (1948-)
Managing partner of Baker Botts law firm; his practice focuses primarily on public offerings, specialized securities transactions, mergers and acquisitions, and venture capital investments
Baker Botts LLP **Ph:** 713-229-1614
1 Shell Plaza **Fax:** 713-229-7714
910 Louisiana St
Houston, TX 77002
www.bakerbotts.com

Smith, Will (1968-)
Actor; singer/rapper (aka Fresh Prince)
Creative Artists Agency **Ph:** 310-288-4545
9830 Wilshire Blvd **Fax:** 310-288-4800
Beverly Hills, CA 90212
www.willsmith.com

Smith, Zadie (1975-)
Author (On Beauty; White Teeth)
Penguin Press Publicity **Ph:** 212-366-2000
375 Hudson St
New York, NY 10014
us.penguingroup.com

Smits, Jimmy (1955-)
Actor
Creative Artists Agency **Ph:** 310-288-4545
9830 Wilshire Blvd **Fax:** 310-288-4800
Beverly Hills, CA 90212
www.nbc.com/The_West_Wing

Smoltz, John (1967-)
Professional baseball player
Atlanta Braves **Ph:** 404-522-7630
PO Box 4064 **Fax:** 404-614-1392
Atlanta, GA 30302
atlanta.braves.mlb.com

Smothers, Dick (1939-)
Comedian (part of the Smothers Brothers comedy team)
William Morris Agency **Ph:** 310-859-4000
1 William Morris Pl **Fax:** 310-859-4462
Beverly Hills, CA 90212
www.smothersbrothers.com

Smothers, Tom (1937-)
Comedian (part of the Smothers Brothers comedy team)
William Morris Agency **Ph:** 310-859-4000
1 William Morris Pl **Fax:** 310-859-4462
Beverly Hills, CA 90212
www.smothersbrothers.com

Smucker, Richard K (1948-)
President and co-CEO (with his brother Tim) of the JM Smucker Co
JM Smucker Co **Ph:** 330-682-3000
1 Strawberry Ln **Fax:** 330-684-6410
Orrville, OH 44667
www.smuckers.com

Smucker, Timothy P (1944-)
Chairman and co-CEO (with his brother Richard) of JM Smucker Co
JM Smucker Co **Ph:** 330-682-3000
1 Strawberry Ln **Fax:** 330-684-6410
Orrville, OH 44667
www.smuckers.com

Smyth, Ryan (1976-)
Professional hockey player
Edmonton Oilers **Ph:** 780-414-4000
11230 110th St **Fax:** 780-409-5890
Edmonton, AB T5G3H7
www.edmontonoilers.com

Snicket, Lemony (1970-)
Author of A Series of Unfortunate Events mystery/humor books; Lemony Snicket is the pseudonym of Daniel Handler
HarperCollins Children's Books **Ph:** 212-261-6500
1350 Ave of the Americas
New York, NY 10019
www.lemonysnicket.com

Snider, Edward M
Chairman/owner of the Philadelphia 76ers basketball team and the Philadelphia Flyers hockey team
Philadelphia Flyers **Ph:** 215-465-4500
Wachovia Center **Fax:** 215-389-9403
3601 S Broad St
Philadelphia, PA 19148
www.philadelphiaflyers.com/team/frontoffice

Snider, Stacey
Chairman of Universal Pictures
Universal Pictures **Ph:** 818-777-1000
100 Universal City Plaza
Universal City, CA 91608
www.universalstudios.com

Snipes, Wesley (1962-)
Actor
United Talent Agency **Ph:** 310-273-6700
9560 Wilshire Blvd 5th Fl **Fax:** 310-247-1111
Beverly Hills, CA 90212

Snoop Dogg (1971-)
Hip-hop artist; actor (real name is Calvin Broadus)
William Morris Agency **Ph:** 310-859-4000
1 William Morris Pl **Fax:** 310-859-4462
Beverly Hills, CA 90212
www.snoopdogg.com

Snow, John W (1939-)
US Secretary of the Treasury
US Dept of the Treasury **Ph:** 202-622-1100
1500 Pennsylvania Ave NW **Fax:** 202-202-2222
Washington, DC 20220
www.ustreas.gov/organization/officials.html

Snow, JT (1968-)
Professional baseball player
Boston Red Sox **Ph:** 617-267-9440
Fenway Park **Fax:** 617-236-6797
4 Yawkey Way
Boston, MA 02215
boston.redsox.mlb.com

Snow, Kate
Co-anchor of ABC News weekend edition of Good Morning America
Good Morning America **Ph:** 212-456-7777
147 Columbus Ave
New York, NY 10023
www.abcnews.go.com/GMA

Snow, Tony (1955-)
White House Press Secretary; former FOX News anchor and talk show host
1600 Pennsylvania Ave NW **Ph:** 202-456-2673
Washington, DC 20500 **Fax:** 202-456-0126

Snowe, Olympia J (1947-)
US Senator from Maine (Republican)
154 Russell Bldg **Ph:** 202-224-5344
Washington, DC 20510 **Fax:** 202-224-1946
snowe.senate.gov

Snyder, Daniel M (1965-)
Owner of the Washington Redskins football franchise
Washington Redskins **Ph:** 703-726-7000
21300 Redskins Park Dr **Fax:** 703-729-7086
Ashburn, VA 20147
www.redskins.com/news/mediaguide/2005Ownership.pdf

Snyder, Gary (1930-)
Poet; also writes prose/essays
Shoemaker & Hoard Publishers **Ph:** 510-595-3664
1400 65th St Suite 250 **Fax:** 510-595-4228
Emeryville, CA 94608
www.shoemakerhoard.com

Snyder, Rick (1959-)
Chairman of the Board and interim CEO of Gateway Inc
Gateway Inc **Ph:** 949-471-7000
7565 Irvine Center Dr **Fax:** 949-471-7001
Irvine, CA 92618
www.gateway.com

Snyder, Vic (1947-)
US Representative from Arkansas (Democrat)
1330 Longworth Bldg **Ph:** 202-225-2506
Washington, DC 20515 **Fax:** 202-225-5903
www.house.gov/snyder

Sobran, Joseph (1946-)
Conservative columnist; former National Review senior editor
Conservative Chronicle **Ph:** 800-888-3039
9 2nd St NW
PO Box 317
Hampton, IA 50441
www.conservativechronicle.com

Sodrel, Mike (1945-)
US Representative from Indiana (Republican)
1508 Longworth Bldg **Ph:** 202-225-5315
Washington, DC 20515 **Fax:** 202-226-6866
sodrel.house.gov

Sohn, Michael N (1940-)
Attorney and former General Counsel of the Federal Trade Commission; his practice focuses on the antitrust aspects of mergers & acquisitions and treble damage class-actions
Arnold & Porter LLP **Ph:** 202-942-5005
555 12th St NW **Fax:** 202-942-5999
Washington, DC 20004
www.arnoldporter.com

Solis, Hilda L (1957-)
US Representative from California (Democrat)
1725 Longworth Bldg **Ph:** 202-225-5464
Washington, DC 20515 **Fax:** 202-225-5467
solis.house.gov

Solmonese, Joe
President of the Human Rights Campaign, an organization working to achieve gay, lesbian, bisexual, and transgender equality; former CEO of EMILY's List
Human Rights Campaign **Ph:** 202-628-4160
1640 Rhode Island Ave NW **Fax:** 202-347-5323
Washington, DC 20036
www.hrc.org

Solomon, Andrew (1963-)
Author of The Noonday Demon: An Atlas of Depression
Simon & Schuster **Ph:** 212-698-7000
1230 Ave of the Americas
New York, NY 10020
www.noondaydemon.com

Solomon, Howard
Chairman & CEO of Forest Laboratories Inc
Forest Laboratories Inc **Ph:** 212-421-7850
909 3rd Ave 23rd Fl **Fax:** 212-750-9152
New York, NY 10022 **TF:** 800-947-5227
www.frx.com

Solomon, Norman (1951-)
Writes the syndicated column Media Beat; also writes books about the media (The Habits of Highly Deceptive Media)
Creators Syndicate Inc **Ph:** 310-337-7003
5777 W Century Blvd Suite 700 **Fax:** 310-337-7625
Los Angeles, CA 90045
www.creators.com/opinion.html

Solovic, Susan
CEO of Small Business Television Network
Small Business Television Network **Ph:** 314-533-7288
20 Allen Ave Suite 344
Saint Louis, MO 63119
www.sbtv.com/about.asp

Solovy, Jerold S (1930-)
Appellate and trial lawyer; specializes in litigating complex business matters and insurance coverage issues
Jenner & Block LLP **Ph:** 312-923-2671
1 IBM Plaza **Fax:** 312-840-7671
330 N Wabash St 40th Fl
Chicago, IL 60611
www.jenner.com

Solow, Robert M, PhD (1924-)
Winner of the 1987 Nobel Prize in Economic Sciences for his contributions to the theory of economic growth
Massachusetts Institute of Technology **Ph:** 617-253-3980
Fax: 617-253-1330
Dept of Economics
50 Memorial Dr
Cambridge, MA 02139
web.mit.edu/globalchange/www/personnel.html

Solzhenitsyn, Aleksandr (1918-)
Russian author and historian; winner of the Nobel Prize in Literature in 1970
ISI Books **Ph:** 302-652-4600
3901 Centerville Rd **Fax:** 302-652-1760
PO Box 4431
Wilmington, DE 19807
www.isi.org/books

Some, Sobonfu
Authority on African spirituality; she is an initiated member of the Dagara tribe of Burkina Faso, and she and her husband (Malidoma Some) teach the ancient wisdom of their tribe
Ancestors Wisdom Spring **Ph:** 916-446-5536
5960 S Land Park Dr Suite 200
Sacramento, CA 95822
www.sobonfu.com

Sommer, Bobbe, PhD
Speaker, consultant, and seminar leader; talks about how to achieve aspirations and goals through positive self-esteem
237 W Alessandro **Ph:** 949-235-9585
San Clemente, CA 92672 **Fax:** 949-361-3606
www.keynotespeaking.com

Sommers, Christina Hoff
Author of Who Stole Feminism? and The War Against Boys
American Enterprise Institute for Public Policy Research **Ph:** 202-862-5800
Fax: 202-862-7177
1150 17th St NW Suite 1100
Washington, DC 20036
www.aei.org

Sone, Hiro
Chef and owner of Terra, a Napa Valley restaurant; also owns a new San Francisco restaurant, Ame
Terra Restaurant **Ph:** 707-963-8931
1345 Railroad Ave
Saint Helena, CA 94574
www.terrarestaurant.com

Sones, Sonya (1952-)
Writer of novels in verse for young adults
Simon & Schuster Books for Young Readers — **Ph:** 212-698-7000
1230 Ave of the Americas
New York, NY 10020
www.sonyasones.com

Sonic Youth
Underground rock band
Creative Artists Agency — **Ph:** 310-288-4545
9830 Wilshire Blvd — **Fax:** 310-288-4800
Beverly Hills, CA 90212
www.sonicyouth.com

Sonnenfeld, Barry (1953-)
Movie director/producer; cinematographer
Creative Artists Agency — **Ph:** 310-288-4545
8930 Wilshire Blvd — **Fax:** 310-288-4800
Beverly Hills, CA 90212

Sonsini, Larry W (1941-)
Attorney known for his expertise is in the areas of corporate law, corporate governance, securities, and mergers & acquisitions; was involved in Google's IPO and Hewlett-Packard's merger with Compaq Computer
Wilson Sonsini Goodrich & Rosati — **Ph:** 650-493-9300 — **Fax:** 650-493-6811
650 Page Mill Rd
Palo Alto, CA 94304
www.wsgr.com

Sontag, Susan (1933-2004)
Author of novels, stories, and essays
Farrar Straus & Giroux — **Ph:** 212-741-6900
19 Union Sq W
New York, NY 10003
www.susansontag.com

Sorenstam, Annika (1970-)
Professional golfer
IMG Inc — **Ph:** 216-522-1200
IMG Center — **Fax:** 216-522-1145
1360 E 9th St Suite 100
Cleveland, OH 44114
www.lpga.com

Soriano, Alfonso (1976-)
Professional baseball player
Washington Nationals — **Ph:** 202-349-0400
RFK Stadium
2400 E Capitol St SE
Washington, DC 20005
washington.nationals.mlb.com

Sorkin, Aaron (1961-)
Writer for TV and movies
Endeavor — **Ph:** 310-248-2000
9601 Wilshire Blvd 3rd Fl — **Fax:** 310-248-2020
Beverly Hills, CA 90210

Soros, George (1930-)
Financier & philanthropist; founder and chairman of the Open Society Institute and the Soros foundations network
Open Society Institute — **Ph:** 212-548-0600
400 W 59th St — **Fax:** 212-548-4679
New York, NY 10019
www.soros.org

Sortun, Ana
Executive chef and owner of Oleana Restaurant in Cambridge, Massachusetts
Oleana Restaurant — **Ph:** 617-661-0505
134 Hampshire St — **Fax:** 617-661-3336
Cambridge, MA 02139
oleanarestaurant.com

Sorvino, Paul (1939-)
Actor
Agency for the Performing Arts — **Ph:** 310-273-0744
9200 Sunset Blvd Suite 900 — **Fax:** 310-888-4242
Los Angeles, CA 90069

Soto, Gary (1952-)
Writes poetry for adults as well as poetry and fiction for children and teens
Harcourt Children's Books — **Ph:** 212-592-1000
15 E 26th St
New York, NY 10010
www.garysoto.com

Soto, Jock
Former dancer with the New York City Ballet; member of the permanent faculty of the NYCB's School of American Ballet
School of American Ballet — **Ph:** 212-769-6600
70 Lincoln Center Plaza — **Fax:** 212-769-4897
New York, NY 10023
www.nycballet.com/about/dancers.html

Souder, Mark (1950-)
US Representative from Indiana (Republican)
2231 Rayburn Bldg — **Ph:** 202-225-4436
Washington, DC 20515 — **Fax:** 202-225-3479
souder.house.gov

Souray, Sheldon (1976-)
Professional hockey player
Montreal Canadiens — **Ph:** 514-932-2582
1275 Saint Antoine St W — **Fax:** 514-932-9296
Montreal, QC H3C5L2
www.canadiens.com

Souter, David H (1939-)
US Supreme Court justice
US Supreme Court Bldg **Ph:** 202-479-3000
1 1st St NE
Washington, DC 20543
www.supremecourtus.gov

Sowell, Thomas, PhD (1930-)
Syndicated columnist; also a senior fellow at the Hoover Institution, with expertise in economics, social decision making, and ethnicity
Hoover Institution on War Revolution & Peace **Ph:** 650-723-1754 **Fax:** 650-723-1687
Stanford University
Stanford, CA 94305
www.tsowell.com

Soyinka, Wole (1934-)
Nigerian playwright; also known for his novels, autobiographical works, poetry, and criticism, and in 1986, he became the first African writer ever to be awarded the Nobel Prize for Literature
Random House Publicity **Ph:** 212-782-9000
1745 Broadway
New York, NY 10019
www.randomhouse.com

Spacek, Sissy (1949-)
Actor
Creative Artists Agency **Ph:** 310-288-4545
9830 Wilshire Blvd **Fax:** 310-288-4800
Beverly Hills, CA 90212

Spacey, Kevin (1959-)
Actor
William Morris Agency **Ph:** 310-859-4000
1 William Morris Pl **Fax:** 310-859-4462
Beverly Hills, CA 90212

Spadafori, Gina
Writes the syndicated column Pet Connection, which provides both expert advice and stories about pets
Universal Press Syndicate **Ph:** 816-932-6600
4520 Main St
Kansas City, MO 64111
www.amuniversal.com/ups/features

Spade, David (1964-)
Comedian; actor
Endeavor **Ph:** 310-248-2000
9601 Wilshire Blvd 3rd Fl **Fax:** 310-248-2020
Beverly Hills, CA 90210
davidspade.com

Spader, James (1960-)
Actor
International Creative Management **Ph:** 310-550-4000
8942 Wilshire Blvd
Beverly Hills, CA 90211
abc.go.com/primetime/bostonlegal

Spanos, Alex G (1923-)
Owner of the San Diego Chargers football franchise; also the founder and chairman of AG Spanos Cos, the nation's largest family-owned construction company
San Diego Chargers **Ph:** 858-874-4500
4020 Murphy Canyon Rd
San Diego, CA 92123
www.chargers.com

Sparks, Nicholas (1965-)
Fiction writer (Message in a Bottle; The Notebook)
Warner Books **Ph:** 212-522-7200
c/o Author Mail
1271 Ave of the Americas
New York, NY 10020
www.nicholassparks.com

Speare, Elizabeth George (1908-)
Author of books for children and young adults (The Witch of Blackbird Pond)
Houghton Mifflin Children's Books **Ph:** 617-351-5000
222 Berkeley St 8th Fl
Boston, MA 02116
www.houghtonmifflinbooks.com

Spears, Britney (1981-)
Pop singer
Creative Artists Agency **Ph:** 310-288-4545
9830 Wilshire Blvd **Fax:** 310-288-4800
Beverly Hills, CA 90212
www.britneyspears.com

Specter, Arlen (1930-)
US Senator from Pennsylvania (Republican)
711 Hart Bldg **Ph:** 202-224-4254
Washington, DC 20510 **Fax:** 202-228-1229
specter.senate.gov

Spelling, Aaron (1923-)
TV & movie producer
Spelling Television **Ph:** 323-965-5700
5700 Wilshire Blvd Suite 575
Los Angeles, CA 90036

Spellings, Margaret (1958-)
US Secretary of Education
US Dept of Education — **Ph:** 202-401-3000
400 Maryland Ave SW — **Fax:** 202-401-0596
Washington, DC 20202
www.ed.gov/news/staff/bios

Spence, Gerry (1929-)
Attorney & former CNBC-TV talk show host; he has never lost a criminal case
Spence Law Firm LLC — **Ph:** 307-733-7290
15 S Jackson St — **Fax:** 307-733-5248
PO Box 548 — **TF:** 800-967-2117
Jackson, WY 83001
www.gerryspence.com

Spencer, LaVyrle (1943-)
Author of romances
Berkley Books Publicity — **Ph:** 212-366-2000
375 Hudson St
New York, NY 10014
us.penguingroup.com

Spencer, Susan (1968-)
48 Hours correspondent
48 Hours — **Ph:** 212-975-4114
524 W 57th St
New York, NY 10019
www.cbsnews.com

Spezza, Jason (1983-)
Professional hockey player
Ottawa Senators — **Ph:** 613-599-0250
Corel Center — **Fax:** 613-599-0358
1000 Palladium Dr
Kanata, ON K2V1A5
www.ottawasenators.com

Spicer, Susan
Chef and co-owner of Bayona Restaurant in New Orleans
Bayona Restaurant — **Ph:** 504-525-4455
430 Dauphine St
New Orleans, LA 70112
www.bayona.com

Spiegelman, Art (1948-)
Cartoonist; his work includes Maus, a Holocaust saga which portrayed Jews as mice and Nazis as cats
Steven Barclay Agency — **Ph:** 707-773-0654
12 Western Ave — **Fax:** 707-778-1868
Petaluma, CA 94952 — **TF:** 888-965-7323
www.barclayagency.com

Spielberg, Steven (1946-)
Filmmaker (producer/director); co-founder of Dreamworks SKG
DreamWorks SKG — **Ph:** 818-733-7000
100 Universal City Plaza
Bldg 5121
Universal City, CA 91608

Spikes, Takeo (1976-)
Professional football player
Buffalo Bills — **Ph:** 716-648-1800
Ralph Wilson Stadium — **Fax:** 716-649-6446
1 Bills Dr
Orchard Park, NY 14127
www.buffalobills.com

Spillane, Mickey (1918-)
Author of the Mike Hammer mystery/detective books; his first book was I, the Jury
Simon & Schuster — **Ph:** 212-698-7000
1230 Ave of the Americas
New York, NY 10020
www.simonsays.com

Spinelli, Jerry (1941-)
Author of books for young readers (Maniac Magee; Wringer; Stargirl)
Random House Children's Books — **Ph:** 212-782-9000
Publicity Dept
1745 Broadway
New York, NY 10019
www.randomhouse.com/kids

Spitzer, Eliot (1959-)
Attorney general of the state of New York
New York State Attorney General — **Ph:** 212-416-8000
120 Broadway
New York, NY 10271
www.oag.state.ny.us

Splichal, Joachim
Master chef and founder, with his wife Christine, of the Patina Group of restaurants
Patina Group — **Ph:** 213-239-2500
400 S Hope St Suite 950
Los Angeles, CA 90071
www.patinagroup.com

Splinter, Michael
President and CEO of Applied Materials
Applied Materials Inc — **Ph:** 408-727-5555
3050 Bowers Ave
Santa Clara, CA 95054
www.appliedmaterials.com

Spoto, Donald, PhD (1941-)
Biographer & theologian; author of The Hidden Jesus and The Reluctant Saint: The Life of Francis of Assisi; has also written biographies of royals and film stars
Penguin Publicity **Ph:** 212-366-2000
375 Hudson St
New York, NY 10014
www.reluctantsaint.tv

Spratt, John M Jr (1942-)
US Representative from South Carolina (Democrat)
1401 Longworth Bldg **Ph:** 202-225-5501
Washington, DC 20515 **Fax:** 202-225-0464
www.house.gov/spratt

Springer, Nancy (1948-)
Author of the Rowan Hood series for young readers
Philomel Books Publicity **Ph:** 212-366-2000
345 Hudson St
New York, NY 10014
us.penguingroup.com

Springs, Shawn (1975-)
Professional football player
Washington Redskins **Ph:** 703-726-7000
21300 Redskin Park Dr **Fax:** 703-726-7086
Ashburn, VA 20147
www.redskins.com

Springsteen, Bruce (1949-)
Singer/songwriter, composer
Creative Artists Agency **Ph:** 212-277-9000
162 5th Ave 6th Fl **Fax:** 212-277-9099
New York, NY 10010
www.brucespringsteen.net

Sproul, RC (1939-)
Founder and chairman of Ligonier Ministries; host of the daily radio program Renewing Your Mind, and has written numerous books as well as magazine articles for evangelical publications
Ligonier Ministries **Ph:** 407-333-4244
PO Box 547500 **TF:** 800-435-4343
Orlando, FL 32854
www.ligonier.org

Spurrier, Steve (1945-)
Football coach
University of South Carolina Athletics Dept **Ph:** 803-777-4202
Rex Enright Athletic Ctr
1300 Rosewood Dr
Columbia, SC 29208
uscsports.collegesports.com

St Clair, Rita
Interior designer; writes the syndicated column Design Line
Tribune Media Services Inc **Ph:** 312-222-4444
435 N Michigan Ave Suite 1500
Chicago, IL 60611
tmsfeatures.com/productlist.htm

St Louis, Martin (1975-)
Professional hockey player
Tampa Bay Lightning **Ph:** 813-301-6600
St Pete Times Forum **Fax:** 813-301-1487
401 Channelside Dr
Tampa, FL 33602
www.tampabaylightning.com

Staake, Bob (1957-)
Artist/illustrator whose humorous drawings appear in magazines, books, greeting cards, and other products
Bob Staake Studio **Ph:** 508-945-0191
274 Main St
Chatham, MA 02633
www.bobstaake.com

Staal, Eric (1984-)
Professional hockey player
Carolina Hurricanes **Ph:** 919-467-7825
RBC Center **Fax:** 919-462-7030
1400 Edwards Mill Rd
Raleigh, NC 27607
www.carolinahurricanes.com

Stabenow, Debbie (1950-)
US Senator from Michigan (Democrat)
702 Hart Bldg **Ph:** 202-224-4822
Washington, DC 20510 **Fax:** 202-228-0325
stabenow.senate.gov

Stackhouse, Jerry (1974-)
Professional basketball player
Dallas Mavericks **Ph:** 214-747-6287
The Pavilion **Fax:** 214-658-7121
2909 Taylor St
Dallas, TX 75226
www.jerrystackhouse.com

Stafford, Rob
Dateline NBC correspondent
Dateline NBC **Ph:** 212-664-4249
30 Rockefeller Plaza
New York, NY 10112
www.msnbc.msn.com/id/3360263

Stahl, Jack L (1954-)
President & CEO of Revlon
Revlon Inc **Ph:** 212-527-4000
625 Madison Ave
New York, NY 10022
www.revlon.com/corporate

Stahl, Lesley (1941-)
60 Minutes correspondent
60 Minutes **Ph:** 212-975-2006
555 W 57th St
New York, NY 10019
www.cbsnews.com

Stahl, Nick (1979-)
Actor
International Creative Management **Ph:** 310-550-4000
8942 Wilshire Blvd
Beverly Hills, CA 90211
www.hbo.com/carnivale

Stahler, Jeff
Editorial cartoonist for The Columbus Dispatch; also creates the comic panel Moderately Confused
Columbus Dispatch **Ph:** 614-461-5000
34 S 3rd St
Columbus, OH 43215
www.unitedfeatures.com

Stairs, Matt (1968-)
Professional baseball player
Kansas City Royals **Ph:** 816-921-8000
Kauffman Stadium **Fax:** 816-921-5775
1 Royal Way
Kansas City, MO 64129
kansascity.royals.mlb.com

Staley, Dawn (1970-)
Professional basketball player
Houston Comets **Ph:** 713-758-7200
Toyota Center **Fax:** 713-758-7396
1510 Polk St
Houston, TX 77002
www.dawnstaley5.com

Staley, Duce (1975-)
Professional football player
Pittsburgh Steelers **Ph:** 412-432-7800
3400 S Water St **Fax:** 412-432-7878
Pittsburgh, PA 15203
www.pittsburghsteelers.com

Staley, Warren R
Chairman of the Board and CEO of Cargill Inc
Cargill Inc **Ph:** 952-742-7575
15407 McGinty Rd
Wayzata, MN 55391
www.cargill.com

Stallone, Sylvester (1946-)
Actor
International Creative Management **Ph:** 310-550-4000
8942 Wilshire Blvd
Beverly Hills, CA 90211
www.sylvesterstallone.com

Stallworth, Donte (1980-)
Professional football player
New Orleans Saints **Ph:** 504-733-0255
5800 Airline Dr **Fax:** 504-731-1768
Metairie, LA 70003
www.neworleanssaints.com

Stamberg, Susan (1938-)
Special Correspondent on NPR; has hosted various shows on NPR
National Public Radio **Ph:** 202-513-2000
635 Massachusetts Ave NW **Fax:** 202-513-3329
Washington, DC 20001
www.npr.org

Stamos, John (1963-)
Actor
Creative Artists Agency **Ph:** 310-288-4545
9830 Wilshire Blvd **Fax:** 310-288-4800
Beverly Hills, CA 90212
www.johnstamos.net

Standley, John T
CEO of Pathmark Stores (supermarket chain)
Pathmark Stores Inc **Ph:** 732-499-3000
200 Milik St **Fax:** 732-499-3072
Carteret, NJ 07008
www.pathmark.com

Stanley, Charles (1932-)
Pastor of the First Baptist Church of Atlanta and founder of In Touch Ministries and the In Touch radio and television programs
In Touch Ministries **Ph:** 770-451-1001
PO Box 7900 **TF:** 800-789-1473
Atlanta, GA 30357
intouch.org

Stanley, Thomas J, PhD
Business author; titles include The Millionaire Next Door (with William Danko)
Andrews McMeel Publishing **Ph:** 800-851-8923
4520 Main St
Kansas City, MO 64111
www.andrewsmcmeel.com

Stantis, Scott
Creator of the comic strip Prickly City
Universal Press Syndicate **Ph:** 816-932-6600
4520 Main St
Kansas City, MO 64111
www.amuniversal.com/ups/features

Stanton, Harry Dean (1928-)
Actor
Bresler Kelly & Assoc **Ph:** 310-479-5611
11500 W Olympic Blvd
Suite 352
Los Angeles, CA 90064

Star, Darren (1961-)
Producer (creator of Sex & the City)
William Morris Agency **Ph:** 310-859-4000
1 William Morris Pl **Fax:** 310-859-4462
Beverly Hills, CA 90212
www.hbo.com/city

Stark, Betsy
Business correspondent for ABC News
ABC News **Ph:** 212-456-7777
77 W 66th St
New York, NY 10023
www.abcnews.go.com/WNT

Stark, Lisa
ABC News correspondent; specializes in reporting on Federal agencies
ABC News **Ph:** 202-222-7700
1717 DeSales St NW
Washington, DC 20036
www.abcnews.go.com/WNT

Stark, Melissa (1974-)
National correspondent for the Today Show (was previously a sidelines commentator on ABC's Monday Night Football)
Today Show **Ph:** 212-664-4249
30 Rockefeller Plaza
New York, NY 10112
www.msnbc.msn.com/id/3079108

Stark, Pete (1931-)
US Representative from California (Democrat)
239 Cannon Bldg **Ph:** 202-225-5065
Washington, DC 20515 **Fax:** 202-226-3805
www.house.gov/stark

Starlin, James P (1949-)
Comic book artist; has written or drawn most of the heroes in the DC and Marvel comic books
Marvel Enterprises Inc **Ph:** 212-576-4000
417 5th Ave
New York, NY 10016
www.starlin.com

Starr, Kenneth (1946-)
Independent Counsel on the Whitewater investigation of President Bill Clinton; now Dean and Professor of Law at Pepperdine University School of Law
Pepperdine University **Ph:** 310-506-4611
School of Law
24255 Pacific Coast Hwy
Malibu, CA 90263
law.pepperdine.edu/academics/faculty

Starr, Paul
Co-founder & co-editor (with Robert Kuttner) of The American Prospect and the founder of Moving Ideas, an online public policy consortium run by The American Prospect
The American Prospect **Ph:** 202-776-0730
2000 L St NW Suite 717 **Fax:** 202-776-0740
Washington, DC 20036
www.prospect.org

Stayskal, Wayne
Editorial cartoonist
Tribune Media Services Inc **Ph:** 312-222-4444
435 N Michigan Ave Suite 1500
Chicago, IL 60611
www.comicspage.com

Stearns, Cliff (1945-)
US Representative from Florida (Republican)
2370 Rayburn Bldg **Ph:** 202-225-5744
Washington, DC 20515 **Fax:** 202-225-3973
www.house.gov/stearns

Steel, Danielle (1947-)
Author of bestselling romance fiction
Random House Publicity **Ph:** 212-782-9000
1745 Broadway
New York, NY 10019
www.daniellesteel.com

Steele, Shari
Executive director and president of the Electronic Frontier Foundation
Electronic Frontier Foundation **Ph:** 415-436-9333
454 Shotwell St **Fax:** 415-436-9993
San Francisco, CA 94110
www.eff.org

Steenburgen, Mary (1953-)
Actor
Gersh Agency **Ph:** 212-997-1818
41 Madison Ave 33rd Fl **Fax:** 212-997-1978
New York, NY 10010

Steenland, Douglas M (1952-)
President & CEO of Northwest Airlines
Northwest Airlines Corp **Ph:** 612-726-2111
2700 Lone Oak Pkwy
Eagan, MN 55121
www.nwa.com/corpinfo

Stefani, Gwen (1969-)
Singer in the rock group No Doubt
United Talent Agency **Ph:** 310-273-6700
9560 Wilshire Blvd 5th Fl **Fax:** 310-247-1111
Beverly Hills, CA 90212
www.gwenstefani.com

Steichen, Edward (1879-1973)
Photographer
Staley-Wise Gallery **Ph:** 212-966-6223
560 Broadway **Fax:** 212-966-6293
New York, NY 10012
www.staleywise.com

Stein, Ben (1944-)
Actor, game show host, writer, lawyer
Endeavor **Ph:** 310-248-2000
9601 Wilshire Blvd 3rd Fl **Fax:** 310-248-2020
Beverly Hills, CA 90210
www.benstein.com

Stein, Ed
Editorial cartoonist for the Denver Rocky Mountain News
Newspaper Enterprise Assn **Ph:** 212-293-8500
200 Madison Ave
New York, NY 10016
www.unitedfeatures.com

Steinbrenner, George (1930-)
Principal owner of the New York Yankees baseball club; also owns an interest in the New Jersey Nets basketball team and the New Jersey Devils hockey team
New York Yankees **Ph:** 718-293-4300
Yankee Stadium
161st St & River Ave
Bronx, NY 10451
newyork.yankees.mlb.com

Steinem, Gloria (1934-)
Feminist; consulting editor & co-founder of Ms Magazine
Ms Magazine **Ph:** 310-556-2515
433 S Beverly Dr **Fax:** 310-556-2514
Beverly Hills, CA 90212

Steiner, David
CEO of Waste Management
Waste Management Inc **Ph:** 713-512-6200
1001 Fannin St Suite 4000
Houston, TX 77002
www.wm.com

Steiner, Ralph (1899-1986)
Photographer
Robert Klein Gallery **Ph:** 617-267-7997
38 Newbury St 4th Fl **Fax:** 617-267-5567
Boston, MA 02116
www.robertkleingallery.com

Steinfeld, Jake (1978-)
Personal fitness trainer and developer of home fitness products
Body by Jake Enterprises Inc **Ph:** 310-571-7101
PO Box 25041 **Fax:** 310-571-7107
Los Angeles, CA 90025
www.bodybyjake.com

Stella, Frank (1936-)
Minimalist painter & sculptor
Paul Kasmin Gallery **Ph:** 212-563-4474
293 10th Ave **Fax:** 212-563-4494
New York, NY 10001
www.paulkasmingallery.com

Stellino, Nick
Chef; host of Nick Stellino's Family Kitchen on PBS
KCTS-TV **Ph:** 206-728-6463
401 Mercer St **Fax:** 206-443-6691
Seattle, WA 98109
www.nickstellino.com

Stephanopoulos, George (1961-)
Chief Washington correspondent for ABC News and anchor of This Week with George Stephanopoulos
ABC News This Week **Ph:** 202-222-7700
1717 DeSales St NW
Washington, DC 20036
www.abcnews.go.com/ThisWeek

Sterling, Donald T (1936-)
Owner of the Los Angeles Clippers basketball team
Los Angeles Clippers **Ph:** 213-742-7500
Staples Center
1111 S Figueroa St Suite 1100
Los Angeles, CA 90015

Stern, David (1942-)
Commissioner of the National Basketball Association (NBA)
National Basketball Assn **Ph:** 212-407-8000
645 5th Ave
New York, NY 10022

Stern, Gerald (1925-)
Poet
WW Norton & Co Inc **Ph:** 212-354-5500
500 5th Ave **Fax:** 212-869-0856
New York, NY 10110
www.nortonpoets.com

Stern, Howard (1950-)
Host of The Howard Stern Show, a morning talk radio/call-in show; also on TV
SIRIUS Satellite Radio **Ph:** 212-584-5100
1221 Ave of the Americas
New York, NY 10020
www.howardstern.com

Stern, Tom
Business owner (executive recruiting) and creator/writer of the comic strip CEO Dad
Stern Executive Search **Ph:** 818-884-2784
4708 Westchester
Woodland Hills, CA 91364
www.sternexec.com

Sternberg, Seymour G
Chairman & CEO of New York Life
New York Life Insurance Co **Ph:** 212-576-7000
51 Madison Ave **Fax:** 212-576-8145
New York, NY 10010
www.newyorklife.com

Sternberg, Stuart
Principal owner of the Tampa Bay Devil Rays baseball franchise
Tampa Bay Devil Rays **Ph:** 727-825-3137
Tropicana Field **Fax:** 727-825-3111
1 Tropicana Dr
Saint Petersburg, FL 33705
tampabay.devilrays.mlb.com

Sterritt, David, PhD (1944-)
Adjunct professor of Language, Literature, and Culture at Maryland Institute College of Art; chair, National Society of Film Critics, and film critic/special correspondent for the Christian Science Monitor
Belvedere Hotel Suite 501-502 **Ph:** 410-385-0123
1 E Chase St
Baltimore, MD 21202
www.davidsterritt.com

Steve Miller Band
Rock group that gained its greatest fame in the 1970's
Monterey Peninsula Artists/Paradigm **Ph:** 831-375-4889
Fax: 831-375-2623
509 Hartnell St
Monterey, CA 93940
www.stevemillerband.com

Stevens, John Paul (1920-)
US Supreme Court justice
US Supreme Court Bldg **Ph:** 202-479-3000
1 1st St NE
Washington, DC 20543
www.supremecourtus.gov

Stevens, Mick
New Yorker cartoonist
Cartoon Bank **Ph:** 914-478-5527
New Yorker Magazine **Fax:** 914-478-5604
28 Wells Ave Bldg 3 4th Fl
Yonkers, NY 10701
www.mickstevens.com

Stevens, Ray (1939-)
Singer/songwriter; his recordings include pop, rock, and country songs, as well as novelty tunes such as The Streak and Ahab the Arab
Clyde Records **Ph:** 615-322-1200
Dept W1 **Fax:** 615-321-5455
1707 Grand Ave
Nashville, TN 37212
www.raystevens.com

Stevens, Robert J
Chairman, president, and CEO of Lockheed Martin
Lockheed Martin Corp **Ph:** 301-897-6105
6801 Rockledge Dr **Fax:** 301-897-6083
Bethesda, MD 20817
www.lockheedmartin.com

Stevens, Ted (1923-)
US Senator from Alaska (Republican)
522 Hart Bldg **Ph:** 202-224-3004
Washington, DC 20510 **Fax:** 202-224-2354
stevens.senate.gov

Stevenson, Bryan (1959-)
Attorney and law professor acclaimed for his work challenging bias against the poor and people of color in the criminal justice system
Equal Justice Initiative of Alabama **Ph:** 334-269-1803
Fax: 334-269-1806
122 Commerce St
Montgomery, AL 36104
www.eji.org/staff.html

Steward, Emanuel (1944-)
Boxing trainer/manager and founder of the Kronk Gym in Detroit; boxing commentator for HBO Sports
Kronk Boxing International Inc **Ph:** 313-532-6971
19244 Bretton Dr
Detroit, MI 48223
www.kronkgym.com

Stewart, Alison
Daytime anchor for MSNBC
MSNBC TV — **Ph:** 201-583-5000
1 MSNBC Plaza
Secaucus, NJ 07094
www.msnbc.msn.com/id/3080263

Stewart, Jon (1962-)
Comedian; host of The Daily Show on Comedy Central
Special Artists Agency — **Ph:** 310-859-9688
9465 Wilshire Blvd Suite 890
Beverly Hills, CA 90212
www.comedycentral.com

Stewart, Lynne (1939-)
Human rights attorney accused of conspiring to support terrorism (she was the defense attorney for a blind sheik who was convicted of terrorism charges in 1995)
Lynne Stewart Defense Committee — **Ph:** 212-625-9696
350 Broadway Suite 700
New York, NY 10013
www.lynnestewart.org

Stewart, Martha (1941-)
Businesswoman/expert on cooking, gardening, homemaking
Martha Stewart Living Omnimedia Inc — **Ph:** 212-827-8000 **Fax:** 212-827-8204
11 W 42nd St
New York, NY 10036
www.marthastewart.com

Stewart, Mary (1916-)
Author of mystery/suspense books; also wrote four books based on the legend of King Arthur
HarperCollins Publishers — **Ph:** 212-207-7000
c/o Author Mail
10 E 53rd St
New York, NY 10022
www.harpercollins.com

Stewart, Patrick (1940-)
Actor
William Morris Agency — **Ph:** 310-859-4000
1 William Morris Pl — **Fax:** 310-859-4462
Beverly Hills, CA 90212
www.patrickstewart.org

Stewart, Rod (1945-)
Singer
Stiefel Entertainment — **Ph:** 310-275-3377
21650 Oxnard St Suite 1925
Woodland Hills, CA 91367
www.rodstewart.com

Stewart, Tony (1971-)
Race car driver
Joe Gibbs Racing — **Ph:** 704-944-5000
13415 Reese Blvd W
Huntersville, NC 28078
www.joegibbsracing.com

Stich, Michael (1968-)
Professional tennis player
SFX Sports Group — **Ph:** 202-686-2000
5335 Wisconsin Ave NW Suite 850 — **Fax:** 202-686-5050
Washington, DC 20015
www.sfxsports.com

Stiefel, Ethan
A principal dancer for American Ballet Theatre
American Ballet Theatre — **Ph:** 212-477-3030
890 Broadway — **Fax:** 212-254-5938
New York, NY 10003
www.abt.org/dancers

Stiles, Julia (1981-)
Actor
Creative Artists Agency — **Ph:** 310-288-4545
9830 Wilshire Blvd — **Fax:** 310-288-4800
Beverly Hills, CA 90212

Stiller, Ben (1965-)
Actor
United Talent Agency — **Ph:** 310-273-6700
9560 Wilshire Blvd 5th Fl — **Fax:** 310-247-1111
Beverly Hills, CA 90212

Stine, Brad
Comedian (Christian comedian)
Michael Smith & Assoc — **Ph:** 615-794-5763
118 Medford Pl — **Fax:** 615-591-5694
Franklin, TN 37064 — **TF:** 866-704-6175
www.bradstine.com

Stine, RL (1943-)
Author of horror books for children (the Goosebumps series) and for older readers (Fear Street)
Scholastic Inc — **Ph:** 212-343-6100
557 Broadway
New York, NY 10012
www2.scholastic.com

Sting (1951-)
Singer/songwriter, composer, actor (born Gordon Matthew Sumner)
Creative Artists Agency — **Ph:** 310-288-4545
9830 Wilshire Blvd — **Fax:** 310-288-4800
Beverly Hills, CA 90212
www.sting.com

Stipe, Michael (1960-)
Singer in the rock group REM; composer; film producer (Saved!)
William Morris Agency **Ph:** 310-859-4000
1 William Morris Pl **Fax:** 310-859-4462
Beverly Hills, CA 90212
www.remhq.com

Stitt, Frank
Chef and owner of restaurants in Birmingham, Alabama
Highlands Bar & Grill **Ph:** 205-939-1400
2011 11th Ave S
Birmingham, AL 35205
www.highlandsbarandgrill.com

Stojakovic, Peja (1977-)
Professional basketball player
Indiana Pacers **Ph:** 317-917-2500
Conseco Fieldhouse **Fax:** 317-917-2599
125 S Pennsylvania St
Indianapolis, IN 46204
www.nba.com/pacers

Stokley, Brandon (1976-)
Professional football player
Indianapolis Colts **Ph:** 317-297-2658
7001 W 56th St **Fax:** 317-297-8971
Indianapolis, IN 46254
www.colts.com

Stolove, Jodi
Creator of the Chair Dancing exercise program
Chair Dancing International Inc **Ph:** 800-551-4386
Fax: 858-793-0747
2658 Del Mar Heights Rd
Del Mar, CA 92014
www.chairdancing.com

Stone, Lisa
Founder, president, and spokesperson of Fit For 2 (pre- and post-natal fitness programs)
325 Hunters Ridge **Ph:** 770-509-8078
Marietta, GA 30068
www.fitfor2.com

Stone, Matt (1971-)
Co-creator and executive producer of South Park (with Trey Parker)
William Morris Agency **Ph:** 310-859-4000
1 William Morris Pl **Fax:** 310-859-4462
Beverly Hills, CA 90212
www.southparkstudios.com

Stone, Oliver (1946-)
Film director/producer
Creative Artists Agency **Ph:** 310-288-4545
9830 Wilshire Blvd **Fax:** 310-288-4800
Beverly Hills, CA 90212

Stone, Sharon (1958-)
Actor
William Morris Agency **Ph:** 310-859-4000
1 William Morris Pl **Fax:** 310-859-4462
Beverly Hills, CA 90212

Stonesifer, Patty
CEO of the Bill & Melinda Gates Foundation
Bill & Melinda Gates Foundation **Ph:** 206-709-3100
Fax: 206-709-3180
PO Box 23350
Seattle, WA 98102
www.gatesfoundation.org

Stoppard, Tom (1937-)
Playwright/screenwriter
Creative Artists Agency **Ph:** 310-288-4545
9830 Wilshire Blvd **Fax:** 310-288-4800
Beverly Hills, CA 90212
www.faber.co.uk/authors.html

Storch, Gerald (1956-)
Chairman and CEO of Toys 'R' Us
Toys 'R' Us Inc **Ph:** 973-617-3500
1 Geoffrey Way
Wayne, NJ 07470
www.toysrusinc.com

Storm, Hannah (1962-)
An anchor of CBS News's The Early Show; was previously an anchor and reporter for NBC Sports
The Early Show **Ph:** 212-975-2824
524 W 57th St
New York, NY 10019
www.cbsnews.com

Stormer, Horst L, PhD (1949-)
Winner of the 1998 Nobel Prize in Physics (on behalf of the Federal Republic of Germany) for his discovery, with Daniel Tsui, of the fractional quantum Hall effect
Columbia University **Ph:** 212-854-3279
Physics Dept **Fax:** 212-854-3379
538 W 120th St
New York, NY 10027
columbia-physics.net

Stossel, John (1947-)
Co-anchor of 20/20
20/20 **Ph:** 212-456-7777
147 Columbus Ave
New York, NY 10023
abcnews.go.com/2020

Stotlar, Douglas (1961-)
President and CEO of CNF Inc, a freight transportation, logistics, supply chain management, and trailer manufacturing company
CNF Inc **Ph:** 650-494-2900
3240 Hillview Ave
Palo Alto, CA 94304
www.cnf.com

Stotts, Terry
Basketball coach
Milwaukee Bucks **Ph:** 414-227-0500
Bradley Center **Fax:** 414-227-0543
1001 N 4th St
Milwuakee, WI 53203
www.nba.com/bucks

Stoudemire, Amare (1982-)
Professional basketball player
Phoenix Suns **Ph:** 602-379-7900
America West Arena **Fax:** 602-379-7990
201 E Jefferson St
Phoenix, AZ 85004
www.nba.com/suns

Stouffer, Linda
News anchor for CNN's Headline News
CNN **Ph:** 404-827-1500
1 CNN Center
Atlanta, GA 30303
www.cnn.com/CNN/anchors_reporters

Stover, Matt (1968-)
Professional football player
Baltimore Ravens **Ph:** 410-547-8100
1101 Russell St **Fax:** 410-547-8112
Baltimore, MD 21230
www.baltimoreravens.com

Stowe, Madeleine (1958-)
Actor
United Talent Agency **Ph:** 310-273-6700
9560 Wilshire Blvd 5th Fl **Fax:** 310-247-1111
Beverly Hills, CA 90212

Stowell, Kent
Founding artistic director (with Francia Russell) and principal choreographer of the Pacific Northwest Ballet
Pacific Northwest Ballet **Ph:** 206-441-9411
301 Mercer St **Fax:** 206-441-2440
Seattle, WA 98109
www.pnb.org/company

Strahan, Michael (1971-)
Professional football player
New York Giants **Ph:** 201-935-8111
Giants Stadium **Fax:** 201-939-4134
East Rutherford, NJ 07073
www.giants.com

Strait, George (1952-)
Country singer
MCA Nashville **Ph:** 615-244-8944
60 Music Sq E **Fax:** 615-880-7440
Nashville, TN 37203
www.georgestrait.com

Strand, Mark (1934-)
Former US Poet Laureate
Knopf Publishing/Author Mail **Ph:** 212-782-9000
1745 Broadway
New York, NY 10019
www.randomhouse.com/knopf

Strand, Paul (1890-1976)
Photographer
Metropolitan Museum of Art **Ph:** 212-535-7710
1000 5th Ave
New York, NY 10028
www.metmuseum.org

Strasser, Todd (1950-)
Author of books for children and young adults, including the Help! I'm Trapped series
Scholastic Inc **Ph:** 212-343-6100
557 Broadway
New York, NY 10012
www.toddstrasser.com

Straub, Peter (1943-)
Author of mystery/fantasy/horror fiction (Ghost Story); has also co-authored books with Stephen King
Random House Publicity **Ph:** 212-782-9000
1745 Broadway
New York, NY 10019
www.peterstraub.net

Straus, Stephen E, MD (1946-)
Director of the National Center for Complementary & Alternative Medicine, National Institutes of Health
National Center for Complementary & Alternative Medicine **Ph:** 301-435-5042 **Fax:** 301-435-6549
31 Center Dr Bldg 31 Rm 5B37
MSC 2182
Bethesda, MD 20892
nccam.nih.gov/about

Streep, Meryl (1949-)
Actor
Creative Artists Agency **Ph:** 310-288-4545
9830 Wilshire Blvd **Fax:** 310-288-4800
Beverly Hills, CA 90212
www.merylstreeponline.net

Street, John F (1944-)
Mayor of Philadelphia
City Hall Suite 215 **Ph:** 215-686-2181
Philadelphia, PA 19107 **Fax:** 215-686-2180
www.phila.gov/mayor

Streisand, Barbra (1942-)
Singer, composer, actor, producer, director
International Creative Management **Ph:** 310-550-4000
8942 Wilshire Blvd
Beverly Hills, CA 90211
www.barbrastreisand.com

Strickland, Ted (1941-)
US Representative from Ohio (Democrat)
336 Cannon Bldg **Ph:** 202-225-5705
Washington, DC 20515 **Fax:** 202-225-5907
www.house.gov/strickland

Strieber, Whitley (1945-)
Author whose work is devoted to close encounter phenomena and related studies
Simon & Schuster **Ph:** 212-698-7000
1230 Ave of the Americas
New York, NY 10020
www.unknowncountry.com

Stringer, Howard
Chairman and CEO of Sony Corp and of Sony Corp of America
Sony Corp of America **Ph:** 212-833-6800
550 Madison Ave
New York, NY 10022
www.sony.com

Strohm, David
General Partner of Greylock, a private venture capital firm
Greylock **Ph:** 650-493-5525
2929 Campus Dr Suite 400 **Fax:** 650-493-5575
San Mateo, CA 94403
www.greylock.com

Stromoski, Rick (1958-)
Cartoonist and humorous illlustrator; creator of the comic strip Soup to Nutz
United Media **Ph:** 212-293-8500
200 Madison Ave
New York, NY 10016
www.unitedfeatures.com

Stronach, Frank
Founder and chairman of Magna International, a major supplier of automotive components, systems, and modules
Magna International Inc **Ph:** 905-726-2462
337 Magna Dr **Fax:** 905-726-7164
Aurora, ON L4G7K1
www.magnaint.com

Strossen, Nadine
Attorney; president of the American Civil Liberties Union
American Civil Liberties Union **Ph:** 212-549-2500
125 Broad St 18th Fl **Fax:** 212-549-2580
New York, NY 10004
www.aclu.org

Stroup, R Keith
A public interest attorney; founder of the National Organization for the Reform of Marijuana Laws (NORML)
National Organization for the Reform of Marijuana Laws **Ph:** 202-483-5500 **Fax:** 202-483-0057
1600 K St NW Suite 501
Washington, DC 20006
www.norml.org

Struss, Karl (1886-1981)
Photographer who won the first Academy Award for cinematography
Amon Carter Museum **Ph:** 817-738-1933
3501 Camp Bowie Blvd
Fort Worth, TX 76107
www.cartermuseum.org

Stuart, Diane (1944-)
Director of the Justice Dept's Office on Violence Against Women
Office on Violence Against Women **Ph:** 202-307-6026 **Fax:** 202-307-3911
US Dept of Justice
810 7th St NW
Washington, DC 20531
www.usdoj.gov/ovw

Stuart, Jill
Fashion designer
550 7th Ave **Ph:** 212-921-2600
New York, NY 10018
www.jillstuart.com

Stuart, Marty (1958-)
Country singer/songwriter
Monterey Peninsula Artists/Paradigm **Ph:** 615-251-4400 **Fax:** 615-251-4401
124 12th Ave S Suite 410
Nashville, TN 37203
www.martystuart.net

Studdard, Ruben (1978-)
Soul/gospel singer; American Idol winner
William Morris Agency **Ph:** 310-859-4000
1 William Morris Pl **Fax:** 310-859-4462
Beverly Hills, CA 90212
www.wma.com/ruben_studdard/summary

Stumpel, Jozef (1972-)
Professional hockey player
Florida Panthers **Ph:** 954-835-7000
BankAtlantic Center **Fax:** 954-835-7700
1 Panther Pkwy
Sunrise, FL 33323
www.floridapanthers.com

Stupak, Bart (1952-)
US Representative from Michigan (Democrat)
2352 Rayburn Bldg **Ph:** 202-225-4735
Washington, DC 20515 **Fax:** 202-225-4744
www.house.gov/stupak

Sturm, Marco (1978-)
Professional hockey player
Boston Bruins **Ph:** 617-624-1900
1 FleetCenter Pl Suite 250 **Fax:** 617-523-7184
Boston, MA 02114
www.bostonbruins.com

Styron, William (1925-)
Author (Confessions of Nat Turner; Sophie's Choice)
Random House Publicity **Ph:** 212-782-9000
1745 Broadway
New York, NY 10019
www.randomhouse.com

Suarez, Ray (1957-)
Senior correspondent on NewsHour with Jim Lehrer
MacNeil/Lehrer Productions **Ph:** 703-998-2138
2700 S Quincy St Suite 250
Arlington, VA 22206
www.pbs.org/newshour/ww/suarez.html

Suggs, Lee (1980-)
Professional football player
Cleveland Browns **Ph:** 440-891-5000
76 Lou Groza Blvd **Fax:** 440-891-5009
Berea, OH 44017
www.clevelandbrowns.com

Sui, Anna
Fashion designer
Anna Sui Showroom **Ph:** 212-768-1004
250 W 39th St 15th Fl **Fax:** 212-302-6199
New York, NY 10018
www.annasui.com

Suits, Julia (1951-)
Artist who draws editorial portraits; also works in other media
Creators Syndicate Inc **Ph:** 310-337-7003
5777 W Century Blvd Suite 700 **Fax:** 310-337-7625
Los Angeles, CA 90045
www.creators.com

Sullivan, John (1965-)
US Representative from Oklahoma (Republican)
114 Cannon Bldg **Ph:** 202-225-2211
Washington, DC 20515 **Fax:** 202-225-9187
sullivan.house.gov

Sullivan, Kathleen M (1955-)
Attorney and Constitutional law specialist
Stanford Law School **Ph:** 650-723-2465
559 Nathan Abbot Way **Fax:** 650-725-0253
Stanford, CA 94305
www.law.stanford.edu

Sullivan, Louis W, MD (1933-)
Former US Secretary of Health & Human Services
National Health Museum **Ph:** 202-737-2670
1155 5th St NW Suite 810
Washington, DC 20036
www.nationalhealthmuseum.org/themuseum

Sullivan, Martin
President and CEO of American International Group (AIG)
American International Group Inc **Ph:** 212-770-7000
70 Pine St
New York, NY 10270
www.aigcorporate.com/corpsite

Sullivan, Mike (1968-)
Hockey coach
Boston Bruins **Ph:** 617-624-1900
1 FleetCenter Pl Suite 250 **Fax:** 617-523-7184
Boston, MA 02114
www.bostonbruins.com

Sullivan, William (1949-)
President and CEO of Agilent Technologies
Agilent Technologies Inc **Ph:** 650-752-5000
395 Page Mill Rd
Palo Alto, CA 94306
www.agilent.com/about/newsroom/execs

Sullum, Jacob (1965-)
Journalist/syndicated columnist; senior editor at Reason, a monthly magazine that covers politics and culture from a libertarian perspective
Creators Syndicate Inc **Ph:** 310-337-7003
5777 W Century Blvd Suite 700 **Fax:** 310-337-7625
Los Angeles, CA 90045
www.creators.com/opinion.html

Sulzberger, Arthur Jr (1951-)
Chairman of the New York Times Co and Publisher of the New York Times
New York Times Co **Ph:** 212-556-1234
229 W 43rd St
New York, NY 10036
www.nytco.com

Summers, Dana
Editorial cartoonist for The Orlando Sentinel; is also creator of the comic strip Bound & Gagged & co-creator, with Ralph Dunagin, of The Middletons
Tribune Media Services Inc **Ph:** 312-222-4444
435 N Michigan Ave Suite 1500
Chicago, IL 60611
www.comicspage.com

Summitt, Pat (1952-)
Women's basketball coach; NCAA's winningest coach
University of Tennessee **Ph:** 865-974-4275
Lady Volunteers
117 Stokely Athletics Ctr
Knoxville, TN 37996
www.coachsummitt.com

Sundin, Mats (1971-)
Professional hockey player
Toronto Maple Leafs **Ph:** 416-815-5700
Air Canada Center
40 Bay St Suite 400
Toronto, ON M5J2X2
www.mapleleafs.com

Sununu, John E (1964-)
US Senator from New Hampshire (Republican)
111 Russell Bldg **Ph:** 202-224-2841
Washington, DC 20510 **Fax:** 202-228-4131
sununu.senate.gov

Sununu, John H, PhD (1939-)
Former governor of New Hampshire; Chief of Staff to President George HW Bush
JHS Assoc Ltd **Ph:** 603-890-1630
24 Samoset Dr
Salem, NH 03079

Surma, John P Jr
Chairman & CEO of US Steel
US Steel Corp **Ph:** 412-433-1121
600 Grant St
Pittsburgh, PA 15219
www.ussteel.com/corp/media/bios.htm

Susman, Stephen D (1941-)
Top trial lawyer and leading dispute resolution practitioner; represents as many defendants as plaintiffs in both commercial and tort cases
Susman Godfrey LLP **Ph:** 713-651-9366
1000 Louisiana Suite 5100 **Fax:** 713-654-6666
Houston, TX 77002
www.susmangodfrey.com

Susser, Allen (1956-)
Chef and owner of Chef Allen's in Aventura, Florida (Miami), which features New World Cuisine using the natural resources of Florida; also a cookbook author
Chef Allen's Restaurant **Ph:** 305-935-2900
19088 NE 29th Ave
Aventura, FL 33180
chefallens.com

Sutherland, Donald (1935-)
Actor
Creative Artists Agency **Ph:** 310-288-4545
9830 Wilshire Blvd **Fax:** 310-288-4800
Beverly Hills, CA 90212

Sutherland, Kiefer (1966-)
Actor
William Morris Agency **Ph:** 310-859-4000
1 William Morris Pl **Fax:** 310-859-4462
Beverly Hills, CA 90212
www.fox.com/24/profiles

Sutter, Darryl (1958-)
Hockey coach
Calgary Flames **Ph:** 403-777-2177
Pengrowth Saddledome **Fax:** 403-777-2195
555 Saddledome Rise SE
Calgary, AB T2G2W1
www.calgaryflames.com

Suvari, Mena (1979-)
Actor
Gersh Agency **Ph:** 310-274-6611
232 N Canon Dr
Beverly Hills, CA 90210

Suzuki, Ichiro (1973-)
Professional baseball player
Seattle Mariners **Ph:** 206-346-4000
Safeco Field **Fax:** 206-346-4050
1250 1st Ave S
Seattle, WA 98134
seattle.mariners.mlb.com

Swaggart, Jimmy (1935-)
Televangelist
Jimmy Swaggart Ministries **Ph:** 225-768-8300
PO Box 262550 **Fax:** 225-769-2244
Baton Rouge, LA 70826
www.jsm.org

Swank, Hilary (1974-)
Actor
Creative Artists Agency **Ph:** 310-288-4545
8930 Wilshire Blvd **Fax:** 310-288-4800
Beverly Hills, CA 90212

Swanson, William H
Chairman and CEO of Raytheon
Raytheon Co **Ph:** 781-522-3000
870 Winter St **Fax:** 781-522-3001
Waltham, MA 02451
www.raytheon.com

Swayze, Patrick (1952-)
Actor
William Morris Agency **Ph:** 310-859-4000
1 William Morris Pl **Fax:** 310-859-4462
Beverly Hills, CA 90212
www.patrickswayze.net

Swed, Mark
Classical music critic
Los Angeles Times **Ph:** 213-237-5000
202 W 1st St **Fax:** 213-237-4712
Los Angeles, CA 90012

Sweeney, John E (1955-)
US Representative from New York (Republican)
416 Cannon Bldg **Ph:** 202-225-5614
Washington, DC 20515 **Fax:** 202-225-6234
www.house.gov/sweeney

Sweeney, John J (1934-)
President of the AFL-CIO
AFL-CIO **Ph:** 202-637-5000
815 16th St NW **Fax:** 202-637-5058
Washington, DC 20006
www.aflcio.org

Sweeney, Mike (1973-)
Professional baseball player
Kansas City Royals **Ph:** 816-921-8000
Kauffman Stadium **Fax:** 816-921-5775
1 Royal Way
Kansas City, MO 64129
kansascity.royals.mlb.com

Swoopes, Sheryl (1971-)
Professional basketball player
Houston Comets **Ph:** 713-758-7200
Toyota Center **Fax:** 713-758-7396
1510 Polk St
Houston, TX 77002
www.wnba.com/comets

Sydor, Darryl (1972-)
Professional hockey player
Tampa Bay Lightning **Ph:** 813-301-6600
St Pete Times Forum **Fax:** 813-301-1487
401 Channelside Dr
Tampa, FL 33602
www.tampabaylightning.com

Sykes, Wanda (1964-)
Comedian
William Morris Agency **Ph:** 310-859-4000
1 William Morris Pl **Fax:** 310-859-4462
Beverly Hills, CA 90212
www.wandasykes.com

Sykora, Petr (1976-)
Professional hockey player
New York Rangers **Ph:** 212-465-6486
Madison Square Garden **Fax:** 212-465-6494
2 Pennsylvania Plaza
New York, NY 10121
www.newyorkrangers.com

Syler, Rene (1963-)
An anchor of CBS News's The Early Show
The Early Show **Ph:** 212-975-2824
524 W 57th St
New York, NY 10019
www.cbsnews.com

Symons, Jeanette
CTO and Vice President of Engineering for Zhone Technologies
Zhone Technologies Inc **Ph:** 510-777-7000
7001 Oakport St
Oakland, CA 94621
www.zhone.com

Syms, Marcy
CEO of Syms Corp, which was founded by her father, Sy Syms
Syms Corp **Ph:** 201-902-9600
1 Syms Way **Fax:** 201-902-9874
Secaucus, NJ 07094
www.syms.com

Syron, Richard F
Chairman & CEO of Freddie Mac, the second largest source of mortgage financing in the US
Freddie Mac **Ph:** 703-903-2000
8200 Jones Branch Dr **Fax:** 703-918-8403
McLean, VA 22102
www.freddiemac.com

Szczerbiak, Wally (1977-)
Professional basketball player
Boston Celtics **Ph:** 617-854-8000
226 Causeway St 4th Fl **Fax:** 617-367-4286
Boston, MA 02114
www.nba.com/celtics

Szep, Paul
Editorial cartoonist/caricaturist
Creators Syndicate Inc **Ph:** 310-337-7003
5777 W Century Blvd Suite 700 **Fax:** 310-337-7625
Los Angeles, CA 90045
www.szep.com

Szymanczyk, Michael E
Chairman and CEO of Philip Morris USA
Philip Morris USA Inc **Ph:** 804-274-2000
615 Maury St
Richmond, VA 23224
www.altria.com

Szymborska, Wislawa (1923-)
Polish-born poet; 1996 Nobel Laureate in Literature
WW Norton & Co Inc **Ph:** 212-354-5500
500 5th Ave **Fax:** 212-869-0856
New York, NY 10110
www.nortonpoets.com

Taback, Simms (1932-)
Illustrator of books for children (I Know an Old Lady Who Swallowed a Fly; Joseph Had a Little Overcoat)
Viking Children's Books Publicity **Ph:** 212-366-2000
345 Hudson St
New York, NY 10014
us.penguingroup.com

Tabak, Lawrence A, DDS, PhD (1951-)
Director, National Institute of Dental & Craniofacial Research, National Institutes of Health
National Institute of Dental & Craniofacial Research **Ph:** 301-496-3571
Fax: 301-402-3288
31 Center Dr
Bethesda, MD 20892
www.nidcr.nih.gov

Taft, Bob (1942-)
Governor of Ohio (Republican)
77 S High St 30th Fl **Ph:** 614-466-3555
Columbus, OH 43215 **Fax:** 614-466-9354
governor.ohio.gov

Tagliabue, Paul (1940-)
Outgoing Commissioner of the National Football League (NFL); has announced his decision to retire in July 2006, provided that a replacement is announced by then
National Football League **Ph:** 212-450-2000
280 Park Ave
New York, NY 10017

Taibbi, Mike
NBC news correspondent, primarily for Dateline NBC
NBC News **Ph:** 212-664-4249
30 Rockefeller Plaza
New York, NY 10112
www.msnbc.msn.com/id/3689499

Talent, James M (1956-)
US Senator from Missouri (Republican)
493 Russell Bldg **Ph:** 202-224-6154
Washington, DC 20510 **Fax:** 202-228-1518
talent.senate.gov

Talese, Gay (1932-)
Journalist/author (Honor Thy Father; Unto the Sons)
Random House Publicity **Ph:** 212-782-9000
1745 Broadway
New York, NY 10019
www.gaytalese.com

Tally, Ted (1952-)
Screenwriter (Silence of the Lambs)
International Creative Management **Ph:** 310-550-4000
8942 Wilshire Blvd
Beverly Hills, CA 90211

Tam, Vivienne (1957-)
Fashion designer
550 7th Ave **Ph:** 212-840-6470
New York, NY 10018 **Fax:** 212-869-4043
www.viviennetam.com

Tamblyn, Amber (1983-)
Actor
Endeavor **Ph:** 310-248-2000
9601 Wilshire Blvd 3rd Fl **Fax:** 310-248-2020
Beverly Hills, CA 90210
www.amtam.com

Tan, Amy (1952-)
Fiction author (Joy Luck Club)
Steven Barclay Agency **Ph:** 707-773-0654
12 Western Ave **Fax:** 707-778-1868
Petaluma, CA 94952 **TF:** 888-965-7323
www.barclayagency.com

Tancredo, Tom (1945-)
US Representative from Colorado (Republican)
1130 Longworth Bldg **Ph:** 202-225-7882
Washington, DC 20515 **Fax:** 202-226-4623
tancredo.house.gov

Tanenbaum, Larry
Chairman of Maple Leaf Sports & Entertainment, the group that owns the Toronto Maple Leafs hockey team and the Toronto Raptors basketball team
Toronto Maple Leafs **Ph:** 416-815-5700
Air Canada Centre
40 Bay St Suite 400
Toronto, ON M5J2X2
www.mapleleafs.com

Tang, Cyrus (1930-)
Founder, chairman, president, and CEO of Tang Industries Inc, a diversified holding company
Tang Industries Inc **Ph:** 702-734-3700
3773 Howard Hughes Pkwy **Fax:** 702-734-6766
Suite 350N
Las Vegas, NV 89109

Tanguay, Alex (1979-)
Professional hockey player
Colorado Avalanche **Ph:** 303-405-1100
Pepsi Center
1000 Chopper Cir
Denver, CO 80204
www.coloradoavalanche.com

Tanner, John S (1944-)
US Representative from Tennessee (Democrat)
1226 Longworth Bldg **Ph:** 202-225-4714
Washington, DC 20515 **Fax:** 202-225-1765
www.house.gov/tanner

Tapper, Jake (1973-)
ABC News correspondent
ABC News **Ph:** 202-222-7700
1717 DeSales St NW
Washington, DC 20036
www.abcnews.go.com/WNT

Tapply, William G (1940-)
Author of the Brady Coyne mystery novels; also writes nonfiction, including articles for Field & Stream
St Martin's Press **Ph:** 212-674-5151
Attn: Publicity Dept
175 5th Ave
New York, NY 10010
www.williamgtapply.com

Taraborrelli, J Randy
Author of celebrity biographies (Frank Sinatra, Michael Jackson, Madonna, Princess Grace, etc.)
Warner Books **Ph:** 212-522-7200
c/o Author Mail
1271 Ave of the Americas
New York, NY 10020
www.jrandy.com

Tarantino, Quentin (1963-)
Film writer, director, producer, actor
William Morris Agency **Ph:** 310-859-4000
1 William Morris Pl **Fax:** 310-859-4462
Beverly Hills, CA 90212

Tartakovsky, Genndy (1970-)
Animator; creator of Dexter's Laboratory and Samurai Jack cartoon series and was producer/director of The Powerpuff Girls
Cartoon Network Studios **Ph:** 818-729-4000
300 N 3rd St
Burbank, CA 91502
www.cartoonnetworkla.com/english/tv_shows/dexter

Tarter, Jill, PhD (1944-)
Astronomer/astrophysicist; a leading researcher in the search for extraterrestrial intelligence (SETI)
SETI Institute **Ph:** 650-961-6633
515 N Whisman Rd
Mountain View, CA 94043
www.seti.org

Tatulli, Mark
Creator of the comic strip Heart of the City
Universal Press Syndicate **Ph:** 816-932-6600
4520 Main St
Kansas City, MO 64111
www.amuniversal.com/ups/features

Taurasi, Diana (1982-)
Professional basketball player
Phoenix Mercury **Ph:** 602-514-8333
America West Arena **Fax:** 602-514-8303
201 E Jefferson St
Phoenix, AZ 85004
www.wnba.com/mercury

Taurel, Sidney
Chairman and CEO of Eli Lilly
Eli Lilly & Co **Ph:** 317-276-3545
Lilly Corporate Ctr
Indianapolis, IN 46285
www.lilly.com

Tauscher, Ellen (1951-)
US Representative from California (Democrat)
1034 Longworth Bldg **Ph:** 202-225-1880
Washington, DC 20515 **Fax:** 202-225-5914
www.house.gov/tauscher

Taylor, Alan, PhD
History professor and author of historical books (William Cooper's Town)
University of California - Davis **Ph:** 530-752-0777
History Dept **Fax:** 530-752-5301
2216 Social Sciences Bldg
1 Shields Ave
Davis, CA 95616
history.ucdavis.edu

Taylor, Andrew C
Chairman and CEO of Enterprise Rent-A-Car, which was founded by his father, Jack Taylor
Enterprise Rent-A-Car Co **Ph:** 314-512-5000
600 Corporate Park Dr **Fax:** 314-512-4706
Saint Louis, MO 63105
www.enterprise.com

Taylor, Charles H (1941-)
US Representative from North Carolina (Republican)
339 Cannon Bldg **Ph:** 202-225-6401
Washington, DC 20515 **Fax:** 202-226-6422
www.house.gov/charlestaylor

Taylor, Chester (1979-)
Professional football player
Minnesota Vikings **Ph:** 952-828-6500
9520 Viking Dr **Fax:** 952-828-6540
Eden Prairie, MN 55344
www.vikings.com

Taylor, Fred (1976-)
Professional football player
Jacksonville Jaguars **Ph:** 904-633-6000
1 Alltel Stadium Pl **Fax:** 904-633-6050
Jacksonville, FL 32202
www.jaguars.com

Taylor, Gene (1953-)
US Representative from Mississippi (Democrat)
2311 Rayburn Bldg **Ph:** 202-225-5772
Washington, DC 20515 **Fax:** 202-225-7074
www.house.gov/genetaylor

Taylor, Glen A
Majority owner of the Minnesota Timberwolves NBA team; an entrepreneur who founded and is chairman of the Taylor Corp, with companies involved in the printing, marketing, and electronics industries
Taylor Corp **Ph:** 507-625-2828
1725 Roe Crest Dr **Fax:** 507-625-2988
North Mankato, MN 56003
www.nba.com/timberwolves

Taylor, James (1948-)
Singer/songwriter
Creative Artists Agency **Ph:** 212-277-9000
162 5th Ave 6th Fl **Fax:** 212-277-9099
New York, NY 10010
www.jamestaylor.net

Taylor, Jason (1974-)
Professional football player
Miami Dolphins **Ph:** 954-452-7000
7500 SW 30th St **Fax:** 954-452-7055
Davie, FL 33314
www.miamidolphins.com

Taylor, Kathryn L
Mayor of Tulsa, Oklahoma
200 Civic Center 11th Fl **Ph:** 918-596-7411
Tulsa, OK 74103 **Fax:** 918-596-9010
www.cityoftulsa.org

Taylor, Maurice (1976-)
Professional basketball player
New York Knicks **Ph:** 212-465-6471
Madison Square Garden **Fax:** 212-465-6498
2 Pennsylvania Plaza
New York, NY 10121
www.nba.com/knicks

Taylor, Mildred D (1943-)
Children's books author (Roll of Thunder, Hear My Cry; Song of the Trees)
Dial Publicity **Ph:** 212-366-2000
345 Hudson St
New York, NY 10014
us.penguingroup.com

Taylor, Paul (1930-)
Modern dance choreographer; founder and artistic director of the Paul Taylor Dance Co
Paul Taylor Dance Co **Ph:** 212-431-5562
552 Broadway 2nd Fl **Fax:** 212-966-5673
New York, NY 10012
www.ptdc.org

Taylor, Penny (1981-)
Professional basketball player
Phoenix Mercury — **Ph:** 602-514-8333
America West Arena — **Fax:** 602-514-8303
201 E Jefferson St
Phoenix, AZ 85004
www.wnba.com/mercury

Taylor, Sean (1983-)
Professional football player
Washington Redskins — **Ph:** 703-726-7000
21300 Redskin Park Dr — **Fax:** 703-726-7086
Ashburn, VA 20147
www.redskins.com

Taylor, Theodore (1921-)
Author of books for children (The Cay; The Maldonado Miracle), young adults (The Weirdo), and adults
Harcourt Children's Books — **Ph:** 212-592-1000
15 E 26th St
New York, NY 10010
www.theodoretaylor.com

Taylor, Travis (1978-)
Professional football player
Minnesota Vikings — **Ph:** 952-828-6500
9520 Viking Dr — **Fax:** 952-828-6540
Eden Prairie, MN 55344
www.vikings.com

Taymor, Julie (1952-)
Stage & film director
Creative Artists Agency — **Ph:** 310-288-4545
9830 Wilshire Blvd — **Fax:** 310-288-4800
Beverly Hills, CA 90212

Teague, Mark
Author/illustrator of children's books (How I Spent My Summer Vacation; Dear Mrs. Larue); has also collaborated with other authors (How Do Dinosaurs Say Goodnight? with Jane Yolen)
Scholastic Inc — **Ph:** 212-343-6100
557 Broadway
New York, NY 10012
www2.scholastic.com

Teasley, Nikki (1979-)
Professional basketball player
Washington Mystics — **Ph:** 202-266-2200
Verizon Center — **Fax:** 202-266-2220
401 9th St NW Suite 750
Washington, DC 20004
www.wnba.com/mystics

Tedeschi, Susan (1970-)
Singer, guitarist, songwriter
Macklem/Feldman Management — **Ph:** 604-734-5945
1505 W 2nd Ave Suite 200
Vancouver, BC V6H3Y4
www.susantedeschi.com

Teichner, Martha
CBS News correspondent
CBS News Sunday Morning — **Ph:** 212-975-4114
Box O
524 W 57th St
New York, NY 10019
www.cbsnews.com

Teixeira, Mark (1980-)
Professional baseball player
Texas Rangers — **Ph:** 817-273-5222
Ameriquest Field in Arlington — **Fax:** 817-273-5294
1000 Ballpark Way — **TF:** 888-968-3927
Arlington, TX 76011
texas.rangers.mlb.com

Tejada, Miguel (1976-)
Professional baseball player
Baltimore Orioles — **Ph:** 410-685-9800
Oriole Park at Camden Yards — **Fax:** 410-547-6279
333 W Camden St
Baltimore, MD 21201
baltimore.orioles.mlb.com

Telnaes, Ann C
Editorial cartoonist; also one of the cartoonists for Six Chix
New York Times Syndicate — **Ph:** 212-499-3300
609 Greenwich St 6th Fl
New York, NY 10014
www.anntelnaes.com

Tempest, Marco
Magician who combines technical savvy with showmanship; his shows include computer-generated imagery, video, music, and stagecraft
Tobias Beckwith Inc — **Ph:** 702-697-7002
3960 Briarcrest Ct — **Fax:** 702-697-7003
Las Vegas, NV 89120
www.marcotempest.com

Templeton, Richard K (1958-)
President & CEO of Texas Instruments
Texas Instruments Inc — **Ph:** 972-995-2011
12500 TI Blvd
Dallas, TX 75243
www.ti.com

Tennant, Rich
Cartoonist and illustrator considered the "father of the computer cartoon"
Universal Press Syndicate **Ph:** 816-932-6600
4520 Main St
Kansas City, MO 64111
www.the5thwave.com/about.html

Teodorescu, Radu
Known as New York's toughest fitness trainer and "trainer to the stars"
Radu Physical Culture **Ph:** 212-581-1995
24 W 57th St
New York, NY 10019
www.radufitness.com

Tepper, Sheri S (1929-)
Author of fantasy fiction
HarperCollins Publishers **Ph:** 212-207-7000
c/o Author Mail
10 E 53rd St
New York, NY 10022
www.harpercollins.com

Terkel, Studs (1912-)
Author (The Good War) and radio broadcasting personality
Chicago Historical Society **Ph:** 312-642-4600
1601 N Clark St **Fax:** 312-266-2077
Chicago, IL 60614
www.studsterkel.org

Terry, Lee (1962-)
US Representative from Nebraska (Republican)
1524 Longworth Bldg **Ph:** 202-225-4155
Washington, DC 20515 **Fax:** 202-226-5452
leeterry.house.gov

Terry, Randall (1959-)
Pro-life Christian activist who was the spokesman for Terry Schiavo's parents; the founder of the anti-abortion group Operation Rescue and president of the Society for Truth and Justice
Society for Truth and Justice **Ph:** 904-819-9450
3501-B N Ponce de Leon Blvd **Fax:** 904-819-9412
Saint Augustine, FL 32084
www.randallterry.com

Tesh, John (1952-)
Musician (piano), television host, syndicated radio show host
Creative Artists Agency **Ph:** 310-288-4545
9830 Wilshire Blvd **Fax:** 310-288-4800
Beverly Hills, CA 90212
www.tesh.com

Tharaldson, Gary
Founder/owner of Tharaldson Lodging Companies, a hotel development and management firm
Tharaldson Lodging Cos **Ph:** 701-235-1060
1202 Westrac Dr SW
Fargo, ND 58103
www.tharaldson.hcareers.com

Thaves, Bob
Creator of the syndicated comic strip Frank & Ernest
Newspaper Enterprise Assn **Ph:** 212-293-8500
200 Madison Ave
New York, NY 10016
www.unitedfeatures.com

The Rock (1972-)
Actor and professional wrestler Dwayne Johnson
United Talent Agency **Ph:** 310-273-6700
9560 Wilshire Blvd 5th Fl **Fax:** 310-247-1111
Beverly Hills, CA 90212
www.wwe.com/superstars/raw/therock

Theismann, Joe (1949-)
Former professional football player (quarterback); analyst on ESPN's Monday Night Football
ESPN **Ph:** 860-585-2000
ESPN Plaza
935 Middle St
Bristol, CT 06010
sports.espn.go.com/espntv/espnGuide

Theodore, Jose (1976-)
Professional hockey player
Colorado Avalanche **Ph:** 303-405-1100
Pepsi Center
1000 Chopper Cir
Denver, CO 80204
www.coloradoavalanche.com

Theron, Charlize (1975-)
Actor
One Entertainment **Ph:** 310-550-9500
9220 Sunset Blvd Suite 306
Los Angeles, CA 90069
www.charlizetheron.com

Theroux, Paul (1941-)
Novelist & short story writer; also writes travel books
Houghton Mifflin Co **Ph:** 617-351-5000
Trade Div
Adult Editorial
222 Berkeley St 8th Fl
Boston, MA 02116
www.houghtonmifflinbooks.com

Therrien, Michel (1963-)
Hockey coach
Pittsburgh Penguins **Ph:** 412-642-1300
1 Chatham Center Suite 400 **Fax:** 412-642-1859
Pittsburgh, PA 15219
www.pittsburghpenguins.com

Thibault, Jocelyn (1975-)
Professional hockey player
Pittsburgh Penguins **Ph:** 412-642-1300
1 Chatham Center Suite 400 **Fax:** 412-642-1859
Pittsburgh, PA 15219
www.pittsburghpenguins.com

Thibault, Mike
Basketball coach
Connecticut Sun **Ph:** 860-862-4000
1 Mohegan Sun Blvd **Fax:** 860-862-4010
Uncasville, CT 06382
www.wnba.com/sun

Third Day
Christian rock group
CAA Nashville **Ph:** 615-383-8787
3310 West End Ave 5th Fl **Fax:** 615-383-4937
Nashville, TN 37203
www.thirdday.com

Thomas, Betty (1948-)
Director/producer
Creative Artists Agency **Ph:** 310-288-4545
9830 Wilshire Blvd **Fax:** 310-288-4800
Beverly Hills, CA 90212

Thomas, Cal (1942-)
Syndicated columnist (political); host of After Hours with Cal Thomas on the FOX News Channel
Tribune Media Services Inc **Ph:** 312-222-4444
435 N Michigan Ave Suite 1500
Chicago, IL 60611
tmsfeatures.com/productlist.htm

Thomas, Clarence (1948-)
US Supreme Court justice
US Supreme Court Bldg **Ph:** 202-479-3000
1 1st St NE
Washington, DC 20543
www.supremecourtus.gov

Thomas, Craig (1933-)
US Senator from Wyoming (Republican)
307 Dirksen Bldg **Ph:** 202-224-6441
Washington, DC 20510 **Fax:** 202-224-1724
thomas.senate.gov

Thomas, E Donnall, MD (1920-)
Winner of the 1990 Nobel Prize in Physiology or Medicine, with Joseph E Murray, for their discoveries concerning organ and cell transplantation in the treatment of human disease; noted for his pioneering work in bone marrow transplantation
Fred Hutchinson Cancer Research Center **Ph:** 206-667-5000
1100 Fairview Ave N
PO Box 19024
Seattle, WA 98109
www.fhcrc.org/research/nobel

Thomas, Helen (1920-)
Veteran reporter; has reported on every president since John F. Kennedy
King Features Syndicate Inc **Ph:** 212-455-4000
888 7th Ave 2nd Fl
New York, NY 10019
www.kingfeatures.com

Thomas, Isiah (1961-)
Former NBA player; president of basketball operations with the New York Knicks
New York Knicks **Ph:** 212-465-6471
Madison Square Garden **Fax:** 212-465-6498
2 Pennsylvania Plaza
New York, NY 10121
www.hoophall.com

Thomas, Joyce Carol (1938-)
Author of books for children (Brown Honey in Broomwheat Tea; I Have Heard of a Land) and for young adults (Marked by Fire)
HarperCollins Children's Books **Ph:** 212-261-6500
1350 Ave of the Americas
New York, NY 10019
www.joycecarolthomas.com

Thomas, Kristin Scott (1960-)
Actor
Creative Artists Agency **Ph:** 310-288-4545
9830 Wilshire Blvd **Fax:** 310-288-4800
Beverly Hills, CA 90212

Thomas, Kurt (1972-)
Professional basketball player
Phoenix Suns **Ph:** 602-379-7900
America West Arena **Fax:** 602-379-7990
201 E Jefferson St
Phoenix, AZ 85004
www.nba.com/suns

Thomas, LaToya (1981-)
Professional basketball player
San Antonio Silver Stars **Ph:** 210-444-5050
1 SBC Center
San Antonio, TX 78219
www.wnba.com/silverstars

Thomas, Pierre
ABC News correspondent; covers the Justice Department and law enforcement issues
ABC News **Ph:** 202-222-7700
1717 DeSales St NW
Washington, DC 20036
www.abcnews.go.com/WNT

Thomas, Rob (1972-)
Singer/composer; lead vocalist in matchbox twenty
Creative Artists Agency **Ph:** 310-288-4545
9830 Wilshire Blvd **Fax:** 310-288-4800
Beverly Hills, CA 90212
www.robthomasmusic.com

Thomas, William M (1941-)
US Representative from California (Republican)
2208 Rayburn Bldg **Ph:** 202-225-2915
Washington, DC 20515 **Fax:** 202-225-8798
billthomas.house.gov

Thomas, Zach (1973-)
Professional football player
Miami Dolphins **Ph:** 954-452-7000
7500 SW 30th St **Fax:** 954-452-7055
Davie, FL 33314
www.miamidolphins.com

Thomasson, Dan
Syndicated political columnist (longtime Washington journalist and former vice president of Scripps Howard Newspapers)
Scripps Howard News Service **Ph:** 202-408-1484
1090 Vermont Ave NW **Fax:** 202-408-5950
Suite 1000
Washington, DC 20005
www.shns.com

Thome, Jim (1970-)
Professional baseball player
Chicago White Sox **Ph:** 312-674-1000
US Cellular Field **Fax:** 312-674-5109
333 W 35th St
Chicago, IL 60616
chicago.whitesox.mlb.com

Thompson, Anne
NBC News chief financial correspondent
NBC News **Ph:** 212-664-4249
30 Rockefeller Plaza
New York, NY 10112
www.msnbc.msn.com/id/3689499

Thompson, Bennie G (1948-)
US Representative from Mississippi (Democrat)
2432 Rayburn Bldg **Ph:** 202-225-5876
Washington, DC 20515 **Fax:** 202-225-5898
benniethompson.house.gov

Thompson, Carol (1951-)
Director of the White House Office of National AIDS Policy
Office of National AIDS Policy **Ph:** 202-456-7320
The White House **Fax:** 202-456-7315
Washington, DC 20502
www.whitehouse.gov/onap/aids.html

Thompson, Craig (1975-)
Comic book artist; creator of the graphic novels Blankets, Carnet de Voyage, and Good-Bye, Chunky Rice
Top Shelf Productions **Ph:** 770-425-0551
PO Box 1282 **Fax:** 770-427-6395
Marietta, GA 30061
www.topshelfcomix.com

Thompson, Emma (1959-)
Actor
William Morris Agency **Ph:** 310-859-4000
1 William Morris Pl **Fax:** 310-859-4462
Beverly Hills, CA 90212

Thompson, Fred (1942-)
US Senator from Tennessee from 1994-2003; former film & TV actor; a visiting fellow at American Enterprise Institute
American Enterprise Institute **Ph:** 202-862-5800
for Public Policy Research **Fax:** 202-862-7177
1150 17th St NW Suite 1100
Washington, DC 20036
www.aei.org

Thompson, Hunter S (1939-2005)
Called the King of Gonzo Journalism; author of Fear & Loathing in Las Vegas
Wylie Agency **Ph:** 212-246-0069
250 W 57th St Suite 2114
New York, NY 10107

Thompson, James R (1936-)
Former governor of Illinois and a member of the 9/11 Commission; attorney (chairman and partner in Winston & Strawn law firm)
Winston & Strawn LLP **Ph:** 312-558-7400
35 W Wacker Dr Suite 4200 **Fax:** 312-558-5700
Chicago, IL 60601
www.winston.com

Thompson, John (1941-)
Head coach of Georgetown University basketball for 27 years
Naismith Memorial Basketball Hall of Fame
1000 W Columbus Ave
Springfield, MA 01105
www.hoophall.com
Ph: 413-781-6500
Fax: 413-781-1939
TF: 877-446-6752

Thompson, John W
Chairman and CEO of Symantec
Symantec Corp
20330 Stevens Creek Blvd
Cupertino, CA 95014
www.symantec.com
Ph: 408-517-8000

Thompson, Ken (1950-)
Chairman, president, and CEO of Wachovia Corp; full name is G Kennedy Thompson
Wachovia Corp
301 S College St Suite 4000
Charlotte, NC 28288
www.wachovia.com
Ph: 704-374-6161
Fax: 704-374-3425

Thompson, Lea
Dateline NBC correspondent and NBC's chief consumer correspondent
Dateline NBC
30 Rockefeller Plaza
New York, NY 10112
www.msnbc.msn.com/id/3360263
Ph: 212-664-4249

Thompson, Mike (1951-)
US Representative from California (Democrat)
231 Cannon Bldg
Washington, DC 20515
mikethompson.house.gov
Ph: 202-225-3311
Fax: 202-225-4335

Thompson, Mike
Editorial cartoonist for the Detroit Free Press
Detroit Free Press
600 W Fort St
Detroit, MI 48226
www.copleynews.com
Ph: 313-222-6400
Fax: 313-222-5981

Thompson, Scott (1959-)
Comedian (Kids in the Hall)/actor
Core Group Talent Agencies
89 Bloor St W 3rd Fl
Toronto, ON M5S1M1
Ph: 416-955-0819
Fax: 416-955-0825

Thompson, Tina (1975-)
Professional basketball player
Houston Comets
Toyota Center
1510 Polk St
Houston, TX 77002
www.wnba.com/comets
Ph: 713-758-7200
Fax: 713-758-7396

Thompson, Tommy G (1941-)
Former US Secretary of Health & Human Services; former Governor of Wisconsin
Akin Gump Strauss Hauer & Feld LLP
Robert S Strauss Bldg
1333 New Hampshire Ave NW
Washington, DC 20036
www.akingump.com
Ph: 202-887-4000

Thomsen, Linda C
Director, Enforcement Div, Securities & Exchange Commission
Enforcement Div
Securities & Exchange Commission
450 5th St NW
Washington, DC 20549
Ph: 202-551-4500

Thornberry, Mac (1958-)
US Representative from Texas (Republican)
2457 Rayburn Bldg
Washington, DC 20515
www.house.gov/thornberry
Ph: 202-225-3706
Fax: 202-225-3486

Thornton, Billy Bob (1955-)
Actor; also writes, directs, produces movies
Creative Artists Agency
9830 Wilshire Blvd
Beverly Hills, CA 90212
www.billybobthornton.net
Ph: 310-288-4545
Fax: 310-288-4800

Thornton, Joe (1979-)
Professional hockey player
San Jose Sharks
HP Pavilion at San Jose
525 W Santa Clara St
San Jose, CA 95113
www.sjsharks.com
Ph: 408-287-7070
Fax: 408-999-5797

Thornton, Zach (1973-)
Professional soccer player
Chicago Fire
980 N Michigan Ave Suite 1998
Chicago, IL 60611
chicago.fire.mlsnet.com
Ph: 312-705-7200
Fax: 312-705-7393

Thune, John (1961-)
US Senator from South Dakota (Republican)
B40E Dirksen Bldg
Washington, DC 20510
www.thune.senate.gov
Ph: 202-224-2321
Fax: 202-228-5429

Thurman, Uma (1970-)
Actor
Creative Artists Agency
9830 Wilshire Blvd
Beverly Hills, CA 90212
Ph: 310-288-4545
Fax: 310-288-4800

Tiahrt, Todd (1951-)
US Representative from Kansas (Republican)
2441 Rayburn Bldg **Ph:** 202-225-6216
Washington, DC 20515 **Fax:** 202-225-3489
www.house.gov/tiahrt

Tibbles, Kevin
NBC News correspondent (based in Chicago)
NBC News **Ph:** 212-664-4249
30 Rockefeller Plaza
New York, NY 10112
www.msnbc.msn.com/id/3689499

Tiberi, Patrick J (1962-)
US Representative from Ohio (Republican)
113 Cannon Bldg **Ph:** 202-225-5355
Washington, DC 20515 **Fax:** 202-226-4523
www.house.gov/tiberi

Tiegs, Cheryl (1947-)
Model
Ford Models **Ph:** 212-219-6500
111 5th Ave **Fax:** 212-966-5028
New York, NY 10003

Tierney, John F (1951-)
US Representative from Massachusetts (Democrat)
120 Cannon Bldg **Ph:** 202-225-8020
Washington, DC 20515 **Fax:** 202-225-5915
www.house.gov/tierney

Tigar, Michael (1941-)
Writer, teacher, and litigator; represented Terry Nichols in the Oklahoma City bombing trial
American University **Ph:** 202-274-4088
Washington College of Law
4801 Massachusetts Ave NW
Rm 206C
Washington, DC 20016
www.wcl.american.edu/faculty/tigar

Tillerson, Rex (1952-)
Chairman and CEO of Exxon Mobil Corp
Exxon Mobil Corp **Ph:** 972-444-1000
5959 Las Colinas Blvd **Fax:** 972-444-1350
Irving, TX 75039
www.exxon.mobil.com

Tillis, Pam (1957-)
Country singer
Bobby Roberts Co **Ph:** 615-859-8899
PO Box 1547 **Fax:** 615-859-2200
Goodlettsville, TN 37070
www.pamtillis.com

Tillman, Spencer (1964-)
Former NFL player, now studio analyst for CBS football
CBS Sports **Ph:** 212-975-4321
51 W 52nd St
New York, NY 10019
cbs.sportsline.com/cbssports/team

Tilly, Jennifer (1958-)
Actor
Binder & Assoc **Ph:** 310-274-9995
1465 Lindacrest Dr
Beverly Hills, CA 90210

Tilove, Jonathan
Newhouse News Service reporter; writes about the impact of immigration and internal migration on American race relations
Newhouse News Service **Ph:** 202-383-7800
1101 Connecticut Ave NW **Fax:** 202-296-9537
Suite 300
Washington, DC 20036
www.newhousenews.com

Tilson Thomas, Michael (1944-)
Conductor; music director of the San Francisco Symphony and artistic director of the New World Symphony, which he founded in 1988; is also Principal Guest Conductor of the London Symphony Orchestra
San Francisco Symphony **Ph:** 415-552-8000
Davies Symphony Hall **Fax:** 415-864-6000
201 Van Ness Ave
San Francisco, CA 94102
www.sfsymphony.org

Tilton, Glenn F (1950-)
Chairman, president, and CEO of UAL Corp and of its principal subsidiary, United Airlines
UAL Corp **Ph:** 847-700-5670
1200 E Algonquin Rd **Fax:** 847-700-2214
Elk Grove Village, IL 60007
www.united.com

Timberlake, Justin (1981-)
*Singer; formerly a member of *NSYNC*
Creative Artists Agency **Ph:** 310-288-4545
9830 Wilshire Blvd **Fax:** 310-288-4800
Beverly Hills, CA 90212
www.justintimberlake.com

Timonen, Kimmo (1975-)
Professional hockey player
Nashville Predators **Ph:** 615-770-7825
Gaylord Entertainment Center **Fax:** 615-770-2341
501 Broadway
Nashville, TN 37203
www.nashvillepredators.com

Tinsley, Bruce
Creator of the comic strip Mallard Filmore
King Features Syndicate Inc **Ph:** 212-455-4000
888 7th Ave 2nd Fl
New York, NY 10019
www.kingfeatures.com

Tinsley, Jamaal (1978-)
Professional basketball player
Indiana Pacers **Ph:** 317-917-2500
Conseco Fieldhouse **Fax:** 317-917-2599
125 S Pennsylvania St
Indianapolis, IN 46204
www.nba.com/pacers

Tippett, Dave (1961-)
Hockey coach
Dallas Stars **Ph:** 214-387-5500
2601 Ave of the Stars **Fax:** 214-387-3599
Frisco, TX 75034
www.dallasstars.com

Tippin, Aaron (1958-)
Country singer
Buddy Lee Attractions **Ph:** 615-244-4336
38 Music Sq East Suite 300 **Fax:** 615-726-0429
Nashville, TN 37203
www.aarontippin.com

Tirico, Mike (1966-)
Sports broadcaster
ESPN **Ph:** 860-585-2000
ESPN Plaza
935 Middle St
Bristol, CT 06010
sports.espn.go.com/espntv/espnGuide

Tisch, Andrew H
Co-Chairman of the Board, Chairman of the Executive Committee and Member of the Office of the President, Loews Corp
Loews Corp **Ph:** 212-521-2000
667 Madison Ave
New York, NY 10021
www.loews.com/loews.nsf/Governance.htm

Tisch, James S
President, CEO, and Member of the Office of the President, Loews Corp
Loews Corp **Ph:** 212-521-2000
667 Madison Ave
New York, NY 10021
www.loews.com/loews.nsf/Governance.htm

Tisch, Jonathan M
Co-Chairman of the Board and Member of the Office of the President, Loews Corp; Chairman and CEO, Loews Hotels
Loews Hotels **Ph:** 212-521-2000
667 Madison Ave
New York, NY 10021
www.loews.com/loews.nsf/Governance.htm

Tkachuk, Keith (1972-)
Professional hockey player
Saint Louis Blues **Ph:** 314-622-2500
Savvis Center **Fax:** 314-622-2582
1401 Clark Ave
Saint Louis, MO 63103
www.stlouisblues.com

Toben, Doreen A
Executive Vice President and CFO of Verizon
Verizon Communications **Ph:** 212-395-2121
1095 Ave of the Americas **Fax:** 212-869-3265
New York, NY 10036
investor.verizon.com/profile

Tobin, James R
President and CEO of Boston Scientific
Boston Scientific Corp **Ph:** 508-650-8000
1 Boston Scientific Pl
Natick, MA 01760
www.bostonscientific.com

tobyMac (1964-)
Christian singer, pop/rock and hip-hop style (performs solo and with dc talk); real name is Toby McKeehan
CAA Nashville **Ph:** 615-383-8787
3310 West End Ave 5th Fl **Fax:** 615-383-4937
Nashville, TN 37203
www.tobymac.com

Toffler, Alvin (1928-)
Considered the first Futurist of the modern age, he predicted the VCR, virtual reality, and cable television; author of several influential business policy books, including Future Shock and The Third Wave
Toffler Assoc **Ph:** 978-526-2444
302 Harbor's Point **Fax:** 978-526-2445
40 Beach St
Manchester, MA 01944
www.toffler.com

Tolan, Peter
Television and movie writer
Creative Artists Agency **Ph:** 310-288-4545
9830 Wilshire Blvd **Fax:** 310-288-4800
Beverly Hills, CA 90212

Tolan, Stephanie S (1942-)
Author of young adult and children's fiction, including Surviving the Applewhites; she also writes and speaks on the subject of exceptionally gifted children
HarperCollins Children's Books **Ph:** 212-261-6500
1350 Ave of the Americas
New York, NY 10019
www.stephanietolan.com

Toles, Tom
Editorial cartoonist for the Washington Post
Universal Press Syndicate **Ph:** 816-932-6600
4520 Main St
Kansas City, MO 64111
www.amuniversal.com/ups/features

Toll, Robert I
Chairman and CEO of Toll Brothers, builders of luxury homes
Toll Brothers Inc **Ph:** 215-938-8000
250 Gibraltar Rd **Fax:** 215-938-8217
Horsham, PA 19044 **TF:** 800-289-8655
www.tollbrothers.com

Tolle, Eckhart (1948-)
Author of The Power of Now; spiritual teacher
New World Library **Ph:** 415-884-2100
14 Pamaron Way **Fax:** 415-884-2199
Novato, CA 94949
www.eckharttolle.com

Tomasson, Helgi (1942-)
Artistic director and resident choreographer for the San Francisco Ballet
San Francisco Ballet **Ph:** 415-861-5600
455 Franklin St
San Francisco, CA 94102
www.sfballet.org

Tome, Carol B
Executive Vice President & CFO of Home Depot
Home Depot Inc **Ph:** 770-384-5735
2455 Paces Ferry Rd **Fax:** 770-384-5736
Atlanta, GA 30339
corporate.homedepot.com

Tomei, Marisa (1964-)
Actor
Creative Artists Agency **Ph:** 310-288-4545
9830 Wilshire Blvd **Fax:** 310-288-4800
Beverly Hills, CA 90212

Tomko, Brett (1973-)
Professional baseball player
Los Angeles Dodgers **Ph:** 323-224-1500
Dodger Stadium **Fax:** 323-224-1269
1000 Elysian Park Ave
Los Angeles, CA 90012
losangeles.dodgers.mlb.com

Tomlin, Lily (1939-)
Actor; comedian
William Morris Agency **Ph:** 310-859-4000
1 William Morris Pl **Fax:** 310-859-4462
Beverly Hills, CA 90212
www.lilytomlin.com

Tomlinson, LaDainian (1979-)
Professional football player
San Diego Chargers **Ph:** 858-574-4500
4020 Murphy Canyon Rd **Fax:** 858-292-2760
San Diego, CA 92123
www.chargers.com

Toms, David (1967-)
Professional golfer
David Toms Foundation **Ph:** 318-798-5437
1545 E 70th St Suite 201 **Fax:** 318-798-1616
Shreveport, LA 71105
www.davidtomsfoundation.com

Toomer, Amani (1974-)
Professional football player
New York Giants **Ph:** 201-935-8111
Giants Stadium **Fax:** 201-939-4134
East Rutherford, NJ 07073
www.giants.com

Toomey, Jim
Creator of the comic strip Sherman's Lagoon
King Features Syndicate Inc **Ph:** 212-455-4000
888 7th Ave 2nd Fl
New York, NY 10019
www.kingfeatures.com

Torre, Joe (1940-)
Baseball manager
New York Yankees **Ph:** 718-293-4300
Yankee Stadium **Fax:** 718-293-8414
161st St & River Ave
Bronx, NY 10451
newyork.yankees.mlb.com

Torres, Jacques
Master Pastry Chef & chocolatier
Jacques Torres Chocolate **Ph:** 718-875-9772
66 Water St **Fax:** 718-875-2167
Brooklyn, NY 11201
www.mrchocolate.com

Torres, Nestor (1957-)
Latin/jazz musician (flute) and composer
c/o Diane Marino **Ph:** 610-668-1223
528 Brookhurst Ave Suite B
Narbert, PA 19072
www.nestortorres.com

Tortorella, John (1958-)
Hockey coach
Tampa Bay Lightning **Ph:** 813-301-6600
St Pete Times Forum **Fax:** 813-301-1487
401 Channelside Dr
Tampa, FL 33602
www.tampabaylightning.com

Torvalds, Linus (1969-)
Creator of the Linux operating system
Open Source Development Labs Inc **Ph:** 503-626-2455 **Fax:** 503-626-2436
12725 SW Millikan Way Suite 400
Beaverton, OR 97005
www.osdl.org

Tose, Maurice B
Founder, chairman, CEO, and president of TeleCommunication Systems, a leader in wireless messaging and location technology
TeleCommunication Systems Inc **Ph:** 410-263-7616 **Fax:** 410-263-7617
275 West St
Annapolis, MD 21401
www.telecomsys.com

Totenberg, Nina (1944-)
NPR's Legal Affairs correspondent
National Public Radio **Ph:** 202-513-2000
635 Massachusetts Ave NW **Fax:** 202-513-3329
Washington, DC 20001
www.npr.org

Towery, Matt (1959-)
Syndicated columnist; has served as campaign chairman for Newt Gingrich and chief strategist for numerous national political campaigns
Creators Syndicate Inc **Ph:** 310-337-7003
5777 W Century Blvd Suite 700 **Fax:** 310-337-7625
Los Angeles, CA 90045
www.creators.com/opinion.html

Towey, Jim
Director of Faith-Based & Community Initiatives
Office of Faith-Based & Community Initiatives **Ph:** 202-456-6708 **Fax:** 202-456-7019
1650 Pennsylvania Ave NW
Washington, DC 20501
www.whitehouse.gov/government/fbci

Towns, Edolphus (1934-)
US Representative from New York (Democrat)
2232 Rayburn Bldg **Ph:** 202-225-5936
Washington, DC 20515 **Fax:** 202-225-1018
www.house.gov/towns

Trachsel, Steve (1970-)
Professional baseball player
New York Mets **Ph:** 718-507-6387
Shea Stadium **Fax:** 718-507-6395
123-01 Roosevelt Ave
Flushing, NY 11368
newyork.mets.mlb.com

Tracy, Brian (1944-)
Corporate performance expert/speaker (leadership, sales, managerial effectiveness, business strategy)
Brian Tracy International **Ph:** 858-481-2977
462 Stevens Ave Suite 202
Solana Beach, CA 92075
www.briantracy.com

Tracy, Jim (1955-)
Baseball manager
Pittsburgh Pirates **Ph:** 412-323-5000
PNC Park **Fax:** 412-323-5009
115 Federal St
Pittsburgh, PA 15212
pittsburgh.pirates.mlb.com

Traquina, Perry M
President & CEO of Wellington Management, an investment management firm
Wellington Management Co LLC **Ph:** 617-951-5000
75 State St
Boston, MA 02109

Traunfeld, Jerry
Executive chef of the Herbfarm restaurant, which features seasonally unique menus
Herbfarm Restaurant **Ph:** 425-485-5300
14590 NE 145th St
Woodinville, WA 98072
www.theherbfarm.com

Travers, Peter
Film critic and senior editor for film at Rolling Stone
Rolling Stone Magazine **Ph:** 212-484-1616
1290 Ave of the Americas
New York, NY 10104

Travis, Debbie
Writes Debbie Travis' House to Home, a syndicated column on decorating; also hosts TV shows on home renovation
King Features Syndicate Inc **Ph:** 212-455-4000
888 7th Ave 2nd Fl
New York, NY 10019
www.kingfeatures.com

Travis, Randy (1959-)
Singer (country and Christian music)
CAA Nashville **Ph:** 615-383-8787
3310 West End Ave 5th Fl **Fax:** 615-383-4937
Nashville, TN 37203
www.randytravis.com

Travolta, John (1954-)
Actor
William Morris Agency **Ph:** 310-859-4000
1 William Morris Pl **Fax:** 310-859-4462
Beverly Hills, CA 90212
www.travolta.com

Trebek, Alex (1940-)
Host of Jeopardy
Jeopardy **Ph:** 310-244-8855
10202 W Washington Blvd **Fax:** 310-244-1513
Culver City, CA 90232
www.jeopardy.com

Trefler, Alan
Founder, CEO, and chairman of Pegasystems; was co-champion of the 1975 World Open Chess Championship
Pegasystems Inc **Ph:** 617-374-9600
101 Main St **Fax:** 617-374-9620
Cambridge, MA 02142
www.pegasystems.com

Trembly, Seth (1982-)
Professional soccer player
Real Salt Lake **Ph:** 801-924-8585
515 S 700 East Suite 2R **Fax:** 801-933-4713
Salt Lake City, UT 84102
www.mlsnet.com/MLS/rsl/

Trever, John
Editorial cartoonist for the Albuquerque Journal
King Features Syndicate Inc **Ph:** 212-455-4000
888 7th Ave 2nd Fl
New York, NY 10019
www.kingfeatures.com

Tribe, Laurence H (1941-)
Professor of constitutional law at Harvard University
Harvard Law School **Ph:** 617-495-4621
420 Hauser Hall **Fax:** 617-495-3383
Cambridge, MA 02138
www.law.harvard.edu

Tritt, Travis (1963-)
Country singer
Monterey Peninsula Artists/Paradigm **Ph:** 615-251-4400 **Fax:** 615-251-4401
124 12th Ave S Suite 410
Nashville, TN 37203
www.travistritt.com

Troise, Joe (1942-)
Co-creator, with Phil Frank, of the comic strip The Elderberries; Troise is the writer and Frank the artist
Universal Press Syndicate **Ph:** 816-932-6600
4520 Main St
Kansas City, MO 64111
www.amuniversal.com/ups/features

Trotta, Liz
Former bureau chief of the Washington Times, now a contributor on FOX News programs
FOX News Channel **Ph:** 212-301-3000
1211 Ave of the Americas
New York, NY 10036
www.foxnews.com/fnctv

Trotter, Charlie
Chef and restaurateur; Charlie Trotter's Restaurant in Chicago is regarded as one of the finest in the world
Charlie Trotter's Restaurant **Ph:** 773-248-6228
816 W Armitage **Fax:** 773-248-6088
Chicago, IL 60614
www.charlietrotters.com

Trotz, Barry
Hockey coach
Nashville Predators **Ph:** 615-770-7825
Gaylord Entertainment Center **Fax:** 615-770-2341
501 Broadway
Nashville, TN 37203
www.nashvillepredators.com

Trudeau, Garry (1948-)
Creator of the syndicated comic strip Doonesbury
Universal Press Syndicate **Ph:** 816-932-6600
4520 Main St
Kansas City, MO 64111
www.doonesbury.com

Trufant, Marcus (1980-)
Professional football player
Seattle Seahawks — **Ph:** 425-827-9777
11220 NE 53rd St — **Fax:** 425-827-9008
Kirkland, WA 98033
www.seahawks.com

Trump, Donald J (1946-)
New York real estate developer whose businesses include casinos, golf clubs, resorts, and entertainment; central figure in The Apprentice TV series
Trump Organization — **Ph:** 212-832-2000
725 5th Ave
New York, NY 10022
www.trump.com

Tsai, Ming
Chef/owner of Blue Ginger in Wellesley, Massachusetts, which features East/West cuisine; is also a cookbook author and has hosted cooking shows on PBS and Food TV
Blue Ginger Restaurant — **Ph:** 781-283-5790
583 Washington St — **Fax:** 781-283-5772
Wellesley, MA 02482
www.ming.com

Tsui, Daniel C, PhD (1939-)
1998 Nobel Prize winner in Physics for his discovery (with Horst Stormer) of the fractional quantum Hall effect
Princeton University — **Ph:** 609-258-4621
Dept of Electrical Engineering — **Fax:** 609-258-6279
Olden St Rm B424
Princeton, NJ 08544
www.ee.princeton.edu/people/Tsui.php

Tubbs Jones, Stephanie (1949-)
US Representative from Ohio (Democrat)
1009 Longworth Bldg — **Ph:** 202-225-7032
Washington, DC 20515 — **Fax:** 202-225-1339
www.house.gov/tubbsjones

Tucci, Joseph M (1947-)
Chairman, president, and CEO of EMC Corp, a leader in products, services, and solutions for information storage and its management
EMC Corp — **Ph:** 617-618-3400
95 Wells Ave 2nd Fl — **Fax:** 617-618-3688
Newton, MA 02459
www.emc.com

Tucci, Stanley (1960-)
Actor
Creative Artists Agency — **Ph:** 310-288-4545
9830 Wilshire Blvd — **Fax:** 310-288-4800
Beverly Hills, CA 90212

Tuchman, Gary
CNN national correspondent
CNN — **Ph:** 404-827-1500
1 CNN Center
Atlanta, GA 30303
www.cnn.com/CNN/anchors_reporters

Tucker, Chris (1972-)
Comic actor
William Morris Agency — **Ph:** 310-859-4000
1 William Morris Pl — **Fax:** 310-859-4462
Beverly Hills, CA 90212

Tucker, Cynthia (1955-)
Editorial page editor at the Atlanta Journal-Constitution and a syndicated columnist
Universal Press Syndicate — **Ph:** 816-932-6600
4520 Main St
Kansas City, MO 64111
www.amuniversal.com/ups/features

Tucker, Darcy (1975-)
Professional hockey player
Toronto Maple Leafs — **Ph:** 416-815-5700
Air Canada Center
40 Bay St Suite 400
Toronto, ON M5J2X2
www.mapleleafs.com

Tucker, Ken
Editor-at-Large and DVD critic for Entertainment Weekly
Entertainment Weekly — **Ph:** 212-522-0059
1675 Broadway
New York, NY 10019
www.kentucker.net

Tulafono, Togiola (1947-)
Governor of American Samoa (Democrat)
American Samoa Government — **Ph:** 684-633-4116
Pago Pago, AS 96799 — **Fax:** 684-633-2269
www.asg-gov.net

Tune, Tommy (1939-)
Broadway dancer, choreographer, singer, and director
International Creative Management — **Ph:** 212-556-5600
40 W 57th St 17th Fl
New York, NY 10019
www.icmtalent.com/musperf/contemporary.html

Turan, Kenneth (1946-)
Movie critic
Los Angeles Times — **Ph:** 213-237-5000
202 W 1st St — **Fax:** 213-237-4712
Los Angeles, CA 90012

Turco, Marty (1975-)
Professional hockey player
Dallas Stars **Ph:** 214-387-5500
2601 Ave of the Stars **Fax:** 214-387-3599
Frisco, TX 75034
www.dallasstars.com

Turgeon, Pierre (1969-)
Professional hockey player
Colorado Avalanche **Ph:** 303-405-1100
Pepsi Center
1000 Chopper Cir
Denver, CO 80204
www.coloradoavalanche.com

Turkoglu, Hedo (1979-)
Professional basketball player
Orlando Magic **Ph:** 407-916-2400
8701 Maitland Summit Blvd **Fax:** 407-916-2884
Orlando, FL 32810
www.nba.com/magic

Turley, James S
Chairman and CEO of Ernst & Young
Ernst & Young LLP **Ph:** 212-773-3000
5 Times Sq
New York, NY 10036
www.ey.com

Turlington, Christy (1969-)
Model
United Talent Agency **Ph:** 310-273-6700
9560 Wilshire Blvd 5th Fl **Fax:** 310-247-1111
Beverly Hills, CA 90212

Turnbull, Charles W (1935-)
Governor of the Virgin Islands (Democrat)
21-22 Kongens Gade **Ph:** 340-774-0001
Saint Thomas, VI 00802 **Fax:** 340-774-1361
www.nga.org

Turner, Josh (1977-)
Country/gospel singer
William Morris Agency **Ph:** 615-963-3000
1600 Division St Suite 300 **Fax:** 615-963-3090
Nashville, TN 37203
www.joshturner.com

Turner, Kathleen (1954-)
Actor
International Creative Management **Ph:** 310-550-4000
8942 Wilshire Blvd
Beverly Hills, CA 90211

Turner, Michael (1960-)
US Representative from Ohio (Republican)
1740 Longworth Bldg **Ph:** 202-225-6465
Washington, DC 20515 **Fax:** 202-225-6754
www.house.gov/miketurner

Turner, Morrie (1923-)
Creator of the comic strip Wee Pals
Creators Syndicate Inc **Ph:** 310-337-7003
5777 W Century Blvd Suite 700 **Fax:** 310-337-7625
Los Angeles, CA 90045
www.creators.com

Turner, Ted (1938-)
Media mogul and philanthropist; chairman of Turner Enterprises and member of the board of directors of Time Warner
Turner Broadcasting System Inc **Ph:** 404-827-1700
1 CNN Center
Atlanta, GA 30348
www.tedturner.com

Turner, Tina (1939-)
Singer
Creative Artists Agency **Ph:** 310-288-4545
9830 Wilshire Blvd **Fax:** 310-288-4800
Beverly Hills, CA 90212
www.officialtina.com

Turow, Scott (1949-)
A practicing attorney & author of legal thrillers (Presumed Innocent)
Farrar Straus & Giroux **Ph:** 212-741-6900
19 Union Sq W
New York, NY 10003
www.scottturow.com

Turturro, John (1957-)
Actor
International Creative Management **Ph:** 310-550-4000
8942 Wilshire Blvd
Beverly Hills, CA 90211

Tuttle, Merlin (1941-)
Founder of Bat Conservation International, which works to teach people about the value of bats and the importance of protecting their habitats
Bat Conservation International **Ph:** 512-327-9721
PO Box 162603 **Fax:** 512-327-9724
Austin, TX 78716

Twain, Shania (1965-)
Country singer
CAA Nashville **Ph:** 615-383-8787
3310 West End Ave 5th Fl **Fax:** 615-383-4937
Nashville, TN 37203
www.shania-twain.com

Twellman, Taylor (1980-)
Professional soccer player
New England Revolution
Gillette Stadium
1 Patriot Pl
Foxborough, MA 02035
www.revolutionsoccer.net
Ph: 508-543-5001
Fax: 508-384-9128

Twiggy (1949-)
Model who became the first supermodel in the 1960s; full name is Twiggy Lawson (born Leslie Hornby)
Ford Models Inc
111 5th Ave
New York, NY 10003
www.twiggylawson.co.uk
Ph: 212-219-6500
Fax: 212-966-5028

Tyler, Anne (1941-)
Author (Accidental Tourist; Breathing Lessons)
Ballantine Books Publicity
1745 Broadway
New York, NY 10019
www.randomhouse.com/BB
Ph: 212-782-9000

Tyler, Liv (1977-)
Actor (daughter of Aerosmith's Steven Tyler)
United Talent Agency
9560 Wilshire Blvd 5th Fl
Beverly Hills, CA 90212
Ph: 310-273-6700
Fax: 310-247-1111

Tyler, Richard (1946-)
Fashion designer
Tyler Trafficante Inc
525 Mission St
South Pasadena, CA 91030
Ph: 626-799-9961
Fax: 626-799-9963

Tynes, Lawrence (1978-)
Professional football player
Kansas City Chiefs
Arrowhead Stadium
1 Arrowhead Dr
Kansas City, MO 64129
www.kcchiefs.com
Ph: 816-920-9300
Fax: 816-920-4315

Tyrese (1978-)
Singer (soul/R&B); full name is Tyrese Gibson
William Morris Agency
1325 Ave of the Americas
New York, NY 10019
www.tyrese.com
Ph: 212-586-5100
Fax: 212-246-3583

Tyrrell, R Emmett Jr (1943-)
Founder & editor in chief of American Spectator; syndicated columnist
Creators Syndicate Inc
5777 W Century Blvd Suite 700
Los Angeles, CA 90045
www.creators.com/opinion.html
Ph: 310-337-7003
Fax: 310-337-7625

Tyson, Eric (1962-)
Personal finance writer, lecturer, and author (Investing for Dummies); writes the syndicated newspaper column Investors' Guide
King Features Syndicate Inc
888 7th Ave 2nd Fl
New York, NY 10019
www.kingfeatures.com
Ph: 212-455-4000

Tyson, John (1954-)
Chairman and CEO of Tyson Foods
Tyson Foods Inc
2210 W Oaklawn Dr
Springdale, AR 72762
ir.tysonfoodsinc.com
Ph: 479-290-4000

U

Udall, Mark (1950-)
US Representative from Colorado (Democrat)
240 Cannon Bldg
Washington, DC 20515
markudall.house.gov
Ph: 202-225-2161
Fax: 202-226-7840

Udall, Tom (1948-)
US Representative from New Mexico (Democrat)
1414 Longworth Bldg
Washington, DC 20515
www.tomudall.house.gov
Ph: 202-225-6190
Fax: 202-226-1331

Udvar-Hazy, Steven F
Founder, chairman, and CEO of International Lease Finance Corp, a subsidiary of AIG that leases aircraft to airlines
International Lease Finance Corp
10250 Constellation Blvd Suite 3400
Los Angeles, CA 90067
www.ilfc.com
Ph: 310-788-1999
Fax: 310-788-1990

Ullman, Myron E III
Chairman and CEO of JC Penney
JC Penney Corp
6501 Legacy Dr
Plano, TX 75024
www.jcpenney.net
Ph: 972-431-1000

Ulrich, Robert J
Chairman and CEO of Target
Target Corp
1000 Nicollett Mall
Minneapolis, MN 55403
investors.target.com
Ph: 612-696-6164

Underwood, Blair (1964-)
Actor
Paradigm Talent & Literary Agency **Ph:** 310-288-8000 **Fax:** 310-288-2000
360 N Crescent Dr
North Bldg
Beverly Hills, CA 90210
www.blairunderwood.com

Underwood, Carrie (1983-)
Country singer
CAA Nashville **Ph:** 615-383-8787
3310 West End Ave 5th Fl **Fax:** 615-383-4937
Nashville, TN 37203
www.carrieunderwoodofficial.com

Unger, Jim (1940-)
Creator of the comic panel Herman
Newspaper Enterprise Assn **Ph:** 212-293-8500
200 Madison Ave
New York, NY 10016
www.unitedfeatures.com

Unser, Al Jr (1962-)
Race car driver (retired)
Sports Management Network **Ph:** 248-335-3535
1668 Telegraph Rd Suite 200 **Fax:** 248-335-3352
Bloomfield Hills, MI 48302
www.sportsmanagementnetwork.com

Updike, John (1932-)
Novelist
Knopf Publishing/Author Mail **Ph:** 212-782-9000
1745 Broadway
New York, NY 10019
www.randomhouse.com/knopf

Upshaw, Gene (1945-)
NFL Hall of Famer and executive director of the National Football League Players Association
National Football League Players Assn **Ph:** 202-463-2200 **Fax:** 202-857-0380
2021 L St NW Suite 600 **TF:** 800-372-2000
Washington, DC 20036

Upton, Fred (1953-)
US Representative from Michigan (Republican)
2183 Rayburn Bldg **Ph:** 202-225-3761
Washington, DC 20515 **Fax:** 202-225-4986
www.house.gov/upton

Urban, Keith (1967-)
Country singer
CAA Nashville **Ph:** 615-383-8787
3310 West End Ave 5th Fl **Fax:** 615-383-4937
Nashville, TN 37203
www.keithurban.net

Uribe, Juan (1979-)
Professional baseball player
Chicago White Sox **Ph:** 312-674-1000
US Cellular Field **Fax:** 312-674-5109
333 W 35th St
Chicago, IL 60616
chicago.whitesox.mlb.com

Urlacher, Brian (1978-)
Professional football player
Chicago Bears **Ph:** 847-295-6600
Halas Hall at Conway Park **Fax:** 847-295-8986
1000 Football Dr
Lake Forest, IL 60045
www.brianurlacher.com

Usher (1978-)
Singer (R&B); full name is Usher Raymond
International Creative Management **Ph:** 310-550-4000
8942 Wilshire Blvd
Beverly Hills, CA 90211
www.usherworld.com

Ustian, Daniel C (1950-)
President and CEO of Navistar, the parent company of International Truck and Engine Corp
Navistar International Corp **Ph:** 630-753-5000
4201 Winfield Rd
Warrenville, IL 60555
www.navistar.com

Vagenas, Peter (1978-)
Professional soccer player
Los Angeles Galaxy **Ph:** 310-630-2200
Home Depot Center **Fax:** 310-630-2250
18400 Avalon Blvd Suite 200
Carson, CA 90746
www.lagalaxy.com

Valenti, Jack (1921-)
Movie industry leader who was head of the Motion Picture Association of America for 38 years; was also special assistant to LBJ during his presidency
William Morris Agency **Ph:** 310-859-4000
1 William Morris Pl **Fax:** 310-859-4462
Beverly Hills, CA 90212

Van Aken, Norman
Chef and owner of Norman's; "the father of New World Cuisine"
Norman's Restaurant **Ph:** 305-446-6767
21 Almeria Ave **Fax:** 305-446-7909
Coral Gables, FL 33134
www.normans.com

Van Allen, James A, PhD (1914-)
Space scientist/astrophysicist who discovered the Earth's radiation belts
University of Iowa **Ph:** 319-335-1699
Dept of Physics & Astronomy **Fax:** 319-335-1753
203 Van Allen Hall
Iowa City, IA 52242
www.physics.uiowa.edu

Van Allsburg, Chris (1949-)
Author and illustrator of children's books (Jumanji; The Polar Express)
Houghton Mifflin Children's Books **Ph:** 617-351-5000
222 Berkeley St 8th Fl
Boston, MA 02116
www.houghtonmifflinbooks.com

Van Amerongen, Jerry
Creator of the comic strip Ballard Street
Creators Syndicate Inc **Ph:** 310-337-7003
5777 W Century Blvd Suite 700 **Fax:** 310-337-7625
Los Angeles, CA 90045
www.creators.com

Van Andel, Jay (1924-2004)
Co-founder, with Rich DeVos, of Amway
Amway Corp **Ph:** 616-787-1000
7575 Fulton St E
Ada, MI 49355
www.amway.com

Van Andel, Steve
Chairman of Alticor Inc; he is the son of Jay Van Andel, who founded Amway with Rich DeVos, and he shares Alticor's Office of the Chief Executive with President Doug DeVos, Rich's son
Alticor Inc **Ph:** 616-787-1000
7575 Fulton St E
Ada, MI 49355
www.alticor.com/people/steve_van_andel.html

Van Der Beek, James (1977-)
Actor
Gersh Agency **Ph:** 310-274-6611
232 N Canon Dr
Beverly Hills, CA 90210

Van Draanen, Wendelin
Author of novels for young readers, including the Sammy Keyes mystery stories
Random House Children's Books **Ph:** 212-782-9000
Publicity Dept
1745 Broadway
New York, NY 10019
www.randomhouse.com/kids

Van Dyke, Dick (1925-)
Actor
William Morris Agency **Ph:** 310-859-4000
1 William Morris Pl **Fax:** 310-859-4462
Beverly Hills, CA 90212

Van Exel, Nick (1971-)
Professional basketball player
San Antonio Spurs **Ph:** 210-444-5000
1 SBC Center **Fax:** 210-444-5003
San Antonio, TX 78219
www.nba.com/spurs

Van Gundy, Jeff (1962-)
Basketball coach
Houston Rockets **Ph:** 713-758-7200
Toyota Center **Fax:** 713-758-7396
1510 Polk St
Houston, TX 77002
www.nba.com/rockets

Van Halen
Rock band (members are Alex Van Halen, guitarist Eddie Van Halen, Michael Sobolewski, and vocalist Sammy Hagar)
William Morris Agency **Ph:** 310-859-4000
1 William Morris Pl **Fax:** 310-859-4462
Beverly Hills, CA 90212
www.van-halen.com

Van Hollen, Christopher Jr (1959-)
US Representative from Maryland (Democrat)
1419 Longworth Bldg **Ph:** 202-225-5341
Washington, DC 20515 **Fax:** 202-225-0375
www.house.gov/vanhollen

Van Horn, Keith (1975-)
Professional basketball player
Dallas Mavericks **Ph:** 214-747-6287
The Pavilion **Fax:** 214-658-7121
2909 Taylor St
Dallas, TX 75226
www.nba.com/mavericks

Van Impe, Jack (1931-)
Televangelist; also has a radio program and produces evangelistic prophecy movies; his message focuses on prophecy in the Bible, particularly in the Book of Revelation
Jack Van Impe Ministries **Ph:** 248-852-2244
PO Box 7004 **Fax:** 248-852-2692
Troy, MI 48007
www.jvim.com

Van Ryn, Mike (1979-)
Professional hockey player
Florida Panthers **Ph:** 954-835-7000
BankAtlantic Center **Fax:** 954-835-7700
1 Panther Pkwy
Sunrise, FL 33323
www.floridapanthers.com

Van Sant, Gus (1952-)
Film director/producer/writer
William Morris Agency **Ph:** 310-859-4000
1 William Morris Pl **Fax:** 310-859-4462
Beverly Hills, CA 90212

Van Sant, Peter (1953-)
48 Hours correspondent
48 Hours **Ph:** 212-975-4114
524 W 57th St
New York, NY 10019
www.cbsnews.com

Van Susteren, Greta (1955-)
Host of FOX's news and interview program On the Record with Greta Van Susteren
FOX News Channel **Ph:** 212-301-3000
1211 Ave of the Americas
New York, NY 10036
www.foxnews.com/fnctv

Van Zandt, Steven (1950-)
Guitarist in Bruce Springsteen's E Street Band; actor (plays Silvio Dante on The Sopranos); aka Little Steven Van Zandt
Shore Fire Media **Ph:** 718-522-7171
32 Court St Suite 1600 **Fax:** 718-522-7242
Brooklyn, NY 11201
www.littlesteven.com

Van Zant
Country rock duo Johnny and Donnie Van Zant
Vector Management **Ph:** 615-269-6600
PO Box 120479 **Fax:** 615-269-6002
Nashville, TN 37212
www.thevanzants.com

Vance, Courtney B (1960-)
Actor
Endeavor **Ph:** 310-248-2000
9601 Wilshire Blvd 3rd Fl **Fax:** 310-248-2020
Beverly Hills, CA 90210
www.nbc.com/Law_&_Order:_Criminal_Intent

Vanderbeek, Jeff
Chairman and managing partner of the New Jersey Devils hockey franchise
New Jersey Devils **Ph:** 201-935-6050
Continental Airlines Arena **Fax:** 201-935-2127
50 Rt 120N
East Rutherford, NJ 07073
www.newjerseydevils.com

Vanderjagt, Mike (1970-)
Professional football player
Dallas Cowboys **Ph:** 972-556-9900
1 Cowboys Pkwy **Fax:** 972-556-9304
Irving, TX 75063
www.dallascowboys.com

Vanderloo, Mark (1968-)
Male model
Wilhelmina Models Inc **Ph:** 212-473-0700
300 Park Ave S 2nd Fl **Fax:** 212-473-3223
New York, NY 10010

Vanney, Greg (1974-)
Professional soccer player
FC Dallas **Ph:** 214-979-0303
14800 Quorum Dr Suite 300 **Fax:** 214-979-1118
Dallas, TX 75254
fc.dallas.mlsnet.com

Vanzant, Iyanla (1953-)
Writes and speaks on spiritual issues that can aid in the development and growth of black women in America (In the Meantime: Finding Yourself and the Love You Want)
Simon & Schuster **Ph:** 212-698-7000
1230 Ave of the Americas
New York, NY 10020
www.simonsays.com

Vardalos, Nia (1962-)
Actor and screenwriter/producer (My Big Fat Greek Wedding)
United Talent Agency **Ph:** 310-273-6700
9560 Wilshire Blvd 5th Fl **Fax:** 310-247-1111
Beverly Hills, CA 90212

Vargas, Elizabeth (1962-)
Co-anchor of World News Tonight and 20/20
ABC News **Ph:** 212-456-7777
147 Columbus Ave
New York, NY 10023
www.abcnews.go.com/2020

Varitek, Jason (1972-)
Professional baseball player
Boston Red Sox **Ph:** 617-267-9440
Fenway Park **Fax:** 617-236-6797
4 Yawkey Way
Boston, MA 02215
boston.redsox.mlb.com

Varmus, Harold E, MD (1939-)
President & CEO of Memorial Sloan-Kettering Cancer Center; former NIH director and co-recipient (with J. Michael Bishop) of the 1989 Nobel Prize for studies of the genetic basis of cancer
Varmus Laboratory **Ph:** 212-639-7317
Memorial Sloan-Kettering Cancer Center **Fax:** 212-717-3125
1275 York Ave
Box 62
New York, NY 10021
www.mskcc.org

Varney, Christine A
Attorney and former commissioner of the Federal Trade Comission (1994-1997); heads Hogan & Hartson's Internet practice group
Hogan & Hartson LLP **Ph:** 202-637-5600
555 13th St NW **Fax:** 202-637-5910
Washington, DC 20004
www.hhlaw.com

Varney, Stuart
Business journalist; business contributor and substitute host for FOX News Channel's Your World with Neil Cavuto
FOX News Channel **Ph:** 212-301-3000
1211 Ave of the Americas
New York, NY 10036
www.foxnews.com/fnctv

Vartan, Michael (1968-)
Actor
Endeavor **Ph:** 310-248-2000
9601 Wilshire Blvd 3rd Fl **Fax:** 310-248-2020
Beverly Hills, CA 90210

Varvel, Gary (1957-)
Editorial cartoonist for the Indianapolis Star
Creators Syndicate Inc **Ph:** 310-337-7003
5777 W Century Blvd Suite 700 **Fax:** 310-337-7625
Los Angeles, CA 90045
www.creators.com

Vasher, Nathan (1981-)
Professional football player
Chicago Bears **Ph:** 847-295-6600
Halas Hall at Conway Park **Fax:** 847-295-8986
1000 Football Dr
Lake Forest, IL 60045
www.chicagobears.com

Vasquez, Gaddi H (1955-)
Director of the Peace Corps
Peace Corps **Ph:** 202-692-2100
1111 20th St NW **Fax:** 202-692-2101
Washington, DC 20526
www.peacecorps.gov

Vass, Bill
Chief Information Officer of Sun Microsystems
Sun Microsystems Inc **Ph:** 650-960-1300
4150 Network Cir
USCA20-210
Santa Clara, CA 95054
www.sun.com

Vaughn, Vince (1970-)
Actor
United Talent Agency **Ph:** 310-273-6700
9560 Wilshire Blvd 5th Fl **Fax:** 310-247-1111
Beverly Hills, CA 90212

Vazquez, Javier (1976-)
Professional baseball player
Chicago White Sox **Ph:** 312-674-1000
US Cellular Field **Fax:** 312-674-5109
333 W 35th St
Chicago, IL 60616
chicago.whitesox.mlb.com

Veciana-Suarez, Ana (1956-)
Miami Herald columnist (syndicated); author
Tribune Media Services Inc **Ph:** 312-222-4444
435 N Michigan Ave Suite 1500
Chicago, IL 60611
tmsfeatures.com/productlist.htm

Vedder, Eddie (1964-)
Singer; vocalist in Pearl Jam
Creative Artists Agency **Ph:** 310-288-4545
9830 Wilshire Blvd **Fax:** 310-288-4800
Beverly Hills, CA 90212

Vedral, Joyce, PhD (1943-)
Fitness personality and author; her fitness plan emphasizes weight training
PO Box 7433 **Ph:** 516-221-9004
Wantagh, NY 11793
www.joycevedral.com

Velasquez, Jaci (1979-)
Singer (Christian & Latin music)
William Morris Agency **Ph:** 615-963-3000
1600 Division St Suite 300 **Fax:** 615-963-3090
Nashville, TN 37203
www.jacivelasquez.com

Velazquez, Nydia M (1953-)
US Representative from New York (Democrat)
2241 Rayburn Bldg **Ph:** 202-225-2361
Washington, DC 20515 **Fax:** 202-226-0327
www.house.gov/velazquez

Velshi, Ali
CNN Business News anchor
CNN New York **Ph:** 212-275-7800
Time Warner Ctr
10 Columbus Cir
New York, NY 10019
www.cnn.com/CNN/anchors_reporters

Vendela (1967-)
Fashion model (full name is Vendela Kirsebom)
William Morris Agency **Ph:** 310-859-4000
1 William Morris Pl **Fax:** 310-859-4462
Beverly Hills, CA 90212

Veneman, Ann M (1949-)
Former US Secretary of Agriculture; now Executive Director of the United Nations Children's Fund (UNICEF)
UNICEF **Ph:** 212-326-7000
3 United Nations Plaza **Fax:** 212-887-7465
New York, NY 10017
www.unicef.org/about/structure

Verplank, Scott (1964-)
Professional golfer
SFX Sports Group **Ph:** 202-686-2000
5335 Wisconsin Ave NW **Fax:** 202-686-5050
Suite 850
Washington, DC 20015
www.pgatour.com

Verve Pipe
Pop rock group
Monterey Peninsula Artists/ **Ph:** 831-375-4889
Paradigm **Fax:** 831-375-2623
509 Hartnell St
Monterey, CA 93940

Vester, Linda (1965-)
Host of DaySide with Linda Vester, FNC's daytime talk show
FOX News Channel **Ph:** 212-301-3000
1211 Ave of the Americas
New York, NY 10036
www.foxnews.com/fnctv

Vetri, Marc
Chef & owner of Vetri Restaurant in Philadelphia
Vetri Restaurant **Ph:** 215-732-3478
1312 Spruce St
Philadelphia, PA 19107
www.vetriristorante.com

Vick, Michael (1980-)
Professional football player
Atlanta Falcons **Ph:** 770-965-3115
4400 Falcon Pkwy **Fax:** 770-965-3185
Flowery Branch, GA 30542
mikevick.com

Vickers, Brian (1983-)
Race car driver
Hendrick Motorsports **Ph:** 704-455-3400
4400 Papa Joe Hendrick Blvd
Charlotte, NC 28262
www.brianvickers.com

Victorine, Sasha (1978-)
Professional soccer player
Kansas City Wizards **Ph:** 816-920-9300
2 Arrowhead Dr **Fax:** 816-920-4774
Kansas City, MO 64129
kc.wizards.mlsnet.com

Vidal, Gore (1925-)
Author (novelist, playwright, and essayist)
Vintage/Anchor Publicity **Ph:** 212-572-2420
1745 Broadway 20th Fl
New York, NY 10019
www.randomhouse.com/vintage

Vidro, Jose (1974-)
Professional baseball player
Washington Nationals **Ph:** 202-349-0400
RFK Stadium
2400 E Capitol St SE
Washington, DC 20003
washington.nationals.mlb.com

Vieira, Meredith (1953-)
Currently moderator of The View and host of Who Wants to be a Millionaire? weedays; is slated to replace Katie Couric on the Today Show when she becomes the anchor of CBS Evening News
The View **Ph:** 212-456-7777
320 W 66th St
New York, NY 10023
abc.go.com/daytime/theview

Vila, Bob (1946-)
Home improvement specialist; host of Bob Vila's Home Again
Bob Vila Cos **Ph:** 617-848-8452
115 Kingston St 3rd Fl **Fax:** 617-848-8401
Boston, MA 02111
www.bobvila.com

Villaraigosa, Antonio R (1953-)
Mayor of Los Angeles
200 N Spring St Rm 305 **Ph:** 213-978-0600
Los Angeles, CA 90012 **Fax:** 213-213-9785
www.lacity.org/mayor

Villella, Edward (1936-)
Dancer; founding artistic director & CEO of the Miami City Ballet
Miami City Ballet **Ph:** 305-929-7000
Ophelia & Juan Js Roca Center
2200 Liberty Ave
Miami Beach, FL 33139
www.miamicityballet.org

Vilma, Jonathan (1982-)
Professional football player
New York Jets **Ph:** 516-560-8100
1000 Fulton Ave **Fax:** 516-560-8198
Hempstead, NY 11550
www.newyorkjets.com

Vilsack, Thomas J (1950-)
Governor of Iowa (Democrat)
State Capitol Bldg **Ph:** 515-281-5211
Des Moines, IA 50319 **Fax:** 515-281-6611
www.governor.state.ia.us

Vinatieri, Adam (1972-)
Professional football player
Indianapolis Colts **Ph:** 317-297-2658
7001 W 56th St **Fax:** 317-297-8971
Indianapolis, IN 46254
www.colts.com

Vinge, Joan D (1948-)
Science fiction author (The Snow Queen)
Warner Books **Ph:** 212-522-7200
c/o Author Mail
1271 Ave of the Americas
New York, NY 10020
www.sff.net/people/jdvinge

Vinton, Will (1948-)
Animator; the creator of the trademarked stopmotion animation technique called Claymation; founded Vinton Studios and Freewill Entertainment animation studios
Freewill Entertainment **Ph:** 503-786-2026
1224 SE River Forest Rd
Portland, OR 97267
www.willvinton.net

Viorst, Judith (1931-)
Poet and author of non-fiction (Necessary Losses) and children's books (Alexander and the Terrible, Horrible, No Good, Very Bad Day)
Simon & Schuster **Ph:** 212-698-7000
1230 Ave of the Americas
New York, NY 10020
www.simonsays.com

Visclosky, Peter J (1949-)
US Representative from Indiana (Democrat)
2256 Rayburn Bldg **Ph:** 202-225-2461
Washington, DC 20515 **Fax:** 202-225-2493
www.house.gov/visclosky

Visnjic, Goran (1972-)
Actor
Endeavor **Ph:** 310-248-2000
9601 Wilshire Blvd 3rd Fl **Fax:** 310-248-2020
Beverly Hills, CA 90210
www.nbc.com/ER

Visser, Lesley (1953-)
TV sports reporter
CBS Sports **Ph:** 212-975-4321
51 W 52nd St
New York, NY 10019
cbs.sportsline.com/cbssports/team

Vitale, Dick (1939-)
Sports broadcaster
ESPN **Ph:** 860-585-2000
ESPN Plaza
935 Middle St
Bristol, CT 06010
espn.go.com/dickvitale

Vitter, David (1961-)
US Senator from Louisiana (Republican)
825A Hart Bldg **Ph:** 202-224-4623
Washington, DC 20510
vitter.senate.gov

Vizcaino, Luis (1974-)
Professional baseball player
Arizona Diamondbacks **Ph:** 602-462-6500
Bank One Ballpark **Fax:** 602-462-6600
401 E Jefferson St
Phoenix, AZ 85004
arizona.diamondbacks.mlb.com

Vizquel, Omar (1967-)
Professional baseball player
San Francisco Giants **Ph:** 415-972-2000
AT & T Park
24 Willie Mays Plaza
San Francisco, CA 94107
sanfrancisco.giants.mlb.com

Voelker, Jim
Chairman, president, and CEO of InfoSpace
InfoSpace Inc **Ph:** 425-201-6100
601 108th Ave NE Suite 1200
Bellevue, WA 98004
www.infospaceinc.com

Voight, Jon (1938-)
Actor
Creative Artists Agency **Ph:** 310-288-4545
9830 Wilshire Blvd **Fax:** 310-288-4800
Beverly Hills, CA 90212

Voight, Karen
Fitness expert and celebrity trainer
Entertaining Fitness Inc **Ph:** 310-264-5800
2225 Broadway Suite B **Fax:** 310-264-5804
Santa Monica, CA 90404
www.karenvoight.com

Voigt, Cynthia (1942-)
Author of books for young adults, including Dicey's Song, Homecoming, and other books in the Tillerman series
Simon & Schuster Books for Young Readers **Ph:** 212-698-7000
1230 Ave of the Americas
New York, NY 10020
www.simonsays.com

Voigt, Deborah (1960-)
Opera & concert singer (soprano)
Columbia Artists Management **Ph:** 212-841-9500
1790 Broadway **Fax:** 212-841-9744
New York, NY 10019
www.deborahvoigt.com

Voinovich, George V (1936-)
US Senator from Ohio (Republican)
317 Hart Bldg **Ph:** 202-224-3353
Washington, DC 20510 **Fax:** 202-228-1382
voinovich.senate.gov

Vokoun, Tomas (1976-)
Professional hockey player
Nashville Predators **Ph:** 615-770-7825
Gaylord Entertainment Center **Fax:** 615-770-2341
501 Broadway
Nashville, TN 37203
www.nashvillepredators.com

Volkow, Nora D, MD (1956-)
Director, National Institute on Drug Abuse, National Institutes of Health
National Institute on Drug Abuse **Ph:** 301-443-6480
Fax: 301-443-8908
6001 Executive Blvd
Rockville, MD 20892
www.nida.nih.gov

von Eschenbach, Andrew, MD
Director of the National Cancer Institute; concurrently, is Acting Commissioner of the US Food & Drug Administration
National Cancer Institute **Ph:** 301-496-5615
31 Center Dr Bldg 31 Rm 11A48 **Fax:** 301-402-0338
MSC 2590
Bethesda, MD 20892
www.nci.nih.gov

Von Fremd, Mike
ABC News correspondent
ABC News **Ph:** 212-456-7777
77 W 66th St
New York, NY 10023
www.abcnews.go.com/WNT

Von Furstenberg, Diane (1946-)
Fashion designer
DVF Studios **Ph:** 212-741-6607
389 W 12th St
New York, NY 10014
www.dvf.com

Von Rhein, John (1945-)
Music critic
Chicago Tribune **Ph:** 312-222-3232
435 N Michigan Ave **Fax:** 312-222-4674
Chicago, IL 60611

Vongerichten, Jean-Georges
Chef & owner of Jean Georges Restaurant in New York; also has other restaurants in New York as well as elsewhere in the US and overseas
Jean Georges Management **Ph:** 212-358-0688
111 Prince St 2nd Fl **Fax:** 212-358-0685
New York, NY 10012
www.jean-georges.com

Vonnegut, Kurt (1922-)
Author and artist
Farber Literary Agency **Ph:** 212-861-7075
14 E 75th St **Fax:** 212-861-7076
New York, NY 10021
www.kurtvonnegut.com

Vredenburgh, Judith
President & CEO of Big Brothers and Big Sisters of America
Big Brothers Big Sisters of America **Ph:** 215-567-7000
Fax: 215-567-0394
230 N 13th St
Philadelphia, PA 19107
www.bbbsa.org

Wachowski, Andy (1967-)
Writer/director/producer (The Matrix, with brother Larry, as the Wachowski Brothers)
William Morris Agency **Ph:** 310-859-4000
1 William Morris Pl **Fax:** 310-859-4462
Beverly Hills, CA 90212

Wachowski, Larry (1965-)
Writer/director/producer (The Matrix, with brother Andy, as the Wachowski Brothers)
William Morris Agency **Ph:** 310-859-4000
1 William Morris Pl **Fax:** 310-859-4462
Beverly Hills, CA 90212

Wade, Dwyane (1982-)
Professional basketball player
Miami Heat **Ph:** 786-777-1000
American Airlines Arena **Fax:** 786-777-1609
601 Biscayne Blvd
Miami, FL 33132
www.nba.com/heat

Waggoner, Robert
Executive chef of the Charleston Grill (contemporary lowcountry cuisine) at the Charleston Hotel in Charleston, South Carolina
Charleston Grill **Ph:** 843-577-4522
224 King St **Fax:** 843-724-8405
Charleston, SC 29401
www.charlestongrill.com

Waghorn, Kerry (1947-)
Caricaturist; creator of Faces in the News
Universal Press Syndicate **Ph:** 816-932-6600
4520 Main St
Kansas City, MO 64111
www.amuniversal.com/ups/features

Wagner, Aly (1980-)
Soccer player on the US National Team
US Soccer Federation **Ph:** 312-808-1300
1801 S Prairie Ave **Fax:** 312-808-1301
Chicago, IL 60616
www.ussoccer.com

Wagner, Billy (1971-)
Professional baseball player
New York Mets **Ph:** 718-507-6387
Shea Stadium **Fax:** 718-507-6395
123-01 Roosevelt Ave
Flushing, NY 11368
newyork.mets.mlb.com

Wagner, Fred
Creator of the comic strip Animal Crackers
Tribune Media Services Inc **Ph:** 312-222-4444
435 N Michigan Ave Suite 1500
Chicago, IL 60611
www.comicspage.com

Wagner, Lawrence M
Chairman and CEO of the Hillman Co, an investment firm with holdings primarily in real estate
Hillman Co **Ph:** 412-281-2620
1900 Grant Bldg **Fax:** 412-338-3520
Pittsburgh, PA 15219

Wagner, Robert (1930-)
Actor
Binder & Assoc **Ph:** 310-274-9995
1465 Lindacrest Dr
Beverly Hills, CA 90210

Wagoner, G Richard (1953-)
Chairman and CEO of General Motors
General Motors Corp **Ph:** 313-556-5000
300 Renaissance Center
Detroit, MI 48265
www.gm.com

Wahlberg, Donnie (1969-)
Actor; singer
IFA Talent Agency **Ph:** 310-659-5522
8730 Sunset Blvd Suite 490 **Fax:** 310-659-3344
Los Angeles, CA 90069
www.donniewahlberg.com

Wahlberg, Mark (1971-)
Actor, model, singer
Endeavor **Ph:** 310-248-2000
9601 Wilshire Blvd 3rd Fl **Fax:** 310-248-2020
Beverly Hills, CA 90210
www.markwahlberg.com

Wainscott, James L
Chairman, president, and CEO of AK Steel
AK Steel Holding Corp **Ph:** 513-425-5000
703 Curtis St
Middletown, OH 45043
www.aksteel.com/news/default.asp?year=2005

Waitley, Denis, PhD (1933-)
Keynote speaker, productivity consultant, and author
Waitley Institute **Ph:** 858-756-4201
PO Box 197 **Fax:** 858-756-9717
Rancho Santa Fe, CA 92067
www.waitley.com

Waits, Tom (1949-)
Singer/songwriter, composer
United Talent Agency **Ph:** 310-248-2000
9560 Wilshire Blvd 5th Fl **Fax:** 310-248-2020
Beverly Hills, CA 90210
www.officialtomwaits.com

Waitt, Ted (1963-)
Businessman (founder and former chairman and CEO of Gateway Inc) and philanthropist
Waitt Family Foundation **Ph:** 858-551-4839
PO Box 1948 **Fax:** 858-551-6871
La Jolla, CA 92038
www.waittfoundation.org

Wakefield, Dan (1932-)
Novelist (Going All the Way), journalist, and screenwriter
Warner Books **Ph:** 212-522-7200
c/o Author Mail
1271 Ave of the Americas
New York, NY 10020
www.danwakefield.com

Wakefield, Tim (1966-)
Professional baseball player
Boston Red Sox **Ph:** 617-267-9440
Fenway Park **Fax:** 617-236-6797
4 Yawkey Way
Boston, MA 02215
boston.redsox.mlb.com

Walcott, Derek (1930-)
Poet; winner of the 1992 Nobel Prize for Literature
Farrar Straus & Giroux **Ph:** 212-741-6900
19 Union Sq W
New York, NY 10003
www.fsgbooks.com

Walden, Greg (1957-)
US Representative from Oregon (Republican)
1210 Longworth Bldg **Ph:** 202-225-6730
Washington, DC 20515 **Fax:** 202-225-5774
www.walden.house.gov

Waldner, Peter
Creator of the comic strip Flight Deck
Creators Syndicate Inc **Ph:** 310-337-7003
5777 W Century Blvd Suite 700 **Fax:** 310-337-7625
Los Angeles, CA 90045
creators.com

Walken, Christopher (1943-)
Actor
International Creative Management **Ph:** 310-550-4000
8953 Wilshire Blvd
Beverly HIlls, CA 90211

Walker, Alice (1944-)
Author of The Color Purple
Random House Publicity **Ph:** 212-782-9000
1745 Broadway
New York, NY 10019
www.randomhouse.com

Walker, Andrew Kevin (1964-)
Film writer
Endeavor **Ph:** 310-248-2000
9601 Wilshire Blvd 3rd Fl **Fax:** 310-248-2020
Beverly Hills, CA 90210

Walker, Antoine (1976-)
Professional basketball player
Miami Heat **Ph:** 786-777-1000
American Airlines Arena **Fax:** 786-777-1609
601 Biscayne Blvd
Miami, FL 33132
www.nba.com/heat

Walker, Brian
With his brother Greg Walker, along with Chance Browne, creates the comic strip Hi & Lois; the three are the sons of the strip's original creators, Mort Walker and Dik Browne
King Features Syndicate Inc **Ph:** 212-455-4000
888 7th Ave 2nd Fl
New York, NY 10019
www.kingfeatures.com

Walker, DeMya (1977-)
Professional basketball player
Sacramento Monarchs **Ph:** 916-928-0000
ARCO Arena **Fax:** 916-928-8109
1 Sports Pkwy
Sacramento, CA 95834
www.wnba.com/monarchs

Walker, Greg (1949-)
With his brother (Brian Walker) and Chance Browne, creates the comic strip Hi & Lois (the three are the sons of the strip's original creators, Mort Walker & Dik Browne); also works on Beetle Bailey, another creation of Mort Walker
King Features Syndicate Inc **Ph:** 212-455-4000
888 7th Ave 2nd Fl
New York, NY 10019
www.kingfeatures.com

Walker, Javon (1978-)
Professional football player
Denver Broncos **Ph:** 303-649-9000
13655 Broncos Pkwy **Fax:** 303-649-9354
Englewood, CO 80112
www.denverbroncos.com

Walker, Jonny (1974-)
Professional soccer player
Columbus Crew **Ph:** 614-447-2739
Columbus Crew Stadium **Fax:** 614-447-4109
1 Black & Gold Blvd
Columbus, OH 43211
columbus.crew.mlsnet.com

Walker, Mort (1923-)
Creator of the comic strips Beetle Bailey and, with Dik Browne, Hi & Lois; founded the Museum of Cartoon Art
King Features Syndicate Inc **Ph:** 212-455-4000
888 7th Ave 2nd Fl
New York, NY 10019
www.kingfeatures.com

Walkup, Robert E (1937-)
Mayor of Tucson, Arizona
PO Box 27210 **Ph:** 520-791-4201
Tucson, AZ 85726 **Fax:** 520-791-5348
www.ci.tucson.az.us/mayor

Wallace, Barbara Brooks
Author of Victorian mystery/melodrama (Peppermints in the Parlor), the Miss Switch books, and other books for young readers
Simon & Schuster Books for Young Readers **Ph:** 212-698-7000
1230 Ave of the Americas
New York, NY 10020
www.barbarabrookswallace.com

Wallace, Ben (1974-)
Professional basketball player
Detroit Pistons **Ph:** 248-377-0100
Palace at Auburn Hills **Fax:** 248-377-4262
4 Championship Dr
Auburn Hills, MI 48326
www.nba.com/pistons

Wallace, Chris (1947-)
Host of FOX News Sunday with Chris Wallace, a Sunday morning public affairs program; also contributes to FNC's political and election news coverage
FOX News Channel **Ph:** 202-824-6300
400 N Capitol St NW Suite 550
Washington, DC 20001
www.foxnews.com/fnctv

Wallace, George (1952-)
Comedian
International Creative Management **Ph:** 310-550-4000
8942 Wilshire Blvd
Beverly Hills, CA 90211

Wallace, Gerald (1982-)
Professional basketball player
Charlotte Bobcats **Ph:** 704-357-0252
100 Hive Dr **Fax:** 704-357-0289
Charlotte, NC 28217
www.nba.com/bobcats

Wallace, Kelly
CNN national correspondent; also frequently hosts Inside Politics Sunday
CNN New York **Ph:** 212-275-7800
Time Warner Ctr
10 Columbus Cir
New York, NY 10019
www.cnn.com/CNN/anchors_reporters

Wallace, Mike (1918-)
Veteran journalist and 60 Minutes correspondent; has announced plans to retire
60 Minutes **Ph:** 212-975-2006
555 W 57th St
New York, NY 10019
www.cbsnews.com

Wallace, Rasheed (1974-)
Professional basketball player
Detroit Pistons **Ph:** 248-377-0100
Palace at Auburn Hills **Fax:** 248-377-4262
4 Championship Dr
Auburn Hills, MI 48326
www.rasheedwallace.com

Wallace, Russ
Creator of the comic panel Natural Selection
Creators Syndicate Inc **Ph:** 310-337-7003
5777 W Century Blvd Suite 700 **Fax:** 310-337-7625
Los Angeles, CA 90045
www.creators.com

Wallace, Rusty (1956-)
NASCAR driver
RWI Racing **Ph:** 704-799-3966
149 Knob Hill Rd
Mooresville, NC 28117
www.rustywallace.com

Waller, Robert James (1939-)
Author of The Bridges of Madison County
Warner Books **Ph:** 212-522-7200
c/o Author Mail
1271 Ave of the Americas
New York, NY 10020
www.twbookmark.com

Wallraff, Barbara
Contributing editor and words columnist at The Atlantic Monthly; writes the syndicated column Word Court, which answers readers questions about language (word origins, grammar, and phraseology)
King Features Syndicate Inc **Ph:** 212-455-4000
888 7th Ave 2nd Fl
New York, NY 10019
www.wordcourt.com

Walsch, Neale Donald
Author of the Conversations with God books
Conversations with God Foundation **Ph:** 541-482-8806
PMB 1150
1257 Siskiyou Blvd
Ashland, OR 97520
www.cwg.org

Walsh, James T (1947-)
US Representative from New York (Republican)
2369 Rayburn Bldg **Ph:** 202-225-3701
Washington, DC 20515 **Fax:** 202-225-4042
www.house.gov/walsh

Walsh, John (1945-)
Host of America's Most Wanted
America's Most Wanted **Ph:** 310-369-1000
FOX Broadcasting Co
10101 W Pico Blvd
Los Angeles, CA 90035
www.amw.com

Walter, Robert D
Founder, chairman, and CEO of Cardinal Health
Cardinal Health Inc **Ph:** 614-757-7700
7000 Cardinal Pl **Fax:** 614-757-6000
Dublin, OH 43017
www.cardinal.com

Walters, Barbara (1931-)
Co-owner, co-executive producer, and co-host of The View; also hosts Barbara Walters Special interview programs
The View **Ph:** 212-456-7777
320 W 66th St
New York, NY 10023
abc.go.com/daytime/theview

Walters, John P (1952-)
Director of the White House Office of National Drug Control Policy (national Drug Czar)
Office of National Drug Control Policy **Ph:** 202-395-6700 **Fax:** 202-395-7521
750 17th St NW
Washington, DC 20503
www.whitehousedrugpolicy.gov

Walters, Kirk
Editorial cartoonist for The Toledo Blade
King Features Syndicate Inc **Ph:** 212-455-4000
888 7th Ave 2nd Fl
New York, NY 10019
www.kingfeatures.com

Walton, Bill (1952-)
Former NBA star; TV sports commentator
Naismith Memorial Basketball Hall of Fame **Ph:** 413-781-6500 **Fax:** 413-781-1939
1000 W Columbus Ave **TF:** 877-446-6752
Springfield, MA 01105
www.billwalton.com

Walton, S Robson
Wal-Mart chairman (son of Wal-Mart founder Sam Walton)
Wal-Mart Stores Inc **Ph:** 479-273-4000
702 SW 8th St
Bentonville, AR 72716
www.walmartstores.com

Waltrip, Darrell (1947-)
Former race car driver; NASCAR television commentator
FOX Sports Net **Ph:** 310-369-1000
10201 W Pico Blvd
Bldg 101
Los Angeles, CA 90035
www.allwaltrip.com

Wambach, Abby (1980-)
Soccer player on the US National Team
US Soccer Federation **Ph:** 312-808-1300
1801 S Prairie Ave **Fax:** 312-808-1301
Chicago, IL 60616
www.ussoccer.com

Wambaugh, Joseph (1937-)
Author who writes about crime (fiction & nonfiction) & police (The Onion Field; The Choirboys)
Bantam Dell Publicity **Ph:** 212-782-9000
1745 Broadway
New York, NY 10019
www.randomhouse.com

Wamp, Zach (1957-)
US Representative from Tennessee (Republican)
1436 Longworth Bldg **Ph:** 202-225-3271
Washington, DC 20515 **Fax:** 202-225-3494
www.house.gov/wamp

Wang, Charles B (1944-)
Majority owner of the New York Islanders hockey franchise and the New York Dragons of the Arena Football League; founder of Computer Associates (retired 2002)
New York Islanders **Ph:** 516-501-6700
1535 Old Country Rd **Fax:** 516-501-6729
Plainview, NY 11803
www.newyorkdragons.com

Wang, Vera (1949-)
Fashion designer
225 W 39th St **Ph:** 212-575-6400
New York, NY 10018
www.verawang.com

Ward, Cam (1984-)
Professional hockey player
Carolina Hurricanes **Ph:** 919-467-7825
RBC Center **Fax:** 919-467-7030
1400 Edwards Mill Rd
Raleigh, NC 27607
www.carolinahurricanes.com

Ward, Hines (1976-)
Professional football player
Pittsburgh Steelers **Ph:** 412-432-7800
3400 S Water St **Fax:** 412-432-7878
Pittsburgh, PA 15203
www.pittsburghsteelers.com

Ward, Jonathan P
Chairman and CEO of ServiceMaster
ServiceMaster Co **Ph:** 630-663-2000
3250 Lacey Rd Suite 600
Downers Grove, IL 60515
corporate.servicemaster.com

Ward, Michael J
Chairman, president, and CEO of CSX
CSX Corp **Ph:** 904-359-3100
500 Water St 15th Fl
Jacksonville, FL 32202
www.csx.com

Ward, Sela (1956-)
Actor
Endeavor **Ph:** 310-248-2000
9601 Wilshire Blvd 3rd Fl **Fax:** 310-248-2020
Beverly Hills, CA 90210
www.fox.com/house

Ware, Chris (1967-)
Cartoonist; creator of the Acme Novelty Library, which is published weekly in New City, a Chicago alternative weekly
Drawn & Quarterly **Ph:** 514-279-2221
PO Box 48056
Montreal, QC H2V4S8
www.drawnandquarterly.com

Warhol, Andy (1928-1987)
Contemporary artist (born Andrew Warhola)
Andy Warhol Museum **Ph:** 412-237-8300
117 Sandusky St **Fax:** 412-237-8340
Pittsburgh, PA 15212
www.warhol.org

Warner, Gertrude Chandler (1890-1979)
Author of The Boxcar Children mysteries
Albert Whitman & Co **Ph:** 847-581-0033
6340 Oakton St **Fax:** 847-581-0039
Morton Grove, IL 60053
www.awhitmanco.com

Warner, John (1927-)
US Senator from Virginia (Republican)
225 Russell Bldg **Ph:** 202-224-2023
Washington, DC 20510 **Fax:** 202-224-6295
warner.senate.gov

Warner, Kurt (1971-)
Professional football player
Arizona Cardinals **Ph:** 602-379-0101
8701 S Hardy Dr **Fax:** 602-379-1819
Tempe, AZ 85284
www.azcardinals.com

Warner, Margaret
Senior correspondent on NewsHour with Jim Lehrer
MacNeil/Lehrer Productions **Ph:** 703-998-2138
2700 S Quincy St Suite 250
Arlington, VA 22206
www.pbs.org/newshour/ww/warner.html

Warner, Ty (1944-)
Founder of Ty Inc, the creator of Beanie Babies
Ty Inc **Ph:** 630-920-1515
280 Chestnut Ave **Fax:** 630-920-1980
Westmont, IL 60559

Warren, Rick (1954-)
Author of The Purpose Driven Life and pioneer of the Purpose-Driven paradigm for church health; founding pastor of Saddleback Church in Lake Forest, California, which has been named the fastest growing Baptist church in history
20 Empire Dr **Ph:** 800-723-3532
Lake Forest, CA 92630
www.purposedrivenlife.com

Warrener, Rhett (1976-)
Professional hockey player
Calgary Flames **Ph:** 403-777-2177
Pengrowth Saddledome **Fax:** 403-777-2195
555 Saddledome Rise SE
Calgary, AB T2G2W1
www.calgaryflames.com

Warsh, Kevin M (1970-)
Member of the Board of Governors of the Federal Reserve System
Federal Reserve System **Ph:** 202-452-3200
20th St & Constitution Ave NW **Fax:** 202-452-2611
Washington, DC 20551
www.federalreserve.gov/bios

Washington, Denzel (1954-)
Actor
International Creative Management **Ph:** 310-550-4000
8942 Wilshire Blvd
Beverly Hills, CA 90211

Wasserman, Dan
Editorial cartoonist for the Boston Globe
Tribune Media Services Inc **Ph:** 312-222-4444
435 N Michigan Ave Suite 1500
Chicago, IL 60611
www.comicspage.com

Wasserman Schultz, Debbie (1966-)
US Representative from Florida (Democrat)
118 Cannon Bldg **Ph:** 202-225-7931
Washington, DC 20515 **Fax:** 202-226-2052
www.house.gov/schultz

Watanabe, Hakubun
Bishop of Buddhist Churches of America
Buddhist Churches of America **Ph:** 415-776-5600
1710 Octavia St **Fax:** 415-771-6293
San Francisco, CA 94109
www.buddhistchurchesofamerica.com

Watanabe, Ken (1959-)
Actor
Endeavor **Ph:** 310-248-2000
9601 Wilshire Blvd 3rd Fl **Fax:** 310-248-2020
Beverly Hills, CA 90210
www.ne.jp/asahi/kensanan/kazuyon

Waters, Alice (1944-)
Executive chef & owner of Chez Panisse Restaurant and Cafe in Berkeley, California
Chez Panisse Restaurant & Cafe **Ph:** 510-548-5525
1517 Shattuck Ave
Berkeley, CA 94709
www.chezpanisse.com

Waters, Maxine (1938-)
US Representative from California (Democrat)
2344 Rayburn Bldg **Ph:** 202-225-2201
Washington, DC 20515 **Fax:** 202-225-7854
www.house.gov/waters

Waterston, Sam (1940-)
Actor
International Creative Management **Ph:** 310-550-4000
8942 Wilshire Blvd
Beverly Hills, CA 90211
www.nbc.com/Law_&_Order

Watson, Carlos
Provides commentary and analysis on various CNN programs on current trends as well as business and legal issues; also writes a column for CNN.com
CNN **Ph:** 404-827-1500
1 CNN Center
Atlanta, GA 30303
www.cnn.com/CNN/anchors_reporters

Watson, Diane E (1933-)
US Representative from California (Democrat)
125 Cannon Bldg **Ph:** 202-225-7084
Washington, DC 20515 **Fax:** 202-225-2422
www.house.gov/watson

Watson, Earl (1979-)
Professional basketball player
Denver Nuggets **Ph:** 303-405-1100
Pepsi Center **Fax:** 303-575-1920
1000 Chopper Cir
Denver, CO 80204
www.nba.com/nuggets

Watson, Emily (1967-)
Actor
William Morris Agency **Ph:** 310-859-4000
1 William Morris Pl **Fax:** 310-859-4462
Beverly Hills, CA 90212

Watson, James D, PhD (1928-)
Chancellor of Cold Spring Harbor Laboratory; 1962 Nobel Prize winner in Physiology or Medicine for the discovery of DNA
Cold Spring Harbor Laboratory **Ph:** 516-367-8455
PO Box 100 **Fax:** 516-367-8496
Cold Spring Harbor, NY 11724
www.cshl.edu

Watson, Paul (1950-)
A co-founder of Greenpeace and founder of the Sea Shepherd Conservation Society, which was established to protect marine wildlife
Sea Shepherd Conservation Society **Ph:** 360-370-5650
Fax: 360-370-5651
PO Box 2616
Friday Harbor, WA 98250
www.seashepherd.org

Watson, Tom (1949-)
Professional golfer
PGA Tour **Ph:** 904-285-3700
100 PGA Tour Blvd
Ponte Vedra Beach, FL 32082
www.pgatour.com/players

Watt, Melvin L (1945-)
US Representative from North Carolina (Democrat)
2236 Rayburn Bldg **Ph:** 202-225-1510
Washington, DC 20515 **Fax:** 202-225-1512
www.house.gov/watt

Wattenberg, Ben (1933-)
Moderator of Think Tank on PBS; nonfiction author; senior fellow at the American Enterprise Institute
Think Tank with Ben Wattenberg **Ph:** 202-530-2550
New River Media
4455 Connecticut Ave NW Suite C-100
Washington, DC 20008
www.pbs.org/thinktank

Watterson, Bill (1958-)
Creator of the comic strip Calvin & Hobbes
Universal Press Syndicate **Ph:** 816-932-6600
4520 Main St
Kansas City, MO 64111
www.ucomics.com

Watts, Andre (1946-)
Concert pianist
CM Artists **Ph:** 212-864-1005
127 W 96th St Suite 13-B **Fax:** 212-864-1066
New York, NY 10025
www.cmartists.com

Watts, Naomi (1968-)
Actor
Creative Artists Agency **Ph:** 310-288-4545
9830 Wilshire Blvd **Fax:** 310-288-4800
Beverly Hills, CA 90212
www.naomiwatts.com

Waugh, Eric (1963-)
Painter/performance artist
Alexandrium Fine Art Inc **Ph:** 514-684-7278
2113 St Regis Blvd Suite G **Fax:** 514-685-1717
Dollard des Ormeaux, QC H9B2M9
www.ericwaugh.com

Waxman, Henry A (1939-)
US Representative from California (Democrat)
2204 Rayburn Bldg **Ph:** 202-225-3976
Washington, DC 20515 **Fax:** 202-225-4099
www.house.gov/waxman

Wayans, Keenen Ivory (1958-)
Movie/television producer/director/writer and actor
William Morris Agency **Ph:** 310-859-4000
1 William Morris Pl **Fax:** 310-859-4462
Beverly Hills, CA 90212

Wayne, Jimmy (1972-)
Country singer
William Morris Agency **Ph:** 615-963-3000
1600 Division St Suite 300 **Fax:** 615-963-3090
Nashville, TN 37203
www.jimmywayne.com

Wayne, Reggie (1978-)
Professional football player
Indianapolis Colts **Ph:** 317-297-2658
7001 W 56th St **Fax:** 317-297-8971
Indianapolis, IN 46254
www.colts.com

Weaver, Jeff (1976-)
Professional baseball player
Los Angeles Angels of Anaheim **Ph:** 714-940-2000
Angel Stadium **Fax:** 714-940-2205
2000 Gene Autry Way
Anaheim, CA 92806
losangeles.angels.mlb.com

Weaver, Sigourney (1949-)
Actor
William Morris Agency **Ph:** 310-859-4000
1 William Morris Pl **Fax:** 310-859-4462
Beverly Hills, CA 90212

Weaver, Wayne (1935-)
Owner of the Jacksonville Jaguars football team; chairman of Shoe Carnival
Jacksonville Jaguars **Ph:** 904-633-6000
1 Alltel Stadium Pl **Fax:** 904-633-6050
Jacksonville, FL 32202
www.jaguars.com

Weaving, Hugo (1960-)
Actor
International Creative Management **Ph:** 310-550-4000
8942 Wilshire Bvd
Beverly Hills, CA 90211

Webb, Brandon (1979-)
Professional baseball player
Arizona Diamondbacks **Ph:** 602-462-6500
Bank One Ballpark **Fax:** 602-462-6600
401 E Jefferson St
Phoenix, AZ 85004
arizona.diamondbacks.mlb.com

Webber, Chris (1973-)
Professional basketball player
Philadelphia 76ers **Ph:** 215-339-7600
Wachovia Center **Fax:** 215-339-7632
3601 S Broad St
Philadelphia, PA 19148
www.nba.com/sixers

Weber, Bob Jr (1957-)
Creator of the comic strip Slylock Fox & Comics for Kids
King Features Syndicate Inc **Ph:** 212-455-4000
888 7th Ave 2nd Fl
New York, NY 10019
www.kingfeatures.com

Weber, Bob Sr (1934-)
Creator of the comic strip Moose & Molly (formerly Moose Miller)
King Features Syndicate Inc **Ph:** 212-455-4000
888 7th Ave 2nd Fl
New York, NY 10019
www.kingfeatures.com

Weddington, Sarah
Attorney who successfully argued Roe v Wade in the US Supreme Court; served as adviser to President Jimmy Carter 1978-1981
Weddington Center **Ph:** 512-478-7163
709 W 14th St
Austin, TX 78701
www.weddingtoncenter.com

Wedge, Eric (1968-)
Baseball manager
Cleveland Indians **Ph:** 216-420-4200
Jacobs Field **Fax:** 216-420-4624
2401 Ontario St
Cleveland, OH 44115
cleveland.indians.mlb.com

Wedge, Michael T
President and CEO of BJ's Wholesale Club
BJ's Wholesale Club **Ph:** 508-651-7400
1 Mercer Rd
Natick, MA 01760
www.bjsinvestor.com

Weeks, Wendell (1959-)
President and CEO of Corning
Corning Inc **Ph:** 607-974-9000
1 Riverfront Plaza
Corning, NY 14831
www.corning.com

Wegman, William (1943-)
Artist (photographs, drawings, paintings, videos); known mainly for his photographs of his weimariners in human clothes
Robert Klein Gallery **Ph:** 617-267-7997
38 Newbury St 4th Fl **Fax:** 617-267-5567
Boston, MA 02116
www.wegmanworld.com

Weider, Betty (1935-)
Former model, later a bodybuilder; a leader in the field of women's health and fitness
Weider Publications LLC **Ph:** 818-884-6800
21100 Erwin St
Woodland Hills, CA 91367
www.bettyweider.com

Weider, Joe (1923-)
Bodybuilder and publisher
Weider Publications Inc **Ph:** 818-884-6800
21100 Erwin St
Woodland Hills, CA 91367

Weight, Doug (1971-)
Professional hockey player
Carolina Hurricanes **Ph:** 919-467-7825
RBC Center **Fax:** 919-462-7030
1400 Edwards Mill Rd
Raleigh, NC 27607
www.carolinahurricanes.com

Weil, Andrew, MD (1942-)
Alternative health practitioner/author/teacher
Knopf Publishing/Author Mail **Ph:** 212-782-9000
1745 Broadway
New York, NY 10019
www.drweil.com

Weill, Sanford I (1933-)
Chairman of Citigroup
CitiGroup Inc **Ph:** 212-559-1000
399 Park Ave **Fax:** 212-793-3946
New York, NY 10043
www.citigroup.com

Weiner, Anthony D (1964-)
US Representative from New York (Democrat)
1122 Longworth Bldg **Ph:** 202-225-6616
Washington, DC 20515 **Fax:** 202-226-7253
www.house.gov/weiner

Weiner, Jonathan (1953-)
Author (The Beak of the Finch)
HarperCollins Publishers **Ph:** 212-207-7000
c/o Author Mail
10 E 53rd St
New York, NY 10022
www.jonathanweiner.com

Weir, Bill
Co-anchor of ABC News' weekend edition of Good Morning America
Good Morning America **Ph:** 212-456-7777
147 Columbus Ave
New York, NY 10023
www.abcnews.go.com/GMA

Weir, Mike (1970-)
Professional golfer
PGA Tour **Ph:** 904-285-3700
100 PGA Tour Blvd
Ponte Vedra Beach, FL 32082
www.mikeweir.com

Weir, Peter (1944-)
Film director and writer
Creative Artists Agency **Ph:** 310-288-4545
9830 Wilshire Blvd **Fax:** 310-288-4800
Beverly Hills, CA 90212

Weis, Charlie (1956-)
Football coach
University of Notre Dame Athletic Dept **Ph:** 574-631-6107
Notre Dame, IN 46556
und.collegesports.com

Weiss, Brian L, MD (1944-)
Practicing psychiatrist and author of Many Lives, Many Masters
Weiss Institute **Ph:** 305-598-8151
PO Box 560788 **Fax:** 305-598-4009
Miami, FL 33256
www.brianweiss.com

Weiss, Hedy
Theater critic
Chicago Sun-Times **Ph:** 312-321-3000
401 N Wabash Ave **Fax:** 312-321-3084
Chicago, IL 60611

Weiss, Melvyn I (1935-)
A leading plaintiffs' lawyer in securities, insurance, environmental, antitrust, and consumer class actions
Milberg Weiss Bershad & Schulman LLP **Ph:** 212-946-9326 **Fax:** 212-273-4396
1 Pennsylvania Plaza 49th Fl
New York, NY 10119
www.milbergweiss.com

Weiss, Michael (1976-)
Figure skater
Stars on Ice **Ph:** 216-436-3708
IMG
1360 E 9th St Suite 100
Cleveland, OH 44114
www.michaelweiss.org

Weisz, Rachel (1971-)
Actor
Creative Artists Agency **Ph:** 310-288-4545
9830 Wilshire Blvd **Fax:** 310-288-4800
Beverly Hills, CA 90212

Welch, Jack (1935-)
Former CEO of GE (retired); author of Jack: Straight from the Gut, which tells about his years at GE and choosing his successor
General Electric Co **Ph:** 203-373-2211
3135 Easton Tpke
Fairfield, CT 06828
www.ge.com/en/company/companyinfo/at_a_glance/bio_welch.htm

Welch, Stanton (1969-)
Choreographer; artistic director of the Houston Ballet
Houston Ballet **Ph:** 713-523-6300
1921 W Bell St
Houston, TX 77019
www.houstonballet.org

Weldon, Curt (1947-)
US Representative from Pennsylvania (Republican)
2466 Rayburn Bldg **Ph:** 202-225-2011
Washington, DC 20515 **Fax:** 202-225-8137
curtweldon.house.gov

Weldon, Dave (1953-)
US Representative from Florida (Republican)
2347 Rayburn Bldg **Ph:** 202-225-3671
Washington, DC 20515 **Fax:** 202-225-3516
weldon.house.gov

Weldon, William C (1948-)
Chairman & CEO of Johnson & Johnson
Johnson & Johnson **Ph:** 732-524-0400
1 Johnson & Johnson Plaza
New Brunswick, NJ 08933
www.investor.jnj.com/governance/bio.cfm

Weller, Jerry (1957-)
US Representative from Illinois (Republican)
108 Cannon Bldg **Ph:** 202-225-3635
Washington, DC 20515 **Fax:** 202-225-3521
weller.house.gov

Welling, Tom (1977-)
Actor
Creative Artists Agency **Ph:** 310-288-4545
9830 Wilshire Blvd **Fax:** 310-288-4800
Beverly Hills, CA 90212

Wells, Bonzi (1976-)
Professional basketball player
Sacramento Kings **Ph:** 916-928-0000
ARCO Arena **Fax:** 916-928-0727
1 Sports Pkwy
Sacramento, TN 95834
www.nba.com/kings

Wells, John (1956-)
TV series producer, writer, director
Creative Artists Agency **Ph:** 310-288-4545
9830 Wilshire Blvd **Fax:** 310-288-4800
Beverly Hills, CA 90212

Wells, Rebecca (1952-)
Author of Divine Secrets of the Ya-Ya Sisterhood
HarperCollins Publishers **Ph:** 212-207-7000
c/o Author Mail
10 E 53rd St
New York, NY 10022
www.ya-ya.com

Wells, Simon (1961-)
Animator; animation director (Prince of Egypt; Who Framed Roger Rabbit)
Endeavor **Ph:** 310-248-2000
9601 Wilshire Blvd 3rd Fl **Fax:** 310-248-2020
Beverly Hills, CA 90210

Wells, Theodore V Jr (1950-)
A top white-collar criminal defense lawyer; has successfully defended Mike Espy (US Agriculture Secretary), Raymond Donovan (US Commerce Secretary), and Michael Milken
Paul Weiss Rifkind Wharton & Garrison LLP **Ph:** 212-373-3089 **Fax:** 212-373-2217
1285 Ave of the Americas
New York, NY 10019
www.paulweiss.com

Wells, Vernon (1978-)
Professional baseball player
Toronto Blue Jays **Ph:** 416-341-1000
1 Blue Jays Way **Fax:** 416-341-1250
Toronto, ON M5V1J1
toronto.bluejays.mlb.com

Welsh, Irvine (1961-)
Fiction writer (Trainspotting; his new book is called Porn)
WW Norton & Co Inc **Ph:** 212-354-5500
500 5th Ave **Fax:** 212-869-0856
New York, NY 10110
www.wwnorton.com/catalog/featured/irvinewelsh

Wendleton, Kate
With Dale Dauten, writes Kate & Dale Talk Jobs
King Features Syndicate Inc **Ph:** 212-455-4000
888 7th Ave 2nd Fl
New York, NY 10019
www.kingfeatures.com

Wenig, Marsha
Yoga instructor and certified yoga therapist; founder of YogaKids
YogaKids International **Ph:** 800-968-0694
2501 Oriole Trail Suite 66
Long Beach, IN 46360
www.yogakids.com

Wenner, Jann S (1946-)
Editor & Publisher of Rolling Stone Magazine
Rolling Stone Magazine **Ph:** 212-484-1616
1290 Ave of the Americas
New York, NY 10104

Werbach, Adam (1973-)
Environmental activist/conservationist; former president of the Sierra Club and former executive director of the Common Assets Defense Fund; founder of Act Now Productions, a producer of videos, films, and commercials
Act Now Productions **Ph:** 415-241-2510
660 York St Suite 102 **Fax:** 415-241-2511
San Francisco, CA 94110

Werner, Tom (1950-)
Independent TV producer and co-founder (with Marcy Carsey) of Carsey-Werner; a co-owner of the Boston Red Sox baseball club
Carsey-Werner LLC **Ph:** 818-655-5598
12001 Ventura Pl 6th Fl
Studio City, CA 91604
www.cwm.com

Wernick, Allan
Writes a syndicated column on Immigration & Citizenship
King Features Syndicate Inc **Ph:** 212-455-4000
888 7th Ave 2nd Fl
New York, NY 10019
www.kingfeatures.com

Wertheimer, Linda (1943-)
Senior National Correspondent; provides analysis and reporting on all NPR News programs
National Public Radio **Ph:** 202-513-2000
635 Massachusetts Ave NW **Fax:** 202-513-3329
Washington, DC 20001
www.npr.org

Wesley, David (1970-)
Professional basketball player
Houston Rockets **Ph:** 713-758-7200
Toyota Center **Fax:** 713-758-7396
1510 Polk St
Houston, TX 77002
www.nba.com/rockets

Wesley, Glen (1968-)
Professional hockey player
Carolina Hurricanes **Ph:** 919-467-7825
RBC Center **Fax:** 919-462-7030
1400 Edwards Mill Rd
Raleigh, NC 27607
www.carolinahurricanes.com

West, Diana
Washington Times columnist; also writes a weekly commentary column syndicated by Newspaper Enterprise Association
Newspaper Enterprise Assn **Ph:** 212-293-8500
200 Madison Ave
New York, NY 10016
www.unitedfeatures.com

West, Kanye (1977-)
Rap artist
Creative Artists Agency **Ph:** 310-288-4545
9830 Wilshire Blvd **Fax:** 310-288-4800
Beverly Hills, CA 90212
www.kanyewest.com

Westbrook, Brian (1979-)
Professional football player
Philadelphia Eagles **Ph:** 215-463-2500
NovaCare Complex **Fax:** 215-339-5464
1 NovaCare Way
Philadelphia, PA 19145
www.philadelphiaeagles.com

Westhead, Paul
Basketball coach
Phoenix Mercury **Ph:** 602-514-8333
America West Arena **Fax:** 602-514-8303
201 E Jefferson St
Phoenix, AZ 85004
www.wnba.com/mercury

Westheimer, Ruth, PhD (1928-)
Sex educator, therapist, and media psychologist; her syndicated column Ask Dr. Ruth provides advice on sex, love, and relationships
King Features Syndicate Inc **Ph:** 212-455-4000
888 7th Ave 2nd Fl
New York, NY 10019
www.drruth.com

Westhoven, Jennifer
New York Stock Exchange correspondent for CNN's Headline News
CNN **Ph:** 404-827-1500
1 CNN Center
Atlanta, GA 30303
www.cnn.com/CNN/anchors_reporters

Westmoreland, Lynn (1950-)
US Representative from Georgia (Republican)
1118 Longworth Bldg **Ph:** 202-225-5901
Washington, DC 20515 **Fax:** 202-225-2515
www.house.gov/westmoreland

Weston, W Galen
Canadian businessman; one of the wealthiest men in the world
George Weston Ltd **Ph:** 416-922-2500
22 St Clair Ave E **Fax:** 416-960-4395
Toronto, ON M4T2S7
www.weston.ca

Westwood, Lee (1973-)
Professional golfer
Gaylord Sports Management **Ph:** 480-483-9500
13845 N Northsight Blvd
Suite 200
Scottsdale, AZ 85260
www.gaylordsports.com

Wetherell, David S
Chairman of CMGI and a member of the company's venture capital affiliate, @Ventures I & II
CMGI Inc **Ph:** 781-663-5001
1100 Winter St Suite 4600
Waltham, MA 02451
www.cmgi.com

Wevers, Olivier
A principal dancer with Pacific Northwest Ballet
Pacific Northwest Ballet **Ph:** 206-441-9411
301 Mercer St **Fax:** 206-441-2440
Seattle, WA 98109
www.olivierwevers.com

Wexler, Robert (1961-)
US Representative from Florida (Democrat)
213 Cannon Bldg **Ph:** 202-225-3001
Washington, DC 20515 **Fax:** 202-225-5974
www.house.gov/wexler

Wexner, Leslie H
Founder, chairman, and CEO of Limited Brands
Limited Brands **Ph:** 614-415-7000
3 Limited Pkwy
Columbus, OH 43230
www.limited.com/investor

Weyrich, Paul (1942-)
Chairman and CEO of the Free Congress Foundation, a conservative think tank
Free Congress Foundation **Ph:** 202-546-3000
717 2nd St NE **Fax:** 202-543-5605
Washington, DC 20002
www.freecongress.org

Whalen, Lindsay (1982-)
Professional basketball player
Connecticut Sun **Ph:** 860-862-4000
1 Mohegan Sun Blvd **Fax:** 860-862-4010
Uncasville, CT 06382
www.wnba.com/sun

Whamond, Dave
Creator of the comic strip Reality Check
United Feature Syndicate **Ph:** 212-293-8500
200 Madison Ave
New York, NY 10016
www.unitedfeatures.com

Whedon, Joss (1964-)
Writer for movies & TV
Creative Artists Agency **Ph:** 310-288-4545
9830 Wilshire Blvd **Fax:** 310-288-4800
Beverly Hills, CA 90212
www.josswhedon.net

Wheeldon, Christopher
Resident choreographer at New York City Ballet
New York City Ballet **Ph:** 212-870-5656
New York State Theater **Fax:** 212-870-7791
20 Lincoln Center
New York, NY 10023
www.nycballet.com/about/cwheeldon.html

Whelan, Gloria (1923-)
Author of Homeless Bird and other books for young readers
HarperCollins Children's Books **Ph:** 212-261-6500
1350 Ave of the Americas
New York, NY 10019
gloriawhelan.com

Whelan, M Edward III
President of the Ethics & Public Policy Center; an attorney and a former law clerk to Supreme Court Justice Antonin Scalia; has served in positions of responsibility in all three branches of the federal government
Ethics & Public Policy Center **Ph:** 202-682-1200
1015 15th St NW Suite 900 **Fax:** 202-408-0632
Washington, DC 20005
www.eppc.org

Whelan, Wendy (1967-)
A principal dancer with the New York City Ballet; has also performed in film and on television
New York City Ballet **Ph:** 212-870-5656
New York State Theater **Fax:** 212-870-7791
20 Lincoln Center
New York, NY 10023
www.nycballet.com/about/dancers.html

Whisenant, John
Basketball coach
Sacramento Monarchs **Ph:** 916-928-0000
ARCO Arena **Fax:** 916-928-8109
1 Sports Pkwy
Sacramento, CA 95834
www.wnba.com/monarchs

Whitacre, Edward E Jr
Chairman and CEO of AT & T Inc; was chairman and CEO of SBC Communications, which acquired AT & T in 2005 and adopted the AT & T name
AT & T Inc **Ph:** 210-821-4105
175 E Houston
San Antonio, TX 78205
sbc.merger-news.com/bios/whitacre.html

Whitaker, Forest (1961-)
Actor
William Morris Agency **Ph:** 310-859-4000
1 William Morris Pl **Fax:** 310-859-4462
Beverly Hills, CA 90212

Whitaker, Julian, MD
Physician and author of several books on health and wellness
Whitaker Wellness Institute **Ph:** 949-851-1550
4321 Birch St Suite 100 **Fax:** 949-851-9970
Newport Beach, CA 92660 **TF:** 800-826-1550
www.drwhitaker.com

White, Armond
New York Press film critic
New York Press **Ph:** 212-244-2282
333 7th Ave 14th Fl **Fax:** 212-244-9864
New York, NY 10001

White, Bill (1932-)
Mayor of Houston
PO Box 1562 **Ph:** 713-247-2200
Houston, TX 77251 **Fax:** 713-247-1067
www.houstontx.gov/mayor

White, Bryan (1974-)
Country singer
Buddy Lee Attractions **Ph:** 615-244-4336
38 Music Sq East Suite 300 **Fax:** 615-726-0429
Nashville, TN 37203
www.bryanwhite.com

White, EB (1899-1985)
Author of books for children (Charlotte's Web, Stuart Little, Trumpet of the Swan)
HarperCollins Children's Books **Ph:** 212-261-6500
1350 Ave of the Americas
New York, NY 10019
www.ebwhitebooks.com

White, Edmund (1940-)
Gay writer (fiction & nonfiction, various genres)
Vintage/Anchor Publicity **Ph:** 212-572-2420
1745 Broadway 20th Fl
New York, NY 10019
www.edmundwhite.com

White, Miles D
Chairman and CEO of Abbott Laboratories
Abbott Laboratories **Ph:** 847-937-6100
100 Abbott Pk Rd
Abbott Park, IL 60064
www.abbottinvestor.com

White, Ruth (1942-)
Writer of fiction for young adults (Sweet Creek Holler, Belle Prater's Boy)
Random House Children's Books **Ph:** 212-782-9000
Publicity Dept
1745 Broadway
New York, NY 10019
www.randomhouse.com/kids

White, Somers
Business speaker/coach/consultant
Somers White Co Inc **Ph:** 602-952-9292
4736 N 44th St **Fax:** 602-840-5970
Phoenix, AZ 85018
www.somerswhite.com

White, Vanna (1957-)
Co-host of Wheel of Fortune
Wheel of Fortune **Ph:** 310-244-1234
Robert Young Bldg **Fax:** 310-244-2233
10202 W Washington Blvd Suite 2000
Culver City, CA 90232
www.wheeloffortune.com

Whitehead, John W (1946-)
Attorney & author; founder of the Rutherford Institute, which gives free legal services to people whose constitutional human rights have been threatened/violated; co-counsel in Paula Jones' sexual harassment suit against Bill Clinton
Rutherford Institute **Ph:** 434-978-3888
PO Box 7482 **Fax:** 434-978-1789
Charlottesville, VA 22906
www.rutherford.org

Whitfield, Ed (1943-)
US Representative from Kentucky (Republican)
301 Cannon Bldg **Ph:** 202-225-3115
Washington, DC 20515 **Fax:** 202-225-3547
www.house.gov/whitfield

Whitfield, Fredricka
CNN news anchor
CNN **Ph:** 404-827-1500
1 CNN Center
Atlanta, GA 30303
www.cnn.com/CNN/anchors_reporters

Whitman, Meg (1956-)
President & CEO of eBay
eBay Inc **Ph:** 408-376-7400
2145 Hamilton Ave **Fax:** 408-376-7401
San Jose, CA 95125
pages.ebay.com/aboutebay.html

Whitney, Ray (1972-)
Professional hockey player
Carolina Hurricanes **Ph:** 919-467-7825
RBC Center **Fax:** 919-462-7030
1400 Edwards Mill Rd
Raleigh, NC 27607
www.carolinahurricanes.com

Wiatt, James
CEO of the William Morris Agency
William Morris Agency Inc **Ph:** 310-859-4000
1 William Morris Pl **Fax:** 310-859-4462
Beverly Hills, CA 90212

Wicker, Roger F (1951-)
US Representative from Mississippi (Republican)
2455 Rayburn Bldg **Ph:** 202-225-4306
Washington, DC 20515 **Fax:** 202-225-3549
www.house.gov/wicker

Wickham, DeWayne
USA Today columnist
USA Today **Ph:** 703-854-3400
7950 Jones Branch Dr
McLean, VA 22108
www.usatoday.com/news/opinion/index.htm

Wie, Michelle (1989-)
Professional golfer
William Morris Agency **Ph:** 212-586-5100
1325 Ave of the Americas **Fax:** 212-246-3583
New York, NY 10019

Wiencek, Henry
Historian and author of An Imperfect God: George Washington, His Slaves, and the Creation of America; also wrote the biographical work, The Hairstons
Farrar Straus & Giroux **Ph:** 212-741-6900
19 Union Sq W
New York, NY 10003
www.fsgbooks.com

Wiesel, Elie (1928-)
Holocaust survivor, human rights activist, educator, author, and winner of the 1986 Nobel Prize for Peace
Elie Wiesel Foundation for Humanity **Ph:** 212-490-7777
Fax: 212-490-6006
529 5th Ave Suite 1802
New York, NY 10017
www.eliewieselfoundation.org

Wieseltier, Leon (1952-)
Literary editor at The New Republic
The New Republic **Ph:** 202-508-4444
1331 H St NW Suite 700 **Fax:** 202-628-9383
Washington, DC 20005

Wiesner, David (1956-)
Children's picture-book author/illustrator (Tuesday; The Three Pigs)
Houghton Mifflin Children's Books **Ph:** 617-351-5000
222 Berkeley St 8th Fl
Boston, MA 02116
www.houghtonmifflinbooks.com/authors/wiesner

Wiest, Diane (1948-)
Actor
International Creative Management **Ph:** 310-550-4000
8942 Wilshire Blvd
Beverly Hills, CA 90211

Wilansky, Heywood
President & CEO of Retail Ventures Inc, the holding company of DSW, Filene's Basement, and Value City Department Stores
Retail Ventures Inc **Ph:** 614-471-4722
3241 Westerville Rd
Columbus, OH 43224

Wilczek, Frank, PhD (1951-)
Winner (with two other scientists) of the 2004 Nobel Prize in Physics for the discovery of asymptotic freedom in the theory of the strong interaction
MIT Dept of Physics **Ph:** 617-253-0284
77 Massachusetts Ave **Fax:** 617-253-8554
Bldg 6-113 Rm 6-305
Cambridge, MA 02139
web.mit.edu/physics/facultyandstaff

Wilder, C John (1958-)
Chairman and CEO of TXU Corp, an electric energy company
TXU Corp **Ph:** 214-812-4600
1601 Bryan St **Fax:** 214-812-8419
Dallas, TX 75201
www.txucorp.com

Wilder, Don
Co-creator, with Bill Rechin, of the comic strip Crock
King Features Syndicate Inc **Ph:** 212-455-4000
888 7th Ave 2nd Fl
New York, NY 10019
www.kingfeatures.com

Wilder, Gene (1933-)
Actor
David Shapira & Assoc **Ph:** 310-967-0480
193 N Robertson Blvd **Fax:** 310-659-4177
Beverly Hills, CA 90211

Wilder, Janos (1954-)
Chef and owner of Janos & J Bar restaurants in Tucson; also opened KAI Restaurant, which the Arizona Republic named Phoenix's Best Southwest Restaurant, at the Sheraton Wild Horse Pass Resort and Spa
Janos Restaurant **Ph:** 520-615-6100
3770 E Sunrise Dr **Fax:** 520-615-3334
Tucson, AZ 85718
www.janos.com

Wilder, L Douglas (1931-)
Mayor of Richmond and former governor of the state of Virginia
900 E Broad St Suite 200 **Ph:** 804-646-7977
Richmond, VA 23219 **Fax:** 804-646-3027
www.ci.richmond.va.us

WilderBrathwaite, Gloria, MD (1964-)
Pediatrician; medical director of the Children's Health Project of DC
Children's Health Project of DC **Ph:** 202-884-3033
111 Michigan Ave NW
Washington, DC 20010
www.childrenshealthfund.org/dc.html

Wilderotter, Maggie
Chairman & CEO of Citizens Communications
Citizens Communications Co **Ph:** 203-614-5600
3 High Ridge Pk
Stamford, CT 06905
www.czn.net/About

Wiley, Richard E
A leading communications attorney and former chairman of the Federal Communications Commission
Wiley Rein & Fielding LLP **Ph:** 202-719-7010
1776 K St NW **Fax:** 202-719-7049
Washington, DC 20006
www.wrf.com

Wilf, Zygmunt
Owner of the Minnesota Vikings football franchise
Minnesota Vikings **Ph:** 952-828-6500
9520 Viking Dr **Fax:** 952-828-6540
Eden Prairie, MN 55344
www.vikings.com

Wilhelm, James A
President and CEO of Standard Parking
Standard Parking Corp **Ph:** 312-274-2000
900 N Michigan Ave Suite 1600 **Fax:** 312-640-6169
Chicago, IL 60611
www.standardparking.com

Wilkens, Lenny (1937-)
Former NBA player, coach; Hall of Fame member as both player and coach
Naismith Memorial Basketball Hall of Fame **Ph:** 413-781-6500
Fax: 413-781-1939
1000 W Columbus Ave **TF:** 877-446-6752
Springfield, MA 01105
www.hoophall.com

Wilkins, Gregory C (1957-)
President & CEO of Barrick Gold Corp, a top Canadian company
Barrick Gold Corp **Ph:** 416-861-9911
Canada Trust Tower
161 Bay St Suite 3700
Toronto, ON M5J2S1
www.barrick.com

Wilkins, Jeff (1972-)
Professional football player
Saint Louis Rams **Ph:** 314-982-7267
1 Rams Way **Fax:** 314-770-9261
Earth City, MO 63045
www.stlouisrams.com

Wilkinson, Bruce (1947-)
Author of The Prayer of Jabez and other spiritual titles; conducts seminars
Multnomah Publishers **Ph:** 541-549-1144
PO Box 1720
Sisters, OR 97759
www.brucewilkinson.com

Wilkinson, Darlene Marie
Author of The Prayer of Jabez for Women; wife of Dr. Bruce Wilkinson, who wrote The Prayer of Jabez
Multnomah Publishers **Ph:** 541-659-1144
PO Box 1720
Sisters, OR 97759
www.darlenewilkinson.com

Wilkinson, Signe
Editorial cartoonist
Philadelphia Daily News **Ph:** 215-854-2000
PO Box 7788
Philadelphia, PA 19101
postwritersgroup.com/wilkinson.htm

Will, George (1941-)
Syndicated columnist (commentary); has also been a contributing analyst on ABC
Washington Post Writers Group **Ph:** 202-334-6375
Fax: 202-334-5669
1150 15th St NW 9th Fl
Washington, DC 20071
www.postwritersgroup.com

Willard, Nancy (1936-)
Poet, novelist, and author of children's books (A Visit to William Blake's Inn; The Tale I Told Sasha)
Vassar College **Ph:** 845-437-5650
English Dept **Fax:** 845-437-7578
124 Raymond Ave
Box 744
Poughkeepsie, NY 12604
www.twbookmark.com

Willems, Mo
Creator of Cartoon Network's Sheep in the Big City, Nickelodeon's The Off-Beats, and the Suzie Kabloozie animated shorts on Sesame Street; also writes books for children
Hyperion Books for Children **Ph:** 212-633-4400
114 5th Ave
New York, NY 10010
www.mowillems.com

Williams, Andy (1927-)
Singer
Andy Williams Moon River Theater **Ph:** 417-334-4500
2500 W Highway 76
Branson, MO 65616
www.andywilliams.com

Williams, Andy (1977-)
Professional soccer player
Real Salt Lake **Ph:** 801-924-8585
515 S 700 East Suite 2R **Fax:** 801-933-4713
Salt Lake City, UT 84102
www.mlsnet.com/MLS/rsl/

Williams, Anthony A (1951-)
Mayor of Washington, DC
1350 Pennsylvania Ave NW **Ph:** 202-727-6263
Washington, DC 20004 **Fax:** 202-727-0505
dc.gov

Williams, Bernie (1968-)
Professional baseball player
New York Yankees **Ph:** 718-293-4300
Yankee Stadium **Fax:** 718-293-8414
161st St & River Ave
Bronx, NY 10451
newyork.yankees.mlb.com

Williams, Brian (1959-)
Anchor and managing editor of NBC Nightly News
NBC Nightly News with Brian Williams **Ph:** 212-664-4249
30 Rockefeller Plaza
New York, NY 10112
www.msnbc.msn.com/id/3689499

Williams, Bruce
Writes the syndicated column Smart Money in which he answers readers' questions on personal finance; also hosts a financial radio talk show
Newspaper Enterprise Assn **Ph:** 212-293-8500
200 Madison Ave
New York, NY 10016
www.unitedfeatures.com

Williams, CK (1936-)
Poet
Farrar Straus & Giroux **Ph:** 212-741-6900
19 Union Sq W
New York, NY 10003
www.fsgbooks.com

Williams, DJ (1982-)
Professional football player
Denver Broncos **Ph:** 303-649-9000
13655 Broncos Pkwy **Fax:** 303-649-9354
Englewood, CO 80112
www.denverbroncos.com

Williams, Eric (1972-)
Professional basketball player
Toronto Raptors **Ph:** 416-366-3865
40 Bay St Suite 400 **Fax:** 416-359-9198
Toronto, ON M5J2X2
www.nba.com/raptors

Williams, Hank Jr (1949-)
Country singer/songwriter
William Morris Agency **Ph:** 615-963-3000
1600 Division St Suite 300 **Fax:** 615-963-3090
Nashville, TN 37203
www.hankjr.com

Williams, Jason (1975-)
Professional basketball player
Miami Heat **Ph:** 786-777-1000
American Airlines Arena **Fax:** 786-777-1609
601 Biscayne Blvd
Miami, FL 33132
www.nba.com/heat

Williams, John (1932-)
Composer of film scores, ceremonial music, and concert works; is also a conductor
Gorfaine/Schwartz Agency **Ph:** 818-260-8500
4111 W Alameda Ave Suite 509
Burbank, CA 91505
www.gsamusic.com/composers.html

Williams, Juan (1954-)
Political contributor and anchor of daytime live coverage for FOX News
FOX News Channel **Ph:** 202-824-6300
400 N Capitol St NW Suite 550
Washington, DC 20001
www.foxnews.com/fnctv

Williams, Lucinda (1953-)
Songwriter/singer (rock & folk)
High Road Touring **Ph:** 415-332-9292
751 Bridgeway 3rd Fl **Fax:** 415-332-4692
Sausalito, CA 94965
www.lucindawilliams.com

Williams, Madieu (1981-)
Professional football player
Cincinnati Bengals **Ph:** 513-621-3550
1 Paul Brown Stadium **Fax:** 513-621-3570
Cincinnati, OH 45202
www.bengals.com

Williams, Maurice (1982-)
Professional basketball player
Milwaukee Bucks **Ph:** 414-227-0500
Bradley Center **Fax:** 414-227-0543
1001 N 4th St
Milwuakee, WI 53203
www.nba.com/bucks

Williams, Michelle (1980-)
Actor
Gersh Agency **Ph:** 310-274-6611
232 N Canon Dr
Beverly Hills, CA 90210

Williams, Miller (1930-)
Poet
University of Illinois Press **Ph:** 217-333-0950
1325 S Oak St **Fax:** 217-244-8082
Champaign, IL 61820
www.press.uillinois.edu

Williams, Montel (1956-)
Television daytime talk show host
Montel Williams Show **Ph:** 212-830-0300
433 W 53rd St **Fax:** 212-262-4602
New York, NY 10019
www.montelshow.com

Williams, Patricia J (1951-)
Columbia University law professor; columnist for The Nation
The Nation **Ph:** 212-209-5400
33 Irving Pl 8th Fl **Fax:** 212-982-9000
New York, NY 10003
www.thenation.com

Williams, Pete
NBC news correspondent covering the Justice Dept & the Supreme Court; was a press official on Capitol Hill and was Congressman Dick Cheney's press secretary and later, Asst Secretary of Defense for Public Affairs
NBC News **Ph:** 202-885-4200
4001 Nebraska Ave NW
Washington, DC 20016
www.msnbc.msn.com/id/3689499

Williams, Ricky (1977-)
Professional football player (currently suspended)
Miami Dolphins **Ph:** 954-452-7000
7500 SW 30th St **Fax:** 954-452-7055
Davie, FL 33314
www.miamidolphins.com

Williams, Robin (1951-)
Comedian and actor
Creative Artists Agency **Ph:** 310-288-4545
9830 Wilshire Blvd **Fax:** 310-288-4800
Beverly Hills, CA 90212

Williams, Roy (1980-)
Professional football player
Detroit Lions **Ph:** 313-216-4000
222 Republic Dr **Fax:** 313-216-4069
Allen Park, MI 48101
www.detroitlions.com

Williams, Roy (1981-)
Professional football player
Dallas Cowboys **Ph:** 972-556-9900
1 Cowboys Pkwy **Fax:** 972-556-9304
Irving, TX 75063
www.dallascowboys.com

Williams, Serena (1981-)
Professional tennis player
IMG Inc **Ph:** 216-522-1200
IMG Center **Fax:** 216-522-1145
1360 E 9th St Suite 100
Cleveland, OH 44114
www.serenawilliams.com

Williams, Ted (1925-)
Photographer
Gallery M **Ph:** 303-331-8400
2830 E 3rd Ave
Denver, CO 80206
www.gallerym.com

Williams, Ted (1918-2002)
Legendary outfielder for the Boston Red Sox
495 Ted Williams Ct **Ph:** 352-746-4767
Hernando, FL 34442 **Fax:** 352-746-2006
www.tedwilliams.com

Williams, Treat (1951-)
Actor
One Entertainment **Ph:** 310-550-9500
9220 Sunset Blvd Suite 306
Los Angeles, CA 90069

Williams, Vanessa (1963-)
Singer, actor; former Miss America
International Creative Management
8942 Wilshire Blvd
Beverly Hills, CA 90211
www.vanessawilliams.de
Ph: 310-550-4000

Williams, Venus (1980-)
Professional tennis player
IMG Inc
IMG Center
1360 E 9th St Suite 100
Cleveland, OH 44114
www.venuswilliams.com
Ph: 216-522-1200
Fax: 216-522-1145

Williams, Vera
Author/illustrator of children's books (A Chair for My Mother; More, More, More Said the Baby)
HarperCollins Children's Books
1350 Ave of the Americas
New York, NY 10019
www.harperchildrens.com
Ph: 212-261-6500

Williams, Walter E, PhD (1936-)
Economics professor at George Mason University; also writes the weekly syndicated column A Minority View
Creators Syndicate Inc
5777 W Century Blvd Suite 700
Los Angeles, CA 90045
www.creators.com/opinion.html
Ph: 310-337-7003
Fax: 310-337-7625

Williams, Woody (1966-)
Professional baseball player
San Diego Padres
Petco Park
PO Box 122000
San Diego, CA 92112
sandiego.padres.mlb.com
Ph: 619-795-5000
Fax: 619-497-5339

Williamson, Corliss (1973-)
Professional basketball player
Sacramento Kings
ARCO Arena
1 Sports Pkwy
Sacramento, CA 95834
www.nba.com/kings
Ph: 916-928-0000
Fax: 916-929-0727

Williamson, Kevin (1965-)
Screenwriter/director (Dawson's Creek, Scream, I Know What You Did Last Summer...)
William Morris Agency
1 William Morris Pl
Beverly Hills, CA 90212
Ph: 310-859-4000
Fax: 310-859-4462

Williamson, Marianne (1953-)
Spiritual/self-help author (A Return to Love; Everyday Grace; A Woman's Worth) and speaker
Hay House Inc
PO Box 5100
Carlsbad, CA 92018
www.marianne.com
Ph: 760-431-7695
Fax: 800-650-5115

Williamson, Michael
Photojournalist who is especially well-known for his pictures of the homeless
Washington Post
1150 15th St NW
Washington, DC 20071
www.washingtonpost.com
Ph: 202-334-6000

Williamson, Mykelti (1960-)
Actor
Agency for the Performing Arts
9200 Sunset Blvd Suite 900
Beverly Hills, CA 90069
Ph: 310-273-0744
Fax: 310-888-4242

Willis, Bruce (1955-)
Actor
Creative Artists Agency
8930 Wilshire Blvd
Beverly Hills, CA 90212
www.brucewillis.com
Ph: 310-288-4545
Fax: 310-288-4800

Willis, Dave
Animator, producer; co-creator of Space Ghost: Coast to Coast and Aqua Teen Hunger Force for Cartoon Network
Cartoon Network
Williams Street
1065 Williams St
Atlanta, GA 30309
www.aquateencentral.com
Ph: 404-885-2263

Willis, Dontrelle (1982-)
Professional baseball player
Florida Marlins
Dolphins Stadium
2267 Dan Marino Blvd
Miami, FL 33056
florida.marlins.mlb.com
Ph: 305-626-7400
Fax: 305-626-7428

Willis, Gerri
Anchor of CNN's Open House
CNN New York
Time Warner Ctr
10 Columbus Cir
New York, NY 10019
www.cnn.com/CNN/anchors_reporters
Ph: 212-275-7800

Wilmington, Michael
Chief movie critic at the Chicago Tribune
Chicago Tribune **Ph:** 312-222-3232
435 N Michigan Ave **Fax:** 312-222-4674
Chicago, IL 60611

Wilpon, Fred
Co-founder and chairman of the board of Sterling Equities; holdings include the New York Mets baseball club
New York Mets **Ph:** 718-507-6387
Shea Stadium **Fax:** 718-507-6395
123-01 Roosevelt Ave
Flushing, NY 11368
sterling-equities.com

Wilson, Adrian (1979-)
Professional football player
Arizona Cardinals **Ph:** 602-379-0101
8701 S Hardy Dr **Fax:** 602-379-1819
Tempe, AZ 85284
www.azcardinals.com

Wilson, Al (1977-)
Professional football player
Denver Broncos **Ph:** 303-649-9000
13655 Broncos Pkwy **Fax:** 303-649-9354
Englewood, CO 80112
www.denverbroncos.com

Wilson, August (1945-)
Playwright (Fences and The Piano Lesson)
Plume Drama Publicity **Ph:** 212-366-2000
375 Hudson St
New York, NY 10014
www.augustwilson.com

Wilson, Brenda
NPR Science Desk correspondent and editor
National Public Radio **Ph:** 202-513-2000
635 Massachusetts Ave NW **Fax:** 202-513-3329
Washington, DC 20001
www.npr.org

Wilson, Brian (1942-)
Songwriter, music producer, musician, singer; a founding member of the Beach Boys
International Creative Management **Ph:** 310-550-4000
8942 Wilshire Blvd
Beverly Hills, CA 90211
www.brianwilson.com

Wilson, Cassandra (1955-)
Jazz singer
Brad Simon Organization **Ph:** 212-730-2132
155 W 46th St 5th Fl **Fax:** 212-730-2895
New York, NY 10036
www.cassandrawilson.com

Wilson, Craig (1976-)
Professional baseball player
Pittsburgh Pirates **Ph:** 412-323-5000
PNC Park **Fax:** 412-323-5009
115 Federal St
Pittsburgh, PA 15212
pittsburgh.pirates.mlb.com

Wilson, Edward O, PhD (1929-)
Sociobiologist and an authority on ants; author of several groundbreaking works, including Sociobiology: The New Synthesis and On Human Nature
Harvard University **Ph:** 617-495-3045
Museum of Comparative Zoology
Entomology Dept MCZ Labs Rm 419
26 Oxford St
Cambridge, MA 02138

Wilson, Eugene (1980-)
Professional football player
New England Patriots **Ph:** 508-543-8200
1 Patriots Pl **Fax:** 508-543-0285
Foxboro, MA 02035
www.patriots.com

Wilson, Heather (1960-)
US Representative from New Mexico (Republican)
318 Cannon Bldg **Ph:** 202-225-6316
Washington, DC 20515 **Fax:** 202-225-4975
wilson.house.gov

Wilson, Joe (1947-)
US Representative from South Carolina (Republican)
212 Cannon Bldg **Ph:** 202-225-2452
Washington, DC 20515 **Fax:** 202-225-2455
joewilson.house.gov

Wilson, Lanford (1937-)
Playwright (Talley's Folly; Fifth of July)
International Creative Management **Ph:** 212-556-5600
40 W 57th St 17th Fl
New York, NY 10019

Wilson, Luke (1971-)
Actor
Creative Artists Agency **Ph:** 310-288-4545
9830 Wilshire Blvd **Fax:** 310-288-4800
Beverly Hills, CA 90212

Wilson, Nancy (1937-)
Singer/song stylist (pop, jazz); host of Jazz Profiles on NPR
John Levy Enterprises Inc **Ph:** 626-398-8179
1828 Coolidge Ave **Fax:** 626-398-7563
Altadena, CA 91001
www.missnancywilson.com

Wilson, Owen (1968-)
Actor
United Talent Agency **Ph:** 310-273-6700
9560 Wilshire Blvd 5th Fl **Fax:** 310-247-1111
Beverly Hills, CA 90212

Wilson, Preston (1974-)
Professional baseball player
Houston Astros **Ph:** 713-259-8000
Minute Maid Park **Fax:** 713-259-8981
501 Crawford St
Houston, TX 77002
houston.astros.mlb.com

Wilson, Rainn (1968-)
Actor
3 Arts Entertainment **Ph:** 310-888-3200
9460 Wilshire Blvd 7th Fl **Fax:** 310-888-3210
Beverly Hills, CA 90212
www.nbc.com/The_Office

Wilson, Ralph C Jr
Owner & chairman of the Buffalo Bills football franchise
Buffalo Bills **Ph:** 716-648-1800
Ralph Wilson Stadium
1 Bills Dr
Orchard Park, NY 14127
www.buffalobills.com

Wilson, Ron (1955-)
Hockey coach
San Jose Sharks **Ph:** 408-287-7070
HP Pavilion at San Jose **Fax:** 408-999-5797
525 W Santa Clara St
San Jose, CA 95113
www.sjsharks.com

Wilson, Tom II
Draws the comic panel Ziggy, the cartoon originally created by his father, Tom Wilson
Universal Press Syndicate **Ph:** 816-932-6600
4520 Main St
Kansas City, MO 64111
www.amuniversal.com/ups/features

Wilson, Woody
Writes the comic strips Judge Parker and Rex Morgan MD
King Features Syndicate Inc **Ph:** 212-455-4000
888 7th Ave 2nd Fl
New York, NY 10019
www.kingfeatures.com

Winans, CeCe (1964-)
Gospel singer
Puresprings Gospel **Ph:** 615-371-1575
5214 Maryland Way Suite 300 **Fax:** 615-371-1571
Brentwood, TN 37027
www.cecewinans.com

Winblad, Ann L
A software industry entrepreneur and technology leader; co-founding Partner of Hummer Winblad Venture Partners
Hummer Winblad Venture Partners **Ph:** 415-979-9600
Fax: 415-979-9601
2 S Park 2nd Fl
San Francisco, CA 94107
www.humwin.com

Winchester, Simon (1944-)
Nonfiction author (Krakatoa; The Professor and the Madman)
HarperCollins Publishers **Ph:** 212-207-7000
c/o Author Mail
10 E 53rd St
New York, NY 10022
www.simonwinchester.com

Winfield, Antoine (1977-)
Professional football player
Minnesota Vikings **Ph:** 952-828-6500
9520 Viking Dr **Fax:** 952-828-6540
Eden Prairie, MN 55344
www.vikings.com

Winfield, Dave (1951-)
Former baseball player; Hall of Fame member
National Baseball Hall of Fame & Museum **Ph:** 607-547-7200
Fax: 607-547-2044
25 Main St **TF:** 888-425-5633
Cooperstown, NY 13326
www.baseballhalloffame.org

Winfrey, Oprah (1954-)
Founder & chairman of Harpo Inc; a television pioneer, philanthropist, magazine founder, creator of Oprah's Book Club, co-founder of Oxygen Media, producer, actor, and owner of Harpo Films, a film production company
Harpo Inc **Ph:** 312-633-1000
110 N Carpenter St
Chicago, IL 60607
www.oprah.com

Winger, Debra (1955-)
Actor
IFA Talent Agency **Ph:** 310-659-5522
8730 Sunset Blvd Suite 490 **Fax:** 310-659-3344
Los Angeles, CA 90069

Winkler, Henry (1945-)
Producer; actor
International Creative Management **Ph:** 310-550-4000
8942 Wilshire Blvd
Beverly Hills, CA 90211

Winkler, Matthew (1955-)
Editor-in-chief of Bloomberg News
Bloomberg News **Ph:** 212-318-2000
731 Lexington Ave
New York, NY 10022

Winn, Randy (1974-)
Professional baseball player
San Francisco Giants **Ph:** 415-972-2000
AT & T Park
24 Willie Mays Plaza
San Francisco, CA 94107
sanfrancisco.giants.mlb.com

Winokur, Barton J
Attorney specializing in mergers & acquisitions and international law; represented Getty Oil in its acquisition by Texaco
Dechert LLP **Ph:** 215-994-2505
Cira Centre **Fax:** 215-994-2222
2929 Arch St
Philadelphia, PA 19104
www.dechert.com

Winship, Peg
Psychotherapist who writes Ask Beth, the nationally syndicated advice column on teens and parenting issues
Creators Syndicate Inc **Ph:** 310-337-7003
5777 W Century Blvd Suite 700 **Fax:** 310-337-7625
Los Angeles, CA 90045
www.creators.com

Winslet, Kate (1975-)
Actor
Creative Artists Agency **Ph:** 310-288-4545
9830 Wilshire Blvd **Fax:** 310-288-4800
Beverly Hills, CA 90212

Winston, George (1949-)
Concert pianist and music producer; also plays guitar and harmonica
Skyline Music **Ph:** 603-586-7171
PO Box 38 **Fax:** 603-586-7068
Jefferson, NH 03583
www.georgewinston.com

Winter, Donald C, PhD
Secretary of the US Navy
US Dept of the Navy **Ph:** 703-695-3131
The Pentagon **Fax:** 703-693-9545
Washington, DC 20350
www.navy.mil

Winters, Brian (1952-)
Basketball coach
Indiana Fever **Ph:** 317-917-2500
Conseco Fieldhouse **Fax:** 317-917-2899
125 S Pennsylvania St
Indianapolis, IN 46204
www.wnba.com/fever

Wirthlin, Richard B, PhD
Founder of WirthlinWorldwide, a strategic opinion research and consulting firm that is now part of Harris Interactive; was strategist & pollster for President Ronald Reagan
Harris Interactive **Ph:** 585-272-8400
135 Corporate Woods
Rochester, NY 14623
www.harrisinteractive.com

Wirtz, William W (1929-)
Owner of the Chicago Blackhawks hockey team
Chicago Blackhawks **Ph:** 312-455-7000
United Center **Fax:** 312-455-7041
1901 W Madison St
Chicago, IL 60612
www.chicagoblackhawks.com

Wise, Gary
Co-creator (with Lance Aldrich) of the comic panel Real Life Adventures
Universal Press Syndicate **Ph:** 816-932-6600
4520 Main St
Kansas City, MO 64111
www.amuniversal.com/ups/features

Wisniewski, David (1953-2002)
Creator of children's books using intricate cut paper illustrations (Golem; Rain Player)
Donna Wisniewski **Ph:** 301-865-5158
4109 Cove Ct
Monrovia, MD 21770
www.davidwisniewski.com

Witherspoon, Reese (1976-)
Actor
Endeavor **Ph:** 310-248-2000
9601 Wilshire Blvd 3rd Fl **Fax:** 310-248-2020
Beverly Hills, CA 90210

Witherspoon, Will (1980-)
Professional football player
Saint Louis Rams **Ph:** 314-982-7267
1 Rams Way **Fax:** 314-770-9261
Earth City, MO 63045
www.stlouisrams.com

Witkin, Joel-Peter (1939-)
Photographer; his pictures are aimed at finding beauty within the grotesque
Fahey/Klein Gallery **Ph:** 323-934-2250
148 N La Brea **Fax:** 323-934-4243
Los Angeles, CA 90036
www.faheykleingallery.com

Witten, Jason (1982-)
Professional football player
Dallas Cowboys **Ph:** 972-556-9900
1 Cowboys Pkwy **Fax:** 972-556-9304
Irving, TX 75063
www.dallascowboys.com

Wittman, Vanessa Ames (1967-)
Executive Vice President & CFO of Adelphia
Adelphia Communications Corp **Ph:** 303-268-6300
5619 DTC Pkwy
Greenwood Village, CO 80111

Woetzel, Damian (1968-)
A principal dancer with the New York City Ballet; has also choreographed a number of ballets
New York City Ballet **Ph:** 212-870-5656
New York State Theater **Fax:** 212-870-7791
20 Lincoln Center
New York, NY 10023
www.nycballet.com/about/dancers.html

Wolcott, Marion Post (1910-1990)
Photographer
Kathleen Ewing Gallery **Ph:** 202-328-0955
1609 Connecticut Ave **Fax:** 202-462-1019
Washington, DC 20009
www.kathleenewinggallery.com

Wolf, Dick (1946-)
Television series creator/writer and executive producer (including the Law and Order programs)
United Talent Agency **Ph:** 310-273-6700
9560 Wilshire Blvd 5th Fl **Fax:** 310-247-1111
Beverly Hills, CA 90212
www.nbc.com/Law_&_Order

Wolf, Frank R (1939-)
US Representative from Virginia (Republican)
241 Cannon Bldg **Ph:** 202-225-5136
Washington, DC 20515 **Fax:** 202-225-0437
www.house.gov/wolf

Wolfe, Sidney, MD
Director of Public Citizen's Health Research Group
Public Citizen's Health Research Group **Ph:** 202-588-1000
1600 20th St NW
Washington, DC 20009

Wolfe, Tom (1931-)
Writer (The Right Stuff; The Electric Kool-Aid Acid Test; Bonfire of the Vanities)
Farrar Straus & Giroux **Ph:** 212-741-6900
19 Union Sq W
New York, NY 10003
www.tomwolfe.com

Wolff, Bobby
Bridge champion; writes the syndicated column The Aces on Bridge
United Feature Syndicate **Ph:** 212-293-8500
200 Madison Ave
New York, NY 10016
www.unitedfeatures.com

Wolff, Josh (1977-)
Professional soccer player
Kansas City Wizards **Ph:** 816-920-9300
2 Arrowhead Dr **Fax:** 816-920-4774
Kansas City, MO 64129
kc.wizards.mlsnet.com

Wolff, Lewis
Co-owner and managing partner of the Oakland Athletics baseball franchise
Oakland Athletics **Ph:** 510-638-4900
Network Assoc Coliseum **Fax:** 510-568-3770
7000 Coliseum Way
Oakland, CA 94621
oakland.athletics.mlb.com

Wolff, Tobias (1945-)
Writer of novels, memoirs, and short stories, including the memoir of childhood, This Boy's Life
Stanford University **Ph:** 650-723-2635
Bldg 460
Margaret Jacks Hall
Stanford, CA 94305
english.stanford.edu

Wolff, Virginia Euwer (1937-)
Author of books for teens (Probably Still Nick Swansen; True Believer; Make Lemonade)
Simon & Schuster Books for Young Readers **Ph:** 212-698-7000
1230 Ave of the Americas
New York, NY 10020
www.simonsays.com

Wolfowitz, Paul D (1943-)
President of the World Bank; former Deputy Secretary of Defense and a leading proponent of the war in Iraq
World Bank Group **Ph:** 202-473-1000
1818 H St NW **Fax:** 202-477-6391
Washington, DC 20433
web.worldbank.org

Wolyniec, John (1977-)
Professional soccer player
Columbus Crew **Ph:** 614-447-2739
Columbus Crew Stadium **Fax:** 614-447-4109
1 Black & Gold Blvd
Columbus, OH 43211
columbus.crew.mlsnet.com

Womack, Lee Ann (1966-)
Country singer
Buddy Lee Attractions **Ph:** 615-244-4336
38 Music Sq East Suite 300 **Fax:** 615-726-0429
Nashville, TN 37203
www.leeannwomack.com

Wonder, Stevie (1950-)
Singer; composer
Creative Artists Agency **Ph:** 310-288-4545
9830 Wilshire Blvd **Fax:** 310-288-4800
Beverly Hills, CA 90212
steviewonder.free.fr

Wong, Janet (1962-)
Author of books for young readers of all ages; also writes poems and stories
Simon & Schuster Books for Young Readers **Ph:** 212-698-7000
1230 Ave of the Americas
New York, NY 10020
www.janetwong.com

Woo, John (1946-)
Movie director and producer
Creative Artists Agency **Ph:** 310-288-4545
9830 Wilshire Blvd **Fax:** 310-288-4800
Beverly Hills, CA 90212

Wood, Audrey
Author/illustrator of books for younger children (King Bidgood's in the Bathtub; Heckedy Peg; The Bunyans); several of her books are illustrated by her husband, Don Wood
Harcourt Children's Books **Ph:** 212-592-1000
15 E 26th St
New York, NY 10010
www.audreywood.com

Wood, Elijah (1981-)
Actor
William Morris Agency **Ph:** 310-859-4000
1 William Morris Pl **Fax:** 310-859-4462
Beverly Hills, CA 90212
www.lordoftherings.net

Wood, Evan Rachel (1987-)
Actor
International Creative Management **Ph:** 310-550-4000
8942 Wilshire Blvd
Beverly Hills, CA 90211

Wood, Gordon S (1933-)
Historian and author (The Americanization of Benjamin Franklin; The Radicalism of the American Revolution)
Penguin Publicity **Ph:** 212-355-2000
375 Hudson St
New York, NY 10014
us.penguingroup.com

Wood, Kerry (1977-)
Professional baseball player
Chicago Cubs **Ph:** 773-404-2827
Wrigley Field **Fax:** 773-404-4129
1060 W Addison St
Chicago, IL 60613
chicago.cubs.mlb.com

Wood, Robert L
Chairman, president, and CEO of Chemtura, a specialty chemicals company formed in 2005 with the merger of Crompton Corp and Great Lakes Chemical Corp
Chemtura Corp **Ph:** 203-573-2000
199 Benson Rd **Fax:** 203-573-3323
Middlebury, CT 06749
www.chemtura.com

Woodard, Alfre (1952-)
Actor
William Morris Agency **Ph:** 310-859-4000
1 William Morris Pl **Fax:** 310-859-4462
Beverly Hills, CA 90212
abc.go.com/primetime/desperate

Woodruff, Bob
Anchor of World News Tonight (currently recovering from injuries suffered in Iraq)
ABC News **Ph:** 212-456-7777
77 W 66th St
New York, NY 10023
www.abcnews.go.com/WNT

Woods, James (1947-)
Actor
International Creative Management **Ph:** 310-550-4000
8942 Wilshire Blvd
Beverly Hills, CA 90211

Woods, Stuart (1938-)
Mystery writer (including the Stone Barrington books)
Putnam Publicity **Ph:** 212-366-2000
375 Hudson St
New York, NY 10014
www.stuartwoods.com

Woods, Tiger (1975-)
Professional golfer; real name is Eldrick Woods
IMG Inc **Ph:** 216-522-1200
IMG Center **Fax:** 216-522-1145
1360 E 9th St Suite 100
Cleveland, OH 44114
www.tigerwoods.com

Woodson, Charles (1976-)
Professional football player
Oakland Raiders **Ph:** 510-864-5000
1220 Harbor Bay Pkwy **Fax:** 510-864-5134
Alameda, CA 94502
www.raiders.com

Woodson, Jacqueline (1963-)
Author of books for young readers, mostly for young adults
GP Putnam's Sons Books for Young Readers **Ph:** 212-366-2000
Publicity Dept
345 Hudson St
New York, NY 10014
www.jacquelinewoodson.com

Woodson, Mike (1958-)
Basketball coach
Atlanta Hawks **Ph:** 404-827-3800
Centennial Tower **Fax:** 404-827-3880
101 Marietta St NW Suite 1900
Atlanta, GA 30303
www.nba.com/hawks

Woodward, Bob (1943-)
A reporter and editor at The Washington Post for 33 years; co-authored All the President's Men with Carl Bernstein; has also written several other books, including (in 2004) Plan of Attack and (in 2003) Bush at War
Simon & Schuster **Ph:** 212-698-7000
1230 Ave of the Americas
New York, NY 10020
www.simonsays.com

Woodward, Joanne (1930-)
Actor
International Creative Management **Ph:** 310-550-4000
8942 Wilshire Blvd
Beverly Hills, CA 90211

Woodward, Lydia
TV writer/producer
Creative Artists Agency **Ph:** 310-288-4545
9830 Wilshire Blvd **Fax:** 310-288-4800
Beverly Hills, CA 90212

Woolsey, Lynn C (1937-)
US Representative from California (Democrat)
2263 Rayburn Bldg **Ph:** 202-225-5161
Washington, DC 20515 **Fax:** 202-225-5163
woolsey.house.gov

Worley, Darryl (1964-)
Country singer
CAA Nashville **Ph:** 615-383-8787
3310 West End Ave 5th Fl **Fax:** 615-383-4937
Nashville, TN 37203
www.darrylworley.com

Wouk, Herman (1915-)
Author (The Caine Mutiny)
Warner Books **Ph:** 212-522-7200
c/o Author Mail
1271 Ave of the Americas
New York, NY 10020
www.twbookmark.com

Wozniak, Steve (1950-)
Co-founder of Apple Computer and designer of early Apple Computer products
Wheels of Zeus Inc **Ph:** 408-358-6030
15595 Los Gatos Blvd **Fax:** 408-358-6090
Los Gatos, CA 95032
www.woz.com

Wright, Charles (1935-)
Poet and poetry editor
Farrar Straus & Giroux **Ph:** 212-741-6900
19 Union Sq W
New York, NY 10003
www.fsgbooks.com

Wright, Chely (1970-)
Country singer
CAA Nashville **Ph:** 615-383-8787
3310 West End Ave 5th Fl **Fax:** 615-383-4937
Nashville, TN 37203
www.chely.com

Wright, Clifford A
Cookbook author; a writer and cook specializing in the regional cuisines of the Mediterranean and Italy
Doe Coover Agency **Ph:** 781-721-6000
PO Box 668 **Fax:** 781-721-6727
Winchester, MA 01890
www.cliffordawright.com

Wright, David
Overseas correspondent for ABC News
ABC News **Ph:** 212-456-7777
77 W 66th St
New York, NY 10023
www.abcnews.go.com/WNT

Wright, Don
Editorial cartoonist for The Palm Beach Post
Tribune Media Services Inc **Ph:** 312-222-4444
435 N Michigan Ave Suite 1500
Chicago, IL 60611
www.comicspage.com

Wright, Frank Lloyd (1867-1959)
Architect
Frank Lloyd Wright Foundation **Ph:** 480-860-2700
Fax: 480-391-4009
Taliesin West
PO Box 4430
Scottsdale, AZ 85261
www.franklloydwright.org

Wright, Jaret (1975-)
Professional baseball player
New York Yankees **Ph:** 718-293-4300
Yankee Stadium **Fax:** 718-293-8414
161st St & River Ave
Bronx, NY 10451
newyork.yankees.mlb.com

Wright, Jeffrey (1965-)
Actor
Creative Artists Agency **Ph:** 310-288-4545
9830 Wilshire Blvd **Fax:** 310-288-4800
Beverly Hills, CA 90212

Wright, Larry
Creator of syndicated comic strip Kit 'N' Carlyle; editorial cartoonist at The Detroit News
Newspaper Enterprise Assn **Ph:** 212-293-8500
200 Madison Ave
New York, NY 10016
www.unitedfeatures.com

Wright, Robert C
Chairman and CEO of NBC Universal
NBC Universal **Ph:** 212-664-4444
30 Rockefeller Plaza **Fax:** 212-664-4085
New York, NY 10022
www.nbcuni.com

Wright, Steven (1955-)
Comedian
United Talent Agency **Ph:** 310-273-6700
9560 Wilshire Blvd 5th Fl **Fax:** 310-247-1111
Beverly Hills, CA 90212
www.stevenwright.com

Wright, Tom
Commissioner of the Canadian Football League
Canadian Football League **Ph:** 416-322-9650
50 Wellington St E 3rd Fl **Fax:** 416-322-9651
Toronto, ON M5E1C8
www.cfl.ca

Wrigley, William Jr (1964-)
Chairman, president, and CEO of Wrigley
Wm Wrigley Jr Co **Ph:** 312-644-2121
410 N Michigan Ave **Fax:** 312-644-0015
Chicago, IL 60611
www.wrigley.com

Wu, David (1955-)
US Representative from Oregon (Democrat)
1023 Longworth Bldg **Ph:** 202-225-0855
Washington, DC 20515 **Fax:** 202-225-9497
www.house.gov/wu

Wuhl, Robert (1951-)
Actor; comedian
Gersh Agency **Ph:** 310-274-6611
232 N Canon Dr
Beverly Hills, CA 90210

Wuntch, Philip
Movie critic
Dallas Morning News **Ph:** 214-977-8222
508 Young St **Fax:** 214-977-8321
Dallas, TX 75202

Wyden, Ron (1949-)
US Senator from Oregon (Democrat)
516 Hart Bldg **Ph:** 202-224-5244
Washington, DC 20510 **Fax:** 202-228-2717
wyden.senate.gov

Wyeth, Andrew (1917-)
Contemporary realist painter
Frank E Fowler **Ph:** 423-821-3081
PO Box 247 **Fax:** 423-821-5779
Lookout Mountain, TN 37350
www.awyeth.com

Wygod, Martin J
Chairman of the Board of Directors of WebMD
WebMD Corp **Ph:** 201-703-3400
669 River Dr **Fax:** 201-703-3401
Center 2
Elmwood Park, NJ 07407
www.webmd.com/corporate

Wyland (1956-)
Marine artist (painter, sculptor, muralist)
Wyland Worldwide Headquarters **Ph:** 949-643-7070 **Fax:** 949-643-7099
5 Columbia
Aliso Viejo, CA 92656
www.wyland.com

Wyle, Noah (1971-)
Actor
International Creative Management **Ph:** 310-550-4000
8942 Wilshire Blvd
Beverly Hills, CA 90211

Wyman, Carolyn
Writes Supermarket Sampler (with Bonnie Tandy Leblang), a weekly column about new grocery store items
Universal Press Syndicate **Ph:** 816-932-6600
4520 Main St
Kansas City, MO 64111
www.amuniversal.com/ups/features

Wynn, Albert R (1951-)
US Representative from Maryland (Democrat)
434 Cannon Bldg **Ph:** 202-225-8699
Washington, DC 20515 **Fax:** 202-225-8714
wynn.house.gov

Wynne, Michael W
Secretary of the US Air Force
US Dept of the Air Force **Ph:** 703-697-7376
Pentagon Rm 4E540 **Fax:** 703-695-8809
Washington, DC 20330
www.af.mil/library/afchain.asp

Wynonna (1964-)
Country singer; originally performed with her mother, Naomi, as The Judds
William Morris Agency **Ph:** 615-963-3000
1600 Division St Suite 300 **Fax:** 615-963-3090
Nashville, TN 37203
www.wynonna.com

X

Xingjian, Gao (1940-)
Novelist, playwright, essayist, director, and painter; the first Chinese writer ever to win the Nobel Prize for Literature (in 2000)
HarperCollins Publishers **Ph:** 212-207-7000
c/o Author Mail
10 E 53rd St
New York, NY 10022
www.harpercollins.com

Y

Yagudin, Alexei (1980-)
Figure skater
Stars on Ice **Ph:** 216-436-3708
IMG
1360 E 9th St Suite 100
Cleveland, OH 44114
www.alexeiyagudin.com

Yamaguchi, Kristi (1971-)
Figure skater
IMG Inc **Ph:** 216-522-1200
IMG Center **Fax:** 216-522-1145
1360 E 9th St Suite 100
Cleveland, OH 44114
www.alwaysdream.org

Yamaguchi, Roy
Founding chef/owner of Roy's restaurants, which feature Hawaiian Fusion cuisine
Roy's Restaurants **Ph:** 949-261-2424
1300 Dove St Suite 105 **Fax:** 949-261-2626
Newport Beach, CA 92660
www.roysrestaurant.com

Yang, Geoffrey Y
A founding partner of Redpoint Ventures, a venture capitalist firm
Redpoint Ventures **Ph:** 650-926-5600
3000 Sand Hill Rd **Fax:** 650-854-5762
Bldg 2 Suite 290
Menlo Park, CA 94025
www.redpoint.com

Yang, Jerry (1968-)
Co-founder and Chief Yahoo of Yahoo! Inc
Yahoo! Inc **Ph:** 408-349-3300
701 1st Ave **Fax:** 408-349-3301
Sunnyvale, CA 94089
docs.yahoo.com/info/pr

Yang, John
ABC News Middle East correspondent
ABC News **Ph:** 212-456-7777
77 W 66th St
New York, NY 10023
www.abcnews.go.com/WNT

Yankelovich, Daniel
Chairman & co-founder (with Cyrus Vance) of Public Agenda; noted social scientist/pollster
Public Agenda **Ph:** 212-686-6610
6 E 39th St **Fax:** 212-889-3461
New York, NY 10016
www.publicagenda.org

Yard, Sherry
Executive pastry chef at Wolfgang Puck's Spago Beverly Hills
Spago Beverly Hills **Ph:** 310-385-0880
176 N Canon Dr **Fax:** 310-385-9690
Beverly Hills, CA 90210
www.wolfgangpuck.com/rest/fine/spago

Yardley, Jonathan (1939-)
Book critic
Washington Post **Ph:** 202-334-6000
1150 15th St NW
Washington, DC 20071

Yashin, Alexei (1973-)
Professional hockey player
New York Islanders **Ph:** 516-501-6700
1535 Old Country Rd **Fax:** 516-501-6729
Plainview, NY 11803
www.newyorkislanders.com

Yawney, Trent (1965-)
Hockey coach; former professional hockey player
Chicago Blackhawks **Ph:** 312-455-7000
United Center **Fax:** 312-455-7041
1901 W Madison St
Chicago, IL 60612
www.chicagoblackhawks.com

Yearwood, Trisha (1964-)
Country singer
William Morris Agency **Ph:** 615-963-3000
1600 Division St Suite 300 **Fax:** 615-936-3090
Nashville, TN 37203
www.trishayearwood.com

Yee, Rodney
Yoga instructor; co-director of Piedmont Yoga Studio in Oakland, California
Piedmont Yoga Studio **Ph:** 510-652-3336
3966 Piedmont Ave
PO Box 11458
Oakland, CA 94611
www.yeeyoga.com

Yelle, Stephane (1974-)
Professional hockey player
Calgary Flames **Ph:** 403-777-2177
Pengrowth Saddledome **Fax:** 403-777-2195
555 Saddledome Rise SE
Calgary, AB T2G2W1
www.calgaryflames.com

Yellen, Janet L, PhD (1946-)
Professor of economics and a former chair of the Council of Economic Advisers (Clinton Administration); former member of the Board of Governors of the Federal Reserve
University of California at Berkeley **Ph:** 510-643-1397
Fax: 510-643-1420
Haas School of Business
545 Student Services Bldg #1900
Berkeley, CA 94720
www.haas.berkeley.edu

Yep, Laurence (1948-)
Author of books for children and young adults, including Dragonwings and Dragon's Gate
HarperCollins Children's Books **Ph:** 212-261-6500
1350 Ave of the Americas
New York, NY 10019
www.harperchildrens.com

Yerba Buena
An 11-piece charanga orchestra based in Seattle; their music is Latin rock/alternative
William Morris Agency **Ph:** 310-859-4000
1 William Morris Pl **Fax:** 310-859-4462
Beverly Hills, CA 90212
www.yerbabuenamusic.com

Yevtushenko, Yevgeny (1933-)
Russian poet & teacher
University of Tulsa **Ph:** 918-631-2856
Dept of English **Fax:** 918-631-3033
365 Zink Hall
Tulsa, OK 74104
www.cas.utulsa.edu/english

Yglesias, Matthew
Columnist for The American Prospect
The American Prospect **Ph:** 202-776-0730
2000 L St NW Suite 717 **Fax:** 202-776-0740
Washington, DC 20036
www.prospect.org

Yoakam, Dwight (1956-)
Country singer/songwriter and actor
William Morris Agency **Ph:** 615-963-3000
1600 Division St Suite 300 **Fax:** 615-963-3090
Nashville, TN 37203
www.dwightyoakam.com

Yolen, Jane (1939-)
Prolific author of children's books (How Do Dinosaurs Say Goodnight; Owl Moon), fantasy, and science fiction; has been called the Hans Christian Andersen of America
HarperCollins Children's Books **Ph:** 212-261-6500
1350 Ave of the Americas
New York, NY 10019
www.janeyolen.com

Yoran, Amit
Entrepreneur, investor, and technology expert; president and CEO of In-Q-Tel and former Director of the National Cyber Security Div at the US Dept of Homeland Security
In-Q-Tel Inc **Ph:** 703-248-3000
PO Box 12407 **Fax:** 703-248-3001
Arlington, VA 22219
www.in-q-tel.org

York, Denise DeBartolo
Chair & owner of the San Francisco 49ers football franchise
San Francisco 49ers **Ph:** 408-562-4949
4949 Centennial Blvd
Santa Clara, CA 95054
www.sf49ers.com

Yost, Ned (1954-)
Baseball manager
Milwaukee Brewers **Ph:** 414-902-4400
Miller Park **Fax:** 414-902-4515
1 Brewers Way
Milwaukee, WI 53214
milwaukee.brewers.mlb.com

Yost, R David
CEO of AmerisourceBergen, the world's leading pharmaceutical distributor
AmerisourceBergen Corp **Ph:** 610-727-7000
1300 Morris Dr Suite 100 **Fax:** 610-727-3600
Chesterbrook, PA 19087
www.amerisourcebergen.com

Young, Andrew (1932-)
Statesman, businessman, ordained minister, human rights activist; former US Congressman, mayor of Atlanta, and Ambassador to the United Nations; top aide to Dr. Martin Luther King, Jr. during the civil rights movement
Good Works International **Ph:** 404-527-8484
303 Peachtree St NE **Fax:** 404-527-3827
Suite 4420
Atlanta, GA 30308
www.goodworksintl.com

Young, CW Bill (1930-)
US Representative from Florida (Republican)
2407 Rayburn Bldg **Ph:** 202-225-5961
Washington, DC 20515 **Fax:** 202-225-9764
www.house.gov/young

Young, Dean
Produces the comic strip Blondie, which he took over from his father, Chic Young, who was Blondie's original creator
King Features Syndicate Inc **Ph:** 212-455-4000
888 7th Ave 2nd Fl
New York, NY 10019
www.blondie.com

Young, Don (1933-)
US Representative from Alaska (Republican)
2111 Rayburn Bldg **Ph:** 202-225-5765
Washington, DC 20515 **Fax:** 202-225-0425
donyoung.house.gov

Young, Ed (1931-)
Illustrator of books for children (Lon Po Po; Cats Are Cats)
Philomel Books Publicity **Ph:** 212-366-2000
345 Hudson St
New York, NY 10014
us.penguingroup.com

Young, Michael (1976-)
Professional baseball player
Texas Rangers **Ph:** 817-273-5222
Ameriquest Field in Arlington **Fax:** 817-273-5294
1000 Ballpark Way
Arlington, TX 76011
texas.rangers.mlb.com

Young, Neil (1945-)
Guitarist and singer; also performs with Crosby Stills & Nash as Crosby Stills Nash & Young
Warner Bros Records **Ph:** 818-846-9090
PO Box 6868 **Fax:** 818-846-8474
Burbank, CA 91510
www.neilyoung.com

Young, Steve (1961-)
Studio analyst for ESPN; former professional football player (quarterback) and member of the Pro Football Hall of Fame
ESPN **Ph:** 860-585-2000
ESPN Plaza
935 Middle St
Bristol, CT 06010
sports.espn.go.com/espntv/espnGuide

Young, Vince (1983-)
Texas Longhorns football player drafted by the Tennessee Titans in 2006
Tennessee Titans **Ph:** 615-565-4000
460 Great Circle Rd **Fax:** 615-565-4006
Nashville, TN 37228
www.titansonline.com

Youssef, Michael (1948-)
Television & radio evangelist (Leading the Way)
Leading the Way **Ph:** 404-841-0100
PO Box 20100
Atlanta, GA 30325
www.leadingtheway.org

Yzerman, Steve (1965-)
Professional hockey player
Detroit Red Wings **Ph:** 313-396-7544
Joe Louis Arena **Fax:** 313-567-0296
600 Civic Center Dr
Detroit, MI 48226
www.detroitredwings.com

Z

Zabor, Rafi (1946-)
Fiction writer (The Bear Comes Home) and occasional jazz drummer
WW Norton & Co Inc **Ph:** 212-354-5500
500 5th Ave **Fax:** 212-869-0856
New York, NY 10110
www.wwnorton.com

Zahn, Paula (1956-)
Anchors Paula Zahn Now, a discussion/interview program on CNN
CNN New York **Ph:** 212-275-7800
Time Warner Ctr
10 Columbus Cir
New York, NY 10019
www.cnn.com/CNN/anchors_reporters

Zakaria, Fareed (1964-)
Editor of Newsweek International; also writes a syndicated column on world affairs
Washington Post Writers Group **Ph:** 202-334-6375
Fax: 202-334-5669
1150 15th St NW 9th Fl
Washington, DC 20071
www.fareedzakaria.com

Zaloom, Paul (1951-)
Puppeteer and satirist
Washington Square Arts & Film **Ph:** 212-253-0333
Fax: 212-253-0330
310 Bowery 2nd Fl
New York, NY 10012
www.paulzaloom.com

Zambrano, Carlos (1981-)
Professional baseball player
Chicago Cubs **Ph:** 773-404-2827
Wrigley Field **Fax:** 773-404-4129
1060 W Addison St
Chicago, IL 60613
chicago.cubs.mlb.com

Zander, Benjamin (1939-)
Conductor of the Boston Philharmonic; also a speaker on the subject of fulfilling potential
Boston Philharmonic **Ph:** 617-236-0999
295 Huntington Ave Suite 210 **Fax:** 617-236-8613
Boston, MA 02115
www.benjaminzander.com

Zander, Edward J
Chairman and CEO of Motorola
Motorola Inc **Ph:** 847-576-5000
1303 E Algonquin Rd **Fax:** 847-576-2101
Schaumburg, IL 60196
www.motorola.com

Zane, Frank (1942-)
Champion bodybuilder and former Mr Olympia
Zane Experience **Ph:** 800-323-7537
PO Box 4088
La Mesa, CA 91944
www.frankzane.com

Zavagnin, Kerry (1974-)
Professional soccer player
Kansas City Wizards **Ph:** 816-920-9300
2 Arrowhead Dr **Fax:** 816-920-4774
Kansas City, MO 64129
kc.wizards.mlsnet.com

Zednick, Richard (1976-)
Professional hockey player
Montreal Canadiens **Ph:** 514-932-2582
1275 Saint Antoine St W **Fax:** 514-932-9296
Montreal, QC H3C5L2
www.canadiens.com

Zelasko, Jeanne (1966-)
Sports commentator
FOX Sports Net **Ph:** 310-369-1000
10201 W Pico Blvd
Bldg 101
Los Angeles, CA 90035

Zelinsky, Paul O
Illustrator of books for children (Doodler Doodling; Knick-Knack Paddywhack!; The Wheels on the Bus); won the Caldecott Medal for his retelling of Rapunzel
HarperCollins Children's Books **Ph:** 212-261-6500
1350 Ave of the Americas
New York, NY 10019
www.paulozelinsky.com

Zellweger, Renee (1969-)
Actor
Creative Artists Agency **Ph:** 310-288-4545
9830 Wilshire Blvd **Fax:** 310-288-4800
Beverly Hills, CA 90212

Zemeckis, Robert (1952-)
Movie producer/director
Rogers & Cowan PR **Ph:** 310-854-8100
Pacific Design Center **Fax:** 310-854-8101
8687 Melrose Ave 7th Fl
Los Angeles, CA 90069

Zerhouni, Elias A, MD (1951-)
Director of the National Institutes of Health
National Institutes of Health **Ph:** 301-496-2433
9000 Rockville Pike **Fax:** 301-402-2700
Bldg 1 Rm 126
Bethesda, MD 20892
www.nih.gov

Zeta-Jones, Catherine (1969-)
Actor
William Morris Agency **Ph:** 310-859-4000
1 William Morris Pl **Fax:** 310-859-4462
Beverly Hills, CA 90212

Zetterberg, Henrik (1980-)
Professional hockey player
Detroit Red Wings **Ph:** 313-396-7544
Joe Louis Arena **Fax:** 313-567-0296
600 Civic Center Dr
Detroit, MI 48226
www.detroitredwings.com

Zewail, Ahmed H, PhD (1946-)
Director of the National Science Foundation Laboratory for Molecular Sciences at CalTech; winner of the 1999 Nobel Prize in Chemistry for his studies of the transition states of chemical reactions using femtosecond spectroscopy
Arthur Amos Noyes Laboratory of Chemical Physics **Ph:** 626-395-6536 **Fax:** 626-792-8456
California Institute of Technology
MC 127-72
1200 E California Blvd
Pasadena, CA 91125
www.its.caltech.edu/~femto

Zhitnik, Alexei (1972-)
Professional hockey player
New York Islanders **Ph:** 516-501-6700
1535 Old Country Rd **Fax:** 516-501-6729
Plainview, NY 11803
www.newyorkislanders.com

Ziegler, Jack (1942-)
New Yorker Magazine cartoonist
Cartoon Bank **Ph:** 914-478-5527
New Yorker Magazine **Fax:** 914-478-5604
28 Wells Ave Bldg 3 4th Fl
Yonkers, NY 10701
www.cartoonbank.com

Ziemer, James L
President and CEO of Harley-Davidson
Harley-Davidson Inc **Ph:** 414-342-4680
3700 W Juneau Ave
Milwaukee, WI 53208
www.harley-davidson.com

Ziglar, Zig (1926-)
Motivational speaker, author, corporate trainer; also writes the syndicated column Message for Daily Living
Ziglar Training Systems **Ph:** 972-233-9191
15303 Dallas Pkwy Suite 550 **Fax:** 972-991-1853
Addison, TX 75001 **TF:** 800-527-0306
www.zigziglar.com

Zillmer, John J
Chairman and CEO of Allied Waste Industries
Allied Waste Industries Inc **Ph:** 480-627-2700
15880 N Greenway Hayden Loop Suite 100
Scottsdale, AZ 85260
www.alliedwaste.com

Zimmer, George (1948-)
Founder & CEO of Men's Wearhouse
Men's Wearhouse Inc **Ph:** 510-657-9821
40650 Encyclopedia Cir **Fax:** 510-623-9764
Fremont, CA 94538
www.menswearhouse.com

Zipes, Douglas P, MD
Noted electrophysiologist; chief of the Cardiology Division at Indiana University School of Medicine
Indiana University Dept of Medicine **Ph:** 317-962-0555
Krannert Institute of Cardiology
1801 N Senate Blvd MPC II * Suite 4000
Indianapolis, IN 46202
internal.medicine.iu.edu/faculty/zipes.html

Zito, Barry (1978-)
Professional baseball player
Oakland Athletics **Ph:** 510-638-4900
Network Assoc Coliseum **Fax:** 510-568-3770
7000 Coliseum Way
Oakland, CA 94621
oakland.athletics.mlb.com

ZOEgirl
Music group (Contemporary Christian)
Jeff Roberts & Associates **Ph:** 615-859-7040
206 Bluebird Dr **Fax:** 615-859-6504
Goodlettsville, TN 37072
www.zoegirlonline.com

Zoellick, Robert B (1953-)
Deputy Secretary of State; formerly the US Trade Representative
US Dept of State **Ph:** 202-647-4000
2201 C St NW
Washington, DC 20520
www.state.gov/s/d

Zollars, William D
Chairman, president, and CEO of YRC Worldwide, one of the largest transportation service providers in the world
YRC Worldwide Inc **Ph:** 913-696-6100
10990 Roe Ave **Fax:** 913-696-6116
Overland Park, KS 66211
www.yrcw.com

Zolotow, Charlotte (1915-)
Author of more than 70 books for young children, including Mr. Rabbit and the Lovely Present (illustrated by Maurice Sendak) and William's Doll (illustrated by William Pene du Bois); she is also a noted editor and publisher
HarperCollins Children's Books **Ph:** 212-261-6500
1350 Ave of the Americas
New York, NY 10019
www.charlottezolotow.com

Zubov, Sergei (1970-)
Professional hockey player
Dallas Stars **Ph:** 214-387-5500
2601 Ave of the Stars **Fax:** 214-387-3599
Frisco, TX 75034
www.dallasstars.com

Zubrus, Dainius (1978-)
Professional hockey player
Washington Capitals **Ph:** 202-266-2200
401 9th St NW Suite 750 **Fax:** 202-266-2210
Washington, DC 20004
www.washingtoncaps.com

Zucker, Jeffrey A (1965-)
CEO of NBC Universal Television Group
NBC Universal Television Group **Ph:** 212-664-4444
Fax: 212-664-3720
30 Rockefeller Plaza
New York, NY 10112
www.nbcuni.com

Zuckerman, Mortimer B (1937-)
Editor-in-chief/columnist for US News & World Report; also chairman/co-publisher of the New York Daily News
US News & World Report **Ph:** 202-955-2000
1050 Thomas Jefferson St NW **Fax:** 202-955-2685
Washington, DC 20007
www.usnews.com

Zukav, Gary
Author of The Seat of the Soul
Seat of the Soul Foundation **Ph:** 541-482-8999
PO Box 339 **Fax:** 541-482-9176
Ashland, OR 97520 **TF:** 888-440-7685
www.zukav.com

Zukerman, Eugenia (1944-)
Musician (flutist); also a published author and a special correspondent for CBS News Sunday Morning, covering classical music, dance, and the arts
International Creative Management **Ph:** 212-556-5600
40 W 57th St 17th Fl
New York, NY 10019
www.eugeniazukerman.com

Subject Headings Table

Page

Actors 499
Advice Columnists
See: Columnists - Lifestyle & Features 529
Animators 505
Artists 505
See also:
Authors & Illustrators - Books for Young Readers 512
Cartoonists - Comic Strips & Panels 525
Cartoonists & Caricaturists - Editorial 527
Photographers 551
Association Executives
See: Organization Leaders 550
Astronauts 506
Attorneys & Judges 506
Authors - Fiction (Adult) 507
See also: Poets 553
Authors - Nonfiction 510
Authors & Illustrators - Books for Young Readers 512
Baseball Players & Managers 514
Basketball Players & Coaches 516
Bobsledders
See: Sports Personalities (Misc) 558
Bodybuilders
See: Fitness Personalities 536
Boxers
See: Sports Personalities (Misc) 558
Business Leaders 519
See also: Sports Team Owners 559
Cartoonists - Comic Strips & Panels 525
Cartoonists & Caricaturists - Editorial 527
Chefs 528
Choreographers
See: Dancers & Choreographers 532
Columnists - Commentary
See: Journalists (Print) 543
Columnists - Lifestyle & Features 529
Comedians 530

Page

Conservationists
See: Organization Leaders 550
Corporate Trainers
See: Motivational Speakers 546
Critics (Art, Books, Film, Music) 531
Cyclists
See: Sports Personalities (Misc) 558
Dancers & Choreographers 532
Directors, Producers, Creators, Writers (Movies & TV) 533
See also: Animators 505
Disc Jockeys
See: Radio Personalities 554
Dramatists
See: Playwrights 553
Economists 535
Fashion Designers 535
Fashion Models 536
Figure Skaters
See: Sports Personalities (Misc) 558
First Ladies
See: US Presidents & Vice Presidents and Their Wives 565
Fitness Personalities 536
Football Players & Coaches 536
Golfers 539
Government & Political Figures (Misc) 540
See also:
Governors 541
Mayors 545
US Presidents & Vice Presidents and Their Wives 565
US Senators & Representatives 565
Governors 541
Gymnasts
See: Sports Personalities (Misc) 558
Hockey Players & Coaches 541
Inventors
See: Scientists & Inventors 556

Page

Journalists (Broadcast)
See:
Radio Personalities 554
Sportscasters 560
Television Anchors & Reporters 560
Journalists (Print) 543
Judges
See: Attorneys & Judges 506
Lawyers
See: Attorneys & Judges 506
Magicians & Illusionists 545
Mayors 545
Models
See: Fashion Models 536
Motivational Speakers 546
Musicians, Singers, Songwriters 547
Olympic Athletes
See: Sports Personalities (Misc) 558
Organization Leaders 550
Photographers 551
Physicians 552
Playwrights 553
Poets 553
Politicians
See: Government & Political Figures (Misc) .. 540
Producers - Movies & TV
See: Directors, Producers, Creators, Writers (Movies & TV) 533
Race Car Drivers 554
Radio Personalities 554
See also: Sportscasters 560
Religious Leaders 556
Scientists & Inventors 556
Screenwriters
See: Directors, Producers, Creators, Writers (Movies & TV) 533
Singers & Songwriters
See: Musicians, Singers, Songwriters 547
Soccer Players 557
Speakers - Motivational
See: Motivational Speakers 546
Spiritual Leaders
See: Religious Leaders 556
Sports Personalities (Misc) 558
See also:
Baseball Players & Managers 514
Basketball Players & Coaches 516
Football Players & Coaches 536
Golfers 539
Hockey Players & Coaches 541
Race Car Drivers 554
Soccer Players 557
Tennis Players 564
Sports Team Owners 559

Page

Sportscasters 560
See also:
Radio Personalities 554
Television Personalities 563
Swimmers
See: Sports Personalities (Misc) 558
Talk Show Hosts
See:
Radio Personalities 554
Television Personalities 563
Televangelists
See: Religious Leaders 556
Television Anchors & Reporters 560
Television Personalities 563
See also: Sportscasters 560
Tennis Players 564
Track & Field Athletes
See: Sports Personalities (Misc) 558
US Presidents & Vice Presidents and Their Wives 565
US Senators & Representatives 565
US Supreme Court Justices
See: Attorneys & Judges 506
Yoga
See: Fitness Personalities 536

Subject Index

Actors

Abraham, F Murray 15
Acevedo, Kirk 16
Affleck, Ben 19
Affleck, Casey 19
Akinnuoye-Agbaje, Adewale 20
Alba, Jessica 20
Alda, Alan 20
Allen, Debbie 22
Allen, Joan 22
Allen, Tim 22
Allen, Woody 22
Alley, Kirstie 23
Ambrose, Lauren 24
Anderson, Gillian 25
Anderson, Pamela 26
Anderson, Richard Dean 26
Andrews, Julie 26
Andrews, Naveen 26
Aniston, Jennifer 27
Ann-Margret 27
Arkin, Alan 29
Arnold, Tom 29
Arquette, Courteney Cox 30
Arquette, David 30
Asner, Ed 31
Attenborough, Richard 31
Aykroyd, Dan 33
Azaria, Hank 33
Bacall, Lauren 34
Bacon, Kevin 34
Baldwin, Alec 35
Bale, Christian 35
Bana, Eric 36
Banderas, Antonio 36
Banks, Tyra 36
Barkin, Ellen 37
Barrymore, Drew 39
Baryshnikov, Mikhail 40
Basinger, Kim 40
Bassett, Angela 41
Bateman, Jason 41
Bates, Kathy 41
Beals, Jennifer 42
Beatty, Warren 43
Beckinsale, Kate 43
Bello, Maria 45
Bellucci, Monica 45
Belushi, Jim 45
Belzer, Richard 45
Benigni, Roberto 46
Bening, Annette 46
Bentley, Wes 47
Bergen, Candice 48
Berry, Halle 50
Bettany, Paul 50
Biel, Jessica 51
Big Boy 51
Binoche, Juliette 52
Black, Jack 53
Blanchett, Cate 54
Bloom, Orlando 55
Bogosian, Eric 57
Bon Jovi, Jon 58
Bosworth, Kate 60
Boyle, Lara Flynn 62
Boyle, Peter 62
Bracco, Lorraine 62
Branagh, Kenneth 63
Bratt, Benjamin 64
Braugher, Andre 64
Brenneman, Amy 65
Bridges, Beau 65
Bridges, Jeff 66
Broderick, Matthew 67
Brody, Adrien 67
Brolin, James 67
Brooks, Mel 68
Brosnan, Pierce 68
Bullock, Sandra 73
Burke, Chris 74
Burnett, Carol 74
Burns, Edward 75
Burstyn, Ellen 75
Buscemi, Steve 76
Butler, Brett 76
Bynes, Amanda 77
Caan, James 77

Actors (Cont'd)

Cage, Nicolas ... 78
Caine, Michael ... 78
Campbell, Neve ... 80
Cantone, Mario ... 81
Carell, Steve ... 82
Carey, Drew ... 82
Carlin, George ... 82
Carrey, Jim ... 83
Carroll, Diahann ... 84
Carter, Helena Bonham ... 84
Caruso, David ... 85
Carvey, Dana ... 85
Cassavetes, Nick ... 86
Castle-Hughes, Keisha ... 87
Cattrall, Kim ... 87
Caviezel, Jim ... 87
Cedric the Entertainer ... 87
Chakiris, George ... 88
Chan, Jackie ... 88
Channing, Stockard ... 89
Chase, Chevy ... 89
Cheadle, Don ... 90
Cher ... 91
Chiklis, Michael ... 91
Chow, Yun-Fat ... 92
Clark, Anthony ... 93
Clarkson, Patricia ... 94
Clayburgh, Jill ... 94
Cleese, John ... 95
Clooney, George ... 95
Close, Glenn ... 95
Collette, Toni ... 99
Connelly, Jennifer ... 101
Connery, Sean ... 101
Connick, Harry Jr ... 101
Conroy, Frances ... 101
Coppola, Sofia ... 103
Corbett, John ... 103
Cosby, Bill ... 104
Costner, Kevin ... 105
Crawford, Michael ... 107
Cromwell, James ... 108
Crosby, Norm ... 108
Cross, Marcia ... 109
Crowe, Russell ... 109
Crudup, Billy ... 109
Cruise, Tom ... 109
Cruz, Penelope ... 110
Cryer, Jon ... 110
Crystal, Billy ... 110
Culkin, Macaulay ... 110
Cumming, Alan ... 111
Curry, Tim ... 112
Curtis, Jamie Lee ... 112
Cusack, Joan ... 112
Cusack, John ... 112
Cuthbert, Elisha ... 113
Dafoe, Willem ... 113
Daly, Tyne ... 114
Damon, Matt ... 114
Danes, Claire ... 114
Daniels, Jeff ... 114
Danner, Blythe ... 115
Danson, Ted ... 115
Danza, Tony ... 115
David, Larry ... 116
Davis, Geena ... 117
Davis, Kristin ... 117
Day-Lewis, Daniel ... 118
De Matteo, Drea ... 119
De Mornay, Rebecca ... 119
DeGeneres, Ellen ... 120
Del Toro, Benicio ... 121
DeLuise, Peter ... 122
Dempsey, Patrick ... 122
DeNiro, Robert ... 122
Depp, Johnny ... 123
Dern, Laura ... 123
DeVito, Danny ... 124
Diaz, Cameron ... 125
DiCaprio, Leonardo ... 125
Dick, Andy ... 125
Diesel, Vin ... 125
Diggs, Taye ... 126
Dillon, Matt ... 126
Dinklage, Peter ... 126
Doherty, Shannen ... 128
Donaldson, Colby ... 128
D'Onofrio, Vincent ... 129
Douglas, Kirk ... 130
Douglas, Michael ... 130
Downey, Robert Jr ... 130
Dreyfuss, Richard ... 131
Driver, Minnie ... 132
Duchovny, David ... 132
Duff, Hilary ... 132
Dukakis, Olympia ... 133
Duke, Patty ... 133
Dunaway, Faye ... 133
Duncan, Michael Clarke ... 133
Dunst, Kirsten ... 134
DuVall, Clea ... 135
Duvall, Robert ... 135
Eads, George ... 136
Eastwood, Clint ... 136
Eckhart, Aaron ... 136
Edwards, Anthony ... 137
Elfman, Jenna ... 139
Elizondo, Hector ... 139
Elliott, David James ... 140
Elwes, Cary ... 140
Eminem ... 141

Actors (Cont'd)

Epps, Omar....142
Essman, Susie....143
Eve....145
Everett, Rupert....145
Falco, Edie....145
Fallon, Jimmy....146
Fanning, Dakota....146
Farrell, Colin....147
Favreau, Jon....147
Ferrell, Will....149
Ferrigno, Lou....149
Field, Sally....149
Fiennes, Joseph....150
Fiennes, Ralph....150
Firth, Colin....150
Fischer, Jenna....150
Fishburne, Laurence....151
Flanery, Sean Patrick....152
Flockhart, Calista....153
Fonda, Bridget....154
Fonda, Jane....154
Fonda, Peter....154
Ford, Harrison....155
Foster, Jodie....156
Fox, Jorja....156
Fox, Matthew....156
Fox, Michael J....157
Foxworthy, Jeff....157
Foxx, Jamie....157
Franz, Dennis....158
Fraser, Brendan....158
Freeman, Morgan....159
Gandolfini, James....163
Garcia, Andy....164
Garner, James....165
Garner, Jennifer....165
Garofalo, Janeane....165
Garrett, Brad....165
Gellar, Sarah Michelle....167
Gere, Richard....167
Giamatti, Paul....168
Gibson, Mel....169
Gifford, Kathie Lee....169
Glenn, Scott....173
Glover, Danny....173
Glover, Savion....173
Goldberg, Whoopi....174
Gooding, Cuba Jr....175
Goodman, John....176
Gossett, Louis Jr....177
Gould, Elliott....177
Grace, Topher....178
Graham, Heather....178
Graham, Lauren....179
Grammer, Kelsey....179
Grant, Hugh....179
Green, Seth....181
Griffin, Kathy....183
Griffith, Andy....183
Griffith, Melanie....183
Griffiths, Rachel....183
Guest, Christopher....185
Gyllenhaal, Jake....187
Gyllenhaal, Maggie....187
Hackman, Gene....188
Hagman, Larry....188
Hall, Michael C....189
Hamilton, Linda....190
Hanks, Tom....191
Hannah, Daryl....191
Harden, Marcia Gay....192
Hargitay, Mariska....193
Harmon, Mark....193
Harrelson, Woody....194
Harris, Ed....194
Harris, Julie....194
Hartnett, Josh....195
Hasselhoff, David....196
Hatcher, Teri....196
Hawke, Ethan....197
Hawn, Goldie....197
Hayek, Salma....197
Hayes, Sean....198
Haysbert, Dennis....198
Heaton, Patricia....199
Heche, Anne....199
Helgenberger, Marg....200
Herman, Pee Wee....202
Herrmann, Edward....202
Hershey, Barbara....203
Hewitt, Jennifer Love....203
Hilton, Paris....205
Hines, Cheryl....205
Hoffman, Dustin....207
Hoffman, Philip Seymour....207
Holbrook, Hal....207
Holloway, Josh....208
Holm, Ian....208
Holmes, Katie....208
Hopkins, Anthony....209
Hopper, Dennis....209
Hounsou, Djimon....210
Houston, Whitney....211
Howard, Ron....211
Hudson, Kate....212
Huffman, Felicity....212
Hughley, DL....212
Hunt, Bonnie....213
Hunt, Helen....213
Hunt, Linda....213
Hunter, Holly....214
Hunter, Rachel....214

Actors (Cont'd)

Hurt, William....214
Huston, Anjelica....214
Ice Cube....215
Ice-T....215
Idle, Eric....215
Imperioli, Michael....216
Innes, Laura....217
Irons, Jeremy....218
Jackman, Hugh....219
Jackson, Joshua....220
Jackson, Samuel L....221
James, Kevin....222
Janney, Allison....223
Johansson, Scarlett....226
Johnson, Don....226
Johnson, Dwayne....226
Jolie, Angelina....229
Jones, James Earl....230
Jones, Tommy Lee....231
Jovovich, Milla....232
Judd, Ashley....232
Kaczmarek, Jane....233
Kanakaredes, Melina....234
Kane, Carol....234
Karn, Richard....235
Keaton, Diane....237
Keener, Catherine....237
Keitel, Harvey....237
Kelly, Moira....239
Kemp, Will....239
Kennedy, Jamie....240
Kidman, Nicole....242
Kilmer, Val....243
Kim, Daniel Dae....243
Kingsley, Ben....245
Kinnear, Greg....245
Klein, Chris....247
Kline, Kevin....248
Knightly, Keira....248
Krasinski, John....252
Krause, Peter....252
Kristofferson, Kris....254
Kudrow, Lisa....255
Kutcher, Ashton....256
Lachey, Nick....257
Lahti, Christine....258
Landau, Martin....258
Lane, Diane....259
Lane, Nathan....259
Lange, Jessica....259
Lansbury, Angela....260
LaPaglia, Anthony....260
Laurie, Hugh....262
Law, Jude....262
Lawrence, Martin....263
Leary, Denis....263
LeBlanc, Matt....264
Ledger, Heath....264
Lee, Jason....265
Leguizamo, John....266
Leigh, Jennifer Jason....266
Leoni, Tea....267
Levy, Eugene....269
Lewis, Jerry....270
Lewis, Juliette....270
Linney, Laura....273
Liotta, Ray....274
Lithgow, John....274
Liu, Lucy....274
LL Cool J....275
Lloyd, Christopher....275
Locklear, Heather....275
Lohan, Lindsay....275
Lohman, Alison....276
Longoria, Eva....276
Lopez, George....276
Lopez, Jennifer....276
Loren, Sophia....277
Love, Courtney....277
Lovitz, Jon....278
Lowe, Rob....278
Lucci, Susan....279
Lupone, Patti....280
Mac, Bernie....281
MacDowell, Andie....282
MacLachlan, Kyle....283
MacLaine, Shirley....283
Macy, William H....283
Madonna....284
Madsen, Michael....284
Maguire, Tobey....285
Mahoney, John....285
Malkovich, John....285
Malone, Jena....286
Mandel, Howie....287
Manheim, Camryn....287
Mantegna, Joe....288
Margulies, Julianna....289
Marshall, Garry....291
Marshall, Penny....291
Marsters, James....291
Martin, Steve....292
Masterson, Mary Stuart....294
Matlin, Marlee....294
McCarthy, Jenny....297
McConaughey, Matthew....298
McCormack, Eric....298
McCrane, Paul....299
McDermott, Dylan....300
McDonald, Audra....300
McDormand, Frances....300
McDowell, Malcolm....300

Actors (Cont'd)

McEntire, Reba 301
McGregor, Ewan 302
McKellen, Ian 303
McShane, Ian 306
Meloni, Christopher 308
Messing, Debra 310
Midler, Bette 311
Miller, Larry 313
Mirren, Helen 314
Mitchell, Brian Stokes 315
Monaghan, Dominic 316
Mo'Nique 317
Montalban, Ricardo 317
Moore, Demi 318
Moore, Julianne 318
Moore, Mandy 318
Moore, Mary Tyler 318
Morales, Esai 319
Moreno, Rita 319
Morris, Kathryn 321
Mortensen, Viggo 321
Moss, Carrie-Anne 322
Mullally, Megan 323
Mulroney, Dermot 324
Muniz, Frankie 324
Murphy, Brittany 325
Murphy, Eddie 325
Murray, Chad Michael 326
Myers, Mike 326
Nabors, Jim 327
Najimy, Kathy 327
Naughton, James 329
Neeson, Liam 329
Neill, Sam 329
Neuwirth, Bebe 330
Newhart, Bob 331
Newman, Paul 331
Newton, Thandie 332
Nicholson, Jack 332
Nimoy, Leonard 333
Nixon, Cynthia 333
Nolte, Nick 334
Norton, Edward 335
Noth, Chris 335
Novak, BJ 335
O'Connell, Jerry 337
O'Donnell, Chris 338
O'Donnell, Rosie 338
Oh, Sandra 338
O'Hurley, John 339
Olmos, Edward James 340
Olsen, Ashley 340
Olsen, Mary-Kate 340
Olyphant, Timothy 340
O'Quinn, Terry 341
Osment, Haley Joel 343
Oz, Frank 345
Pacino, Al 345
Palance, Jack 346
Palminteri, Chazz 346
Paltrow, Gwyneth 347
Pantoliano, Joe 347
Paquin, Anna 347
Parker, Mary-Louise 348
Parker, Sarah Jessica 348
Parton, Dolly 349
Patinkin, Mandy 350
Patric, Jason 350
Paxton, Bill 351
Pearce, Guy 351
Peet, Amanda 352
Penn, Robin Wright 353
Penn, Sean 353
Perrineau, Harold 355
Perry, Matthew 355
Peters, Bernadette 355
Petersen, William 356
Pfeiffer, Michelle 357
Phillippe, Ryan 357
Phillips, Lou Diamond 358
Phoenix, Joaquin 358
Pierce, David Hyde 359
Pitt, Brad 360
Piven, Jeremy 360
Plummer, Christopher 361
Poitier, Sidney 361
Ponce, Carlos 362
Portman, Natalie 364
Presley, Elvis 365
Preston, Kelly 366
Priestley, Jason 367
Prinze, Freddie Jr 367
Pullman, Bill 368
Quaid, Dennis 368
Quaid, Randy 368
Queen Latifah 369
Quinn, Aidan 369
Ramis, Harold 371
Reagan, Ronald 373
Redford, Robert 373
Redgrave, Vanessa 373
Reese, Della 374
Reeve, Christopher 374
Reeves, Keanu 374
Reiner, Rob 376
Reiser, Paul 376
Reubens, Paul 202
Reynolds, Burt 377
Reynolds, Debbie 377
Rhames, Ving 377
Rhea, Caroline 377
Ribisi, Giovanni 378

Actors (Cont'd)

Ricci, Christina 378
Rickman, Alan 379
Rigby, Cathy 380
Ripa, Kelly 381
Robbins, Tim 382
Roberts, Doris 382
Roberts, Julia 382
Rock, Chris 385
Rockwell, Sam 385
Rodriguez, Freddy 385
Rodriguez, Michelle 386
Rogers, Mimi 387
Romano, Ray 388
Romijn, Rebecca 388
Rossellini, Isabella 390
Roth, Tim 390
Rourke, Mickey 391
Rowlands, Gena 391
Rush, Geoffrey 393
Russell, Kurt 393
Russo, Rene 393
Ryan, Meg 394
Ryder, Winona 395
Saget, Bob 396
Sandler, Adam 398
Sarandon, Susan 399
Schroder, Rick 405
Schwarzenegger, Arnold 407
Schwimmer, David 407
Seagal, Steven 408
Selleck, Tom 410
Sevigny, Chloe 411
Seymour, Jane 411
Shalhoub, Tony 412
Shandling, Garry 412
Shatner, William 413
Sheen, Charlie 414
Sheen, Martin 414
Shepard, Sam 414
Sheridan, Nicolette 414
Shields, Brooke 415
Short, Martin 416
Shue, Elisabeth 416
Silverstone, Alicia 418
Simmons, Henry 418
Sims, Molly 419
Sinise, Gary 420
Sisto, Jeremy 420
Sizemore, Tom 420
Slater, Christian 420
Smith, Anna Deavere 422
Smith, Jada Pinkett 422
Smith, Kevin 423
Smith, Maggie 423
Smith, Will 424
Smits, Jimmy 424
Snipes, Wesley 425
Snoop Dogg 425
Sorvino, Paul 427
Spacek, Sissy 428
Spacey, Kevin 428
Spade, David 428
Spader, James 428
Stahl, Nick 431
Stallone, Sylvester 431
Stamos, John 431
Stanton, Harry Dean 432
Steenburgen, Mary 432
Stein, Ben 433
Stewart, Patrick 435
Stiles, Julia 435
Stiller, Ben 435
Stone, Sharon 436
Stowe, Madeleine 437
Streep, Meryl 438
Streisand, Barbra 438
Sutherland, Donald 440
Sutherland, Kiefer 440
Suvari, Mena 440
Swank, Hilary 441
Swayze, Patrick 441
Sykes, Wanda 441
Tamblyn, Amber 443
Theron, Charlize 446
Thomas, Kristin Scott 447
Thompson, Emma 448
Thompson, Fred 448
Thompson, Scott 449
Thornton, Billy Bob 449
Thurman, Uma 449
Tilly, Jennifer 450
Tomei, Marisa 452
Tomlin, Lily 452
Travis, Randy 454
Travolta, John 454
Tucci, Stanley 455
Tucker, Chris 455
Turner, Kathleen 456
Turturro, John 456
Tyler, Liv 457
Underwood, Blair 458
Van Der Beek, James 459
Van Dyke, Dick 459
Van Zandt, Steven 460
Vance, Courtney B 460
Vardalos, Nia 460
Vartan, Michael 461
Vaughn, Vince 461
Visnjic, Goran 463
Voight, Jon 464
Wagner, Robert 465
Wahlberg, Donnie 465

Actors (Cont'd)

Wahlberg, Mark....465
Walken, Christopher....466
Ward, Sela....469
Washington, Denzel....470
Watanabe, Ken....470
Waterston, Sam....470
Watson, Emily....470
Watts, Naomi....471
Weaver, Sigourney....471
Weaving, Hugo....472
Weisz, Rachel....473
Welling, Tom....474
Whitaker, Forest....476
Wiest, Diane....478
Wilder, Gene....478
Williams, Michelle....481
Williams, Robin....481
Williams, Treat....481
Williams, Vanessa....482
Williamson, Mykelti....482
Willis, Bruce....482
Wilson, Luke....483
Wilson, Owen....484
Wilson, Rainn....484
Winfrey, Oprah....484
Winger, Debra....485
Winkler, Henry....485
Winslet, Kate....485
Witherspoon, Reese....485
Wood, Elijah....487
Wood, Evan Rachel....487
Woodard, Alfre....487
Woods, James....488
Woodward, Joanne....488
Wright, Jeffrey....489
Wuhl, Robert....489
Wyle, Noah....490
Zaloom, Paul....493
Zellweger, Renee....494
Zeta-Jones, Catherine....494

Advice Columnists

See: Columnists - Lifestyle & Features pg 529

Animators

Bakshi, Ralph....35
Catmull, Ed....87
Csupo, Gabor....110
Davies, Rob....116
Groening, Matt....184
Gustafson, Mark....187
Hannan, Peter....192
Hertzfeldt, Don....203
Johnson, Traci Paige....228
Judge, Mike....232
Keane, Glen....236
Klasky, Arlene....247
Kricfalusi, John....253
Lasseter, John A....261
MacFarlane, Seth....282
Maiellaro, Matt....285
McCracken, Craig....299
Moore, Steve....318
Parker, Trey....348
Schiff, Brad....403
Selick, Henry....410
Stone, Matt....436
Tartakovsky, Genndy....443
Vinton, Will....463
Wells, Simon....474
Willems, Mo....480
Willis, Dave....482

Artists

See also: Authors & Illustrators - Books for Young Readers pg 512; Cartoonists - Comic Strips & Panels pg 525; Cartoonists & Caricaturists - Editorial pg 527; Photographers pg 551

Agam, Yaacov....19
Azarian, Mary....33
Bantock, Nick....36
Basquiat, Jean-Michel....40
Bearden, Romare....42
Bennett, Olivia....46
Bourgeois, Louise....60
Calder, Alexander....78
Catlett, Elizabeth....87
Chagall, Marc....88
Conrad, Paul....101
Dali, Salvador....114
de Kooning, Willem....119
Engelbreit, Mary....141
Ernst, Max....143
Falconer, Ian....146
Gerstein, Mordicai....168
Gilliam, Sam....170
Gorey, Edward....177
Haring, Keith....193
Hirschfeld, Al....205
Hockney, David....206
Kahlo, Frida....233
Kinkade, Thomas....245
Klein, Yves....247
Kline, Franz....247
Krasner, Lee....252
Kruger, Barbara....254
Lassen, Christian Riese....261
Lawrence, Jacob....263
Lomas Garza, Carmen....276
MacDonald, Richard....282
Magritte, Rene....284

Artists (Cont'd)

Max, Peter 295
Merrill, Christine 309
Miro, Joan 314
Mondrian, Piet 317
Moss, Geoffrey 322
Nechita, Alexandra 329
Neiman, LeRoy 329
O'Keeffe, Georgia 339
Oliphant, Pat 339
Picasso, Pablo 358
Pindell, Howardena 359
Pollock, Jackson 362
Ray, Man 372
Richeson, Clee 379
Ringgold, Faith 380
Rockwell, Norman 385
Rothko, Mark 391
Schutz, Stephen 406
Segal, George 409
Sheeler, Charles 413
Staake, Bob 430
Stella, Frank 433
Suits, Julia 439
Vonnegut, Kurt 465
Warhol, Andy 469
Waugh, Eric 471
Wright, Frank Lloyd 489
Wyeth, Andrew 489
Wyland 490

Association Executives

See: Organization Leaders pg 550

Astronauts

Aldrin, Buzz 21
Collins, Eileen 99
Glenn, John 173
Jemison, Mae 224
Lovell, James A Jr 277
Lucid, Shannon 279
Pogue, William R 361
Ride, Sally 380
Schmitt, Harrison H 404

Attorneys & Judges

Alito, Samuel A Jr 21
Allred, Gloria 23
Alvarez, Cesar L 24
Angelos, Peter G 26
Archer, Dennis W 28
Baker, James A III 35
Baron, Frederick M 38
Bartlit, Fred H Jr 40
Bell, Griffin B 44
Ben-Veniste, Richard 45
Bennett, Robert S 47
Berman, Steve W 49
Bernick, David M 49
Birnbaum, Sheila L 52
Black, Roy 53
Blake, Jonathan D 54
Bloom, Lisa 55
Boggs, Thomas Hale Jr 57
Boies, David 57
Bowman, Richard A 61
Brafman, Ben 63
Breyer, Stephen G 65
Brogan, Stephen J 67
Brown, Joe 69
Bruce, Carol Elder 71
Bugliosi, Vincent 73
Burchfield, Bobby R 74
Cabraser, Elizabeth J 78
Chesley, Stanley M 91
Chu, Morgan 92
Ciresi, Michael V 93
Clifford, Robert A 95
Coffee, John C Jr 97
Conn, David 101
Coulter, Ann 105
Craig, Greg 106
Crier, Catherine 108
Culvahouse, Arthur B Jr 111
Dannhauser, Stephen J 115
Darden, Christopher 115
Davidson, Gordon K 116
Dees, Morris S 120
Dershowitz, Alan 123
Dunner, Donald R 134
Ecohawk, John E 137
Edelman, Marian Wright 137
Ennico, Cliff 142
Epstein, Richard 142
Essen, Richard J 143
Estrich, Susan 144
Fahner, Tyrone C 145
Feinberg, Kenneth R 148
Fieger, Geoffrey 149
Fielding, Fred F 150
Fiske, Robert B Jr 151
Fitzgerald, Patrick J 151
Foley, Thomas S 154
Ford, Jack 155
Gary, Willie E 165
Geragos, Mark 167
Ginsberg, Benjamin L 171
Ginsburg, Ruth Bader 171
Gonzales, Alberto 175
Gorelick, Jamie S 177
Gorton, Slade 177
Grace, Nancy 177

Attorneys & Judges (Cont'd)

Graham, Fred....178
Greco, Michael S....180
Guilfoyle, Kimberly....186
Guthrie, Savannah....187
Hausfeld, Michael D....197
Hayes, Eddie....197
Hiepler, Mark....203
Hill, Anita....204
Hynes, Patricia M....215
Jamail, Joseph D III....222
Jones Reynolds, Star....231
Jordan, Gregory B....231
Jordan, Vernon E Jr....231
Judge Judy....232
Kantor, Mickey....234
Karas, Beth....234
Katz, Joel A....236
Kendall, David E....239
Kennedy, Anthony M....239
Kennedy, Robert F Jr....240
Lancaster, Ralph I Jr....258
Lee, William F....265
Lerach, William S....267
Lessig, Lawrence....268
Leving, Jeffery M....269
Lipton, Martin....274
Luskin, Robert D....280
MacKinnon, Catharine A....283
Marshall, Thurgood....291
Masry, Edward....293
McCartan, Patrick F....297
Meese, Edwin III....307
Melton, Howell W Jr....308
Mendelson, Alan C....308
Mesereau, Thomas....309
Meserve, Richard A....310
Metcalfe, Walter L Jr....310
Millstein, Ira M....314
Milone, Francis M....314
Mitchell, George J....315
Mobley, Stacey J....316
Mondale, Walter F....317
Moore, Roy S....318
Morgenthau, Robert M....320
Motley, Ronald L....322
Neufeld, Peter....330
Nolan, Beth....334
O'Donnell, Pierce....338
Ogletree, Charles J....338
Olson, Ronald L....340
Olson, Theodore B....340
O'Quinn, John M....341
Papantonio, Mike....347
Phillips, Carter G....358
Phillips, John R....358
Pirkey, Louis T....360
Podesta, John....361
Politan, Vinnie....362
Popeo, R Robert....363
Reasoner, Harry M....373
Reich, Steven F....375
Rill, James F....380
Roberts, John G Jr....382
Romero, Anthony D....388
Rubin, Ellis S....392
Russo, Thomas A....394
Sayler, Robert N....401
Scalia, Antonin....401
Scheck, Barry....402
Scheindlin, Judith....402
Schwartz, Herbert F....406
Seligman, Nicole K....410
Shapiro, Robert L....412
Shapiro, Steven....412
Sherman, Mickey....415
Shernoff, William....415
Shestack, Jerome J....415
Smaltz, Donald....421
Smith, Walter J....424
Sohn, Michael N....425
Solovy, Jerold S....426
Sonsini, Larry W....427
Souter, David H....428
Spence, Gerry....429
Spitzer, Eliot....429
Starr, Kenneth....432
Stein, Ben....433
Stevens, John Paul....434
Stevenson, Bryan....434
Stewart, Lynne....435
Strossen, Nadine....438
Stroup, R Keith....438
Sullivan, Kathleen M....439
Susman, Stephen D....440
Thomas, Clarence....447
Thompson, James R....448
Tigar, Michael....450
Tribe, Laurence H....454
Varney, Christine A....461
Weddington, Sarah....472
Weiss, Melvyn I....473
Wells, Theodore V Jr....474
Whelan, M Edward III....476
Whitehead, John W....477
Wiley, Richard E....479
Williams, Patricia J....481
Winokur, Barton J....485

Authors - Fiction (Adult)

See also: Poets pg 553

Achebe, Chinua....16
Adams, Richard....17

Authors - Fiction (Adult) (Cont'd)

Allende, Isabel 23
Alvarez, Julia 24
Amis, Martin 25
Anderson, Kevin J 25
Ansay, A Manette 27
Anthony, Piers 27
Archer, Jeffrey 28
Atwood, Margaret 31
Auchincloss, Louis 32
Auel, Jean 32
Auster, Paul 32
Baldacci, David 35
Banks, Lynne Reid 36
Banks, Russell 36
Bantock, Nick 36
Banville, John 36
Barker, Clive 37
Barnes, Linda 38
Barrett, Andrea 39
Barth, John 39
Beattie, Ann 42
Bellow, Saul 45
Benchley, Peter 45
Berendt, John 47
Berg, Elizabeth 48
Berger, Thomas 48
Berriault, Gina 50
Binchy, Maeve 52
Bova, Ben 60
Bradbury, Ray 62
Bradford, Barbara Taylor 62
Braun, Lilian Jackson 64
Braun, Matt 64
Breslin, Jimmy 65
Briscoe, Connie 66
Brooks, Terry 68
Brown, Dan 69
Brown, Rita Mae 70
Brown, Sandra 70
Buckley, Christopher 73
Burke, James Lee 74
Bushnell, Candace 76
Butler, Octavia E 77
Butler, Robert Olen 77
Byatt, AS 77
Canin, Ethan 80
Cannell, Stephen J 80
Card, Orson Scott 81
Carey, Peter 82
Carroll, James 84
Chabon, Michael 88
Cherryh, CJ 91
Child, Lee 91
Cisneros, Sandra 93
Clancy, Tom 93
Clark, Carol Higgins 93
Clark, Mary Higgins 94
Clarke, Arthur C 94
Coben, Harlan 96
Coelho, Paulo 96
Collins, Jackie 99
Connell, Evan S 101
Connelly, Michael 101
Connolly, John 101
Conroy, Pat 101
Cook, Robin 102
Cook, Thomas H 102
Coonts, Stephen 102
Cornwell, Patricia 104
Coulter, Catherine 105
Coupland, Douglas 105
Crews, Harry 108
Crichton, Michael 108
Cunningham, Michael 111
Cussler, Clive 112
Dailey, Janet 113
Danticat, Edwidge 115
Deaver, Jeffery 119
Delaney, Samuel R 121
DeLillo, Don 121
DeMille, Nelson 122
Didion, Joan 125
Doctorow, EL 127
Doerr, Anthony 127
Doyle, Roddy 131
Dunne, Dominick 134
Dunne, John Gregory 134
Eco, Umberto 137
Ellroy, James 140
Enger, Leif 141
Ephron, Nora 142
Erdrich, Louise 142
Esquivel, Laura 143
Eugenides, Jeffrey 144
Evans, Nicholas 144
Evans, Richard Paul 144
Fielding, Helen 150
Fisher, Carrie 151
Flagg, Fannie 152
Ford, Richard 155
Forsyth, Frederick 155
Fowles, John 156
Francis, Dick 157
Franzen, Jonathan 158
Frayn, Michael 158
Frazier, Charles 159
French, Marilyn 159
Fuentes, Carlos 161
Gabaldon, Diana 162
Gaiman, Neil 162
Gaines, Ernest J 162
Garcia Marquez, Gabriel 164

Authors - Fiction (Adult) (Cont'd)

George, Elizabeth....167
Gibbons, Kaye....168
Gibson, William....169
Glass, Julia....172
Godwin, Gail....173
Goldman, William....174
Gordimer, Nadine....176
Gordon, Mary....176
Grafton, Sue....178
Grass, Gunter....180
Grau, Shirley Ann....180
Grimes, Martha....183
Grisham, John....184
Guterson, David....187
Guy, Rosa....187
Haley, Alex....189
Hamilton, Jane....190
Harris, Thomas....194
Hegi, Ursula....199
Heller, Jane....200
Helprin, Mark....201
Herbert, Brian....202
Higgins, Jack....204
Hijuelos, Oscar....204
Hillerman, Tony....205
Hoffman, Alice....207
Holeman, Linda....207
Hunter, Evan....214
Irving, John....218
Isaacs, Susan....218
Ishiguro, Kazuo....219
Jackson, Lisa....220
Jakes, John....222
James, PD....222
Jenkins, Jerry B....224
Jin, Ha....225
Jong, Erica....231
Joyce, Brenda....232
Karon, Jan....235
Kellerman, Faye....238
Kellerman, Jonathan....238
Keneally, Thomas....239
Kennedy, William....240
Keyes, Daniel....242
Kidd, Sue Monk....242
Kincaid, Jamaica....243
King, Stephen....245
Kingsolver, Barbara....245
Kingston, Maxine Hong....245
Klein, Joe....247
Kluger, Richard....248
Koontz, Dean....250
Krantz, Judith....252
Krentz, Jayne Ann....253
Kundera, Milan....255
Labiner, Norah....256
LaHaye, Tim....257
Lahiri, Jhumpa....257
Lamb, Wally....258
Lamott, Anne....258
Lawrence, Martha C....263
Le Carre, John....263
Le Guin, Ursula K....263
Leavitt, David....263
Lee, Harper....265
Lehane, Dennis....266
Leonard, Elmore....267
Lessing, Doris....268
Lethem, Jonathan....268
Letts, Billie....268
Levin, Ira....269
Lippman, Laura....274
Lodge, David....275
Lurie, Alison....280
Lustig, Arnost....280
Mahfouz, Naguib....285
Mailer, Norman....285
Maron, Margaret....290
Martini, Steve....292
Mason, Bobbie Ann....293
Matthiessen, Peter....295
Maupin, Armistead....295
Maynard, Joyce....296
McBain, Ed....296
McCaffrey, Anne....296
McCarthy, Cormac....297
McCrumb, Sharyn....299
McCullough, Colleen....299
McDermott, Alice....300
McEwan, Ian....301
McGahern, John....301
McGuane, Thomas....302
McIntyre, Vonda....303
McLaughlin, Emma....304
McMillan, Terry....305
McMurtry, Larry....305
Merullo, Roland....309
Michael, Judith....311
Miller, Sue....313
Millhauser, Steven....313
Mistry, Rohinton....315
Mitchard, Jacquelyn....315
Mitchell, David....315
Moore, Michael....318
Morgan, Marlo....320
Morgan, Robert....320
Morrison, Toni....321
Mosley, Walter....322
Munro, Alice....324
Murakami, Haruki....324
Murray, Sabina....326
Naipaul, VS....327

Authors - Fiction (Adult) (Cont'd)

Oates, Joyce Carol 336
O'Brien, Edna.................................337
Oe, Kenzaburo.................................338
Ondaatje, Michael..............................341
Ozick, Cynthia.................................345
Paley, Grace 346
Paretsky, Sara.................................347
Parker, Robert B...............................348
Patchett, Ann..................................349
Patterson, James...............................350
Patterson, Richard North 350
Perry, Anne...................................355
Picoult, Jodi 359
Piercy, Marge..................................359
Pilcher, Rosamunde.............................359
Plain, Belva...................................360
Potok, Chaim..................................364
Price, Reynolds 366
Price, Richard.................................366
Proulx, Annie..................................367
Pynchon, Thomas...............................368
Quindlen, Anna................................369
Redfield, James 373
Rendell, Ruth..................................376
Rice, Anne....................................378
Ridley, John 380
Robbins, Tom..................................382
Roberts, Nora..................................383
Roberts, Willo Davis 383
Robinson, Marilynne............................384
Roth, Philip...................................390
Rushdie, Salman...............................393
Russo, Richard.................................393
Salinger, JD...................................396
Salvatore, RA 397
Sandford, John.................................398
Saramago, Jose 399
Schwarz, Christina.............................407
Sebold, Alice..................................409
Seth, Vikram..................................411
Shaara, Jeff 411
Sheldon, Sidney 414
Shields, David.................................415
Shreve, Anita 416
Shteyngart, Gary...............................416
Siddons, Anne Rivers 417
Slouka, Mark 421
Smiley, Jane 421
Smith, Lee....................................423
Smith, Zadie..................................424
Solzhenitsyn, Aleksandr.........................426
Sparks, Nicholas...............................428
Spencer, LaVyrle...............................429
Spillane, Mickey 429
Steel, Danielle 432
Stewart, Mary..................................435
Straub, Peter 437
Strieber, Whitley...............................438
Styron, William................................439
Tan, Amy 443
Tapply, William G..............................443
Tepper, Sheri S 446
Theroux, Paul..................................446
Turow, Scott...................................456
Tyler, Anne 457
Updike, John...................................458
Vidal, Gore....................................462
Vinge, Joan D..................................463
Vonnegut, Kurt 465
Wakefield, Dan.................................466
Walker, Alice..................................466
Waller, Robert James 468
Wambaugh, Joseph 469
Wells, Rebecca 474
Welsh, Irvine 474
White, Edmund.................................477
Wolfe, Tom 486
Wolff, Tobias..................................486
Woods, Stuart 488
Wouk, Herman 488
Xingjian, Gao 490
Zabor, Rafi....................................493
Zukerman, Eugenia.............................495

Authors - Nonfiction

Albom, Mitch 20
Altea, Rosemary.................................23
Alterman, Eric 24
Applebaum, Anne 28
Askins, Renee...................................31
Atkinson, Rick 31
Baldrige, Letitia.................................35
Ball, Edward 36
Ban Breathnach, Sarah 36
Barry, Dave 39
Beamer, Lisa....................................42
Beattie, Melody 43
Bennett, William J 47
Berg, A Scott 48
Birnbach, Lisa 52
Blanchard, Ken 54
Blum, Deborah 56
Bolles, Richard Nelson...........................58
Bradshaw, John.................................62
Breslin, Jimmy..................................65
Browne, Sylvia..................................71
Bryson, Bill.....................................72
Buchwald, Art 73
Bugliosi, Vincent.................................73
Burrough, Bryan.................................75
Burrows, Edwin G 75
Cahill, Thomas..................................78

Authors - Nonfiction (Cont'd)

Canfield, Jack 80
Canton, James 81
Caro, Robert A 83
Chittister, Joan 92
Chopra, Deepak 92
Coles, Robert 98
Collins, James C 99
Connell, Evan S 101
Coulter, Ann 105
Covey, Stephen R 106
Cramer, Richard Ben 107
D'Adamo, Peter J 113
Dalai Lama 113
Danko, William 114
Dass, Ram 115
De Angelis, Barbara 119
Diamond, Jared 124
Dobson, James C. 127
Dower, John W 130
Duffy, Karen 132
Dyer, Wayne 135
Edelman, Ric 137
Ellis, Joseph 140
Farah, Joseph 146
Fisher, Mary 151
Fleischman, John 152
Fox, Michael 156
Franken, Al 158
Frommer, Arthur 160
Fuentes, Carlos 161
Glink, Ilyce 173
Goodwin, Doris Kearns 176
Gordon, Mary 176
Gourevitch, Philip 177
Graham, Katharine 178
Gray, John 180
Greene, Bob 181
Greenfield, Lauren 182
Greider, William 182
Groopman, Jerome 184
Halberstam, David 188
Hansen, Mark Victor 192
Hartmann, Thom 195
Havel, Vaclav 197
Hay, Louise L. 197
Heady, Robert K 198
Hedrick, Joan D. 199
Heller, Rachael F 200
Heller, Richard F 200
Howe, Neil 211
Hubbard, Barbara Marx 211
Huffington, Arianna 212
Isaacson, Walter 218
Ivins, Molly 219
Jenkins, Jerry B. 224
Johnson, Spencer 228
Junger, Sebastian 232
Kagan, Robert 233
Katzen, Mollie 236
Kaysen, Susanna 236
Kennedy, David M 240
Kiyosaki, Robert T 247
Klein, Joe 247
Klein, Naomi 247
Kluger, Richard 248
Korda, Michael 250
Krakauer, Jon 252
Kriegel, Robert 253
Kushner, Harold S 256
Kuttner, Robert 256
LaHaye, Tim 257
Lama, His Holiness the Dalai 258
Lamott, Anne 258
Landis, Robyn 259
Lapham, Lewis H 260
Larson, Edward J 261
Lebowitz, Fran 264
Lechter, Sharon L 264
Leckey, Andrew 264
Lewis, CS 270
Lewis, David Levering 270
Love, Susan 277
Lucado, Max 278
Lynch, Thomas 280
Mackay, Harvey 282
MacLaine, Shirley 283
Maltin, Leonard 286
Matthiessen, Peter 295
McCourt, Frank 299
McCullough, David 299
McGraw, Phil 302
McPhee, John 306
Menand, Louis 308
Miles, Jack 311
Millman, Dan 314
Moore, Thomas 318
Morgenstern, Julie 320
Morris, Edmund 320
Murkoff, Heidi 325
Myss, Caroline 327
Naipaul, VS 327
Naisbitt, John 327
Nasar, Sylvia 328
Nhat Hanh, Thich 332
Noonan, Peggy 334
Novak, Michael 335
Nuland, Sherwin B. 336
Null, Gary 336
Opdyke, Irene Gut 341
Orman, Suze 342
Ornish, Dean 342
Ornstein, Norman J 342

Authors - Nonfiction (Cont'd)

O'Rourke, PJ....342
Ozick, Cynthia....345
Paglia, Camille....346
Peck, M Scott....352
Pelzer, Dave....353
Perricone, Nicholas....355
Peters, Tom....356
Pfaff, William....357
Philbrick, Nathaniel....357
Phillips, Bill....357
Pinker, Steven....359
Pollitt, Katha....362
Popcorn, Faith....363
Prager, Dennis....365
Preston, Richard....366
Price, Reynolds....366
Pritikin, Robert....367
Rakove, Jack N....370
Ramsey, Dave....371
Reed, Ishmael....374
Reeves, Richard....374
Reich, Robert B....375
Roberts, Cokie....382
Roberts, Monty....383
Roizen, Michael....387
Rooney, Andy....389
Rule, Ann....392
Rushdie, Salman....393
Sacks, Oliver....395
Sanders, Mark D....398
Sawhney, Mohanbir....401
Scheuer, Michael....403
Schiff, Stacy....403
Schlessinger, Laura....403
Schlosser, Eric....404
Sears, Barry....409
Sedaris, David....409
Senge, Peter....410
Shields, David....415
Siegel, Bernie....417
Siegel, Marc K....417
Solomon, Andrew....426
Sommers, Christina Hoff....426
Sontag, Susan....427
Sowell, Thomas....428
Spoto, Donald....430
Stanley, Thomas J....431
Starr, Paul....432
Strieber, Whitley....438
Talese, Gay....442
Taraborrelli, J Randy....443
Taylor, Alan....444
Terkel, Studs....446
Theroux, Paul....446
Thompson, Hunter S....448
Tolle, Eckhart....452
Vanzant, Iyanla....460
Vidal, Gore....462
Viorst, Judith....463
Wakefield, Dan....466
Walsch, Neale Donald....468
Warren, Rick....470
Wattenberg, Ben....471
Weil, Andrew....472
Weiner, Jonathan....473
Weiss, Brian L....473
Whitaker, Julian....477
White, Edmund....477
Whitehead, John W....477
Wiencek, Henry....478
Wiesel, Elie....478
Wilkinson, Bruce....479
Wilkinson, Darlene Marie....479
Williams, Patricia J....481
Williamson, Marianne....482
Wilson, Edward O....483
Winchester, Simon....484
Wolfe, Tom....486
Wood, Gordon S....487
Woodward, Bob....488
Zukav, Gary....495

Authors & Illustrators - Books for Young Readers

Ada, Alma Flor....16
Adoff, Arnold....18
Adoff, Jaime....18
Alda, Arlene....20
Alexander, Lloyd....21
Almond, David....23
Applegate, KA....28
Ardagh, Philip....28
Avi....33
Azarian, Mary....33
Babbitt, Natalie....34
Banks, Lynne Reid....36
Bauer, Joan....42
Bennett, Cherie....46
Berenstain, Jan....47
Berenstain, Stan....47
Black, Holly....53
Block, Francesca Lia....55
Blos, Joan W....56
Blume, Judy....56
Bond, Michael....58
Bonners, Susan....59
Boynton, Sandra....62
Brashares, Ann....64
Brett, Jan....65
Bridwell, Norman....66
Brown, Marc....70
Brown, Marcia....70

Authors & Illustrators - Books for Young Readers (Cont'd)

Brown, Margaret Wise 70
Bunting, Eve 74
Byars, Betsy 77
Cabot, Meg 78
Cannon, Janell 80
Carle, Eric 82
Chambers, Aidan 88
Cleary, Beverly 94
Clements, Andrew 95
Cofer, Judith Ortiz 97
Cole, Joanna 98
Colfer, Eoin 99
Collier, Bryan 99
Cooney, Caroline B 102
Cooper, Susan 102
Cormier, Robert 104
Creech, Sharon 108
Curtis, Christopher Paul 112
Curtis, Jamie Lee 112
Cushman, Karen 112
Dahl, Roald 113
Danziger, Paula 115
Davis, Kenneth C 117
dePaola, Tomie 123
Dessen, Sarah 124
DiCamillo, Kate 125
DiTerlizzi, Tony 127
Draper, Sharon M 131
Duncan, Lois 133
Egielski, Richard 138
Emberley, Ed 140
Falconer, Ian 146
Farmer, Nancy 146
Feiffer, Jules 148
Fleischman, John 152
Fleischman, Paul 152
Fleischman, Sid 152
Fleming, Denise 152
Fox, Paula 157
Freedman, Russell 159
Fritz, Jean 160
Gaiman, Neil 162
Gammell, Stephen 163
Gantos, Jack 163
Geisel, Theodore 166
George, Jean Craighead 167
Gerstein, Mordicai 168
Giblin, James Cross 169
Giff, Patricia Reilly 169
Gilliland, Jillian 170
GrandPre, Mary 179
Greenfield, Eloise 182
Grimes, Nikki 184
Guevara, Susan 186
Haddix, Margaret Peterson 188
Haley, Gail E 189
Halse Anderson, Laurie 190
Hamilton, Virginia 190
Handford, Martin 191
Henkes, Kevin 201
Hesse, Karen 203
Hill, Eric 204
Hinton, SE 205
Holeman, Linda 207
Holt, Kimberly Willis 208
Horvath, Polly 210
Hyman, Trina Schart 215
Jacques, Brian 222
Jenkins, Steve 224
Johnson, Traci Paige 228
Juster, Norton 232
Kadohata, Cynthia 233
Keats, Ezra Jack 237
Keith, Harold 238
Kerr, ME 241
Kirk, David 246
Koertge, Ron 249
Konigsburg, EL 250
Korman, Gordon 250
Kunhardt, Dorothy 255
Kunhardt, Edith 255
Kuskin, Karla 256
L'Engle, Madeleine 267
Lester, Julius 268
Lewis, CS 270
Lipsyte, Robert 274
Lobel, Arnold 275
Lomas Garza, Carmen 276
Lowry, Lois 278
Lynch, Chris 280
Macaulay, David 281
MacLachlan, Patricia 283
Martin, Ann M 291
Martin, Bill Jr. 291
Martinez, Victor 292
Marzollo, Jean 293
Maynard, Joyce 296
Mazer, Norma Fox 296
McCully, Emily Arnold 299
McDermott, Gerald 300
McKinley, Robin 304
McKissack, Frederick L 304
McKissack, Patricia C 304
Meltzer, Milton 308
Munsch, Robert 324
Murphy, Jim 325
Myers, Walter Dean 326
Na, An 327
Naylor, Phyllis Reynolds 329
Neville, Emily Cheney 331
Nixon, Joan Lowery 333
Nolan, Han 334

Authors & Illustrators - Books for Young Readers (Cont'd)

Numeroff, Laura 336
Nye, Naomi Shihab 336
Osborne, Mary Pope 343
Page, Robin 346
Palatini, Margie 346
Parish, Herman 347
Park, Barbara 347
Park, Linda Sue 348
Pascal, Francine 349
Paterson, Katherine 350
Paulsen, Gary 351
Peck, Richard 352
Peck, Robert Newton 352
Pierce, Tamora 359
Pike, Christopher 359
Pilkey, Dav 359
Pinkney, Andrea Davis 360
Pinkney, Jerry 360
Pinkwater, Daniel 360
Plum-Ucci, Carol 361
Prelutsky, Jack 365
Pullman, Philip 368
Ransome, James E 371
Rathmann, Peggy 372
Rennison, Louise 376
Rey, HA 377
Reynolds, Peter H 377
Rinaldi, Ann 380
Ringgold, Faith 380
Roberts, Willo Davis 383
Rohmann, Eric 387
Rowling, JK 391
Ryan, Pam Munoz 394
Rylant, Cynthia 395
Sachar, Louis 395
Say, Allen 401
Schoenherr, John 404
Scieszka, Jon 407
Sendak, Maurice 410
Shannon, David 412
Shulevitz, Uri 416
Simon, Seymour 419
Singer, Marilyn 419
Sleator, William 421
Slobodkina, Esphyr 421
Small, David 421
Snicket, Lemony 424
Sones, Sonya 427
Speare, Elizabeth George 428
Spinelli, Jerry 429
Springer, Nancy 430
Stine, RL 435
Strasser, Todd 437
Taback, Simms 442
Taylor, Mildred D 444
Taylor, Theodore 445
Teague, Mark 445
Thomas, Joyce Carol 447
Tolan, Stephanie S 452
Van Allsburg, Chris 459
Van Draanen, Wendelin 459
Viorst, Judith 463
Voigt, Cynthia 464
Wallace, Barbara Brooks 467
Warner, Gertrude Chandler 469
Whelan, Gloria 476
White, EB 477
White, Ruth 477
Wiesner, David 478
Willard, Nancy 479
Willems, Mo 480
Williams, Vera 482
Wisniewski, David 485
Wolff, Virginia Euwer 486
Wong, Janet 487
Wood, Audrey 487
Woodson, Jacqueline 488
Yep, Laurence 491
Yolen, Jane 492
Young, Ed 492
Zelinsky, Paul O 494
Zolotow, Charlotte 495

Baseball Players & Managers

Aaron, Hank 15
Abreu, Bobby 16
Affeldt, Jeremy 18
Alomar, Sandy 23
Alou, Felipe 23
Alou, Moises 23
Anderson, Garrett 25
Aquino, Greg 28
Baez, Danys 34
Bagwell, Jeff 34
Baker, Dusty 35
Batista, Miguel 41
Bay, Jason 42
Beckett, Josh 43
Bell, Buddy 44
Bell, David 44
Beltran, Carlos 45
Beltre, Adrian 45
Benitez, Armando 46
Berkman, Lance 48
Biggio, Craig 51
Blalock, Hank 54
Bochy, Bruce 57
Bonds, Barry 58
Boone, Aaron 59
Bradley, Milton 62
Brock, Lou 67
Burnett, AJ 74

Baseball Players & Managers (Cont'd)

Burrell, Pat ... 75
Cabrera, Miguel ... 78
Cameron, Mike ... 79
Carpenter, Chris ... 83
Casey, Sean ... 86
Castilla, Vinny ... 86
Castillo, Luis ... 86
Chacon, Shawn ... 88
Chavez, Eric ... 90
Clemens, Roger ... 95
Colon, Bartolo ... 100
Cordero, Francisco ... 103
Counsell, Craig ... 105
Cox, Bobby ... 106
Cruz, Jose Jr ... 110
Damon, Johnny ... 114
Davis, Doug ... 117
Delgado, Carlos ... 121
DeRosa, Mark ... 123
Dotel, Octavio ... 129
Drese, Ryan ... 131
Drew, JD ... 131
Dunn, Adam ... 134
Durham, Ray ... 135
Edmonds, Jim ... 137
Erstad, Darin ... 143
Escobar, Kelvim ... 143
Feliz, Pedro ... 148
Finley, Steve ... 150
Floyd, Cliff ... 153
Fogg, Josh ... 153
Ford, Lew ... 155
Franco, Julio ... 157
Francona, Terry ... 157
Gagne, Eric ... 162
Garciaparra, Nomar ... 164
Gardenhire, Ron ... 164
Garner, Phil ... 165
Giambi, Jason ... 168
Gibbons, John ... 168
Gibson, Bob ... 169
Giles, Brian ... 170
Giles, Marcus ... 170
Girardi, Joe ... 171
Glaus, Troy ... 172
Glavine, Tom ... 172
Gonzalez, Luis ... 175
Green, Shawn ... 181
Griffey, Ken Jr ... 183
Guardado, Eddie ... 185
Guerrero, Vladimir ... 185
Guillen, Carlos ... 186
Guillen, Jose ... 186
Guillen, Ozzie ... 186
Hafner, Travis ... 188
Halladay, Roy ... 189
Harang, Aaron ... 192
Hargrove, Mike ... 193
Helton, Todd ... 201
Hernandez, Ramon ... 202
Hillenbrand, Shea ... 204
Hoffman, Trevor ... 207
Hudson, Tim ... 212
Huff, Aubrey ... 212
Hunter, Torii ... 214
Hurdle, Clint ... 214
Ibanez, Raul ... 215
Isringhausen, Jason ... 219
Jenkins, Geoff ... 224
Jeter, Derek ... 225
Johnson, Randy ... 228
Jones, Andruw ... 229
Jones, Chipper ... 229
Jones, Jacque ... 229
Kendall, Jason ... 239
Kent, Jeff ... 241
Kim, Byung-Hyun ... 243
Kolb, Dan ... 249
Konerko, Paul ... 250
Koskie, Corey ... 251
La Russa, Tony ... 256
Lee, Carlos ... 264
Lee, Derrek ... 265
Leyland, Jim ... 271
Lidge, Brad ... 272
Lidle, Cory ... 272
Lieber, Jon ... 272
Little, Grady ... 274
Lo Duca, Paul ... 275
Loaiza, Esteban ... 275
Lofton, Kenny ... 275
Lopez, Javy ... 276
Loretta, Mark ... 277
Lowe, Derek ... 278
Lowell, Mike ... 278
Macha, Ken ... 282
Mackowiak, Rob ... 283
Maddon, Joe ... 284
Maddux, Greg ... 284
Mantle, Mickey ... 288
Manuel, Charlie ... 288
Maroth, Mike ... 290
Marquis, Jason ... 290
Martinez, Pedro ... 292
Martinez, Victor ... 292
Matheny, Mike ... 294
Matsui, Hideki ... 294
Matsui, Kazuo ... 294
McCarver, Tim ... 297
Melvin, Bob ... 308
Mesa, Jose ... 309
Millar, Kevin ... 311

Baseball Players & Managers (Cont'd)

Morgan, Joe....320
Morris, Matt....321
Moyer, Jamie....322
Mulder, Mark....323
Narron, Jerry....328
Nathan, Joe....329
Nevin, Phil....331
Ordonez, Magglio....342
Ortiz, David....343
Ortiz, Russ....343
Oswalt, Roy....344
Overbay, Lyle....344
Pavano, Carl....351
Peavy, Jake....351
Pena, Wily Mo....353
Penny, Brad....353
Percival, Troy....354
Perez, Oliver....354
Perlozzo, Sam....355
Pettitte, Andy....357
Piazza, Mike....358
Pierre, Juan....359
Posada, Jorge....364
Prior, Mark....367
Pujols, Albert....368
Radke, Brad....369
Ramirez, Aramis....370
Ramirez, Manny....370
Randolph, Willie....371
Renteria, Edgar....376
Rhodes, Arthur....378
Ripken, Cal Jr....381
Rivera, Mariano....381
Robinson, Frank....384
Robinson, Jackie....384
Rodriguez, Alex....385
Rodriguez, Ivan....385
Rogers, Kenny....386
Rolen, Scott....387
Rollins, Jimmy....388
Romero, JC....388
Rowand, Aaron....391
Ryan, Nolan....394
Sanders, Reggie....398
Santana, Johan....399
Schilling, Curt....403
Schmidt, Jason....404
Scioscia, Mike....407
Sexson, Richie....411
Sheets, Ben....414
Sheffield, Gary....414
Showalter, Buck....416
Smoltz, John....424
Snow, JT....425
Soriano, Alfonso....427
Stairs, Matt....431
Suzuki, Ichiro....440
Sweeney, Mike....441
Teixeira, Mark....445
Tejada, Miguel....445
Thome, Jim....448
Tomko, Brett....452
Torre, Joe....452
Trachsel, Steve....453
Tracy, Jim....453
Uribe, Juan....458
Varitek, Jason....461
Vazquez, Javier....461
Vidro, Jose....462
Vizcaino, Luis....464
Vizquel, Omar....464
Wagner, Billy....465
Wakefield, Tim....466
Weaver, Jeff....471
Webb, Brandon....472
Wedge, Eric....472
Wells, Vernon....474
Williams, Bernie....480
Williams, Ted....481
Williams, Woody....482
Willis, Dontrelle....482
Wilson, Craig....483
Wilson, Preston....484
Winfield, Dave....484
Winn, Randy....485
Wood, Kerry....487
Wright, Jaret....489
Yost, Ned....492
Young, Michael....492
Zambrano, Carlos....493
Zito, Barry....495

Basketball Players & Coaches

Abdul-Jabbar, Kareem....15
Abdur-Rahim, Shareef....15
Adelman, Rick....18
Adubato, Richie....18
Allen, Ray....22
Alston, Rafer....23
Anderson, Derek....25
Anthony, Carmelo....27
Arenas, Gilbert....28
Armstrong, Darrell....29
Arroyo, Carlos....30
Artest, Ron....30
Auerbach, Red....32
Barkley, Charles....37
Barry, Brent....39
Beard, Alana....42
Bell, Raja....45
Bibby, Mike....50
Bickerstaff, Bernie....51

Basketball Players & Coaches (Cont'd)

Billups, Chauncey 52
Bird, Larry 52
Bird, Sue 52
Blount, Mark 56
Bogans, Keith 57
Bogues, Muggsy 57
Boozer, Carlos 59
Bosh, Chris 59
Bowen, Bruce 61
Boykins, Earl 61
Brand, Elton 64
Brown, Larry 69
Brown, Mike 70
Brown, PJ 70
Bryant, Joe 72
Bryant, Kobe 72
Butler, Caron 77
Camby, Marcus 79
Carlisle, Rick 82
Carter, Vince 85
Casey, Dwane 86
Cassell, Sam 86
Catchings, Tamika 87
Cato, Kelvin 87
Chancellor, Van 89
Cheaney, Calbert 90
Cheeks, Maurice 90
Claxton, Speedy 94
Cowens, Dave 106
Coyle, Pat 106
Crawford, Jamal 107
Croshere, Austin 109
Curry, Eddy 112
Daniels, Antonio 114
D'Antoni, Mike 115
Davis, Baron 117
Davis, Ricky 118
DeForge, Anna 120
Delk, Tony 122
Deng, Luol 122
Dickau, Dan 125
Dixon, Tamecka 127
Donovan, Anne 129
Douglas, Katie 130
Duhon, Chris 133
Duncan, Tim 133
Dunleavy, Mike 134
Dunleavy, Mike Sr 134
Erving, Julius 143
Feaster, Allison 147
Ferdinand, Marie 149
Finley, Michael 150
Ford, Cheryl 154
Fortson, Danny 156
Francis, Steve 157
Frank, Lawrence 157
Fratello, Mike 158
Frazier, Walt 159
Garnett, Kevin 165
Gasol, Pau 165
Ginobili, Manu 171
Gooden, Drew 175
Goodson, Adrienne 176
Griffin, Eddie 183
Griffith, Yolanda 183
Hamilton, Richard 190
Hammon, Becky 191
Harpring, Matt 193
Harrington, Al 194
Haslem, Udonis 196
Havlicek, John 197
Hayes, Jarvis 197
Hill, Bob 204
Hill, Brian 204
Hill, Grant 204
Hinrich, Kirk 205
Holdsclaw, Chamique 207
Howard, Dwight 211
Howard, Josh 211
Hudson, Troy 212
Hughes, Dan 212
Hughes, Larry 212
Iguodala, Andre 216
Ilgauskas, Zydrunas 216
Iverson, Allen 219
Jackson, Bobby 220
Jackson, Jim 220
Jackson, Lauren 220
Jackson, Marc 220
Jackson, Phil 221
Jackson, Stephen 221
James, LeBron 222
Jamison, Antawn 222
Jaric, Marko 223
Jefferson, Richard 224
Johnson, Avery 226
Johnson, Joe 227
Johnson, Magic 227
Johnson, Shannon 228
Jones, Damon 229
Jones, Eddie 229
Jordan, Eddie 231
Jordan, Michael 231
Karl, George 235
Kidd, Jason 242
Kirilenko, Andrei 245
Knight, Bob 248
Knight, Brevin 248
Korver, Kyle 251
Kukoc, Toni 255
LaFrentz, Raef 257
Laimbeer, Bill 258

Basketball Players & Coaches (Cont'd)

Lenard, Voshon 266
Lennox, Betty 267
Leslie, Lisa 268
Lewis, Rashard 271
Mabika, Mwadi 281
Maggette, Corey 284
Magloire, Jamaal 284
Malone, Moses 286
Maravich, Pete 288
Marbury, Stephon 288
Marion, Shawn 289
Marshall, Donyell 291
Martin, Kenyon 292
Mason, Desmond 293
McConnell Serio, Suzie 298
McDyess, Antonio 300
McGrady, Tracy 302
McHale, Kevin 303
McMillan, Nate 305
McWilliams-Franklin, Taj 306
Melvin, Chasity 308
Mihm, Chris 311
Miles, Darius 311
Miller, Andre 312
Miller, Brad 312
Miller, Kelly 313
Miller, Mike 313
Ming, Yao 314
Mitchell, Sam 315
Mobley, Cuttino 316
Mohammed, Nazr 316
Montgomery, Mike 317
Mourning, Alonzo 322
Mutombo, Dikembe 326
Nash, Steve 328
Nolan, Deanna 334
Nowitzki, Dirk 336
Odom, Lamar 338
Ohlde, Nicole 338
Okafor, Emeka 339
Okur, Mehmet 339
O'Neal, Jermaine 341
O'Neal, Shaquille 341
Parker, Tony 348
Payton, Gary 351
Penicheiro, Ticha 353
Pierce, Paul 359
Popovich, Gregg 363
Powell, Elaine 365
Prince, Tayshaun 367
Radmanovic, Vladimir 369
Randolph, Zach 371
Redd, Michael 373
Richardson, Jason 379
Richardson, Quentin 379
Ridnour, Luke 380
Riley, Pat 380
Rivers, Doc 381
Robinson, Crystal 384
Robinson, David 384
Rose, Jalen 389
Russell, Bill 393
Sales, Nykesha 396
Salley, John 397
Saunders, Flip 400
Scott, Byron 407
Simmons, Bobby 418
Skiles, Scott 420
Sloan, Jerry 421
Smith, Joe 422
Smith, Katie 423
Smith, Tangela 424
Stackhouse, Jerry 430
Staley, Dawn 431
Stojakovic, Peja 436
Stotts, Terry 437
Stoudemire, Amare 437
Summitt, Pat 440
Swoopes, Sheryl 441
Szczerbiak, Wally 442
Taurasi, Diana 443
Taylor, Maurice 444
Taylor, Penny 445
Teasley, Nikki 445
Thibault, Mike 447
Thomas, Isiah 447
Thomas, Kurt 447
Thomas, LaToya 448
Thompson, John 449
Thompson, Tina 449
Tinsley, Jamaal 451
Turkoglu, Hedo 456
Van Exel, Nick 459
Van Gundy, Jeff 459
Van Horn, Keith 459
Wade, Dwyane 465
Walker, Antoine 466
Walker, DeMya 466
Wallace, Ben 467
Wallace, Gerald 467
Wallace, Rasheed 467
Walton, Bill 468
Watson, Earl 470
Webber, Chris 472
Wells, Bonzi 474
Wesley, David 475
Westhead, Paul 475
Whalen, Lindsay 476
Whisenant, John 476
Wilkens, Lenny 479
Williams, Eric 480
Williams, Jason 480

Basketball Players & Coaches (Cont'd)

Williams, Maurice....481
Williamson, Corliss....482
Winters, Brian....485
Woodson, Mike....488

Bobsledders

See: Sports Personalities (Misc) pg 558

Bodybuilders

See: Fitness Personalities pg 536

Boxers

See: Sports Personalities (Misc) pg 558

Business Leaders

See also: Sports Team Owners pg 559

Abele, John....15
Ackerman, F Duane....16
Adair, Charles E....16
Adami, Norman....17
Adams, KS "Bud" Jr....17
Adderley, Terence E....18
Albrecht, Chris....20
Albrecht, Mark....20
Alesio, Steven....21
Alford, Harry C....21
Allen, Paul G....22
Allison, Herbert M Jr....23
Altabef, Peter....23
Alvarado, Linda G....24
Alvarez, Antonio C II....24
Amos, Daniel....25
Anderson, Bradbury H....25
Anderson, Paul M....26
Andreas, G Allen....26
Andreessen, Marc L....26
Annenberg, Walter H....27
Anschutz, Philip F....27
Ansin, Edmund Newton....27
Archibald, Nolan....28
Arison, Micky....29
Arpey, Gerard J....30
Ash, Mary Kay....30
Avent, Sharon Hoffman....32
Babrowski, Claire....34
Ballmer, Steven A....36
Barnes, Brenda C....38
Barrett, Colleen....39
Barrett, Craig R....39
Barth, John....40
Battista, Richard....41
Bechtel, Riley P....43
Belda, Alain JP....44
Belkin, Steven....44
Bendixen, Sergio....46
Benhamou, Eric....46
Benmosche, Robert H....46
Benson, Kevin E....47
Bentas, Lily H....47
Berg, Jeffrey....48
Bern, Dorrit J....49
Bernauer, David W....49
Bernick, Howard B....49
Bernstein, Steven....49
Betty, Garry....50
Bewkes, Jeffrey L....50
Beyster, J Robert....50
Bezos, Jeffrey P....50
Black, Cathleen P....53
Blank, Arthur M....54
Blankfein, Lloyd....54
Bloch, Henry....55
Bloomberg, Michael R....56
Bodenheimer, George....57
Bollenbach, Stephen F....58
Bonnie, Shelby....59
Bovender, Jack O Jr....60
Boyd, Jeffery H....61
Boyle, Gertrude....62
Boyle, Timothy....62
Brandon, David A....64
Bravo, Rose Marie....64
Breen, Edward....65
Bren, Donald L....65
Brenneman, Greg....65
Brin, Sergey....66
Broad, Eli....66
Brown, Colin W....68
Buckley, George W....73
Buffett, Warren E....73
Burd, Steven A....74
Busch, August A III....76
Bush, Fredy....76
Buss, Jerry....76
Butt, Charles C....77
Butte, Amy S....77
Cafaro, Debra A....78
Callahan, Robert F Jr....79
Camilleri, Louis C....79
Cammarata, Bernard....79
Campbell, James....80
Campbell, Kirk....80
Cappiello, Frank....81
Carell, Monroe J Jr....82
Carey, Chase....82
Carsey, Marcy....84
Case, Stephen M....86
Casper, Stephen P....86
Castagna, Vanessa....86
Castro-Wright, Eduardo....87
Catmull, Ed....87
Catz, Safra....87

Subject Index

Business Leaders (Cont'd)

Cerf, Vinton G 88
Chabraja, Nicholas 88
Chambers, John T 88
Chenault, Kenneth I 90
Cherkasky, Michael G 91
Chernin, Peter 91
Chu, James 92
Claflin, Bruce L 93
Clark, Dick 93
Clark, Richard 94
Cohen, Ben 97
Cohen, Betty 97
Cohen, Richard B 97
Colligan, Ed 99
Comper, F Anthony 100
Connor, Christopher 101
Cook, Richard 102
Cook, Scott D 102
Coppola, Michael 103
Corbett, Luke 103
Correll, AD 104
Cote, David M 105
Coxe, Tench 106
Craig, Jenny 106
Crowe, James 109
Crowell, Andrew E 109
Culp, H Lawrence 110
Dahlberg, Ken 113
D'Alessandro, David F 113
Dan, Michael 114
Darbee, Peter 115
Davenport, Lynn P 116
David, George A 116
Davidson, Richard K 116
Davidson, William M 116
Davis, Claude E 117
Davis, Clive 117
Davis, Erroll B Jr 117
Dayton, Sky 118
Deaton, Chad C 119
Decker, Dwight W 120
Decker, Susan 120
Dell, Michael 122
Deromedi, Roger K 123
Desmond-Hellmann, Susan 124
Deutsch, Donny 124
DeVos, Doug 124
DeVos, Richard M 124
Diller, Barry 126
Dillon, David B 126
Dimon, James 126
Disney, Anthea 126
Disney, Roy E 127
Doerr, L John 127
Dolan, Charles F 128
Dolan, Peter R 128
Doley, Harold E Jr 128
Donald, Arnold W 128
Dooner, John 129
Dougan, Brady W 129
Duques, Henry 135
Dyer, Colin 135
Dyson, Esther 135
Earl, Robert I 136
Ebersol, Dick 136
Eckert, Robert A 136
Edelman, Ric 137
Edwardson, John 138
Ejabat, Mory 139
Eller, Timothy 139
Ellison, Lawrence J 140
Engelbreit, Mary 141
Engen, Travis 141
Engibous, Thomas J 141
Eresman, Randy 142
Ergen, Charles W 142
Ernst, Mark 143
Eskew, Michael L 143
Essner, Robert 144
Evanson, Paul 144
Fairbank, Richard 145
Falco, Randy 145
Falk, Thomas 146
Faraci, John V 146
Farr, David 146
Farrell, W James 147
Farris, G Steven 147
Feld, Kenneth 148
Fennessy, Richard A 149
Fetter, Trevor 149
Fettig, Jeff 149
Filo, David 150
Fireman, Paul B 150
Fisher, Donald G 151
Fishman, Steven 151
FitzSimons, Dennis J 151
Flynn, Timothy P 153
Flynt, Larry 153
Foley, William 154
Foote, William 154
Ford, Eileen 154
Ford, Scott 155
Ford, William Clay 155
Ford, William Clay Jr 155
Forsee, Gary D 155
Frankfort, Lew 158
Franklin, Martin 158
Freston, Thomas E 159
Fribourg, Paul J 159
Friedman, Jane 160
Friedman, Rachelle 160
Frost, Richard W 161

Business Leaders (Cont'd)

Fu, Cary T....161
Fudge, Ann....161
Fuld, Richard S Jr....161
Gadiesh, Orit....162
Gallup, Patricia....163
Ganzi, Victor....164
Gates, Bill....166
Gattinella, Wayne....166
Geffen, David L....166
George, Richard L....167
Gilbert, Daniel....169
Gilliland, Sam....170
Gillings, Dennis B....170
Gilman, Kenneth....171
Giuliani, Rudy....172
Glaser, Robert....172
Goldberg, Danny....174
Golisano, B Thomas....174
Goodnight, James H....176
Goolsby, OB Jr....176
Gordon, Ellen....176
Gorman, Leon A....177
Gorog, Chris....177
Grant, Hugh....179
Gratton, Robert....180
Graves, Earl G Sr....180
Grazer, Brian....180
Green, Richard C....181
Greenberg, Jerry A....181
Greenfield, Jerry....182
Grey, Brad....182
Grinney, Jay....184
Grinstein, Gerald....184
Gross, Bill....184
Grove, Andrew S....185
Haas, Bob....187
Hackett, James....187
Hagan, Michael J....188
Hall, Donald J Jr....189
Halmi, Robert Jr....189
Hammergren, John H....191
Hanrahan, Paul....192
Hanway, H Edward....192
Haque, Promod....192
Harding, Scott....192
Harrington, Richard J....194
Harrison, E Hunter....195
Harrison, Shelley A....195
Harrison, William B Jr....195
Hay, Lewis III....197
Hearn, Timothy J....198
Hearst, George R Jr....198
Hefner, Christine....199
Hefner, Hugh....199
Hess, John....203
Heyer, Steven J....203
Hill, David....204
Hoffman, Ronald....207
Hollander, Joel....208
Holliday, Charles O Jr....208
Honeycutt, Van B....209
Horn, Alan....209
Houghton, James R....210
Howard, Ron....211
Huber, David R....211
Huey, John....212
Hughes, Catherine L....212
Huizenga, H Wayne....213
Huntsman, Jon M....214
Hurd, Mark V....214
Iacocca, Lee....215
Icahn, Carl....215
Iger, Robert A....215
Ilitch, Marian....216
Ilitch, Michael....216
Immelt, Jeffrey R....216
Ingram, Martha R....217
Irani, Ray....218
Ireland, Jay....218
Isdell, E Neville....219
Jackson, Mike....220
Jacobs, Irwin M....221
Jacobs, Jeremy M....221
Jacobs, Paul E....221
Jeffries, Michael....224
Jenkins, Charlie Jr....224
Jenness, James....225
Jobs, Steve....225
Johnson, Abigail....226
Johnson, Edward C III....226
Johnson, H Fisk....227
Johnson, John D....227
Johnson, Robert L....228
Johnson, William R....228
Johnston, Larry....228
Jones, John P III....230
Jones, Robert G....230
Joos, David W....231
Jordan, Michael H....231
Josefowicz, Gregory....231
Judge, Jonathan J....232
Jung, Andrea....232
Kapor, Mitchell....234
Karatassos, Pano....235
Karatz, Bruce....235
Karmanos, Peter Jr....235
Karmazin, Mel....235
Katen, Karen....236
Katzenberg, Jeffrey....236
Kearney, Chistopher J....237
Keegan, Robert....237
Kelleher, Herbert D....238

Business Leaders (Cont'd)

Kellner, Larry....238
Kelly, Gary C....238
Kelly, Robert....239
Kennedy, Parker....240
Kent, Philip I....241
Kerger, Paula....241
Kerkorian, Kirk....241
Kerr, David W....241
Ketchum, Mark D....242
Khosla, Vinod....242
Kiely, W Leo....242
Killinger, Kerry....243
Kim, James J....243
Kimmel, Sidney....243
King, Mark....244
Kirsch, Steve....246
Kirsch, William S....246
Kline, Lowry....248
Klose, Kevin....248
Kluge, John W....248
Knauss, Donald R....248
Knight, Philip H....248
Koch, Charles G....249
Kohler, Herbert V Jr....249
Kovacevich, Richard M....251
Krasny, Michael P....252
Krause, Roy G....252
Krawcheck, Sallie L....253
Krehbiel, Frederick A....253
Kullman, Ellen....255
Lack, Andrew R....257
Lacy, Alan J....257
Lafley, Alan G....257
Lampert, Edward S....258
Landon, Allan R....259
Lane, Robert W....259
Lanni, J Terrence....260
Lanza, Frank....260
Larchet, Patti....260
Lauder, Leonard A....261
Lauder, William P....261
Lavin, Leonard H....262
Lawler, Joseph....262
Laybourne, Geraldine....263
Lazarus, Shelly....263
Lee, Debra....265
Lenny, Richard H....267
Lentz, Nathanael V....267
Leonsis, Ted....267
Lepore, Dawn G....267
Lerner, Randolph D....268
Lesar, David J....268
Levine, Howard....269
Levinson, Arthur....269
Lewent, Judy C....270
Lewinter, Mel....270
Lewis, Aylwin B....270
Lewis, Edward....270
Lewis, Kenneth D....270
Liang, Christine....271
Liddy, Edward M....271
Ligon, Austin....272
Lindner, Carl H....273
Liveris, Andrew N....275
Logue, Ronald E....275
Lorberbaum, Jeffrey S....276
Loveman, Gary....277
Lovett, Richard....277
Lucas, George....278
Lundgren, Terry....279
Lynch, Peter L....280
Lyne, Susan....280
Lynton, Michael....281
MacInnis, Frank....282
Mack, John....282
Mackey, John....282
Maffei, Gregory B....284
Magerko, Maggie H....284
Malcolm, Steven....285
Malone, John....286
Maloof, Gavin....286
Maloof, Joe....286
Manoogian, Richard A....288
Mark, Reuben....289
Marriott, JW Jr....290
Marriott, Richard....290
Mars, John F....290
Marshall, Jon A....291
Mas, Jorge....293
Maughan, Rex....295
Mays, L Lowry....296
McCann, James F....296
McCaughey, Gerald....297
McCaw, John E Jr....298
McClure, Charles G "Chip"....298
McCourt, Frank....299
McCoy, Dustan....299
McDaniel, Raymond....300
McGeary, Roderick C....301
McGill, Steve....302
McGovern, Patrick J....302
McGrath, Eugene....302
McGrath, Joseph....302
McGrath, Judy....302
McGraw, Harold III....302
McGuire, William W....303
McKelvey, Andrew J....303
McKenna, Dennis....303
McKinnell, Henry A....304
McLane, Drayton Jr....304
McMahon, Vince....305
McNair, Robert C....305

Business Leaders (Cont'd)

McNealy, Scott....306
McNerney, W James....306
Mehta, Sonny....307
Meijer, Doug....307
Meijer, Hank....307
Melman, Richard....307
Messman, Jack L....310
Meyer, Barry M....310
Meyer, Ron....310
Michaels, Jack D....311
Miller, Alan....312
Miller, Avram....312
Miller, Jonathan....312
Miller, Larry H....313
Ming, Jenny....314
Mitchell, William....315
Mobley, Stacey J....316
Molendorp, Dayton H....316
Monfort, Charles....317
Montgomery, Larry....317
Montrone, Paul....317
Moonves, Leslie....318
Moore, Ann S....318
Moore, Darla D....318
Moore, Gordon E....318
Moore, J Stuart....318
Moran, James M....319
Moran, Patricia G....319
Moreno, Arturo....319
Morgan, James....320
Morgridge, John P....320
Morris, Doug....320
Morris, Michael G....321
Morris, Peter....321
Mudd, Daniel H....323
Mulcahy, Anne M....323
Muller, Edward R....323
Mulva, James J....324
Munger, Charles T....324
Munk, Peter....324
Murdoch, K Rupert....324
Murphy, John V....325
Murphy, Steve....325
Myers, Bruce C....326
Nardelli, Robert L....328
Nassetta, Christopher J....328
Nelson, Marilyn Carlson....330
Neubauer, Joseph....330
Neuharth, Al....330
Newhouse, Donald E....331
Newhouse, Samuel I Jr....331
Niblock, Robert....332
Nieporent, Drew....333
Noddle, Jeffrey....333
Nooyi, Indra K....334
Novak, David....335
O'Brien, James J....337
Odland, Steve....337
Olson, Peter....340
Omidyar, Pierre....341
O'Neal, Stan....341
O'Reilly, David J....342
Orfalea, Paul J....342
Ormond, Paul A....342
Otellini, Paul....344
Otis, Clarence Jr....344
Owens, James W....344
Ozzie, Ray....345
Page, Larry....345
Palmisano, Samuel J....346
Pamplin, Robert B Jr....347
Park, CS....347
Parker, Douglas W....348
Parker, Mark....348
Parrett, William G....348
Parsons, Richard D....349
Pascal, Amy....349
Paulson, Henry M Jr....351
Peek, Jeffrey M....352
Pellett, Nancy C....352
Peluso, Michelle....352
Penske, Roger....353
Perdue, David A....354
Perdue, James A....354
Perelman, Ronald O....354
Perenchio, Jerry....354
Perez, Antonio....354
Perot, Ross....355
Peterson, Donald K....356
Peterson, Peter G....356
Pierce, Harvey R....359
Pilgrim, Bo....359
Plank, Raymond....360
Pollock, Robert B....362
Popeil, Ronald M....363
Porter, Michael E....363
Poses, Frederic....364
Post, Jeffrey....364
Pressler, Paul S....366
Ptak, Frank....368
Rainwater, Gary....370
Rajamannar, MV....370
Ratcliffe, David M....372
Redstone, Shari....374
Redstone, Sumner M....374
Reid, Travis....375
Rein, Jeffrey A....375
Reinemund, Steven S....375
Renwick, Glenn M....376
Reynolds, Robert....377
Rhodes, William....378
Rice, Linda Johnson....378

Business Leaders (Cont'd)

Richenhagen, Martin............................379
Riggio, Leonard................................380
Rivet, Jeannine M..............................381
Roberts, Brian L...............................382
Roberts, Leonard H.............................383
Robertson, Michael L...........................383
Rodale, Ardath.................................385
Rodkin, Gary...................................385
Rogel, Steven R................................386
Rogers, Edward S...............................386
Rohr, James E..................................387
Rooney, Therese A..............................389
Rose, Robert E.................................389
Rosen, Uzi.....................................389
Rosensweig, Dan................................390
Rosenthal, Daniel D............................390
Roski, Edward P Jr.............................390
Ross, Scott....................................390
Rowe, John W...................................391
Rowling, Robert B..............................391
Rubin, Robert E................................392
Ruiz, Hector...................................392
Russell, Herman J..............................393
Russo, Patricia F..............................393
Rust, Edward B Jr..............................394
Ryan, Arthur F.................................394
Ryan, Patrick G................................394
Ryan, Patrick T................................394
Ryan, Thomas M.................................394
Ryder, Thomas O................................394
Sabia, Michael J...............................395
Sall, John.....................................397
Sammons, Mary..................................397
Sandler, Marion O..............................398
Sanger, Stephen................................398
Santana, Jose..................................399
Sargent, Ronald................................399
Savage, Frank..................................400
Scardino, Marjorie M...........................401
Schar, Dwight..................................402
Scher, Laura...................................402
Schleyer, William T............................403
Schmidt, Eric E................................404
Schnatter, John H..............................404
Schneider, Donald J............................404
Schnieders, Richard J..........................404
Schuessler, John...............................405
Schultz, Howard................................405
Schulze, Richard M.............................406
Schutz, Stephen................................406
Schwab, Charles R..............................406
Schwab, Leslie B...............................406
Schwartz, Jonathan.............................406
Schwartz, Ted..................................406
Scott, Walter Jr...............................408
Seidenberg, Ivan...............................409
Semel, Terry...................................410
Serra, Matthew.................................411
Shapira, David S...............................412
Sharer, Kevin..................................413
Shaye, Robert K................................413
Sidhu, Sanjiv S................................417
Silverman, Henry R.............................418
Simmons, Russell...............................418
Sinegal, James D...............................419
Skinner, James A...............................420
Sloan, Harry...................................421
Smith, Daniel E................................422
Smith, Frederick W.............................422
Smucker, Richard K.............................424
Smucker, Timothy P.............................424
Snider, Stacey.................................425
Snyder, Daniel M...............................425
Snyder, Rick...................................425
Solomon, Howard................................426
Solovic, Susan.................................426
Soros, George..................................427
Spielberg, Steven..............................429
Splinter, Michael..............................429
Stahl, Jack L..................................431
Staley, Warren R...............................431
Standley, John T...............................431
Steenland, Douglas M...........................433
Steiner, David.................................433
Sternberg, Seymour G...........................434
Stevens, Robert J..............................434
Stewart, Martha................................435
Storch, Gerald.................................436
Stotlar, Douglas...............................437
Stringer, Howard...............................438
Strohm, David..................................438
Stronach, Frank................................438
Sullivan, Martin...............................439
Sullivan, William..............................439
Sulzberger, Arthur Jr..........................440
Surma, John P Jr...............................440
Swanson, William H.............................441
Symons, Jeanette...............................441
Syms, Marcy....................................441
Syron, Richard F...............................442
Szymanczyk, Michael E..........................442
Tang, Cyrus....................................443
Taurel, Sidney.................................444
Taylor, Andrew C...............................444
Taylor, Glen A.................................444
Templeton, Richard K...........................445
Tharaldson, Gary...............................446
Thompson, John W...............................449
Thompson, Ken..................................449
Thomsen, Linda C...............................449
Tillerson, Rex.................................450
Tilton, Glenn F................................450

Business Leaders (Cont'd)

Tisch, Andrew H 451
Tisch, James S 451
Tisch, Jonathan M 451
Toben, Doreen A 451
Tobin, James R 451
Toffler, Alvin 451
Toll, Robert I 452
Tome, Carol B 452
Torvalds, Linus 453
Tose, Maurice B 453
Traquina, Perry M 453
Trefler, Alan 454
Trump, Donald J 455
Tucci, Joseph M 455
Turley, James S 456
Turner, Ted 456
Tyson, John 457
Udvar-Hazy, Steven F 457
Ullman, Myron E III 457
Ulrich, Robert J 457
Ustian, Daniel C 458
Van Andel, Jay 459
Van Andel, Steve 459
Vass, Bill 461
Voelker, Jim 464
Wagner, Lawrence M 465
Wagoner, G Richard 465
Wainscott, James L 466
Waitt, Ted 466
Walter, Robert D 468
Walton, S Robson 468
Wang, Charles B 469
Ward, Jonathan P 469
Ward, Michael J 469
Warner, Ty 469
Weaver, Wayne 472
Wedge, Michael T 472
Weeks, Wendell 472
Weill, Sanford I 473
Welch, Jack 473
Weldon, William C 474
Weston, W Galen 475
Wetherell, David S 476
Wexner, Leslie H 476
Whitacre, Edward E Jr 476
White, Miles D 477
Whitman, Meg 477
Wiatt, James 478
Wilansky, Heywood 478
Wilder, C John 478
Wilderotter, Maggie 479
Wilhelm, James A 479
Wilkins, Gregory C 479
Wilpon, Fred 483
Winblad, Ann L 484
Winfrey, Oprah 484
Wirthlin, Richard B 485
Wittman, Vanessa Ames 486
Wood, Robert L 487
Wozniak, Steve 488
Wright, Robert C 489
Wrigley, William Jr 489
Wygod, Martin J 490
Yang, Geoffrey Y 490
Yang, Jerry 490
Yoran, Amit 492
Yost, R David 492
Zander, Edward J 493
Ziemer, James L 494
Zillmer, John J 494
Zimmer, George 494
Zollars, William D 495
Zucker, Jeffrey A 495

Cartoonists - Comic Strips & Panels

Adams, Scott 17
Alcaraz, Lalo 20
Aldrich, Lance 20
Amend, Bill 24
Anderson, Brad 25
Armstrong, Robb 29
Armstrong, Tom 29
Ayers, Chuck 33
Baldwin, Mike 35
Barrows, Allison 39
Basset, Brian 41
Batiuk, Tom 41
Bell, Darrin 44
Bell-Lundy, Sandra 45
Bender, Carole 45
Bender, Jack 45
Bentley, Stephen 47
Billingsley, Ray 51
Blake, Bud 54
Boldman, Craig 57
Bolle, Frank 58
Bolling, Ruben 58
Borgman, Jim 59
Brady, Pat 63
Breathed, Berkeley 65
Breen, Steve 65
Brigman, June 66
Brookins, Gary 67
Brown, Chester 68
Browne, Chance 71
Browne, Chris 71
Cabrera, Rob 78
Campbell, Jenny 80
Cantu, Hector 81
Casson, Mel 86
Castellanos, Carlos 86
Chast, Roz 89

Cartoonists - Comic Strips & Panels (Cont'd)

Cho, Frank 92
Church, Jok 93
Clark, Todd 94
Clowes, Daniel 96
Cochran, Tony 96
Condron, Bob 100
Conley, Darby 100
Coverly, Dave 106
Crane, Brian 107
Cravens, Greg 107
Crumb, Robert 110
Curfman, Greg 111
Davis, Jim 117
Deering, John 120
Delainey, Gary 121
Detorie, Rick 124
Dickenson, Steve 125
Donnelly, Liza 129
Duffy, JC 132
Dumas, Jerry 133
Dunagin, Ralph 133
Dunham, Chip 133
Eastman, Kevin 136
Eisman, Hy 139
Eliot, Jan 139
Elrod, Jack 140
Evans, Greg 144
Fagan, Kevin 145
Frank, Phil 157
Fredericks, Fred 159
Fry, Michael 161
Gary, Charlos 165
Gately, George 166
Gianni, Gary 168
Gilbert, David 169
Gilchrist, Brad 170
Gilchrist, Guy 170
Gilligan, Paul 170
Glasbergen, Randy 172
Goldberg, Stan 174
Grace, Bud 177
Griffith, Bill 183
Groening, Matt 184
Guisewite, Cathy 186
Guren, Peter 187
Harrell, Rob 193
Harris, Jeff 194
Hart, Johnny 195
Heath, Mark 198
Heir, Theron 200
Hinds, Bill 205
Hoest, Bunny 206
Holbrook, Bill 207
Hollander, Nicole 208
Janz, Matt 223
Johnson, Jimmy 227
Johnston, Lynn 229
Keane, Bil 236
Keefe, Jim 237
Key, Ted 242
Killian, Mike 243
Kirkman, Rick 246
Kochalka, James 249
Kovaleski, John 252
LaBan, Terry 256
Laird, Peter 258
Larson, Julie 261
Lazarus, Mell 263
LeDoux, Harold 264
Lee, Stan 265
Lee, Vic 265
Lewis, T 271
Locher, Dick 275
Lorenz, Lee 277
MacIntosh, Craig 282
Mallett, Jef 286
Mankoff, Robert 287
Marciuliano, Francesco 289
Marlette, Doug 290
Martin, Joe 292
McCoy, Glenn 299
McDonnell, Patrick 300
McEldowney, Brooke 300
McFarlane, Todd 301
McGarry, Steve 301
McGruder, Aaron 302
McPherson, John 306
Meddick, Jim 306
Mignola, Mike 311
Millar, Jeff 311
Miller, Wiley 313
Millionaire, Tony 314
Montague-Reyes, Karen 317
Moore, Steve 318
Mora, Gene 319
Morgan, Mike 320
Myers, Russell 326
Nolan, Graham 334
Panter, Gary 347
Parisi, Mark 347
Parker, Brant 348
Pastis, Stephan 349
Peirce, Lincoln 352
Peters, Mike 356
Piccolo, Rina 358
Piraro, Dan 360
Price, Hilary 366
Raeside, Adrian 369
Rasmussen, Gerry 371
Rechin, Bill 373
Rehr, Henrik 375
Reiner, John 375

Cartoonists - Comic Strips & Panels (Cont'd)

Roberts, Patrick....383
Rose, John....389
Rubin, Leigh....392
Ryan, Tom K....394
Sakai, Stan....396
Sansom, Chip....399
Scaduto, Al....401
Scancarelli, Jim....401
Scarpelli, Henry....402
Schmich, Mary....404
Schneider, Howie....404
Schorr, Bill....405
Schulz, Charles....406
Scott, Jerry....408
Shulock, Margaret....416
Smith, Jeff....422
Spiegelman, Art....429
Stahler, Jeff....431
Stantis, Scott....432
Starlin, James P....432
Stern, Tom....434
Stevens, Mick....434
Stromoski, Rick....438
Summers, Dana....440
Tatulli, Mark....443
Telnaes, Ann C....445
Tennant, Rich....446
Thaves, Bob....446
Thompson, Craig....448
Tinsley, Bruce....451
Toomey, Jim....452
Troise, Joe....454
Trudeau, Garry....454
Turner, Morrie....456
Unger, Jim....458
Van Amerongen, Jerry....459
Wagner, Fred....465
Waldner, Peter....466
Walker, Brian....466
Walker, Greg....467
Walker, Mort....467
Wallace, Russ....467
Ware, Chris....469
Watterson, Bill....471
Weber, Bob Jr....472
Weber, Bob Sr....472
Whamond, Dave....476
Wilder, Don....478
Wilson, Tom II....484
Wilson, Woody....484
Wise, Gary....485
Wright, Larry....489
Young, Dean....492
Ziegler, Jack....494

Cartoonists & Caricaturists - Editorial

Aislin....19
Alcaraz, Lalo....20
Anderson, Kirk....25
Anderson, Nick....25
Ariail, Robert....28
Asay, Chuck....30
Auth, Tony....32
Babin, Rex....34
Beattie, Bruce....43
Bennett, Clay....46
Benson, Steve....47
Bish, Randy....52
Bok, Chip....57
Borgman, Jim....59
Branch, John....63
Breen, Steve....65
Britt, Chris....66
Brookins, Gary....67
Cagle, Daryl....78
Carlson, Stuart....82
Catalino, Ken....87
Conrad, Paul....101
Corrigan, Patrick....104
Curtis, Stacy....112
Davies, Matt....116
Day, Bill....118
Deering, John....120
Duffy, Brian....132
Feiffer, Jules....148
Gamble, Ed....163
Gorrell, Bob....177
Handelsman, Walt....191
Heller, Joe....200
Higgins, Jack....204
Hitch, David....206
Holbert, Jerry....207
Horsey, David....210
Hulme, Etta....213
Jones, Clay....229
Jones, Taylor....230
Keefe, Mike....237
Kelley, Steve....238
Koterba, Jeff....251
Landgren, Don Jr....259
Litton, Drew....274
Locher, Dick....275
Lowe, Chan....278
Luckovich, Mike....279
MacKay, Graeme....282
Margulies, Jimmy....289
Markstein, Gary....290
Marlette, Doug....290
McCoy, Glenn....299
McKee, Rick....303
Menees, Tim....308
Morin, Jim....320

Cartoonists & Caricaturists - Editorial (Cont'd)

Mosher, Terry....321
Moss, Geoffrey....322
Ohman, Jack....338
Oliphant, Pat....339
Payne, Henry....351
Peters, Mike....356
Pett, Joel....356
Pett, Mark....356
Powell, Dwane....365
Raeside, Adrian....369
Rall, Ted....370
Ramirez, Michael....370
Ramsey, Marshall....371
Ritter, Mike....381
Rogers, Rob....387
Sack, Steve....395
Sargent, Ben....399
Schorr, Bill....405
Shelton, Mike....414
Sheneman, Drew....414
Siers, Kevin....417
Smith, Mike....423
Stahler, Jeff....431
Stayskal, Wayne....432
Stein, Ed....433
Suits, Julia....439
Summers, Dana....440
Szep, Paul....442
Telnaes, Ann C....445
Thompson, Mike....449
Toles, Tom....452
Trever, John....454
Varvel, Gary....461
Waghorn, Kerry....465
Walters, Kirk....468
Wasserman, Dan....470
Wilkinson, Signe....479
Wright, Don....489

Chefs

Adams, Jamie....17
Adams, Jody....17
Amernick, Ann....24
Antunes, Joel....28
Auden, Bruce....32
Avondoglio, Kirk....33
Baker, Mark....35
Barker, Ben....37
Barker, Karen....37
Batali, Mario....41
Bayliss, Rick....42
Bittman, Mark....53
Blitz, Marty....55
Blumer, Bob....56
Bouley, David....60
Boulot, Philippe....60
Boulud, Daniel....60
Bourdain, Anthony....60
Brown, Alton....68
Caggiano, Biba....78
Carsberg, Scott....84
Cary, Kathy....85
Chiarello, Michael....91
Choy, Sam....92
Colicchio, Tom....99
Daelemans, Kathleen....113
de Cavel, Jean-Robert....119
De Laurentiis, Giada....119
Deen, Paula....120
Del Grande, Robert....121
Denton, Jody....123
Des Jardins, Traci....123
Desaulniers, Marcel....123
DiSpirito, Rocco....127
Donna, Roberto....128
Dooher, Donna....129
Douglas, Tom....130
Ducasse, Alain....132
Earles, Johnny....136
Eismann, Jonathan....139
English, Todd....141
Feniger, Susan....149
Flay, Bobby....152
Florence, Tyler....153
Galloping Gourmet....163
Gand, Gale....163
Garten, Ina....165
Gerin, Jean-Louis....167
Ginsburg, Art....171
Goin, Suzanne....173
Gray, Todd....180
Hamersley, Gordon....190
Harrison, Clifford....194
Hayward, Sam....198
Hefter, Lee....199
Higgins, Greg....203
Jeanty, Philippe....224
Joho, Jean....229
Kahan, Paul....233
Karatassos, Pano....234
Kashiba, Shiro....235
Keller, Hubert....238
Kelly, Melissa....238
Kerr, Graham....241
Kinkead, Bob....245
Kornick, Michael....251
Lacroix, Jean-Marie....257
Lagasse, Emeril....257
Lomonaco, Michael....276
Lukins, Sheila....279
Lynch, Barbara....280
Malouf, Waldy....286

Chefs (Cont'd)

Manion, John 287
Matsuhisa, Nobuyuki 294
Mavrothalassitis, George 295
McClelland, Frank 298
McGrath, Robert 302
Milliken, Mary Sue 313
Moulton, Sara 322
Mr Food 322
Murphy, Tamara 325
Nischan, Michel 333
O'Connell, Patrick 337
Ogden, Bradley 338
Oliver, Jamie 340
Oringer, Ken 342
Osteen, Louis 343
Palmer, Charlie 346
Peck, Carole 352
Peel, Mark 352
Pellegrini, Luciano 352
Pence, Caprial 353
Pepin, Jacques 354
Pernot, Guillermo 355
Perrier, Georges 355
Portale, Alfred 363
Pouillon, Nora 365
Prudhomme, Paul 367
Puck, Wolfgang 368
Raichlen, Steven 370
Rathbun, Kent 372
Rathbun, Kevin 372
Ray, Rachael 372
Ripert, Eric 381
Rockenwagner, Hans 385
Romano, Michael 388
Rosengarten, David 390
Ruta, Frank A. 394
Samuelsson, Marcus 397
Schlesinger, Chris 403
Schlow, Michael 404
Schreiber, Cory 405
Serrano, Julian 411
Siu, Russell WJ 420
Sone, Hiro 426
Sortun, Ana 427
Spicer, Susan 429
Splichal, Joachim 429
Stellino, Nick 433
Stitt, Frank 436
Susser, Allen 440
Torres, Jacques 452
Traunfeld, Jerry 453
Trotter, Charlie 454
Tsai, Ming 455
Van Aken, Norman 459
Vetri, Marc 462
Vongerichten, Jean-Georges 464
Waggoner, Robert 465
Waters, Alice 470
Wilder, Janos 478
Wright, Clifford A. 489
Yamaguchi, Roy 490
Yard, Sherry 491

Choreographers

See: Dancers & Choreographers pg 532

Columnists - Commentary

See: Journalists (Print) pg 543

Columnists - Lifestyle & Features

Alkon, Amy 21
Archerd, Army 28
Arnet, Danielle 29
Barry, Dave 39
Bazer, Mark 42
Beck, Marilyn 43
Bennett, Cherie 46
Berger, Dan 48
Berko, Malcolm 48
Bigar, Jacqueline 51
Black, Linda 53
Blonz, Ed 55
Brazelton, T Berry 64
Brothers, Joyce 68
Brun, Christine 71
Burness, Tad 74
Burns, Scott 75
Burros, Marian 75
Cameron, W Bruce 79
Carrell, Al 83
Carrell, Kelly 83
Carter, Chip 84
Carter, Jonathan 85
Carter, Tim 85
Cohen, Harlan 97
Cohen, Randy 97
Cole, Harriette 98
Cruz, Humberto 110
Dale, Steve 113
Dauten, Dale 116
Debnam, Betty 120
Deitz, Susan 121
Denton, Stephanie 123
Dickinson, Amy 125
Donohue, Paul 129
Dr Ruth 131
Ebert, Roger 136
Eberts, Marge 136
Edelman, Ric 137
Ennico, Cliff 142
Erickson, Donna 143
Farmer, Eunice 146

Columnists - Lifestyle & Features (Cont'd)

FitzGerald, Tom 151
Flowers, Paulette 153
Fox, Michael 156
Friedman, Amy 160
Frommer, Arthur 160
Gardner, David 164
Gardner, Tom 164
Gellman, Marc 167
Gilliland, Jillian 170
Gisler, Peggy 171
Glink, Ilyce 173
Gott, Peter 177
Graedon, Joe 178
Graedon, Teresa 178
Gray, John 180
Grove, Lloyd 185
Hamilton, Gene 190
Hamilton, Katie 190
Harney, Kenneth 193
Hartman, Tom 195
Heady, Robert K 198
Heloise 200
Hirsch, Lynda 205
Hobica, George 206
Hoffman, Ken 207
Howard, Margo 211
Hunt, Mary 213
Jones, Jeanne 230
Kennedy, Joyce Lain 240
Kinsolving, Carey 245
Kornheiser, Tony 251
Kovel, Ralph 252
Kovel, Terry 252
Kristof, Kathy 253
Landers, Ann 259
Lank, Edith 260
Last, Eugenia 261
Lavin, Cheryl 262
Leblang, Bonnie Tandy 264
Leckey, Andrew 264
Mackay, Harvey 282
Magliozzi, Ray 284
Magliozzi, Tom 284
Mammana, Dennis 287
Margolis, Matthew 289
Martin, Ellen James 291
Martin, Judith 292
McAllister, Rallie 296
McDonough, Kevin 300
McKay, Peter 303
McMahon, Tom 305
Meeks, Larry 307
Merin, Jennifer 309
Miss Manners 314
Mullen, Jim 323
Myers, David W 326
Nelson, Stephanie 330
Newman, Steve 331
Nicholson, Susan 332
Novak, Lindsey 335
Perkins, Ed 354
Phillips, Jeanne 358
Pope, Edwin 363
Post, Peggy 364
Preston, Marilynn 366
Price, Deb 366
Rimm, Sylvia 380
Rubenstein, Atoosa 392
Saunders, Jeraldine 400
Savage, Terry 400
Schwabach, Bob 406
Schwabach, Joy 406
Seamans, Andy 409
Seniuk, Lasha 410
Shales, Tom 412
Shepherd, Chuck 414
Sichelman, Lew 417
Sikorsky, Bob 417
Singletary, Michelle 420
Smith, Liz 423
Smith, Stacy Jenel 423
Smith, Steve 423
Spadafori, Gina 428
St Clair, Rita 430
Travis, Debbie 454
Tyson, Eric 457
Wallraff, Barbara 468
Wendleton, Kate 474
Wernick, Allan 475
Westheimer, Ruth 475
Williams, Bruce 480
Winship, Peg 485
Wolff, Bobby 486
Wyman, Carolyn 490
Ziglar, Zig 494

Comedians

Adams, Orny 17
Allen, Tim 22
Anderson, Louie 25
Arnold, Tom 29
Attell, Dave 31
Barr, Roseanne 39
Becker, Rob 43
Behar, Joy 44
Belzer, Richard 45
Bernhard, Sandra 49
Brady, Wayne 63
Burnett, Carol 74
Butler, Brett 76
Cantone, Mario 81
Carey, Drew 82

Comedians (Cont'd)

Carlin, George ... 82
Carrot Top ... 84
Carvey, Dana ... 85
Cedric the Entertainer ... 87
Chappelle, Dave ... 89
Cho, Margaret ... 92
Chong, Tommy ... 92
CK, Louis ... 93
Clark, Anthony ... 93
Collins, Bobby ... 99
Cosby, Bill ... 104
Coulier, Dave ... 105
Crosby, Norm ... 108
Crystal, Billy ... 110
DeGeneres, Ellen ... 120
Dick, Andy ... 125
Engvall, Bill ... 141
Essman, Susie ... 143
Fallon, Jimmy ... 146
Ferrell, Will ... 149
Foxworthy, Jeff ... 157
Foxx, Jamie ... 157
Franken, Al ... 158
Gallagher ... 162
Garlin, Jeff ... 164
Garofalo, Janeane ... 165
Garrett, Brad ... 165
Goldberg, Whoopi ... 174
Goldthwait, Bobcat ... 174
Gottfried, Gilbert ... 177
Griffin, Kathy ... 183
Hammond, Darrell ... 191
Harvey, Steve ... 196
Herman, Pee Wee ... 202
Hughley, DL ... 212
Idle, Eric ... 215
Izzard, Eddie ... 219
James, Kevin ... 222
Johnson, Jay ... 227
Kennedy, Jamie ... 240
Klein, Robert ... 247
Larry the Cable Guy ... 260
Lawrence, Martin ... 263
Leary, Denis ... 263
Leguizamo, John ... 266
Leifer, Carol ... 266
Leno, Jay ... 267
Lewis, Jerry ... 270
Liebman, Wendy ... 272
Lopez, George ... 276
Lovitz, Jon ... 278
Mac, Bernie ... 281
MacDonald, Norm ... 282
Maher, Bill ... 285
Mandel, Howie ... 287
Martin, Steve ... 292
Mason, Jackie ... 293
Mercer, Roy D ... 309
Miller, Dennis ... 312
Miller, Larry ... 313
Mo'Nique ... 317
Murphy, Eddie ... 325
Nealon, Kevin ... 329
Newhart, Bob ... 331
O'Donnell, Rosie ... 338
Penn & Teller ... 353
Poundstone, Paula ... 365
Rhea, Caroline ... 377
Rickles, Don ... 379
Rivers, Joan ... 381
Rock, Chris ... 385
Rodriguez, Paul ... 386
Romano, Ray ... 388
Rudner, Rita ... 392
Saget, Bob ... 396
Sandler, Adam ... 398
Schimmel, Robert ... 403
Seinfeld, Jerry ... 409
Shandling, Garry ... 412
Shore, Pauly ... 416
Short, Martin ... 416
Sinbad ... 419
Slayton, Bobby ... 421
Smirnoff, Yakov ... 421
Smothers, Dick ... 424
Smothers, Tom ... 424
Spade, David ... 428
Stewart, Jon ... 435
Stine, Brad ... 435
Sykes, Wanda ... 441
Thompson, Scott ... 449
Tomlin, Lily ... 452
Tucker, Chris ... 455
Wallace, George ... 467
Williams, Robin ... 481
Wright, Steven ... 489
Wuhl, Robert ... 489

Conservationists

See: Organization Leaders pg 550

Corporate Trainers

See: Motivational Speakers pg 546

Critics (Art, Books, Film, Music)

Acocella, Joan ... 16
Adams, Thelma ... 17
Alterman, Eric ... 24
Ansen, David ... 27
Artner, Alan ... 30
Barclay, Dolores ... 37
Barnes, Clive ... 38

Critics (Art, Books, Film, Music) (Cont'd)

Bianculli, David....50
Brantley, Ben....64
Browne, David....71
Caro, Mark....83
Corliss, Richard....104
Corrigan, Maureen....104
Danto, Arthur C....115
Denby, David....122
DeRogatis, Jim....123
Dirda, Michael....126
Dunning, Jennifer....134
Ebert, Roger....136
Edelstein, David....137
Eichman, Erich....138
Franklin, Nancy....158
Gleiberman, Owen....172
Habes, Bob....187
Hoberman, J....206
Holden, Stephen....207
Holland, Bernard....208
Horwitz, Jane....210
Husni, Samir A....214
Kauffmann, Stanley....236
Kisor, Henry....246
Kitman, Marvin....246
Klawans, Stuart....247
Knight, Christopher....248
Kot, Greg....251
Lane, Anthony....259
Lawson, Terry....263
Leonard, John....267
Lyons, Jeffrey....281
Maltin, Leonard....286
Maslin, Janet....293
McDonough, Kevin....300
Medved, Michael....307
Menand, Louis....308
Mondello, Bob....317
Mr Magazine....322
Poniewozik, James....362
Reed, Rex....374
Reich, Howard....375
Rodriguez, Rene....386
Roeper, Richard....386
Rozen, Leah....392
Sachs, Lloyd....395
Santoro, Gene....399
Schwarzbaum, Lisa....407
Segal, Lewis....409
Seitz, Matt Zoller....410
Shales, Tom....412
Shalit, Gene....412
Siegel, Joel....417
Smith, Roberta....423
Sterritt, David....434
Swed, Mark....441
Travers, Peter....453
Tucker, Ken....455
Turan, Kenneth....455
Von Rhein, John....464
Weiss, Hedy....473
White, Armond....477
Wieseltier, Leon....478
Wilmington, Michael....483
Wuntch, Philip....489
Yardley, Jonathan....491

Cyclists

See: Sports Personalities (Misc) pg 558

Dancers & Choreographers

Abdul, Paula....15
Ailey, Alvin....19
Allen, Debbie....22
Ananiashvili, Nina....25
Ann-Margret....27
Arpino, Gerald....30
Askegard, Charles....31
Balanchine, George....35
Barbee, Victor....37
Baryshnikov, Mikhail....40
Bocca, Julio....56
Bourne, Matthew....60
Brown, Trisha....70
Carreno, Jose Manuel....83
Chakiris, George....88
Chaya, Masazumi....90
Corella, Angel....103
Cunningham, Merce....111
Derricks, Marguerite....123
Ferri, Alessandra....149
Flatley, Michael....152
Glover, Savion....173
Gomes, Marcelo....174
Hubbe, Nikolaj....211
Inaba, Carrie Ann....216
Jamison, Judith....223
Jansen, JoAnn....223
Jasperse, John....223
Joffrey, Robert....225
Jones, Bill T....229
Kage, Jonas....233
Karaty, Dan....235
Kemp, Will....239
Kent, Julie....241
Kirstein, Lincoln....246
Kistler, Darci....246
Kries, Jennifer....253
Kubovy, Itamar....254
Kudelka, James....254
Kudelka, Marty....255
Liang, Edwaard....271

Dancers & Choreographers (Cont'd)

MacLaine, Shirley....283
Malakhov, Vladimir....285
Maldonado, Chuck....285
Martins, Nilas....293
Martins, Peter....293
Maxwell, Carla....295
McKayle, Donald....303
McKenzie, Kevin....304
Mitchell, Arthur....315
Morris, Mark....321
Nakamura, Kaori....328
Nichols, Kyra....332
Nissinen, Mikko....333
Ortega, Kenny....342
Parsons, David....349
Robbins, Jerome....382
Robinson, Cleo Parker....384
Robinson, Fatima....384
Robson, Wade....384
Rooney, Michael....389
Russell, Francia....393
Soto, Jock....427
Stiefel, Ethan....435
Stowell, Kent....437
Taylor, Paul....444
Tomasson, Helgi....452
Tune, Tommy....455
Villella, Edward....463
Welch, Stanton....473
Wevers, Olivier....476
Wheeldon, Christopher....476
Whelan, Wendy....476
Woetzel, Damian....486

Directors, Producers, Creators, Writers (Movies & TV)

See also: Animators pg 505

Allen, Woody....22
Altman, Robert....24
Anderson, Paul Thomas....26
Apted, Michael....28
Attenborough, Richard....31
Ball, Alan....36
Beatty, Warren....43
Bellisario, Donald....45
Bender, Lawrence....46
Benigni, Roberto....46
Bertolucci, Bernardo....50
Bochco, Steven....56
Branagh, Kenneth....63
Brooks, James L....68
Brooks, Mel....68
Brown, David....69
Bruckheimer, Jerry....71
Bullock, Sandra....73
Burns, Edward....75
Burns, Ken....75
Burton, Tim....76
Cameron, James....79
Cannell, Stephen J....80
Carpenter, John....83
Carsey, Marcy....84
Cassavetes, Nick....86
Chase, David....89
Clark, Dick....93
Coen, Ethan....96
Coen, Joel....97
Columbus, Chris....100
Coolidge, Martha....102
Coppola, Francis Ford....103
Coppola, Sofia....103
Costner, Kevin....105
Crane, David....107
Crowe, Cameron....109
Darabont, Frank....115
David, Larry....116
de Bont, Jan....119
De Palma, Brian....119
DeLuise, Peter....122
Demme, Jonathan....122
DeNiro, Robert....122
DeVito, Danny....124
Donner, Richard....129
Douglas, Michael....130
Dugan, Dennis....133
Eastwood, Clint....136
Edwards, Blake....137
Egoyan, Atom....138
Emmerich, Roland....141
English, Diane....141
Ephron, Nora....142
Eszterhas, Joe....144
Fager, Jeffrey....145
Farrelly, Bobby....147
Farrelly, Peter....147
Fontana, Tom....154
Forman, Milos....155
Foster, Jodie....156
Frears, Stephen....159
Friedkin, William....159
Ganis, Sid....163
Geffen, David L....166
Gibson, Mel....169
Goldsman, Akiva....174
Grazer, Brian....180
Greenspan, Bud....182
Guest, Christopher....185
Hall, Barbara....189
Hampton, Christopher....191
Hanks, Tom....191
Heckerling, Amy....199
Hewitt, Don....203

Directors, Producers, Creators, Writers (Movies & TV) (Cont'd)

Howard, Ron....211
Hughes, John....212
Ivory, James....219
Jackson, Peter....221
Jarmusch, Jim....223
Jewison, Norman....225
Jonze, Spike....231
Katzenberg, Jeffrey....236
Kauffman, Marta....236
Kaufman, Philip....236
Kelley, David E....238
King, Michael Patrick....244
Koepp, David....249
LaGravenese, Richard....257
Landis, John....259
Leder, Mimi....264
Lee, Ang....264
Lee, Spike....265
Levinson, Barry....269
Liman, Doug....272
Lonergan, Kenneth....276
Lucas, George....278
Lumet, Sidney....279
Lynch, David....280
Lyne, Adrian....280
Lynn, Jonathan....280
Madden, John....283
Maiellaro, Matt....285
Mamet, David....287
Mann, Emily....287
Mann, Michael....287
Marshall, Garry....291
Marshall, Penny....291
May, Elaine....295
McG....301
Mendes, Sam....308
Michaels, Lorne....311
Minghella, Anthony....314
Mischer, Don....314
Moore, Michael....318
Morris, Errol....320
Newell, Mike....331
Nichol, Joseph McGinty....332
Nichols, Mike....332
Nimoy, Leonard....333
Oz, Frank....345
Parker, Trey....348
Penn, Sean....353
Petersen, Wolfgang....356
Polanski, Roman....362
Pollack, Sydney....362
Ramis, Harold....371
Ratner, Brett....372
Redford, Robert....373
Reiner, Rob....376
Reitman, Ivan....376
Ridley, John....380
Robbins, Tim....382
Rodriguez, Robert....386
Romanek, Mark....388
Ross, Gary....390
Rudin, Scott....392
Russell, Jay....393
Sayles, John....401
Schumacher, Joel....406
Scorsese, Martin....407
Scott, Ridley....408
Scott, Tony....408
Seagal, Steven....408
Shepard, Sam....414
Sherman-Palladino, Amy....415
Shyamalan, M Night....417
Silver, Joel....417
Singer, Bryan....419
Singleton, John....420
Smith, Kevin....423
Sonnenfeld, Barry....427
Sorkin, Aaron....427
Spelling, Aaron....428
Spielberg, Steven....429
Star, Darren....432
Stiller, Ben....435
Stipe, Michael....436
Stone, Matt....436
Stone, Oliver....436
Streisand, Barbra....438
Tally, Ted....442
Tarantino, Quentin....443
Taymor, Julie....445
Thomas, Betty....447
Thornton, Billy Bob....449
Tolan, Peter....451
Van Sant, Gus....460
Vardalos, Nia....460
Wachowski, Andy....465
Wachowski, Larry....465
Walker, Andrew Kevin....466
Wayans, Keenen Ivory....471
Weir, Peter....473
Wells, John....474
Werner, Tom....475
Whedon, Joss....476
Whitaker, Forest....476
Williamson, Kevin....482
Willis, Dave....482
Winkler, Henry....485
Wolf, Dick....486
Woo, John....487
Woodward, Lydia....488
Zemeckis, Robert....494

Disc Jockeys

See: Radio Personalities pg 554

Dramatists

See: Playwrights pg 553

Economists

Altman, Stuart 24
Arrow, Kenneth J 30
Asmus, Barry 31
Barfield, Claude E. 37
Becker, Gary S. 43
Bernanke, Ben S 49
Bies, Susan Schmidt 51
Bourguignon, Francois 60
Buchanan, James M Jr 72
Calfee, John E 78
Calomiris, Charles 79
Canton, James 81
Chimerine, Lawrence 91
Coase, Ronald H 96
Debreu, Gerard 120
Dent, Harry S Jr 123
Eberstadt, Nicholas 136
Fogel, Robert W 153
Friedman, Milton 160
Fuchs, Victor 161
Glassman, James K 172
Goodman, John C. 176
Hahn, Robert W 188
Hall, Robert E 189
Hassett, Kevin A 196
Heckman, James J 199
Helms, Robert P 200
Howe, Neil 211
Hubbard, R Glenn 211
Kahneman, Daniel 233
Klein, Lawrence R 247
Kohn, Donald L. 249
Kosters, Marvin H 251
Kotlikoff, Laurence J. 251
Kroszner, Randall S. 254
Kudlow, Lawrence 255
Lazear, Edward P 263
Lerman, Robert 268
Lindsey, Lawrence B 273
Lucas, Robert E Jr 279
Makin, John H 285
Marron, Donald B. 290
McFadden, Daniel L. 301
Meltzer, Allan H 308
Merton, Robert C 309
Meyer, Laurence H. 310
Moon, Marilyn 317
Mundell, Robert A 324
North, Douglass C 335
Olson, Mark W. 340
Penner, Rudolph G 353
Peterson, George E 356
Prescott, Edward C 365
Rajapatirana, Sarath 370
Reinhardt, Uwe E 376
Reynolds, Alan 377
Reynolds, Don 377
Roberts, Paul Craig 383
Romer, Paul M. 388
Rubin, Robert E 392
Rukeyser, Louis 392
Samuelson, Paul A. 397
Saving, Thomas R 401
Schelling, Thomas C 402
Scholes, Myron S 404
Sharpe, William F. 413
Shaw, Kathryn L. 413
Shilling, A Gary 415
Smith, Vernon 424
Solow, Robert M 426
Sowell, Thomas 428
Warsh, Kevin M. 470
Williams, Walter E. 482
Yellen, Janet L. 491

Fashion Designers

Allard, Linda 22
Armani, Giorgio 29
Azria, Max 33
Barnes, Jhane 38
Blahnik, Manolo 53
Bouwer, Marc 60
Buchman, Dana 73
De La Renta, Oscar 119
Herrera, Carolina 202
Hilfiger, Tommy 204
Jacobs, Marc 221
Johnson, Betsey 226
Kamali, Norma 233
Karan, Donna 234
Klein, Calvin 247
Lagerfeld, Karl 257
Lauren, Ralph 262
Madden, Steve 283
McCartney, Stella 297
McClintock, Jessica 298
McQueen, Alexander 306
Miller, Nicole 313
Mizrahi, Isaac 316
Oldham, Todd 339
Posen, Zak 364
Rowley, Cynthia 391
Saint Laurent, Yves 396
Simmons, Kimora Lee 418
Stuart, Jill 438
Sui, Anna 439
Tam, Vivienne 442
Tyler, Richard 457
Von Furstenberg, Diane 464
Wang, Vera 469

Fashion Models

Alexis, Kim 21
Alt, Carol 23
Aubry, Gabriel 31
Ballou, Tyson 36
Banks, Tyra 36
Brinkley, Christie 66
Bundchen, Gisele 74
Burke, Brooke 74
Canadas, Esther 80
Crawford, Cindy 107
Dillon, Kate 126
Duffy, Karen 132
Emme 141
Frederique 159
Hall, Jerry 189
Harlow, Shalom 193
Hilton, Paris 205
House, Yoanna 210
Hunter, Rachel 214
Hutton, Lauren 214
Ireland, Kathy 218
Jovovich, Milla 232
Klum, Heidi 248
Laughlin, Natalie 262
Lima, Adriana 272
Lundquist, Alex 279
Macpherson, Elle 283
Miller, Marisa 313
Moss, Kate 322
Murphy, Carolyn 325
Ribeiro, Caroline 378
Romijn, Rebecca 388
Rossellini, Isabella 390
Russo, Rene 393
Schenkenberg, Marcus 402
Schiffer, Claudia 403
Shaw, Jason 413
Sims, Molly 419
Tiegs, Cheryl 450
Turlington, Christy 456
Twiggy 457
Vanderloo, Mark 460
Vendela 462

Figure Skaters

See: Sports Personalities (Misc) pg 558

First Ladies

See: US Presidents & Vice Presidents and Their Wives pg 565

Fitness Personalities

Austin, Denise 32
Baptiste, Baron 36
Bass, Clarence 40
Blanchard, Mark 54
Blanks, Billy 55
Cole, Scott 98
Columbu, Franco 100
Cooper, Kenneth H 102
Creavalle, Laura 107
Cruise, Jorge 109
Curry, Susie 112
Draper, Dave 131
Ferrigno, Lou 149
Finger, Alan 150
Francis, Bev 157
Friedrich, Cathe 160
Gasper, Gay 165
Gern, Francesca 168
Greene, Bob 181
Grimes, MaDonna 183
Haney, Lee 191
Johnson, Jill 227
Kest, Bryan 241
Kries, Jennifer 253
La Lanne, Jack 256
Lana, Wai 258
Lee, Cyndi 264
Little, Tony 274
Miller, Gin 312
Missett, Judi Sheppard 315
Mylrea, Mindy 326
Oliva, Sergio 339
Pearl, Bill 351
Phillips, Bill 357
Preston, Marilynn 366
Price, Joan 366
Prickett, Charlene 367
Rhee, Jhoon 378
Richard, Margaret 378
Saffell, Janis 396
Sansone, Leslie 399
Sarcev, Milos 399
Schwarzenegger, Arnold 407
Scott, Carol 407
Scott, Larry 408
Simmons, Richard 418
Steinfeld, Jake 433
Stolove, Jodi 436
Stone, Lisa 436
Teodorescu, Radu 446
Vedral, Joyce 461
Voight, Karen 464
Weider, Betty 472
Weider, Joe 472
Wenig, Marsha 474
Yee, Rodney 491
Zane, Frank 493

Football Players & Coaches

Abraham, John 16

Football Players & Coaches (Cont'd)

Aikman, Troy 19
Akers, David 20
Alexander, Shaun 21
Allen, Larry 22
Allen, Marcus 22
Alstott, Mike 23
Bailey, Champ 35
Barber, Ronde 37
Barber, Tiki 37
Barlow, Kevan 37
Barnett, Nick 38
Belichick, Bill 44
Bennett, Drew 46
Biletnikoff, Fred 51
Billick, Brian 51
Bledsoe, Drew 55
Bly, Dre 56
Boldin, Anquan 57
Boller, Kyle 58
Bowden, Bobby 61
Bradshaw, Terry 63
Brady, Tom 63
Brees, Drew 65
Briggs, Lance 66
Brooking, Keith 67
Brooks, Aaron 67
Brooks, Derrick 67
Brown, Chris 68
Brown, Josh 69
Brown, Kris 69
Brown, Sheldon 70
Brown, Willie 70
Bruce, Isaac 71
Brunell, Mark 72
Bruschi, Tedy 72
Bryant, Paul W 72
Buchanon, Phillip 73
Bulger, Marc 73
Bulluck, Keith 74
Burleson, Nate 74
Burress, Plaxico 75
Bush, Reggie 76
Butler, Jerametrius 77
Callahan, Bill 79
Carney, John 83
Carr, David 83
Carr, Lloyd 83
Carroll, Pete 84
Carter, Cris 84
Chambers, Chris 88
Childress, Brad 91
Chrebet, Wayne 92
Clark, Danny 93
Clayton, Michael 94
Clements, Nate 95
Coker, Larry 98
Colbert, Keary 98
Coles, Laveranues 98
Collinsworth, Cris 100
Coughlin, Tom 105
Cowher, Bill 106
Crennel, Romeo 108
Croom, Sylvester 108
Cross, Randy 109
Crumpler, Alge 110
Culpepper, Daunte 111
Cundiff, Billy 111
Darling, James 115
Davis, Domanick 117
Dawkins, Brian 118
Dawson, Phil 118
Dayne, Ron 118
Del Rio, Jack 121
Delhomme, Jake 121
Dierdorf, Dan 125
Dillon, Corey 126
Ditka, Mike 127
Driver, Donald 132
Droughns, Reuben 132
Drummond, Eddie 132
Duckett, TJ 132
Dungy, Tony 133
Dunn, Warrick 134
Dwight, Tim 135
Edwards, Donnie 138
Edwards, Herm 138
Elam, Jason 139
Elway, John 140
Esiason, Boomer 143
Evans, Lee 144
Farrior, James 147
Faulk, Marshall 147
Favre, Brett 147
Feeley, AJ 148
Feely, Jay 148
Fisher, Jeff 151
Fitzgerald, Larry 151
Fletcher, London 153
Foster, DeShaun 156
Fox, John 156
Franks, Bubba 158
Fujita, Scott 161
Gamble, Chris 163
Garcia, Jeff 164
Gates, Antonio 166
Gibbs, Joe 169
Glenn, Aaron 173
Glenn, Terry 173
Glover, La'Roi 173
Goings, Nick 173
Gonzalez, Tony 175
Graham, Shayne 179

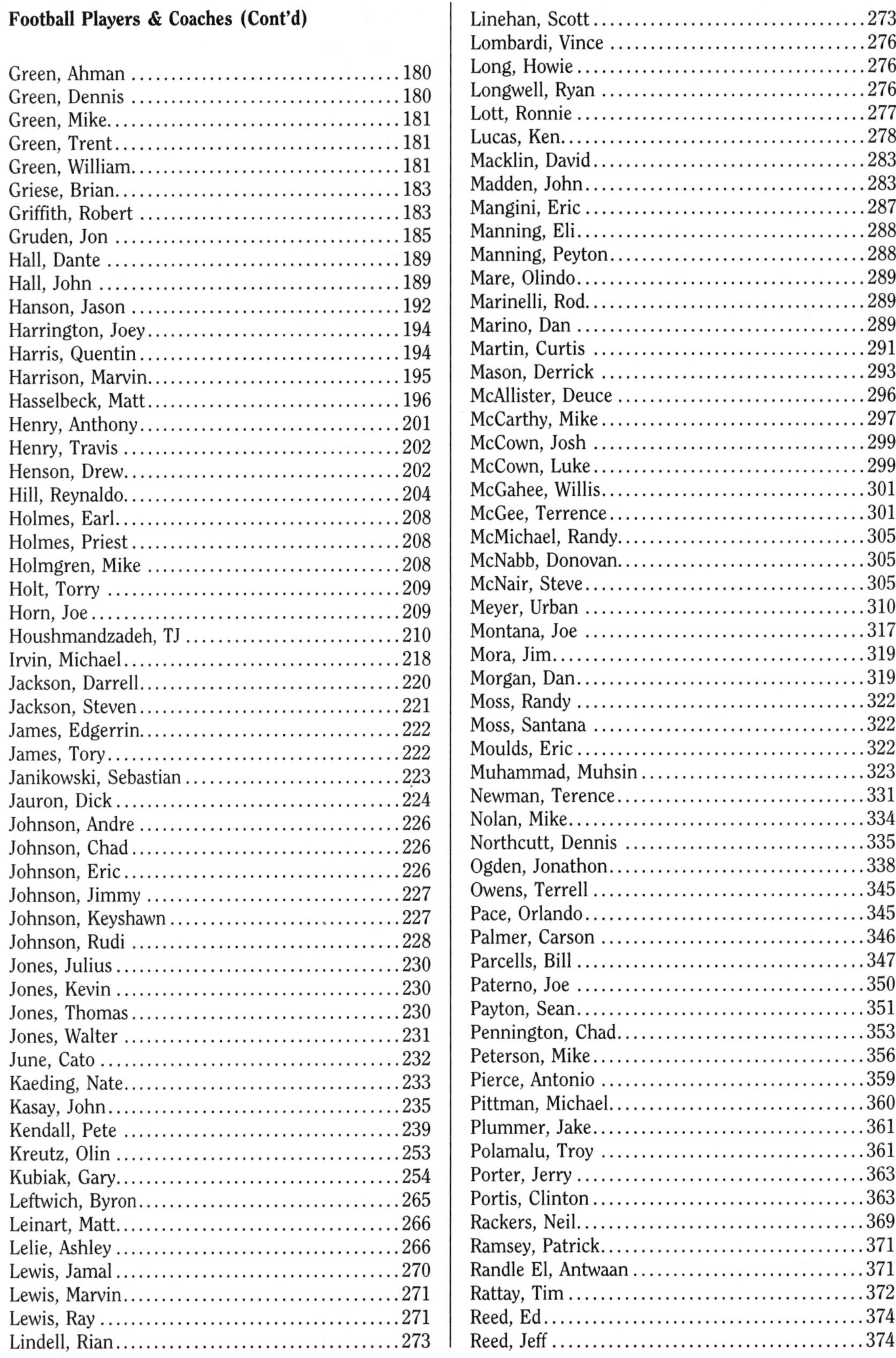

Football Players & Coaches (Cont'd)

Green, Ahman 180
Green, Dennis 180
Green, Mike 181
Green, Trent 181
Green, William 181
Griese, Brian 183
Griffith, Robert 183
Gruden, Jon 185
Hall, Dante 189
Hall, John 189
Hanson, Jason 192
Harrington, Joey 194
Harris, Quentin 194
Harrison, Marvin 195
Hasselbeck, Matt 196
Henry, Anthony 201
Henry, Travis 202
Henson, Drew 202
Hill, Reynaldo 204
Holmes, Earl 208
Holmes, Priest 208
Holmgren, Mike 208
Holt, Torry 209
Horn, Joe 209
Houshmandzadeh, TJ 210
Irvin, Michael 218
Jackson, Darrell 220
Jackson, Steven 221
James, Edgerrin 222
James, Tory 222
Janikowski, Sebastian 223
Jauron, Dick 224
Johnson, Andre 226
Johnson, Chad 226
Johnson, Eric 226
Johnson, Jimmy 227
Johnson, Keyshawn 227
Johnson, Rudi 228
Jones, Julius 230
Jones, Kevin 230
Jones, Thomas 230
Jones, Walter 231
June, Cato 232
Kaeding, Nate 233
Kasay, John 235
Kendall, Pete 239
Kreutz, Olin 253
Kubiak, Gary 254
Leftwich, Byron 265
Leinart, Matt 266
Lelie, Ashley 266
Lewis, Jamal 270
Lewis, Marvin 271
Lewis, Ray 271
Lindell, Rian 273
Linehan, Scott 273
Lombardi, Vince 276
Long, Howie 276
Longwell, Ryan 276
Lott, Ronnie 277
Lucas, Ken 278
Macklin, David 283
Madden, John 283
Mangini, Eric 287
Manning, Eli 288
Manning, Peyton 288
Mare, Olindo 289
Marinelli, Rod 289
Marino, Dan 289
Martin, Curtis 291
Mason, Derrick 293
McAllister, Deuce 296
McCarthy, Mike 297
McCown, Josh 299
McCown, Luke 299
McGahee, Willis 301
McGee, Terrence 301
McMichael, Randy 305
McNabb, Donovan 305
McNair, Steve 305
Meyer, Urban 310
Montana, Joe 317
Mora, Jim 319
Morgan, Dan 319
Moss, Randy 322
Moss, Santana 322
Moulds, Eric 322
Muhammad, Muhsin 323
Newman, Terence 331
Nolan, Mike 334
Northcutt, Dennis 335
Ogden, Jonathon 338
Owens, Terrell 345
Pace, Orlando 345
Palmer, Carson 346
Parcells, Bill 347
Paterno, Joe 350
Payton, Sean 351
Pennington, Chad 353
Peterson, Mike 356
Pierce, Antonio 359
Pittman, Michael 360
Plummer, Jake 361
Polamalu, Troy 361
Porter, Jerry 363
Portis, Clinton 363
Rackers, Neil 369
Ramsey, Patrick 371
Randle El, Antwaan 371
Rattay, Tim 372
Reed, Ed 374
Reed, Jeff 374

Football Players & Coaches (Cont'd)

Reid, Andy....375
Rice, Jerry....378
Robinson, Dunta....384
Roethlisberger, Ben....386
Rolle, Samari....387
Saban, Nick....395
Sams, BJ....397
Sapp, Warren....399
Sauerbrun, Todd....400
Schottenheimer, Marty....405
Scobee, Josh....407
Scott, Bryan....407
Shanahan, Mike....412
Sharpe, Shannon....413
Sharper, Darren....413
Shell, Art....414
Sheppard, Lito....414
Shields, Will....415
Shockey, Jeremy....416
Shula, Don....416
Simmons, Brian....418
Simms, Chris....418
Simms, Phil....418
Smith, Aaron....422
Smith, Derek....422
Smith, Jimmy....422
Smith, Lovie....423
Smith, Rod....423
Spikes, Takeo....429
Springs, Shawn....430
Spurrier, Steve....430
Staley, Duce....431
Stallworth, Donte....431
Stokley, Brandon....436
Stover, Matt....437
Strahan, Michael....437
Suggs, Lee....439
Taylor, Chester....444
Taylor, Fred....444
Taylor, Jason....444
Taylor, Sean....445
Taylor, Travis....445
Theismann, Joe....446
Thomas, Zach....448
Tillman, Spencer....450
Tomlinson, LaDainian....452
Toomer, Amani....452
Trufant, Marcus....455
Tynes, Lawrence....457
Upshaw, Gene....458
Urlacher, Brian....458
Vanderjagt, Mike....460
Vasher, Nathan....461
Vick, Michael....462
Vilma, Jonathan....463
Vinatieri, Adam....463
Walker, Javon....467
Ward, Hines....469
Warner, Kurt....469
Wayne, Reggie....471
Weis, Charlie....473
Westbrook, Brian....475
Wilkins, Jeff....479
Williams, DJ....480
Williams, Madieu....481
Williams, Ricky....481
Williams, Roy....481
Williams, Roy....481
Wilson, Adrian....483
Wilson, Al....483
Wilson, Eugene....483
Winfield, Antoine....484
Witherspoon, Will....486
Witten, Jason....486
Woodson, Charles....488
Young, Steve....492
Young, Vince....493

Golfers

Azinger, Paul....33
Beem, Rich....44
Calcavecchia, Mark....78
Clarke, Darren....94
Couples, Fred....105
Creamer, Paula....107
Daly, John....114
Daniel, Beth....114
DiMarco, Chris....126
Els, Ernie....140
Faldo, Nick....146
Faxon, Brad....147
Furyk, Jim....161
Garcia, Sergio....164
Gulbis, Natalie....186
Harmon, Butch....193
Hoch, Scott....206
Inkster, Juli....217
Irwin, Hale....218
Kite, Tom....246
Langer, Bernhard....260
Lehman, Tom....266
Leonard, Justin....267
Love, Davis III....277
Mallon, Meg....286
Maltbie, Roger....286
Mayfair, Billy....295
Mediate, Rocco....307
Mickelson, Phil....311
Miller, Johnny....312
Mize, Larry....316
Nicklaus, Jack....333
Norman, Greg....334
Pak, Se Ri....346

Subject Index

Golfers (Cont'd)

Palmer, Arnold....346
Park, Grace....348
Perry, Chris....355
Price, Nick....366
Sabbatini, Rory....395
Singh, Vijay....419
Sorenstam, Annika....427
Toms, David....452
Verplank, Scott....462
Watson, Tom....471
Weir, Mike....473
Westwood, Lee....475
Wie, Michelle....478
Woods, Tiger....488

Government & Political Figures (Misc)

See also: Governors pg 541; Mayors pg 545; US Presidents & Vice Presidents and Their Wives pg 565; US Senators & Representatives pg 565

Abraham, Spencer....16
Addington, David S....18
Albright, Madeleine....20
Annan, Kofi....27
Armey, Dick....29
Baker, James A III....35
Barnhart, Jo Anne B....38
Barreto, Hector V....39
Ben-Veniste, Richard....45
Bennett, William J....47
Blakey, Marion C....54
Bodman, Samuel....57
Bolten, Joshua B....58
Bolton, John R....58
Brailer, David J....63
Brown, Harold....69
Browner, Carol....71
Brzezinski, Zbigniew....72
Buchanan, Patrick J....73
Carmona, Richard H....82
Carville, James....85
Chao, Elaine L....89
Chertoff, Michael....91
Clark, Wesley....94
Clarke, Richard....94
Cohen, William S....97
Cox, Christopher....106
Cuomo, Mario....111
D'Amato, Alfonse....114
Daschle, Tom....115
Dean, Howard....119
Diaz, Nils J....125
Dole, Bob....128
DuPont, Pete....134
Edwards, John....138
Everson, Mark W....145
Ferraro, Geraldine....149
Fielding, Fred F....150
Fitzgerald, Patrick J....151
Foley, Thomas S....154
Friedman, Kinky....160
Gillespie, Ed....170
Gingrich, Newt....171
Giuliani, Rudy....172
Gonzales, Alberto....175
Gorelick, Jamie S....177
Gorton, Slade....177
Gutierrez, Carlos M....187
Hadley, Stephen....188
Hagee, Michael W....188
Halperin, Morton....190
Hamilton, Lee H....190
Harvey, Francis J....195
Havel, Vaclav....197
Helms, Jesse....200
Indyk, Martin S....217
Inman, Bobby R....217
Jackson, Alphonso R....220
Johanns, Mike....225
Johnson, Stephen L....228
Kemp, Jack....239
Kerrey, Bob....241
Kirkpatrick, Jeane J....246
Kissinger, Henry....246
Leavitt, Michael O....263
Lehman, John F....266
Libby, I Lewis....271
Marron, Donald B....290
Matalin, Mary....294
McCurry, Mike....300
Meese, Edwin III....307
Mineta, Norman Y....314
Mitchell, George J....315
Mosbacher, Robert Jr....321
Moseley, T Michael....321
Mueller, Robert S III....323
Mullen, Michael G....323
Nader, Ralph....327
Negroponte, John D....329
Nicholson, R James "Jim"....332
Nunn, Sam....336
O'Keefe, Sean....339
Olson, Theodore B....340
Pace, Peter....345
Panetta, Leon....347
Pason, Greg....349
Paulison, R David....350
Pellett, Nancy C....352
Perot, Ross....355
Podesta, Anthony T....361
Podesta, John....361
Pollack, Kenneth M....362

Government & Political Figures (Misc) (Cont'd)

Portman, Rob....364
Potter, John E....364
Powell, Colin....365
Press, Bill....365
Reed, Ralph E Jr....374
Reich, Robert B....375
Rice, Condoleezza....378
Richards, Ann....379
Roemer, Timothy J....386
Rove, Karl....391
Rudman, Warren B....392
Rumsfeld, Donald H....392
Scarlett, Lynn....402
Schlesinger, James R....403
Schroeder, Pat....405
Shriver, Maria....416
Snow, John W....425
Snow, Tony....425
Spellings, Margaret....429
Spitzer, Eliot....429
Stuart, Diane....438
Sununu, John H....440
Thompson, Carol....448
Thompson, Fred....448
Thompson, James R....448
Thompson, Tommy G....449
Towery, Matt....453
Towey, Jim....453
Vasquez, Gaddi H....461
Walters, John P....468
Winter, Donald C....485
Wolfowitz, Paul D....487
Wynne, Michael W....490
Young, Andrew....492
Zoellick, Robert B....495

Governors

Acevedo-Vila, Anibal....16
Baldacci, John....35
Barbour, Haley....37
Blagojevich, Rod R....53
Blanco, Kathleen....54
Blunt, Matt....56
Bredesen, Phil....65
Bush, Jeb....76
Camacho, Felix....79
Carcieri, Don....81
Corzine, Jon....104
Daniels, Mitch....114
Douglas, James H....129
Doyle, Jim....130
Easley, Michael F....136
Ehrlich, Robert L Jr....138
Fitial, Benigno....151
Fletcher, Ernie....152
Freudenthal, David D....159
Granholm, Jennifer....179
Gregoire, Christine....182
Guinn, Kenny....186
Heineman, Dave....200
Henry, Brad....201
Hoeven, John....206
Huckabee, Michael D....212
Huntsman, Jon M Jr....214
Kaine, Tim....233
Kempthorne, Dirk....239
Kulongoski, Ted....255
Lingle, Linda....273
Lynch, John....280
Manchin, Joe III....287
Minner, Ruth Ann....314
Murkowski, Frank....325
Napolitano, Janet....328
Owens, Bill....344
Pataki, George E....349
Pawlenty, Tim....351
Perdue, Sonny....354
Perry, Rick....355
Rell, M Jodi....376
Rendell, Edward G....376
Richardson, Bill....379
Riley, Robert....380
Romney, Mitt....388
Rounds, Mike....391
Sanford, Mark....398
Schwarzenegger, Arnold....407
Schweitzer, Brian....407
Sebelius, Kathleen....409
Taft, Bob....442
Tulafono, Togiola....455
Turnbull, Charles W....456
Vilsack, Thomas J....463

Gymnasts

See: Sports Personalities (Misc) pg 558

Hockey Players & Coaches

Aebischer, David....18
Alfredsson, Daniel....21
Amonte, Tony....25
Antropov, Nik....28
Arnott, Jason....29
Babcock, Mike....34
Barnaby, Matthew....38
Belfour, Ed....44
Berard, Bryan....47
Bertuzzi, Todd....50
Blake, Rob....54
Bondra, Peter....58
Bouwmeester, Jay....60
Bowman, Scotty....61
Boyle, Dan....61

Subject Index

Hockey Players & Coaches (Cont'd)

Brind'Amour, Rod 66
Brisebois, Patrice 66
Brodeur, Martin............ 67
Brown, Curtis............ 69
Burke, Sean............ 74
Carbonneau, Guy 81
Carlyle, Randy 82
Chara, Zdeno 89
Cheechoo, Jonathan............ 90
Chelios, Chris............ 90
Clement, Bill 95
Cloutier, Dan 96
Cole, Erik............ 98
Comrie, Mike 100
Conroy, Craig............ 101
Crosby, Sidney............ 108
Datsyuk, Pavel 115
Davidson, John 116
Demitra, Pavol............ 122
Desjardins, Eric............ 124
DiPietro, Rick............ 126
Domi, Tie............ 128
Draper, Kris 131
Drury, Chris 132
Dvorak, Radek 135
Elias, Patrik............ 139
Emery, Ray 141
Erat, Martin 142
Esche, Robert............ 143
Fedorov, Sergei 148
Fedotenko, Ruslan 148
Ference, Andrew 149
Fleury, Marc-Andre 153
Foote, Adam 154
Forsberg, Peter 155
Friesen, Jeff............ 160
Gaborik, Marian............ 162
Gagne, Simon 162
Gainey, Bob............ 162
Gallant, Gerard 163
Gelinas, Martin 167
Giguere, Jean-Sebastien............ 169
Gionta, Brian 171
Gomez, Scott 175
Gonchar, Sergei............ 175
Grahame, John 179
Granato, Cammi 179
Granato, Tony 179
Gretzky, Wayne 182
Grier, Mike 182
Guerin, Bill............ 185
Hamrlik, Roman............ 191
Handzus, Michal............ 191
Hanlon, Glen 191
Hartley, Bob 195
Hasek, Dominik............ 196
Hatcher, Derian............ 196
Havlat, Martin 197
Heatley, Dany............ 199
Hecht, Jochen 199
Hejduk, Milan............ 200
Hinote, Dan............ 205
Hitchcock, Ken 206
Holik, Bobby............ 208
Horton, Nathan 210
Hossa, Marian............ 210
Howe, Gordie 211
Iginla, Jarome 215
Jagr, Jaromir 222
Johnson, Greg 226
Jokinen, Olli 229
Joseph, Curtis 232
Jovanovski, Ed 232
Kaberle, Tomas 233
Kapanen, Sami............ 234
Kariya, Paul............ 235
Kasparaitis, Darius 236
Keenan, Mike 237
Khabibulin, Nikolai 242
Kiprusoff, Miikka 245
Kitchen, Mike............ 246
Koivu, Saku 249
Kolzig, Olaf............ 250
Kovalchuk, Ilya 251
Kovalev, Alex 252
Kozlov, Vyacheslav............ 252
Kuba, Filip............ 254
Lamoriello, Lou............ 258
Lang, Robert............ 259
Langenbrunner, Jamie 260
Lapointe, Martin 260
Laviolette, Peter 262
Lecavalier, Vincent............ 264
Leclair, John............ 264
Leetch, Brian 265
Legace, Manny............ 265
Lehtinen, Jere 266
Lehtonen, Kari............ 266
Lemaire, Jacques............ 266
Lemieux, Mario 266
Lidstrom, Nicklas 272
Linden, Trevor 273
Lindros, Eric............ 273
Lundqvist, Henrik 279
Luongo, Roberto............ 279
MacLean, Doug 283
MacTavish, Craig............ 283
Madden, John............ 283
Malhotra, Manny............ 285
Maltby, Kirk 286
Marchant, Todd............ 289
Marleau, Patrick 290

Hockey Players & Coaches (Cont'd)

Martin, Jacques 292
McCabe, Bryan 296
McCarty, Darren 297
Mellanby, Scott 307
Miller, Ryan 313
Modano, Mike 316
Modin, Fredrik 316
Murray, Bryan 325
Nabokov, Evgeni 327
Nash, Rick 328
Naslund, Markus 328
Nedved, Petr 329
Niedermayer, Scott 333
Nieuwendyk, Joe 333
O'Neill, Jeff 341
Ovechkin, Alexander 344
Ozolinsh, Sandis 345
Parrish, Mark 349
Peca, Michael 352
Perreault, Yanic 355
Phaneuf, Dion 357
Poti, Tom 364
Primeau, Keith 367
Pronger, Chris 367
Quenneville, Joel 369
Rafalski, Brian 370
Rathje, Mike 372
Raycroft, Andrew 372
Recchi, Mark 373
Redden, Wade 373
Renney, Tom 376
Ricci, Mike 378
Richards, Brad 379
Roberts, Gary 382
Roenick, Jeremy 386
Roloson, Dwayne 388
Rolston, Brian 388
Roy, Patrick 391
Rucinsky, Martin 392
Ruff, Lindy 392
Sakic, Joe 396
Salei, Ruslan 396
Samsonov, Sergei 397
Sanderson, Geoff 398
Satan, Miroslav 400
Sather, Glen 400
Sedin, Daniel 409
Sedin, Henrik 409
Selanne, Teemu 410
Shanahan, Brendan 412
Shaw, Brad 413
Simon, Chris 418
Skoula, Martin 420
Smyth, Ryan 424
Souray, Sheldon 427
Spezza, Jason 429
St Louis, Martin 430
Staal, Eric 430
Stumpel, Jozef 439
Sturm, Marco 439
Sullivan, Mike 439
Sundin, Mats 440
Sutter, Darryl 440
Sydor, Darryl 441
Sykora, Petr 441
Tanguay, Alex 443
Theodore, Jose 446
Therrien, Michel 447
Thibault, Jocelyn 447
Thornton, Joe 449
Timonen, Kimmo 450
Tippett, Dave 451
Tkachuk, Keith 451
Tortorella, John 453
Trotz, Barry 454
Tucker, Darcy 455
Turco, Marty 456
Turgeon, Pierre 456
Van Ryn, Mike 460
Vokoun, Tomas 464
Ward, Cam 469
Warrener, Rhett 470
Weight, Doug 472
Wesley, Glen 475
Whitney, Ray 477
Wilson, Ron 484
Yashin, Alexei 491
Yawney, Trent 491
Yelle, Stephane 491
Yzerman, Steve 493
Zednick, Richard 493
Zetterberg, Henrik 494
Zhitnik, Alexei 494
Zubov, Sergei 495
Zubrus, Dainius 495

Inventors

See: Scientists & Inventors pg 556

Journalists (Broadcast)

See: Radio Personalities pg 554; Sportscasters pg 560; Television Personalities pg 563

Journalists (Print)

Alter, Jonathan 24
Alterman, Eric 24
Applebaum, Anne 28
Applegate, Jane 28
Asim, Jabari 31
Atkinson, Rick 31
Barnes, Fred 38
Barone, Michael 38

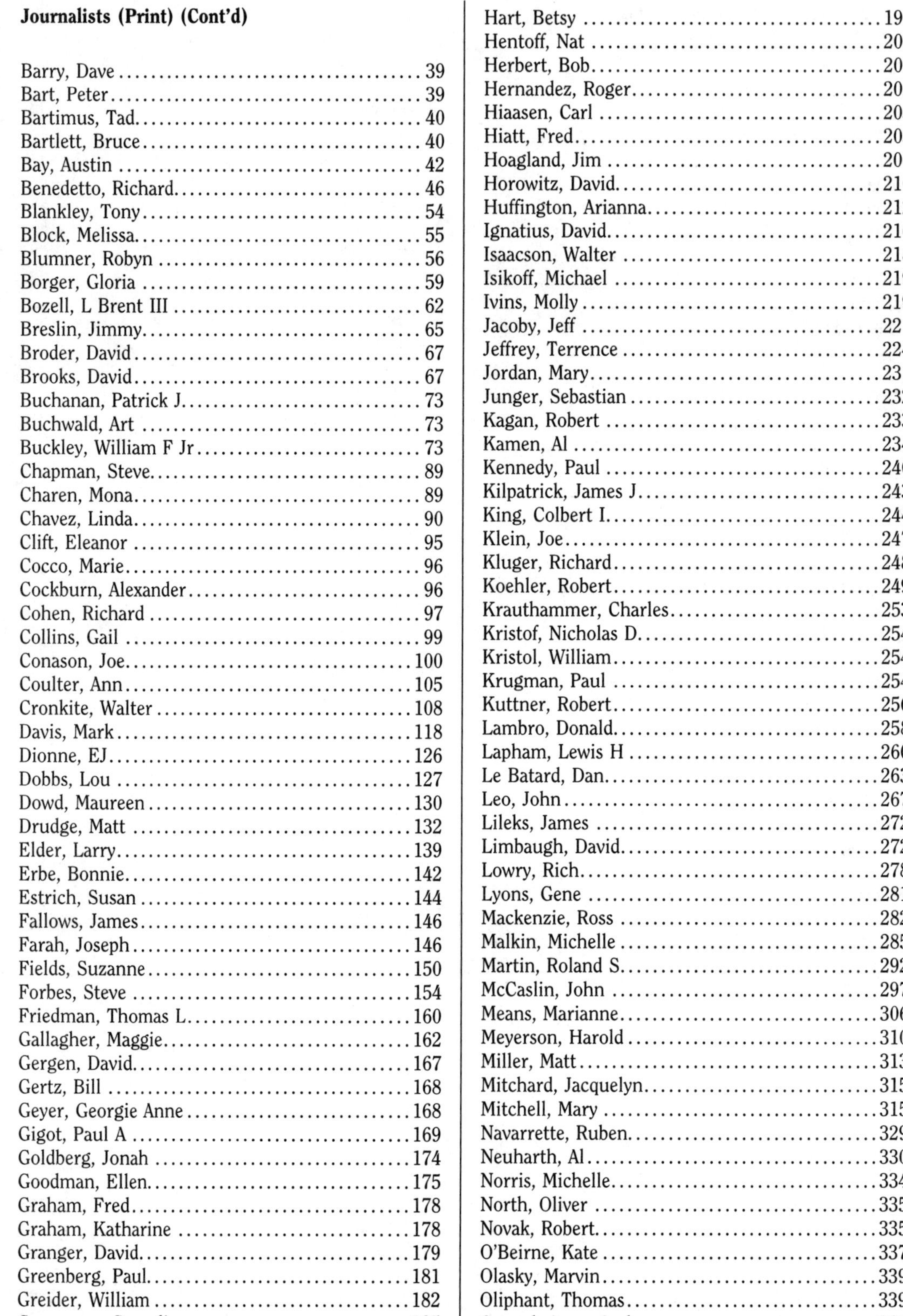

Journalists (Print) (Cont'd)

Barry, Dave....39
Bart, Peter....39
Bartimus, Tad....40
Bartlett, Bruce....40
Bay, Austin....42
Benedetto, Richard....46
Blankley, Tony....54
Block, Melissa....55
Blumner, Robyn....56
Borger, Gloria....59
Bozell, L Brent III....62
Breslin, Jimmy....65
Broder, David....67
Brooks, David....67
Buchanan, Patrick J....73
Buchwald, Art....73
Buckley, William F Jr....73
Chapman, Steve....89
Charen, Mona....89
Chavez, Linda....90
Clift, Eleanor....95
Cocco, Marie....96
Cockburn, Alexander....96
Cohen, Richard....97
Collins, Gail....99
Conason, Joe....100
Coulter, Ann....105
Cronkite, Walter....108
Davis, Mark....118
Dionne, EJ....126
Dobbs, Lou....127
Dowd, Maureen....130
Drudge, Matt....132
Elder, Larry....139
Erbe, Bonnie....142
Estrich, Susan....144
Fallows, James....146
Farah, Joseph....146
Fields, Suzanne....150
Forbes, Steve....154
Friedman, Thomas L....160
Gallagher, Maggie....162
Gergen, David....167
Gertz, Bill....168
Geyer, Georgie Anne....168
Gigot, Paul A....169
Goldberg, Jonah....174
Goodman, Ellen....175
Graham, Fred....178
Graham, Katharine....178
Granger, David....179
Greenberg, Paul....181
Greider, William....182
Grumman, Cornelia....185
Halberstam, David....188
Hart, Betsy....195
Hentoff, Nat....202
Herbert, Bob....202
Hernandez, Roger....202
Hiaasen, Carl....203
Hiatt, Fred....203
Hoagland, Jim....206
Horowitz, David....210
Huffington, Arianna....212
Ignatius, David....216
Isaacson, Walter....218
Isikoff, Michael....219
Ivins, Molly....219
Jacoby, Jeff....221
Jeffrey, Terrence....224
Jordan, Mary....231
Junger, Sebastian....232
Kagan, Robert....233
Kamen, Al....234
Kennedy, Paul....240
Kilpatrick, James J....243
King, Colbert I....244
Klein, Joe....247
Kluger, Richard....248
Koehler, Robert....249
Krauthammer, Charles....253
Kristof, Nicholas D....254
Kristol, William....254
Krugman, Paul....254
Kuttner, Robert....256
Lambro, Donald....258
Lapham, Lewis H....260
Le Batard, Dan....263
Leo, John....267
Lileks, James....272
Limbaugh, David....272
Lowry, Rich....278
Lyons, Gene....281
Mackenzie, Ross....282
Malkin, Michelle....285
Martin, Roland S....292
McCaslin, John....297
Means, Marianne....306
Meyerson, Harold....310
Miller, Matt....313
Mitchard, Jacquelyn....315
Mitchell, Mary....315
Navarrette, Ruben....329
Neuharth, Al....330
Norris, Michelle....334
North, Oliver....335
Novak, Robert....335
O'Beirne, Kate....337
Olasky, Marvin....339
Oliphant, Thomas....339
Oppenheimer, Andres....341
O'Reilly, Bill....342

Journalists (Print) (Cont'd)

O'Rourke, PJ....342
Page, Clarence....345
Parker, Kathleen....348
Payne, Les....351
Peirce, Neal....352
Peretz, Martin....354
Perez, Miguel....354
Pfaff, William....357
Pitts, Leonard Jr....360
Podhoretz, John....361
Pollitt, Katha....362
Prager, Dennis....365
Press, Bill....365
Pruden, Wesley....367
Quindlen, Anna....369
Ramos, Jorge....371
Raspberry, William....372
Rather, Dan....372
Reese, Charley....374
Reeves, Richard....374
Remnick, David....376
Rich, Frank....378
Rios, Delia M....381
Roberts, Cokie....382
Roberts, Paul Craig....383
Roberts, Steven V....383
Rodriguez, Richard....386
Rooney, Andy....389
Rusher, William....393
Russell, Mark....393
Salinas, Maria Elena....396
Samuelson, Robert....397
Sanchez, Marcela....398
Sartwell, Crispin....400
Saunders, Debra....400
Scheer, Robert....402
Schlafly, Phyllis....403
Schlosser, Eric....404
Schorr, Daniel....405
Schram, Martin....405
Shapiro, Ben....412
Shields, Mark....415
Shribman, David....416
Sobran, Joseph....425
Solomon, Norman....426
Sowell, Thomas....428
Starr, Paul....432
Steinem, Gloria....433
Sullum, Jacob....439
Thomas, Cal....447
Thomas, Helen....447
Thomasson, Dan....448
Tilove, Jonathan....450
Towery, Matt....453
Tucker, Cynthia....455
Tyrrell, R Emmett Jr....457
Veciana-Suarez, Ana....461
Wenner, Jann S....474
West, Diana....475
Wickham, DeWayne....478
Will, George....479
Williams, Patricia J....481
Winkler, Matthew....485
Yglesias, Matthew....491
Zakaria, Fareed....493
Zuckerman, Mortimer B....495

Judges

See: Attorneys & Judges pg 506

Lawyers

See: Attorneys & Judges pg 506

Magicians & Illusionists

Amazing Kreskin....24
Blaine, David....53
Burton, Lance....75
Copperfield, David....103
Gunnarson, Dean....186
Harary, Franz....192
Houdini, Harry....210
McBride, Jeff....296
Penn & Teller....353
Randi, James....371
Tempest, Marco....445

Mayors

Abramson, Jerry E....16
Anderson, Rocky....26
Autry, Alan....32
Barnes, Kay....38
Barrett, Tom....39
Begich, Mark....44
Bloomberg, Michael R....56
Bright, Bobby N....66
Brown, Byron....68
Brown, Jerry....69
Cashell, Robert....86
Chavez, Martin J....90
Cicilline, David N....93
Coleman, Michael B....98
Cook, John....101
Cornett, Mick....104
Dailey, Jim....113
Daley, Richard M....113
DeStefano, John Jr....124
Diaz, Manuel A....125
Driscoll, Matthew J....131
Duffy, Robert J....133
Dyer, Buddy....135
Ellis, C Jack....140
Fahey, Mike....145

Mayors (Cont'd)

Frankel, Lois J ... 158
Franklin, Shirley ... 158
Gonzales, Ron ... 175
Goodman, Oscar B ... 176
Gordon, Phil ... 176
Hannemann, Mufi ... 192
Hardberger, Phil ... 192
Herenton, Willie W ... 202
Hession, Dennis P ... 203
Hickenlooper, John ... 203
Holden, Kip ... 207
Iorio, Pam ... 218
Isaac, Teresa Ann ... 218
Jackson, Frank G ... 220
James, Sharpe ... 222
Jennings, Gerald D ... 225
Joines, Allen ... 229
Jones, Samuel L ... 230
Kilpatrick, Kwame M ... 243
Kincaid, Bernard ... 243
Levy, Robert W ... 269
Littlefield, Ron ... 274
Mallory, Mark ... 286
Marks, John ... 289
Mayans, Carlos ... 295
McCrory, Patrick ... 299
McLin, Rhine L ... 305
Menino, Thomas M ... 309
Miller, Laura ... 313
Moncrief, Mike ... 316
Munson, David R ... 324
Nagin, C Ray ... 327
Newsom, Gavin C ... 332
Nickels, Greg ... 333
Oberndorf, Meyera E ... 337
O'Connor, Bob ... 337
O'Malley, Martin ... 340
O'Neill, Beverly ... 341
Palmer, Douglas H ... 346
Perez, Eddie A ... 354
Peterson, Bart ... 356
Peyton, John ... 357
Potter, Tom ... 364
Purcell, Bill ... 368
Reed, Stephen R ... 374
Riley, Joseph P Jr ... 380
Rybak, RT ... 394
Sanders, Jerry ... 398
Slay, Francis G ... 421
Street, John F ... 438
Taylor, Kathryn L ... 444
Villaraigosa, Antonio R ... 463
Walkup, Robert E ... 467
White, Bill ... 477
Wilder, L Douglas ... 479
Williams, Anthony A ... 480

Models

See: Fashion Models pg 536

Motivational Speakers

Alessandra, Tony ... 21
Amos, Wally ... 25
Aun, Michael A ... 32
Austin, Emory ... 32
Bach, David ... 34
Ball, Jim ... 36
Bethel, Sheila Murray ... 50
Blanchard, Ken ... 54
Bleier, Rocky ... 55
Boyd, Ty ... 61
Broome, Michael ... 68
Brown, Les ... 69
Burrus, Daniel ... 75
Canfield, Jack ... 80
Chopra, Deepak ... 92
Cole, Scott ... 98
Crum, Thomas ... 110
Cummuta, John ... 111
Dent, Harry S Jr ... 123
Dyer, Wayne ... 135
Ennico, Cliff ... 142
Fisher, Mary ... 151
Fripp, Patricia ... 160
Greshes, Warren ... 182
Hahn, Scott ... 188
Haney, Lee ... 191
Hansen, Mark Victor ... 192
Harmon, Merle ... 193
Harrell, Keith ... 193
Hennig, James F ... 201
Holst, Art ... 208
Hopkins, Tom ... 209
Howe, Neil ... 211
Hutson, Don ... 214
Johnson, Spencer ... 228
Kennedy, Danielle ... 240
King, Bernice A ... 244
Kriegel, Robert ... 253
Mackay, Harvey ... 282
Maxwell, John C ... 295
McNally, David ... 305
Mitchell, W ... 315
Morgenstern, Julie ... 320
Naisbitt, John ... 327
Orman, Suze ... 342
Peters, Tom ... 356
Putnam, Howard ... 368
Qubein, Nido ... 368
Reynolds, Don ... 377
Robbins, Anthony ... 382
Rohn, Jim ... 387

Motivational Speakers (Cont'd)

Sanborn, Mark 397
Schwarzkopf, H Norman 407
Siegel, Bernie 417
Slutsky, Jeff 421
Sommer, Bobbe 426
Tracy, Brian 453
Waitley, Denis 466
White, Somers 477
Zander, Benjamin 493
Ziglar, Zig 494

Musicians, Singers, Songwriters

3 Doors Down
50 Cent 15
Abdul, Paula 15
Adams, Bryan 17
Adams, Oleta 17
Adams, Yolanda 17
Adkins, Trace 18
Aerosmith 18
Aguilera, Christina 19
Aiken, Clay 19
Allan, Gary 22
Amos, Tori 25
Andrews, Julie 26
Anthony, Marc 27
Armstrong, Kit 29
Ashanti 30
Audioslave 32
Ax, Emanuel 33
Bacharach, Burt 34
Bacon, Kevin 34
Badu, Erykah 34
Barbieri, Gato 37
Barenaked Ladies 37
Battle, Kathleen 41
Beck 43
Belafonte, Harry 44
Bell, Joshua 45
Bennett, Tony 47
Benson, George 47
Bentley, Dierks 47
Bergman, Marilyn 48
Bernstein, Leonard 49
Berry, Chuck 50
Big & Rich 51
Bjork 53
Black, Clint 53
Black Eyed Peas 53
Blige, Mary J 55
Blunt, James 56
Bocelli, Andrea 56
Bolton, Michael 58
Bon Jovi, Jon 58
Bono 59
Bowie, David 61
Branch, Michelle 63
Braxton, Toni 64
Brickman, Jim 65
Bridgewater, Dee Dee 66
Brightman, Sara 66
Brooks, Garth 68
Brooks & Dunn 68
Brown, James 69
Buble, Michael 72
Buffett, Jimmy 73
Byrd, Tracy 77
Caedmon's Call 78
Camp, Jeremy 79
Campbell, Glen 80
Carey, Mariah 82
Carpenter, Mary Chapin 83
Carreras, Jose 83
Carroll, Diahann 84
Carter, Deana 84
Channing, Carol 89
Chapman, Steven Curtis 89
Charles, Ray 89
Cher 91
Chestnutt, Mark 91
Church, Charlotte 93
Clapton, Eric 93
Clarkson, Kelly 94
Cole, Natalie 98
Cole, Paula 98
Combs, Sean "Diddy" 100
Connick, Harry Jr 101
Corea, Chick 103
Corgan, Billy 103
Costello, Elvis 104
Crawford, Michael 107
Cray, Robert 107
Crouch, Andrae 109
Crow, Sheryl 109
Cyrus, Billy Ray 113
Daniels, Charlie 114
Davis, Chip 117
Dido 125
Diffie, Joe 126
Dion, Celine 126
Dixie Chicks 127
Domingo, Placido 128
Duarte, Chris 132
Duff, Hilary 132
Dylan, Bob 135
Edmonds, Kenneth "Babyface" 137
Elliott, Missy 140
Eminem 141
Enya 142
Eschenbach, Christoph 143
Estefan, Gloria 144
Etheridge, Melissa 144

Musicians, Singers, Songwriters (Cont'd)

Evanescence ... 144
Evans, Sara ... 144
Eve ... 145
Feinstein, Michael ... 148
Fleming, Renee ... 152
Fogerty, John ... 153
Franklin, Aretha ... 158
Furtado, Nelly ... 161
Gabriel, Peter ... 162
Garfunkel, Art ... 164
Geldof, Bob ... 166
Gill, Vince ... 170
Goldsmith, Jerry ... 174
Goo Goo Dolls ... 175
Gracin, Josh ... 178
Grant, Amy ... 179
Gray, Macy ... 180
Green Day ... 181
Griggs, Andy ... 183
Groban, Josh ... 184
Hamlisch, Marvin ... 190
Harris, Emmylou ... 194
Hawkins, Sophie B. ... 197
Henley, Don ... 201
Hill, Faith ... 204
Horner, James ... 209
Hornsby, Bruce ... 209
Houston, Whitney ... 211
Ice Cube ... 215
Ice-T ... 215
Iglesias, Enrique ... 215
Iglesias, Julio ... 216
Indigo Girls ... 216
Isaak, Chris ... 219
Ja Rule ... 219
Jackson, Alan ... 220
Jackson, Janet ... 220
Jackson, Michael ... 220
Jagger, Mick ... 222
Jamiroquai ... 222
Jarreau, Al ... 223
Jars of Clay ... 223
Jewel ... 225
John, Elton ... 226
Jones, George ... 229
Jones, Norah ... 230
Jones, Quincy ... 230
Jones, Tom ... 230
Keith, Toby ... 238
Kelis ... 238
Kelly, R. ... 239
Kelly, Sarah ... 239
Kenny G ... 240
Keys, Alicia ... 242
Kid Rock ... 242
King, BB ... 244
King, Carole ... 244
KISS ... 246
Klugh, Earl ... 248
Knopfler, Mark ... 249
Knowles, Beyonce ... 249
Kochalka, James ... 249
Korn ... 250
Krall, Diana ... 252
Kravitz, Lenny ... 253
Kristofferson, Kris ... 254
LaBelle, Patti ... 256
Lachey, Nick ... 257
Lambert, Miranda ... 258
lang, kd ... 259
Larsen, Blaine ... 260
Lauper, Cyndi ... 262
Lavigne, Avril ... 262
Lee, Tommy ... 265
Lennox, Annie ... 267
Levine, James ... 269
Lewis, Ramsey ... 271
Lin, Lucia ... 273
Linkin Park ... 273
LL Cool J ... 275
Lockhart, Keith ... 275
Loggins, Kenny ... 275
Lonestar ... 276
Los Lobos ... 277
Love, Courtney ... 277
Loveless, Patty ... 277
Lovett, Lyle ... 277
Ludacris ... 279
Lupone, Patti ... 280
Lynn, Loretta ... 281
Ma, Yo-Yo ... 281
Madonna ... 284
Manilow, Barry ... 287
Mannheim Steamroller ... 287
Manson, Marilyn ... 288
Marley, Ziggy ... 290
Marsalis, Branford ... 290
Marsalis, Wynton ... 291
Martin, Ricky ... 292
Master P ... 293
matchbox twenty ... 294
Mathis, Johnny ... 294
Matsui, Keiko ... 294
Mattea, Kathy ... 294
Matthews, Dave ... 295
McBride, Martina ... 296
McCartney, Paul ... 297
McDonald, Audra ... 300
McDonald, Michael ... 300
McEntire, Reba ... 301
McFerrin, Bobby ... 301
McGrath, Mark ... 302

Musicians, Singers, Songwriters (Cont'd)

McGraw, Tim 302
McLachlan, Sarah 304
McPartland, Marian 306
Medeski Martin & Wood 306
Mehta, Zubin 307
Mellencamp, John 307
Merchant, Natalie 309
MercyMe 309
Messina, Jo Dee 310
Metheny, Pat 310
Meyer, Edgar 310
Midler, Bette 311
Midori 311
Mighty Mighty Bosstones 311
Milsap, Ronnie 314
Mitchell, Joni 315
Moby 316
Montgomery, John Michael 317
Montgomery Gentry 317
Moore, Mandy 318
Morissette, Alanis 320
Mos Def 321
Nabors, Jim 327
Nakai, R Carlos 328
Naughton, James 329
Nelly 330
Nelson, Willie 330
Neville, Aaron 331
Newman, Randy 331
Newsboys 331
Newton, Wayne 332
Nichols, Joe 332
Norman, Bebo 334
Norman, Jessye 334
Nugent, Ted 336
Oliveira, Elmar 340
Ono, Yoko 341
O'Riley, Christopher 342
Orrico, Stacie 342
Osbourne, Ozzy 343
Osmond, Donny 343
Osmond, Marie 343
Outkast 344
Paisley, Brad 346
Paris, Twila 347
Parton, Dolly 349
Patinkin, Mandy 350
Patty, Sandi 350
Pearl Jam 351
Perlman, Itzhak 355
Peters, Bernadette 355
Petty, Tom 357
Phish 358
Point of Grace 361
Ponce, Carlos 362
Portman, Rachel 364
Presley, Elvis 365
Presley, Lisa Marie 365
Previn, Andre 366
Queen Latifah 369
Raitt, Bonnie 370
Rascal Flatts 371
Red Hot Chili Peppers 373
Reed, Lou 374
Reese, Della 374
Relient K 376
Rhymes, Busta 378
Richards, Keith 379
Rimes, LeAnn 380
Robinson, Smokey 384
Rogers, Kenny 387
Ronstadt, Linda 388
Sanborn, David 397
Sanders, Mark D 398
Sandoval, Arturo 398
Sansone, Maggie 399
Santana, Carlos 399
Sawyer Brown 401
Secada, Jon 409
Seger, Bob 409
Setzer, Brian 411
Severinsen, Doc 411
Shakira 412
Shankar, Ravi 412
SHeDaisy 413
Shelton, Blake 414
Shore, Howard 416
Simon, Carly 418
Simon, Paul 419
Simpson, Ashlee 419
Simpson, Jessica 419
Skaggs, Ricky 420
Slatkin, Leonard 420
Smith, Michael W 423
Smith, Will 424
Snoop Dogg 425
Sonic Youth 427
Spears, Britney 428
Springsteen, Bruce 430
Stefani, Gwen 433
Steve Miller Band 434
Stevens, Ray 434
Stewart, Rod 435
Sting 435
Stipe, Michael 436
Strait, George 437
Streisand, Barbra 438
Stuart, Marty 438
Studdard, Ruben 439
Taylor, James 444
Tedeschi, Susan 445
Tesh, John 446

Musicians, Singers, Songwriters (Cont'd)

Third Day....447
Thomas, Rob....448
Tillis, Pam....450
Tilson Thomas, Michael....450
Timberlake, Justin....450
Tippin, Aaron....451
tobyMac....451
Torres, Nestor....453
Travis, Randy....454
Tritt, Travis....454
Turner, Josh....456
Turner, Tina....456
Twain, Shania....456
Tyrese....457
Underwood, Carrie....458
Urban, Keith....458
Usher....458
Van Halen....459
Van Zandt, Steven....460
Van Zant....460
Vedder, Eddie....461
Velasquez, Jaci....462
Verve Pipe....462
Voigt, Deborah....464
Wahlberg, Donnie....465
Waits, Tom....466
Watts, Andre....471
Wayne, Jimmy....471
West, Kanye....475
White, Bryan....477
Williams, Andy....480
Williams, Hank Jr....480
Williams, John....480
Williams, Lucinda....480
Williams, Vanessa....482
Wilson, Brian....483
Wilson, Cassandra....483
Wilson, Nancy....484
Winans, CeCe....484
Winston, George....485
Womack, Lee Ann....487
Wonder, Stevie....487
Worley, Darryl....488
Wright, Chely....488
Wynonna....490
Yearwood, Trisha....491
Yerba Buena....491
Yoakam, Dwight....491
Young, Neil....492
Zander, Benjamin....493
ZOEgirl....495
Zukerman, Eugenia....495

Olympic Athletes

See: Sports Personalities (Misc) pg 558

Organization Leaders

Abshire, David M....16
Adamson, Rebecca....18
Afkhami, Mahnaz....19
Alford, Harry C....21
Apted, Michael....28
Armey, Dick....29
Askins, Renee....31
Barlow, John Perry....37
Barnes, Michael D....38
Bauer, Gary....41
Bergman, Marilyn....48
Bettman, Gary....50
Birch, Glynn....52
Boles, Anita....57
Bond, Julian....58
Borden, Enid....59
Boyle, Father Gregory J....61
Bozell, L Brent III....62
Brady, James....63
Brady, Sarah....63
Brey-Casiano, Carol A....65
Buchanan, Angela "Bay"....72
Buchanan, Patrick J....73
Chavez, Cesar E....89
Claybrook, Joan....94
Clohessy, David....95
Colson, Chuck....100
Combs, Roberta....100
Cooper, Matthew T....102
Cousteau, Jacques....105
Cousteau, Jean-Michel....105
Cronin, John....108
Cruise, Sister Tricia....109
Dees, Morris S....120
DeMuth, Christopher....122
Dobson, James C....127
Douglass, John W....130
Downs, Hugh....130
DuPont, Pete....134
Ecohawk, John E....137
Edelman, Marian Wright....137
Eisenberg, Alan....138
Fahey, John M Jr....145
Farrakhan, Louis....147
Fehr, Donald....148
Fortson, Tom....156
Franz, Wanda....158
Fuller, Linda....161
Fuller, Millard....161
Gaddy, C Welton....162
Gandy, Kim....163
Ganis, Sid....163
Garber, Don....164
Gates, Henry Louis Jr....166
Gates, Melinda....166
Gerard, Leo W....167

Organization Leaders (Cont'd)

Gingrich, Candace 171
Glickman, Dan 173
Gordon, Bruce 176
Graham, Franklin 178
Greco, Michael S. 180
Grosvenor, Gilbert 184
Gulati, Sunil 186
Hagelin, John 188
Halperin, Morton 190
Hamre, John J 191
Helton, Mike 201
Hilgeman, Georgia K 204
Hoffa, James P 207
Holmes, Joan 208
Howse, Jennifer L. 211
Hunt, Helen LaKelly 213
Hunter, Bill 213
Insulza, Jose Miguel 217
Isaacs, Amy 218
Jackson, Jesse 220
Jacobson, Michael F. 221
Jones, Larry 230
Keene, David 237
Kennedy, Robert F Jr 240
King, Coretta Scott 244
King, Dexter Scott 244
King, Martin Luther Jr 244
LaPierre, Wayne Jr 260
Levin, Joseph J Jr 269
Lomax, Michael 276
Luck, Jo 279
MacCormack, Charles F 281
Mahfood, Robin 285
Mas, Jorge 293
Maxwell, Kay J 295
McCarthy, Colman 297
McGuire, Jack 303
Mittermeier, Russell A 316
Nader, Ralph 327
Neas, Ralph G. 329
Novelli, William D 335
Nunn, Sam 336
O'Leary, Dennis S. 339
O'Steen, David N. 343
Parker, Star 348
Pasierb, Steve 349
Perkins, Tony 354
Pope, Carl 363
Pope, Lois 363
Richards, Cecile 379
Roberts, Carter 382
Robinson, Ron 384
Rodriguez, Arturo 385
Roemer, Timothy J 386
Romero, Anthony D 388
Rotenberg, Marc 390
Saskin, Ted 400
Schatz, Thomas 402
Schlafly, Phyllis 403
Schroeder, Pat 405
Schultz, William F 405
Seager, John 408
Selig, Allan H "Bud" 410
Slaughter, John B 420
Solmonese, Joe 426
Soros, George 427
Steele, Shari 432
Stern, David 433
Stonesifer, Patty 436
Stroup, R Keith 438
Sweeney, John J 441
Tagliabue, Paul 442
Terry, Randall 446
Tuttle, Merlin 456
Upshaw, Gene 458
Valenti, Jack 458
Veneman, Ann M 462
Vredenburgh, Judith 465
Watson, Paul 471
Werbach, Adam 474
Weyrich, Paul 476
Whelan, M Edward III 476
Whitehead, John W 477
Wolfe, Sidney 486
Wright, Tom 489
Yankelovich, Daniel 491
Young, Andrew 492

Photographers

Abbott, Berenice 15
Adams, Ansel 17
Alda, Arlene 20
Almond, Joan 23
Arma, Tom 29
Avedon, Richard 32
Avery, Sid 33
Barney, Tina 38
Beard, Peter 42
Bernhard, Ruth 49
Bourke-White, Margaret 60
Brandt, Bill 64
Brassai 64
Brundege, Barbara 71
Carter, Keith 85
Cartier-Bresson, Henri 85
Citret, Mark 93
Cramer, Charles 107
Cunningham, Imogen 111
Curtis, Edward S. 112
Davidson, Bruce 116
Davis, Lynn 118
Demarchelier, Patrick 122

Photographers (Cont'd)

Dzerigian, Steve 135
Eisenstaedt, Alfred 139
Erwitt, Elliott....143
Feininger, Andreas....148
Frank, Robert....157
Friedlander, Lee 160
Frye, Michael 161
Geddes, Anne 166
Giacomelli, Mario....168
Gilpin, Laura 171
Goldin, Nan....174
Greenfield, Lauren....182
Guzy, Carol....187
Henry, Carol....201
Jablonski, Patrick....219
Jones, Dewitt 229
Kenna, Michael 239
Klein, Steven 247
Kolbrener, Bob 250
LaChapelle, David....257
Lange, Dorothea 259
Leibovitz, Annie....266
Lerner, Nathan 268
Lyon, Danny....281
Mann, Sally....287
Mapplethorpe, Robert....288
Morse, Ralph....321
Muench, David....323
Muench, Marc 323
Mydans, Carl....326
Nelson, Kendall....330
Newman, Arnold....331
Penn, Irving 353
Perkins, Lucian....354
Ritts, Herb....381
Rolston, Matthew 388
Rosenblum, Walter....389
Ross, Alan 390
Schatz, Howard....402
Seliger, Mark 410
Sheeler, Charles 413
Sherman, Cindy 414
Steichen, Edward 433
Steiner, Ralph 433
Strand, Paul 437
Struss, Karl....438
Wegman, William....472
Williams, Ted....481
Williamson, Michael 482
Witkin, Joel-Peter....486
Wolcott, Marion Post 486

Physicians

Agatston, Arthur S....19
Alexander, Duane F....21
Battey, James F Jr 41
Brailer, David J....63
Brazelton, T Berry....64
Brown, Michael S....70
Bruner, Joseph P 72
Carmona, Richard H....82
Carson, Ben....84
Chopra, Deepak....92
Coburn, Tom 96
Collins, Francis....99
Cooley, Denton A....102
Cooper, Kenneth H....102
DeBakey, Michael E....120
Dulbecco, Renato 133
Edelman, Gerald M 137
Fauci, Anthony S 147
Fineberg, Harvey V 150
Gayle, Helene....166
Gerberding, Julie L 167
Goldstein, Joseph L....174
Gott, Peter....177
Groopman, Jerome....184
Guillemin, Roger 186
Gupta, Sanjay....186
Healy, Bernadine....198
Heimlich, Henry....200
Ho, David....206
Hodes, Richard J....206
Hoffman, Ronald L....207
Insel, Thomas R 217
Jarvik, Robert....223
Jemison, Mae 224
Johnson, Timothy....228
Kandel, Eric 234
Katz, David L....236
Katz, Stephen I....236
Koop, C Everett....250
Kornberg, Arthur 251
Li, Ting-Kai....271
Lindberg, Donald AB....273
Love, Susan....277
MacKinnon, Roderick....283
McAllister, Rallie....296
McClellan, Mark B 298
Murad, Ferid....324
Nabel, Elizabeth G....327
Novello, Antonia 336
Nuland, Sherwin B....336
Ochsner, John L 337
O'Leary, Dennis S....339
Ornish, Dean 342
Perricone, Nicholas 355
Pettigrew, Roderic I....357
Prusiner, Stanley B 367
Richardson, Dot....379
Rodgers, Griffin P....385
Roizen, Michael....387

Physicians (Cont'd)

Rosenfeld, Isadore....389
Sacks, Oliver....395
Salk, Jonas....396
Schwartz, David A....406
Senay, Emily....410
Siegel, Bernie....417
Siegel, Marc K....417
Sieving, Paul A....417
Smith, Hamilton O....422
Smith, Hugh C....422
Straus, Stephen E....437
Sullivan, Louis W....439
Tabak, Lawrence A....442
Thomas, E Donnall....447
Varmus, Harold E....461
Volkow, Nora D....464
von Eschenbach, Andrew....464
Whitaker, Julian....477
WilderBrathwaite, Gloria....479
Wolfe, Sidney....486
Zerhouni, Elias A....494
Zipes, Douglas P....494

Playwrights

Albee, Edward....20
Auburn, David....32
Ayckbourn, Alan....33
Bogosian, Eric....57
Edson, Margaret....137
Ensler, Eve....142
Feiffer, Jules....148
Fo, Dario....153
Foote, Horton....154
Frayn, Michael....158
Friel, Brian....160
Fugard, Athol....161
Guare, John....185
Hampton, Christopher....191
Hare, David....193
Kushner, Tony....256
Larson, Jonathan....261
Levin, Ira....269
Lonergan, Kenneth....276
Lucas, Craig....278
Mamet, David....287
Mann, Emily....287
Marber, Patrick....288
Margulies, Donald....289
May, Elaine....295
McNally, Terrence....306
Miller, Arthur....312
Nicholson, William....332
Parks, Suzan-Lori....348
Pinter, Harold....360
Rabe, David....369
Sagal, Peter....396
Schenkkan, Robert....402
Shaffer, Peter....412
Shepard, Sam....414
Simon, Neil....419
Smith, Anna Deavere....422
Soyinka, Wole....428
Stoppard, Tom....436
Wilson, August....483
Wilson, Lanford....483

Poets

Ai....19
Angelou, Maya....27
Ashbery, John....30
Carruth, Hayden....84
Clifton, Lucille....95
Codrescu, Andrei....96
Collins, Billy....99
Creeley, Robert....108
Cummings, EE....111
Dennis, Carl....122
Dove, Rita....130
Dunn, Stephen....134
Giovanni, Nikki....171
Gluck, Louise....173
Graham, Jorie....178
Grimes, Nikki....184
Hall, Donald....189
Hass, Robert....196
Heaney, Seamus....198
Hirshfield, Jane....205
Kapell, Dave....234
Kinnell, Galway....245
Kinsella, John....245
Koertge, Ron....249
Komunyakaa, Yusef....250
Kumin, Maxine....255
Kunitz, Stanley....255
Levine, Philip....269
Lynch, Thomas....280
Madsen, Michael....284
Meredith, William....309
Merwin, WS....309
Morrison, Lillian....321
Mueller, Lisel....323
Muldoon, Paul....323
Nelson, Marilyn....330
Nye, Naomi Shihab....336
Peacock, Molly....351
Piercy, Marge....359
Pinsky, Robert....360
Pollitt, Katha....362
Ponsot, Marie....363
Prelutsky, Jack....365
Rich, Adrienne....378
Schutz, Susan Polis....406

Poets (Cont'd)

Silverstein, Shel 418
Snyder, Gary 425
Sones, Sonya 427
Soto, Gary 427
Stern, Gerald 434
Strand, Mark 437
Szymborska, Wislawa 442
Viorst, Judith 463
Walcott, Derek 466
Williams, CK 480
Williams, Miller 481
Wright, Charles 488
Yevtushenko, Yevgeny 491

Politicians

See: Government & Political Figures (Misc) pg 540

Producers - Movies & TV

See: Directors, Producers, Creators, Writers (Movies & TV) pg 533

Race Car Drivers

Andretti, John 26
Andretti, Marco 26
Andretti, Mario 26
Andretti, Michael 26
Biffle, Greg 51
Burton, Jeff 75
Busch, Kurt 76
Castroneves, Helio 87
Cheever, Eddie Jr 90
Earnhardt, Dale 136
Earnhardt, Dale Jr 136
Edwards, Carl 137
Fittipaldi, Christian 151
Foyt, AJ 157
Gibbs, Joe 169
Gordon, Jeff 176
Green, Jeff 181
Harvick, Kevin 196
Hornish, Sam Jr 209
Jarrett, Dale 223
Johnson, Jimmie 227
Kahne, Kasey 233
Kenseth, Matt 241
LaBonte, Bobby 257
Marlin, Sterling 290
Martin, Mark 292
Mayfield, Jeremy 295
McMurray, Jamie 305
Mears, Casey 306
Nemechek, Joe 330
Newman, Ryan 331
Parsons, Benny 349
Patrick, Danica 350
Penske, Roger 353
Petty, Kyle 357
Petty, Richard 357
Roush, Jack 391
Sadler, Elliott 395
Stewart, Tony 435
Unser, Al Jr 458
Vickers, Brian 462
Wallace, Rusty 468
Waltrip, Darrell 468

Radio Personalities

See also: Sportscasters pg 560

Abramson, Larry 16
Adams, Noah 17
Adler, Margot 18
Agar, Jerry 19
Albom, Mitch 20
Arnold, Elizabeth 29
Ashbrook, Tom 30
Banks, Doug 36
Bartley, Dick 40
Beck, Glenn 43
Bianculli, David 50
Big Boy 51
Big Tigger 51
Blasingame, Jim 55
Block, Melissa 55
Bohannon, Jim 57
Boortz, Neal 59
Bradley Hagerty, Barbara 62
Bridgewater, Dee Dee 66
Brinker, Bob 66
Brodesser, Claude 67
Browne, Joy 71
Bruno, Tony 72
Calhoun, Coyote 79
Campbell, Ben 80
Carr, Howie 83
Chadwick, Alex 88
Child, Fred 91
Codrescu, Andrei 96
Colmes, Alan 100
Conan, Neal 100
Cooper, Kenneth H 102
Corley, Cheryl 103
Corrigan, Maureen 104
Curwood, Steve 112
Daly, Carson 114
David, Ted 116
Davis, Mark 118
Dees, Rick 120
Dobson, James C 127
Drudge, Matt 132
Edell, Dean 137
Edelman, Ric 137

Radio Personalities (Cont'd)

Edelstein, David....137
Egan, Brian....138
Elder, Larry....139
Farah, Joseph....146
Flanders, Laura....152
Flatow, Ira....152
Flintoff, Corey....153
Franken, Al....158
Gallagher, Mike....162
Gardner, David....164
Gardner, Tom....164
Garner, Blair....165
Garofalo, Janeane....165
Geronimo, Don....168
Glass, Ira....172
Griswold, Tom....184
Gross, Terry....184
Grosvenor, Vertamae....185
Handel, Bill....191
Hannity, Sean....192
Hansen, Liane....192
Harrigan, Irv....194
Harris, Richard....194
Hartmann, Thom....195
Harvey, Paul....195
Harvey, Steve....196
Hendrie, Phil....201
Hoffman, Ronald L....207
Horowitz, David....210
Howard, Clark....211
Hudson, Mac....212
Humphries, Rusty....213
Imus, Don....216
Ingraham, Laura....217
Innes, Scott....217
Insana, Ron....217
Joyner, Tom....232
Kasell, Carl....235
Kasem, Casey....235
Keillor, Garrison....237
Kennedy, Robert F Jr....240
Kevoian, Bob....242
King, Larry....244
Komando, Kim....250
Kraddick, Kidd....252
Larson, Lars....261
Leykis, Tom....271
Liasson, Mara....271
Liddy, G Gordon....272
Limbaugh, Rush....272
Lionel....273
Littlefield, Bill....274
Magliozzi, Ray....284
Magliozzi, Tom....284
Malloy, Mike....286
Marr, Tom....290
Martino, Tom....292
Masters, Roy....293
McChesney, John....298
McPartland, Marian....306
Medved, Michael....307
Mercer, Roy D....309
Miller, Matt....313
Miller, Stephanie....313
Muller, Mancow....324
Myss, Caroline....327
Nathan, Alan....328
Neighmond, Patricia....329
Noory, George....334
Norris, Michelle....334
North, Oliver....335
O'Meara, Mike....341
O'Reilly, Bill....342
O'Riley, Christopher....342
Osgood, Charles....343
Overby, Peter....344
Owens, Ronn....344
Papantonio, Mike....347
Parshall, Janet....349
Pinkwater, Daniel....360
Prager, Dennis....365
Quivers, Robin....369
Ramsey, Dave....371
Reagan, Michael....373
Rehm, Diane....375
Resnick, John....377
Reynolds, Joey....377
Rhodes, Randi....378
Ritchie, Fiona....381
Roberts, Cokie....382
Rogers, Neil....387
Rome, Jim....388
Sagal, Peter....396
Samuelson, Orion....397
Savage, Michael....400
Schlessinger, Laura....403
Schorr, Daniel....405
Seacrest, Ryan....408
Siegel, Robert....417
Simeone, Lisa....418
Simon, Scott....419
Smerconish, Michael....421
Smiley, Tavis....421
Smith, Harry....422
Stamberg, Susan....431
Stern, Howard....434
Terkel, Studs....446
Totenberg, Nina....453
Wertheimer, Linda....475
Wilson, Brenda....483

Subject Index

Religious Leaders

Adler, Margot 18
Ankerberg, John 27
Avanzini, John 32
Barnett, Tommy 38
Becket, Candace 43
Benedict XVI 46
Chittister, Joan 92
Copeland, Kenneth 102
Coughlin, Daniel 105
Crouch, Andrae 109
Dalai Lama 113
Dass, Ram 115
Dobson, James C 127
Dollar, Creflo A Jr 128
Duplantis, Jesse 134
Edgar, Robert W 137
Evans, Tony 144
Falwell, Jerry 146
Farrakhan, Louis 147
Fortson, Tom 156
Gaddy, C Welton 162
Garlington, Joseph 165
Gellman, Marc 167
George, Bob 167
Graham, Billy 178
Graham, Franklin 178
Graham, Jack 178
Hagee, John 188
Hammond, Mac 191
Hanby, Mark 191
Hartman, Tom 195
Hayford, Jack 198
Hinckley, Gordon B 205
Hinn, Benny 205
Jackson, Jesse 220
Jenkins, Jerry B 224
Jentzsch, Heber 225
Kaplan, Joel S 234
Kennedy, D James 240
King, Bernice A 244
King, Martin Luther Jr 244
Lama, His Holiness the Dalai 258
Laurie, Greg 262
Lerner, Michael 268
Levitt, Zola 269
Long, Eddie L 276
Lucado, Max 278
McDowell, Josh 300
McManus, Erwin 305
Meyer, Joyce 310
Moore, Roy S 318
Mother Angelica 322
Murillo, Mario 325
Nhat Hanh, Thich 332
Osteen, Joel 343
Pacwa, Father Mitch 345
Paulk, Earl 350
Phelps, Fred 357
Prather, Hugh 365
Roberts, Oral 383
Roberts, Richard 383
Robertson, Pat 384
Robison, James 384
Rogers, Adrian 386
Schorsch, Ismar 405
Schrag, Jim 405
Schuller, Robert H 405
Some, Sobonfu 426
Sproul, RC 430
Stanley, Charles 431
Swaggart, Jimmy 441
Van Impe, Jack 460
Watanabe, Hakubun 470
Youssef, Michael 493

Scientists & Inventors

Adams, Julian 17
Agarwal, Deborah A 19
Altman, Sidney 24
Axel, Richard 33
Ballard, Robert 36
Berg, Jeremy 48
Berners-Lee, Tim 49
Binder, Alan 52
Bishop, J Michael 52
Blonz, Ed 55
Blum, Deborah 56
Borysenko, Joan 59
Boyer, Paul D 61
Brewer, Eric A 65
Brown, Michael S 70
Buck, Linda B 73
Caplan, Arthur 81
Cech, Thomas R 87
Cerf, Vinton G 88
Chu, Steven 92
Clarke, Arthur C 94
Cordova, France 103
Corey, Elias James 103
Cousteau, Jacques 105
Cray, Seymour 107
Curl, Robert F 112
Davis, Raymond Jr 118
Deisenhofer, Johann 121
Diaz, Nils J 125
Doherty, Peter C 128
Drexler, K Eric 131
Dulbecco, Renato 133
Dyson, Freeman 135
Edelman, Gerald M 137
Engelbart, Douglas 141
Fenn, John B 149
Fineberg, Harvey V 150

Scientists & Inventors (Cont'd)

Fossey, Dian ... 156
Galdikas, Birute ... 162
Gates, Bill ... 166
Giacconi, Riccardo ... 168
Glauber, Roy J ... 172
Goldstein, Joseph L ... 174
Goodall, Jane ... 175
Grady, Patricia A. ... 178
Grandin, Temple ... 179
Gray, William M ... 180
Greengard, Paul ... 182
Gross, David J ... 184
Grubbs, Robert H ... 185
Guillemin, Roger ... 186
Hagelin, John ... 188
Hall, John L ... 189
Harrison, Shelley A ... 195
Heeger, Alan J ... 199
Horner, Jack ... 209
Horvitz, H Robert ... 210
Ignarro, Louis J ... 216
Jackson, Shirley Ann ... 221
Jarvik, Robert ... 223
Jastrow, Robert ... 224
Johnson, Lonnie ... 227
Kahn, Robert E ... 233
Kandel, Eric ... 234
Kilby, Jack ... 242
Kleinrock, Leonard ... 247
Kohn, Walter ... 249
Kornberg, Arthur ... 251
Krim, Mathilde ... 253
Kurzweil, Ray ... 256
Landis, Story C ... 259
Laughlin, Robert B ... 262
Lee, David M. ... 264
Lindberg, Donald AB ... 273
Lowman, Meg ... 278
MacDiarmid, Alan ... 281
MacKinnon, Roderick ... 283
Mammana, Dennis ... 287
Marcus, Rudolph A. ... 289
Margulis, Lynn ... 289
Mayfield, Max ... 296
Meserve, Richard A ... 310
Miller, Rand ... 313
Minsky, Marvin ... 314
Mullis, Kary B ... 324
Murad, Ferid ... 324
Nye, Bill ... 336
Olah, George A ... 339
Osheroff, Douglas D. ... 343
Perl, Martin L ... 355
Phillips, William D. ... 358
Politzer, H David ... 362
Popeil, Ronald M. ... 363
Richardson, Robert C ... 379
Roberts, Lawrence G. ... 383
Rodriguez, Eloy ... 385
Romero, John ... 388
Rose, Irwin ... 389
Rowland, F Sherwood ... 391
Salk, Jonas ... 396
Schrock, Richard R ... 405
Smith, Hamilton O ... 422
Stormer, Horst L ... 436
Tarter, Jill ... 443
Torvalds, Linus ... 453
Tsui, Daniel C ... 455
Tuttle, Merlin ... 456
Van Allen, James A. ... 459
Varmus, Harold E. ... 461
Watson, James D. ... 471
Wilczek, Frank ... 478
Wilson, Edward O. ... 483
Wozniak, Steve ... 488
Zewail, Ahmed H ... 494

Screenwriters

See: Directors, Producers, Creators, Writers (Movies & TV) pg 533

Singers & Songwriters

See: Musicians, Singers, Songwriters pg 547

Soccer Players

Adu, Freddy ... 18
Albright, Chris ... 20
Armas, Chris ... 29
Arnaud, Davy ... 29
Barrett, Wade ... 39
Beckerman, Kyle ... 43
Broome, Paul ... 68
Buddle, Edson ... 73
Busch, Jon ... 76
Cannon, Joe ... 80
Carroll, Brian ... 84
Conrad, Jimmy ... 101
Crawford, Matt ... 107
Cunningham, Jeff ... 111
Curtin, Jim ... 112
De Rosario, Dwayne ... 119
Dempsey, Clint ... 122
Denton, Eric ... 123
Djorkaeff, Youri ... 127
Donovan, Landon ... 129
Dunivant, Todd ... 134
Dunseth, Brian ... 134
Freeman, Hunter ... 159
Garcia, Juan Pablo ... 164
Garcia, Nick ... 164
Garlick, Scott ... 164

Subject Index

Soccer Players (Cont'd)

Gaven, Eddie....166
Gbandi, Chris....166
Gomez, Christian....174
Gomez, Herculez....175
Gros, Joshua....184
Guevara, Amado....185
Guzan, Brad....187
Hamm, Mia....190
Hartman, Kevin....195
Heaps, Jay....198
Hejduk, Frankie....200
Henderson, Chris....201
Hendrickson, Ezra....201
Jewsbury, Jack....225
Johnson, Eddie....226
Jones, Cobi....229
Joseph, Shalrie....232
Kreis, Jason....253
Lilly, Kristine....272
Magee, Mike....284
Mapp, Justin....288
Marshall, Tyrone....291
Martins, Thiago....293
Mathis, Clint....294
Meola, Tony....309
Mina, Roberto....314
Moreno, Alejandro....319
Moreno, Jaime....319
Noel, Fabrice....333
Noonan, Pat....334
Nunez, Ramo....336
O'Brien, Ronnie....337
Olsen, Ben....340
Onstad, Pat....341
Oughton, Duncan....344
Palencia, Juan Francisco....346
Parkhurst, Michael....348
Pope, Eddie....363
Quaranta, Santino....368
Ralston, Steve....370
Ramirez, Ramon....371
Razov, Ante....373
Reis, Matt....376
Rimando, Nick....380
Rolfe, Chris....387
Sanneh, Tony....398
Scurry, Briana....408
Sealy, Scott....409
Sequeira, Douglas....411
Thornton, Zach....449
Trembly, Seth....454
Twellman, Taylor....457
Vagenas, Peter....458
Vanney, Greg....460
Victorine, Sasha....462
Wagner, Aly....465
Walker, Jonny....467
Wambach, Abby....468
Williams, Andy....480
Wolff, Josh....486
Wolyniec, John....487
Zavagnin, Kerry....493

Speakers - Motivational

See: Motivational Speakers pg 546

Spiritual Leaders

See: Religious Leaders pg 556

Sports Personalities (Misc)

See also: Baseball Players & Managers pg 514; Basketball Players & Coaches pg 516; Football Players & Coaches pg 536; Golfers pg 539; Hockey Players & Coaches pg 541; Race Car Drivers pg 554; Soccer Players pg 557; Tennis Players pg 564

Ali, Muhammad....21
Armstrong, Lance....29
Browning, Kurt....71
Cohen, Sasha....97
De la Hoya, Oscar....119
Devers, Gail....124
Dragila, Stacy....131
Edwards, Torri....138
Eldredge, Todd....139
Fleming, Peggy....152
Foreman, George....155
Gordeeva, Ekaterina....176
Greene, Maurice....181
Hawk, Tony....197
Holyfield, Evander....209
Johnson, Dwayne....226
Johnson, Lawrence....227
Jones, Marion....230
Keibler, Stacy....237
Kerrigan, Nancy....241
King, Don....244
Krayzelburg, Lenny....253
Kwan, Michelle....256
Lawler, Jerry....262
Lee, Jeanette....265
Lewis, Carl....270
Ohno, Apolo....338
Richardson, Dot....379
Riley, Dawn....380
Runyan, Marla....393
Steward, Emanuel....434
The Rock....446
Weiss, Michael....473
Yagudin, Alexei....490
Yamaguchi, Kristi....490

Sports Team Owners

Adams, KS "Bud" Jr 17
Alexander, Leslie 21
Allen, Paul G 22
Angelos, Peter G 26
Anschutz, Philip F 27
Arison, Micky 29
Attanasio, Mark 31
Belkin, Steven 44
Benson, Tom 47
Bidwell, William V 51
Bisciotti, Steve 52
Blank, Arthur M 54
Bowlen, Pat 61
Brown, Michael 70
Burns, Harmon E 75
Buss, Jerry 76
Cohan, Christopher 97
Cohen, Alan 97
Colangelo, Jerry J 98
Cuban, Mark 110
Davidson, William M 116
Davis, Al 116
DeVos, Richard M 124
DeWitt, William O Jr 124
Dolan, Charles F 128
Dolan, Lawrence 128
Edwards, N Murray 138
Ellman, Steve 140
Elway, John 140
Ford, William Clay 155
Frontiere, Georgia 161
Gilbert, Daniel 169
Giles, Bill 170
Gillett, George N Jr 170
Glass, David D 172
Glazer, Malcolm I 172
Golisano, B Thomas 174
Grousbeck, Wyc 185
Heisley, Michael 200
Henry, John W 201
Hicks, Thomas O 203
Hotchkiss, Harley 210
Huizenga, H Wayne 213
Hunt, Lamar 213
Ilitch, Marian 216
Ilitch, Michael 216
Irsay, James 218
Jacobs, Jeremy M 221
Johnson, Robert Wood IV 228
Jones, Jerry 230
Karmanos, Peter Jr 235
Kohl, Herbert H 249
Kraft, Robert J 252
Kroenke, E Stanley 254
Laurie, William J 262
Lee, Debra 265
Leipold, Craig L 266
Lemieux, Mario 266
Leonsis, Ted 267
Lerner, Randolph D 268
Lindner, Carl H 273
Loria, Jeffrey H 277
Lurie, Jeffrey 280
Magowan, Peter A 284
Maloof, Gavin 286
Maloof, Joe 286
Mara, Wellington T 288
McCaskey, Michael 297
McCaw, John E Jr 298
McClatchy, Kevin S 298
McConnell, John H 298
McLane, Drayton Jr 304
McNair, Robert C 305
Melnyk, Eugene 308
Miller, Larry H 313
Modell, Art 316
Montgomery, David 317
Moores, John 319
Moreno, Arturo 319
Naegele, Robert O Jr 327
Pohlad, Carl R 361
Pollin, Abe 362
Ratner, Bruce 372
Reinsdorf, Jerry 376
Richardson, Jerry 379
Rogers, Edward S 386
Rooney, Daniel M 389
Roski, Edward P Jr 390
Samueli, Henry 397
Sarver, Robert 400
Shinn, George 415
Simon, Herbert 419
Simon, Melvin 419
Snider, Edward M 424
Snyder, Daniel M 425
Spanos, Alex G 428
Steinbrenner, George 433
Sterling, Donald T 433
Sternberg, Stuart 434
Tanenbaum, Larry 443
Taylor, Glen A 444
Vanderbeek, Jeff 460
Wang, Charles B 469
Weaver, Wayne 472
Werner, Tom 475
Wilf, Zygmunt 479
Wilpon, Fred 483
Wilson, Ralph C Jr 484
Wirtz, William W 485
Wolff, Lewis 486
York, Denise DeBartolo 492

Sportscasters

See also: Radio Personalities pg 554; Television Personalities pg 563

Arute, Jack....30
Baddoo, Terry....34
Barkley, Charles....37
Berman, Chris....48
Bernstein, Bonnie....49
Bradshaw, Terry....63
Brando, Tim....64
Brown, James....69
Buck, Joe....73
Carillo, Mary....82
Carter, Cris....84
Cellini, Vince....87
Clement, Bill....95
Cohn, Linda....97
Collinsworth, Cris....100
Corso, Lee....104
Costas, Bob....104
Criqui, Don....108
Cross, Randy....109
Davidson, John....116
Deford, Frank....120
Dierdorf, Dan....125
Ditka, Mike....127
Enberg, Dick....141
Esiason, Boomer....143
Fowler, Chris....156
Gammons, Peter....163
Gumbel, Greg....186
Harlan, Kevin....193
Harmon, Merle....193
Irvin, Michael....218
Johnson, Gus....227
Johnson, Jimmy....227
Lampley, Jim....258
Levy, Steve....269
Long, Howie....276
Lundquist, Verne....279
Macatee, Bill....281
Madden, John....283
Marino, Dan....289
Mayne, Kenny....296
McCarver, Tim....297
McEnroe, John....301
McEnroe, Patrick....301
Merchant, Larry....309
Morgan, Joe....320
Myers, Chris....326
Nantz, Jim....328
Patrick, Dan....350
Potvin, Denis....364
Saunders, John....400
Scott, Stuart....408
Scully, Vin....408
Sharpe, Shannon....413
Shriver, Pam....416
Simms, Phil....418
Steward, Emanuel....434
Theismann, Joe....446
Tillman, Spencer....450
Tirico, Mike....451
Visser, Lesley....463
Vitale, Dick....463
Walton, Bill....468
Waltrip, Darrell....468
Young, Steve....492
Zelasko, Jeanne....493

Swimmers

See: Sports Personalities (Misc) pg 558

Talk Show Hosts

See: Radio Personalities pg 554

Televangelists

See: Religious Leaders pg 556

Television Anchors & Reporters

Abrams, Dan....16
Allen, Ron....22
Amanpour, Christiane....24
Andrews, Wyatt....26
Angle, Jim....27
Asman, David....31
Aspell, Tom....31
Assuras, Thalia....31
Attkisson, Sharyl....31
Avila, Jim....33
Axelrod, Jim....33
Baier, Bret....34
Barnes, Fred....38
Bartiromo, Maria....40
Bash, Dana....40
Bashir, Martin....40
Battista, Bobbie....41
Bazell, Robert....42
Begala, Paul....44
Berman, John....49
Bernhard, Lisa....49
Bittermann, Jim....53
Blakemore, Bill....54
Bleier, Scott....55
Blitzer, Wolf....55
Bradley, Ed....62
Brancaccio, David....63
Braver, Rita....64
Brokaw, Tom....67
Brown, Bob....68
Brown, Campbell....68
Brown, Dara....69
Browne, Patti Ann....71
Brzezinski, Mika....72

Television Anchors & Reporters (Cont'd)

Burns, Eric 75
Bury, Chris 76
Buttner, Brenda.... 77
Cafferty, Jack 78
Cameron, Carl 79
Carlson, Gretchen.... 82
Carlson, Tucker.... 82
Carroll, Jason.... 84
Caruso-Cabrera, Michelle 85
Carville, James.... 85
Cavuto, Neil 87
Centanni, Steve.... 88
Chen, Julie 90
Chetry, Kiran.... 91
Choi, Sophia.... 92
Claman, Liz.... 93
Cochran, John 96
Cohn, Scott.... 98
Collins, Heidi 99
Cooper, Anderson.... 102
Corderi, Victoria 103
Cosby, Rita 104
Costello, Carol 104
Costello, Tom.... 105
Couric, Katie 105
Cowan, Lee 106
Cramer, James.... 107
Crier, Catherine.... 108
Cronkite, Walter 108
Crowley, Candy 109
Crowley, Monica 109
Cummins, Jim 111
Cuomo, Christopher 111
Curry, Ann.... 112
Dahler, Don.... 113
David, Ted 116
Dawson, Pat 118
Deutsch, Donny.... 124
Dhue, Laurie.... 124
Dobbs, Lou 127
Donvan, John.... 129
Doocy, Steve.... 129
Dotson, Bob 129
Douglass, Linda.... 130
Dow, Harold 130
Downs, Hugh 130
Ellerbee, Linda.... 139
Ellis, Rehema 140
Engel, Richard.... 141
Ensor, David.... 142
Epperson, Sharon.... 142
Erbe, Bonnie.... 142
Faber, David 145
Farnsworth, Elizabeth.... 146
Faw, Bob 147
Feyerick, Deborah.... 149
Fletcher, Martin 153
Folbaum, Rick 153
Fortin, Judy 156
Franken, Bob 158
Frazier, Stephen 159
Gangel, Jamie.... 163
Geist, Bill.... 166
Gharib, Susie 168
Gibson, Charles.... 169
Gibson, John.... 169
Goldberg, Bernard 173
Goldman, Stan.... 174
Goler, Wendell.... 174
Gomez, Rebecca 175
Green, Lauren 181
Greenfield, Jeff.... 182
Gregory, David.... 182
Griffeth, Bill 183
Grove, Amanda 185
Gupta, Sanjay.... 186
Guthrie, Savannah.... 187
Haines, Mark 188
Halperin, Mark.... 190
Hansen, Chris 192
Harris, Dan 194
Hartman, Steve.... 195
Hayes, Erin 197
Hays, Kathleen.... 198
Hazelton, Ron 198
Hegedus, Mike.... 199
Hemmer, Bill 201
Herera, Sue.... 202
Herridge, Catherine.... 202
Hill, ED.... 204
Hobson, Mellody 206
Holt, Lester.... 208
Huddy, Juliet 212
Hume, Brit 213
Ifill, Gwen 215
Insana, Ron.... 217
Iovanna, Carol 218
James, Sara.... 222
Jamieson, Bob 222
Jansing, Chris 223
Jarrett, Gregg.... 223
Jennings, Peter 225
Jerrick, Mike.... 225
Johns, Joe 226
Kagan, Daryn 233
Kangas, Paul.... 234
Karas, Beth 234
Karl, Jonathan.... 235
Kasich, John.... 236
Keating, Phil.... 237
Keenan, Terry.... 237
Kelly, Greg 238

Television Anchors & Reporters (Cont'd)

Kernan, Joe....241
Keteyian, Armen....242
Kilmeade, Brian....243
King, John....244
Knoller, Mark....248
Kondracke, Morton....250
Koppel, Andrea....250
Kotb, Hoda....251
Kristol, William....254
Kroft, Steve....254
Krulwich, Robert....254
Kurtz, Howard....256
Lagattuta, Bill....257
Larson, John....261
Lauer, Matt....261
Lee, Mike....265
Lehrer, Jim....266
Lewis, Dana....270
Lewis, George....270
Liesman, Steve....272
Lin, Carol....272
Lisovicz, Susan....274
Litke, Mark....274
Mabrey, Vicki....281
MacCallum, Martha....281
Maceda, Jim....282
Magnus, Edie....284
Malveaux, Suzanne....287
Mankiewicz, Josh....287
Martin, David....291
Mathisen, Tyler....294
Matthews, Chris....294
McCuddy, Bill....299
McDowell, Dagen....300
McFadden, Cynthia....301
McGinnis, Susan....302
McIntyre, Jamie....303
McKenzie, John....304
McLaughlin, John....304
McLaughlin, Sean....304
Meade, Robin....306
Meier, Randy....307
Mendenhall, Preston....308
Meserve, Jeanne....309
Miklaszewski, Jim....311
Miller, Keith....312
Mitchell, Andrea....315
Mitchell, Russ....315
Moos, Jeanne....319
Moran, Terry....319
Moriarty, Erin....320
Morrell, Geoff....320
Morrison, Keith....321
Muir, David....323
Muller, Judy....323
Murphy, Ann Pleshette....325
Murphy, Dennis....325
Myers, Lisa....326
Nance, John J....328
Napolitano, Andrew....328
Nasr, Octavia E....328
Nguyen, Betty....332
Novotny, Monica....336
O'Beirne, Kate....337
O'Brien, Miles....337
O'Brien, Soledad....337
O'Donnell, Kelly....338
O'Donnell, Norah....338
Olbermann, Keith....339
Oliver, Meg....340
O'Neill, Roger....341
O'Reilly, Bill....342
Osgood, Charles....343
Osunsami, Steve....344
Overmyer, Steve....344
Paul, Christi....350
Pelley, Scott....352
Phillips, Julian....358
Phillips, Kyra....358
Phillips, Stone....358
Pinkerton, Jim....360
Plante, Bill....361
Potter, Ned....364
Press, Bill....365
Price, Dave....366
Quick, Becky....369
Quinn, Brigitte....369
Quinones, John....369
Raddatz, Martha....369
Ramos, Jorge....371
Rather, Dan....372
Ratigan, Dylan....372
Reagan, Ron....373
Reid, Chip....375
Reynolds, Dean....377
Ritter, Bill....381
Rivera, Geraldo....381
Robach, Amy....381
Roberts, Chuck....382
Roberts, Deborah....382
Roberts, John....382
Roberts, Robin....383
Roberts, Troy....383
Robertson, Nic....384
Roker, Al....387
Rooney, Andy....389
Rooney, Brian....389
Rose, Charlie....389
Rosen, James....389
Ross, Brian....390
Roth, Richard....390
Russert, Tim....393

Television Anchors & Reporters (Cont'd)

Sabine, Charles....395
Safer, Morley....395
Salinas, Maria Elena....396
Sanders, Kerry....398
Savidge, Martin....400
Sawyer, Diane....401
Scarborough, Joe....401
Schadler, Jay....402
Schieffer, Bob....403
Schlesinger, Richard....403
Schneider, William....404
Sciutto, Jim....407
Scott, Jon....408
Scott, Willard....408
Seemungal, Martin....409
Seigenthaler, John....409
Sellers, Bob....410
Senay, Emily....410
Sesno, Frank....411
Shawn, Eric....413
Sherr, Lynn....415
Shipman, Claire....415
Shriver, Maria....416
Shuster, David....417
Sieberg, Daniel....417
Simon, Bob....418
Smith, Harry....422
Smith, Larry....423
Smith, Shepard....423
Snow, Kate....425
Spencer, Susan....429
Stafford, Rob....430
Stahl, Lesley....431
Stark, Betsy....432
Stark, Lisa....432
Stark, Melissa....432
Stephanopoulos, George....433
Stewart, Alison....435
Storm, Hannah....436
Stossel, John....436
Stouffer, Linda....437
Suarez, Ray....439
Syler, Rene....441
Taibbi, Mike....442
Tapper, Jake....443
Teichner, Martha....445
Thomas, Cal....447
Thomas, Pierre....448
Thompson, Anne....448
Thompson, Lea....449
Tibbles, Kevin....450
Trotta, Liz....454
Tuchman, Gary....455
Van Sant, Peter....460
Van Susteren, Greta....460
Vargas, Elizabeth....460
Varney, Stuart....461
Velshi, Ali....462
Vester, Linda....462
Vieira, Meredith....462
Von Fremd, Mike....464
Wallace, Chris....467
Wallace, Kelly....467
Wallace, Mike....467
Warner, Margaret....469
Watson, Carlos....470
Wattenberg, Ben....471
Weir, Bill....473
Westhoven, Jennifer....475
Whitfield, Fredricka....477
Williams, Brian....480
Williams, Juan....480
Williams, Pete....481
Willis, Gerri....482
Woodruff, Bob....487
Wright, David....489
Yang, John....491
Zahn, Paula....493
Zukerman, Eugenia....495

Television Personalities

See also: Sportscasters pg 560

Abdul, Paula....15
Allen, Ted....22
Arnold, Tom....29
Banks, Tyra....36
Barker, Bob....37
Barrow, Andrea....39
Batali, Mario....41
Behar, Joy....44
Bergeron, Tom....48
Big Tigger....51
Bloom, Lisa....55
Burke, Brooke....74
Casablanca, Ted....85
Colmes, Alan....100
Cowell, Simon....106
Crier, Catherine....108
Daly, Carson....114
Davis, Paige....118
DeGeneres, Ellen....120
Douglas, Kyan....130
Dr Phil....131
Ebert, Roger....136
Ennico, Cliff....142
Filicia, Thom....150
Flay, Bobby....152
Ford, Jack....155
Ginsburg, Art....171
Grace, Nancy....177
Graham, Fred....178
Guilfoyle, Kimberly....186

Television Personalities (Cont'd)

Gumbel, Bryant 186
Hannity, Sean 192
Hart, Mary 195
Hasselbeck, Elisabeth 196
Hayes, Eddie 197
Hazelton, Ron 198
Irwin, Steve 218
Jackson, Randy 221
Johanson, Sue 226
Johnson, Timothy 228
Jones Reynolds, Star 231
Judge Judy 232
Karn, Richard 235
Katz, David L 236
Kimmel, Jimmy 243
King, Larry 244
Kolls, Rebecca 250
Kressley, Carson 253
Kudlow, Lawrence 255
Kurtis, Bill 255
Lagasse, Emeril 257
Leno, Jay 267
Letterman, David 268
Lipton, James 274
Lowell, Christopher 278
Maher, Bill 285
Maltin, Leonard 286
McGraw, Phil 302
McHale, Joel 303
McMahon, Ed 305
Miller, Stephanie 313
Mr Food 171
Nathan, Joan 329
Norville, Deborah 335
O'Brien, Conan 337
Oliver, Jamie 340
Orman, Suze 342
Osmond, Donny 343
Pauley, Jane 350
Pennington, Ty 353
Philbin, Regis 357
Podhoretz, John 361
Politan, Vinnie 362
Povich, Maury 365
Probst, Jeff 367
Rhea, Caroline 377
Ripa, Kelly 381
Rivers, Joan 381
Roberts, Cokie 382
Rogers, Fred 386
Rome, Jim 388
Sajak, Pat 396
Salley, John 397
Saralegui, Cristina 399
Scheindlin, Judith 402
Seacrest, Ryan 408
Smiley, Tavis 421
Stern, Howard 434
Stewart, Jon 435
Trebek, Alex 454
Vester, Linda 462
Vieira, Meredith 462
Vila, Bob 463
Walsh, John 468
Walters, Barbara 468
White, Vanna 477
Williams, Montel 481
Winfrey, Oprah 484

Tennis Players

Agassi, Andre 19
Ashe, Arthur 30
Blake, James 54
Bryan, Bob 72
Bryan, Mike 72
Capriati, Jennifer 81
Carillo, Mary 82
Clijsters, Kim 95
Craybas, Jill 107
Davenport, Lindsay 116
Dent, Taylor 123
Evert, Chris 145
Federer, Roger 147
Fish, Mardy 151
Frazier, Amy 159
Ginepri, Robby 171
Graf, Steffi 178
Granville, Laura 179
Henin-Hardenne, Justine 201
Hewitt, Lleyton 203
Hingis, Martina 205
Jenkins, Scoville 224
King, Billie Jean 244
Kournikova, Anna 251
Mauresmo, Amelie 295
McEnroe, John 301
McEnroe, Patrick 301
Nadal, Rafael 327
Noah, Yannick 333
Philippoussis, Mark 357
Pierce, Mary 359
Rafter, Patrick 370
Roddick, Andy 385
Safina, Dinara 396
Sampras, Pete 397
Seles, Monica 410
Sharapova, Maria 413
Shaughnessy, Meghann 413
Shriver, Pam 416
Smith, Stan 423

Tennis Players (Cont'd)

Stich, Michael 435
Williams, Serena 481
Williams, Venus 482

Track & Field Athletes

See: Sports Personalities (Misc) pg 558

US Presidents & Vice Presidents and Their Wives

Bush, Barbara 76
Bush, George HW 76
Bush, George W 76
Bush, Laura Welch 76
Carter, Jimmy 85
Carter, Rosalynn 85
Cheney, Lynne V 90
Cheney, Richard 90
Clinton, Bill 95
Clinton, Hillary Rodham 95
Eisenhower, Dwight D 139
Eisenhower, Mamie Doud 139
Ford, Betty 154
Ford, Gerald R 155
Gore, Albert Jr 177
Gore, Tipper 177
Johnson, Lady Bird 227
Johnson, Lyndon B 227
Kennedy, John Fitzgerald 240
Mondale, Walter F 317
Nixon, Richard M 333
Quayle, Dan 368
Reagan, Nancy 373
Reagan, Ronald 373

US Senators & Representatives

Abercrombie, Neil 15
Ackerman, Gary L. 16
Aderholt, Robert 18
Akaka, Daniel K 20
Akin, Todd 20
Alexander, Lamar 21
Alexander, Rodney M 21
Allard, Wayne 22
Allen, George 22
Allen, Thomas H 22
Andrews, Robert E 26
Baca, Joe 34
Bachus, Spencer 34
Baird, Brian 35
Baker, Richard 35
Baldwin, Tammy 35
Barrett, J Gresham 39
Barrow, John 39
Bartlett, Roscoe G 40
Barton, Joe 40
Bass, Charles F 40
Baucus, Max 41
Bayh, Evan 42
Bean, Melissa L 42
Beauprez, Bob 43
Becerra, Xavier 43
Bennett, Robert F 46
Berkley, Shelley 48
Berman, Howard L 48
Berry, Marion 50
Biden, Joseph R Jr 51
Biggert, Judy 51
Bilirakis, Michael 51
Bingaman, Jeff 52
Bishop, Rob 52
Bishop, Sanford D Jr 53
Bishop, Timothy 53
Blackburn, Marsha W 53
Blumenauer, Earl 56
Blunt, Roy 56
Boehlert, Sherwood L 57
Boehner, John A 57
Bond, Kit 58
Bonilla, Henry 58
Bonner, Jo 59
Bono, Mary 59
Boozman, John 59
Bordallo, Madeleine Z 59
Boren, Dan 59
Boswell, Leonard L 60
Boucher, Rick 60
Boustany, Charles W Jr 60
Boxer, Barbara 61
Boyd, Allen 61
Bradley, Jeb E 62
Brady, Kevin 63
Brady, Robert A 63
Brown, Corrine 69
Brown, Henry E Jr 69
Brown, Sherrod 70
Brown-Waite, Ginny 71
Brownback, Sam 71
Bunning, Jim 74
Burgess, Michael C 74
Burns, Conrad 74
Burr, Richard 75
Burton, Dan 75
Butterfield, GK Jr 77
Buyer, Steve 77
Byrd, Robert C 77
Calvert, Ken 79
Camp, Dave 79
Campbell, John 80
Cannon, Christopher 80
Cantor, Eric 81
Cantwell, Maria 81

Subject Index

US Senators & Representatives (Cont'd)

Capito, Shelley Moore ... 81
Capps, Lois ... 81
Capuano, Michael E ... 81
Cardin, Benjamin L ... 81
Cardoza, Dennis ... 81
Carnahan, Russ ... 83
Carper, Thomas ... 83
Carson, Julia ... 84
Carter, John R ... 85
Case, Ed ... 86
Castle, Michael N ... 86
Chabot, Steve ... 88
Chafee, Lincoln D ... 88
Chambliss, Saxby ... 88
Chandler, Ben ... 89
Chocola, Chris ... 92
Christensen, Donna ... 92
Clay, William L ... 94
Cleaver, Emanuel ... 95
Clinton, Hillary Rodham ... 95
Clyburn, James E ... 96
Coble, Howard ... 96
Coburn, Tom ... 96
Cochran, Thad ... 96
Cole, Tom ... 98
Coleman, Norm ... 98
Collins, Susan ... 99
Conaway, Mike ... 100
Conrad, Kent ... 101
Conyers, John Jr ... 101
Cooper, Jim ... 102
Cornyn, John ... 104
Costa, Jim ... 104
Costello, Jerry F ... 105
Craig, Larry E ... 106
Cramer, Bud ... 106
Crapo, Mike ... 107
Crenshaw, Ander ... 108
Crowley, Joseph ... 109
Cubin, Barbara ... 110
Cuellar, Henry ... 110
Culberson, John ... 110
Cummings, Elijah ... 111
Davis, Artur ... 117
Davis, Danny ... 117
Davis, Geoff ... 117
Davis, Jim ... 117
Davis, Jo Ann ... 117
Davis, Lincoln ... 118
Davis, Susan A ... 118
Davis, Tom ... 118
Dayton, Mark ... 118
Deal, Nathan ... 119
DeFazio, Peter A ... 120
DeGette, Diana ... 121
Delahunt, William ... 121
DeLauro, Rosa ... 121
DeLay, Tom ... 121
DeMint, Jim ... 122
Dent, Charles W ... 122
DeWine, Mike ... 124
Diaz-Balart, Lincoln ... 125
Diaz-Balart, Mario ... 125
Dicks, Norman D ... 125
Dingell, John D ... 126
Dodd, Christopher J ... 127
Doggett, Lloyd ... 127
Dole, Elizabeth H ... 128
Domenici, Pete ... 128
Doolittle, John T ... 129
Dorgan, Byron L ... 129
Doyle, Mike ... 130
Drake, Thelma D ... 131
Dreier, David ... 131
Duncan, John J Jr ... 133
Durbin, Richard J ... 135
Edwards, Chet ... 138
Ehlers, Vernon J ... 138
Emanuel, Rahm ... 140
Emerson, Jo Ann ... 140
Engel, Eliot L ... 141
English, Phil ... 141
Ensign, John ... 142
Enzi, Mike ... 142
Eshoo, Anna G ... 143
Etheridge, Bob ... 144
Evans, Lane ... 144
Everett, Terry ... 145
Faleomavaega, Eni FH ... 146
Farr, Sam ... 146
Fattah, Chaka ... 147
Feeney, Tom C ... 148
Feingold, Russell D ... 148
Feinstein, Dianne ... 148
Ferguson, Mike ... 149
Filner, Bob ... 150
Fitzpatrick, Mike ... 151
Flake, Jeff ... 152
Foley, Mark ... 154
Forbes, J Randy ... 154
Ford, Harold Jr ... 155
Fortenberry, Jeff ... 156
Fortuno, Luis G ... 156
Fossella, Vito J ... 156
Foxx, Virginia ... 157
Frank, Barney ... 157
Franks, Trent ... 158
Frelinghuysen, Rodney ... 159
Frist, Bill ... 160
Gallegly, Elton ... 163
Garrett, Scott ... 165
Gerlach, Jim ... 168

US Senators & Representatives (Cont'd)

Gibbons, Jim....168
Gilchrest, Wayne T....169
Gillmor, Paul E....171
Gingrey, Phil....171
Gohmert, Louie....173
Gonzalez, Charles A....175
Goode, Virgil H Jr....175
Goodlatte, Robert W....175
Gordon, Bart....176
Graham, Lindsey....179
Granger, Kay....179
Grassley, Charles E....180
Graves, Sam....180
Green, Al....180
Green, Gene....181
Green, Mark....181
Gregg, Judd....182
Grijalva, Raul M....183
Gutierrez, Luis V....187
Gutknecht, Gil....187
Hagel, Charles....188
Hall, Ralph M....189
Harkin, Tom....193
Harman, Jane....193
Harris, Katherine....194
Hart, Melissa A....195
Hastert, J Dennis....196
Hastings, Alcee L....196
Hastings, Doc....196
Hatch, Orrin G....196
Hayes, Robin....197
Hayworth, JD....198
Hefley, Joel....199
Hensarling, Jeb....202
Herger, Wally....202
Herseth, Stephanie....202
Higgins, Brian....203
Hinchey, Maurice D....205
Hinojosa, Ruben....205
Hobson, David L....206
Hoekstra, Peter....206
Holden, Tim....207
Holt, Rush....209
Honda, Michael M....209
Hooley, Darlene....209
Hostettler, John N....210
Hoyer, Steny H....211
Hulshof, Kenny....213
Hunter, Duncan....213
Hutchison, Kay Bailey....214
Hyde, Henry J....214
Inglis, Bob....217
Inhofe, James M....217
Inouye, Daniel K....217
Inslee, Jay....217
Isakson, Johnny....219
Israel, Steve....219
Issa, Darrell E....219
Istook, Ernest Jim....219
Jackson, Jesse Jr....220
Jackson Lee, Sheila....221
Jefferson, William J....224
Jeffords, James M....224
Jenkins, William....224
Jindal, Bobby....225
Johnson, Eddie Bernice....226
Johnson, Nancy L....228
Johnson, Sam....228
Johnson, Tim....228
Johnson, Timothy V....228
Jones, Walter B....231
Kanjorski, Paul E....234
Kaptur, Marcy....234
Keller, Ric....238
Kelly, Sue....239
Kennedy, Edward M....240
Kennedy, Mark R....240
Kennedy, Patrick....240
Kerry, John F....241
Kildee, Dale E....243
Kilpatrick, Carolyn C....243
Kind, Ron....243
King, Peter T....244
King, Steve....245
Kingston, Jack....245
Kirk, Mark Steven....246
Kline, John P....247
Knollenberg, Joe....248
Kohl, Herbert H....249
Kolbe, Jim....249
Kucinich, Dennis....254
Kuhl, John R "Randy" Jr....255
Kyl, Jon....256
LaHood, Ray....258
Landrieu, Mary....259
Langevin, James R....260
Lantos, Tom....260
Larsen, Rick....261
Larson, John B....261
Latham, Tom....261
LaTourette, Steve....261
Lautenberg, Frank R....262
Leach, Jim....263
Leahy, Patrick J....263
Lee, Barbara....264
Levin, Carl....269
Levin, Sander M....269
Lewis, Jerry....270
Lewis, John....270
Lewis, Ron....271
Lieberman, Joseph I....272
Lincoln, Blanche L....273

US Senators & Representatives (Cont'd)

Linder, John 273
Lipinski, William O 274
LoBiondo, Frank A 275
Lofgren, Zoe 275
Lott, Trent 277
Lowey, Nita M 278
Lucas, Frank D 278
Lugar, Richard G 279
Lungren, Daniel E 279
Lynch, Stephen F 280
Mack, Connie IV 282
Maloney, Carolyn B 286
Manzullo, Donald 288
Marchant, Kenny 288
Markey, Edward J 289
Marshall, James C 291
Martinez, Mel R 292
Matheson, Jim 294
Matsui, Doris 294
McCain, John 296
McCarthy, Carolyn 297
McCaul, Michael 297
McCollum, Betty 298
McConnell, Mitch 298
McCotter, Thaddeus G 298
McCrery, Jim 299
McDermott, Jim 300
McGovern, James P 302
McHenry, Patrick 303
McHugh, John M 303
McIntyre, Mike 303
McKeon, Buck 304
McKinney, Cynthia 304
McMorris, Cathy 305
McNulty, Michael R 306
Meehan, Martin T 307
Meek, Kendrick 307
Meeks, Gregory W 307
Melancon, Charlie 307
Menendez, Robert 308
Mica, John L 310
Michaud, Mike 311
Mikulski, Barbara A 311
Millender-McDonald, Juanita 312
Miller, Brad 312
Miller, Candice S 312
Miller, Gary G 312
Miller, George 312
Miller, Jeff 312
Mollohan, Alan B 316
Moore, Dennis 318
Moore, Gwen 318
Moran, James 319
Moran, Jerry 319
Murkowski, Lisa 325
Murphy, Timothy F 325
Murray, Patty 326
Murtha, John P 326
Musgrave, Marilyn N 326
Myrick, Sue 326
Nadler, Jerrold 327
Napolitano, Grace Flores 328
Neal, Richard E 329
Nelson, Ben 330
Nelson, Bill 330
Neugebauer, Randy 330
Ney, Bob 332
Northup, Anne Meagher 335
Norton, Eleanor Holmes 335
Norwood, Charlie 335
Nunes, Devin 336
Nussle, Jim 336
Obama, Barack 337
Oberstar, James L 337
Obey, David 337
Olver, John W 340
Ortiz, Solomon P 343
Osborne, Tom 343
Otter, CL "Butch" 344
Owens, Major R 344
Oxley, Michael G 345
Pallone, Frank Jr 346
Pascrell, Bill 349
Pastor, Ed 349
Paul, Ron 350
Payne, Donald M 351
Pearce, Steve 351
Pelosi, Nancy 352
Pence, Mike 353
Peterson, Collin C 356
Peterson, John 356
Petri, Thomas E 356
Pickering, Chip 358
Pitts, Joseph R 360
Platts, Todd Russell 361
Poe, Ted 361
Pombo, Richard W 362
Pomeroy, Earl 362
Porter, Jon 363
Price, David 366
Price, Tom 366
Pryce, Deborah 367
Pryor, Mark 367
Putnam, Adam 368
Radanovich, George 369
Rahall, Nick 370
Ramstad, Jim 371
Rangel, Charles B 371
Reed, Jack 374
Regula, Ralph 375
Rehberg, Dennis 375
Reichert, Dave 375

US Senators & Representatives (Cont'd)

Reid, Harry....375
Renzi, Rick....376
Reyes, Silvestre....377
Reynolds, Thomas M....377
Roberts, Pat....383
Rockefeller, Jay....385
Rogers, Harold....386
Rogers, Mike....387
Rogers, Mike D....387
Rohrabacher, Dana....387
Ros-Lehtinen, Ileana....389
Ross, Mike....390
Rothman, Steven R....391
Roybal-Allard, Lucille....391
Royce, Ed....392
Ruppersberger, Dutch....393
Rush, Bobby L....393
Ryan, Paul....394
Ryan, Timothy J....394
Ryun, Jim....395
Sabo, Martin Olav....395
Salazar, John T....396
Salazar, Ken....396
Sanchez, Linda T....398
Sanchez, Loretta....398
Sanders, Bernard....398
Santorum, Rick....399
Sarbanes, Paul S....399
Saxton, Jim....401
Schakowsky, Janice D....402
Schiff, Adam....403
Schmidt, Jean....404
Schumer, Charles E....406
Schwartz, Allyson Y....406
Schwarz, Joe....407
Scott, David....408
Scott, Robert C....408
Sensenbrenner, Jim Jr....410
Serrano, Jose E....411
Sessions, Jeff....411
Sessions, Pete....411
Shadegg, John....411
Shaw, E Clay Jr....413
Shays, Christopher....413
Shelby, Richard C....414
Sherman, Brad....414
Sherwood, Don....415
Shimkus, John....415
Shuster, Bill....416
Simmons, Rob....418
Simpson, Mike....419
Skelton, Ike....420
Slaughter, Louise M....421
Smith, Adam....422
Smith, Christopher H....422
Smith, Gordon....422
Smith, Lamar....423
Snowe, Olympia J....425
Snyder, Vic....425
Sodrel, Mike....425
Solis, Hilda L....426
Souder, Mark....427
Specter, Arlen....428
Spratt, John M Jr....430
Stabenow, Debbie....430
Stark, Pete....432
Stearns, Cliff....432
Stevens, Ted....434
Strickland, Ted....438
Stupak, Bart....439
Sullivan, John....439
Sununu, John E....440
Sweeney, John E....441
Talent, James M....442
Tancredo, Tom....443
Tanner, John S....443
Tauscher, Ellen....444
Taylor, Charles H....444
Taylor, Gene....444
Terry, Lee....446
Thomas, Craig....447
Thomas, William M....448
Thompson, Bennie G....448
Thompson, Mike....449
Thornberry, Mac....449
Thune, John....449
Tiahrt, Todd....450
Tiberi, Patrick J....450
Tierney, John F....450
Towns, Edolphus....453
Tubbs Jones, Stephanie....455
Turner, Michael....456
Udall, Mark....457
Udall, Tom....457
Upton, Fred....458
Van Hollen, Christopher Jr....459
Velazquez, Nydia M....462
Visclosky, Peter J....463
Vitter, David....463
Voinovich, George V....464
Walden, Greg....466
Walsh, James T....468
Wamp, Zach....469
Warner, John....469
Wasserman Schultz, Debbie....470
Waters, Maxine....470
Watson, Diane E....470
Watt, Melvin L....471
Waxman, Henry A....471
Weiner, Anthony D....473
Weldon, Curt....473
Weldon, Dave....474

US Senators & Representatives (Cont'd)

Weller, Jerry....474
Westmoreland, Lynn....475
Wexler, Robert....476
Whitfield, Ed....477
Wicker, Roger F....478
Wilson, Heather....483
Wilson, Joe....483
Wolf, Frank R....486
Woolsey, Lynn C....488
Wu, David....489
Wyden, Ron....489
Wynn, Albert R....490
Young, CW Bill....492
Young, Don....492

US Supreme Court Justices
See: Attorneys & Judges pg 506

Yoga
See: Fitness Personalities pg 536